Anthropology

A Global Perspective

Eighth Edition

Anthropology

A Global Perspective

Eighth Edition

Raymond Scupin
Lindenwood University

Christopher R. DeCorse
Syracuse University

Boston   Columbus   Indianapolis   New York   San Francisco   Amsterdam
Cape Town   Dubai   London   Madrid   Milan   Munich   Paris   Montréal   Toronto
Delhi   Mexico City   São Paulo   Sydney   Hong Kong   Seoul   Singapore   Taipei   Tokyo

Editorial Director: Dickson Musslewhite
Publisher: Charlyce Jones-Owen
Editorial Assistant: Maureen Diana
Program Manager: Rob DeGeorge
Project Manager: Richard DeLorenzo
Procurement Specialist: Mary Ann Gloriande
Permissions Specialist: Brooks Hill-Whilton
Image Permissions Specialist: Jen Simmons/Lumina Datamatics, Inc.
Cover Art Director: Maria Lange
Cover image: Shutterstock
Director, Digital Studio: Sacha Laustein
Media Product Manager: David Alick
Media Project Manager: Amanda Smith
Full-Service Project Management and Composition: Tracy Duff/Lumina Datamatics, Inc.

Credits and acknowledgments borrowed from other sources and reproduced with permission appear in the appropriate Credits sections at the end of the book.

Library of Congress Cataloging-in-Publication Data
Scupin, Raymond.
    Anthropology : a global perspective / Raymond Scupin, Christopher R. DeCorse. — Eighth edition.
        pages cm
    Includes bibliographical references and index.
    ISBN 978-0-13-400486-0—ISBN 0-13-400486-8
    1. Anthropology. I. DeCorse, Christopher R. II. Title.
    GN25.S39 2016
    301—dc23

                                                        2014044490

10 9 8 7 6 5 4 3 2 1

Student Edition
ISBN-10: 0-13-400486-8
ISBN-13: 978-0-13-400486-0

Instructor's Review Copy:
ISBN-10: 0-13-400500-7
ISBN-13: 978-0-13-400500-3

Á La Carte
ISBN-10: 0-13-400512-0
ISBN-13: 978-0-13-400512-6

Contents

Boxes

Anthropologists at Work

John Hawks: Physical (or Biological) Anthropologist

Kelley Hays-Gilpin: Archaeologist

Bonnie Urciuoli: Linguistic Anthropologist

Scott Atran: Cultural Anthropologist

A. Peter Castro: Applied Anthropologist

Scott Madry: Google Earth and Armchair Archaeology

George Fletcher Bass: Underwater Archaeologist

Jane Goodall and Dian Fossey: Primatologists in the Field

Donald Johanson: Paleoanthropologist

Grahame Clark and the Mesolithic

Nancy Rosenberg: Gender, Food, Globalization and Culture

Russell Bernard: Saving Languages

Gabriella Coleman: The Ethnography of Hackers and Geeks

Eric Wolf: A Global Anthropologist

Susan Brownell: Ethnography in China

Akbar Ahmed: Globalization and the Islamic World

Clyde Collins Snow: Forensic Anthropologist

John McCreery: Applying Anthropology in Japan

Critical Perspectives

Engendering Archaeology: The Role of Women in Aztec Mexico

Historical Archaeology

Underwater Archaeology

Planetary-Level Extinctions

Creationism, Intelligent Design, and Evolution

What's in a Name? Primate Classification and Taxonomy

Interpreting the Fayum Fossils

The Piltdown Fraud

Race and Genetics: The Human Genome Project

Joseph Arthur de Gobineau and the Aryan Master Race

Could Early Hominins Speak? The Evolution of Language

The Origins of Maize

War before Civilization?

Contacts between Two Worlds?

The Downfall of the Moche

Key National Symbols

The Anthropology of the "Self"

Human Aggression: Biological or Cultural?

Were There Matriarchal States?

Graduation: A Rite of Passage in U.S. Society

Globalization and McDonald's

The Elgin Marbles

Ethical Controversies in El Dorado

Preface

Educational Goals and Orientation of This Text

The world has become a small place. Global communications, international trade, geopolitical events, and ease of travel have brought people from different cultures into more intimate contact than ever before, forcing this generation of students to become more knowledgeable about societies other than their own. This textbook is grounded in the belief that enhanced global awareness is essential for people preparing to take their place in the interconnected world of the twenty-first century. Anthropology is ideally suited to introduce students to this global perspective. Through exploring the range of human diversity, the subfields of anthropology help liberate students from narrow, parochial views and enable them to appreciate the full sweep of the human condition.

The anthropological perspective, which stresses critical thinking, the evaluation of competing hypotheses, and the skills to generalize from specific data, is fundamental to a well-rounded education. This text engages readers in anthropology by delving into both classic and current research. It reflects a commitment to anthropology's holistic and integrative approach, demonstrating how the four basic subfields of anthropology—biological anthropology, archaeology, linguistics, and cultural anthropology—together yield a comprehensive understanding of humanity. Insights from each of the subfields are woven together to reveal how anthropologists unlock the working of a particular society or discover the threads that unite human societies in the past and present. In examining anthropological research, this text often draws on research from other disciplines, including an array of findings from biology, paleontology, history, psychology, sociology, political science, religious studies, and research in other areas that shed light on anthropological inquiry. Exploring interactions between anthropology and other fields further underscores anthropology's unique, holistic perspective that sparks the critical imagination that brings the learning process to life.

The comparative approach, another cornerstone of anthropology, is also highlighted throughout the text. When anthropologists assess fossil evidence, artifacts, languages, or cultural beliefs, they weigh the evidence from a comparative perspective, even as they acknowledge the unique elements of each case, society, or culture. Anthropologists draw on examples from across both time and space. The text consequently casts an inquiring eye on materials from numerous geographical regions and historical eras to enrich student understanding. In evaluating human evolution, prehistoric events, language divergence, or developments in social structure, anthropologists must rely on a diachronic approach, and draw on models that accommodate change through time.

Three Unifying Themes of This Text

In the previous edition of this textbook, we emphasized three unifying themes that structured the material presented. These have been retained and expanded in this eighth edition. The first two themes we introduce students to are the *diversity of human societies* and cultural patterns the world over and the *similarities that make all humans fundamentally alike*. To achieve these two objectives, we pay as much attention to universal human characteristics as we do to local cultural contexts and conditions. We emphasize the growing interconnectedness of humanity and both the positive and negative consequences of this reality. We draw on anthropological studies to discover how people are responding to the process of globalization.

The third theme, which we emphasize more prominently in this edition, focuses on the interconnections between the sciences and humanities within anthropology. We call this the *synthetic-complementary approach*, which views the scientific method and the methods in the humanities as complementary and suggests that one is incomplete without the other. This theme had been mentioned in previous editions, but we make it much more of a centerpiece in this one. This third important theme dovetails with the two other themes, demonstrating how human behavior is unique to a specific culture, and yet is also universal. This point resonates with an observation made by the late Eric Wolf. In another anthropology textbook published decades ago, Wolf emphasized that anthropology has always had one foot in the sciences and the other foot in the humanities. This observation is even truer today. Wolf said, "Anthropology is both the most scientific of the humanities and the most humanistic of the sciences" (1964, 88). Wolf was kind enough to give us suggestions in developing this textbook, and we would like to carry on the tradition that he emphasized in his work.

Some anthropologists have argued that the scientific approach is not suitable for assessing and interpreting human behavior and culture, whereas others believe that the humanistic approach is not appropriate for developing general cross-cultural and causal explanations about human behavior and culture. This has led to textbooks that focus on either one approach or the other. In this book, we highlight how the interpretive-humanistic perspective is complementary to the scientific method, which seeks general cross-cultural and causal explanations for human behavior and culture. The interpretive-humanistic perspective provides insight into the specifics of human behavior within different cultures, whereas the scientific approach offers a method to test causal explanations that allow for insight into universal aspects of human behavior.

What's New to This Edition

- Learning objectives and summaries added to all chapters.
- New discussion of obsidian hydration and revised discussion of archaeological and paleoanthropological methods.
- Substantially revised presentation of primate and hominin classification integrating genetic data.
- Updated information on new fossil and archaeological evidence on early hominin origins, including the Denisovans.
- Revised and expanded discussion of the genetic evidence and evolutionary models for the emergence of *Homo sapiens* with new illustrations.
- New Critical Perspectives box in the Human Variation chapter called "Joseph Arthur de Gobineau and the Aryan Master Race" that explores the use of Nazi pseudoscience to meet political ends.
- Revised and expanded discussion of modern human variation, including epigenetic and cultural factors.
- Updated discussion of the new evidence for the FOX2P gene in Neandertals in the Critical Perspectives box "Could Early Hominins Speak? The Evolution of Language."
- New and expanded discussions of domestication and early agriculture in different world areas.
- New and expanded discussions of the theories of state formation and the origins of civilizations in different world areas.
- New Anthropologist at Work boxes illustrating current research directions of a linguistic anthropologist who explores race and ethnicity issues and corporate culture and a cultural anthropologist who is examining the world of hackers and geeks dealing with the Internet.

- New discussions of Pierre Bourdieu on agency and forms of economic, social, and cultural capital.
- New discussion of the ethics of anthropological research in war zones and its controversies.
- New reorganization of chapters 14–19 to highlight the different environments, subsistence and demographic conditions, technology, economics, social structures including family, gender, and age, politics, warfare, law, religion, art, and music found in different forms of societies throughout the world.
- New discussion of the research on human cooperation and the development of prosocial norms in economics and religious traditions.
- New discussion of polyandry based on recent cross-cultural research.
- New discussion of universalistic religious traditions including Hinduism, Buddhism, Judaism, Catholicism, Protestantism, and Islam.
- New discussions of art and music as studied by anthropologists and ethnomusicologists in different societies, including agricultural, industrial, and postindustrial states.
- New discussions of the recent research on the *burakumin* people of Japan.
- New discussion of John Hartigan's research on the Mexican genome reflecting a different concept of race compared to the U.S. folk model.
- New Anthropologists at Work box on Akbar Ahmed and his research on globalization and the Islamic World.
- New discussion of John Bowen's research on secularization and Islam in France.
- New discussions of "Engaged Anthropology" within the context of Applied Anthropology.
- New discussions of cardiac disease in India and acupuncture in the United States as research topics in medical anthropology.

Features of This Text

Boxes

Critical Perspectives boxes highlight specific anthropological questions, focusing on how information is collected and evaluated. Students are placed in the role of an anthropologist and engaged in the analysis of particular problems and their interpretation. A popular feature since the first edition, Critical Perspectives boxes push students to critically evaluate evidence when considering scientific and philosophical questions that have no easy answers. We have added a new Critical Perspectives box for this eighth edition. By probing beneath the surface of various assumptions and hypotheses, students discover both the excitement and challenge of anthropological investigation.

Anthropologists at Work boxes, profiling prominent anthropologists, humanize many of the issues covered in the chapters. These boxes—another carryover from the first edition—go behind the scenes to trace the personal and professional development of some of today's leading anthropologists. We have added three new boxes in this area focusing on Bonnie Urciuoli's work as a linguistic anthropologist, Gabriella Coleman's fascinating ethnographic research on hackers and geeks on the Internet, and Akbar Ahmed's research on globalization and the Islamic world.

Pedagogical Aids

For sound pedagogical reasons, we have retained some features in this eighth edition of *Anthropology: A Global Perspective*. Each chapter opens with a Chapter Outline and Learning Objectives that will help guide students to the most important issues addressed in that chapter. And each chapter ends with Summary and Learning Objectives that address issues covered in it; students can use these to help comprehend the material they have read. In addition, each chapter ends with a list of Key Terms that will help students focus on important concepts introduced in the chapter.

Support for Instructors and Students

Instructor's Manual: For each chapter in the text, this valuable resource provides a detailed Chapter Outline, Learning Objectives from the text, Lecture and Discussion Topics, Classroom Activities, and Research and Writing Topics. For easy access, this manual is available for download at **www.pearsonhighered.com/irc**

Text Bank: Test questions in multiple-choice, true/false, and essay formats are available for each chapter. For easy access, this test bank is available for download at **www.pearsonhighered.com/irc**

MyTest: This computerized software allows instructors to create their own personalized exams, edit any or all of the existing test questions, and add new questions. Other special features of the program include random generation of test questions, creation of alternate versions of the same test, scrambling question sequence, and test preview before printing. For easy access, this software is available at **www.pearsonhighered.com/irc**.

PowerPoint Presentation Slides for Anthropology: These PowerPoint slides combine text and graphics for each chapter to help instructors convey anthropology principles in a clear and engaging way. For easy access, they are available for download at **www.pearsonhighered.com/irc**.

Acknowledgments

A textbook like this one requires the enormous effort of many people. First, we would like to offer thanks to our colleague Christina Dames, who is a recent graduate of the University of Missouri, Columbia anthropology program and a faculty member at Lindenwood University. She provided in-depth research assistance on the production of this textbook, helping to update the materials in many areas.

We would also like to thank the following reviewers for their valuable comments on the various editions of this textbook: Susan Abbott-Jamieson, University of Kentucky; Kelly D. Alley, Auburn University; Barbara Gallatin Anderson, Southern Methodist University; Robert Bee, University of Connecticut; Harumi Befu, Stanford University; John E. Blank, Cleveland State University; Barry Bogin, University of Michigan—Dearborn; Donald E. Brown, University of California—Santa Barbara; Tom Brutsaert, Syracuse University; Robert Carmack, State University of New York—Albany; A. H. Peter Castro, Syracuse University; Miriam S. Chaiken, New Mexico State University; Gail W. Cromack, Onondaga Community College; James Duvall, Contra Costa College; Allen S. Ehrlich, Eastern Michigan University; Michele Ruth Gamburd, Portland State University; Josef Gamper, Monterey Peninsula College; Alan Goodman, Hampshire College; Leonard Greenfield, Temple University; Joan Gross, Oregon State University; Raymond Hames, University of Nebraska; W. Penn Handwerker, Humboldt State University; Richard D. Harris, University of Portland; Robert W. Hefner, Boston University; Robert Hitchcock, University of New Mexico, Albuquerque; Benita J. Howell, University of Tennessee—Knoxville; Arian Ishaya, DeAnza Community College; Howard Kress, University of Connecticut; Norris Johnson, University of North Carolina—Chapel Hill; Rita S. Kipp, Kenyon College; Nancy B. Leis, Central Michigan University; William Leons, University of Toledo; James Lett, Indian River Community College; Kenneth E. Lewis, Michigan State University; Scott Madry, University of North Carolina—Chapel Hill; Ester Maring, Southern Illinois University—Carbondale; Ann P. McElroy, State University of New York—Buffalo; Robert R. McIrvin, University of North Carolina—Greensboro; Nancy P. McKee, Washington State University; Barry H. Michie, Kansas State University; David Minderhout, Bloomsburg University; Katherine Moore, Bentley College; Robert Moorman, Miami-Dade Community College—North; James Myers, California State University—Chico; Tim O'Meara, World Bank Pacific Islands; Thomas O'Toole, St. Cloud

State University; John W. Page, Kirkland, Washington; Curt Peterson, Elgin Community College; Leonard Plotnicov, University of Pittsburgh; D. Tab Rasmussen, Washington University—St. Louis; James L. Ross, University of Akron; Susan D. Russell, Northern Illinois University; L. Schell, State University of New York—Albany; Edwin S. Segal, University of Louisville; David H. Spain, University of Washington; John Townsend, Syracuse University; Robert B. Townsend, College of Lake County; Trudy Turner, University of Wisconsin–Milwaukee; Stephen A. Tyler, Rice University; Virginia J. Vitzthum, University of California—Riverside; Alaka Wali, University of Maryland; Dustin Wax, University of Nevada, Los Vegas, William Wedenoja, Southwest Missouri State University; Melford S. Weiss, California State University–Sacramento; Ronald K. Wetherington, Southern Methodist University; Aubrey Williams, University of Maryland; Pamela Willoughby, University of Alberta; and Larry Zimmerman, University of South Dakota.

In particular for this eighth edition, we would like to thank Anna Bellisari, Wright State University; Andrew Kramer, University of Tennessee; Bruce P. Wheatley, University of Alabama–Birmingham; Daniel J. Wescott, University of Missouri; Robert R. Paine, Texas Tech University. We would like to thank John Hawks at the University of Wisconsin at Madison for his evaluation of the hominin evolution chapter. His expertise in the most current hypotheses within paleoanthropology and genetics was extremely helpful.

We also extend thanks to all colleagues who sent us photos and information for use in the biography boxes.

We are grateful for the unwavering support given to this project by Pearson. Without the moral support and encouragement of our acquisition editor Charlyce Owens-Jones, Richard DeLorenzo Project Manager, Permissions editor Brooks Hill-Whilton at Pearson and Senior Project Manager at Lumina Datamatics Tracy Duff, Jen Simmons Photo researcher at Lumina Datamatics, and Carol Ann Ellis this project would have been much harder to complete.

Our warmest appreciation goes to our families, whose emotional support and patience throughout the publication of the eight editions of this text truly made this book possible.

Anyone with comments, suggestions, or recommendations regarding this text is welcome to send e-mail messages to the following addresses: *rscupin@lindenwood.edu* or *crdecors@maxwell.syr.edu*.

Raymond Scupin

Christopher R. DeCorse

REVEL™

Educational technology designed for the way today's students read, think, and learn

When students are engaged deeply, they learn more effectively and perform better in their courses. This simple fact inspired the creation of REVEL: an immersive learning experience designed for the way today's students read, think, and learn. Built in collaboration with educators and students nationwide, REVEL is the newest, fully digital way to deliver respected pearson content.

REVEL enlivens course content with media interactives and assessments—integrated directly within the authors' narrative—that provide opportunities for students to read about and practice course material in tandem. This immersive educational technology boosts student engagement, which leads to better understanding of concepts and improved performance throughout the course.

Learn more about REVEL: www.pearsonhighered .com/REVEL

About the Authors

Raymond Scupin is Professor of Anthropology and International Studies at Lindenwood University. He is currently the Director at the Center for International and Global Studies at Lindenwood. He received his B.A. degree in history and Asian studies, and anthropology, from the University of California—Los Angeles. He completed his M.A. and Ph.D. degrees in anthropology at the University of California—Santa Barbara. Dr. Scupin is truly a four-field anthropologist. During graduate school, he did archaeological and ethnohistorical research on Native Americans in the Santa Barbara region. He did extensive ethnographic fieldwork in Thailand with a focus on understanding the ethnic and religious movements among the Muslim minority. In addition, Dr. Scupin taught linguistics and conducted linguistic research while based at a Thai university.

Dr. Scupin has been teaching undergraduate and graduate courses in anthropology for more than 30 years at a variety of academic institutions, including community colleges, research universities, and a four-year liberal arts university. Thus, he has taught a very broad spectrum of undergraduate students. Through his teaching experience, Dr. Scupin was prompted to write this textbook, which would allow a wide range of undergraduate students to understand the holistic and global perspectives of the four-field approach in anthropology. In 1999, he received the Missouri Governor's Award for Teaching Excellence. In 2007, Dr. Scupin received the Distinguished Scholars Award at Lindenwood University.

Dr. Scupin has published many studies based on his ethnographic research in Thailand. He returned to Thailand and other countries of Southeast Asia to update his ethnographic data on Islamic trends in that area, an increasingly important topic in the post-9/11 world. He is a member of many professional associations, including the American Anthropological Association, the Asian Studies Association, and the Council of Thai Studies. Dr. Scupin has recently authored *Religion and Culture: An Anthropological Focus, Race and Ethnicity: The United States and the World*, and *Peoples and Cultures of Asia*, all published by Pearson Prentice Hall.

Christopher R. DeCorse received his B.A. in anthropology with a minor in history from the University of New Hampshire, before completing his M.A. and Ph.D. degrees in archaeology at the University of California—Los Angeles. His theoretical interests include the interpretation of ethnicity and culture change in the archaeological record, archaeology and popular culture, and general anthropology. Dr. DeCorse has excavated a variety of prehistoric and historic period sites in the United States, the Caribbean, and Africa, but his primary area of research has been in the archaeology, history, and ethnography of West Africa. Dr. DeCorse has taught archaeology and general anthropology in undergraduate and graduate programs at the University of Ghana, Indiana University of Pennsylvania, and Syracuse University, where he is currently professor and past chair of the Department of Anthropology. His academic honors and awards include: the Daniel Patrick Moynihan Award for Outstanding Teaching, Research and Service; the William Wasserstrom Award for Excellence in Graduate Teaching; and the Syracuse University Excellence in Graduate Education Faculty Recognition Award.

Dr. DeCorse is particularly interested in making archaeology more accessible to general audiences. In addition to the single-authored physical anthropology and archaeology textbook *The Record of the Past: An Introduction to Physical Anthropology and Archaeology*, he coauthored with Brian Fagan, the eleventh edition of *In the Beginning: An Introduction to Archaeology*, both published by Prentice Hall. Dr. DeCorse's academic publications include more than 60 articles, book chapters, and research notes in a variety of publications, including *The African Archaeological Review, Historical New Hampshire, Historical Archaeology*, the *Journal of African Archaeology*, and *Slavery and Abolition*. A volume on his work in Ghana, *An Archaeology of Elmina: Africans and Europeans on the Gold Coast 1400–1900*, and an edited volume, *West Africa during the Atlantic Slave Trade: Archaeological Perspectives*, were published in 2001. His most recent book (2008), *Small Worlds: Method, Meaning, and Narrative in Microhistory*, coedited with James F. Brooks and John Walton, deals with the interpretation of the past through the lense of microhistory.

Chapter 1
Introduction to Anthropology

 ## Learning Objectives

After reading this chapter you should be able to:

1.1 Compare and contrast the four major subfields of anthropology.

1.2 Describe how the field of anthropology is holistic, interdisciplinary, and global.

1.3 Explain how the scientific method is used in anthropological explanations.

1.4 Discuss how the field of anthropology bridges both the sciences and the humanities.

1.5 Describe why any student should study anthropology.

First contact. To science-fiction writers, *first contact* refers to the first meeting between humans and extraterrestrial beings. To anthropologists, the phrase refers to the initial encounters between peoples of different societies. For thousands of years, peoples throughout the world have had first contacts with each other. Today, "first contacts" are happening at every moment—through e-mail, smartphones, and the Web, as well as by the ease of international travel. What do we observe at these "first contacts"? How do we understand diverse peoples of the world? How can we explain human behaviors? In a globalized world, these questions are growing more and more important. As we shall see in this chapter, anthropology incorporates four major subfields that seek to understand different aspects of humanity in much the same way that future space travelers might investigate extraterrestrials.

Anthropologists use a variety of field methods, techniques, and theoretical approaches to conduct their investigations, which have two major goals: to understand the *uniqueness and diversity* of human behavior and human societies around the world and to discover the *fundamental similarities* that connect human beings throughout the world in both the past and the present. To accomplish these goals, anthropologists undertake systematic case studies of human populations across the globe.

These studies have broadened our understanding of humanity, from the beginning of human societies to the present. This chapter introduces the distinctive approaches used in anthropology to achieve these goals.

Anthropology: The Four Subfields

1.1   Compare and contrast the four major subfields of anthropology.

The word *anthropology* is derived from the Greek words *anthropo*, meaning "human beings" or "humankind," and *logia*, translated as "knowledge of" or "the study of." Thus, we can define **anthropology** as the study of humankind. This definition in itself, however, does not distinguish anthropology from other disciplines. After all, historians, psychologists, economists, sociologists, and scholars in many other fields systematically study humankind in one way or another. Anthropology stands apart because it combines four subfields that bridge the natural sciences, the social sciences, and the humanities. These four subfields—biological anthropology, archaeology, linguistic anthropology, and cultural anthropology—constitute a broad approach to the study of humanity the world over, both past and present. Figure 1.1 shows these subfields and the various specializations that make up each one. A discussion of these subfields and some of the key specializations in each follows.

The subfields of anthropology initially emerged in Western society in an attempt to understand non-Western peoples. When Europeans began exploring and colonizing the world in the fifteenth century, they encountered native peoples in the Americas, Africa, the Middle East, and Asia. European travelers, missionaries, and government officials described these non-Western cultures, providing a record of their physical appearances, customs, and beliefs. By the nineteenth century, anthropology had developed into the primary discipline for understanding these non-Western societies and cultures. The major questions that these nineteenth-century anthropologists sought to answer dealt with the basic differences and similarities of human societies and cultures and with the physical variation found in peoples throughout the world. Today, anthropologists do not solely focus their attention on non-Western cultures: They are just as likely to examine cultural practices in an urban setting in the United States as to conduct fieldwork in some far-off place. However, anthropologists continue to grapple with the basic questions of human diversity and similarities through systematic research within the four subfields described below.

Biological Anthropology

Biological anthropology, (also referred to as physical anthropology) is the branch of anthropology concerned with humans as a biological species. As such, it is the subfield most closely related to the natural sciences. Biological anthropologists conduct research in two major areas: human evolution and modern human variation. The investigation of human evolution presents one of the most tantalizing areas of anthropological study. Research has now traced the African origins of humanity back over six million years, while fieldwork in other world areas has traced the expansion of early human ancestors throughout the world. Much of the evidence for human origins consists of **fossils**, the fragmentary remains of bones and living materials preserved from earlier periods. The study of human evolution through analysis of fossils is called **paleoanthropology** (the prefix *paleo* from the Greek word

Excavation of a human skull from an ancient burial

Figure 1.1 The four core subfields of anthropology and applied anthropology.

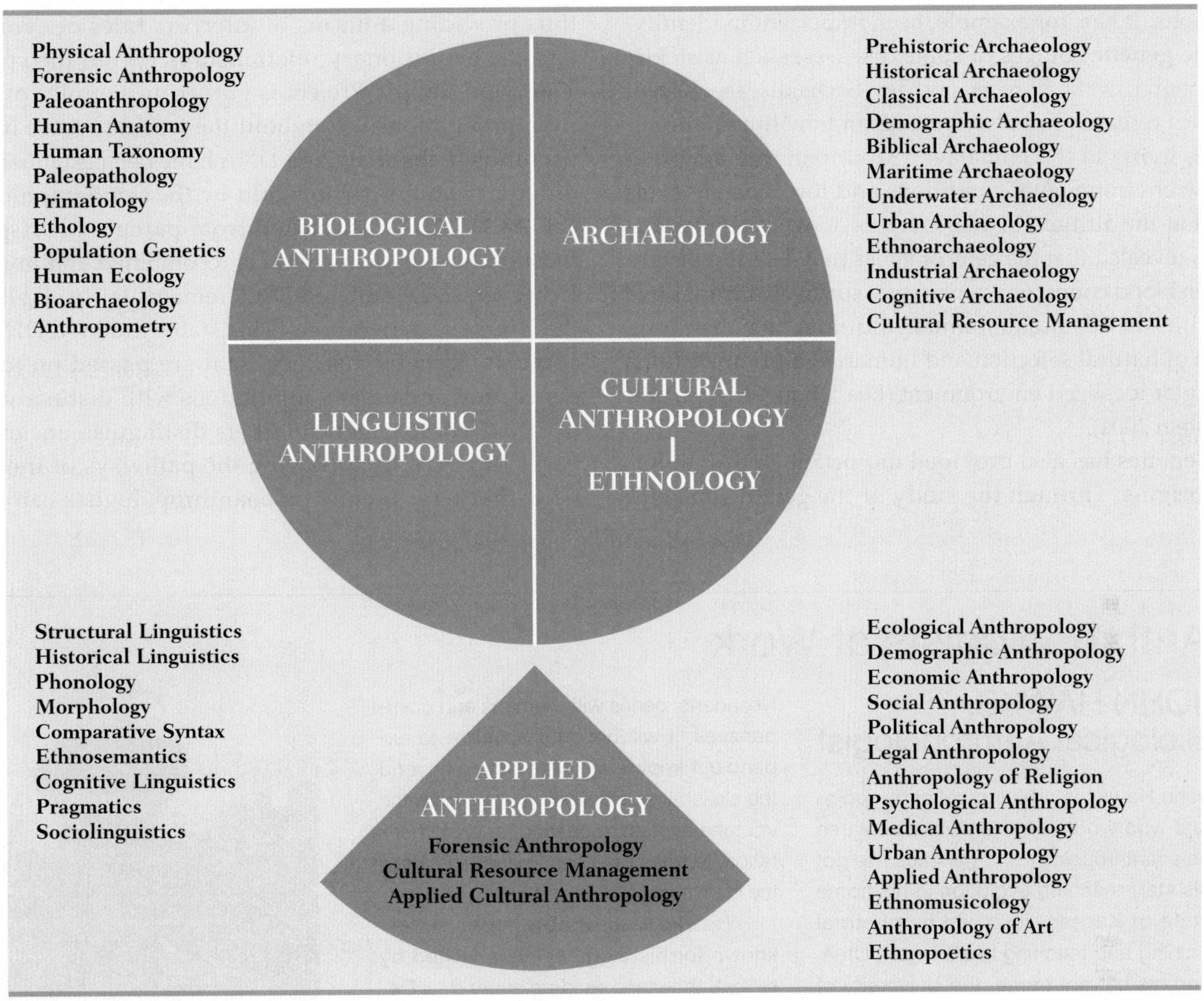

Physical Anthropology
Forensic Anthropology
Paleoanthropology
Human Anatomy
Human Taxonomy
Paleopathology
Primatology
Ethology
Population Genetics
Human Ecology
Bioarchaeology
Anthropometry

Prehistoric Archaeology
Historical Archaeology
Classical Archaeology
Demographic Archaeology
Biblical Archaeology
Maritime Archaeology
Underwater Archaeology
Urban Archaeology
Ethnoarchaeology
Industrial Archaeology
Cognitive Archaeology
Cultural Resource Management

BIOLOGICAL ANTHROPOLOGY

ARCHAEOLOGY

LINGUISTIC ANTHROPOLOGY

CULTURAL ANTHROPOLOGY | ETHNOLOGY

Structural Linguistics
Historical Linguistics
Phonology
Morphology
Comparative Syntax
Ethnosemantics
Cognitive Linguistics
Pragmatics
Sociolinguistics

APPLIED ANTHROPOLOGY

Forensic Anthropology
Cultural Resource Management
Applied Cultural Anthropology

Ecological Anthropology
Demographic Anthropology
Economic Anthropology
Social Anthropology
Political Anthropology
Legal Anthropology
Anthropology of Religion
Psychological Anthropology
Medical Anthropology
Urban Anthropology
Applied Anthropology
Ethnomusicology
Anthropology of Art
Ethnopoetics

palaios means "old" or "ancient"). Paleoanthropologists use a variety of scientific techniques to date, classify, and compare fossilized bones to determine the links between modern humans and their biological ancestors. These paleoanthropologists may work closely with archaeologists when studying ancient tools and activity areas to learn about the behavior of early human ancestors.

Other biological anthropologists explore human evolution through **primatology**, the study of primates. **Primates** are a diverse order of mammals that share an evolutionary history with humans and, therefore, have many physical characteristics in common with us. Many primatologists observe primates such as chimpanzees, gorillas, gibbons, and orangutans in their natural habitats to ascertain the similarities and differences between these other primates and humans. These observations of living primates provide insight into the behaviors of early human ancestors.

Another group of biological anthropologists focuses their research on the range of physical variation within and among different modern human populations. These anthropologists study human variation by measuring physical characteristics—such as body size, variation in blood types, or differences in skin color—or various genetic traits. Their research aims at explaining *why* such variation occurs, as well as documenting the differences in human populations.

Skeletal structure is also the focus of anthropological research. Human *osteology* is the particular area of specialization within biological anthropology dealing with the study of the human skeleton. Such studies have wide-ranging applications, from the identification of murder victims from fragmentary skeletal remains to the design of ergonomic airplane cockpits. Biological anthropologists are also interested in evaluating how disparate physical characteristics reflect evolutionary adaptations to different environmental conditions, thus shedding light on why human populations vary.

An increasingly important area of research within biological anthropology is *genetics*, the study of the biological "blueprints" that dictate the inheritance of physical characteristics. Genetics research examines a wide variety of questions. It has, for example, been important in identifying the genetic sources of some diseases, such as sickle-cell anemia, cystic fibrosis, and Tay-Sachs disease. Recent genetics research has also focused on how human populations living in the Himalayan Mountains are adapting to new environmental conditions and low oxygen levels found at the altitude of 4,000 meters above sea level. Research revealed that the gene or genes that determine high-oxygen blood count for women gave survival and adaptive capacities in this high mountain altitude, demonstrating a case of natural selection and human evolution within a particular localized environment (Beall, Song, Elston, and Goldstein 2004).

Genetics has also provided important clues into human origins. Through the study of the genetic makeup of modern humans, biological anthropologists have calculated the genetic distance among modern humans, thus providing a means of inferring rates of evolution and the evolutionary relationships within the species. The Genographic Project is gathering samples of DNA from populations throughout the world to trace human evolution. Labs analyzing DNA have been established in different regions of the world by the Genographic Project. As DNA is transmitted from parents to offspring, most of the genetic material is recombined and mutated. However, some mutated DNA remains fairly stable over the course of generations. This stable mutated DNA can serve as "genetic markers" that are passed on to each generation and create populations with distinctive sets of DNA. These genetic markers distinguish ancient lineages of DNA. By following the pathways of these genetic markers, genetic paleoanthropologists can blend

Anthropologists at Work

JOHN HAWKS, Biological Anthropologist

John Hawks is a biological anthropologist who works on the border between paleoanthropology and genetics. He got his start teaching evolution in his home state of Kansas, followed by doctoral training and teaching in Michigan, Utah, and his current home, the University of Wisconsin. He studies the relationships between the genes of living and ancient people, to discover the ways that natural selection has affected them. In 2007, Hawks and his co-workers scanned the genome, finding evidence for widespread selection on new, advantageous mutations during the last 40,000 years (Hawks et al. 2007). The breadth of this selection across the genome indicated that human evolution actually accelerated as larger populations and new agricultural subsistence exerted strong pressures on ancient people. Far from slowing down our evolution, culture had created new opportunities for adaptive change in the human population.

Hawks made substantial contributions examining the Neandertal genome. The availability of genetic evidence from ancient bones has transformed the way we study these ancient people. By comparing Neandertal genes with humans and chimpanzees, it will become possible to expand our knowledge of evolution beyond the skeletal record, finding signs from the immune system, digestion, and pigmentation, to traits like hearing and ultimately, the brain itself.

Hawks is probably most widely known for his blog, which is visited by several thousand readers every day. Describing new research from an expert's perspective, he has shown the power of public outreach as an element of the scientific process. This element of his work has made him a leader in the "open science" movement, trying to expand public accessibility to scientific research and open access to scientific data.

Hawks says that a biological anthropologist has to use evidence from the fossil record and has to be trained in human anatomy—especially *bone* anatomy, or osteology. Biological anthropologists have to know the anatomical comparisons between humans and other primates, and the way these anatomies relate to habitual behaviors. The social and ecological behaviors of primates vary extensively in response to their unique ecological circumstances. Understanding the relationship of anatomy, behavior, and

John Hawks

environment gives biological anthropologists a way to interpret ancient fossils and place them in their environmental context. However, Hawks' scientific work hasn't been limited to genetics and fossils. He has become more and more interested in the problems of cultural transmission and information theory.

Hawks welcomes everyone who is interested in human evolution based on a scientific approach to go to his blog at http://johnhawks.net/weblog/hawks/hawks.html.

Children of different nationalities and cultures

archaeology, prehistoric, and linguistic data with paleoanthropological data to trace human evolution. The Genographic Project traces both mitochondrial DNA (passed from mother to offspring in long lineages of maternal descent) and the Y chromosome (passed from father to son). These data have helped provide independent evidence for the African origins of the modern human species and human ancestors. This evidence will be discussed in later chapters on the evolution of modern humans. Individuals can join the project and submit samples of their own DNA to trace their genetic linkage to ancient populations at https://genographic.national-geographic.com.

Archaeology

Archaeology, the branch of anthropology that examines the material traces of past societies informs us about the culture of those societies—the shared way of life of a group of people that includes their values, beliefs, and norms. **Artifacts**, the material products of former societies, provide clues to the past. Some archaeological sites reveal spectacular jewelry like that found by the film character Indiana Jones or in the treasures of a pharaoh's tomb. Most artifacts, however, are not so spectacular. Despite the popular image of archaeology as an adventurous, even romantic pursuit, it usually consists of methodical, time-consuming, and—sometimes—somewhat tedious research. Archaeologists often spend hours sorting through ancient trash piles, or **middens**, to discover how members of past societies ate their meals, what tools they used in their households and

in their work, and what beliefs gave meaning to their lives. They collect and carefully analyze the broken fragments of pottery, stone, glass, and other materials. It may take them months or even years to fully complete the study of an excavation. Unlike fictional archaeologists, who experience glorified adventures, real-world archaeologists thrive on the intellectually challenging adventure of systematic, scientific research that enlarges our understanding of the past. While excavation, or "scientific digging," and fieldwork remains the key means of gathering archaeological data, a host of new techniques are available to help archaeologists locate and study archaeological sites. One innovative approach increasingly used in archaeology employs the GIS (Geographic Information Systems), a tool that is also increasingly used by environmental scientists and geologists, as well as geographers. Archaeologists can use the GIS linked to satellites to plot the locations of ancient settlements, transportation routes, and even the distribution of individual objects, allowing them to study the patterns and changes represented (Tripcevich and Wenke 2010).

Archaeologists have examined sites the world over, from campsites of the earliest humans to modern landfills. Some archaeologists investigate past societies whose history is primarily told by the archaeological record. Known as *prehistoric archaeologists*, they study the artifacts of groups such as the ancient inhabitants of Europe and the first humans to arrive in the Americas. Because these researchers have no written documents or oral traditions to help interpret the sites they examine and the artifacts they recover, the archaeological record provides the primary source of information for their interpretations of the past. *Historical archaeologists*, on the other hand, work with historians in investigating the societies of the more recent past. For example, some historical archaeologists have probed the remains of plantations in the southern United States to gain an understanding of the lifestyles of enslaved Africans and slave owners during the nineteenth century. Other archaeologists, called *classical archaeologists*, conduct research on ancient civilizations such as in Egypt, Greece, and Rome.

There are many more areas of specialization within archaeology that reflect the geographic area, topic, or time period on which the archaeologist works (see Figure 1.1). Examples of these specializations include industrial archaeology, biblical archaeology, medieval and postmedieval archaeology, and Islamic archaeology. Underwater archaeologists are unique in being distinguished from other archaeologists by the distinctive equipment, methods, and procedures needed to excavate under water. They investigate a wide range of time periods and sites throughout the world, ranging from sunken cities to shipwrecks. Another field of archaeology is called ethnoarchaeology.

Archaeologists excavating the site of Elmina in coastal Ghana.

Ethnoarchaeology is the study of artifacts and material record of modern peoples to understand the use and symbolic meaning of those artifacts.

In another novel approach, still other archaeologists have turned their attention to the very recent past. For example, in 1972, William L. Rathje began a study of modern garbage as an assignment for the students in his introductory anthropology class. Even he was surprised at the number of people who took an interest in the findings. A careful study of garbage provides insights about modern society that cannot be ferreted out in any other way. Whereas questionnaires and interviews depend upon the cooperation and interpretation of respondents, garbage provides an unbiased physical record of human activity. Rathje's pioneering "garbology project" is still in progress and, combined with information from respondents, offers a unique look at patterns of waste management, consumption, and alcohol use in contemporary U.S. society (Rathje 1992).

Linguistic Anthropology

Linguistics, the study of language, has a long history that dovetails with the discipline of philosophy, but is also one of the integral subfields of anthropology. **Linguistic anthropology** focuses on the relationship between language and culture, how language is used within society, and how the human brain acquires and uses language. Linguistic anthropologists seek to discover the ways in which languages are different from one another, as well as how they are similar. Two wide-ranging areas of research in linguistic anthropology are structural linguistics and historical linguistics.

Structural linguistics explores how language works. Structural linguists compare grammatical patterns or other linguistic elements to learn how contemporary languages mirror and differ from one another. Structural linguistics has also uncovered some intriguing relationships between language and thought patterns among different groups of people. Do people who speak different languages with distinct grammatical structures think and perceive the world differently from each other? Do native Chinese speakers think or view the world and life experiences differently from native English speakers? Structural linguists are attempting to answer this type of question.

Linguistic anthropologists also examine the connections between language and social behavior in different cultures. This specialty is called **sociolinguistics**. Sociolinguists are interested both in how language is used to define social groups and in how belonging to a particular group leads to specialized kinds of language use. In Thailand, for

Anthropologists at Work

KELLEY HAYS-GILPIN, Archaeologist

Conservation of the past, the deciphering of gender in the archaeological record, and the meaning of rock art are just a few of the intriguing topics that Kelley Hays-Gilpin has addressed in more than two decades of research. Hays-Gilpin is an archaeologist with a research focus on the prehistoric American Southwest, particularly the history and archaeology of the Pueblo peoples. Like many modern archaeologists, her career has included work in both cultural resource management and university teaching (see Chapter 25). Her doctoral work focused on early decorated ceramics in the Four Corners region in the Southwest, and she began her career with the Navajo Nation Archaeology Department in Flagstaff, Arizona. Hays-Gilpin worked on collections salvaged from archaeological sites destroyed by development projects or threatened by construction. Currently, she teaches archaeology, ceramic analysis, and rock art courses at Northern Arizona University in Flagstaff, located just hours from the Petrified Forest National Park and significant rock art sites.

Although concerned with the interpretation of past technology and adept at ceramic classification, Hays-Gilpin has consistently sought to push the interpretation of archaeological data to extract deeper meaning than archaeologists usually propose. Beginning with her doctoral work, she became increasingly interested in the study of ideology, symbols, and gender in the archaeological record. Through the comparative study of pottery, textiles, and rock art, she used ancient art as a means of understanding cultural continuity and change. This research furthered her understanding of modern Native American perceptions of, and concerns about, the past. For Hays-Gilpin, the significance of ancient objects to contemporary indigenous people—having conversations about ancestors and making connec-

tions between the past and present—is of crucial importance. It is about being able to glean messages from the past that help us live better lives in the present, including such matters as how to grow food in the desert and how to help others understand and appreciate their heritage.

Hays-Gilpin co-authored an interdisciplinary study of *Prehistoric Sandals from Northeastern Arizona: The Earl H. Morris and Ann Axtell Morris Research*, published in 1998. It draws on the research of three generations of women engaged in the study of essentially the same group of archaeological materials from sites in northeastern Arizona. While it provides a detailed examination of a particular collection, the study also affords insight into changing perceptions of archaeological interpretation. Also published in 1998 was Hays-Gilpin's co-edited volume, *Reader in Gender Archaeology*, which helped establish the legitimacy of gendered approaches to the study of the archaeological record.

For archaeologists, rock art—paintings and engravings—provides a unique source of information, offering clues to prehistoric subsistence, ideology, and religion. Yet the interpretation of these prehistoric creations is challenging, and they have often received less attention than they deserve. Hays-Gilpin's *Ambiguous Images: Gender and Rock Art* (2004), which won the Society for American Archaeology's 2005 book prize, provides a significant contribution to the relatively unexplored field of gender in rock art. Hays-Gilpin demonstrates that rock art is one of the best lines of evidence available to understand the ritual practices, gender roles, and ideological constructs of prehistoric peoples.

In addition to her current academic position, Hays-Gilpin holds the Edward Bridge Danson Chair of Anthropology at the Museum of Northern Arizona, where she is director of the Hopi Iconography Project. This project, a collaborative effort between the

Kelley Hays-Gilpin

museum and the Hopi Tribe's cultural preservation office, explores Hopi cultural continuity over centuries, if not millennia, through pottery, rock art, mural painting, baskets, and textiles. More important, the project is exploring ways in which Hopi traditions can help shape a sustainable future for Hopi communities through subsistence farming, craft production, public health programs, and cultural revitalization.

For Hays-Gilpin, the study of archaeology must emphasize teamwork and reward team players. She feels that archaeologists are not in competition with one another, but rather in competition with the forces that are destroying the archaeological record faster than it can be studied. Her research and career epitomize this approach to archaeology. Hays-Gilpin advocates monitoring and reporting on sites that have been threatened with destruction, and she continues work on many collections that have resided in museums for as much as a century. Her work has led her to collaborate with a network of archaeologists, cultural anthropologists, art historians, linguistic anthropologists, and Hopi artists. Her interdisciplinary approach to the past exemplifies modern archaeology's holistic and inclusive requirements—quite a contrast to its more narrowly specialized traditions. With this new approach, Hays-Gilpin has helped to redefine the discipline of archaeology.

Anthropologist Christina Dames doing linguistic research in West Kalimantan, Borneo, Indonesia

example, there are 13 forms of the pronoun *I*. One form is used with equals, other forms come into play with people of higher status, and some forms are used when males address females (Scupin 1988).

Another area of research that has interested linguistic anthropologists is historical linguistics. **Historical linguistics** concentrates on the comparison and classification of different languages to discern the historical links among them. By examining and analyzing grammatical structures and sounds of languages, researchers are able to discover rules for how languages change over time, as well as which languages are related to one another historically. This type of historical linguistic research is particularly useful in tracing the migration routes of various societies through time by offering multiple lines of evidence—archaeological, paleoanthropological, and linguistic. For example, through historical linguistic research, anthropologists have corroborated the Asian origins of the Native American populations.

Cultural Anthropology

Cultural anthropology is the subfield of anthropology that examines contemporary societies and cultures throughout the world. Cultural anthropologists do research in all over the world, from the tropical rainforests of the Democratic

Anthropologists at Work

BONNIE URCIUOLI, Linguistic Anthropologist

Bonnie Urciuoli completed her B.A. in English at Syracuse University. She completed her M.A. and Ph.D. at the University of Chicago. Her doctorate combined the study of both anthropology and linguistics. She has done research in New York City as a linguistic consultant on a Columbia University-sponsored project with Puerto Rican and African-American teenagers; with grants from the Ford Foundation and the Spencer Foundation. In this project she studied Puerto Rican families in Manhattan and the Bronx, examining patterns of Spanish-English bilinguals and related language ideologies. She has taught linguistics and anthropology at Indiana University and, since 1988, at Hamilton College in Clinton, New York. Based on her research on Puerto Rican bilingualism in New York City, Urciuoli began examining the intersection of race, class and linguistic identity, which resulted in several articles and a 1996 book recently re-issued and entitled *Exposing Prejudice: Puerto Rican Experiences of Language, Race, and Class*. In this

book Urciuoli describes how Puerto Rican migrants struggle to adjust to the mainly English-speaking majority. She discusses the history and relationship of the United States and Puerto Rico, in which Puerto Rico has often been referred to as a "backward" and "undeveloped" society. These negative characterizations have consequences for the Puerto Rican migrants who come to the United States and find themselves as a discriminated racial underclass. With Urciuoli's focus on language, she notes how Puerto Rican English is often described as "broken" or "ungrammatical" and how prejudice connects to language and influences discrimination in obtaining jobs and achievements in education. The Puerto Rican migrants are urged to get rid of their accent in order to succeed in business and in education. When Puerto Rican migrants do speak English with teachers, employers, and others, their experience is often fraught with fear and anxiety. Urciuoli studies how "accents," "pronunciation," "tone," and "word choice'" are perceived by people of various ethnic backgrounds, including the Puerto Ricans. Her book indicates that language prejudices are

Bonnie Urciuoli

prevalent in the United States and have a definite influence on how ethnic minorities are treated.

Urciuoli's current research began when she met Latino students from working-class backgrounds at the rural and the largely white affluent student population at Hamilton College in upstate New York. These Latino students were very similar to the Puerto Rican teenagers she encountered in New York City, who were the topic of her book *Exposing Prejudice*. Urciuoli has been publishing articles about how colleges market *multiculturalism* and *diversity* as part of their image, while Latino students and those of other minority groups who provide that diversity often experience social and academic struggles. At times, these Latino students are categorized and diagnosed as having "language interference," or "learning disorders" (Urciuoli 2003). Currently, Urciuoli is conducting in-depth interviews with these Latino students about their educational experiences, which will become her new book on this topic.

Urciuoli has also contributed some unique linguistic anthropological research of the Internet. In an essay entitled "Skills and Selves in the New Workplace" published in the *American Ethnologist*, Urciuoli analyzes the language of Internet corporate Web sites that market skills-related services. She investigates the language that the cor-

porate world uses in which students or workers have to position themselves when seeking and performing their jobs. Corporations include key terms such as *skills*, *communication*, *team*, and *leadership* in their advertisements, workshops, and literature on the Internet. Urciuoli seeks to understand how students and workers are supposed to manage their "selves" in the corporate environment. The corporate world presents "skills" as quantifiable, testable, and subject to ratings. In the early days of the industrial revolution, "skills" were related to the tasks that were needed to perform in the factory. However, currently, the corporate language used tends to construct diverse "soft skills" as easily assessed and unproblematic for evaluating the market value of one's own self in relation to leadership, teamwork, or other management performance criteria. Educational institutions in the United States have

been influenced by what the corporate world deems important for skill development. Students and workers have to market themselves as having a "bundle of skills" in order to become successful. Corporate Web sites and workshops emphasize how students and workers are responsible for developing these "soft skills." However, in reality these diverse skills are not as easily tested and assessed as presented in these corporate advertisements and literature. It is important to realize that this essay was published in 2008, just as the American economy was entering a devastating recession. Since that time, many students have been striving to market themselves for the American economy by developing and presenting these "bundles of skills" for success. Bonnie Urciuoli has contributed toward an understanding of this process with her linguistic anthropological analysis of the Internet.

Republic of the Congo and Brazil to the Arctic regions of Canada, from the deserts of the Middle East to the urban areas of China. The first professional cultural anthropologists conducted research on non-Western or remote cultures in Africa, Asia, the Middle East, Latin America, and the Pacific Islands and on the Native American populations in the United States. Today, however, many cultural anthropologists have turned to research on their own cultures in order to gain a better understanding of their institutions and cultural values.

Cultural anthropologists (sometimes the terms *sociocultural anthropologist* and *ethnographer* are used interchangeably with *cultural anthropologist*) use a unique research strategy in conducting their fieldwork in different settings. This research strategy is referred to as **participant observation** because cultural anthropologists learn the language and culture of the group being studied by participating in the group's daily activities. Through this intensive participation, they become deeply familiar with the group and can understand and explain the society and culture of the group as insiders. We discuss the methods and techniques of cultural anthropologists at greater length in Chapter 14.

The results of the fieldwork of the cultural anthropologist are written up as an **ethnography**, a description of a society. A typical ethnography reports on the environmental setting, economic patterns, social organization, political system, and religious rituals and beliefs of the society under study. This description is based on what

anthropologists call *ethnographic data*. The gathering of ethnographic data in a systematic manner is the specific research goal of the cultural anthropologist. Technically, **ethnology** refers to anthropologists who focus on the cross-cultural aspects of the various ethnographic studies done by the cultural anthropologists. Ethnologists analyze the data that are produced by the individual ethnographic studies to produce cross-cultural generalizations about humanity and cultures. Many cultural anthropologists use ethnological methods to compare their research from their own ethnographic fieldwork with the research findings from other societies throughout the world.

Applied Anthropology

The four subfields of anthropology (biological anthropology, archaeology, linguistic anthropology, and cultural anthropology) are well established. However, anthropologists also recognize a fifth subfield. **Applied anthropology** is the use of anthropological data from the other subfields to address modern problems and concerns. These problems may be environmental, technological, economic, social, political, or cultural. Anthropologists have played an increasing role in the development of government policies and legislation, the planning of development projects, and the implementation of marketing strategies. Although anthropologists are typically trained in one of the major subfields, an increasing number are finding employment outside of universities

Anthropologists at Work

SCOTT ATRAN, Cultural Anthropologist

Born in 1952 in New York City, Scott Atran went to Columbia University as a Westinghouse mathematics scholar. At a student demonstration against the Vietnam War in 1970, he met the famous anthropologist Margaret Mead, and she invited him to work as her assistant at the American Museum of National History. In 1970, Atran also traveled to the Middle East for the first time, conducting fieldwork in Palestinian villages. As a graduate student in 1974, Atran organized a famous debate at the Abbaye de Royaumont in France on the nature of universals in human thought and society, with the participation of some well-known scholars such as the linguist Noam Chomsky, the psychologist Jean Piaget, the anthropologists Claude Lévi-Strauss and Gregory Bateson, and the biologists François Jacob and Jacques Monod, a conference which many consider a milestone in the development of the field known as cognitive science.

Atran continued observing societies as he traveled overland from Portugal to China, via Afghanistan and Pakistan. Landing again in the Middle East, he conducted ethnographic research on kinship and social ties, land tenure, and political economy among the Druze, a religious group in Israel and Lebanon. Later, Atran became a pioneer in the study of the foundations of biological thinking in Western science and other Native American Indian groups such as the Itzá Maya in Mexico. This research became the basis of his well-known books *Cognitive Foundations of Natural History: Towards an Anthropology of Science*, *The Native Mind and the Cultural Construction of Nature*, and *Plants of the Petén Itzá Maya*, which illustrate how people throughout the world classified biological species of plants and animals in very similar ways.

Later, Atran began an investigation of the cognitive and evolutionary foundations of religion, which resulted in his widely acclaimed book *In Gods We Trust: The Evolutionary Landscape of Religion* In this book Atran explores the psychological foundations of religion and how it has become a universal feature of all human societies. He has also contributed toward an understanding of the characteristics associated with suicide bombers and political and religious terrorism in different areas of the world. Atran has been funded by the National Science Foundation and other agencies to study the phenomena of terrorism; this has included fieldwork and interviews with al-Qaeda associates and other militant groups, as well as with political leaders in conflict zones in Europe, the Middle East, Central and Southeast Asia, and North Africa. His recent book *Talking to the Enemy: Faith, Brotherhood and the (Un)Making of Terrorists* is based on this long-term research. In March, 2010, Atran testified before the Senate Armed Services Subcommittee on Emerging Threats and Capabilities today on "Pathways to and from Violent Extremism: The Case for Science-Based Field Research."

Atran has taught at Cambridge University, Hebrew University in Jerusalem, and the École des hautes études en sciences sociales (School for the Advanced Studies of the Social Sciences) in Paris. He is currently a research director in anthropology at the Centre national de la recherche scientifique (The Center for Scientific Research, CNRS) based in Paris and is a member of the Jean Nicod Institute at the École normale supérieure. He is also visiting professor of psychology and public policy at the University of Michigan, presidential scholar in sociology at the John Jay College of Criminal Justice in New York City, and co-founder of ARTIS Research and Risk Modeling. Most recently Atran has become senior fellow and co-founder of the Centre for the Resolution of Intractable Conflicts, at Harris Manchester College and the Department of Social Anthropology, Oxford University.

Atran's broadly interdisciplinary scientific studies on human reasoning

Scott Atran

processes and cultural management of the environment, and on religion and terrorism, have been featured around the world in science publications, such as *Science*, *Nature*, *Proceedings of the National Academy of Sciences USA*, and *Brain and Behavioral Sciences*, as well as the popular press, including features stories with BBC television and radio, National Public Radio, *The Wall Street Journal*, and *Newsweek*. He has been the subject of a cover story in *The New York Times Magazine* ("Darwin's God," 2007) and has written numerous op-eds for the *New York Times* and the magazine *Foreign Policy*.

Atran has teamed up with psychologists and political scientists, including Douglas Medin and Robert Axelrod, to experiment extensively on the ways scientists and lay people categorize and reason about nature, on the cognitive and evolutionary psychology of religion, and on the role of sacred values in political and cultural conflict. Based on recent fieldwork, he has testified before the U.S. Congress and has repeatedly briefed National Security Council staff at the White House on paths to violent extremism among youth in Southeast and South Asia, the Middle East, North Africa, and Europe. Atran has utilized his knowledge and research as a cultural anthropologist to help understand some of the basic questions of human life and also to contribute to solving some of our current problems with globally sponsored political and religious terrorism.

and museums. Although many anthropologists see at least some aspects of their work as applied, it is the application of anthropological data that is the central part of some researchers' careers. Indeed, approximately half of the people with doctorates in anthropology currently find careers outside of academic institutions.

Each of the four major subfields of anthropology has applied aspects. Biological anthropologists, for example, sometimes play a crucial role in police investigations, using their knowledge of the human body to reconstruct the appearance of murder victims on the basis of fragmentary skeletal remains or helping police determine the mechanisms of death. Archaeologists deal with the impact of development on the archaeological record, working to document or preserve archaeological sites threatened by the construction of housing, roads, and dams. Some linguistic anthropologists work with government agencies and indigenous peoples to document disappearing languages or work in business to help develop marketing strategies. Cultural anthropologists, such as A. Peter Castro (see "Anthropologists at Work: A. Peter Castro: Applied Anthropologist"), have played a key role in the planning of government programs so that they take peoples' cultural beliefs and needs into consideration. These applied aspects of anthropological research are highlighted in Chapter 25.

Anthropologists at Work

A. PETER CASTRO, Applied Anthropologist

Conflict over use of the environment is a theme that unites A. Peter Castro's work as an applied cultural anthropologist, including his more than two decades of service as a consultant for the Near East Foundation, the Food and Agriculture Organization of the United Nations (FAO), the United States Agency for International Development (USAID), the United Nations Development Program (UNDP), CARE, and other organizations. Conflict is a ubiquitous aspect of human existence. While disputes may be an important means for people to assert their rights, interests, and needs, conflicts can escalate into violence that threatens both lives and livelihoods. Castro has used his perspective, skills, and knowledge as a cultural anthropologist to address issues related to understanding and dealing with environmental conflicts in participatory and peaceful ways. Besides his ongoing work as a consultant, he incorporates conflict issues into his classes in the anthropology department of the Maxwell School of Citizenship and Public Affairs at Syracuse University, where he is an associate professor.

Castro's interest in environmental conflicts reflects his rural California upbringing, where farm worker unionization struggles, debates about offshore oil development, and conflicts over housing and commercial expansion were everyday occurrences. He credits his professors at the University of California, Santa Barbara, where he obtained his undergraduate and graduate degrees, with giving him the inspiration and training to use cultural anthropology to address pressing social and environmental issues. As an undergraduate, Castro was a research assistant on a number of applied anthropology projects. In classes and through long discussions outside of class, he learned invaluable lessons about issues in health care and agricultural programs and about the importance of linking local, national, and global dimensions of human and environmental crises. Castro's Ph.D. advisor, David Brokensha, has a distinguished record as an applied anthropologist and was instrumental in providing opportunities for Castro to develop contacts in international agencies. Brokensha was one of the founders of the Institute for Development Anthropology, a nonprofit research and educational organization dedicated to applying anthropological theories and methods to improve the condition of the world's poor.

Castro's early work as an applied anthropologist for international organizations focused on practical aspects of planning, managing, and evaluating community forestry programs and

Peter Castro with Darfur people

projects. Although conflict between communities and public forest administrators often propelled the rise of such programs and projects, conflict itself was not initially seen by officials and technical officers as a topic of concern. Nonetheless, Castro found that, whether carrying out applied ethnographic fieldwork on deforestation in Kenya for the USAID or preparing a literature-based review of indigenous forest management practices for the FAO, one needed to take such issues into account. For example, it was apparent that conservation efforts in Kenya could not be understood without relating them to long struggles involving different rural groups, government agencies, commercial interests, and other stakeholders. In addition, Castro discovered through ethnographic interviews and archival research that conflicting parties had sometimes in the past negotiated agreements calling for their co-management of local resources that still had relevance today (for example, see Castro's book

(continued)

Facing Kirinyaga: A Social History of Forest Commons in Southern Mount Kenya, 1995). Castro's concern with integrating historical analysis, as well as conflict analysis, into international development planning is illustrated in his edited collection of articles on the theme "Historical Consciousness and Development Planning" in the interdisciplinary journal *World Development* (1998).

The importance of dealing with environmental conflicts became starkly clear when Castro was asked by UNDP in 1992 to serve as team leader for the midterm evaluation of Bangladesh's Social Forestry Project, a countrywide effort being implemented at a cost of $46 million. The project was supposed to create the capacity for Bangladesh's Forestry Department to engage in community-oriented training, tree planting, and resource protection. While the project had many accomplishments, it also had severe problems in many areas due to lack of public participation. Sadly, a project meant to address long-standing conflicts served to intensify them. The evaluation mission

identified these issues, but because the UNDP could not compel changes, it terminated the project early in some tribal areas where conflict was becoming particularly intense.

Castro worked as a consultant for FAO, writing and editing a number of publications aimed at providing information and practical training on natural resource conflict management. He co-edited a useful book with Antonio Engel called *Negotiation and Mediation Techniques for Natural Resource Management* in 2007. Most recently, Castro is a consultant for the Near East Foundation. He served as lead trainer for workshops on collaborative natural resource conflict management in Zalingei, Central Darfur State, Sudan (in August–September 2012) and in Sévaré, Mopti Region, Mali, in September 2013. Both areas have suffered from conflict. For more than a decade Darfur has suffered from large-scale violence and instability. National political instability and violence in Mali's north and west have had a severe impact on Mopti, including its world-renowned tourist

areas at Djenné and in the Dogon area. The Near East Foundation has projects aimed at contributing to livelihood restoration and peace-building. Trainees at the workshop included local members of the Near East Foundation staff, as well as members from local partner organizations and other NGOs. The Near East Foundation has reported that this training has already directly contributed to several successfully mediated and negotiated agreements in local land conflicts.

Castro is also involved in research on climate change. His research culminated in the co-authored book *Climate Change and Threatened Communities: Vulnerability, Capacity and Action*, edited by A. Peter Castro, Dan Taylor and David W. Brokensha. The book presents 15 case studies from different regions, including two that Castro wrote on highland Ethiopia and on central Darfur (co-authored by Yassir Hassan Satti). Castro's work as an applied anthropologist has been recognized throughout the world.

Holistic Anthropology, Interdisciplinary Research, and the Global Perspective

1.2 Describe how the field of anthropology is holistic, interdisciplinary, and global.

Anthropology is an interdisciplinary, holistic field. Most anthropologists receive some training in each of four subfields of anthropology. However, because of the huge amount of research undertaken in these different subfields—more than 300 journals and hundreds of books are published every year—no one individual can keep abreast of all the developments across the discipline. Consequently, anthropologists usually specialize in one of the four subfields. Nevertheless, most anthropologists are firmly committed to a **holistic** approach to understanding humankind—a broad, comprehensive account that draws on all four subfields under the umbrella of anthropology. This holistic approach integrates the analyses of biological, environmental, psychological, economic, historical, social, and cultural conditions of humanity. In other words, anthropologists study the physical characteristics of humans,

including their genetic endowment, as well as their prehistoric, historic, and social and cultural environments. Through collaborative studies among the various specialists in the four subfields, anthropologists can ask broadly framed questions about humanity.

Anthropology does not limit itself to its own four subfields to realize its research agenda. Although it stands as a distinct discipline, anthropology has strong links to other social sciences. Cultural anthropology, for instance, is closely related to sociology. In the past, cultural anthropologists examined the traditional societies of the world, whereas sociologists focused on modern societies. Today, cultural anthropologists and sociologists explore many of the same societies using similar research approaches. For example, both rely on statistical and nonstatistical data whenever appropriate in their studies of different types of societies.

As we shall discover in later chapters, cultural anthropology also overlaps the fields of psychology, economics, and political science. Cultural anthropologists draw on psychology when they assess the behavior of people in other societies. Psychological questions bearing on perception, learning, and motivation all figure in ethnographic fieldwork. Additionally, cultural anthropologists or ethnologists probe the economic and political behavior and thoughts of people in various societies, using these data for comparative purposes.

Finally, anthropology dovetails considerably with the field of history, which, like anthropology, investigates the human past. Every human event that has ever taken place in the world is a potential topic for both historians and anthropologists. Historians describe and explain human events that have occurred throughout the world; anthropologists place their biological, archaeological, linguistic, and ethnographic data in the context of these historical developments. An important area of anthropological research that overlaps with history is the field of ethnohistory. **Ethnohistory** is the study of the history of a particular ethnic group. Ethnohistory may be based on written historical documents, or more often oral narratives that are recorded by ethnographers working in various regions of the world.

Through the four subfields and the interdisciplinary approach, anthropologists have emphasized a *global perspective*. The global perspective enables anthropologists to consider the biological, environmental, psychological, economic, historical, social, and cultural conditions of humans at all times and in all places. Anthropologists do not limit themselves to understanding a particular society or set of societies, but attempt to go beyond specific or local conditions and demonstrate the interconnections among societies throughout the world. This global perspective is used throughout this text to show how anthropologists situate their findings in the interconnecting worldwide context.

Anthropological Explanations

1.3 **Explain how the scientific method is used in anthropological explanations.**

A fundamental question faced by anthropologists is how to evaluate the particular social, cultural, or biological data they gather. Human knowledge is rooted in personal experience, as well as in the beliefs, traditions, and norms maintained by the societies in which people live. This includes such basic assumptions as putting on warm clothing in cold weather and bringing an umbrella if it is going to rain, for example. Yet, it also includes notions about how food should be prepared, what constitutes "appropriate" behavior, and what the appropriate social and cultural roles are for men and women.

Religion constitutes another source of human knowledge. Religious beliefs and faith are most often derived from sacred texts, such as the Bible, Qur'an, and Talmud, but they are also based on intuitions, dreams, visions, and extrasensory perceptions. Most religious beliefs are

cast in highly personal terms and, like personal knowledge, span a wide and diverse range. People who do not accept these culturally coded assumptions may be perceived as different, abnormal, or nonconformist by other members of their society. Yet, ethnographic and cross-cultural research in anthropology demonstrates that such culturally constituted knowledge is not as general as we might think. This research indicates that as humans, we are not born with this knowledge. Such knowledge tends to vary both among different societies and among different groups within the same society.

Popular perceptions about other cultures have often been based on ethnocentric attitudes. **Ethnocentrism** is the practice of judging another society by the values and standards of one's own society. To some degree, ethnocentrism is a universal phenomenon. As humans learn the basic values, beliefs, and norms of their society, they tend to think of their own culture as preferable, and as what is normal, while ranking other cultures as less desirable. Members of a society may be so committed to their own cultural traditions that they cannot conceive of any other way of life. They often view other cultural traditions as strange or alien, perhaps even inferior, crazy, or immoral.

Such deeply ingrained perceptions are difficult to escape, even for anthropologists. Nineteenth-century anthropologists, for example, often reinforced ethnocentric beliefs about other societies. The twentieth century saw the co-opting of anthropological data to serve specific political and social ends. As the twentieth century progressed, however, anthropologists increasingly began to recognize the biases that prevented the interpretation of other cultures in more valid, systematic ways.

The Scientific Method

Given the preceding concerns, it is critical to understand how anthropological interpretations are evaluated. In contrast to personal knowledge and religious faith, anthropological knowledge is not based on traditional wisdom or revelations. Rather, anthropologists employ the **scientific method**, a system of logic used to evaluate data derived from systematic observation. Researchers rely upon the scientific method to investigate both the natural and the social worlds because the approach allows them to make claims about knowledge and to verify those claims with systematic, logical reasoning. Through critical thinking and skeptical thought, scientists strive to suspend judgment about any claim for knowledge until it has been verified.

Testability and *verifiability* lie at the core of the scientific method. There are two ways of developing testable propositions: the inductive method and the deductive method. In the **inductive method**, the scientist first makes observations and collects data (see Figure 1.2).

Figure 1.2 Deductive and inductive research methods

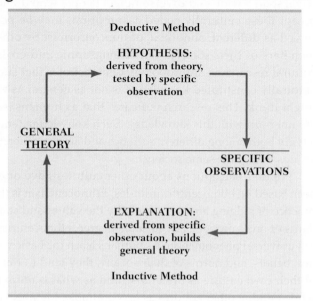

The data collected are referred to as variables. A **variable** is any piece of data that changes from case to case. For example, a person's height, weight, age, and sex all constitute variables. Researchers use the observations about different variables to develop hypotheses about the data. A **hypothesis** is a testable proposition concerning the relationship between particular sets of variables in the collected data. The practice of testing hypotheses is the major focus of the scientific method, as scientists test one another's hypotheses to confirm or refute them. If a hypothesis is found to be valid, it may be woven together with other hypotheses into a more general theory.

Theories are statements that explain hypotheses and observations about natural or social phenomena. Because of their explanatory nature, theories often encompass a variety of hypotheses and observations. One of the most comprehensive theories in anthropology is the theory of evolution (see Chapter 3). This theory explains diverse hypotheses about biological and natural phenomena, as well as discoveries by paleoanthropologists and geneticists.

In contrast to the inductive method, the **deductive method** of scientific research begins with a general theory from which scientists develop testable hypotheses. Data are then collected to evaluate these hypotheses. Initial hypotheses are sometimes referred to as "guesstimates" because they may be based on guesswork by the scientist. These hypotheses are tested through experimentation and replication. As with the inductive method, scientists test and retest hypotheses and theories to ensure the reliability of observations made.

Through these methods, researchers do not arrive at absolute truths. Theories may be invalidated or falsified by contradictory observations. Yet, even if numerous observations and hypotheses suggest that a particular theory is true, the theory always remains open to further testing and evaluation. The systematic evaluation of hypotheses and theories enables scientists to state their conclusions with a certainty that cannot be applied to personal and culturally construed knowledge.

Despite the thoroughness and verification that characterize the research, anthropological explanations have limitations. Anthropologists must grapple with a myriad of complex, interwoven variables that influence human society and biological processes. The complexities of the phenomena being studied make it difficult to assess all of the potential variables, and disagreements about interpretations are common. Consequently, conclusions are frequently presented as tentative and hypothetical. The point here, however, is not that progress is impossible. Anthropological evidence can be verified or discarded by making assumptions explicit and weeding out contradictory, subjective knowledge. Inadequate hypotheses are rejected and replaced by better explanations. Explanations can be made stronger by drawing on independent lines of evidence to support and evaluate theories. This process makes the scientific method much more effective than other means of acquiring knowledge.

Humanistic Interpretive Approaches in Anthropology

1.4 **Discuss how the field of anthropology bridges both the sciences and the humanities.**

The scientific method is not the only means used by anthropologists to study different societies and cultures. Anthropologists also employ a more humanistic-interpretive approach as they study cultures. Think of this analogy: When botanists examine a flower, they attempt to understand the different components of the plant within a scientific framework; they analyze the biochemical and physical aspects of the flower. However, when painters, poets, or novelists perceive a flower, they understand the plant from an aesthetic standpoint. They might interpret the flower as a symbolic phenomenon that represents nature. The scientist and the humanist use different approaches and perspectives when examining the natural world. Anthropologists employ a humanistic-interpretive approach in many circumstances.

James Peacock uses another type of analogy to discuss the difference between the scientific and the humanistic-interpretive approaches in anthropology (1986). Peacock draws from the field of photography to construct his analogy. He discusses the "harsh light" of the rigor of scientific analysis, used to study the biological and material conditions of a society, versus the "soft focus" used when interpreting the symbols, art, literature, religion, or music of different societies. Peacock concludes that both the "harsh light" and the "soft focus" are vital ingredients of the anthropological perspective.

Cultural anthropologists utilize the humanistic-interpretive method as they conduct ethnographic research. However, archaeologists also employ these same methods when examining artifacts from ancient societies. When cultural anthropologists or archaeologists examine various practices and institutions in different societies, they often find that an outsider cannot easily comprehend these phenomena. In order to comprehend these different practices and institutions, cultural anthropologists or archaeologists often have to interpret these phenomena, just as one might interpret a literary, poetic, or religious text. Cultural beliefs and practices may not be easily translatable from one society to another. Cultural anthropologists or archaeologists frequently find practices and institutions that have meaning and significance only within a specific language and culture. Cultural anthropologists or archaeologists endeavor to understand cultural practices or institutions that may have rich, deep, localized meaning within the society being examined, but that are not easily converted into transcultural or cross-cultural meaning. We focus more thoroughly on this humanistic-interpretive approach in Chapter 13 on anthropological explanations.

Thus, in addition to its interconnections with the natural and social sciences, the discipline of anthropology is aligned with the humanistic fields of inquiry. This is particularly true with respect to the field of cultural anthropology, as these researchers are involved in the study of different contemporary cultures. When participating in the life and experience of people in various societies, ethnographers must confront a multitude of different behaviors and values that may have to be translated and interpreted. As mentioned above, archaeologists also confront this type of problem when studying past cultures and civilizations from different regions of the world. Similar issues confront linguistic anthropologists as they translate and understand various languages.

Many anthropologists explore the creative cultural dimensions of humanity, such as myth, folklore, poetry, art, music, and mythology. **Ethnopoetics** is the study of poetry and how it relates to the experiences of people in different societies; for example, a provocative study of the poetry of a nomadic tribe of Bedouins in the Middle East has yielded new insights into the concepts of honor and shame in this society (Abu-Lughod 1987). Another related field, **ethnomusicology**, is devoted to the study of musical traditions in various societies throughout the world. Ethnomusicologists record and analyze music and the traditions that give rise to musical expression, exploring similarities and differences in musical performance and composition.

Ethnomusicologist Dale Olsen completed a fascinating study of Japanese music in South America. There are Japanese minority populations in the countries of Peru, Brazil, Argentina, Paraguay, and Bolivia. Olsen has studied the musical forms, both popular and classical, of these Japanese minorities and how they reflect the maintenance of ethnicity and culture in South America (2004). Other anthropologists study the art of particular societies, such as pottery styles among Native American groups.

Studies of fine art conducted by anthropologists have contributed to a more richly hued, global portrait of humankind. Artistic traditions spring up in all societies, and anthropologists have shed light on the music, myths, poetry, literature, and art of non-Western and other remote peoples. As a result, we now have a keener appreciation of the diverse creative abilities exhibited by humans throughout the world. As anthropologists analyze these humanistic and artistic traditions, they broaden our understanding of the economic, social, political, and religious conditions that prevail within these societies.

One fundamental difference exists between the scientific and the humanistic-interpretive aspects of anthropology. This difference pertains to the amount of progress one can achieve within these two different but complementary enterprises. Science has produced a cumulative increase in its knowledge base through its methodology. Thus, in the fields of astronomy, physics, chemistry, biology, and anthropology, there has been significant progress in the accumulation of knowledge; we know much more about these fields of science than our ancestors knew in the fifteenth or even the nineteenth century. As a result of scientific discoveries and developments, the scientific knowledge in these areas has definitely become more effective in offering explanations regarding the natural and social world. As we shall see in Chapter 13 on anthropological explanations, anthropologists today have a much better understanding of human behavior and culture than did anthropologists in the nineteenth century. Through the use of the scientific method, anthropology has been able to make strides in assessing human behavior and cultural developments.

In contrast, one cannot discuss the progress in the humanities in the same manner. Myth, literature, music, and poetry have not progressed in the way that scientific explanations have. One certainly cannot say that the literature or music of the twenty-first century has progressed beyond that of the time periods of Sophocles, Shakespeare, Dante, Bach, or Beethoven. As we shall see, the various humanistic endeavors involving beliefs, myths, and artistic expression in small-scale and ancient civilizations are extremely sophisticated and symbolically complex, and one cannot assess modern societies as "superior" or more "progressive" in those domains.

The essence of anthropology consists of understanding and explaining human behavior and culture with endeavors monopolized by no single approach. Such an enlarged perspective within anthropology requires peaceful coexistence between scientism and humanism, despite their differences. In a recent discussion of this issue within anthropology, Anne Campbell and Patricia Rice suggest that many anthropologists do not agree with one another's assumptions from either a humanistic or a scientific perspective because of their philosophical commitments to one or the other area (Campbell and Rice 2003). However, anthropologists recognize these differences among themselves, and this is helpful, to a great degree, in making progress in our field because we continue to criticize and challenge one another's assumptions and orientations, which results in a better understanding of both the scientific explanations and the humanistic understandings within our field.

What we are going to find in this textbook is that the many great syntheses of anthropological knowledge require the fusion of both the scientific and the humanistic perspectives. When the archaeologist studies the precision and beauty embodied in the 4,500-year-old pyramids of the Egyptian civilization, he (or she) finds that their inspiration came partly from the mathematics of numbers considered sacred and divine and partly from the emulation of nature. Both scientific and humanistic approaches enable anthropologists to study the sacred and the mundane aspects of nature and culture. When anthropologists combine the scientific and humanistic approaches, they can discover what is transcultural and universal and what is unique to specific societies. This is the major goal of anthropological research: to determine the similarity and differences of humans in the past and the present.

Why Study Anthropology?

1.5   Describe why any student should study anthropology.

Students sometimes question the practical benefits of their educational experience. Hence, you might ask, "Why study anthropology?" First, anthropology contributes to a general liberal arts education, which helps students develop intellectually and personally, as well as professionally. Studies indicate that a well-rounded education contributes to a person's success in any chosen career, and because of its broad interdisciplinary nature, anthropology is especially well suited to this purpose (Briller and Goldmacher 2008). Because students of anthropology can see the "whole picture," they may be able to generate creative solutions to the problems that face humanity today. Anthropology students have diverse and widely applicable skill sets that include research, critical thinking, speaking foreign languages, and an understandings of law, politics, history, biology and economics, just to name a few. Further, anthropology students understand fundamental aspects of what it means to be human—an understanding that can be applied to multiple areas of life.

Critical Thinking and Global Awareness

In the context of a liberal arts education, anthropology and anthropological research cultivate critical thinking skills. As we noted earlier, the scientific method relies on constant evaluation of, and critical thinking about, data collected in the field. By being exposed to the cultures and lifestyles of unfamiliar societies, students may adopt a more critical and analytical stance toward conditions in their own society. Critical thinking skills enhance the reasoning abilities of students wherever life takes them.

Anthropology also creates an expanding global awareness and an appreciation for cultures other than our own. In this age of rapid communication, worldwide travel, and increasing economic interconnections, young

This photo shows three blind Yalunka musicians from Sierra Leone in West Africa. Ethnomusicologists study musical traditions from every area of the world.

people preparing for careers in the twenty-first century must recognize and show sensitivity toward the cultural differences among peoples, while understanding the fundamental similarities that make us all distinctly human. In this age of cultural diversity and increasing internationalization, sustaining this dual perception of underlying similar human characteristics and outward cultural differences has both practical and moral benefits. Nationalistic, ethnic, and racial bigotry are rife today in many parts of the world, yet our continuing survival and happiness depend upon greater mutual understanding. Anthropology promotes a cross-cultural perspective that allows us to see ourselves as part of one human family in the midst of tremendous diversity. Our society needs not just citizens of some local region or group but also, and more importantly, world citizens who can work cooperatively in an inescapably multicultural and multinational world to solve our most pressing problems of bigotry, poverty, and violence.

In addition, an anthropology course gives students a chance to delve into a discipline whose roots lie in both the sciences and the humanities. As we have seen, anthropology brings to bear rigorous scientific methods and models in examining the causes of human evolution, behavior, and social relationships. But anthropologists also try to achieve a humanistic understanding of other societies in all their rich cultural complexity. Anthropology casts a wide net, seeking an understanding of ancient and contemporary peoples, biological and societal developments, and human diversity and similarities throughout the world.

Viewing life from the anthropological perspective, students will also gain a greater understanding of their personal lives in the context of the long period of human evolution and development. In learning about behavior patterns and cultural values in distant societies, students question and acquire new insights into their own behavior. Thus, anthropology nurtures personal enlightenment and self-awareness, which are fundamental goals of education.

While these general goals are laudable, the study of anthropology also offers more pragmatic applications (Omohundro 1998). As seen in the discussion of applied anthropology, all of the traditional subfields of anthropology have areas of study with direct relevance to modern life. Many students have found it useful to combine an anthropology minor or major with another major. For example, given the increasingly multicultural and international focus of today's world, students preparing for careers in business, management, marketing, or public service may find it advantageous to have some anthropology courses on their résumés. The concepts and knowledge gleaned from anthropology may enable students to find practical applications for dealing with issues of cultural and ethnic diversity and multiculturalism on a daily basis. Similarly, policymakers in federal, state, and local governments may find it useful to have an understanding of historic preservation issues and cultural resource management concerns. In education, various aspects of anthropology—including the study of evolution, the human past, and non-European cultures and the interpretation of cultural and social phenomena—are increasingly being integrated into elementary and secondary school curricula. Education majors preparing for the classroom can draw on their background in anthropology to provide a more insightful context for some of these issues.

Summary and Review of Learning Objectives

1.1 Compare and contrast the four major subfields of anthropology.

Anthropology consists of four subfields: biological anthropology, archaeology, linguistic anthropology, and cultural anthropology or ethnology. Each of these subfields uses distinctive methods to examine humanity in the past and in all areas of the world today. Biological anthropologists investigate human evolution and the physical variation of modern human populations throughout the world. Archaeologists study the past by analyzing artifacts (material remains) of past societies. Linguistic anthropologists focus their studies on languages, seeking out historical relationships among languages, pursuing clues to the evolution of particular languages, and comparing one language with another to determine differences and similarities. Cultural anthropologists conduct fieldwork in human societies to examine people's lifestyles. They describe these societies in written studies called ethnographies, which highlight behavior and thought patterns characteristic of the people studied. In examining societies, cultural anthropologists use systematic research methods and strategies, primarily participant observation, which involves participating in the daily activities of the people they are studying.

1.2 Describe how the field of anthropology is holistic, interdisciplinary, and global.

Through the combination of the four subfields in anthropology, many different variables are investigated, ranging from biological factors such as genetics to material artifacts, language, and culture to provide a holistic view of humankind. Anthropology is inherently interdisciplinary and connects with other fields of research such as biology, psychology, economics, history, political science, and sociology, as well as the fine arts and humanities. By its nature, anthropology takes a global approach with its studies of humanity everywhere throughout the world, both past and present.

1.3 Explain how the scientific method is used in anthropological explanations.

Central to anthropological inquiry is the systematic collection and evaluation of data. This includes employing both inductive and deductive methods to evaluate hypotheses and develop theories. Theories explain natural or social phenomena. The conclusions reached are always open to re-evaluation and further testing in light of new data. In this way, faulty interpretations and theories are discarded.

1.4 Discuss how the field of anthropology bridges both the sciences and the humanities.

Anthropologists draw on the scientific method to investigate humanity, while recognizing the limitations of science in grasping the subtleties of human affairs. Yet, anthropology is also a humanistic discipline that focuses on such cultural elements as art, music, and religion. By bridging the sciences and the humanities, anthropology enables us to look at humanity's biological and cultural heritage with a broad perspective.

1.5 Describe why any student should study anthropology.

For students, anthropology creates a global awareness and a deep appreciation of humanity past and present. By evaluating anthropological data, students develop critical thinking skills. And the process of anthropological inquiry—exploring other cultures and comparing them to one's own—sheds light on one's personal situation as a human being in a particular time and place.

Key Terms

anthropology, p. 2
applied anthropology, p. 9
archaeology, p. 5
artifacts, p. 5
biological anthropology, p. 2
cultural anthropology, p. 8
deductive method, p. 14
ethnoarchaeology, p. 6
ethnocentrism, p. 13
ethnography, p. 9
ethnohistory, p. 13

ethnology, p. 9
ethnomusicology, p. 15
ethnopoetics, p. 15
fossils, p. 2
historical linguistics, p. 8
holistic, p. 12
hypothesis, p. 14
inductive method, p. 13
linguistic anthropology, p. 6
linguistics, p. 6
middens, p. 5

paleoanthropology, p. 2
participant observation, p. 9
primates, p. 3
primatology, p. 3
scientific method, p. 13
sociolinguistics, p. 6
structural linguistics, p. 6
theories, p. 14
variable, p. 14

Chapter 2
The Record of the Past

 Learning Objectives

After reading this chapter you should be able to:

2.1 Define paleoanthropology and discuss what we can learn about the past from fossil evidence.

2.2 Discuss what the archaeological record can tell us about past societies.

2.3 Discuss the basic techniques used to locate archaeological sites and fossil localities.

2.4 Discuss the basic techniques of archaeological excavation.

2.5 Compare and contrast how archaeologists and paleoanthropologists date their discoveries.

2.6 Discuss the challenges of interpreting the past and how these are overcome.

19

Why study the human past? During the early history of anthropology, the answer to this question was straightforward. The study of fossils and artifacts of the past sprang out of a curiosity about the world and the desire to collect and organize objects. This curiosity was, in part, a reflection of the increasing interest in the natural world that arose with the Western scientific revolution beginning in the fifteenth century (see Chapter 3). For early collectors, however, the object was often an end in itself. Items were placed on shelves to look at, with little or no interest expressed in where the fossils might have come from or what the artifacts and their associated materials might tell about the people that produced them. Collectors of this kind are called **antiquaries**.

Early antiquarian collections often incorporated many different items in addition to fossils and archaeological materials. For example, the museum of Olaus Wormius, a seventeenth-century Danish scholar, included uniquely shaped stones, seashells, ethnographic objects, and curiosities from around the world, in addition to fossils and ancient stone tools. While these objects were sometimes described and illustrated with great care, they were not analyzed or interpreted to shed light on the evolution of life or on the lifeways of ancient humans. Of course, ancient coins, metal artifacts, and jewelry were recognized for what they were, but stone tools and even ancient pottery were generally regarded as naturally occurring objects or the work of trolls, elves, and fairies (Stiebing 1994).

By the late eighteenth century, scholars started to move beyond the simple description of objects to an increasing appreciation of the significance of fossil remains and the material traces of ancient human societies. This appreciation fell within the context of a host of new observations in the natural sciences, including many about the geological record and the age of the Earth. In 1797, an English country gentleman named John Frere published an account of some stone tools he had found in a gravel quarry in Suffolk. Although brief, the description is tantalizing in terms of the changing attitude toward traces of the past. Fossilized bones of extinct animals and stone tools—actually Paleolithic hand axes—were found at a depth of more than 12 feet in a layer of soil that appeared undisturbed by more recent materials. Frere correctly surmised that the tools were "from a very remote period indeed, even beyond that of the present world" (Daniel 1981:39). This was a recognition of prehistoric archaeology.

The nineteenth century saw the first fossil finds of ancient human ancestors. They included the bones found in the Neanderthal Valley of Germany in 1856, now recognized as an archaic human species, *Homo neanderthalensis*, or Neandertal man (see Chapter 5). Although this was a historic discovery, the significance of the fossils was not realized at the time. The initial interpretations were diverse. Some scholars correctly interpreted the finds as an early human ancestor, but others variously dismissed the bones as those of a Cossack soldier, an elderly Dutchman, a powerfully built Celt, or a pathological idiot (Trinkaus and Shipman, 1993)! Information continued to accumulate, however, and by the end of the nineteenth century, the roots of modern archaeological and paleoanthropological study were well established.

Here we examine the material record of the past and some of the techniques used by modern anthropologists to locate, recover, and date their discoveries. On one hand, this includes the bones and preserved remains used by paleoanthropologists to trace human origins. On the other hand, it deals with the material traces of human behavior that archaeologists focus on to interpret past cultures. In reality, the subdisciplines are often intertwined. Paleoanthropologists use excavation and surveying techniques similar to those used by archaeologists—or they rely on archaeologists—to locate and recover their finds. As to be discussed in Chapter 25, archaeological methods have also played an important role in forensic anthropology.

This book provides an overview of some of the techniques used by paleoanthropologists and archaeologists in their research. It also deals with some of the major questions that have been addressed by anthropologists, including the evolution of the human species, the human settlement of the world, the origins of agriculture, and the rise of complex societies and the state. In reading these discussions, it is important to remember that interpretations are constantly being revised. New fossils are constantly uncovered and archaeological sites exposed. Improved methods also modify the amount and kind of information available to researchers. Each of these discoveries adds to the amount of information available to interpret the past—and to evaluate and revise existing interpretations.

Answering Questions

Few modern archaeologists or paleoanthropologists would deny the thrill of finding a well-preserved fossil, an intact arrow point, or the sealed tomb of a king, but the romance of discovery is not the primary driving force for these scientists. In contrast to popular movie images, modern researchers are likely to spend more time in a laboratory or in front of a computer than looking for fossils or exploring lost cities. Their most fundamental desire is to reach back in time to understand our past more fully.

Although anthropologists make an effort to document the record of bygone ages as completely as possible, they clearly cannot locate every fossil, document every archaeological site, or even record every piece of information about each artifact recovered. Despite decades of research, only a minute portion of such important fossil localities as those in the Fayum Depression in Egypt and Olduvai Gorge in

Tanzania have been studied (see Chapter 4). In examining an archaeological site or even a particular artifact, many different avenues of research might be pursued (see the box "Engendering Archaeology: The Role of Women in Aztec Mexico" below). For example, when investigating pottery from a particular archaeological site, some archaeologists might concentrate on the technical attributes of the clay and the manufacturing process (Rice 1987). Others might focus on the decorative motifs on the pottery and how they relate to the myths and religious beliefs of the people who created them. Still other researchers might be most interested in the pottery's distribution (where it was found) and what this conveys about ancient trade patterns.

Research is guided by the questions about the past that the anthropologists want to answer. In order to formulate these, the researchers review existing data that help place their research in a wider context. Anthropologists also begin by being well grounded in the different theoretical perspectives of anthropology that shape their questions. With this background, anthropologists plan a research project. This is done in a systematic way, as outlined in the discussion of the scientific method in Chapter 1. To ensure that the data recovered are relevant to their questions, paleoanthropologists and archaeologists begin a project by preparing a **research design** in which the objectives of the project are set out and the strategy for recovering the relevant data is outlined. The research design must take into account the types of data that will be collected and how those data relate to existing anthropological knowledge. Within the research design, the anthropologist specifies what methods will be used for the investigation, what regions will be surveyed, how much of a site will be excavated, and how the artifacts will be analyzed. Generally, the research design is then reviewed by other anthropologists, who recommend it for funding by various government agencies or private research foundations.

Critical Perspectives

Engendering Archaeology: The Role of Women in Aztec Mexico

The interpretation of the material record poses a challenge to archaeologists. It provides excellent evidence on some subjects—ancient technology, diet, hunting techniques, and the plan of an ancient settlement—but some topics are more difficult to address. What were the marriage customs, the political system, or the religious beliefs of the ancient inhabitants of a site? These factors are by nature nonmaterial and are not directly preserved archaeologically. Even documentary records may offer only limited insight on some topics.

In a fascinating study of gender among the Aztec of ancient Mexico, archaeologist Elizabeth Brumfiel utilized both the archaeological and the documentary record to provide new insights into the past (Brumfiel 1991, 2005). The Aztec civilization was flourishing in central Mexico when the Spanish reached the Americas. It had emerged as the principal state in the region by the fifteenth century, eventually dominating an area stretching from the Valley of Mexico to modern-day Guatemala,

Aztec codex showing women weaving.

some 500 miles to the southwest. The capital, Tenochtitlán, was an impressive religious center built on an island in Lake Texcoco. The city's population numbered tens of thousands when the Aztec leader, Montezuma, was killed during fighting with Spanish conquistadors led by Hernán Cortés in 1520. Within decades of the first Spanish contact, the traces of the Aztec empire had crumbled and been swept aside by European colonization.

Records of the Aztec civilization survive in documentary accounts recorded by the Spanish. The most comprehensive is a monumental treatise on Aztec life, from the raising of children to religious beliefs, written by Fray Bernardino de Sahagún (Brumfiel 1991). It is the most exhaustive record of a Native American culture from the earliest years of European contact. For this reason, it has been a primary source of information about Aztec life and culture.

Brumfiel was particularly interested in reconstructing the roles of women in Aztec society. Sahagún's description of women focuses on weaving and food preparation. Regrettably, as Brumfiel points out, his work offers little insight into how these endeavors were tied to other economic, political, and religious activities. In addition, Sahagún does not comment on some of his own

(continued)

illustrations that show women involved in such undertakings as healing and marketing. Interpretations based solely on Sahagún's descriptions seemed to marginalize women's roles in production as nondynamic and of no importance in the study of culture change.

To obtain a more holistic view of women in Aztec society, Brumfiel turned to other sources. The Aztecs also possessed their own records. Although most of them were sought out and burned by the zealous Spanish priests, some Aztec codices survive. These sources indicate that textiles were essential as tribute, religious offerings, and exchange. Many illustrations also depict women in food production activities. In addition to various categories of food, the codices show the griddles, pots, and implements used in food preparation.

Independent information on these activities is provided by the archaeological record. For example, the relative importance of weaving can be assessed by the number and types of spindle whorls (perforated ceramic disks used to weight the spindle during spinning) that are found in large numbers on archaeological sites. Archaeological indications of dietary practices can be inferred from ceramic griddles, cooking pots, jars, and stone tools used in the gathering and preparation of food.

Brumfiel notes that the most interesting aspect of archaeological data on both weaving and food preparation is the variation. Given the static model of women's roles seen in the documentary records, a uniform pattern might be expected in the archaeological data. In fact, precisely the opposite is true. Evidence for weaving and cooking activities varies in different sites and over time. Brumfiel suggests that the performance of these activities was influenced by a number of variables, including environmental zones, proximity to urban markets, social status, and intensified agricultural production.

Food preparation, essential to the household, was also integral to the tenfold increase in the population of the Valley of Mexico during the four centuries preceding Spanish rule. As population expanded during the later Aztec period, archaeological evidence indicates that there was intensified food production in the immediate hinterland of Tenochtitlán. Conversely, the evidence for weaving decreases, indicating that women shifted from weaving to market-oriented food production. These observations are not borne out at sites farther away from the Aztec capital, though. In more distant sites, women intensified the production of tribute cloth with which the Aztec empire transacted business.

Brumfiel's research provides insights into the past that neither archaeological nor documentary information can supply on its own. She was fortunate to have independent sources of information that she could draw on to interpret and evaluate her conclusions. Her interpretation of Aztec life provides a much more dynamic view of women's roles. The observations are also consistent with the view of the household as a flexible social institution that varies with the presented opportunities and constraints. Brumfiel's work underscores the importance of considering both women's and men's roles as part of an interconnected, dynamic system.

Points to Ponder

1. In the absence of any documentary or ethnographic information, how can archaeologists examine gender in past societies?
2. Can we automatically associate some artifacts with men or with women?
3. Think of examples of how interpretations of gender would vary in different cultural and archaeological settings.

Paleoanthropological Study

2.1 Define paleoanthropology and discuss what we can learn about the past from fossil evidence.

As discussed in the preceding chapter, paleoanthropology is the field within biological anthropology that focuses on human evolution and the behavior of early human ancestors. As will be discussed in Chapter 5, the behavior, diet, and activities of these early humans were very different from those of modern humans. Determining their behavior, as well as the age of the finds and the environment in which early humans lived, is dependent on an array of specialized skills and techniques. Understanding depends on the holistic, interdisciplinary approach that characterizes anthropology.

As in all anthropological research, a paleoanthropological project begins with a research design outlining the objectives of the project and the methodology to be employed. This would include a description of the region and the time period to be examined, the data that will be recovered, and an explanation of how the proposed research would contribute to existing knowledge.

For example, researchers might target geological deposits of a specific location and age for examination because of the potential to discover the origins of the common ancestors of humans and apes (see Chapter 4), the earliest branches on the human lineage, or the fossil record of the first modern humans (see Chapter 5).

The initial survey work for a paleoanthropological project often relies on paleontologists and geologists, who provide an assessment of the age of the deposits within the region to be studied and the likely conditions that contributed to their formation. Clues about the age may be determined through the identification of distinctive geological deposits and associated floral and faunal remains (see the discussion of dating methods and faunal correlation later in this chapter). Such information also helps in the reconstruction of the paleoecology of the region and, hence, the environment in which early human ancestors lived. **Paleoecology** (*paleo*, from the Greek, meaning "old," and *ecology*, meaning "study of environment") is the study of ancient environments.

Based on the information provided by paleontologists and geologists, more detailed survey work is undertaken to locate traces of early humans. Looking for such traces

Figure 2.1 Only a small number of the creatures that have lived are preserved as fossils. After death, predators, scavengers, and natural processes destroy many remains, frequently leaving only fragmentary traces for researchers to uncover.

has been likened to looking for a needle in a haystack, except in this case the "looking" involves the scrutiny of geological deposits and the careful excavation of buried skeletal remains and associated material. This stage of the research may draw on the skills of the archaeologist, who is trained to examine the material remains of past societies (see later discussion of "Archaeological Excavation").

Fossils and Fossil Localities

Much of paleoanthropological research focuses on the locating and study of fossil remains. Fossils are the preserved remains, impressions, or traces of living creatures from past ages. They form when an organism dies and is buried by soft mud, sand, or silt (Figure 2.1). Over time this sediment hardens, preserving the remains of the creature within. Occasionally, conditions may be such that actual portions of an organism are preserved—fragments of shells, teeth, or bones. But most fossils have been altered in some way, the decayed parts of bone or shell having been replaced by minerals or surrounding sediment. Even in cases in which fragments of bone or shell are present, they have often been broken or deformed and need to be carefully reconstructed. The challenge faced by paleoanthropologists is what criteria to use to distinguish species from a number of closely related taxa on the basis of fragmentary skeletal remains. The unraveling of the genetic codes of living species has also led to debate over the classification. Despite the imperfection of the fossil record, a striking history of life on Earth has survived.

Paleoanthropologists refer to places where fossils are found as **fossil localities**. These are spots where predators dropped animals they had killed, places where creatures were naturally covered by sediments, or sites where early humans lived. Of particular importance in interpreting fossil localities is the **taphonomy** of the site—the study of the variety of natural and behavioral processes that led to the formation of the deposits uncovered. As seen in Figure 2.2, the taphonomy of an individual fossil locality may be complex and the unraveling of the history that contributed to its formation very challenging indeed (Blumenschine

1995; Lyman 2010). The fossil locality may include traces of the activities of early humans—the artifacts resulting from their behavior, tool manufacture, and discarded food remains, as well as the remains of the early humans themselves. On the other hand, these traces may have been altered by a host of disturbances, including erosion by wind and rain, as well as destruction and movement by wild animals.

Only a small number of the once-living creatures are preserved in the fossil record. After death, few animals are left to lie peacefully, waiting to be covered by layers of sediment and preserved as fossils. Many are killed by predators that scatter the bones. Scavengers may carry away parts of the carcass, and insects, bacteria, and weather quickly destroy many of the remains that are left. As a result, individual fossil finds are often incomplete. Some areas might not have had the right conditions to fossilize and preserve remains, or the remains of early human ancestors that may be present might be so fragmentary and mixed with deposits of other ages that they are of limited use. Another consideration is the accessibility of fossil deposits. Fossils may be found in many areas, but they often lie buried under deep deposits that make it impossible for researchers to study them and assess their age and condition. In other instances, however, erosion by wind or water exposes underlying layers of rock that contain fossils, thus providing the

Figure 2.2 A variety of different activities and events contribute to the formation of an individual fossil locality. These include the activities of early human ancestors, but also such natural processes as decomposition and decay, erosion by wind and rain, and movement of bones and artifacts by animals. Paleoanthropologists must try to decipher these different factors in interpreting the behavior of early human ancestors.

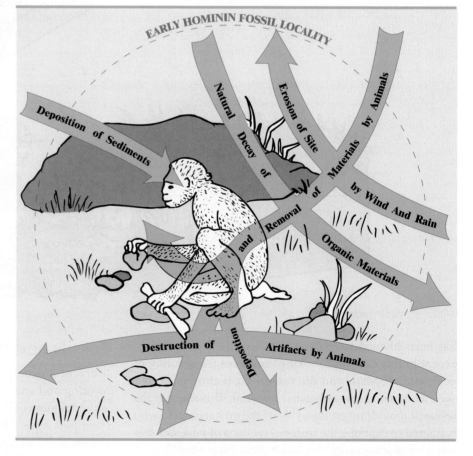

paleoanthropologist the chance to discover them—even as they are weathering away.

Once a fossil locality is found, systematic excavations are undertaken to reveal buried deposits. In excavating, paleoanthropologists take great pains to record a fossil's context. **Context** refers to a fossil's or artifact's exact position in relation to the surrounding sediments and any associated materials. Only if the precise location and associations are known can a fossil be accurately dated and any associated archaeological and paleontological materials be fully interpreted.

After fossils have been removed from the ground, the detailed analysis of the finds begins. This starts with the careful cleaning of fossil remains and associated materials. Fossils are generally preserved in a hardened, mineralized deposit, and cleaning may be tedious and time-consuming. Careful study of fine-grained sediments sometimes reveals the preservation of minute fossils of shellfish, algae, and pollen. Improved techniques, such as computer and electronic scanning equipment, have revealed that images of the delicate structure in bones or the interior of a skull may be preserved in a fossil. Artifacts and faunal remains from the excavations are labeled and carefully described, and any fossil remains of early humans are reconstructed.

Drawing on all of the geological, paleontological, archaeological, and physical anthropological information, the paleoanthropologist then attempts to place the discoveries in the context of other discoveries and interpretations. The anatomical characteristics of the fossils of the early humans will be compared to other fossils to try to assess their evolutionary relationship, and the other data will be brought to bear on the reconstruction of the ancient environment and models of the way they lived. As more evidence is uncovered, the original interpretation may be confirmed, reinterpreted, or declared false in light of the new findings.

Archaeological Research

2.2 Discuss what the archaeological record can tell us about past societies.

As seen in Chapter 1, archaeology is the subdiscipline of anthropology that deals with the study of past human cultures through the material traces they left behind. Culture is a fundamental concept in the discipline of anthropology. In popular use, most people use the word *culture* to refer to "high culture": Shakespeare's works, Beethoven's symphonies, Michelangelo's sculptures, gourmet cooking, imported wines, and so on. Anthropologists, however, use the term in a much broader sense. **Culture** is a shared way of life that includes the material products and nonmaterial products (values, beliefs, and norms) that are transmitted within a particular society from generation to generation. This view of culture includes agricultural practices, social organization, religion, political systems, science, and sports. Culture encompasses all aspects of human activity, from the fine arts to popular entertainment, from everyday behavior to the most deeply rooted religious beliefs. Culture contains the plans, rules, techniques, and designs for living.

In seeking to understand past cultures through their physical traces, archaeologists face an inherent difficulty. By its very nature, culture is *nonmaterial*—that is, it refers to intangible products of human society (such as values, beliefs, religion, and norms) that are not preserved archaeologically. Hence, archaeologists must rely on the artifacts—the physical remains of past societies. This residue of the past is called material culture. **Material culture** consists of the physical products of human society (ranging from weapons to clothing). The earliest traces of material culture are stone tools dating back more than two-and-a half million years: simple choppers, scrapers, and flakes. Modern material culture consists of all the physical objects that a contemporary society produces or retains from the past, such as tools, streets, buildings, homes, toys, medicines, and automobiles. Archaeologists investigate these material traces of societies to examine the values, beliefs, and norms that represent the patterned ways of thinking and acting within past societies. In the study of the more recent past, archaeologists may be able to draw on observations of contemporary peoples, written records, or oral traditions to aid in their interpretation of the archaeological materials found (see the box "Historical Archaeology").

Archaeological interpretation has historically been strongly influenced by cultural anthropology theory (Lamberg-Karlovsky 1989; Trigger 2006). *Cultural anthropology*—the study of modern human populations—helps archaeologists understand how cultural systems work and how the archaeological record might reflect portions of these systems. On the other hand, archaeology offers cultural anthropology a time depth that cannot be obtained through observations of living populations. The archaeological record provides a record of past human behavior. Clearly, it furnishes important insights into past technology, providing answers to such questions as "When did people learn to make pottery?" and "How was iron smelted?" However, artifacts also offer clues to past ideals and belief systems. Consider, for example, what meanings and beliefs are conveyed by such artifacts as a Christian cross, a Jewish menorah, or a Hopi kachina figure. Other artifacts convey cultural beliefs in more subtle ways. Everyday items, such as the knife, fork, spoon, and plate used in Americans' meals, are not the only utensils suitable for the task; indeed, food preference itself is a culturally influenced choice.

Critical Perspectives

Historical Archaeology

Some archaeologists have the luxury of written records and oral histories to help them locate and interpret their finds. Researchers delving into ancient Egyptian sites, the ancient Near East, Greek and Roman sites, Chinese civilization, Mayan temples, Aztec cities, Islamic sites, biblical archaeology, and the settlements of medieval Europe can all refer to written sources ranging from religious texts to explorers' accounts and tax records.

Why dig for archaeological materials if written records or oral traditions can tell the story? Although such sources may provide a tremendous amount of information, they do not furnish a complete record (Deetz 1996; Noel Hume 1983; Orser 2004). Whereas the life story of a head of state, records of trade contacts, or the date of a temple's construction may be preserved, the lives of many people and the minutiae of everyday life were seldom written down. In addition, documentary sources are often biased by the writer's personal or cultural perspective. For example, much of the written history of Native Americans, sub-Saharan Africans, Australian Aborigines, and many other indigenous peoples were recorded by European missionaries, traders, and administrators, who frequently provided only incomplete accounts viewed in terms of their own interests and beliefs.

Information from living informants and oral traditions may also provide important information about some populations, particularly societies with limited written records. In recognizing the significance of such nonwritten sources, however, it is also necessary to recognize their distinct limitations. The specific roles oral traditions played (and continue to play) varied in different cultural settings. Just as early European chroniclers

Archaeologist Merrick Posnansky interviewing the chief of the town of Hani, Ghana. Researchers can use knowledge gathered from living informants to help interpret archaeological finds.
Source: Courtesy of Merrick Posnansky, UCLA.

viewed events with reference to their own cultural traditions, so oral histories are shaped by the worldviews, histories, and beliefs of the various cultures that employ them. Interpreting such material may be challenging for individuals outside the originating cultures. The study of the archaeological record may provide a great deal of information not found in other sources and provide an independent means of evaluating conclusions drawn on the basis of other sources of information (see the box "Engendering Archaeology: The Role of Women in Aztec Mexico"). For example, it has proven particularly useful in assessing change and continuity in indigenous populations during the past 500 years (DeCorse 2001; Lightfoot 2005).

In the Americas, during the past several decades, an increasing amount of work has concentrated on the history of immigrants who arrived in the last 500 years from Europe, Asia, Africa, and other world areas. Archaeological studies have proven of great help in interpreting historical sites and past lifeways,

as well as culture change, sociopolitical developments, and past economic systems. Among the most significant areas of study is the archaeology of slavery (Ferguson 1992; Singleton 1999). Although living in literate societies, slaves were prohibited from writing, were often illiterate, and thus left a very limited documentary record of their own. Archaeological data have been used to provide a much more complete picture of plantation life and slave society.

Points to Ponder

1. What are some different sources of "historical" information—written and orally preserved accounts—that you can think of? How are these different from one another in terms of the details they might provide?

2. Consider a particular activity or behavior important to you (for example, going to school, participating in a sport, or pursuing a hobby). How would evidence of the activity be presented in written accounts, oral histories, and the archaeological record?

The objectives of archaeological research vary tremendously in terms of the time periods, geographical areas, and research questions considered. Many researchers have examined the themes dealt with in this book: the behavior of early human ancestors, the initial settlement of the

Americas, the origins of agriculture, and the emergence of complex political systems. However, other archaeologists have turned their attention to the more recent past and have examined the archaeological record of European colonization over the past 500 years and nineteenth-century

Anthropologists at Work

GEORGE FLETCHER BASS: Underwater Archaeologist

George Fletcher Bass is one of the pioneers of underwater archaeology—a field that he actually did not set out to study and, indeed, a field that was virtually unrecognized as a discipline when he entered it. Although he was always fascinated with the sea and diving, Bass began his career working on land sites, earning a master's degree in Near Eastern archaeology at Johns Hopkins University in 1955. He then attended the American School of Classical Studies at Athens and excavated at the sites of Lerna, Greece, and Gordion, Turkey. Following military service in Korea, Bass began his doctoral studies in classical archaeology at the University of Pennsylvania. It was there, in 1960, that he was asked by Professor Rodney S. Young if he would learn to scuba dive in order to direct the excavation of a Bronze Age shipwreck discovered off Cape Geldonya, Turkey. Bass's excavations of this site marked the first time an ancient shipwreck was excavated in its entirety under the water.

During the 1960s, Bass went on to excavate two Byzantine shipwrecks off Yassi Ada, Turkey. At these sites he developed a variety of specialized methods for underwater excavation, including new mapping techniques, a submersible decompression chamber, and a two-person submarine. In 1967, his team was the first to locate an ancient shipwreck using side-scan sonar. In addition to setting standards for underwater archaeological research, these excavations captured popular imagination and revealed shipwrecks as time capsules containing a spectacular array of artifacts, many unrecovered from terrestrial sites (Throckmorton 1962; Bass 1963, 1973).

After completing his doctorate in 1964, Bass joined the faculty at the University of Pennsylvania. He remained there until 1973, when he left to found the Institute of Nautical Archaeology (INA), which has been affiliated with Texas A&M University since 1976. Under his guidance, the INA has become one of the world's premier programs in underwater archaeology. The institute has conducted research throughout the world on shipwrecks and sites of a diversity of time periods. Bass has continued to focus on shipwrecks in Turkey, where he is an honorary citizen of the town of Bodrum. Some of his more recent projects include a fourteenth-century B.C. wreck with a cargo of copper, ivory, tin, glass, and ebony, and a medieval ship with a large cargo of Islamic glass (Bass et al. 2004). Bass has written or edited more than a dozen books and is the author of over 100 articles. Through his publications, he has introduced both ar-

Dr. George Bass, after a dive.

chaeologists and the wider public to the potential and excitement of underwater archaeology.

Because of his unique contribution to underwater archaeology, Bass has been widely recognized and has received awards from the National Geographic Society, the Explorers' Club, the Archaeological Institute of America, and the Society for Historical Archaeology. President George W. Bush presented him with the National Medal for Science in 2002.

American society; they have even shed light on modern society by sifting through garbage bags and landfills.

The Archaeological Record

The preservation of archaeological materials varies (Lucas 2012; Schiffer 1987). Look at the objects that surround you. How long would these artifacts survive if left uncared for and exposed to the elements? As is the case with the fossil record, the archaeological past is a well-worn and fragmentary cloth rather than a complete tapestry. Stone artifacts endure very well, and thus it is not surprising that much of our knowledge of early human lifeways is based on stone tools. Ceramics and glass may also survive very well, but iron and

copper corrode, and organic materials, such as bone, cloth, paper, and wood, generally disappear quickly.

In some cases, environmental conditions that limit insect and microbial action and protect a site from exposure to the elements may allow for the striking preservation of archaeological materials. Some of the most amazing cases are those in which items have been rapidly frozen. An illustration of this kind of preservation is provided by the discovery in 1991 of the 5,300-year-old frozen remains of a Bronze Age man by hikers in Italy's Tyrol Mountains (Fowler 2000). With the body were a wooden backpack, a wooden bow, 14 bone-tipped arrows, and fragments of clothing. In other instances, underwater sites, waterlogged environments, very dry climate, or rapid burial

Critical Perspectives

Underwater Archaeology

Sunken ships, submerged settlements, and flooded towns: This wide variety of sites of different time periods in different world areas shares the need for specialized techniques to locate, excavate, and study them (Bass 2005; Menotti 2004). Although efforts were occasionally made in the past to recover cargoes from sunken ships, it was only with the invention and increasing accessibility of underwater breathing equipment during the twentieth century that the systematic investigation of underwater sites became feasible. Often artifacts from underwater sites are better preserved and so present a wider range of materials than those from land. Even more important,

Remains of the Mary Rose.

underwater sites are immune to the continued disturbances associated with human activity that are typical of most land sites. Shipwrecks can be compared to time capsules, containing a selection of artifacts that were in use in a certain context at a specific time. Archaeologists working on land seldom have such clearly sealed archaeological deposits.

A tantalizing example of an underwater archaeological project is the excavation and raising of the preserved remains of the *Mary Rose*, the pride of the young English Navy and the flower of King Henry VIII's fleet. The 700-ton warship, which was probably the first English warship designed to carry a battery of guns between its decks, foundered and sank in Portsmouth harbor on a warm July afternoon in 1545. Henry VIII, camped with his army at Southsea Castle, is said to have witnessed the disaster and heard the cries of the crew. In the 1970s, the site of the *Mary Rose* was rediscovered and was systematically explored by volunteer divers from around the world. The ship produced a spectacular array of over 14,000 artifacts, ranging from massive cannons to musical instruments, famed English longbows, and navigational equipment. Finds from the *Mary Rose* and the preserved portions of the hull can be seen at the Mary Rose Ship Hall and Exhibition at the Her Majesty's Naval Base, Portsmouth, England (Marsden 2003, 2009).

Most people associate underwater archaeology with sunken ships, and

this, in fact, represents an important part of the subdiscipline. However, rising sea levels or natural disasters may also submerge cities and towns. Research on settlements now underwater is providing increasing insight into early human settlement (Bass 2005; Menotti 2004). As in the case of shipwrecks, the lack of oxygen and the sealed nature of the archaeological materials present special challenges in excavation, but also remarkable preservation. Such is the case of Port Royal, Jamaica, a flourishing trade center and infamous gathering place for pirates during the seventeenth century. In 1692, a violent earthquake and tidal wave submerged or buried portions of the city, preserving a record for future archaeologists. Excavations at the site spanning the last three decades have recovered a wealth of materials from seventeenth-century life (Hamilton and Woodward 1984).

Points to Ponder

1. Archaeological excavation on land is a meticulous and careful process. Discuss how excavation and recording methods would have to be modified to conduct archaeological research underneath the water.
2. Given the unique location and preservation found at underwater sites, why might they be more appropriate or important than land sites for considering certain types of research questions?

---

may create conditions for excellent preservation. Such unique instances provide archaeologists with a much more complete record than is usually found.

Places of past human activity that are preserved in the ground are called **archaeological sites**. Sites reflect the breadth of human endeavor. Some are settlements that may have been occupied for a considerable time—for example, a Native American village or an abandoned gold-mining town in the American West. Other sites reflect specialized activities—for instance, a ceremonial center, a burial ground, or a place where ancient hunters killed and butchered an animal.

Much of the archaeologist's time is devoted to the study of artifacts—any object made or modified by humans. They include everything from chipped stone tools and pottery to plastic bottles and computers. Nonmovable artifacts, such as an ancient fire hearth, a pit dug in the ground, or a wall, are called **features**. In addition to artifacts and features, archaeologists examine items recovered from archaeological sites that were not produced by humans, but nevertheless provide important insights into the past. Animal bones, shells, and plant remains recovered from an archaeological site furnish information on both the past climatic conditions and the diet of the early

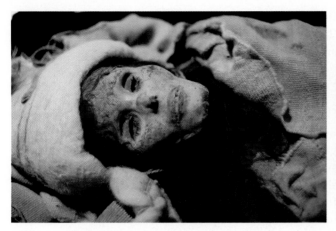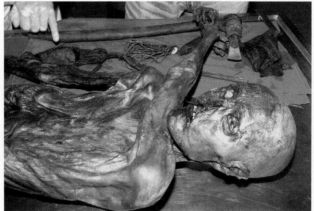

In some cases, environmental conditions may allow for amazing preservation, as illustrated by the 4,000-year-old naturally mummified remains of a woman discovered in the arid hills near the Chinese city of Ürümqi (left) and the 5,300-year-old frozen remains of a man found in Italy's Tyrol mountains (right).

inhabitants. The soil of a site is also an important record of past activities and the natural processes that affected a site's formation. Fires, floods, and erosion all leave traces in the earth for the archaeologist to discover. All of these data may yield important information about the age, organization, and function of the site being examined. These non-artifactual organic and environmental remains are referred to as **ecofacts**.

As is the case with the recovery of fossils, the archaeologist takes special care to record the *contexts* in which archaeological materials are found: the artifacts' specific location in the ground, and associated materials. Without a context, an artifact offers only a limited amount of information. By itself, a pot may be identified as something similar to other finds from a specific area and time period, but it provides no new information. If, however, it and similar pots are found to contain offerings of a particular kind and are associated with female burials, a whole range of other inferences may be made about the past. By removing artifacts from sites, laypersons unwittingly cause irreparable damage to the archaeological record.

Locating Sites and Fossil Localities

2.3 **Discuss the basic techniques used to locate archaeological sites and fossil localities.**

In 1940, schoolboys retrieving their dog from a hole in a hillside near Montignac, France, found themselves in an underground cavern. The walls were covered with delicate black and red paintings of bison, horses, and deer. The boys had discovered Lascaux Cave, one of the finest known examples of Paleolithic cave art. Chance findings

such as this sometimes play a role in the discovery of archaeological remains, as well as paleoanthropological research, but researchers generally have to undertake a systematic examination, or **survey**, of a particular area, region, or country to locate archaeological sites or fossil localities. They will usually begin by examining previous descriptions, maps, and reports of the area for references to archaeological sites. Informants who live and work in the area may also be of great help in directing archaeologists to discoveries.

Of course, some archaeological sites are more easily located than others: the great pyramids near Cairo, Egypt; Stonehenge in southern England; and the Parthenon of Athens have never been lost. Though interpretations of their precise use may differ, their impressive remains are difficult to miss. Unfortunately, many sites, particularly some of the more ancient, are more difficult to locate. The settlements occupied by early humans were usually small, and only ephemeral traces are preserved in the ground. In many instances, they may be covered under many feet of sediment. Examination of the ground surface may reveal scatters of artifacts, discolorations in the soil, or exposed fossils, which provide clues to buried deposits. Sometimes nature inadvertently helps researchers, as erosion by wind or rain may expose sites. Archaeologists can also examine road cuts, building projects, and freshly plowed land for archaeological materials. Fossils are often deeply buried, resting beneath layers of sediment, making locating them especially difficult. For this reason, paleoanthropologists often cannot employ many of the techniques archaeologists use to locate shallower archaeological deposits.

In the field, the researcher defines what areas will be targeted for survey. These areas will be determined by the research design, but also by environmental and

Electrical resistivity survey directed by Matthew Johnson under way at Bodiam Castle, East Sussex, England. Photograph taken by Dr. David Underhill.

topographical considerations, as well as the practical constraints of time and money. Surveys can be divided into *systematic* and *unsystematic* approaches (Renfrew and Bahn 2012). The latter is easier as the researcher simply walks over trails, riverbanks, and plowed fields in the survey area and takes note of any archaeological material. In a similar way, paleoanthropologists searching for fossils may examine places where buried sediments have been exposed by erosion. This approach avoids the problem of climbing through thick vegetation or rugged terrain. Unfortunately, it may also produce a biased sample of the archaeological remains present; ancient land uses might have little correspondence with modern trails or plowed fields.

Researchers use many different methods to ensure more systematic results. In some instances, a region, valley, or site is divided into a *grid*, which is then walked systematically. In other instances, transects may provide useful information, particularly where vegetation is very thick. In this case, a straight line, or *transect*, is laid out through the area to be surveyed. Fieldworkers then walk along this line, noting changes in topography, vegetation, and artifacts.

Subsurface Archaeological Testing and Survey

Because many archaeological sites are buried in the ground, many surveys incorporate some kind of subsurface testing. This may involve digging auger holes or shovel test pits at regular intervals in the survey, the soil from which is examined for any traces of archaeological material. This technique may provide important information on the location of an archaeological site, its extent, and the type of material represented.

Today, many different technological innovations allow the archaeologist to prospect for buried sites without lifting a spade. The utility of these tools can be illustrated by the magnetometer and resistivity meter. The **proton magnetometer** is a sensor that can detect differences in the soil's magnetic field caused by buried features and artifacts. A buried foundation will give a different reading from an ancient road, both being different from the surrounding undisturbed soil. As the magnetometer is systematically moved over an area, a plan of buried features can be created.

Electrical **resistivity** provides similar information, though it is based on a different concept. A resistivity meter is used to measure the electrical current passing between electrodes that are placed in the ground. Variation in electrical current indicates differences in the soil's moisture content, which in turn reflects buried ditches, foundations, or walls that retain moisture to varying degrees.

Although at times yielding spectacular results, techniques such as magnetometer and resistivity surveys are not without their limitations. Buried metal at a site may confuse the magnetic readings of other materials, and a leaking hose wreaks havoc with a resistivity meter. Both techniques may produce confusing patterns as a result of shallowly buried geological features such as bedrock.

Remote Sensing

An archaeologist was once heard to say that "one ought to be a bird to be a field archaeologist," and indeed, the perspective provided by **aerial photography**, sometimes called "aerial archaeology," has been a boon to archaeologists. Experiments with aerial photography occurred prior to World War I, but it was during the war that its potential importance to archaeological surveys was recognized (Daniel 1981:165). Pilots noticed that some sites, invisible on the ground, were dramatically seen from the air. The rich organic soils found in archaeological sites, subtle depressions in the ground surface, or slight differences in vegetation resulting from buried features may be dramatically illustrated in aerial photographs. More recent

Anthropologists at Work

SCOTT MADRY: Google Earth and Armchair Archaeology

The value of aerial photography and high-tech satellite imagery in archaeology is well demonstrated, but the cost of such resources has often placed them beyond the reach of most archaeologists. But this situation is changing. Once the purview of governments and space programs, high-altitude images are becoming both more common and of more general interest, and archaeologists are reaping the benefits.

A case in point is Google Earth, a popular desktop program that provides satellite imagery, allowing users to zoom in on specific locales and even track their own movements. The program is useful in getting directions and checking out vacation spots, as well as an aid in planning for a variety of nonprofit and public benefit organizations. Archaeologist Scott Madry became curious about the potential use of Google Earth in his long-term research on the archaeology of Burgundy, France (Madry 2007). Madry is interested in the application of aerial photography, remote sensing, and geographic information systems technology to understanding the interaction between the different cultures and the physical environment over the past 2,000 years. While he found that the images available on Google Earth were of limited use in his research area, the data available

Satellite photo of the Nile River in Egypt illustrates the stark contrast between the river's floodplain and the surrounding desert. At the southern edge of the image is Luxor, which includes the ruins of the ancient Egyptian city of Thebes. Archaeologists are increasingly able to use space-age technology to locate archaeological features.

for a neighboring region that shared a similar environment and culture history provided dramatic images of archaeological sites. Although many of these sites had been previously identified, the results demonstrated the potential of Google Earth as an archaeological research tool.

Google Earth is not the perfect solution for every research situation. The coverage is dependent on the images available and is of variable quality. Consequently, it is of limited use for some areas. Even in cases where good images are available, thick vegetation and tree cover may limit the use of both satellite images and aerial photography. Finally, while the images provided by Google Earth may help in locating and mapping sites, archaeologists still need to excavate.

technological innovations, such as the use of infrared, false color photography, help identify differences in vegetation and make abandoned settlements and patterns of past land use more apparent. Aerial photography has proven very important in locating sites, but it is also of particular use in mapping and interpretation (Brophy and Cowley 2005; Kruckman 1987).

Of increasing use to archaeologists are photographs or images taken from extremely high altitudes by satellites or space shuttles. The scale of these pictures sometimes limits their use, and their cost sometimes makes them beyond the reach of many researchers (Madry 2003; Madry et al. 2003). The potential application of such sophisticated techniques, however, has been well demonstrated. National Aeronautics and Space Administration (NASA) scientists, working with archaeologists, have been able to identify ancient Mesopotamian and Mayan settlements and farmlands that had not been located with other techniques. *Space imaging radar*, which can detect features buried under six feet of sand, proved helpful in identifying ancient caravan routes on the Arabian Peninsula. These routes enabled researchers to locate the lost city of Ubar, a trade center that was destroyed around 100 A.D., and the city of Saffara on the

Aerial photography often allows the identification of archaeological sites that may be invisible on the ground. This aerial photograph of a recently plowed cornfield in Perry County, southern Illinois, led to the discovery of the Grier Site. Subsequent excavation revealed an ancient Native American site that had been occupied for thousands of years; the burials date to about 1000 B.C.
Source: Courtesy of Larry Kruckman, Indiana University of Pennsylvania.

Indian Ocean (Clapp 1998). As this technology becomes both more refined and more affordable, it will provide an increasingly important resource for archaeologists (see box "Anthropologists at Work: Scott Madry).

Archaeological Excavation

2.4   Discuss the basic techniques of archaeological excavation.

Archaeological surveys provide invaluable information about the past. The distribution of sites on the landscape offers knowledge about the use of natural resources, trade patterns, and political organization. Surveys also help define the extent of specific sites and allow for a preliminary assessment of their age and function. These data are invaluable in interpreting regional developments and how individual sites form part of a larger picture. For example, changes in settlement patterns have been used to assess the development of sociopolitical complexity and state level societies (see Chapter 9). However, depending on the project's research objectives, an archaeologist may want more detailed information about individual sites. Once an archaeological site has been located, it may be targeted for systematic archaeological excavation (Figure 2.3).

Excavation is costly, time-consuming, and also destructive. Once dug up, an archaeological site is gone forever; it can be "reassembled" only through the notes kept by the archaeologist. For this reason, archaeological excavation is undertaken with great care. Although picks and shovels, or even bulldozers, may occasionally come into play, the tools used most commonly are the trowel, whisk broom, and dustpan. Different techniques may be required for different kinds of sites. For example, more care might be taken in excavating the remains of a small hunting camp than a nineteenth-century house in an urban setting covered with tons of modern debris. On underwater sites, researchers must contend with recording finds using

specialized techniques while wearing special breathing apparatus (see the boxes "Underwater Archaeology" and "George Fletcher Bass: Underwater Archaeologist"). Nevertheless, whatever the site, the archaeologist carefully records the context of each artifact uncovered, each feature exposed, and any changes in surrounding soil.

Work usually begins with clearing the site and preparing a detailed site plan. A grid is placed over the site. This is usually fixed to a **datum point**, some permanent feature or marker that can be used as a reference point and will allow the excavation's exact position to be relocated. As in the case of other facets of the research project, the research design determines the areas to be excavated. Excavations of *midden* deposits, or ancient trash piles, often provide insights into the range of artifacts at a site, but excavation of dwellings might provide more information into past social organization, political organization, and socioeconomic status.

A question often asked of archaeologists is how deep they have to dig to "find something." The answer is, "Well, that depends." The depth of any given archaeological deposit is contingent upon a wide range of variables, including the type of site, how long it was occupied, the types of soil represented, and the environmental history of the area. In some cases, artifacts thousands or even hundreds of thousands of years old may lie exposed on the surface. In other cases, flooding, burial, or cultural activities may cover sites with thick layers of soil. A clear illustration of this is seen in *tells* (settlement mounds) in the Near East, which sometimes consist of archaeological deposits covering more than 100 square acres hundreds of feet deep.

Dating Methods

2.5   Compare and contrast how archaeologists and paleoanthropologists date their discoveries.

How old is it? This simple question is fundamental to the study of the past. Without the ability to temporally order

Figure 2.3 Excavation, archaeological plan, and artist's reconstruction of an eighteenth-century slave cabin at Seville Plantation, St. Anne's, Jamaica. The meticulous recording of excavated artifacts and features allows archaeologists to reconstruct the appearance of past settlements. In this case, eighteenth-century illustrations and written descriptions helped the artist add features, such as the roof, that were not preserved archaeologically.
Source: Courtesy of Douglas V. Armstrong, Syracuse University.

fossils, archaeological sites, and artifacts, there is no way to assess evolutionary change, cultural developments, or technological innovations. Paleoanthropologists and archaeologists employ many different dating techniques. Some of these are basic to the interpretation of both the fossil record and archaeological sites. Others are more appropriate for objects of certain ages or for particular kinds of materials (for example, volcanic stone, as opposed to organic material). Hence, certain techniques are more typically associated with archaeological research than paleoanthropological research, and vice versa. In any given project, several different dating techniques are used in

Archaeologists taking notes from an excavation.

Relative Dating Relative dating refers to dating methods that determine whether one particular fossil, artifact, fossil locality, or site dates before or after another. Relative dating methods do not provide an actual date, just an age relative to something else. The most basic relative dating method is **stratigraphic dating**, a technique pioneered by the seventeenth-century Danish scientist Niels Stensen (1638–1687). Today, Stensen is better known by the Latinized version of his name, Nicholas Steno. Steno was the first person to suggest that the hard rock where fossils are found had once been soft sediments that had gradually solidified. Because sediments had been deposited in layers, or *strata*, Steno argued that each successive layer was younger than the layers underneath. Steno's **law of supraposition** states that in any succession of rock layers, the lowest rocks have been there the longest and the upper rocks have been in place for progressively shorter periods. This assumption forms the basis of stratigraphic dating.

Steno was concerned with the study of geological deposits, but stratigraphic dating is also of key importance in dating archaeological materials (Figure 2.4). An

conjunction with one another to independently validate the age of the materials being examined. Dating methods can be divided into two broad categories that incorporate a variety of specific dating techniques: relative dating and numerical dating. Accurate dating of discoveries depends upon both methods. The following discussion is not exhaustive, but rather intended to illustrate the different kinds of dating methods that have been employed.

Excavation of a burial in Warszawa, Poland.

SOURCE: Courtesy of **Marek E. Jasinski,** Institute of Historical Studies, Archaeology Programme Norwegian University of Science and Technology.

Figure 2.4 Archaeological materials and the remnants of human occupation often accumulate to striking depths. This hypothetical profile illustrates the potentially complex nature of the archaeological record and how different techniques might be combined to date discoveries.

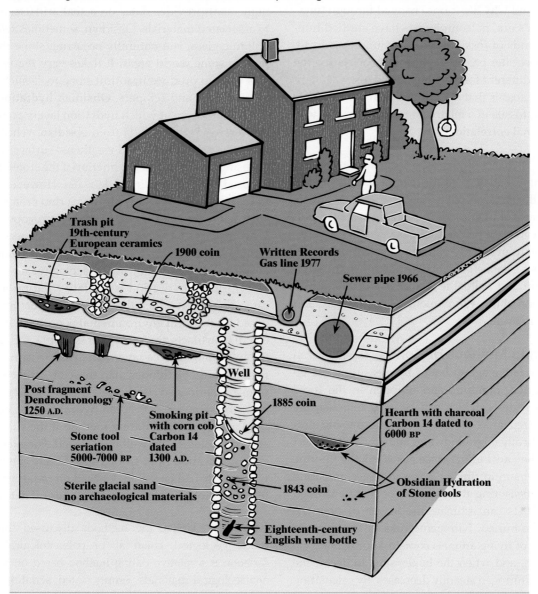

archaeological site presents a complex layer cake of stratigraphic levels representing the accumulation of cultural material, such as trash and housing debris, as well as natural strata resulting from flooding, the decomposition of organic material, and the like. Layers associated with human occupation often accumulate to striking depths.

Like all relative dating methods, stratigraphic dating does not allow researchers to assign an actual numerical age to a fossil or artifact. Rather, it indicates only whether one fossil is older or younger than another within the same stratigraphic sequence. This technique is essential to paleoanthropological and archaeological interpretation because it allows researchers to evaluate change through time. However, researchers must take notice of any disturbances that may have destroyed the order of geological or archaeological deposits. Disturbances in

the Earth's crust, such as earthquakes and volcanoes, can shift or disrupt stratigraphic layers. Archaeological sites may be ravaged by erosion, burrowing animals, and human activity.

Faunal Succession One of the first people to record the location of fossils systematically was William Smith (1769–1839), the "father" of English geology (Winchester 2002). An engineer at a time when England was being transformed by the construction of railway lines and canals, Smith noticed that as rock layers were exposed by the construction, distinct fossils occurred in the same relative order again and again. He soon found that he could arrange rock samples from different areas in the correct stratigraphic order solely on the basis of the fossils they contained. Smith had discovered the principle of faunal succession (literally, "animal" succession). A significant scientific milestone, Smith's observations were made 60 years before Darwin proposed his evolutionary theories to explain how and why life-forms changed through time.

Since Smith's era, paleontologists have studied hundreds of thousands of fossil localities around the world. Fossils from these sites provide a means of correlating the relative ages of different fossil localities and also cast light on the dating of fossils that are not found in stratigraphic context. Placing fossils in a relative time frame in this way is known as **faunal correlation**.

Palynology

Remains of plant species, which have also evolved over time, can be used for relative dating as well. **Palynology** is the study of pollen grains, the minute male reproductive parts of plants. By examining preserved pollen grains, we can trace the adaptations vegetation underwent in a region from one period to another. In addition to helping scientists establish the relative ages of strata, studies of both plant and animal fossils offer crucial clues to the reconstruction of the environments where humans and human ancestors lived.

Relative Dating Methods of Bones

Scientists can determine the relative age of bones by measuring the elements of fluorine, uranium, and nitrogen in the fossil specimens. These tests, which can be used together, are sometimes referred to as the *FUN trio*. Fluorine and uranium occur naturally in groundwater and gradually collect in bones after they are buried. Once absorbed, the fluorine and uranium remain in the bones, steadily accumulating over time. By measuring the amounts of these absorbed elements, scientists can estimate the length of time the bones have been buried. Nitrogen works in the opposite way. The bones of living animals contain approximately 4 percent nitrogen, and when the bones start to decay, the concentration of nitrogen steadily decreases. By calculating the percentage of nitrogen remaining in a fossilized bone, scientists can calculate its approximate age.

The FUN trio techniques all constitute relative dating methods because they are influenced by local environmental factors. The amounts of fluorine and uranium in groundwater differ from region to region, and variables such as temperature and chemicals present in the surrounding soil affect the rate at which nitrogen dissipates. Because of this variation, relative concentrations of fluorine, uranium, and nitrogen in two fossils from different areas of the world may be similar despite the fact that they differ significantly in age. The techniques are thus of greatest value in establishing the relative age of fossils from the same deposit. These methods have been supplanted by more modern, numerical dating methods but they were historically important in establishing the relative ages of fossil finds (see "The Piltdown Fraud" in Chapter 5).

Obsidian Hydration

Obsidian hydration is a relative dating method that has proven very useful in dating artifacts made from obsidian. It is a particularly useful technique as it provides dates on actual artifacts, as opposed to associated materials. Obsidian, sometimes referred to as volcanic glass, is a naturally occurring stone that is common in some world areas. It flakes very regularly and so was used to produce beautiful stone tools such as knives, spear points, and scrapers. **Obsidian hydration** dating is based on the rate at which hydration layers accumulate on the surface of tools made from obsidian. When an obsidian artifact is made, the old weathered surface is flaked off, exposing the unweathered interior of the stone. This newly exposed surface contains little water. However, over time, the surface absorbs water, forming a rind or layers that can be measured using a high powered microscope. As the water is absorbed at a regular rate, the thickness of the hydration layers provides an indication of the relative ages of obsidian artifacts within an archaeological site.

Obsidian hydration is a relative dating method because the rate at which the hydration layers form is influenced by the local environmental conditions in which the obsidian artifacts are found. For example, the thickness of the hydrated surface layers on artifacts from a very dry region would be thinner than those on artifacts recovered from a waterlogged site, despite the fact that the sites might be of the same age. Obsidian hydration can, however, be used as a numerical dating method if the site conditions and chronologies are well understood. For example, if obsidian hydration rates from a specific site can be tied to a well-established chronology based on radiocarbon dating, they will provide quite accurate numerical dates.

Seriation

Unlike the methods discussed thus far that utilize geological, chemical, or paleontological principles, seriation is a relative dating method based on the study of archaeological materials. Simply stated, **seriation** is a dating technique based on the assumption that any particular artifact, attribute, or style will appear, gradually increase in popularity until it reaches a peak, and then progressively decrease. Systematic change in style can be seen in a wide range of material cultural, ranging from stone tools to clothing fashions and automobile designs. Archaeologists measure changes in artifact types by comparing the relative percentages of certain attributes or styles in different stratigraphic levels in a site or across different sites. Using the principle of increasing and decreasing popularity of attributes, archaeologists are then able to place the artifacts in a relative chronological order. Seriation was particularly important for chronologically ordering ceramics and stone tools before the advent of many of the numerical dating techniques discussed later.

The principles of seriation can be illustrated by examining stylistic changes in New England gravestones of the seventeenth, eighteenth, and nineteenth centuries. Unlike

Figure 2.5 The seriation of gravestones in a New England cemetery by archaeologist James Deetz illustrates the growth and gradual decline in popularity of a closely dated series of decorative motifs.
Source: From In Small Things Forgotten by James Deetz. Copyright © 1996 by James Deetz. Used by permission of Doubleday, a division of Random House, Inc.

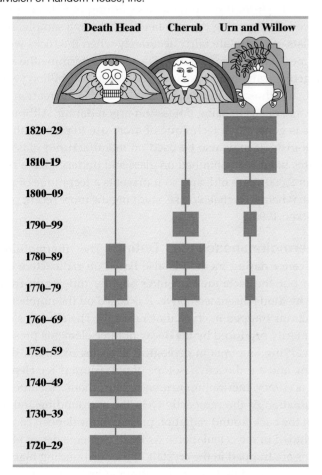

many artifacts, gravestones can be closely dated, and so can be used to evaluate the principle of seriation. Archaeologist James Deetz charted how designs on dated colonial gravestones changed through time (Deetz 1996). His study of gravestones in Stoneham Cemetery, Massachusetts, as illustrated in Figure 2.5, demonstrates the validity of the method. In the course of a century, death's-head motifs were gradually replaced by cherub designs, which in turn were replaced by urn and willow decorations. The study also illustrates how local variation in beliefs and trade patterns may influence the popularity of an attribute.

Numerical or Absolute Dating

In contrast to relative dating techniques, numerical dating methods (sometimes also referred to as "absolute" or "chronometric" methods) provide actual ages. For recent time periods, historical sources such as calendars and dating systems that were used by ancient peoples provide numerical dates. Mayan and Egyptian sites, for example,

can often be dated by inscriptions carved into the monuments themselves (see the discussion of Writing Systems in Chapter 9). However, such written records only extend back a few thousand years, and these sources are not available for many regions. Researchers have consequently explored a variety of methods to establish the age of fossil finds and archaeological discoveries.

During the nineteenth century, scientists experimented with many methods designed to pinpoint the numerical age of the Earth itself. A number of these methods were based on observations of the physical world. Studies of erosion rates, for instance, indicated that it had taken millions of years to cut clefts in the earth like the Grand Canyon in the United States. Other strategies were based on the rates at which salt had accumulated in the oceans, the Earth had cooled, and geological sediments had formed (Prothero 1989). By observing current conditions and assuming a standard rate at which these processes had occurred, scientists calculated the amount of time represented. These early approaches were flawed, however, by a limited understanding of the complexity of natural processes involved and the range of local conditions. Therefore, these techniques at best provide only crude relative dating methods. In contrast to these early researchers, today's scientists have a wide variety of highly precise methods of dating paleontological and archaeological finds (Aitken 1990; Brothwell and Pollard 2001).

Several of the most important numerical dating techniques used today are based on *radioactive decay*, a process in which *radioisotopes*, unstable atoms of certain elements, break down or decay by throwing off subatomic particles and energy over time. These changes can produce either a different isotope of the same element or another element entirely. In terms of dating, the significance of radioactive decay is that it occurs at a set rate regardless of environmental conditions, such as temperature fluctuations, amount of groundwater, or the depth below surface. The amount of decay that has taken place can be measured with a device called a *mass spectrometer*. Hence, by calculating how much decay has occurred in a geological specimen or an artifact, scientists can assign a numerical age to it.

Radiocarbon Dating   Radiocarbon dating, also known as carbon-14 dating, is perhaps the best known and most common numerical dating technique used by archaeologists. It is of particular importance because it can be used to date any organic matter that contains carbon, including fragments of ancient wooden tools, charcoal from ancient fires, and skeletal material. The technique of using radioactive decay as a dating tool was pioneered by Willard Libby, who received the 1960 Nobel Prize in chemistry for his work on radiocarbon dating.

Radiocarbon dating, as its name implies, is based on the decay of carbon-14 (^{14}C), a radioactive (unstable) isotope of carbon that eventually decays into nitrogen. The concentration of carbon-14 in a living organism is comparable to that of the surrounding atmosphere and is absorbed by the organism as carbon dioxide (CO_2). When the organism dies, the intake of CO_2 ends. Thus, as the carbon-14 in the organism begins to decay, it is not replaced by additional radiocarbon from the atmosphere.

Like other radioisotopes, carbon-14 decays at a known rate that can be expressed in terms of its *half-life*, the interval of time required for half of the radioisotope to decay. The half-life of carbon-14 is 5,730 years. By measuring the quantity of carbon-14 in a specimen, scientists can determine the amount of time that has elapsed since the organism died.

The use of accelerator mass spectrometry (AMS), which makes it possible to determine the number of individual atoms of ^{14}C remaining in a sample, has allowed for more precise dating and also for the dating of much smaller samples. Dates of up to 80,000 years old have been obtained, but the technique is generally limited to dating materials less than about 60,000 years old (Plastino et al. 2001; Taylor and Southon 2007). The minuscule amounts of radiocarbon remaining in materials older than this make measurement difficult. Because of the time period represented, radiocarbon is of limited use to paleoanthropologists who may be dealing with fossil finds millions of years old. However, radiocarbon dating is of great importance to archaeologists who deal with materials of more recent age.

Potassium-Argon and Fission-Track Dating

Several isotopes that exhibit radioactive decay are present in rocks of volcanic origin. Some of these isotopes decay at very slow rates over billions of years. Two radiometric techniques that have proven of particular help to paleoanthropologists and archaeologists studying early human ancestors are potassium-argon and fission-track dating. These methods do not date fossil material itself. Rather, they can be used to date volcanic ash and lava flows that are associated with fossil finds. Fortunately, many areas that have produced fossil discoveries were volcanically active in the past and can be dated by using these techniques. These methods have been employed at such fossil localities as the Fayum Depression in Egypt (see Chapter 4), Olduvai Gorge in Tanzania, and Hadar, Ethiopia (see Chapter 5).

In **potassium-argon dating**, scientists measure the decay of a radioisotope of potassium, known as potassium-40 (^{40}K), into an inert gas, argon (^{40}Ar). During the intense heat of a volcanic eruption, any argon present in a mineral is released, leaving only the potassium. As the rock cools, the potassium-40 begins to decay into argon. Because the half-life of ^{40}K is 1.3 billion years, the potassium-argon method can be used to date very ancient finds, and has thus been important in dating fossils of early human ancestors. Although this technique has been used to date

volcanic rocks a few thousand years old, the amount of argon is so small that it is more commonly used on samples dating over 100,000 years (McDougall and Harrison 1999).

Fission-track dating is based on the decay of a radioactive isotope of uranium (^{238}U) that releases energy at a regular rate. In certain minerals, microscopic scars, or tracks, from the spontaneous splitting of ^{238}U are produced. By counting the number of tracks in a sample, scientists can estimate fairly accurately when the rocks were formed. Fission-track dating is used to determine the age of geological samples between 300,000 and 4.5 billion years old, and thus it can provide independent confirmation on the age of strata using potassium-argon dating. Although this is generally a technique of more use to paleoanthropologists, it may also be used on manufactured glasses. Dates have been obtained on glass and pottery glazes less than 2,000 years old, and so it presents a technique of potential help to archaeologists studying the more recent past (Aitken 1990).

Thermoluminescence Dating

The **thermoluminescence dating** method is also based on radioactive decay, but the technique operates slightly differently from the methods discussed above. It is based on the number of electrons trapped in crystalline minerals. The electrons are primarily produced by the decay of three elements present in varying amounts in geological deposits: uranium, thorium, and a radioactive isotope of potassium (^{40}K). Hence, for accuracy, thermoluminescence dates should include an evaluation of the radioactivity in the surrounding soil so that the background radiation present in the deposit can be included in the calculations. As these elements decay, electrons are trapped in the crystals of the surrounding matrix. In order to be dated using the technique, artifacts must have been heated, as in the case of the firing of ceramics. Heating releases any trapped electrons; decay subsequently begins again, and electrons once again start to accumulate in the crystal matrix of the object. By calculating the rate at which electrons have accumulated and measuring the number of electrons trapped in a sample, the age can be determined.

The importance of thermoluminescence dating lies in the fact that it can be used to date artifacts themselves, as opposed to associated stratigraphic deposits, as with potassium argon dating. Thermoluminescence dating has been particularly useful in dating ceramics—one of the most common artifacts found on sites dating to the last 10,000 years. It has, however, also been used in cases where stone tools have been heated during their manufacture or time of use (some stone becomes easier to work with if heated). Similarly, it has been used in cases where the clay or stone of a hearth area has been heated; the key once again is that the sample has been heated at the time of use or manufacture to set the amount of accumulated electrons to zero. Dates of tens or hundreds of thousands of years have been obtained on stone tools (Aitken et al. 1993). The method has also proven very useful in differentiating modern fakes from ancient ceramic objects.

Dendrochronology Dendrochronology is a unique type of numerical dating based on the annual growth rings found in some species of trees (Figure 2.6). Because a ring corresponds to a single year, the age of a tree can be determined by counting the number of rings. This principle was recognized as early as the late eighteenth century by the Reverend Manasseh Cutler, who used it to infer that a Native American mound site in Ohio was at least 463 years old. The modern science of dendrochronology was pioneered in the early twentieth century by A. E. Douglass, using well-preserved wood from the American Southwest.

Today tree-ring dating is a great deal more sophisticated than counting tree rings. In addition to recording annual growth, tree rings also preserve a record of environmental history: thick rings represent years when the tree received ample rain; thin rings denote dry spells. In more temperate regions, the temperature and the amount of sunlight may affect the thickness of the rings. Trees of the same species in a localized area will generally show a similar pattern of thick and thin rings. This pattern can then be overlapped with patterns from successively older trees to build up a master dendrochronology sequence. In the American Southwest, a sequence using the bristlecone pine has now been extended to almost 9,000 years ago. Work on oak sequences in Ireland and Germany has been used to create a master dendrochronology sequence dating back over 10,000 years.

The importance of this method is manifest. Dendrochronology has proven of great significance in areas such as the American Southwest, where the dry conditions often preserve wood. The growth rings in fragments of wood from archaeological sites can be compared to the master dendrochronology sequence, and the date the tree

Figure 2.6 Dendrochronology is based on the careful examination of distinct patterns of thin and thick growth rings that preserve a record of a region's environmental history. As illustrated here, samples of wood from different contexts may be pieced together to provide a master dendrochronology. Fragments of wood from archaeological sites can then be compared to this dendrochronology to determine the period in which the tree lived.

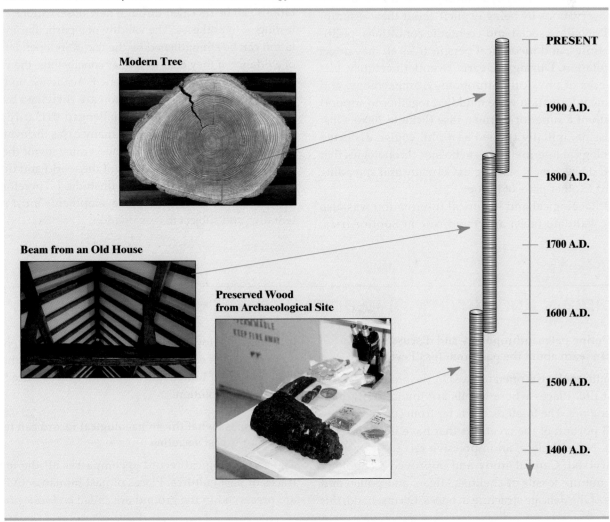

was cut down can be calculated. Even more important, dendrochronology provides an independent means of evaluating radiocarbon dating. Fragments dated by both techniques confirm the importance of radiocarbon as a dating method. However, wood dated by both techniques indicates that carbon-14 dates more than 3,000 years old are increasingly younger than their actual age. The reason for this lies in the amount of carbon-14 in the Earth's atmosphere. Willard Libby's initial radiocarbon dating calculations were based on the assumption that the concentration was constant over time, but we now know that it has varied. Dendrochronologies have allowed scientists to correct, or calibrate, radiocarbon dates, rendering them more accurate.

Interpretations About the Past

2.6 Discuss the challenges of interpreting the past and how these are overcome.

Views of the past are, unavoidably, tied to the present. As we discussed in Chapter 1, anthropologists try to validate their observations by being explicit about their assumptions. Prevailing social and economic conditions, political pressures, and theoretical perspectives all may affect interpretation. During the early twentieth century, bits and pieces of physical anthropology, archaeology, and linguistic information were muddled together to support the myth of a superior German race (Pringle 2006). Gustav Kossina, initially trained as a philologist, distorted archaeological interpretations to bolster chronologies that showed development starting in Germany and spreading outward to other parts of Europe.

Archaeological and historical information was also used to validate racist apartheid rule in South Africa.

South African textbooks often proffered the idea that black, Bantu-speaking farmers migrating from the north and white and Dutch-speaking settlers coming from the southwest arrived in the South African hinterland at the same time. This interpretation had clear relevance to the present: Both groups had equal claim to the land. However, archaeological evidence knocked out the foundations of this contrived history (Hall 1988). Archaeological evidence indicates that the ancestors of the black South Africans had moved into the region by 200 A.D., 1,500 years before the initial European settlement.

In these cases, versions of the past were constructed with dangerous effects on the present. More commonly, errors in interpretation are less intentional and more subtle. All researchers carry their own personal and cultural biases with them. Human societies are complex, and how this complexity is manifested archaeologically varies. These factors make the evaluation of interpretations challenging, and differences of opinion frequently occur.

Although there is no formula that can be used to evaluate all paleoanthropological and archaeological materials, there are useful guidelines. As seen in the preceding chapter, a key aspect of anthropological research is a systematic, scientific approach to data. Outmoded, incorrect interpretations can be revealed through new observations and the testing of hypotheses. The validity of a particular interpretation can be strengthened by the use of independent lines of evidence; if they lead to similar conclusions, the validity of the interpretation is strengthened. Academic books and articles submitted for publication are reviewed by other researchers, and authors are challenged to clarify points and strengthen observations. In many cases the evaluation of a particular theory or hypothesis must await the accumulation of data. Many regions of the world and different aspects of the past are virtually unstudied. Therefore, any theories about these areas or developments must remain tentative and subject to reevaluation.

Summary and Review of Learning Objectives

2.1 Define paleoanthropology and discuss what we can learn about the past from fossil evidence.

Paleoanthropologists often use fossils, the preserved traces of past life. Places where fossils are found are termed *fossil localities*. The fossil record is far from complete; only a small portion of the creatures that have lived are preserved. Nevertheless, an impressive record of past life has survived. Careful study and improved technology reveal minute fossils of shellfish, algae, and pollen and images of the delicate structure in bones. On one hand, this

information allows for the reconstruction of the environments in which early human ancestors lived. On the other hand, fossils of human ancestors are used to trace human origins and evolution.

2.2 Discuss what the archaeological record can tell us about past societies.

The archaeological record encompasses all the material traces of past cultures. Places of past human activity that are preserved in the ground are called *archaeological sites*.

Sites contain artifacts (objects made or modified by humans), as well as other traces of past human activity and a record of the environmental conditions that affected the site. In studying archaeological materials, archaeologists are particularly interested in the context, the specific location of finds and associated materials. Understanding the context is of key importance in determining the age, uses, and meanings of archaeological materials.

2.3 Discuss the basic techniques used to locate archaeological sites and fossil localities.

Archaeological sites and fossil localities provide important information about the past. They may be located in many different ways. Often traces of a site may survive on the ground, and local informants, maps, and previous archaeological reports may be of help. To discover sites, archaeologists may survey large areas, looking for any indications of archaeological remains. Technological aids such as aerial photographs and satellite imagery may help locate sites. Surface examinations may be supplemented by subsurface testing, as well as tools such as the magnetometer or resistivity meter to help archaeologists identify artifacts and features beneath the ground. Fossils are often deeply buried, resting beneath layers of sediment, making locating them especially difficult. For this reason, paleoanthropologists often cannot employ many of the techniques archaeologists use to locate shallower archaeological deposits.

2.4 Discuss the basic techniques of archaeological excavation.

Depending on a project's objectives, archaeological sites may be targeted for excavation, which can be thought of a "scientific digging." Excavation is always undertaken with great care, and the material recovered carefully recorded. Although picks and shovels may sometimes be used, hand trowels and dust brooms remain the most important tools. Before excavation, a site is divided into a grid, which allows for the context of each artifact to be carefully noted.

The depth of an excavation depends on a number of variables, including the type of site, the length of occupation, the soils present, and the area's environmental history.

2.5 Compare and contrast how archaeologists and paleoanthropologists date their discoveries.

Dating of fossils and archaeological materials is of key importance in the interpretation of the past. Without the ability to place finds in their relative ages, there is no way of assessing evolutionary change, technological innovations, or cultural developments. Paleoanthropologists and archaeologists use many different dating techniques that can be classified as either relative or absolute dating methods. Methods such as stratigraphic dating, faunal succession, and obsidian hydration provide only relative ages for finds in the same deposits. In contrast, numerical dating techniques like radiocarbon dating, potassium-argon dating, and dendrochronology can be used to assign actual numerical ages to finds.

2.6 Discuss the challenges of interpreting the past and how these are overcome.

Interpretations of the past are inevitably influenced by the present. At times interpretations about the past have been used to support political ends, as seen in Nazi Germany and the apartheid policies of South Africa. Researchers try to avoid biases by employing systematic, scientific methodology. Theories can be revealed as false through testing and replaced by more convincing arguments. These, in turn, can be negated or strengthened by exploring new lines of evidence. Archaeological theories, often derived from cultural anthropology, help archaeologists conceptualize how cultures work and what aspects of a past culture might be preserved archaeologically. Ultimately, this reflection provides a more complete explanation of the dynamics of past cultures and culture change.

Key Terms

aerial photography, p. 30
antiquaries, p. 20
archaeological sites, p. 28
context, p. 25
culture, p. 25
datum point, p. 32
dendrochronology, p. 39
ecofacts, p. 29
faunal correlation, p. 36
faunal succession, p. 36

features, p. 28
fission-track dating, p. 38
fossil localities, p. 24
law of supraposition, p. 34
material culture, p. 25
obsidian hydration, p. 36
paleoecology, p. 22
palynology, p. 36
potassium-argon dating, p. 38
proton magnetometer, p. 30

radiocarbon dating, p. 37
relative dating, p. 34
research design, p. 21
resistivity, p. 30
seriation, p. 36
stratigraphic dating, p. 34
survey, p. 29
taphonomy, p. 24
thermoluminescence dating, p. 38

Chapter 3
Evolution

 ## Learning Objectives

After reading this chapter you should be able to:

3.1 Explain how cosmologies regarding human origins differ from scientific views of evolution.

3.2 Discuss how the scientific revolution provided the context for the theory of evolution.

3.3 Explain how Darwin's view of natural selection and evolution differed from earlier scientific views.

3.4 Discuss Gregor Johann Mendel's principles of inheritance.

3.5 Discuss how Mendel's principles of inheritance have changed in light of a better understanding of molecular genetics.

3.6 Define and discuss how evolution takes place.

3.7 Discuss how and why new species arise.

3.8 Briefly outline the evidence for the evolution of life on Earth and how evolutionary relationships are evaluated.

One of the major questions biological anthropologists grapple with is the origins of humankind. The fossil record preserves evidence of past life on Earth, tracing a progression of simple one-celled organisms to increasingly diverse forms. A small portion of the fossil record relevant to human evolution is presented in Chapters 4 and 5. How did these different forms of life emerge and new species arise? The biological explanations for this process is the focus of this chapter.

Theories concerning the evolution of life date back to the ancient Greeks, but it was only during the nineteenth century that the first comprehensive theories of evolution were developed. They were made possible through discoveries in many different areas. The acceptance of evolutionary theory is based on research in many fields. Indeed, the value of evolutionary theory is its utility as a unifying explanation for a wide variety of phenomena. Before examining the scientific basis for our understanding of evolution, it is useful to consider other explanations of human origins.

Cosmologies and Human Origins

3.1 Explain how cosmologies regarding human origins differ from scientific views of evolution.

The most profound questions are the ones that perplex us the most. Where did we come from? Why are we here? What is our place in the universe? These questions have been shared by many people throughout history. Most cultures have developed explanations that provide answers to these fundamental questions. **Cosmologies** are conceptual frameworks that present the universe (the *cosmos*) as an orderly system. They often include answers to these basic questions about human origins and the place of humankind in the universe, usually considered the most sacred of all cosmological conceptions.

Cosmologies account for the ways in which supernatural beings or forces formed human beings and the planet we live on. These beliefs are transmitted from generation to generation through ritual, education, laws, art, and language. For example, the Navajo people of the southwestern United States believe that the Holy People, supernatural and sacred, lived below ground in 12 lower worlds. A massive underground flood forced the Holy People to crawl through a hollow reed to the surface of the Earth, where they created the universe. A deity named Changing Woman gave birth to the Hero Twins, called Monster Slayer and Child of the Waters. Human mortals, called Earth Surface People, emerged, and First Man and First Woman were formed from the ears of white and yellow corn.

In the tradition of Taoism, male and female principles known as *yin* and *yang* are the spiritual and material sources for the origins of humans and other living forms. Yin is considered the passive, negative, feminine force or principle in the universe, the source of cold and darkness, whereas yang is the active, positive, masculine force or principle, the source of heat and light. Taoists believe that the interaction of these two opposite principles brought forth the universe and all living forms out of chaos. These examples illustrate just two of the highly varied origin traditions held by different people around the world.

Western Traditions of Origins

In Western cultural traditions, the ancient Greeks had various mythological explanations for human origins. One early view was that Prometheus fashioned humans out of water and earth. Another had Zeus ordering Pyrrha, the inventor of fire, to throw stones behind his back, which in turn became men and women. Later Greek views considered biological evolution. The Greek philosopher Thales of Miletus (c. 636–546 B.C.) attempted to understand the origin and the existence of the world without reference to mythology. He argued that life originated in the sea and that humans initially were fishlike, eventually moving onto dry land and evolving into mammals.

The most important cosmological tradition affecting Western views of creation is recounted in the biblical Book of Genesis, which is found in Greek texts dating back to the third century B.C. This Judaic tradition describes how God created the cosmos. It begins with "In the beginning God created the heaven and the earth" and describes how creation took six days during which light, heaven, Earth, vegetation, Sun, Moon, stars, birds, fish, animals, and humans originated. Yahweh, the Creator, made man, Adam, from "dust" and placed him in the Garden of Eden. Woman, Eve, was created from Adam's rib. Later, as Christianity spread throughout Europe, this tradition became the dominant cosmological explanation of human origins.

In Europe before the Renaissance, the Judeo-Christian view of creation provided the only framework for understanding humanity's position in the universe. The versions of creation discussed in the biblical text fostered a specific concept of time: a linear, nonrepetitive, unique historical framework that began with divine creation. These events were chronicled in the Bible; there was no concept of an ancient past stretching far back in time before human memory. This view led some theologians to attempt to calculate the precise age of the Earth on the basis of information in the Bible, such as references to births and deaths and the number of generations mentioned. One of the best known of these calculations was done by Archbishop James Ussher of Ireland (1581–1656). By calculating the number of generations mentioned in the Bible

This painting by Michelangelo in the Sistine Chapel represents the idea of spiritual creation, the dominant worldview in Western cosmology for centuries.

and drawing of classical writers, Ussher dated the beginning of the universe to the year 4004 B.C. Thus, according to Bishop Ussher's estimate, the Earth was approximately 6,000 years old.

The biblical account of creation led to a static, fixed view of plant and animal species and the age of the Earth. Because the Bible recounted the creation of the world and everything on it in six days, medieval theologians reasoned that the various species of plants and animals must be fixed in nature. God had created plant and animal species to fit perfectly within specific environments and did not intend for them to change. They had been unaltered since the time of the divine creation, and no new species had emerged. This idea regarding the permanence of species influenced the thinking of many early scholars and theologians.

The Scientific Revolution

3.2   Discuss how the scientific revolution provided the context for the theory of evolution.

In Europe during the Renaissance (after c. 1450 A.D.), scientific discoveries began to challenge conceptions about both the age of the Earth and humanity's relationship to the rest of the universe. Copernicus and Galileo presented the then novel idea that the Earth was not circled by the celestial bodies, but rather was just one of several planets revolving around the sun. As this idea became accepted, humans could no longer view themselves and their planet as the center of the universe, which had been the traditional belief. This shift in cosmological thinking set the stage for entirely new views of humanity's links to the rest of the natural world. New developments in the geological sciences began to radically revise the estimates of the age of the Earth, which contradicted a literal reading of the biblical account of creation. These and other scientific discoveries in astronomy, biology, chemistry, physics, and mathematics dramatically transformed Western thought, including ideas about humankind (Henry 2002).

Among the most dramatic ideas to result from the scientific revolution was the theory of evolution, which sees plant and animal species originating through a gradual process of development from earlier forms. Although it is not intended to contradict cosmologies, it is based on a different kind of knowledge. Cosmological explanations frequently involve divine or supernatural forces that are, by their nature, impossible for human beings to observe. We accept and believe in them, on the basis of faith. Scientific theories of evolution, in contrast, are derived from the belief that the universe operates according to regular processes that can be observed. The scientific method is not a rigid framework that provides indisputable answers. Instead, scientific theories are propositions that can be evaluated by testing and observation. Acceptance of the theory of evolution is based on observations in many areas of geology, paleontology, and biology.

Catastrophism versus Uniformitarianism

The pre-Renaissance view of a static universe and of an Earth a few thousand years old with unchanging species posed problems for early geologists and naturalists (a term used at that time to refer to biologists), who were beginning to study the thick layers of stone that cover the earth and the fossilized remains they contained. Many of the forms of life represented in these fossils were unlike any living species. How long had it taken to form these thick deposits of soil and stone? How old were the remains of the strange creatures represented in the fossil remains? The geological record did not fit within the time frame that a literal reading of the biblical account of creation allowed.

As evidence for the great antiquity of the Earth and for many extinct animal species accumulated, some scholars proposed theories that attempted to reconcile the geological and fossil records with the biblical account of Genesis. One interpretation was presented by Georges Chrétien Léopold Frédéric Dagobert Cuvier (1769–1832), a French naturalist who is sometimes called the father of zoology (Rudwick 1997). Georges Cuvier, as he is more commonly known, studied the fossil record, including the remains of extinct, prehistoric elephant-like animals called *mammoths* in the vicinity of Paris. He also noted the successive replacement of fossil species through time. However, he saw species as fixed and unchanging. He proposed the geological theory known as **catastrophism**, which reasoned that the Earth had been created and destroyed multiple times. The extinct species represented in the fossil record had disappeared through a series of catastrophes of divine origin. Some species of animals might survive these events, just as the account of creation in the Book of Genesis recounted that animals collected by Noah and taken aboard the ark survived the biblical flood. The new species of animals that appeared in the following layers represented a new creation event. Catastrophism became the best-known geological explanation consistent with the literal interpretation of the biblical account of creation.

Other geologists challenged catastrophism and the rigidity of nature through scientific studies. They noted evidence that suggested the Earth changed through gradual, natural processes that were still observable. This view, which provided the basis for later geological interpretations, became known as **uniformitarianism** (Repcheck 2003). One of the first proponents of this perspective was the French naturalist and keeper of the king's gardens, Georges-Louis Leclerc, the Comte de Buffon (1707–1788). In 1774, Buffon theorized that the Earth changed through gradual, natural processes that were still observable. He proposed that rivers had created canyons, waves had changed shorelines, and other forces had transformed the features of the Earth. After being criticized by theologians, Buffon attempted to coordinate his views with biblical beliefs. He suggested that the six days of creation described in the Bible should not be interpreted literally. Buffon rather suggested that these passages actually refer to six *epochs* representing a gradual period of creation rather than 24-hour days. Each epoch consisted of thousands of years in which the Earth and different species of life were transformed. Although Buffon's interpretation allowed more time for geological changes in the Earth's past, there was no geological evidence for the six epochs of gradual creation.

As information on the geological record accumulated, the uniformitarian view eventually became the mainstream position in geology. In 1795, James Hutton, in his landmark book *Theory of the Earth*, explained how natural processes of erosion and deposition of sediments had formed the various geological strata of the Earth. Hutton observed that these natural processes must have taken thousands of years. In his book, he estimated that the Earth was at least several million years old. In 1833, the English scholar, Charles Lyell (1797–1875), noted by some as the father of modern geology, reinforced the uniformitarian view. In his *Principles of Geology*, Lyell discussed natural processes, such as volcanoes, earthquakes, glaciers, erosion, and decomposition that shaped the geological landscape. More importantly, in a readable and comprehensive way, he observed that these processes were still observable and had been constant—uniform—over time. He also argued that scientists could deduce the age of the Earth from the rate at which sediments are deposited and by measuring the thickness of rocks. Through these measurements, Lyell also concluded that the Earth was millions of years old.

Modern geologists have a far better understanding of geological processes and much more sophisticated means of dating the Earth. As will be discussed later, the age of the Earth is now estimated to be billions, rather than millions, of years, divided into five major ages and many other periods and epochs (see page 62). Although many of the views of Buffon, Hutton, and Lyell have been superseded, they were historically important in challenging traditional views of a static universe with fixed species. Their fundamental points concerning the consistent and ongoing natural processes that have shaped the geological landscape have been reaffirmed by modern research. The uniformitarian view thus set the stage for an entirely new way of envisioning the universe, the Earth, and the living forms on the planet.

Theory of Evolution

3.3 Explain how Darwin's view of natural selection and evolution differed from earlier scientific views.

The scientific revolution also led to changing perspectives regarding the origin of species and humankind's place in nature. There were discoveries of archaeological remains and contacts with the non-Western populations that were unmentioned in any written records including the Bible and classical Greek and Roman writings. Where did the Native American Indians come from? Were they one of the lost tribes of Israel referred to in the Bible, or were they created separately and without souls, as some sixteenth-century scholars suggested (Adovasio and Page, 2002, 5)? Antiquarians—as collectors of artifacts and curiosities of the past were sometimes called—of the eighteenth and nineteenth centuries increasingly began to recognize archaeological materials that predated written history. The relative ages of both fossils and archaeological materials could be dated by their stratigraphic positions (see relative dating methods in Chapter 2), suggesting periods older than the historically known Greek and Roman civilizations. There were also many discoveries of fossil remains clearly unlike any living species. Scholars, including many clergy, documented systematic change through time in the fossil species represented (see discussion of faunal succession in Chapter 2). How were these finds to be explained? Scholars started to question the fixity of species and a literal interpretation of the biblical account of creation. They suggested that plants and animals had evolved—changed through time—through natural processes.

Evolution refers to the process of change in the genetic makeup of a species over time. It is used to explain the emergence of new species. Evolutionary theory holds that existing species of plants and animals have emerged over millions of years from simple organisms. Although the theory of evolution is usually associated with Charles Darwin, the idea that modern plants and animals could change was posited by a number of scholars prior to the mid-1800s. Georges-Louis Leclerc, the Comte de Buffon (1707–1788), who had argued that the Earth changed through gradual, natural processes, also underscored the changing nature of species and their ability to adapt to local environmental conditions. Erasmus Darwin (1731–1802), an eighteenth-century physician and Charles Darwin's grandfather, also suggested evolutionary concepts. However, none of these early theorists suggested a unified theory that *explained* evolution. They proposed no reasonable mechanism for evolution and, consequently, most people could not accept these ideas.

A more comprehensive early theory that attempted to explain evolution was posited by a French chemist and biologist, Jean-Baptiste Pierre Antoine de Monet, Chevalier de Lamarck (1744–1829). Lamarck proposed that species could change as a result of dynamic interactions with their environment. As a result of changing environmental conditions, behavioral patterns of a species would alter, increasing or decreasing the use of some physical structures. As a result of these changing physical needs, the *besoin* (the force for change within organisms) would be directed to these areas, modifying the appropriate structures and enabling the animals to adapt to their new environmental circumstances. In other words, if a particular animal needed specialized organs to help in adaptation, these organs would evolve accordingly. In turn, because the characteristics made the animal better suited to its environment, these new structures would be passed on to their offspring (Mayr 1982).

The most famous example used by Lamarck was the long necks of giraffes. He suggested that this distinctive feature evolved when a short-necked ancestor took to browsing on the leaves of trees instead of on grass. Lamarck speculated that the ancestral giraffe, in reaching up, stretched its neck. The force for change was directed to the giraffe's neck, and it was increased in length. This physical characteristic was passed on to the giraffe's offspring. The offspring of this ancestral giraffe stretched still farther. As this process repeated itself from generation to generation, the present long neck of the giraffe was eventually achieved.

Because evolution takes place as a result of physical characteristics acquired in the course of a creature's lifetime, Lamarck's theory is referred to as the *inheritance of acquired characteristics* or *use-disuse theory*. Variations of Lamarck's view of inheritance were used by many nineteenth-century scientists to explain how physical characteristics originated and were passed on. Today, however, this theory is rejected for several reasons. First, Lamarck overestimated the ability of a plant or an animal to adapt or change to meet new environmental conditions. In addition, we now know that physical traits acquired during an organism's lifetime cannot be inherited by the organism's offspring. In order for traits to be passed on, they must be encoded in genetic information contained within the sex cells (see later discussion). For example, a weightlifter's musculature, an acquired characteristic, will not be passed on to his or her children. Nevertheless, Lamarck's ideas illustrate early theories that attempted to explain evolutionary change. His work is notable in proposing a unified theory of how evolution takes place and also because of the emphasis it placed on the interaction between organisms and their environments.

Darwin, Wallace, and Natural Selection

Two individuals strongly influenced by the scientific revolution were Charles Robert Darwin (1809–1882) and Alfred Russel Wallace (1823–1913), nineteenth-century British naturalists. Through their careful observations and their identification of a plausible mechanism for evolutionary change, they transformed perspectives of the origin of species. Impressed by the variation in living species and their interaction with the environment, Darwin and Wallace independently developed an explanation of why this variation occurs and the basic mechanism of evolution. This

Charles Darwin (1809–1882). Darwin is known for identifying natural selection as a key evolutionary process.

HMS *Beagle* in South America. Charles Darwin's trip around the world on the *Beagle* gave him the opportunity to study many different animals in varied environments.

mechanism is known as **natural selection**, which can be defined as genetic change in a population resulting from differential reproductive success. This is now recognized as one of the four principal evolutionary processes.

Beginning in 1831, Darwin traveled for five years aboard the British ship HMS *Beagle* on a voyage around the world. During this journey, he collected numerous plant and animal species from many different environments. In the 1840s and 1850s, Wallace observed different species of plants and animals during an expedition to the Amazon and later continued his observations in Southeast Asia and on the islands off Malaysia. Darwin and Wallace arrived at the theory of natural selection independently, but Darwin went on to present a thorough and completely documented statement of the theory in his book *On the Origin of Species*, published in 1859. The volume's full title gives a fair idea of its focus: *On the Origin of Species by Means of Natural Selection, or the Preservation of Favored Races in the Struggle for Life*.

In their theory of natural selection, Darwin and Wallace emphasized the enormous variation that exists in all plant and animal species. They combined these observations with those of Thomas Malthus (1766–1834), a nineteenth-century English clergyman and political economist whose work focused on human populations. Malthus was concerned with population growth and the constraints that limited food supplies had on population size. Darwin and Wallace realized that similar pressures operate in nature. Living creatures produce more offspring than can generally be expected to survive and reproduce. For example, for the thousands of tadpoles that hatch from eggs, few live to maturity. Similarly, only a small number of the seeds from a maple tree germinate and grow into trees. In recognizing the validity of this fact, Darwin and Wallace realized that there would be *selection* in which organisms survived. What factors would determine their survival?

Variation within species and reproductive success are the basis of natural selection. Darwin and Wallace reasoned that certain individuals in a species may be born with particular characteristics or traits that make them better able to survive. For example, certain plants within a species may naturally produce more seeds than others, or some frogs in a single population may have coloring that blends in with the environment better than others, making them less likely to be eaten by predators. With these advantageous characteristics, certain members of a species are more likely to reproduce and, subsequently, pass on these traits to their offspring. Darwin and Wallace called this process *natural selection* because nature, or the demands of the environment, actually determines which individuals (and, therefore, which traits) survive. This process, repeated countless times over millions of years, is the means by which species change or evolve over time.

Examples of Natural Selection

One problem Darwin faced in writing *On the Origin of Species* was a lack of well-documented examples of natural selection at work. Most major changes in nature take place over thousands or millions of years. As a result, the process of natural selection is often too slow to be documented in a researcher's lifetime. However, when animals or plants are exposed to rapid changes in their environment, we can actually observe natural selection in action.

A classic case of natural selection is illustrated by the finches of the Galapagos Islands, located about 500 miles off the coast of South America. These birds were studied by Charles Darwin when he visited the islands during his travels on the HMS *Beagle*. Volcanic in origin and cut off

Alfred Russel Wallace (1823–1913). Along with Charles Darwin, Wallace is credited with identifying natural selection as a mechanism for evolutionary change.

from the South American mainland, the Galapagos have a diversity of species related to, but distinct from, those of South America. Darwin was struck by how the geographic isolation of a small population could expose its members to new environmental conditions where different adaptive features might be favored. Darwin described the variation in the islands' finches. In general, the birds have rather dull plumage and are quite similar, except in the size and shape of their beaks—a feature that is closely related to the ways in which the birds obtain their food. Some species of finch, for example, have short, thick beaks that they use to eat seeds, buds, and fruits, while others have long, straight beaks and subsist primarily on nectar from flowers.

The finches of the island of Daphne Major in Galapagos were the focus of a long-term research project by Peter and Rosemary Grant, beginning in 1973 (Grant 1999; Weiner 1994). The island is small enough to allow researchers to study the island's flora and fauna intensively and provide an unambiguous demonstration of natural selection in

operation. The Grants and their students focused on two species of finch—the medium ground finch and the cactus finch. Over time, every finch on the island was captured, carefully measured and weighed, and also tagged so that each bird could be identified in the field. The diet of the birds was documented and the availability of food resources charted. A dramatic change in the finches' food resources occurred between mid-1976 and early 1978 as a result of a drought. The lack of rainfall led to a decrease in the food supplies favored by smaller-beaked finches. The remaining food consisted of larger, harder seeds that were difficult for finches with small beaks to break open. On the other hand, finches with larger, heavier beaks were able to more easily crack and extract food from hard-shelled seeds. Not surprisingly, many of the finches with smaller beaks died of starvation during the drought.

The variation in beak size is a good illustration of how natural selection may act on different species, but it also illustrates the significance of variation within individual species. Of the more than 1,000 medium ground finches found on the island at the beginning of the Grants' study, only 180 remained after the drought. Notably, the finches that survived had a larger average beak size than that of the population prior to the drought. As beak size is an inherited characteristic, the new generations of birds born after the drought also had a larger average beak size. This case study illustrates how natural selection can eliminate maladaptive traits from a population and select for features that help ensure survival and, ultimately, reproductive success for some members of a species. Many modern scientists believe that new species emerge when small populations become isolated from the parent group and encounter new selective pressures that may favor different characteristics.

Natural selection is currently viewed as one of four major forces in the evolution of species. It enabled Darwin to explain the mechanisms of biological evolution, and it remains a powerful explanation for the development of living species of plants and animals. Before turning to the other processes that influence evolution, we will consider the way traits are passed on from one generation to the next.

The photos of different dogs, a Cockapoo, Dachshund, and German Shepard, exhibit the wide variation in physical characteristics that may be found within the same species.
Source: Courtesy of Rodney Livingston (left), C. R. DeCorse (center), and Shutterstock (Right).

The finches of the Galapagos Islands provide an excellent example of natural selection at work. The beaks of the various species of finch are used for exploiting different kinds of foods. If environmental conditions suddenly change, some characteristics may be more favored than others.

Principles of Inheritance

3.4   Discuss Gregor Johann Mendel's principles of inheritance.

Darwin contributed to the modern understanding of biological evolution by thoroughly documenting the *variation* of living forms and by identifying the key process of natural selection. Like most nineteenth-century scientists, however, he did not understand *heredity*, or how specific traits are passed on from one generation to the next. Darwin reasoned that during the reproductive process, the parental substances are mixed to produce new traits in the parents' offspring. These conclusions were based in part on his experiments with plants and animals, in which he had observed that the offspring often had characteristics from both parents. Darwin was unclear about how these traits were transmitted, but he reasoned that as with a metal alloy, such as bronze, which is a mixture of tin and copper, the traits of an offspring represented a blending of parental substances. Today, we know that inherited characteristics are not a mixture of parental substances, such as with the mixing of fluids or metal alloys. Rather, traits are passed from parents to offspring in individual "particles" or packages—what we now refer to as genes.

Mendel and Modern Genetics

Modern understanding of heredity emerged through the studies of an Austrian monk named Gregor Johann Mendel (1822–1884). During the 1860s, Mendel began a series of breeding experiments with pea plants that revolutionized biological thought. Although his findings were not recognized until the twentieth century, Mendel laid the groundwork for what is today known as the science of *genetics*, the biological subfield that deals with heredity. In

compiling his rules of heredity, Mendel discredited earlier theories of inheritance. He was the first to conclusively demonstrate that traits are inherited in discrete packages of information that were not mixed during reproduction. The principles he laid out as a result of this work are useful in understanding inheritance in humans, as well as all other biological organisms.

Mendel's most important experiments involved the crossbreeding of pea plants. In order to discern patterns of inheritance, Mendel focused on traits that could each be expressed in only one of two ways. Height and seed color are two examples: He studied plants that were either tall *or* dwarf or plants that produced either green *or* yellow peas. He initially focused his experiments on one characteristic or trait at a time, carefully cross-pollinating *purebred* plants, plants that were similar with regard to one of his traits. Mendel crossed purebred tall pea plants with purebred dwarf, or short plants. In this way, he was able to study the traits that appeared in *hybrids*, the offspring resulting from tall and dwarf plants. He could then evaluate the proportion of characteristics found in successive generations. Mendel drew several important conclusions from these experiments.

Mendel's Principle of Segregation   By following the results of cross-pollination through several generations, Mendel discovered a distinct pattern of reproduction. The first generation of hybrid plants—that is, plants produced by parents having purebred tall and purebred dwarf characteristics—were all tall. However, when he crossbred these hybrid plants, the next generation contained both tall and dwarf plants. Thus, the dwarf variety that seemed to

Gregor Johann Mendel (1822–1884). Through his study of pea plants, Mendel laid the foundation for the understanding of heredity.

disappear in the first generation of hybrids reappeared in the second generation (see Figure 3.1).

Significantly, the ratio of tall to dwarf plants in the second hybrid generation was always approximately 3 to 1 (three tall plants to one dwarf plant). Mendel conducted similar experiments focusing on other characteristics and obtained similar results. This led Mendel to reject the earlier notions of inheritance, such as blending. None of the pea plants exhibited mixed characteristics: All of the plants were either tall or short; all of the peas were either green or yellow.

The fact that the three-to-one ratio reappeared consistently convinced Mendel that the key to heredity lay deep within the pea plant seeds. Mendel correctly concluded that the particles responsible for passing traits from parents to offspring occurred in pairs, each offspring receiving half of a pair from each parent. During fertilization, the particles of heredity, what we now call genes, from each parent are combined. The observation that units of heredity (or genes) occur in pairs and that offspring receive half of a pair from each parent is the basis of the *principle of segregation*, Mendel's first principle of inheritance.

Dominant and Recessive Traits   Mendel also observed that certain traits prevailed over others. He labeled the prevailing traits **dominant**. In contrast, he labeled as **recessive** those traits that were unexpressed in one generation but expressed in following generations. In pea plants, he found that tall was dominant and dwarf was recessive.

Figure 3.1 illustrates why recessive traits can disappear in one generation and appear in the next. In the first generation, a purebred tall plant and a purebred dwarf plant are crossbred. The pairs of genetic information in the purebred tall plants only contain genetic material for tallness (*TT*), and the purebred dwarf plants only contain information for the dwarf trait (*tt*). When these purebred plants are crossbred, the offspring receive genetic material from each parent (*Tt*). Only the tall trait appears in the offspring because tall is the dominant trait and the dwarf characteristic is recessive. However, when these hybrid plants are crossbred, the recessive trait reappears. As Figure 3.1 illustrates, the crossing of two hybrid parents (*Tt*) produces four possible combinations: one *TT*, two *Tt*, and one *tt*. The single offspring that only has the tall characteristic (*TT*) as well as those that inherited both tall and dwarf characteristics (*Tt*) appear tall, the dwarf characteristic being recessive. The offspring that inherit two recessive particles (*tt*) exhibit the recessive trait. This accounts for the 3-1 ratio that Mendel observed in the offspring of two hybrid plants. Mendel concluded that the particle containing the recessive trait, which is masked by the dominant trait in

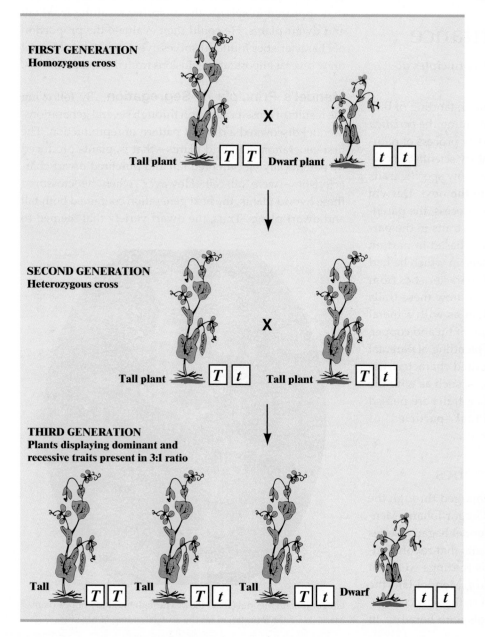

FIRST GENERATION
Homozygous cross

Tall plant T T Dwarf plant t t

SECOND GENERATION
Heterozygous cross

Tall plant T t Tall plant T t

THIRD GENERATION
Plants displaying dominant and recessive traits present in 3:1 ratio

Tall T T Tall T t Tall T t Dwarf t t

Figure 3.1 In one of his experiments, Mendel crossbred plants that were purebred (homozygous) for particular traits, as illustrated here by the tall and dwarf pea plants. As tallness is a dominant trait, all the offspring of this cross were tall. In the third generation, however, the recessive traits reappear, or segregate.

one generation, can reappear if it occurs in both parents. Mendel's theory explained how hybrid parents expressing only the dominant trait could produce offspring exhibiting the recessive trait. Purebred parents could pass on only the dominant or recessive trait, whereas hybrid parents could pass on either one.

The alternate forms of the same genes, such as "tall" or "dwarf," are referred to as **alleles**. When an organism has two of the same kinds of alleles, it is referred to as **homozygous** for that gene. Thus, homozygous tall plants are *TT* (purebred dominant for tallness), whereas homozygous dwarf plants are *tt* (purebred recessive for shortness). In contrast, when an organism has two different alleles, it is **heterozygous** for that gene. Thus, the *Tt* hybrids are heterozygous plants, possessing both tall and dwarf alleles. When a heterozygous plant expresses only characteristics of one allele such as tallness, that allele is dominant. The allele whose expression is masked in a heterozygote (for example, shortness) is a recessive allele. Thus, two organisms with different allele combinations for a particular trait may have the same outward appearance: *TT* and *Tt* pea plants will appear the same.

Biologists distinguish between the genetic constitution and the outward appearance of an organism. The actual genetic makeup of an organism is referred to as its **genotype**; the external, observable characteristics of that organism that are shaped in part by the organism's genetic makeup, as well as its unique life history, are called its **phenotype**. Genotype and phenotype are illustrated in Figure 3.2.

Principle of Independent Assortment

The preceding experiments all focused on one physical trait. In subsequent studies, Mendel investigated the outcomes of fertilization between pea plants that differed in two ways, such as in both plant height and color of the pea, in order to evaluate whether the two characteristics were linked. As in the previous experiments, the offspring of purebred (homozygous) parents exhibited only the dominant characteristics. When Mendel cross-fertilized these hybrids, however, the offspring displayed the characteristics present in the purebred generation in a ratio of 9:3:3:1, as illustrated in Figure 3.3.

This experiment indicated that no two traits are always passed on together. Mendel concluded that during the reproductive process, the particles determining different traits separate from one another and then *recombine* to create variation in the next generation. Thus, in the experiments by Mendel discussed above, plants produced peas that were yellow and round, yellow and wrinkled, green and wrinkled, and green and round. Mendel referred to the fact that individual traits (such as height or color) occur independently of one another as the *principle of independent assortment*.

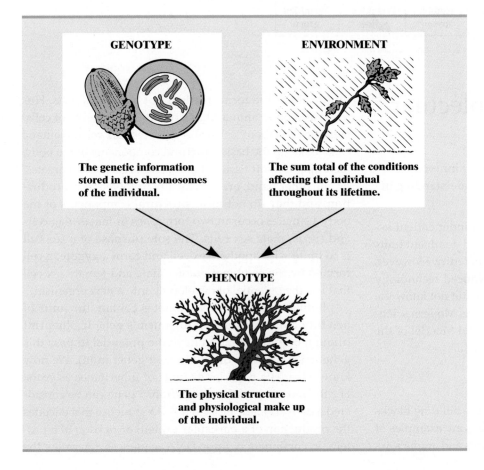

Figure 3.2 The genotype interacts with the external environment to produce the phenotype.
Source: From *The Illustrated Origin of Species* by Charles Darwin, abridged by Richard Leakey (Rainbird/Faber & Faber, 1979). Reprinted by permission of the Robert Harding Picture Library.

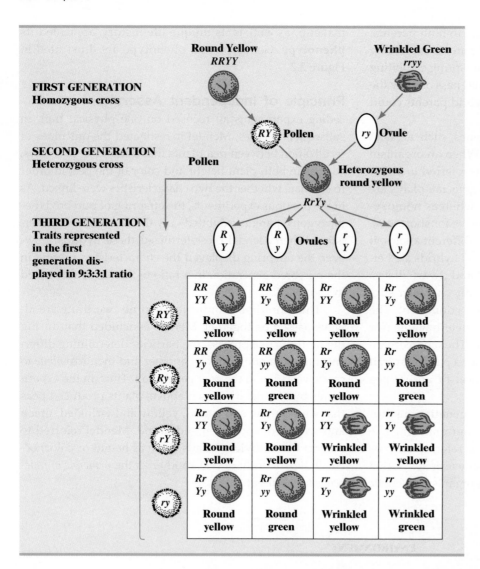

Inheritance and Molecular Genetics

3.5 Discuss how Mendel's principles of inheritance have changed in light of a better understanding of molecular genetics.

Mendel's principles of segregation and independent assortment and the concepts of recessive and dominant traits are still viewed as key mechanisms of heredity. However, because Mendel did not have the advanced technology needed to investigate cellular biology, he did not know the inner workings of the units of inheritance. Modern scientists have a better understanding than did Mendel of the dynamics of heredity at the cellular level.

Cells and Genes

Heredity is encoded in cells, which are the building blocks of all living things. Bacteria and amoebas are examples of single-celled organisms; in contrast, plants and animals are multicellular life-forms made up of billions of cells. Humans and other animals have two different forms of cells: **somatic cells** (body cells) and **gametes** (sex cells). Somatic cells make up the basic structural components of the body, including the soft tissues, bones, and organs. The gametes, on the other hand, are specifically involved in reproduction, and they do not form structural components of the body. Gametes occur in two forms: *ova* or female egg cells and *sperm*, male sex cells. The sole purpose of a sex cell is to unite with another sex cell and form a **zygote**, a cell formed by the combination of a male and female sex cell that has the potential of developing into a new organism.

Both somatic cells and gametes contain the units of heredity that constitute an organism's genetic blueprint (though only the gametes have the potential to pass this genetic information on to the next generation). We now know Mendel's particles or units of inheritance as *genes*. For the purposes of this discussion, a **gene** can be considered a deoxyribonucleic acid (DNA) sequence that encodes the production of a particular protein or portion of a protein. In combination, these DNA sequences determine the physical characteristics of an organism. Genes, discrete units of hereditary information, may be made up of hundreds, or even thousands, of DNA sequences.

The Role of DNA

Molecules of **deoxyribonucleic acid** (DNA) are the secret of a cell's genetic blueprint. The DNA molecule looks like a spiral ladder or, more poetically, like a *double helix* (Figure 3.4). The sides of the ladder consist of sugar (deoxyribose) and phosphate, and the rungs are made up of four nitrogen bases: adenine, thymine, guanine, and cytosine. The DNA bases are arranged in sequences of three, called *codons*. These sequences determine the assembly of different amino acids. For example, the combination and arrangement of the bases guanine, thymine, and cytosine encode the amino acid glutamine. *Amino acids* are chemicals joined together in chains to produce different proteins—chemical compounds that are fundamental to the makeup and running of the body's cells. There are 20 different kinds of amino acids that can, in differing combinations and amounts, produce millions of different proteins basic to life.

Figure 3.4 This illustration shows the chemical structure of DNA. The DNA molecule forms a spiral ladder of sugar (S) and phosphate (P) linked by four nitrogen bases: adenine (A), guanine (G), thymine (T), and cytosine (C).

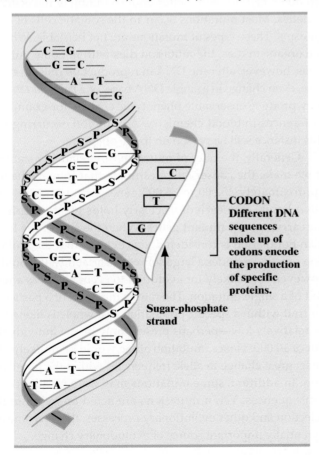

CODON
Different DNA sequences made up of codons encode the production of specific proteins.

Sugar-phosphate strand

Mitosis and Meiosis

At certain times, cells divide to form new cells. Gametes and somatic cells divide in different ways, a fact that is very significant in terms of their differing roles. Strands of DNA containing heredity information are contained in each living cell, but while both kinds of cells contain an organism's genetic code, only the gametes provide a means of passing this information on to an offspring through reproduction. Normally, the DNA molecules exist as single, uncoiled, thread-like strands within each cell. The minute DNA threads contained within each human somatic cell are estimated to be as much as 6 feet long. During cell division the DNA becomes tightly coiled and forms discrete structures called *chromosomes*. The single DNA threads replicate by forming a double strand, one strand being an exact copy of the original. Each species has a specific number of chromosomes that make up their somatic cells. Humans have 23 pairs of chromosomes or 46 chromosomes in all.

When somatic cells divide to produce new cells—a process biologists call **mitosis**—they replicate themselves to produce identical cells. Somatic cells have complete pairs of chromosomes. Mitosis is simply a process for making identical cells within a single individual. In contrast, sex cells, or gametes, are produced through the process of **meiosis**—two successive cell divisions that produce cells with only *half* the number of chromosomes (23 in the case of humans). Meiosis reduces the amount of genetic material to half to prepare for sexual reproduction. During fertilization when two sex cells are joined together, they reproduce a new organism with a complete complement of chromosomes (46 in humans).

The process of meiosis is very important in terms of evolution because it necessitates genetic recombination. Offspring of sexually reproducing species are not identical copies of their parents, but rather unique individuals who have received contributions of genetic material from each parent. It is during meiosis and sexual reproduction that Mendel's principles of segregation and independent assortment operate. This reshuffling of genetic material does not change allele frequencies by itself. It ensures, however, that the entire range of traits present in a species is produced and can subsequently be acted on by evolutionary forces.

Polygenic Inheritance

Mendel's experiments with pea plants discussed above focused on the investigation of physical traits that were controlled by alleles at one genetic locus and had phenotypic expressions that were distinct: Plants were either tall or dwarf; the peas either green or yellow. There were no plants of varying height or of mixed green and yellow color. Today these are called *Mendelian traits* or *traits of simple inheritance*. More than 4,500 human traits are inherited in this manner. The A, B, and O blood types in humans are an example; individuals have one or another of these blood groups; they do not have a mixture.

While some human characteristics are inherited as discrete traits, the majority are passed on in a more complicated fashion. In contrast to Mendelian traits, many physical characteristics in humans have phenotypic expressions that form a gradation and are influenced by alleles at more than one genetic locus. Traits that display a graded series determined by genes at multiple genetic loci are referred to as *polygenic* or *continuous traits*. They include many of the most visible aspects of human features, such as height, skin color, and hair color; consequently, they were often used as the basis for racial classifications. None of these traits fall into perfectly bounded categories. Unlike pea plants, humans occur in a variety of heights (and sizes) and have a wide range of natural hair colors.

Epigenetic Factors

To complicate matters further, genes and their expression are influenced by many other factors (Jablonka and Lamb 2006). Although DNA provides the fundamental genetic blueprint, other factors influence the expression of genetic traits. In some cases, the genetic directions provided by genes may be turned "on" or "off," modifying the effect the genes have without modifying the DNA sequence. For example, skin, muscle, and brain cells all contain the same DNA; they have same genetic blueprint, but appear different because their genes are turned on or off in varied ways. These modifications that are external to the DNA sequence are referred to as **epigenetic**, which literally means "above" or "on top of" genes. The complex interaction of DNA with these varied factors during cellular development makes it impossible to predict what a person will be like solely by mapping the sequences of their DNA.

Population Genetics and Evolution

3.6 **Define and discuss how evolution takes place.**

To understand the process of evolution fully, we cannot focus on individuals. A person's genetic makeup, fixed during conception, remains with that individual throughout his or her lifetime. Although people mature and change in appearance, they do not *evolve* in a biological sense.

Evolution refers to change in the genetic makeup of a *population* of organisms. A **population** here refers to a group of individuals who can potentially interbreed. To understand evolution, a scientist must consider all the genes in a population. This assortment of genes is known as the **gene pool**. Any particular gene pool consists of

different allele frequencies, the relative amounts of the alternate forms of genes that are present.

In terms of genetics, evolution can be defined as the process of change in allele frequencies between one generation and the next. Alteration of the gene pool of a population is influenced by four evolutionary processes, one of which, natural selection, has already been discussed in relation to the work of Charles Darwin and Alfred Wallace. The other three processes are mutation, gene flow, and genetic drift. In addition, cultural, behavioral and epigenetic factors also influence the genetic makeup of a *population* and thus are potential sources of evolutionary change. These various factors are discussed in the following paragraphs.

Mutations

Mutations are alterations of genetic material at the cellular level. They can occur spontaneously during the cell replication process, or they can be induced by environmental factors such as radiation. Although we frequently think of mutations as harmful, they introduce variation into the gene pool and may create new, advantageous characteristics. Mutation serves as the primary force behind evolution because it is the *only* source of new genetic variation. The other evolutionary processes act on the genetic variation introduced through mutation. Maladaptive characteristics introduced by mutation are quickly eliminated by natural selection.

The role of mutation was only recognized during the twentieth century with better understanding of molecular genetics. Most mutations occur in the somatic cells of organisms. These types of mutations are not heritable. When the organism dies, the mutation dies with it. Some mutations, however, alter the DNA in reproductive cells. In this case, even change in a single DNA base, or a *point mutation*, may produce observable phenotypic change, for example, differences in blood chemistry. A mutation occurring in this instance will be passed on to the offspring.

Generally, the rates of mutations are relatively stable. If we make the conservative estimate that humans have approximately 20,000 to 25,000 genes with hundreds of DNA bases, then each of us clearly holds great potential for carrying new mutant genes. When the size of the human population is considered, it is evident that the mutation process provides a large source of variability. It would, however, be unlikely for evolution to occur solely as a result of a single mutation. The rate of mutation of a particular trait within a specific population as a whole is likely to be relatively low—perhaps present only in one individual out of 10,000. Hence, mutation alone would be unlikely to effect great change in allele frequencies within the population. In addition, some mutations may have no adaptive consequences. Yet, if mutations are acted on by natural selection and other evolutionary processes, they become a potentially important source of evolutionary change.

Gene Flow

Gene flow is the exchange of alleles between populations as a result of interbreeding. When this exchange occurs, new genetic material may be introduced, changing the allele frequencies in a population. The process of gene flow has affected most human societies. Migrants from one society enter a new region and intermarry with the local population. Through reproduction, they transmit new genes into the population. In this way, new mutations arising in one population can be transmitted to other members of the species.

In addition to providing a mechanism for introducing new genetic material, gene flow can act to decrease variation between populations. If two distinct populations continue to interbreed, they will become progressively similar genetically. Migration and connections between different populations have long been a feature of human societies and among early human ancestors. This genetic interconnectedness explains why new human species have not emerged: There has been sufficient gene flow between populations to prevent the creation of substantial genetic distance.

With the development of modern transportation, gene flow occurs on a worldwide scale. In this context, however, it is useful to remember that many cultural or social factors play a role in gene flow in human populations. Religious practices, socioeconomic status, and ethnicity may all influence the selection of mates (see discussion of cultural and behavioral factors below and in Chapter 6).

Genetic Drift

Genetic drift is evolutionary change resulting from random sampling phenomena that eliminate or maintain certain alleles in a gene pool. It includes the influence of chance events that may affect evolutionary change that are in no way influenced by individuals' genetic makeup. For example, in any population, only a small sample of the potential array of genetic material is passed on from one generation to the next. Every human being produces hundreds of thousands of gametes, each representing a different genetic combination, yet people produce only a few offspring. The chance selection of genetic material that occurs during reproduction results in minor changes in allele frequencies from one generation to the next. Chance events, such as death by disease or accident, also bring about change in allele frequencies. For example, if only ten individuals within a population carry a particular genetic trait and all of them die as a result of accident or disease, this genetic characteristic will not be passed on to the next generation.

Because evolution occurs in populations, change resulting from genetic drift is influenced by the size of the population as well as the relative allele frequencies represented. In larger populations, random events, such as accidental deaths, are unlikely to have as significant an effect on the population's gene pool. In smaller populations, however, such events can substantially alter the genetic variation present. A particular kind of genetic drift, known as the **founder effect**, results when only a small number of individuals in a population pass on their genes to the following generation. Such a situation might result when a famine decimates a large group or when a small migrant population moves away and establishes a new settlement in an isolated area. In these instances, the founding members of the succeeding generation will have only a portion—a sample—of the full range of the genetic material that was present in the original population. Because early human ancestors and human populations lived in small bands of people, perhaps consisting of family groups, genetic drift was likely an important evolutionary force.

Natural Selection

Natural selection provides the key to evolution. It can be defined as genetic change in a population, as reflected in allele frequencies and as a result of differential reproductive success. The other evolutionary forces already discussed are important in creating variation in allele frequencies within and between populations, but they provide no direction.

As illustrated in the case of Darwin's finches on the Galapagos Islands, certain alleles (as expressed in particular physical traits such as long or short beaks) may be selected for by environmental factors. They may enable an organism to resist disease better, obtain food more efficiently, or avoid predators more effectively. Individuals with such advantages will, on average, be more successful in reproducing and will thereby pass on their genes to the next generation at higher rates. Evolutionary "success" can be evaluated in relative terms; if the environment changes, natural selection pressures also change.

In the case of the finches, the larger- and smaller-beaked varieties were initially equally successful (or "fit"), but as food resources were depleted by drought, the individuals with heavier beaks were favored. This shift in allele frequencies in response to changing environmental conditions is called **adaptation**. Through evolution, species develop characteristics that allow them to survive and reproduce successfully in particular environmental settings. The specific environmental conditions to which a species is adapted is referred to as its **ecological niche**.

Cultural, Behavioral and Epigenetic Factors

Mutations, gene flow, genetic drift, and natural selection have long been regarded as the primary evolutionary processes; they influence the genetic material present, its exchange, and distribution. However, other cultural, behavioral and epigenetic factors interact with these processes and so influence the genetic makeup of a population and thus are potential sources of evolutionary change.

One factor is an organism's interactions with its surroundings. Plant and animal species may alter their environment, something that may affect their adaptability and influence natural selection. For example, through grazing or predation, a species may change the distribution of other plant or animal species, changing the types of species represented and the availability of food resources. As these changes alter the environment, they also alter the characteristics that are being selected for by natural selection, and thus the direction of evolutionary change. The process by which organisms modify their environment is referred to *niche construction*. These modifications are not necessarily in the best interest of the species.

More than any other species, human societies dramatically impact the environments in which they live. Activities such as the hunting and gathering of food resources, land clearing, and water control modify the distribution of previously occurring plant and animal species. For example, as land is cleared for farming, plant species better suited to these changing conditions become more common. This, in turn, may lead to further changes in plant distribution and morphology. Significantly, these changes are unintentional, unplanned consequences of these activities (see discussions of modern human variation in Chapter 6 and coevolution in Chapter 8).

In modern societies, industrialization, urbanization and pollution have dramatic implications for human health and reproduction. Overcrowding, combined with poor knowledge of sanitation, food storage, and personal hygiene has contributed to nutritional deficiencies, the spread of infectious diseases, reduced growth rates, and decline in reproductive success, all of which have implications in evolutionary terms. In some instances, human cultural practices influence evolutionary processes even more directly, inhibiting gene flow and so contribute to genetic drift within a population. For example, restrictive marriage practices and laws prohibiting marriage between people of certain groups restrict the exchange of genes within a population. These factors are further discussed in Chapter 6.

Epigenetic Factors and Evolution As discussed previously, epigenetic changes refer to modifications of the genetic code that are external to DNA sequences. As in the case of mutations, most epigenetic changes occur in the somatic cells of organisms or, in sperm and egg cells, are erased when the two combine to form a fertilized egg. Consequently, those changes are not heritable. However, it is possible that epigenetic changes in parents' sperm and egg cells may be passed on to the next generation. While epigenetic inheritance has not been demonstrated in human populations, a strong case can be made for it having played a role in evolution (Jablonka and Lamb 2006).

How Do New Species Originate?

3.7 Discuss how and why new species arise.

Evolutionary change is a dynamic, complex process. Although it is useful to discuss the preceding processes and factors as distinct variables, they all interact to affect evolutionary change. Mutation provides the ultimate source of new genetic variants, whereas gene flow, genetic drift, and natural selection alter the frequency of the new allele. Behavior and cultural factors further influence its distribution. The key consideration is change in the genetic characteristics of a population from one generation to the next. Over time, this change may produce major differences among populations that were originally very similar.

Measuring Evolutionary Change

To measure evolutionary change, researchers find it useful to evaluate evolutionary processes operating on a population by comparing allele frequencies for a particular trait to an idealized, mathematical model known as the **Hardy-Weinberg theory of genetic equilibrium**. This model, developed independently by G. H. Hardy and W. Weinberg, sets hypothetical conditions under which none of the evolutionary processes is acting and no evolution is taking place. The model makes several important assumptions. It presumes that no mutation is taking place (there are no new alleles); there is no gene flow (no migration or movement in or out of the population); no genetic drift (a large enough population is represented that there is no variation in allele frequencies due to sampling); and that natural selection is not operating on any of the alleles represented. The model also assumes that mating is randomized within the population so that all individuals have equal potential of mating with all other individuals of the opposite sex.

Given these assumptions, there will be no change in allele frequencies from one generation to the next. If examination of genotype frequencies within a population matches the idealized model, no evolution is taking place, and the population is said to be in Hardy-Weinberg equilibrium. If study suggests the genotype frequencies are not the same as the predicted model, then we know that at least one of the assumptions must be incorrect. Further research can then be undertaken to identify what the source of evolutionary change is. In practice, determining which evolutionary processes are acting on a population is challenging. Different evolutionary processes may act against one another, giving the appearance that none is operating. Small amounts of change may also go unrecognized. Nevertheless, the Hardy-Weinberg theory provides a starting point for evaluating evolutionary change.

Speciation

One of the most interesting areas of research in evolutionary theory is how, why, and when new species arise. This is known as the study of **speciation**. Generally, biologists define a **species** as a group of organisms that have similar physical characteristics, can potentially interbreed with one another to produce fertile offspring, and who are reproductively isolated from other populations.

Phyletic Gradualism   According to this perspective of evolution, speciation occurs when there is an interruption in gene flow between populations that formerly were one species but became isolated by geographic barriers. In geographic isolation, these populations may reside in different types of environments, and natural selection, mutation, or genetic drift may lead to increasingly different allele frequencies. Eventually, through evolutionary change, these two populations become so different genetically that they are no longer the same species. Darwin hypothesized that speciation was a gradual process of evolution occurring very slowly as different populations became isolated. This view is called *gradualism*, or **phyletic gradualism**.

Punctuated Equilibrium   Beginning in the early twentieth century, some scientists challenged the gradualistic interpretation of speciation, arguing that new species might appear rapidly. Paleontologists (fossil specialists) Stephen Jay Gould and Niles Eldredge (1972) proposed a theory known as **punctuated equilibrium**. When examining ancient fossil beds, paleontologists discovered that some plants or animals seemed to exhibit little change over millions of years. These creatures appeared to remain in a state of equilibrium with their habitats for long geological periods, which were

A characteristic of a species is that its members can successfully interbreed only with one another. The mule is the offspring of a female horse and a male donkey, two clearly distinct species. As mules are always sterile, however, the reproductive isolation of the two species is maintained.

interrupted by major changes, or punctuations, leading to rapid speciation.

Punctuated equilibrium and gradualism (see Figure 3.5) present extreme perspectives of the rate at which evolution occurs, but the two views are not incompatible. Indeed, neither Darwin nor Gould and Eldredge suggested particular rates that were the same in all cases (Gingerich 1984). The fossil record provides examples of both cases (Bown and Rose 1987; Levinton 1988). The particular rate of change in a particular species depends on its specific adaptive features and the surrounding environmental conditions. Most paleontologists, biologists, and anthropologists agree that both types of evolution have occurred under different circumstances during different geological epochs. As our understanding of the fossil record increases, we will be better able to specify when and where speciation and evolution occurred rapidly and when and where they occurred gradually.

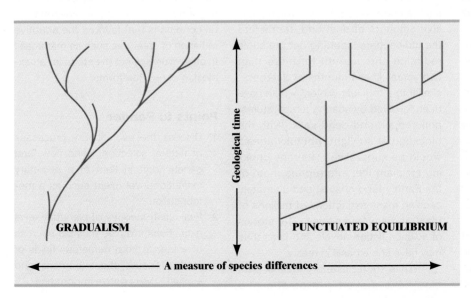

GRADUALISM   **PUNCTUATED EQUILIBRIUM**

Geological time

A measure of species differences

Figure 3.5 An illustration of two models of evolution. Gradualism implies a gradual, steady rate of speciation, while punctuated equilibrium suggests evolutionary change as a series of stops and starts. The two perspectives are not inconsistent with each other, and the fossil record provides evidence of both.

Adaptive Radiation

Adaptive radiation is the rapid diversification and adaptation of an evolving population into new ecological niches. It provides a useful illustration of the evolutionary process and the factors that influence rates of evolutionary change. As we have seen, organisms have tremendous reproductive potential, yet this potential is generally limited by the availability of food, shelter, and space in the environment. Competition with other organisms and natural selection limit the number of offspring that live. Eventually, organisms may utilize all the resources available in a particular ecological niche, making competition for food and other resources intense. Some individuals in a population may move into new environmental niches or explore new territories where resources are more available and chances for survival greater. In these new environments, with limited competition and abundant food, they may expand rapidly.

Critical Perspectives

Planetary-Level Extinctions

Most scientists today accept that periods of dramatic extinction, followed by the rapid evolution of new species and, successively, by long periods of relative stasis, occurred in the evolution of life. These major punctuations date long before the emergence of even the most distant human ancestors. Among the most notable are the Cretaceous-Tertiary extinction event of 65 million years ago that resulted in the disappearance of most species of dinosaurs, and an even more dramatic Permian-Triassic event that may have witnessed the extinction of most life on Earth around 251 million years ago. Estimates of similar events occurring in the Earth's past range from five major events to over twenty (Benton 2003; Raup and Sepkoski 1984; Raup 1999). In the case of the five major events, it is estimated that 50 to 90 percent of life on Earth became extinct. What could cause these dramatic events?

A variety of theories have been proposed, including the possible impact of large-scale volcanic activity, drop in sea levels, long-term stress on the ecosystem (from a variety of factors), and a gamma ray burst from a supernova (Macleod 2001). Increasing evidence, however, indicates that meteorite strikes may have been a major contributing factor in these extinctions. The evidence includes the presence of large concentrations of iridium in geological deposits dating to the Cretaceous-Tertiary boundary, the period of time that witnessed the extinction of the dinosaurs. Iridium is only found in extraterrestrial objects such as meteorites,

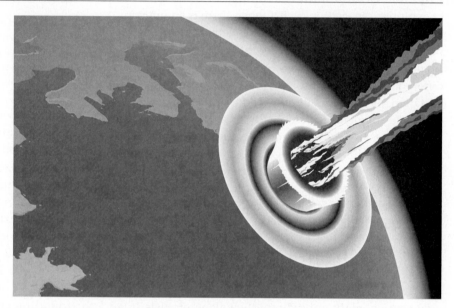

Meteor hitting the Earth.

asteroids, and comets. Evidence for meteorite strikes also includes craters, such as the one found at the tip of the Yucatán Peninsula in the Gulf of Mexico. This crater, which is a mile wide and a mile deep, dates back 65 million years. A meteor strike large enough to cause such a crater would have thrown massive amounts of dust and debris into the atmosphere, shutting out the sun's radiation and warmth for more than two years. These months of darkness, similar to a "nuclear winter," would have been followed by soaring temperatures, polluted air, and dead seas. With the blockage of sunlight, photosynthesis would be suppressed, thereby choking off plant life, interrupting most of the Earth's food chains, and ultimately causing mass extinctions of millions of plant and animal species. The stories of science fiction novels and films thus may have some basis in reality.

While such planetary level events may have played a dramatic and catastrophic role in the survival of some species, as Stephen Jay Gould (1985) pointed out, the disastrous conditions would also have created conditions conducive to new forms of life. Thus, although a meteorite impact may have resulted in the demise of the dinosaurs, it might have produced new environmental conditions that favored the adaptive radiation of creatures such as mammals. In other words, it set the stage for an explosion of new life-forms.

Points to Ponder

1. Discuss the evolutionary processes of natural selection, gene flow, and genetic drift in light of a planetary extinction-level event such as a meteor strike.

2. Evaluating theories of planetary-level extinctions involves multiple sources of evidence from numerous fields of study. Discuss these sources and evaluate their relative importance.

The creatures of the Galapagos Islands, discussed earlier with regard to Darwin's studies, provide an illustration of adaptive radiation. Located 500 miles off the coast of South America, the islands present an amazing diversity of flora and fauna. The islands' species are similar to those found on the South American mainland where they originated. Yet, while similar, they are also distinct in many respects. Darwin reasoned that the island was initially colonized by a few representatives of the mainland species. The newly formed volcanic islands had no life-forms and the arriving, mainland colonists, unfettered by competition, quickly expanded in the new niche. Because the various environments of the islands were different from those of the mainland, the descendants of the original arrivals evolved traits favorable to the exploitation of the new conditions and, therefore, increased chances of reproductive success.

The adaptive radiation of many species is recorded in the fossil record. For example, at the beginning of the Mesozoic Era when reptiles first adapted to land environments, they were able to expand into a vast array of ecological niches with little competition. Environmental change may also create conditions favorable for the adaptive radiation of some species. Even natural disasters that lead to the extinction of many species may provide opportunity for others, as described in the box on Planetary-Level Extinctions. Such conditions favor species that have the ability to exploit the changing conditions, and this likely explains the expansion of the placental mammals at the beginning of the Cenozoic Era. Evolutionary processes acting on the expanding population may produce many new varieties and species adapted to ecological niches different from the parent population, ultimately leading to new species.

The Evolution of Life

3.8 Briefly outline the evidence for the evolution of life on Earth and how evolutionary relationships are evaluated.

Modern scientific findings indicate that the universe as we know it began to develop between 13 billion and 14 billion years ago. At approximately 4.6 billion years ago, the sun and Earth formed, and about a billion years later, the first life appeared in the sea. Through evolution, living forms developed adaptive characteristics, survived, and reproduced. Geological forces and environmental changes, bringing about both gradual and rapid changes, led to new forms of life.

From studying the fossilized bones and teeth of different creatures, paleontologists have tracked the evolution of living forms throughout the world. They document the fossil record according to geological time, which is divided into *eras*, which are subdivided into *periods*, which in turn are composed of *epochs* (see page 62).

Analogy and Homology

How do paleontologists determine evolutionary relationships? Two useful concepts in discussing the divergence and differentiation of living forms are homology and analogy. **Homology** refers to traits that have resulted from a common evolutionary origin, though they may differ in form and function. For example, a human hand bears little resemblance to a whale's fin. Humans and whales live in very different environments, and the hand and fin perform in very different ways. Careful examination of human and whale skeletons, however, reveals many structural similarities that can be explained by a common, albeit distant, evolutionary relationship (see Figure 3.6). Thus, the hand and the fin are referred to as homologous. To understand the evolutionary relatedness of different species, researchers focus on homologous features.

Yet, not all features result from shared evolutionary origins. **Analogy** refers to similarities in organisms that have no evolutionary relationship. Analogous forms result from *convergent evolution*, the process by which two unrelated types of organisms develop similar physical characteristics. These resemblances emerge when unrelated organisms adapt to similar environmental niches. For example, hummingbirds and hummingbird moths resemble each other physically and have common behavioral characteristics. However, they share no direct evolutionary descent.

Figure 3.6 The structural similarities between the human hand and the whale's fin are an example of homology: features that share a common evolutionary origin but which may differ in form and function.

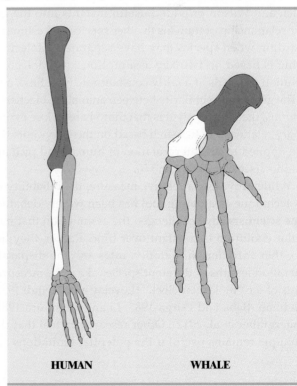

HUMAN   **WHALE**

Blood Chemistry and DNA

The majority of information on the evolution of life and human origin is provided by the information found in the fossil record. In recent years, however, studies of the genetic makeup of living organisms have received increasing attention. It is striking to note that despite the tremendous diversity of life, the DNA codes for the production of proteins—with few exceptions—dictate the joining of the same amino acids in all organisms, from the simplest one-celled plants and animals to humans. This semblance of genetic building blocks provides additional evidence for the common origin of all life.

Study of the differences and similarities in the arrangement of genetic material for living animals provides important insights into evolutionary relationships. Similarities in the DNA of different species indicate that they inherited genetic blueprints (with minor modifications) from a common ancestor. In most instances, this information has provided independent confirmation of conclusions about evolutionary relationships based on the study of skeletal characteristics and fossil remains. In some instances, however, physical characteristics may be confused because of convergent evolution. Study of genetic information and blood chemistry helps to avoid this confusion.

Genetic material of living animals has also been used to estimate when different species diverged. A technique known as *molecular dating* was developed by Vincent Sarich and Allan Wilson of the University of California, Berkeley (1967). The technique involves comparing amino acid sequences or, more recently, using what is called *DNA hybridization* to compare DNA material itself. As a result, Sarich and Wilson provided useful insights into the genetic relationship of humans to other species and estimates regarding when species may have separated. Molecular dating is based on two key assumptions: (1) Molecular evolution proceeds at a fairly constant rate over time, and (2) The greater the similarity between animals in biochemical terms, the more likely it is that they share a close evolutionary relationship. Research based on these concepts has been applied to the interpretation of human and primate evolution (see Chapters 4 and 5).

While providing a relative measure, the reliability of this technique as a dating tool has been widely debated. Some scientists have challenged the assumption that molecular evolution is constant over time. Rather, they believe that variation in mutation rates and the disparate generation lengths of different species skew the measurements of the "molecular clock" (Lovejoy and Meindl 1972; Goodman, Baba and Darga 1983; Li and Tanimura 1987; Langergraber et al. 2012). Other researchers feel that the technique remains useful if the potential limitations are taken into consideration. Future work may help to resolve these issues.

Plate Tectonics and Continental Drift

In examining the evolution and distribution of living forms, it is important to consider the role of geological processes. The formation of natural features, such as continents, mountains, and oceans, provides an important mechanism for restricting or encouraging gene flow. **Plate tectonics** is the complex geological process that brings about the drift of continents. The outer shell of the Earth is made up of plates that are in constant motion caused by the movement of molten rocks deep within the Earth. According to scientific investigation, the continents move a few centimeters a year (Tarling 1985). Over millions of years, the continents have sometimes drifted together and then separated, a process known as **continental drift**.

Determining the precise location of different continents at specific geological time periods has helped scientists to understand evolutionary connections among different species of plants and animals. Scientists hypothesize that until about 200 million years ago, the Earth's landmass was one gigantic, interconnected continent that is referred to as *Pangaea*. During the Mesozoic era, Pangaea began to break apart, forming two supercontinents. The southern supercontinent, known as *Gondwana*, consisted of what are now South America, Africa, Antarctica, Australia, and India. The northern continent, consisting of North America, Greenland, Europe, and Asia, is known as *Laurasia* (see Figure 3.7).

Throughout the Mesozoic and Cenozoic eras, the supercontinents continued to move. South America separated from Africa; North America, Greenland, and Europe divided; and Africa joined with Eurasia. Forty million years ago, North America separated from Europe. By 20 million years ago, the continued fracturing and movements of the geological plates resulted in the gradual migration of the continents to their present locations.

Examination of continental drift has helped paleontologists and other scientists understand the distribution of different plant and animal species. For example, the same types of fossil reptiles have been recovered from Mesozoic deposits in North America and the Gobi Desert in Asia, a good indication that these landmasses were connected at that time. In contrast, the separation of South America from other continents during the Cenozoic era supports the fossil and biological evidence for the divergence of primates from Africa, Asia, and Europe and primates from the Americas (see Chapter 4).

Figure 3.7 Understanding the geological process of continental drift—the movement of continents as a result of plate tectonics—helps paleontologists understand the distribution of fossil species.

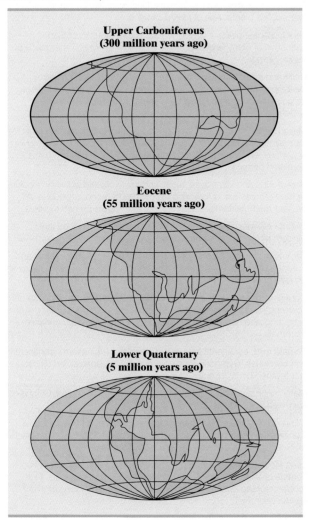

Upper Carboniferous
(300 million years ago)

Eocene
(55 million years ago)

Lower Quaternary
(5 million years ago)

The Paleontological Record

The Precambrian and Paleozoic Eras The fossil evidence shows that by the end of the Precambrian, simple forms of life resembling modern bacteria, including some species that may have been able to *photosynthesize*, had emerged. Various species of algae have been dated to more than one billion years ago. (see Table 3.1). Beginning with the Paleozoic, which dates from approximately 541 million to 252 million years ago, deposits of fossils became more abundant, enabling paleontologists to follow the adaptive radiation of jellyfish, worms, fish, amphibians, and early reptiles.

The Mesozoic Era The Mesozoic (252 million to 65 million years ago) marks the adaptive radiation of reptiles. This era is divided into the Triassic, Jurassic, and Cretaceous periods. The Mesozoic is known as the Age of Reptiles. Unlike earlier forms of life, reptiles could exist entirely outside the water. They were the first successful land animals and reigned as the dominant species in this new environment. Many of the snakes, lizards, and turtles found in Mesozoic formations are similar to contemporary species. Of all the species that lived during the Mesozoic, the dinosaurs are the most well known today. They included the giant carnivore (meat eater) *Tyrannosaurus*; larger, plant-eating creatures such as the *Brachiosaurus*; and numerous other species, both large and small.

Although reptiles were the dominant animals of the Mesozoic, paleontologists have found fossils of many other organisms from this same era. For example, bird fossils, some even showing the outlines of feathers, have been preserved from the Jurassic period. The paleontological record demonstrates beyond a doubt that a direct evolutionary relationship exists between reptiles and birds. One classic fossil example is *Archaeopteryx*, an animal about the size of a crow, with small wings, teeth, and a long, reptilian tail.

Near the end of the Cretaceous period, many animals became extinct. Changing climatic conditions, competition from newly evolving mammals, and, possibly, extraterrestrial episodes led to the demise of many reptile species, including the dinosaurs, as well as many other organisms.

The Cenozoic Era The Cenozoic Era (65 million years ago to the present), or the Age of Mammals, was characterized by the dominance and adaptive radiation of mammals. This era is divided into two periods, the Tertiary, which encompassed 63 million years, and the Quaternary, which covers the last two million years. During the Cenozoic, various species of mammals came to occupy every environmental niche. Some, such as whales and dolphins, adapted to the sea. Others, such as bats, took to the air. Most mammals, however, are represented by a diverse array of land animals, including dogs, horses, rats, bears, rabbits, apes, and humans. One of the major evolutionary advantages that enabled mammals to radiate so rapidly was their reproductive efficiency. In contrast to reptiles, which lay eggs that are vulnerable to predators, most mammals retain their eggs internally within the female. The eggs are thus protected and nourished until they reach an advanced stage of growth. Consequently, a much higher percentage of the young survive into adulthood, when they can reproduce. It is the early Cenozoic period that witnessed the evolution of earliest primates, the order of which humans are part.

Table 3.1 A Record of Geologic Time

Era	Period	Epoch	Millions of Years Ago	Geological Conditions and Evolutionary Development
Cenozoic (Age of Mammals)	Quaternary	Holocene	0.0117	End of last Ice Age; warmer climate. Decline of woody plants; rise of herbaceous plants. Age of *Homo sapiens*.
		Pleistocene	2.6	Four Ice Ages; glaciers in Northern hemisphere; uplift of Sierras. Extinction of many large mammals and other species. Emergence of genus *Homo*.
	Tertiary	Pliocene	5.3	Uplift and mountain building; volcanoes; climate much cooler. Development of grasslands and flowering plants; decline of forests. Large carnivores; many grazing mammals; australopithecines appear.
		Miocene	23	Major continents in approximately their current locations; mountain formation. Climate drier, cooler. Flowering plants continue to diversify. Many forms of mammals; anthropoid primates flourish; earliest hominoid primates.
		Oligocene	33	Rise of Alps and Himalayas; most land low; volcanic activity in Rockies. Spread of forests and flowering plants; rise of monocotyledons. All present mammal families represented; anthropoid primates evolve.
		Eocene	56	Climate warmer. Gymnosperms and flowering plants dominant. Modern birds; first true primates appear.
		Paleocene	65	Climate mild to cool; continental seas disappear; North America and Europe still joined. Age of Mammals begins; likely emergence of the first primate ancestors.
Mesozoic (Age of Reptiles)	Cretaceous		145	Continents start to separate; formation of Rockies; swamps. Rise of flowering plants; gymnosperms decline. Dinosaurs peak, then become extinct; toothed birds become extinct; first modern birds; primitive mammals.
	Jurassic		201	Climate mild; continents low; inland seas; mountains form; continental drift continues. Gymnosperms common. Large, specialized dinosaurs; first toothed birds; insectivorous marsupials.
	Triassic		252	Many mountains and deserts form; continental drift begins. Gymnosperms.
Paleozoic (Age of Ancient Life)	Permian		298	Continents merge as Pangaea; glaciers; formation of Appalachians. Conifers diversify; cycads evolve. Modern insects appear; mammal-like reptiles; extinction of many Paleozoic invertebrates.
	Carboniferous		358	Lands low; great coal swamps; climate warm and humid, then cooler. Forests of ferns, club mosses, horsetails, and gymnosperms. First reptiles; spread of ancient amphibians; many insect forms; ancient sharks abundant.
	Devonian		419	Glaciers; inland seas. Terrestrial plants well established; first forests; gymnosperms and bryophytes appear. Age of Fishes; amphibians and wingless insects appear; many trilobites.
	Silurian		443	Continents mainly flat. Vascular plants appear; algae dominant in aquatic environment. Fish evolve; terrestrial arthropods.
	Ordovician		485	Sea covers continents; climate warm. Marine algae dominant; terrestrial plants appear. Invertebrates dominant; fish appear.
	Cambrian		541	Climate mild; lands low; oldest rocks with abundant fossils. Algae dominant in aquatic environment. Age of Marine Invertebrates; most modern phyla represented.
Precambrian	Proterozoic		2,500	Planet cooled; glaciers; Earth's crust forms; mountains form. First multicellular forms of life appear; primitive algae and fungi, marine protozoans; marine invertebrates appear toward end of period.
Origin of the Earth; Origin of the Universe			4 billion 13 to 14 billion	Evidence of first prokaryotic cells.

Critical Perspectives

Creationism, Intelligent Design, and Evolution

Despite the increasing scientific evidence supporting evolution, not all segments of American and Western society have accepted the geological, genetic, and fossil data that are the basis of evolutionary theory (Petto and Godfrey 2007; Young and Largent 2007). Various versions of creation that rely on literal interpretations of the Bible are taught by some Christian, Jewish, and Islamic groups, as well as other religious denominations. For example, many members of the Old Order Amish (discussed in Chapter 10) accept an extreme literal reading of the biblical passage that refers to "four corners of the Earth held up by angels" and believe that the Earth is a two-dimensional flat plane. Members of the International Flat Earth Society have similar beliefs about a flat Earth (Scott 2004). These views reflect the ancient Hebrew description in the biblical passages referring to the Earth as a flat disk floating on water with the heavens held up by a dome (or firmament) with the sun, moon, and stars attached to it.

In the nineteenth century, some individuals attempted to reconcile a literal reading of the account of creation in Genesis 1:22 by translating the Hebrew term *day* as periods of time thousands or millions of years long, rather than 24-hour days (Sedley 2007). Some contemporary creationists' teachings expose similar views; they are sometimes referred to as "day-age" creationists. However, the vast majority of activists in the campaign against teaching evolution call themselves "progressive creationists." The Progressive Creationists accept the modern scientific view of the Big Bang and that the Earth is billions of years old, but do not accept the theory of evolution. They believe that God not only created the Big Bang, but also created separate "kinds" of plants and animals with genetic variations that resulted in the development of contemporary species of living organisms.

A group of creationists that have actively campaigned against the teaching of evolution call themselves "scientific creationists," represented by the Institute for Creation Research. This group proposes a biblically based explanation for the origins of the universe and of life. They reject modern physics, chemistry, and geology concerning the age of the Earth. They argue that the entire universe was created within a period of six days, based on the account in Genesis 1:2. They believe that the universe was spontaneously created by divine fiat 6,000 to 10,000 years ago, challenging evidence for billions of years of geological history and fossil evidence. These creationists explain the existence of fossilized remains of ancient life by referring to a universal flood that covered the entire Earth for 40 days. Surviving creatures were saved by being taken aboard Noah's ark. Creatures that did not survive this flood, such as dinosaurs, became extinct. This creationist view is taught in some of the more fundamentalist denominations of Protestantism, Judaism, and Islam.

Scientific creationists read the texts and theories presented by biologists, geologists, and paleontologists and then present their arguments against the evolutionary views. They do very little, if any, direct biological or geological research to refute evolutionary hypotheses (Rennie 2002). Their arguments are based on biblical sources mixed with misinterpretations of scientific data and evolutionary hypotheses. The cosmological framework espoused by the scientific creationists is not based on any empirical findings. For example, scientists around the world find no physical evidence of a universal flood. Local floods did occur in the Near East and may be related to the story of Noah that appears in the Bible (and in earlier Babylonian texts). But to date, no evidence exists for a universal flood that had the potential to wipe out human populations worldwide or to cause the extinction of creatures such as dinosaurs (Isaak 2007).

A more recent form of creationism has been referred to as "intelligent design creationism" (Gross and Forest 2004; Petto and Godfrey 2007). The historical roots of this conceptual stance go back to philosophers such as Plato and Aristotle in the Greek tradition, who suggested that a spiritual force structured the universe and society. These ideas were Christianized by Saint Thomas Aquinas (1225–1274) and European scholars during the medieval period. In the nineteenth century, theologian William Paley (1743–1805) argued that one could see proof of God's existence by examining the Earth and the remarkable adaptations of living organisms to their environments, using the famous analogy that if we found a watch, we would have to assume that there was a watchmaker—we can see God's plan as we observe the natural world (1803). Two contemporary theorists who support this position are Lehigh University's biochemist Michael Behe, author of *Darwin's Black Box* (1996), and philosopher and mathematician William Dembski, professor of science and theology at Southern Seminary in Louisville, Kentucky, author of the book *Intelligent Design* (1999).

Debates between intelligent design proponents and other researchers have been extensive and, at times, quite spirited (Rennie 2002; Shanks 2004; Shanks and Joplin 1999). Critics of intelligent design creationism note that Behe, Dembski, and their followers concede that microevolution and macroevolution has occurred, but contend that some biological phenomena and the complexity of life cannot be explained by modern science and that this complexity itself is proof that there must be an intelligent supernatural designer. Although most scientists would not rule out the possibility of supernatural creation, they do require evidence. In this respect, intelligent design has failed to provide a more compelling argument of human origins than evolutionary theory.

Given these diverse perspectives, is there any common ground between

(*continued*)

religious explanations of human origins and scientific theories? Surveys indicate that a surprising number of Americans assume that the creation-evolution controversy is based on a dichotomy between believers in God and secular atheists who are antireligious. This is incorrect. There are many varieties of both religious perspectives and evolutionary explanations, many of them compatible. Scientists and others who accept evolution are not necessarily atheists (Pennock 2003; Scott 2004). One major view of evolution is known as *theistic evolution*, which promotes the view that God creates through the evolutionary processes. Supporters of this perspective accept the modern scientific findings in astronomy, biology, genetics, and fossil and geological evidence, but see God as intervening in how evolution takes place. Theistic evolution is the official view accepted by the Roman Catholic Church; it was reiterated by Pope John Paul II in 1996. In this statement, John Paul II emphasized that evolution was not just "theory," but was based on an enormous amount of empirical evidence, or "facts." The Roman Catholic theological position is that although humans may indeed be descended from earlier forms of life, God created the human soul. Other contemporary mainstream Protestant, Jewish, Muslim, Hindu, and Buddhist scientists also accept theistic evolution. This position sees no conflict between religion and science and reflects a continuum between the creationist and evolutionary views.

Another view of evolution is sometimes referred to as *materialist evolutionism* or *philosophical materialism*. Scientists and philosophers who hold this view believe that the scientific evidence for evolution results in a proof

of atheism. Charles Darwin recorded in his memoirs how he vacillated between muddled religious faith, atheism, and what he later accepted as agnosticism (the belief that one cannot know as humans whether God exists or not) (Desmond and Moore 1991). Survey polls demonstrate that most Americans believe materialist evolutionism is the dominant view among scientists, despite the fact that this is not the case. Because it challenges religious interpretations, it is one of the primary reasons why some fundamentalist religious-based groups have opposed the teaching of evolution in public schools in the United States.

In actuality, there are scientists who accept theistic evolution or other spiritual views along with scientific theories. For example, one of the leading critics of intelligent design creationism is the practicing Roman Catholic biologist at Williams College, Kenneth Miller. Miller has authored a book called *Finding Darwin's God: A Scientist's Search for Common Ground between God and Evolution* (2000). In this book, Miller draws on biology, genetics, and evolutionary data to challenge intelligent design proponents' claims that the complexity of life demonstrates an intelligent designer. Paul Davies, a Protestant theologian and philosopher who authored the book *The Fifth Miracle* (2000) about faith and the evolution of life, is also critical of the intelligent design creationist model and relies on the empirical findings in science and evolution to refute their claims.

These individuals and other scientists accept theistic views of evolution, but emphasize that scientific understanding of the universe and life must be based on the methods of *naturalism*. This *methodological naturalism* requires the scientist to rely on "natural"

or "materialist" (biological and physical) explanations rather than spiritual or theological explanations for examining the universe and evolution, *but it does not compel one to accept atheism*. In fact, many major philosophers and scientists, such as anthropologist Eugenie Scott (former director of the National Center for Science Education) and the famed Albert Einstein, argued that one cannot prove or disprove the existence of God through the use of science. Methodological naturalism does not result in a conflict between faith and science. Rather, faith and science are viewed as two separate spheres and modes of understanding the world. This method of naturalism coincides with the teachings of the Roman Catholic position and many mainstream Protestant, Jewish, Muslim, Hindu, and Buddhist traditions.

Evolutionary explanations and other scientific theories often fail to satisfy our deep spiritual questions and moral concerns. While science can give us some basic answers about the universe and life, it cannot reveal spiritual insights. And yet, a scientific perspective does tend to leave us in a state of "spiritual awe" as described by Darwin in the famous closing passage of the *Origin of Species*: "There is grandeur in this view of life."

Points to Ponder

1. How can accounts of creation such as that found in Genesis 1:2 be evaluated empirically?

2. Have any of the scientific creationist claims convinced you of the falsity of evolution?

3. Do you think that faith and science are compatible when assessing the scientific record regarding evolution?

Summary and Review of Learning Objectives

3.1 Explain how cosmologies regarding human origins differ from scientific views of evolution.

Cosmologies are conceptual frameworks that present the universe (the *cosmos*) as an orderly system. They often include explanations of human origins and the place of humankind in the universe. Cosmological explanations

frequently involve divine or supernatural forces that are, by their nature, impossible for human beings to observe. We accept them and believe in them, on the basis of faith. Scientific theories of evolution, in contrast, are derived from the belief that the universe operates according to regular processes that can be observed. The scientific method is not a rigid framework that provides indisputable answers. Instead, scientific theories are propositions that can be evaluated by future testing and observation. Acceptance of the theory of evolution is based on observations in many areas of geology, paleontology, and biology.

3.2 Discuss how the scientific revolution provided the context for the theory of evolution.

In Europe during the Renaissance (after c. 1450 A.D.), scientific discoveries began to challenge concepts about both the age of the Earth and humanity's relationship to the rest of the universe. Astronomers such as Copernicus and Galileo discovered that the earth was not the center of the universe and along with other planets revolved around the sun. Geologists initiated research that demonstrated that the age of the earth was much older than described in religious texts such as the Bible. These findings provided the historical context for the development of the theory of evolution.

3.3 Explain how Darwin's view of natural selection and evolution differed from earlier scientific views.

Evolution refers to the process of change in the genetic makeup of a species over time. It is used to explain the emergence of new species. Theories regarding the evolution of plants and animal species were proposed by a number of scholars prior to the mid-1800s. However, none of these early theorists suggested a unified theory that explained evolution and, consequently, most people could not accept these ideas. Research by Charles Robert Darwin (1809–1882) and Alfred Russel Wallace (1823–1913) independently identified natural selection as a key mechanism for explaining change in a species over time. Natural selection is now recognized as one of the four principal evolutionary processes.

3.4 Discuss Gregor Johann Mendel's principles of inheritance.

Principles of inheritance refer to how specific traits are passed on from one generation to the next. Modern understanding of heredity emerged through the studies of an Austrian monk named Gregor Johann Mendel (1822–1884). Through the study of successive generations of pea plants, Mendel made several important observations. He demonstrated that traits are inherited in discrete packages of information that are not mixed during reproduction. The observation that units of heredity (or genes) occur in pairs and that offspring receive half of a pair from each parent is the basis of the principle of segregation. Mendel also observed that certain traits prevailed over others. He labeled the prevailing traits "dominant" and those traits that were unexpressed in one generation but expressed in following generations "recessive." Mendel referred to the fact that individual traits occur independently of one another as the principle of independent assortment.

3.5 Discuss how Mendel's principles of inheritance have changed in light of a better understanding of molecular genetics.

Mendel's principles of segregation and independent assortment and the concepts of recessive and dominant traits are still viewed as important aspects of heredity. However, using more advanced technology, modern scientists have a better understanding of the dynamics of heredity at the cellular level. Mendel's experiments focused on the investigation of physical traits in pea plants that were controlled by alleles at one genetic locus and had phenotypic expressions that were distinct: Plants were either tall or dwarf; the peas either green or yellow. There were no plants of varying height or of mixed green and yellow color. Today these are called Mendelian traits or traits of simple inheritance. While some human characteristics are inherited as discrete traits, the majority are passed on in a more complicated fashion. In contrast to Mendelian traits, many physical characteristics in humans have phenotypic expressions that form a gradation and are influenced by alleles at more than one genetic locus. Traits that display a graded series determined by genes at multiple genetic loci are referred to as polygenic or continuous traits. They include many of the most visible aspects of human features, such as height, skin color, and hair color.

3.6 Define and discuss how evolution takes place.

Evolution refers to the process of change in the genetic makeup of a species over time. It is used to explain the emergence of new species. Alteration of the gene pool of a population is influenced by four evolutionary processes: mutation, gene flow, genetic drift and natural selection. In addition, cultural, behavioral and epigenetic factors may further influence the genetic makeup of a population and thus are potential sources of evolutionary change. Evolutionary change is a dynamic, complex process. Although it is useful to discuss the preceding processes and factors as distinct variables, they all interact to affect evolutionary change. The key consideration is change in the genetic characteristics of a population from one generation to the next. Over time, this change may produce major differences among populations that were originally very similar.

3.7 Discuss how and why new species arise.

The study of speciation, or how and why new species arise, is one of the most interesting areas of research in evolutionary theory. A species is a group of organisms that have similar physical characteristics, can potentially interbreed with one another to produce fertile offspring, and that are reproductively isolated from other populations. Punctuated equilibrium and gradualism present extreme perspectives of the rate at which evolution and the process of speciation occur. According to phyletic gradualism, speciation occurs when there is an interruption in gene flow between populations that formerly were one species but became isolated. Gradually, through evolutionary change, these two populations become so different genetically that they became separate species. In contrast, punctuated equilibrium views evolution as occurring at variable rates; some species remaining in a state of equilibrium with their habitats for long geological periods, which were then interrupted by major changes, or punctuations, leading to rapid speciation. The fossil record provides examples of both, and most scientists agree that both types of evolution have occurred.

3.8   Briefly outline the evidence for the evolution of life on Earth and how evolutionary relationships are evaluated.

From studying the fossilized remains of different creatures, paleontologists have tracked the evolution of living forms throughout the world. They document the fossil record according to geological time, which is divided into *eras*, which are subdivided into *periods*, which in turn are composed of *epochs*. Paleontologists and anthropologists determine evolutionary relationships using both the fossil evidence and the genetic make-up of modern organisms. Prior to the advent of modern genetic studies, evolutionary relationships were inferred on the basis of organisms' physical characteristics. A useful concept in discussing the evolutionary relationships of living forms is homology. Homology refers to traits that have resulted from a common evolutionary origin, though they may differ in form and function. For example, a human hand bears little resemblance to a whale's fin. Careful examination of human and whale skeletons, however, reveals many structural similarities that can be explained by a common, albeit distant, evolutionary relationship. The majority of information on the evolution of life and human origin is provided by the information found in the fossil record. In recent years, however, studies of the genetic make-up of living organisms have received increasing attention. Study of the differences and similarities in the arrangement of genetic material for living animals provides important insights into evolutionary relationships. Similarities in the DNA of different species indicate that they inherited genetic blueprints (with minor modifications) from a common ancestor. Through the use of molecular dating, the genetic material of living animals has also been used to estimate when different species diverged. In most instances, this information has provided independent confirmation of conclusions about evolutionary relationships based on the study of skeletal characteristics and fossil remains.

Key Terms

adaptation, p. 55
adaptive radiation, p. 58
alleles, p. 51
analogy, p. 59
catastrophism, p. 45
continental drift, p. 60
cosmologies, p. 43
deoxyribonucleic acid (DNA), p. 53
dominant, p. 50
ecological niche, p. 55
epigenetic , p. 54
evolution, p. 46
founder effect, p. 55

gametes, p. 52
gene, p. 52
gene flow, p. 55
gene pool, p. 54
genetic drift, p. 55
genotype, p. 51
Hardy-Weinberg theory of genetic equilibrium, p. 56
heterozygous, p. 51
homology, p. 59
homozygous, p. 51
meiosis, p. 53
mitosis, p. 53

mutations, p. 54
natural selection, p. 46
phenotype, p. 51
phyletic gradualism, p. 57
plate tectonics, p. 60
population, p. 54
punctuated equilibrium, p. 57
recessive, p. 50
somatic cells, p. 52
speciation, p. 57
species, p. 57
uniformitarianism, p. 45
zygote, p. 52

Chapter 4
The Primates

Learning Objectives

After reading this chapter you should be able to:

4.1 Discuss characteristics shared by all primates.

4.2 Explain the basis for primate taxonomy.

4.3 Discuss what fossil evidence reveals about primate evolution.

4.4 Describe the importance of social organization among the primates.

4.5 Discuss human origins in light of primate evolution, and describe how humans are both similar to and different from other primate species.

Humans are members of the mammalian order **Primates**, a diverse group of animals that also includes monkeys, prosimians, and apes. While a diverse group, primates share a number of key characteristics, such as large brain size, keen vision, dexterous hands, and a generalized skeleton that allows for great physical agility. Primates also tend to have smaller litters than other animals, devoting more care and attention to the rearing of their offspring. These traits are more prominent in some primates, while hardly evident in others. Similar features can also be found in many nonprimates. For example, the lion has very efficient eyesight, and the tree squirrel is exceedingly agile. However, the unique *combination* of traits found in the primates distinguishes them from other animals.

As humans are primates, examination of both living and fossil primate species is key to understanding human origins. We can trace the striking similarities among primates to a series of shared evolutionary relationships. Many people hold a common misconception about human evolution—the mistaken belief that humans descended from modern apes such as the gorilla and chimpanzee. This is a highly inaccurate understanding of Charles Darwin's thesis and contemporary scientific theories of human evolution, as well as the available fossil evidence. Gorillas and chimpanzees are not human ancestors. Rather, like humans, the gorilla and chimpanzee represent the end points of their own distinct evolutionary lineages (see Table 4.1 and Figure 4.2). As primates, however, they share a distant common ancestor (now extinct) with other primates.

Examinations of primate fossils afford insight into the evolutionary stages through which human ancestors passed, while examination of living primate species provides insight into primate adaptations to different environments, behavior, and possible commonalities with early human ancestors. Primate *paleontologists* and *paleoanthropologists* study fossil bones and teeth of early primates to trace lines of human evolution dating back millions of years. Meanwhile, *primatologists* concentrate on living, nonhuman primates, working to discover subtle similarities and differences among these creatures. As researchers weave together the fossil record and conclusions from primatological observations, they discern the tapestry of human evolution—how it occurred and what makes humans physically and behaviorally distinct from other primate species.

Primate Characteristics

4.1 **Discuss characteristics shared by all primates.**

Primate characteristics incorporate a wide variety of physical and anatomical traits that represent adaptations to a variety of environments, particularly **arboreal** adaptations—that is, life in the trees (Campbell 2007;

Fleagle 2013; Richard 1985). They include features related to locomotion and movement, diet, vision, and maturation. As discussed in the following chapter, many of these features were likely important in the adaptive abilities of early human ancestors.

Movement and Locomotion

Among the most important physical characteristics of primates is their generalized skeletal structure that allows for a great deal of flexibility in movement. Consider, for example, the *clavicle*, or collarbone, a feature found in early mammals. This skeletal element has been lost in faster, more specialized land animals, such as the dog and the horse, that have more rigid skeletons. In primates, the clavicle provides both support and flexibility, enabling them to rotate their shoulders and arms to perform a range of movements. In the wild, this skeletal structure gives primates the ability to reach for branches and food while roaming through treetops, or to manipulate objects. Humans, of course, do not live in trees. However, their generalized primate skeleton is what allows them to drive cars, catch baseballs, and throw spears. There is also a tendency toward upright posture in all primates. Though most pronounced in humans, all primates can stand; upright walking is occasionally found in nonhuman species such as the chimpanzee and orangutan.

Dexterity in the digits (fingers and toes) of the feet and hands, another key primate trait, makes it easy for primates to grasp and manipulate objects. All primates (except for the callitrichids) have sensitive pads and nails on their fingertips rather than claws, and many have five digits on their hands and feet. Primate digits are *prehensile* or highly effective for grasping. Consequently, in contrast to cats or rodents with claws, primates climb by wrapping their hands and feet around branches. A particularly important aspect of the primate hand is the **opposable thumb**, found in humans and many other primates (Figure 4.1). Humans can touch the tips of each of their fingers with the thumb, an ability that makes them adept at manipulating small objects. Some primates do not have opposable thumbs, but all members of the Primate order share a high degree of digit mobility.

Dentition, Eyesight, and Brain Size

Dentition or the number, form, and arrangement of teeth, serves as a distinguishing characteristic of many types of animals. Because they are strong and are often better preserved in the fossil record than other parts of the skeleton, teeth are particularly valuable evidence for paleontologists who use them to identify extinct primates. Compared to other mammals, primates have multipurpose teeth that can be used for either cutting or crushing foods. The dental structure of primates is generally consistent with an **omnivorous** diet

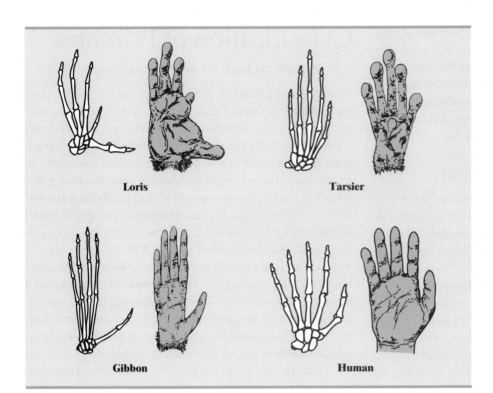

Figure 4.1 Examples of primate hands. Although they vary in form, they share a high degree of manual dexterity.

Loris

Tarsier

Gibbon

Human

made up of a variety of foods, from plants, fruits, nuts, and seeds to insects and other animals.

Different teeth perform different functions. Their shape varies from one primate species to another as a result of evolutionary adaptations to particular food-processing situations (Swindler 2002). The anterior (front) teeth, including the incisors and canines, are used to transfer food into the mouth. They are designed for cutting, tearing, and biting. The posterior (back) teeth, including the molars and premolars, are more specialized for breaking down food by crushing or grinding. This basic dental configuration is present in most mammals and the majority of primates. However, depending on their adaptations, the number and form of the various teeth is different in different species. For example, the canine teeth of a carnivore, such as a lion, are pronounced and the premolars pointed; they are better suited for biting and tearing meat. In contrast, the molars of plant-eating animals, like cows and horses, are broad and flat for masticating fibrous plant material.

Unlike lions or horses, primate teeth are not overly specialized with regard to size and shape. Human teeth, for example, exhibit some differences—our canines are clearly different in shape from our molars—but they are all relatively the same size. This makes them multipurpose teeth suitable for eating just about everything. Although individual primate species tend to exploit specific kinds of foods, particularly fruits, leaves, and insects, some species will also eat and kill small birds and amphibians. Chimpanzees have also been known to kill and eat other mammals. Primates' unspecialized dentition indicates an evolutionary trend throughout their history toward an omnivorous diet.

Vision   Refined vision also sets primates apart. Whereas many animals are highly dependent on *olfaction*, the sense of smell, primates, having large eyes oriented to the front and protected by bony structures, rely heavily on vision. This visual orientation favors *binocular* and *stereoscopic vision* in which the visual fields of the eyes overlap, transmitting images to both sides of the brain. Primates benefit from enhanced depth perception as a result. Evolution has also made the retina of primates' eyes sensitive to different wavelengths of light, producing color vision in most primates. Primates depend upon their highly developed visual sense to identify food and coordinate grasping and leaping.

This visual acuity has important adaptive implications. On one hand, it would have facilitated life in an arboreal environment, making it easy for primates to move through the trees. On the other hand, acute vision would have also enhanced primates' food-getting ability, including the gathering of seeds and berries (Sussman 1991). It could have also facilitated hunting (Cartmill 1997). Eyes oriented to the front are a characteristic generally found in predators, and this trait would have allowed primates to effectively hunt for insects, amphibians, or other creatures.

Complexity of the Brain   Distinguishing primates even more than the preceding characteristics are the size and complexity of the brain. This is a trend among the placental mammals in general, but particularly notable among the primates. Relative to body size, primates have larger brains than any other land animal; only the brains of some marine mammals are of comparable relative size (Fleagle 2013). In primates, the *neocortex*, the surface portion of the brain associated with sensory messages and voluntary control of movement, features a large number of convolutions, or folds, that maximize the surface area. This implies development of the brain functions associated with the processing and integration of both motor and sensory functions. As they evolved, these larger, complex brains undoubtedly helped primates to locate and extract food and to avoid predators (Jolly 1985).

Reproduction and Maturation

In contrast to most other animals, primates reproduce few offspring, and these undergo long periods of growth and development. The gestation period for primates—that is, the length of time the young spend in the mother's womb—is longer than that of nonprimate animals of comparable size. Primate offspring are born helpless and unable to survive on their own. For this reason, they have long periods of maturation, during which they remain highly dependent on their parents and other adults. As an example, a kitten reaches full adulthood at one year, whereas a baboon takes seven or eight years to reach maturity. Humans, in contrast, have a period of infancy that lasts six years. Full adulthood, characterized by the appearance of the third molars, or "wisdom teeth," is reached at 20 years of age.

This protracted maturation process has adaptive advantages. Parents invest much more time in the care and rearing of their offspring, ensuring greater survival rates. Living in social groups, immature primates learn complex tasks, primarily by observing their mothers and fathers, but also by observing others in their social group. Through this *social learning*, primates gain the skills needed to locate food and shelter and to elude predators.

Classification of Primates

4.2 Explain the basis for primate taxonomy.

Primates are placed in a distinct group on the basis of their shared physical characteristics. Individual species—groups of individuals that can potentially interbreed and are reproductively isolated from other populations—share even more specific traits. These categories are useful to researchers. **Taxonomy**, the science of classification, gives scientists a convenient way of referring to, and comparing, living and extinct organisms. Modern taxonomy is based on the work of the Swedish scientist Carl von Linné, also known as Carolus Linnaeus (1707–1778). Linnaeus created a system of Latin names to categorize plants and animals based on their similarities. The Linnaean system follows a hierarchical pattern (see Table 4.1), ranging from large categories, such as *kingdoms* that encompass creatures sharing overarching characteristics, to small groups, or *species*, whose members can all potentially interbreed.

Human beings belong to the kingdom Animalia, one of several major divisions of nature. Members of this kingdom are mobile, complex organisms that sustain themselves by eating plants and other animals. Other categories, or *taxa*, are based on more specific criteria (see Table 4.1). For example, humans have backbones, a feature that places them in the subphylum Vertebrata, while the presence of body hair and mammary glands further identifies them as members of the class Mammalia (mammals). Classes are subdivided into a number of orders; humans belong to the order Primates. Like other mammals, primates are warm-blooded animals that possess hair for

---

Table 4.1 Classification Relevant to Human Ancestry

The classification of living organisms is hierarchical. Membership in a kingdom is determined by very basic characteristics. Classification into other categories is based on increasingly specific criteria. The words *primate*, *anthropoid*, *hominoid*, and *hominid* are used to refer to members of the categories Primates, Anthropoidea, Hominoidea, and Hominidae. Superfamily names generally end in *-oidea*, family names in *-idae*, and subfamily names in *-inae*.

Category	Taxon	Common Description
Kingdom	Animalia	Animals
Phylum	Chordata	Animals with notochords
Subphylum	Vertebrata	Animals with backbones
Superclass	Tetrapoda	Four-footed vertebrates
Class	Mammalia	Vertebrates with body hair and mammary glands
Order	Primates	All prosimians, monkeys, apes, and humans
Suborder	Anthropoidea	All monkeys, apes, and humans
Infraorder	Catarrhini	Old World anthropoids
Superfamily	Hominoidea	Apes and humans
Family	Hominidae	orangutans, chimpanzees, gorillas, and humans
Subfamily	Homininae	chimpanzees, gorillas, and humans
Tribe	Hominini	Bipedal apes including humans
Genus	*Homo*	Humans and their immediate ancestors
Species	*Homo sapiens*	Modern humans

Critical Perspectives

What's in a Name? Primate Classification and Taxonomy

Scientists have traditionally used physical characteristics that reflect shared adaptive histories in classifying primates into various families, genera, and species (see Table 4.1, Figure 4.2). However, the unraveling of genetic codes has revealed the specific genetic links between living species. While the two approaches have yielded similar, if not identical, divisions they are not always the same.

Let's consider the classification of humans, chimpanzees, gorillas, and orangutans. On the one hand, the African apes (chimpanzees and gorillas) and orangutans, which have certain physical traits in common, were traditionally placed in their own family, Pongidae; the pongids. Humans, on the other hand, followed another evolutionary line, making them distinct in appearance, distinctive in terms of their upright posture, and very different in terms of their behavioral adaptations. In contrast to other primates, humans have larger brains and lack the thick body hair found in other primate species. Humans also have developed a complex culture—material

objects and nonmaterial concepts—that they use to interact with the environment. For this reason, scientists placed humans and their immediate ancestors in the family Hominidea; the hominids. The separation of the hominids from the pongids makes sense both in light of their distinct evolutionary histories and human cultural development.

However, molecular studies of genetic material of living primates, as well as the careful study of ape and human anatomy, indicate that in actuality, humans and the African apes are more closely related than either group is to the orangutans (Andrews and Martin 1987). As a result, a variety of new classification schemes emerged over the past two decades that attempt to represent the close genetic relatedness between humans and their closest living relatives, and the implications that this has for the understanding of evolutionary relationships.

One solution has been to place the orangutans, chimpanzees, and gorillas, as well as humans and their ancestors, into the family Hominidae, which is further divided into two subfamilies: Subfamily Ponginae is used to refer to the orangutans, while subfamily Homininae includes the gorillas, chimpanzees, and

humans, a grouping that reflects their close genetic relatedness. Humans and their ancestors are then placed in their own tribe, Hominini (hominins) to denote their unique characteristics.

This classification schema has significant implications for the discussion of human evolution. The classification more accurately reflects the genetic relatedness of the different species, and for that reason is used in this book. However, the new terminology is more cumbersome and potentially confusing, as previously used terms have different meanings in the new scheme. The term *hominid* had been used to denote the split of the human family from the rest of the apes. In the revised classification, Hominidae includes both humans and the African apes, with humans, gorillas, and chimpanzees each making up their own tribe within the subfamily.

Points to Ponder

1. Review the different approaches to primate classification. Outline how and why these perspectives differ.
2. A key objective taxonomy is to facilitate comparison. Discuss how the revision of taxonomic systems is, or is not, useful.

Order	Suborder	Infraorder	Superfamily	Family	Subfamily	Tribe	Common Term
P R I M A T E S	Prosimii						Loris Lemur Tarsier
	Anthropoidea	Platyrrhini					New World monkey
		Catarrhini	Cercopithecoidea				Old World monkey
			Hominoidea	Hylobatidae			Gibbon
				Hominidae	Ponginae		Orangutan
					Homininae	Gorillini	Gorilla
						Panini	Chimpanzee Bonobo
						Hominini	Human

insulation and nourish their young with milk from mammary glands. However, primates' refined visual sense, manual dexterity, distinctive skeletal structure, and large brain size differentiate them from other mammals.

Although all primates share certain basic characteristics, there is a great deal of variation among species. There

is some disagreement among primatologists about how particular species are related to one another and how the order should be divided. Linnaeus developed his classification system to facilitate the comparison of organisms a century before Darwin introduced his theory of evolution. Consequently, Linnaeus did not consider evolutionary relationships in his taxonomies. However, after Darwin's publication of *On the Origin of Species* in 1859, biologists increasingly applied theories of evolution to systems of classification, giving rise to a number of scientific disputes about the basis of classification. Scientists initially focused on physical similarities among species, traits that most likely emerged as evolutionary adaptations to specific environments. More recently, the actual genetic links can be determined through the study of DNA. With increasing research into the genetic codes of living primates, genetic relatedness has become more important in taxonomy (see the box "What's in a Name?").

Primate Subdivisions

The order Primates is divided into two suborders: Prosimii, or prosimians, and Anthropoidea, or anthropoids. The prosimians include modern lemurs, lorises, and tarsiers, all of which are found exclusively in Asia, Africa, and Madagascar. The anthropoids, comprising all monkeys, apes, and humans, can be separated into two smaller divisions, or infraorders: Platyrrhini, referring to all monkeys found in the Americas; and Catarrhini, or anthropoid primates of Europe, Asia, and Africa. The catarrhines are subdivided into the superfamilies Cercopithecoidea, consisting of the Old World monkeys; and Hominoidea, which includes apes and humans. The hominoids are further divided into two families consisting of the Hylobatidae, the gibbons and siamangs of Asia; and the Hominidae, which includes humans and the so-called "Great Apes," the chimpanzees, gorillas, and orangutans. Humans and the African apes, along with their ancestors, are placed in subfamily Homininae because of their close genetic relatedness, while the more distantly related orangutans are placed in the separate subfamily Ponginae. Researchers have further broken down the Homininae subfamily, to include three separate tribes: the Hominini (humans and their ancestors), Panini (chimps), and Gorillini (gorillas). While this terminology can be challenging to understand, and has been made somewhat more confusing by recent changes in classification (See the box "What's in a Name?"), classification is of key importance in providing scientists a means of describing individual species and fossil finds. Paleoanthropologists have taken a particular interest in members of the subfamily Homininae because these are the primates most closely related to humans.

Classification of Fossil Primates

Biologists and primatologists sometimes disagree about the classification of living organisms. However, paleontologists and paleoanthropologists face even more daunting challenges in classifying extinct species because they must base their conclusions solely on characteristics preserved in the fossil record, such as skeletal structure and dentition. Natural variations within populations, the vagaries of climatic and geological changes, and the ravages of time all make identifying species on this basis exceedingly difficult (Conroy 1990; Hartwig 2002).

In the past, scientists have placed great emphasis on the skull, or *cranium*, in distinguishing fossil primates from one another. The cranium provides important clues to an extinct animal's vision, diet, cognitive abilities, and posture. However, as increasing numbers of fossils have been recovered, paleontologists have looked more closely at the *postcranial skeleton*, all the bones of the body excluding the skull (Strasser and Dagosto 1988). By examining the postcranial skeleton, we can determine a great deal about a primate's posture and locomotion, which, in turn, tells us about the animal's adaptations to specific environments. As we bring together all this information, we can discern much more clearly how fossil primates looked and functioned in their environments.

The fossil record for certain periods is sketchy, at best. For example, we know that the Paleocene epoch of the Tertiary period was likely an important period with regard to the emergence of the first primates. Unfortunately, only a limited number of well-preserved fossils from this period have been located, making reconstruction of primate evolution difficult. Because of the fragmentary nature of some finds, identification to the species level is not possible, and their specific evolutionary relationships remain uncertain. As more information is obtained, some interpretations of primate evolution will likely see a great deal of revision.

Evolution of the Primate Order

4.3   Discuss what fossil evidence reveals about primate evolution.

The physical characteristics that define Order Primates, as well as those of individual primate species, can be clearly seen in living populations, but they are also preserved in the fossil record. Methods of locomotion, refinements in vision, and the evolution of the brain necessitate specific bone and muscle structures that are visible in the skeleton. Similarly, the structure and organization of the brain can be inferred through the examination of the *crania*, or skulls, of fossilized species. Behavioral patterns, such as extended periods of infant dependency or primate social organization, are best viewed through the observation of living species. However, some activities, such as chimpanzee tool use (discussed later) or the behavior of early human ancestors (see Chapter 7), can be obtained from the archaeological record. Observation of modern primate species may also facilitate the reconstruction of the behaviors of fossil species that occupied similar environments. These evolutionary trends can be traced through the lines of primates from the Eocene to the present day.

There are approximately 250 species of living primates, representing the products of millions of years of adaptation. Scientists speculate that the first primate ancestors probably evolved during the radiation of the placental mammals during the Paleocene epoch of the early Tertiary period, approximately 65 million to 56 million years ago (see Table 3.1, Figure 4.2). However, the oldest clearly recognizable primates date to the Eocene epoch (56 to 33 million years ago). Species of ancestral prosimian primates emerged as the earliest forms of primates, followed by the anthropoids. While these early creatures resembled modern primates in some respects, particularly in the shape and arrangement of their teeth, they were unlike any living species. Notably, in some instances, the number of fossil species during certain time periods is greater than in the case of their modern counterparts. Because modern primates inhabit environments similar to those occupied by extinct species, the study of modern-day primates casts light on the adaptive characteristics of earlier primate species. Modern nonhuman primates embody some of the same adaptive features found in fossil species and, in this way, reflect the evolutionary phases through which the primates passed over millions of years.

Many placental mammals appeared during the middle Paleocene and are known from fossil remains in Asia, Europe, Africa, and America. However, candidates for ancestral primates are fragmentary and widely debated. Possible relatives are represented by a number of different genera, collectively referred to as *plesiadapiforms* (Clemens 1974; Gingerich 1986). Although they have sometimes been classified as a distinct suborder of archaic Primates, plesiadapiforms more likely represent a distinct group of mammals near the root of the primate family tree (see Figure 4.2, Table 3.1). Certain aspects of plesiadapiform dentition distinguish these creatures from earlier animals. These features bear some similarities to later primates, but the plesiadapiforms also exhibit distinctive adaptations to particular environmental niches. These adaptations include specialized teeth, cranial structure, and limb bones unlike those of any later primates, indicating that the plesiadapiforms are not precursors of any primate groups that come after them.

The status of other fossil species as early primate ancestors remains equally tenuous. The discovery of 60-million-year-old fossil teeth near the Atlas Mountains of Morocco lends support to the theory that early primates emerged in Africa (Gingerich 1990). These teeth define a previously unknown species, *Altialasius koulchii*, tiny creatures probably weighing no more than 3.5 ounces. Yet, given the fragmentary nature of the finds, the precise relationship of this species to primates is uncertain. These creatures may be precursors of anthropoid primates, or they may represent a side branch, such as the

Primates most likely evolved from creatures similar in appearance to modern tree shrews, shown here.

plesiadapiforms. It is important to note that North America was still attached to Europe during the early Tertiary period, and animals, including primate ancestors, could have moved easily between the continents. The earliest primates may have evolved in other parts of the world, including North America, Europe, and Asia, as well as Africa. To provide the context for the emergence of the earliest human ancestors, the evolution of the primates is briefly reviewed.

Prosimians

The prosimians, which appeared at the beginning of the Eocene, were the first true primates. These early prosimian primates flourished: More than 200 widely distributed species are represented. Researchers have located the most complete prosimian fossil finds in North America and Europe, but more fragmentary examples of prosimian fossils have been discovered in Asia and Africa (Fleagle 2013). Paleoanthropologist Elwyn Simons (1972) has described these early prosimians as "the first primates of modern aspect," signaling their important place in primate evolution.

In examining the cranial structure of the Eocene prosimians, scientists have found striking evidence to indicate that these animals relied much more upon vision than on their sense of smell. Consider the *endocast*—a cast of the brain—of *Tetonius*, a 50-million-year-old prosimian found in Wyoming (Radinsky 1967). Although the olfactory portions of the brain are small compared to earlier creatures, the occipital and temporal lobes (the sections of the cerebrum associated with vision) are relatively large. From its large eyes, researchers deduce that *Tetonius* was **nocturnal**—that is, it searched for food at night when other animals were sleeping. Present-day (extant) nocturnal animals have large eyes to take in the greater amounts of light needed for night vision. A nocturnal orientation can be inferred in extinct animals whose crania reveal large orbits (spaces in the skull for eyes).

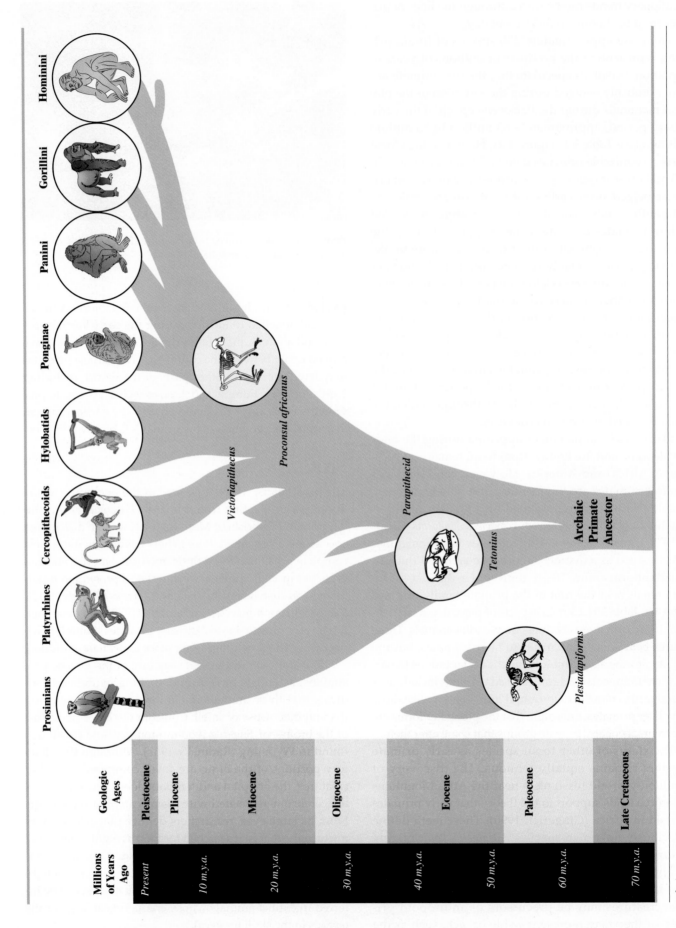

Figure 4.2 One interpretation of primate evolutionary relationships.

Scientists have unearthed few postcranial skeletons of the early prosimians, but the available finds suggest that these creatures were evolving toward the more generalized skeletal structure that characterizes later primates. With slender limbs and modified hands and feet, these primates most likely had some of the locomotor and grasping abilities of modern species. And in some species, nails were replacing claws (Dagosto 1988). These characteristics, which were retained as *primitive characteristics* in modern prosimians, suggest that these creatures were related to later species. Interestingly, some fossil prosimians also exhibit features that resemble the most primitive characteristics in the anthropoid primates, such as the orbits of the eye and the structure of foot and leg bones. However, the skeletal structures of some of these species also exhibit many distinctive features. These adaptations, or *derived characteristics*, include specialized teeth, cranial structures, and limb bones, making their relationship to living primates uncertain.

Modern Prosimians Modern prosimians have changed relatively little from their ancestors and reside in small, isolated populations. They include the lemurs and indris of Madagascar (an island off the east coast of Africa), the loris-

Ring-tailed lemurs from Madagascar are an example of a living prosimian species.

es of tropical Southeast Asia and Africa, and the tarsiers of Southeast Asia.

A heightened visual sense makes most of the living prosimians well adapted to a nocturnal lifestyle. They do not have color vision. Like their fellow primates, however, they possess stereoscopic vision and enlarged brains relative to other animals, which help them to coordinate leaping and food gathering in their arboreal environment. A keen sense of smell, more highly developed than that of the anthropoid primates, helps them to seek out food and shelter at night.

Like other primates, the prosimians use the five dexterous digits on their hands and feet to grasp objects and move easily through trees. Some *prosimii*, such as the indris, move by vertical clinging and leaping from branch to branch in an upright position, springing with their hind legs and landing with their arms and legs. All of the living prosimians have nails instead of claws on their digits, but some have retained grooming claws on their hind feet that are used to clean their fur. Because of the extensive destruction of the tropical rain forests in which the prosimians live, all are endangered animals.

Evolution of the Anthropoids

As many of the early prosimians gradually became extinct at the end of the Eocene epoch, new types of primates emerged in tropical forest environments. Among these new primates were creatures that were the ancestors of modern anthropoids, including humans. Scientists divide the anthropoids into two groups based on their evolutionary relatedness. These two categories are the infraorders platyrrhini (including all monkeys from the Americas, or New World monkeys) and catarrhini (which includes both the cercopithecoids, the Old World monkeys from Europe, Asia, and Africa; and the hominoids, including apes and humans).

The evolution of the higher primates is closely tied to plate tectonics and continental drift, examined in Chapter 3. During the late Cretaceous period, approximately 65 million years ago, North America and Europe were joined, allowing free migration of primates between what later became the European, African, and Asian continents and the Americas. About 40 million years ago, the Americas separated from Europe, Asia, and Africa, ending contact between primates from the Eastern and Western hemispheres. This geological development resulted in disparate lines of primate evolution. Platyrrhines evolved in southern Mexico and Central and South America, and cercopithecoids developed in Africa and Asia. We shall first examine the monkeys in the Americas and then turn to the evolution of monkeys and hominoids in Europe, Asia, and Africa.

Evolution of the Platyrrhines The fossil record for the evolution of superfamily platyrrhini, including all the monkeys in the Americas, is sparse and consists only of fragmentary fossil evidence from Bolivia, Colombia, Argentina, and Jamaica. Indeed, all of the primate fossils found in South America would fill no more than a shoe box (Fleagle 2013). Paleontologists, therefore, have not been able to reconstruct a detailed account of how anthropoid evolution proceeded in the Americas. Current interpretations favor the theory that the platyrrhines evolved from African anthropoid primates, a theory consistent with the limited fossil evidence and shared similarities in dentition and biochemical characteristics. In particular, some of the early African anthropoid primates from the family parapithecidae resemble South American monkeys (see later discussion of catarrhines).

Although African origins for the platyrrhines present the most likely interpretation of the available fossil evidence, scientists remain puzzled about how ancestral anthropoids may have arrived in South America from Africa. Uncertainty surrounds much of our understanding of continental drift during this period, making it difficult to date precisely when various landmasses separated. South America is believed to have been an island continent during most of the early Cenozoic era and separated from Africa. Periods of low sea levels during the Oligocene era (33 million to 23 million years ago) may have exposed landmasses and created areas of relatively shallow water in the

South Atlantic. Yet, the movement of ancestral platyrrhines between the continents would still have likely involved crossing open water. Transportation over large expanses of water on floating masses of vegetation has been used to explain the movement of some species, and, in fact, ocean currents would have been favorable to an African–South American crossing. It has, however, been questioned whether this method of dispersal is consistent with primate dietary and climatic requirements and whether transport over large bodies of water would have been possible.

North and Central America have also been suggested as the home of the ancestral platyrrhines, but there is no fossil evidence to bolster such an interpretation (Fleagle 2013). Paleogeographical reconstructions would also seem to confound this theory, as they suggest that during the Oligocene era, the distance between South America and landmasses to the north was even greater than that between South America and Africa. However, the geological history of the Caribbean is poorly known. Another candidate for the platyrrhine origins is Antarctica. Though it was joined to South America during the appropriate time period, the absence of any information on the evolution of mammalian species on Antarctica makes this scenario impossible to evaluate.

Modern Monkeys of the Americas The monkeys of the Americas encompass more than 50 different species—including the marmosets, the tamarins, the sakis, and the squirrel, howler, spider, and wooly monkeys—having a tremendous range in physical appearance and adaptations (Jolly 1985). One feature that distinguishes anthropoids from the Americas from those originating in Europe, Asia, or Africa is the shape of the nose. The former monkeys have broad, widely flaring noses with nostrils facing outward. The latter anthropoids have narrow noses with the nostrils facing downward.

Monkeys from the Americas are almost exclusively arboreal, spending their days in trees and coming to the ground only to move from one tree to another. Their elongated limbs are ideal for grasping tree branches. As **quadrupeds**, they use all four limbs for locomotion. In addition, many of these monkeys have developed a unique grasping, or *prehensile*, tail. Prehensile tails serve as a fifth limb, enabling some platyrrhines to hang from branches and feed with their other limbs. This unusual tail also gives the monkeys greater coordination and balance as they move through trees. Most monkeys from the Americas eat a varied, omnivorous diet that includes fruits, insects, and small animals.

Evolution of the Catarrhines Compared to the meager fossil findings of monkeys from the Americas, paleontologists have unearthed extensive anthropoid remains from Europe, Asia, and Africa. Specimens of superfamily Catarrhini have been recovered from all over these continents, including many regions that primates no longer inhabit. Among the most significant fossil localities are those in the Fayum Depression in

A spider monkey hanging from its prehensile tail. Platyrrhine primates with prehensile tails are found only in the Americas.

A male baboon's open mouth displays his prominent canine teeth. The larger canine teeth of male baboons compared to females illustrates sexual dimorphism.

early anthropoid primates may represent a distinct branch early in the anthropoid line (Kay 2000).

Genus *Apidium*, a group of closely related species, are particularly well-known parapithecids. They have been identified in hundreds of fragments of fossilized bones that allow for some reconstruction of what the creature may have been like. *Apidium* is a small, quadrupedal primate with a short snout. They had 36 teeth, the same number found in modern American monkeys. Apidium's comparatively small orbits indicate that *Apidium* was **diurnal**, that is, active during the day. Postcranial bones, such as the long hind legs and flexible ankles, lead researchers to believe that *Apidium* was an effective leaper and possibly adapted to an arboreal environment.

Cercopithecoids   To trace the earliest potential ancestors of Old World monkeys (superfamily cercopithecoidea) of Europe, Asia, and Africa, paleontologists turn to the Miocene deposits in northern and eastern Africa, pegged at 23 million to 5.3 million years ago. Unfortunately, Miocene fossil remains are highly fragmentary, and many species are only known on the basis of their teeth. They represent a diversity of species, none of which can be conveniently related to any modern species or even subfamilies. They are classified as an ancestral subfamily of fossil monkeys known as the *Victoriapithecinae* that predates the diversification of the modern subfamilies of cercopithecoids (cercopithecinea and colobinea, discussed later).

An early representative of cercopithecoidea is *Victoriapithecus*, a small-to-medium-sized monkey (between 10 and 55 pounds) described on the basis of fossils recovered near Lake Victoria in Kenya (Fleagle 2013). *Victoriapithecus* and related genera had a number of characteristics of modern cercopithecoid species. For example, the chewing surfaces of *Victoriapithecus* molars had distinctive patterns of cusps and ridges that are found in extant species. In addition, males and females had different-sized canine teeth, a feature *Victoriapithecus* had in common with all monkeys of Europe, Asia, and Africa. However, some of the more derived features found in later monkeys were absent from *Victoriapithecus*. Thus, these primates cannot be placed in any modern subfamily. Rather, because they represent a transitional form between earlier catarrhines and modern monkeys, they make up their own subfamily of extinct primitive monkeys, the *Victoriapithecinae*.

Remains of many other species of monkeys have been found in fossil beds of the Pliocene and Pleistocene epochs (5.3 million years of age up to the recent past). The majority of these extinct species can be conveniently organized into the same subfamilies as living monkeys, providing continuity with modern species.

Modern Monkeys of Europe, Asia, and Africa
Modern-day cercopithecoids encompass an extremely diverse group, consisting of some 70 or 80 different species scattered throughout sub-Saharan Africa, southern Asia, and northern

Egypt, an extremely arid region rich in fossil-bearing strata dating from 45 million to 31 million years ago. Anthropoid fossils abound in the upper part of the formation, dating back about 37 million years ago. During this period, the Fayum was a lush tropical forest, ideal for primates; an amazing variety of plant and animal fossils have been unearthed in this once-fertile region (Simons and Rasmussen 1990).

Parapithecids   Among the most interesting of the early anthropoid primates are representatives of the family Parapithecidae. However, scientists have not determined the precise relationship of these animals to later primates. Skeletal and dental structures of certain parapithecids resemble those of platyrrhines or squirrel monkeys now living in Central and South America (Kay 2000). Discovering these features in African fossils, researchers conjectured that parapithecids may have emerged sometime near the divergence of the anthropoids from the Americas and those from Europe, Asia, and Africa. However, the parapithecids exhibit many specialized, derived dental traits that suggest evolutionary adaptations leading away from the lines of later anthropoids. One theory holds that these

Japan. Next to humans, they are the most widely distributed primate group. These monkeys include different species of macaques, langurs, savanna and hamadryas baboons, geladas, colobus monkeys, and proboscis monkeys. Like the anthropoids of the Americas, these monkeys are quadrupedal. Although primarily arboreal, some, such as the savanna baboons, are terrestrial. Unlike their American counterparts, these monkeys do not have prehensile tails; however, some do use their tails as aids in communication and balance.

These monkeys break down into two subfamilies: cercopithecinea and colobinea. Most of the cercopithecines live in Africa, but some, such as the macaques, are also found in Asia. The colobines include the langurs of Asia and the African colobus monkeys. The two subfamilies differ most with respect to nutrition. The cercopithecines have a slightly more varied diet, feeding on many types of vegetation and fruit. Their cheek pouches act like storage bins; these pouches can be filled with food intended to be eaten in another place. In contrast, the colobines subsist primarily on leaves; often referred to as "leaf-eating monkeys," they have specialized teeth, stomachs, and intestines that enable them to digest the woody, cellulose parts of plants. Compared to the cercopithecines, the colobines are less mobile, often residing in the trees where they feed.

Pronounced **sexual dimorphism**, in which males and females of the same species exhibit separate characteristics unrelated to sexual reproduction, distinguishes many

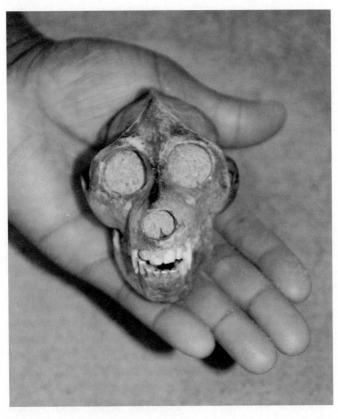

Skull of *Aegyptopithecus zeuxis*, an Oligocene anthropoid, excavated from the Fayum Depression in Egypt.

cercopithecine monkeys. The male baboon, for example, has a much larger body and larger canine teeth than the female. These differences arise as a result of rivalry among males for females. Species in which competition for sexual mates is limited exhibit little sexual dimorphism, whereas species characterized by intense competition display the most dramatic dimorphism (Kay et al. 1988). Other features, including relative differences in the size of the testes and sexual swelling in females during ovulation, also correlate with mating rivalry and patterns of social organization.

Emergence of the Hominoids

The evolution of the anthropoids set the stage for the appearance of the first representatives of superfamily hominoidea and, consequently, the emergence of more immediate human ancestors. Consider representatives of the genus *Aegyptopithecus*, discovered in the Fayum region in Egypt and dating from approximately 33 million years ago. The fossil evidence for *Aegyptopithecus* includes a skull, numerous jaw fragments, and several limb bones. *Aegyptopithecus* is believed to have been comparable in size to a modern howler monkey, which weighs only 13 to 18 pounds (Fleagle 1983; Conroy 1990). The postcranial bones reflect the skeletal structure of an arboreal quadruped. The dentition of *Aegyptopithecus* also offers several useful insights. Dental structure, for example, indicates that this early ape subsisted on a diet of fruit and leaves. Researchers have also noted a great deal of variation in the size of canine teeth, which may indicate that the species was sexually dimorphic. Drawing on analogies with modern primates, scientists infer that *Aegyptopithecus* lived in social groups in which competition over females was intense.

Aegyptopithecus resembles primitive monkeys and prosimians in several key respects, including its small brain and diminutive skeletal structure. However, other features, such as its 32 teeth—the same number found in humans and apes—suggest that *Aegyptopithecus* may represent an ancestor of later hominoids.

Hominoid Evolution The fossil record sheds little light on the period spanning the time when *Aegyptopithecus* flourished through the early Miocene, some 10 million years later. However, we can state with certainty that the Miocene (23 million to 5.3 million years ago) brought apes to the fore (Begun 2010). According to the fossil evidence, the earliest forms of protoapes evolved in Africa before 18 million years ago. After that, Africa was connected to Europe and Asia through the Arabian Peninsula, enabling hominoids to migrate to these other continents. The fossil evidence indicates that the late Miocene apes adapted to an impressive variety of geographic and climatic conditions in Europe, the Middle East, Asia, and Africa.

A study of various Miocene fossil species spotlights the intermediate stages through which modern hominoids may have passed. However, determining the exact lineages leading to specific living species is complicated. Scientists attempting to classify Miocene apes are hampered by two problems: the vast number of species and fragmentary fossil evidence. The number and variety of fossil species is significantly greater than the number of living representatives. Researchers categorize these apes primarily on the basis of their teeth, which prompted some to nickname them the "dental apes." This method of identification has one major weakness, however; convergent evolution in similar environmental settings (say, the tropical forests of present-day Africa and the tropical forests of contemporary South Asia) may have produced nearly identical dentition in primates of markedly different ancestry.

As in the case of the other ancestral primates discussed, Miocene fossils represent creatures that were quite distinct from any living species. The postcranial bones of Miocene apes and protoapes reveal a number of ape-like and monkey-like trait combinations dissimilar from any found in living hominoids. This leads researchers to speculate that these fossil species engaged in locomotive and behavior patterns unlike any exhibited by modern species (Fleagle 1983). Nevertheless, it is worthwhile to underscore that these fossil species were hominoids, possessing characteristics that clearly place them closer to modern apes and humans than Old World Monkeys.

Ancestors of Modern Hominoids   Early researchers studying the middle and late Miocene apes attempted to trace clear ancestral lines back in time to specific modern hominoids, including the families hylobatidae (siamangs and gibbons) and hominidae (orangutans, chimpanzees, gorillas, and humans). As we will see, the phylogeny of none of these species is clear. Various fossil specimens dating back as far as the Oligocene and Miocene have occasionally been classified as ancestral to modern species. However, these identifications were based on very superficial similarities between fossil and extant species. Looking closely at specific features, we see that these extinct creatures were far more primitive, lacking a number of refined cranial and postcranial skeletal developments found in living species. The evolutionary ancestry of these various species has become increasingly complicated as new finds are made, and current research casts doubt on whether a "neat and tidy" picture will ever emerge. The Miocene hominoids and modern nonhuman hominoids are discussed briefly later. Human evolution is treated in more detail in Chapter 5.

Possible ancestors of nonhuman hominoids are found in deposits of the Miocene and Pliocene epochs in Africa, Europe, and Asia. In the case of the Asian and African material, it is tempting to make connections between some of these finds and the modern hominoids living in these regions. Yet, the diversity of the species that seem to be represented, combined with the fragmentary nature of the fossil

finds, make interpretations of their relationship to later species tenuous. The first examples of fossil species with clear similarities to modern species do not appear until the Pleistocene epoch, less than 2 million years ago (see Table 3.1).

African Hominoids   Miocene hominoids that may prefigure modern homininae (orangutans, chimpanzees, gorillas, and humans) are from Africa. These finds include fossil material 23 to 14 million years old, incorporating material earlier in age than that from Asia and Europe. Fossil species are primarily known from Kenya, the best described of which are representatives of the genus *Proconsul*. The finds mostly consist of teeth, but a few fragments of skulls, limb bones, and vertebrae have been recovered, and these show considerable variation. The best-known early Miocene protoape, *Proconsul africanus* (Figure 4.3), has been reconstructed, offering a good illustration of the mix of features found in some of the Miocene primates. This protoape's pronounced snout, or muzzle, contrasted significantly with the more diminutive snout in the majority of later monkeys and apes. Yet, the auditory region of the brain in *P. africanus* was indistinguishable from that of living apes and monkeys from Eurasia and Africa. Other regions of the brain also mirrored those of living monkeys, but much of the sensory and mental development seen in living apes was absent (Falk 1983).

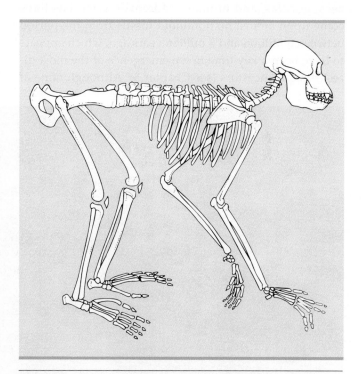

Figure 4.3 A reconstructed skeleton of *Proconsul africanus* based on finds from East Africa.

The best-known early Miocene protoape, *Proconsul* illustrates the mix of features found in some of the Miocene primates.
Source: Adapted from Roger Lewin, *Human Evolution: An Illustrated Introduction*, Blackwell Scientific Publications, 1989, p. 58. Used by permission of Blackwell Science Ltd.

Examining the postcranial skeleton of *P. africanus*, researchers have also noted similarities to both apes and monkeys (Walker and Pickford 1983; Beard et al. 1986). Weight estimates for *Proconsul* range from 10 to 150 pounds. Available evidence also suggests varying environmental adaptations and locomotive patterns. The size and structure of the leg bones (especially the fibula) and the configuration of the foot resembled those of apes. Like living apes, *P. africanus* lacked a tail. However, the arrangements of the arm and hand bones had more in common with some monkeys than with apes. Despite these similarities, *P. africanus* lacked many of the more specialized features of modern apes or monkeys. While a quadrupedal creature adapted to an arboreal environment, *P. africanus* lacked the swinging and leaping capabilities of apes and monkeys.

For several decades two *Proconsul* species (*africanus* and *major*) were thought to be ancestral to modern chimps and gorillas (see Figure 4.4). This relationship to a modern species, however, was based on size and geographic distribution, not shared morphological characteristics (Fleagle 2013). Further studies demonstrate that *Proconsul*, as well as other Miocene apes, were far more primitive in structure than living species. Furthermore, molecular dating studies of modern primates lead experts to believe that *Proconsul* lived long before the divergence of the different homininae lineages leading to modern chimpanzees, gorillas, and humans. Moreover, scientists have come upon almost no hominoid fossils from the period between 8 million and 4 million years ago, which appears to have been a key time in the emergence of the most direct human ancestors (see Chapter 5). Although none of these species can be pointed to as the specific ancestor of modern homininae, *Proconsul* species likely represent hominoid ancestors near the divergence of hylobatids and hominids (see Figure 4.2).

Asian Hominoids The Asian Miocene fossils, ranging geographically from Turkey to China, incorporate the greatest diversity among the Miocene hominoids. The best-known examples are the sivapithecines, dating from about 16 million to 7 million years ago. These also include a closely related genus referred to as *Lufengpithecus*, named after the site in China where many examples have been recovered. The dentition and facial anatomy of the sivapithecines bear some resemblance to those of modern apes, particularly the orangutan. For this reason, they had sometimes been viewed as potential ancestors. However, in light of more fossil finds, paleoanthropologists now agree that the sivapithecines were a highly specialized species. Recent finds in Turkey, India, and Pakistan suggest that sivapithecines may have moved on all fours, like modern chimpanzees and gorillas, rather than spending a great deal of time climbing trees, as do modern orangutans. Dental wear indicates the diet of sivapithecines was fruit rather than seeds or grasses. These hominoids appear to have thrived in a variety of environments, including tropical forests as well as drier, open bushlands.

Gigantopithecus Some of the Asian Miocene apes were quite remarkable, including several species of enormous, extinct hominoids classified as genus *Gigantopithecus*—the name suggesting their gigantic size (Ciochon et al. 1990).

Figure 4.4 Drawing on fossils of extinct species and associated remains of other plants and animals, researchers are able to reconstruct the appearance and behavior of ancient primates, as in this reconstruction of *Gigantopithecus*.
Source: Denis Finnin, American Museum of Natural History

These massive creatures were first identified on the basis of their teeth, which were being sold in Chinese shops as "dragon bones". Very fragmentary gigantopithecine fossils have been found in China, Vietnam, Pakistan, and northern India. The earliest gigantopithecine are from late Miocene fossil localities (dating from approximately 5 million years ago), and the most recent are from Pleistocene caves dating from less than 1 million years ago. Judging from the fossil remains, the gigantopithecines towered over other primates; no doubt, their huge teeth and jaws presented an intimidating sight. The larger of the two species, *G. blacki*, may have reached a height of 6 to 9 feet and a weight of 600 pounds.

The dentition of *Gigantopithecus* resembles that of *Sivapithecus*; both share such features as thick enamel and low, flat cusps. These similarities suggest that the gigantopithecines descended from the earlier apes. Judging from the large teeth and thick, heavy mandibles, paleontologists theorize that *Gigantopithecus* subsisted on a diet of hard, fibrous plants such as bamboo. This hypothesis gained support recently when scientists discovered microscopic traces of plant residue called *phytoliths* on fossil teeth. These deposits may be consistent with a diet of bamboo.

The oversized features of *Gigantopithecus* have prompted speculation that this creature may be an ancestor of an as-yet-undiscovered Abominable Snowman residing in the frozen heights of the Himalayas. Most primatologists believe, however, that *Gigantopithecus* represents a highly specialized form of hominoid that diverged from the other lines and became extinct about 1 million years ago.

European Hominoids Of the African, Asian, and European finds, the final category is perhaps the most enigmatic. Hominoid fossils are known from France, Italy, Greece, and Austria, notably incorporating ranges now uninhabited by primates. Like detectives with too many suspects and not enough evidence, paleontologists' efforts to trace hominoid evolution is not helped by these scattered finds. As a group they are more restricted in time than the Asian and African material, roughly dating between 9 and 13 million years ago. They seem to incorporate several genera, the most well-known of which is *Dryopithecus*. The dentition of this species bears some similarities to the sivapithecine, suggesting some relationship to the Asian hominoids. Other finds, however, especially a series from Greece designated *Ouranopithecus*, have been seen by some researchers as having affinities with the African material. Thus, the evolutionary relationships of these species to other taxa remain uncertain.

Paleontologists discovered significant fossils in Spain of a primate that some researchers have viewed as a link between the various ape species of gorillas, chimpanzees, orangutans, and humans. This creature, named *Pierolapithecus catalaunicus*, has some physical traits that seem to connect it with early hominids. For example, *P. catalaunicus* had a very flat face with nostrils that are in almost the same plane as its eye sockets. Its face would resemble that of a modern gorilla. Yet, the wrist bones and vertebrae indicate that *Pierolapithecus* would have been able to brachiate (discussed later), in contrast to a gorilla which is a knuckle walker. Most likely these creatures spent most of their time in the trees. Paleoanthropologists believe that this creature existed in both Africa and Europe during the Miocene epoch about 13 million years ago (Moyá-Solá et al. 2004).

The Extinction of Most Miocene Apes During the early Miocene, ape species proliferated, but most became extinct for reasons that still elude scientists (Conroy 1990). By the middle Miocene (approximately 16 million to 10 million years ago), ape species became dramatically less common compared to monkeys, reversing the earlier trend. Apes all but disappear in the fossil assemblages of the late Miocene (10 million to 5.3 million years ago), and, as yet, there have not been any fossil finds of apes in Eurasia and Africa after the Miocene. In contrast, the middle Miocene fossil record provides evidence of abundant and diverse species of monkeys and the radiation of African monkeys into Eurasia. At the end of the Miocene, the specialized bipedal apes, the hominins, made their appearance (see Chapter 5).

Global climatic and ecological changes undoubtedly played a role in the extinction of the Miocene apes. Although it is difficult to generalize about a time period spanning 20 million years, the trend in continental climates was toward drier and cooler conditions (Conroy 1990). Sixteen million years ago, the tropical rain forests of Africa were replaced by more open woodlands and savannahs. In the circum-Mediterranean region, the climate became more temperate and seasonal.

Many of the Miocene apes probably had difficulty adjusting to the cooler, drier climates. It is only in the less temperate, more tropical regions of Asia and Africa that apes continued to survive. However, some of the hominoids became more terrestrial, successfully adjusting to the new, open environments. It is these species that became the precursors of modern apes and humans.

Modern Apes

The modern apes, descendants of the Miocene hominoids, are found only in Asia and Africa. In Asia, the surviving species include the gibbon, the siamang, and the orangutan. The African hominoids are the chimpanzee and the gorilla.

The gibbon's long arms and powerful shoulder muscles allow it to negotiate its arboreal environment by brachiating, an arm-over-arm suspensory locomotion used to move from branch to branch. Gibbons can swing through the trees like acrobats, covering up to 30 feet in a single motion.

The Gibbon and Siamang

Modern representatives of the family Hylobatidae, including the siamang and the gibbon, are the most specialized and the smallest of the living apes. They are also the most numerous, inhabiting the evergreen forests throughout Southeast Asia. There are several species of gibbon, which weigh between 11 and 14 pounds. The siamang is larger, weighing up to 25 pounds. The hylobatids savor a diverse diet, ranging from fruits and leaves to spiders and termites, although the choice of food depends on local environments and the time of year.

All the hylobatids have relatively short trunks; extremely long, slender arms; curved fingers (see Figure 4.1); and powerful shoulder muscles. These characteristics enable them to negotiate their arboreal environment through brachiation. *Brachiation* refers to arm-over-arm suspensory locomotion used to move from branch to branch. Many primates can easily hang from tree branches with one hand while feeding or wrestling with a playmate with the other. However, brachiating primates, such as the gibbon, swing through the trees like acrobats, covering up to 30 feet in a single motion.

The gibbons and siamangs live in monogamous family groups consisting of male-female pairs and as many as four immature offspring. These young may stay in the family group for up to ten years. Foraging for food together or individually, families sometimes range over large areas and fiercely defend their territories. The hylobatids are noisy, often calling and vocalizing to signal their presence to other groups.

The Orangutan

The orangutan, a member of the subfamily ponginae and the only large Asian ape alive today, lives exclusively in the heavily forested regions of the Indonesian islands of Borneo and Sumatra. They are among the most intelligent primates. Like the African great apes, discussed later, orangs have been observed making and using simple tools to extract insects and nuts (van Schaik 2003). Orangutans are large, sexually dimorphic apes. Males weigh about 150 pounds, whereas females reach about half that size. Because of their large size, orangs are not as agile as the lesser apes, like the gibbon. Nevertheless, their long arms and fingers allow them to move quite efficiently through the trees. When traveling long distances, they occasionally drop to the ground and move in a quadrupedal fashion. The orangutan has a distinctive *noyau* (small group) social organization, in which adult males and females do not live in large social groups or pairs. Instead, adult females, together with their immature offspring, range over comparatively small areas searching for leaves, fruits, and seeds. Adult males, in contrast, cover larger areas, often encountering several females with whom they may mate.

Orangutans, the largest living Asian ape, live in the heavily forested regions of the Indonesian islands of Borneo and Sumatra. This photo shows a young orangutan in captivity.

Increasingly, these shy, mostly solitary creatures are facing extinction in many areas as development eliminates their ranges and the depletion of the tropical rain forests continues apace, particularly as a result of plantation farming and agribusiness. At one time, over 200,000 orangutans may have inhabited the tropical forests of Asia, but today the orangutan is an endangered species. Presently, fewer than 50,000 orangutans may survive in Borneo and Sumatra, their number having dramatically dropped during the last decade. An illegal trade in these animals is still booming, with baby orangs selling for as little as $200 or $300. Unless this trend is reversed, the creatures may face extinction within the next two decades.

The Gorilla   The tribes panini (chimps) and gorillini (gorillas) are the nonhuman representatives of the homininae subfamily. As with the orangutan, the habitats of these great apes are being threatened by humans. Today these apes—all confined to restricted areas in Africa—are listed as endangered species. However, given the thick vegetation and remote areas in which they live, it is difficult to get

Male gorilla pounding its chest. The gorilla is the largest living primate.

Source: From Marvin Harris, *Culture, People, Nature: An Introduction to General Anthropology.* Copyright ©1988. All rights reserved. Reprinted by permission of Allyn & Bacon.

accurate population estimates. About 40,000 lowland gorillas (the type usually seen in zoos) may live in the forests of western and central Africa. In the lake areas of East Africa, only a few hundred mountain gorillas remain.

The gorilla is the largest living primate (Schaller 1976; Richard 1985). The adult male weighs up to 400 pounds; the female grows to about 200 pounds. Although they can climb, gorillas are the most terrestrial of all primates, besides humans, because of their great size. On the ground, they use an unusual quadrupedal form of locomotion called **knuckle walking**. Rather than supporting their forelimbs with the palms of their hands (as do most other primates), knuckle walkers rest their hands on the ground in a curled position, with the tops of their curled middle and index fingers bearing their weight. Big-boned creatures, gorillas also have large, powerful jaws and chewing muscles for eating a wide variety of terrestrial vegetation such as roots, shoots, and bark. Yet, despite their tremendous size and strength, they are shy, gentle creatures.

Gorillas thrive in social groups of about 12 animals, although the group's size may range from 2 to 20, and lone males are occasionally seen. Groups are dominated by an older male, or silverback. Observing mountain gorillas over a long period, Dian Fossey discovered that their groups consist of unrelated females and immature males (see the box "Primatologists in the Field: Jane Goodall and Dian Fossey" on page 85). Female gorillas may transfer from one group to another once or many times during their lives. This pattern differs markedly from other primate groups, which are made up of related individuals. Males appear to transfer less frequently than females, and when leaving a group they generally do not join another. New groups may form when females join a lone male.

The Chimpanzee   Chimpanzees, the living representatives of tribe panini, inhabit a broad belt across equatorial Africa from the west coast to Lake Tanganyika in the east. Two species of chimpanzees have been identified in Africa: the "common" chimpanzee (*Pan troglodytes*) and the "pygmy" or bonobo chimpanzee (*Pan paniscus*). At present, bonobos are found only in a small forested area of central Africa, whereas the common chimp inhabits both rainforests and mountain forests, as well as dry woodland regions. Like gorillas, chimpanzees are knuckle walkers whose anatomy suits this form of locomotion. However, chimps also spend a good deal of time swinging in the trees and feeding on a wide range of fruit and vegetation. Primatologists have discovered that chimps occasionally hunt, eating birds and small mammals (Goodall 1986). Chimps and gorillas are recognized as the most intelligent of all the apes. Studies indicate that from a genetic standpoint, chimpanzees and humans are over 98 percent identical (Jones, Martin, and Pilbeam 1992).

An infant chimpanzee (*Pan troglodytes*) in northeastern Sierra Leone.Genetically, the chimpanzee and the gorilla are almost identical to humans.

The fluid nature of chimpanzee social life makes the day-to-day experiences of a chimpanzee far more varied than those of most other primates (Goodall 1986). Chimpanzees band together in less structured social organizations than those of other primates. A chimpanzee community may number from 15 individuals to several dozen, but adults of both sexes may forage alone or band together into groups of between 4 and 10. There is no overall leader, and the makeup of the smaller feeding groups is constantly changing. Chimpanzee communities are defined by groups of males that generally maintain friendly relations and utilize the same feeding range. Primatologist Jane Goodall (1986) has observed that male-female sexual bonding among chimpanzees is extremely varied. One female may mate with a number of males in the group. In other cases, a male and a receptive female may form a temporary sexual bond, or *consortship*, and travel together for several days.

Among the most notable aspects of chimpanzee behavior is tool use. Wild chimps have long been noted to use simple tools, such as blades of grass or twigs, to extract termites from their nests (Goodall 1986). These natural implements may be modified by bending, stripping them of leaves, or breaking them to appropriate length. At times, chimps may fabricate tools at other locations for future use. Studies have also noted chimps using stones to crack open nuts (Mercader et al. 2002). Stones are carried from tree to tree and reused. This activity, which is a significant food source, leaves behind piles of nut shells, stone flakes, and tools with distinctive wear patterns. Materials such as these are visible archaeologically and are, in some ways, analogous to tool sites associated with early human ancestors, suggesting these sites may be associated with the cracking of hard-shelled nuts by early hominids.

Like other living primates, chimpanzees represent modern representatives of their own evolutionary line. Yet, because of their genetic similarity to humans and their complex behavioral patterns—including tool use—they have often served as inspirations for behavioral models of early human ancestors. Other aspects of chimpanzee behavior are examined below and in Chapter 5 with regard to primate models of early hominin behavior.

Primate Behavior

4.4   Describe the importance of social organization among the primates.

Modern primates have complex learning abilities and engage in multifaceted social activities. Some primates of the same species exhibit disparate forms of social organization and behavior because of differing ecological circumstances. On the other hand, the behavior of some primates varies within the species, even when they live in similar environmental conditions. In this fact lies the increasing sense that nonhuman primate species possess what some might recognize as the rudiments of human "culture"—behavioral practices passed on from generation to generation that are not rooted in genetics or adaptations to particular environments. In studying these creatures, primatologists have identified a number of concepts that are useful in describing primate behaviors.

Social Groups   Most primates congregate in social groups or communities, sometimes known as *troops*. Living in groups confers many advantages, including a more effective defense against predators, enhanced food gathering, more intensive social learning, greater assistance in rearing offspring, and increased reproductive opportunities. By ensuring these things, primates make sure that infants receive adequate care, nourishment, and protection, and they bolster their reproductive success.

A cornerstone of primate life is the relationship between mothers and infants. Many animals virtually ignore

Anthropologists at Work

JANE GOODALL AND DIAN FOSSEY: Primatologists in the Field

For many years, our ideas about the behaviors of nonhuman primates came from observations of animals in captivity. Not surprisingly, removed from their natural environments and often secluded from other animals, these primates did not exhibit normal behavior patterns. By observing primates in the wild, we can obtain a much more accurate picture of their activities and responses. Such studies, though, pose special problems. Animals like chimpanzees and gorillas live in secluded areas that are heavily forested and difficult to reach. They keep their distance from humans, making close observation challenging. In addition, primates are long-lived (chimpanzees and gorillas may reach ages of more than 50 years), which makes it difficult for researchers to draw conclusions about maturation and long-term social relations. Today, we know a great deal about the behavior of chimpanzees, gorillas, and other primates in their natural habitats. This information was gathered through the persistence of many primatologists, but the pioneering work of two researchers—Jane van Lawick Goodall and Dian Fossey—deserves special note.

Jane Goodall was born in Bournemouth, England, in 1934. As a child, she was fascinated by living creatures. In one of her books, *In the Shadow of Man*, she recounts how at age four she crept into a henhouse and patiently waited five hours to see how a chicken laid an egg. At age eight, Goodall decided that when she grew up she would go to Africa and live with wild animals. This long-standing desire took her to Kenya in the late 1950s, where she met Louis Leakey, noted for his research on human origins (see Chapter 5). Leakey encouraged Goodall's interest in African wildlife, suggesting that she study chimpanzees. At that time, almost nothing was known about the behavior of wild chimpanzees. Only one study had been

Dian Fossey's patience eventually allowed her to make careful observations of mountain gorillas. Her tragic death in the field has been recounted in the film *Gorillas in the Mist.*

carried out, and that had lasted less than three months, far too short a period to gather much meaningful information. Leakey secured funding for Goodall to study chimpanzees in an isolated area near Lake Tanganyika in East Africa.

Arriving in Gombe National Park in 1960, Goodall found the chimpanzees frustratingly uncooperative. It took her more than six months to overcome their deeply rooted fear of humans. Goodall's work (1971, 1990) on the Gombe chimps has now spanned more than fifty years, providing invaluable insight into chimpanzee behavior. She was the first to observe chimpanzees manufacturing simple tools to extract termites—a favorite food—from their nests. She has documented the long-term bonds between mother and child and the complexity of social relations. Goodall was also the first to spot the darker side of chimpanzee behavior, including occasional instances of cannibalism, murder, and warfare. We owe these important observations about the social behavior of chimps to Goodall's extraordinary commitment. Hers is the longest ongoing study of any primate group. Today, Goodall spends a great deal of time on conservation work to try to assist in preserving the habitat for chimpanzees and other primates in the wild.

Another key contributor to primate studies was Dian Fossey, who spent 18 years documenting the life of the mountain gorillas of Parc des Virungas, Zaire, and Parc des Volcans, Rwanda (Fossey 1983). Dian Fossey was born in 1936 in San Francisco. She had always dreamed of visiting Africa to study the wildlife, a dream she fulfilled in 1963 when she borrowed enough money for a seven-week safari to observe the mountain gorillas of Mount Mikeno, Zaire. While in East Africa, Fossey sought out Louis Leakey, who was then supporting Jane Goodall's work. Convinced of Fossey's commitment, Leakey was instrumental in obtaining funding for her to initiate research for a long-term study of the mountain gorilla.

Fossey faced particularly difficult problems in her studies. The habitat of the mountain gorilla is threatened by the extension of cultivation and herd lands. In addition, the area is hunted by people from nearby African settlements, who often use snares to capture animals like the antelope; tragically, gorillas are sometimes caught in these traps. In other cases, gorillas themselves have been the target of poachers who have cultivated a thriving market in gorilla body parts. Some tribes use gorilla ears, tongues, testicles, and small fingers to make virility potions. Gorilla heads and hands have sometimes been sold as gruesome souvenirs to European tourists for about twenty dollars apiece. Fossey estimated that two-thirds of gorilla deaths were the result of poaching.

Fossey adopted a strong stand against poachers, practicing what she called "active conservation." She destroyed traps, raided temporary shelters used by poachers, and herded gorillas away from areas where hunters proliferated. In 1985, she was brutally murdered in her cabin at the Karisoke Research Center in Rwanda. Some of her experiences are recounted in the book *Gorillas in the Mist*, published shortly before her death and subsequently made into a movie.

Significantly, Goodall and Fossey had received no formal training in primatology before beginning their fieldwork. Although later granted a doctorate from Cambridge University, Goodall had only a secondary school education and experience in business when she first went to Kenya. Fossey had been an occupational therapist before going to Africa, and she garnered official recognition for her work only after years of field experience. With their extraordinary courage and commitment, these women overcame tremendous obstacles to undertake their research.

The work of researchers like Goodall and Fossey has greatly broadened our knowledge of the behavior of living primates, but this knowledge is accumulating far too slowly. The fossil record indicates that primates once ranged over a much wider portion of the globe than they do today. Many species that are now extinct suffered from environmental changes over the past 30 million years; however, the perilous position of some modern primates can be laid directly at the doorstep of humans. In many areas, primates are still hunted for food. Expanding human settlements and the destruction of forests directly endanger nonhuman primates, threatening the very survival of animals like the mountain gorilla of central Africa, the lion-tail macaque of India, the golden-lion tamarin of Brazil, and many others. The work of researchers like Goodall and Fossey highlights the plight of humankind's closest living relatives and may awaken people to the myriad preventable threats these creatures face.

---

their offspring after birth. However, as mentioned earlier, primates tend to have longer periods of maturation than other animals. During infancy, primates are cared for by their mothers, often forming a lasting bond (Harlow and Harlow 1961). This mother-infant attachment is particularly strong among the anthropoid apes, and it may continue throughout a primate's lifetime. We find poignant examples of chimps tenderly caring for an injured infant or mother in Jane Goodall's studies of chimpanzees in the wild (Goodall 1986). These close attachments undergird primate social organization.

Dominance Hierarchy A social order known as **dominance hierarchy** characterizes group organization in many primate species (Fedigan 1983). Dominance refers to the relative social status or rank of a primate, which is determined by its ability to compete successfully with its peers for objects of value such as food and sexual partners. In most primate groups, a specific dominance or rank hierarchy is based on size, strength, and age. In general, males dominate females of the same age, and older, stronger individuals acquire a higher rank than younger and weaker ones. Certain females may dominate others because they are better able to compete for food, thus enhancing their reproductive success. Each member of the group must learn its rank in the hierarchy and act accordingly. Even species like the chimpanzee that do not have single, dominant group leaders are organized into a dominance hierarchy. Once the order of dominance is established in the group, this hierarchical structure serves to head off conflict and socially disruptive activities. In some ecological circumstances, such as a harsh savannah, the dominance hierarchy is extremely rigid. Under more forgiving conditions, such as a forested region, the hierarchy is more loosely structured. In either case, the dominance hierarchy reduces chaotic behaviors and promotes orderly, adaptive conduct.

Primatologists have observed that dominance hierarchies inhibit outright aggression and conflict (Richard 1985; Goodall 1986). Goodall describes some circumstances in which violence and aggression erupt in chimpanzee communities. Adult males patrol the perimeters of their home range looking for trespassers. Though chimpanzee males rarely cross into the home ranges of other communities, when trespassing does occur, the patrol party viciously attacks the outsider. In one incident witnessed by Goodall, a number of adult males split off from their community and moved from one area of their home range in Gombe National Park to another area. During a three-year period, the original group attacked and killed most of the members of this renegade community. Goodall concludes that when a dominance hierarchy is disrupted or when dominance hierarchies are not well developed (as, for instance, when chimps break away from one community to form another), violence and warfare may result.

Affiliative Behavior As part of group living, primates also engage in various kinds of affiliative behavior that help resolve conflicts and promote group cohesion. This conduct, which may involve interpersonal behavior such as hugging, kissing, and sex, can be illustrated by **social grooming**. Whereas other animals groom themselves, social grooming is unique to primates. Chimpanzees will sit quietly as other members of the troop carefully pick through their hair, removing ticks, fleas, dirt, and other debris. Social grooming not only promotes hygiene, but also reduces conflict and friction between males and females and between young and old in the troop. Grooming works like a "social cement," bonding together members of the troop by maintaining social interaction, organization, and order among them all (Jolly 1985; Falk 2000; Strier 2003).

Primate Sexual Behavior   Male-female sexual behavior among primates does not follow a single pattern; rather, it varies according to environmental circumstances and the particular species of primate. As in the case of the gibbon, there may be monogamous sexual bonds between one male and one female. However, most of the higher primates do not form close, singular sexual bonds. Primatologists usually find in a group a single dominant adult male that has exclusive access to females. Sex may be used to cement alliances (Small 1993; Smuts 1995). Sometimes, female gorillas may side with a young dominant male against an older one (Fossey 1983; Campbell 1987). While sex may be an important means of solidifying social networks, it is also fun. The bonobos, or pygmy chimps, like humans, appear to separate sex from reproduction, enjoying it as a pleasurable activity (Small 1993). They engage in a variety of positions; males and females may rub their genital areas against one another for enjoyment, and French kiss. Sex appears as an important means of releasing tension and avoiding conflict. Such social subtleties and nuances in behavior, especially pronounced among the anthropoid primates, distinguish primate behavior from that of other species.

Communication   Primates are great communicators. Conveying or passing on information includes autonomic, unintentional responses, such as olfactory (odor-related) signals or raised body hair that may indicate fear or threat. Communication among primates also encompasses various intentional acts, such as the examples of affiliative behavior discussed previously. Primates complement these modes of communication with a diversity of calls, facial expressions, and gestures that convey a variety of meanings. As noted above, the gibbons are particularly noisy, often calling and vocalizing to signal their presence to other groups. However, other primate species also make a variety of sounds that are used in specific contexts. When threatened, baboons make a loud barking sound, and chimps utter a distinctive grunt when hungry.

Primates often combine body movements, vocalizations, and facial gestures into *displays*—repetitive behaviors that signal one another and other animals. In making these displays, primates express basic emotions, such as fear and affection, as well as convey threats, greetings, courtship signals, and warnings of impending danger. The primates communicate through grunts, hoots, ground slapping, head bobbing, screams, scent marking (among prosimians), and facial gestures (among anthropoids

of Eurasia and Africa). Examples of displays can be illustrated in the behaviors of many real primates, but the quintessential primate display is epitomized by the chest pounding and a roar like the fictional great ape King Kong of the movies. The more intelligent apes, especially the gorillas and chimpanzees, draw on a more highly developed repertoire of communication tools.

The Human Primate

4.5   **Discuss human origins in light of primate evolution, and describe how humans are both similar to and different from other primate species.**

As members of the order Primates, humans share many physical and anatomical similarities, as well as some behavioral characteristics, with other primate species. Like other primates, modern humans can rotate their arms fully, grasp branches, and stand erect. Humans' sensory organs also bear a striking similarity to those of some of the other primates. Humans, as well as apes and monkeys, have keen visual acuity, including stereoscopic, binocular, and color vision. They also have diminished olfactory abilities compared to other animals. Thus, humans, apes, and monkeys all appear to perceive the external world in much the same way. The striking resemblance between the skeletons of a chimpanzee and a human being clearly identifies humans and chimpanzees as fellow primates. Yet, humans also possess physical and mental abilities that make them unique.

One of the most striking differences between humans and other primates is the human ability to walk upright on two legs. Chimps, gorillas, and orangutans may stand upright for short periods, but only humans maintain a completely erect posture and consistently walk upright on two legs. The human pelvis, legs, and feet provide the balance and coordination that make this type of movement possible. Because human hands are not needed for locomotion, they have evolved into highly precise organs for the manipulation of objects. Human hands have short finger bones (or phalanges) compared to other primates (see Figure 4.1). This trait further enhances humans' manual dexterity. We examine the adaptive aspects of *bipedalism* (walking on two legs) and the implications these physical abilities had for the behavior of early human ancestors in Chapter 5.

Another distinctive human characteristic is their brain size. Although all primates have large brains relative to body size, the human brain is three times as large as we would expect for a primate of this size and build (Passingham 1982). The human cerebrum, referred to in common usage as the "gray matter," and its outer covering, the neocortex (the section that controls higher brain functions), are far more highly developed than those of other primates. These features have important implications for human's ability to engage in complex learning, abstract thought, and the storing and processing of information.

Human social organization also likely had important implications for human evolution. As seen above, most primates congregate in social groups, and this was likely true for early human ancestors. Living in groups confers many advantages, including greater opportunities for social learning. The protracted period of dependence and maturation characteristic of humans—longer than any other primate—make this aspect of human behavior particularly important. This longer period of dependency provides extended opportunity for social learning and passing information such as strategies for obtaining food, how to avoid predators, and tool manufacture. The size and complexity of the human brain, together with the long period of maturation, stand as the most significant differences between humans and other primates. These features are expressed in human's extraordinary capacity to learn, to their imaginative social interactions, and to their facility—unique among all life-forms—to use and produce symbols, language, and culture.

Summary and Review of Learning Objectives

4.1 Discuss characteristics shared by all primates.

Primates are a diverse group of animals that includes prosimians, monkeys, apes, and humans. While a diverse group, primates share a number of key characteristics, including large brain size, keen vision, dexterous hands, and a generalized skeleton that allows for great physical agility. Primates also tend to have smaller litters than other animals, devoting more care and attention to the rearing of their offspring. Some of these traits are prominent in some primates and hardly evident in others. Similar features can also be found in many non-primates. However, the unique combination of traits found in the primates distinguishes them from other animals. Study of the genetic codes of living primates also demonstrates their shared evolutionary relationships.

4.2 Explain the basis for primate taxonomy.

Taxonomy, the science of classification, gives scientists a convenient way of referring to, and comparing, living and extinct organisms. Modern taxonomy is based on the work of the Swedish scientist Carolus Linnaeus (1707–1778). The Linnaean system follows a hierarchical pattern, ranging from large categories, such as kingdoms that encompass creatures sharing overarching characteristics, to smaller groups that share more specific traits. The smallest categories consist of species—groups of individuals that can potentially interbreed and are reproductively isolated from other populations. Members of individual species share the most features. Primates, including humans, are placed into groups on the basis of their shared physical characteristics and evolutionary relatedness. Linnaean classification was originally based on visible physical similarities and differences between species. However, with increasing research into the genetic codes of living primates, genetic relatedness has become a more important basis for taxonomy.

4.3 Discuss what fossil evidence reveals about primate evolution.

The physical characteristics that define order Primates can be clearly seen in living populations, but they are also preserved in the fossil record. Methods of locomotion, refinements in vision, and the evolution of the brain necessitate specific bone and muscle structures that are visible in the skeleton. Similarly, the organization of the brain can be inferred through the examination of the *crania*, or skulls, of fossilized species. Behavioral patterns, such as extended periods of infant dependency or primate social organization, are best viewed through the observation of living species, but some clues may also be provided by the archaeological record. Scientists speculate that the first primate ancestors probably evolved during the Paleocene epoch of the early Tertiary period (70 million to 55 million years ago). However, the oldest clearly recognizable primates date to the Eocene epoch (55 to 34 million years ago). Species of ancestral prosimian primates emerged as the earliest forms of primates, followed by the anthropoids. While these early creatures resembled modern primates, they were unlike any living species. Modern nonhuman primates embody some of the same adaptive features found in fossil species and, in this way, reflect the evolutionary phases through which the primates passed over millions of years.

4.4 Describe the importance of social organization among the primates.

Direct information on primate social organization and behavior primarily come from the observation of living species. Social organization and behaviors learned in social settings are important in primate life and were likely also of key importance in human evolution. Primates display disparate forms of social organization and behavior, both between and within the species. This variation suggests that nonhuman primate species possess what might be described as the rudiments of human "culture"—behavioral practices passed on from generation to generation that are not rooted in genetics or adaptations to particular environments. Most primates congregate in social groups or communities. This confers many advantages, including a more effective defense against predators, enhanced food gathering, more intensive social learning, greater assistance in rearing offspring, and increased reproductive opportunities. By ensuring these things, primates make sure that infants receive adequate care, nourishment, and protection, and they bolster their reproductive success.

4.5 Discuss human origins in light of primate evolution, and describe how humans are both similar to and different from other primate species.

As members of the order primates, humans share many physical and anatomical similarities, as well as some behavioral characteristics, with other primate species. Like other primates, humans have a skeletal structure that allows for great flexibility in movement. Humans' sensory organs also bear a striking similarity to those of some of the other primates. Yet, humans also possess physical and mental abilities that make them unique. One of the most striking human characteristics is the human ability to walk upright on two legs. Other primates may stand upright for short periods, but only humans maintain a completely erect posture and consistently walk upright on two legs. Because human hands are not needed for locomotion, they have evolved into highly precise organs for the manipulation of objects. Another distinctive human characteristic is their brain size. The human cerebrum, and its outer covering, the neocortex, are far more highly developed than those of other primates. These features have important implications for humans' ability to engage in complex learning, abstract thought, and the storing and processing of information. Finally, their varied and complex social organizations also make humans distinct. Most primates congregate in social groups, and this was likely true for early human ancestors. The protracted period of dependence and maturation characteristic of modern humans--longer than any other primate--make this aspect of human behavior particularly important. These features are expressed in humans' extraordinary capacity to learn, to their imaginative social interactions, and to their facility—unique among all life-forms—to use and produce symbols, language, and culture.

Key Terms

arboreal, p. 68
dentition, p. 68
dexterity, p. 68
diurnal, p. 77
dominance hierarchy, p. 86

knuckle walking, p. 83
nocturnal, p. 73
omnivorous, p. 68
opposable thumb, p. 68
primates, p. 68

quadrupeds, p. 76
sexual dimorphism, p. 78
social grooming, p. 86
taxonomy, p. 70

Chapter 5
Hominin Evolution

Learning Objectives

After reading this chapter you should be able to:

5.1 Explain the principal trends in hominin evolution and within genus *Homo*.

5.2 Describe the fossil evidence for early hominin evolution.

5.3 Discuss the challenges paleoanthropologists face in interpreting the fossil record and explain why their interpretations sometimes change.

5.4 Describe and discuss the different models for the emergence of anatomically modern humans.

5.5 Describe how new genomic research and molecular dating have helped anthropologists interpret human evolution.

5.6 Discuss the different theories regarding the relationship of *Homo sapiens neanderthalensis* and *Homo sapiens*.

The evolution of primates in the Miocene and Pliocene epochs serves as a backdrop for the emergence of early human ancestors. By the Miocene epoch (23 million to 5.3 million years ago), primates in various forms—the precursors of modern prosimians, monkeys, and apes—proliferated in many geographic regions. Sometime in the late Miocene or early Pliocene, new and distinct forms of primates of the subfamily Hominidae emerged. Classified as members of the tribe hominini or **hominins** (see the box "What's in a Name?" in Chapter 4, page 71), these varied species present a range of distinctive features in their teeth, jaws, and brains that represent adaptations to varying environments. However, they all share the structural anatomy needed for **bipedalism**—the ability to walk upright on two legs. It is this characteristic that separates the hominins from other primates and collectively identifies them as the species most directly related to modern humans.

Paleoanthropologists have advanced numerous interpretations of hominin evolution over the past century. Although opinions diverge on the proper naming and classification of individual fossil specimens, paleoanthropologists are in broad agreement about the evolution of the human species from a small-brained bipedal ape, the Hominini lineage branching off from the other primates approximately six to ten million years ago. For the purposes of this discussion, we primarily focus on two genera of hominins: *Australopithecus*, which emerged first, and genus *Homo*. Both of these groups include a number of different species, some of which have at times been placed in separate genera. Going back over six million years, the australopithecines are the older group, and they are only known from African fossil finds. The earliest representatives of the species are *A. anamensis* and *A. afarensis*. Australopithecine fossils date from roughly six million to one million years ago. After that, there is no trace of this genus in the fossil record, leading paleoanthropologists to conclude that they became extinct at about that time.

The first representatives of genus *Homo*, the genus that includes modern humans, first appear in the fossil record just over two million years ago. There is a consensus among anthropologists that genus *Homo* evolved from the australopithecines, though interpretations vary as to which australopithecine species gave rise to the new genus. The earliest members of the *Homo* line to be identified in the fossil record are the species *H. habilis* and *H. rudolfensis*, dating between 2.2 million and 1.6 million years ago. What distinguishes the first representatives of genus *Homo* from the australopithecines is a trend toward larger brain size. *H. habilis* is followed in the fossil record by *H. erectus* (including finds sometimes designated *H. ergaster*), which is known from finds in Africa dating 1.8 million years old. *Homo erectus*, in turn, evolved into *H. sapiens*, the species that encompasses modern humans, during the past 400,000 years. Members of genus *Homo* coexisted with some of the later australopithecine species between 2.2 million and 1 million years ago.

Trends in Hominin Evolution

5.1 **Explain the principal trends in hominin evolution and within genus *Homo*.**

The hominins are members of the order primates. As such, they share the basic primate characteristics discussed in Chapter 4, including a generalized skeleton, a high degree of manual dexterity, and prolonged infant dependency. But the hominins evolved with distinctive, derived characteristics. As noted, the first and most significant of these is bipedalism, a feature found in all hominins. Other distinctive features include the reduction of face, jaw, and anterior teeth and a trend toward increasing cranial capacity in genus *Homo*. Changes in these attributes are preserved in the fossil remains of early hominins, and the evolutionary relationships of different species are traced on the basis of the similarities and differences present in individual finds. These characteristics are exemplified in modern humans and least pronounced in earlier hominin species.

The evolution of certain physical, social, and cultural characteristics of hominins is difficult to trace because the characteristics are not preserved in the fossil record. For example, unlike other surviving primates, modern humans are not completely covered with hair. Loss of body hair, as well as characteristics such as skin color and the prevalence of sweat glands, might be a relatively recent phenomenon (see discussion in Chapter 6), but we can find no indication of these developments in fossilized remains. Other trends, such as degrees of social complexity and the origins of human culture, are also of great importance, but such features cannot be directly inferred from fossil remains. Rather, they are evaluated on the basis of early hominins' tools, food remains, and living sites, topics examined in Chapter 7.

Bipedalism

Hominins are the only primates that are fully bipedal. As discussed in Chapter 4, although gorillas, chimpanzees, orangutans and other primates can stand upright, they spend most of their time on all fours. As with other types of locomotion, bipedalism is reflected in skeletal structure and so its evolution can be traced in the fossil record. For example, the hips and knees of hominins differ markedly from those of knuckle walkers like the chimpanzee Paleoanthropologists also focus on the position of the **foramen magnum**, the opening in the base of the skull through which the spinal cord passes. In quadrupedal animals, this aperture is at the back of the skull, which allows the head to extend out in front of the body. In contrast, the foramen magnum in bipedal creatures is on the bottom of the skull, sitting squarely above the body. Structures of the skull associated with bipedalism are especially important because the postcranial bones of many fossil hominins have not been preserved.

Bipedalism stands as the earliest and most important trend in hominin evolution. Initially, many paleoanthropologists believed that the earliest hominins, the australopithecines, were not proficient at bipedalism, perhaps moving with a swinging, slouched gait like that of chimpanzees or gorillas. These interpretations were based on limited fossil finds and have not been supported by more recent studies. Fossil remains of the oldest known hominins, in fact, indicate that these creatures walked as well as modern humans (Figure 5.1). Our best scientific guess places the appearance of bipedalism in hominins sometime between six million and ten million years ago, a period of time that is unfortunately poorly represented in the fossil record.

Why Bipedalism? Although bipedal posture can be clearly inferred on the basis of skeletal remains, it is more difficult to reconstruct the behavior of early hominins and

thus evaluate how upright posture may have been beneficial. The adaptive aspects of bipedalism—how it may have enhanced the survival and reproductive success of early hominins—are not immediately apparent. Bipedalism, for example, is a relatively slow means of locomotion. Nor does the skeletal and muscle structure needed for bipedalism provide the most effective way of climbing or moving through trees—clearly, disadvantages in terms of avoiding predators. Upright posture also places added stress on the lower back, hips, and legs and makes it more difficult to supply the brain with blood. In light of these seeming disadvantages, there has been a great deal of debate regarding how this feature was adaptive, and why was it selected for in early hominins.

While there is ongoing debate about the origins of bipedalism, two overarching points can be made. First, bipedal locomotion probably evolved as a result of a confluence of factors rather than a single adaptive characteristic. As discussed later, thermoregulation models may provide the most plausible explanation for the origins of bipedalism. Perspectives, however, vary and researchers have suggested different views of how walking upright may have been adaptive. Secondly, bipedalism clearly had important social, as well as behavioral, consequences. Once developed, this type of locomotion served early

Figure 5.1 Drawing of Lucy's knee bones and hips compared with those of humans and apes. Lucy's skeletal structure is almost identical to that of modern humans, indicating that, like humans, *A. afarensis* was fully bipedal.

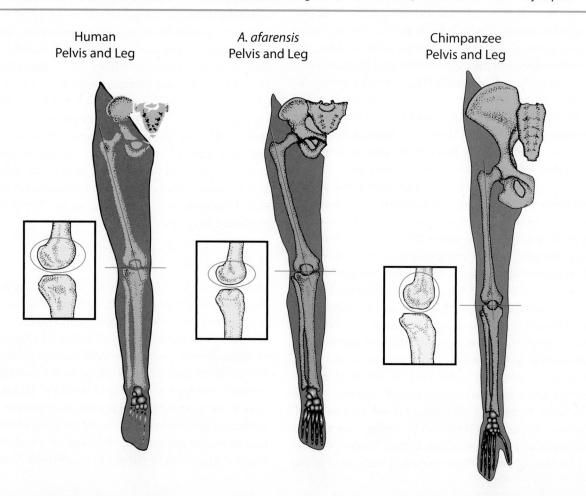

Human
Pelvis and Leg

A. afarensis
Pelvis and Leg

Chimpanzee
Pelvis and Leg

hominins well in a variety of ways by freeing their hands for such tasks as tool use, transporting food, and carrying infants. These activities, in turn, would have facilitated a number of important social and cultural innovations.

Tool Use One of the early theories regarding the origins of bipedalism suggested that it evolved because it freed the hands to make tools. Because early hominins lacked sharp teeth and strong jaws, the ability to use tools would have given them access to a greater variety of food sources, thus ensuring increased survival and ultimate reproductive success (Washburn 1960; Pilbeam 1972; Shipman 1984). This would have been an important adaptive advantage. Unfortunately, the existing evidence does not support this hypothesis. The earliest tools, simple stone choppers, date just over 2.6 million years ago, whereas the origin of bipedalism can be traced back at least 6 to 10 million years ago. More importantly, however, the capability for tool manufacture is not dependent on bipedalism. Rather, it is dependent on cognitive abilities and the manual dexterity needed to manipulate objects. Modern nonhuman primates, such as chimpanzees and orangutans, make simple tools of twigs and grass to extract food from tight spots, and similar improvised tools may have been made by early hominin ancestors regardless of their ability to walk upright (see Chapter 7). Even with tools, the slower-moving bipedal hominins would have been inviting targets for predators.

Transport of Food and Offspring Similar limitations confront the transport of offspring or food as selective factors in the emergence of bipedalism. Carrying food or infants could, theoretically, have facilitated food use and infant care (Hewes 1961; Isaac 1978a). Yet, in light of observed primate behavior, the importance of transport as a selective pressure is ambiguous at best. As with other primates, the offspring of early hominin ancestors likely were able to cling tightly to the mother. This would have allowed the female to move freely in search of food or to find safety. Bipedalism would have allowed infants to be carried, but this advantage would seem to be greatly outweighed by the inability to move quickly through the trees to elude predators. The added potential of dropping an infant would further seem to reduce any possible adaptive advantage. Likewise, food carrying would seem to have limited adaptive significance because animals tend to consume food where it is found. Any benefits of being able to transport food or offspring by hand would seem to be offset by slower, less mobile movement that would not have afforded an effective means of avoiding predators.

Provisioning and More Rather than focusing on a single behavior that may have been adaptive, clues to the origins of bipedalism may lie in thinking about the unique *combination* of activities and social interactions that bipedalism may imply. Paleoanthropologist Owen Lovejoy

(1981, 1984) suggested that the evolution of bipedalism turned on more than merely the ability to carry objects or use tools. Because it involved the modification of a wide range of biological and behavioral traits, it must have conferred some adaptive advantage on early hominins, even before they had fully developed the physical capabilities for bipedalism. Lovejoy posits that the crucial advantage may have been the ability to transport food back to a mate by walking upright and using simple implements, such as broad leaves, to maximize the amount of food that could be carried. Provisioning by the male would have allowed the female to increase the quality and quantity of time devoted to infant care. This intensification of parental attention, in turn, would have promoted the survival of infants and, therefore, the species. Taking the theory a step further, Lovejoy asserts that food sharing and the cooperation that underlies this behavior may have produced a reproductive strategy that favored sexual fidelity and close, long-term relations between a male and a female. While plausible, assessing Lovejoy's interpretations concerning early hominin behavior on the basis of fragmentary fossils remains very difficult indeed, and many researchers have critiqued his suggestions. A major criticism is that there is no evidence that early hominins favored sexual fidelity or close, long-term, male-female relations, things that by nature are difficult to assess on the basis of the fossil record.

Thermoregulation Models More recent theories have considered the unique adaptive advantages that bipedal locomotion may have conferred in the environment in which early hominins evolved—possibly the semi-open savannas and mixed woodlands of East and Central Africa, regions that have produced many of the early hominin fossil finds (Wheeler 1991). Food resources in this mixed savanna-woodland environment would have been scattered and selection would have favored endurance, rather than speed, in locomotion. A combination of attributes in humans makes us very efficient at bipedal locomotion, particularly with regard to endurance running or jogging (Bramble and Lieberman 2004; Lieberman et al. 2007). Less heat is generated in the legs of bipeds. In addition, the ligaments in the legs and feet (the Achilles tendon, for example) allow humans to release energy like a spring as they move forward. Our flexible chests and anatomy also make for stable bipedal movement.

An interrelated aspect of the thermodynamic model also considers the possible benefits of sweat glands and the loss of body hair (Wheeler 1992, 1994). Sweat cools the body; less body hair and more exposed skin would have further facilitated cooling. These features would have provided an adaptive advantage to movement under the hot equatorial sun, and so may have been selected for in early hominins. Early hominins may have been able to move during the hottest times of the day, times when predators such as lions rest. Modern humans have substantially less body hair than other primates and also sweat more than any other animal. Modern apes such as the chimpanzees and gorillas sweat, though not as much as humans, and it is likely that early hominins sweated.

As a consequence of these varied attributes, bipedal hominins, while slower moving than some four-legged (quadrupedal) animals over short distances, would have moved more efficiently over *longer* distances, something that would have allowed them to travel greater distances in search of food. Humans are not simply able to walk upright; we excel at walking. In fact, Daniel Lieberman and Dennis Bramble (2007) have observed that with our steady pace, humans can outdistance almost all other mammals over long distances, particularly when it is hot. Indeed, it has been noted that the modern San people of southern Africa sometimes employ persistence hunting, literally chasing animals until they collapse (Liebenberg 2006). These interrelated traits may have conferred important adaptive advantages on early hominins; their bipedal stature, combined with efficient vision, would also have facilitated their ability to identify food resources.

While these interpretations are plausible, and they may explain why bipedalism emerged, the movements of early hominins across the savanna and their behaviors are difficult, if not impossible to assess on the basis of the archaeological record. Nor does the fossil provide a record of features such as body hair and sweat glands, so it is unknown how sweaty or hairy early hominins might have been. It is, therefore, difficult to fully evaluate the thermoregulation model. Sorting out all of the variables and which ones played the most prominent roles in the development of bipedalism continues to challenge anthropologists.

Figure 5.2 This illustration shows the ape and the human jaw. In the human jaw the teeth are not parallel, but flare away from each other at the back of the mouth.

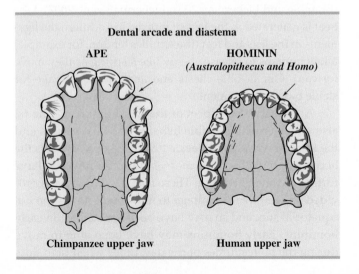

Dental arcade and diastema

APE

HOMININ
(*Australopithecus and Homo*)

Chimpanzee upper jaw

Human upper jaw

Reduction of the Face, Teeth, and Jaws

We also see in hominin evolution a series of interrelated changes primarily associated with diet and food-processing requirements. The oldest fossil hominins have a protruding, or *prognathic*, face, the jaw extending out farther than in modern humans. In addition, the canine teeth of early hominins, while smaller than those of other apes, are large compared with those of humans. In this respect, they can be seen as transitional between earlier species and later human ancestors. To accommodate these larger canines, which extend beyond the other teeth, there are gaps between the teeth of the opposing jaw. This feature, called *diastema*, is characteristic of the early hominins, as well as living apes and monkeys such as the gorilla and baboon, but absent in humans (see Figure 5.2). Finally, the teeth of early hominins are arranged in a U-shaped pattern, and the teeth on opposite sides of the mouth are parallel. This arrangement is similar to that found in modern gorillas, orangutans, and chimps. In contrast, in the human jaw the teeth are not parallel, but flare away from each other at the back of the mouth.

Approximately two million years ago, these characteristics started to become less pronounced in hominins. As noted in Chapter 4, primate teeth including those of hominin species can generally handle an omnivorous diet with ease. However, hominin teeth, with flat molar crowns and thick tooth enamel, are highly specialized for grinding. Early primates, as well as living prosimians and anthropoids, had large canine and incisor teeth that are well suited to cutting and slicing. In contrast, the size of these teeth is greatly reduced in later hominin species. Early representatives of the genus *Homo* have smaller canines, and the gaps associated with larger canine teeth disappear. In humans, the canine teeth retain a distinctive shape, but they are almost the same size as the other teeth. Of all the hominins, the faces of modern humans are the least protruding.

Some of the other hominin species have teeth and cranial structures that suggest adaptations to specialized diets. In particular, the robust australopithecines (*A. robustus, A. boisei* and *A. aethiopicus* discussed later) developed massive chewing muscles and extremely large molars compared with those of modern humans. This strong dentition earned one species, *Australopithecus boisei*, the nickname "nutcracker man." Scientists believe that these features most likely evolved in response to a diet of coarse, fibrous vegetation. Paleoanthropologists cite several key skeletal structures in the jaw and the cranium as evidence of this creature's powerful chewing capacity. Thick, enlarged jaws and cheekbones provided attachments for these huge muscles. Some australopithecine fossil specimens have a **sagittal crest**, a bony ridge along the top of the skull that grows larger as more chewing muscles reach up along the midline of the cranium.

In contrast to the australopithecines, evolving *Homo* species may have consumed a more varied diet based on gathering vegetation, hunting animals, and scavenging. This theory corresponds with the size and contour of their molars—similar to those of modern humans—and the absence of such features as sagittal crests, which accompany specialized chewing muscles.

Increase in Cranial Capacity

The defining characteristic of genus *Homo* is a tendency toward increased cranial capacity and the complexity of the brain. Like the changes in dentition, growth in cranial capacity first appears in hominins dating from about two million years ago. Before that, the size and organization of the hominin brain underwent comparatively little change. Early australopithecines such as *A. afarensis* (which lived some three million to four million years ago) had a cranium about the size of a softball, barely surpassing that of a modern chimpanzee. Hominin cranial capacity remained fairly constant at this size for 2 million years, averaging just over 400 cubic centimeters (cc). Then, sometime after two million years ago, members of the genus *Homo* began to show a steady increase in cranial size. The cranial capacity of *H. habilis*, the first representative of the genus, was over 600 cc. The brain in *Homo erectus* averaged 1,000 cc, and the modern human brain measures, on average, 1,350 cc, a threefold increase from the australopithecines. Significantly, this constitutes an increase in both *relative* and *absolute* size. Even taking into account that modern humans are substantially larger than australopithecines, the relative size of the hominin brain more than doubled in the last two million years (McHenry 1982).

Changes in the cranial capacity of early hominins undoubtedly influenced physical and social developments, which are less easily studied through fossil remains. For instance, increasing brain size almost certainly prompted numerous modifications in hominin diet, the use of tools, the evolution of language, and the intricacies of social organization. Greater sophistication in any of these areas may have improved early hominins' chances of survival.

Fossil Evidence for Hominin Evolution

5.2 Describe the fossil evidence for early hominin evolution.

In *On the Origin of Species*, Charles Darwin devoted relatively little attention to human evolution, noting simply, "Much light will be thrown on the origin of man and his history" (Darwin 1859). In the mid-nineteenth century, when Darwin was writing his treatise, scientists had scant fossil evidence for hominin origins. Since Darwin's time, however, thousands of hominin fossils have been recovered, most of them in Africa. The Hominid Vault of the Kenya National Museum alone contains hundreds of hominin specimens from Kenya and Tanzania, and more than 1,500 other specimens have been recovered from South African sites. Specimens range from isolated teeth to nearly complete skeletons. Although paleoanthropologists have uncovered many spectacular finds, some discoveries merit special attention because they prompted anthropologists to modify theories of human evolution. In this section, we examine several of the most important fossil finds, beginning with the first hominin ancestors. The locations of some of these key discoveries are illustrated in Figure 5.3.

The Oldest Hominins

Fossil evidence for the evolution of the first hominins—from the period between six million and ten million years ago when the transition to bipedalism first occurred—remains very incomplete. The classification of these discoveries and their relationship to later species are uncertain, though some intriguing finds have been discovered. Among the most promising locales are a series of sites in Kenya, particularly the areas around Lake Turkana, Lake Baringo, and the Tugen Hills in the Rift Valley region. The Middle Awash area of Ethiopia also has great potential. Geological deposits in each of these areas span the relevant time periods, and well-preserved fossil deposits are represented. Notably, several exciting discoveries have also been made in Chad in Central Africa, a region that had not previously produced hominin remains.

Sahelanthropus tchadensis The Chad discoveries are especially notable because they occur some 1,500 miles farther west than any other early hominin find. This specimen, named *Sahelanthropus tchadensis*, consists of a complete, though distorted, cranium dated to approximately six million to seven million years ago, making it the oldest possible hominin (Brunet et al. 2002; Wolpoff et al. 2006). The dentition and cranium possess features that are a mixture of ape and hominin characteristics. In particular, the teeth are smaller than those of apes and do not extend below the other teeth, making it more comparable to later hominins. The limited information on the post-cranial skeleton prevents the full assessment of how *S. tchadensis* may have moved. However, the shape and orientation of the foramen magnum suggests the ability to walk upright. Until more information becomes available, the evolutionary relationship of *Sahelanthropus tchadensis* to species will remain uncertain. Nevertheless, this fossil discovery from Chad has important implications regarding the evolution of the early hominins as it affords insight into the distribution and diversity of species present when hominin species were emerging.

Figure 5.3 Map of African fossil finds.

Source: Figure, "Map of African fossil finds," from Roger Lewin, *In the Age of Mankind: A Smithsonian Book of Human Evolution,* Smithsonian Books, 1988, p. 71. (Art by Phil Jordan and Julie Scheiber). Reprinted by permission of Phil Jordan and Associates, Inc.

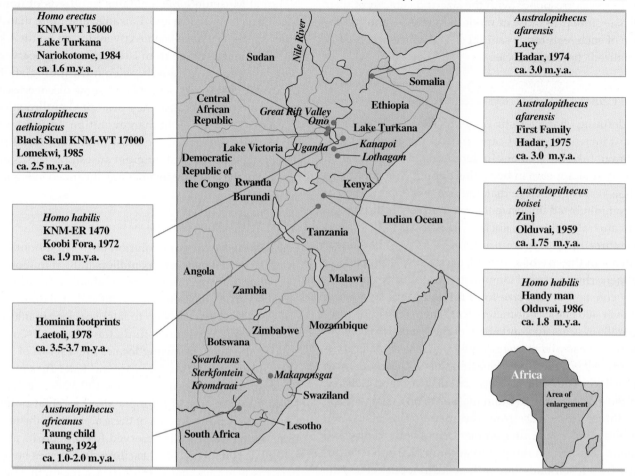

Orrorin tugenensis Fossil evidence for another early hominin ancestor is *Orrorin tugenensis,* represented by fossilized teeth and a few pieces of postcranial bone found from the Tugen Hills in Kenya (Aiello and Collard 2001; Pickford et al. 2002; Wong 2003). The researchers who discovered these finds have suggested that this species is an ancestor of later hominins. This is very significant as the fossil locality where the remains were discovered has been securely dated to between 5.7 million and 6.1 million years ago. If recognized as a hominin, the Tugen Hills finds would indeed be those of *orrorin* which means "original man" in the local African language. In some respects, Orrorin presents features more similar to later human ancestors than australopithecine species (discussed later). Orrorin's teeth, for example, are small like modern human's. This has led some researchers to suggest this species as a more direct human ancestor, something that would move later australopithecine species to a side branch of human evolution (Reynolds and Gallagher 2012). However, because of the fragmentary nature of these fossils and the uncertainty of their classification, their hominin status remains uncertain.

Ardipithecus ramidus Other potential hominin ancestors come from a series of fossil localities in the Middle Awash area of Ethiopia. This region, located at the intersection of the Rift Valley, the Red Sea, and the Gulf of Aden, has produced some of the most spectacular fossil finds, including Lucy and other examples of *Australopithecus afarensis* that will be discussed later. Fossil localities in the Middle Awash excavated by a number of researchers over the past two decades have produced a large number of fossil fragments that collectively represent some of the earliest potential hominin ancestors yet recovered. They have been given their own genus, *Ardipithecus,* divided into two different species (White et al. 2009). The more recent of these, named *A. ramidus* ("Ground ape at the root"), lived about 4.4 million years ago. The older of the two species, *A. kadabba,* has been dated to approximately 5.6 million years old (Haile-Selassie et al. 2004). It is known from very fragmentary remains, and may be ancestral to *A. ramidus.*

A. ramidus is of particular interest because it may have lived slightly after the divergence of the tribe hominini and the African apes; the gorilla (gorillini) and chimpanzee

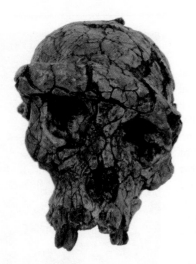
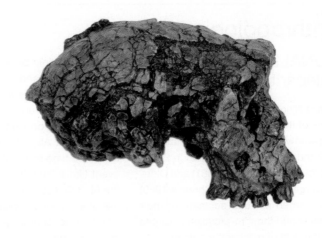

The *Sahelanthropus* skull, found in Chad and dated to approximately six million to seven million years ago, is especially notable since it occurs some 1,500 miles farther west than any other early hominin find. It also ranks as one of the oldest possible hominins ancestors.

(panini). In some respects, *A. ramidus* is quite different from both the African apes and later hominin species, such as the australopithecines. The cranial capacity of these Middle Awash creatures is quite small—at least as small as that of other early hominins—but the form of the cranium is also more ape-like, and the canine teeth are larger. The placement of the cranium over the spinal column, the shape of the pelvis, and the structure of the limb bones are, however, consistent with bipedal locomotion—the hallmark of the hominins (Lovejoy et al. 2009). Yet unlike other hominin species, *Ardipithecus* had a grasping big toe. This is a feature well adapted for locomotion in the trees found in nonhominin species such as the gorilla and chimpanzee. This combination of features has led some researchers to argue that *Ardipithecus* should not be given hominin status (Stanford 2012).

Australopithecus anamensis: Early Hominins from Lake Turkana

The region around Lake Turkana in northern Kenya has also yielded a host of important fossil finds, including the discoveries of *Australopithecus aethiopicus*, *Homo habilis*, and *Homo erectus* (discussed subsequently). Some of the earliest widely recognized hominin remains are represented by a number of finds made over the past 30 years at Kanapoi, southwest of Lake Turkana, and Allia Bay, on the eastern side of Lake Turkana, including the remains of a species designated *Australopithecus anamensis* (Leakey et al. 1995).

The fossils of *A. anamensis* are fragmentary, including teeth and jaw fragments and some postcranial bones. The age of the finds is placed between 3.9 million and 4.2 million years ago. The leg bones are consistent with bipedal— hominin—posture, but the finds also present some distinctive attributes. Like *Ardipithecus*, the skull and the teeth are quite primitive. The external ear openings are also unlike more recent hominins. However, in contrast to

the *Ardipithecus* remains, the molar enamel on the teeth of these specimens is thick and, thus, more analogous to more recent hominin species. Hence, the finds may represent a transitional link between species such as early *Ardipithecus* and the australopithecines. Because of their similarity to later finds, they have been placed in genus *Australopithecus* but have been assigned a new species designation, *A. anamensis*, in recognition of their distinctive attributes. The relationship of these finds to *Australopithecus afarensis* is still being evaluated, but most researchers place them near the base of the branches leading to genus *Homo* and the later australopithecines.

Australopithecus afarensis

During the 1970s, a joint American–French team of paleoanthropologists led by Donald Johanson and Maurice Taieb made several exciting hominin finds in the well-preserved geological beds near the Great Rift Valley in the Hadar area of the Afar region of Ethiopia (Johanson et al. 1982; see the box "Donald Johanson: Paleoanthropologist"). This valley has experienced extensive mountain-building and volcanic activity over the last several million years, and erosion has brought many fossils to the surface where they await discovery by researchers.

Because many subtle differences distinguish the dentition of the various Hadar finds, Johanson initially believed that more than one species was represented. After subsequent study of the remains, however, Johanson and his colleagues concluded that the discoveries all belong to a single hominin species, which they designated *Australopithecus afarensis* (Johanson, White, and Coppens 1978; Bower 1991). The researchers argue that the differences they discerned are the result of natural variation and sexual dimorphism within the species. Some scholars, however, still maintain that more than one species is represented.

Anthropologists at Work

DONALD JOHANSON: Paleoanthropologist

Born in Illinois in 1943, Donald Johanson is one of the world's most influential and best-known paleoanthropologists. His firsthand accounts of research in Ethiopia (Johanson and Edey 1981) and Olduvai Gorge (Johanson and Shreeve 1989) have earned popular acclaim for their readable and thought-provoking insights into the field of paleoanthropology.

In 1973, Johanson, in conjunction with French geologist Maurice Taieb, began research in an area known as Hadar in the Afar triangle of northeastern Ethiopia. At that time the region had been largely unexplored by paleoanthropologists. Although the present climate is arid and inhospitable, the fossil record indicates that the region supported a variety of life-forms four million to three million years ago. In Hadar, Johanson and his fellow researchers uncovered many finds that cast light on early hominins and their environment.

Two spectacular finds in Hadar have received particular attention. The first, uncovered in 1974, was a strikingly complete (40 percent) skeleton of an early hominin affectionately referred to as "Lucy." The second find, unearthed in 1975 at a site designated AL 333, consisted of a remarkable collection of hundreds of hominin bones, representing at least 13 adults and children. Additional research at the site revealed additional discoveries. Given the proximity of the finds, Johanson believes that all the creatures at AL 333 may have died at the same time in a sudden catastrophic event like a flash flood. Both Lucy and the AL 333 discoveries were representative of a previously undescribed species, which Johanson named *Australopithecus afarensis*.

In 1978, Johanson, in conjunction with paleoanthropologist Timothy White, reinterpreted the prevailing notions about hominin ancestry. They surveyed existing information and integrated it with Johanson's finds from Hadar. Then, they restructured the hominin family tree, placing *A. afarensis* at the base, with two branches, one sprouting toward the genus *Australopithecus* and the other giving rise to the genus *Homo*. Although more recent discoveries have led to the conclusion that the hominins may be divided into more than two branches, the majority of paleoanthropologists accept *A. afarensis* as one of the earliest known hominins.

Some of Johanson's interpretations have been called into question. Other researchers have challenged his classification of *A. afarensis*, arguing

Donald Johanson (far left) with other paleoanthropologists analyzing hominin fossils from the Afar region of Ethiopia.

that the fossils represent more than one species. His major critics include paleoanthropologists Mary and Richard Leakey, known for their own research at Olduvai Gorge, Laetoli, Koobi Fora, and Lake Turkana. Johanson has observed: "Frustrating as it is, the distantly tantalizing truths about our origins will probably not be revealed before we ourselves are buried under the earth. But that will not stop me from testing and retesting new hypotheses, exploring further possibilities" (Johanson and Shreeve 1989: 133).

The *Australopithecus afarensis* fossils discovered at Hadar and Laetoli (see later discussion) have been dated between three million and four million years ago, making these some of the earliest well-described hominin remains. The fossils are remarkably primitive in comparison to later australopithecines; from the neck up, including the cranium and jaw, *A. afarensis* is definitely ape-like. The upper body also has features, such as curved figures, that would have made it well adapted for climbing and moving through an arboreal environment. However, the abundant lower limb bones and the pelvic orientation, as well as the position of the hips and knees, indicate that *A. afarensis* was a fully erect, bipedal creature (Lovejoy 1988). This mélange of postcranial features has led researchers to debate whether *A. afarensis* was ground dwelling or still spent a great deal of time in the trees. Such interpretive disagreements underscore the challenges researchers face in analyzing fragmentary remains of nonliving species.

Lucy   Among the most spectacular finds made by Johanson's team at Hadar was a fossilized skeleton of an ancient hominin that was almost 40 percent intact, making it among the earliest and most complete fossil hominins recovered. This find, scientifically designated *Australopithecus afarensis*, became popularly known as "Lucy" (named after a Beatles song, "Lucy in the Sky with Diamonds"). Lucy had a small cranium (440 cc) and large canine teeth. In fact, Lucy's skull resembles that of a modern chimpanzee. However, below the neck the anatomy of the spine, pelvis, hips, thigh bones, and feet clearly shows that Lucy walked on two feet (Lovejoy 1988). Lucy was a fairly small creature, weighing approximately 75 pounds, and she stood about 3.5 to 4 feet tall.

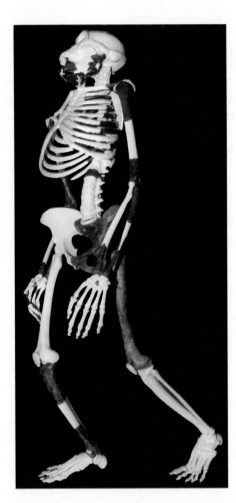

Reconstruction of *Australopithecus afarensis* based on skeletal remains recovered by Donald Johanson at Hadar, Ethiopia, in 1974.

The Dikika Baby Another fascinating find from Hadar is the popularly named "Dikika baby" or "Lucy's baby." Excavated by paleoanthropologist Zeresenay Alemseged in 1999 at a site called Dikika, just a couple of miles from where the Lucy find was discovered, the fossil remains were encased in stone and took five years of careful excavation to extract. Like the Lucy discovery, the Dikika find is the well-preserved remains of an *A. afarenis*, but whereas Lucy was an adult, the Dikika fossil is of a 3-year-old child (Alemseged et al. 2006). The find consists of an almost complete skull, the entire torso, much of the legs, and parts of the arms.

The completeness of this find is especially exciting because the smaller bones of young children are even more unlikely to survive the ravages of time than are those of adults. The young age of the Dikika baby and the completeness of the find afford unique insight into the growth and development of the species, as well as the physical attributes of the species, which includes features, such as the shoulder blades, that have been poorly preserved in other *A. afarensis* finds. While just an infant, the Dikika baby possesses the definitely bipedal features that characterize adult examples such as Lucy. In addition, the structure of the bones of the hands and shoulder blades may suggest

A. afarensis was well suited to an arboreal environment. The arm sockets in particular are oriented upward, more like those of a gorilla than those of later hominins and humans. This would support interpretations that have underscored the species adaptation to an arboreal environment.

The Laetoli Footprints

The site of Laetoli, some 30 miles south of Olduvai Gorge in northern Tanzania, has produced a number of fossil finds, including possible examples of *Australopithecus afarensis*, the fossil species described at Hadar. However, the site is best known for the remarkable discovery of fossilized footprints. Thousands of footprints of various species of ancient animals are preserved in an ancient layer of mud covered with volcanic ash. However, a remarkable finding by Mary Leakey in 1978 revealed footprints clearly left by fully bipedal creatures approximately 3.5 million years ago (Leakey and Hay 1979). The evidence consists of a trail more than 75 feet long made by three hominins. Studies of these footprints have revealed that the mode of locomotion for these early hominins was fully bipedal and comparable to that of modern humans. The presence of bipedal species at this time period had been well established on the basis of fossil evidence. However, the Laetoli footprints provide independent, and indisputable, evidence of the existence of a bipedal creature 3.5 million years ago.

A hominin footprint fossilized in volcanic ash at Laetoli, Tanzania is shown next to a modern foot. Dated at over 3.5 million years, the trail of footprints at the site provides dramatic evidence that early hominins such as *Australopithecus afarensis* were fully bipedal.

Australopithecus africanus

Australopithecus africanus is primarily known from fossil finds in southern Africa dating between two million and three million years ago. The species lived after those discussed in the preceding sections. However, it possessed a smaller cranial capacity than more recent examples of genus *Homo*. An adult *A. africanus* had a cranial capacity that averaged around 450 cc, probably weighed between 40 and 60 pounds, and was between 3.5 and 4.75 feet tall. Although the age of the South African finds are challenging to date, these gracile australopithecines are dated to between two million and three million years ago on the basis of fossils of extinct animals of known age found in the same deposits.

Taung child   *A. africanus* is memorable as the first described example of an australopithecine. The Taung child, found in 1924, was named *Australopithecus africanus*, the "southern ape of Africa," by its discoverer. The discovery was a remarkable combination of coincidence and luck. The man responsible for the find was Raymond Dart, an Australian-born anatomist living in South Africa. In 1924, Dart was given a box of fossils from the rubble of a limestone quarry near the town of Taung, South Africa. The rubble included the front of a skull, a jaw, and an endocranial cast of a bipedal creature that was clearly very different from modern humans. On the basis of the teeth, Dart judged the creature to have been quite young at death, and he called his discovery the "Taung child" (Dart 1925, 1967). Today, the individual is estimated to have been between three and four years old at the time of death.

Although *A. africanus* had certain ape-like features, it also exhibited a number of unique characteristics. For example, the foramen magnum was farther forward in the Taung child than in modern apes, indicating that this creature's head was balanced above the spine. In other words, it moved with the upright posture characteristic of a biped—a key hominin characteristic. The brain of the Taung child was very small, hardly larger than that of a chimpanzee. Its structure, however, differed from that of apes and was more highly developed in some regions. The canine teeth were much closer in size to a human child's than to an infant ape's, and lacked the diastema found in apes' teeth. Dart astounded the scientific world by announcing that the Taung child was a hominin, an intermediate link between humans and earlier primates.

Other *A. africanus* Finds   At the time of its discovery, many paleoanthropologists challenged Dart's conclusions, arguing that the Taung child was really an ape. Contemporary evolutionary theories suggested that large cranial capacity was the critical characteristic of hominin evolution, and critics pointed out that the cranial capacity of Dart's find was too small for it to have been ancestral to humans

(see the box "The Piltdown Fraud"). But Dart's critics were proven wrong. In the decades following the discovery of the Taung child, a number of similar finds were made in South Africa. During the 1940s, Dart excavated additional fossils from Makapansgat Cave. Scottish paleontologist Robert Broom (1938) also came upon a number of similar fossils at Sterkfontein. Some of these new finds were adult specimens of creatures like the Taung child. With their humanlike dentition, bipedal capabilities, and small cranial capacity, they were unquestionably hominins. These discoveries clearly established the Taung child as a hominin and *Australopithecus* as a valid genus.

The Robust Australopithecines: Branches on the Family Tree

While a number of fossil finds present possible, albeit debated, ancestors of modern humans, a variety of discoveries have revealed creatures decidedly unlike us who likely represent side branches on the human family tree. These include several species that have been collectively classed as robust australopithecines. They include three different species, *A. robustus*, *A. boisei*, and *A. aethiopicus*, dated between 2.7 million and 1 million years ago. Their specific taxonomic designations, however, have been widely debated and an increasing number of researchers place them in a separate species, *Paranthropus* (Tattersall 1998; Stringer and Andrews 2005). *Paranthropus* translates as "alongside humans," a name that signals their distinct ancestry from modern humans. Nevertheless, while possessing a number of distinct features, they are also clearly bipedal and are, therefore, closely related to hominin species that were ancestral to humans. The identification of robust australopithecine species presents an increasingly complex picture of evolution that emphasizes diversity within the hominins and what paleoanthropologists emphasize as "bushiness." That is, instead of a neat, ladder-like, unidirectional evolution of bipedal

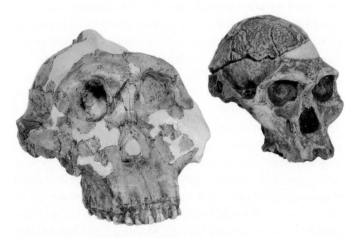

Australopithecine skulls: The example at left is a robust form; a gracile form is at right.

Critical Perspectives

The Piltdown Fraud

One of the most bizarre stories in the history of paleoanthropology involves the fossil known as the "Piltdown man." Widely discussed and debated for several decades, this discovery was eventually exposed as an elaborate fraud. Although it does not figure in current theories of hominin evolution, we examine the Piltdown man controversy because the alleged specimen was accepted as a legitimate human ancestor during the early decades of the twentieth century and influenced interpretations of human evolution (Weiner 1955; Blinderman 1986). This cautionary tale illustrates the efficiency of modern scientific techniques, but also serves as a warning about how scientists can be swayed by their own preconceived ideas.

Piltdown man was "discovered" in 1912 in a gravel quarry near Sussex, England, by a lawyer and amateur geologist named Charles Dawson. The quarry had previously produced the bones of extinct animals dating to the early Pleistocene (approximately 1.8 million years ago). The supposed hominin remains uncovered there consisted of the upper portion of the cranium and jaw. The skull was very large, with a cranial capacity of about 1,400 cc, which placed it within the range of modern humans. However, the lower jaw was ape-like, the canine teeth large and pointed. This picture of early hominins mirrored popular early twentieth-century notions of the unique intellectual capabilities of humanity. Humans, so the interpretation

went, evolved their large brains first, with other characteristics appearing later. In fact, available fossil evidence points to just the opposite evolutionary pattern.

Piltdown man was officially classified as *Eoanthropus dawsoni* ("Dawson's dawn man") and accepted by the scientific community as the earliest known representative of humans found in western Europe. A number of paleoanthropologists in France, Germany, and the United States remained skeptical about the findings, but they were unable to disprove the consensus of the English scientific community. As time went by, however, more hominin fossils were discovered, and none of them exhibited the combination of an ape-like jaw and a large, human-like cranium seen in the Piltdown find.

With contradictory evidence mounting, skepticism grew in the paleoanthropological community concerning the legitimacy of the Piltdown fossils. Finally, in the early 1950s, scientists completed a detailed reexamination of the Piltdown material. Using fluorine analysis (see Chapter 2), they discovered that the skull and jaw were of relatively recent vintage; the jaw, in fact, was younger than the skull. In reality, the Piltdown fossil consisted of a human skull from a grave a few thousand years old attached to the jaw of a recently deceased adolescent orangutan. The ape-like teeth embedded in the jaw had been filed down to resemble human teeth. The place where the jaw joined the skull was also broken away so that it would not be immediately evident that

the jaw and skull did not go together. To complete the ruse, the jaw was stained with a chemical to match the color of the skull.

Clearly, whoever perpetrated the Piltdown hoax had some knowledge of paleoanthropology. By the time the hoax was unmasked, most of the people who could have been implicated had died (Blinderman 1986). Putting aside the question of who was responsible for the hoax, we now recognize that paleoanthropological research between 1912 and the 1950s was definitely harmed by the Piltdown find, because the scientific community pursued a false path in hominin research. The initial acceptance of the Piltdown fraud as legitimate may partially explain why the Taung child, one of the most startling hominin fossil discoveries of the early twentieth century, was relegated to relative obscurity for so many years.

Points to Ponder

1. What lessons does the Piltdown fraud provide for the way paleoanthropological research should proceed and how findings should be validated?
2. The recovery methods and the limited information on the context of the find clearly contributed to the success of the Piltdown fraud. Contrast the details of the Piltdown discovery with more recent finds at Olduvai Gorge, Tanzania, or Hadar, Ethiopia.
3. Can you think of other cases in which researchers' theoretical perspectives have affected their interpretation of the evidence?

hominins from an early ancestor to modern humans, multiple species of hominins—some of them not ancestral to modern humans—roamed Africa at the same time. The fact that many of these species became extinct raises questions about the selective pressures that led to their demise and what ensured the adaptive success of human ancestors.

Robust Australopithecines from South Africa

The first remains of robust species of australopithecine were found in South Africa, following the discovery of the Taung child. In addition to the Taung child and adult

examples of *Australopithecus africanus*, the South African cave sites produced distinct hominin remains more recent in age (Broom 1938, 1949). These specimens have a large, broad face and enormous teeth and jaws. Because of this variation, Dart, Broom, and other researchers gave these discoveries a number of new genus and species designations, placing then in the genus *Paranthropus*. Although differences of opinion still exist about their exact relationship to other species, for convenience they are here referred to as *Australopithecus robustus* to distinguish them from the more delicate, or gracile, *A. africanus*.

South African examples of *A. robustus* are poorly dated, but available evidence suggests that they are more recent than *A. africanus,* perhaps dating between two million and one million years ago. *A. robustus* was not necessarily taller or heavier than *A. africanus.* In fact, the body sizes of the gracile *A. africanus* and robust forms may have been similar (McHenry 1988). Rather, the term *robust* refers to the distinctive features of the skull and heavy dentition of *A. robustus.* A particularly distinct feature found in *A. robustus* but absent in *A. africanus* is a sagittal crest, a bony ridge running along the top of the skull that is associated with the species' massive chewing muscles. Collectively these features indicate that *A. robustus* likely relied heavily on a diet of tough, fibrous foods.

Australopithecus boisei: The "Nutcracker Man"

Following the initial discovery of hominin fossils in South Africa, many additional finds came to light. One of the most exciting of these, called *Australopithecus boisei,* was the first of many discoveries made in eastern Africa by paleoanthropologists Louis and Mary Leakey. *Australopithecus boisei* was found in the Olduvai Gorge, a 30-mile canyon stretching across the Serengeti Plain of Tanzania. In 1959, Mary Leakey recovered an almost complete fossil skull from the gorge. The find was a robust australopithecine, but a species that was even more robust than the examples known from South Africa. The teeth of *A. boisei* were distinctly hominin in form, but were much larger than those of any other hominin species, a feature that earned *A. boisei* the nickname "Nutcracker Man." Louis Leakey (1959) named the discovery *Zinjanthropus boisei,* but less formally dubbed it "Zinj." Similarities in the dentition place it with the robust forms from South Africa and give it its designation as a robust australopithecine.

At the time of its discovery in the 1950s, Zinj was a particularly exciting find because it increased the range and number of potential human ancestors that had existed, revealing the complex history of hominin evolution. However, what made the find especially notable was that it was the first early hominin find to be well dated using a numerical dating technique: potassium-argon. The earlier hominin fossil finds from South Africa had been difficult to date. Scientists could not precisely determine the conditions that formed the different fossil localities represented. The South African cave deposits had been eroded and disturbed by nature, mixing fossils of varying ages. In contrast, the fossil deposits at Olduvai Gorge lie in undisturbed strata, occupying the same relative positions in which they were originally deposited. In addition, the area around Olduvai Gorge was volcanically active in the past. As a result, deposits of *tuff,* a porous rock formed from volcanic ash, created distinct layers within the Olduvai deposits. These volcanic layers can be dated by using the potassium-argon

method (see Chapter 2). Potassium-argon dates on tuffs above and below Zinj placed the fossil's age at approximately 1.75 million years old. This date, and additional dates on other fossil finds, revolutionized paleoanthropology by finally providing numerical ages for specific fossil specimens.

Australopithecus aethiopicus: The "Black Skull"

The incomplete puzzle of hominin ancestry was filled in with one more piece in 1985, this one dug out of the fossil beds west of Lake Turkana, Kenya, at a fossil locality known as Lomekwi I. Discovered by English paleoanthropologist Alan Walker, the find consists of the fragments of an australopithecine dating to approximately 2.5 million years ago. Because the fossil had been stained blue-black by manganese in the soil, it became known as the "Black Skull," or, by its Kenya National Museum catalogue number, KNM-WT 17000 (Walker et al. 1986). Another example of the same species may be represented by more incomplete remains found earlier in the Omo River valley of Ethiopia.

The Black Skull is a robust australopithecine, but of a type far more robust than *A. robustus* and *A. boisei,* which are more recent in age. It also has some features resembling the older australopithecines, such as *A. afarensis,* but absent in more recent robust australopithecines. For example, the cranium of the Black Skull is small, comparable in size and shape to that of the older *A. afarensis* fossils. The movement of the *A. aethiopicus* jaw is also similar to that of *A. afarensis.* Yet the face is large, prognathic, and very robust, boasting massive teeth and a pronounced sagittal crest. This suggests a different evolutionary lineage from the other robust australopithecines and, thus, presents a more complex picture of the hominin family tree. Because of its distinct combination of features, some researchers place it in a separate genus, *Paranthropus aethiopicus* (Stringer and Andrews 2005).

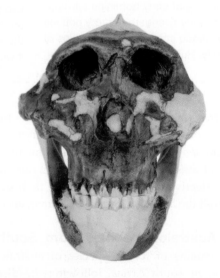

Australopithecus boisei, nicknamed the "Nutcracker Man". Note the prominent jaw and sagittal crest.

The Origins of Genus *Homo*

If the robust australopithecines are shirttail relations in the human family tree, what species present the most likely precursors of genus *Homo*? Our earliest ancestors are represented by a number of tantalizing finds that suggest the earliest members of our own species first emerged over two million years ago. The earliest known accepted representatives of the genus include two species, *Homo habilis* and *Homo rudolfensis*, distinguished from the australopithecines by their larger cranial capacity. The first representatives of these species came to light at Olduvai Gorge in the 1960s, with more recent discoveries coming from Koobi Fora, Kenya (Simons 1989b; Leakey et al. 2012). The various *H. habilis* remains from Olduvai and Koobi Fora date from between 2.3 million and 1.4 million years ago, while the best dated example of *H. rudolfensis* dates to between 1.8 million and 1.9 million years ago. Hence, the temporal range of these hominins overlap with each other, as well as those of the robust australopithecines and the earliest *Homo erectus* finds, making it difficult to infer their evolutionary relationships. *Homo habilis* and *H. rudolfensis* may represent distinct evolutionary lineages separate from those leading to modern humans. Yet, their larger cranial capacity clearly separates them from the australopithecines.

Homo habilis: "The Handyman" Fragmentary finds of *H. habilis* were first made by Louis and Mary Leakey in the 1960s. The discovery of Zinj in 1959 and the revolutionary dating of the find using potassium-argon, sparked a flurry of activity at Olduvai Gorge. Between 1960 and 1964, the Leakeys and their colleagues excavated the fragmentary remains of approximately 20 fossil hominins (Leakey 1961). Some were clearly *Homo erectus* (discussed later); others appeared comparable to the Zinj find. However, still other fossils pointed to the existence of a creature dating more than two million years old that was unlike any of the known australopithecines or more recent representatives of genus *Homo*. The distinguishing characteristic of the new species was its cranial capacity, which Louis Leakey estimated at close to 640 cc, significantly larger than that of any australopithecines, but still substantially smaller than that of *H. erectus*. The Leakeys named the creature *Homo habilis*, or "handyman," feeling that it was this species that must be responsible for the simple Oldowan stone tools that had been recovered at Olduvai Gorge.

Critics initially challenged the inclusion of *H. habilis* within genus *Homo*, maintaining that the fragmentary fossils fell within the normal cranial range of the australopithecines. However, studies of more complete finds confirm their somewhat larger cranial capacity, and so membership in genus *Homo* would seem justified. Oldowan tools have been found in contexts predating the appearance of *H. habilis* in the fossil record and also in association with other hominin species. Hence, these earliest known representatives of genus *Homo* cannot be credited with the earliest known use of stone tools. Nonetheless, *H. habilis* remains notable for its larger cranial capacity, the hallmark of genus *Homo*.

Homo rudolfensis: KNM-ER 1470 The Leakeys' son, Richard, made a series of exciting discoveries at Koobi Fora on the eastern shores of Lake Turkana, Kenya. Excavations produced several specimens that have been classified as *Homo habilis*. Among the finds, however, was a relatively complete skull that has been classified with the new species name *Homo rudolfensis*. Discovered in 1972 by Bernard Ngene and dated between 1.8 million and 1.9 million years ago, the fossil is known by its Kenya National Museum catalogue number, KNM-ER 1470. The skull has a cranial capacity of 775 cc, at the upper range of the known *H. habilis* fossils. It also possesses a flatter and broader face with thickly enameled cheek teeth. On the basis of these differences, the 1470 skull and related finds have been designated as a different species *H. habilis*: *Homo rudolfensis* (Leakey et al. 2012). Some researchers have, however, questioned this classification and so far no reliable postcranial remains have been found for *H. rudolfensis*. Thus, further evidence will be needed to determine the actual connection between *H. habilis* and *H. rudolfensis*.

Homo erectus

H. habilis is followed in the fossil record by *Homo erectus* (including finds labeled *H. ergaster*), which in turn is followed by *H. sapiens*, the species that encompasses modern humans. *Homo erectus* was a highly successful and widely dispersed species. Well-dated fossil finds identified as *H. erectus* range in age between 1.9 million and 140,000

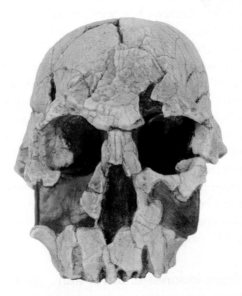

Homo rudolfensis, the KNM-ER 1470 skull. Found at Lake Turkana in 1972 it is one of the oldest representatives of genus Homo.

years ago. However, dates obtained on *H. erectus* fossils and associated animal bones from the sites of Ngandong and Sambungmacan, Java, suggest that pockets of *H. erectus* populations may have existed as recently as 40,000 to 70,000 years ago, though the depositional histories of these fossil localities are uncertain and the direct dating of the fossils is problematic (Yokoyama et al. 2008). Fossil finds bearing *H. erectus* features have been recovered from Kenya, Tanzania, Zambia, Algeria, Morocco, Georgia in southeastern Europe, China, and Indonesia, indicating that the species had the widest distribution of any hominin species with the exception of *Homo sapiens*.

Many of the discoveries now regarded as representatives of *H. erectus* were initially known by a variety of other genus and species names, including *Pithecanthropus erectus* and *Sinanthropus pekinensis*. However, more recent consensus has recognized the majority of the variation represented in the different finds as within the range that occurs in a single species. Some of the examples of *H. erectus* share many similarities with modern humans, illustrating both the interrelatedness of the species with *H. sapiens* and the challenges of classification. Some researchers have argued that the finds possessing the more modern characteristics should be designated by a separate species name, *H. ergaster*, including very early finds from Africa such as the Turkana Boy. Other researchers have argued that some of more recent *H. erectus* fossils should simply be regarded as archaic *H. sapiens*.

Turkana Boy

Turkana Boy The oldest remains of *H. erectus* have been found in Africa. One of the most complete finds, known as "Turkana boy," was recovered at the Nariokotome site near Lake Turkana in Kenya. This discovery consists of the relatively complete skeleton of an 8-year-old boy about 5 feet tall. The skeleton indicates that, below the neck, Turkana boy was physically comparable to modern humans. The cranium has a brain capacity of about 900 cc, which falls into the range of other *H. erectus* finds (Stringer and Andrews 2005). More recently, fossils that may date from the same period as Nariokotome have been found outside Africa. For example, fossil evidence from Dmanisi in the southeastern European nation of Georgia has been dated at 1.7 million years ago (Balter and Gibbons 2000; Vekua et al. 2002). A relatively complete skull from Dmanisi indicates a brain size of only 600 cc and other characteristics, which overlap with those of the earlier hominin species *H. habilis* or *H. rudolfensis*. This suggests a possible transitional creature between earlier *Homo* and *H. erectus*.

Finds from Indonesia: Java Man

Finds from Indonesia: Java Man The first examples of fossils now generally categorized as *H. erectus* were made in Asia, discovered in 1891 by the Dutch doctor Eu-

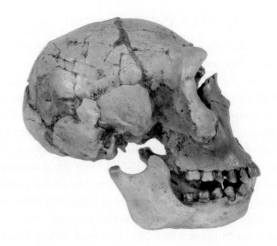

Homo ergaster skull dated to about 1.8 million years old is sometimes classified as the African variety of *H. erectus*.

gene Dubois. At the time, this was the first bona fide discovery of a pre-*Homo sapiens* hominin. Digging near Trinil in northern Java (an Indonesian island), Dubois found a leg bone, two molars, and the top of a hominin cranium. The leg was indistinguishable from that of a modern human, but the cranium was small and flat, and had heavy brow ridges, compared with modern humans. Dubois named his find *Pithecanthropus erectus* ("erect ape-man"), but today the species is classified as *Homo erectus*.

Dubois (1894) viewed his find as a missing link between humans and modern apes, but this view betrayed faulty understanding of Darwin's theory of evolution. Darwin's "missing link" referred to a common ancestor of the human and ape lineages; he never proposed a direct link between modern humans and apes, which represent the end points of distinct evolutionary lines. Other scientists correctly placed *Pithecanthropus* as an intermediary form on the evolutionary track between *Homo sapiens* and an earlier hominin ancestor.

Discoveries in China: Peking Man

Discoveries in China: Peking Man Following Dubois' discoveries, information about similar creatures accumulated at an increasing rate during the first decades of the twentieth century. Many of the most important finds came from Zhoukoudian, about 30 miles southwest of Beijing (then spelled Peking in English transliteration), China. In 1929, a team of researchers led by Chinese geologist W. C. Pei found a skull embedded in limestone during an excavation. Pei showed the skull to Davidson Black, a Canadian anatomist, who concluded that the skull represented an early form of human. Black labeled the creature *Sinanthropus pekinensis*, commonly known as "Peking man."

His curiosity piqued, Black undertook additional work at the site, which eventually produced 6 skulls, 12 skull fragments, 15 pieces of lower jaw, 157 teeth, and miscellaneous pieces of postcranial skeletons. Also unearthed at the site were traces of charcoal (possibly the remains of cooking fires) and stone tools. Anatomist Franz Weidenreich succeeded Black at the medical college and prepared casts, photos, and drawings of the Zhoukoudian fossils. Before the Japanese invasion during World War II, Weidenreich fled China with these reproductions—a fortuitous move for science, because the actual fossils were lost during the war and have never been recovered. Recent dating of the stratum where the Zhoukoudian fossils were recovered suggests that Peking man lived between 460,000 and 230,000 years ago.

Other *Homo erectus* Finds In addition to more finds in China, discoveries were made in other areas. Forty years after Dubois' excavations in Java, anthropologist G. H. R. Koenigswald uncovered the remains of comparable early hominins in the same area. Initially, scientists, working with few finds and lacking comparative specimens, speculated that each of these discoveries constituted a new evolutionary branch. We now know that, despite their disparate locations, these early discoveries are all representatives of a single genus and species, today classified as *Homo erectus*. In many respects, *Homo erectus* is identical to modern humans, although the postcranial skeleton is generally heavier and more robust. What most sets this species apart from *Homo sapiens* is the cranium, which lacks the high, vaulted appearance of that of modern humans and has a smaller average brain capacity.

Interpreting the Fossil Record

5.3 Discuss the challenges paleoanthropologists face in interpreting the fossil record and explain why their interpretations sometimes change.

Several sources of evidence indicate that the earliest human ancestors evolved in Africa. The oldest hominin species, as well as the earliest fossil evidence for anatomically modern humans, are from Africa. Climatic conditions on the African continent during the Pliocene and Pleistocene were warm, and they would have been well suited to evolving hominins. Our closest genetic relatives, the chimpanzee and gorilla, also come from Africa, suggesting a large primate genetic pool. Finally, the earliest stone tools, represented by the Oldowan tradition, are also known to be from Africa. Although the recent discovery and dating of early representatives of genus *Homo* from Asia have raised questions concerning when hominins migrated out of Africa, the overwhelming evidence for hominin origins remains Africa.

While the geographical origins of the hominins may be somewhat clear, it is more challenging to chart the hominin

family tree. As illustrated in the preceding discussion of fossil finds, as paleoanthropologists have unearthed increasing numbers of early hominin fossils their interpretations of hominin evolution have become increasingly complex. Initially, scientists drew a straight evolutionary line from *Australopithecus africanus* to *Homo erectus* and on to *Homo sapiens*. But a number of finds clearly demonstrate that in several instances more than one species of hominin roamed the Earth at the same time. How were these different species related, and how do they relate to the evolution of *Homo sapiens*?

Fundamental to tracing hominin evolution is the question of which features should be used to classify genera and species. Because the size and complexity of the brain are the most distinctive physical characteristics of modern humans, increasing cranial capacity is clearly an important feature in examining the evolution of genus *Homo*. Yet, the range of cranial capacities overlaps among hominins, making it difficult to use this as the basis for distinguishing discrete species (Armelagous and van Gerven 2003; Tattersall 1986). Study of modern species—including humans— demonstrates that there is, in fact, a great deal of variation within species in features such as cranial capacity, body size, and skeletal structure. For example, chimps from Tanzania's Gombe National Park display an astonishing degree of variation in size and skeletal structure (Bower 1990). Modern humans are equally diverse in their physical characteristics. In interpreting fragmentary hominin fossils from widely separated localities, we must take into account such natural variation within species.

In the preceding discussion of the fossil evidence for hominin evolution, the names designating specific genera and species are intended to provide a simplified overview of some of the principal discoveries. The names used here are widely accepted appellations used by paleoanthropologists, but they are not universally agreed on. Perspectives of hominin classification lie between two extremes. Some scientists, who can be called *splitters*, argue that some species designations do not reflect all the species represented. For instance, some researchers have argued that the *A. afarensis* finds from Hadar do not constitute a single, sexually dimorphic species, but at least two distinct species. Others in this camp contend that further divisions are called for within the gracile and robust australopithecines (Tattersall 1986, 1998). In fact, as we saw previously, many researchers place the robust australopithecines (including *A. aethiopicus*, *A. robustus*, and *A. boisei*) into a separate genus from *Australopithecus* called *Paranthropus*. Concerns about the differences between the early and late examples of *H. erectus* have led to the reclassification of some of the former as *H. ergaster*. Some researchers have called for further divisions.

At the opposite extreme from the splitters are the *lumpers*, who maintain that current taxonomic designations place too much emphasis on differences among individuals and do not sufficiently consider the variation that might be expected within species. This position is best advocated by C. Loring Brace (Brace and Montagu 1965; Brace 1967, 1989). Brace asserts that the information available on *Homo habilis*, *A. afarensis*, and *A. aethiopicus* is insufficient to categorize each as a distinct species, and he advocates including them with other genus and species. For example, *H. habilis*, *H. ergaster*, and other finds might all be included with *Homo erectus*.

At this point, it is useful to underscore that the different perspectives presented by lumpers and splitters include a great deal of consensus about the differences present in the individual fossil finds. The divergence in opinion is about what the differences in the fossil finds imply about taxonomic classification and the process of speciation. Unfortunately, the ultimate defining aspect of a species, the ability to interbreed, is not something that can be assessed on the basis of fossil evidence.

Changing Views

Many interpretations of hominin evolution have been advanced through the years. Some of these, explored in the following section, are illustrated in Figure 5.4 . When they were proposed, they represented valid attempts to explain the available fossil evidence. Like all sciences, paleoanthropology proceeds by formulating hypotheses and then

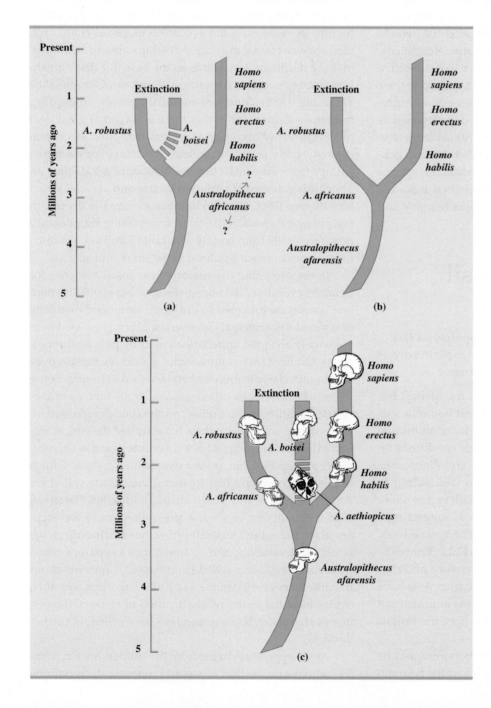

Figure 5.4 Changing interpretations of hominin evolution: (a) Various theories during the 1960s and 1970s placed *A. africanus* in a position ancestral to *Homo* or to both *Homo* and later australopithecines. The robust australopithecines were placed on their own side branch; (b) In 1979, Johanson and White named a new species, *A. afarensis*, which they placed at the base of the hominin family tree leading to both *Australopithecus* and *Homo*. *A. africanus* was moved to a side branch leading to the robust australopithecines; (c) In 1985, the discovery of *A. aethiopicus* made the picture more complex, suggesting that all of the australopithecines cannot be located on a single side branch. More recent discoveries have led to further revision (see Figure 5.5).

testing them against empirical data. In contrast to most sciences, however, the data from the fossil record cannot be obtained by laboratory experiments. Rather, paleoanthropologists must await the next unpredictable fossil find. As new evidence is uncovered, new hypotheses are developed, and old ones are modified or discarded. As the number of fossil species represented has increased and our understanding of the fossil record has become more refined, the interpretations have had to account for more variation and thus have become increasingly complex (see Figure 5.5).

A. *africanus* as Ancestor A number of theories propounded in the 1960s and 1970s placed *A. africanus* at the base of the hominin family tree, as illustrated in Figure 5.4(a) . These interpretations of evolution basically held that hominins developed along two main branches. As the most sophisticated of the australopithecines, *A. africanus* was considered the most likely to have given rise to the genus *Homo* and was, therefore, placed at the bottom of the branch leading to *Homo habilis*, *Homo erectus*, and ultimately *Homo sapiens*. The robust australopithecines (including various species sometimes classified in genus *Paranthropus*) occupied their own branch, eventually becoming extinct around one million years ago. Because of their large teeth and specialized chewing apparatus, the robust australopithecines were not viewed as directly ancestral to *Homo*. In some interpretations, *A. africanus* was located at the base of the

hominin tree, positioned as a possible ancestor of both the later australopithecines and genus *Homo*. Other variations saw *P. boisei* and *P. robustus* on separate branches entirely.

The Discovery of *Australopithecus afarensis*
Following the discovery of Lucy and other *A. afarensis* fossils at Hadar in the 1970s, Donald Johanson and Timothy White proposed a new interpretation of hominin evolution, which is illustrated in Figure 5.4(b) Variations of this interpretation were incorporated into many models in the following decade. Johanson and White hypothesized that the genus *Australopithecus* began with *A. afarensis*, dated at about four million to three million years ago. They contended that *A. afarensis* was the common ancestor of all subsequent hominin species. In their scheme, one of the branches from *A. afarensis* leads to *A. africanus* and *A. robustus*. The other major branch leads toward the evolution of *Homo habilis* and succeeding species of genus *Homo*, culminating in modern *Homo sapiens* (Johanson and White 1979). Many paleoanthropologists concurred with this model of hominin evolution until the mid-1980s.

Revised Interpretations Interpretations of the late 1980s and 1990s had to grapple with a new spate of discoveries. With the discovery of the Black Skull in 1985, a relatively neat picture of human evolution grew more clouded and more complex. Johanson and White had placed

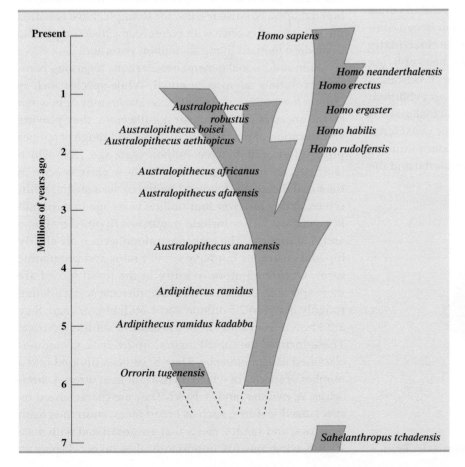

Figure 5.5 More recent discoveries have extended the hominin family tree further back in time. New branches have also been added, making the hominin family tree look more like a bush.

A. boisei at the end of the extinct line of australopithecines, a sort of hyper-robust form of *A. robustus* (Figure 5.4(b). This was a logical conclusion, given the available fossil evidence at the time. Unfortunately, *A. aethiopicus* does not fit into this neat picture. It has certain characteristics found in *A. boisei* but not in *A. africanus* and *A. robustus*, yet *A. aethiopicus* is as old as *A. africanus*. Scientists wishing to insert the Black Skull into the Johanson and White evolutionary tree would be hard pressed to explain how certain features appeared in *A. aethiopicus*, disappeared in *A. africanus* and *A. robustus*, and then reappeared in *A. boisei* (Johanson and Shreeve 1989). A more logical and workable interpretation places *A. boisei* and *A. robustus* on branches of their own. Other limbs would lead to *A. africanus* and genus *Homo*, as pictured in Figure 5.4(c) .

Current Perspectives

As new finds and additional information relevant to hominin ancestry have come to light, the interpretation of human phylogeny has become ever more challenging. More recent discoveries have added new species as well as extended the hominin family tree even further back in time. New branches have also been added, making our family tree look increasingly bush-like (Quintyn 2009; White 1995; Wolpoff et al. 2006; Wood 2002). Current models of hominin evolution must now take into account older and more primitive species like *Ardipithecus ramidus* and *Australopithecus anamensis*. Interpretations of fossil finds must also be reconciled with increasing information from a completely different source: genetic data. As discussed later and in Chapter 4, study of the genetic relatedness of living primate species has implications for both the classification of hominin finds and the interpretation of their evolutionary history. The extraction of DNA from fossil material has also provided new information that has to be considered in tracing evolutionary relationships of modern humans and their closest ancestors, such as the Neandertal and the Denisovans, which we will address later.

Australopithecus afarensis, best known from discoveries in Hadar, Ethiopia.

Acceptance of new species and a more branching view of hominin evolution have led to the reanalysis and reinterpretation of earlier finds (see Figure 5.4). Some researchers have underscored variation within fossils formerly recognized as single species. Hence, splitting has become somewhat more fashionable than lumping. This is particularly true within genus *Homo*. Fossils commonly designated *H. erectus* span from 1.8 million years to less than 140,000 years old. Although some differences in the structure of the cranium are present in these varied finds, *H. erectus* has been generally been seen as an extremely well-adapted and long-lived species. However, some scientists have argued that some of the earliest *H. erectus* finds from Africa, as well as more recent finds from other world areas, possess distinctive features that merit a separate species designation, *Homo ergaster*. They see these fossils as having characteristics more transitional to *H. sapiens*. Consequently, they would place *H. ergaster* more directly ancestral to *Homo sapiens* than other *H. erectus* finds, which would be placed in a separate lineage. Similarly, as we saw above, fossils formerly categorized as *H. habilis* are now classified by some researchers as *H. rudolfensis*.

Despite the seemingly confusing array of interpretations, the diversity of finds uncovered provides insight into human origins. While a number of possible hominin ancestors may be represented, the varied fossil finds are nonetheless consistent with a model of human phylogeny that traces the evolution of genus *Homo* from small-brained bipedal apes. No discoveries, for example, have revealed the presence of species with cranial capacities comparable to modern humans living six million years ago.

Some additional general observations regarding hominin evolution can also be noted. While species such as *Orrorin tugenensis* and *Ardipithecus ramidus* may or may not be the ancestors of later australopithecines, they provide an indication of the types of features and range of species present four million to six million years ago, from which later species may have emerged. These early species in the fossil record are followed by the earliest australopithecines, dating just over four million years ago to three million years ago. They include *A. afarensis* (typified by Lucy) and *A. anamensis*. The early australopithecines are clearly bipedal creatures, but have small brains and prognathic faces. Occurring more recently in the fossil record are more specialized, derived australopithecine species dating roughly between 2.5 million and 1 million years ago; they are known from finds in both east and southern Africa. These include the robust australopithecines, sometimes classified as *Paranthropus*. They have been divided into a number of species of which there are at least three: *A. aethiopicus*, *A. robustus*, and *A. boisei*. They are characterized by specialized features, such as broad faces, enormous teeth and jaws, and sagittal crests that are associated with massive chewing muscles. Importantly, they do not display an increase in cranial capacity compared to the earlier australopithecines. These features suggest that the robust australopithecines represent a specialized adaptation that makes them unlikely candidates for human ancestors.

Early representatives of the genus *Homo* appear in the fossil record at the same time as the robust australopithecines and, thus, coexisted with them. Most of the known specimens (*H. habilis* and *Homo rudolfensis*) are from East Africa, but possible representatives have also been found in South Africa. This group of fossils has a number of important characteristics—including larger cranial capacity, change in the shape of the cranium, and smaller teeth—that place them as intermediaries between earlier australopithecines and the large-brained *Homo erectus*.

Missing Pieces in the Fossil Record All of the preceding views of hominin evolution are based on excavated fossils. Part of the problem with these interpretations—and the continuing need for revision—lies in the fact that our perception of the fossil record is woefully incomplete. The currently known fossils do not begin to represent the extent and diversity of extinct species. It has been estimated that less than 3 percent of the primate species that once roamed the Earth have been recognized in the fossil record (Martin 1990). Some scholars have long contended that australopithecines like Lucy emerged after the split between the *Australopithecus* and *Homo* lineages. In other words, the australopithecines represent a separate hominin branch, and the early part of the *Homo* lineage is still poorly known (Shipman 1986a). Given the fact that fossils of hominins dating earlier than four million years ago are fragmentary and their ancestry uncertain, any number of scenarios might be posited but cannot currently be evaluated because of the lack of fossil remains.

A tantalizing illustration of our inadequate knowledge of the fossil record is underscored by fossil finds such as *Sahelanthropus tchadensis*, discussed earlier, and other fragmentary remains found at a site near Koro Toro in Chad in 1995. Until these discoveries, the majority of the early hominins located had been recovered from sites in eastern and southern Africa, ranging from South Africa to Ethiopia. Consequently, models of hominin evolution focused on these finds and generally assumed that the hominins evolved in these areas. However, the distribution of hominins in Central and West Africa is poorly known. These regions lack the extensive, and more thoroughly explored, exposures of Pliocene and Pleistocene deposits that have been studied in other parts of Africa. The presence of the Chad finds, far beyond what had been considered the geographic distribution of early hominins, raises questions about how much we *do not know*.

It is likely that future discoveries will continue to extend the human lineage further back in time and produce an increasingly "bushy" hominin family tree, and models of hominin lineages will continue to be revised. Further research may also lead the search for human ancestry in entirely new directions. This perspective recognizes the inadequacy of the fossil record and the incomplete nature of the available data. Of course, it also lacks explanatory value and, as a result, is a somewhat unsatisfactory conclusion. Despite the limited information, the majority of paleoanthropologists prefer to speculate on the potential relationships of the known fossil species. These reconstructions allow us to think about how the human species may have emerged. While debate regarding interpretation of individual finds and their place in human ancestry will continue, new information is gradually providing greater insight.

Genetic Differences and Hominin Evolution

The preceding discussion of hominin phylogeny has focused on information gleaned from the fossil record—actual traces of early hominins recovered from the ground. During the past several decades some researchers have increasingly approached the study of human evolution from a completely different direction. As noted in Chapter 4 (see the box "What's in a Name?" (page 71), scientists have studied the similarities and differences in chromosomes and DNA sequencing of living primates and determined the genetic relatedness of individual species. Genetic information has shed new light on hominin evolution, aiding in both the formulation of new hypotheses and their evaluation.

The genetic data on living primates has led to a reassessment of the way in which both living and fossil species are classified. Scientists traditionally placed humans and their immediate ancestors in the family Hominidae—the **hominids**—because of their upright posture, distinctive appearance, and unique behavioral adaptations. The so-called "Great Apes," including chimpanzees, gorillas and orangutans, were placed in the separate family of Pongidae. However, comparing genetic data from modern humans and nonhuman primates, researchers have demonstrated that the base pairs in the DNA sequences of chimpanzees and humans are 95 percent the same (Britten 2002). There is slightly more distance between humans and gorillas, but genetically the similarities between the two species still approaches 100 percent. This similarity in genetic code indicates a closer evolutionary relationship among chimpanzees, gorillas and humans than there is between any of these species and any of the other primates, including the orangutan. Consequently, taxonomic classification has been revised. Family *Hominidea* (the hominids) now includes both subfamily *Ponginae*, consisting of the Orangutan, and subfamily *Homininae*, including the chimpanzee, gorilla and humans (respectively referred to as the tribes *Panini*, *Gorillini*, and *Hominini*). This classification more accurately reflects the genetic relatedness of the different species. Yet, it is somewhat confusing as previously used terms have different meanings.

Drawing upon the genetic data from living primates, researchers have gone a step further and attempted to infer the amount of time it took for evolution to produce the amount of genetic distance between various species. This is based on determining the rate at which mutation, and ultimately, the process of speciation, takes place. Genetic research suggests the separation of the human and chimpanzee lineages approximately five million to six million years ago (Kumar et al. 2005; Yang 2002). The genetic information, therefore, would appear to complement the fossil evidence, which provides evidence of species that lived near the time of the divergence of chimpanzees and humans (*Ardipithecus ramidus* and *kadabba*).

Genetic data provides new and, importantly, independent data that can be used to assess the relative genetic distance between different primate species and the possible times of their evolutionary divergence. Researchers have also used DNA to examine the origins of modern humans and their dispersal out of Africa, as well as the relationship of Neandertals to modern humans (discussed later in "Neandertals and Modern Humans" and the "Denisovans"). Yet, genetic data provides no clues to how ancestral hominins adapted to different environments, their feeding habits, their geographic range, their lifeways, or any of the myriad other questions that concern paleoanthropology. Clues to human origins, therefore, will continue to also depend upon discoveries pried from the fossil record.

From *Homo erectus* to *Homo sapiens*

5.4 **Describe and discuss the different models for the emergence of anatomically modern humans.**

Scientists cannot pinpoint which selective pressures prompted *H. erectus* to evolve into *H. sapiens*. Fossils of *H. erectus* (including finds designated *H. ergaster*) range in age from 1.9 million to less than 140,000 years old. The longevity of the species is a testament to how well *H. erectus* adapted to different environmental conditions, having ranged across the diverse climates from Africa and southern Europe to Asia. Presumably, *H. sapiens* must have had some adaptive advantage over earlier hominin species, but no consensus has emerged about what specific selective pressures were involved. Among the physical changes found in *H. sapiens* are a larger brain and full speech capabilities, which undoubtedly sparked concomitant behavioral consequences. Many of the distinctive characteristics seen in *H. sapiens* stem from cultural factors as well. As will be seen in Chapter 7, *H. erectus* made increasing

use of socially learned technology to interact with and control the environment. This trend intensifies in later human populations.

Many hominin remains from the period between 400,000 and 200,000 years ago are difficult to classify because they exhibit physical traits characteristic of both *H. erectus* and *H. sapiens*. These hominins, which can be alternately viewed as either advanced *H. erectus* or early *H. sapiens*, can be referred to as **transitional forms**. The discovery of finds that do not fit neatly into taxonomic categories is not surprising. As we saw in Chapter 4, related species have many similar characteristics that reflect their evolutionary relationships. Transitional forms illustrate these relationships and offer physical evidence of the process of speciation.

Transitional Forms

In examining the transition from *H. erectus* to *H. sapiens*, we need to cast a critical eye on the physical characteristics that distinguish the two species. *Homo erectus* shares many physical features with modern humans; in fact, the postcranial skeletons are essentially the same, except for the generally heavier, more massive structure of *H. erectus* bones. The major differences between the two species appear in the skull. The skulls of *Homo sapiens* are high and vaulted, providing a large cranial capacity. In contrast, the skulls of *H. erectus* feature a **postorbital constriction**, meaning that the front portion of the skull narrows behind the eye sockets and the high forehead of *H. sapiens* is absent. Lacking the high vaulted cranium of *H. sapiens*, the skull of *H. erectus* is widest toward the base.

Other distinctive characteristics of *H. erectus* make scientists believe that these creatures had strong jaw and neck muscles. These traits include a slight ridge at the back of the skull and heavy eyebrow ridges, structural features that have disappeared in modern humans. *Homo erectus* also exhibits a *prognathic* face, the nose and teeth extending toward the front. This is an attribute of early hominins and living, nonhuman primates that is absent in *H. sapiens*. The anterior teeth of *H. erectus* are relatively small compared to those of earlier *Homo* species, but large in comparison to those of modern humans.

Transitional forms bearing various combinations of *H. erectus* and *H. sapiens* features have been discovered in Europe, Asia, and Africa. The mosaic of physical characteristics found in some specimens has sparked debate over how to designate species most appropriately. This debate can be illustrated by the Petralona cranium, uncovered in eastern Greece in 1960 (Day 1986). Scientists have debated the age of the find (claims ranging from one million years old to 120,000 years old have been made), yet the consensus leans toward an age of approximately 350,000 years old. The species designation of this fossil has also been widely contested. The Petralona cranium exhibits many of the classic *H. erectus* characteristics, including thick bones, pronounced brow ridges, and a low cranial vault. However, the cranial capacity is estimated at approximately 1,200 cc, placing it at the uppermost limits of *H. erectus* and within the lower range of the more recent species of genus *Homo*, including both *H. neanderthalensis* and *H. sapiens*.

The Evolution of *Homo sapiens*

Although researchers generally agree that *H. erectus* evolved into *H. sapiens*, there is substantial disagreement about how, where, and when this transition occurred. Early interpretations were based on limited information and often emphasized the uniqueness of individual finds. Currently, there is growing consensus that anatomically modern humans first evolved in Africa and then spread out to other world areas. A variety of competing interpretations continue to be evaluated. For the purposes of this discussion, two contrasting models are presented: the Multiregional Evolutionary Model and the Replacement Model. Supporting evidence for each of these perspectives has been presented, and the varied models each have their supporters. A third set of interpretations, consisting of Hybridization and Assimilation Models, which attempt to reconcile the two opposing extremes in various ways have also been presented.

Multiregional Evolutionary Model As noted earlier, *Homo erectus* has the widest distribution of any hominin species other than modern humans. According to the **multiregional evolutionary model** of modern human origins, the gradual evolution of *H. erectus* into archaic *H. sapiens* and, finally modern *H. sapiens* took place concurrently in the various parts of Asia, Africa, and Europe over the past 2.5 million years (as illustrated in Figure 5.6a). In this view, the transition from *H. erectus* to *H. sapiens* was within a single human species. Through natural selective pressures and genetic differences, local *H. erectus* populations developed particular traits that varied from region to region; consequently the variation in physical characteristics noted in modern human populations is deeply rooted in the past (Wolpoff and Caspari 1997). Early variations of this model, initially proposed in the early twentieth century, suggested the parallel evolution of *H. sapiens* in different regions. More recent perspectives, however, underscored that *gene flow*—the widespread sharing of genes through interbreeding—between populations in the different regions prevented the evolution of distinct species. The emergence of *H. sapiens* was, therefore, a widespread phenomenon, although different regional populations continued to exhibit distinctive features.

Working from the multiregional evolutionary model, we would expect to see a great deal of regional genetic continuity, meaning that the fossil finds from a particular geographic area should display similarities from the earliest representatives of *H. erectus* to those of modern populations. Supporters of this model argue that such continuities do indeed exist. For example, skeletal remains of early *H. sapiens* from different regions of China, North Africa, and Europe resemble modern populations in those areas in some respects (Bednarik 2011; Smith 1984; Thorne and Wolpoff 1992; Wolpoff and Caspari 2002). Certain distinctive features can be identified in the cranium, dentition, jaws, and particular features of the postcranial skeleton. Researchers favoring this interpretation further note regional continuity in the archaeological records of different world areas.

Replacement Model The **replacement model,** or the "recent African origin of modern humans model," has increasingly garnered support among researchers (Liu et al. 2006; Stringer 1985; Stringer and Andrews 2005). It holds that *H. sapiens* evolved in one area of the world first (Africa) and migrated to other regions, as illustrated in Figure 5.6b. It is called the replacement model because it assumes that *H. sapiens* were contemporaries of the earlier *H. erectus* but eventually replaced them without significant interbreeding. According to the replacement hypothesis, *H. sapiens* populations all descended from a single common ancestral group. Thus, although the modern and archaic species overlapped in their spans on Earth, they were highly distinctive, genetically different evolutionary lineages. Consequently, there is minimal diversity among modern humans and the regional differences in modern human populations are relatively recent developments.

Some researchers believe that fossil evidence supporting the replacement hypothesis may be found in the homeland of all hominins: Africa. The earliest known examples of anatomically modern *H. sapiens* come from Ethiopian sites dating 150,000 to 190,000 years ago (McDougall et al. 2005; White et al. 2003). In the replacement view, these remains are evidence of the earliest representatives of modern *H. sapiens*, the species first evolving in Africa and then spreading out of Africa to other areas.

While the preceding scenario remains plausible, the evidence is not without limitations. The fossil evidence from Africa remains fragmentary, and a fuller understanding of the distribution of early modern humans is desirable. Genetic data also provides challenges to this perspective. The replacement model was originally given a great deal of support by studies of mitochondrial DNA in modern humans undertaken in the 1980s, which suggested that the maternal line of all living women can be traced to a single female living in Africa about 200,000 years ago. This would clearly support a recent African origin of modern humans. While additional genetic data support an African origin, studies have also suggested that there was at least some interbreeding

Figure 5.6 Three different interpretations of the emergence of *H. sapiens*. The multiregional evolutionary model (a) suggests regional continuity and the gradual evolution of all *H. erectus* and archaic *H. sapiens* populations into modern humans, gene flow between populations (here represented by horizontal arrows) preventing the emergence of distinct species. In contrast, supporters of the replacement model (b) see modern humans as evolving in Africa and spreading out, replacing earlier hominin populations. Various hybridization and assimilation models (c) allow for varying degrees of gene flow between *Homo sapiens* and earlier populations of archaic *H. sapiens* via gene flow or genetic admixture.

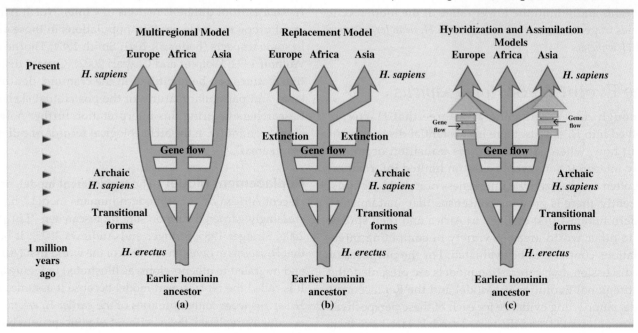

between anatomically modern *H. sapiens* and earlier archaic species, such as the Neandertals (discussed later), affording a more complex picture of our genetic history.

Hybridization and Assimilation Models It is possible, perhaps likely, that neither of the preceding models for the emergence of anatomically modern humans is completely correct. Neither fully accounts for all of the fossil and genetic evidence. The processes involved in the emergence of modern humans were likely more complex and encompassed more variables than can be neatly wrapped up in either of the two overarching perspectives (Gunz et al. 2009; Lahr and Foley 1994; Stringer 2001). Emergent human populations may have incorporated a great deal of physical diversity—as well as behavioral, social, and linguistic differences. Further, it is unlikely that migrations (out of Africa or elsewhere) were unidirectional affairs involving the movement of homogeneous populations. Many different migrations via different routes, recolonization of previously occupied territories, and gene flow with other populations were more probable. Understanding of such variables provides insight into not only the emergence of modern humans, but also the source of the diversity underlying present-day populations.

A number of more recent interpretations of modern human origins have attempted to reconcile the conflicting aspects of the multiregional and replacement models, as well as the varied factors noted above (Gibbons 2011). These have been referred to by a variety of names. The proposed interpretations can, however, be collectively referred to as **hybridization and assimilation models** in that they allow for varying degrees of gene flow between *H. sapiens* and earlier populations of archaic *H. sapiens*. Gene flow or genetic admixture between anatomically modern humans and indigenous premodern populations occurred as a result of population migrations and varying degrees of interbreeding between different populations.

As is the case with the replacement model, these perspectives generally accept the relatively recent African origin of anatomically modern humans. All of these perspectives can be differentiated from the multiregional model that assumes the emergence of modern humans in more than one area. In these hybridization and assimilation scenarios, anatomically modern *H. sapiens* emerged in Africa first, after about 200,000 years ago, and then migrated outward into other world areas. As a result of interbreeding, anatomically modern humans hybridized with earlier archaic populations, eventually replacing them. In fact, fossil evidence from the Near East, as well as Europe and East Asia, indicates that different hominin species overlapped in time and space, while fossils that seem to represent admixtures of *H. sapiens* and Neandertal features have also been identified (Soficaru and Trinkaus 2006). Finally, genetic data indicates at least some interbreeding between modern human ancestors and archaic *Homo sapiens*. These interpretations underscore a greater amount of gene flow than the replacement model allows. Hence hybridization or assimilation models may more correctly represent the complex and gradual nature of the processes represented.

Genetic Data and Modern Human Origins

5.5 **Describe how new genomic research and molecular dating have helped anthropologists interpret human evolution.**

As discussed previously with regard to the tracing of primate and earlier hominin ancestry, researchers have also brought biochemical techniques to bear on the question of modern human origins. The genetic research also stands as a good example of the degree of scrutiny—and debate—that new theories attract and the importance of relying on different sources of data (Relethford 2003).

The genetic make-up of modern humans provides a record of the genetic history of our species. When individuals from different groups interbreed, the offspring's DNA is provided by each of the parents (see discussion of DNA in Chapter 3). This admixture of DNA is subsequently passed down through the following generations, all the way to modern humans. The genetic data obtained have increasingly proven consistent with an African origin of *H. sapiens* (Deshpande et al. 2009). Yet in some cases, different kinds of genetic data have been seen as consistent with both the replacement and multiregional models (Ayala 1995; Frayer et al. 1993; Harding et al. 1997; Harris and Hey 1999).

Human genetic variation reflects geographical origins: individuals from one region will, generally, be more genetically similar than individuals from a distant region (see the box on Race and Genetics: The Human Genome Project in Chapter 6). Yet, the study of the genetic make-up of modern humans, as well as the study of DNA extracted from the fossilized bones of archaic humans such as the Neandertals and denisovians (discussed later) also provides a record of the complexity of gene flow in ancient populations; populations were never "pure" in a genetic sense. Study of genetic material has also provided clues to gene flow over the more recent past. For example, it may provide a record of Arab and trans-Atlantic slave trades (Hellenthal et al. 2014). Two specific types of genetic markers have been examined with specific regard to the emergence of modern humans: mitochondrial DNA and Y-chromosomal DNA. These are notable in reflecting, respectively female and male genetic ancestry.

Mitochondrial Eve

Among the genetic studies that have received the most popular media attention is the use of mitochondrial DNA (mtDNA) from modern humans to understand human origins. Working at the University of California, Berkeley in the 1980s, a team of researchers studied the mitochondrial DNA of modern women (Cann et al. 1987; Stoneking et al. 1987; Wilson and Cann 1992). On the basis of the studies, which were widely publicized, they argued that modern humanity could be traced back to a single African female who lived between 200,000 and 130,000 years ago (popularly referred to in the media as "Eve"). This method provided important insights, but interpretation of the data is challenging and remains a source of debate.

The strength of the technique lies in the distinctive characteristics of mtDNA. This type of DNA is located in the portion of the cell that helps convert cellular material into the energy needed for cellular activity. In contrast to nuclear DNA (see Chapter 3), mtDNA is not carried by the (male) sperm when it fertilizes the egg. The genetic code embedded in mtDNA, therefore, is passed on only through the female. Thus, individuals' mtDNA is not altered by recombination during reproduction. Each of us inherits this type of DNA from our mother, our mother's mother, and so on, along a single, maternal genealogical line. The variation present in human female mtDNA is the result of accumulated mutations that have occurred. By determining the rate at which mutations have occurred, the time at which the human lineage diverged from that of earlier human ancestors can be determined. The greater amount of mutation present, the greater amount of time was needed for them to accumulate.

The study by the Berkeley team focused on the mtDNA of 147 women from Africa, Asia, Europe, Australia, and New Guinea (Cann et al. 1987). The accumulation of random mutations in the different populations displayed distinctive patterns. Significantly, the mtDNA of the African women tended to be more diverse, or heterogeneous, suggesting that mutations present had a long time to accumulate. In other populations, the mtDNA was more uniform, or homogeneous, a sign that they had not had as much time to accumulate mutations. Assuming a constant mutation rate, the researchers inferred a maternal line in Africa dating back to between 200,000 and 130,000 years ago. Linking these data to the replacement model of human origins, they further suggested that these anatomically modern humans moved out of Africa, replacing the earlier *H. erectus* populations throughout the world.

Mitochondrial DNA studies provide tantalizing clues to modern human origins. There is still, however, debate about the methods used and the interpretation of the results obtained (Cyran and Kimmel 2010; Mountain 1998; Templeton 1993, 2002). More recent research has demonstrated that mutation rates across the mitochondrial genome vary and that the mutation rate has also varied through time (Henn et al. 2009; Ho et al. 2005; Howell et al. 2003; Soares et al. 2010). Despite the vibrant debate and media hype that at times characterized the mtDNA data, the projected age of a shared female ancestor in the different studies is broadly similar, insofar as they have yielded estimates ranging from 100,000 to 200,000 years ago. The mtDNA data also favors the replacement model, with Africa as the ultimate place of origin of later anatomically human populations. Yet here the likely complexity of the movement of early human populations out of Africa, and their interactions with early hominin populations should again be underscored.

Paternal Genetic Ancestry

Researchers have also studied paternal genetic ancestry through information encoded on the Y chromosome. Humans have two types of sex chromosomes: X and Y. Females have two X chromosomes, while males have an X and a Y. A child's gender depends on whether a father's sperm contains an X or a Y chromosome, which combines with an X chromosome from the mother during reproduction (see Chapter 3). Consequently, studies of Y chromosomes provide a genetic record of paternal ancestry. As in the case of mtDNA, the mutation rate of Y chromosomes calculated on the basis of genetic data from modern humans has been used to infer the time when modern humans emerged as well as the relatedness of different human populations.

Y-chromosomal Adam is the popular name given to the most recent common patrilineal ancestor of all living humans. The mutation rate in Y chromosomes is quite high, making assessment of the age of this patrilineal ancestor challenging. Estimates have varied in different studies, some contrasting with the estimated reached in mtDNA studies (Hammer et al. 1998; Hammer and Zegura 2002). However, more recent calibrations of both the mtDNA data and the Y-chromosome data have yielded relatively consistent results (Poznik 2013). Although the estimates of Y-chromosomal Adam range from 100,000 to 200,000 years old, the studies are consistent with the mtDNA data that suggest a relatively recent, African origin for modern humans. However, the data also suggest movement back into Africa following the initial expansion of modern humans out of Africa.

Archaic and Anatomically Modern *Homo sapiens*

5.6 **Discuss the different theories regarding the relationship of *Homo sapiens neanderthalensis* and *Homo sapiens*.**

Although debate continues over the classification of certain hominins dating between 200,000 and 400,000 years ago, there is much more agreement over later finds. For the most part, all hominin fossils dating to the last 200,000 years are classified as *H. sapiens*.

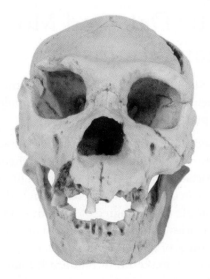

Homo heidelbergensis, first discovered near Heidelberg, Germany in 1908.

This is not to say that *H. sapiens* populations of 200,000 years ago were identical to modern humans, or that all of the finds represented possess the same physical characteristics. However, the distinctive features noted are all considered within the range of variation found within a single species. To simplify our discussion, hominins of the last 200,000 years can be divided into two categories: **archaic *Homo sapiens*** and **anatomically modern *Homo sapiens***. Archaic *H. sapiens* can be viewed as transitional forms on the evolutionary lineage extending from *H. erectus* to modern *H. sapiens*, possessing features characteristics of both species. Indeed, some finds dating before 200,000 years ago, including the Petralona cranium noted above, have been labeled archaic *H. sapiens*. At the other extreme, hominin fossils with archaic *H. sapiens* features overlap with those of anatomically modern *Homo sapiens*, finds that possess all of the characteristics found in modern humans.

Generally, anatomically modern humans are more delicate than *Homo erectus* and archaic examples of *Homo sapiens*. However, modern humans encompass a great deal of variation and in some cases their post-cranial anatomy may be quite robust. The major distinguishing features between archaic *Homo sapiens* and anatomically modern *Homo sapiens* are in the skull. In contrast to archaic specimens, anatomically modern *Homo sapiens* have a pronounced forehead, the skull extending upwards rather than back from the eyes. The teeth are also somewhat smaller, resulting in a more prominent chin. The earliest examples of anatomically modern humans are known from African finds dating between 190,000 and 160,000 years ago, with the first examples dating as recently as 40,000 years ago in other regions. The oldest African finds consist of two partial skulls and post-cranial bones from Omo, Ethiopia, dated to 195,000 years ago. Other early

A fossilized skull of an anatomically modern *Homo sapiens* from the Cro-Magnon rock shelter, France. Features such as the domed skull and clearly defined chin are characteristic of modern humans.

examples are represented by slightly more complete finds excavated at Herto in Ethiopia's Afar Triangle (White et al. 2003). The Herto finds include three crania consisting of two adult males and a six-year-old child. The finds possess some archaic features but were regarded by their discoverers as direct ancestors of modern *Homo sapiens.*

In contrast to the preceding cases, finds possessing features seen in earlier *H. erectus* populations continue to be present, though to a lesser degree. The mosaic of features that characterizes archaic *H. sapiens* takes clear shape in remains unearthed at the Broken Hill Mine in Kabwe, Zambia. These finds, initially classified as *Homo rhodesiensis* (Rhodesian man), are now more widely accepted as *Homo heidelbergensis.* The Kabwe finds consist of a cranium and the postcranial bones of three or four individuals, dated to at least 125,000 years ago (Begun 2012; Rightmire 1993). On the one hand, the thickness of the bone, heavy brow ridges, and sloping forehead of the cranium are characteristic of *H. erectus*. Also like *H. erectus,* the Kabwe skull is widest at the base. On the other hand, the cranial capacity is large (1,280 cc), and the postcranial skeleton bears a strong resemblance to *H. sapiens*. Similar remains have been found at other southern African, East African, and North African sites. The Kabwe find once again raises the question of which features best differentiate species, or if separate species designations are justified.

Homo sapiens neanderthalensis

The best-known example of an archaic *H. sapiens* is *H. sapiens neanderthalensis,* also known popularly as "Neandertal man." Neandertal fossils dating between 200,000 and 30,000 years ago have been discovered in Europe and the Middle East, and it is possible that Neandertals may have

coexisted with anatomically modern humans in Europe as recently as 24,000 years ago (Duarte et al. 1999). In the past, climatic conditions in this area spanned a more extreme range than they do today. The southern regions had warmer, milder climates, and the northern regions were partially glaciated and extremely cold.

The Neandertal physique has become the quintessential image of "cave men" in popular culture. They have often been portrayed as second-rate hominins, swept to extinction by quicker-thinking modern humans (Brace 1964; for readable, fictional portrayals, see Auel 1981; Golding 1981). This depiction stems, in part, from an early find of a skeleton of an elderly individual whom scientists later determined had suffered from arthritis. In fact, Neandertals were quite literally thick-skulled and had the heavy brow ridges seen in *H. erectus*. In the classic Neandertal, the mid-portion of the face protruded as if the nose and surrounding features were pulled forward (Figure 5.7).

Figure 5.7 A comparison of the skulls of *H. erectus, H. sapiens neanderthalensis,* and modern *H. sapiens*. The most distinctive feature of the latter is the high vaulted forehead and the prominent chin.

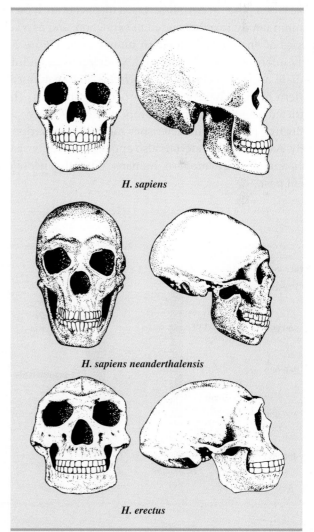

H. sapiens

H. sapiens neanderthalensis

H. erectus

The front teeth of Neandertals were larger than those of modern humans. Often, Neandertals teeth bear evidence of heavy wear (some were actually worn down to stubs), which leads researchers to believe that the teeth may have been used by Neandertals in much the same way as tools.

Yet despite the above features, the image of Neandertals as brutish creatures is misleading. The large Neandertal cranial capacity ranged from 1,200 to 2,000 cc and could accommodate a brain as large as, or even larger than, that of a modern human. Moreover, studies of Neandertal endocasts indicate that the structure and intellectual capacities of the Neandertal brain mirrored those of modern humans (Holloway 1985). Artifacts used by these populations reflect a much more complex range of adaptive skills than do those of pre-*H. sapiens* hominins (see Chapter 7).

Neandertals and Modern Humans Ever since the first Neandertal skulls were found in the nineteenth century, scientists have pondered the links between Neandertals and modern humans (Figure 5.8). They have, alternatively, been seen as: a transitional species between *Homo erectus* and modern humans; a distinct branch on the hominin family tree that ended in extinction; and as a subspecies of anatomically modern humans (see Figure 5.8). Early interpretations that viewed Neandertals as an intermediate ancestor between *Homo erectus* and anatomically modern humans have been discarded (Figure 5.8a). Their restricted geographic range (Europe and Middle East) and distinctive physical characteristics make this scenario unlikely. As noted, Neandertals also appear to have coexisted with anatomically modern humans until the relatively recent past.

A growing consensus among anthropologists holds that Neandertals had distinctive physical features that separate them from anatomically modern *H. sapiens*, but no one has come up with a cogent, widely accepted theory to explain which selective pressures produced these features (Trinkaus 2006). Researchers tend to favor the hypothesis that a "pre-Neandertal" population, possibly originating in another region and migrating to the classic Neandertal area, underwent severe natural selection in response to the cold environment of Europe. Fossil finds interpreted as reflecting pre-Neandertal characteristics have been found dating back at least 300,000 years. In this view, natural selection and lack of gene flow with other archaic *H. sapiens* populations produced the distinctive Neandertal characteristics.

In Heidelberg, Germany, some fossil evidence indicates that an early form of Neandertal was evident in Europe. This individual became known as *Homo heidelbergensis* and some paleoanthropologists have hypothesized that this species gave rise to the Neandertals in Europe and in Africa to modern *Homo sapiens* (Stringer and Andrews 2005). *H. heidelbergensis* has smaller teeth and jaws and a very large brain (1,300 cc) that differs from *H. erectus*, but larger teeth, jaws, and a prognathic face with large brow ridges make this creature much different from *Homo sapiens* (Rightmire 1997).

The site of Atapuerca in northern Spain has been important in understanding the early Neandertal (Bermúdez de Castro et al. 2004). The Atapuerca site is deep within an extensive cave system that has yielded over 2,500 human fossils. The paleoanthropologists have been divided on how to classify some of the hominin fossils. Some have seen the fossils as a late form of *heidelbergensis*, whereas others perceived them within the category of an early

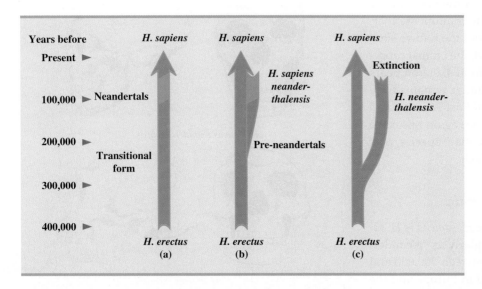

Figure 5.8 Three interpretations of the evolutionary relationships between Neandertals and modern humans: (a) unilinear evolution, (b) pre-Neandertals, and (c) separate lineages.

H. neanderthalensis (Stringer and Andrews 2005). Nevertheless, these fossils that are dated as early as 300,000 years ago indicate a complex picture of an early "bushy" transitional period of human evolution in Europe.

Clues to the Neandertals' relatedness to modern humans comes from molecular testing of genetic material extracted from Neandertal bones recovered at three sites that indicates substantial differences between the Neandertals and modern humans, while estimates of the separation of the Neandertal and modern human lineages range from 370,000 to 500,000 years ago (Noonan 2006; Green et al. 2010; Hawks 2013). While these data, based on mitochondrial DNA, must be regarded as tentative, they clearly suggest significant genetic distance between humans and Neandertals. Yet, initial findings that indicated Neandertals did not contribute to the mitochondrial DNA pool of modern populations (Krings et al. 1997) has been reevaluated in light of the recent work that suggests that Neandertal DNA in non-African modern European populations may range from 1 percent to 4 percent (Green 2010; Hawks 2013). Analysis of mtDNA from a Neandertal tooth discovered in Belgium has further shown that the Neandertals made up a very diverse population (Hodgson et al. 2010; Orlando et al. 2006; Hawks 2013).

The perceived variation in Neandertal DNA and the inclusion of Neandertal DNA in some modern human populations is particularly significant in light of the previous discussion of hybridization and assimilation models in the emergence of modern humans: Although the distinctiveness of the Neandertal genetic make-up is clear, the evidence for some Neandertal DNA in modern humans suggests some interbreeding (Hawks 2013).

Denisovans or the Denisova hominins

The intricate picture of the emergence of modern humans and their relationship to archaic human populations has been made all the more complex by the fossil and archaeological evidence that is emerging on the **Denisovans,** or the **Denisova hominins**, a previously unknown hominin species or subspecies that was contemporaneous with modern humans and Neandertals. The site from which hominin remains are known is in the Denisova cave in Siberia, Russia. Archaeological data suggests that the site was occupied from over 125,000 years ago up until modern times (Dalton 2010; Krause et al. 2010; Hawks 2013). Archaeological excavations suggest possible occupation by both Neandertals and modern humans. The site is consequently of interest in tracing Neandertal and modern human interactions.

The most tantalizing information, however, was provided by genetic data recovered from bones recovered from the site dating to between 30,000 and 48,000 years ago. Mitochondrial DNA extracted from the bones revealed a pattern unlike either that found in modern humans or Neandertals. The mtDNA signature has been described as the "Denisova hominin," apparently an extinct hominin species or subspecies. Additional study of the nuclear genome suggests that the Denisovans share a common origin with Neandertals, and that they interbred with the ancestors of modern-day Melanesians and Australian Aborigines. Additional study of the genomic data, suggests interbreeding with another, unknown human lineage distinct from the Neandertals and modern humans (Pennisi 2013; Hawks 2013). Discoveries such as these begin to hint at the complex history of human interactions and the questions that remain for researchers to answer.

Summary and Review of Learning Objectives

5.1 Explain the principal trends in hominin evolution and within genus *Homo*.

Hominini (the hominins) is the tribe of order primates that includes modern humans and their immediate ancestors. Although hominin species share certain general features with all primates, they also evince several distinct characteristics. Changes in these attributes are preserved in hominin fossils, and the evolutionary relationships of different species are traced on the basis of the similarities and differences present in individual finds. Bipedalism, the ability to walk upright, is the most important trend in hominin evolution—Hominins are the only primates that are fully bipedal. Fossil evidence indicates that bipedalism is the earliest hominin trait, evolving sometime between six million and ten million years ago. Although bipedal posture can be inferred on the basis of skeletal remains, it is more difficult to evaluate why it was selected for in early hominin species. Other trends include a tendency toward the reduction of face, jaw and anterior teeth and, within genus *Homo*, a trend toward increasing cranial capacity. These features appear more recently, primarily during the past two million years. These characteristics are exemplified in modern humans and least pronounced in earlier hominin species. Sweat glands and reduction in body hair may also have been selected for in early hominins. However, while these traits are readily apparent in modern humans, they are impossible to assess on the basis of fossil evidence. Some hominin species have teeth and cranial structures that suggest adaptations to specialized diets. In particular, the robust australopithecines developed massive chewing muscles and extremely large molars compared with those of modern humans, suggesting a distinct evolutionary history from more direct human ancestors.

5.2 Describe the fossil evidence for early hominin evolution.

Thousands of hominin fossils have been recovered; all of the earliest remains came from Africa. There is debate regarding the classification and evolutionary relationships of individual fossil finds. However, the fossil record is consistent with the evolution of the human species from a small-brained bipedal ape, the hominini lineage branching off from the other homininae primates approximately six to ten million years ago. Intriguing finds that may represent the oldest hominins have been discovered in Kenya, Ethiopia, and Chad. However, these remains are incomplete and their relationships to later species are still being debated. This discussion has focused on two genera: *Australopithecus*, which includes species that may be ancestral to humans as well as extinct side branches; and genus *Homo*, which includes modern humans and their closest ancestors. Paleoanthropologists believe that *A. anamensis* may be a species that lived close to the base of the hominin family tree, with at least three branches: two branches leading to later australopithecine species, and one to genus *Homo* and modern humans. The first representatives of genus *Homo*, the genus that includes modern humans, first appear in the fossil record just over two million years ago. The earliest members of genus *Homo* to be identified in the fossil record are the species *H. habilis* and *H. rudolfensis*, dating between 2.3 million and 1.4 million years ago. Consequently, members of genus *Homo* coexisted with some of the later australopithecine species between 2.2 million and 1 million years ago. What distinguishes the first representatives of genus *Homo* from the australopithecines is a trend toward larger brain size. *H. habilis* is followed in the fossil record by *H. erectus*, known from finds in Africa dating 1.8 million years old. *Homo erectus*, in turn, evolved into *H. sapiens*, the species that encompasses modern humans, during the past 400,000 years.

5.3 Discuss the challenges paleoanthropologists face in interpreting the fossil record and explain why their interpretations sometimes change.

Like all sciences, paleoanthropology proceeds by formulating hypotheses and then testing them against empirical data. In contrast to most sciences, however, the data from the fossil record cannot be obtained by laboratory experiments. Rather, paleoanthropologists must await the next unpredictable fossil find. As new evidence is uncovered, new hypotheses are developed and old ones are modified or discarded. As the number of fossil species represented has increased and our understanding of the fossil record has become more refined, interpretations have had to account for more variation and thus have become increasingly complex. Initially, scientists drew a straight evolutionary line from the earliest known human ancestors to modern humans. A number of finds, however, clearly demonstrate that in several instances more than one species of hominin roamed the Earth at the same time. To account for these discoveries, new branches have been added, making our family tree look increasingly bush-like. New discoveries have also extended the hominin family tree even further back in time. Researchers sometimes disagree about the classifications of individual finds. Splitters argue that some species designations do not reflect all the species represented. At the opposite extreme, lumpers maintain that current taxonomic designations place too much emphasis on differences among individuals and do not sufficiently consider variation within species. To complicate things further, current models of hominin evolution must also be reconciled with increasing information provided by genetic data. Despite this seemingly confusing array of interpretations, the diversity of finds uncovered provides insight into human origins. While a number of possible hominin ancestors may be represented, the varied fossil finds are nonetheless consistent with a model of human phylogeny that traces the evolution of genus *Homo* from small-brained bipedal apes. Future discoveries will continue to extend the human lineage further back in time and models of specific hominin lineages will continue to be revised.

5.4 Describe and discuss the different models for the emergence of anatomically modern humans.

Although researchers agree that *H. erectus* evolved into *H. sapiens*, there is substantial disagreement about how, where, and when this transition occurred. Early interpretations were based on limited information and often emphasized the uniqueness of individual finds. Currently, there is growing consensus that anatomically modern humans first evolved in Africa and then spread out to other world areas. A variety of competing interpretations continue to be evaluated of exactly how this took place. These include two contrasting perspectives referred to as the Multiregional Evolutionary Model and the Replacement Model. A third set of interpretations, consisting of Hybridization and Assimilation Models, that attempt to reconcile the two opposing extremes in various ways, has also been presented. Supporting evidence for each of these perspectives has been presented and each have their supporters.

5.5 Describe how new genomic research and molecular dating have helped anthropologists interpret human evolution.

Researchers have increasingly approached the study of human evolution by studying the similarities and differences in the chromosomes and DNA sequencing of living primates and modern humans, as well as genetic material recovered from fossils. The genetic data from living primates led to a reassessment of the way in which both living and fossil species are classified, as illustrated by the change in subfamily *Homininae* to include the chimpanzee, gorilla and humans (respectively referred to as the tribes *Panini*, *Gorillini*, and *Hominini*). Researchers have further attempted to infer the amount of time it took for evolution to produce the amount of genetic distance between various species. Genetic research into mutations rates suggests the separation of the human and chimpanzee lineages approximately five million to six million years ago. Genetic research has also focused on more recent human ancestry. Two specific types of genetic markers have been examined with specific regard to the emergence of modern humans: mitochondrial DNA and Y-chromosomal DNA. These are notable in reflecting, respectively, female and male genetic ancestry. While they remain the focus of a great deal of debate, the genetic data obtained have increasingly proven consistent with an African origin of *H. sapiens*. The study of the genetic make-up of modern humans, as well as the study of DNA extracted from the fossilized bones of archaic humans such as the Neandertals and Denisovans also provides a record of the complexity of gene flow in ancient populations.

5.6 Discuss the different theories regarding the relationship of *Homo sapiens neanderthalensis* and *Homo sapiens*.

H. sapiens neanderthalensis, popularly known as "Neandertal man," is the best-known example of an archaic *H. sapiens*. Neandertal fossils dating between 200,000 and 30,000 years ago have been discovered in Europe and the Middle East. Ever since their initial discovery, scientists have pondered the links between Neandertals and modern humans. Neandertals have, alternatively, been seen as: a transitional species between *Homo erectus* and modern humans; a distinct branch on the hominin family tree that ended in extinction; and as a subspecies of anatomically modern humans. Early interpretations that viewed Neandertals as an intermediate ancestor between *Homo erectus* and anatomically modern humans have been discarded. The restricted geographic range of the Neandertals (Europe and Middle East) and their distinctive physical characteristics make this scenario unlikely. As noted, Neandertals also appear to have coexisted with anatomically modern humans until the relatively recent past. Current consensus tends to regard Neandertals as an archaic subspecies of *H. sapiens* that disappeared as a result of intensive selective pressures and genetic drift. Some additional clues to the Neandertals' relatedness to modern humans come from genetic material extracted from Neandertal bones. This indicates substantial differences between the Neandertals and modern humans, while estimates of the separation of the Neandertal and modern human lineages range from 370,000 to 500,000 years ago. Yet research also indicates some interbreeding took place between Neandertals and anatomically modern humans. Estimates of Neandertal DNA in non-African modern European populations range from 1 percent to 4 percent. The inclusion of Neandertal DNA in some modern human populations is particularly significant in light of hybridization and assimilation models of the emergence of modern humans: Although the distinctiveness of the Neandertal genetic make-up is clear, the evidence for some Neandertal DNA in modern humans suggests some interbreeding.

Key Terms

anatomically modern *Homo sapiens*, p. 114
archaic *Homo sapiens*, p. 114
bipedalism, p. 91
Denisovans or Denisovan hominins, p. 117
foramen magnum, p. 91

hominids, p. 109
hominins, p. 91
hybridization and assimilation models, p. 112
multiregional evolutionary model, p. 111
postorbital constriction, p. 110

replacement model, p. 111
sagittal crest, p. 94
transitional forms, p. 110

Chapter 6
Human Variation

 ## Learning Objectives

After reading this chapter you should be able to:

6.1 Identify the different sources of human variation.

6.2 Provide examples of how physical characteristics in human populations may represent adaptations arising from natural selection.

6.3 Discuss how environmental factors may be sources of evolutionary change.

6.4 Discuss how cultural factors may be sources of evolutionary change.

6.5 Explain the challenges faced in dividing human populations into different races and why modern anthropologists avoid these classifications.

6.6 Discuss how contemporary anthropologists assess the relationship between intelligence and race.

6.7 Discuss current approaches to human variation.

Biological anthropologists study humans as a biological species. As we saw in Chapter 5, *Homo sapiens* populations migrated throughout the world, settling in varied climatic and environmental settings. Yet, despite the fact that modern humans have a wider geographic distribution and live in more diverse environments than any other primate group, we all bear a striking degree of genetic similarity. While human populations are widely distributed and have experienced some reproductive isolation, we are more alike than we are different. Certainly no population has become so genetically isolated as to constitute a separate species. Rather, modern human populations are the product of a tremendous amount of gene exchange.

Yet, although modern humans represent a single species, we clearly are not all alike. As a species, humans exhibit a great deal of *phenotypic variation*—individuals' external, observable characteristics, which are shaped in part by both their genetic makeup and unique life histories (see Chapter 3). Ongoing research into the human genome has provided dramatic insight into the genetic basis of human diversity. It has, however, also underscored the complexity of the processes involved, and the role non-genetic factors play in shaping human evolutionary history (Jablonka and Lamb 2006). The challenge of identifying the sources of human diversity and how this diversity should be viewed are the focus of this chapter. Explaining how and why humans are both similar and different is a major focus of biological anthropology.

Sources of Human Variation

6.1   Identify the different sources of human variation.

Consider the dramatic differences that distinguish human populations. What are the reasons for these variations? Differences in many physical characteristics, including variation in height, skin color, hair texture, and facial features, represent genetically inherited characteristics and are readily discernible. However, we can also note environmental variables that influence variation, such as darker skin color from sun tanning or increase in lung capacity resulting from life at high elevations. Finally, we can think of geographic and cultural factors that might restrict interbreeding and gene flow across different populations, and so influence the genetic make-up of a population. These few examples illustrate how varied factors interact to produce human variation.

To understand variation among human populations, we must consider three primary sources of variation: (1) *evolutionary processes* affecting genetic diversity within and between populations; (2) *environment*—the variation among individuals and populations that springs from their unique life experiences and interactions with the environment; and (3) *culture*—the variation stemming from disparate cultural beliefs and practices inculcated during an individual's formative years and reinforced throughout life. Each of these sources of variation may play a role in long-term evolutionary change in a species, as well as an individual's external, observable characteristics. These sources of variation will be discussed in turn.

Genetics and Evolution

The genetic makeup of modern humans allows for a great deal of potential variation. Genetically determined human traits can frequently be expressed in different ways. As discussed in Chapter 3, a population's total complement of genes is referred to as a *gene pool*. In *Homo sapiens*, as well as in animal populations, genes may have two or more alternate forms (or *alleles*)—a phenomenon called **polymorphism** (literally, "many forms"). These differences are expressed in various physical characteristics, ranging from hair and eye color to less visible differences in blood chemistry. Many of these traits vary in their expression in different world areas. For example, we associate certain hair texture and skin color with populations in specific geographic areas. Species made up of populations that can be distinguished regionally on the basis of discrete physical traits are called **polytypic**.

Four fundamental evolutionary processes have long been recognized and were examined in Chapter 3. They are: mutation, natural selection, gene flow, and genetic drift. *Mutations*, which are random changes in the genetic code, bring about changes in allele frequencies. Mutations may result in evolutionary change only if they occur in the sex cells of individuals, enabling this change to be passed on to succeeding generations. Mutations are important in explaining human variation because they are ultimately the source of all genetic variation. They may be beneficial, detrimental, or neutral in terms of an organism's reproductive success. The evolutionary process that determines which new mutations will enter a population is *natural selection*. Through natural selection, traits that diminish reproductive success will be eliminated, whereas traits enhancing the ability to reproduce will become more widespread.

Although natural selection has favored certain traits in human populations, it does not explain all genetic variation. Some physical characteristics, such as eye color, confer no discernible reproductive advantages. We might therefore expect such neutral traits to be evenly distributed throughout human populations as a result of *gene flow*, the interbreeding of human populations, yet this is not the case. The nonrandom distribution of neutral traits illustrates *genetic drift*, random processes of selection that alter allele frequencies. Genetic drift is particularly useful in explaining differences among genetically isolated populations. Archaeological data suggest that Paleolithic populations may have consisted of small bands of between 30 and 100 individuals, groups in which change arising from genetic drift may have been a particularly important factor.

As discussed in Chapter 3, the study of molecular genetics has revealed that genes and their expression are also influenced by epigenetic factors. While DNA provides the fundamental genetic blueprint, directions provided by genes may be turned "on" or "off," modifying the effect the genes have without modifying the DNA sequence. These modifications that are external to the DNA sequence are referred to as *epigenetic*, which literally means "above" or "on top of" genes.

The Physical Environment

Humans are highly sensitive to changes in their environment, and environment is thus an important factor in human variation. Environment may affect the individual during his or her lifetime, as well as cause long-term evolutionary change in populations. The environment influences human variation by promoting or restricting growth and development. Physical differences among humans may arise as a result of how well the requirements for growth are met. We can examine the effects of the physical environment by studying how individuals with similar genetic makeup develop in different environmental settings. If, for example, identical twins were separated at birth and reared in different regions of the world, any physical variation between them could be attributed to their disparate physical environments. Environment also influences human populations. Study of genetic variation in human populations has revealed how natural selection has played a role in adaptations to specific environments.

Culture

Many of the visible features that distinguish human populations are cultural. People differ in the customs and beliefs that guide the way they eat, dress, and build their homes. Such differences are superficial: If a child born in one region of the world is raised in another culture, he or she will learn and embrace the customs and beliefs of the adopted culture. Human behavior and culture may, however, influence human genetic makeup in a variety of ways. As discussed in Chapter 3, plant and animal species alter the environments in which they live, something that may affect their adaptability and influence natural selection. The process by which organisms modify their environment is referred to *niche construction*. These modifications are not necessarily in the best interest of the species. More than any other species, human societies dramatically impact the environments in which they live. Plant and animal domestication, land clearing, and industrialization are human activities that have dramatically affected the environment. Overcrowding, combined with poor knowledge of sanitation, food storage, and personal hygiene has contributed to nutritional deficiencies, the spread of infectious disease, decline in growth rates, and diminished reproductive success, all of which have implications in evolutionary terms. Significantly, these changes are unintentional, unplanned consequences of these activities (see discussion of coevolution in Chapter 8.).

Culture may even more directly influence human genetic variation through religious beliefs, social organization, marriage practices, or prejudices that restrict intermarriage among different groups and thus, inhibit gene flow. Many human cultures maintain rules of *endogamy*—that is, marriage to someone within one's own group—thereby restricting gene flow. Cultural beliefs also determine diet, living conditions, and the environment in which people work; these effects, in turn, either promote or hamper human growth and development. As will be seen in our discussion of race, social and cultural factors influence both human variation and our perception of it.

Evaluating Reasons for Variation

Although we know that genetic, environmental, and cultural factors all contribute to human variation, it is often difficult to assess the relative importance of each. All three influences, in combination, yield the characteristics found in an individual, as well as in populations. We can see the intertwined nature of these sources of variation by examining body height. How tall a person grows clearly stems, in part, from his or her genetic makeup. This can be illustrated by certain African, Philippine, and New Guinean populations that have mean heights of less than five feet. This average is much lower than that of most other human populations. Studies indicate that the relatively short stature in these populations is caused by a deficiency in a hormone that stimulates growth, a genetic trend (Shea and Gomez 1988).

At the same time, however, height varies significantly even among populations that are genetically similar. One way to account for this is to examine variation in environmental factors, such as the amount of sunlight a person is exposed to, the average daily temperature, differences in health and nutrition, and rates of exposure to disease. Consider seasonal changes in growth rates: Children living in temperate climates grow more quickly during the spring and summer than during the fall and winter, while children in tropical climates experience growth spurts during the dry season rather than during the rainy season (Bogin 1978). In both instances, scientists conjecture that more rapid growth correlates with greater exposure to sunlight, although precisely how this works remains unclear. One theory holds that the increased sunlight in certain seasons stimulates the body's production of Vitamin D, which promotes bone growth.

Finally, cultural factors can also affect people's health and, as a consequence, their growth. In some cultures, for example, certain social groups have greater access than others to food, shelter, and protection against childhood diseases, all of which affect growth rates. Underprivileged children whose basic nutritional needs are often unsatisfied will not grow as tall as those born into a society with material abundance.

Because of the complex interrelationships among genetic, environmental, and cultural influences, the relative importance of each of these elements can be deciphered only through detailed analysis of specific human populations.

Adaptive Aspects of Human Variation

6.2 **Provide examples of how physical characteristics in human populations may represent adaptations arising from natural selection.**

Natural selection has played a key role in the evolution of the human species, as well is in variation among modern humans. As scientists explore human origins, they have posited a variety of ways in which natural selection may have contributed to some of the differences observed in modern human populations. If natural selection promoted these differences, there should be evidence to substantiate this assertion. Unfortunately, since soft tissues are not preserved in the fossil record, the validity of many of these theories can often only be evaluated indirectly. How then do we assess the effects of natural selection? One way is to look at how different physical characteristics enable modern humans to adapt to disparate environmental conditions. In addition, the unraveling of the human genome has provided insight into the genetic basis of human variation and some of the adaptive features represented (see the box "Race and Genetics").

Body Hair and Sweat Glands

One of the striking physical differences between humans and other primates is our lack of body hair. Modern humans are also formidable at sweating, with some two

million sweat glands spread across our bodies. Our relatively hairless skin is covered with sweat glands, which other primates lack. What led to these differences? The answer may lie in the environments in which our early human ancestors evolved. It is likely that early hominins had relatively light-colored skin covered with hair, much like modern chimpanzees and gorillas, our closest living biological relatives (Mukhopadhyay, Henze, and Moses 2014; Relethford 2013: 385; Jurmain, Kilgore, Trevathan, and Ciochon 2014). Light skin color and thick body hair are well suited to forest and wooded environments. However, as early hominins moved out into more open savannas, this would have been a disadvantage. Here human ancestors would have faced higher temperatures, greater energy expenditure to obtain food and, subsequently, increased risk of heat stroke and heat exhaustion. The solution was to sweat more, which cools the body through evaporation (Jablonski and Chaplin 2000; Jablonski 2012; Wheeler 1992, 1994).

Unfortunately, the earliest of our hominin ancestors were likely poor at sweating. As is the case with modern chimpanzees and gorillas, they probably had relatively few sweat glands, which were primarily located on the palms of their hands and the soles of their feet. In some cases, however, individuals may have been born with more than the typical number of sweat glands. The loss of body hair would have further facilitated cooling. These individuals would have been able to sweat more, remain cooler, and thus maximize the time they could spend foraging for food. This, ultimately, better ensured their reproductive success. As seen in the discussion of bipedalism in Chapter 5, the success of our hominin ancestors may partly be a consequence of their ability to search for food and hunt when other creatures could not.

Skin Color

Among the most striking physical differences in modern human populations is skin color, which varies tremendously among individuals and multiple shades of skin color are found in populations in different world areas. Although human skin color may appear dramatically different in different individuals, it is a physical characteristic that exhibits **continuous variation**; that is, the differences cannot be divided into discrete, readily definable colors, but exhibit a continuous spectrum of variation from one extreme to another. The basis for this variation is complex. Skin color is a *polygenic* trait that is a consequence of variation in the alleles of more than one gene. The specific genetic loci involved, the precise manner of inheritance, and the evolutionary factors that may have contributed to variation in skin color have been the focus of wide-ranging debate (Jablonski and Chaplin 2000; Jablonski 2012).

Differences in Skin Color   A number of factors combine to give human skin its color. The most important of these is *melanin*, the dark pigment that primarily determines the lightness or darkness of skin and which is responsible for variations of tan, brown, and black skin color (Parra 2007; Relethford 2013). Melanin is produced by cells known as *melanocytes*, located in the bottom layers of the skin. Interestingly, all modern humans have about the same number of melanocytes. However, their arrangement and the amount of melanin they produce underlie variation in skin color. These factors are, to some extent, genetically controlled (Szabo 1967; Lamason 2005; Relethford 2013). People with lighter skin have less melanin, which allows the white tissues beneath the skin (the *epidermis*) to show through.

A variety of other variables also influence skin color. *Hemoglobin*, a protein that contains iron, gives red blood cells their color. In people with less melanin in their skin, this red color shows through more strongly, tinting their skin pink. *Carotene*, an orange-yellow pigment that confers a yellowish tinge, is contained in certain foods, so people with a large amount of carotene in their diet may have an orange tone in their skin. However, the presence of carotene is not what gives a yellowish cast to the skin of individuals of Asian descent. Rather, this skin tone is the result of a thickening of the exterior layers of skin. Finally,

skin color is also directly influenced by the environment. Exposure to the ultraviolet radiation in sunlight stimulates the production of melanin, yielding what we call a tan. Thus, variation in an individual's skin color stems from the interaction of both genetic and environmental factors (Williams-Blangero and Blangero 1992).

Adaptive Aspects of Skin Color   While reasons for the variation in skin color are complex, adaptive aspects of light and dark skin color may have played a role in the presence of light and dark skin color in different human populations. Analysis of the distribution of skin pigmentation reveals a distinctive pattern. In most world areas, skin color is generally darker in populations closer to the equator (Birdsell 1981; Relethford 2013; Jablonski 2012). Further north and south of the equatorial zone, skin coloration is progressively lighter (see Figure 6.1). This observation was particularly true before the large population migrations of the last 500 years.

Scientists who have studied the distribution patterns of skin pigmentation hypothesize that natural selection played a decisive role in producing varying shades of skin color. Several adaptive aspects of pigmentation suggest why skin color may have been favored by natural selection. First, darker skin confers advantages in a tropical environment, the regions of Africa where early humans

Figure 6.1 Variation in human skin color prior to the major population movements of the past 500 years shows the clustering of darker skin color toward the equator.

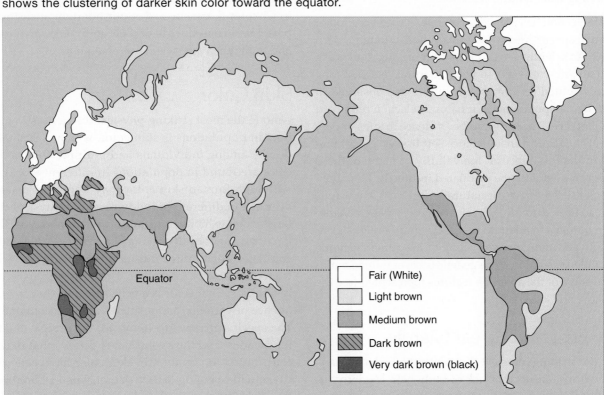

evolved. Melanin provides protection from ultraviolet (UV) radiation in sunlight, which has been shown to have a number of detrimental effects (Relethford 2013; Jablonski 2012). Prolonged exposure to the sun can cause sunburn, sunstroke, and skin cancer. More importantly, it can significantly decrease folate levels (Jablonski and Chaplin 2000; Jablonski 2012). Folate, a member of the Vitamin B complex, is essential for normal fetal development. Low folate levels in mothers have been correlated with embryonic defects, such as spina bifida and anencephaly (the absence of a full brain or spinal cord). Even an hour of exposure to intense sunlight is sufficient to reduce folate levels by half in light-skinned individuals. As *Homo sapiens* evolved in the tropical equatorial zones, darker skin pigmentation was likely highly adaptive.

If the adaptive advantages of darker skin are clear-cut, why do some human populations have light-colored skin? Research suggests that darker skin is not advantageous in all environmental settings. As early humans moved into more temperate regions with less sunlight, other selective pressures, especially the need for Vitamin D, conferred an adaptive advantage on lighter skin pigmentation. We know today that when human skin is exposed to UV radiation in sunlight, the UV rays stimulate the synthesis of Vitamin D. This is important because insufficient levels of Vitamin D can result in deficiency diseases such as rickets, which is caused by the decalcification of bone. Because of this decalcification, body weight and muscle activity will ultimately deform the bone. Pelvic deformity in women and the associated increase in infant mortality rates would have been a significant adaptive disadvantage. Vitamin D also has other significant functions in regulating thousands of genes that may prevent cancer and provide natural antibiotics (Mukhopadhyay et al. 2014; Relethford 2013; Jurmain et al. 2014). With this in mind, physical anthropologists conjecture that the production of optimal levels of Vitamin D may have had a hand in the distribution of light skin. Lower regional UV levels closely correspond with fairer skin coloration (Jablonski and Chaplin 2000; 2010; Jablonski 2012).

People who inhabited equatorial regions with ample exposure to sunlight evolved darker skin pigmentation to avoid the deleterious effects of UV radiation. In contrast, people who lived in cold, cloudy climates would have increased chances of survival and, ultimately, reproductive success if they had lighter skin that absorbed higher levels of UV radiation and were consequently able to synthesize more Vitamin D. Over time, natural selection favored darker skin in the tropics and lighter skin in regions with lower levels of sunlight and the associated UV radiation (Jablonski 2012).

Recent studies have increasingly revealed the genetic basis of skin color. Research has linked polymorphisms of at least two genes to dark pigmentation in human populations; variations of three other genes are linked to lighter skin in European populations, but not in East Asian groups (Lamason 2005; Norton et al. 2007). This variation in the genes suggests skin color has been acted on by natural selection in varied ways in human populations.

Body Build

The influence of natural selection and environment on human body and limb forms is especially pronounced. These interrelationships were first noted by the nineteenth-century English zoologist Carl Bergmann. He observed that in mammal and bird populations, the larger members of the species predominate in the colder parts of a species range, whereas the smaller representatives are more common in warmer areas. This pattern also holds true for human populations.

Bergmann explained these findings in reference to the ways birds and mammals dissipate heat. Bergmann's rule states that smaller animals, which have larger surface areas relative to their body weights, lose excess heat efficiently and, therefore, function better at higher temperatures. Larger animals, which have a smaller surface area relative to their body weight, dissipate heat more slowly and are, therefore, better adapted to cold climates. The same applies to humans: People living in cold climates tend to have stocky torsos and heavier average body weights, whereas people in warmer regions have more slender frames on average.

Building on Bergmann's observations about heat loss, the American zoologist J. A. Allen did research on protruding parts of the body, particularly arms and legs. Allen's rule maintains that individuals living in colder areas generally have shorter, stockier limbs. Longer limbs, which lose heat more quickly, typify populations in warmer climates. Bergmann's and Allen's rules are illustrated by the contrasting body builds of a man from Tanzania and Native American woman (See photograph page 126).

Bergmann's and Allen's observations can be partially explained by natural selection: Certain body types are more adaptive in some climatic settings than others (Mukhopadhyay et al. 2014; Relethford 2013; Jurmain et al. 2014). However, developmental acclimatization also affects body and limb size, according to studies conducted among modern U.S. groups descended from recent migrants from Asia, Africa, and, primarily, Europe (Newman and Munro 1955). Researchers discovered that individuals born in warmer states generally developed longer limbs and more slender body types than did those from colder states. As these developments occurred within such a short time (a few generations at most), they could not be attributed to evolutionary processes. Laboratory experiments with animals produced similar findings. Mice raised in cold

A Samburu man from Kenya in East Africa (left) and a Native American Eskimo woman (right), illustrating how body weight and shape vary according to both Bergmann's rule and Allen's rule.

conditions developed shorter, stouter limbs than did mice growing up in warmer settings (Riesenfeld 1973; Serat et al. 2008).

Cranial and Facial Features

Because the human skull and facial features vary tremendously in shape, numerous theories explaining this variation have been advanced over the centuries. In the nineteenth century, many people embraced *phrenology*, the belief that a careful study of the bumps of the cranium could be used to "read" an individual's personality or mental abilities, or even the future. Other nineteenth-century theories posited a relationship between race, cranial shape, and facial features. For example, nineteenth-century theorists argued that African skulls were smaller than European skulls, ignoring the amount of overlap between the groups or the amount of variation within the groups. None of these beliefs has withstood scientific scrutiny (Mukhopadhyay et al. 2014; Relethford 2013: 385; Jurmain et al. 2014).

Why, then, do skull shapes vary? As with body build, the shape of the skull and face may represent adaptations to the physical environment. By examining hundreds of populations, researchers have found a close correlation between skull shapes and climate. People living in colder climates tend to have rounded heads, which conserve heat better, whereas people in warmer climates tend to have narrow skulls (Beals et al. 1984). Other studies have considered the environmental factors that may have favored specific nose types. Studies indicate that higher, narrower nasal openings have more mucous membranes, surfaces that moisten inhaled air. People living in drier climates tend to have more mucous membranes, regardless of whether the environment is hot or cold. Of course, these observations are generalizations regarding populations; many individual exceptions can also be noted.

Biochemical Characteristics

Research on human variation has revealed less obvious differences among populations than skin color, body build, and facial appearance. Variation occurring in dozens of less visible features—such as blood type, the consistency of earwax, and other subtle biochemical traits—also illustrates evolutionary processes at work. It is easy to imagine how natural selection may have affected the distribution of some of these features. Consider, for example, resistance to disease. If a lethal illness were introduced into a population, individuals with a natural genetic resistance would have an enhanced chance of survival. With increased odds of reproducing, these individuals' genetic blueprints would quickly spread throughout the population (Motulsky 1971).

History offers many tragic examples of one population inflicting disease on another that had no natural immunity. For example, when Europeans first came in contact with indigenous peoples of the Americas and the South Pacific, they carried with them the germs that cause measles and smallpox. Because these diseases had afflicted European populations for centuries, most Europeans had adapted natural immunities to them. When the diseases were introduced into populations that had never been exposed to them, however, plagues of catastrophic proportions ensued. Many Native American Indian and Polynesian populations were decimated by the spread of diseases brought to their lands by Europeans.

Blood Types Among the most studied biochemical characteristics are blood group systems, particularly the ABO system. This represents the phenotypic expression of three alleles—A, B, and O. A and B are both dominant, whereas O is recessive. These different alleles are a good illustration of polymorphism in a simple genetic trait. They are expressed in four phenotypes: type A (genotypes AA and AO); type B (genotypes BB and BO); type AB (genotype AB); and type O (genotype OO).

The three blood-group alleles are found throughout the world in varying frequencies from population to population. Type O is by far the most common, ranging from over 50 percent in areas of Asia, Australia, Africa, and Europe to 100 percent among some Native American Indian groups. Type A occurs throughout the world, but generally in smaller percentages than does type O. Type B has the lowest frequency. Believed to have been totally absent from native South American groups, type B is most common in Eurasia and can be tracked in a clinal distribution outward into Europe in the west and Asia in the east (see discussion of clines on page 139).

Anthropologists, citing the nonrandom distribution of blood types, conclude that natural selection may have favored certain gene frequencies, keeping the percentage of individual alleles stable in particular populations. This natural selection might have something to do with resistance to disease. Each blood type constitutes a different antigen on the surface of red blood cells. An *antigen* is a substance that promotes the production of *antibodies*, proteins that combat foreign substances entering the body. The presence of these different antigens and antibodies is the reason doctors need to know a person's blood type before giving a blood transfusion. Type A blood has anti-B antibodies, and vice versa. Type O incorporates antibodies that fight against proteins in both type A and type B. People with blood type B (with anti-A antibodies) are better able to fight off diseases such as syphilis, which resemble type A antigens on a biochemical level. Similarly, scientists have posited links between blood types and resistance to many infectious diseases, including bubonic plague, smallpox, and typhoid fever. Before the advent of modern medical technology, natural resistance to these diseases would have conferred critical adaptive advantages.

Sickle-Cell Anemia

By studying population genetics and evolutionary change within populations, scientists have gained important insights into genetic diseases, those diseases arising from lethal genes that cause severe disabilities. One such disease, sickle-cell anemia, produces an abnormal form of *hemoglobin*, the blood molecule that carries oxygen in the bloodstream. In individuals with sickle-cell anemia, the abnormal hemoglobin molecules rupture and collapse into a sickle-like shape, inhibiting the distribution of oxygen. Individuals afflicted with sickle-cell anemia often die in childhood.

If natural selection operates on human characteristics, why did it fail to eliminate such a lethal gene? It did not, because under some conditions the sickle-cell gene can confer adaptive advantages, protecting carriers of the gene from malaria, an infectious disease spread by mosquitoes. Researchers discovered a high correlation between the distribution of the sickle-cell gene and regions where malaria is present. In these malarial areas, the gene may be present in up to 40 percent of the population, including portions of Africa, the Mediterranean, the Arabian Peninsula, and India. Malaria is a potentially fatal disease, and individuals without the sickle-cell gene (or access to modern medical treatment) exposed to it tend to die in high numbers. Investigators found, however, that the blood of those who carry the sickle-cell gene is sufficiently inhospitable to the malaria parasite to confer on sickle-cell carriers genetic resistance to the disease. Thus, although sickle-cell carriers may contract malaria, they are less likely to die from it (see Figure 6.2).

It works like this: Recalling from Chapter 3 Mendel's *principle of segregation*, we note that there are three genotypes—homozygous dominant (AA), heterozygous (Aa), and homozygous recessive (aa). Because people who are homozygous for sickle-cell anemia usually die before reproducing (Motulsky 1971), only individuals who are heterozygous for the trait are likely to transmit the disease to the next generation. Two heterozygous parents have a 25 percent chance of having a child who manifests the disease. Although heterozygous individuals are carriers of the sickle-cell trait, they are better able to survive the threat of malaria than are individuals who do not carry the sickle-cell gene. Studies confirm that heterozygous carriers of sickle-cell anemia have higher fertility rates than noncarriers in regions where malaria is common (Mukhopadhyay et al. 2014). Consequently, the survival of those with heterozygous genotypes balances the deaths of those who are homozygous recessive for the trait. The sickle-cell gene, therefore, is transmitted from generation to generation as an evolutionary adaptation in areas where malaria is prevalent.

Balanced Polymorphism In the case of sickle-cell anemia, a lethal recessive gene confers partial protection against malaria. When homozygous and heterozygous genes exist in a state of relative stability, or equilibrium, within a population, this is known as **balanced polymorphism**. In equatorial Africa, 40 percent of the population carries the sickle-cell gene, constituting an evolutionary

Figure 6.2 Geographic distribution of sickle-cell anemia and its relationship to the distribution of malaria.

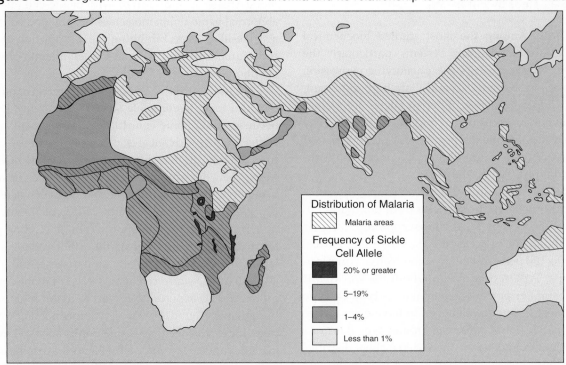

Distribution of Malaria
☒ Malaria areas

Frequency of Sickle
Cell Allele

■ 20% or greater

■ 5–19%

■ 1–4%

□ Less than 1%

A scanning electron micrograph of a deformed red blood cell (left) in sickle-cell anemia, a hereditary blood disease. To the right of the sickle cell is a normal, biconcave red blood cell.

trade-off. Natural selection has created this balanced polymorphism to protect the African populations, but at a high cost: the deaths of some people.

By examining the sickle-cell gene in regions without malaria, we also see an example of how natural selection acts against a harmful genetic trait. Approximately 2 percent to 6 percent of African-Americans carry the sickle-cell gene—a greater percentage than that found in individuals of non-African origin in the United States, but far lower than incidences of sickle-cell anemia among African populations (Workman et al. 1963). In part, this can be explained by gene flow between African-Americans and other

populations not affected by the sickle-cell gene. However, statistical studies point to another reason. Unlike Africa, the United States does not have high levels of malarial infection; therefore, the gene represents a severe liability. It is no longer favored by natural selection and is therefore, gradually being eliminated from the gene pool.

Lactase Deficiency

Humans also vary in how well they digest particular foods. Most extensively studied is variation in the production of a digestive enzyme called *lactase*, which is responsible for the digestion of *lactose*, the sugar found in milk. All human infants can digest milk. Milk from domesticated cattle has also been important in many human populations for the last 8,000 years. Yet, the majority of humans lack the genetic coding that continues to produce lactase after about four years of age, a tendency also seen in other mammals. Without lactase, milk ferments in the intestine, causing diarrhea and cramps. This condition is referred to as **lactase deficiency**. Contrary to popular advertising, milk is not necessarily good for you, at least not as adults. In fact, for millions of human beings, milk consumption leads to severe discomfort (Hollox 2005). The majority of adults in Asian and African populations do not drink milk because they are not able to digest it properly.

Variation in lactase production among human populations is a result of conditions that favored the ability to digest lactose. The ability to produce lactase is especially common among populations that have a history of *pastoralism*, the reliance on domesticated animals such as cows, sheep, and goats. Such animals provide plenty of milk to drink. In this cultural environment, natural selection favored individuals best able to make use of all available sources of nutrition. Consequently, it is not surprising that populations with long associations with milk-producing, domesticated cattle, are typically more lactose tolerant. African pastoralists such as the Fulani, for example, produce significantly more lactase than do other African populations who do not raise dairy animals (Relethford 2013; Mukhopadhyay et al. 2014).

European populations, among the world's most lactose-tolerant populations, are partly descended from Middle Eastern pastoralists. Milk from domesticated cattle was likely an important food resource in Europe over the past 8,000 years. This long reliance on milk is reflected in the modern populations. Diversity in European cattle milk genes closely mirrors areas that have revealed locations of early European farming sites (more than 5,000 years old) that were likely associated with early cattle raising. This suggests a close correspondence between the domestication of cattle and evolution of lactose tolerance (Beja-Pereira 2003). The presence of this adaptive trait also provides an illustration of how human behavior unintentionally interacts with genetic processes to effect evolutionary change (Jablonka and Lamb 2006: 292-298; Mukhopadhyay et al. 2014; Relethford 2013; Jurmain, et al. 2014).

Effects of the Physical Environment

6.3   Discuss how environmental factors may be sources of evolutionary change.

We have highlighted the role of evolutionary processes in human variation, but we have also noted how differences in physical surroundings affect these processes and their physical expression in humans. Think back to the differences between genotype and phenotype. Varying environmental conditions may produce vastly different appearances (*phenotypes*) in organisms of very similar genotypes. For example, if we take two plants with identical genetic makeup (*genotypes*) and plant one in a fertile, well-irrigated field and the other in a stony, poorly watered area, the resulting plants will look completely different despite their genetic similarity. Humans have settled in an amazing range of environmental zones, and the physical environment plays a comparable role in causing differences in human populations. Notably, human populations have sometimes adapted to similar environmental differences in different ways.

Acclimatization is the physiological process of becoming accustomed to a new environment (Frisancho 1979). Individuals that visit or move to a high altitude, for example, may initially have difficulty breathing, but after living in this environment for some time their bodies will acclimatize and they will be able to breathe easier. This physiological adjustment is temporary: When these individuals return to lower altitudes, their bodies and breathing will revert to their earlier states. This type of acclimatization can be differentiated from **developmental acclimatization**. In this case, individuals born or raised in certain environmental conditions may develop nonreversible physical characteristics, such as larger lungs or body build.

High-Altitude Adaptations

People living in high-altitude environments such as the Himalaya or Andes Mountains provide clear illustrations of acclimatization. Because of the lower barometric pressure at high altitude, people take in less oxygen, making the air feel "thinner." So, at high elevations, most humans experience dizziness and breathing difficulties, which are symptoms of *hypoxia*, or oxygen deficiency (Mukhopadhyay et al. 2014; Relethford 2013: 389; Jurmain et al. 2014: 391; 425-427). Yet, people raised in high-altitude environments, or people who are acclimatized to these environments, do not have these reactions. They have adapted to lower amounts of oxygen in different ways, particularly greater lung capacity, which promotes greater oxygen exchange. We attribute this adaptation to high altitudes to developmental acclimatization, because children born in lowland environments who are raised at higher elevations develop many of the same physical characteristics as those born in the latter environment (Beall 2007).

High-altitude adaptations provide a dramatic example of acclimatization. However, as in some of the other physical characteristics examined, other factors have also been shown to come into play. In some cases, natural selection has played a role in the selection of genes useful to people living in these high- altitude environments. A recent study of Tibetans and Nepalese Sherpa who live at the high altitudes of the Himalayas has shown that they have genes that allow them to maintain relatively low hemoglobin concentrations at high altitude (Jeong et al. 2013). Consequently Tibetans have a lower risk of complications, such as thrombosis, compared with other humans, something that enhances their ability to thrive at high altitudes. Based on the genetic data from modern populations, researchers have suggested that these genetic adaptations for life at high elevations originated approximately 30,000 years ago in peoples related to modern Sherpa. These genes were subsequently passed on to more recent migrants from lower elevations via interbreeding, and then amplified by natural selection in modern Tibetans.

Native Americans in the Andes Mountains. People raised in high-altitude environments become acclimatized to these conditions in a variety of ways.

Cultural Factors in Human Evolution

6.4 Discuss how cultural factors may be sources of evolutionary change.

While humankind has evolved in a biological sense, humans have increasingly adapted to new conditions using culture, inhabiting the breadth of environmental and ecological zones across the globe. When learned behaviors are passed on from generation to generation, these behaviors inevitably interact with genetic inheritance (Jablonka and Lamb 2006: 292-292). Consequently, social and cultural factors directly influence human variation in a variety of ways.

In some cases, the impact of cultural practices on gene flow and genetic inheritance are quite clear. Although humans can theoretically choose a mate from among any potential spouses within geographic limits, culture often circumscribes those choices. In the Middle East, for example, Christians, Jews, and Muslims live in close proximity to one another, yet most marry within their own religious group. Sometimes, these cultural sanctions take on the force of law. For example, at one time both South Africa and certain regions of the United States had laws prohibiting marriage between whites and blacks. Such cultural practices inhibit gene flow and contribute to genetic drift within a population. The Amish, an Anabaptist Christian community in Pennsylvania and the Midwestern United

States, provide a dramatic example. The Amish live in a number of closed communities that severely restrict interaction with outsiders and are genetically isolated. As the majority of modern-day Amish are descended from a few hundred eighteenth-century founders, genetic disorders

Members of an Amish community. The Amish, a religious community in Pennsylvania and the Midwest, severely restrict interaction with other cultures. Religion, ethnicity, and perceived cultural differences can curb gene flow among human populations.

that are quite rare in other populations are common in some Amish communities. These include metabolic disorders, dwarfism, and an unusual distribution of blood types (Morton et al. 2003). These are clearly maladaptive traits that can contribute to higher mortality rates.

Humans have also had dramatic impact on the environments in which we live, activities that also affect genetic processes. Lactase deficiency and the inability to digest milk were discussed above with regard to adaptive selection in populations that have a history of pastoralism. In these settings, milk from domesticated animals such as cows, sheep, and goats provided plenty of milk to drink, and natural selection favored individuals best able to make use of all available sources of nutrition. The ability to produce lactase, the digestive enzyme needed to digest milk, is a genetically determined characteristic. Consequently, in this cultural setting, selection favored individuals able to take advantage of these additional nutritional resources, and lactose tolerance became more common in populations practicing pastoralism. Once developed, the trait also had the benefit of allowing for increased calcium intake, something that helps prevent Vitamin D deficiencies and associated ailments such as rickets (Jablonka and Lamb 2006: 295).

The point here, however, is that the selective pressures that gave rise to this trait—domestication and associated increase in the availability of milk—were produced by human behaviors. In fact, the role of human behavior and lactase production is more complex than simply the association of lactose tolerance and pastoralism. There are also different degrees of lactose tolerance in different populations that historically practiced pastoralism. This variation is also likely the result of cultural preferences. In some cases, cultures such as those in northern Europe favored the use of cattle for their milk and have the highest rates of lactose tolerance. Others cultures such as those in southern Europe consumed milk in the form of cheese, or utilized cattle for their meat. These populations have a lesser ability to digest milk, but it is still greater than in groups that do not practice pastoralism (Jablonka and Lamb 2006: 295).

The example of lactose production in populations associated with pastoralism provides an example of human interaction with the environment that produced an adaptive advantage; the ability to digest milk provided increased nutrition for some populations. The impact of human behavior on the environment is, however, not always for the best. Sickle-cell anemia, a genetic disorder common in some world areas, was also discussed before in terms of natural selection. Individuals afflicted with sickle-cell anemia often die in childhood. This clearly maladaptive trait was not eliminated from populations because it confers partial protection against malaria, a potentially fatal disease. Yet, while providing a benefit, the case of sickle-cell anemia and malaria also provides a negative example of human behavior in the advent of a genetic trait. In certain parts of Africa, the spread of malaria was the result of the adoption of slash-and-burn agriculture. This agricultural practice, common in many agricultural societies, involves cutting down trees and then burning them. The ashes are left behind to fertilize the land. The deforestation associated with slash-and-burn agriculture created small clearings and pools of water, which in turn attracted mosquitoes, and with mosquitoes came malaria. Human agricultural practices, hence, provided a partial explanation for the initial spread of malaria in some areas.

Many other examples of the dramatic impacts of human behavior and their potential impact on genetic processes can also be noted. Nowhere is the impact of culture more pronounced than in modern urban societies.

The Impact of Modern Urban Life

Urbanization—the concentration of populations into large urban centers—has altered human lifestyles in dramatic and significant ways. Certain issues must be addressed whenever large numbers of people live together in a small area: How will they be supplied with food and water? How will sanitation needs be met? Will crowded living conditions enhance life or make it barely tolerable? Different cultures have worked through these issues with varying degrees of success. In some cities, overcrowding combined with poor knowledge of sanitation, food storage, and personal hygiene has contributed to nutritional deficiencies and the spread of infectious disease and reduced growth rates. Factors such as these explain why archaeological data seem to suggest that health actually declined in some human populations with the advent of food production and the rise of the first cities (see discussions in Chapters 8 and 9).

Daily life in modern American cities exposes people to air pollution, contaminated water, high noise levels, and other environmental hazards, all of which aggravate physiological stress. Toxic waste, brought on by the improper disposal of hazardous chemicals, poses a problem of immense proportions in the United States. An example of the threat to human health and development is Love Canal, near Niagara Falls, New York, which was used as a dumping ground for chemical waste between 1940 and 1953 (Vianna and Polan 1984; Paigen et al. 1987). Studies have shown that women who lived close to the dump site gave birth to infants with lower average weights than babies born to women in other areas. Further research demonstrated that children raised near Love Canal were shorter than children of the same age raised elsewhere. This tendency was most pronounced in children who lived near Love Canal for the longest period of time.

Lower birth rates and reduced growth rates may be just the tip of the iceberg. As awareness of the threat of toxic waste increases, links to a host of other health hazards, neurological disorders, and cancer rates are being identified. The long-term implications of phenomena such as these for our genetic history can only be guessed.

The Concept of Race

6.5 Explain the challenges faced in dividing human populations into different races and why modern anthropologists avoid these classifications.

The varied elements of human variation and the complexity of their interpretation are perhaps nowhere highlighted more dramatically than by the differences between popular perceptions and scientific studies of race. Although humans present a diverse bunch, dividing human populations into discrete racial categories or classifications is extremely problematic. Many attempts at racial classifications have been made, but these have failed because they proved too rigid

An Ainu elder male. The Ainu, an ethnic group in northern Japan, are generally distinguished from other Japanese by such physical features as lighter skin and higher-bridged noses—attributes frequently associated with European populations. The distribution of characteristics like these confounds attempts at racial classification.

to account for either the tremendous variation found within individual races or the shared similarities between these supposedly different groups. For this reason, modern anthropologists generally avoid using racial classifications, but rather focus on the specific characteristics represented.

The term *race* was likely derived from the Latin root *ratio*, with a meaning similar to "species" or "kind" (of thing). Physical characteristics, such as skin pigmentation, nose shape, and hair texture, have prompted people throughout history to classify humans into different "races." Although the diversity of human populations is undeniable, delineating specific races has little practical or scientific value in studying human variation (MacEachern 2012; Lieberman and Scupin 2012; Templeton 2013). As we shall see, physical characteristics do not divide humans into readily discernible groups or races; clearly bounded, racially distinct populations are not found in the real world.

Further, the word *race* is a loaded term in part because people use the word differently in different contexts (MacEachern 2012). Classification of physical characteristics serves only to label particular categories of phenomena arbitrarily selected by the researcher—or the individual. Humans in both the past and present have used various racial classifications to categorize people and have developed stereotypes about the behavior and mental abilities of different "racial categories." Racial categories have subsequently been used as justification for the discrimination or the marginalization of certain groups. Racial classifications can also be used as self-defined categories in census data or in other contexts to refer to styles of music, dance, or literature.

Perhaps most importantly with regard to the current discussion, racial classifications do not *explain* the reason for the observed variation. In the following discussion, we examine early racial classifications because incorrect and faulty ideas stemming from some classifications are still widespread. The varied criteria used in these early classifications and the numbers of races identified—ranging from 3 to 30—underscore the limited use of the concept. Table 6.1 summarizes some of these early racial classification systems.

Ancient Classification Systems

Humans have likely always been conscious of the differences between us. Archaeologists have found indications of racial classifications in ancient depictions of people in rock paintings in Europe and other world areas (Jochim 1998). Later civilizations with written texts, including ancient Egypt, Greece, Rome, India, China, and the Near East, used a variety of *folk taxonomies*, informal and unscientific racial classifications, based on skin color or other physical features, as well as cultural characteristics. As early as 3,000 B.C., the ancient Egyptians divided all human populations into one of four categories: red for Egyptians, yellow for people to the east, white for people to the north, and black

Critical Perspectives

Race and Genetics: The Human Genome Project

The Human Genome Project, a 13-year project initiated in 1990 and completed in 2003, was a joint effort coordinated by the U.S. Department of Energy and the National Institutes of Health. Its primary objective was the daunting task of mapping the genetic loci of all of the approximately 20,000 to 25,000 human genes and to determine the sequences of the estimated three billion base pairs that make up human DNA. In addition, the project explored the ethical, legal, and social issues of the research, as well as the scientific implications. Although the project has been completed, analysis of the vast amount of information recovered will continue for years to come. The current and potential benefits of the research include applications in the diagnosis of diseases, the creation of new energy sources (biofuels), the monitoring of pollutants, the study of evolution, research into human migration and origins, and the use of genetic information in forensics.

This groundbreaking study of the genetic makeup of modern humans has also dramatically changed the understanding of who we are as a species and the commonality of all human populations. The project research further challenges concepts of "race" and has underscored the limitations of the term in understanding variation in modern human populations. As discussed in this chapter, race is a complicated topic. While in some contexts, the term has been used to indicate physical characteristics, such as skin pigmentation, nose shape, and hair texture, in other settings it may refer to a variety of religious, cultural, social, national, historical, or linguistic criteria. From a scientific perspective, racial classifications fail because they do not account for

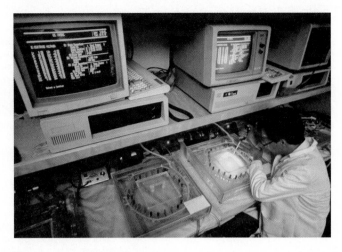

Genome Project lab equipment.

the tremendous variation within different so-called races, or the shared similarities between these supposedly different groups (Molnar 2006). For these reasons, the majority of anthropologists today find dividing different populations into distinctive racial categories or classifications extremely problematic. The Human Genome Project underscored the shared similarities of human populations and the arbitrary nature of racial classification (Jorde and Wooding 2004; Royal and Dunston 2004).

Criticisms of the concept of race are not new. But the Human Genome Project brings new information to this discussion, which forces the reappraisal of attempts at racial classifications. It makes it clear that human variation is far more nuanced and complex than single traits, such as skin color, suggest. The study does show a correspondence in genetic makeup with shared geographic origin or heredity. Some of these characteristics include features traditionally used in racial classifications. But these correlations are imperfect, and genetic variation is distributed in a continuous overlapping fashion across populations. That is, while individuals from the widely separated geographical areas of Europe, Asia, and sub-Saharan Africa may have distinct genetic patterns, such clear differences become blurred as other populations are included. For example, if a South Asian sample is included, there is a significant amount of overlap with the other

groups. In addition, individuals within each of the groups also encompass a great deal of variation, frequently possessing some, but not all, of the characteristics shared by other members of the group.

The Human Genome Project and other research indicate that human genetic variation does reflect geographical origins. Individuals from one regional area will, in general, be more genetically similar than individuals from a distant region. However, because of the long history of gene flow between populations, human variation is distributed in a continuous fashion and cannot be partitioned into discrete groups. Populations were never "pure" in a genetic sense, and divisions of race were never neatly bounded.

Points to Ponder

1. Discuss different definitions of race that you have heard or read about. How are these categories different or similar?
2. What are some of the characteristics or features other than genetic differences that explain variation in human populations?
3. What aspects of human ancestry do you think the Human Genome Project will help us understand?

for Africans to the south. Later, in the biblical book of Genesis, a similar classification scheme appears in a tale chronicling the distribution of the human population:

And the sons of Noah that went forth from the ark were Shem, Ham and Japheth: … these are the three sons of Noah: and of them was the whole earth overspread. (Genesis 9:18–19)

Table 6.1 How Many Races Are There?

Historically, there have been many attempts to classify races. These classifications are dependent on the criteria selected. The great disagreement among scientists over the number and characteristics of different races is a good indication of the limited usefulness of the concept. Examples of different racial classifications and their basis are contained in the table. Other researchers have suggested completely different races and definitions.

Origin of Theory	Number of Races	Description	Basis of Classification
Ancient Egyptians, 14th century B.C.	4	Egyptians (red), Easterners (yellow), people from the north (white), and people from the south (black)	Skin color
Carolus Linnaeus, 1735	4	Europeans (white), North American Indians (red), Asiatics (yellow), Africans (black)	Skin color
Johann Blumenbach, 1781	5	Caucasian, Ethiopian, Mongolian, Malay, Native American	Skin color, hair color, facial features, and other physical traits
J. Deniker, 1900	29	Adriatic, Ainu, Assyroid, Australian, Berber, Bushman, Dravidian, Ethiopian, Littoral-European, Western-European, Northern-European, Eastern-European, Ibero-Insular, Indo-Afghan, Indonesian, Melanesian, Negrito, Negro, Polynesian, Semite, South American, North American, Central American, Patagonian, Eskimo, Lapp, Ugrian, Turkish, Mongol	Hair color and texture, eye color
William Boyd, 1950	6	European, African, Asiatic, American Indian, Australoid, Early European	Blood groups
Carleton Coon, Stanley Garn, & Joseph Birdsell, 1950	30	Murrayian, Ainu, Alpine, Northwestern European, Northeastern European, Lapp, Forest Negro, Melanesian, Negrito, Bushman Bantu, Sudanese, Carpentarian, Dravidian, Hamite, Hindu, Mediterranean, Nordic, North American Colored, South African Colored, Classic Mongoloid, North Chinese, Southeastern Asiatic, Tibeto-Indonesian, Mongoloid, Turkic, American Indian Marginal, American Indian Central, Ladino, Polynesian, Neo-Hawaiian	Evolutionary trends, body build, and special surface features, such as skin color and facial structure
Stanley Garn, 1961	9	Africans, Amerindian (Native Americans), Asiatics, Australians, Europeans, Indians, Melanesian-Papuans, Micronesians, Polynesians	Geographic boundaries restricting gene flow
Walter Bodmer, 1976	3	Africans, Caucasians, Easterners (including Australians and Pacific Islanders)	Major geographical groups
Current Perspectives	Modern researchers reject simplistic typological classifications of race and focus their efforts on specific characteristics and explaining why there is variation in particular traits.		

The descendants of Shem (the Semites) were the ancient Israelites. The descendants of Ham ventured to the south and the east, and the descendants of Japheth moved north. The word *Ham* originally meant "black" and referred to the black soil of the Nile delta, but its meaning was eventually changed to describe the skin color of Ham's descendants. According to the Bible, Ham had seen his father naked in a drunken sleep and was cursed and sent off to the south to become the father of the black people. At the end of Genesis, the descendants of Ham are condemned to be "servants of servants unto [their] brethren" (Genesis 9:25). During the era of slavery, many Westerners cited this passage as the justification for an entrenched system of racial discrimination (Leach 1988; Braude 1997; Davis 1997).

By correlating physical characteristics with cultural differences, ancient classification systems such as these assumed erroneously that populations which shared certain physical traits, especially skin color, also shared other physical characteristics and behaviors. These beliefs gave rise to many popular misconceptions and generalizations concerning the values, traditions, and behaviors of different peoples. Based on contemporary scientific research on DNA, genetics, linguistics, prehistory, historical, and anthropological data, there is no scientific evidence to substantiate the claims of the biblical beliefs about the sons of Noah (Cavalli-Sforza, Menozzi, and Piazza 1994; Brooks, Jackson, and Grinker 2004).

Early "Scientific" Studies of Race

During the 1500s when European explorers began to make contact with different peoples and cultures, various forms of "scientific" classifications began to appear. Earlier ideas based on blood and essential essences influenced these models of scientific racism. In these interpretations, the skin color of the varied peoples in the Americas, Africa, the Middle East, and Asia were associated with particular essences, behaviors, and mental developments. Europeans measured these civilizations in comparison with their own and thus, designated them as "savage" and "barbaric." Europeans began to rank the people they discovered according to differences in skin colors, with nonwhite peoples at the bottom. With this rationale to support them, biased treatment, colonization, and slavery of non-Western peoples could occur freely.

One of the earliest scientific efforts to organize human variation into racial categories was undertaken by the Swedish scientist Carolus Linnaeus, who developed the taxonomic system still used to classify organisms (see the discussion of taxonomy in Chapter 3). Linnaeus' classification of humans, created in 1735, divided *Homo sapiens* into four races based on skin color: *Homo europaeus* (white Europeans), *Homo americanus* (red North American Indians), *Homo asiaticus* (yellow Asians), and *Homo afer* (black Africans). His classification of humans was influenced by ancient and medieval theories, as well as European perceptions of their superiority. For example, he classified the American Indians with reddish skin as choleric, with a need to be regulated by customs. Africans with black skin were relaxed, indolent, negligent, and governed by caprice. In contrast, Europeans with white skin were described as gentle, acute, inventive, and governed by laws (Lieberman and Scupin 2012).

In 1781, a German scientist, Johann Blumenbach, devised a racial classification system that is still sometimes used in popular, unscientific discussions of race. He divided humans into five distinct groups—Caucasian, Mongolian, Malay, Ethiopian, and Native American—corresponding to the colors white, yellow, brown, black, and red, respectively. Blumenbach based his racial typology primarily on skin color as well as geography, but he considered other traits as well, including facial features, chin form, and hair color. Although Blumenbach emphasized the unity of all humanity, his typologies were modified during the nineteenth and early twentieth centuries as the three races of mankind, the Caucasoid, Mongoloid, and Negroid as a means of justifying slavery, colonialism, and racism throughout the world (Lieberman and Scupin 2012; Fluehr-Lobban 2006). Later, a number of physical anthropologists in the United States and Europe, such as Samuel Morton, Ernst Haeckel, Rudolph Virchow, and others, began to assert that the Caucasian race had larger brains and higher intellectual capacities than non-Caucasians (Shipman 1994; Wolpoff and Caspari 1997; Lieberman and Scupin 2012).

Limitations of Early Classification Systems

Because early researchers such as Linnaeus and Blumenbach created their typologies before Darwin and Mendel had published their findings, they did not incorporate the modern principles of natural selection, heredity, and population genetics. For example, Mendel's principle of independent assortment holds that physical traits are not linked together in the process of reproduction and transmission of genetic material. In other words, there is no "package" of characteristics that is passed on to members of different "races." Thus, blond hair and blue eyes are not consistently found in tandem, just as a specific skin color and hair texture are not linked to each other. Rather, these traits are independent of one another, leading to varying combinations in different individuals. Variation in the combination of traits makes it impossible to classify races according to well-defined criteria that hold for entire populations.

Continuous Variation and Classification   Early scientists, just as modern researchers, encountered another fundamental problem in distinguishing races. Instead of falling into discrete divisions, many characteristics exhibit a spectrum from one extreme to another, a phenomenon called *continuous variation*. Figure 6.3 illustrates this concept by showing the overlap of different skin colors, as measured by reflected light. If skin color is to be used as the primary criterion for determining race, how, then, do we divide the races? Inevitably, any boundaries we draw are entirely arbitrary.

If races constituted fundamental divisions within the human species, such differences would be readily measurable; in fact, they are not. As scientific information has accumulated, the picture has become increasingly complicated and the boundaries more obscure. Some people have attempted to explain continuous variation as a function of *mongrelization*, or interbreeding. This notion follows the logic that at some point in the past, the races were "pure," but the lines separating one race from another have become blurred by recent interbreeding. Such ideas reveal a naïve understanding of the human past. As has been discussed in Chapters 3 and 5, human history is characterized by a tremendous amount of migration and intermixing that must be accounted for. Although gene flow may have been more restricted in some groups than in others, human populations have always interbred. Consequently, different races would have been impossible to distinguish during any time period.

Geographical Races

By the mid-twentieth century, anthropologists had recognized the arbitrary nature of different racial classifications and took a more biological approach. Unlike earlier theorists, they did not rely on single, arbitrarily defined characteristics, such as skin pigmentation. Instead, in developing classification systems, they focused on the influences evolutionary forces may have had on geographically isolated human populations. Stanley Garn (1971), for example, divided modern humans into what he called *geographical races*, populations isolated from one another by natural barriers such as oceans, mountains, and deserts.

Figure 6.3 Variation in skin color, as measured by the amount of reflected light. The measurements cannot be divided into natural divisions, thus illustrating the arbitrary nature of racial classification.

Source: From *The Human Species: An Introduction to Biological Anthropology* by John Relethford. Copyright ©1990 by Mayfield Publishing Company. Reprinted by permission of the publisher.

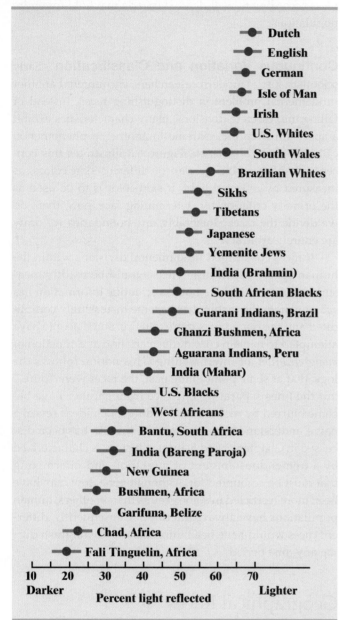

He reasoned that because of these barriers most people in each population married within their own gene pool. Garn's taxonomy divided humans into nine geographical races: Amerindian, Polynesian, Micronesian, Melanesian-Papuan, Australian, Asiatic, Indian, European, and African. These were further divided into smaller local races and micro-races that reflected restricted gene flow among smaller populations.

Garn's approach sought to frame the classification of human races in evolutionary terms. However, critics

pointed out that even these divisions imply stronger similarities among the races than actually exist. Some of Garn's supposed races exhibit an enormous amount of variation. Consider, for example, the "Mediterranean race," which extends, according to Garn, from Morocco in the far western Mediterranean to the Saudi Arabian peninsula thousands of miles to the east. It is difficult to imagine the culturally diverse groups included in this vast area as a discrete breeding population. Even more importantly, the degree of difference between this group and others is no greater than the variation contained within the group itself (Molnar 2006).

Heredity and Intelligence

6.6   Discuss how contemporary anthropologists assess the relationship between intelligence and race.

Before leaving the discussion of race and human variation, one other area of research needs to be examined: the study of intelligence. In no area of study have the varying effects of genes, environment, and culture been more confused. **Intelligence** can be defined as the capacity to process and evaluate information for problem solving. It can be contrasted with **knowledge**—the storage and recall of learned information. Heredity undoubtedly plays a role in intelligence; this is confirmed by the fact that the intelligence of genetically related individuals (for example, parents and their biological children) displays the closest correlation. Yet other environmental, social, and cultural factors also come into play. The interpretation of the varying roles of these different factors has further been confused by the challenges involved in measuring intelligence, and attempts to link these measurements to flawed concepts of races.

Following Darwin's publications on human evolution, many writers grounded allegedly "scientific" racist philosophies on misinterpretations of his theory. Nineteenth-century English thinkers, such as Herbert Spencer and Francis Galton, believed that social evolution worked by allowing superior members of society to rise to the top while inferior ones sank to the bottom. These views reinforced the false belief that particular groups of people, or races, had quantifiably different intellectual capacities.

Problems in Measuring Intelligence

Most scientists agree that intelligence varies among individuals. Yet it has been difficult to measure intelligence objectively because tests inevitably reflect the beliefs and values of a particular cultural group. Nevertheless, a number of devices have been developed to measure

Critical Perspectives

Joseph Arthur de Gobineau and the Aryan Master Race

At times, racial classifications have been used to justify **racism**, an ideology that advocates the superiority of certain supposed races and the inferiority of others, which leads to prejudice and discrimination against particular populations. Often with limited scientific grounding, such perspectives twist scientific information to meet political and social objectives

In 1853, racist beliefs coalesced in a four-volume treatise by the French aristocrat Joseph Arthur de Gobineau titled *Essai sur l'inéégalitéé des races humaines (Essay on the Inequality of the Races of Humanity).* In this work, Gobineau described the whole of human history as a struggle among the various "races" of humanity. He argued that each race had its own intellectual capacity, either high or low, and that there were stronger and weaker races. Gobineau promoted the conquest of so-called "weaker races" by allegedly stronger ones.

Gobineau opened his book with the statement that everything great, noble, and fruitful in the works of humanity springs from the Aryan family, the so-called "super race." Just prior to Gobineau's writings, it had been discovered by Western linguists that the languages of the Greeks, Germans, Romans (Latin), and Persians were all related to the ancient Sanskrit "Aryan" language family. Laying a thin foundation on this linguistic classification, Gobineau argued that a single "super" race of Aryans had led to the development of all the major civilizations of the

The extermination of millions of Jews by the Nazis before and during World War II was justified by unscientific theories of race that had no basis in empirical fact.

world. He suggested that the Aryan super race spread out to create, first, the Hindu civilization, then the Egyptian, Assyrian, Greek, Chinese, Roman, German, Mexican, and Peruvian civilizations (Montagu 1997; Banton 1998). Gobineau argued that these civilizations declined because of "racial mixing." Following the biblical narrative about Noah's sons, he argued that the superior Aryan race were the white descendants of Japhet. The Aryans were superior to the sons of Shem, the Semites. The Hamites were the descendants of Ham, an inferior race of blacks residing in Africa.

In the 1930s, drawing on Gobineau's ideas, Nazi racist ideology based on the presumed superiority of a pure "Aryan race" was used to justify the annihilation of millions of Jews and other "non-Aryan" peoples in Europe. Nazi pseudoscientists undertook expeditions across the globe and misconstrued actual scientific data to support the idea of Germany's primary position as a successor to

the Aryan civilization. These racist beliefs have no basis in actual fact. Human groups never fit into such neat categories, and there was never an Aryan master race. Even staunch advocates of Nazi ideology found it difficult to define precisely which physical characteristics supposedly distinguished one "race" from another. Many Jewish people living in Europe during the Holocaust possessed the same physical features as those associated with so-called "Aryans," Germans, or other Europeans.

Points to Ponder

1. Consider Gobineau's ideas of a master race in light of what you know about modern human variation. What problems do you see with it?
2. Many of the ideas regarding an Aryan master race were clearly fanciful. Why did so many people believe them?
3. Can you think of other cases where pseudoscientific information has been used to foster political aims?

intelligence, the most prominent among them being the intelligence quotient (IQ) test, invented by French psychologist Alfred Binet in 1905. Binet's test was brought to the United States and modified to become the Stanford-Binet test. The inventors warned that the test was valid only when the children tested came from similar cultural

environments; yet the IQ test was used in the late nineteenth century at Ellis Island to weed out undesireables and "mentally deficient" peoples such as Italians, Poles, Jews, and other Europeans.

These IQ tests are widely used today for tracking students in the U.S. educational system, sparking controversy among educators and social scientists alike. In a controversial book called *The Bell Curve: Intelligence and Class Structure in American Life* (1994), Richard Herrnstein and Charles Murray argue that research supports the conclusion that race is related to intelligence. Utilizing a bell-curve statistical distribution, they place the IQ of people with European ancestry at 100. People of East Asian ancestry exceed that standard slightly, averaging 103; people of African descent fall below that standard, with an average IQ of 90. Their findings imply that IQ scores are related to genetic differences among races.

A number of scientists have noted the faulty reasoning used by Herrnstein and Murray, as well as by others who have attributed IQ differences between African-Americans and European Americans to so-called racial groupings. If there truly were IQ score differences between African-Americans and European Americans, then African-Americans with more European ancestry ought to have higher IQ scores than those with less European ancestry. However, in a major IQ study of hundreds of African-Americans whose European ancestry was determined through blood testing, Scarr and Weinberg (1978) found no significant relationship between IQ scores and the degree of European admixture.

These test-score disparities indicate that cultural and social patterns are the more significant variables. African-Americans are no less intelligent than other groups, but carrying a legacy of disadvantage, many contend with a cultural environment that discourages self-confidence and achievement. Most anthropological research on this topic indicates that when differences in socioeconomic status and other factors were controlled for, the difference between African-Americans and European Americans was insignificant (Molnar 2006). In Japan, a group of people known as the *burakumin* (see Chapter 23 pages 555), who exhibit no major physical differences between themselves and other Japanese people but who have been subject to prejudice and discrimination for centuries in their society, tend to score lower on IQ tests than other Japanese (Molnar 2006). This indicates the strong influence of socioeconomic factors in measuring IQ. Additional studies show that educational enrichment programs boost IQ scores (Molnar 2006). Much research has determined that IQ scores increase within every generation of every population by three to five points, indicating the profound influence of social and educational conditions on IQ scores. The other major criticism of Herrnstein, Murray, and like-minded theorists is that they reify "race" as if races were based on clear-cut and distinct genetic groups, ignoring the enormous variation within these so-called races (MacEachern 2012; Lieberman and Scupin 2012).

In a recent evaluation of the question of IQ, race, and the environment, psychologist Richard Nisbett of the University of Michigan relies on numerous studies, statistical, historical, and experimental to refute the notion that IQ is deeply encoded in our genes (2009). In his book *Intelligence and How to Get It* (2009), Nisbett writes about how class differences are much more important than race or heredity in influencing IQ scores. When poor children are adopted into upper-class homes, their IQ scores rise by 12 to 18 points. Nisbett suggests that IQ scores are expandable depending on the enrichment of children's environments. He records an enormous amount of data demonstrating the rapid trend in upward IQ scores. The average IQ score in 1917 would amount to only 73 on today's IQ test, and half the population would be considered mentally retarded by today's measurements. IQ scores have risen remarkably over time, indicating that environmental and educational factors are much more important than heredity in determining intelligence.

Most psychologists agree that intelligence is not a readily definable characteristic like height or hair color. Psychologists view intelligence as a general capacity for "goal-directed adaptive behavior," that is, behavior based on learning from experience, problem solving, and reasoning (Myers 2012). Though this definition of intelligence would be acceptable to most social scientists, we now recognize that some people are talented in mathematics, others in writing, and still others in aesthetic pursuits such as music, art, and dance. Because abilities vary from individual to individual, psychologists such as Howard Gardner question the view of intelligence as a single factor in the human makeup. Based on cross-cultural research, Gardner (2004) has concluded that intelligence does not constitute a single characteristic but rather amounts to a mix of many differing faculties. According to Gardner, each of us has distinct aptitudes for making music, for spatially analyzing the visual world, for mastering athletic skills, and for understanding ourselves and others—a type of social intelligence. Not surprisingly, Gardner concludes that no single test can possibly measure what he refers to as "multiple intelligences."

The majority of psychologists and other scientists concur with Gardner's findings that intelligence spans a wide and diverse range of cognitive processes and other capacities. The IQ test ranks people according to their performance of various cognitive tasks, especially those that relate to scholastic or academic problem-solving. Yet it cannot predict how successfully a person will adapt to specific environmental situations or even handle a particular job. Throughout the world, people draw on various forms of intelligence to perform inventive and creative tasks, ranging from composing music to developing efficient hunting strategies. Before we call someone "intelligent," we have to know what qualities and abilities are important in that person's environment.

Current Approaches to Human Variation

6.7 Discuss current approaches to human variation.

Taxonomies that classify humans into separate races, even those based on modern scientific observations, fall short because they are too static to encompass the dynamic nature of human interaction and the consequences of varying environmental and evolutionary forces. Any criterion selected as the basis for classification is necessarily arbitrary. The physical characteristics that have historically been used to distinguish one race from another form an extremely small part of a human's total genetic makeup. There is so much variation among individuals within populations that the classification schemes become extremely blurred and break down. For these reasons, the anthropologists studying human variation steer clear of defining race. Instead, they focus on explaining variation in specific traits.

Clinal Distribution

Because many physical traits vary independently of one another, some researchers have found it useful to examine single traits, or unitary variables. In many contemporary studies of biological variation, scientists plot the distribution of individual traits on maps by zones known as **clines**. A map of **clinal distribution** can be likened to a weather map. It traces a continuous, progressive gradation from one geographic region to another. Rather than simply stating whether it is going to be hot or cold, weather maps detail the temperatures in different parts of the country. Lines tracing temperatures identify approaching storm fronts, and special designations indicate areas experiencing heat waves. Weather maps graphically represent the intersection of a range of variables that explain weather patterns beyond the local level. Similarly, plotting the distribution of individual traits in human populations sheds light on the genetic, environmental, and cultural factors that influenced their distribution. Using mathematical models to analyze evolutionary processes in a gene pool, scientists have tracked specific physical traits within a population.

Anthropologist Joseph Birdsell (1981) conducted a classic clinal distribution study of blond, or tawny, hair among Australian Aborigines. While conducting fieldwork, Birdsell noted that the majority of Aborigines had dark brown hair, but some had tawny hair. Significantly, the tawny hair trait was not evenly distributed throughout the Aborigine population, but was concentrated in certain areas. A map of the percentages of tawny-haired individuals in each region revealed the spread of the trait (Figure 6.4). In some areas of the western desert, 100 percent of the people had tawny hair. Farther away from the western desert, fewer tawny-haired people were to be found. Birdsell speculated that a mutation or, more likely, repeated mutations produced light-colored hair in some individuals. In certain areas, the light-colored hair replaced the original dark brown hair color, for reasons that are unclear. Over time, through gene flow with surrounding groups, the new trait spread outward. The clinal distribution of tawny hair offers a graphic illustration of microevolutionary change over time within one human population.

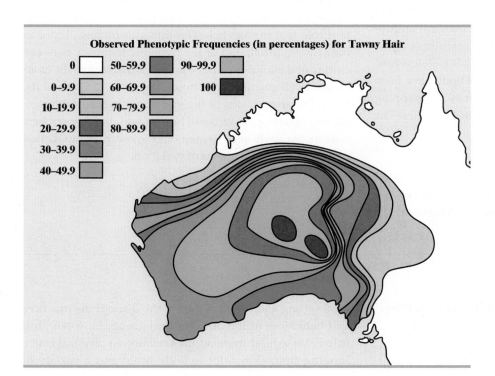

Observed Phenotypic Frequencies (in percentages) for Tawny Hair

0	50–59.9
0–9.9	60–69.9
10–19.9	70–79.9
20–29.9	80–89.9
30–39.9	90–99.9
40–49.9	100

Figure 6.4 A clinal distribution map of tawny hair color in Australia. The trait probably originated in the western desert, where it is most common. The percentage of tawny hair decreases in waves spreading out from this area. This is an example of a study focusing on one genetic trait.
Source: From *Human Evolution* by Joseph B. Birdsell. Copyright ©1975, 1981 by Harper & Row, Inc. Reprinted by permission of Addison-Wesley Educational Publishers, Inc.

This approach can be used to examine other differences in human populations, but it also further underscores the problems inherent in attempts at the classification of human races. When plotted individually, the varying distribution of physical traits is readily apparent. Notably, the clinal distributions of other physical characteristics in Australian Aborigines differ from that for tawny hair color. This further indicates the limited explanatory value of classifications based on individual or constellations of physical characteristics.

Multivariate Analysis

In addition to univariate approaches that focus on a single trait, **multivariate analysis** examines the interrelationships among a number of different traits. Such studies are extremely complex, and scientists using this approach must decide which physical traits and which variables should be examined. Biologist R. C. Lewontin adopted a multivariate approach in his study of human variation. Lewontin (1972) probed the distribution of physical traits that vary in human populations, including those that have been considered distinctive to certain races, such as skin color and hair texture. In focusing on how the distribution of these traits compares to common divisions by race, he noted that traits used to identify races do not accurately reflect human variation. Observed differences among Africans, Caucasians, Mongoloids, South Asians, Oceanians, Australian Aborigines, and Native Americans (divisions that approximate Garn's geographical races) account for only about 6 percent of the total amount of variation in human populations. Almost 94 percent of human variation of physical traits occurs *within* each of these different "races." Lewontin's genetic findings have been confirmed by many other contemporary studies in biological anthropology that underscore the very limited usefulness of the concept of race (Mukhopadhyay et al. 2014; Relethford 2013; Jurmain et al. 2014). These observations have been further borne out by recent research such as the mapping of the human genome (see the box Race and Genetics: The Human Genome Project).

Current Perspectives

Sorting out the varied reasons for variation in human populations is clearly complex. Recent studies and the unwrapping of the human genome have provided dramatic insights, yet have further revealed the complexity of the processes involved. In light of this complexity, it is not surprising that modern researchers examine the varied aspects of human variation in terms of specific characteristics, their origins, and their interactions rather than trying to delineate distinctive subspecies or races.

Dramatic insights into the genetic makeup of modern humans have been provided by the Human Genome Project, which was jointly coordinated by the U.S. Department of Energy and the National Institutes of Health (see the box Race and Genetics: The Human Genome Project). The project mapped the genetic loci of all of the estimated 20,000 to 25,000 human genes and determined the sequences of the estimated three billion base pairs that make up human DNA. With this information in hand, it seemed that the genetic basis of human variation and an individual human's genetic identity would be revealed in their entirety. However, while the results of the project have in some respects proven to be even more exciting than anticipated, revealing a host of connections, intersections and nuances in humanity's genetic ancestry, the research has also underscored that viewing genes and genetic processes as the sole explanation of human variation is not valid (Jablonka and Lamb 2006: 4-8). A human's appearance cannot be understood simply by reading the genetic code in their DNA. This has led to a reassessment of the roles of the processes of mutation, natural selection, gene flow, and genetic drift that have traditionally been seen as the principal source of evolutionary change.

This reassessment does not mean that these traditional evolutionary processes are not of great importance, and they do provide key mechanisms for evolutionary change. However, researchers are increasingly aware of the important role that human behavior and culture has played in human evolution, and of the dynamic feedback between culture and evolution. This was well illustrated in the cases of sickle-cell anemia and lactose intolerance. As seen in the preceding discussions of the varied genetic, environmental, and behavioral sources of human variation, researchers now increasingly seek to map out the complex interaction of these numerous sources of variation.

Summary and Review of Learning Objectives

6.1 Identify the different sources of human variation.

Human beings evince tremendous variation. Many of the observable differences are the result of cultural variations and are superficial; individuals taken from one cultural setting and raised in another will adopt the practices and behaviors of the new cultural group. However, humans also exhibit tremendous variation in physical traits, ranging from skin color to body build and a variety of biochemical characteristics. These traits are the products of the dynamic interaction of evolutionary processes affecting genetic diversity within and between populations, the physical environment, and cultural variables. The four principal processes of evolution that influence the genetic makeup of a population are mutations, natural selection, gene flow, and genetic drift. In addition to these processes, genes and their expression are also influenced by epigenetic factors that are external to the DNA sequence. The physical environment also influences human variation by promoting or restricting growth and development. Humans dramatically impact the environments in which they live, activities that may have evolutionary implications. Culture may even more directly influence human genetic variation through practices that inhibit gene flow. Although we know that all of these factors contribute to human variation, it is challenging to assess their relative importance.

6.2 Provide examples of how physical characteristics in human populations may represent adaptations arising from natural selection.

Studies suggest that many genetically controlled traits may be the result of natural selection. For example, having darker skin may have been an advantage in tropical Africa, where early humans evolved. Melanin, which is found in greater concentration in darker skin, provides protection from ultraviolet (UV) radiation in sunlight, which has been shown to have a number of detrimental effects, including sunburn, sunstroke, and skin cancer. Most importantly, it decreases folate levels, a factor that causes higher numbers of birth defects and so directly affects reproductive success. As early humans moved into temperate regions with less sunlight, other selective pressures, especially the need for Vitamin D, conferred an adaptive advantage on lighter skin pigmentation. Reduced production of Vitamin D is associated with deficiency diseases such as rickets and increased infant mortality rates. As Vitamin D production is stimulated by UV radiation, people who lived in colder, cloudy climates would have had improved chances of survival if they had lighter skin that absorbed higher levels of UV radiation and, thus, synthesized more Vitamin D. Over time, natural selection favored darker skin in the tropics and lighter skin in regions with less sunlight. The influence of natural selection and the environment can also be seen in human body and limb forms, which in part may relate to thermoregulation. This characteristic can be illustrated by Bergmann's rule that states that smaller animals, which have larger surface areas relative to their body weights, lose excess heat efficiently and, thus, function better at higher temperatures. Larger animals, which have a smaller surface area relative to their body weight, dissipate heat more slowly and so are better adapted to cold climates. The same principal applies to humans: People

living in cold climates tend to have stocky torsos and heavier average body weights, whereas people in warmer regions have more slender frames. Adaptive features can also be seen in sweat glands, body hair, cranial and facial features, biochemical characteristics such as blood groups, and lactose tolerance.

6.3 Discuss how environmental factors may be sources of evolutionary change.

Humans are highly sensitive to changes in their physical surroundings and environment is consequently an important factor in human variation. Environment may affect the individual during his or her lifetime, as well as long-term evolutionary change in populations. Adaptive features resulting from natural selection may arise as a result of how well the requirements for growth are met in certain environments. Acclimatization refers to the physiological process through which humans become accustomed to a new environment. This physiological adjustment is temporary: When these individuals leave the new environment, they revert to their earlier states. This type of acclimatization can be differentiated from developmental acclimatization. In this case, individuals born or raised in certain environmental conditions may develop nonreversible physical characteristics.

6.4 Discuss how cultural factors may be sources of evolutionary change.

Human behavior and culture may also influence human genetic makeup. Species alter the environments in which they live, something that may affect their adaptability and so influence natural selection. The process by which organisms modify their environment is referred to as niche construction. More than any other species, human societies dramatically impact the environments in which they live. Human activities such as plant and animal domestication, land clearing, and industrialization have dramatically impacted the environment. Culture may even more directly influence human genetic variation through religious beliefs, social organization, marriage practices, or prejudices that restrict intermarriage among different groups and, thus, inhibit gene flow. Cultural beliefs also determine diet, living conditions, and the environment in which people work; these effects, in turn, either promote or hamper human growth and development.

6.5 Explain the challenges faced in dividing human populations into different races and why modern anthropologists avoid these classifications.

Physical characteristics, such as skin pigmentation, nose shape, and hair texture, have prompted people throughout history to classify humans into different "races." Although human populations clearly encompass a great deal of diversity, physical characteristics cannot be used to divide humans into readily discernible groups or races. Instead of falling into discrete divisions, many characteristics exhibit a spectrum from one extreme to another, a phenomenon called continuous variation. Different characteristics also sort independently of one another and so do not provide the same divisions. Inevitably, any boundaries we draw are entirely arbitrary. If races constituted fundamental divisions within the human species, such differences would be readily measurable; in fact, they are not. Many attempts at racial classifications have been made, but these have failed because they proved too rigid to account for either the tremendous variation found within individual races or the shared similarities between these supposedly different groups. The varied criteria used in different classifications of human races and the dramatically different numbers of races identified—ranging from 3 to 30—underscore the limited use of the concept. Even more importantly, identifying different races does not explain the reason for the observed variation. The word *race* is also of limited use because the word is used differently in different contexts. It may be used as justification for the discrimination or the marginalization of certain groups. Racial classifications can also be used as self-defined categories in census data or in other contexts to refer to styles of music, dance, or literature. For these reasons, modern anthropologists avoid using racial classifications, but rather focus on the distribution and study of specific traits and the explanation of the processes that may have produced them.

6.6 Discuss how contemporary anthropologists assess the relationship between intelligence and race.

Another aspect of human variation is intelligence, which can be defined as the capacity to process and evaluate information for problem solving. It can be contrasted with knowledge—the storage and recall of learned information. Although individuals vary in their intelligence, researchers generally agree that environmental and cultural factors influence intelligence much more than hereditary or genetic factors. A consensus among educators and social scientists holds that rather than being a singular trait, intelligence is actually a mix of different faculties that cannot be measured by one culturally coded test. The interpretation of the varying roles of these different factors has further been confused by the challenges involved in measuring intelligence, and attempts to link these measurements to flawed concepts of races.

6.7 Discuss current approaches to human variation.

Modern studies of human variation focus on explaining why such variation occurs. Because many physical traits vary independently of one another, some researchers have found it useful to examine single traits, or unitary variables. Plotting the distribution of individual traits in human populations sheds light on the genetic, environmental, and cultural factors that influenced their distribution. In contrast, multivariate analysis examines the interrelationships among a number of different traits. Such studies are extremely complex, and scientists using this approach must decide which physical traits and which variables should be examined. Dramatic insights into the genetic makeup of modern humans have been provided by the Human Genome Project, which was jointly coordinated by the U.S. Department of Energy and the National Institutes of Health. The project mapped the genetic loci that make up human DNA. The results of the project have revealed a host of connections, intersections and nuances in humanity's genetic ancestry, as well as the importance of cultural, environmental, cultural, and epigenetic factors in human variation. In light of this complexity, it is not surprising that modern researchers examine the varied aspects of human variation in terms of specific characteristics, their origins, and their interactions rather than trying to delineate distinctive subspecies or races.

Key Terms

acclimatization, p. 129
balanced polymorphism, p. 127
clinal distribution, p. 139
clines, p. 139
continuous variation, p. 123

developmental acclimatization, p. 129
intelligence, p. 136
knowledge, p. 136
lactase deficiency, p. 128
multivariate analysis, p. 140

polymorphism, p. 121
polytypic, p. 121
racism, p. 137

Chapter 7
The Paleolithic

 ## Learning Objectives

After reading this chapter you should be able to:

7.1 Discuss the sources of information on early hominin behavior and the challenges archaeologists face when interpreting the behaviors and lifestyles of the oldest hominins.

7.2 Describe how the behavior of *Homo erectus* and the earliest representatives of genus *Homo* differed from that of earlier hominins.

7.3 Describe the changes in the tool traditions that distinguish the Middle Paleolithic

period and discuss the hominin species that may have produced them.

7.4 Describe the changes in the archaeological record that distinguish the Upper Paleolithic period and discuss what these technological changes may imply about the lives of early humans.

7.5 Discuss the contrasting theories regarding the initial human settlement of the Americas and the archaeological evidence that supports or refutes each perspective.

In the preceding chapters, we saw how physical anthropologists have used fossils and molecular genetics to trace the evolution of humans as a biological species over the past 10 million years. During this period of time, different hominin species evolved, including some that were the ancestors of modern humans. In addition to changes in physical characteristics, there were also changes in how these early human ancestors lived. Behavior, including tool manufacture and use, hunting strategies, and social organization, played an increasingly important role in their adaptation to the environment. Archaeologically, we also start to see things that imply behaviors and cultural developments beyond mere subsistence. These nonutilitarian aspects of the archaeological record include stylistic variation in stone tools, the beginning of art, and possible evidence of religious beliefs. This is the real story of human origins.

How did these early human ancestors behave? What tools did they use? What social organizations did they have? Interpreting the behavior of earliest hominins, researchers face a daunting task as early hominin behavior can be inferred only indirectly. Observations of modern nonhuman primates may offer some insights into the range of hominin behavior, and provide a potential means of modeling early hominin activities. Beginning about three and a half million years ago, information can also be obtained from archaeological materials, including the tools they made, the fossilized bones of the animals they ate, and the living sites they left behind. In particular, a great deal of information comes from the study of stone tools, or *lithics*, because these survive very well even after being buried in the ground for millions of years. Researchers refer to the earliest stone tools produced by pre-*Homo sapiens* hominins as **Lower Paleolithic** implements, referring to the earliest part of the Old Stone Age (roughly between 2.6 million and 300,000 years ago).

Exemplifying the Lower Paleolithic are the Oldowan and Acheulean stone tool traditions. The archaeological record associated with the emergence of *Homo sapiens* (beginning after about 300,000 years ago) becomes increasingly sophisticated and diverse. This time period, primarily divided on the basis of changes in stone tool technology, is referred to as the **Middle Paleolithic** and the **Upper Paleolithic** (or the *Middle* and *Late Stone Age*). The Middle and Upper Paleolithic periods saw a burst of creative energy and technological innovations that distinguish them from the Lower Paleolithic.

The Upper Paleolithic also witnessed the expansion of modern humans across the globe, with migrations into areas such as the Americas, Australia, and the islands of the Pacific Ocean that had previously been unoccupied by hominins. Some of these movements were facilitated by changing climatic conditions during the past 100,000 years that dropped sea levels and exposed land masses that had previously been underwater. Humans developed specialized technologies to live in varied environmental conditions ranging from the African deserts to the high Arctic.

While many clues to the human past have been gleaned, the material record often presents only a shaded view of the dynamic behaviors it represents. New discoveries, methods, and theories make the interpretation of the human past an exciting endeavor. Thus, archaeologists and paleoanthropologists must bring to the field a keen sense of imagination, a detective's acuity, and the patience to piece together the lifeways of our long-dead human ancestors.

Lifestyles of the Earliest Hominins

7.1 Discuss the sources of information on early hominin behavior and the challenges archaeologists face when interpreting the behaviors and lifestyles of the oldest hominins.

What was life like for early hominins? Understanding the behaviors of the oldest of human ancestors is frustrated by the limited amount of information afforded by the archaeological record, which only begins six million or seven million years after the origins of bipedalism and when the first hominins appeared. There are no artifacts, features, or archaeological sites associated with the oldest hominin finds. In many instances, the oldest hominin fossil localities, the places where fossils are found, likely do not represent living areas, but rather places where early hominins were naturally buried and preserved. Hence, these localities provide little insight into how early hominins lived. How can researchers gain insight into the activities of the earliest human ancestors?

Primate Models of Early Hominin Behavior

To help understand what the social life and behaviors of early hominins may have been like, some researchers have turned to the study of living nonhuman primates. Primate models of early hominins have been made possible by long-term primate studies, such as those conducted by Jane Goodall and Dian Fossey noted in Chapter 4. Although the behaviors of human ancestors did not mirror those of any living primate, studies of modern primates potentially shed light on how environmental factors may have led to bipedalism and shaped other aspects of early hominin behavior (Kinsey 1987; de Waal 2001; Pickering and Domínguez-Rodrigo 2010; Sayers and Lovejoy 2008). The mother-infant bonds, friendships, and complex patterns of social interactions found in higher primates may also offer insights into early hominin behavior.

While researchers have examined a variety of nonhuman primates in developing models of early hominin behaviors, chimpanzees have received particular attention. Of the living primates, chimpanzees have the closest evolutionary relationship to humans. In addition, because of the complexity of their behavior, researchers have drawn possible parallels between chimpanzee social organization, food-getting practices and tool use, and the activities of early hominins.

The Gathering Hypothesis, proposed by Nancy Tanner (1987), drew on behaviors observed in modern chimpanzees to understand how gathering may have played a crucial role among early hominins. Drawing upon observations of living chimpanzees, Tanner argued that gathering and tool use by females were of key importance in obtaining plant foods among early hominins, and further argued that this may have been an important selective pressure in the emergence of bipedalism. As seen in Chapter 4, modern chimpanzees have been observed using simple tools, such as sticks or folded blades of grass to extract termites from their nests, and they regularly use stones to crack open nuts (Mercader 2002; Toth et al. 2004; Toth and Schick 2009).

The way in which tools are manufactured and how this behavior is learned are also of particular interest. Field observations reveal female chimpanzees to be more consistent and more proficient tool users than males. Female chimps commonly share food with their young, and mothers

have been observed rewarding their daughters for learning how to use tools. Tanner suggested that early hominins may have engaged in similar social dynamics in tool use, strategies for the acquisition of food, and in feeding the young.

Observations of chimpanzee hunting—of monkeys, immature bush pigs, baboons, and other species—have also been well documented. It has been suggested that this social hunting, and the cooperation it entails, is more complex than that of social carnivores and thus, is potentially a means of understanding the emergence of hunting in early hominins and their social organization (Boesch and Boesch 1989). Jill Pruetz and Paco Bertolini (2007) observed wild chimpanzees hunting bushbabies (small prosimians) in Senegal. The chimpanzees made tools out of branches pulled from living trees; the branches were then trimmed of side branches and the ends, the points sometimes sharpened using their teeth. These implements were effectively used as spears that were forcibly thrust into bushbaby burrows. Notably, this tool-assisted hunting was primarily done by females and immature chimpanzees. In other observations, the majority of observed chimpanzee hunting has been done by males. These findings were used to further underscore the potential importance of tool use among female hominins in the evolution of the earliest tool technologies (Pruetz and Bertolini 2007: 414).

Recent critiques, however, have cautioned against taking primate models of early hominin behavior too far (Pickering and Domínguez-Rodrigo 2010; Sayers and Lovejoy 2008). At least in some instances, claims of the uniqueness of chimpanzee behavior and the appropriateness of making comparisons with early hominins are unjustified. While indicating the potential range of early hominin behavior, some of the activities observed among chimpanzees, including tool use, food transport, and social learning, are not restricted to chimpanzees or to the primates and, in fact, have counterparts throughout the animal kingdom. Hence, chimpanzee behavior is not particularly distinct. More importantly, the presence of these behaviors in nonhuman primates does not reveal the unique behaviors that likely characterized early hominins. For example, despite the evidence for hunting among chimpanzees, they rarely scavenge the carcasses of animals killed by other predators. Yet, as discussed later, this is a feature which seems to have been an important characteristic of early hominin behavior. Rather than commonalities with other primates, it is perhaps the uniqueness of early hominin behavior that is of key importance in understanding their development.

A young female chimpanzee uses a stick to dig insects out of a fallen tree. Study of nonhuman primate behavior may provide clues to the behavior of early hominins.

The Archaeological Record

The archaeological record provides an important, indeed, to a large extent *the* source of information on early hominin behavior. As noted in Chapter 5, bipedalism freed hominins' hands for other tasks, such as tool use, food gathering, and infant care. There is no question that tools had important consequences for early hominins, allowing them to exploit a wider range of food, defend themselves more effectively, and generally perform many tasks that they would not have been able to do otherwise. For example, tools would have allowed early hominins to cut through the tough hides of animal carcasses, the meat of which could then be used as food.

Unfortunately, the evidence for the initial use of tools is ephemeral. The first tools were very likely *unmodified* pieces of wood, stone, bone, or horn that were picked up to perform specific tasks and then discarded soon afterwards. Frustratingly for researchers, artifacts of this kind are unlikely to be preserved or recognized in archaeological contexts. On one hand, wood, bone and horn do not survive as well as stone, and tools of these materials have rarely been recovered in Lower Paleolithic contexts. On the other hand, the simplicity of early tools, as well as their brief periods of use, makes them difficult to identify.

Who made and used the first tools is also a source of debate. Although it is perhaps tempting to associate the manufacture of the first tools with the larger-brained members of our own genus *Homo*, the oldest stone tools clearly predate the earliest representative of the genus. The oldest evidence for stone tool use, albeit limited, comes from cut marks left on two bones recovered in Dikika, Ethiopia and dated to roughly 3.4 million years ago (McPherron et al. 2010). The oldest well dated stone tools date back just over 2.6 million years ago (Semaw et al 2003). In contrast, the earliest representative of genus *Homo*, *H. habilis*, does not appear in the fossil record until some 300,000 or 400,000 years later. Hence, evidence for tool use would appear to long predate the first representatives of genus *Homo*.

During later periods, species that have been interpreted as potential ancestors of genus *Homo* (such as *Australopithicus africanus* and *A. garhi*, an early hominin recovered in Ethiopia, have similarly been identified as the most likely toolmakers. While this may have been the case, other early hominins may have made and used simple tools. In particular, stone tools have been found in association with some of the robust australopithecines, including *A. robustus*, *A. boisei*, and *A. aethiopicus* (Sussman 1994). In this context, it is worthwhile to again note the preceding discussion regarding nonhuman primate behavior. Studies of modern chimpanzees have demonstrated that they have the cognitive abilities to manufacture simple stone tools and will use them to obtain desired food. It would not be surprising that various species of early hominins made similar use of tools.

The First Tools The oldest recognizable tools are rudimentary stone implements found in Africa dating back almost 2.6 million years ago from a site in Gona, Ethiopia (de Heinzelin 1999; Semaw et al. 2003). These types of tools were first identified by Louis and Mary Leakey at Olduvai Gorge in Tanzania, East Africa, an area that has also been the site of many important hominin fossil finds. The Leakeys called this stone tool technology the **Oldowan industry**, using another version of the name *Olduvai* (Toth and Schick 2004). The Oldowan marks the beginning of the Lower Paleolithic. Oldowan tools are basically naturally shaped river cobbles or angular blocks of stone that have intentionally sharpened edges. The cobbles, perhaps measuring four or five inches across, were sharpened by using another rock as a hammer stone to break off chips or flakes in a process called **percussion flaking** (Figure 7.1a). As flakes were removed, they left behind a sharp edge that could be used for cutting and scraping, producing a crude pebble tool or chopper (Figure 7.1b). The flakes themselves also had sharp edges that could also be used as tools (Potts 1991, 1993). Tools with flaking on one side are termed *unifacial*; those with flaking on two sides are termed *bifacial*.

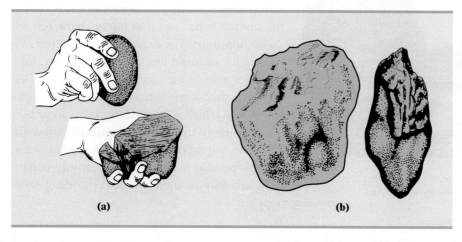

(a)   (b)

Figure 7.1 Oldowan industry: (a) the percussion flaking method, in which a hammer stone is used to remove flakes from a stone to produce a chopper tool; (b) an Oldowan chopper.

Pebble tools and flakes are the most distinctive Oldowan implements, but other artifacts have also been found. Some of these tools would have required little or no modification. For example, the hammer stones used to manufacture stone tools or to crack open bones to extract the nutritious marrow from inside, are no more than natural stones of convenient size. Their battered surfaces are the only indication of their use. Some stones recovered from archaeological sites bear no obvious evidence of use. Called *manuports*, archaeologists know that they were handled by early hominins because they are found together with other artifacts in places where such stones do not naturally occur, in some instances having likely been carried several kilometers.

How Were Tools Used? Because the Oldowan tools are very simple, even trained researchers sometimes find it challenging to tell which stones were manufactured by early hominins and which were broken by natural forces. In general, archaeologists note that the flaking in manufactured tools follows a more regular, consistent pattern than in stones in which a sharp edge is produced by natural processes. In addition, through **experimental studies** paleoanthropologists and archaeologists may actually duplicate the processes that may have been used by hominins to create tools, striking flakes off a cobble to produce a chopper, for example. Experimenting with these replica tools, researchers have discovered the types of tasks that they may have been used for, including cutting through hides, dismembering animals, and whittling wood (Toth and Schick 2004).

Researchers also conduct **use-wear and residue studies** to help decipher how early tools were used. When a person uses a stone tool, the tool's edge becomes nicked and dull (just like your razor blades). Distinctive patterns of *use-wear* can be associated with specific types of use. For example, cutting or sawing motions leave behind different wear patterns than scraping or chopping. By comparing the edges of stone tools used in experimental studies with the edges of stone tools recovered archaeologically, researchers can obtain clues as to how ancient tools were used. In addition, the material the tool has been used to cut or chop may leave a distinctive polish or *residue*. In examining 56 stone artifacts from Koobi Fora, dating to 1.5 million years ago, Lawrence Keeley and Nicholas Toth (1981) determined that four of these tools had been used to cut meat, and five others bore residues of plant matter. In the South African caves, the polishes on some animal bones have been interpreted by researchers as possible evidence that they were used for an activity, such as digging, that would have smoothed the bones' surfaces (Brain 1981).

Indirect evidence of early hominin activities and tool use also comes from the fossilized remains of animals found in archaeological sites (Potts 1988; Toth and Schick 2004). The types of animals represented provide an indication of the environments in which the hominins lived, as well as the animals that were likely exploited for food. For example, certain species might be more indicative of an open savanna-like environment than of a tropical forest. In addition, by examining the marks on the bones or the ways in which the bones were broken, researchers are able to discern how animals were butchered and what parts of an animal were used for food. **Cut marks** produced by stone tools are distinct from other marks, such as those that might be left on a bone by a predator's teeth or natural weathering. Cut marks left on animal remains by stone tools indicate how the tools were used to cut and scrape soft flesh off the bone. The distinctive ways in which some bones were broken also suggests that hominins cracked open long bones to expose the marrow, presumably with the help of stone tools. The marrow would have provided an important food source. As noted above, cut marks on bones from Dikika, Ethiopia, dating to almost 3.4 million years ago currently provide the earliest evidence for hominin tool use. These observations of the how and when of early tool use have important implications for models of early hominin subsistence and behavior discussed later.

Oldowan Sites and Early Hominin Behavior

Stone tools, manuports, and faunal remains provide important clues about the lifestyles of early hominins, particularly when they are found in an archaeological context and associated with other artifacts (see Chapter 2). Most Oldowan archaeological sites are relatively small and, in some cases, might only consist of a few hundred artifacts and fossilized bones. The earliest archaeological sites are from areas that have also revealed important hominin fossils: Hadar and Omo in Ethiopia; the Lake Turkana area in Kenya; South Africa; and Olduvai Gorge, Tanzania. At Olduvai, tools have been found in clusters along with discarded animal bones and flakes cast off from tool manufacture. In one case, more than 40,000 bones and 2,600 stones were found together (Domínguez-Rodrigo et al. 2007).

There is no question that these artifacts and sites were produced by hominins, but what does this information actually tell us about early hominin behavior? Piecing together the meaning of early hominin sites is challenging and interpretations have prompted a great deal of debate. In addition to the activities of early hominins, natural processes of decay and erosion, as well as movement and modification by carnivores modify the materials present and their arrangement. As new data have accumulated, views of early hominin activities have dramatically changed.

The changing perspectives illustrate the various sources of information researchers have drawn on to reconstruct early hominin behavior, as well as the ways in which scientific theories are evaluated in light of the evidence.

Man the Hunter or Woman the Gatherer? One of the first interpretations of early hominin behavior proposed has been referred to as the "Man the Hunter" hypothesis. This interpretation was developed by Glynn Isaac and Mary Leakey during the 1960s and 1970s when some of the first archaeological evidence on early hominin material culture was coming to light (Lee and DeVore 1968; Leakey 1971; Isaac 1978b). According to this perspective, hunting—facilitated by bipedalism, increased cranial capacity, and tool use—was the key to early hominin life. In a model that assumed a great deal of social complexity, Isaac and Leakey conjectured that the Olduvai archaeological sites represented *home bases*, locations where hominins actually lived. They argued that males brought back meat, particularly from large animals, to the home base to be shared with other adults (especially females) and children who had remained in camp. In this view, food sharing, prolonged infant care, and the social interaction that occurred at the home base prefigured the kind of social arrangements that characterize modern human societies. Drawing an analogy to contemporary human hunting-and-gathering populations, such as the Ju/'hoansi or !Kung San of Southern Africa, this model provides an idealized interpretation of human lifestyles stretching back two million years.

Many researchers increasingly viewed the man-the-hunter model as problematic, however. Critics pointed out that this interpretation of hominin activity places far too much emphasis on the role of the male and too little on that of the female (Dahlberg 1981; Tanner 1981; Fedigan 1986). Drawing upon observations of modern hunter-gatherers, critics argued that plants—fruits, seeds, and vegetables—and not meat were more likely to have been the major food source for early hominins. In contemporary human hunter-gatherer populations, women generally collect plant resources and play the key role in providing food. This type of organization—rather than male hunting—was suggested as a more likely model for early hominin subsistence.

Current Perspectives Subsequent research criticized aspects of the preceding theories for assuming that early hominin behavior paralleled that of modern humans (Gould 1980; Binford 1985; Potts 1988). Reanalyzing the data from early hominin localities and material from new sites, researchers have produced very different interpretations of early hominin life. Current theories do not assume the high degree of social complexity posited by the home-base model. By their very nature, early hominins—bipedal apes—were unlike any living primate and certainly far removed from modern humans in terms of their behaviors.

Indeed, the distinctive adaptive strategies and behaviors of these early human ancestors were probably the very features that distinguished them from other primate species. Although modern human diet and subsistence strategies as well as those of living primates may be used as models, the uniqueness of the early hominins always needs to be kept in mind.

Some clues to the social organization of early hominin groups may be informed by studies of their skeletal remains. A notable aspect of pre-genus *Homo* hominins (the australopithecines) revealed by their skeletal remains is the high degree of sexual dimorphism—males being significantly larger than females. In living primates, sexual dimorphism is associated with species in which males compete for females (see discussion in Chapter 4). Hence, the sexual dimorphism noted in australopithecine species may imply that males competed for females (Wrangham 1987). Drawing further parallels with modern primates' social organization and food-getting strategies, early hominins may have lived in multi-male and female groups of 30 or so individuals. The size of the groups may have fluctuated, depending on the availability of food resources.

Groups of 30 individuals could account for the concentrations of faunal remains, tools, and flakes seen archaeologically at early hominin sites. A number of studies have, however, underscored that the formation processes and activities represented were likely different at different fossil localities and sites (Domínguez-Rodrigo et al. 2007; Schick 1986). Larger concentrations of artifacts and bones, such as the Olduvai sites, may indicate "favored places" for early hominins. These were not huts or simple shelters; rather they were places where hominins gathered because of their proximity to water or food, the presence of shade, or a protected area. Stone and food might have been transported to these areas for potential use. In other cases, sites may represent scavenging or kill sites that were occupied or used for much briefer periods of time. While less evocative than earlier models, these observations are a more realistic assessment of creatures whose behavior was likely dramatically different from our own.

Diet and Subsistence The available evidence suggests that meat as well as fruits and grains were important in early hominins' diets, although their relative significance remains uncertain. The bulk of the archaeological data comes from faunal remains. Noting the portions of the animals that the fossilized bones represent, Lewis Binford (1985) suggested that the majority of the bones found at hominin sites were not the product of hunting forays but rather the remains of animals killed by other predators that were subsequently scavenged by hominins. The bones are predominantly the ends of leg bones, horn, and crania—not the choice cuts of meat one would expect a hunter to bring home but very consistent with the remains that might be scavenged from a kill site. Chopping marks, such as might have resulted from the dismembering of a carcass, are rare. The majority are consistent with the cutting or scraping of meat from the bones. Binford's interpretation gains additional support from microscopic studies of bones showing that, at least in some cases, cut marks from tools overlie carnivore tooth marks (Potts and Shipman 1981; Shipman 1986b).

More recent evidence from faunal remains has further underscored the use of animal protein and, possibly, scavenging as an aspect of early hominin behavior (Blumenschine 1995; Semaw et al. 2003). Studies of shattered bones from archaeological sites have revealed percussion marks that likely indicate that the bones were intentionally broken by early hominins—probably to extract bone marrow. Bone marrow would have been an important food source. Long bones containing marrow frequently survive intact on lion and leopard kills, so they may have been readily available to early hominins at kill sites.

While the opportunistic scavenging of meat from kill sites may have been one aspect of early hominin subsistence, the possibility of early hominin hunting has not been ruled out. Some researchers have suggested that the animal bones recovered from sites represent hominin hunting or the capability of hominins to drive off predators from kill sites (Domínguez-Rodrigo 2002; Domínguez-Rodrigo and Pickering 2003). This model is supported by studies that suggest that the portions of meat recovered were not simply the bones left by other predators but, rather, the more nutritious portions of the carcass. Whether hunters or scavengers, the size of the animals represented and the amount of bone present indicates that Oldowan hominins made far more extensive use of meat than living primates such as chimpanzee or baboons, perhaps a good indication of their distinctive subsistence strategies.

Although there is clear evidence for the opportunistic consumption of meat, plant foods were also likely an important component of early hominins' diets. Based on the study of living primates, it might, in fact, be suggested that early hominins relied heavily upon plant food. Modern species, ranging from monkeys to the chimpanzee, may complement their diets with insects or smaller animals, but foods such as leaves, fruits, and vegetable matter predominate (Tanner 1987). Unfortunately, plant remains are poorly preserved archaeologically and offer no direct evidence of early hominin diets. Indirect evidence for the exploitation of plant foods comes from the study of hominin teeth, though the specific types of plants exploited may have varied in different species. The massive molars of the robust australopithecines, for example, would have been ideally suited for chewing plant material. Striations, pitting, and wear on their teeth are also consistent with the wear that might be associated with the processing of roots, tubers, and seeds. In contrast, the smaller teeth of other australopithecines may suggest a more varied diet. In the absence of more information, it is impossible to state with any degree of certainty how important plant foods were in comparison to meat.

The Life and Times of Genus *Homo*

7.2 Describe how the behavior of *Homo erectus* and the earliest representatives of genus *Homo* differed from that of earlier hominins.

As seen in Chapter 5, the first representatives of genus *Homo* are known from African fossil finds dating back just over two million years ago. These species are believed to represent the evolutionary branch leading to modern humans. *H. habilis* (the "handy man"), known from discoveries in Kenya, Tanzania, and South Africa, dates between 1.6 and 2.2 million years ago. The oldest *Homo erectus* fossils (including finds that some researchers have designated *H. ergaster*), represented by the Turkana boy find, are slightly more recent, at 1.8 million years ago. More than anything else, genus *Homo* is characterized by greater cranial capacity compared to other hominins. Physically, the postcranial skeleton of *H. erectus* resembled that of modern humans, but the species' cranial capacity, while less than modern humans', was greater than that of earlier hominins. In addition, the shape and arrangement of later *H. erectus* skulls (including examples sometimes classified as *H. heidelbergensis*) has led some researchers to believe that these protohumans may have been the first hominins with both the physical and mental capacities for speech (see the box "Could Early Hominins Speak? The Evolution of Language").

These changes in physical characteristics undoubtedly underlaid a myriad of behavioral, social, and cultural developments. A number of innovations in tool technology may be associated with the evolution of the genus *Homo*, and these are discussed later. However, perhaps the best indication of the success of the genus is illustrated by the fact that *H. erectus* had the widest distribution of any hominin aside from *Homo sapiens*. Fossil discoveries classified as *H. erectus* range from widely dispersed sites in Africa (including Kenya, Tanzania, and South Africa), to Eurasia, Indonesia, and China, eastern Asia, and the Caucus Mountains of southern Russia (and presumably the areas in between), indicating that these areas had been settled by one million years ago. The occupation of Europe was slightly later, with current findings dating later than about 800,000 years ago. Significantly, these areas are not simply widely separated in space, but are also located in varied environmental zones ranging from tropical African savannahs to cold and temperate forests in Europe and Asia.

Critical Perspectives

Could Early Hominins Speak? The Evolution of Language

The ability to communicate is a key aspect of human adaptation, and the origin of human speech has been widely debated. Primates, in general, are effective communicators (see Chapter 4). Apes and monkeys utilize an array of howls, screams, hoots, grunts, and facial gestures that are used to signal one another and other animals (Arbib et al. 2008). The apes most closely related to humans, gorillas and chimpanzees, draw upon an even more highly developed repertoire of communication tools. It is, therefore, likely that early hominins such as *Ardipithecus ramidus* and *Australopithecus anamnesis* were able to communicate in similar ways, but it is unlikely that they were able to speak. While all of the questions are far from addressed, increasing evidence suggests that it may have only been with the emergence of our own species, *Homo sapiens,* that the full range of speaking abilities appeared. Evidence consists of both the cognitive and physical abilities to speak.

Indications of the cognitive abilities of early hominins come from the study of **endocasts**, the casts of the interior of the cranium, which can be likened to a blueprint of the surface of the brain. As discussed earlier, the evolution of hominins was accompanied by increasing cranial capacity (brain size) within the genus *Homo*. It was, however, not solely the increase in cranial capacity that was significant, but also the shape and organization of the brain. Several areas of the brain play important roles in the human capacity for speech. The expansion of the hominin brain corresponded with the increasing size of the cerebral cortex, the outer layer of brain related to higher cerebral functions, such as memory and symbolic capacities. Other areas of the brain particularly related to linguistic abilities are *Broca's area* and *Wernicke's area*, both located in the left hemisphere. Studies of fossil endocasts have suggested that *Homo habilis'* brains indicate more development in

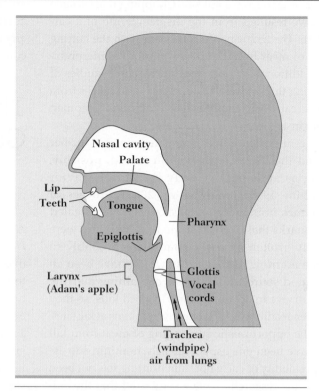

Figure 7.2 The physiology of speech making, which is unique to humans.

these areas than is found in apes and the australopithecines, and *Homo erectus'* brains are even more developed, being comparable to those of modern humans in shape (Coolidge and Wynn 2009:103-105; Tobias 1998; Wynn 1998; also see Gannon et al. 1998). If this is the case, then it is possible that *H. erectus* had at least some of the cognitive abilities needed for speech, though they lacked the physical capabilities for speech found in modern humans. They may, however, have had pre-adaptations that, in turn, may have resulted in future language capacities (Clegg 2004).

Various anatomical and physiological features also contribute to human speech abilities. Although primates, especially the apes, have lips, mouths, and tongues, no primate other than humans has the full physical anatomy for speech. Human vocal organs form an irregular tube connecting the lungs, windpipe, and *larynx*, the voice box containing the vocal cords. The larynx holds air in the lungs and controls its release. These vocal organs work in conjunction with our tongue, lips, and nose to produce speech. This allows humans to articulate sounds and manipulate their sequence.

Many of the features that are of key importance in human speech, such as the tongue and larynx, are not preserved in fossils. Their development and evolution are, therefore, difficult to assess, and the available information is somewhat indirect. One potential source of information that is sometimes preserved in fossil remains is the hyoid bone, a small bone in the throat that is connected to the larynx and the other structures needed for speech. The shape of the human hyoid bones is quite distinct from those of other primates, such as the chimpanzee. A hyoid bone from an *Australopithecus afarensis* appears chimpanzee-like in appearance, suggesting that hominins at this point in time (three to four million years ago) did not have the physical capabilities for speech. Finds of archaic *Homo sapiens* (*H. heidelbergensis*), however, possess hyoid bones that are human-like in form, possibly suggesting that archaic humans had the physical capability for speech some 530,000 years ago (Martinez et al. 2008).

The capability for speech can also be determined by the position of the larynx, which is inferred by the shape of the base of the cranium. In humans, the larynx is lower than in other animals. This position allows humans to generate a wider array of sounds needed for speech. The low placement of the larynx corresponds with the shape of the base of the cranium, which is curved. In contrast, the bases of the crania of animals with high larynxes, such as modern chimpanzees, are flatter. The cranial bases of the australopithecines are comparable in shape to those of modern apes, suggesting a highly placed larynx and the related lack of range in sound production. The bases of *Homo erectus* skulls are also quite curved. This inferred placement of the *larynx* suggests that the physical capabilities for speech only fully appeared in *Homo sapiens*.

Insight into the genetic basis of human speech was revealed by the recent discovery of the FOXP2 gene that is connected with the embryonic development of the areas of the brain associated with linguistic capacities (Lieberman 2007; Hawks 2013). The FOXP2 gene is located on human chromosome 7. All normal humans have two copies of chromosome 7 and two copies of FOXP2. In a long-term study of a family, a genetic mutation was identified that leaves them with only one working copy of FOXP2. Individuals within the family have problems with motor control and cognitive deficits. They consequently are unable to control their tongue properly for speaking and have difficulty repeating two-word sequences. FOXP2 is a gene that turns other genes on and off and, consequently, there is no one-to one-correspondence between it and a single trait; in other words, it is not *the* "language" gene. However, it is obvious that the mutation that led to the development of the FOXP2 gene was definitely important in the evolution of the human capacity for language; it was likely among a series of genetic mutations that contributed to language capabilities in modern humans.

In a fascinating new development, anthropologist Svante Pääbo and his colleagues at the Max Planck Institute for Evolutionary Anthropology in Leipzig, Germany, extracted DNA from Neandertal skeletal remains and discovered that the Neandertal FOXP2 genes carries the same two mutations of amino acids as those carried by modern *Homo sapiens* (Krause et al. 2007; Maricic et al. 2012; Hawks 2013). This indicates that Neandertal may have been carrying an ancestral FOXP2 mutation prior to modern *Homo sapiens*, suggesting that Neandertal may have delivered the language capacity to modern *Homo sapiens* through interbreeding sometime before the common ancestor of the two species, around 300,000 years ago. Modern *Homo sapiens* have a derived form of the FOXP2 mutation (Hawks 2013).

With the preceding clues in mind, it remains difficult to identify the critical stage in the evolution of communication from simple vocalizations or a sign-based communication, to complex, symbolic language. Yet, language undoubtedly greatly facilitated human adaptation and creativity. Richard Klein has, in fact, suggested that there was a big-bang scenario for the evolution of language and brain development (2003). He argues that there must have been a sudden alteration in the organization of the *Homo sapiens* brain, resulting from a genetic mutation around 50,000 years ago. This organizational change, he suggests, is expressed in the array of cultural innovations that characterize the Upper Paleolithic. Words and grammar facilitated the cultural and technological changes that allowed modern humans to be so successful in adapting to different environments around the world. Klein suggests that more archaic representatives of genus *Homo* such as the Neandertals could not have had anything approximating human culture. Examples of Neandertal artifacts like stone tools and jewelry are explained as borrowings from the more advanced *Homo sapiens*. Other researchers disagree, noting the evidence for speech capabilities and the richness of the Middle Paleolithic archaeological record (McBrearty and Brooks 2000).

Although anthropologists may disagree regarding the timing and origins of language capabilities in humans, the capacity for language was probably the last major step in our biological evolution (Klein 2003, Mellars 2006, Mithen 1996; Deacon 1997, Lieberman 2007). Since that time, human history has been dominated by *cultural* rather than *biological* evolution. This cultural evolution and the subsequent developments in adaptation and creativity could not have occurred before a fully evolved language capacity.

Points to Ponder

1. Discuss the evidence that exists for the evolution of both the cognitive and physical abilities for speech. What are some of the challenges faced in interpreting these data?
2. Consider the importance of verbal communication in your life. Examine how and why the abilities for speech may have had a dramatic impact on early hominin populations.

H. erectus was not simply mobile, but equipped with the cognitive abilities to adapt to widely different climates (see Figure 7.3).

The Archaeological Record and the Acheulean Industry

In contrast to the scant traces of earlier hominin behavior, the archaeological record after approximately a million and half years ago is somewhat more substantial and the tools more readily recognizable. Yet, the interpretation of hominin activities still depends on material excavated from relatively few sites, widely scattered in time and space, which likely represent varied functions and activities. As is the case with archaeological evidence for earlier hominins' behavior, a principal source of information comes from stone tools.

There were a number of significant changes in stone tool technology during the period of time associated with the evolution of the genus *Homo*. After their first appearance 2.6 million years ago, Lower Paleolithic tool traditions changed very slowly. The simple Oldowan pebble tools

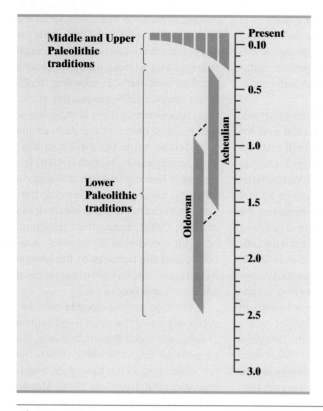

Figure 7.3 A chart outlining the relative chronologies of Lower, Middle, and Upper Paleolithic technologies. The Oldowan and Acheulean industries of the Lower Paleolithic were simple and long lasting. They were followed by Middle and Upper Paleolithic industries, which became increasingly more complex and varied.

and flakes remained the characteristic artifacts one million years after their first appearance. However, approximately 1.6 to 1.7 million years ago, some changes began to appear, including tools with more advanced flaking that may have served as drills and proto-bifaces (tools with flaking on two sides, somewhat like simple arrow heads). These increasingly sophisticated implements are referred to as the *developed Oldowan*, to distinguish them from the simpler Oldowan tools. Also during this period, a new tool tradition emerged, the **Acheulean industry** (see Figure 7.4).

Along with the Oldowan, this is the other major stone tool industry that marks the Lower Paleolithic.

Acheulean tools have been found in sites dating between 1.8 million and 250,000 years ago. The industry is named after the town of Saint-Acheul, France, where some of the first discoveries were made. However, the earliest examples have been found in Africa. These new tool types did not immediately replace early forms; the simple Oldowan choppers continue in the archaeological record. The flaking methods seen in developed Oldowan and Acheulean tools are similar to the manufacturing methods seen in earlier Oldowan tools. In this respect, they represent the further development and elaboration of the Oldowan. But the new and varied types of implements that characterize the Acheulean would have provided a more varied tool kit.

As is the case with the earlier Oldowan finds, the hominins responsible for these technological innovations are uncertain. Acheulean and developed Oldowan tools have been associated with *Homo habilis*, as well as *Homo erectus*. However, the earlier portion of this time period also includes fossil evidence for the robust australopithecines (*A. aethiopicus*, *A. boisei*, and *A. robustus*). Most significantly, both *H. habilis* and *A. boisei* are associated with Oldowan and early Acheulean tools at Olduvai Gorge. Later Acheulean tools are found with transitional or archaic forms of *H. sapiens* such as the Neandertals. Given these associations, the resolution of who made and used the tools will remain open (Camps and Chauhan, 2009).

Hand Axes and Other Tools Like the Oldowan choppers, Acheulean tools were produced by percussion flaking, but they exhibit more complexity. Most characteristic of the Acheulean is the *hand axe*, a sharp, bifacially flaked stone tool shaped like a large almond, which would have been effective for a variety of chopping and cutting tasks (see Figure 7.5a). Unlike Oldowan pebble tools and flakes, which consisted of irregularly flaked natural cobbles, the hand axe was fashioned by removing many flakes to produce a specific form. In other words, the toolmaker

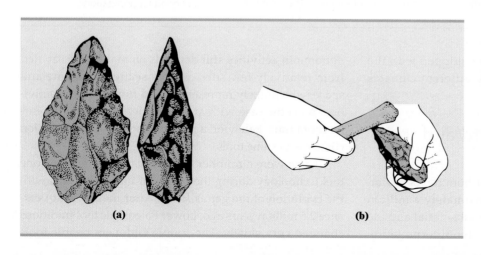

(a)   (b)

Figure 7.4 In later Acheulean technology, the characteristic hand axes (a) were made by the soft-hammer method (b).

Work space

Work space

Hearth

Work space

Figure 7.5 A hypothetical reconstruction of a shelter of stones and saplings as it may have appeared approximately 300,000 years ago at Terra Amata, France.

Source: Adapted from Henry de Lumley, "A Paleolithic Camp at Nice." Copyright ©1969 by Scientific American, Inc. Illustration by Eric Mose. Reprinted by permission of the artist, Eric Mose.

had to be able to picture a specific shape in a stone. This may indicate a significant advance in cognitive abilities (Wynn 1995).

Hand axes are very consistent in their form. Despite variations in material, examples from throughout Africa and Europe are remarkably similar. As in the case of the Oldowan, flakes are also an important component of Acheulean assemblages. Many bear evidence of additional flaking and reshaping, suggesting that they were modified for use. More recent hand axes, dating after about 600,000 years ago, are somewhat more regular in shape and more delicately flaked than earlier examples. This careful flaking was accomplished using a more refined manner of percussion flaking, called the *soft hammer* method, pictured in Figure 7. 4a. In this technique, flakes were struck with an appropriately shaped piece of softer material, such as a bone or antler, rather than a hammer stone. This method allowed for more accurate flaking and produced shallower, more controlled flakes than a hammer stone. Toward the end of the Acheulean, some of the stone tools prefigure the more sophisticated methods of manufacture that characterize the Middle and Upper Paleolithic industries discussed later. These later Acheulean stone tool assemblages have fewer hand axes and large flaked tools. Rather, they are characterized by smaller implements that were shaped from more carefully prepared flakes.

There is a significant gap in Acheulean stone tool distribution. Researchers have found that the distinctive Acheulean hand axes do not occur in archaeological assemblages east of northern India, including China and Indonesia, areas that have produced significant *H. erectus* finds. Stone tool assemblages are, instead, characterized by large choppers and flaked tools. These are not the simple Oldowan choppers, but bifacially flaked tools as sophisticated in their manufacture as hand axes. Why hand axes do not appear in these Asian assemblages is uncertain. Some

researchers have suggested that the initial *H. erectus* populations in Asia may not have been familiar with the hand-axe technology, possibly representing a population that migrated out of Africa before the technology was developed (Schick and Toth 1993). Alternatively, the lack of hand axes may represent distinctive tool requirements or the result of the use of an alternative type of material for tools. Paleoanthropologist Geoffrey Pope has proposed that the absence of hand axes in Asian collections may reflect a reliance on bamboo, which commonly grows in precisely the areas where hand axes are not represented (Pope 1989). Bamboo, a material that would make strong and durable tools, is unfortunately poorly preserved in archaeological contexts, making it difficult to evaluate its use.

Acheulean hand axes are very common on some archaeological sites, at times literally occurring by the hundreds (see photo of Olorgesailie, Kenya). This suggests that they were a handy tool to have around, but how were they actually used? Some hand axes measure six inches or so in length and could be conveniently hand held, but others are quite large, measuring over a foot from base to tip. Such large implements would seem to be very unwieldy. Experimental studies indicate that hand axes could have made excellent all-purpose tools, possibly fulfilling a variety of chopping, cutting, and butchering tasks. The battered edges on some hand axes are consistent with this type of use.

The first tools of materials other than stone are also contemporaneous with late Acheulean tools. The earliest spears date to 400,000 years ago. These lack any kind of stone tip and are simply wooden shafts with pointed ends (Schick and Toth 1993; Thieme 1997). While hand axes are superficially similar in appearance to gigantic arrowheads, their large size would have made it impractical to use them as spear points or stabbing weapons. Smaller, stone projectile points do not appear until much later. Given the time period represented, the preservation of wood is

The archaeological site of Olorgesailie, Kenya, one of the most informative Acheulean sites in Africa, dates to approximately 700,000–900,000 years ago. A walkway at the site allows visitors to view Paleolithic tools exposed on the surface. A cleaver or cutting tool is shown on the right.

Source: Courtesy of Pamela Willoughby, University of Alberta.

unlikely, and examples of spears are known from few sites. The most well-documented wooden spears were found at Clacton-on-Sea, England (circa 300,000 years old) and Schöningen, Germany (circa 400,000 years old); although they were not embedded in the bones of an animal, they may have been used for hunting. Artifacts made from materials other than stone include flaked pieces of bone and elephant ivory, some of which duplicate stone hand axes in form. Other non-lithic artifacts have been found, but these are generally nondescript and do not afford much insight into life during the Lower Paleolithic. As was pointed out in the discussion of early hominin tool use, implements of other materials were very likely used during this period, but they did not survive archaeologically.

Living Sites The archaeological sites of early genus *Homo* are associated with varied activities, including areas of possible tool manufacture, living areas, and butchering sites. Caves are particularly promising areas of investigation for archaeologists as such areas would have provided natural shelters. Some of the most significant *H. erectus* finds have been recovered from cave deposits, as is the case with the "Peking Man" finds discussed in Chapter 5. In addition, caves also may preserve deep, unbroken sequences of artifactual material. Yet, caves also present their own interpretive difficulties, representing a variety of animal activities and formation processes, as is the case with many of the South African caves associated with early hominin finds (discussed in Chapter 5).

Open-air *H. erectus* sites have also been the focus of archaeological research. In southern Europe, Torralba and Ambrona in Spain and Terra Amata on the French Riviera have produced large assemblages of tools, as well as possible evidence for structures that may shed light on the behaviors of the more recent *H. erectus* populations (de Lumley 1969; Laville et al. 1980; Villa 1983). Interpreting the Terra Amata finds, Henry de Lumley suggested they

may include evidence of simple shelters constructed over a framework of posts braced with rocks (see Figure 7.7). These sites have also provided important insights into diet and food procurement as discussed later.

Fire The ability to produce, or at least to manipulate fire may have been an important development for early members of genus *Homo*. The use of fire is particularly significant as it would have increased the variety of foods that could have been exploited, served as a means of protection, and as a source of warmth as *Homo erectus* migrated into colder climates. Although possible evidence for fire dates back as much as 1.5 million years ago, the earliest evidence is sometimes ambiguous. Some supposed hearths may be natural features or organic deposits, not traces of fire. On the other hand, even if the archaeological evidence for fire is indisputable, the question of whether it represents controlled use of fire by hominins is sometimes unclear.

The earliest evidence for the use of fire, dating back 1 million to 1.5 million years ago, comes from Africa, including the sites of Swartkrans in South Africa, Koobi Fora and Chesowanja in Kenya, and the site of Gadeb in Ethiopia. The evidence consists of deposits of baked earth, traces of charred organic material, and heated stone artifacts (Brain, C. K., 1981; Clark and Harris 1985; Alperson-Afil and Goren-Inbar, 2010). It is possible that natural occurrences of burning vegetation and brush fires might produce similar features. However, researchers have demonstrated that the evidence for heating is both more intense and more localized than it would be in the case of natural occurrences such as brush fires, but consistent with a hearth or fire pit. If this is, in fact, evidence for the use of fire, it would mean that early *H. erectus* populations had the use of fire when they first migrated out of Africa.

More recent evidence for the use of fire comes from the Lower Paleolithic Acheulean site of Gesher Benot Ya'aqov, Israel, initially occupied about 790,000 years ago. The site

Elephant tusks *in situ* at the site of Ambrona, Spain. The evidence from this site indicates the careful butchering of meat and a detailed knowledge of food resources.

is especially notable as the evidence is found throughout the site's 100,000 years of occupation. This suggests more than simply the use of fire, but the ability to control fire and, perhaps even make it (Alperson-Afil 2008). Other Acheulean sites have also produced evidence of fire. The cave site of Zhoukoudian, China, which yielded the remains of *H. erectus*, also preserved an array of animal bones and possibly traces of fire hearths dating roughly 500,000 to 240,000 years ago (Binford and Ho 1985; Weiner et al. 1998). The evidence for fire includes dark lenses of soil and charred animal bones. The latter provides the most compelling evidence and may suggest that meat was cooked or roasted. The dark soil stains may be indications of fire, but analysis has not confirmed if they are, in fact, wood ash.

Diet and Subsistence   The question of whether the early members of genus *Homo* were efficient hunters or proficient scavengers has remained a source of debate. As was the case with the earlier Oldowan material, there was an early assumption that the bones found at Acheulean sites reflected hominin hunting. Currently, however, the available evidence leaves the issue unresolved. The consensus is that the majority of bones in *H. erectus* sites likely do not represent hunting; in some instances, scavenging is clearly represented, and in others, the bones would appear to relate solely to carnivore activities. Definitive evidence for hunting does not appear until about 250,000 years ago in association with archaic or modern *Homo sapiens* (Villa et al. 2005).

While perhaps not representative of hunting, the recovered faunal remains do indicate an increasing

knowledge of food resources and the ability to exploit them. The sites of Ambrona and Torralba in Spain, dated to approximately 400,000 years ago, provide some of the most complete evidence of Lower Paleolithic activities. Located within sight of each other, the two sites have produced a wide assortment of animal remains, including horse, deer, wild ox, lion, hyena, and especially large numbers of elephant. There is clear evidence for butchering, using Acheulean tools over a long period of time. Given the large number of bones, the sites represent more than simply the opportunistic scavenging of carnivore kills, but rather reflect detailed knowledge of the opportunities for provisioning that this area offered. Hominins may have opportunistically preyed or scavenged animals that were trapped or died in the water (Schick and Toth 1993; Villa et al. 2005).

Beyond animal resources, several sites have provided clear evidence of the range of food resources exploited, although it is impossible to assess their relative importance. The availability of a wide variety of naturally occurring plant foods, such as berries, tubers, and fruits, makes it plausible that these things would have played an important role in hominin diets, and evidence has been recovered from a few sites. Excavations at the 790,000-year-old site of Gesher Benot Ya'aqov, Israel recovered a variety of organic remains, including nuts, fruits, and seeds (Melamed 1997). Similarly, the occupants of Terra Amata, France appeared to have enjoyed a varied diet, consuming such large animals as extinct species of deer, elephant, boar, rhinoceros, and wild ox, as well as oysters, mussels, limpets, and fish drawn from the Mediterranean. The relatively meager amount of seeds recovered archaeologically may reflect both poor preservation and the archaeological methodologies employed. While it is true that organic materials are often poorly preserved, specialized techniques that might recover traces of plant remains are not always employed. The evidence that is available serves to underscore the varied nature of the resources that hominins likely exploited.

The Middle Paleolithic

7.3 Describe the changes in the tool traditions that distinguish the Middle Paleolithic period and discuss the hominin species that may have produced them.

The Middle Paleolithic (beginning approximately 300,000 years ago), referred to as the *Middle Stone Age* in Africa, is the period of time associated with archaic *Homo sapiens* and the emergence of anatomically *H. sapiens*. It is followed by the Upper Paleolithic, or *Late Stone Age,* beginning approximately 50,000 years ago. Note, however, that these periods are separated on the basis of variations in tool types and manufacturing techniques; the chronological divisions used here are intended to provide only the crudest of guidelines. The actual appearance of characteristic Middle or Upper Paleolithic tools varies in different world areas and is often defined on the basis of differing characteristics. The earliest dated finds come from Africa and cluster between 200,000 and 300,000 years ago (McBrearty and Brooks, 2000). Yet, even here sites with Middle Stone Age industries have been dated both earlier and later.

The association of specific Middle Paleolithic tool traditions with specific hominin populations has also proven problematic. In some cases, tools defined as Middle Paleolithic have been associated with *H. erectus* remains, while in later contexts identical tools have been found with both archaic and modern *H. sapiens* (McBrearty and Brooks, 2000). Notably, evidence for the survival of *Homo sapiens neanderthalensis* has been extended up to just 30,000 years ago or less, clearly indicating coexistence with *Homo sapiens* for some time. The overlap of Middle Paleolithic industries with the Acheulean at one end and industries described as Upper Paleolithic on the other, as well as their association with varied hominin species, would appear to be inconsistent with a dramatic, "big bang" model of the emergence of anatomically modern humans and their culture (see the box "Could Early Hominins Speak? The Evolution of Language").

The archaeological record of the past 200,000 years becomes increasingly sophisticated and diverse. While the Acheulean finds are more evenly flaked and symmetrical than the crude Oldowan tools, they still represent a relatively small number of tool types that are remarkably uniform, almost repetitive, in appearance. In contrast to the relatively slow change in the Oldowan and Acheulean tool traditions during the preceding million years, the Middle Paleolithic displays greater complexity and an increasing array of local variation.

Changes in Technology and Subsistence

Percussion flaking gained greater refinement during the Middle Paleolithic. Tools consist of small flaked implements; the hand axes and large flakes that characterized the Acheulean disappear. Middle Paleolithic technological innovations can be illustrated by the **Levalloisian technique**. Using this method, the toolmaker first shaped a stone into a regular form or *core* by striking flakes off the exterior. Additional pieces were then struck off from one side to form a flat striking platform. From this prepared core, the toolmaker struck the edge to produce flakes that were fashioned into scrapers, points, and knives. The Levalloisian technique created longer cutting edges relative to the size of the stone, allowing for a more economical use of the stone. Tools were also more standardized and could be produced in less time than with earlier methods.

Regional innovations in stone tool technology can be seen in Middle Paleolithic finds throughout the world. The increasing amount of local variation reflects subtle changes in techniques and the raw materials used to make the tools, but it also likely indicates the varying needs of individuals adapting to different environments. In Africa, for example, there are a variety of innovations in tool technology during this period. These are extremely variable, making them difficult to define and to identify the earliest representative industries. Some of the most sophisticated Middle Stone Age (as the Middle Paleolithic is called in Africa) percussion-flaking techniques from Africa can be seen in material from the Kapthurin Formation Kenya, where Acheulean implements were replaced by Middle Stone Age artifacts more than 280,000 years ago (McBrearty and Tryon, 2006). The site reveals a trend away from larger, cruder forms to smaller, more carefully flaked implements such as small scrapers, shaped flakes, and points. Some archaeological evidence indicates that more refined tool kits may have facilitated the first settlement of portions of Africa that had not been extensively occupied earlier, including the arid northeastern regions (Clark 1970:107; Bailey et al. 1989). Similar trends toward smaller, more carefully flaked tools are found in other areas. In Europe and the Near East, the Middle Paleolithic includes sites associated with the Neandertals, the archaic *H. sapiens* who inhabited Europe prior to 30,000 years ago (discussed later).

During the Middle Paleolithic, fire hearths become common in the archaeological record and are found in sites ranging from Africa to Europe. The association of these features with hominin living areas is indisputable. Their regularity suggests that the manipulation of fire was well accomplished by these populations. As noted, this would have had important implications in terms of diet and food processing, as well as warmth and protection from animals.

Diet and Subsistence As is the case with earlier archaeological evidence, there is debate about how these refined tools were used, particularly with regard to the question of hunting or scavenging. The distribution of faunal remains, including the prevalence of bones from parts of animals that would more likely have been scavenged, suggests that the opportunistic scavenging of meat remained an important aspect of Middle Paleolithic subsistence. Yet, there is also unambiguous evidence for hunting. As noted, the first spears made their appearance at the end of the Lower Paleolithic, and they were likely an important weapon for Middle Paleolithic populations. At the Klasies River site in South Africa, a weapon tip was found embedded in the vertebra of a large buffalo, providing clear evidence for hunting (Singer and Wymer 1982). Some faunal remains from this site suggest that varied hunting strategies were employed with different species. Buffalo are represented by the bones of either very young or very old animals, suggesting that the weaker or slower were preyed on. On the other hand, eland are represented by the bones of large numbers of fit, adult animals. It has been suggested that this distribution may indicate that animals were killed in large numbers, perhaps by driving them off a cliff or trapping them.

Evidence from African finds also suggests the exploitation of a diversity of other resources. At the Klasies River site, shellfish are common in some of the living areas and were likely gathered. Fish bones also occur at Klasies and in other Middle Paleolithic African sites. Plant remains, possibly processed, are also represented in deposits from the Klasies site. The archaeological remains from sites near Katanda in the Republic of the Congo and at Blombos Cave in South Africa include possible bone projectile points and harpoons that could have been used for hunting or, in the case of the harpoons, for fishing (Yellen et al. 1995). Such varied evidence complements the ever-increasing variety seen in Middle Paleolithic stone tool assemblages in Africa and other parts of the world. Collectively, this information indicates more varied and sophisticated technological innovations likely geared toward the exploitation of specific regional food resources. These specialized adaptations to local conditions are illustrated by the Neandertals.

The Neandertals

Neandertals, the archaic *H. sapiens* who inhabited Europe and the Middle East between 200,000 and 30,000 years ago, are perhaps the quintessential representatives of the Middle Paleolithic. They fashioned implements whose versatility far surpassed earlier technologies. The Middle Paleolithic stone tool industry associated with Neandertal populations (also associated with anatomically modern *Homo sapiens* in some contexts) is known as the **Mousterian**, which is named after a rock shelter at Le Moustier, France, where it was first described. Produced by the Levalloisian technique, Mousterian implements could have been used for cutting, leather working, piercing, food processing, woodworking, hunting, and producing weapons (Binford and Binford 1966; Bordes 1968).

The Neandertals were probably the first human ancestors to adapt fully to the cold climates of northern Europe. Though direct evidence is lacking, their technology must have included the manufacture of at least rudimentary clothes; otherwise, they would not have survived the cold winters. These may have consisted of simple wraps or cloaks made of animal skins; no evidence for sewing exists until the Upper Paleolithic. Clues to Neandertal life have come from archaeological excavation caves and rock shelters, as well as open-air sites that may have served as temporary camps during the summer months. Archaeologists cite remains of charcoal deposits and charred bones as indications that Neandertals utilized fire not only for warmth, but also for cooking and, perhaps, for protection against dangerous animals.

There is evidence that the scavenging of carcasses killed by predators and the gathering of plant resources continued. But there is also evidence that the Neandertals were efficient hunters who stalked both small and large game, including such extinct creatures as European elephants, elk, bison, and huge bears that stood between 9 and 12 feet tall and weighed up to 1,500 pounds. Their lifestyle must have been carefully attuned to the seasonal resources available. In the cold climate of Ice Age Europe, the storage of food for the winter months was probably of great importance. Neandertals likely faced a hard life. The comparison of healed fractures found on Neandertal bones with those of other populations revealed similarities with one group in particular—modern rodeo riders. The skeletal remains of Neandertals indicate numerous examples of broken bones, particularly to the upper body. This may reflect the perils of hunting large animals at close range (Berger and Trinkaus 1995).

Neandertal Ritual Beliefs Study of Neandertal sites has also given archaeologists some of the most tantalizing hints of activities beyond hunting and gathering and the struggle for subsistence—possible evidence that Neandertals practiced rituals. Regrettably, much of this evidence, portrayed in countless movies, novels, and caricatures has been more circumstantial than archaeologists would like. Among the most notorious of the speculative discoveries are the cave bear bones found in association with Neandertal

Shanidar Cave in northern Iraq is the site of some of the most fascinating discoveries of Neandertal remains.
Source: Courtesy of Stafford Clarry.

artifacts in Drachenloch (Dragon's) Cave, Switzerland. Initially excavated by amateur archaeologist Emil Bächler between 1917 and 1921, the remains of a number of cave bear skulls were said to have been found in an arrangement of stone slabs—a discovery that was interpreted as a crude shrine. Some writers have used these discoveries to paint a complex picture of Neandertal rituals. Despite the romantic appeal of a Neandertal "cave bear cult," these interpretations lack the most important thing archaeologists need to glean insights into such complex issues as prehistoric ritual beliefs: clearly documented *archaeological context* (Chase and Dibble 1987; Tattersall, 1995; Trinkaus and Shipman 1994). The Drachenloch Cave finds were not excavated by trained archaeologists, and no plans or photographs of the discovery were made at the time of excavation (Rowley-Conwy 1993). Without this information, interpretation of a Neandertal shrine remains entirely speculative. In the absence of clear associations between the bear bones and the tools, this evidence suggests only that Neandertals visited a cave in which bears may have hibernated and occasionally died.

More convincing than the evidence for a bear cult are discoveries suggesting that Neandertals were the first hominins to intentionally bury their dead. Finds at a number of sites, including Shanidar, Iraq; Teshik-Tash, Uzbekistan; La Chapelle-aux-Saints, France; and Kebara, Israel have been interpreted as intentional burials (Solecki 1971; Rowley-Conwy 1993). Of these finds, the evidence for

burial is most compelling at the French and Israeli sites. In both instances, the skeleton of a Neandertal man was found in a pit that seems to be too regular in shape to have been formed naturally.

Other skeletal evidence suggests that Neandertals may have cared for individuals with disabilities. At the Shanidar site, for example, archaeologists identified the remains of one individual who had the use of only one arm, the result of an accident or a birth defect. Despite that disability, this individual lived a relatively long life. Although no set of ritual beliefs or social altruism can be definitely inferred on the basis of these finds, they do indicate the growing group communication, social complexity, and awareness that distinguish humans.

Modern *Homo sapiens* and Their Cultures

7.4 Describe the changes in the archaeological record that distinguish the Upper Paleolithic period and discuss what these technological changes may imply about the lives of early humans.

The archaeological record of the last 50,000 years is principally associated with anatomically modern *H. sapiens*. Between 50,000 and 10,000 years ago, human populations migrated throughout the globe, adapting both physically and culturally to conditions in disparate regions. Physically, these peoples resembled modern humans in most respects. Their fossilized skeletons do not have the heavy, thick bones, large teeth, and prominent brow ridges seen in archaic forms. The high, vaulted shape of their crania is modern, too, with dimensions similar to those of present-day humans. From the cold climates of northern Asia to the deserts of Africa, groups of *H. sapiens* shared similar characteristics as part of a single human species. Like modern populations, however, these early groups likely exhibited variation in physical traits, such as skin color, body build, and facial features that represent adaptations to local environmental conditions and selective pressures (see Chapter 6).

Archaeological sites associated with anatomically modern *H. sapiens* display a flowering of cultural expressions in everything from tool making and home building to social arrangements and subsistence strategies. If the Middle Paleolithic represents an impressive array of innovations compared to the Lower Paleolithic, the Upper Paleolithic is even more stunning in its appearance. Upper Paleolithic sites look dramatically different in terms of the richness and diversity of the material culture present and the variety of sites represented. The inhabitants of these varied settlements had highly efficient subsistence strategies that gave them free time for experimentation and innovation. This period witnessed the full development of Paleolithic art, as well as the expansion of humans into the Americas and Australia, continents that had previously been unoccupied by hominins.

The Material Record of *Homo sapiens*

Anatomically modern *H. sapiens* populations crafted increasingly complex tools and developed strategies suited to meet the needs of life in varied environments. These innovations are reflected in an array of different stone tool traditions. Whereas the Lower and Middle Paleolithic can be described in terms of a few tool industries and characteristic tools, Upper Paleolithic industries are represented by a myriad of different local and regional designations that reflect distinct local styles and tool kits. For example, European archaeologists divide the Upper Paleolithic period into the Chatelperronian, Aurignacian, Gravettian, Solutrean, and Magdalenian stone industries, with each encompassing tremendous variation in stone tool types. Stone tool production made a major technological advance with increasingly fine techniques for producing *blades* (long, narrow flakes that had uses as knives, harpoons, and spear points). Among the most striking examples of Upper Paleolithic percussion flaking are Solutrean projectile points, dated to 20,000 years ago. These implements, often measuring several inches long, probably functioned as spear points. Yet, the flaking is so delicate and the points so sharp that it is difficult to imagine them fastened to the end of a spear. Some researchers have ventured a guess that they may have been made as works of art, not tools for everyday use.

Upper Paleolithic peoples produced a number of specialized stone tools, such as *borers* (drills) and *burins* (chisel-like tools for working with bone or ivory). Tools like these facilitated the manufacture of the bone, antler, and ivory artifacts that became increasingly common during the Upper Paleolithic. Although the absence of artifacts of bone and ivory in earlier time periods may, in part, be the result of poorer preservation of organic materials in sites of greater antiquity, there is no question that Upper Paleolithic peoples became adept at working with a variety of materials. Upper Paleolithic sites have produced bone needles for sewing clothing, fibers for making rope, evidence of nets, and trapping equipment. This period is also distinguished by the increasing evidence for **composite tools**,

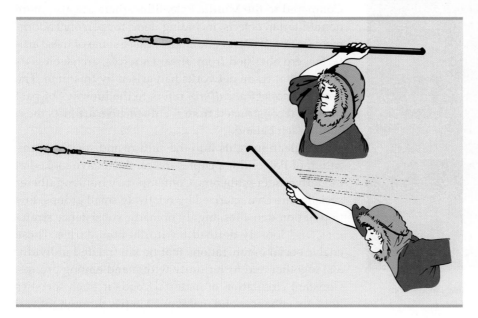

Figure 7.6 An innovation of the Upper Paleolithic was the spear thrower, or atlatl, a device that extended the hunter's arm, enabling him to make a more powerful throw.

implements fashioned from several pieces. For example, consider the harpoon, which might consist of a wooden shaft slotted for the insertion of sharp stone flakes, and a detachable point. Spear throwers, or *atlatls*, that extended the reach of the hunter's arm were invented during this period, too. A particularly important innovation, these long, thin pieces of wood or ivory enabled Upper Paleolithic hunters to hurl projectiles much faster than they could by hand.

Diet and Subsistence Upper Paleolithic technology indicates that early *H. sapiens* were efficient hunters. Many archaeological sites contain bones from mammoths, giant deer, musk ox, reindeer, steppe bison, and other animals. In addition, piles of animal bones have been discovered at the bottom of high cliffs. In reconstructing the meaning of these finds, archaeologists conjecture that *H. sapiens* hunters stampeded the animals off cliffs to be killed and butchered by waiting hunters below. Archaeologists have also found the remains of traps that Upper Paleolithic hunters used to snare animals. Upper Paleolithic people gathered plants to supplement their diet and probably to use for medicinal purposes. However, because of the small size of Upper Paleolithic living areas and the limited amount of plant remains recovered from archaeological sites, we can sketch only an incomplete picture of diet. Given the technological innovations noted, however, it might be inferred that the exploitation of varied resources in diverse environments became increasingly efficient.

Shelters In the Upper Paleolithic period, technology clearly advanced to the point where people were proficient at building shelters, some quite elaborate. These structures have earlier counterparts, such as those in the Lower

Reconstruction of an Upper Paleolithic tent dwellings made from animal skins based on evidence from Dordogne, France.

Paleolithic at Terra Amata, discussed previously. During the Upper Paleolithic, however, evidence for reuse and indications of longer settlement occupation become more commonplace. Among the more spectacular are five shelters from a 15,000-year-old site at Mezhirich in Ukraine, constructed from bones of mammoths, an extinct species of elephant (Gladkih et al. 1984). The mammoths' jaws formed the shelter's base, and ribs, tusks, and other bones were used for the sides. Inside, archaeologists discovered work areas, hearths, and accumulations of artifacts. Storage pits located between the structures indicate that the shelters were inhabited for long periods. Scientists speculate that the settlement may have been occupied by more than 50 people.

Ethnicity and Social Organization

Advances in tool making took different forms around the world. Some of this regional variation stemmed from specialized technologies suited to particular environments; in other cases, tool-making technology was driven by the specific types of stone available in a region. Yet regional differences may also reflect something more: patterns of culture, ethnicity, and individual expression. Archaeologist James Sackett (1982), who studied the classic Middle and Upper Paleolithic finds in France, notes that tools serving the same function seem to exhibit a great deal of variation. Many Upper Paleolithic artisans fashioned their stone tools in distinctive styles that vary from region to region, possibly signaling the first traces of ethnic and cultural divisions in human populations. Just as we often associate particular styles in dress, decoration, and housing with specific ethnic groups, archaeologists rely on expressions of ethnic identity preserved in material remains to piece together the lifestyles of earlier peoples. A sense of imagination comes through in Upper Paleolithic artifacts as well. Compared to the Middle Paleolithic, there are also more nonutilitarian objects, including items for personal adornment (White 1982). In addition, because some of these artifacts were obtained from distant sources, archaeologists believe that trade networks had arisen by this time. The term *archaeological cultures* refers to the lifeways of past peoples reconstructed from the distinctive artifacts these cultures left behind.

To glean insights into the culture and social organization of Paleolithic peoples, researchers have looked at modern hunter-gatherers. Contemporary hunter-gatherer societies are characterized by relatively small groups, low population densities, highly nomadic subsistence strategies, and loosely defined territorial boundaries. These enable social organizations that tie kin (related individuals) together and foster unity within and among groups. Constant circulation of material goods in such societies not only enhances and maintains kin ties through mutual obligations, but also inhibits the accumulation of wealth by any individual in the society. This enables these societies to remain *egalitarian*; they have very small differences in wealth among individuals. People of the same sex, age, and capabilities have the same access to goods and authority in these types of societies.

The most common form of political organization among ethnographically documented hunter-gatherer societies is the **band**, a fairly small group of people tied together by close kinship relations. A band is the least complex form of political system and most likely the oldest. Each band is politically independent of the others and has its own internal leadership. Most of the leaders in the bands are males, but females also take some important leadership roles. Leaders are chosen because of their skills in hunting, food collecting, communication, decision making, or other personal abilities. Political leaders, however, generally do not control the group's economic resources or exercise political power as they do in other societies, and there is little, if any, social stratification between political leaders and others in the band. Because band societies are highly egalitarian, with no fundamental differences between those with, and those without, wealth or political power, leaders of bands must lead by persuasion and personal influence rather than by coercion or withholding resources. Leaders do not maintain a military or police force and, thus, have no definitive authority.

Although it is tempting to draw a similar picture of Paleolithic hunters, the analogy is not without limitations. The archaeological record of the Paleolithic is consistent with small kin-based groups. Yet, archaeological information on Paleolithic hunter-gatherers suggests that their subsistence strategies varied substantially and probably included the beginnings of some of the complexity, socioeconomic inequality, and more sedentary lifestyles that characterize more recent periods (Price and Brown 1985).

Upper Paleolithic Art

In addition to their other technological accomplishments, Upper Paleolithic peoples created an impressive array of artwork, including paintings, incised carving, three-dimensional sculptures, jewelry, and a variety of nonutilitarian objects. Possible evidence for art has been recovered from earlier Lower and Middle Paleolithic contacts. While tentative, the findings are suggestive of later developments. In particular, beads and other ornaments occur in sites dating back 130,000 years (McBrearty and Brooks, 2000:521–528). Incisions on bone and the use of pigment on artifacts may also suggest aesthetic sensibilities (Cain 2006; Tyron and

McBrearty 2002). A possible female figurine associated with Acheulean artifacts was found at the Berekhat site in the Golan Heights (d'Erico and Nowell 2000). While it is debatable if the stone represents a female figure or a naturally shaped stone, the artifact does possess three incised lines which clearly indicate at least some human modification.

A variety of possible examples of similar art objects have been noted in other Middle Paleolithic contexts. It is, however, only during the Upper Paleolithic or Late Stone Age that such items become common, and they are sometimes striking in nature. These include sculptures in bone, ivory, and stone found throughout Europe that depict human and animal figures. Among the most notable of these finds are female figures, speculatively dubbed "Venus" figurines (see Figure 7.7). Rock paintings, done with mineral pigments such as ochre, also appear. Magnificent abstract and naturalistic renderings of animals and humans dressed in the hides of animals decorate the walls of caves in Spain and France. These murals, or cave paintings, may have been drawn to celebrate a successful hunt or to ensure a better future. Because some of them are located deep in underground caves, researchers have speculated that this art held profound spiritual and religious significance, possibly having figured in to religious ceremonies. Yet their purpose is difficult to determine. It is possible that these evocative cave murals could have been painted solely as an expression of the artist's (or artists') view of life (Halverson 1987).

Upper Paleolithic burial

Figure 7.7 The archeological record of the Upper Paleolithic becomes progressively more elaborate, including more sophisticated stone tools and nonutilitarian items such as those pictured here. The large projectile point at left is a Solutrean laurel leaf spear point. The two female figures at top are examples of Venus figurines.

Source: W. J. Sollas, *Ancient Hunters and their Modern Representatives*, Macmillan, 1911.

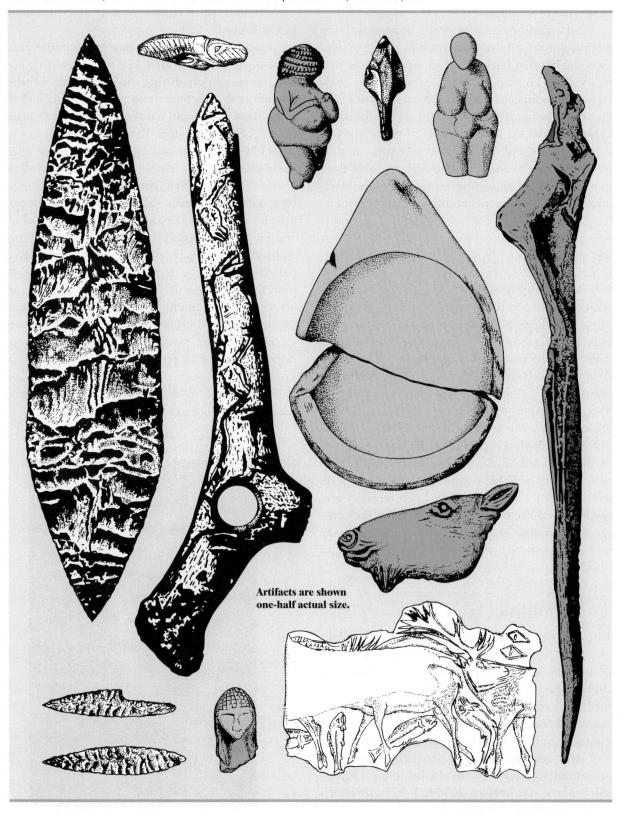

Artifacts are shown one-half actual size.

The Migration of Upper Paleolithic Humans

7.5 Discuss the contrasting theories regarding the initial human settlement of the Americas and the archaeological evidence that supports or refutes each perspective.

Upper Paleolithic hunter-gatherers developed specialized technologies that allowed them to adapt to diverse environments in ways their precursors could not have imagined. Efficient subsistence strategies and varied tool kits facilitated adaptations to varied climatic and environmental conditions, including the frigid north. It is also likely that simple watercraft, such as dugout canoes, aided in the expansion of anatomically modern *Homo sapiens* out of Africa and the first settlement of some areas, such as the Indian Ocean rim, Australia, and the Americas. At home in such a wide variety of environments, *H. sapiens* Upper Paleolithic populations occupied the entire globe, including areas such as North and South America and Australia that had never before been occupied by hominins.

The movement of Upper Paleolithic populations was also helped by changes in world climatic conditions during the past 100,000 years. During the latter part of the Pleistocene, or Ice Age (see Chapter 3, Table 3.1), when climatic conditions were much cooler and wetter than they are now, the northern regions of Asia, North America, and Europe were covered by huge sheets of ice, or glaciers, that extended from the polar ice caps. The vast amount of water frozen in these glaciers lowered sea levels around the world by hundreds of feet, exposing vast tracts of land, known as *continental shelves*, that were previously (and are still) beneath the sea. Many regions of the world surrounded by water today were connected to other land areas when these low-lying landmasses were exposed by lower water levels. These "land bridges" allowed *H. sapiens* to migrate from one region to another over land that is now covered by seawater.

Upper Paleolithic Hunters in the Americas

A variety of information indicates that the first humans came to the Americas from Asia. Physical similarities between Asians and Native Americans, bolstered by genetic and linguistic data, clearly establish the Asian origin of Native American populations (Ward 1999). Some researchers have suggested that the data are indicative of three waves of migration. Linguist Joseph Greenberg (1986) divided Native American languages into three broad groups: Aleut-Eskimo, Na-Dene, and Amerind. He

further suggested that these linguistic groups represent three migrations from Asia. Because Amerind is the most widespread and linguistically diversified, Greenberg contends that it has had more time to evolve and is the earliest wave. Aleut-Eskimo, in contrast, is confined to a comparatively small number of Native American groups, an indication that these are the most recent arrivals. The Na-Dene speakers are representative of the intermediating migration. Some researchers have suggested that the data can be explained by a single migration, an interpretation supported by the relatively limited genetic variation among widely dispersed Native American populations.

Although most anthropologists agree that the primary settlement of the Americas was by Asian populations, there has been a great deal of disagreement about precisely how and when this took place. The theory that has predominated for some time hypothesizes a land migration from Siberia into modern Alaska over a low-lying land bridge that is now the Bering Strait. Today, the Bering Strait is a frigid body of water connecting the Pacific and Arctic Oceans. Between 75,000 and 10,000 years ago, however, glaciers lowered sea levels worldwide and exposed areas that are today covered with water. The Bering Strait was transformed into a landmass, known as Beringia that was more than 1,000 miles wide (Hopkins 1982). Recent studies of sediment cores recovered from the now-sunken landmass indicate that Beringia was a region that would have been very habitable to migrating humans (Hoffecker et al. 2014). Upper Paleolithic hunters

Figure 7.8 Migration routes to the Americas: (a) Many theories have suggested initial human migration from Asia via exposed land in Beringia (now the Bering Strait) and south through ice-free corridors into North and South America; (b) more recent interpretations have suggested that settlement could have occurred along the coast using watercraft.

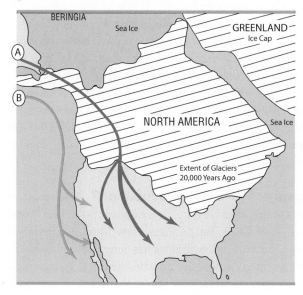

would have moved across Canada southward through an ice-free corridor between the glaciated areas into North and South America.

Alternatively, more recent theories have suggested that initial settlement could have been by sea. As will be discussed later, the first human settlers of regions such as the island continent of Australia must have arrived via watercraft approximately 40,000 years ago. Additional data further suggest that watercraft of some kind, the ability to carry drinking water, and reliance on coastal marine resources may have been well established in areas such as the Indian Ocean rim and the coast of southeast Asia by 75,000 years ago (Bulbeck 2007). Therefore, the possibility that the Americas were initially settled by people using simple watercraft during a similar time period is not improbable. In this model, Upper Paleolithic populations would have skirted along the coasts of what is now Siberia, Alaska, and western Canada, southward into the remainder of North and South America. The exposure of Beringia to lower sea levels and an ice-free corridor that are required for land migration would not be necessary.

If there has been debate about the "how" of human arrival in the Americas, the question of "when" has been even more contentious. This question is one that could be resolved by archaeological data. Unfortunately, the available archaeological data is often limited and its evaluation challenging. Relevant sites have proven difficult if not impossible to locate. Beringia and areas of the coast that may have been exposed during the Ice Age and may have been visited by Upper Paleolithic settlers are now beneath the sea, and critical areas of the land route were glaciated. In this context, it is also worth noting that any archaeological sites associated with these early arrivals are likely very insubstantial. Human populations likely traveled in small, migratory bands (whether by land or sea) and their sites would have limited visibility. While locating sites in these settings is not impossible, it is certainly challenging.

In considering the timing of human settlement of the Americas, researchers have embraced one of two major perspectives concerning the peopling of the Americas: the Clovis-first hypothesis and the pre-Clovis hypothesis. The **Clovis-first hypothesis** holds that the first humans arrived in the Americas about 12,000 years ago. The **pre-Clovis hypothesis** pegs this migration at a much earlier date, perhaps 30,000 to 40,000 years ago.

Clovis or Pre-Clovis Occupation? The term *Clovis* refers to a distinctive type of stone spear point first found at Blackwater Draw, near Clovis, New Mexico. Clovis spear points, measuring several inches long, have flaked channels, or *flutes*, down the middle, which may have made them easier to attach to the spear shaft. Clovis points have been recovered from across North America and are

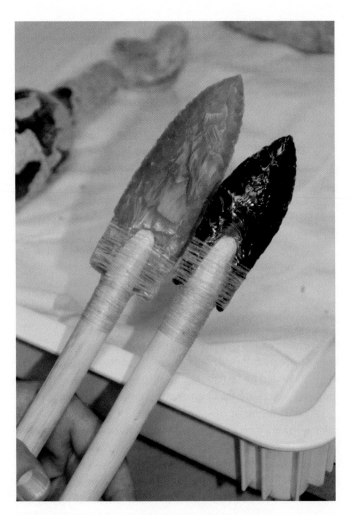

Clovis spear points shown as the may have been attached to spear shafts.

closely dated to between about 11,200 and 10,900 years ago (Haynes 1991). Clovis artifacts clearly establish the human settlement of America after 12,000 years ago. In the Clovis-first hypothesis, these tools are interpreted as the work of Paleo-Indians, the first migrants to enter North America from Asia. They are presumed to have arrived in the Canadian Yukon approximately 12,000 years ago, a figure based on estimates of how long it would have taken migratory hunters to reach the Clovis sites identified in the United States. The Clovis people, in turn, gave rise to later Native American cultures. The Clovis-first hypothesis was the most commonly accepted view of the Upper Paleolithic settlement of the Americas for most of the twentieth century.

In the past two decades, the pre-Clovis hypothesis that humans inhabited the Americas earlier than 12,000 years ago has gained increasing support. Archaeologists questioned the rapid spread of early Paleo-Indian cultures throughout the Americas that the Clovis-first hypothesis required. Could humans have migrated from Alaska and put down roots in such disparate areas as Maine and the southernmost tip of South America in a relatively short period of 1,000 or 2,000 years? Some studies suggested that the rate of migration proposed by Clovis-first proponents is unrealistically fast (Whitley and Dorn 1993). The

Researchers examining the Monte Verde site in Chile, which was very important in demonstrating the pre-Clovis settlement of the Americas.

problem the proponents of the pre-Clovis hypothesis faced was the lack of well-dated, pre-Clovis archaeological sites.

Debate over the pre-Clovis occupation of the Americas has focused on two key criteria: (1) clear indication of human occupation and (2) accurate dates of over 12,000 years ago (Dillehay and Meltzer 1991; Meltzer 1993; Taylor 1995). Although a number of archaeological sites in North and South America had been dated to between 12,000 and 40,000 years ago, their interpretation and ages were frequently seen as debatable, and they were not generally accepted as evidence of pre-Clovis settlement. This has, however, changed, and an increasing number of sites indicate pre-Clovis occupation. Two sites serve to illustrate the types of finds represented: the Meadowcroft Rockshelter, near Pittsburgh, Pennsylvania, and Monte Verde in Chile.

Excavations at the Meadowcroft Rockshelter were undertaken by archaeologist James Adovasio over a period of six years (Adovasio and Page 2002). The site recovered Paleo-Indian tools dated to 14,500 years ago, 3,000 to 4,000 years before Clovis; deeper levels produced even earlier dates of 19,000 years ago. Although this would seem to present evidence of pre-Clovis occupations, a number of criticisms were raised regarding the proposed age of the site. One of these was that the material used for carbon-14 dating was contaminated by disturbance or mixed with older, geological carbon. The possibility of contamination is always a concern in archaeological research, but this seems unlikely given the careful field methods used in the excavation of the site. Of more concern is the limited artifactual evidence associated with the oldest dates; the

Paleo-Indian bison kill in the western United States. Early humans in North America probably depended on a wide variety of plants and animals. Kill sites such as these, however, suggest at least a partial reliance on large animals.

earliest is a fragment of bark that the excavators believe was trimmed to make a basket. While an important site, the excavations provided less compelling evidence than some researchers would like of pre-Clovis occupation.

An exciting pre-Clovis site from South America was discovered in Monte Verde, Monte Verde, Chile. It has been the focus of research by archaeologist Tom Dillehay (2000) since 1976. Because of the moist soil in the area, preservation is much better than is generally seen at other Paleo-Indian sites. Dillehay found the remains of 42 plants and the bones of rodents, fish, and larger animals that had been hunted by human settlers, as well as flaked stone tools. There were also traces of a row of huts, built of wooden frames with hide coverings, which may have housed between 30 and 50 people. Some of the stone tools had been brought from 60 miles away. Most significant of all, radiocarbon dating has established the age of the Monte Verde artifacts at between 12,000 and 13,000 years ago. Subsequent excavations of simpler stone tools from earlier strata may push this date back beyond 30,000 years ago.

Information from sites such as the Meadowcroft Rockshelter and Monte Verde has cast increasing doubt on the Clovis-first scenario. Settlement of the Americas by small migratory groups at least 17,000 years ago is likely, a period that is consistent with at least some of the information suggested by mitochondrial DNA and other genetic dating (Ward 1999; Seielstad et al. 2003). It is possible that settlement by small groups occurred earlier, but their presence on the landscape was limited and so their archaeological traces are ephemeral.

Homo sapiens in Asia, Australia, and Oceania

The occupation of Asia by hominins extends back several hundred thousand years, as we saw with the discoveries of *H. erectus* in Indonesia and China. But this settlement did not extend to Japan, Australia, Tasmania, or the islands of the Pacific; instead, these areas began to be populated only during the Upper Paleolithic with the advent of *H. sapiens*.

Like the settlement of the Americas, the date of the first arrival of human populations in Japan is still an open question. Lower sea levels during the Pleistocene produced expanses of dry land linking Japan to the Asian mainland and allowed migration. Yet, few early sites have been located. Archaeologists excavating at Fukui Cave in northern Kyushu have discovered several stone tools and flakes dated to more than 31,000 years ago (Aikens and Higuchi 1981).

The Initial Settlement of New Guinea and Australia Archaeological research pins the earliest human settlement in Australia to 50,000 years

The Moai statues of Easter Island dated between 1250 and 1500 A.D. represent an organized labor project by a well-developed society in the Pacific Islands.

ago, perhaps somewhat earlier. At that time, Australia was connected by a continental shelf to New Guinea, but there were no land bridges between the Australia–New Guinea landmass and the Southeast Asia mainland. Scientists, therefore, speculate that the first humans arrived in Australia by simple rafts or boats, but to date no evidence of these vessels has been uncovered. There are signs of human occupation by 35,000 to 40,000 years ago over most of the continent, with the possible exception of Australia's central desert (White and O'Connell 1982; White 1993). The earliest finds from the island of Tasmania, located south of Australia, are somewhat more recent, dating to between 30,000 and 35,000 years ago.

On the basis of stone tool industries and skeletal remains, some Australian archaeologists have postulated that the continent was settled by two waves of immigrants. The earliest of the arrivals are represented by the finds at Bobongara on New Guinea's Huon Peninsula, dated to about 45,000 years ago. The diagnostic stone tools at this site consist of crude axes, weighing 4 to 5 pounds that were made by striking large, irregular flakes off river cobbles (White 1993).

The Bobongara finds can be contrasted with later tools (dated after about 26,000 years ago) from sites such as Nawamoyn and Malangangerr in northern Australia and Nombe in the New Guinea highlands. Some of the stone tools from these sites were partly shaped by grinding the edges against other stones. As will be seen in Chapter 8, this *ground stone technique* does not become common in other world areas for another 10,000 years. Citing these discoveries, some researchers have argued that these different stone tool technologies might represent other immigrant populations.

Searching for support of this theory, researchers have turned to physical anthropology and skeletons of early Australians. The earliest human remains in Australia, dating back some 20,000 years, come from Lake Mungo in the southeastern interior of the continent. The skulls of the two individuals represented are described as delicate. They have frequently been contrasted with finds at another site, Kow Swamp, which dates somewhat later. Scientists have identified more than 40 burials at Kow Swamp, and compared to the Lake Mungo remains, the skulls are generally heavier and have sloping foreheads. On the basis of these differences, some researchers postulate that these remains reflect two different migratory populations. This view can only be classified as highly speculative, however, since the Lake Mungo remains represent only two individuals. The two collections do share many similarities, and perhaps if more individuals had been found at Lake Mungo, they might appear to be closer in heritage (Habgood 1985).

Pacific Frontiers The Pacific Islands, or Oceania, were the last great frontier of human habitation. The Pacific Ocean covers one-third of the earth's surface, broken only occasionally by islands and coral reefs. The islands, spread over thousands of miles, are usually divided into three groups: Melanesia, which includes the smaller islands immediately north and east of Australia; Micronesia, which is farther north and includes the islands of Guam, Naura, Marshall, and Gilbert; and Polynesia, which includes widely scattered islands such as Tahiti, Hawaii, and Easter Island east of the preceding groups. The achievements of the early settlers of these regions are all the more remarkable considering that many of the islands are not visible from other bodies of land. Nevertheless, humans had settled hundreds of the islands long before the arrival of the first European mariners in the sixteenth century.

Not surprisingly, the earliest evidence for human settlement comes from the larger islands of Melanesia, closer to New Guinea. Archaeological evidence from the Bismarck and Solomon Islands places the first evidence for human occupation at about 30,000 years ago. Like the early settlements of New Guinea and Australia, this evidence consists of stone tools associated with hunting-and-gathering adaptations. The settlement of the smaller islands of Melanesia, as well as those of Micronesia and Polynesia, was substantially later, perhaps beginning no more than 3,000 or 4,000 years ago (Irwin 1993). These settlers were farmers who brought domesticated animals and root crops with them (see). They also brought pottery and a shell tool technology.

Summary and Review of Learning Objectives

7.1 Discuss the sources of information on early hominin behavior and the challenges archaeologists face when interpreting the behaviors and lifestyles of the oldest hominins.

The behaviors and lifestyles of the earliest hominins are challenging to interpret, as their appearance in the fossil record long predates the first archaeological clues. The oldest archaeological sites and first indications of stone tool use date back only about 3.5 million years, perhaps 6 million or 7 million years after the emergence of our earliest hominin ancestors. In addition, the fossil localities where the oldest hominins have been found probably do not represent living sites or activities areas, but rather places where hominins were naturally buried and preserved. To glean some insight, researchers have turned to the behaviors of modern nonhuman primates, which may

offer some insights into the range of early hominin behavior and provide a potential means of modeling early hominin activities. Critics, however, have cautioned against taking primate models of early hominin behavior too far, as the behavior of these creatures was likely quite different from that of humans and other living primates. After about 3.5 million years ago, the archaeological record provides more information on early hominin behavior, including the tools they made, the fossilized bones of the animals they ate, and the living sites they left behind.

7.2 Describe how the behavior of *Homo erectus* and the earliest representatives of genus *Homo* differed from that of earlier hominins.

In contrast to the earliest hominins, the activities of later hominin species—including *H. erectus*, the species that precedes *H. sapiens*—are more readily identifiable.

Evidence for *Homo erectus* behavior includes Acheulean tool technology, characterized by hand axes, as well as the first wooden spears and flaked pieces of bone and elephant ivory. Archaeological sites associated with *H. erectus* represent varied activities, including areas of possible tool manufacture, living areas, and butchering sites. *H. erectus* archaeological finds have been recovered from both cave deposits and open-air sites, while evidence for the first simple structures is associated with more recent *H. erectus* populations. The ability to produce, or at least to manipulate fire may have been an important development for early members of genus *Homo*. This is particularly significant as the use of fire would have increased the variety of foods that could have been exploited, served as a means of protection, and as a source of warmth. Although bones of a variety of animals are found at sites associated with *H. erectus*, the majority likely do not represent hunting; in some instances, scavenging or carnivore activity is clearly represented. Yet, while perhaps not representative of hunting, the recovered remains indicate an increasing knowledge of food resources and the ability to exploit them. Beyond animal resources, evidence suggests that *H. erectus* exploited a variety of other naturally occurring food resources such as shellfish, nuts and berries. The development of more elaborate stone tools, simple shelters, and the use of fire, as well as the ability to exploit varied food resources likely facilitated the movement of *H. erectus* out of Africa into other world areas.

7.3 Describe the changes in the tool traditions that distinguish the Middle Paleolithic period and discuss the hominin species that may have produced them.

The Middle Paleolithic, beginning approximately 300,000 years ago, is the period of time associated with archaic *Homo sapiens* and the emergence of anatomically *H. sapiens*. It is followed by the Upper Paleolithic, beginning approximately 50,000 years ago. These periods, however, represent variations in tool types and manufacturing techniques; the chronological divisions provide only the crudest of guidelines. The first appearance of both Middle and Upper Paleolithic tools varies in different world areas. The earliest Middle Paleolithic tools come from Africa, where the earliest dates cluster between 200,000 and 300,000 years ago. Yet, even here dated sites with Middle Stone Age industries vary widely in age. Middle Paleolithic tool traditions are also associated with different hominin populations. In some cases, tools defined as Middle Paleolithic have been found with *H. erectus* remains, while in later contexts identical tools have been found in association with both archaic and modern *H. sapiens*. Compared to the preceding Lower Paleolithic period, the archaeological record of the Middle Paleolithic is increasingly sophisticated and diverse. The technological innovations

can be illustrated by the Levalloisian technique. Using this method, the toolmaker first shaped a stone into a regular form or *core* by striking flakes off the exterior. Additional pieces were then struck off from one side to form a flat striking platform. This technique created longer cutting edges relative to the size of the stone, allowing for a more economical use of the stone, the efficient production of scrapers, projectile points, and knives. Regional innovations in stone tool technology can be seen in Middle Paleolithic finds throughout the world. The increasing amount of local variation reflects subtle variation in techniques and the raw materials used to make the tools, but it also likely indicates the varying needs of individuals adapting to different environments.

7.4 Describe the changes in the archaeological record that distinguish the Upper Paleolithic period and discuss what these technological changes may imply about the lives of early humans.

The Upper Paleolithic is the period of time primarily associated with anatomically modern *Homo sapiens*. It can be dated to between 50,000 and 10,000 years ago, though the distinctive artifacts represented have been dated substantially earlier in some areas, particularly Africa. Upper Paleolithic sites look dramatically different in terms of the richness and diversity of the material culture present and the variety of sites represented. Regional stone tool industries reflect increasingly specialized adaptations to local environmental conditions, but may also hint at ethnic and cultural differences. There is also increased evidence for tools made of bone, ivory and wood, including the first evidence for bone needles. These artifacts indicate that early *H. sapiens* were efficient hunters. Many archaeological sites contain bones from mammoths, giant deer, musk ox, reindeer, steppe bison, and other animals. People also gathered plants to supplement their diet and probably for medicinal purposes. Upper Paleolithic sites also include a variety of shelters, some quite elaborate. The Upper Paleolithic witnessed a dramatic increase in the amount of nonutilitarian artifacts, such as necklaces, pendants and full development of Paleolithic art. This efficient and varied tool kit facilitated the expansion of humans into the Americas and Australia, continents that had previously been unoccupied by hominins.

7.5 Discuss the contrasting theories regarding the initial human settlement of the Americas and the archaeological evidence that supports or refutes each perspective.

A great deal of evidence indicates that the Americas were settled by anatomically modern *Homo sapiens* migrating from Asia. Yet, archaeological information on these migrations remains scanty, leading to disagreements about precisely when and how they occurred. Land migration via a land bridge in the area of the modern-day Bering Sea has long been favored, but movement along the Pacific Rim and down the western coasts of North and South America using simple watercraft is being increasingly considered as a means of population movement. Two major perspectives concerning the peopling of the Americas can be outlined: the Clovis-first hypothesis and the pre-Clovis hypothesis. The term *Clovis* refers to a distinctive type of stone spear point first found near Clovis, New Mexico. Clovis artifacts clearly demonstrate human settlement across North America, and are closely dated to between 11,200 and 10,900 years ago. In the Clovis-first hypothesis, these tools are interpreted as the work of Paleo-Indians—the first migrants to enter North America from Asia. They are presumed to have arrived in the Canadian Yukon via the Bering Land Bridge and, in turn, gave rise to later Native American cultures. The Clovis-first hypothesis was the most commonly accepted view of the Upper Paleolithic settlement of the Americas for most of the twentieth century. The pre-Clovis hypothesis pegs initial human settlement at a much earlier date, perhaps 30,000 to 40,000 years ago. Debate over the pre-Clovis occupation of the Americas has focused on demonstrating clear and well-dated evidence of human occupation. Although a number of archaeological sites in North and South America have been dated to between 12,000 and 40,000 years ago, their interpretation and ages were debated and they were not generally accepted as evidence of pre-Clovis settlement. This has, however, changed, and an increasing number of sites indicate pre-Clovis occupation.

Key Terms

Acheulean industry, p. 152
band, p. 161
Clovis-first hypothesis, p. 164
composite tools cut marks, p. 159
endocasts, p. 150

experimental studies, p. 147
Levalloisian technique, p. 156
Lower Paleolithic, p. 144
Middle Paleolithic, p. 144
Mousterian, p. 157

Oldowan industry, p. 146
percussion flaking, p. 146
pre-Clovis hypothesis, p. 164
Upper Paleolithic, p. 144
use-wear and residue studies, p. 147

Chapter 8
The Origins of Domestication and Settled Life

Chapter Outline

Learning Objectives

After reading this chapter you should be able to:

8.1 Discuss the changes that characterize the Epipaleolithic, Mesolithic, and Archaic and how these periods can be seen as laying the foundation for domestication.

8.2 Explain what transformations in human subsistence and culture are implied by the term "Neolithic."

8.3 Compare and contrast theories of agricultural origins.

8.4 Review domestication in various world areas, and discuss how these transformations were different.

8.5 List and discuss the major consequences of domestication for prehistoric peoples.

During the past 50,000 years, humans have undergone minimal changes in their physical characteristics. As seen in Chapter 6, modern human populations are the product of a tremendous amount of gene exchange, and certainly no population has become so genetically isolated as to constitute a separate species. In contrast, human cultural and technological adaptations have grown substantially more sophisticated. The most significant of these shifts relates to *subsistence*, the manner in which humans obtain food and nourishment. As discussed in the previous chapter, Upper Paleolithic populations were probably relatively mobile, *nomadic* people who hunted migratory herd animals and gathered other naturally occurring plant and animal resources. These hunter-gatherers drew extensively from their environment, but likely made limited effort to alter or modify it intentionally. This pattern gradually changed. People started to explore new subsistence strategies and to experiment with growing plants and breeding animals for food. This culminated with a shift from hunting and gathering to *food production*. People no longer relied on naturally occurring food resources; rather, they grew and raised the food they needed.

The end of the Pleistocene epoch, approximately 12,000 years ago, was a period of environmental change. Climatic conditions became warmer, marking the transition to the Holocene, the current geological epoch. Rather than moving around in pursuit of large animals, humans started to make more intensive use of smaller game animals and wild plants within localized areas. The fishing and the gathering of marine resources also yielded valuable food sources as people became less mobile and increasingly focused their energies on the exploitation of plants and animals within particular regional environments. This change, reflected in new technologies and alterations in the archaeological record, occurred at different times in different world areas. Archaeologists refer to the period marking this shift to broad-spectrum, collecting subsistence strategies variously as the Epipaleolithic, Mesolithic, or Archaic. In time, people also started to experiment with planting crops and raising wild animals in captivity, practices that set the stage for one of the most dramatic changes in human history: the beginning of food production. This transformation is generally referred to as the **Neolithic**. Within a remarkably short period of time—10,000 years—most human populations went from relying on hunted and gathered resources to foods they grew and raised themselves. This chapter explores the how and why of this exciting transformation.

The End of the Paleolithic: Changes in Climate and Culture

8.1 Discuss the changes that characterize the Epipaleolithic, Mesolithic, and Archaic and how these periods can be seen as laying the foundation for domestication.

Between the late Pleistocene and the early Holocene (see Table 3.1 in Chapter 3 on page 62), the gradual warming of the Earth's temperature caused the great glaciers of the Pleistocene to melt. Sea levels rose in coastal areas, and lands that had been compressed under the glaciers rose. Landmasses, such as Beringia and portions of the continental shelves that had facilitated the human settlement of the Americas and Australia, were now covered with water. As the Earth's climate changed, many species of plants and animals became extinct. For example, Pleistocene megafauna like the mammoth and the mastodon disappeared. Yet others adapted to the new conditions and even expanded in the new environments. As the ice sheets melted in North America, Europe, and Asia, thick forests replaced the *tundra*, the vast treeless plains of the Arctic regions. These climatic changes enabled human populations to live in northern areas that previously had been uninhabitable.

The reshaping of the Earth's environment prompted new patterns of technological development. As large game became extinct in Europe and North America, for example, humans increasingly relied upon smaller game, fish, and gathered plants to satisfy nutritional needs in a strategy that represented a subtle change to a focus on a wider subsistence base and a more intensive exploitation of localized resources. This is referred to as **broad-spectrum collecting**. Because of variation in local environments, many specialized regional patterns and technologies developed, which makes it difficult to generalize about developments worldwide. These new subsistence strategies have been referred to as the **Epipaleolithic** in Southwest Asia, the **Mesolithic** in Europe, and the **Archaic** in the Americas.

Epipaleolithic, Mesolithic, and Archaic Technology

The transition to broad-spectrum collecting began in different regions at different times and had varying consequences. In some areas relatively permanent settlements emerged, whereas in other regions people continued to maintain relatively mobile nomadic lifestyles. Some ethnographically known hunting-and-gathering populations, such as the !Kung San of southern Africa or the Inuit in Alaska, still heavily rely on naturally occurring plant and animal resources.

The tool technologies associated with the Epipaleolithic, Mesolithic, and Archaic are highly varied, at least partly representing specialized tools needed in varied environments. In general, they differ markedly from those of the Paleolithic; typically they are smaller and more specialized than Paleolithic implements. Some of the most common Epipaleolithic and Mesolithic tools are known as **microliths**, small flakes of stone that were used for a variety of purposes. Frequently, they were incorporated into composite tools, forming harpoon barbs, knife blades, and sickles (see Figure 8.2). The bow and arrow had appeared in the Upper Paleolithic, and later Mesolithic and Archaic peoples made extensive use of this technological innovation, which allowed hunters to kill game from a greater distance and with more accuracy than did spears.

A new type of stone tool, *ground stone*, also became common in many societies. Some of these implements were probably unintentional products of food processing. To make seeds and nuts more palatable, people pulverized them between a handheld grinding stone and a larger stone slab, or even a large rock. This activity shaped the hand stones and wore depressions, or grooves, into the stone slabs. Using a similar grinding process, Mesolithic peoples intentionally made some stones into axes, gouges, and *adzes* (specialized tools to shape wood). Tools with similar functions had been produced by percussion flaking during the Paleolithic, but ground-stone tools tended to be much stronger.

This increasingly sophisticated stone-working technology allowed for a great many innovations in such activities as the harvesting of resources and the shaping of wood for building. Although watercraft were apparently developed in at least some regions during the Upper Paleolithic (as indicated by the human settlement of Australia), ground-stone tools would have made it easier to cut down and hollow out logs to make dugout canoes. Vessels of this type would have improved mobility and enabled people to exploit more diverse ocean, lake, and river resources. Ground-stone sinkers and fishhooks made from shell, bone, or stone attest to the development and importance of tools specifically used to exploit aquatic resources.

The new subsistence strategies and technologies developed during the Epipaleolithic, Mesolithic, and the Archaic mark important transformations in human culture (Hayden 2009; Zeder 2012). They are also significant in laying the foundation for the cultural changes and adaptive strategies that occurred during the Neolithic. The specific plants and animals and the subsistence

Ground-stone tools. These types of tools, found in Mesolithic and Neolithic sites, are different from earlier Paleolithic tools that were produced by flaking.

strategies that followed varied in different world areas. Examples of some of these transformations are discussed later.

The Epipaleolithic in Southwest Asia In Southwest Asia, the end of the Upper Paleolithic is referred to as the Epipaleolithic. In Israel, Lebanon, Palestine, Jordan, Syria, Turkey, Iraq, and Iran—the area known as the *Fertile Crescent*—scientists have chronicled a gradual trend toward the exploitation of a variety of resources. This area extends along a curve from the Red Sea, north along the eastern edge of the Mediterranean Sea, then southeast through the Zagros Mountains of Iran and Iraq, down to the Persian Gulf (Figure 8.1). It includes a number of distinct environmental zones, ranging from high mountains to the fertile Tigris and Euphrates River valleys. Here, early hunter-gatherers found a wide range of natural resources. This region provides some of the earliest evidence for the manipulation of wild plants. Early Epipaleolithic sites, such as Ohalo II in northern Israel, provides evidence for sedentary communities and the utilization or storage of over 100 plant species, such as emmer wheat, wild barley, and acorns, 20,000 years ago.

Archaeologically, one of the best-known late Epipaleolithic cultures of Southwest Asia is the Natufian, located in the eastern portion of the Fertile Crescent in what is today part of Israel, Palestine, and portions of Jordan. Dating to approximately 14,500 to 11,500 years ago, the Natufian is characterized by increasing reliance on wild animals and plants (Mellaart 1975; Henry 1984; Moore and Hillman 2000; Monro 2009). The Natufians settled in villages where they cultivated wild grains and cereal grasses. Archaeologists have discovered a number of items that confirm these new dietary practices, from mortars, pestles, and ground-stone bowls to sharp flint blades that were inserted into bone handles and used to cut grains (Figure 8.2). Archaeologists know how these blades were used because a distinctive residue, called **silica gloss**, was left by the plant stalks. Among the plants exploited by the Natufians were wild barley and various species of legumes that provided a rich source of protein (Miller 1992).

Natufian society also demonstrates the increasing elaboration associated with more permanent settlement. Whereas early Natufian sites were established in natural rock shelters, some later settlements were quite substantial, incorporating houses with stone foundations, paved floors, and storage chambers. Variation in the material wealth found in graves suggests that there was some differentiation in social status. Imported items, such as seashells, salt, and obsidian (a volcanic glass), attest to the Natufians' expanding trade contacts as well. These data suggest greater social complexity than that of earlier societies.

The European Mesolithic

European Mesolithic sites display a variety of subsistence strategies, reflecting a range of adaptations to various local conditions. Northern European sites such as Meiendorf and Stellmoor in northern Germany include extensive evidence of reindeer kills. On the other hand, sites in France, Britain, and Ireland display reliance on a greater diversity of animals (Price and Brown 1985). Archaeological evidence for Mesolithic subsistence strategies and how archaeologists interpret this information can be illustrated by the well-studied British site of Star Carr, dating to about 10,000 years ago. Meticulous excavation by archaeologist J. G. D. Clark between 1949 and 1951 produced traces of many different activities (Clark 1979; Fagan 2001; Milner 2006). Large piles of refuse, or *middens,* contained bones of wild game such as elk, pig, bear, and especially red deer. Discovered tools included projectile points fashioned from elk and red deer antlers and stone microliths, which may have been used for scraping hides or shaping

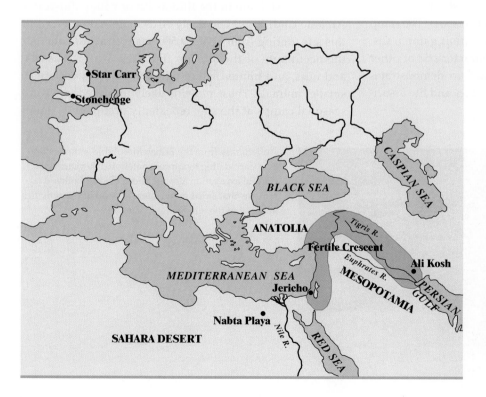

Figure 8.1 Sites of domestication in Southwest Asia, Europe, and the Nile Valley that are mentioned in the text.

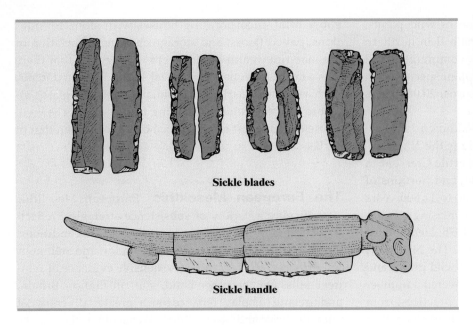

Figure 8.2 A hypothetical reconstruction of a Natufian sickle, showing stone blades set in a bone handle. Traces of silica gloss, a distinctive polish resulting from cutting plant stems, have been found on stone blades, suggesting how they were used.

Source: Based on D. A. E. Garrod and D. M. A. Bate, *The Stone Age of Mount Carmel* (New York: Oxford University Press, 1937), and James Mellaart, *The Earliest Civilizations of the Near East* (London: Thames and Hudson, 1975).

Sickle blades

Sickle handle

antlers. The careful excavations also produced a host of *organic remains*, such as plants and smaller fragments of bone, that provide further insight into the resources utilized at the site.

Though researchers agree that Star Carr was a small, intermittently occupied camp, opinions about its precise function have varied. Clark saw it as a winter settlement of several families of men, women, and children, who used a period of semi-settled existence to replace equipment expended during other, more mobile seasons (Clark 1979). More recent evidence supports the view that the site had a more specialized function, perhaps serving as a hunting camp or butchering station used for very short periods at different times of the year (Andresen et al. 1981). The camp may have been optimally located to exploit game trails. Such seasonal occupation may be characteristic of other Mesolithic sites. In either scenario, Star Carr demonstrates the intensive exploitation of local resources and the associated technologies.

The Archaic in the Americas   The changes and diversity in adaptations noted at Old World Epipaleolithic and Mesolithic sites also characterize Archaic sites in the Americas. The specific technologies and resources involved are different, but the experimentation and intensive exploitation of local resources are similar. American Archaic sites are usually categorized on the basis of geographic divisions, such as the Western Archaic, the Great Lakes Archaic, and the Northern Archaic (Thomas 1999). In turn, these categories are subdivided into regional traditions (distinguished by different tool complexes) and temporal periods (that is, Early, Middle, and Late).

The Koster site in the Illinois River valley illustrates Archaic traditions. The Early Archaic remains found at this site, dating from about 9,500 years ago, indicate that the occupants of the site ate fish, freshwater mussels, and nuts, and hunted white-tailed deer and a variety of smaller animals. These remains likely indicate there were seasonal camps at the site, repeatedly occupied by small

Antler mask from the British Mesolithic settlement of Star Carr, dating to approximately 10,000 years ago. Careful excavation also produced a host of other remains that aided in the interpretation of the activities and diet of the inhabitants of the site.

Anthropologists at Work

Grahame Clark and the Mesolithic

Grahame Clark (1907–1995) was one of the most influential archaeologists of the twentieth century. Drawing on his exhaustive knowledge of the archaeological record, he placed the British Mesolithic in a wider context and effectively created a view of a world prehistory. Also an active and inspiring teacher, Clark invigorated the Cambridge University archaeology department and made it one of the leading programs in the world. His research set a standard for fieldwork that pioneered interdisciplinary collaborative research, now taken for granted. His life's work illustrates the changing views and archaeological perceptions of the Mesolithic, as well as the emergence of archaeology in the twentieth century as the scientific study of the past (Fagan 2001).

Clark's interest in archaeology began when he was a boy in Sussex Downs, England, where prehistoric archaeological sites abound. There he roamed the hills looking for artifacts. As an adolescent at Marlborough College (which in the United States would be called a private preparatory school), he continued his collecting and also visited archaeological excavations, including the famous Windmill Hill Neolithic site. This informal education served him well. Clark wrote papers and gave lectures on archaeology, developing a lifelong curiosity about the ancient world. When he was still at Marlborough, he published four papers in the Natural History Society *Reports*. The first dealt with the classification and description of the artifacts he collected on his field trips. The young Clark was determined to become a professional archaeologist.

The period between the World Wars was a time of changing perspectives. The field of prehistoric archaeology was still a relatively new discipline. Much of the work that had been undertaken in the preceding century had focused on the description, classification, and dating of archaeological finds. There were still relatively few professional archaeologists, and much of the work on British and European Paleolithic, Mesolithic, and Neolithic sites was done by amateur archaeologists. As Clark was developing his interests, a new generation of archaeologists was starting to synthesize the information from sites and to interpret, rather than simply describe, their finds.

Grahame Clark entered Cambridge University in 1926, which at the time was one of the few places one could go for undergraduate training in archaeology. He studied history during his first two years but retained his resolve to be an archaeologist. He subsequently studied cultural anthropology, physical anthropology, and archaeology, three of the four major subdisciplines of anthropology covered in this book. This breadth of background is reflected in the holistic perspective he later brought to his research. While an undergraduate, he published several papers, including detailed artifact studies. His knowledge, scholarly abilities, and tenacity were recognized, and Clark became the first candidate to be registered for a doctorate in archaeology at Cambridge University.

Grahame Clark (right) in the field.

His doctoral dissertation topic was the British Mesolithic.

At the time, the Mesolithic was ill defined archaeologically. The prevailing view saw the classic Upper Paleolithic peoples disappearing and eventually being replaced by Neolithic farmers, with the two archaeological periods separated by a hiatus. The simple archaeological artifacts placed chronologically in between were seen by some as degraded examples of the classic Upper Paleolithic industries. Clark undertook a systematic study of all the Mesolithic artifacts he could find, including materials from all over Britain and Europe. He recognized the Mesolithic's unique characteristics and the role of environmental change. He interpreted the Mesolithic tool kit as an innovation designed to exploit new subsistence strategies at the end of the Pleistocene, developments that, in turn, set the stage for food production.

Although Clark's view of the Mesolithic has been enhanced by more recent research, his view of the Mesolithic as a transitional period of experimentation and intensive exploitation of local resources remains central to our understanding of Mesolithic life.

---

bands of hunter-gatherers over several centuries. The Early Archaic finds contrast dramatically with the Middle Archaic finds from Koster, which date from around 7,000 years ago. This period is characterized by larger and much more permanent settlements, including sturdy houses made of log supports covered with branches and clay. The occupants subsisted on many of the same foods as in the preceding period, but they concentrated more on easily obtainable resources found within a few miles of their settlement. The site may have been occupied for most, if not all, of the year.

Some North American Archaic sites prefigure the technological and social complexity typical of later food-producing societies. For example, the Poverty Point sites in the lower Mississippi Valley in Louisiana, which are dated to between 3,300 and 2,200 years ago, include the remains of naturally available foods and stone tools typical of other Archaic sites, but also include fired clay balls (Gibson 2000). These clay balls were likely used as *cooking stones* that could be heated in a fire and dropped into wooden bowls or baskets to cook food. These balls provide the earliest evidence of fired clay in North America. Even more striking are the vast earthworks of six concentric octagonal ridges and mounds found at the Poverty Point site. The earthworks, which cover some 500 acres, provide evidence of organizational capabilities and ritual expression more typical of later food-producing societies.

The Neolithic: Origins of Food Production

8.2 **Explain what transformations in human subsistence and culture are implied by the term "Neolithic."**

The Neolithic, or "New Stone" Age, beginning before 10,000 years ago in some world areas, marks one of the most pivotal changes in human history: the shift from food gathering to food production. The term "Neolithic" is generally used to indicate the beginning of domestication, but an array of other terms is used when referring to specific regional traditions. As is the case in the change from the Paleolithic to the Mesolithic and Archaic periods, the transition to the New Stone Age initially took place gradually. New technologies and subsistence strategies did not simply replace older ones; farming populations continued to exploit naturally occurring resources. Indeed, modern agricultural populations still do a limited amount of hunting and gathering. Yet, the advent of agriculture had important consequences; among these changes was a trend toward larger, more settled communities and population growth. The need to maintain and care for crops and domesticated animals would have almost necessitated peoples' proximity to their farms and a more settled existence. The consequences of domestication are treated in more detail below.

The origins of the manipulation of wild plants and animals began during the Epipaleolithic, Mesolithic, and Archaic. During this period, human populations experimented with new types of subsistence activities, including the practice of growing plants, known as **cultivation**. Some groups deliberately collected seeds for planting, not just for consumption. In addition, certain populations began to tame wild animals like dogs or wolves to have as companions and to help in hunting (Pennisi 2002). Dogs were likely the first domesticated animal, having been tamed by Upper Paleolithic hunters and gatherers. Recent studies of DNA from remains found in archaeological sites in the Near East and Siberia suggest dogs were domesticated over 30,000 years ago (Druzhkova et al. 2013; von Holdt 2010). Archaeologically, the remains of domesticated dogs have been found in sites in Europe and Israel dating 10,000 to 14,000 years ago. Other groups sought to capture wild varieties of sheep, goats, cattle, and horses and to travel with these animals to suitable pastures as the seasons changed.

Eventually, some populations came to rely upon certain cultivated plants more than others. They also concentrated their energies on raising particular animals. In doing this, they selected certain species over others and raised individual plants or animals with specific characteristics. In other words, these populations engaged in **artificial selection**, a process similar to natural selection in which people encourage the reproduction of certain plants or animals and prevent others from breeding. In effect, these human populations were modifying the reproductive patterns of certain plants and animals to propagate characteristics better suited to their own needs. Gradually, this process yielded plants and animals that were distinct from wild species and dependent upon humans. This process is referred to as **domestication**.

To some extent, the domestication of plants and animals may have occurred in an unplanned way. When people gathered wild seeds, the larger seeds on the stem were easier to pick. Similarly, people likely kept more docile, easily tamed animals rather than the more aggressive members of the species. In some world areas about 10,000 years ago, these processes of artificial selection promoted societies that placed great emphasis on domesticated plants and animals. Because people had to remain in certain areas to tend their crops, they began to put down roots for a more permanent home.

Evidence for Domestication

Much of what we know about domestication comes from the archaeological record. Because wild and domesticated species differ physically, researchers can trace the transition to domestication by examining plant and animal remains (Ucko and Dimbleby 1969; Struever 1970; Cowan and Watson 1992; Smith 1995). For example, wild species of grains, such as wheat and barley, have fragile *rachis*, the portion of the stem where the seeds are attached. This feature is advantageous in the wild because the seeds easily fall to the ground, where they can germinate and reproduce. In contrast, on domesticated plants, seeds tend to cling to the stems, attached with firm rachis. This does not enhance the plants' reproductive success in the wild, but it does facilitate harvesting by humans. Domesticated plants also have larger edible parts, as a rule, which is something early farmers would have favored.

Increasing knowledge about both plant domestication and the exploitation of wild species is a result of intensifying awareness among researchers of the need to recover plant remains from excavations through more refined recovery techniques. A great deal of information has been obtained by the use of a technique known as **flotation**. When placed in water, soil from an excavation sinks, whereas organic materials, including plant remains, float to the surface. These can then be skimmed off and examined for identifiable fragments. Other information may be obtained by studying the stomach contents of well-preserved bodies and *coprolites*, or fossilized feces.

Flotation being done by an archaeologist. Specialized techniques such as this are used to recover plant remains that shed light on the use of both wild and domesticated plants.

Although archaeologists can easily distinguish some plant species in the wild from those that were domesticated, the domestication of animals is more difficult to discern from archaeological evidence, even though many features distinguish wild animals from domesticated ones. Unlike their wild counterparts, domesticated cattle and goats produce more milk than their offspring need; this excess is used by humans. Wild sheep do not produce wool, and undomesticated chickens do not lay extra eggs. Unfortunately, however, the animal remains—primarily skeletons—found at archaeological sites often exhibit only subtle differences between wild and domesticated species. Researchers have traditionally considered reduction in jaw or tooth size as an indication of domestication in some species, for example, the pig and dog. Other studies have attempted to identify changes in bone shape and internal structure. Although providing possible insights, such approaches are problematic when the diversity within animal species is considered because the particular characteristics used to identify "domesticated" stock may fall within the range found in wild herds.

A different approach to the study of animal domestication is to look for possible human influence on the makeup and distribution of wild animal populations, for example,

changing ratios in the ages and sexes of the animals killed by humans (Wilson and Payne 1982) Archaeological evidence from Southwest Asia shows that Paleolithic hunters, who hunted wild goats, sheep and gazelles as a staple of their lifestyle, initially targeted a variety of animals, but killed those that yielded the largest amount of meat with the least effort. However, by the Natufian period, the faunal record indicates that hunting strategies had intensified. Having killed the larger, more desirable animals, humans increasingly hunted all age groups of animals such as the gazelle, as well as smaller animals that required more effort to trap or kill. They also made more intensive use of the gazelle carcasses, in terms of utilizing all of the meat present. This information supports an intensification trend across the Epipaleolithic period that culminates in the transition to agriculture (Monroe 2009).

Other Archaeological Evidence In the absence of direct evidence from plant and animal remains, archaeologists examining the origins of food production at times can indirectly infer a shift to domestication. For example, the food-processing requirements associated with food production are different from those needed for hunting and gathering. Hence, specific technological innovations, such as grinding stones used for processing grains, are found more frequently at Neolithic sites. In addition, Neolithic peoples had to figure out ways to store food crops: Since agricultural production is seasonal, seeds and grains had to be stored from one season to the next, for both planting and food. Thus, during the Neolithic, structures used as granaries became increasingly common, allowing for the stockpiling of large food supplies against periods of famine. Agricultural peoples constructed large and small granaries or storage bins and pits out of such diverse materials as wood, stone, brick, and clay. Remnants of these storage structures are found archaeologically. Sherds of pottery, too, often give clues to Neolithic communities. Whereas nomadic hunter-gatherers could not easily carry heavy clay pots in their search for new herds and food sources, the settled agrarian lifestyle encouraged the development of pottery, which would facilitate both the cooking and storing of food.

Generalizations about farming cannot be made solely on the basis of indirect evidence such as pottery, however, as the same artifact inventory is not associated with the transition to domestication in all cultural settings. In many instances, evidence for domestication precedes the use of pottery. For example, in some sites in Southwest Asia, domesticated barley appears before the use of pottery (Miller 1992). Conversely, some of the earliest pottery yet discovered, some 10,500 years old, was produced by the Jomon culture of Japan, a sedentary hunting-and-gathering society (Aikens and Higuchi 1981).

Distribution of Wild Species Archaeology does not provide all of the answers. Plant and animal remains are

Chinese Ceramics dating to the 3rd Millennium B.C. Pottery is one of the innovations characteristic of the Neolithic.
Source: Courtesy of the Everson Museum of Art, Syracuse, New York.

often poorly preserved or nonexistent. Furthermore, finding early plant or animal remains at a particular site does not necessarily mean that the plant was domesticated there. The species may have originally been domesticated elsewhere and introduced to the area where the remains were discovered.

One way researchers trace the provenance of a domesticated species is to pinpoint the areas where related wild species are currently found. Because wild species served as the breeding stock for domesticated varieties, domestication probably occurred in these areas. For example, wild species of tomato have been identified in South America, making that a prime candidate as the site of initial cultivation. Domesticated lettuce, which is presently grown in many regions of the world, probably derived from prickly lettuce, a wild species of the same genus that is native to Asia Minor. The origin of domesticated cattle has been traced to *Bos primigenius*, the wild ox, an animal native to Europe, Asia, and Africa that became extinct in Europe in the early seventeenth century.

Molecular Genetics The study of the DNA of modern plants and animals is also proving to be an increasingly important resource in understanding the domestication of some species. As discussed in Chapter 5, the study of mitochondrial DNA has provided useful insights into the origins of modern humans. The amount of mutation present gives an indication of the genetic similarity and differences between populations, as well as the time period they likely separated in their evolutionary history. Similar

techniques have been applied to some domesticated species (Jones 2002; Pennisi 2002). For example, mitochondrial DNA evidence suggests that the dog was domesticated by Upper Paleolithic peoples from several lineages of wolves, probably initially in the Near East (von Holdt et al. 2010).

Other studies have focused on the complicated issue of the domestication of cattle. There are two distinct groups of domesticated cattle: the taurine varieties found in Europe, Southwest Asia, and North Africa, and the zebu, found principally in South Asia. These varieties can interbreed, so they do not represent distinct species, but when and where were they domesticated? Genetic evidence suggests that all cattle were derived from *Bos primigenius*, a wild ancestor now extinct. The zebu and taurine varieties appear to have separated over 200,000 years ago, while North African and Southwest Asia/European varieties appear to have separated 20,000 to 26,000 years ago. As these periods of time long predate any evidence for domestication, the different varieties must have been domesticated separately: the zebu in South Asia and the taurine varieties in North Africa and Southwest Asia/Europe.

Ethnographic Studies We can also discover clues to domestication in ethnographic data. On one hand, observation of modern hunter-gatherers indicates how wild resources are utilized, what subsistence patterns are, and what practices may have led to or facilitated the domestication. On the other hand, many modern cultures make varying use of wild, as well as domesticated plants and animals. Observations of these practices may provide insight into the subsistence patterns of Upper Paleolithic or Mesolithic populations that first started to experiment with the manipulation of plants and animals.

The cross-cultural study of plant use in modern populations is termed *ethnobotany*; the study of the interrelationship between ancient plants and human populations is called **paleoethnobotany**. In one example of this kind of approach, archaeologist Merrick Posnansky (1984) examined what he refers to as "the past in the present." He observes that in addition to domesticates, modern farmers in Ghana, West Africa, harvest more than 200 species of wild plants on a seasonal basis. The farmers also trap wild animals, such as the grass cutter, or cane rat, to supplement their diet. Posnansky draws a parallel between these practices and similar activities by early farmers based on finds at nearby archaeological sites some 3,500 years old.

As the early inhabitants of the region faced similar subsistence challenges in a comparable environmental setting, Posnansky speculates that studies of modern farmers may provide insights into the options available to ancient farmers and the mechanisms that eventually led to domestication.

Why Did Domestication Occur?

8.3 Compare and contrast theories of agricultural origins.

Today, we take food production for granted. The vast majority of the world's population depends upon crops and animals domesticated and cared for by humans for sustenance. In contrast, hunting and gathering accounts for a comparatively small part of our diet. Yet the reasons for domestication initially taking place are unclear.

Although the benefits of food producing may seem clear from a modern perspective, the transition to a reliance upon domesticated foods was not necessarily an obvious choice for Upper Paleolithic and Mesolithic hunter-gatherers. In contrast to hunting and gathering, agriculture takes much more time and energy. The soil has to be tilled, seeds must be planted, and the crops need protection from weeds and pests. Moreover, agriculture demands patience. Several months may elapse from the time a crop is planted until it can be harvested. Tree crops like bananas and plantains may not bear fruit until almost a year after planting. In addition, agricultural production is a risky enterprise. Despite the considerable effort that people invest in planting, weeding, and protecting crops, the harvest may still fail, producing enormous hardships for the entire society.

Hunting and gathering, in comparison, represents a highly successful subsistence strategy. Compared to the farmers' investment in labor, hunter-gatherers spent a comparatively limited amount of time procuring food. Ethnographic studies of groups like the Bushmen and San of southern Africa indicate that they may have invested only between twelve and nineteen hours a week in the search for food (Diamond 1987; Lee 1969). Although figures may vary, this method clearly afforded them a great deal more leisure time than their agrarian neighbors had, particularly in settings with ample amounts of naturally occurring food. Undoubtedly, as seen in Chapter 7, humans were hunter-gatherers for the vast majority of their history; as recently as 500 years ago, 15 percent of the world's populations still subsisted by that means (Murdock 1968).

The disadvantages of agricultural production, then, would appear to outweigh the benefits, yet most of our hunting-and-gathering ancestors made the transition to agriculture. For this reason, researchers have considered a variety of theories as to why this transition took place. An early theory of the nineteenth century credited a solitary, unknown genius with suddenly coming up with the idea of planting seeds; this innovation, then, led to agricultural civilizations. Such a simplistic scenario is clearly unlikely. Gathering information from a number of world regions, archaeologists have formulated several provocative theories to explain the transition to agriculture.

The Oasis Theory

In the 1930s, V. Gordon Childe (1936, 1952) advanced one of the first scientific theories concerning the move to domestication. Childe suggested that at the end of the Pleistocene a major climatic change transformed the environment in regions like Southwest Asia that led to new subsistence strategies. Severe droughts, he argued, forced humans to concentrate their settlements around fertile oases. Animals would also have been attracted to these oases and in these settings, humans and animals would have interacted, laying the foundation for domestication. Initially, the animals would have just been used for their meat, but eventually humans realized the benefits of using them for their hides, wool, milk, and labor. Having developed a symbiotic relationship, the process of artificial selection and domestication in which humans selected for the traits they found beneficial would have followed. According to Childe, once invented, agriculture enabled humans to maintain a reliable food supply in extreme conditions, and the concept of food production spread rapidly to other regions. Childe called this presumed period of dramatic change the Neolithic "revolution."

Popularly known as the *oasis theory*, Childe's interpretation was seen as a plausible explanation by archaeologists for a number of years. Human familiarity with both plant and animal species was certainly a factor in domestication. Changing environmental conditions, which Childe hypothesized as a driving mechanism behind agricultural origins, has also been revisited in varied ways by researchers up until the present, as discussed later with regard to the population and demographic stress models. However, Childe's interpretation primarily focused on the process of animal domestication and said relatively little about the domestication of plants. He also lacked the archaeological evidence for the clustering of human and animal populations around oases or a full understanding of the environmental conditions in the late Pleistocene. In fact, rather than a period of increased dryness, southwest Asia likely experienced wetter conditions during this time.

The Readiness Hypothesis

A different theory, developed by archaeologist Robert Braidwood, was based on finds excavated in Southwest Asia during the 1940s and 1950s. Braidwood undertook fieldwork specifically to evaluate Childe's theory and to examine the origins of agriculture. His archaeological data provided a crucial assessment of Childe's theories. Braidwood found no evidence for the concentration of human and animal populations around oases at the end of the Pleistocene, or for a dramatic Neolithic revolution. Critiquing Childe's interpretation, he further noted that climatic conditions comparable to those at the end of the Pleistocene had existed in this region at several time periods dating back at least 75,000 years. If agriculture was developed in response to environmental pressures such as these, as Childe suggested, why had domestication not occurred earlier? Braidwood (1960) hypothesized rather that agriculture was a gradual progression that arose as a result of humans being's increasing familiarity with the varied plants and animals around them. After a long period, this resulted in domestication:

> *Around 8000 B.C. the inhabitants of the hills around the Fertile Crescent had come to know their habitat so well that they were beginning to domesticate the plants and animals they had been collecting and hunting. At slightly later times human cultures reached the corresponding level in Central America and perhaps in the Andes, in southeastern Asia, and in China. From these "nuclear" zones cultural diffusion spread the new way of life to the rest of the world.* (Braidwood 1960: 6)

Braidwood's statement may present a plausible description of agricultural origins, but like Childe's theory, Braidwood's hypothesis does not explain what prompted hunter-gatherers to adopt agriculture as a way of life. Formulated prior to detailed studies of modern hunter-gatherers, Braidwood's view assumed that the benefits of domestication were readily evident, and adoption depended on human ingenuity. Underlying his model is a sweeping assumption about human nature or psychology—that earlier peoples were not ready to

innovate or develop agriculture for some unexplained reason. This theory, sometimes referred to as the *readiness hypothesis*, does not answer two key questions: how and why domestication originated when it did.

A Push Toward Domestication? The Environment, Population Growth, and Demographic Stress

More recent models of the origins of agriculture have sought to explain the factors that may have pushed hunters and gatherers to adopt agriculture. Beginning in the late 1960s, a number of interpretations have been influenced by economist Ester Boserup's (1965) theories about the relationships among population, labor, and resources. Although Boserup initially set out to explain changes in complex agricultural practices, her ideas can be applied equally well to the origins of domestication. She speculated that societies will intensify their cultivation practices only when they are forced to by rising population pressure on the available resources. Making the transition from simple to intensive agriculture requires such a substantial increase in labor that the results may not warrant the effort. History attests to this statement. Many hunting-and-gathering societies were familiar with intensive agriculture, but did not adopt these practices because of the vast increase in labor needed to succeed. In this view, then, agricultural production would not have made sense for populations who enjoyed reliable food resources and experienced insufficient population growth to make these resources inadequate. At some point, however, population pressures may have forced people to adopt food-production techniques. Researchers differ in their interpretations of what factors may have caused these pressures.

Archaeologist Lewis Binford (1968) linked increasing population pressure to environmental change. Binford noted that at the end of the Pleistocene period, sea levels began to rise with the melting of the world's glaciers in the temperate regions. He reasoned that rising sea levels would have forced coastal peoples to migrate into interior regions, where other populations had already settled, as well as more marginal, less desirable areas. In Binford's view, this population movement led to increased competition for naturally occurring food resources and demographic stress. In response to these demographic and environmental shifts, populations had to explore new options to secure food and, consequently, began to systematically cultivate the land. Thus, Binford contended, population pressure prompted the development of agriculture.

Archaeologist Mark Cohen (1977) formulated another hypothesis that attributes the push toward domestication to population growth. Cohen underscored the growth of hunter-gatherer populations and their expansion into new territories during the Upper Paleolithic. He suggested that by the end of the Paleolithic era, hunting-and-gathering societies had spread to all parts of the world. During their migrations they gradually expanded the amount and variety of wild food resources they could draw upon for sustenance. Eventually, these populations were using nearly all of the naturally available food. As populations continued to grow and territorial expansion left very few unpopulated areas for nomadic hunter-gatherers to explore, the need to feed greater numbers of people gave rise to agrarianism.

Studying data from Mesoamerica and Southwest Asia, archaeologist Kent Flannery (1965, 1973) further elaborated the mechanisms through which humans adopted agriculture. He argued that the critical push for domestication took place in marginal zones outside of the optimal resources areas, the areas where the most food resources could be naturally obtained. The transition to cultivation and, eventually, domestication, took place when humans in these peripheral zones introduced plants to environmental zones *outside* the areas where the plants normally flourished. According to Flannery's hypothesis, transplantation might have stemmed from population growth, or from a human desire to exploit certain resources on a more permanent basis. Under these circumstances, humans would have had to invest extra time to nurture plants removed from their natural environment. This, then, resulted in domestication.

More recent work by Brian Hayden (2010) focuses on the importance of risk reduction as an important aspect of domestication. He notes that the range of technologies that emerged in the Mesolithic, including more efficient fishing technologies (nets, weirs, and fish hooks), mass food processing technologies, and the capabilities for long-term storage, allowed for the production of agricultural surpluses, a phenomenon that laid the foundation for increasingly complex hierarchical societies that emerged during the Neolithic. Societies developed strategies that provided interconnections with family members and other members of the community that could share food and help provide sustenance in times of scarcity. These ties were strengthened by social structures and ritual activities such as feasting. In this context, strategies that secured food resources were encouraged.

Coevolution

The preceding varied perspectives share an emphasis on human decision in the move to a reliance on domestication. One archaeologist, David Rindos (1984), criticized other interpretations of the origins of domestication for placing too much emphasis on conscious or intentional human selection. He examined the question of domestication from a biological, evolutionary framework. He argued that humans *unintentionally* promoted the survival and dispersal of certain types of plants through such activities

as weeding, storing, irrigating, and burning fields. Human agents unintentionally selected and germinated specific varieties of plants and adopted certain behaviors that created a link between agricultural yields and population growth. As particular species of plants became more common because of these practices, human reliance on them increased. This, in turn, led to further changes in both plant distribution and morphology, as well as human behavior. Thus, in Rindos's perspective, human agricultural practices and biological changes in cultivated plants evolved simultaneously.

Rindos's research usefully underscores the potential role of unconscious human choice in the process of domestication. However, while recognizing the significance of these observations, other archaeologists have emphasized that human learning, cognition, culture, and conscious processes are just as crucial in explaining the origins of agriculture. For example, Michael Rosenberg (1990) points out that cultural norms regarding property and territorial arrangements in hunter-gatherer populations were a conscious societal development. Similarly, he believes that such deliberate cultural choices affected the transition to agriculture. Similar points have been made by other researchers, such as Melinda Zeder (2011) who has underscored the ability of humans to invent new behaviors that would have maximized the utilization of new food resources and, more significantly, the ability to pass on these socially learned behaviors to succeeding generations. While human behavior and changes in the environments within which they interacted resulted in changes in plant and animal interactions, these uniquely human abilities made the process of domestication far more dramatic that that seen in nature (see the discussion of niche construction in Chapter 3, Page 56).

Agricultural Origins in Perspective

Anthropologists have increasingly recognized that the transition from food gathering to food production represented a complex interplay of factors, and that the trajectories to domestication were not necessarily the same in all world areas. The origins of domestication may have been somewhat unintentional, to the extent that human settlement and behaviors did impact the environment and certain plants thrived in these new conditions. However, the archaeological records of the Mesolithic, Archaic and the Epipaleolithic are indicative of populations that both understood their environments and developed the technologies to exploit them. Knowledge and the need for reliable food sources would have provided incentives for the exploration and development of new technologies and food production.

None of the preceding models seem to fully explain domestication in all settings in all parts of the world. Many archaeologists would likely agree that population growth and demographic stress are plausible driving forces behind domestication. Some researchers have, however, criticized the population-pressure models, arguing that population pressures alone would not make people abandon hunting and gathering in favor of intensive agriculture (Hassan 1981). The major problem with these models, however, is the challenge involved in assessing the archaeological data. Evaluating past human and animal populations and demographic stress, and their relationship to the appearance of agriculture is difficult. Although archaeologists would concur that population densities did increase at the end of the Pleistocene, there is less consensus of whether this population surge occurred before or after the transition to food production. Recent work seems to lend increasing support to at least some of the assertions made in population models in certain world areas (Bar-Yosef 2011). Full evaluation of these theories will, however, rely on future research of the phenomena involved.

Domestication in Different Regions of the World

8.4 Review domestication in various world areas, and discuss how these transformations were different.

Although archaeologists have not reached consensus concerning the exact reasons for domestication, information on where early domestication took place is being revealed by ongoing research. With these data in hand, researchers agree that the process was much more intricate, gradual, and varied than the "revolution" envisioned by some early theorists. Historically known agricultural populations exhibit a great deal of variation in terms of the plants represented, the specific cultivation practices represented, and the extent to which they rely on specific crops (Denham 2005). This diversity in expression was likely also true in the past.

Discussions of the transition to domestication have traditionally spotlighted southwest Asia and, to a lesser extent, China and Mesoamerica (Harlan 1971; Smith 1995). This is understandable, as these are areas where some of the first archaeological evidence pertaining to domestication was recovered, and they still represent some of the earliest and best documented examples of the transition to food production. However, the origins and diffusion of domestication are complex and worldwide in scope. Although domestication occurred earlier in some areas than in others, it took place independently in many regions and involved a vast number of species (Figure 8.3). Evidence for the indigenous domestication of plants and animals is found on each of the continents, with the exception of Antarctica and Australia.

A great deal of research remains to be done to identify those regions where early agriculture emerged. Currently, there are far more gaps in our understanding than well-described scenarios. Hence, a great deal of archaeological research considers questions of "when" and "where." However, researchers have also been increasingly concerned with examining the complex social and cultural contexts in which domestication took place (Barker 2006; Bellwood 2005; Cauvin 2000; Denham et al. 2007). The following discussions briefly review the transition to food production in different world areas. These few examples serve to highlight some of the distinctive aspects of early domestication and the particular challenges faced in its interpretation. These few illustrations do not begin to cover the diversity of settings represented in what was a varied and wide-ranging transformation in human subsistence.

Southwest Asia

As discussed above with regard to the Epipaleolithic, archaeological sites in the modern countries of Israel, Lebanon, Palestine, Jordan, Syria, Turkey, Iraq, and Iran—a region sometimes referred to as the *Fertile Crescent*—documents the gradual change from hunting and gathering to domestication (Figure 8.1). This early transition, marked by a gradual shift from a reliance on wild plants and animals to domesticated species, is similar to the pattern of early agricultural origins in many other world areas, though played out with a variety of other ways.

The Fertile Crescent was an ideal setting for early agriculturalists: The region boasted naturally occurring species of wheat and barley, as well as sheep and goats, which subsequently all became successful domesticates. The manipulation of wild plants by the Natufians and the other Epipaleolithic populations of southwest Asia, paved the way for later farming communities (Henry 1984, 1989; Hole 2009; Bar-Yosef 2011). Some research has suggested the potential role of periodic dry phases in pushing people toward agriculture, an idea consistent with some of the population and demographic stress models of agricultural origins discussed previously. Over time, these populations display an increasing reliance upon various combinations of domesticated plants and animals. After several thousand years, a distinct pattern of village life—based on wheat, barley, peas, beans and lentils, sheep, goats, pigs, and cattle—appeared. These Neolithic societies continued the elaboration of material culture initiated in earlier periods.

One of the most famous of these Neolithic settlements is Jericho, which exemplifies these developments. Jericho flourished long before the time of Joshua and the Israelites, as described in the Bible (Kenyon 1972). It emerged as one of the first large settlements in the region. The site is located in an area that would have had dependable water sources and land suitable for cultivation, features of

Figure 8.3 A world map showing areas of early plant domestication and some of the species represented.
Source: Adapted from Arthur Gettis, et al., *Introduction to Geography*, 5th ed. Copyright ©1995 The McGraw-Hill Companies. Used by permission of the McGraw-Hill Companies.

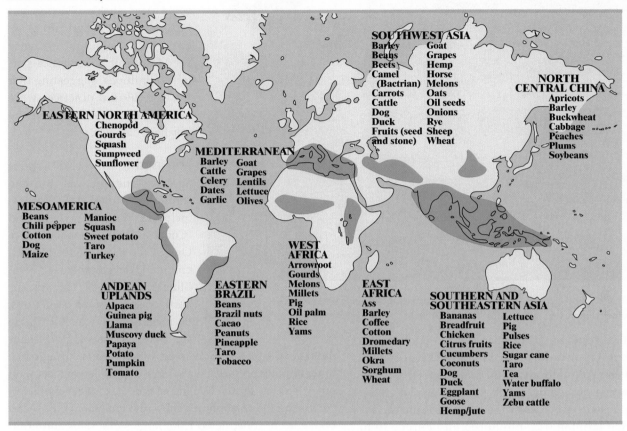

SOUTHWEST ASIA
Barley, Beans, Beets, Camel (Bactrian), Carrots, Cattle, Dog, Duck, Fruits (seed and stone), Goat, Grapes, Hemp, Horse, Melons, Oats, Oil seeds, Onions, Rye, Sheep, Wheat

NORTH CENTRAL CHINA
Apricots, Barley, Buckwheat, Cabbage, Peaches, Plums, Soybeans

EASTERN NORTH AMERICA
Chenopod, Gourds, Squash, Sumpweed, Sunflower

MEDITERRANEAN
Barley, Cattle, Celery, Dates, Garlic, Goat, Grapes, Lentils, Lettuce, Olives

MESOAMERICA
Beans, Chili pepper, Cotton, Dog, Maize, Manioc, Squash, Sweet potato, Taro, Turkey

WEST AFRICA
Arrowroot, Gourds, Melons, Millets, Pig, Oil palm, Rice, Yams

ANDEAN UPLANDS
Alpaca, Guinea pig, Llama, Muscovy duck, Papaya, Potato, Pumpkin, Tomato

EASTERN BRAZIL
Beans, Brazil nuts, Cacao, Peanuts, Pineapple, Taro, Tobacco

EAST AFRICA
Ass, Barley, Coffee, Cotton, Dromedary, Millets, Okra, Sorghum, Wheat

SOUTHERN AND SOUTHEASTERN ASIA
Bananas, Breadfruit, Chicken, Citrus fruits, Cucumbers, Coconuts, Dog, Duck, Eggplant, Goose, Hemp/jute, Lettuce, Pig, Pulses, Rice, Sugar cane, Taro, Tea, Water buffalo, Yams, Zebu cattle

crucial importance to early farmers (Kenyon 1972). The earliest settlement at Jericho was most likely a temporary seasonal camp that gradually became a more permanent settlement. By 10,000 years ago, Jericho had emerged as a sizable town with permanent mud-brick structures containing finely plastered floors and walls. A massive stone wall with towers and what may be a defensive ditch were built around portions of the settlement. Among the more striking discoveries at the site were human skulls that had been covered with modeled clay representing facial features with shells inserted for eyes. Dated to approximately 9,500 years ago, these objects and ones like them, appear to have figured prominently in the ritual life of these early farming communities (Kuijt 2000). The long occupation at Jericho, consisting of substantial villages built on the same spot over thousands of years, provides an excellent illustration of a *tell*, a type of archaeological site that became increasingly common during the Neolithic.

The Eastern Fertile Crescent Extensive remnants of the Neolithic transition have also been found in the eastern Fertile Crescent as well. In the valley steppeland areas of the Zagros Mountains and surrounding hills of modern day Iran and Iraq, archaeologists have uncovered extensive evidence of a way of life based on cultivation

and *pastoralism*, a subsistence strategy that has as its core the rearing of domesticated animals. By 10,000 years ago, Neolithic farming villages dotted the entire region.

Agriculture spread rapidly to the lowland area of the Mesopotamian plain, which was flooded each spring by the Tigris and Euphrates Rivers. The annual flooding enabled crops to mature before the soil was completely dried out, and it gave rise to one of humankind's most important innovations, *irrigation systems,* to maintain crop growth from season to season. Ali Kosh, in southern Iran, is one of the earliest farming sites in this region (Smith 2005). Archaeologists have discovered sequential phases of human occupation dating back 9,500 years. The earliest settlements may have been seasonal, the people relying upon wild animals, fish, and waterfowl for sustenance. Over time, however, the region's inhabitants gradually began cultivating or domesticating plants and animals, including sheep, emmer wheat, and barley. Signs of irrigation and domesticated cattle appeared about 7,500 years ago.

Europe

Although considered a discrete area here, Europe actually comprises a variety of different climatic, topographical, and cultural regions, ranging from the mild Mediterranean

Excavated remains of the great tower of early Jericho, a thriving Neolithic settlement that developed from a temporary camp used by Mesolithic hunter-gatherers.

climates in the south to the frigid areas of Sweden, northwestern Russia, and northern Poland. The area was equally diverse culturally and climatically in the past. Mesolithic hunting-and-gathering populations exploited the diversity of resources in these varied climes. There is clear evidence that farming was introduced into Europe from southwestern Asia. The earliest dates on the domesticated species represented occur in southwest Asia, as do their likely progenitors.

Although it seems clear that agriculture was initially introduced, it is less clear how this took place. Did migrating farming populations move into the area from the regions to the east? Or did the *idea* of agriculture spread? Traditional views held that early farmers expanded in a wave from southwestern Asia and Anatolia, displacing earlier Mesolithic populations (Evans and Rasson 1984; Dennell 1992). Although current evidence suggests that most crops, including barley, peas, lentils, vetch, and rye, were introduced, there was a great deal of variation in the timing and manner of adoption. In addition, the local domestication of some crops, such as oats and peas, cannot be ruled out.

Surveying the available data, we can discern three different patterns of agricultural adoption (Dennell 1992). First, in some areas, such as southeastern and central Europe, evidence for domestication appears suddenly and is frequently associated with village settlement and pottery. In the second pattern, the evidence for farming appears gradually; there is no clear distinction between Mesolithic and Neolithic settlements. This pattern holds true for western Europe, the British Isles, and much of the Mediterranean coast. Domesticated grains, legumes, and livestock turn up in different combinations and at different times,

eventually giving rise to true farming communities only after hundreds of years. Third, in some areas, such as Sweden and Finland, a shift to agriculture occurs gradually, but the evidence for Mesolithic subsistence patterns continues, suggesting that the agricultural practices were not initially successful in the northern climates.

Megaliths By 6,000 years ago, agriculture was thriving throughout most of Europe, including Britain and Ireland (Cooney 2000; Thomas 1999). One of the most interesting and enigmatic developments of Neolithic Europe was the appearance of large stone structures, or **megaliths** (Greek for "large stones"). Archaeological sites dating to the period show traces of large houses, fragments of well-made pottery, and evidence of trade contacts with other regions. Distinctive burial complexes also characterize this period. Elaborate tombs with chambers for several bodies were constructed from large stone slabs and boulders. These structures were the earliest megaliths. Later megalithic structures were much more elaborate and intricately designed, consisting of circular patterns of ditches and huge, upright stones (Pitts 2001).

Among the most famous megalithic structures is Stonehenge, located on Salisbury Plain in southern England. Popular wisdom credits the massive stone monument to the Druids, a religious sect in Britain during the first century B.C. In fact, Stonehenge long predates the Druids. Archaeological research reveals that work on Stonehenge first began around 3000 B.C. and spanned the next 2,000 years. As illustrated in the chapter-opening photo, a circle of 30 vertical stones, each weighing more than 25 tons, marks the center of the site. Running across the tops of these stones is a series of 30 stones, each weighing about 6 tons.

No one has yet pinpointed why Stonehenge and other megaliths were constructed. The uniqueness of the sites and their associated artifacts, underscore their probable, if unknown, religious functions (Parker Pearson 2012). Burials have been excavated from within Stonehenge, and this may further suggest the site served as a burial ground, perhaps for individuals with higher social status. Studies by English astronomers Gerald Stanley Hawkins (1965) and Sir Fred Hoyle (1977) suggested that many of the stone's structures mark astronomical observations. For example, viewed from the center of Stonehenge, outlying stones indicate the summer and winter solstices; other alignments point to positions of the moon and possibly other celestial bodies. The astronomers suggested that the knowledge of the heavens expressed in Stonehenge may indicate the site's importance in predicting the seasons of the year for agricultural planting. These astronomical interpretations garnered a great deal of popular interest, and they continue to captivate attention today. However, at least some of the purported astronomical alignments are based on features that archaeological data indicate would not have been in use at the same time.

Apart from the interpretation of specific features and their uses, these imposing monuments are important because they clearly demonstrate a growing social complexity in Neolithic Europe. Regardless of the builders and the structures' purpose, their construction would have necessitated a great deal of cooperation and organization. They may have served to reinforce the social, economic, and religious authority of the people who directed their construction. In this respect, they prefigure the complexity seen in later, state-level societies.

East Asia

Agricultural practices unrelated to those in the southwestern Asia emerged independently in the far eastern part of the continent, and are represented by a suite of different domesticates. As in other world areas, the advent of domestication was likely preceded by a period of experimentation with naturally occurring plants and animals. And once domesticates initially appeared, in many instances farmers continued to exploit natural occurring resources (Morrison 2006). Recent discoveries, particularly in China, present some of the most interesting and tantalizing insights into early agriculture. Yet, many areas have not been studied in detail, and much more work remains to be done to understand the origins and diversity of domestication in Asia. One of the interpretive problems faced by researchers

The West Kennet Long Barrow in southern England. Dating between 3600–2500 BC, it provides an example of an early Megalith.
Source: Courtesy of Christopher R. DeCorse

is agreeing on what characteristics distinguish wild from domesticated plants. For example, in some cases, rice grains have been recovered from very early contexts. It is, however, uncertain if these represent domesticated plants or the gathering of naturally occurring, wild varieties.

China Many questions regarding the origins of domestication in China remain, but increasing evidence has confirmed initial suggestions that the Chinese river valleys were early centers of domestication. Some researchers have long asserted that Chinese agricultural beginnings, including the early domestication of rice and millet, date prior to 9,000 years ago (Chang 1970, 1975; Crawford 1992). Recent research has confirmed this supposition and possibly pushed the origins of domestication back even further (Boaretto et al. 2009; Prendergast et al. 2009; Wang et al. 2010), making the origins of the Chinese Neolithic potentially as early or earlier than some of the evidence from southwestern Asia. Sites with pottery dating before 8,500 years ago are generally assumed by archaeologists to be early Neolithic, although in many cases actual plant remains are absent.

Perhaps the most important of the Asian domesticates is rice, which is now said to feed half of the world's population. It is now grown in all world areas, but it is especially important in the history and cultures of Asia. Compared to the world's other major grain crops, wheat (discussed above with regard to the Fertile Crescent) and maize (domesticated in the Americas), rice produces more food energy and protein per acre. Consequently, rice can support more people on the same amount of land (Chang and Luh 1991). This makes it clear why rice is important today and why it was likely equally important in the past.

Several areas of China have produced early evidence for rice dating back 10,000 years or more. These include sites in the Yangtze River valley, the Huai River Valley, and the Shandong Province further to the north (Boaretto et al. 2009; Prendergast et al. 2009; Wang et al. 2010). Currently, the earliest possible evidence comes from Yuchanyan Cave south of the Yangtze River. The occupation of this site spans the late Pleistocene to the early Holocene (which began 12,000 years ago) and so covers the time period that may have been of key importance in early agricultural transitions. The site preserved a variety of wild foods, illustrating the diversity of resources exploited, including many species of birds, fish, and shell fish, as well as bears, boar, deer, and tortoises. Also included in the finds are several rice grains and fragments of at least two ceramic vessels determined to be between 18,300 and 15,430 years old by radiocarbon dating. Both of these finds are tantalizing: the former providing the region's earliest possible evidence of domestication and the latter some of the world's oldest pottery. However, some researchers feel that, while the rice may indicate consumption, it may represent a wild rather than domesticated variety. Regardless, these dates, along with the associated ceramics, suggest the presence of early settled communities, and future research may reveal earlier evidence of domestication.

In northern central China, the earliest direct evidence for domestication currently dates between 8,500 and 7,000 years ago, somewhat later than in the south. Rice, although an important staple today, appears to have become common only after the appearance of other domesticates. Green foxtail millet, a wild grass, was the ancestor of domesticated foxtail millet, a crop which became a staple in the region. Domesticated animals are represented by the pig, the dog, and possibly the chicken. Villages of this early period supported a mixed economy dependent on plant and animal husbandry, as well as the continued exploitation of fish, wild game, nuts, and berries.

These early societies were the forerunners of later cultures such as Yangshao, which flourished throughout much of the Yellow River valley between 5000 and 3000 B.C Yangshao sites are typically more than five times the size of those of the preceding period (Crawford 1992). In addition to earlier domesticates, domesticated animals such as cattle, sheep, and goats were raised. Significantly, these societies were still not entirely dependent upon domestication; hunting, gathering, and fishing continued to supplement their diet. Yangshao farming villages comprised fairly substantial dwellings that were built partly below ground. Special areas were designated for the manufacture of pottery, and cemeteries were located outside the village.

Southeast Asia and Japan Evidence for early domestication is more limited in southern China and southeastern Asia. It appears to occur somewhat later and, at least in some cases, represents the spread of domesticates, such as rice, from other areas. The site of Spirit Cave in northern Thailand, excavated in the 1960s, was initially interpreted as providing evidence for early domestication as far back as 11,000 years ago (Solheim 1971). Reassessment, however, rather suggests that early plant remains more likely represents the utilization of wild varieties of almonds, betel, beans, and water chestnuts, that may have been used for food or as condiments (Gorman 1969, 1977).

More compelling evidence for the use of domesticates dates later, primarily from sites further to the south. Rice appears to have spread throughout Vietnam and Thailand in Southeast Asia by 3000–2000 B.C. Some of the earliest evidence comes from the site of Khok Phanom Di, eastern central Thailand (Bentley et al. 2007). Domesticated rice was recovered from some of the earliest levels. However, it occurs in limited quantities and it is possible that it was not grown locally but, rather, brought from other areas. Notably, as in a number of the other cases examined, hunting and gathering seems to have continued in Thailand

and other parts of Asia long after the initial introduction of domesticates (Bellwood 2005).

A similar continuation of broad-spectrum collecting appears to have been the case in Korea until about 4,000 years ago and in Japan until somewhat later, perhaps 2,400 years ago. After this period, domesticates from the Asian mainland, probably China, then spread through Korea and Japan, and beyond into the islands of Southeast Asia and the Pacific. Subsequently, rice cultivation became very important throughout these regions. Rice propelled the development of societies throughout Malaysia and the Indonesian islands, culminating in the evolution of complex agricultural societies.

Vegiculture in Melanesia, Micronesia, and Polynesia In New Guinea in the Pacific islands (Melanesia, Micronesia, and Polynesia) rice appears, but taro and yam, along with tree crops such as breadfruit, coconut, and banana, appear to have been more important, and they may represent the earliest domesticates. Researchers, however, face a particular challenge in tracing the origins of domesticated root crops, such as taro and yam. It is, unfortunately, very difficult to distinguish domesticated from wild varieties of root crops, and the archaeological remains needed to clear up this mystery are typically very fragmentary (Sauer 1952). In many areas, root crops are propagated by dividing and replanting living plants, an activity referred to as **vegiculture**. It is, therefore unclear, if early farmers utilized seeds from the plants or relied on vegiculture from an early date. Notably, some modern domesticates can no longer reproduce using seeds under normal conditions but are dependent on human intervention. This has led some researchers to suggest that vegiculture has always been the predominant method of planting in some places (Denham 2005). So, whereas experts suspect that root crops were exploited very early in areas such as Southeast Asia, they are unable to specify the precise time period of domestication. In New Guinea, the initial cultivation of wild taro, yams, and bananas, is hypothesized to date prior to 7,000 to 6,500 years ago.

South Asia

South Asia, or southern Asia, spans the area south of the Himalayan mountain range, encompassing the modern countries of Bangladesh, Bhutan, India, Nepal, and Pakistan. This region has revealed fascinating glimpses into the human past, including insights into both the origins of agriculture and early civilizations. As yet, however, the available information on the history of domestication and agriculture in the region is very limited. This restricted view contrasts dramatically with the fuller, though still fragmentary, pictures available for some world areas. The story of domestication on the subcontinent is, hence, one that will be told on the basis of future work.

At the present time, some of the most direct evidence for the early use of domesticated plants in the region relates to species that were domesticated elsewhere and subsequently introduced into the Indian subcontinent. Wheat and barley, which originated in southwest Asia, appears in the Ganges River valleys after about 5,500 years ago, and in south-central India after about 4,000 years ago (Fuller 2011: 350, 356). Domesticated species of rice from China, a very important staple in the region today, may also have arrived in the Ganges River valley 4,000 years before the present.

Although the introduction of domesticated plant species and the associated methods of farming were clearly important in south Asian agricultural traditions, emerging evidence suggests that the cultivation of indigenous species may have taken place in several areas of the subcontinent prior to, or concurrently with, the arrival of introduced crops (Fuller 2011). Given the limited archaeological data on actual plant remains, many of the clues regarding early domestication have been provided by examination of the distributions of the likely wild progenitors of domesticated species. These include species that, in general, have not been extensively studied. Potential candidates for indigenous domestication include mung bean, horse gram, local varieties of millet, chickpeas, and pigeon pea, as well as indigenous species of rice. In the absence of actual plant remains, indirect indications of agriculture are also provided by the appearance of larger, sedentary villages that are suggestive of farming. Indications of important, potentially independent areas of early cultivation come from five regions: the Deccan Plateau in south central India, the Middle Ganges River Valley, the Mahanadi River Valley, the Saurashtra Peninsula in northwest India, and the Himalayan foothills of the Punjab region.

Some of the earliest potential evidence for agriculture, including possible evidence for the domestication of indigenous species of rice, comes from the north in the Middle Ganges and the Mahanadi River valleys. Indicators of domestication consist of settled villages, pottery making and rice from sites in the Ganges floodplain. The earliest of these sites date between 10 and 11,000 years ago, which makes them comparable in age to some of the early farming sites of China and southwestern Asia. However, given the information at hand, it is unclear if the Indian rice recovered was gathered from naturally occurring stands or cultivated. It is also unclear if it represents a domesticated variety (Fuller 2000: 356).

Evidence for domesticated rice, as well as for other potential domesticates and evidence for settled communities indicative of farming, become more common between 5000 to 4000 years ago, at least in portions of the subcontinent. Research seems to suggest that prior to this period substantial hunter-gatherer settlements were limited. This would seem to suggest that agricultural origins began with more mobile and, perhaps, sparser populations (Fuller 2011: 359). This scenario contrasts with models proposed for areas such as southwest Asia where demographic stress among settled hunter-gatherer populations has been seen as one of the possible driving forces for the origins of agriculture.

Although fragmentary, the available information from South Asia indicates a great deal of early experimentation with cultivation and, possibly, independent indigenous domestication. The possibility also remains that domestication of local species arose after the introduction of farming from other areas. Future work will likely push the origins for domestication in this world area back further in time.

Africa

As discussed in preceding chapters, research in Africa has been very important in revealing the history of all humankind. However, information on the origins of domestication in Africa, as well as much of the continent's more recent prehistoric past, is not as well documented as it is for many other parts of the world. The continent is vast, some three and a half times the size of the United States, and it encompasses a diversity of climatic zones, ranging from desert to tropical rain forests. Agricultural practices and the species represented are extremely varied, and this diversity was undoubtedly present in the past. However, only limited research has been undertaken in some regions, and basic chronologies are therefore lacking. To some extent, the tropical climates that predominate in portions of the continent may have contributed to the poor preservation of plant and animal remains that might provide insight into the origins of domestication. In particular, root crops such as yam are unlikely to survive archaeologically. However, research strategies and recovery techniques, such as flotation, specifically aimed at the recovery of plant remains have not often been employed. It is, therefore, more likely that the absence of research and the lack of appropriate techniques explain the limited recovery of early domesticates.

The absence of information from Africa is unfortunate because the evidence that has been gleaned thus far indicates that several independent areas of domestication are represented. These include plants from varied ecological zones in a broad swath extending from the sub-Saharan West Africa forests and forest margins to northeastern Africa. Several dozen species of indigenous domesticated plants have been identified, including many crops that are still of considerable importance in Africa. Utilization of a variety of domesticates introduced from other areas has also clearly been very important. In addition to providing insight into early domesticates, observations of modern African subsistence strategies have been of interest to researchers; modern African societies maintain a wide variety of hunting and gathering, and agricultural practices, making the region a key area of study for researchers probing the transition to food production (Clark and Brandt 1984).

Indications of the transition toward broad spectrum collecting that preceded the origins of agriculture in other world areas are well represented. Indeed, microliths and some of the specialized tools typically associated with broad spectrum collecting during the Epipaleolithic, Mesolithic and Archaic in other world areas occur far earlier in portions of Africa, in some instances dating 60 to 70 thousand years ago (Phillipson 1993: 63-68). While not an indicator of early agriculture, this does suggest that intensive exploitation naturally occurring localized resources had spanned much of the Late Stone Age, as the Upper Paleolithic is referred to in Africa. The archaeological record presents a varied picture and archaeologists have generally avoided generalized terms such as the Mesolithic and Neolithic, but rather employ a variety of more localized terminology to describe the varied archaeological traditions represented.

As in other world areas, the transition to agriculture in Africa likely represented a mosaic of different adaptations and subsistence strategies. Intensification and broad spectrum collecting provided the foundation for the gradual transition to agriculture in some areas. Yet there is also evidence of the migration and expansion of African agriculturalists from their original living areas into new territories, bringing a range of cultural and technological innovations with them. In some, cases, hunting and gathering adaptations continued up until the present: the !Kung San of southern Africa, and the Efé, Mbuti, and Aka peoples of the central African forest represent continuations of this subsistence strategy (see Chapter 15, pages 326).

Pastoralism in the Sahara The earliest evidence for agricultural origins in Africa currently comes from the northern half of the continent, including the large region now covered by the Sahara Desert. Changing environmental conditions at the end of the Pleistocene may at least partly explain a move from hunting and gathering subsistence to domestication. From around 65,000 years ago until the start of the Holocene (about 12,000 years ago) the western Sahara Desert was hyper-arid, at least as dry as today and perhaps drier. This began to change during the Holocene when the rains of tropical Africa began to move northward, bringing sufficient moisture for a wide variety of sahelian grasses, trees and bushes to grow, and for a few small animals to exist, mostly hares and small gazelle, but also a few small carnivores. Even with the rains it was still very dry; the annual rainfall was no more than 100–150 mm per year, and it was unpredictable and punctuated with numerous droughts, some of which caused the desert to be abandoned for lengthy periods.

In this setting of environmental change, people experimented with new subsistence strategies. Evidence for an early focus on pastoralism, a strategy based on domesticated animals, comes from a number of Saharan archaeological sites. These developments are best illustrated by discoveries in Nabta Playa, located in the far south of Egypt (Wendorf and Schild 2000). Nabta Playa is a large geological depression, which during the early Holocene (approximately 12,000–5500 years ago) was dotted with settlements. The region was intermittently and seasonally filled with water, which encouraged people to come there. Today it contains dozens, perhaps hundreds, of archaeological sites. After about 9,000 years ago, these settlements became somewhat more permanent, but were likely still only occupied seasonally. Archaeological finds from these seasonal camps includes pottery, as well as cattle bones. However, a dependence on the gathering of naturally occurring foods, such as wild grasses and sorghum, continued.

Researchers have suggested that the cattle at Nabta Playa must represent domesticated varieties as they could not have survived in the dry environment without human assistance. However, this has been a source of debate, as indigenous wild cattle were present in portions of the Sahara and were an important food source for hunter-gather groups. Genetic evidence indicates that cattle were domesticated independently in Africa (Blench and MacDonald 2000). A date for the initial domestication is, however, still open for debate. If the 9,000- year-old evidence from Nabta Playa represents domesticated cattle, this would make it comparable in age with the appearance of domesticated cattle in other world areas such as southwest Asia.

Stronger evidence for domestication dates after eight thousand years ago. At this time, wetter environmental conditions allowed the further expansion of people into the Sahara, and semi-permanent and permanent settlements dating to this period have been identified in Egypt's western desert (Wendorf and Schild 1984). Excavations at these sites have yielded remains of domesticated cattle, barley, well-made pottery, and storage pits. At Nabta Playa sheep or goats appear from approximately 7,000 years ago. Other sites in Egypt, of more recent age, have produced the remains of emmer wheat, flax, lentils, chickpeas, sheep, and goats. Whereas these later plant and animal domesticates are not indigenous and indicate a southwestern Asian origin, the associated tool kits are distinctly African (Harlan 1992). To the west, additional evidence for domesticated cattle of approximately the same age comes from sites in northern Chad and Niger.

In the far western Sahara, the earliest evidence for the extensive use of domesticated plants dates between 3,000 and 4,000 years ago. Beginning slightly prior to this period, climatic conditions became less arid and more suitable for human settlement than they are today. At the earliest sites, artifacts such as grinding stones suggest that plant foods were being processed, even though few actual plant remains or residue have been recovered. Some of the most telling evidence for domestication comes from Dhar Tichett in Mauretania, an archaeological site where impressions of bulrush millet and sorghum were preserved in pottery sherds dating after 4000 years ago (Holl 2009; Munson 1981). Additional evidence for domesticated plants, as well as cattle, sheep, and goats comes from sites in the savannah regions south of the Sahara in Mali, Chad, and northern Nigeria. Notably, as in the Saharan cases discussed, the primary focus seems to have been pastoralism, rather than the cultivation of plants.

Domestication in Sub-Saharan West Africa Information from sub-Saharan Africa reveals many regional traditions that effectively made use of a host of wild plant and animal resources. In contrast to northern Africa, the current evidence suggests that the transition to food production seems to have occurred somewhat later. The plethora of naturally occurring animal and plant resources in these areas may have been sufficient to meet the subsistence needs of the indigenous hunting-and-gathering populations. However, the current picture is very incomplete, and this view may be substantially modified in light of future work.

A wide variety of plants are currently cultivated in West Africa, including a number that were likely domesticated from indigenous species. Examination of the distribution of modern wild species suggests the initial domestication of sorghum, African rice, millets, oil palm, and over 60 species of yam took place within the region. This includes crops from several environmental zones and more localized areas. Millet, for example, was likely first manipulated in the arid savanna regions to the north, discussed previously, while yams were more likely cultivated along the forest-savanna margin. Archaeological excavations have, frustratingly, yielded very limited direct insight; the vast majority of information is indirect. Evidence for larger and more permanent settlements, ceramics, ground-stone artifacts, and microliths that have typically been associated with the beginning of domestication in other world areas occur in many portions of the West African forest and forest margins. Some of the earliest evidence hints at the development of yam cultivation in eastern West Africa (Cameroon, Nigeria, and Benin) by 7,000 or 8,000 years ago (Phillipson 1993: 147).

Similar evidence dates somewhat later in areas farther to the west. Some of the best evidence is represented by Kintampo complex sites in modern Ghana and Côte d'Ivoire (D'Andrea and Casey 2002). These early settlements, dated to between 3,000 and 4,000 years ago, are typified by the presence of microliths, polished stone axes, grinding stones, pottery, and distinctive terracotta grinders or rasps. A more sedentary lifestyle is also illustrated by more sizable settlement sites and house remains. Direct evidence for domesticates was long limited to a few finds

of uncertain context. However, well-dated finds of pearl millet have more recently been recovered. Notably, these dates are similar in age to those obtained on pearl millet in some of the western Saharan sites. Also, evidence for animal husbandry in Kintampo sites has long been debated. This consists of the remains of sheep or goats, and possibly cattle and guinea fowl. Wild resources were also exploited including the oil palm and hackberry. The intensification of agriculture, trade, craft production, and settled life found in the Kintampo sites may represent similar, through locally adapted, patterns in other portions of the forest and the forest–savanna margin.

Northeast Africa A review of the origins of domestication in Africa must include some mention of northeast Africa, particularly Ethiopia and Eritrea, if only to underscore the frustratingly limited amount of information available on what must have been an important area for early agriculture, and indigenous domestication. The current information of its early history is largely indirect, primarily coming from linguistic and botanical information. Imported domesticates such as wheat and barley that originated in southwest Asia have been cultivated for a sufficiently long period to allow for a large number of varieties to be developed, including some unique to the region. Domesticated cattle may have arrived in Ethiopia between 5,000 and 6,000 years ago. Later archaeological sites in Ethiopia and Eritrea, dating 4,000 to 2,000 years ago include evidence for domesticated cattle, goats or sheep, horse, barley, chickpeas, and beans (Blench and MacDonald 2000; Schmidt et al. 2008). Rock art sites in Ethiopia, Somalia, and Eritrea attest to domesticated cattle, but these sites are poorly dated (Schmidt et al. 2008). Notably, Ethiopia was likely the farthest southern extent of ox-drawn plow agriculture, introduced from southwest Asia.

Even more tantalizing is the evidence for the indigenous domestication of an impressive number of crops such as cereal teff, noog (an oil plant), finger millet, ensete (false banana), coffee, and chat (another stimulant). As the natural varieties of these plants are indigenous to this region, they were likely domesticated there. Linguistic evidence also supports the early domestication of cereal plants, as well as herding, possibly prior to 6,000 years ago (Ehret 1980). East African sites to the south provided successively later dates for both plant and animal domesticates. These varied threads provide important avenues for future research.

The Origins of Domestication in the Americas

In the Americas, the transition from the Paleoindian period (the Upper Paleolithic) to a pattern of broad spectrum collecting, marked by the Archaic period, began around 9,000 years ago. These Archaic peoples laid the foundation for later agricultural societies. An amazing diversity of plants were domesticated in the Americas, including many that are now of world-wide importance. These crops include corn (maize), squash, various species of beans, potatoes, pumpkin, tomatoes, sunflower, peanuts, cacao, and tobacco.

As seen in other world areas, this shift in subsistence strategies encompasses a wide range of cultures and tool technologies. Many American cultures, reflecting numerous regional variations and spanning a great many environmental zones, developed subsistence strategies based on domesticated crops that flourished locally. In describing these adaptations, archaeologists generally use specific names rather than the generic *Neolithic*. A hunting and gathering mode of subsistence also continued in some areas and, in some instances, supported quite elaborate cultures. Three discrete areas are of note with regard to independent, indigenous domestication. These areas are the Mesoamerica, the Peruvian highlands of South America, and the eastern United States.

Mesoamerica presents the earliest evidence for domestication in the Americas, as well as the place of origin of a number of key species. Mesoamerica extends from the northern boundary of present-day Mexico to the southern borders of Nicaragua and Costa Rica. As in the past, the region today encompasses a great deal of environmental and cultural diversity. Early cultivation techniques and domesticates likely also varied, a factor that needs to be considered when reaching general conclusions about the advent of agriculture in the region. At present, all of the early evidence for plant cultivation and domestication comes from Mexico, much of it from dry cave sites; these data, then, can represent only a small portion of the variation probably present in the wider region (Flannery 1985; McClung de Tapia 1992; Smith 2000).

Early Archaic populations subsisted on a varied diet provided by hunting and gathering. Beginning around 10,000 years ago, however, the populations increasingly cultivated wild species. The first domesticates appear to have been squash and bottle gourds, the earliest evidence coming from the Mexican site of Guilá Naquitz in the Oaxaca Valley. The bottle gourd has a hard outer rind that makes it useful for containers, and the seeds are also edible. Restudy of this site has yielded evidence for the domestication of these species 8,000 to 10,000 years ago (Smith 2000). The earliest current evidence for domesticated maize dates significantly later, after around 6,500 years ago. Other domesticates, including squash, grain amaranth, chili peppers and, finally, beans occur later.

A great deal of debate has surrounded both maize's wild progenitor and the plant's role in Archaic subsistence (see the box, "The Origins of Maize"). Both an extinct species of wild maize and teosinte, a species of wild grass that still grows in many parts of Mesoamerica, have been proposed as possible ancestors of the domesticated species. Current botanical and genetic evidence suggest that teosinte is the probable ancestor. The transition from hunting and gathering to a reliance on domestication has been seen as a rather slow process, Archaic populations gradually making increased use of domesticated plants and transitioning to agriculture. However, the Archaic reliance on a relatively mobile hunting and gathering subsistence pattern seems to have continued well after initial domestication, perhaps only occurring after the domestication of maize.

Once it made its appearance, maize agriculture was widely dispersed. In addition to the recovery of plant remains, archaeologists have tracked changes in Mesoamerican subsistence strategies by examining artifacts such as stone-grinding slabs, locally called *metates*, and hand-grinding stones, known as *manos*. They have also noted the construction of food storage facilities and the permanent settlement of large populations in village farming communities. This pattern of intensive agriculture based on maize eventually took hold in various regions of Mesoamerica, subsequently spreading to both North and South America.

South America

As in other portions of the Americas, prehistoric South America encompassed a diversity of cultural and ecological settings for the development of early agriculture (Pearsall 1992). These included distinct systems that involved both indigenous domesticates and species introduced from Mesoamerica, as well as subsistence economies that continued to rely heavily on gathered resources. Agricultural practices were adapted to the low-altitude cultivation of manioc (a root crop), maize, and beans. Others evolved in mid-altitudes and focused on maize, peanuts, and beans. And in the high-altitude settings of the Andes Mountains a number of minor tubers and cereals were exploited, but these were dominated by the potato. These varied patterns present a complex mosaic, and there is no complete picture for the domestication of any one crop.

Indications of early agricultural developments in South America have been found in a number of areas, but many of the better-known sites are located in Peru. Following the Pleistocene, Archaic people exploited varied local resources through this area. In the coastal regions, they found sustenance in fish and other marine resources. In the Peruvian highlands and steep mountain slopes, which are cut by varied microenvironments, the early inhabitants exploited quite different resources. Here early highland hunting-and-gathering populations first subsisted on animals like the giant sloth and smaller species of wild game, plus a variety of wild plants. Finds of more recent age from a number of sites indicate an Archaic subsistence based

Critical Perspectives

The Origins of Maize

One of the most important domesticated plants from the Americas is maize *(Zea mays)*, more popularly referred to as corn. After originating in Mesoamerica, maize cultivation spread throughout much of North and South America, where it became the principal staple of many Native American populations. Following the arrival of the Europeans in the fifteenth century, the plant was taken from the Americas and introduced throughout the world, and it is now an important food crop in Europe, Asia, and Africa. The origins of the plant and its evolutionary ancestry have long been the focus of a great deal of research and debate. The identification of the wild ancestor of maize provides a good illustration of the kind of evidence researchers must draw on to trace the evolutionary history of a plant (Smith 1995).

Archaeological data have provided a scattered record of the origins and spread of maize. The evidence from the Tehuacan Valley, Mexico, now includes almost 21,000 cobs and cob fragments, 797 kernels, and many fragments of husks, leaves, tassel fragments, and roots that present a remarkable record of the plants' evolution spanning almost 7,000 years (MacNeish 1970; Smith 1995). The earliest finds come from the lowest levels of the San Marcos and Coxcatlán caves located in the Tehuacan Valley. These early plants are quite unlike modern varieties. Their cobs are less than two inches long, and they characteristically have eight rows of six to nine kernels, each partially enclosed by soft husk-like sheaths. More recent cobs are successively larger, with increasing numbers of kernels that lack the husk-like coverings.

Although the evolutionary history of maize might seem very well documented, the archaeological evidence failed to conclusively reveal the wild ancestor from which domesticated maize originated. Some researchers initially believed that the early cobs from the San Marcos and Coxcatlán caves actually predated the domestication of *Zea mays* and, in fact, represented the plant's wild, now extinct ancestor. Other

Domesticated species of plants and animals differ physically from wild varieties. In this photograph, the oldest maize cobs (at left) can be readily distinguished from the larger, more recent examples (right).

scientists disagreed and proposed that a variety of a wild grass, called *teosinte*, was the progenitor of domestic maize. Teosinte is an annual grass that still grows in Mexico.

We now know that teosinte is the wild ancestor of maize. The conclusive evidence was provided by several lines of research. Careful reanalysis of the cobs recovered archaeologically from San Marcos Cave revealed that the cobs clearly had features of a domesticated plant. In particular, the plants lacked any means of dispersing their seeds and, consequently, no means of reproducing naturally. Humans would have had to strip the kernels from the cobs and plant them. Hence, the plants were completely dependent on humans to propagate and were domesticated in the fullest sense.

In addition, researchers located a modern variety of maize, called Argentine popcorn, which shares many of the features found in the early cobs from San Marcos and Coxcatlán caves. This domesticated plant is still grown in limited quantities in Argentina. Unlike modern maize, the plant is relatively short, three to four feet high, with one to five branches. Ears occur at the ends of the branches and along their length, each plant producing ten to fifteen small ears, hardly larger than those found on teosinte. Researchers believe that this plant may be a relic of the initial dispersal of

domesticated maize into South America from Mesoamerica.

To try to identify the ancestor of maize, botanists traced the distribution of modern teosinte; there are several species in Mexico and Central America, some of which occur only in remote and inaccessible areas. The morphological and genetic similarities of these plants to domestic *Zea mays* strongly indicate that this variety of teosinte is the progenitor of maize and thus the likely geographical region where initial domestication took place. Analysis of the genetic material of one of these varieties, *Zea mays parviglumis*, known from the Mexican highlands, indicates this to be the most likely ancestor of domesticated maize (Matsuoka 2002).

Points to Ponder

1. What are the different lines of evidence that allowed the ancestor of domesticated maize to be identified? What are the strengths and limitations of each of these explanations?

2. What factors might make the discovery of the evolutionary history of other plant species more difficult to determine?

3. If you were designing a research project to examine the origins of domesticated wheat, what are some of the methodological concerns you would consider?

upon hunting camelids (guanacos and vicuñas closely related to llamas), and deer, and gathering wild plants (Pearsall 1992).

Many of the earliest finds of cultivated plants are from the highlands, perhaps supporting interpretations that some of the early domesticated species may have originated there. Archaic communities undoubtedly experimented with a variety of wild plants, and dates of 10,000 years ago or more have been proposed for the appearance of some domesticates. The first secure dates, however, appear to be somewhat later, suggesting that the earliest domesticated species—including potatoes, tomatoes, cotton, and different species of beans—first appeared between 7,000 and 8,000 years ago. Notably, in some areas, the evidence for the use of many crops appears to precede the presence of ceramics. In fact, the abundant remains of cotton dating between 2000 B.C. and 1500 B.C. have given this period the name "Cotton Preceramic." Introduced plant species from Mesoamerica also become of key importance throughout the continent.

The Americas had relatively few wild animal species suitable for domestication; the main domesticates came from South America. They include the llama, alpaca, guinea pig, and Muscovy duck. There are varied interpretations for the age and process of their domestication. The llama and alpaca appear to have been domesticated by 5,000 to 6,000 years ago. These are domesticated camelid species that were initially exploited for their meat and hides. The llama became important as a pack animal, the only indigenous example from the Americas, while the alpaca became especially valued for its wool. Dates for the domestication of the guinea pig, a small rodent unrelated to pigs, vary wildly, but it certainly dates back to 3,000 years ago (Lavallée 1990). The guinea pig was used for its meat, and small enclosures, guinea pig runs, have been identified archaeologically.

North America

Researchers long viewed North America as peripheral to the domestication center located in Mesoamerica. Maize, introduced from Mesoamerica, in fact became the most important domesticate in later, Native North American societies. Yet the inhabitants of North America domesticated other plants on their own before the arrival of introduced domesticates (Smith 1989, 1995). Archaeologists have uncovered evidence from archaeological sites in Alabama, Arkansas, Illinois, Kentucky, Missouri, Ohio, and Tennessee that various starchy and oily seeds were domesticated in what has been termed the *Eastern Agricultural Complex* (Ford 1985; Keegan 1987).

Species of plants that appear to have been independently domesticated in North America include goosefoot (*Chenopodium berlandieri*), marsh elder (*Iva annua*), sunflower (*Helianthus annus*), erect knotweed (*Polygonum erectum*), maygrass (*Phalaris caroliniana*), and a potentially indigenous variety of gourd (*Cucurbita pepo*). As in other areas, the manipulation of wild plants likely began first, with Archaic hunters and gatherers cultivating wild species. Domesticated plants, indicated by the presence of larger seeds than those found in wild varieties, have been recovered from sites dating between 4,000 and 5,000 years ago. The domesticated species include plants that could have been used for food, as well as oil, cosmetics, and (in the case of the gourd) containers. The productivity and potential importance of these species as food resources are collectively lower than maize, however, and this likely explains why maize becomes increasingly important after its introduction. Yet, although the importance of these local species was overshadowed by introduced domesticates, a description of the lower Mississippi River in the 1720s makes it clear that *Chenopodium* was still grown by Native Americans at that time. Unfortunately, this early North American domesticate is now extinct.

The cultivation of Mesoamerican domesticates, such as maize and beans, spread into eastern North

Native American cultures developed a wide variety of agricultural practices suitable for many different environments. Farming communities, such as those at the Cliff Palace ruins in Colorado, flourished for hundreds of years by making effective use of the limited water available.

America during the period between 800 and 1100 A.D. (Smith 1989). Gradually, maize became the most important crop in farming communities throughout North America. In what is now the southwestern United States, maize cultivation led to specialized dry-land farming practices in Pueblo cultures such as the Hohokam, the Anasazi, and the Mogollon. These practices included irrigation methods and precise planting and harvesting schedules organized around rainy seasons. An array of agricultural technologies that promoted the cultivation of maize, beans, and squash diffused throughout the Midwest, the Southeast, and eventually the Northeast, culminating in the Adena and Hopewell cultures (in the eastern United States) and the immense Mississippian cultural complex with its center at Cahokia, now in Illinois.

Consequences of Domestication

8.5   List and discuss the major consequences of domestication for prehistoric peoples.

Although no one can pinpoint the precise reasons for the domestication of plants and animals, these activities clearly had far-reaching consequences. In many ways, the Neolithic looks very familiar from a modern vantage. Settlements sometimes included houses with beds, fireplaces and chairs. Animals were penned in adjacent areas, and terraces marked the presence of nearby fields. Many of the tools that were used are also recognizable: hoes, axes, pottery, and knives. These similarities with aspects of modern life serve to underscore the dramatic changes that occurred in human societies with domestication. Life during the Neolithic became increasingly distant from the hunting and gathering societies of the Epipaleolithic, Mesolithic, and Archaic. These Neolithic transformations include changes in population, health, material complexity, and sociopolitical organization. These changes are discussed next.

Human Settlement and Population Growth

In contrast to earlier hunter and gathering societies, farming communities are typically larger and more sedentary. Because farmers had to remain near their fields and maintain their livestock, they often remained in the same settlements year round. Occupying houses for longer periods of time, people also invested more time in the construction of their dwellings. Tents or more hastily constructed structures were replaced by houses of wood and clay, stone, or mud blocks. These features provide for a much more visible archaeological record as well as clear testament to changing living conditions.

A major consequence of domestication was population growth. Agriculture supports larger populations by making food supplies more stable and reliable. Even more significantly, agriculture yields more food per acre of land, which allows a given region to support a larger population. More sedentary lifestyles and the higher-calorie diets associated with domestication likely resulted in an overall increase in birth rates.

As a result of these factors, the number of humans rose dramatically during the Neolithic, producing a surge in world population that constituted a major demographic shift in human history. Prehistoric population sizes are difficult to estimate, but some researchers estimate that the world's population rose from perhaps 30 million at the end of the Paleolithic to 300 million by the year 1 A.D., a tenfold increase (Hassan 1981; also see Bocquet-Appel 2011).

Health and Nutrition

Although agriculture promoted population growth, it did not necessarily improve the quality of life in Neolithic societies. In fact, in many instances, the advent of domestication actually contributed to a decline in human health (Cohen and Armelagos 1984; Larsen 1995). The larger settlements of the Neolithic increasingly brought people into contact with one another, facilitating the spread of infectious disease. In some cases, people also became dependent upon particular domesticated plants like corn, to the exclusion of most other foodstuffs. This restricted diet did not fulfill nutritional requirements as well as that of hunter-gatherers, which encompassed a wider variety of both plants and animals. Reliance on one crop rather than on a variety of wild resources also boosted the risk of famine.

Research indicates that many agricultural populations appear to have suffered from nutritional problems and dietary stress. Indicators of a person's health and nutrition are preserved in his or her skeleton. Signs of physiological stress brought on by food shortages show up in *Harris lines*, lines in long bones indicating periods of arrested growth, and in *enamel hypoplasias*, deficiencies in tooth enamel. Calculations of prehistoric people's average height and age of death also shed light on changes in general health. Many of these indications of dietary stress are found on the skeletons of individuals of the Neolithic period, indicating that many agricultural populations underwent chronic and life-threatening malnutrition and disease, especially during infancy and childhood. This is not to say that earlier Paleolithic and Mesolithic populations did not experience food stress: They did. However, surveying prehistoric skeletal information worldwide, more signs of stress and other health and nutritional problems appear in sedentary Neolithic communities.

Critical Perspectives

War before Civilization?

As we consider life during the Neolithic, the images that most commonly come to mind are of a peaceful people who lived a rugged lifestyle, exploited natural resources, and were united in a shared goal of survival. Although hunting large game animals would have required both courage and implements capable of inflicting fatal wounds, we seldom consider that these weapons were turned against other human beings. In a book entitled *War Before Civilization*, archaeologist Lawrence H. Keeley (1996) questions this pacifist view. In a far-ranging study that moves from the archaeological record of the Mesolithic and Archaic to the complex societies of Mesoamerica and the Nile Valley, Keeley convincingly demonstrates that archaeological evidence on early human societies provides ample demonstration of warfare, murder, and mayhem.

Keeley's own experience as an archaeologist began as a college freshman excavating a prehistoric Native American village site in San Francisco Bay, California. The site contained many burials of individuals who had met violent deaths, as evidenced by the stone projectile points embedded in their skeletons. This evidence suggests that the killings in the population were at least four times the percentage of those in the United States and Europe during the war-filled twentieth century. Despite this fact, the general view at the time was that the native peoples of California were exceptionally peaceable.

The situation in coastal California was not unique. Keeley examined archaeological data and descriptions of conflicts in non-Western societies and found that the circumstances in other world areas and other time periods were equally, if not more, violent. Early farming communities and early agricultural states provide numerous illustrations of conflict and warfare. Excavations of a fortification ditch at Crow Creek, South Dakota (1325 A.D.) revealed the skeletal remains of nearly 500 men, women, and children who had been scalped, mutilated, and left exposed to scavengers before being interred. Studies of early

Neolithic settlements (6,000 to 7,000 years old) in Europe and Britain, including sites excavated by Keeley, show that the first farmers to colonize central and northwestern Europe built villages fortified with palisades and ditches. Some of these settlements bear clear evidence of archery attacks, destruction by fire, and brutal deaths. The defensive sites seem to have been located along the margins of territories, possibly as protection against earlier hunting-and-gathering Mesolithic populations. The early Maya civilizations of Mesoamerica were frequently at war, as evidenced by fortifications and numerous murals showing warriors and captives. Some of the earliest written records include chronicles of conquests and military victories.

If evidence for conflict and warfare is so prevalent in early societies, why have archaeologists generally failed to discuss this aspect of our past? The explanation provides a good illustration of how research objectives and designs shape the interpretations we reach. Keeley argues that archaeologists have essentially "pacified the past" and "shared a pervasive bias against the possibility of prehistoric warfare" (Keeley 1996: vii). Preconceived perceptions and methodologies aimed at answering other questions prohibited researchers from looking for evidence of conflict or recognizing relevant data that were uncovered. Given his own grounding in traditional views of the past, Keeley himself was actually surprised when his research on early European Neolithic sites revealed evidence of fortifications. His work at the site of Darion had earlier revealed defensive features, yet he noted that subconsciously he had not really believed his own arguments concerning the evidence for fortifications, and he assumed that Darion's fortifications were an aberration (Keeley 1996: viii). With a particular view of the past in mind, defensive sites have often been described by the more neutral terms *enclosures* or *symbolic features*, and the significance of violent death in pre-Columbian Native American populations is left unexplored.

Keeley further points out that anthropological views of non-Western,

preindustrial societies, which serve as analogies for the behavior of prehistoric peoples, were similarly biased. Ethnographic descriptions of conflicts were colored by views of modern warfare. Because battles involving multiple combatants are the characteristic events and primary goals of contemporary conflicts, it was these features that ethnographers recorded. Of course, battles in tribal societies involved far fewer people, and they often stopped after a relatively small number of casualties. While these observations may seem to support a more peaceful view of nonindustrialized societies and less violent images of prehistoric peoples, they fail to take into account the numbers of people killed in raids, ambushes, and surprise attacks on villages that represent the major component of tribal warfare. Keeley concludes:

> Primitive war was not a puerile or deficient form of warfare, but war reduced to its essentials: killing enemies with a minimum risk, denying them the means of life via vandalism and theft (even the means of reproduction by the kidnapping of their women and children), terrorizing them into either yielding territory or desisting from their encroachments and aggressions *(Keeley 1996: 175)*.

Popular imagery of the peaceful, noble savage fails to recognize in prehistoric societies the same rapaciousness that characterizes our own, and thus robs them of some of their humanity. Sadly, the evidence from the past holds the same catalog of deaths, violence, and destruction as exists today.

Points to Ponder

1. Discuss Keeley's ideas. What other interpretations might explain the archaeological evidence he discusses besides warfare and conflict?

2. Think about your own images of Paleolithic hunter-gatherers and views of ethnographically known hunter-gatherers. How are these views different from the ones presented by Keeley?

3. Do you think Keeley makes his case?

Increasing Material Complexity

Archaeologically, the Neolithic takes shape through an explosion of artifacts. Most Neolithic settlement sites have huge trash mounds, or *middens*, containing food remains, broken tools, and other garbage. Sorting through these artifacts and the detritus of these societies reveals an increasingly sophisticated material culture. There were dramatic changes in technology specifically associated with food production and consumption, including tools used for farming, cooking, and food storage, as well as the construction of irrigation systems and terraces for farming. While fired ceramics and pottery are occasionally associated with pre-agricultural, hunting and gathering populations, pottery is ubiquitous on Neolithic sites. Clay was shaped into an array of vessel forms and was also used to make pots, pipes, lamps, and sculptures. Plants cultivated by humans included cotton and flax, which were then woven into cloth. Ritual structures and ornamentation also became more elaborate. There were also innovations in transportation technology; in areas such as southwest Asia, people used the wheel to construct carts that could be pulled by oxen. The first metal working also takes place.

Sociopolitical Organization

The advent of domestication also had dramatic impacts on how human societies were organized. As they grew in size, they also became increasingly complex. Paleolithic cultures, consisting of small bands of people reliant on hunting and gathering, were generally egalitarian: People of the same sex and capabilities had more or less equal shares in the benefits of social living, even as they acknowledged that some were better hunters or more gifted leaders than others. In contrast, during the Mesolithic and the Neolithic, there was a clear trend toward greater social stratification. Certain members of these societies acquired more influence than others in societal decision making, such as how to allocate agricultural surpluses, and were thus able to accumulate more wealth. Another marked change was the emergence of full-time craft specialists, individuals who concentrated on the manufacture of tools, pottery, and other goods.

During the Neolithic, artifacts and material culture that can be associated with different individuals within a given society increasingly display a greater amount of variation. Things such as housing, burials, and personal adornment appear increasingly varied in different contexts: in some cases they seem to have been more elaborate, exotic, or rare, including items from far away, while in other cases the artifacts were very simple and modest. These differences can be seen as indicators of growing divisions on the basis of wealth, prestige, and status in early agricultural societies. These developments set the stage for momentous changes in human social and political life, as we shall see in the next chapter.

Summary and Review of Learning Objectives

8.1 Discuss the changes that characterize the Epipaleolithic, Mesolithic, and Archaic and how these periods can be seen as laying the foundation for domestication.

The terms Epipaleolithic, Mesolithic, and Archaic refer to a period when human populations increasingly focused on a wider subsistence base and the more intensive exploitation of localized resources, a subsistence strategy that has been referred to as broad-spectrum collecting. They are transitional periods between the earlier Upper Paleolithic and the later Neolithic periods. Earlier Upper Paleolithic populations were nomadic people who hunted migratory herd animals and gathered naturally occurring plant and animal resources. This pattern gradually changed at the end of the Pleistocene epoch, approximately 12,000 years ago. At this time climatic conditions became warmer, marking the transition to the Holocene, the current geological epoch. Rather than moving around in pursuit of large animals, humans made more intensive use of smaller game animals, fishing, and wild plants within localized areas. They became less mobile and increasingly focused on the exploitation of resources within particular regional environments. Because of variation in local environments, many specialized regional patterns and technologies developed. These changes, reflected in the archaeological record, occurred at various times in different areas, making it difficult to generalize about developments worldwide. Hence, this transition is variously referred to as the Epipaleolithic in Southwest Asia, the Mesolithic in Europe, and the Archaic in the Americas. As time went on, people started to explore new subsistence strategies and to experiment with growing plants and breeding animals for food, as opposed to relying on naturally occurring resources. This shift from hunting and gathering to food production marks the beginning of the Neolithic.

8.2 Explain what transformations in human subsistence and culture are implied by the term "Neolithic."

The Neolithic, or "New Stone" Age, beginning before 10,000 years ago in some world areas, marks a pivotal change in human history: the shift from food gathering to food production. The term "Neolithic" is generally used to indicate the beginning of domestication, but a variety of terms is used by archaeologists when referring to specific regional traditions. As is the case in the change from the Paleolithic to the Mesolithic and Archaic periods, the transition to the Neolithic occurred gradually. New technologies and subsistence strategies did not simply replace older ones; farming populations continued to exploit naturally occurring resources. Yet, the advent of agriculture had important consequences. Among these changes was a trend toward larger, more settled communities and population growth. The need to maintain and care for crops and domesticated animals would have necessitated peoples' proximity to their farms and a more settled existence. The food-processing requirements associated with food production are also different from those needed for hunting and gathering. Hence, specific technological innovations, such as grinding stones for processing grains, are found more frequently at Neolithic sites. In addition, Neolithic peoples had to store food crops: Seeds and grains had to be kept from one season to the next, for planting and food. Pottery, too, is often associated with Neolithic communities. Whereas nomadic hunter-gatherers could not easily carry heavy clay pots, the settled agrarian lifestyle encouraged the development of pottery, which would facilitate both the cooking and storing of food. These features are visible archaeologically.

8.3 Compare and contrast theories of agricultural origins.

The reasons for the transition to agriculture have been widely debated. On the one hand, domestication provides more regular food supplies, allowing for growth in human populations. On the other hand, hunter–gatherers actually invest much less time in subsistence activities than do food producers. Theories of domestication have sought to explain the factors that pushed hunters and gatherers to adopt agriculture. Interpretations, such as those by Lewis Binford, Mark Cohen, and others have been influenced by economist Ester Boserup's theories about the relationships among population, labor, and resources, which argue that societies intensify their cultivation practices only when they are forced to by rising population pressure on the available resources. Drawing on this idea, these theories propose a link between increasing population pressure and environmental change. Binford, for example, reasoned that rising sea levels at the end of the Pleistocene period forced coastal peoples to migrate into interior regions, where other populations had already settled. This population movement led to increased competition for naturally occurring food resources and demographic stress. In response, people explored new options to secure food and began to cultivate the land. Binford's model, as well as those of many other researchers, emphasizes human decisions in the move to domestication. Archaeologist David Rindos criticized these interpretations for placing too much emphasis on conscious or intentional human selection. He examined the question of domestication from a biological, evolutionary framework. He argued that humans unintentionally promoted the survival and dispersal of certain types of plants through such activities as weeding, storing, irrigating, and burning fields. Human agents selected and germinated specific varieties of plants and adopted certain behaviors that created a link between agricultural yields and population growth. As particular species of plants became more common because of these practices, human reliance on them increased. This, in turn, led to further changes in both plant distribution and morphology, as well as human behavior. Anthropologists have increasingly recognized that the transition from food gathering to food production likely represented a complex interplay of factors and that the trajectories to domestication were not necessarily the same in all world areas.

8.4 Review domestication in various world areas, and discuss how these transformations were different.

Discussion of the origins of food production has often highlighted the evidence for early domestication in southwest Asia and, to a lesser extent, China and Mesoamerica. In fact, these areas did produce some of the first archaeological evidence pertaining to domestication, and they still represent some of the earliest examples of the transition to food production. However, the origins and diffusion of domestication are complex and worldwide in scope. Although domestication occurred earlier in some areas than in others, it took place independently in many regions, and it involved a vast number of species. The way in which the transition to food production occurred also varied in different settings. In many instances, new technologies and subsistence strategies did not simply replace older ones; farming populations continued to exploit naturally occurring resources. In other cases, new innovations appear to have spread and become accepted quite rapidly. A great deal of research remains to be done to identify those regions where early agriculture emerged. Currently, there are far more gaps in our understanding than well-described scenarios. Hence, a great deal of archaeological research considers questions of "when" and "where." The evidence from the Americas, Europe, and across Asia illustrates the domestication of an amazing diversity of both plant and animal species, and a wide range of cultural settings. These highlight some of the distinctive aspects of early domestication and the particular challenges faced in its interpretation.

8.5 List and discuss the major consequences of domestication for prehistoric peoples.

Food production had dramatic consequences. These transformations include changes in population, health, material complexity, and social stratification. Because farmers had to remain near their crops, Neolithic peoples became more sedentary than earlier hunting-and-gathering populations. Agriculture supports larger populations by making food supplies more stable and reliable. Even more significantly, agriculture yields more food per acre of land, which allows a given region to support a larger population. More sedentary life styles and the higher-calorie diets associated with domestication likely also resulted in an overall increase in birth rates. As a result of these factors, population rose dramatically during the Neolithic, producing a surge of people across the world that constituted a major demographic shift. This transition was not without disadvantages. Diseases associated with larger population concentrations and the tendency to focus on growing one crop gave rise to poorer health and deficiency diseases. The Neolithic period is also marked by increasingly sophisticated material culture, social stratification, and political complexity. Clay was shaped into an array of vessel forms, and pottery is ubiquitous on Neolithic sites. Plants such as cotton were woven into cloth. There were also other technological innovations such as carts that could be pulled by animals, metal working, and art. Societies also became more complex. In contrast to preceding periods, the Neolithic is marked by greater social stratification. Some members of these societies acquired more influence than others in societal decision making and were thus able to accumulate more wealth. Another marked change was the emergence of full-time craft specialists, individuals who concentrated on the manufacture of tools and other goods. These trends set the stage for the emergence of states in many world areas.

Key Terms

Archaic, p. 171
artificial selection, p. 176
broad-spectrum collecting, p. 171
cultivation, p. 176
domestication, p. 176

Epipaleolithic, p. 171
flotation, p. 176
megaliths, p. 184
Mesolithic, p. 171
microliths, p. 172

Neolithic, p. 171
paleoethnobotany, p. 179
silica gloss, p. 173
vegiculture, p. 186

Chapter 9

The Rise of the State and Complex Society

 Learning Objectives

After reading this chapter you should be able to:

9.1 Discuss the different characteristics that have been used to define civilizations and the limitations of these definitions.

9.2 Discuss the different sources of information that archaeologists draw on to study early states.

9.3 Discuss some of the challenges and limitations of the different theories of state formation.

9.4 Discuss where some of the first agricultural states were located and their characteristics.

9.5 Discuss different theories of why states collapse.

The pyramids of ancient Egypt, the monumental ruins of Mesoamerica, the tombs of Chinese emperors; perhaps no aspect of the past has captivated popular attention more than ancient civilizations. This chapter examines the origins of these societies, why they arose, and how archaeologists study them. As we saw in Chapter 8, the advent of domestication during the Neolithic brought many changes to human societies, including more settled communities, population growth, craft specialization, increased social stratification, and growing sociopolitical complexity. Gradually, as permanent settlements expanded, people in many regions of the world developed techniques, such as irrigation, plow cultivation, and the use of fertilizers, which allowed fields to be cultivated year after year. These intensive agricultural practices produced food surpluses, which contributed to population growth and further changes in human societies. Beginning approximately 5,500 years ago in some world areas, these developments coalesced in the appearance of complex societies commonly called *civilizations*.

A key aspect of this growing sociopolitical complexity was institutionalized government, or the **state**, run by full-time officials. The intensification of agricultural production was accompanied by the rise of agricultural states in Southwest Asia, Egypt, India, China, and later in Greece, Rome, Byzantium, Southeast Asia, sub-Saharan Africa, and feudal Europe. In the Americas, early complex societies are represented by Teotihuacán, and later Olmec and Mayan sites in Mesoamerica; the Andean empires of South America; and the Mississippian complex sites in North America. The location of some of these early civilizations is highlighted in Figure 9.1 on page 213.

The State and Civilization

9.1 **Discuss the different characteristics that have been used to define civilizations and the limitations of these definitions.**

How do we define civilization and the state? V. Gordon Childe, whose theories on domestication were discussed in Chapter 8, also wrote on the origin of complex societies. He believed that the rise of "civilization" could be easily defined by the appearance of ten specific features, including: urban centers of between 7,000 and 20,000 inhabitants; a highly specialized division of labor, with economic roles other than those pertaining to agricultural production; a ruling class of religious, civil, and military leaders; extensive food surpluses; monumental architecture; the use of numbers and writing systems for record keeping; developments in arithmetic, geometry, and astronomy; sophisticated art expressed in a variety of materials; long-distance trade; and an institutionalized form of political organization based on force—the state (Childe 1950).

Childe's definition serves to underscore many of the criteria that are often used by archaeologists to characterize and study complex societies. Yet, a survey of the archaeological and historical information that is now available reveals that such neat definitions as Childe's are too rigid to define the diversity in the societies under study. Early states were quite varied in terms of the cultural settings in which they emerged and in terms of their specific features. In fact, all of the characteristics noted by Childe are rarely present in the earliest societies that have been termed *civilizations*. Alternative interpretations that list what features are the key ingredients of civilization create more problems than they solve: None provide definitions that are equally applicable in all settings. In this text, the term *civilization* is used in a general way to indicate a complex society with some of the features noted by Childe. In studying the development of early societies, today's anthropologists generally focus on the specific features represented, such as their economic development, technology, trade, and art, rather than all-encompassing definitions.

Types of Political Systems

Of particular interest to anthropologists are the changes in sociopolitical organization that characterize these early societies; the rise of the *state*. In order to distinguish different kinds of political organization, many anthropologists use variations of a fourfold classification system first developed by anthropologist Elman Service (1971), which divides societies into bands, tribes, chiefdoms, and states. As we saw in Chapter 7, a *band* is the least complex in terms of sociopolitical organization—and the oldest—form of political system. Paleolithic populations were likely organized into bands, and this type of social organization is also the most common among ethnographically known hunter-gatherer societies. Band organization is based upon close kinship relations, perhaps consisting of an extended family and having no more than 100 members. Bands were typically egalitarian: People of the same sex and capabilities had more or less equal shares in the benefits of social living, even as they acknowledged variation in peoples' skills or abilities.

Tribes are more complex societies with political institutions that unite larger groupings of people into a political system. Tribes do not have centralized, formal political institutions, but they do have *sodalities*, groups based on kinship, age, or gender that provide for a more complex political organization. **Chiefdom** political systems are more complex than tribal societies in that they are more formalized and centralized. Chiefdoms establish centralized authority over populations through a variety of economic, social, and religious institutions. Despite their size and complexity, however, chiefdoms are still fundamentally organized by kinship principles. Although chiefdoms have different levels of status and political authority, the people within these levels are related to one another through kinship ties. Eric Wolf (1982) has referred to bands, tribes, and chiefdoms as *kin-ordered societies*.

The *state* is structurally distinguished from the preceding types of political organization on the basis of an institutionalized bureaucracy or government. States have centralized political systems that establish power and authority over large populations in different territories. While the ruler of a state may be an inherited position, state systems are not based on kinship. Because early states were more complex and highly organized than prestate societies, they could not rely solely on kinship to define different status positions. Land ownership and occupation became more important than kinship in organizing society. In the highly centralized agricultural societies, the state itself replaced kin groups as the major integrating principle. State bureaucracies govern society on behalf of ruling authorities through procedures that plan, direct, and coordinate political processes.

The fourfold classification system outlined above is not without some of the ambiguities faced in Childe's definition of civilization; political organizations form more of a continuum than four neat divisions, and many societies do not neatly fit into an individual category (McIntosh 1999; Johnson and Earle 2000; Pauketat 2007; Smith 2004; Yoffee 2005). It is also important to remember that this classification scheme is not a progressive, hierarchical typology. That is, states, which seem more familiar from a modern vantage, are not inherently "better" than bands or tribes. Rather, each of these categories is a simplification of the varied forms of human societies that existed in the past and the present, each with their own cultural practices and traditions. Finally, from an archaeological perspective, it is especially challenging to assess many of the features that are relevant to these classifications. And there are many debates as to whether this or that society was a chiefdom or a state, let alone what more nuanced aspects of sociopolitical structures they may have had. However, the classification serves to facilitate comparison and organize information. It is used flexibly, with the dynamic nature of human societies in mind.

Agricultural States

Early states were characterized by a high degree of social inequality, settings in which a relatively small portion of the population had political authority and controlled access to goods and services. They are most distinguished by their uniqueness; the first states emerged at times when the majority of the world's population still lived in small agricultural communities. The creation of food surpluses, along with better food-storage technologies, led to new forms of economic relations. Mastery in early states was based primarily on the control of agricultural surpluses,

often managed by complex administrative systems. For this reason, the term **agricultural states** is often used to describe these early state-level societies. Many people were freed from working in the fields to pursue functions unrelated to farming. This was the beginning of specialization. New, full-time occupations emerged: Craftsworkers produced stone and metal tools, clothing, jewelry, pottery, and art. Other workers engaged in commerce, government, religion, education, the military, and other sectors of the economy.

The increasing division of labor influenced both rural and urban areas. Farm laborers were not only involved in essential food production; they also turned to crafts production to supplement their income. Over time, some agricultural villages began to produce crafts and commodities not just for their own consumption, but for trade with other villages and with the urban centers. With increasing long-distance trade, regional and local marketplaces began to emerge. Foodstuffs and other commodities produced by peasants, artisans, and craftsworkers were bought and sold in these marketplaces. Through these activities, rural villages became involved in widespread trading alliances and marketing activities. In early cities, such as Ur, Teotihuacán, and Tikal, markets were centrally located, offering both imported and domestically manufactured items, as well as food. In addition, marketplaces arose throughout the countryside. Taxes on these goods ensured a steady flow of goods from villages to towns to regional and national capitals.

The power of the rulers in agricultural states was often expressed in sumptuous palaces, monumental architecture, and luxuriant lifestyles. The opulent lifestyle of these rulers can be dramatically contrasted with that of the other classes. It was in early states that slavery and the state-sanctioned use of force to enforce laws became common. The leaders of the state often sanctioned their positions through the manipulation of religious institutions and symbols. The division between the supernatural and social institutions that we acknowledge today had little meaning in these cultural settings (Trigger 1993; also see discussion of religion in agricultural societies in Chapter 19).

Primary and Secondary States One distinction that archaeologists make when discussing the origin and development of state societies is between *primary states* and *secondary states* (Spencer and Redmond 2004; Liu 2009; Stanish 2001; Parkinson and Galaty 2007; Yoffee 2005). Primary states refer to those agricultural states that developed independently without influence from external influences from other early states. Secondary states, on the other hand, are societies that arose later, perhaps in response to initial developments in a neighboring primary state. Anthropologists are particularly interested in the emergence of primary states, as these present the opportunity to examine the distinctive conditions that led to state development.

Primary agricultural states emerged in many parts of the world. Six of the earliest were in Mesopotamia (3500 B.C.); the Egyptian Old Kingdom (3500 B.C.); China (2500 B.C.); the Indus River Valley, India (2500 B.C.); and in both Mexico and Peru (300 B.C.). Later, secondary agricultural states flourished in many other areas, including Greece and Rome, tropical Africa, Southeast Asia, and, to a lesser extent, North America. These societies exhibited many of the signs of complexity, social stratification, and specialization that Childe used to define civilization, and some of these features are discussed later (Connah 2001; Liu 2009; Spencer and Redman 2004; Stanish 2001; Tainter 1990; Trigger 1993; Yoffee 2005). Yet, it is also important to underscore that as more is learned about these early societies, their diversity of form and organization becomes increasingly apparent. While some commonalities are apparent (for example, the development of comparatively larger settlements and the presence of monumental architecture), the specifics of these features are quite distinct in the different world areas represented.

Studying Complex Societies

9.2 Discuss the different sources of information that archaeologists draw on to study early states.

Archaeologists draw on many sources of information to reconstruct the nature of early agricultural states. Variations in such features as **settlement patterns**, site characteristics, and increasing amounts of trade materials can, for example, be associated with different forms of political organization or social stratification. In addition, for the first time, researchers can draw on written sources produced by ancient peoples themselves to help interpret the past. Depending on a researcher's theoretical orientation and research design, a project may focus on certain aspects of a prehistoric state, perhaps on the link between the control of agricultural land and status differentiation, or the expression of religious beliefs in art and architecture.

Settlement Patterns and Organization

Important clues about the scale and complexity of an ancient society can be gleaned by studying the size and distribution of settlements. The world's first cities developed from Neolithic villages. With the emergence of state societies, larger urban settlements, or *cities*, became focal points of government, trade, and religious life. The first states were linked to the control or dominance of particular territories that often incorporated settlements of different size and function. By collecting information on these different types of settlements, archaeologists can locate the centers of ancient states, define sites with specialized functions, infer political divisions, and try to understand how these early societies operated.

In Chapter 2, we saw how archaeologists gather information on past settlements through ground surveys, remote sensing techniques such as aerial photography, and excavation. In addition to locating sites accurately, determining their age is of great importance; without this information, developments at a particular time cannot be evaluated. Drawing on these resources, archaeologists can map the distribution of early settlements and chart changes in their size and distribution through time. This information may provide clues into the origin and development of early political systems.

A concept that illustrates how the arrangement of settlements on the landscape may allow archaeologists to infer the political organization of past societies is illustrated by the use of central place theory. This theory was developed by the German geographer Walter Christaller (1933). Surveying the contemporary distribution of towns in southern Germany in the 1930s, Christaller hypothesized that given uniform topography, resources and opportunities, the distribution of sites in a region would be perfectly regular. Political and economic centers would be located an equal distance from one another; each in turn would be surrounded by a hierarchical arrangement of smaller settlements, all evenly spaced. Implicit in this theory is the assumption that this hierarchical arrangement of settlements represents a network of economic relations, with goods and services, and their administration, centralized in the largest settlements. The archaeological implications of the theory are clear: The largest archaeological site in a region might be assumed to be the capital, regional centers would be represented by slightly smaller sites, and village sites would be even smaller.

Of course, Christaller's idealized plan is altered by many factors. In reality, the locations of natural resources and topography are not uniform. Differences in the types of resources present, their distribution, and the presence or absence of rivers that would facilitate transportation all influence the locations of settlements. The size of sites of the same level or function may vary. Nevertheless, the study of both modern and ancient settlements confirms the basic premise of central place theory: Major centers are located some distance from one another and surrounded by sites in a hierarchically nested pattern. More nuanced models have provided more sophisticated ways of conceptualizing that influence settlement distribution and the organization of ancient states (Crumley 1976; Renfrew and Cooke 1979; Evans and Gould 1982; Nakoinz 2010).

Evidence for Administration In addition to size, archaeologists use a host of other indicators to determine the position of sites in a settlement hierarchy. The primary center of the state can be expected to have more indications of administration, higher status, and more centralized authority than other settlements in the region. These features might be represented by monumental architecture, administrative buildings, archives, and storage facilities. Record keeping was very important in agricultural states, and some of these records survive. People sometimes used seals to impress clay sealings with marks of ownership and authority. Such artifacts might be expected to be particularly prevalent in political, economic, or religious centers (Smith 1990). Features such as these may suggest a site's role as a primary center, even if it is smaller in size than other settlements.

The archaeological record also provides indications of administration outside of the primary center. There may be evidence of centralized administration, such as that just noted, but to a lesser extent. Road systems and carefully maintained pathways might link settlements within a state. A feature that seems associated with many early states is the establishment of outposts in key locations along their margins (Algaze 1993). Such outposts may have served to defend territory, secure access to resources, gain influence in peripheral areas, or facilitate trade.

Monumental Architecture

No archaeological discoveries captivate popular imagination more than the temples, palaces, and tombs of past civilizations. Aside from the obvious advantage of helping archaeologists locate sites, monumental architecture preserves information about the political organization, ritual beliefs, and lifeways of ancient people. As seen in Chapter 8,

A ziggurat in Ur in Southwest Asia. Sumerian ziggurats, such as this, served as places of worship.

megalithic monuments such as Stonehenge were erected by pre-state societies. However, the surplus of wealth, high-density populations, and organization harnessed by states made monumental architecture one of the most striking legacies of early societies. The great temples, pyramids, and palaces of ancient civilizations were the work of thousands of skilled artisans, laborers, and slaves, who quarried and transported huge stones and sculpted numerous artworks. In many respects, they represent the constellation of skills that these early societies possessed. Although some buildings may have had civil functions, the purpose of most monumental constructions in agricultural states was intertwined with religious conceptions and beliefs. While massive, and clearly intended for display, these were often not "public" structures in the sense that all members of the society had access to them. Rather, in most instances, they were reserved for elites or religious leaders.

Monumental architecture also served dramatically different functions in different cultural settings. For example, the *ziggurats* of Southwest Asia may have primarily been shrines used by priests (Charvát et al. 2002; Crawford 1993). Constructed between 5,000 and 2,500 years ago by the Sumerian, Babylonian, and Assyrian civilizations in what is today the countries of Iraq, Iran, and Kuwait, these structures were massive step pyramids, each level successively smaller than the one beneath it. They were multicolored and had extensive architectural details, including glazed inlaid decorations. The massive ziggurat in the Sumerian city of Babylon is said to have had seven levels with flights of steps leading up to a temple or shrine at the summit. Some of the features of these early structures have been identified archaeologically. However, as the ziggurats were constructed of mud blocks, in many cases their upper levels are poorly preserved. The use of the upper levels of ziggurats for shrines is described by the classical Greek writer Herodotus (Crawford 1993: 73, 85).

In contrast to the ziggurat, the pyramids of the Egyptian Old Kingdom dating from between 2,686 B.C. and 2,181 B.C. served a quite different purpose. Based on beliefs of resurrection and life in an afterworld, the pyramids were built as burial chambers for the pharaohs. They contained many material items that the pharaoh had used or needed in life, and would need in the afterworld: Beds, chairs, clothing, weapons, pottery, and even food was included with the burial goods. The first pyramid was built under the direction of Pharaoh Djoser approximately 4,680 years ago (Smith 2004). It is the smallest of the royal pyramids constructed at the capital at Memphis, near modern Cairo. The pyramid of Djoser was followed by more complex structures, culminating with the Great

Pyramid at Giza, which is 481 feet tall and covers 13 acres at its base. The Great Pyramid dates to the reign of Pharaoh Khufu, or Cheops, approximately 4,600 years ago (Romer 2007). Next to the Great Pyramid, two smaller pyramids made of quarried limestone blocks were built by later pharaohs. Like the Sumerian ziggurats, the pyramids were not isolated features, but part of ritual landscape that included an array of temples, causeways and other features.

Monument construction was also prevalent among the early civilizations in the Americas. Some of the best-known are palaces, temples, and pyramid complexes built by the Maya (Coe 2011; Sharer 2006). The Mayan center of Tikal in the tropical forest of Guatemala, was one of the largest cities in the Americas when it flourished between 200 and 900 A.D. Estimates of the settlement's population vary greatly, ranging between 10,000 and 90,000 people. The city's ruins are spectacular. They contain more than 300 palaces, ceremonial and civic buildings, and pyramids. some standing over 230 feet high. At the top of these structures were temples decorated with carvings made from a plaster or cement called *stucco*. Some of these carvings represent *nagual*, animal spirits that lived apart from humans, but could at certain times merge with the human soul. Mayan religious beliefs in half-human–half-jaguar figures, snakes, eagles, alligators, and other spirit beings are preserved in their religious structures.

Specialization

Specialization has received particular attention from archaeologists, as it has often been viewed as a consequence of agriculture that was a key aspect of state formation. Agricultural surplus freed people to undertake nonsubsistence-related pursuits, such as pottery manufacture, weaving, and metal working. In state societies, more people were able to concentrate full time on these specialized tasks, supported by the food surplus made available by intensive agriculture. To some extent, this was simply the modification or elaboration of existing technologies. For example, stone tools such as axes, hammers, knives, and scrapers were refined for more prolonged use or to meet more varied needs. However, a variety of new technologies also appeared. The craftsmanship and artwork found in agricultural civilizations represent a dramatic shift in the scale of technology and the organization of production compared with that of earlier, smaller-scale societies. Many technological innovations were dramatically expressed in myriad pieces of artwork and monumental construction.

Among the most ubiquitous artifacts on Neolithic sites are broken fragments of pottery. Ceramics can be used for a multitude of purposes, ranging from food storage and consumption to ritual purposes and decoration. Although pottery dates back to the beginnings of the Neolithic—earlier in some cases—the production of ceramics became

Funerary Urns, Veracruz Olmec Culture, 800–600 B.C. Earthenware with red slip glaze.
Source: Courtesy of the Everson Museum of Art, Syracuse, New York.

increasingly elaborate in early states. Ceramics are also quite durable and survive well in the ground, so they are commonly found in archaeological contexts. Whereas earlier archaeological sites had often been primarily marked by scatters of stone artifacts, archaeological sites associated with the early civilizations of Mesopotamia, Mesoamerica, China, and other world areas are often covered with hundreds of thousands of ceramic sherds.

In many parts of the Old World, pottery was increasingly fired in *kilns*: specialized ovens that allowed pottery to be heated to higher temperatures, making it more durable. In Southwest Asia, the first kilns have been dated to approximately 8,000 years ago (Bienkowski and Millard 2010: 233). Some of the world's oldest *pottery wheels* date 2,000 or 3,000 years later—a period of time that corresponds with the emergence of early states (Roux and Pierre de Miroschedji 2009). The pottery wheel is a device that can be used for shaping ceramic vessels, allowing them to be produced quicker and with more regularity in shape than if they are made entirely by hand. Pottery wheels became widely used in the later Neolithic societies of Europe and Asia. An amazing diversity of ceramic pottery bowls, jugs, jars, dishes, and other items were produced, often decorated with a multitude of geometric designs, as well as naturalistic representations of animals, plants, and people.

Many key technological developments are associated with early agricultural civilizations. In the Old World, a particularly important innovation was the beginning of *metallurgy*, the ability to extract metals from their ores. Gold, copper, and iron had long been utilized by Paleolithic and earlier Neolithic populations in many parts of the world (Photo 1989). However, in these cases, people used naturally occurring pieces of these metals, such as gold nuggets, meteoric iron, or pieces of native copper. These materials were limited, and people had to primarily rely on stone or wood to fashion tools. With the development of metallurgy, large amounts of metals could be extracted from ores. Copper, tin, and iron ores were smelted and then forged or cast into a diversity or ornaments

Ancient glass beads from Mesopotamia, Egypt, and China. Many technological innovations, as well as increasing craft specialization, are associated with early agricultural states.
Source: Collection of The Corning Museum of Glass, Corning, New York.

and implements, enabling some agricultural peoples to create more durable tools, as well as more efficient weapons. By 2,000 to 3,000 years ago, iron smelted from ore was being produced from Southwest Asia, to sub-Saharan Africa and Asia (Miller and van Der Merwe 1994; Muhly, 2003; Wagner 1993: 335–340).

Across the world, early agricultural civilizations produced an array of intricate carvings, massive sculptures, woven textiles, beads, and other artwork. The world's oldest glass objects are also associated with early agricultural states of Southwest Asia. Elaborate watercolors called *frescoes*, painted on plaster walls, decorated some of the early palaces and houses. Collectively, these innovations testify to the impressive development of both technology and the arts in early agricultural civilizations (Berrin and Pasztory 1993).

In settlements of state societies, craft specialists were often concentrated in particular areas, and many archaeological sites bear evidence of specialized workshops or areas for craft production. Different crafts often have their own distinctive technology and materials. Consequently, these areas can sometimes be readily identified archaeologically. Researchers have uncovered extensive areas used for *obsidian* flaking, jade working, weaving, sewing, leatherworking, potting, metalworking, and even beer brewing.

The preceding discussion has focused on increasing craft specialization. However, the surplus agricultural resources found in early states also freed people for other specialized roles, including accountants, administrators, scribes, soldiers, and rulers. In some societies, one's craft specialization or profession was closely linked to social position and status. Archaeological data—depicting ancient life, art, and sculpture—attest to both these different activities and the varied status these jobs accorded.

Status and Social Ranking

Written accounts and illustrations, often depicting the wealth and power of rulers, underscore the disparities that existed between the rich and the poor in early agricultural states. The kind of food, housing, clothing, and material goods people had access to was rigidly controlled. Many of these distinctions are recognizable archaeologically in palace complexes, the presence of exotic trade items, and greater-than-average concentrations of wealth. For example, Teotihuacán, which flourished in Mexico between about 100 and 650 A.D., was a planned city with perhaps as many as 120,000 inhabitants at its peak, making it one of the largest cities in the world at that time (Carballo 2011; Millon 1976; Millon 1993; Sanders et al. 2003). Neither the houses nor their furnishings were uniform; larger compounds with lavish interior decoration suggest a great deal of variation in both wealth and status.

Important indications of status differences may also be expressed in mortuary remains (Brown 1971; Carr 1995; Chapman et al. 1981). Archaeologists often study *grave goods*, artifacts associated with a body, to evaluate status. Surveying variation in the materials from different graves from a given population, researchers may gain insights into the deceased's social standing. A dramatic case in point is provided by ancient Egypt. The amount of labor invested in the Egyptian pyramids, which served as tombs for the pharaohs, indicates the both importance of the pharaoh and the organizational power of the state. The treatment of the pharaoh's body was also different. Initially, the practice of mummification was something only reserved for the ruling elite. Later, during the New Kingdom, mummification became the desired means of burial for all Egyptians. However, even then the preparation of the body, the care taken, and the associated burial goods were much better in

Glass portrait of King Amenhotep II, Egypt, 1426–1400 B.C. Art in early agricultural states often highlighted the power and authority of the rulers. Collection of The Corning Museum of Glass, Corning, New York, purchased with the assistance of the Museum Endowment Fund.

the pharaoh's case than with other members of the population. In some early agricultural civilizations, servants were put to death and buried with a ruler, along with a wealth of grave goods. It is logical to assume that the graves of higher status individuals within a society will be more impressive and have a wider array of valuable goods than those of commoners. It is, however, important to recognize other differences within cultural groups, such as age, occupation, and gender in assessing these differences.

In some cases, a person's status may be inferred directly from skeletal remains. Using this information, biological anthropologists are often able to determine the age, sex, and health of an individual, and this information may provide clues to a person's social standing. As discussed in Chapter 8, the transition to agriculture brought about dramatic changes in peoples' diets, not all of them for the better (Cohen and Armelagos 1984; Larsen 1995). In some cases, people became dependent upon particular domesticated plants like corn, to the exclusion of most other foodstuffs. This contributed to decreasing nutrition and dietary stress, consequences that were often felt by the less elite members of a society (Goodman et al. 1984).

Trade and Exchange

Trade—the exchange of goods and services—has long been a feature of human societies; it did not begin with the appearance of early states. During the Upper Paleolithic, valuable raw materials, such as obsidian and shells, were traded over long distances (Renfrew et al. 1966; Frahm 2012). During the Neolithic, some individuals began to concentrate on trade full time, and exchange networks extended over ever-growing areas (Blake and Knapp 2005; Frahm 2013). With the emergence of early states, however, trade and trade networks burgeoned, often controlled by state bureaucracies. Expanded mercantile exchange is indicated by the appearance of standardized weights and measures as well as monetary systems, including coinage. Documentary records also frequently list trade contacts and the costs and amounts of materials exchanged.

More information about early exchange networks comes from the trade materials themselves. Certain kinds of raw materials, or *artifacts*, may be characteristic of a particular region. Resources were not evenly distributed throughout the landscape, and items such as precious stones, metals, and amber were frequently traded over long distances. Raw materials might have been exchanged for finished products such as pottery, hides, beads, and cloth. As some of these items have survived, they provide an archaeological record of past exchange (Baugh and Ericson 1994; Brumfiel and Earle 1987). By plotting the distribution of these commodities, an archaeologist may be able to trace past trade networks. Typically, the availability of a trade material decreases as distance from the source increases. Hence, it is logical to assume that as one moves away from a resource or production center, archaeological sites will contain fewer examples of that particular type of trade item. Yet, interpretation of this information is less straightforward than one might think. Simply counting the instances of a particular artifact at sites fails to consider the site size or function, the variation in preservation, and the amount of archaeological work that has been undertaken (Renfrew and Bahn 2000). To assess this trade successfully, archaeologists need to consider these variables.

Some trade materials can be readily recognized as exotic imports. At times, coins, sealings, or manufacturers' marks on such artifacts as pottery may even indicate specific sources. But the origin of some artifacts is less clear. Pottery styles can be copied, and stones of diverse origin can look quite similar. To identify an artifact's origins, archaeologists use a number of techniques of varying sophistication. The simplest method is to examine an object such as a stone or potsherd under low magnification for rocks, minerals, or other inclusions that can be linked to a particular location.

A much more sophisticated technique, referred to as **trace element analysis**, involves the study of the elements found in different raw materials or artifacts (Tite 1972; Pollard et al. 2007). The basic chemical configuration of certain kinds of metals or stones is broadly similar—all obsidian, for example, contains silicon, oxygen, and calcium—but certain elements may be present in very small quantities. These trace elements may occur in quite different concentrations in materials from different sources. Therefore, if their presence in artifacts is plotted, it may provide a means of assessing distribution patterns. Trace element analysis has proven to be a very valuable technique for tracing the origins of a wide variety of different trade materials. The cost and specialized equipment needed has often limited its use by many researchers. However, the increasing availability of devices such as the portable or handheld *X-ray fluorescence* (XRF) machine has dramatically increased the feasibility of these types of studies. The handheld XRF emits high intensity X-rays. When an artifact or fragment of obsidian is subjected to these fluorescent X-rays, distinctive to different elements are emitted, allowing the different elements to be identified. Because this technique is not destructive and is relatively inexpensive, it can be used in a variety of settings.

The Archaeology of Religion

Allusion to the importance of religion in early states has pervaded the preceding discussion. As state societies emerged, political power and religion became closely intertwined (see discussion in Chapter 19). Religion was often an important factor in validating the authority of the rulers and unifying the peoples within the state. Because there was no separation between the state and religious authority, religions in early agricultural states are sometimes referred to as *ecclesiastical religions*. Monuments and ritual structures such as ziggurats, temples, and pyramids are potent testaments to both religious beliefs and to the status afforded to religious leaders. Evidence for ancient religion has, consequently, often been the focus of the archaeological study of early states (Barnes 1995; Budge 1900; Dunand and Zivie-Coche 2005; Insoll 2004, 2011; Pauketat et al. 2002).

Ancient religion is, perhaps, one of the most fascinating aspects of archaeological study. It is also one of the most challenging. As is the case with other areas of research such as trade or status, important insights into ancient religion may be provided by written texts. When available, these sources may offer a great deal of information (Allen 2001; Budge 1895). Yet such descriptions are often lacking, and in many cases written texts only present certain aspects of religious practices. In such cases archaeologists must infer religious beliefs from material culture, and this is difficult. A standard joke among archaeologists when confronting an artifact whose function is unknown is to describe it as a "ritual object," an explanation that serves to underscore the challenge of inferring the complex, non-material aspects of past cultures.

Although the study of past religions is difficult, insights may be drawn from a number of different sources. Often religious beliefs are given physical expression in places of worship. These locations may have architectural features,

spatial arrangements, decorative elements, and artifacts distinct from other buildings at a site. In many cultures, worship involved offerings or animal and human sacrifices, traces of which may be preserved. Archaeological finds may also include representations of deities, ritual figures, or symbols that convey religious beliefs. At times, individual artifacts may provide important clues. Such is the case with the Moche, a small state in the valleys of coastal Peru that reached its zenith between about 100 and 750 A.D. (see the box The Downfall of the Moche page 222). Archaeologists used remarkably detailed depictions of rituals on Moche pottery and murals to interpret material recovered archaeologically (Donnan and Castillo 1992). Finally, some of the most tantalizing indications of past belief systems are provided by burials. The manner of interment, grave goods, and funerary objects provides insight into mortuary rituals and, ultimately, some of the most important of human belief systems.

An interesting example of the unique insights that can be provided by archaeological data is illustrated by the Aztec New Fire Ceremony. During the fifteenth and sixteenth centuries, the Aztec state dominated the region of central Mexico and Guatemala. It was the dominant state in this area at the time the Spanish arrived in the early sixteenth century. The New Fire Ceremony is one of the few Aztec rituals documented in both the archaeological and historical records (Elson and Smith 2001). The Spanish described the ceremony as an imperial Aztec ritual celebrating the renewal of the cosmos. It included specific activities such as fasting, ritual cleansing, bloodletting and, most notably, the destruction of old household items. Piles of discarded artifacts associated with the ceremony have been identified archaeologically, verifying the practice in a variety of locations. Archaeological data, however, indicate that the New Fire Ceremony was celebrated by other peoples before the rise of the Aztec. The fact that this ceremony predates the rise of Aztec authority has led researchers to suggest that the New Fire Ceremony was an ancient ritual that was appropriated by the Aztec empire as a means of ritually legitimizing their authority (Elson and Smith 2001: 170).

Religion was a central feature of agricultural states, and it would be impossible to interpret monuments like the pyramids of Egypt, the temples of the Moche, or the daily lives of the Aztec without examining the unique belief systems of which they were a part. Consequently, the study of past religions and reconstructions of ancient rituals is an important focus of anthropological research.

Written Language

The advent of state-level organization gives archaeologists a source of information not available to researchers working on earlier periods: written sources. Writing appears independently in several world areas, including

Mesoamerica, Egypt and the Nile Valley, Southwest Asia, China, the Indus River Valley, and the Aegean (Daniels and Bright 1995). In each of these regions, writing systems were developed 2,000 to 5,000 years ago. As noted, Childe considered writing to be fundamental to the definition of civilization, and there is no question that writing systems would have been advantageous in a variety of ways (Hooker 1990). However, surveying early states, archaeologist Bruce Trigger (1993) notes that there are no obvious differences in the social, political, and economic organization of societies that had writing and those that did not. In the absence of writing, information was sometimes chronicled by special oral historians who recounted traditions, rulers' names, and important events. This is the case with many of the societies of sub-Saharan Africa. Although there are several examples of indigenous writing systems from Africa, these are relatively recent and very limited in terms of their use. Oral traditions, rather, provide the most important means of passing on information to following generations (DeCorse 1996).

Anthropologists have explored the origins of writing and its effects on society. Writing systems may have originated in agricultural states in response to commercial and political needs—for example, as a means of keeping accounts for taxation. This is an observation borne out by the fact that the majority of early texts from around the world deal with rather mundane aspects of record keeping. But as complex civilizations developed, writing systems became linked with historical, literary, and religious expression. They also chronicled the achievements of the rulers. Often their specific functions varied in different cultural settings. Undoubtedly, literacy afforded great social and economic power to the official bureaucrats, lawyers, and priests of large-scale political states (Goody 1987).

Written records may provide information on administration, ruling dynasties, political divisions, trade contacts, and locations of settlements. Because of the amount of information such sources provide, archaeologists working in some regions may gear their work toward locating and interpreting early libraries or archives. This is particularly true of research in Southwest Asia, where many records are preserved on clay tablets, and also in Egypt where many records were inscribed in stone or on surviving pieces of papyrus (a paper-like material made from the papyrus plant) and pieces of art. Apart from the information preserved in the records themselves, repositories such as libraries indicate the degree of centralized authority and bureaucratic organization that was present.

Writing Systems Writing systems in early agricultural states developed independently and are quite distinct in terms of the specific systems employed and the information they provide. Simple pictures, sometimes referred to as *pictographs*, were the precursors of several early writing systems. Pictographs utilize symbols (simple drawings of the things they represent) and ideograms (which represent ideas or more abstract concepts). Pictographic symbols and ideograms are still used today, exemplified in signs indicating male and female restrooms, nonsmoking areas, or pedestrian crosswalks. In some cases, as in ancient Egyptian, Sumerian, and Chinese civilizations, pictographs were developed into more elaborate *ideographic* or **logographic writing systems**, which use pictures or symbols to represent complete words. Of course, many symbols are required to represent all the words in a language. These writing systems can be contrasted with writing systems that represent sounds, which are then used in combinations to construct words.

The Chinese writing system developed from a logographic writing system. The Chinese characters, estimated to number between 70,000 and 125,000, have been conventionalized, but it is still easy to recognize their ideographic origins (DeFrancis 1984). In the Chinese system, the individual symbols represent complete words (technically called *morphemes*) that have meaning. There is no connection between sounds (*phonemes*) and their written expression. This means that the speakers of the varied Chinese dialects, such as Mandarin, Cantonese, or Hakka, can readily read the same text without difficulty. Thus, writing has been one of the strongest cultural forces in unifying Chinese culture.

Several **hieroglyphic writing** systems also evolved from an ideographic type of picture writing. Hieroglyphic writing simplifies a picture into a symbol that has a direct relationship to the sound of a word. People in different parts of the world, like the Egyptians and Maya, developed hieroglyphic systems independently of one another (Loprieno 1995; Coe and Van Stone 2005).

In another form of writing, called *syllabic writing*, the characters themselves express nothing but a sequence of sounds. These sounds make up the syllables of the language. Syllabic writing is more efficient than ideographic or hieroglyphic writing because it uses a smaller number of characters. The ancient Semitic writing systems such as Arabic and Hebrew were syllabic systems. One modern language that still involves a mostly syllabic writing system is Japanese (although Japanese writing also includes Chinese characters).

Eventually, in the Mediterranean region, *alphabetic writing systems* evolved from syllabic forms. In alphabetic writing, there is a sign for each sound (technically each phoneme) of the language rather than one for each word or for each syllable. This is the most efficient writing system because most languages have only 12 to 60 total sounds. Hence, an alphabetic writing system can, with the fewest possible units, record every possible utterance in the language. The Greek writing system is the first to be considered fully alphabetic because it has a separate written symbol for each vowel and consonant. From the Greek system, the Romans adapted the Latin alphabet, which became the basis of the writing system of Western Europe and, eventually, of English.

Theories about State Formation

9.3 Discuss some of the challenges and limitations of the different theories of state formation.

Agricultural states arose independently in different world areas at different times and not at all in some regions. Why did these early states emerge? As in the case for the transition to domestication, the reasons for state formation are not entirely obvious. While writing, architecture, and numerous technological innovations can be considered beneficial, the advantages of state-level society were not equally shared by all. While the opulent palaces and wealth of the ruling elite are readily apparent, commoners sacrificed some of their personal rights to the state, which collected tribute and taxes, used force to maintain its authority, and in many cases institutionalized slavery.

Not surprisingly, there are varied perspectives regarding the emergence of early states, and there has been a great deal of debate regarding the question of why states formed. As a review of the preceding information indicates, states were complex both in terms of their sociopolitical organization and the ways in which they are represented archaeologically. Empirical evaluation of causal factors on the basis of archaeological information is challenging (Bell 1994: 100-116; Crumley 1995; Roscoe 2013). What are the key attributes that are the measure of a state? If we cannot adequately define it, how can its origins be examined? Two overarching factors are of particular and interrelated importance. The first is scale. Although states shared some features with earlier Paleolithic and Neolithic societies, they tended to be larger. This is true with regard to the settlement sites represented, including the first truly urban centers–or cities, as well as the extent of the surrounding territories over which states extended their influence. Secondly, states maintained centralized political authority. Although a variety of populations might be represented and other social institutions might be present, the authority of the state cuts across these divisions and unified the polity.

To explain state formation, researchers have posited an array of theories (Lenski 1966; Carneiro 1970; Service 1975; Cohen and Service 1978; Haas 1982; Deihl 2000; Roscoe 2013). For convenience, these can be divided into three contrasting perspectives: integrationist (sometimes referred to as *voluntaristic* or *functionalist*) theories; conflict theories (sometimes called *coercive*); and multi-causal (or *multivariant*) theories. **Integrationist theories** of state formation assume that society as a whole benefited from state organization or, in other words, the state was a positive, integrative response that arose by consensus to meet conditions that a society faced. The special benefits that certain individuals or groups in a society may have obtained were balanced by the key organizational or managerial functions they performed, which enabled the society to survive and prosper. In contrast, **conflict theories** emphasize domination and exploitation. These models see state organization as having arisen as a result of the ability of certain individuals or groups to monopolize or control people and/or resources. State organization, therefore, was advantageous only to a society's dominant elite and, in general, very costly to subordinate groups like the peasantry.

Integrationist and conflict theories are not necessarily either-or scenarios (Allardt 1968; Cohen 1978; Roscoe 2013; Spencer and Redmond 2004). Evidence regarding early states reveals evidence to support both integrationist and coercive perspectives. In reality, it was likely a combination of factors that contributed to the development of these political formations. Many interpretations have, consequently, considered **multi-causal** (or *multivariant*) reasons for state formation. Given the contrasting information from different world areas, it also seems clear that the constellation of factors that led to state formation were not the same in all cultural settings.

Integrationist or Voluntaristic Perspectives

Integrationist perspectives suggest that the state arose as a result of collective action for the general benefit of society, for example, the construction of canals for irrigation and defensive works, or the exploitation of natural resources. A theory often used to illustrate an integrationist view of state formation is the hydraulic hypothesis developed by Karl Wittfogel (1957) on the basis of his work in China. Wittfogel observed that many early states developed in river valleys, areas that would have provided both farmland and sufficient water for growing crops. His **hydraulic hypothesis** proposed that the development of the state was linked to the need to effectively manage water resources in these areas. Wittfogel suggested that expansion of intensive agriculture created problems, such as disputes among landowners and the need to build and operate irrigation canals, dikes, and other devices related to the control of water resources. Labor also had to be recruited, mobilized, fed, and organized. To resolve these problems, people developed centralized bureaucracies.

While water resources were undeniably important in early farming communities as a driving force behind early state formation, the hydraulic hypothesis was not borne out by more recent archaeological evidence. Many of the irrigation projects associated with agricultural civilizations, such as those in early Mesopotamia, Mesoamerica,

In areas such as the Nile Valley, the *shaduf*, a bucket on a long weighted pole, was used to bring water to irrigation channels. The construction and control of water resources may have played an important role in the origin of early states.

South America, and China, appear to have been organized locally without centralized governments (Adams 1966; Chang 1986). In the central highlands of Mexico and elsewhere, archaeological research has also demonstrated the construction of irrigation canals by pre-state societies (Sanders and Price 1968). In many of these cases, state-level societies did not emerge. In contrast, in such areas as Egypt and India, the state bureaucracy had developed prior to the initiation of large-scale irrigation. Therefore, instead of large-scale irrigation contributing to the rise of the state, it was actually a later consequence of state development. Thus, in a wide variety of cases, the advent of irrigation does not correspond with state formation.

Trade and Exchange   Other integrationist perspectives can be illustrated by theories that emphasize the role of trade in the emergence of the state (Rathje 1971; Wright and Johnson 1975). In these scenarios, the organizational requirements needed to produce trade items and to manage trade were a major driving force. At least in some cases, early civilizations seemed to have flourished in areas where some essential resources were lacking. For example, obsidian used in the manufacture of stone tools, metal ores,

or other key resources might be absent. Viewing trade from an integrationist perspective, the ability to control these resources and related craft specialization would have been very advantageous. The bureaucracies associated with the control of these resources and the increasing labor specialization linked with the production of trade items led to a concomitant rise in administrative specialization.

As in the case with the hydraulic hypothesis, the timing of trade and craft specialization does not seem to work in terms of the genesis of early states. Although it is clear that trade was important, it is also clear that it was not the primary cause in the rise of state societies. Increased understanding of pre-state exchange systems and techniques such as trace element analysis have made the picture of early exchange far more complex than was previously thought (Sabloff and Lamberg-Karlovsky 1975). Inter- and intraregional trade long predates state formation in many instances, and increased trade may be more a consequence of state society than a reason for state formation.

Conflict or Coercive Theories

Conflict theories of state formation are as equally varied as integrationist perspectives, and subsume a number of distinct perspectives. Conflict perspectives are similar, however, in that these models stress conflict, coercion and dominance as key aspects of state formation (Roscoe 2013). The earliest of these perspectives was articulated in the nineteenth century by Friedrich Engels, who drew on the work of Karl Marx and anthropologist Lewis Henry Morgan (Claessen and Skalnik 1978; also see Chapter 13). In Engel's perspective, agricultural surpluses led to increasing social stratification, particularly the division between those who farmed the land and those who lived off of the agricultural surpluses that were produced. The need of the latter group to protect their accumulated wealth led to increasing social stratification and, eventually, the state.

Anthropologist Morton Fried (1967) also developed a conflict model that focuses upon agricultural resources and growing social stratification. According to Fried, as populations grew, vital resources such as land became increasingly scarce, causing various groups to compete for these resources. Ultimately, this competition led to domination by a particular group, which then enjoyed privileged access to land and other economic resources. This dominant group constructed the state to maintain its privileged position. To accomplish this, the state—the ruling elite—used force and repression against subordinate groups. Thus, in Fried's view, the state is inherently coercive and utilizes force to perpetuate the economic and political inequalities in a society.

Other researchers have similarly underscored the evidence for stratification and domination by a ruling elite during the earliest phases of state formation. For example,

Jonathan Haas (1982) uses data from various world areas to underscore the role of conflict and coercion. Though Haas notes that the process of state formation included some integrative functions, he concludes that the elites dominated economic resources to the point that they could exert repressive and coercive power over the rest of the population. For example, Haas observes that the large-scale monument construction of state societies required a ruling elite class that coerced peasants to pay tribute and provide labor to the state. The ruling elite could use its control over economic resources to mobilize large-scale labor projects. Haas does not believe that simpler types of political organizations, such as chiefdoms, could extract this labor and tribute from their populations.

Archaeologist Elizabeth Brumfiel (1983) approaches conflict from another direction. Drawing on evidence from the Aztec state in Mesoamerica, she hypothesized that coercion and repression evolve from political factors rather than from the economic determinants proposed by Fried and Haas. Brumfiel focuses on the political networks and the elimination of competition utilized by various Aztec leaders to consolidate the authority of one ruling group. During one phase of political competition, the rulers centralized their authority through organizational reforms that reduced the power of subordinate rulers and nobles. Brumfiel maintains that these manipulations are important preconditions for state formation and coercion.

Warfare and Circumscription

A different perspective of the role of conflict in state formation is provided by anthropologist Robert Carneiro (1970). In particular, Carneiro sought to explain why early agricultural states emerged in some settings and not others. His theory focuses on the availability of environmental resources and warfare. Drawing on specific examples from research in South America, as well as other world areas, Carneiro hypothesized that population growth in a region with clearly defined boundaries, such as a narrow valley surrounded by high mountains, leads to land shortages, resulting in increased competition and warfare among villages. In this context, efficient military organization and the ability to seize and control agricultural lands would have been advantageous. In such cases, one group eventually became powerful enough to dominate other populations. Members of this dominant group subsequently became the state administrators who ruled over the less powerful groups.

These settings where environmental resources were limited, or *circumscribed*, can be contrasted with situations where there was ample agricultural land; in such cases, defeated populations and those seeking new farmland could simply move into new areas. Thus, the state only emerged in regions where land was in short supply and competition for scarce resources existed.

Carneiro (1970) further suggested that population centers could be confined, or *circumscribed,* by factors other than environment and geography. Circumscription, for example, would also have occurred when an expanding population was surrounded by other powerful societies. This "social circumscription" would have prevented weaker groups from simply migrating into surrounding regions where they would be able to enjoy greater autonomy. Surrounded by stronger polities, they too would be pushed to develop stronger centralized authority.

Criticisms of Conflict Approaches Some theorists have been critical of conflict models. Drawing on various archaeological data, Elman Service (1975) and other researchers concede that inequality and conflict are basic aspects of state development, but they emphasize the enormous conflict-reducing capacities of state systems that coordinate and organize diverse groups of people. Service argues that the archaeological record does not indicate extensive class-based conflict in pre-state societies that subsequently would have led to state formation. Following theorists such as Max Weber, critics further note that state systems tend to become coercive or repressive only when they are weak. Service further argued that strong centralized state systems provide benefits to all social groups and thereby gain political legitimacy and authority that reduce the degree of repression and coercion needed to maintain order. In this sense, Service views state societies as differing only in degree from chiefdom societies.

Some writers have also questioned the fundamental theoretical underpinning of conflict theories, which assumes that human ambition, greed, and exploitation are universal motivating factors (Tainter 1990). If such characteristics are common to all societies, why didn't food surpluses, status differentiation, and class conflict appear in all societies? Hunting-and-gathering populations have social mechanisms that maintain egalitarian relationships and hinder individual ambition. If class conflict is a universal explanation of state formation, "How did the human species survive roughly 99 percent of its history without the state?" (Tainter 1990:35).

Multicausal (or *Multivariant*) Theories of State Formation

Review of the preceding factors indicates that the reasons for state formation are more complex than can be explained by a single causal factor. Not surprisingly, many researchers have long drawn on aspects of both integrationist and conflict theories to reach a full understanding of the dynamics of state formation. Instead of focusing on one variable, such as irrigation or coercion, these theories attempt to understand the links among variables in the social system. Some of these perspectives drew on cultural ecology, a theoretical perspective that focused on how sociocultural systems adapt to their environmental settings. (See discussion of cultural ecology in Chapter 13.)

Theories based on *systems models* of state formation have emphasized the requirements of agricultural states to organize large populations; to produce, extract, and exchange economic resources; to maintain military organizations; and to manage information (Cohen 1978; Dye 2009; Flannery 1972; Wright 1977). A case in point is the perspective of Robert McCormack Adams (1966; 1981), which was based on his fieldwork in Iraq. Adams underscored that there was no single factor that resulted in state formation. Rather, states arose as a consequence of a variety of interrelated conditions, including social organization, the environment, craft specialization, and population growth. Once the state arose, this fostered additional transformations, such as further territorial expansion and continued population growth.

Conclusions about Early State Formation

The reasons for state formation are clearly complex and do not lend themselves to explanations reliant on a single cause. Rather, they likely involved a range of demographic, social, political, economic, environmental, and cultural factors. Although integrationist factors are present in early societies, these seem difficult to reconcile with the archaeological information available. Conflict theories are perhaps somewhat more satisfactory, in that they do a better job of explaining the driving forces behind the emergence of states, and thus why states appeared in some places and not others. Yet some of the conditions noted seem to fit some world areas, but not others. Systems models, in contrast, are attractive in incorporating the spectrum of variables that might be present.

In truth, none of the theories surveyed above are quite as simple as they have been presented; they rather are meant to highlight the different factors that may have come into play in state formation. The majority of the theories reviewed recognize the importance of a variety of both integrative and conflict factors in state formation. On the one hand, it is clear that the organizational and managerial capabilities of state society are worthwhile. On the other, it may be noted that the benefits of stratification are not as advantageous to all members of a population, as some integrationist theories hypothesize.

One of the most challenging aspects of evaluating different theories of state formation returns to the problem of the different terminology and definitions employed. Anthropologist Paul Roscoe has recently underscored this by observing that the various integrationist and conflict theories are often aimed at explaining different aspects of ancient societies. Although often equally subsumed under the label "state," he underscores the difference between the "political community" (the totality of individuals who make up the body politic) and the political center (the apparatus of government). While these concepts are clearly interrelated, they deal with different aspects of societies. Roscoe observes that aims of a political community are often shared and voluntaristic; for example, the need to unite for protection and defense. On the other hand, the objectives of the political center (the ruling elite) are characteristically coercive and aimed at maintaining, or securing, their power and authority.

Hierarchy or Heterarchy? Human societies are complex affairs, and the workings of past social systems are difficult to untangle. This complexity has been underscored by many researchers. For example, in reviewing complex societies, archaeologist Carole Crumley notes the complexity of the different variables involved, but also the varied ways they interact across different scales within societies. She observes that models or early states have often assessed complexity in terms of hierarchy: increasing stratification in terms of status and differentiation in power relations. Although it is clear that such stratification does characterize power relations in some cases, Crumley emphasizes the networks of *heterarchical* relations that may operate at the same time. Religious and kinship relations may intersect in various cross-cutting ways with political organization. While hierarchical organizations represent vertical differences, heterarchy can be thought of as horizontal, cross-cutting hierarchical power relations.

Particularly in the case of complex societies like states, status—a person's position in a society—may reflect his or her amount of wealth, power, or prestige, or a combination of all three. One individual, for example, might be a ritual practitioner, with others recognized as important merchants, architects, or administrators. Their social standings, and how those might be represented in material preserved archaeologically, are quite different. These types of nuanced distinctions are also true with regard to settlements. Three cities might have all been similar in size, and so appear quite similar when viewed archaeologically. However, their size and the relative importance it represents might derive from different factors: One might have been an administrative center, one a manufacturing center, and the third a harbor valued as a trade center. Study of ethnographic and archaeologically known societies in Africa, in particular, indicate that the rigidly hierarchical models of complex societies found in some world areas are not applicable in many cases (MacIntosh 1999). These observations underscore the complexity of past social relations. However, they also highlight the ambiguity of concepts such as band, tribe, chiefdom, and state, which many researchers feel do not fully capture the varied nature of past human societies.

Critical Perspectives

Contacts between Worlds?

How interconnected was the ancient world? There have been many theories concerning trans-Atlantic and trans-Pacific contacts long before Christopher Columbus's voyages of discovery and the maritime expansion of Europe in the late fifteenth century. At times, these theories have been based on quite scanty evidence. And some have been quite fantastic.

Many of the early European settlers in the Americas simply could not believe that Native Americans built the massive earthen and stone monuments they encountered and suggested that they were the work of Phoenicians, one of the Lost Tribes of Israel, or a lost race of mound builders. More recently, zoologist Barry Fell (1980) proposed that America was settled by colonists from Europe and North Africa sometime between 3000 and 1000 B.C. Still other theories have proposed that inhabitants of the mythical continents of Atlantis or Mu settled the Americas and left traces behind (Williams 1991). In a very speculative work, Jeffrey Goodman (1981) proposed that civilizations worldwide are related to an original culture that arose in California, which he asserts was the original Garden of Eden. Goodman contended that from this location, humans settled the rest of the Americas and crossed to the mythical continents of Atlantis and Mu to enter Europe and Asia. In an even more radical vein, popular writer Erich Von Daniken (1970) has argued that extraterrestrial beings colonized Earth and were the impetus for early human civilizations.

Archaeologists and physical anthropologists who have examined these ideas are skeptical. As we saw in preceding chapters, there is substantial evidence for human evolution in Africa, the expansion of anatomically modern humans throughout the world, and the rise of a diversity of agricultural societies in many areas. The consensus regarding the peopling of the Americas is that the initial human settlement was by Asian populations during the Upper Paleolithic, possibly via a land bridge in the area of the Bering Strait or via watercraft along the coast. Dental and skeletal evidence, as well as genetic information from Native American populations, is consistent with an Asian origin. There have been no generally accepted archaeological discoveries connecting ancient Israelites or Phoenicians with the early settlement of the Americas. Nor have geologists or archaeologists found any evidence of lost continents such as Atlantis and Mu. Certainly, archaeologists have not identified any evidence of spaceships!

In his entertaining book *Frauds, Myths, and Mysteries: Science and Pseudoscience in Archaeology*, archaeologist Kenneth Feder (2014) reviews many of the myths, mysteries, and frauds that have been perpetrated about the past. He notes that many people often seem more prone to believe speculations rather than scientifically verified evidence. Because the past cannot be experienced directly, people are drawn to speculative, fantastic, or entertaining accounts of what occurred.

Other theories concerning pre-Columbian intercontinental contacts are more plausible. Anthropologist George Carter (1988) suggested that plants and animals spread from Asia to America before the age of Columbus. Evidence, such as pottery designs, artwork, and plants, has also led some archaeologists to hypothesize pre-Columbian diffusion across the Pacific (Jett 1978). Archaeologist Betty J. Meggers (1980), for example, theorized the pre-Columbian diffusion of culture traits from Japan to Ecuador on the basis of similarities in pottery chronologies and decorative styles in the two areas.

While possible, these theories are difficult to prove. Similarities in material culture do not necessarily indicate the actual movement of people or the diffusion of ideas. Humans are naturally inventive and, in disparate world areas, may come up with quite similar ideas. Although Near Eastern, Egyptian, and Mesoamerican pyramids look somewhat similar, they appear to be based upon the universal and practical means of monument construction. There are a finite number of ways to construct a high tower with stone blocks. For this reason, children from widely different cultural settings often construct pyramids when playing with blocks.

Archaeologists need a compelling amount of evidence to evaluate and support a new theory. This is particularly true if the proposed interpretation is inconsistent with other existing theories and evidence. At this point, however, it is important to emphasize that this does not mean that archaeologists have absolutely proven that Atlantis did not exist or that Phoenicians did not visit the Americas before Columbus. Or, for that matter, that the Earth was colonized by extraterrestrials. Archaeologists just need more evidence.

Columbus and his crew were not the first Europeans to reach the Americas. The pre-Columbian Viking presence in North America was long considered unlikely. However, persistent research and the archaeological excavations have demonstrated the Viking settlement of Greenland and the northeast coast of Canada beginning in the 10th century A.D.—beating Columbus by several hundred years (Ingstad and Ingstad 2001). Many different theories regarding the initial human settlement of the Americas, the origins of agriculture, and the rise of complex societies have been proposed by archaeologists. These theories are still widely debated, despite the fact that some of them have a good deal more supporting evidence than some of the more fanciful ideas discussed previously. Anthropologists evaluate different theories on the basis of the data available. These make some interpretations more likely than others. Some theories can be discarded. However, reevaluation and reassessment of interpretations can always be undertaken in light of new evidence.

Points to Ponder

1. What ideas have you heard regarding connections between distant civilizations?

2. What types of evidence would convince you of connections between civilizations? How would you go about assessing information about these ideas?

3. What would it take to convince you that extraterrestrial creatures brought civilization to Earth?

4. What does an extraterrestrial origin imply about the abilities of humans to develop their own civilizations?

Figure 9.1 Early states present an abundance of technology, craft specialization, and artistic achievement. The states shown here represent some of the earliest states in the world.

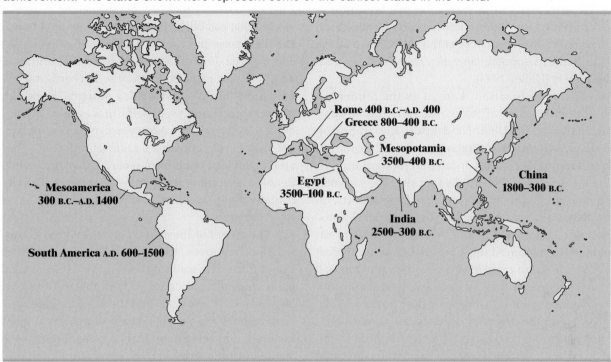

States in Different World Areas

9.4   Discuss where some of the first agricultural states were located and their characteristics.

Theories regarding state formation address one of the most interesting, as well as one of the most frustrating, questions regarding ancient civilizations. Theories about the development of the state will continue to be debated for years to come. Apart from ongoing theorizing, information on early civilizations has provided tremendous insight into the past. Ongoing research around the world illustrates an amazing range of past societies and indicates that there are many more mysteries left to uncover.

As in the case of agricultural origins, archaeological research on early states and civilizations has concentrated on some world areas more than others. Southwest Asia (Mesopotamia) and Egypt have been the focus of extensive research dating back to the early nineteenth century. As a result, these regions figured prominently in early models of state formation and civilization (Childe 1936, 1952). In some interpretations, civilization was seen as having largely developed in these areas and then spread elsewhere. These regions do indeed provide some of the earliest indications of state-level societies, as well as detailed archaeological information. The later agricultural states of the Mediterranean, including classical Greece and Rome, have also long captivated attention. In the Americas,

Mesoamerican civilizations have been the focus of both early work and ongoing research.

Many other areas have been far less thoroughly investigated. Yet, research around the globe has increasingly revealed an amazing diversity of early civilizations. Work in East Asia, South Asia and Africa, in particular, has provided insights into the origins of early civilizations in these areas. It is not possible to survey all of them, but the following discussion provides some idea of the diversity of the civilizations represented.

Civilizations in Southwest Asia

Some of the earliest agricultural civilizations in the world emerged in Southwest Asia. As noted, this region was the focus of early research, and the work undertaken provides some of the most substantive information available on early states, including the distribution of settlements on the landscape, as well as large-scale excavations of individual sites. Research, however, continues to reveal more information. The use of satellite imagery, for example, promises to provide a much fuller understanding of early settlements and their relationship to early state formation (Menze and Ur 2011).

As discussed in Chapter 8, Southwest Asia includes the Fertile Crescent, notable for its early evidence of both plant and animal domestication. Beginning about 8,000 years ago, irrigation from the Euphrates River allowed for the significant expansion of grain agriculture. Also of key importance was the utilization of domesticated cattle, both as draft animals for plow agriculture and their milk. By about 6,000 years ago, increasingly intensive agricultural practices provided the foundation for early agricultural states. The first civilizations arose at the base of the Zagros Mountains in the Mesopotamian valley near the Tigris and Euphrates rivers (Dalley 1998).

The earliest civilization, known as the Sumerian Empire, contained some of the world's first urban centers, such as Uruk, Ur, Ubaid, and Eridu, the origins of which extend back to agricultural settlements of the fourth or fifth millennium B.C. Uruk, located in modern Iraq, is sometimes described at the world's first city. The site consists of a massive settlement mound, or tell, many portions of which have not been investigated. By about 5,500 years ago, the town had grown in size, becoming the largest settlement in the region. At this time, it may have covered close to 250 acres and contained a population of tens of thousands of people. It was, by far, the largest settlement in the region. Its significance, however, does not rest solely on its size, but in the diversity of functions represented. There were administrative areas, temples, and ritual spaces, along with distinct locations for pottery production, metal working, and stone carving. It is this multiplicity of function that differentiates Uruk from earlier, large Neolithic settlements such as Jericho. The monumental ruins at Uruk also include early ziggurats, monumental structures made up of a series of platforms with temples at the top where priests conducted rituals. The influence of Uruk on surrounding areas is manifest in Uruk-style architecture, ceramics, and other artifacts.

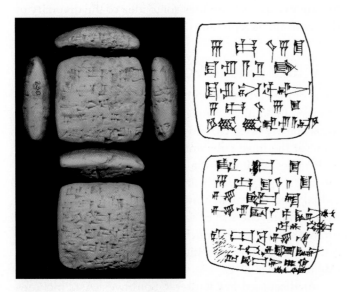

A cuneiform tablet: A composite of images showing the obverse, reverse and sides of tablet. The inscriptions record flour and animal offerings, the workmen used, and the name of the scribe.
Source: Courtesy of Special Collections Research Center, Syracuse University Libraries.

Another of the major cities of early Mesopotamia was Ur, in southern Mesopotamia, which eclipsed Uruk. By 2100 B.C., the city had become the center of an extensive empire that established an extensive regional bureaucracy to collect taxes and tribute. The breadth of political control and organization of labor surpassed that found at Uruk. This is in part revealed by extensive records in cuneiform, one of the world's first writing systems. Beginning with pictographic symbols, cuneiform was used in Mesopotamian society for some 3,000 years until disappearing from use in the last centuries B.C. (Englund 1998). Preserved on clay tablets, cuneiform records provide a remarkably detailed account of the empire's workings. The city of Ur contained very elaborate temples and places, as well as a royal cemetery.

The rulers of these early states exerted control over surrounding areas, through political authority and the use of force. The walls and defensive works around these early cities are indicative of both the ability to organize large scale labor projects and the need for defense. Cuneiform records also provide details of military organization, victories, and conquests. These are the records of the first armies. In time, however, the costs of maintaining political domination over a vast region, coupled with large-scale population growth, overtaxed Ur's economic and physical resources. In 2000 B.C., the empire collapsed. Archaeologists have concluded that in the 1,000 years following the fall of Ur, the number of settlements in Mesopotamia declined by 40 percent (Tainter 1990).

Later agricultural states in northern Mesopotamia included Babylon (2000–323 B.C.) and Assyria (1920–1780 B.C.). These empires established widespread trade routes throughout the Middle East. They maintained political control over extensive rural regions, requiring peasants to provide surplus food and labor for monument construction. Babylon's ruler, Hammurabi, developed the first written legal codes to maintain a standardized system of political rules for the Babylonian empire. Other agricultural peoples of Southwest Asia were the Phoenicians, the Arameans, and the Hebrews, who settled the kingdom of Israel in about 1000 B.C. In addition, in the country now known as Iran, the Persian civilization rose to conquer much of the Middle East in the sixth century B.C.

The agricultural civilizations of the Middle East influenced one another through the rapid spread of technology and culture. Craft specialization and long-distance trade was extensive and is well represented by trade materials throughout the region and far beyond. For example, via extensive caravan routes, the Bedouins carried goods from port cities in the Arabian Peninsula across the desert to cities such as Damascus, Jerusalem, and Cairo. Contacts among the civilizations were further enhanced by the movement of trading ships in the Mediterranean. Because of these economic and cultural connections, these civilizations had broad knowledge of metallurgy, highly developed writing and coinage systems, and an extensive network of roads, as well as sophisticated ecclesiastical religions with full-time priests.

Early Asian Civilizations

As briefly outlined with regard to the origins of domestication, East Asia presents a varied picture of independent cultural developments. The domestication of a variety of plant and animal species preceded the emergence of agricultural states, some of which are better known than others. The earliest primary state societies appeared in China during the second and third millennia B.C., making their origins similar in age to Uruk in Southwest Asia. The civilizations of Southeast Asia, including that of the Khmer, appear to date later and have been viewed as secondary states that may have at least partly arisen as a result of external influences, particularly from South Asia. However, the limited archaeological information of the agricultural societies that preceded these states makes it difficult to fully evaluate their origins.

China The earliest civilizations in China were located in the Yellow and Yangzi river valleys. Agricultural communities in these areas became widespread 9,000 to 10,000 years ago. These early sites are followed by settlements that display increasing evidence of urbanization, specialization, social stratification, and trade. Some of the earliest indications of growing complexity come from north central China. In the Yangzi River Valley, sites such as Chengtoushan reveal evidence of urban centers, fortifications, and elite graves dating to circa 4000 B.C. Further north, from the central plains to the north of the Yellow River, sites associated with the Longshan culture also bear evidence of increasing social stratification (Dematte 1999; Liu 2009). These late Neolithic sites set the stage for the Xia (circa 1700–1500 B.C.) and Shang (circa 1500–1045 B.C.) dynasties that straddled the Yellow River Valley. These dynasties are poorly known from much later written sources and, more recently, from archaeological research. The political organization of the Xia and Shang periods laid the stage for a series of dynasties spanning the next two millennia (Chang 1986).

Excavations at Erlitou, an archaeological site likely associated with the Xia dynasty, have revealed substantial evidence for craft specialization, as well as social stratification, including the remains of a palace complex. Elites were buried in coffins with elaborate bronzes, jade carvings, and pottery. Archaeological research at Anyang, the last Shang capital, indicates that the site was massive and covered 25 square kilometers (9.7 square miles). Other Shang sites, such as Zhengzhou and Huanbei, have revealed equally impressive remains such as palace and ritual complexes, kilns, workshops, and stratified burial areas. These urban centers were divided into residential, craft, and royal neighborhoods, each with distinctive structures. The cities had walled fortresses designed to keep out nomadic invaders such as Mongol pastoralists from regions farther north.

Notably, some of the material from Erlitou, and especially the later Shang sites, include traces of written symbols. The roots of this pictographic writing go back to the Neolithic, and examples have been recovered from Longshan sites. The inscriptions occur on bones that were likely used in divination. Animal bones were heated, and the number and direction of the resulting cracks were used to divine the future. The results of these divinations were then recorded on the bones. By the Shang dynasty, the early pictographic symbols had become a fairly standardized means of representing objects and ideas. This pictographic writing evolved into modern Chinese characters. Consequently, early inscriptions can be at least partially translated.

The Chinese dynasties expanded their territories through much of the area covered by modern China and beyond. The Han Dynasty (206 B.C.–A.D. 220) was particularly important in expanding political control via military force and in formalizing state administration. Some of the features of modern China date back to this early Chinese dynasty. Among the territories that were incorporated into China were portions of northern Korea, which was occupied by Han armies in 108 B.C. Chinese authority, and especially cultural influences, shaped later Korean agricultural states. The Han influence also extended to the west, with trade connections that reached all the way to the Mediterranean.

Southeast Asia It is clear that a number of agricultural states emerged in Southeast Asia. Unfortunately, they remain relatively poorly known, as archaeological research that would reveal their origins and underpinnings in earlier Neolithic societies has not been undertaken. While not well documented throughout the region, domesticates, principally introductions from China, were being cultivated by 5,000 years ago, though the exploitation of naturally occurring plants and animals seems to have continued. The current evidence for complexity, as well as for the emergence of early states, dates substantially later than in the Chinese examples to the north. Chinese texts hint that that the first states may have emerged in Southeast Asia 2,000 years ago (Higham 2005). Wet-rice cultivation and extensive irrigation projects provided the basis for historically documented state societies such as the Khmer Empire of Cambodia (800–1435), Pagan Dynasty of Burma (1044–1287), the Ayudhyan Dynasty of Thailand (1350–1760), and the Majapahit Kingdom of Indonesia (1350–1425).

The Khmer civilization is among the best-known and most extensive of the Southeast Asian empires. It controlled much of lowland Cambodia, and portions of Thailand and Laos, between about 800 and 1435 (Higham 2005). The capital city of the Khmer was at Angkor in northwest Cambodia. Angkor is a modern term that refers to a large urban center that contained more than 20,000 temples and religious structures, including the enormous mausoleum of Angkor Wat. The Khmer rulers, who were considered semi-divine, are said to have had a bureaucratic staff of 300,000 priests and were supported by the tribute of millions of peasants (Sardesai 1989).

Interpretations of the origins of Angkor as well as other Southeast Asian states, have often underscored influences from the civilizations of South Asia. There are unmistakable influences of Indian cultures in the architecture of Angkor. The written texts and inscriptions are typically in Sanskrit, the language of Hinduism, and they are written in an Indian script. The kings of Angkor also had Indian names. Connections with South Asia are, therefore, clear. Reevaluation of historic inscriptions has, however, revealed narratives that were written in the Khmer language and refer to local deities. This has led some researchers to reevaluate the indigenous foundations of Khmer civilization. Archaeological evidence has provided further indications of earlier hints of complexity that may have provided a foundation for state formation.

South Asia: The Indus Valley

The Indus Valley, or Harappan, civilization of South Asia arose in the Indus River Valley in what is now northwestern India and Pakistan. As discussed in the preceding chapter, the story of domestication on the Indian subcontinent is very incomplete, as is the nature of the associated agricultural societies. A relatively mobile pattern of hunting and gathering seems to have continued to be the predominant type of subsistence pattern practiced in most of the region. Evidence for more settled villages, suggestive of farming, do not occur in most of the subcontinent until between 5,000 to 4,000 years ago. However, in the far northwest, the site of Mehrgarh, located some 125 miles west of the Indus Valley in western Pakistan, provides evidence of more settled agricultural communities by 9,000 years ago. The Mehrgarh site, as well as the plant remains from the early Harrapan sites (5,000 to 4,200 years ago), suggests a heavy reliance on wheat and barley; introductions from Southwest Asia (Fuller 2011:358; Meadow 1996). There are also similarities in ceramics and other artifacts that further suggest connections with Mesopotamia. This suggests that the Neolithic foundation of the Indus Valley civilization may have rested on domesticates and possibly farming patterns introduced from the west. However, given the lack of archaeological evidence on both Neolithic and early Harrapan sites, this will have to be evaluated in light of future research.

Although less well known than the early cultures of Southwest Asia and China, the Indus Valley Civilization provides early indications of complexity. It is known from several sites in western India and Pakistan (Chakrabarti 1999; Wright 2010). Of these, Harappa and Mohenjo Daro are the two best-known settlements, but there were several other major towns or cities that have not been fully studied. Both Harappa and Mohenjo Daro developed on the Indus River in what is today the country of Pakistan. The site of Harappa was the first settlement excavated and the Harrapan Civilization is named after that site.

In terms of evidence for urbanization, monumental architecture, craft specialization, and long-distance trade, the Indus Valley sites reveal many of the same trends noted in the other early civilizations discussed. During their apogee these were among the largest cities in Asia. Mohenjo Daro may have had a population of nearly 35,000. The city was well planned and laid out in a grid, with single-room apartments, multiroom houses, courtyards, and the ancient world's most sophisticated sewer and plumbing systems. In the center of the city stood an enormous mound constructed of mud brick that was protected by fortifications. Close to this ceremonial and political center were a large public bathhouse and a bathing pool that may have been used for ritual purposes. Craft specializations included stone carving and metallurgy (copper, bronze, lead, and tin). An early innovation may have been bullock carts, some of the world's earliest wheeled vehicles.

A writing system, known as the Indus script, is known from hundreds of inscriptions on stone, monuments, and a variety of artifacts (Parpola 1994). Most inscriptions are very brief, four or five characters in length, the longest only containing 17 symbols. There had long been debate about the significance and meaning of these symbols, which were undeciphered. Some researchers have argued that it represents a written language and that, therefore, the Harappans were a literate society. A variety of recent claims of interpretations have been made, though opinions still seem to vary as to their significance. As there are relatively few inscriptions, all of which are quite brief, it is perhaps unlikely that it will provide detailed information on the civilization. Regardless of their specific interpretation, they illustrate another aspect of complexity in this early state.

Agricultural Civilizations in Africa

Africa spans a massive area and incorporates tremendous environmental and cultural variation. As seen in the review of agricultural origins, agricultural societies based on both introduced and indigenous plants, as well as societies based on pastoralism, became widespread in Africa, providing the base for a variety of later agricultural states. What is striking about these societies is the diversity of political systems represented. These range from Ancient Egyptian civilization, which was a very centralized, hierarchical state, to other, complex societies that appear to have been more heterarchical in organization. Equally striking is the varied amount of archaeological work that has been done in different areas. More than 50 years ago, George Murdock observed that archaeologists had perhaps "only lifted an ounce of earth on the Niger for every ton carefully sifted on the Nile" (Murdock 1959:73). This statement is almost as true now as it was then. Ancient Egypt, which was concentrated in the lower Nile Valley, has captivated the attention of researchers for more than two centuries and it has been the focus of extensive archaeological research. In contrast, very little work has been done in many portions of sub-Saharan Africa, making our view of early civilizations in these areas quite fragmentary.

The Nile Valley The earliest evidence for state formation in Africa comes from the lower Nile Valley in what is today Egypt. Ancient Egypt is also undeniably the best-known African civilization, its pyramids, tombs, and temples having long been the focus of both academic research and popular imagination. The treasures of the pharaohs, such as those of Tutankhamun (fourteenth century B.C.), are spectacular by any standard. The degree of centralized political authority represented epitomizes the concept of hierarchical state organization.

As discussed in Chapter 8, there is wide-ranging evidence for the indigenous domestication of plants and pastoralism in different parts of Africa. However, the key domesticates in the lower Nile Valley appear to have been introductions from Southwest Asia (Phillipson 1993). By 7,000 years ago, agricultural settlements, such as Merimde in the Nile Delta, include evidence of cattle, sheep, goats, pigs, dogs, barley, wheat, and flax. In the following millennium, the material culture of these early agricultural populations became increasingly elaborate. Surrounded by desert, population was highly concentrated in the Nile's fertile floodplain.

The origins of the Egyptian state can be traced back to the unification of Upper and Lower Egypt in about 3100 B.C. Although there were periods of instability, it was remarkably long lived, spanning more than 3,000 years. Hieroglyphic writing seems to have developed independently in the Nile Valley and it provides a detailed record of some aspects of ancient Egyptian society, including the ruling dynasties. On the basis of this documentary record, archaeologists have traditionally divided the history of ancient Egypt into a long series of periods based on the various recorded dynasties.

The state was organized around the rulers, called pharaohs, who were believed to possess supernatural authority. A highly centralized bureaucracy evolved to collect

Egyptian paintings demonstrate that the pharoahs of Egypt had an exalted political status.

taxes in the form of agricultural goods, raw materials, and labor. A variety of specialized occupations emerged, including priests, scribes, administrators, architects, and craftsmen. Urban areas, such as Memphis and Thebes, with populations of more than 100,000, sprang up next to the Nile River, where agricultural production exceeded that of Mesopotamia. In contrast to the Sumerian cities, urban centers such as Thebes and Memphis were cut off from surrounding nomadic tribes by desert regions; thus, they did not have to construct walled fortresses to maintain security.

Egyptian civilization dominated the Nile Valley, extending its influence well to the south into Nubia (discussed later). Military campaigns were also launched to extend Egyptian control into Southwest Asia. Ancient Egyptian trade materials are found throughout the eastern Mediterranean. The authority of the Egyptian state gradually declined during the first millennium B.C., however, when at different times it was ruled by Nubian, Persian, and Greek leaders. The dynastic period was finally brought to a close when Egypt became a colony of the Roman Empire in 30 B.C.

Nubia The fertile floodplain of the Nile, which was so important to the people of ancient Egypt, was also invaluable to people living to the south in the upper Nile. This area was known to the ancient Egyptians as Kush or Nubia, and it is today part of the country of Sudan. This region was clearly controlled by pharonic Egypt at various times during its history. However, there is also evidence for independent developments. It has been the focus of less archaeological research and it also lacks the detailed documentary records that are provided by Egyptian hieroglyphic texts. The full picture of the early Nubian states is, therefore, much more fragmentary in comparison to that of ancient Egypt.

Evidence of one of Nubia's earliest civilizations is provided by the site of Kerma, located 500 kilometers north of Khartoum. Kerma may have been the capital of the Nubian state of Kush that is referred to in Egyptian texts of the Middle Kingdom. The town's ruins include a spectacular monumental mud-brick structure called a *deffufa*. Large *tumuli* (burial mounds), containing hundreds of human sacrificial victims, and associated settlement areas are also indicative of the town's importance. Although some Egyptian influences are evident at Kerma, it was clearly an indigenous state, the origins of which can be traced back to the second or third millennium B.C.

A number of other civilizations are associated with Nubia, among the best-known being Meroë, which flourished between 500 B.C. and 300 A.D. Meroë is located south and east of Kerma, above the fifth cataract of the Nile. Unique characteristics of Meroitic civilization include temples to the lion-god Apedemek, a distinct system of kingship, and a unique form of writing. Used from about the second century B.C. to the fourth century A.D., the Meroitic script remains undeciphered today. Meroë reached its peak after 300 B.C., when trade connections were made with Egypt and the classical Greco-Roman world. The civilization declined rapidly during the third century A.D.

Great Zimbabwe A number of agricultural states emerged independently in other parts of Africa. One of the best-known of these is represented by Great Zimbabwe and related sites in southeastern Africa. Great Zimbabwe, situated near the Zambezi River, lent its name to the modern nation of Zimbabwe. The Great Zimbabwe dates to between 1250 and 1450 AD. It contains more than 200 large stone buildings in its center. A temple or ritual enclosure within the city is the largest prehistoric structure found in sub-Saharan Africa. It consists of a great circular building

surrounded by walls 24 feet high. These imposing remains were surrounded by less-permanent structures made of timber and clay, which archaeologists believe may have housed 20,000 people (Pikirayi 2001).

Archaeologist Graham Connah (2001) has described Great Zimbabwe as "the best-known and most ill-used archaeological site in Africa." Early ethnocentric European theories suggested that the site was a copy of the Queen of Sheba's palace, perhaps built by a group of lost white settlers. Poorly done, early digging at the site destroyed much of the information that could have been obtained by systematic archaeological excavation. Yet, more recent work indicates that Great Zimbabwe can best be understood as a continuation of indigenous African cultural traditions. The origins of Great Zimbabwe begin with twelfth century A.D. Iron Age sites, and the settlement itself gained prominence between the thirteenth and fifteenth centuries. Archaeological data suggest continuities with the Bantu-speaking Shona people who still occupy the area.

Great Zimbabwe was a center of an extensive empire. Sites with similar wall construction, ceremonial structures, and artifacts are found throughout the modern nations of Zimbabwe and South Africa. The most important economic activities included cultivation of cereal crops, cattle raising, gold mining, and long-distance trade along the East African coast. The artistic achievements of this civilization can be seen in soapstone sculptures of crocodiles, birds, and other animals.

The East African Coast Settlements had developed in coastal Kenya and Tanzania by the first century A.D. Their origins are clearly indigenous, but trade connections with the civilizations of northern Africa, the Indian Ocean, and

The Great Zimbabwe civilization (1250–1450 C.E.) was a very complex state with enormous stone walls surrounding a temple enclosure.

the African hinterland clearly contributed to their growth during the early second millennium A.D. Arabic and classical Greek references indicate a long period of contact with peoples to the north and east going back at least 2,000 years. The arrival of Persian Gulf settlers may date back to the ninth century A.D., with Indian colonists arriving five centuries later. Gold from Zimbabwe, as well as raw materials and slaves, likely provided impetus for the expansion of trade connections throughout the region. Archaeological materials from these sites include trade goods from as far away as China.

The extent of some of these settlements is quite impressive, as illustrated by Gedi on the Kenyan coast. This town, which flourished between the thirteenth and the sixteenth centuries A.D., covers approximately 45 acres. The ruins of the town include impressive stone-walled structures, mosques, and Islamic tombs. Examples of other coastal settlements can be seen at Kilwa and Lamu. These are only a few examples, however; an estimated 173 towns on the coast have stone ruins (Kusimba 1999). Some of these settlements provided the basis for early states, some of which include clearly external influences such as the use of Arabic and the Islamic faith.

West Africa West Africa includes tremendous environmental and cultural diversity. Indications of increasing complexity during the first millennium B.C. and the first millennium A.D. are found in both the marginal savanna areas south of the Sahara and the West African forest. Many areas have not been well studied by archaeologists. Generally, the region seems to have developed larger and more nucleated settlements than the eastern part of the continent.

Increasing trade contacts, iron smelting, and political complexity in what is today the modern countries of Senegal and Gambia are evidenced by the appearance of tumuli and megaliths. Examples of the latter are the sites of Kerbach and Wasu, which have circles of carefully dressed stones. Archaeological survey has revealed that these features have an extensive distribution (McIntosh 2013). The complexity represented likely provided the basis for the later, historically known kingdoms of the western savanna. Further east in the Inland Niger Delta, the site of Jenné-jeno also provides evidence of urban origins in West Africa prior to the development of long distance trade across the Sahara (McIntosh 2005).

Much more is known about the later West African states of ancient Ghana and Mali, which flourished in the western savanna. Both of these states are known from Arabic accounts, in which Ghana is mentioned from the eighth to tenth centuries A.D. The origins of Mali may date back almost as far, but Mali reached its apogee later and eclipsed Ghana. The wealth of ancient Mali was well known beyond West Africa, and Malian cities such as Timbuktu were familiar to European writers of the period.

Megaliths at the site of Wassu, The Gambia, West Africa.

Unfortunately, although the capitals of ancient Mali and Ghana have tentatively been located, excavation has not yet provided a clear picture of their origins.

Indications of urbanization and state-level sociopolitical organization also come from the forest and savanna margins of southwestern Nigeria, an area that is today occupied by the Yoruba people. Settlements such as Benin include massive earthworks that enclose hundreds of square miles. Ife, another early Yoruba site, contained a large palace complex and many other monuments with stone and terra-cotta sculptures (Connah 2001). Ife was a major political and ceremonial center where artisans produced bronze castings of religious figures. The artwork presents a high degree of technological sophistication and craft specialization before the end of the first millennium A.D. Another striking feature of ancient Ife is the potsherd pavements that covered the roads and walkways within the town. These were made of broken pieces of pots, placed on their edges and arranged into decorative patterns. Although the settlements of Benin and Ife are historically known, documented in African oral traditions and early European accounts, their origins extend back to the first millennium A.D.

Even more tantalizing indications of early complexity in Nigeria come from the site of Igbo-Ukwu, dated to the tenth century A.D. The elaborate metal objects found at the site are associated with shrines and the tomb of what appears to have been an individual of high status. Unfortunately, the associated settlement and surrounding sites have not been examined. The Igbo-Ukwu site is of particulate note as the Igbo people present fairly high density populations, yet lack the usual indicators of centralized political authority.

A great deal of information has appeared about African states in the past few decades. Recent archaeological work has, for example, revealed earthworks similar to those found in Nigeria in the southern forest of Ghana (Chouin and DeCorse 2010). However, the lack of archaeological work on settlement sites and surrounding areas makes it difficult to evaluate the full extent of these features and what resources may have been important. Other regions, such as the central African, are virtually unknown.

Empires of the Americas

Following the emergence of an agricultural system based on the production of maize, beans, and squash, a series of indigenous complex societies developed in Mesoamerica and South America (see the box "Contacts between Two Worlds?"). In lowland Mesoamerica, a sedentary farming civilization known as the Olmec thrived from about 1500 to 400 B.C. The Olmec civilization is sometimes regarded as the "mother culture" of Mesoamerica, because many of the features represented appear in later Mesoamerican civilizations such as those of the Maya and Aztec. Olmec achievements include large-scale monument construction, hieroglyphic writing, a calendar system, and sophisticated iconography. Warfare and human sacrifice, darker aspects of Mesoamerican societies, are also represented.

These varied cultural accomplishments indicate that Olmec society was highly organized; yet whether it represents state- or chiefdom-level political organization has been widely debated (Coe 1977; Service 1978a). Much of the disagreement centers on the role of the principal Olmec sites of San Lorenzo and the slightly later site of LaVenta,

both located in modern-day Mexico. Each of these sites possesses impressive monumental architecture, palaces, and sculptures. Yet, while clearly impressive, it is unclear how many people lived in these areas. Lack of domestic architecture led some scholars to view them as ritual centers that lacked the urban concentrations found in early states in other areas. However, continued work suggests that there were likely associated residential communities, consisting of both elite populations and commoners, albeit poorly known.

There has also been disagreement regarding the Olmecs' position as the "mother culture" of Mesoamerican civilizations. Criticism of the Olmecs' role is based on the fact that many of the features represented appear to occur earlier in other areas. Parallels in many aspects of Olmec culture, including architecture and ritual practices, occur widely in Mesoamerica, suggesting that the features seen in the Olmec area are representative of earlier, widespread beliefs. This perspective is more consistent with the developments in widely separated areas such as Teotihuacan, located far to the north. Regardless of whether or not Olmec sites represent *the* mother culture of Mesoamerica, they provide clear illustration of many of the features found in early states throughout the region.

Teotihuacán Teotihuacán in the central highlands of Mexico was a major city that became the center of an agricultural empire of perhaps one million inhabitants. Most archaeologists believe that this empire eventually incorporated both Mayan lowland and highland ceremonial centers. Its influence is manifest in artistic styles, texts, and a diversity of cultural influences throughout much of Mesoamerica.

Some estimates have placed the population of Teotihuacán itself as high as 150,000 inhabitants by 200 A.D. (Millon 1993). The settlement was, undoubtedly, one of the largest cities anywhere in the ancient world; its boundaries extended over an area of about eight square miles. Teotihuacán was divided into quarters and district neighborhoods, with as many as 2,200 apartment houses and 400 craft workshops. It also had more than 75 temples and ritual structures, including the Pyramid of the Sun and the Pyramid of the Moon. The Pyramid of the Sun is the largest monument in pre-Columbian America.

The Pyramid of the Moon looms over the ancient city of Teotihuacán in central Mexico. The city, which may have had a population of 150,000 by 200 A.D., included residential complexes and craft centers, as well as dozens of temples and religious structures.

The inhabitants of the Valley of Mexico developed a highly effective pattern of cultivation known as *chinampas*. The valley contained many lakes and swamps that were used as gardens. In chinampas cultivation, farmers dug up the muddy bottom from lakes and swamps and planted maize, beans, and squash in this rich soil. This system of cultivation was extremely productive and allowed farmers to plant and harvest several times a year to support dense populations.

The dramatic decline of the Teotihuacán civilization, which occurred about 650 A.D., is still being investigated by archaeologists. The evidence from artifacts suggests that the flow of goods into the city from outlying regions was abruptly reduced. The city and its monuments were systematically burned circa 550 A.D. The population dropped within 50 years to one-fourth its former size (Tainter 1990). This decline was followed by a period of political fragmentation that enabled other groups, such as the Toltec and eventually the Aztec, to dominate the region politically. The Aztec settled in the city of Tenochtitlán, located at the current site of Mexico City. By 1400, they had established political control over an empire of 25 million people.

The Classic Maya   Another major civilization, known as the Maya, arose in lowland Mesoamerica around 300 B.C. and dominated the Yucatan peninsula throughout the first millennium A.D. The Maya have been the focus of a great deal of archaeological research. The Mayan calendar is also well known. As a result, it is one of the better understood Mesoamerican civilizations.

The Maya developed a diversified agricultural system that was a combination of slash-and-burn horticulture, intensive horticulture based on hillside terracing, and large-scale irrigation agriculture. The Mayan population has been estimated at 3 million (Coe, Snow, and Benson 1986). From large ceremonial centers, such as Tikal in northern Guatemala and Palenque in Mexico, the Maya maintained extensive trade networks with peoples throughout the region. In these centers, an elite class emerged that traced its royal lineages back to various deities.

Archaeologists agree that the Mayan centers, with hieroglyphic writing, knowledge of astronomy, calendars, priests, and large monuments, were states. Mayan society was very hierarchical. Mayan kings ruled with divine authority, and sometimes were venerated as gods themselves. Lower-ranked lords and officials were clearly of lesser ritual and political status, but lived in their own palaces and residential areas. The Mayan kings and officials were the unambiguous leaders in ritual, warfare, building decisions, and diplomacy. It is, however, unclear if the Maya had the well-established administrative bureaucracies found in areas such as South Asia and the Nile Valley.

Andean Civilizations

Agricultural societies became widespread in South America, providing the basis for a number of complex societies. However, in western South America, sites in Chile and Peru indicate that the first larger, settled communities boasting early indications of complexity practiced some cultivation but were still heavily reliant on natural resources. In northern Peru, intensive farming, associated with growing populations, pottery production, and weaving, had been adopted by 3,800 years ago. Mounds, courtyards, and walled enclosures also appear, which has led some archaeologists to postulate the beginnings of social stratification and increasing sociopolitical organization. The most massive of these structures is the site of Sechin Alto, located on Peru's desert coast. It is a massive mound of complex faces with stonework and stucco friezes. Construction seems to have been initiated by about 1,400 B.C and continued intermittently for a thousand years.

The Andean civilizations of Peru—including Moche (100 to 800 A.D.) in the north, Tiahuanaco (200–1100 A.D.) in the south near Lake Titicaca, and the Incan empire (1476–1534)—developed intensive agriculture based on elaborate systems of irrigation and canals. The Andean peoples, like the Mesoamericans, relied on mixed patterns of agriculture, involving slash-and-burn cultivation in some areas and more intensive agriculture in others, to support large urban centers. The major food crops were maize, potatoes, and a plant called quinoa, the seeds of which are ground for flour. The most important domesticated animals were the llama, which provided both meat and transportation, and the alpaca, which produced wool for textile production.

As with Teotihuacán, Andean cities became the centers of regional states. The empire of Huari dominated almost the entire central Andean region and developed

The Inca fortress of Sacsahuaman, Peru. Conflict theorists point to the massive labor requirements used to construct monumental structures to underscore the exploitative nature of state societies.

Critical Perspectives

The Downfall of the Moche

By 2,000 years ago, a number of small state-level societies had emerged in northwestern South America along the coast and hinterland of present-day Peru. The best known is that of the Moche, which was centered in the Moche and nearby Chicama valleys. At its peak, the state controlled satellite communities in neighboring territories, eventually extending its influence hundreds of miles to the north and south (Donnan and McClelland 1979).

The archaeological record provides a rich testament to the wealth and power of the Moche. Ceremonial complexes, such as those near the modern city of Trujillo, include adobe-brick temple platforms, pyramids, and associated room complexes that may have served as palaces. In 1987, the riches found in an undisturbed tomb of a Moche warrior-priest near the modern village of Sipán led some to dub the discovery a "King Tut of the New World." Although the Moche possessed no writing system, the interpretation of the Sipán tomb and other Moche sites is aided by exquisite depictions of Moche life on pottery vessels.

The Moche kingdom flourished for almost 800 years. However, by 600 A.D., the classic Moche ceremonial centers were abandoned, and power shifted to other areas. Archaeological excavations and recent photographs taken by the space shuttle *Challenger* have provided insights into what may have caused this collapse (Moseley and Richardson 1992). Excavations during the 1970s provided part of the answer to the Moche mystery. Prior to that time Moche ceremonial structures were known, but no one had found any settlements, leading archaeologists to believe that the populations that had built the monumental structures had lived elsewhere. Deep excavations at Moche sites during 1972, however, revealed residences, civic buildings, and high-status cemeteries buried under almost 30 feet of sand—evidence that the Moche centers had been destroyed at their peak of prosperity.

Interpretations of the archaeological findings have been aided by recent insights into the environmental conditions that may have ravaged the Moche sites and buried them with sand. Between 500 and 600 A.D., the Moche region experienced devastating rainfall and large-scale flooding characteristic of a climatic phenomenon today known as *El Niño*. During normal climatic conditions, a cold stream of water known as the Humboldt or Peru Current flows through the Pacific Ocean along the west coast of South America. This cold water limits rainfall along the coast, producing the America's driest desert in northern Chile and Peru. During an *El Niño* event, which may last 18 months, this pattern suddenly changes, with disastrous consequences. Warm water flows along the coast, and the normally arid coastland is beset with torrential rains and flooding, while severe drought plagues the usually wetter highlands of Peru and Bolivia. Archaeological evidence indicates that floodwaters, possibly from one or more *El Niño* events, destroyed Moche settlements and stripped as much as 15 feet from some sites. Although the Moche survived the flooding, by 600 A.D. sand dunes engulfed irrigation canals, fields, and architecture.

Recent studies of photographs taken by the space shuttle *Challenger* in 1983 and earlier satellite photos have helped explain the dune encroachment (Moseley and Richardson 1992). The high-altitude photographs of the Peruvian coast link the formation of new beach ridges and dune systems to earthquakes and *El Niño*. The *Challenger* photographs indicate that a new beach ridge formed between 1970 and 1975. The ridge's appearance was linked to the Rio Santa earthquake of 1970, which caused massive landslides that dumped huge amounts of earth into the dry river valleys. The torrential rains of the *El Niño* event of 1972–1973 carried this debris into the ocean, where strong currents deposited it in a new beach ridge. The ridge, in turn, provided the sand for the dunes that swept inland. Events such as these undoubtedly occurred in the past.

The available evidence seems to support the theory that *El Niño* events, possibly exacerbated by earthquakes, may have contributed to the downfall of the Moche state. Additional evidence suggests that there may have been periods of extreme drought prior to 600 A.D. The combination of these environmental disasters beyond human control could have seriously undermined the state's ability to produce the agricultural surplus it needed to survive. In the absence of any means of overcoming these problems, the downfall of the Moche state may have been inevitable.

Points to Ponder

1. What other evidence could be used to evaluate this interpretation of the collapse of the Moche state?

2. Even if excellent evidence for environmental disasters is uncovered, can other reasons for the collapse of the Moche be ruled out?

3. Is it likely that it will be possible to create general models that will explain the collapse of societies in all cultural and environmental settings?

4. Do you think that study of ancient states offers any insights into problems facing modern societies?

locally based urban centers to control outlying provinces. In addition, vast trading links produced interconnections with many regions. Tiahuanaco controlled a large rural area characterized by massive construction and irrigation projects that required large amounts of state-recruited labor. These empires collapsed by 1100 A.D. (Tainter 1990).

Later, the Inca settled in the urban capital of Cuzco and consolidated imperial domain over all of modern-day Peru and adjacent areas. Supported by a well-organized militia and an efficient state organization dominated by a divine emperor, the Inca ruled over a population of 6 million.

The Collapse of State Societies

9.5 Discuss different theories of why states collapse.

Perhaps no aspect of early agricultural states is more intriguing than the question of why they ceased to function. As discussed in the chapter opening, no agricultural states exist today. Lost ruins, palaces hidden in tropical forests, and temples buried beneath shifting sand captivate the attention of archaeologists and the public alike. These images grip our attention all the more because of the lusterless prospect that the downfall of these ancient societies offers insight into the limitations of our own civilization. As Joseph Tainter notes: "Whether or not collapse was the most outstanding event of ancient history, few would care for it to become the most significant event of the present era" (Tainter 1990:2).

In looking at their demise, it is important to note that many early agricultural states were exceedingly successful. They flourished in many different world areas for hundreds of years. Ancient Egypt, which spanned a period of 3,000 years, is particularly notable, but many early civilizations lasted longer than the 200-odd years the United States has been in existence. The apparent success of these states makes the reasons for their collapse all the more enigmatic. What accounts for the loss of centralized authority, the decline in stratification and social differentiation, the interruption of trade, and the fragmentation of large political units that seem to document the end of many different civilizations? These features extend beyond the end of specific governments or political systems; rather, they seem to reflect the breakdown of entire cultural systems.

Reasons for Collapse

In examining the downfall of complex societies, writers have posited many different theories. Among the earliest were notions that collapse was somehow an innate, inevitable aspect of society, to be likened to the aging of a biological organism. Plato, for example, wrote that "since all created things must decay, even a social order...cannot last forever, but will decline" (quoted in Tainter 1990:74). Although romantically appealing, such interpretations lack explanatory value and cannot be evaluated by empirical observation.

More recent scholars have sought a more precise understanding of the factors that contributed to collapse. Many theories have focused on the depletion of key resources as a result of human mismanagement or climatic change. In an agricultural state, conditions that interfered with or destroyed the society's ability to produce agriculture surplus would have had serious consequences. If the

society was unable to overcome this depletion, collapse would result (Diamond 2005; Tainter 2006). Reasons such as this have been posited as contributing to the collapse of complex societies such as Mesopotamia (Adams 1981), Egypt (Butzer 1984), and Mesoamerica (Haas 1982). The role of environmental degradation in the collapse of one society is examined in more detail in the box "The Downfall of the Moche" (page 222).

In some cases, researchers have suggested that resource depletion may be the result of sudden catastrophic events, such as earthquakes, volcanic eruptions, or floods that have an impact on agricultural lands as well as other resources. One of the most well-known theories of this kind links the destruction of Minoan civilization in the Mediterranean to the eruption of the Santorini volcano on the island of Thera (Marinatos 1939).

Other theories have suggested that conditions within societies have led to collapse. Many of these theories stress the tension or conflict resulting from social stratification. For example, mismanagement, excessive taxes, demands for food and labor, or other forms of exploitation by a ruling class are seen as instigating revolts or uprisings by the disaffected peasant class. Without the support of the peasants, the political system cannot function and the state collapses (Yoffee 1979; Guha 1981; Lowe 1985).

Alternatively, some researchers have viewed collapse as the result of the societies' failure to respond to changing conditions. For example, the late anthropologist Elman Service (1960:97) argued: "The more specialized and adapted a form in a given evolutionary stage, the smaller its potential for passing to the next stage." Underlying this interpretation is the assumption that successful adaptation to a particular environmental or cultural setting renders a society inflexible and unable to adapt to changing conditions. In this setting, less complex societies with greater flexibility overthrew older states.

Anthropologist Joseph Tainter notes in a survey that most of the models that have been presented focus on specific case studies, not on the understanding of collapse as a general phenomenon. He points out that most researchers assume that the decline in complexity associated with collapse is a catastrophe: "An end to the artistic and literary features of civilization, and the umbrella of service and protection that an administration provides, are seen as fearful events, truly paradise lost" (Tainter 1990:197). Tainter argues that, in reality, collapse represents a logical choice in the face of declining returns. When people's investment in complexity fails to produce benefits, they opt for disintegration.

Anthropological explanations concerning the collapse of agricultural states can be evaluated in light of ethnographic, historical, and archaeological evidence. Upon surveying information from different states, it appears that reasons for collapse are exceedingly complex (Tainter 2006). The specific manifestation varies in individual settings, just as the specific features that define states differ. Adequate appraisal is dependent upon the existence of a great deal of information about the society under study, including its technological capabilities, population, agricultural yields, and internal and external warfare, as well as climatic conditions in the region. The difficulty involved in assessing competing models is perhaps best illustrated by the fact that very different hypotheses have often been used to explain the decline of the same society.

Anthropologists are committed to offering more comprehensive explanations of the collapse of various agricultural societies using more refined and sophisticated technologies and methods as they develop in the future.

In Chapters 21 and 22, we discuss how contemporary globalization trends, beginning with European colonialism in the 1500s, have resulted in dramatic transformations in these various agricultural societies. We need to understand conditions of these societies as much as possible in order to offer more comprehensive explanations of globalization and its impact on them today.

Summary and Review of Learning Objectives

9.1 Discuss the different characteristics that have been used to define civilizations and the limitations of these definitions.

In anthropological literature, civilization is a term generally used to refer to a complex society associated with the origins of urbanization and state formation. However, various features have been used as defining characteristics, including some or all of the following: urban centers; food surpluses; specialized division of labor; sociopolitical stratification; monumental architecture; record-keeping systems; developments in arithmetic, geometry, and astronomy; sophisticated art; long-distance trade; and state level political organization. There is, however, no agreed-upon list of which of these features are the key defining characteristics of a civilization. For this reason, the term is only used in a general way to indicate a complex society with some of the preceding features.

9.2 Discuss the different sources of information that archaeologists draw on to study early states.

Many different kinds of archaeological information can be drawn on to examine early states. They include the study of settlement patterns and settlement distribution on the landscape, architectural features, indications of administration or centralized authority, monumental architecture, evidence of craft specialization, and indicators of status differences. These variables may provide clues to the origins, extent, and structure of early state systems. In some cases, written records may also be used, a source of information that researchers working on earlier periods did not have.

9.3 Discuss some of the challenges and limitations of the different theories of state formation.

A great deal of debate remains regarding the reasons for state formation. The explanations are clearly complex, and they likely involve a range of demographic, social, political, economic, environmental, and cultural factors. The various

theories surveyed highlight some of the different factors that may have come into play in state formation. The majority of the theories, however, recognize the importance of a variety of variables. A challenging aspect of evaluating state formation stems from the different terminology and definitions employed. Some anthropologists have underscored this concern by observing that the various theories are often aimed at explaining different aspects of ancient societies. Although often equally subsumed under the label "state," distinction should be made between the "political community" (the totality of individuals who make up the body politic) and the political center (the apparatus of government). While these concepts are interrelated, they deal with different aspects of societies. The aims of a political community are often shared and voluntaristic. However, the objectives of the political center (the ruling elite) are characteristically coercive and aimed at maintaining its power and authority. Different theories are also challenged by their failure to explain the complexity of the social systems represented. There is a diversity of different variables involved, but they also interacted in varied ways. Some researchers have also underscored the need to consider different models of complexity. Hierarchy, expressed in increasing social stratification and differentiation in power relations, does characterize power relations in some cases. However, a variety of heterarchical relations may operate at the same time. These observations highlight the ambiguity of concepts such as band, tribe, chiefdom, and state that do not capture the varied nature of past human societies.

9.4 Discuss where some of the first agricultural states were located and their characteristics.

Archaeologists have conducted research in many different areas of the world in order to evaluate models of state formation. These studies have provided many examples of the origins of the state and revealed a variety of differences in their timing, characteristics, and cultural expressions. As in the case of agricultural origins, archaeological research on early states and civilizations has concentrated on some world areas more than others. Southwest Asia (Mesopotamia) and Egypt have been the focus of extensive research dating back to the early nineteenth century. As a result, these regions figured prominently in early models of state formation and civilization. In some interpretations, civilization was seen as having largely developed in these areas and then spread elsewhere. These regions do provide some of the earliest indications of state-level societies, as well as detailed archaeological information. The later agricultural states of the Mediterranean, including classical Greece and Rome, have also long captivated attention. In the Americas, Mesoamerican civilizations have been the focus of both early work and ongoing research. Many other areas have been far less thoroughly investigated. Yet, research around the globe has increasingly revealed an amazing diversity of early civilizations. Work in East Asia, South Asia and Africa, in particular, has provided insights into the origins of early civilizations in these areas.

9.5 Discuss different theories of why states collapse.

Many early states were very successful, spanning thousands of years. What accounts for the loss of centralized authority, the decline in stratification and social differentiation, the interruption of trade, and the fragmentation of large political units that seem to document the end of many ancient civilizations? These features extend beyond the end of specific governments; rather, they reflect the breakdown of entire cultural systems. Writers have posited many different theories. Among the earliest were notions that collapse was somehow an innate, inevitable aspect of society, to be likened to the aging of a biological organism. More recent scholars have sought a more precise understanding of the factors that contributed to collapse. Many theories have focused on the depletion of key resources as a result of human mismanagement or climatic change. Reasons such as this have been posited as contributing to the collapse of complex societies such as Mesopotamia, Egypt, and Mesoamerica. In other cases, researchers have suggested that resource depletion may be the result of sudden catastrophic events, such as earthquakes, volcanic eruptions, or floods that have an impact on agricultural lands as well as other resources. Other theories have suggested that conditions within societies, such as class conflict, led to collapse. Alternatively, some researchers have viewed collapse as the result of the societies' failures to respond to changing conditions. Reasons for the downfall of complex societies are clearly complex and varied in different cultural settings.

Key Terms

agricultural states, p. 200
chiefdom, p. 199
conflict theories, p. 208
hieroglyphic writing, p. 207

hydraulic hypothesis, p. 208
integrationist theories, p. 208
logographic writing systems, p. 207
multi-causal, p. 208

settlement pattern, p. 201
state, p. 199
trace element analysis, p. 205
tribes, p. 199

Chapter 10
Culture

Chapter Outline

Learning Objectives

After reading this chapter you should be able to:

10.1 Discuss the basic characteristics and components of *culture* as understood by anthropologists.

10.2 Discuss how humans acquire their culture.

10.3 Discuss how anthropologists understand the sharing of culture.

10.4 Discuss the components of nonmaterial culture studied by anthropologists.

10.5 Describe how culture results in differences among people in various societies.

10.6 Describe how culture leads to universal similarities among people in widely separated societies.

The Characteristics of Culture

10.1 Discuss the basic characteristics and components of *culture* as understood by anthropologists.

As mentioned in Chapter 2, culture is a fundamental concept within the discipline of anthropology. E. B. Tylor, the first professional anthropologist, proposed a definition of culture that includes all of human experience:

Culture . . . is that complex whole which includes knowledge, belief, arts, morals, law, custom, and any other capabilities and habits acquired by man as a member of society. (1871:1).

This view suggests that culture includes tools, weapons, fire, agriculture, animal domestication, metallurgy, writing, the steam engine, glasses, airplanes, computers, penicillin, nuclear power, rock and roll, video games, designer jeans, religion, political systems, subsistence patterns, science, sports, and social organizations. Thus, as mentioned in Chapter 2 culture includes all aspects of human activity, from the fine arts to popular entertainment, from everyday behavior to the development of sophisticated technology. It contains the plans, rules, techniques, designs, and policies for living. Tylor was using the term *culture* as a general phenomenon for all of humanity that was different from our physical or biological characteristics. The fundamental aspect of culture recognized by anthropologists today is that it is distinct from our human biological characteristics or genetics.

This nineteenth-century definition of culture has some terminology that would not be acceptable to modern anthropologists. For example, it relies on the word *man* to refer to what we currently would refer to as *humanity*. In addition, nineteenth-century theorists such as Tylor tended to think of "culture" as equivalent to "civilization," which implicitly suggested that there was an increase, accumulation, or growth in "culture" and "civilization" as societies progressed and evolved. This is not the meaning of culture that contemporary anthropologists maintain. Cultures are not evolving in some simplistic manner from early civilizations to modern civilizations as the nineteenth-century anthropologists believed. As we will discuss, humans have had different languages, beliefs, values, dietary habits, and norms or "cultures" that are associated with various regions in the past as well as the present.

Notice that Tylor's definition includes the word *society*. In general terms, society refers to an organized group of animals within a specific territory. In particular, it refers to the patterns of relationships among the animals within that territory. Biologists often refer to certain types of insects, herd animals, and social animals such as monkeys and apes as living in societies.

In the past, anthropologists attempted to make a simple distinction between society and culture. **Society** was said to consist of the patterns of relationships among people within a specified territory, and culture was viewed as the byproducts of those relationships. This view of society as distinguishable from culture was derived from ethnographic studies of small-scale societies. In such societies, people within a specific territory were believed to share a common culture. However, contemporary anthropologists have found this notion of shared culture to be too simplistic and crude. For example, modern anthropologists conduct ethnographic research in complex societies. Within these societies there are many distinctive groups that maintain different cultural traditions. Culture is not a uniform by-product of society—within societies there are varieties of culture. Even in small-scale societies, the idea that all people share a collective "culture" is also too crude and simplistic. As we shall see in this chapter, this conception of shared culture often resulted in gross stereotypes of, and extreme generalizations about, groups of people and their behavior.

Many anthropologists adopt the hybrid term *sociocultural system*—a combination of the terms *society* (or *social*) and *culture*—to refer to what used to be called "society" and the byproduct "culture." As we shall see in later chapters, many anthropologists use the term *sociocultural system* as the basic conceptual framework for analyzing ethnographic research.

Culture is Learned

10.2 Discuss how humans acquire their culture.

The unique capacity for culture in the human species depends upon learning. We do not inherit our culture through our genes in the way we inherit our physical characteristics. We obtain our culture through the process of enculturation. **Enculturation** is the process of social interaction through which people learn and acquire their culture. We will study this process in more detail in the next chapter. Humans acquire their culture both consciously, through formal learning, and unconsciously, through informal interaction. Anthropologists distinguish among several types of learning. One type is known as **situational learning**, or trial-and-error learning, in which an organism adjusts its behavior on the basis of direct experience. The costs and risks of situational learning can be quite high. Imagine if you only based your decisions about food on trial and error—you might encounter a number of foods that are poisonous or inedible. It would be very risky. Fortunately, humans are capable of learning from one another.

The young psychologist B.F. Skinner using conditioning to train a pigeon. This is an example of situational learning.

Learning from one another is called **social learning**. It occurs when one organism observes another organism respond to a stimulus and then adds that response to its own collection of behaviors. Thus, the organism need not have the direct experience; it can observe how others behave and then imitate or avoid those behaviors (Rendell et al. 2010). Obviously, humans learn by observing classmates, teachers, parents, friends, and the media. Within social situations, children and adults can make inferences about what is observed and perceived. Other social animals also learn in this manner. For example, wolves learn hunting strategies by observing pack members. Similarly, chimpanzees observe other chimps fashioning twigs with which to hunt termites and then imitate those behaviors. Recently, some primatologists and anthropologists have suggested that nonhuman primates have "culture" based upon how they learn socially from one another and have variations of behavior from one group to another (Sapolsky 2006; Laland et al. 2009). However, it appears that nonhuman animals, including primates, do not intentionally or deliberately teach one another as humans do (Tomasello et al. 2005). In addition, as we will discuss later and in Chapter 12 on language, these nonhuman primates do not appear to have a core aspect of what most anthropologists view as an important criteria for designating a "culture," and that is the ability to symbolize (Rossano 2010; Konner 2010).

Symbols and Symbolic Learning

Humans do not engage in social learning only through direct observation. Instead, humans can learn about things that are not immediately observable by using symbols. **Symbolic learning** is based on our linguistic capacity and ability to use and understand **symbols**, arbitrary meaningful units or models we use to represent reality. An example of the arbitrary aspects of symbolism would be the colors red, yellow, and green for traffic lights in the United States (Sahlins 1976). Traffic lights could be other colors in different societies, but in the United States, they take this arbitrary form. Sounds such as "cat," "dog," "tree," "one," "two," and "three" in English are symbolic and arbitrary because, as we know, the sounds that symbolize those words in languages such as Chinese, Navajo, or Russian can be completely different. However, linguistic anthropologists know that symbols do not just refer to items such as animals or numbers. Symbolic communication and language can be used to represent abstract ideas and values. Symbols are the conceptual devices that we use to communicate abstract ideas to one another. We communicate these symbols through language. For example, children can learn to distinguish and name coins such as pennies, nickels, and quarters, and to use this money as a symbolic medium of exchange. The symbols of money in the United States or other societies are embedded within a host of many other symbols. Symbols do not stand in isolation from one another; instead, they are interconnected within linguistic symbol systems that enable us to provide rules and meanings for objects, actions, and abstract thought processes. The linguistic capacity that we are born with gives us the unique ability to make and use symbolic distinctions.

Humans learn most of their behaviors and concepts through symbolic learning. We do not have to depend

A chimp with a crumpled leaf made to drink water. Chimps learn much through social learning by observing one another.

A Vietnamese elder man teaching a child the written language. This is an example of symbolic learning.

upon situational learning or observations of others to perceive and understand the world and one another. We have the uniquely human ability to abstract the essence of complex events and patterns, creating images through symbols, and bestowing meaning and making inferences about these meanings.

Through the ability to symbolize, humans can learn, create meanings, and infer from those meanings in order to transmit culture. Parents do not have to depend on demonstrations to teach children. As children mature, they can learn abstract rules and concepts involving symbolic communication. Through oral traditions and text, humans can transmit this information across vast distances and through time. Symbolic learning has almost infinite possibilities in terms of absorbing and using information in creative ways. Most of our learning as humans is based on this symbolic-learning process.

Symbols and Signs   Symbols are arbitrary units of meaning, in contrast to **signs**, which are directly associated with concrete physical items or activities. Many nonhuman animals can learn signs. For example, a dog can learn to associate the ringing of a bell (a physical activity) with drinking water. You can teach the dog to drink when you ring the bell. Hence, both humans and other animals can learn signs and apply them to different sorts of activities or to concrete items.

Symbols are different from signs in that they are not directly associated with any concrete item or physical activity; they are much more abstract. A symbol's meaning is not always obvious. However, many symbols are powerful and often trigger behaviors or emotional states. For example, the designs and colors of the flags of different countries represent symbolic associations with abstract ideas and concepts (see "Critical Perspectives:

Key National Symbols"). In some flags, the color red may symbolize blood; in others, it may symbolize revolution. In many countries, the desecration of the national flag, itself a symbol, is considered a crime. When the symbols associated with particular abstract ideas and concepts that are related to the national destiny of a society are violated, powerful emotions may be aroused.

The ability to symbolize, to create symbols and bestow meaning on them, enhances our learning capacities as humans in comparison with other types of animals. Anthropologist Leslie White maintained that the most distinctive feature of being human is the ability to create symbols:

It is impossible for a dog, horse, or even an ape, to have any understanding of the meaning of the sign of the cross to a Christian, or of the fact that black (white among the Chinese) is the color of mourning. No chimpanzee or laboratory rat can appreciate the difference between Holy water and distilled water, or grasp the meaning of Tuesday, 3, or sin. (1971:23–24).

Symbols and Culture   The human capacity for culture is based on our linguistic and cognitive ability to symbolize. Culture is transmitted from generation to generation through symbolic learning and the ability to make inferences regarding our symbols and language (Bloch 2012). (In Chapter 12, we discuss the relationship between language and culture.) Through the transmission of culture, we learn how to subsist, how to socialize, how to govern our society, and what gods to worship. Culture is the historical accumulation of symbolic knowledge that is shared by a society. This symbolic knowledge is transmitted through learning, and it can change rapidly from parents to children and from one generation to the next. Generally, however, people in societies go to great lengths to conserve their cultural and symbolic traditions. The persistence of cultural and symbolic traditions is as widespread as cultural change.

Culture is Shared

10.3 Discuss how anthropologists understand the sharing of culture.

Culture consists of the shared practices and understandings within a society. To some degree, culture is based on shared meanings that are to some extent "public" and thus, beyond the mind of any individual (Geertz 1973). Some of this culture exists before the birth of an individual into the society, and it may continue (in some form) beyond the death of any particular individual. These publicly shared meanings provide designs or recipes for surviving and contributing to the society. On the other hand, culture is also within the minds of individuals. For example, we mentioned that children learn the symbolic meanings of the different coins and bills that constitute money. The children figure out the meanings of money by observing practices and learning the various symbols that are public. However, children are not just passive assimilators of that cultural knowledge. Cognitive anthropologists such as Roy D'Andrade and Naomi Quinn emphasize **schemas**, or cultural models that are internalized by individuals and have an influence on decision making and behavior. They emphasize how culture is acquired by and modeled as schemas within individual minds and can motivate, shape, and transform the symbols and meanings (Quinn and Holland 1987; D'Andrade 1989, 1995).

Contemporary anthropologists recognize that cultural understandings are not shared equally by all members of a society (Fox and King 2002; Barth 2002; de Munck 2000). Even in small-scale societies, culture is shared differently by males and females or by young and old. Some individuals in these societies have a great deal of knowledge regarding agriculture, medical practices, or religious beliefs; those beliefs and that knowledge are not equally distributed. In our complex industrialized society, culture consists of a tremendous amount of information and knowledge regarding technology and other aspects of society. Different people learn different aspects of culture, such as repairing cars or television sets, understanding nuclear physics or federal tax regulations, or composing music. Hence, to some extent, culture varies from person to person, from subgroup to subgroup, from region to region, from age group to age group, and from gender to gender. Contemporary anthropologists also note how culture is "contested," referring to how people question and may fundamentally disagree and struggle over the specifics of culture. Yet despite this variation, some common cultural understandings allow members of society to adapt, to communicate, and to interact with one another.

Without some of these common understandings, a society could not exist.

One recent anthropological understanding of culture is sometimes referred to as the epidemiological approach pioneered by Dan Sperber and his colleagues (Sperber 1996, Sperber and Hirschfeld 1999, Bloch 2012, Ross 2004). These anthropologists draw on the fields of cognitive science and cognitive psychology to discuss how culture propagates like a contagious disease from one person to another. Thus, religious beliefs, cooking recipes, folktales, and even scientific hypotheses are ideas or representations within the human mind that spread among people in a shared environment. Chains of communication propagate these beliefs or cultural representations within a population. As in the spread of a contagious disease, some representations take hold and are maintained in particular populations, while other beliefs or representations do not resonate with specific groups and become extinct. Also, some beliefs or representations spread and are retained more easily within a population because they are more easily acquired than other beliefs. For example, some folktales or religious narratives are easily maintained within a population in contrast to highly complex abstract mathematical formulae and narratives based on the findings within science. As we will see in Chapter 11, this epidemiological approach to culture is widely used by cognitive anthropologists to study how culture is transmitted and retained within populations.

Aspects of Culture

10.4 Discuss the components of nonmaterial culture studied by anthropologists.

Within a broad and refined understanding, contemporary anthropologists have tried to isolate the key elements that constitute culture. Two of the most basic aspects of culture are material and nonmaterial culture.

As mentioned in Chapter 2, material culture consists of the physical products of human society (ranging from weapons to clothing styles), whereas **nonmaterial culture** refers to the intangible products of human society (values, beliefs, and norms). As we discussed in Chapter 7, the earliest traces of material culture are stone tools associated with early hominins. They consist of a collection of very simple choppers, scrapers, and flakes. Modern material culture consists of all the physical objects that a contemporary society produces or retains from the past, such as tools, streets, buildings, homes, toys, medicines, and automobiles. Cultural anthropologists investigate the material culture of the societies they study, and they also examine the relationship between the material culture and the nonmaterial culture: the values, beliefs, and norms that represent the patterned ways of thinking and acting within a society. Archaeologists, meanwhile, are primarily concerned with interpreting past societies by studying their material remains.

Values

Values are the standards by which members of a society define what is good or bad, holy or unholy, beautiful or ugly. They are assumptions that are widely shared within the society. Values are a central aspect of the nonmaterial culture of a society and are important because they influence the behavior of the members of a society. The predominant values in the United States include individual achievement and success, efficiency, progress, material comfort, equality, freedom, science, rationality, nationalism, and democracy, along with many other assumptions (Williams 1970; Bellah et al. 1985, 2000). Although these values might seem normal to Americans, they are not accepted values in all societies. For instance, just as American society tends to emphasize individualism and self-reliance, other societies, such as the Old Order Amish in the United States, instead stress cooperation and community interest.

Critical Perspectives

Key National Symbols

Societies throughout the world have drawn upon important cultural symbols as a means of distinguishing their community from others. Some of these cultural symbols are secular or nonreligious in meaning, whereas others have religious connotations. Anthropologist Victor Turner (1967) described symbols as "multivocal," suggesting that they have multiple meanings for people within a society. He also said that symbols have the characteristic of "condensation," having the ability to unify many things and actions into a single formation.

National symbols such as flags have the potential for expressing deeply felt emotions in condensed forms. Flags, with their great public visibility, have been an extremely important symbolic medium of political communication throughout the centuries. In U.S. society, the flag is a key secular symbol reflecting deeply felt community ties.

The word swastika (*svastika*) is a Sanskrit word and ancient symbol of the earliest traditions of Hinduism and Buddhism; it is associated with "well-being" and "goodness." The swastika is used in many Hindu and Buddhist rituals and religious icons. However, the swastika was used as a symbol in the German flag during the Nazi regime (1933-1945) and has become stigmatized, as it is linked with anti-Semitism, violence, and hatred. The Nazi Party and Adolf Hitler selected the swastika as their symbol because it was linked as with the "Aryan

Virgin of Guadalupe

race," the purported superior race of the ancient Indians and the Nordic race of northern Europe, including the Germans. These racist notions regarding the Aryan race and Nordic race have been debunked by modern science. However, the swastika symbol is used by hate groups such as the Klu Klux Klan and neo-Nazi groups in the United States. The use of the swastika is outlawed in modern Germany.

Various religious symbols have produced fundamental meanings and metaphors for many countries throughout the world. For example, the symbols associated with the Virgin Mary in Roman Catholicism have developed into national symbols of unity for some countries. In Mexico, the symbolism associated with the Virgin of Guadalupe has served to unify different ethnic communities (Wolf 1958; Kurtz 1982;

Ingham 1986; Beatty 2006). After Spain had colonized the indigenous Indian communities of Mexico beginning in the sixteenth century, many of the Indians, such as the Aztecs, were converted to Roman Catholicism. According to Mexican tradition, the Virgin Mary appeared before a Christianized Indian, Juan Diego, in 1531 in the form of a brown-skinned Indian woman.

Tepeyac, the place where the apparition occurred, was the sacred site of an Aztec fertility goddess, Tonantzin, known as Our Lady Mother. Aztec cosmology contained many notions regarding the virgin births of deities. For example, Huitzilopochtli, the deity believed to have led the Aztecs to their home in Tenochtitlán, had been miraculously conceived by the Aztec mother goddess. Thus, Aztec religious beliefs regarding Tonantzin somewhat paralleled Catholic teachings about Mary.

During the Virgin's appearance, Tonantzin commanded Juan Diego to inform the bishop of Mexico that a shrine should be built at the spot. The Shrine of the Virgin of Guadalupe is today a huge church, or basilica. Over the altar, Juan Diego's cloak hangs, embossed with the image of a young, dark-skinned woman wearing an open crown and flowing gown, standing on a half-moon that symbolizes the Immaculate Conception.

The Virgin of Guadalupe became a potent symbol that has endured throughout generations, assuming different meanings for different social groups. To the Indians of Mexico, the Virgin embodies both Tonantzin and the newer Catholic beliefs and aspirations concerning eternal salvation. To the mestizos, people with mixed Spanish and Indian ancestry, she represents the supernatural mother who gave them a place in both the indigenous and the colonial worlds. To Mexicans in general, the Virgin represents the symbolic resolution of the many conflicts and problems that resulted from violent encounters between the Europeans and the local population (Kurtz 1982). The Guadalupe shrine has become one of the most important pilgrimage sites in Mexico. In 2002, the late Pope John Paul II made a trip to Mexico to canonize Juan Diego as a saint in the Roman Catholic Church. The Vatican's recognition of this important hybrid religious figure helped reinforce the importance of this national symbol for Mexico (Beatty 2006).

National symbols, whether religious or secular, have played extremely important roles in mobilizing people and countries in times of transition and struggle. These national symbols reflect the deep feelings that tie peoples together in what some scholars have referred to as "imagined communities" (Anderson 1991). People share some basic key symbols with millions of people in an "imagined community" or nation regardless of whether they know one another as individual persons. Regardless of whether these communities are imagined or not, such symbols are key aspects of culture that are likely to be retained by societies worldwide in the twenty-first century.

Points to Ponder

1. What kinds of feelings and emotions do you have when you hear your national anthem played as you watch your flag?
2. Can you think of any other examples of national symbols that have played a role in world history or politics?
3. Are there any disadvantages of national symbols that have influenced various societies?
4. Could international symbols be developed that would draw all of humanity together?

Beliefs

Beliefs held by the members of a society are another aspect of nonmaterial culture. Beliefs are cultural conventions that concern true or false assumptions, including specific descriptions of the nature of the universe and humanity's place in it. Values are generalized notions of what is good and bad; beliefs are more specific and, in form at least, have more content. "Education is good" is a fundamental value in American society, whereas "Grading is the best way to evaluate students" is a belief that reflects assumptions about the most appropriate way to determine educational achievement.

Most people in a given society assume that their beliefs are rational and firmly grounded in common sense. As we saw in Chapter 1, however, some beliefs may not necessarily be scientifically accepted. For example, our intuitive and commonsense understandings may lead us to conclude that the Earth is flat and stationary. When we look around us, the plane of the Earth looks flat, and we do not feel as if the Earth is rotating around the Sun. Yet, our cognitive intuitions and commonsense beliefs about these notions are contradicted by the knowledge gained by the scientific method.

Some anthropologists in the past have referred to the worldview of a particular society. A *worldview* was believed to consist of various beliefs about the nature of reality that provided a people with a more or less consistent orientation toward the world. Worldviews were viewed as guides to help people interpret and understand the reality surrounding them. Early anthropologists believed, for example, that the worldviews of the traditional Azande of East Africa and the traditional Navajos of the southwestern region of the United States included meaningful beliefs about witches (Evans-Pritchard 1937; Kluckhohn 1967). In these societies, witchcraft was believed to cause illnesses in some unfortunate individuals. On the other hand, in societies such as that of Canada, medical doctors diagnosed illnesses using the scientific method and believed illnesses were caused by viruses, bacteria, or other material forces. These early anthropologists maintained that such differing beliefs about illness reflected the different worldviews of these societies. However, modern anthropologists remain very skeptical about these notions of worldviews shared by entire cultures. This notion suggested that cultures were very homogeneous. Presently, anthropologists concur that the concept of a people sharing a worldview is highly questionable. Through systematic ethnographic research with different types of people within a society, contemporary anthropologists discover a great deal of variation in cultural beliefs.

In particular circumstances in a society, some beliefs may be combined into an ideology. An **ideology** consists of cultural symbols and beliefs that reflect and support the interests of specific groups within society (Yengoyan 1986; Comaroff and Comaroff 1991:22). Certain groups promote ideologies for their own ends as a means of maintaining and justifying economic and political authority. Different economic and political systems—including capitalism, socialism, communism, democracy, and totalitarianism—are based on differing ideologies. For example, many political leaders in capitalist societies maintain the ideology that individuals should be rewarded monetarily based on their own self-interest. In contrast, leaders in socialist societies have adopted the ideology that the well-being of the community or society takes precedence over individual self-interest.

In some societies, especially complex ones with many different groups, an ideology may produce **cultural hegemony**, the ideological control by one dominant group over values, beliefs, and norms. For example, one dominant ethnic group may impose its cultural beliefs on subordinate groups. In the United States, the dominant ethnic group in the eighteenth and nineteenth centuries, white Anglo-Saxon Protestants, was able to impose its language, cultural beliefs, and practices on the Native Americans in U.S. society. In many areas of the world, minority groups often accept the ideologies of the economically and politically dominant groups through the process of cultural hegemony. Some anthropologists have noted that subordinate groups may accept the ideology of the dominant group even if it is to their disadvantage. For example, in the past some Native Americans or African-Americans accepted the belief that white Americans were superior because they appeared to have many more opportunities to acquire wealth and political power than they did. Thus, the ideological culture of the dominant group becomes the "taken-for-granted" natural order and reality of the minority groups. In other cases of cultural hegemony, subordinate groups begin to resist the ideological foundations of the dominant group. For example, anthropologist Lila Abu-Lughod studied how Bedouin women of the Arab world resisted the imposition of the male-dominated ideologies in Egypt (1990).

Norms

Norms—a society's rules of right and wrong behavior—are another aspect of nonmaterial culture. Norms are shared rules or guidelines that define how people "ought" to behave under certain circumstances. Norms are generally connected to the values, beliefs, and ideologies of a society. For example, we have seen that in U.S. culture, individualism is a basic value, reflected in the prevailing beliefs. It is not surprising, then, that U.S. society has many norms based upon the notion of individual initiative and responsibility. Individuals are admonished to work for their own self-interest and not to become a burden to their families or community. Older Americans, if self-sufficient, are not supposed to live with their children. Likewise, self-sufficient young adults beyond a certain age should not live with their parents. These individualistic norms reflect the values of U.S. society and contrast with norms existing in other societies. In many agricultural societies, it would be considered immoral to allow aging parents to live outside the family. In these populations, the family is a moral community that should not be separated. Rather than individualism, these norms emphasize communal responsibility within the family unit.

Folkways   Norms guiding ordinary usages and conventions of everyday life are known as **folkways**. Members of a society frequently conform to folkways so readily that they are hardly aware these norms exist. For example, if a Chinese anthropologist were to ask an American why Americans eat with knives and forks, why Americans allow dating between single men and women without chaperones, or why American schoolchildren are not allowed to help one another on exams, he or she might get vague and uninformative answers, such as, "Because that's the way it is done," or, "It's the custom," or even, "I don't know." Cultural anthropologists are accustomed to receiving these kinds of answers from the members of the society they are studying. These folkway norms or standards of etiquette are so embedded in the society that they are not noticeable unless they are openly violated.

Folkways help ensure that social life proceeds smoothly by providing guidelines for an individual's behavior and expectations of other people's behavior. At the same time, folkways allow for some flexibility. Although most people conform to folkways most of the time, folkways are sometimes violated, but these violations are not severely punished. Thus, in U.S. society, people who eat with chopsticks rather than with knives and forks or who do not keep their lawns neatly mowed are not considered immoral or depraved, nor are they treated as criminals.

Mores   Mores (pronounced MOR-ays) are much stronger norms than are folkways. Members of society believe that their mores are crucial for the maintenance of a decent and orderly way of life. People who violate mores are usually severely punished, although punishment for the violation of mores varies from society to society. It may

Saudi Arabian women in full Islamic dress as they are in a public market buying gold jewelry.

not all anthropologists agree that there are concise, clear-cut distinctions among these terms. The terms are used only to help us understand the complex symbolic aspects of nonmaterial culture.

Ideal versus Real Culture

When discussing values, beliefs, and norms, cultural anthropologists often distinguish between ideal culture and real culture. **Ideal culture** consists of what people say they do or should do, whereas **real culture** refers to their actual behaviors. Cultural anthropologists have discovered that the ideal culture frequently contrasts with people's actual behavior. For instance, a foreign anthropologist may learn that Americans cherish the value of equal opportunity, yet in observing Americans, the anthropologist might encounter many cases in which people from different economic, class, racial, ethnic, and religious backgrounds are treated in a highly unequal manner. In later chapters, we discuss how some societies are structured around kinship ties and principles of lineage such as patrilineal and matrilineal descent. Anthropologists often discover, however, that these kinship and descent principles are violated by the actual practices of people (Kuper 1988). Thus, in all societies, anthropologists find that there are differences between the ideal and real cultural practices of individuals.

take the form of ostracism, vicious gossip, public ridicule, exile, loss of one's job, physical beating, imprisonment, commitment to a mental asylum, or even execution. For example, in some Islamic societies such as Iran and Saudi Arabia, the manner in which a woman dresses in public is considered morally significant. If a woman violates the dress code in these societies, she may be arrested by religious police and detained. Government and religious regulations control how Saudi women have to dress. They have to wear the *abaya* (a full black cloak), the *hijab* (head scarf), and the *niqab* (face veil). As we shall see later in the text, in hunting-and-gathering societies, individuals who do not share goods or resources with others are often punished by gossip, ridicule, and occasionally ostracism.

Not all norms can be neatly categorized as either folkways or mores. Distinguishing between the two is especially difficult when dealing with societies other than our own. In reality, norms fall at various points on a continuum, depending upon the particular circumstances and the society under consideration. The prohibition of public nudity may be a strong norm in some societies, but it may be only a folkway or pattern of etiquette in others. Even within a society, rules of etiquette may come to have moral significance. For example, as discussed before, the proper form of dress for women in some societies is not just a matter of etiquette, but has moral or religious connotations.

Values, beliefs, and norms are used by many social scientists when referring to nonmaterial culture. However,

Cultural Diversity

10.5 **Describe how culture results in differences among people in various societies.**

Throughout history, humans have expressed an interest in cultural diversity. People have recognized differences in values, norms, beliefs, and practices everywhere. Whenever different groups have come into contact with one another, people have compared and contrasted their respective cultural traditions. Societies often differentiated themselves from one another based on these variant cultural patterns. For example, one of the first Western historians, Herodotus, a Greek scholar of the fifth century B.C., wrote about the different forms of behavior and belief in societies, such as that of Egypt. He described how the Egyptians behaved and thought differently from the Greeks.

Writings on the diversity of cultures have often been based on ethnocentric attitudes. As we saw in Chapter 1, *ethnocentrism* is the practice of judging another society by the values and standards of one's own society. It appears that ethnocentrism is a universal phenomenon (Brown 2012). As humans learn the basic values, beliefs, and norms of their society, they tend to think of their own group and culture as preferable, ranking other cultures as less desirable. In fact, members of a society become so committed to particular cultural traditions that they cannot conceive of any other way of life. They often view other cultural traditions as strange, alien, inferior, crazy, or immoral.

The study of cultural diversity became one of the principal objectives of anthropology as it developed as a profession in the nineteenth century. But like earlier writers, nineteenth-century anthropologists often reinforced ethnocentric beliefs about other societies (see Chapter 13). In the twentieth century, however, anthropologists began to recognize that ethnocentrism prevents them from viewing other cultures in a scientific manner.

To combat the problem of ethnocentrism, twentieth-century anthropologists developed the concept of cultural relativism. **Cultural relativism** is the view that cultural traditions must be understood within the context of a particular society's responses to problems and opportunities. Cultural relativism is a method or procedure for explaining and interpreting other people's cultures. Because cultural traditions represent unique adaptations and symbolic systems for different societies, these traditions must be understood by anthropologists as objectively as possible. In order to do an ethnographic study, anthropologists must suspend their own judgments and examine the other society in terms of its history and culture. Cultural relativism offers anthropologists a means of investigating other societies without imposing ethnocentric assumptions. Cultural anthropologists attempt to understand the logic of the people they are studying. Perhaps that logic does not make sense from the anthropologists' perspective, but the task is to understand and explain the reasoning of the population studied.

Although cultural relativism provides a sound methodological basis for ethnographic research, it may involve some serious ethical problems. For example, many cultural anthropologists have found themselves in societies in which cultural practices may produce physical harm to people. How do cultural anthropologists refrain from making a value judgment about such harmful cultural practices as infanticide, child or spousal abuse, torture, or murder? This issue is an ever-present problem for anthropologists and deserves careful thought. Anthropologists do not argue that any practice or culture is as good or worthy as another. In fact, one of the major goals in anthropology is to improve conditions and enhance human rights for all people. After learning about different practices and traditions in other societies throughout this text, the moral issues raised by cultural relativism are discussed in Chapter 25.

Food and Diversity

To understand the difference between human biological and cultural behaviors, we can simply observe the variety of ways in which different societies satisfy a basic biological drive such as hunger. Although humans are omnivorous animals with the ability to digest many types of plants and animals for nutrition, there are many differences in eating behaviors and food preferences throughout the world. Food is not just a source of nutrition and oral pleasure. It becomes an aesthetic experience, a mechanism of sharing, a center of celebration, and sometimes a statement about one's own ethnic, religious, and cultural identity (Appadurai 1981; Rozin 2010).

In general, American culture labels animals as either edible or inedible. Most Americans would be repulsed by the thought of eating insects and insect larvae, but many societies consider them to be delicacies. American culture also distinguishes between pets, which are not eaten, and farm animals, such as chickens, cows, and pigs, which can be eaten. In the United States, horses are considered pets or work animals, and there are no industries for raising them for human consumption. Yet, horsemeat is a regular part of the continental European diet. The French, Belgians, Dutch, Germans, Italians, Poles, and other Europeans consume significant quantities of horsemeat each year (Harris 1985).

Anthropologists explain differences in dietary preferences in various ways. For example, Mary Douglas offered an explanation of why the Jewish people have prohibitions against eating pork. She described this prohibition in her book *Purity and Danger: An Analysis of the Concepts of Pollution and Taboo* (1966) by suggesting that all societies have symbolic classifications of certain objects or foods that are unclean, tabooed, polluted, or dirty, as well as those that are clean, pure, or undefiled. To illustrate her ideas regarding the classification of matter or foods, Douglas examined the ancient Israelites' classification of animals and taboos against eating certain animals such as pigs and shellfish, as described in Leviticus in the Bible. Douglas argues that like other humans, the ancient Israelites classified reality by placing things into distinct "mental boxes." However, some things do not fit neatly into discrete mental boxes. Some items are anomalous and ambiguous; thus they fall between the basic categories used to define cultural reality.

These anomalous items are usually treated as unclean, impure, unholy, polluting, or defiling.

In explaining how these processes influenced the classification of animals among the ancient Israelites, Douglas alludes to the descriptions in the first chapter of the Bible, Genesis, where God creates the animals with specific characteristics: Birds with feathers are soaring in the sky; fish with scales and fins are swimming in the water; and creatures with four feet are walking, hopping, or jumping on the land. However, some animals did not easily fit into the cultural categories used for the classification of animals. Animals that combined elements of different realms were considered ambiguous, and therefore unclean or unholy. For example, terrestrial animals that move by "swarming upon the earth," such as insects, were declared unclean and were prohibited from being eaten. Animals that have cloven hooves and chew cud, such as sheep, goats, and cattle, were considered clean and could be eaten. However, pigs have cloven hooves but do not chew cud and, therefore, failed to fit into the cultural classification of reality accepted by the ancient Israelites. Consequently, pigs were considered unclean and polluting, and were prohibited in the ancient Israelite diet. Shellfish and eels were also unclean animals because they swim in the water, but lack fins and scales. These anomalous creatures fell outside of the systematic classification of animals. Douglas maintains that the dietary laws of Leviticus represented an ideal construction of reality that represented God's plan of creation, which was based on perfection, order, and holiness. This became integral to the worldview of the ancient Israelites and affected their dietary preferences.

The late anthropologist Marvin Harris hypothesized that cultural dietary preferences frequently have an adaptive significance (1977, 1985). In seeking the origins of the pig taboo, Harris emphasized, as did Douglas, that among the ancient Israelites, pigs were viewed as abominable animals not suited for human consumption. Yet, many societies show no aversion to the consumption of pork. Pigs have been a primary source of protein and fat throughout China and Europe. In some societies in the Pacific Islands, pigs are so highly regarded they are treated as members of the family (but they are also eaten). One medical explanation for the dietary prohibition is that the pig is an unclean animal and that it carries diseases such as trichinosis, which is caused by a type of tapeworm. Harris, however, considered these explanations to be unsatisfactory. Regarding cleanliness, Harris acknowledged that because pigs cannot sweat, in hot, dry climates such as the Middle East, they wallow in their excrement to keep cool. He noted, however, that other animals, such as goats and chickens, can also be dirty, but they are eaten. Similarly, Harris emphasized that many other animals, such as cows, which are widely consumed, also carry diseases.

Ultimately, Harris explained the origins of the pig taboo in Judaism (and later Islam) by analyzing the ecological conditions of the Middle East. He maintained that this dietary restriction represented a cultural innovation that helped the societies of this region to adapt. About 1200 B.C., the ancient Israelites had settled in a woodland area that had not been cultivated. As they rapidly cut down trees to convert areas to irrigated agricultural land, they also severely restricted areas suitable for raising pigs on natural forage. Eventually, pigs had to be fed grains as supplements, which made them extremely costly and direct competitors with humans. Moreover, they required artificial shade and moisture to keep cool. In addition, pigs were not useful for pulling plows, producing milk, or providing hides or wool for clothing.

Chinese man with pig

Anthropologist at Work

NANCY ROSENBERGER: Gender, Food, Globalization, and Culture

After earning her university degree, Nancy Rosenberger traveled to northeastern Japan to teach English. She had majored in English and had never taken an anthropology or Japanese course in her life! While living in Japan, Rosenberger became fascinated with Japanese culture and language and wanted to study more. By chance, she read an article about the famous anthropologist Lévi-Strauss in a popular magazine by an anthropology professor named Aram Yengoyan. The global questions about culture and society which anthropologists ask intrigued her. Several years later, Rosenberger studied anthropological theory under Professor Yengoyan at the University of Michigan, where she earned her doctorate in cultural anthropology.

Rosenberger's main topic of research has been Japan and the changing position of women. For her Ph.D. dissertation, she investigated middle-aged women and the way they expressed their dissatisfaction, not in words, but through bodily aches and pains which they labeled as menopausal problems. Since 1993, she has conducted a longitudinal study of 55 Japanese women who were single and between the ages of 25 and 35 when she first met them. Rosenberger has since followed these women into middle age. She was particularly interested in this cohort because they are highly affected by the globalization of media and individualized consumption in Japan, but they also learned post-war Japanese values emphasizing group responsibility. These women's personal decisions about delaying marriage and having one or no children have changed Japan in big ways, yet they deal with contradictions. Work and educational institutions have not changed so much, and Japanese women have had to compromise in order to maintain relationships with husbands, children, and parents. All of this research material contributed to Rosenberger's book, *Gambling with Virtue: Japanese Women and the Search for Self in a Changing Nation* (2001).

Rosenberger has continued her research on these Japanese women and has a new book coming out entitled *Dilemmas of Adulthood: Nuances of Long-term Resistance among Japanese Women*, which traces the ambiguous feelings that include both the resistance and compliance of the Japanese women in this longitudinal study. For comparative purposes, Rosenberger also did research in Korea and Thailand on young, single women and saw how similar global ideas combine with local values and situations. She discovered that in these countries, women gain independence from global ideas and processes, but they still cope with entrenched gender inequality.

In 2001, Rosenberger began applied research for the local Hunger Task Force in Oregon. With her colleague, Joan Gross, she interviewed low-income people in two rural communities about questions of food security—whether they had enough nutritious and culturally appropriate food. In their study, Rosenberger and Gross found that people had enough food, but the food that they could afford through retail stores and food banks was not very nutritious, especially if they were diabetic or obese. They also found that these people are victims of a globalized food system that produces much processed food, but takes the control of food production out of local hands. Rosenberger has continued to work on local food issues with an organization called Ten Rivers Food Web which encourages the production and distribution of local food across three counties, and links affluent and low-income people with local foods.

In 2005, Rosenberger took her new interest in food and culture to Uzbekistan on a Fulbright scholarship to study in Central Asia. She is presently writing a book on food, nationalism, and class, gender, and ethnic differences in

Nancy Rosenberger

Uzbekistan called *Seeking Food Rights: Nation, Inequality and Repression in Uzbekistan*. In this book, she explores the class, gender, and ethnic differences that emerge through food in Uzbekistan, even though leaders attempt to unite the nation through a national cuisine. Rosenberger has found that the Uzbek people are hospitable and proud of their identity; they want to share their national cuisine with plenty of meat. However, poor people, particularly those who live in the Uzbekistan countryside, cannot be full citizens in this way. Ironically, while globalization overwhelms much of the world, the leaders of Uzbekistan have tightened their borders to keep out globalized food. McDonald's is nonexistent in this country, but people do desire more food choices. In the main city in Uzbekistan, Rosenberger saw a hamburger shop set up in a park that advertised "Madonna's" on a red sign with golden arches—an example of the creative mixtures that people construct from global culture.

Rosenberger's interest in food has also transferred back to Japan. She notes that the global world is one of risk, as is our food supply because it is produced and comes from all over the world. Japan is highly dependent upon food imports, many from the United States, and increasingly from China. In 2007, when some Japanese became ill from poison pot stickers made in

China, the local media went wild with accusations of "global food terror." Individual Japanese felt powerless, and fears of their Chinese neighbors welled up over food. All of this made local Japanese food more popular, and profited a group of organic farmers with whom Rosenberger was doing research in Japan. These organic farmers live consciously in resistance to global capitalism, practice self-sufficiency to the fullest extent possible, and sell their food only in face-to-face relationships. In 2012 Rosenberger conducted in-depth interviews with over 40 organic farmers in Japan, particularly in the Northeast (Tohoku) and around Tokyo. One important question she addressed was: How do farmers who were affected by Fukushima radiation respond to the situation of radiation in their food and fields? Another important question was: How have organic farmers changed in Japan from the 1970s to the 2010s? Future publications will highlight this research.

Rosenberger emphasizes that cultural anthropology has fostered a fascinating career for herself. Through it, she has talked in depth with many interesting people in a variety of countries and walks of life. She enjoys alerting students to both the inequalities in the world and the creativity that people bring in blending their local ways with global forces.

According to Harris, despite the increasing costs associated with pig raising, people were still tempted to raise them for nutritional reasons. He hypothesized that the pig taboo was established to inhibit this practice through religious authorities and texts that redefined the pig as an unclean animal. Neighbors of the ancient Israelites, such as the Egyptians, began to share the abhorrence of the pig. The pig taboo was later incorporated into the Islamic religious text, the Qur'an, so that today both Muslims and Jews are forbidden to eat pork.

Thus, according to Harris's hypothesis, in the hot, dry regions of the world where pigs are poorly adapted and extremely costly to raise, the meat of the pig came to be forbidden. He emphasized the practical considerations of pig raising, including the fact that they are hard to herd and are not grazing animals like goats, sheep, or cattle. In contrast, in the cooler, wetter areas of the world that are more appropriate for pig raising, such as China and New Guinea, pig taboos are unknown, and pigs are the prized foods in these regions.

Both Douglas and Harris offer insights into the development of the dietary preferences of Jews and Christians. While Douglas explores the important symbolic significance of these preferences, Harris examines the cost effectiveness and practical aspects of these food taboos. Anthropologists such as Harris and others have been studying dietary diversity, such as why some people prohibit the eating of beef, whereas other people have adopted it as an integral aspect of their diet. Food preferences illustrate how humans the world over have universal needs for protein, carbohydrates, minerals, and vitamins but obtain these nutrients in different ways, depending upon the dietary preferences established within their culture. Anthropologists Sidney Mintz and Christine DuBois have summarized how other anthropologists have studied food and eating habits around the world and how these developments are associated with ecological conditions, technological requirements, biological factors, but also with patterns of identity, gender, class differences, and ritual and religious beliefs (2002).

Anthropologists have continued to explore these numerous dimensions of food and eating habits in many different societies. For example, Daniel Fessler and C. D. Naverette looked at a broad cross-cultural sample of food taboos (2003). They found that food taboos are overwhelmingly associated with meat and animal products compared with fruits or vegetables. Animal foods are viewed as much more dangerous than fruits and vegetables with respect to disease or death. The high cost of trial-and-error learning about which animal foods would be harmful would be counterproductive in any cultural tradition; thus, food taboos associated with animals tend to become more pervasive than prohibitions against fruits or vegetables. Research on the cultural aspects of food is an important arena for contemporary anthropological research.

Dress Codes and Symbolism

Although some cultural differences may relate to the environmental adaptations of societies emphasized by some anthropologists, much more of our cultural diversity is a consequence of symbolic creations. Symbols provide the basis of meaningful shared beliefs within a society. Because of our inherent cultural capacity, we tend to be meaning-seeking creatures. In addition to the satisfaction of biological needs, we have needs for meaning and significance in our personal and social lives.

The importance of symbols as a source of cultural diversity can be seen in the dress codes and hairstyles of different societies. In most situations, the symbolism of clothing and hairstyles communicates different messages, ranging from political beliefs to identification with specific ethnic or religious groups. The tartan of a Scottish clan, the black leather jacket and long hair of a motorcycle gang member in the United States, and the veil of an Islamic woman in Saudi Arabia all provide a symbolic vocabulary that creates cultural diversity.

Many examples of clothing styles can be used to illustrate how symbols contribute to cultural diversity. Consider, for instance, changing dress codes in the United States. During the 1960s, many young people wore jeans, sandals, and beads to symbolize their rebellion against what they conceived as the conformist inclinations of American society. By the 1980s, many of the same people were wearing three-piece "power suits" as they sought to advance up the corporate ladder.

An example of how hairstyles can create meaningful symbolic codes can be seen in a group known as the Rastafarians (sometimes known as Rastas or Rastaman) of Jamaica. The majority of the people of Jamaica are of African descent. During the eighteenth and nineteenth centuries, they were brought to Jamaica by European slave traders to work on plantations. The Rastafarians are a specific religious group that believes Haile Selassie (1892–1975), the former emperor of Ethiopia whose original name was Ras Tafari, was the black Messiah who appeared in the flesh for the redemption of all blacks exiled in the world of white oppression. Rastafarian religion fuses Old Testament teachings, Christian mysticism, and Afro-Jamaican religious beliefs. The Rastafarian movement originated as a consequence of harsh economic, political, and living conditions in the slums of Jamaica.

In the 1950s, during the early phase of the Rastafarian movement, some male members began to grow their hair in "locks" or "dreadlocks" to symbolize their religious and political commitments. This hairstyle became well known in Western society through reggae music and Rasta musicians such as the late Bob Marley. Rastafarians derive the symbolism of their dreadlock hairstyle from the Bible. They view the unshaven man as the natural man and invoke Samson as one of the most important figures in the Bible. Dreadlocks also reflect a dominant symbol within the Rastafarian movement—the lion. The lion is associated with Haile Selassie, one of whose titles was the "Conquering Lion of Judah." To simulate the spirit of the lion, some Rastas do not cut their hair, sometimes growing their locks 20 inches or more.

In addition, the dreadlock hairstyle has a deeper symbolic significance in Jamaican society, where hair was often referred to as an index of racial and social inequality. Fine, silky hair was considered "good," whereas woolly, kinky hair was frowned upon (Barrett 1977). The white person with fine, silky hair was considered higher on the social ladder than was the typical African descendant in Jamaica. Thus, the Rastafarian hairstyle is a defiant symbol of resistance to the cultural values and norms of Jamaican society.

Bob Marley (1945–1981).

Rastafarian dreadlocks and long beards symbolize savagery, wildness, danger, disorder, and degeneration. They send the message that Rastafarians are outside of Jamaican society. Many Jamaicans view the dreadlocks as unkempt, dangerous, and dirty, yet to the Rastafarians, dreadlocks symbolize power, liberation, and defiance. Through their hairstyle, they announce to society that they do not accept the values, beliefs, and norms of the majority of the people. Some young people in the United States have grown dreadlocks to symbolize their resistance to the dominant norms, beliefs, and values of the majority culture emphasizing capitalism and individual competition.

Thus, to a great extent, culture consists of a network of symbolic codes that enhance values, beliefs, worldviews, norms, and ideologies within a society. Humans go to great lengths to create symbols that provide meaning for individuals and groups. These symbolic meanings are a powerful source of cultural diversity. When anthropologists study these symbolic codes and meanings, they often draw upon the humanistic-interpretive approach to comprehend these phenomena.

Ethnicity

One important aspect of culture is the recognition of one's own group as distinct from another, based on different values, beliefs, norms, and other characteristics. When referring to these differences, anthropologists use the terms *ethnic group* and *ethnicity*. **Ethnicity** is based upon perceived differences in ancestral origins or descent and upon shared historical and cultural heritage. An **ethnic group** is a collectivity of people who believe they share a common history, culture, or ancestry. For example, a small ethnic group known as the Old Order Amish maintains very strong ethnic boundary markers in U.S. society (Hostetler 1980; Kephart and Zellner 1994). Amish ethnicity originated in Switzerland during the sixteenth century. The Old Order Amish descended from a group of Anabaptists who split off with their own leadership during the Protestant Reformation. After this split, the Amish began to define themselves as different from other Anabaptists, Protestants, and Catholics, and they faced a great deal of persecution from the religious authorities (Kephart and Zellner 1994; Kraybill 2001). Eventually, the Amish fled to the United States in the 1700s, settling first in Lancaster, Pennsylvania. From there, they have grown in number and live in 20 different states in the United States. Today, the Amish population is about 227,000 with about 50,000 in Ohio, 40,000 in Pennsylvania, and smaller numbers in 17 different states. There are no longer any Amish living in Europe.

The Old Order Amish in the United States emphasize their ethnic difference through language by speaking a German dialect within their communities. The Amish dress in a traditional manner similar to that prescribed by the cultural codes of the 1600s. Men wear hats and have long beards; women have long hair, which is always covered by a hat in public. Based upon their interpretation of the Bible, the Amish strive to maintain a conservative, traditional way of life that forbids the adoption of modern technology such as electricity, automobiles, or television. They do not allow their children to be educated beyond the eighth grade so that they are not exposed to modern U.S. culture. The Amish have an extremely emotional attachment to their ethnicity and culture. These sentiments are deeply rooted within Amish culture and are evident in their language, dress, and traditional style of life, which distinguishes them from other North Americans.

We will discuss many different ethnic groups throughout the various chapters in this text, and in Chapter 23 we elaborate on how anthropologists have developed methods to investigate the complexities of ethnicity, ethnic groups, and ethnic movements around the world.

Cultural Universals

10.6 Describe how culture leads to universal similarities among people in widely separated societies.

As previously discussed, early anthropologists emphasized the realities of cultural diversity in their research and writings. Some anthropologists, however, began to recognize

Donald E. Brown

that humans throughout the world share some fundamental behavioral characteristics. George Murdock, an anthropologist who devoted himself to cross-cultural analysis, compiled a lengthy list of cultural universals from hundreds of societies. **Cultural universals** are essential behavioral characteristics of societies, and they are found all over the world. Murdock's list of cultural universals includes such basics as language, cooking, family, folklore, games, community organization, decorative art, education, ethics, mythology, food taboos, numerals, personal names, magic, religious rituals, puberty customs, toolmaking, and sexual restrictions. Although the specific content and practices of these universals may vary from society to society, the fact that these cultural universals exist underlies the essential reality that modern humans are of one biological family and one species.

In an influential book titled *Human Universals* (1991), anthropologist Donald E. Brown suggests that in their quest to describe cultural diversity, many anthropologists have overlooked basic similarities in human behavior and culture. This has led to stereotypes and distortions about people in other societies, who are viewed as "exotic," "inscrutable," and "alien."

Following in Murdock's footsteps, Brown describes many human universals. In one imaginative chapter, Brown creates a group of people he refers to as the "Universal People," who have all the traits of any people in any society throughout the world. The Universal People have language with complex grammar to communicate and think abstractly; kinship terms and categories to distinguish relatives and age groupings; gender terms for male and female; facial expressions to show basic emotions; a concept of the self as subject and object; tools, shelter, and fire; patterns for childbirth and training; families and political groupings; conflict; etiquette; morality, religious beliefs, and worldviews; and dance, music, art, and other aesthetic standards. Brown's depiction of the Universal People clearly suggests that these and many other aspects of human behavior result from certain problems that threaten the physical and social survival of all societies. For a society to survive, it must have mechanisms to care for children, adapt to the physical environment, produce and distribute goods and services, maintain order, and provide explanations of the natural and social environments. In addition, many universal behaviors result from fundamental biological characteristics common to all people.

Anthropologists have discovered that culture can be both diverse and universal. The challenge for anthropology is to understand the basis of both this diversity and this universality. To paraphrase the late anthropologist Clyde Kluckhohn: Every human is like all other humans, some other humans, and no other human. The major objective of cultural anthropology is to investigate the validity of this statement.

Summary and Review of Learning Objectives

10.1 Discuss the basic characteristics and components of *culture* as understood by anthropologists.

Culture consists of the material (technology, tools, weapons, etc.) and nonmaterial (values, beliefs, and norms) components that are distinct from our human biological inheritance or genetics.

10.2 Discuss how humans acquire their culture.

Humans acquire their culture through situational, social, and symbolic learning. Symbolic learning is the most important aspect of cultural transmission. Language and symbols enable humans to transmit culture across time and space. Children and adults learn and make inferences within the context of symbols and language to acquire their culture.

10.3 Discuss how anthropologists understand the sharing of culture.

Culture consists of the shared practices and understandings within a society. To some degree, culture is based on shared meanings that are to some extent "public" and thus, beyond the mind of any individual. However, culture is also carried within the mind of individuals. Through systematic ethnographic research contemporary anthropologists have found that culture is not shared by everyone equally within a society, but is distributed among different individuals. This has led to less generalizations and stereotypes about various cultures throughout the world.

10.4 Discuss the components of nonmaterial culture studied by anthropologists.

Nonmaterial culture includes values, beliefs, and norms. Values are the standards by which members of a society define what is good or bad, holy or unholy, beautiful or ugly.

They are assumptions that are widely shared within the society. Beliefs are specific cultural conventions that concern true or false assumptions, including specific descriptions of the nature of the universe and humanity's place in it. Norms are a society's rules of right and wrong behavior; they are another aspect of nonmaterial culture. Norms include folkways or etiquette rules and "mores" or specific rules regarding morality that are sanctioned within a society.

10.5 Describe how culture results in differences among people in various societies.

Ethnographic research by anthropologists on hundreds of societies on topics such as food, dress, and material and nonmaterial components of culture have shown that there is an enormous amount of cultural diversity throughout the world.

10.6 Describe how culture leads to universal similarities among people in widely separated societies.

While cultural diversity is obvious, anthropologists have also found many human universals that produce similarities for humans in widely separate societies. Language, cooking, norms, folklore, religion, and hundreds of other universals exist in the different cultures of the world. Thus, anthropologists have been engaged in exploring both the diversity and the similarity of human cultures throughout the world.

Key Terms

Chapter 11
The Process of Enculturation: Psychological and Cognitive Anthropology

 Learning Objectives

After you have read this chapter you should be able to:

11.1 Discuss the relationship between biology and culture and how anthropologists regard the nature/nurture questions of humanity.

11.2 Explain the difference between nonhuman animal behavior and human behavior.

11.3 Discuss how anthropologists study enculturation and its relationship to personality formation.

11.4 How have anthropologists used the psychoanalytic approach to study personality and culture?

11.5 Explain how anthropologists understand incest avoidance and the incest taboo.

11.6 What have anthropologists learned about enculturation and sexuality?

11.7 Discuss the relationship between enculturation and cognition.

11.8 Discuss what cognitive anthropologists have learned about universals and human thought processes.

11.9 How does evolutionary psychology contribute to an understanding of human universals?

11.10 Discuss what anthropologists have discovered about human emotions.

11.11 Discuss the new field of neuroanthropology.

11.12 Discuss the limitations of enculturation in examining human behavior.

In the previous chapter, we explored the concept of culture as it reflects the differences and similarities in human behavior and thought around the world. This chapter focuses on how anthropologists study the relationship between the individual and culture, or the process of enculturation. Recall from Chapter 10 that enculturation is the process of social interaction through which people learn their culture. In this chapter, we will discuss the different approaches that anthropologists have taken to study the process of enculturation. One of the earliest approaches in this field is **psychological anthropology**. Unlike psychologists, who tend to study people within the psychologists' own societies, psychological anthropologists observe people and the process of enculturation in many different types of societies (Henrich, Heine, Norenzayan 2010). Their research findings are then used as the basis of cross-cultural studies to determine how and why behavior, thoughts, and feelings differ and are similar from society to society. In this chapter, we will also discuss the approaches of **cognitive anthropology**, which is the study of cognition and cultural meanings through specific methodologies such as psychological experiments, computer modeling, and other techniques to elicit underlying unconscious factors that structure human-thinking processes.

Psychological anthropologists and cognitive anthropologists study the development of personality characteristics and individual behaviors in a given society and how they are influenced by enculturation. In their studies, anthropologists need to question basic assumptions regarding human nature: Is human nature primarily a matter of biological influences or of cultural factors? In order to study this question, psychological and cognitive anthropologists focus on the enculturation process and precisely how this process influences personality characteristics, sexual behavior, thinking and cognition, and emotional development. This chapter considers some of the major research by psychological and cognitive anthropologists on the process of enculturation.

Biology versus Culture

11.1 Discuss the relationship between biology and culture and how anthropologists regard the nature/nurture questions of humanity.

Before we explore the specific aspects of psychological anthropology, we need to consider some questions. One fundamental concept that anthropologists reflect upon is what is frequently referred to as "human nature." Two questions immediately arise when discussing this concept: If there are basic similarities or universal patterns of human behavior, does that mean that human nature is biologically transmitted through heredity? If this is the case, to what extent can culture or learning change human nature to produce variation in behavior within different societies? These two questions have led to a controversy in anthropology, with some anthropologists emphasizing the biological influences on human behavior while others emphasize the social or cultural influences on behavior.

Today, however, most anthropologists realize that neither biological nor cultural influences exist in absolute, pure form. Modern anthropologists, therefore, adopt a biocultural or *interactionist perspective*, which combines the effects of biology and culture to explain human behavior. Anthropologists recognize that human behavior depends upon both our biological endowment and what we learn from our society or culture. What interactionists care about is the interrelationship between the biological and the learned factors in any behavior. For example, anthropologists Kathryn Coe and Craig Palmer, along with Nancy Aiken, argue that humans communicate valuable information that is important to survival and the future success of descendants (biological concerns) through cultural mechanisms such as storytelling (Coe et al. 2006).

Instincts and Human Nature

11.2 **Explain the difference between nonhuman animal behavior and human behavior.**

Anthropologists often address this question about human nature: To what extent is human nature similar to the nature of other animals? For example, according to the traditional view of humans, the human body is "animal-like" or "machine-like," and the human mind is separate from the body. For many Westerners, this image of humans has been used to distinguish humans from other types of animals.

Human Beings as Animals

What do we mean when we say that humans are animal-like? This statement can create misunderstandings because of the different meanings we give to the word *animal*. On the one hand, we distinguish animals scientifically from plants and minerals. This system of classification places humans in the animal category. On the other hand, *animal* is sometimes used in a derogatory or pejorative sense. For example, in one of the earliest uses of the word in written English, Shakespeare wrote:

> *His intellect is not replenished, hee is only an animal, onely sensible in the duller parts. (Love's Labour's Lost, IV, ii)*

This is the negative meaning of the term that we associate with films such as *Animal House*, referring to "uncivilized," "irrational," "unthinking," and "brutish" behaviors. In attempting to understand humans fully, anthropologists emphasize only the scientific meaning of the word *animal*. Anthropologists maintain that humans are partly like all animals, partly like certain types of animals, and partly like no other animal.

Because we humans are part of the animal kingdom, we share certain characteristics with all animals. We have to consume certain amounts of carbohydrates, proteins, and minerals to survive, just as other animals do. We cannot photosynthesize and process our own foods from within, as plants do. In addition, we share certain characteristics with particular types of animals. For example, like other mammals, we have body hair, and human mothers have the capacity to suckle their offspring with milk produced after birth. Similarly, like other primates such as chimpanzees and gorillas, we have stereoscopic, color vision; we have nails instead of claws; we are extremely sociable; and our infants experience a long period of dependence on adults.

Despite these similarities with other animals, humans are unquestionably the most complex, intelligent, and resourceful creatures on the planet. Humans have spread and adapted to every continent, becoming the most widely dispersed animal on the Earth. We have been the most creative species in our abilities to adjust to different conditions, ranging from tropical rainforests to deserts to rural agricultural areas to urban environments.

Instincts in Animals

Anthropologists have often asked this question: What gives the human species its tremendous flexibility in adjusting to these different environments? One way of answering this question is to compare the fundamental behaviors of human and nonhuman animals. Many animals inherit **instincts**, genetically-based innate behaviors, that allow them to take advantage of the specific conditions in their environment. Instinctive behaviors occur widely within the animal kingdom. For example, certain species of birds migrate during the winter season. Temperature changes or differences in ultraviolet radiation from the sun trigger biochemically based, inborn hormonal reactions that act on neurological mechanisms, stimulating all normal individuals within a particular species of bird to fly in a certain direction. This behavior enables the birds to find sufficient feeding grounds for survival during the winter season. But these birds are also influenced by external factors such as temperature and other environmental conditions that contribute to their behavior; their "instincts" alone do not "determine" their behavior.

Another example of these species-specific instincts is the nest-building behavior of certain bird populations. In an experiment, scientists isolated as many as five generations of weaver finches and did not supply them with nest-building materials. (Weaver finches are small, brightly colored, seed-eating birds that construct complicated nests with side entrances.) When the scientists released the sixth generation of finches, however, these birds automatically built nests identical to those of their ancestors.

Bears hibernating, salmon swimming upstream to lay eggs during a specific season, spiders spinning perfect webs, and infant turtles and alligators walking unaided toward the water after hatching from eggs are other examples of instinctive behaviors. These behaviors can be thought of as a kind of innate knowledge with which these animals are born that enables them to adapt, survive, and produce offspring. However, the behavior of these animals is not influenced solely by instincts. This will be emphasized in the next section.

A weaver finch bird building a nest. This is an example of an instinctive behavior.

Instincts and Learned Behaviors

As emphasized above, the fact that some animal behaviors are instinctive does not mean that environment has nothing to do with these behaviors. Although some animal behavior such as a spider weaving a web is near-perfect when it first appears, typically the development of most animal behavior involves a continuous interaction between the organism and the environment.

This does not mean that nonhuman animals do not learn their complex behaviors, however. For example, most birds have to learn the particular songs that they sing for various purposes after being exposed to the songs of their particular species. However, when biologists study bird song, they find that there is a very complex process that involves both nature and nurture in learning these songs that help birds communicate with one another. For example, song learning by birds varies from species to species. Some species do not need to be exposed to the specific vocalizations to reproduce them in near-perfect form. A particular species of dove sings a species-specific type of "coo" in perfect form even when reared with other species of doves. In contrast, parrots can learn to imitate any song they hear. But generally, many other birds, such as chaffinches and other species, need to be exposed to the adult song during their early months to acquire the specific vocalization for their particular species (Catchpole and Slater 1995; Hinde and Stevenson-Hinde 1987; Marler and Slabbekorn 2004). In fact, much of animal behavior is a result of both genetically based neurological capacities and "nurture," or learning that provides the animals with the experience they need to adapt and survive within the world.

Most ethologists (scientists who study animal behavior) agree that complex instincts in different types of animals can be classified as exhibiting a *closed* or a more *open* type of genetic program. Closed types of instincts remain fairly stable, even when environmental conditions change, whereas open types respond more sensitively to changing circumstances. For example, many species of birds that migrate, such as geese, have changed their migratory behavior in response to climate changes. Thus, even behaviors that are genetically based can be modified to some degree by experience and by specific environmental conditions.

Do Humans Possess Instincts?

Because humans are part of the animal kingdom, this question arises: Do we have any instinctive behaviors? This question is difficult to answer because we use the word *instinct* in different contexts. Sometimes, we refer to athletes as having the right kind of instincts in going toward the basket or goal line. Upon further reflection, however, it is obvious that basketball or football players who respond in an automatic way to a play situation do so only after practicing for long hours and developing the coordination and skillful moves necessary for competitive sports. Because athletic skills are learned, they are not comparable to the instinctive behaviors of animals. We also use the term *instinct* to refer to some intuitive processes. For example, we have all heard about relying upon our instincts in making difficult decisions. Usually, when we refer to our "gut instincts," what we really mean are our "intuitions." Some "cognitive intuitions" may very well be based on "innate predispositions" that develop as a result of our brain and neurological developments, as well as early learning in infancy. However, as mentioned earlier, closed instincts are genetically prescribed behaviors that rigidly determine behavior, whereas our intuitions are internal feelings and cognitive states that tend to motivate us in certain directions. It appears that some of our intuitions are more like open instincts, which involve a great deal of learning from the environment. As Matt Ridley, a well-known biologist, who emphasizes an interactionist understanding of human behavior, states, "Instincts, in a species like the human one, are not immutable genetic programmers; they are predispositions to learn" (1996:6).

Thus, we can ask these questions: Do humans have any closed instincts like those of other nonhuman animals? Do we have any automatic, biologically controlled behaviors? Because of the wide range of behaviors shown by humans, most anthropologists, psychologists, and other social scientists concur that humans do not have any instincts that automatically motivate and drive our behavior.

We do have some genetically determined behaviors called simple reflexes, or involuntary responses, such as being startled by a loud noise, blinking our eyes, breathing, and throwing out our arms when we lose our balance. These reflexive behaviors are automatic responses to environmental conditions, and we do them unconsciously. But these are not comparable to the complex behaviors related to the closed instincts of some other species. Some anthropologists, however, influenced by evolutionary psychology, hypothesize that humans have some genetically prepared behaviors that have enabled us to adapt to varying conditions in our evolutionary history. As mentioned above, evolutionary psychologists do think that humans have "cognitive intuitions" that predispose certain "forms of thinking and perhaps action." Yet, they do not view these cognitive intuitions as automatically motivating and driving human behavior; instead, these cognitive intuitions are definitely shaped by experience and learning, as well as by brain and neurological developments while we are young children. Psychologist David Myers has followed the research on "intuitions" for many years and concludes that although we as humans rely on our intuitions for many decisions and actions we take, our intuitions can be very faulty guides for understanding the reality around us (Myers 2002).

Drives

We humans have basic, inborn **drives**—biological urges such as hunger, thirst, and sex—that need satisfaction. These drives are important for the survival of the species. Yet, again, these drives are not comparable to the closed instincts of nonhuman animals. We are not programmed to satisfy them in a rigid, mechanical manner. Rather, the ways in which we satisfy such drives are learned through experience. We do not automatically build a spider's web to capture our food; we have to learn to find food in ways that vary widely in many different types of environments. And unlike some other animals, we may choose to override rather than to satisfy these drives. For example, people can ignore the hunger drive by going on hunger strikes as a political protest or opting to fast for dietary or religious reasons.

If we do not have closed instincts that rigidly prescribe our behavior, what do we have that makes us so successful and creative? The answer is that we have the capacity for flexibility in creating conditions and providing solutions for human survival. Some animals have a closed biogram, a genetically closed behavioral complex that is related to their adaptations to their specific environment niche. In contrast, humans have an open biogram, an extremely flexible genetic program that is shaped by learning experiences.

Culture versus Instinct

Our unprecedented success in adapting to different conditions reflects not only our open biograms, but also the influence of human culture. Our capacity for culture, an inherent aspect of the human mind, has enabled us to modify our behaviors and to shape and adjust to our natural environment. The *capacity* for culture is genetically programmed through the human brain and nervous system. But as we emphasized in Chapter 10, culture is not transmitted biologically through genetic programming. Instead, it is learned through the enculturation process and is passed on from generation to generation. Culture frees us from relying upon the slow process of natural selection to adapt to specific environments.

Most genes do not specifically encode for narrowly defined types of human behavior. We are not genetically programmed to build shelters in a certain manner, to devise patterns of economic distribution, to get married, to vote for a president, to carry out a revolution, or to believe in a particular religion. These are learned behaviors based on the enculturation processes that make up the economic, social, political, and religious practices and concepts of a particular society. Without culture, we would not be able to adjust to the tremendous range of environments throughout the world. We would not be able to adapt to Arctic conditions, hunt animals and collect plants, herd cattle, plant crops, or drive a car. The development of the human mind, with the capacity for culture, represents the greatest revolutionary breakthrough in the evolution of life.

Enculturation: Culture and Personality

11.3 Discuss how anthropologists study enculturation and its relationship to personality formation.

Enculturation is a lifelong process, and it links individuals with the specific culture to which they are exposed. Immediately after they are born, infants begin to absorb their language and culture—the etiquette, mores, values, beliefs, and practices of their society—through both unconscious and conscious learning—situational, social, and symbolic.

Enculturation is a vital foundation of our humanity. Virtually helpless at birth, an infant needs care and is completely dependent on others for survival. Through the interaction of enculturation with biologically based predispositions, a person acquires his or her **personality**, the fairly stable patterns of thought, feeling, and action associated with a specific person. Personality includes cognitive, emotional, and behavioral components. The cognitive component of personality consists of thought patterns, memory, belief, perception, and other intellectual capacities. The emotional component includes emotions such as love, hate, envy, jealousy, sympathy, anger, and pride. The behavioral component consists of the skills, aptitudes, competence, and other abilities or potentials that are developed throughout the course of a person's life.

Early Studies of Enculturation

During the 1930s and 1940s, a number of anthropologists began to research enculturation to learn about the influence of culture on personality development. At this time, some social scientists suggested that biology and race are the most influential determinants of human behavior (see Chapter 23). In Germany, for example, social scientists who were members of the Nazi Party promoted the idea that because of biological characteristics, some races are superior to others in respect to behavior and thought. Cultural anthropologists in the United States began to challenge this view of biological or racial determinism through research on enculturation (Boas 1940; Benedict and Weltfish 1943; Degler 1991; Konner 2002). In particular, two women anthropologists, Ruth Benedict and Margaret Mead, became pioneers in early psychological anthropology. They published extensively and became prominent in this area of research. Both of these anthropologists maintained that each society and culture has a unique history. After studying processes such as child rearing and enculturation, they proposed that every culture is characterized by a dominant personality type. Culture, they argued, is essentially "personality writ large." The field studies they did became the basis of what was then called culture-and-personality theory.

Benedict and Culture Types   One classic example of the application of culture-and-personality theory is Benedict's analysis of the Plains and Pueblo Native American Indian societies. In an essay titled "Psychological Types in the Cultures of the Southwest" (1928) and in a classic book, *Patterns of Culture* (1934), Benedict classified Pueblo societies as having an Apollonian (named for the Greek god Apollo) culture. The Pueblo cultural ethos stressed gentleness, cooperation, harmony, tranquility, and peacefulness. According to Benedict, these values explain why members of Pueblo societies were "moderate." The Pueblo rarely indulged in violence, and they avoided the use of drugs and alcohol to transcend their senses.

In contrast, Benedict characterized the Plains societies as Dionysian (after the Greek god Dionysius). She described how the values and ethos of the Plains groups were almost the direct opposite of those of the Pueblo. The Plains Indians were involved in warfare and violence, and their ritual behavior included the use of drugs, alcohol, fasting, and physical self-torture and mutilation to induce religious ecstasy. Benedict extended her analysis

Ruth Fulton Benedict and Plains Indians

to such groups as the Kwakiutl Native American peoples and the Dobu of Melanesia. She referred to the Kwakiutl as "megalomaniacs" and the Dobuans as "paranoid," fearing and hating one another. In each case, she claimed that the group's values and ethos had created a distinctive cultural personality. In Benedict's analysis, individual personalities were formed through enculturation and the values, beliefs, and norms of different societies led to variations in culture. In other words, Benedict believed that the culture of a particular society can be studied by studying the personality of its bearers. She thought that the patterning or configuration of a particular culture is simply reflected in an individual's personality.

Mead in Samoa   Margaret Mead was one of the most influential contributors to the field of culture and personality. Although most of her ethnographic reports focused on fairly isolated, small-scale societies located in the Pacific islands, she addressed issues that concerned U.S. society, particularly adolescence, child care, and relationships between males and females. At the age of 23, Mead went to the islands of American Samoa to study adolescent development. In the United States and other societies, adolescence was usually identified with emotional conflict and rebellion against parental authority. Her mentor, Franz Boas (see Chapter 13), wanted her to investigate this aspect of life in Samoa to determine whether this pattern of adolescent development was universal. The central research question that Mead was to investigate was: To what extent are adolescent problems the product of physiological changes occurring at puberty or the result of cultural factors?

Mead resided in Samoa for nine months and interviewed 68 Samoan girls (25 of these in depth) in three villages. She concluded that, in contrast to U.S. society, adolescence in Samoa was not characterized by problems between the young and the old. She attributed the difference between the two societies to different sets of values, which produced different cultural personalities. In her book *Coming of Age in Samoa* (1928), she argued that Samoan society emphasized group harmony and cooperation. These values arose, according to Mead, from Samoan child-rearing practices. Samoan children were raised in family units that included many adults. Therefore, youngsters did not develop strong emotional ties to any one adult. Consequently, she argued, emotional bonds were relatively shallow.

For this reason, Mead continued, Samoan society was more permissive than U.S. society. Children learned privately and often secretly about sexuality, and adolescents learned freely but had hidden, clandestine premarital sex. In addition, Mead contended that Samoan society shared a common set of values and standards. Therefore, Samoan children were not exposed to conflicting values and differing political and religious beliefs, as were U.S. adolescents.

Margaret Mead with a young Samoan female.

For these reasons, Mead concluded, Samoan children experienced a much easier transition from adolescence into adulthood than did their counterparts in the United States.

The Culture-and-Personality School: An Evaluation   The anthropological tradition represented by Mead and Benedict stimulated more careful research regarding personality and culture. Much of the data provided by these early psychological anthropologists was important in understanding the enculturation process. As a result of these early studies, we now have a better understanding of personality formation, thought, behavior, and emotional development within different human societies.

Despite these accomplishments, the culture-and-personality school has been criticized on many fronts. One major shortcoming cited is the practice of characterizing an entire society in terms of one dominant personality. Culture-and-personality theorists assumed that all members of a given society share the same cultural knowledge. This assumption produced highly stereotyped presentations of various cultures and peoples. In fact, culture and knowledge are distributed differently and unequally within society. Some people have knowledge of a culture's values, beliefs, and ideologies that others do not have. As discussed in Chapter 10, people do not all share the same culture; culture is variously distributed among different individuals. Thus, defining an entire society as a single personality creates cultural stereotypes, rather than a realistic portrait of a people. Benedict, for example, neglected many data that suggested that both the Plains and the Pueblo societies exhibited Apollonian and Dionysian behaviors.

The culture-and-personality school has also been criticized for focusing entirely on the nonmaterial aspects of culture. Theorists such as Benedict went so far as to argue that cultural values are completely autonomous from material conditions (Hatch 1973). Therefore, they did not include such factors as technology or the physical environment in their explanations of human behavior. Again using Benedict as an example, the fact that traditional Plains Indians were primarily bison-hunting groups, whereas the Pueblo peoples were agriculturalists in a semiarid desert, was not included in her analysis, yet this fact was obviously important in their societies.

A final criticism of the culture-and-personality theorists is their perceived tendency to attribute human behavior entirely to cultural factors. Of course, their emphasis on cultural determinants, rather than biological determinants, reflects the attempt to criticize the biological and racist determinism prevalent during that period. During the time period when the Nazi movement and other racist causes were emphasizing biological and racial determinism, Benedict and Mead, along with their mentor Franz

Boas, were illustrating the importance of culture in shaping and influencing human behavior. However, one controversy developed in anthropology in the 1980s with the late Australian anthropologist Derek Freeman's criticism of Margaret Mead. This controversy illustrated the global dimension and reach of anthropology worldwide.

The Freeman–Mead Controversy

In 1983, Freeman attracted a great deal of international attention when he published a controversial book titled *Margaret Mead and Samoa: The Making and Unmaking of an Anthropological Myth*. Having conducted fieldwork in Samoa intermittently since 1940, Freeman concluded that Mead's findings were largely erroneous. Whereas Mead had portrayed the Samoan people as lacking strong passions, aggression, warfare (warfare had been suppressed by the government, but it did exist well into the colonial period when Mead was there), a sense of sin or guilt, rape, suicide, and other behaviors associated with intense emotions, Freeman claimed to find all of these behaviors.

Freeman challenged Mead by asserting that strong emotional ties did exist between parents and children in Samoan society. He also challenged Mead's conclusions concerning casual attitudes toward sexuality. Pointing out that Samoa had converted to Christianity during the 1830s, Freeman asserted that most Samoans had puritanical views toward sexuality. He found that virginity for girls was highly valued, casual sexual liaisons were prohibited, and adultery was severely punished. Furthermore, government records indicated that the incidence of rape in Samoa (proportionate to population size) was twice as high as that in the United States.

Freeman also rejected Mead's claims for an easy transition from adolescence to adulthood. He noted that adolescents were harshly punished by their parents for any transgressions. He presented charts illustrating that offenses and delinquent behaviors among Samoans peaked at the age of 16, especially for males. Thus, Freeman concluded that adolescents in Samoa go through a period of deviance and rebellion against their elders in the same way that other adolescents around the world do. Freeman asserted that hormonal changes, as well as cultural influences, have consequences for adolescent behavior everywhere. Samoan adolescents are not much different from adolescents elsewhere.

How could two anthropologists studying the same people arrive at such radically different conclusions? Instead of residing with a Samoan family, Mead lived with an American family and conducted interviews intermittently. However, Freeman does concede that Mead had an incredible amount of energy and tried to find out as carefully as possible what these young females thought and how they behaved when they frequently visited the back porch of her household. Although she was appointed by the Samoan chiefs as an important high-status *taupou* (a ceremonial position as a village virgin), Freeman claimed that because she was a young woman, she did not interview many of the significant chiefs. Of the 25 females she interviewed, half were not past puberty and, therefore, could not serve as models of the transition from adolescence to adulthood.

Freeman argued that the major reason for Mead's misinterpretation of Samoan society was her extreme reliance on the model of cultural determinism of theorists such as Benedict. Thus, Mead's portrayal of Samoa as a society without adolescent problems supported the claims of her close colleagues at that time, who maintained that biology had little influence on behavior. In contrast, Freeman emphasized a biocultural or interactionist approach, which focuses on both biological and cultural influences. He argued that the biological changes that accompany adolescence inevitably affect adolescent behavior.

The Freeman–Mead debate remains a major controversy in anthropology. Supporters of Mead point out that Freeman studied Samoa years and even decades after Mead did. Because societies are not static, it is possible that Samoan values and lifestyles had changed by the time of Freeman's work. Freeman wrote two more recent books, *Margaret Mead and the Heretic: The Making and Unmaking of an Anthropological Myth* (1997) and *The Fateful Hoaxing of Margaret Mead* (1999), in which he emphasized how Mead was strongly influenced by the ideas of cultural determinism. He believed that Mead overlooked any type of biological influences on behavior.

However, other anthropologists of Samoa, such as Paul Shankman, note that Mead did not discount biology entirely; she merely rejected the extreme biological deterministic views of their time (Shankman 1998, 2001, 2009a, 2009b). In addition, Freeman tended to emphasize public morality or "ideal culture" based on what people said, rather than what they actually did. Also, Freeman overlooked Mead's very precise 1930 study of Samoan social organization and culture, which is still viewed as a classic intensive ethnographic work today by Samoan specialists. In the recent book *The Trashing of Margaret Mead: Anatomy of an Anthropological Controversy*, Shankman assesses the Mead–Freeman controversy and the international media event that developed about anthropological issues (2009b). In Shankman's assessment, he provides an in-depth understanding of both Mead and Freeman's perspectives and how their personal histories within anthropology resulted in misinterpretations and exaggerations about Samoan culture and society. In addition, Shankman emphasizes that Freeman had neglected the fact that Mead did take an interactionist approach to understanding Samoan behavior and culture. This resulted in Freeman's misrepresentation of Mead's analysis and perspective. Shankman discusses the impact of the Mead–Freeman debate on contemporary Samoan society. Since neither Mead nor Freeman discussed how globalization has transformed and created numerous problems such as high suicide rates for young people, medical problems such as obesity and diabetes, along with poverty, the relevance of the debate has become marginal to the Samoans today. Overall, the Mead–Freeman controversy resulted in a complex debate within and outside of anthropology. As the controversy has matured, a number of anthropologists have refined their understanding of both the realities of, and the myths about, Samoan culture and have developed a more nuanced biocultural or interactionist approach to assessing enculturation issues (Shankman 2009b, 2013).

Childhood Acquisition of Cultural Knowledge

Despite limitations of early research on enculturation and on culture and personality, pioneering women anthropologists such as Margaret Mead, Ruth Benedict, and others were the first to systematically examine the effects of childhood training on personality development. Male ethnographers had not paid much attention to this subject. This innovative research has resulted in a much improved understanding of the techniques of childhood training and enculturation throughout the world. Since then, a number of studies of childhood training by psychological anthropologists have contributed to this area of research. Anthropologist Meredith Small in her books *Our Babies, Ourselves: How Biology and Culture Shape the Way We Parent* (1998) and *Kids: How Biology and Culture Shape the Way We Raise Our Children* (2001) summarizes how biological factors interact with learning in enculturation processes in many different societies throughout the world. In these two books, Small emphasizes that biology intersects with culture in infant and child development, but that we are neurologically "unfinished" and brain growth is inextricably connected with social and cultural development.

Japanese Childhood Enculturation   Some contemporary ethnographic research projects focus on the type of childhood training and enculturation that influence the learning of basic concepts of a particular culture. One study, conducted by Joy Hendry (1992, 2013), focused on how children in Japan become enculturated. According to the Western stereotype, Japanese society is characterized as "collectivistic," rather than "individualistic." A related stereotype is that Japanese society is a "consensus" or "conformist" society, with everyone submitting to the norms of the group. Hendry's ethnographic research on whether these stereotypes are correct focused on how children learn their initial concepts of Japanese culture and adjust to group behaviors.

Hendry found that small children are extremely important in Japanese culture. Babies are afforded every possible individual attention. For example, many highly educated mothers give up their careers to dedicate themselves to full-time nurturing once a child is born. The child is to be kept in a secure, harmonious household. A tiny child is often strapped to a mother's back or front while the mother works, shops, and performs daily routines. Also, an adult will lie down with a child at bedtime until he or she falls asleep and in some cases, sleeps all night with the child. From an American perspective, it appears that the child is totally indulged, but the child learns a great many routine tasks such as eating, washing, dressing, and toilet training through repetition until the child can do these tasks on his or her own.

During this early phase of enculturation, children learn two basic cultural concepts: *uchi*, or inside of the house, including the people inside, and *soto*, the outside world. Human beings are categorized by these concepts, and various behaviors in a Japanese household, such as removing shoes before entering the house, reinforce the inside/outside dichotomy. *Uchi* is associated with safety, security, and cleanliness. *Soto* is where danger may lurk; big dogs, strangers, or even demons and ghosts may be outside. For the first few years of their lives, children play with siblings and cousins and then gradually with close neighbors. They are allowed to play in the immediate neighborhood from as early as two years of age if it is a safe environment, and they begin to build up a new set of "inside" personal relations with neighbors who live nearby.

At the age of four or five, children are introduced to group life with outsiders in a kindergarten or day nursery. At first, the children cry for a while and refuse to join in, but eventually they become involved with the new group of fellow kindergartners, and this becomes a new *uchi* group for them. They learn to cooperate with one another in the group and begin to develop an identity appropriate for group life. However, Hendry emphasized that the children do not lose their individuality. Each child is treated as an individual by the teacher, who obtains a great deal of background knowledge about the child. (Parents fill out forms regarding their child's strengths and weaknesses, likes and dislikes, siblings, and other details.) In addition, the teacher visits each child's home at least once during the academic year. Thus, along with learning to cooperate with their new *uchi* group, these children also become familiar with their own individuality and the individual characteristics of their peers. When engaging in group activities, whether in games, sports, learning activities, or other responsibilities, the children teach each other personal skills and abilities so that the entire group will benefit.

In addition, Hendry notes the intricacies of the interrelation between the inner self (*tatemae* or face) and harmony.

Children are taught that group harmony is predicated upon how one presents themselves to others, which is based on the empathic understanding of what it means to feel hurt. These young children learn to empathize with the feelings of others and are taught that selfishness is an "an unrestrained state." Hendry points out that a child's behavior is disapproved of if it stems merely from self-interest (and does not consider either the needs of others or the implications of such behavior on others). This is related to the important interrelation between the inner self (*tatemae* or face) and group harmony.

Hendry concluded that even though Japanese children learn to participate in many group-oriented activities, they do not completely lose their sense of individuality. Although Japanese society does not emphasize individualism in the same way U.S. society does, with its connotations of self-assertion and individual rights, Japanese children develop their own sense of self in respect to their individual talents and abilities. One of the conclusions based on the new types of psychological anthropology studies such as Joy Hendry's is that children are not just passive recipients in the enculturation process. Instead, they are active contributors to the meaning and outcome of interactions with other members of society.

The child is viewed as an active agent in this new conception of enculturation and learns to choose and design appropriate responses to specific social situations and contexts as he or she is exposed to them. Psychological anthropologists are contributing to a better understanding of how children acquire cultural knowledge through exposure and active participation in everyday social interaction.

A Japanese mother and child.

Psychoanalytic Approaches in Anthropology

11.4 How have anthropologists used the psychoanalytic approach to study personality and culture?

Sigmund Freud's Influence

A number of psychological anthropologists have been influenced by the concepts and ideas of Sigmund Freud, the founder of psychoanalysis and psychiatry. Freud (1856–1939), a Viennese physician trained in the natural sciences, viewed human behavior as a reflection of innate emotional factors. His theory of human behavior emphasizes the importance of emotions in the development of an individual's personality. He tried to demonstrate that a great deal of emotional life is unconscious; that is, people are often unaware of the real reasons for their feelings and actions. Freud postulated that the personality is made up of three sectors: the *id, ego,* and *superego.*

Freud believed that all humans are born with unconscious, innate drives for sex and aggression. These unconscious desires are part of the **id**. According to Freud, these drives promote the seeking of immediate pleasure and the avoidance of pain. The id represents the basic needs of humans, needs that exist in the unconscious. Freud maintained that the id is rooted in the biological organism and is present at birth; the newborn is basically a bundle of needs. But the sexual and the aggressive drives are often frustrated by society. This frustration frequently results in what Freud termed *repression*, wherein the energy created by these sexual and aggressive drives of the id is redirected into socially approved forms of expression.

Eventually, the second part of the personality, the *ego*, becomes differentiated from the id. The **ego** represents the conscious attempt to balance the innate pleasure-seeking drives of the human organism with the demands and realities of the society. The ego is the "conscious" part of the personality and is sometimes referred to as the "reality part" of the personality.

Finally, the human personality develops the superego, which is the presence of culture within the individual. The **superego** is based on the internalized values and norms of society, which create the individual's conscience. The superego develops first in response to parental demands, but gradually the child learns that he or she has to respond to the society and culture at large. For example, Freud hypothesized that all male children are driven by an unconscious desire to have an affectionate and sexual relationship with their mother. This unconscious desire leads to hostility toward their natural father, the authority figure within the family. Freud called this the *Oedipus complex*. This desire is frustrated by the morality and norms of society, the superego, and the enculturation process. These emotional feelings become repressed, and the mature ego of the individual emerges to intervene between these desires and the dictates of society.

Freud's hypotheses were highly controversial in his own lifetime and remain so today. Although his theories are based on limited examples from his European medical and psychoanalytic practice, he extended his conclusions to include all of humanity. Freud's early scientific work was in neurology and brain science, and he believed that all of his findings regarding the human psyche would eventually be reduced to neurological patterns and development within the brain (1891). For example, Freud experimented with the drug cocaine himself in the early twentieth century, and although he abandoned the use of this drug because of its negative consequences, his experiments did increase scientific findings about the effects of cocaine and other drugs on the brain (Konner 2002). Freud's conceptions regarding enculturation have been modified by some modern anthropologists who study the role of childhood experiences in the formation of personality. However, Freud's theories of emotional development and the role of the unconscious in personality represent significant contributions to anthropological research on enculturation.

Anthropologists inspired by the Freudian approach attempt to study the relationship among the unconscious thoughts, emotions, and motives of humans. In some cases, they collaborate with psychiatrists to study dreams, symbols, fantasy life, interrelations among family members, and sexual relations (Paul 1989, 1996; Herdt and Stoller 1990).

Understanding Incest Avoidance and the Incest Taboo

11.5 Explain how anthropologists understand incest avoidance and the incest taboo.

One of the topics addressed by anthropologists is incest. During their studies of interrelationships among family members and sexual relations in various societies, psychological anthropologists noted the widespread avoidance of incestuous behavior. They have developed various hypotheses to understand what are referred to as incest avoidance and the incest taboo. Freud offered a mythical explanation for the origins of the incest taboo in his book *Totem and Taboo* (1913). In this book, Freud proposed that the incest taboo is a result of the Oedipus complex and the rivalry between fathers and sons. According to Freud, in the earliest families, the sons rebelled against their fathers, resulting in what he referred to as Primal Patricide. Having killed their fathers, the sons felt a sense of guilt, so they developed the incest taboo prohibiting sexual relations within the family. Although anthropologists no longer take Freud's myth of the Primal Patricide seriously, there is no question that Freud's notions once had an influence on thinking about the problems of incest avoidance and the incest taboo.

Anthropologists have been studying these issues regarding incest and the family for a long time and have developed a number of different hypotheses to explain the worldwide prevalence of the incest taboo. **Incest** involves sexual relations or marriage between certain relatives. **Incest avoidance** refers to the shunning of sexual relations and marriage between certain relatives. Incest avoidance is a universal phenomenon (Brown 1991). This appears to be valid for humans, and it is also widely found throughout the animal kingdom (Bischof 1972; Murray and Smith 1983; Pusey 2004). The **incest taboo** is based on strong cultural norms that prohibit sexual relations or marriage between certain relatives. Although incest avoidance is found universally, incest taboos are not. Anthropologists find that some societies view incest with disgust and revulsion; these societies have strong prohibitions or taboos against incest. Yet in other societies, people view incest as such an incredible and even laughable behavior that no taboo is called for (Van den Berghe 1979).

Marriage and sex between parent and child and between brother and sister is forbidden in almost all societies, although certain exceptions do exist. Ancient Egyptians, Hawaiians, and Incas institutionalized incestuous brother-sister marriages within their ruling classes. This phenomenon is known as royal incest. The purpose of this practice was to maintain the ruling family's economic wealth and political power. For most people in most societies, however, marriages within the immediate family are forbidden.

Biological Explanations of Incest Avoidance

One ancient and widely held view of the basis for incest avoidance is that inbreeding within the immediate family causes genetic defects. This view is connected with the observation that abnormal or defective negative traits that are carried within the family would be accentuated by inbreeding.

The problem here is that inbreeding itself does not cause harmful genes to exist; it only causes these harmful genes to proliferate in a rapid fashion if they already exist within the immediate family. In fact, recent studies of cousin marriage have indicated that inbreeding actually produces mostly positive genetic influences. Obviously, as mentioned before, harmful genes can result in negative consequences in cousin marriages; however, according to the recent scientific findings in the human genome project, every individual has approximately 1,000 harmful genes out of about 25,000 genes. Anthropologists find that populations apparently can be highly inbred for many generations and survive quite well. Although harmful genetic consequences are found within some inbred populations, anthropologists are seeking alternative explanations of the universality of incest avoidance (Wolf and Durham 2004).

Marital Alliance and the Incest Taboo

Rather than focusing on biological tendencies, some anthropologists have concentrated on the social consequences of inbreeding. In an early explanation, E. B. Tylor (1889) hypothesized that incest taboos originated as a means of creating alliances among different small-scale societies. Marriages outside of one's group create kinship alliances that encourage cooperation and improve chances for survival. Tylor coined the phrase "marry out or be killed out" to summarize his argument that if people did not create these social alliances, dire consequences would follow, including warfare among the different groups. Anthropologists Leslie White and Claude Lévi-Strauss have presented variations of this functionalist hypothesis (White 1959; Lévi-Strauss 1969). The problem with these hypotheses is that they explain the origins of marrying outside of one's group, rather than incest taboos (Van den Berghe 1980; Wolf 2004).

Another type of explanation was proposed by Malinowski, who viewed the incest taboo as a mechanism that functions to sustain the family as an institution (1927). Malinowski argued that brother-sister, father-daughter, or mother-son marriages or sexual relations would generate status-role conflict and rivalry within the family, leading to dysfunctions and possible dissolution. The incest taboo thus serves to reduce family friction and conflict and to maintain harmony within the family. Obviously, this view is closest to the traditional Freudian perspective on the incest taboo.

Childhood Familiarity Hypothesis

Another explanation of the origin and perpetuation of incest avoidance is known as the *childhood familiarity hypothesis*, which proposes that siblings that were raised together in the family do not become erotically involved or sexually attracted to one another because of a biological tendency. Children living in close association with one another would develop mutual sexual aversion and avoid incest.

A number of psychological anthropological studies appear to support this hypothesis. Arthur Wolf studied a marriage pattern in Taiwan called "minor marriage"

(known locally as *sim-pua* marriage), in which a very young girl was adopted into the family of her future husband. The boy and the future bride were then raised in a sibling type of relationship. The purpose of this system was to allow the girl to adjust to her new family through a long association with her husband's kin. Wolf (1970, 2004) interviewed many people who were involved in these arranged relationships and found that most of them were dissatisfied both sexually and romantically with their spouses. Both males and females were inclined to have extramarital relations, and divorce rates were higher than normal. These conclusions appear to support the childhood familiarity hypothesis.

Another study, conducted in Israel, also presented evidence to support this hypothesis. When European Jews first settled in what was then known as Palestine in the early twentieth century, they established collective communities known as kibbutzim. Within these kibbutzim, children were separated from the family into peer groups of six to eight children to be raised and socialized together. Children in these peer-group settings had sibling-like relationships with one another. To examine the childhood

Israeli children in Kibbutz

familiarity hypothesis, Israeli anthropologist Yonina Talmon (1964) studied the second generation of three kibbutzim. She discovered that there were no married couples who had known each other from peer groups in the kibbutzim. Although as small children these individuals may have shown a sexual interest in members of the opposite sex within their peer groups, this interest diminished after maturity. A later comprehensive study of 211 kibbutzim by anthropologist Joseph Shepher (1983) found that of 2,769 married couples, only 14 marriages were from the ranks of the peer groups. Moreover, every one of these 14 marriages had been dissolved through separation or divorce.

Incest Avoidance: Biocultural or Interactionist Perspectives

Today, most anthropologists agree that incest avoidance likely occurs for a variety of reasons. From an evolutionary perspective, the rule of marrying outside one's family would help to create alliances. It would also induce greater genetic diversity, thereby enhancing the adaptation and survival of different populations. In an extensive cross-cultural analysis of mating systems, Melvin Ember (1975) hypothesized that populations expanding as a result of agricultural development began to notice the spread (not the creation) of harmful genes as a result of inbreeding and, therefore, created incest prohibitions. And, additionally, as Malinowski had suggested, incest avoidance would support family roles and functions.

The fact that incest does occur, coupled with the existence of institutionalized incestuous marriage practices in the royal families of some societies, indicates that incest avoidance cannot be reduced to a biological instinct. Humans are not biologically programmed to avoid incest in any mechanistic fashion. The most comprehensive explanation of incest has to take into account generalized biological tendencies along with sociocultural factors.

In a refinement of the childhood familiarity hypothesis, Paul Roscoe (1994) offers an interactionist explanation of incest avoidance. He suggests that relatives who are raised in close association with one another develop a strong emotional bond, or kinship amity—culturally based values that lead to a sense of mutual support and intense feelings of affection. In contrast, sexual arousal and sexual relations are connected to some degree with aggressive impulses, which have a physiological and a neurological basis. Thus, sexual-aggressive impulses are depressed between close kin, who have developed kinship amity. In addition, according to Roscoe's hypothesis, kinship amity can be extended to distant kin through enculturation, resulting in an incest taboo that prohibits sex between more distant relatives. Interactionist explanations such as Roscoe's, combining both biological and cultural factors, are producing insightful hypotheses regarding incest avoidance (Chapais 2008; Turner and Maryanski 2005).

Despite the fact that incest avoidance is found universally and is likely tied to biological processes, many social workers and psychologists note that we appear to be in the midst of an epidemic of incest in the United States. By one estimate, one in twenty women may be a victim of father-daughter sexual abuse (Russell 1986). Anthropologist Mark T. Erickson has been exploring this incidence of incest using a model based on evolutionary psychology and medicine (1999). He suggests that within contemporary societies, as the family unit has become more fragile with weaker kinship attachments, incest is likely to occur more frequently. In the cases of incest that do occur between father and daughter, the father is usually a person who has been sexually abused himself and has not developed close kinship and familial attachments with his children. An extreme lack of nurturance and mutual bonding between family members increases the likelihood of incest arising within families. Erickson's findings suggest that the incest avoidance biological processes can be stunted and distorted, leading to tragic results in contemporary societies.

Critical Perspectives

The Anthropology of the "Self"

One topic that is currently inspiring a great deal of cross-cultural research is the issue of the individual, or the concept of the "person" within society. More specifically, many anthropologists are addressing these questions: Do people in different societies view themselves as *individuals*, *selves*, or *persons* who

(continued)

are separate from their social group? If not, can we assume that people in these societies are *self-motivated* or *self-interested* in pursuing various goals? We usually make this assumption to explain our own behaviors and those of other people in our own society, but can we use this assumption to explain the behavior of people in other societies?

In the West, we tend to regard people as individuals who feel free to pursue their self-interests, to marry or not to marry, and to do what they want with their private property. Individualism is stressed through cultural beliefs and ideologies that serve as a basis for our economic, social, political, legal, and religious institutions. But is this sense of individualism a "natural" condition, or is it a byproduct of our distinctive social and historical development? One way of answering this question is through cross-cultural research. If we find that other people do not think in these terms, then we can assume that our thoughts about the self, mind, and individual are conditioned by our historical and cultural circumstances.

One early theorist who influenced modern anthropological research on these questions was Marcel Mauss, a French sociologist who argued that the concept of the "self" or "person" as separate from the "role" and "status" within society arose in relationship to modern capitalist society ([1938]1985). Relying upon the ethnographic research of anthropologists such as Franz Boas, he theorized that the concept of the individual person had developed uniquely in the West through the evolution of Roman law, Christian ideas of morality, and modern philosophical thought.

For example, according to Mauss, during the medieval period in Europe, it would have been unheard of to think of an individual as completely separate from the larger social group. Medieval Christianity portrayed the individual as merely an element in God's creation, which was referred to as the "great chain of being." All elements in the universe were arranged in a hierarchy from God to angels, humans, animals, trees, rocks, and other inorganic materials. All these elements had distinct values, depending on their distance from God. To modern Westerners, these

views appear strange and outmoded. However, according to some anthropologists, our view of ourselves as independent from groups and environments may be just as strange.

Influenced by Mauss, French anthropologist Louis Dumont (1970) argued that modern Western notions of individualism differ from those of other societies, such as India. In his book *Homo Hierarchicus*, he contrasted Western individualism with Indian Hindu conceptions that value social hierarchy. He pointed out that Hindu philosophy treats individuals as members of caste groups, which are linked to one another in a social hierarchy. Thus, from the Hindu vantage point, individuals cannot be thought of as separate from their social environment.

Francis Hsu, a Chinese-American anthropologist, maintained that the Chinese concept of self is radically different from that of the West (1981). Hsu argued that whereas individualism permeates all U.S. values and institutions, in China the individual is inclined to be socially and psychologically dependent on others. He contrasted the individual-centeredness of American society with the situation-centeredness of Chinese society. He concluded that the individual in China is strongly encouraged to conform to familistic and group norms.

Hsu argued that the situation-centeredness of Chinese society is partly responsible for its lack of economic and political development in the 1940s and 1950s. In contrast, he believed that the individualism of American society has encouraged capitalist enterprise and democratic institutions. However, he also believed that the American concern for self and individualism has led to rampant materialism and consumerism and to a lack of concern for the overall good of society.

Dorinne Kondo makes a similar argument regarding the Western notion of the self in comparison to the Japanese conception of the self (1990). Kondo refers to the Western notion of the autonomous, private self that moves across different social contexts, whereas the Japanese self is always viewed in a relational, socially bounded context. When the Japanese participate in

workplace and neighborhood activities embedded within networks and hierarchies, they cannot conceive of their private "self." Even within their households, individuals are constrained by their neighbors. On the other hand, do Westerners or Americans, as students or workers feel they have complete control of their own self and their destiny (de Munck 2000)? Marilyn Strathern, an anthropologist who does research in New Guinea, posits that the Mt. Hagener populations she studies do not conceive of themselves as individuals or bounded units, but as "dividuals," or partible assemblages of the multiple social relations in which they participate (Strathern 1984, 1988). Diane Mines, who does research in India, uses the term "dividuals" to refer to Indians who are members of hierarchical ranked caste groups (2009).

As we can see, psychological anthropologists differ over the degree to which culture influences the concept of the self. In some cases, these descriptions of different concepts of self may be exaggerations by anthropologists working in very different kinds of societies. Melford Spiro and some other psychological anthropologists think that humans everywhere have similar concepts regarding the self (Spiro 1993). These different understandings reflect various assumptions and conclusions based on philosophical commitments. They need to be evaluated and criticized by anthropologists based on the most significant research findings available in biological, cross-cultural, and specific findings within ethnographic research.

Points to Ponder

1. To what extent are your views of yourself as a distinct individual influenced by prevailing social norms?
2. Do you think that people throughout the world hold similar views? Why or why not?
3. Do you agree with Hsu's analysis of the benefits and shortcomings of widespread individualism?
4. What would be the advantages and disadvantages of a system that emphasizes the overall society, rather than the individual?

Enculturation and the Sex Drive

11.6 What have anthropologists learned about enculturation and sexuality?

Human sexuality is a subject that connects the biological and cultural aspects of the individual and culture. The sex drive, sexual maturation, and sexual activity have different meanings for individuals, depending on the societal and cultural contexts. What are considered "normal," "abnormal," or "deviant" patterns of sexuality differ from one society to another.

Anthropologists have studied enculturation and its consequences for sexual practices in varying societies. Like hunger, sex is a natural biological drive or urge for humans universally. However, this drive is channeled in certain directions through the process of enculturation.

Codes of Sexual Behavior

Societies differ with respect to how permissive or restrictive their codes or norms regarding sexuality are. Some societies approve of premarital and extramarital sexual relations, whereas others strictly segregate males from females to prohibit such relations. In some societies, sexual activity begins very early for both males and females to prepare for marriage. For example, with the Lepcha of Sikkim (a small kingdom north of India in the Himalayan Mountains), girls have their first sexual experience before puberty. In Lepcha society, sexual activity is considered as much a necessity as food or drink, and like food or drink, for the most part it does not matter from whom one receives it, though one is naturally grateful to those who provide it (Lindholm and Lindholm 1980). The Lepcha have a great deal of sexual freedom and appear to have very little sexual jealousy.

The antithesis of this permissive pattern of sexuality is found in some Arab societies of the Middle East. In Saudi Arabia, girls and women are strictly segregated from boys and men. Young girls begin wearing a cloak and veil at the age of puberty. Saudi Arabian society prohibits the mixing of males and females and to this end provides separate institutions for education, work, and other public facilities. In Saudi society, a family's honor is judged by its control over the sexuality of its daughters. Brides are expected to be virgins, and, to guarantee this, families prevent daughters from interacting with boys. Sexual segregation and the dress code are strongly enforced by religious police in Saudi society.

Other highly restrictive attitudes and patterns of sexuality were found in societies such as the Inis Beag Islanders of Ireland, studied by anthropologist John Messenger (1971). Sex was never discussed openly at home or near children.

Parents gave no sexual instruction to children. Messenger reported that the Inis Beag people lacked basic knowledge regarding sexual matters: For example, there seemed to be a general ignorance of the ability of females to have orgasms, any expression of male or female sexuality is considered deviant, and it was believed that sexual activity weakens men. Females and males were separated at an early age. Dancing was permitted, but there was no touching or contact between males and females. Dirty jokes and nudity were strongly frowned on. Messenger reported that there was little evidence of any premarital sex or any sexual foreplay between married people. Generally, people married very late in life, and there was a high percentage of celibate males in the population. Through these ethnographic examples, anthropologists have found that sexual behavior and practice varies widely throughout the world.

Sexuality and Culture

Though there is an enormous range of scientific evidence to suggest that homosexuality is an inherited disposition influenced by genes, neurological developments, and heredity, anthropologists continue to investigate both the biology and the cultural aspects of this form of sexuality. In exploring sexuality in other societies, psychological anthropologists have examined homosexuality by using a comparative, cross-cultural approach. Homosexuality was a well-accepted pattern of behavior in ancient societies such as those of the Greeks and Romans. Many societies have had institutionalized cultural roles for people who are not classified as either male or female. In the country of Oman, anthropologist Unni Wikan (1991) describes individuals known as *xaniths*, who are transsexuals and represent a third gender. In some islands of Southeast Asia such as Bali and Java, third-gender individuals known as *waria*, a combination of the words *wanita* (woman) and *pria* (man) are not only accepted, but also have important roles to play in the society (Brown 1976, Murtagh 2013). In Thailand, a third gender is represented by what are known as *kathoeys* (Nanda 2000; Jackson 1995; Barmé 2002). *Kathoeys* are primarily transsexual males who dress in women's clothes and take on a feminine role in Thai society. Many Buddhists in Thailand believe that one becomes a *kathoey* as a result of a *karmic* destiny influenced by one's reincarnation. This *karmic* destiny is inherited and is unalterable.

In some Native American Indian societies, certain males wore female clothing, and some devoted themselves to offering sexual services to male warriors. These individuals were referred to as *berdaches* by Europeans and were regarded as different from both males and females. These individuals, many of whom were homosexuals, also provided resources and took care of other subsistence activities for their neighbors and relatives in the society (Callender and Kochems 1983; Roscoe 1994). Within these

Native American societies, the distinction between homosexuals and heterosexuals was not made in the same way as in Western European and U.S. culture. The sexuality of the members of this third gender was not central to their identities or roles within society. Instead, the central characteristic of this third gender was the occupational role. Traditionally, these individuals did not face prejudice and discrimination and were accepted as a natural third gender within their society.

Anthropologist Serena Nanda (1990, 2000) has done an extensive ethnographic study of the *hijras* of India, who are viewed as neither men nor women. They are born as males, but some undergo an operation in which their genitals are surgically removed. This operation transforms them, not into females (because they cannot give birth) but into *hijras*, a third gender. The *hijras* are followers of a particular Hindu goddess, Bahuchara Mata or Shiva, and earn their living by performing at various types of religious ceremonies. They dress like females and to some extent exaggerate feminine behavior, but they also indulge in certain male-only behaviors, such as smoking a *hookah* (water pipe) and cigarettes. Within the cultural context of Indian society, the *hijras* are considered neither deviant nor unnatural, but rather simply an additional form of gender (Murtagh 2013).

Anthropologists have described a variety of male homosexual practices among the highland societies of Papua New Guinea. Among peoples such as the Etoro and the Sambia, male homosexuality is incorporated into initiation rituals. In these societies, there appear to be no distinctions among heterosexual, homosexual, and bisexual individuals. Gilbert Herdt (1987) describes how prepubescent Sambian males are initiated into male secret societies and engage in strictly homosexual activities with the older males of these societies. They are obligated to perform regular oral intercourse on the older males and believe that obtaining the gift of semen from their seniors will enable them to become strong, vigorous warriors. These boys are forbidden to engage in any heterosexual relationships for about ten years. Following this lengthy period, they marry and, from that time onward, take up heterosexual relationships with their wives, but then they have homosexual relationships with the young men undergoing their initiation puberty rites of passage.

The United States has gone through different cycles of restrictiveness and permissiveness regarding the cultural norms that influence sexual practices (D'Emilio 1988). In the early history of the United States, Puritan norms equated sexuality with sinful behavior. Later, in the nineteenth century, American society reinforced restrictive Puritan attitudes. But the 1920s were a more liberal, permissive era with regard to sexual attitudes. The 1950s proved to be once again a more restrictive period, but this was followed by the sexual revolution of the 1960s. American society is extremely complex, and many different norms and attitudes are represented with respect to sexuality. The restrictive legacy of Puritanism still exists within some groups, as evidenced by the various legal statutes in some states regarding homosexual practices. Most recently, a number of states within the United States have approved same-sex marriage, which reflects new changes in American attitudes regarding homosexuality.

Enculturation and Cognition

11.7 Discuss the relationship between enculturation and cognition.

Anthropologists have been exploring thinking processes, or cognition, among different peoples in various societies as it relates to enculturation. One assumption held widely by early social scientists was that people in small-scale or so-called primitive societies have different forms of cognition than people in civilized societies. This assumption was challenged by a number of anthropologists who focused on cognitive development from a cross-cultural perspective.

Structuralism

Following World War II, French anthropologist Claude Lévi-Strauss founded a field of study known as *structuralism*. The primary goal of structuralism is to investigate the thought processes of the human mind in a universal context; consequently, it is a field that overlaps with psychological anthropology. Structuralists are interested in the unconscious and conscious patterns of human thinking. In one of his first major books, *The Savage Mind* (1966), Lévi-Strauss discussed how peoples living in small-scale societies use the same unconscious thinking and logical reasoning processes that people in large-scale, complex societies do. He proposed that there is a universal logical form in human thought and cognition around the world.

Drawing on the field of linguistics, Lévi-Strauss argued that thinking is based on *binary oppositions*. In other words, humans classify the natural and social world into polar types (binary oppositions) as a stage of reasoning. For example, foods are classified as raw versus cooked or hot versus cold. From these binary contrasts, coherent patterns of thought are developed. In addition, he suggests that the fundamental binary structural distinctions between "nature" and "culture" are found in all societies. He demonstrated how religious mythologies universally invoke symbols that have a dual aspect, representing nature and culture. Lévi-Strauss focused on such diverse phenomena as kinship, mythology, cuisine, and table manners to discover the hidden structural logic underlying these diverse cultural ideas and practices. Within all of these practices and beliefs, Lévi-Strauss maintains that there are important logical and deep structural distinctions between nature and culture. Even though the rules and norms that structure these ideas and practices may appear arbitrary, Lévi-Strauss believed that a "deep universal structure" underlies these cultural phenomena. Thus, this universal structure of the mind produces similar thinking and cognition throughout the world.

Jean Piaget and Lev Vygotsky

Jean Piaget (1896–1980), a Swiss psychologist, spent more than a half-century studying the ways in which children think, perceive, and learn. His research has influenced the anthropological perspective on cognition and enculturation. Piaget believed that the process of thinking and reasoning was related to the biological process of neural changes that influence the brain. He used experiments that focused not only on what children learn, but also on how they understand the world. Piaget identified four major stages of cognitive development: the sensorimotor, preoperational, concrete-operational, and formal-operational stages. Piaget hypothesized that these stages reflect biological maturation, as well as enculturation. As each child progresses through these stages, he or she acquires more information and begins to organize and perceive reality in new and different ways.

Piaget suggested that certain innate categories regulate and order our experience of the world. Although he was certainly aware that the learning of values, norms, and beliefs is not the same from society to society, he believed that humans everywhere progress in the same sequence through the various stages described above. Later in his research career, Piaget recognized that the stages he posited had fuzzy borders and that the precise age at which each stage of cognitive development is reached varies from individual to individual, depending on innate mental capacities and the nature of the enculturation experience.

Piaget's model of learning has had a widespread influence on anthropologists' understanding of enculturation. He posited that learning comprises the complementary processes of *assimilation* and *accommodation*, which differentiate between how new information or knowledge is understood vis-à-vis existing mental models or schemas. He discusses assimilation as how new knowledge is adjusted to fit into existing schemas without changing very much. But eventually, accommodation takes place in the learning process and the schemas do change in order to adjust to the new knowledge and information. This Piagetian perspective influenced the late French anthropologist (and sociologist) Pierre Bourdieu, who studied tribes and peasants in Algeria as well as the French society, education, and culture (1977, 1984). Bourdieu referred to how existing mental schemas

were modified by the social and cultural environment and were produced and reproduced to form a *habitus* or internalized dispositions that influenced and shaped cognition and behavior (Lizardo 2004).

Russian psychologist Lev Vygotsky followed the work of Piaget and emphasized the biological aspects of thinking and cognition, but because he was living in the Soviet Union, he was influenced by thinkers such as Karl Marx on how social relationships had an impact on thinking and behaving (Gopnik, Meltzoff, and Kuhl 1999; Konner 2002, 2010). Vygotsky accepted some of the stages of cognitive development proposed by Piaget. However, he argued that the stages in the development of thought and reasoning did not represent sharp distinctions, but rather were more continuous and also were shaped by linguistic, social, and cultural contexts. For example, he thought that literacy could have an important influence on cognition and perception. Unfortunately, Vygotsky died as a young man of 38, and his students were forbidden to conduct further research on the relationship between biology and culture because the Soviet Union under Joseph Stalin banned the teaching of evolutionary biology due to its conflict with Marxist doctrines.

Inuit boy

Piaget and Vygotsky and their research have influenced numerous psychological anthropologists and their approach to understanding cognition, the human mind, and enculturation. British anthropologist Maurice Bloch (1977, 1985, 2012) has suggested that many cultural universals are the result of biopsychological factors shared by all humans that interact with the practical conditions of the world. For example, Bloch postulates that all humans have the intuitive capabilities to perceive time and space in the same way. Time and space are fundamental concepts that enable humans to adapt to the practical conditions of the world. These practical conditions include changes in seasons, climatic and environmental characteristics, and the overall effects of natural aging processes. In Bloch's view, despite our intuitive understandings, people can learn to conceptualize time and space in radically different ways, depending on religious beliefs and worldviews. For example, in the Hindu tradition, people perceive time cyclically in relationship to the creation and destruction of the universe, which take place over millions of years. In the Judeo-Christian tradition, people perceive time in a more linear fashion from the time of creation to the present. However, in both the Hindu and the Judeo-Christian cultures, in everyday, practical circumstances, people perceive time both cyclically and linearly in relation to the cycle of seasonal changes or to the life cycle of an individual through biological aging.

Many other anthropologists have been testing Piaget's and Vygotsky's theories throughout the world to determine whether their stages are indeed universal. As we will see shortly, their theories have had an enormous impact upon contemporary explanations of cognition and thought within the field of cognitive anthropology. One conclusion emphasized in this research by cognitive anthropologists is that we humans share very similar cognitive and reasoning processes whether we live in the forests of New Guinea or the city of New York. Yet, all our cognitive processes are influenced by the culture and language that we are exposed to as children and throughout our lives. All people use similar patterns of logic and develop an understanding of cause-and-effect relationships. People everywhere develop classification systems through similar processes of abstraction and generalization. The differences among cultural groups lie in the content of the values, beliefs, and norms of society.

Cognitive Anthropology

11.8 **Discuss what cognitive anthropologists have learned about universals and human thought processes.**

A number of anthropologists have been pursuing the understanding of human psychology through the fields of cognitive anthropology and evolutionary psychology. As mentioned in the introduction of this chapter, *cognitive anthropology* is the study of cognition and cultural meanings through specific methodologies such as experiments, computer modeling, and other techniques to elicit underlying unconscious factors that structure human thinking processes. Cognitive anthropology developed in the 1950s and 1960s through the systematic investigation of kinship terminologies within different cultures. However, more recently, cognitive anthropology has drawn on the findings within the field of cognitive science, the study of the human mind based upon computer modeling (D'Andrade 1995; de Munck 2000, Kronenfeld et al. 2011). Cognitive anthropologists have developed experimental methods and various cognitive tasks to use among people they study in their fieldwork so as to better comprehend human psychological processes and their relationship to culture. Through cognitive anthropology, we have learned that the human mind organizes and structures the natural and social world in distinctive ways.

For example, cognitive anthropologists have been doing research on how humans classify and perceive colors in the natural world. Color is a very complex phenomenon for scientists and anthropologists. To physicists, color is determined by wavelengths of light. To biologists, color involves the neural responses in the human eye and the brain and is related to the ability of humans to adapt and survive in nature. Color can also be symbolic and represent our feelings and emotions, and as we saw in Chapter 10, this symbolism varies from culture to culture. Early philosophers and scientists such as Aristotle, René Descartes, and Isaac Newton believed that there were seven basic colors. Later, anthropologists and linguists began to ask questions such as these: Do people classify and categorize colors in an arbitrary manner based on their language and culture? Or do people classify, categorize, and perceive colors in similar ways throughout the world? Cognitive anthropologists Brent Berlin and Paul Kay have been studying the basic color terms of different societies since the 1960s. They analyzed the color-naming practices of informants from 98 globally distributed language groups and found that societies differ dramatically in the number of basic color terms they possess, from two in some New Guinea tribes to eleven in English in the United States. They showed, however, that despite this difference, all color terms used by diverse societies follow a systematic pattern (1969).

A language with only two color terms will divide the color spectrum between white and black. If a language contains three terms, the spectrum will be black, red, and white. A language with four terms will have black, red, white, and then green, yellow, or blue. A language with six terms will have black, white, red, yellow, green, and blue. These are the focal colors that become universal (Kay, Regier, and Cook 2005).

Berlin and Kay suggested that this pattern indicates an evolutionary sequence common to all languages. Red is adopted after white and black. In general, a language does not adopt a term for brown unless it already has six color terms. English, most Western European languages, Russian, Japanese, and several others add four color terms—gray, pink, orange, and purple—after brown is classified. Berlin and Kay correlate the evolution of color terms with the evolution of society. Societies with only two color terms have a simple level of technology, whereas societies with eleven basic color terms have a complex technology.

The evidence from Berlin and Kay's study suggests that color naming is not at all arbitrary. If color terms were selected randomly, there would be thousands of possible color systems. In fact, there are only 33 possible color-naming systems. Recently, Paul Kay and other colleagues reported that statistical tests from more than 100 languages in both industrial and nonindustrial societies demonstrated that there are strong universal tendencies in color classification and naming (Kay et al. 2005). In other words, to some extent, color perception transcends culture and language.

However, other anthropologists and psychologists have done some research that indicates that color is influenced by language and culture. British anthropologists and psychologists Debi Roberson, Ian Davies, and Jules Davidoff did research among members of the Berinomo tribe of Papua New Guinea and found that they do not distinguish blue from green, but they do distinguish between shades of green (*nul* and *wor*) that are not shared by Western peoples. Also, these researchers found some tribal members who, with training, could learn to distinguish blue from green, unlike other members of the tribe (Roberson, Davies, and Davidoff 2000, Roberson, Davidoff, and Shapiro 2005). This research tends to illustrate that color names do influence the perception of color in some cases. It appears that learning does play a role in how children perceive and categorize colors (Roberson 2010). Yet, these findings do not completely refute the empirical findings of Berlin, Kay, and other anthropologists.

Although much more research needs to be done on the perception and classification of colors, these findings do not support the conclusion that color classification is completely arbitrary. Instead, the vast majority of psychologists and anthropologists concur that the physiological basis of color vision is the same for all humans (and some primates) with normal color vision. Additionally, recent studies indicate that prelinguistic infants and toddlers within different language groups distinguish the same color categories (Franklin et al. 2005). On the other hand, anthropologists recognize that cognitive higher-order

processing and linguistic learning may have an influence on color perception, and as is well known, the symbolic representation and meaning of colors do vary from society to society (Sahlins 1976; Lucy and Shweder 1979).

In a cognitive anthropological study, James Boster concluded that as with colors, people from different societies classify birds in similar ways. Boster (1987) found that the South American Jivaro Indian population classified species of native birds in a manner corresponding to the way scientists classify those birds. To discover whether this pattern of classification was random, Boster had university students with no scientific training and no knowledge of South American birds classify those birds. The students did so with the exact criteria used by both the Jivaro Indians and the Western scientists. Most recently, two cognitive anthropologists working in Honduras found that insects were classified by Honduran farmers in the same way that scientists do worldwide (Bentley and Rodrigúez 2001). Despite variations in classifications found within groups and individuals within societies, cognitive anthropologists such as Scott Atran (1990, 1998, Atran and Medin 2008, Kronenfeld, et al. 2011) have shown that plants and animals are categorized and classified in universally similar taxonomies. These taxonomies are ordered according to the distinctive morphological features of the various plants and animals in nature. Despite variant cultures in different regions of the world, the human mind appears to organize the natural world in nonarbitrary ways.

These findings in cognitive anthropology suggest that the human mind organizes reality in terms of **prototypes**, distinctive classifications that help us map and comprehend the world. If reality was inherently unorganized and could be perceived in any way, then color naming and animal and plant classification would be completely arbitrary. The results of this research support the notion that people the world over share certain cognitive abilities and that language and culture are as likely to reflect human cognition as they are to shape it. It suggests that evolution selected certain fundamental visual-processing and category-building abilities for humans everywhere (Lakoff 1987; Lakoff and Johnson 2000; D'Andrade 1995, Atran et al. 2002, Atran and Medin 2008).

Cognitive anthropologists have discovered that not only do humans think in prototypes, but also we use *schemas* to help us understand, organize, and interpret reality. As mentioned above, the concept of schemas was introduced by Jean Piaget to discuss a particular "cognitive structure which has reference to a class of similar action sequences" (de Munck 2000:77). Schemas are constructed out of language, images, and logical operations of the human mind in order to mediate and provide meaning to social and cultural reality. Thus, schemas are more complex than prototypes or taxonomic categories. And schemas may vary from one culture to the next. For example, the schemas *writing* in English and *kaku* in Japanese have some similarities, and these terms are usually translatable between the languages. They both refer to making some marks with an implement across a surface. The schema *writing* in English, however, always entails the act of writing in a language, whereas *kaku* can refer to writing or doodling or drawing a picture (D'Andrade 1995). Cognitive anthropologists find that like taxonomies, schemas are organized into hierarchies and aid in our adapting to, and coping with, cognitive and cultural complexities.

In addition to prototypes, taxonomies, and schemas, cognitive anthropologists investigate how *narratives* are used to coordinate thought processes. **Narratives** are stories or events that are represented within specific cultures. There are certain types of narratives, such as the story of Little Red Riding Hood, which are easily retained by an individual's memory and told over and over again within a society. Thus, certain forms of narrative have easily recognizable plots and can be distributed widely within a society (Sperber 1996). Other forms of narratives, such as a formal proof in mathematics or logic or an evolutionary biological explanation in science, are much more difficult to distribute widely. Cognitive anthropologists are studying religious mythologies, folktales, and other types of narratives to determine why some are effortlessly transmitted, spread quickly, and used to produce cultural representations that endure for generations. Cognitive anthropological research has been fruitful in providing biocultural or interactionist models of the ways that humans everywhere classify, organize, understand, interpret, and narrate their natural social and cultural environment.

Evolutionary Psychology

11.9 How does evolutionary psychology contribute to an understanding of human universals?

A recent development that draws on cognitive anthropology and attempts to emphasize the interaction of nature (biology) and nurture (learning and culture) in understanding and explaining enculturation, human cognition, and human behavior is the field known as **evolutionary psychology**. Some anthropologists draw on ethnographic research, psychological experiments, and evolutionary psychology to demonstrate how the human brain developed and how it influences thinking processes and behavior. These anthropologists question the traditional premise that the human mind is a passive instrument that soaks up the cultural environment like a sponge. Instead, they view the human mind as designed by evolution to actively adjust to the culture and environment.

Anthropologists who have been influenced by evolutionary psychologists reason that if the human body is a product of evolutionary forces, then the human brain was produced by the same forces. It is, therefore, useful to consider the effects of natural selection acting during the long period of the Paleolithic in order to better understand how humans think, learn, interact, and behave across the globe and throughout time. These anthropologists suggest that the mind and culture co-evolved. They believe that natural selective forces must have shaped the mind and behavior. Consequently, because natural selective forces are highly specific, some evolutionary psychologists hypothesize that the human brain is divided into specialized cognitive domains or *modules*, or independent units, which contain various functions that enabled our ancestral humans to adapt to Paleolithic conditions. These specific modules within the brain predispose humans to perceive, think, and behave in certain ways to allow for adaptation. In other words, there are genetically induced "evolved predispositions" that have consequences for human perception, thinking, emotions, and behavior today. For example, in Chapter 12, we review the research indicating that the human brain has a language-learning module that enables children to learn their language without learning the explicit complex rules of grammar for communication.

Aside from the language-learning module, anthropologists, in a book entitled *The Adapted Mind* (1992), edited by Jerome Barkow, Leda Cosmides, and John Tooby, have hypothesized that modules in the brain enable humans to understand intuitively the workings of nature, including motion, force, and how plants and animals function. The authors refer to psychological research that demonstrates how infants distinguish objects that move around (such as balls) from living organisms (such as people and animals) that are self-propelled. These anthropologists theorize that innate, specialized modules in the human brain help develop an intuitive understanding of biology and physics. Just as children learn their language without learning the formal grammatical rules, humans can perceive, organize, and understand basic biological and physical principles without learning formal scientific views. Children at very early ages have intuitive notions, or "theories," about persons, animals, plants, and artifacts. They have an intuitive understanding of the underlying properties and behavioral expectations of these phenomena from early stages of infancy. In addition, young children at two years old or so have the ability to comprehend how other people have intentions. In other words, these young children have an intuitive "theory of mind" and can determine how other people have thoughts and intend to use them in communication or behavior (Boyer 1998, 2001).

Evolutionary psychologists further contend that the mind uses different rules to process different types of information. For example, they suggest there are innate modules that help humans interpret and predict other people's behavior and modules that enable them to understand basic emotions such as happiness, sadness, anger, jealousy, and love. In addition, these specialized modules influence male-female relationships, mate choice, and cooperation or competition among individuals.

In *The Adapted Mind* (1992), anthropologist Jerome Barkow asks why many people like to watch soap operas. He answers that the human mind is designed by evolution to be interested in the social lives of others—rivals, mates, relatives, offspring, and acquaintances. To be successful in life requires knowledge of many different phenomena and social situations, evolutionary psychologists argue, and innate predispositions influence how we sense, interpret, think, perceive, communicate, and enable adaptation and survival in the world.

Evolutionary psychologists tend to emphasize the commonalities and similarities in culture and behavior found among people in different parts of the world. Thus, they are interested in the types of human universals described by anthropologist Donald E. Brown (see Chapter 10). Although evolutionary psychologists do not ignore learning or culture, they hypothesize that innate modules or mechanisms in the brain make learning and enculturation happen (Nettles 2009).

Many evolutionary psychologists believe that some of the evolved predispositions that are inherited may not be as adaptive today as they were during the time of the Paleolithic. For example, humans during that period had to worry more about avoiding the danger of wild animals and other groups and about getting enough salt and sugar to eat for survival, but such evolved predispositions may not help humans adapt to modern society.

Some anthropologists have criticized evolutionary psychology for not emphasizing the richness and complexity of cultural environments. At present, however, many anthropologists are using the methods of cognitive anthropology and evolutionary psychology to understand human nature and culture. The field of evolutionary psychology is in its infancy and will most likely grow to offer another biocultural or interactionist perspective on human thought and behavior.

Enculturation and Emotions

11.10 Discuss what anthropologists have discovered about human emotions.

One significant question asked by psychological anthropologists is: To what degree does enculturation influence emotions? Obviously, different language groups have different terms for emotions, but do the feelings of anger, happiness, grief, and jealousy vary from society to society?

Do some societies have unique emotions? For example, Catherine Lutz, in her book *Unnatural Emotions: Everyday Sentiments on a Micronesian Atoll and Their Challenge to Western Theory* (1988), suggested that many of the emotions exhibited by the Ifaluk people in the Pacific islands are not comparable to American or Western emotions. She noted that the Ifaluk emotion words *song* (justifiable anger) and *fago* (compassion/love/sadness) have no equivalent in English emotion terms, and that anthropologists need to examine the linguistic and cultural context to interpret what emotions mean from culture to culture. Lutz does admit that there are some basic emotions that are universal based on biological and physiological factors (1988:210). However, she cautions anthropologists to comprehend these basic emotions in relationship to the cultural context of the society under study.

Psychological anthropologists have been conducting research on the topic of emotions since the early research of Benedict and Mead. As discussed earlier in the chapter, Benedict and Mead argued that each culture is unique and that people in various societies have different personalities and, consequently, different types of emotions. These different emotions are a result of the unique kind of enculturation that has shaped the individual's personality. In their view, the enculturation process is predominant in creating varying emotions among different societies. In other words, culture determines not only how people think and behave, but also how they feel emotionally.

In contrast, other early psychological anthropologists focused on universal biological processes that produce similar emotional developments and feelings in people throughout the world. According to this perspective, emotions are seen as instinctive behaviors that stimulate physiological processes involving hormones and other chemicals in the brain. In other words, if an individual feels "anger," this automatically raises his or her blood pressure and stimulates specific muscle movements. In this view, emotional developments are part of the biology of humans universally, and thus emotions are experienced in the same way everywhere.

Many psychological anthropologists have emphasized a biocultural or interactionist approach, taking both biology and culture into account in their studies of emotions (Hinton 1999). A study conducted by Karl Heider (1991) focused on three different ethnic groups in Indonesia: the Minangkabau in West Sumatra, the Minangkabau Indonesians, and the Javanese. Heider systematically described the vocabulary of emotions that each of these groups used to classify their feelings of sadness, anger, happiness, fear, surprise, love, contempt, shame, and disgust, along with other feelings. Through intensive interviews and observations, Heider determined whether the vocabulary of emotions is directly related to specific emotional behaviors.

Following his ethnographic study, Heider concluded that four of the emotions—sadness, anger, happiness, and surprise—tend to be what he classifies as basic cross-cultural emotions. In other words, these emotions appear to be universally understood and stable across cultures. Other emotions, however, such as love, fear, and disgust, appear to vary among these societies. For example, love among the Minangkabau and Minangkabau Indonesians is mixed with the feeling of pity and is close to sadness. Fear is also mixed with guilt, and feelings of disgust are difficult to translate across cultural boundaries. Heider emphasizes that his study is preliminary and needs much more analysis and reanalysis; nevertheless, it is an interesting use of the interactionist approach to the study of emotions.

Daniel Fessler also explored how both biology and culture contribute to the development of human emotions (1999). Fessler did ethnographic work among the Bengkulu, an ethnic group in Sumatra, a major island in Indonesia. He discusses the importance of two emotions, *malu* and *bangga*, exhibited in many situations by the Bengkulu. *Malu* appears to be quite similar to *shame* in English. Bengkulu who feel *malu* withdraw from social interaction, stoop, and avert their gaze. People who feel *malu* are described as those who have missed religious services, did not attend to the sick, did not send their children to school, drank alcohol, ate during times of fasting, or violated other norms. *Bangga* is the linguistic expression of the emotion that people feel when they do something well and have had success, such as doing well in baking cakes, winning an election, hosting a large feast, being skilled in oratory, or feeling good about their physical appearance or house and furnishings. *Bangga* seems to be most similar to the emotion term *pride* in English. Fessler notes that *malu* and *bangga* appear to be exact opposites of one another, and both emotions provide individuals with an assessment of their relationship to the rest of the group. He suggests that these two emotions are universal and that they have evolved in connection with attempts to coordinate one's mind and behavior for cooperation and competition within groups of people. Fessler emphasizes that though these emotions may be displayed and elaborated in different ways in various cultures, they reflect a universal, pan-human experience.

In *Thinking Through Cultures: Expeditions in Cultural Psychology* (1991), psychological anthropologist Richard Shweder emphasizes that ethnographic research on emotions has demonstrated the existence of both universal and culturally specific aspects of emotional functioning among people in different societies. He uses a piano keyboard as an analogy to discuss emotional development in children. Children have something like a universal emotional keyboard, with each key being a separate emotion: disgust, interest, distress, anger, fear, contempt, shame, shyness, guilt, and so forth. A key is struck whenever a situation such as loss, frustration, or novelty develops. All children recognize and can discriminate among basic emotions by a young age. However, as adults, the tunes that are played on the keyboard vary with experience. Some keys are not struck at all, whereas others are played frequently. Shweder concludes, "It is ludicrous to imagine that the emotional functioning of people in different cultures is basically the same. It is just as ludicrous to imagine that each culture's emotional life is unique" (1991:252). Psychological anthropologists recognize that a biocultural or interactionist approach that takes into account human biological factors and cultural variation is necessary to comprehend the enculturation process and emotional development.

Neuroanthropology

11.11 Discuss the new field of neuroanthropology.

A new field of neuroanthropology has emerged with its first major book published by MIT Press, edited by Daniel Lende and Greg Downey, entitled *The Encultured Brain: An Introduction to Neuroanthropology* (2012). These anthropologists are working with neuroscientists to explore the connections among neurology, culture, cognition, emotions, and behavior. The various authors demonstrate that the contemporary research in cognitive neuroscience has to take cultural variability into account in order to provide more comprehensive explanations of humanity. Some of the chapters deal with comparisons between the brains of nonhuman primates and humans. Compared to nonhuman primates, the human brain is extremely plastic and structured for intensive social interaction and culture. Other chapters focus on case studies dealing with human memory, skill acquisition, habits, and variations in cultural practices. A fascinating chapter by Greg Downey focuses on brain activation and its involvement in practitioners of *capoiera*, a Brazilian art form that combines martial arts and dance. He draws on evidence that demonstrates that even unconsciousness brain activity is connected with cultural factors related to the practice of *capoiera*.

In an essay by a pioneer of neuroanthropology, Stephen Reyna describes what he calls "neuronal culture," neural memory networks that store the contents of cultural categories within the brains of individuals. These neural memory networks enable individuals to link and interpret experiences from the past in order to adapt to immediate realities (2012). Reyna stresses that this neuroanthropological approach emphasizes the process of enculturation and how neurological linkages demonstrate both the similarity and differences among humans throughout the world, the major goal of anthropological research.

In another original research project in neuroanthropology, Scott Atran has teamed with Gregory C. Berns to employ functional magnetic resonance imaging (fMRI) to explore a number of issues related to religion and violence (Berns and Atran 2012). With the use of fMRI, this research team has been investigating brain activation and how sacred values trigger emotional responses consistent with sentiments that coincide with absolute morality and outrage (Berns and Atran 2012; Berns, Bell, Capra, Prietula, Moore, Ginges, Atran 2012). Specifically, when individuals are confronted with statements that are contrary to their sacred values, the amygdala, the region of the brain associated with physiological arousal, produces heightened affective emotional responses, resulting in experiences of moral outrage and potential violence (Berns et al. 2012). This research team is also investigating how altruism within one's own group, concepts of honor, and norms may be associated with various brain activation that are connected with violence and warfare.

In another area of neuroanthropology, some researchers have been investigating individual and collective memory. This research is focused on how nations, ethnic communities, and individuals remember, manipulate, invent, and construct their pasts. These anthropologists have been coordinating research with cognitive psychologists, historians, and neuroscientists on collective memory and its relationship to individual memory and brain activity (Boyer and Wertsch 2009; Anastasio, Ehrenberger, Watson, Zhang 2012). Both individual and collective memories are by nature elusive, selective, and difficult to quantify, but these researchers attempt to demonstrate how individual and collective memories become consolidated and retained. While most of the memory research in the past by anthropologists and historians was anti-psychological, these new research efforts are collaborative and include the findings in cognitive psychology and neurology (Boyer and Wertsch 2009; Anastasio et al. 2012). For example this research details what is known at both the neurological and psychological level regarding "flashbulb memories," such as memories of traumatic events such as 9/11, and how they are connected with collective shared memories. The research in this area includes the use of neuroimaging as a means of enhancing what is known from brain states for identifying individual and collective memories. Although neuroanthropology is in its infancy, with future improvements in fMRI technology and more refined techniques, it may be possible to explore precise linkages between neurology, culture, emotions, and human behavior.

The Limits of Enculturation

11.12 Discuss the limitations of enculturation in examining human behavior.

When we consider enculturation or socialization, we are confronted with this question: Are humans only robots who respond rigidly to the demands of their innate drives,

their genes, and the norms of their culture? If our behavior depends so much upon the enculturation process, what becomes of human concepts such as freedom and free will? Do people in our society or others have any personal choice over their behavior, or is all behavior and thought shaped by innate drives and the norms of these societies?

Unique Biological Tendencies

In actuality, although enculturation plays a major role in producing personality and behavioral strategies within society, there are a number of reasons why enculturation is not completely determinative. First, people are born with different innate tendencies (not hard-wired genetically controlled instincts) for responding to the environment in a variety of ways. Our individual behavior is partially a result of our own genetics and biological constitution, which influences our hormones, our metabolism, and other aspects of our physiology. All societies have people who differ with respect to temperament because of these innate tendencies. Enculturation cannot produce people who respond to environmental or cultural pressures in a uniform manner.

Individual Variation and Agency

Second, enculturation is never a completely uniform process. Enculturation experiences are blended and synthesized in unique ways by individuals. Even in the most isolated, small-scale societies, young people behave differently from their parents. Furthermore, not all people in a particular society are socialized or enculturated in exactly the same manner. As we have emphasized in the contemporary understanding of culture, anthropologists recognize that the vast amounts of information transmitted through enculturation often lead to variations in what children are taught in different families and institutions.

In addition, norms do not dictate behavior in any rigid manner. People in any society are always confronted with contradictory norms, and society is always changing, affecting the process of enculturation. Enculturation rarely provides people with a precise blueprint for the behavioral responses needed in the many situations they face.

Thus, enculturation is an imprecise process. People may internalize the general program for behavior—a series of ideal norms, rules, and cultural guidelines for action—but how these general principles apply in any specific set of concrete circumstances is difficult or impossible to specify. Anthropologists have been emphasizing the fact that human behavior involves "agency." **Agency** is the process of intentional conscious (self-aware) choices that humans make that may alter their social or cultural world (Bourdieu 1977, Smith 2013). Individuals have multiple motives and intentions related to their sociocultural environment that both constrain and enable opportunities for agency and action. In some cases, people obey social and cultural rules completely, whereas in others they violate or ignore them. Enculturation provides the historically developed cultural forms through which the members of society share meanings and symbols and relate to one another. But in reality, people maneuver within these cultural forms, choosing their actions to fulfill both their own needs and the demands of their society.

Summary and Review of Learning Objectives

11.1 Discuss the relationship between biology and culture and how anthropologists regard the nature/nurture questions of humanity.

Psychological anthropologists attempt to understand similarities and differences in behavior, thought, and feelings among societies by focusing on the relationship between the individual and culture, or the process of enculturation. One question that psychological anthropologists focus on is the degree to which human behavior is influenced by biological tendencies versus learning. Today, most anthropologists have adopted a biocultural or interactionist approach that emphasizes both biology and culture as influences on enculturation and human behavior.

11.2 Explain the difference between nonhuman animal behavior and human behavior.

Many nonhuman animals have closed instincts that rigidly structure their behavior patterns, allowing for survival and adaptation in specific environmental conditions. These closed instincts have been selected by environmental factors over millions of years of evolution. It does not appear that humans have closed instincts. Instead, humans have the unique capacity for culture, which enables them to modify and shape their behavior to adapt to different environmental conditions. Without enculturation, humans are unable to think, behave, and develop emotionally in order to function in society.

11.3 Discuss how anthropologists study enculturation and its relationship to personality formation.

The early studies of enculturation, called culture-and-personality studies, focused on culture as if it were an integrated type of personality. These early studies by pioneers such as Ruth Benedict and Margaret Mead provided some important data regarding enculturation processes, but they often exaggerated the significance of cultural determinants of human behavior. However, these efforts led to a more systematic examination of enculturation and childhood training. These studies have refined our understanding of childhood training in many different types of societies.

11.4 How have anthropologists used the psychoanalytic approach to study personality and culture?

The theories of Sigmund Freud have had an influence on psychological anthropology. His model of enculturation and personality development has been used by a number of psychological anthropologists to investigate human behavior. In some cases, anthropologists collaborate with psychoanalysts to study dreams, sexual fantasies, family relations, and topics such as incest. Incest, incest avoidance, and the incest taboo have been studied thoroughly within anthropology, leading to insightful explanations for these phenomena.

11.5 Explain how anthropologists understand incest avoidance and the incest taboo.

Today, most anthropologists agree that incest avoidance likely occurs for a variety of reasons. From an evolutionary perspective, the rule of marrying outside one's family would help to create alliances. It would also induce greater genetic diversity, thereby enhancing the adaptation and survival of different populations. In an extensive cross-cultural analysis of mating systems, Melvin Ember (1975) hypothesized that populations expanding as a result of agricultural development began to notice the spread (not the creation) of harmful genes as a result of inbreeding and, therefore, created incest prohibitions. And, additionally, as Malinowski had suggested, incest avoidance would support family roles and functions. The fact that incest does occur, coupled with the existence of institutionalized incestuous marriage practices in the royal families of some societies, indicates that incest avoidance cannot be reduced to a biological instinct. Humans are not biologically programmed to avoid incest in any mechanistic fashion. The most comprehensive explanation of incest has to take into account generalized biological tendencies along with sociocultural factors.

11.6 What have anthropologists learned about enculturation and sexuality?

Enculturation's relationship to sexual practices and norms has been a topic of research in psychological anthropology. A wide variation of sexual practices and norms in different parts of the world has been described. These practices and norms, including widely distributed patterns of homosexual behavior and acceptance of a third gender beyond male and female, indicate how enculturation influences the sex drive in human communities.

11.7 Discuss the relationship between enculturation and cognition.

The relationship between enculturation and cognition has also been a field of study within psychological anthropology. Structuralist anthropology, developed by Claude Lévi-Strauss, focuses on the relationship between culture and thought processes. Lévi-Strauss hypothesized that the human mind is structured to produce underlying patterns of thinking that are universally based.

The early studies of Jean Piaget and Lev Vygotsky on the development of cognitive processes have also influenced psychological anthropology. Many researchers are actively engaged in testing Piaget's and Vygotsky's model of cognitive development in different societies.

11.8 Discuss what cognitive anthropologists have learned about universals and human thought processes.

Cognitive anthropologists have been drawing from the fields of computer modeling and psychological experimentation in laboratories to examine cognition. They have examined how humans classify colors, animals, and plants. They find that humans classify and categorize colors, animals, and plants in very similar ways throughout the world. Cognitive anthropologists have discovered that human thought processes are based on prototypes, schemas, and narratives in all societies.

11.9 How does evolutionary psychology contribute to an understanding of human universals?

Evolutionary psychologists have hypothesized that humans have some genetically prepared innate predispositions that evolved during the Paleolithic that have a wide-ranging universal influence on cognition, emotions, and human behavior. Their research has been a leading example of interactionist research in psychological anthropology that has provided some rich hypotheses regarding human behavior, cognition, and emotions. Many evolutionary psychologists believe that some of the evolved predispositions that are inherited may not be as adaptive today as they were during the time of the Paleolithic. For example, humans during that period had to worry more about avoiding the danger of wild animals and other groups and about getting enough salt and sugar to eat for survival, but such evolved predispositions may not help humans adapt to modern society.

11.10 Discuss what anthropologists have discovered about human emotions.

Emotional development is another area of study in psychological anthropology. Researchers are trying to understand how emotions such as sadness, happiness, fear, anger, and contempt are similar and different from one society to another. Their findings indicate that there are both universal and specific cultural variations with respect to emotional development in different societies.

11.11 Discuss the new field of neuroanthropology.

A new field of neuroanthropology has emerged as anthropologists work with neuroscientists to explore the connections among neurology, culture, cognition, emotions, and behavior. Anthropologists emphasize that the contemporary research in cognitive neuroscience has to take cultural variability into account in order to provide more comprehensive explanations of humanity. Anthropologists are exploring the relationships among neurology, memory, and both individual memory and collective memory, to discover how nations, ethnic communities, and individuals remember, manipulate, invent, and construct their pasts.

11.12 Discuss the limitations of enculturation in examining human behavior.

In actuality, although enculturation plays a major role in producing personality and behavioral strategies within society, there are a number of reasons why enculturation is not completely determinative. First, people are born with different innate tendencies (not hard-wired genetically controlled instincts) for responding to the environment in a variety of ways. Our individual behavior is partially a result of our own genetics and biological constitution, which influences our hormones, our metabolism, and other aspects of our physiology. All societies have people who differ with respect to temperament because of these innate tendencies. Enculturation is never a completely uniform process. Enculturation experiences are blended and synthesized in unique ways by individuals. Even in the most isolated, small-scale societies, young people behave differently from their parents. Furthermore, not all people in a particular society are socialized or enculturated in exactly the same manner. In addition, norms do not dictate behavior in any rigid manner. People in any society are always confronted with contradictory norms, and society is always changing, affecting the process of enculturation. Enculturation rarely provides people with a precise blueprint for the behavioral responses needed in the many situations they face.

People may internalize the general program for behavior—a series of ideal norms, rules, and cultural guidelines for action—but how these general principles apply in any specific set of concrete circumstances is difficult or impossible to specify. Anthropologists have been emphasizing the fact that human behavior involves "agency." Agency is the process of intentional conscious (self-aware) choices that humans make that may alter their social or cultural world. Individuals have multiple motives and intentions related to their sociocultural environment that both constrain and enable opportunities for agency and action. In some cases, people obey social and cultural rules completely, whereas in others they violate or ignore them. Enculturation provides the historically developed cultural forms through which the members of society share meanings and symbols and relate to one another. But in reality, people maneuver within these cultural forms, choosing their actions to fulfill both their own needs and the demands of their society.

Key Terms

agency, p. 265
cognitive anthropology, p. 244
drives, p. 247
ego, p. 252
evolutionary psychology, p. 262

id, p. 252
incest, p. 253
incest avoidance, p. 253
incest taboo, p. 253
instincts, p. 245

narratives, p. 262
personality, p. 247
prototypes, p. 261
psychological anthropology, p. 244
superego, p. 252

Chapter 12
Language

Learning Objectives

After reading this chapter you should be able to:

12.1 Compare and contrast how the laboratory studies of nonhuman animal communication differs from what is found in the studies of nonhuman animals in the wild.

12.2 Discuss what makes human languages unique in comparison with nonhuman animal communication.

12.3 Describe what anthropologists conclude about the evolution of language.

12.4 Discuss how linguistic anthropologists study language.

12.5 Explain how children acquire their languages.

12.6 Discuss the relationship between language and culture.

12.7 Describe how anthropologists study the history of languages.

12.8 Describe what the field of sociolinguistics tells us about language use.

12.9 Discuss other forms of communication humans use beside language.

In Chapter 10, we discussed how the capacity for culture enables humans to learn symbolically and to transmit symbols from generation to generation. **Language** is a system of *symbols* with standard meanings. Through language, members of a society are able to communicate with one another; it is an integral aspect of culture. Language allows humans to communicate what they are experiencing at any given moment, what they have experienced in the past, and what they are planning for in the future. Like culture, the language of any particular individual exists before the person's birth and is publicly shared *to some extent* by the members of a society. For example, people born in the United States are exposed to an English-speaking language community, whereas people in Russia learn the Russian language. These languages provide the context for symbolic understanding within these different societies. In this sense, language, as part of culture, transcends the individual. Without language, humans would have difficulty transmitting culture. Without culture, humans would lose their unique "humanity."

When linguists refer to language, they usually mean spoken language. Yet, spoken language is only one form of communication. **Communication** is the act of transferring information to others. As we will discover in this chapter, many nonhuman animals have basic communication skills. We will discuss current anthropologists' understanding of how animal communication has evolved into human language. We will also discover that humans communicate with one another in ways other than language.

Nonhuman Communication

12.1 Compare and contrast how the laboratory studies of nonhuman animal communication differs from what is found in the studies of nonhuman animals in the wild.

Teaching Apes to Sign

Psychologists and other scientists have conducted a considerable amount of research on animal communication. Some of the most interesting and controversial research has been done on chimpanzees and gorillas, animals that are close genetically, physiologically, and developmentally to humans. The study of nonhuman animal communication has implications for understanding how the ability to symbolize and language evolved. In 1966, psychologists Allen and Beatrice Gardner adopted a female chimpanzee named Washoe and began teaching her American Sign Language (ASL, or Ameslan), a nonvocal form of communication used by the deaf. The ASL used by deaf humans is not an "artificial language" for deaf people. ASL is a complex language that evolved over 150 years in the United States and is very similar to spoken language, with complex grammar and abstract symbolic representations. After four years with the Gardners, Washoe was able to master over 150 signs. They reported that Washoe was able to combine signs to invent new signs. This was truly a remarkable feat for a chimpanzee, and it challenged the traditional assumption that only humans have the capacity for using symbols (Gardner and Gardner 1969; Gordon 2004).

At the Yerkes Regional Primate Research Center at Emory University in Atlanta, Georgia, in the 1970s, a chimpanzee named Lana was taught to communicate through a color-coded computer keyboard using *lexigrams* (graphic symbols). Researchers concluded that Lana was able to use and combine signs in the computer language. For example, she referred to a cucumber as a "green banana" and to an orange as an "apple that is orange" (Rumbaugh 1977). David and Ann Premack, psychologists at the University of California, Santa Barbara, taught a chimpanzee named Sarah to manipulate colored plastic discs and different shapes to form simple sentences and ask for objects (Gordon 2004). Eventually, primatologist Roger Fouts, who had been Allen Gardner's graduate student, took over the care of Washoe and spent some 30 years with her and other chimpanzees. During this period, Fouts observed Washoe communicating signs from the ASL with other chimpanzees. He has spent considerable time and research on chimpanzee communication abilities and linguistic capacities, recorded in his book *Next of Kin: What Chimpanzees Have Taught Me about Who We Are* (1997). He found that these chimps could produce category words for certain types of foods: Celery was "pipe food"; watermelon was "candy drink"; and radish, a food first tasted by Washoe, was "hurt cry food." Also, when he introduced Washoe to a newly adopted chimpanzee named Louis, Fouts signed in ASL, "I HAVE BABY FOR YOU." Washoe signed back "BABY, BABY, BABY!" and hooted for joy. In his book, Fouts argues that chimpanzee communication and linguistic capacities are very similar to human language capacities and differ only in *degree*.

In a widely publicized study in the 1970s, Francine Patterson taught Koko, a female gorilla, to use some 1,000 ASL words. Koko was billed as the world's first "talking" gorilla (Patterson and Cohn 1978; Patterson and Linden 1981). At the age of four, Koko was given an intelligence test based on the Stanford–Binet Intelligence Scale and scored an 85, only slightly below the score of an average human child. In addition, according to Patterson, Koko demonstrated the capacity to lie, deceive, swear, joke, and combine signs in new and creative ways. Koko also asked for, and received, a pet kitten to nurture (Gordon 2004).

Ape Sign Language Reexamined

These studies of ASL sign use by apes challenged traditional ideas regarding the gap between humans and other types of animals. They are not, however, without their critics. One source of criticism is based on work done at Columbia University by psychologist Herbert Terrace (1986). Terrace began examining the previous ape language studies by training a chimpanzee named Nim Chimpsky (named after the well-known linguist discussed later, Noam Chomsky). Videotapes of the learning sessions were used to carefully observe the cues that may have been emitted by the trainers. Terrace also viewed the videotapes of the other studies on chimpanzee communication.

Terrace's conclusions challenged some of the earlier studies. Videotape analysis revealed that Nim rarely initiated signing behaviors, signing only in response to gestures given by the instructors, and that 50 percent of his signs were simply imitative. Unlike humans, Nim did not learn the two-way nature of conversation. Nim also never signed without expecting some reward. In addition, Nim's phrases were random combinations of signs. And Nim never signed to another chimpanzee who knew ASL unless a teacher coached him. Finally, the videotapes of the other projects showed that prompters gave unconscious signals to the chimpanzees through their body gestures.

Terrace's overall conclusions indicate that chimpanzees are highly intelligent animals that can learn many signs. They cannot, however, understand syntax, the set of grammatical rules governing the way words combine to form sentences. An English-speaking child can systematically place a noun before a verb followed by an object without difficulty. A chimpanzee cannot use these types of grammatical rules to structure sentences. Terrace concludes that although chimpanzees have remarkable intellectual capacities and excellent memories, they do not have the syntactical abilities of humans to form sentences.

Terrace's work did not end the ape language debate. Sue Savage-Rumbaugh has tried to eliminate the methodological problem of giving ambiguous hand signs to train chimpanzees at the Yerkes laboratory at Emory University. Terrace had suggested that the researchers such as Patterson and Rumbaugh were cuing their subjects with their own signs to respond to specific signs. In her book *Ape Language: From Conditioned Response to Symbol* (1986), Savage-Rumbaugh reports on a 10-year-old *bonobo*, or "pygmy" chimpanzee (a different species of chimpanzee from the common chimpanzee) named Kanzi, who learned to communicate with lexigrams, the graphic, geometric word-symbols that act as substitutes for human speech; 250 lexigrams are displayed on a large keyboard. At the age of two and a half, Kanzi spontaneously reached for the keyboard, pointed to the lexigram for *chase*, and ran away. Savage-Rumbaugh observed him repeatedly touch the lexigram for *chase* and scamper off. By age six, Kanzi had mastered a vocabulary of 90 symbols.

Psychologist Sally Boysen at the Ohio State University and researcher Tetsuro Matsuzawa at Kyoto University in Japan have been doing research not only on the language abilities of chimpanzees, but also on their numerical

Joyce Butler and Nim

abilities (Boysen and Bernston 1989). The chimpanzees studied are reported to have learned how to count from zero to nine and also to "read" Japanese characters (kanji) or English words. However, these researchers do not conclude that these chimpanzees have grammar or syntactical abilities.

Ethological Research on Ape Communication

In addition to doing laboratory research on animal communication, *primatologists* study the behavior of primates in their natural environment and have conducted a number of impressive field studies. **Ethologists**, scientists who study animal behavior, find that many types of animals have *call systems*—certain sounds or vocalizations that produce specific meanings—that are used to communicate for adaptive purposes. Animals such as prairie dogs, chickens, various types of monkeys, and chimpanzees have call systems.

In a primatological study of gorillas in central Africa, George Schaller isolated 22 vocalizations used by these primates. This compares with 20 vocalizations used by howler monkeys, 30 used by Japanese macaque monkeys, and nine used by gibbons (Schaller 1976). Like these other vocalizations, the gorilla sounds are associated with specific behaviors or emotional states, such as restful feeding, sexual behavior, play, anger, and warnings of approaching threats. Infant gorillas also emit certain sounds when their mothers venture off. Schaller admits that some vocalizations were not accompanied by any specific type of behavior or stimulus.

Chimpanzee Communication: Jane Goodall

The most impressive long-term investigation of chimpanzees in their natural environment was carried out by Jane Goodall, a primatologist who studied the chimpanzees of the Gombe Game Reserve in Africa since 1960. Goodall has gathered a great deal of information on the vocalizations used by these chimps. Her observations demonstrated that the chimpanzees use a great variety of calls, which are tied directly to emotional states such as fear, annoyance, and sexual excitement. She concludes that "the production of a sound in the absence of the appropriate emotional state seems to be an almost impossible task for the chimpanzee" (Goodall 1986:125).

Goodall found that the chimps use "intraparty calls," communication within the group, and "distance calls," communication with other groups. Intraparty calls include pant-grunts directed to a higher-ranking individual within the group as a token of respect and barks, whimpers, squeaks, screams, coughs, and other sounds directed toward other chimps in the immediate group. Distance calls serve a wider range of functions, including drawing attention to local food sources, announcing the precise location of individuals in the home territory, and, in times of distress, bringing help from distant allies. Other current primatological studies indicate that chimpanzee vocalization such as pant-hoots are context-specific and are not limited to predation or other behaviors (Crockford and Boesch 2003). Further research is needed to discover whether the chimps use these vocalizations to distinguish among different types of foods and dangers in the environment.

Although primate communication in the wild indicates that they do not use symbolic language or anything close to ASL, nevertheless the laboratory studies that have trained chimpanzees and gorillas to use ASL clearly demonstrate that the gap between primate communication and human language may be reduced. Whether they indicate that apes can use true human symbolic language remains undecided and controversial. Although recent neurological research on chimpanzees has shown that they have areas in their brain with linguistic capacities and potentialities similar to those of humans, more research needs to be done on primate communication to investigate this phenomenon (Gannon et al. 1998; Small 2001; Gordon 2004). Primatologist Michael Tomasello and colleagues have done studies that indicate that modern chimps lack the capacity for sharing and making inferences about the intentions of one another (2005). These primatologists suggest that this lack of capacity for sharing intentions and interest in cooperation with others for pursuing goals is a major difference between nonhuman primates and humans.

Jane Goodall with infant chimpanzee

Most anthropologists and psychologists have concluded that apes show the ability to manipulate linguistic symbols when the symbols are hand gestures or plastic symbols. However, the fact that they do not have the capacity to transmit symbolic language beyond the level of a two-year-old human child does not mean that they are *failed humans*. Chimps are perfectly good at being chimps. It would appear that humans have many different sorts of linguistic capacities. Whether they are different in *degree* or in *kind* is a topic that has divided the primatologists, linguistic anthropologists, and psychologists who assert differing claims based upon their evidence in the field or the laboratory. We will explore this aspect of linguistic capacities in humans later in this chapter.

Animal Communication and Human Language

12.2 Discuss what makes human languages unique in comparison with nonhuman animal communication.

Both laboratory and field studies of animal communication offer fascinating insights into the question of what distinguishes human communication from animal communication. Many Western philosophers such as Plato and René Descartes have identified speech and language as the major distinction between humans and other animals. Modern studies on animal communication, however, suggest that the language gap separating humans from other animals is not as wide as it once appeared. These studies also indicate that fundamental differences exist between animal communication and human languages. The question is not whether animals can communicate; we know that almost every animal can. The real question is: How does animal communication differ from human communication? In searching for an answer to this question, linguistic anthropologists have identified a number of distinctive characteristics of human languages. The four most important features are productivity, displacement, arbitrariness, and combining sounds (Hockett and Ascher 1964).

Productivity

Human languages are inherently flexible and creative. Users of human languages, even small children, can create sentences never heard before by anyone. There are no limits to our capability to produce messages that refer to the past, present, or future. We can express different thoughts, meanings, and experiences in infinite ways. In contrast, animal communication systems in

natural settings are rigid and fixed. The sounds of animal communications do not vary and cannot be modified. The offspring of chimpanzees will always use the same pattern of vocalization as the parents. In contrast, the highly flexible nature of human languages allows for efficient and creative uses of symbolic communication. William von Humboldt, a nineteenth-century linguist, used the phrase "the infinite use of finite media" to suggest the idea of linguistic productivity (von Humboldt [1836] 1972; Pinker 1994).

Displacement

It is clear from field studies, and to some extent from laboratory studies, that the meaning of a sound or vocalization of a nonhuman animal is closely tied to a specific type of stimulus. For example, the chimpanzee's vocalization is associated with a particular emotional state and stimulus. Thus, a growl or scream as a warning to the group cannot be made in the absence of some perceived threat. Similarly, animals such as parrots and mynah birds can learn to imitate a wide variety of words, but they cannot substitute or displace one word for another. In contrast, the meanings of sounds in human languages can refer to people, things, or events that are not present, a feature called "displacement." We can discuss things that are not perceived by our visual or auditory capacities.

This capacity for displacement enables humans to communicate with one another using highly abstract concepts. Humans can express their objectives in reference to the past, present, and future. They can discuss spiritual or hypothetical phenomena that do not exist concretely. They can discuss past history through myth or specific genealogical relations. Humans can refer to what will happen after death through myth or theological concepts such as heaven or spiritual enlightenment. Displacement allows humans to plan for the future through the use of foresight. Obviously, this linguistic ability for displacement is interrelated with the general symbolic capacities that are shared by humans, providing the basis of culture, as discussed in Chapter 10. Symbolic capacities allow humans to manipulate abstract concepts to develop complex beliefs and worldviews.

Arbitrariness

The arbitrariness of sounds in a communication system is another distinctive feature of human languages. Words seldom have any necessary connection with the concrete objects or abstract symbols they represent. In English, we say one, two, and three to refer to the numbers, whereas the Chinese say *yi*, *er*, and *san*. Neither language has the "correct" word for the numbers because there is no correct word. "Ouch" is pronounced "*ay*" in Spanish and "*ishkatak*" in the Nootkan Indian language. A German shepherd dog does not have any difficulty understanding the bark of a French poodle. An English speaker, however, will have trouble understanding a Chinese speaker. A chimpanzee from West Africa will have no difficulty communicating with a chimpanzee from East Africa (although primatologists do find different behavior patterns, such as toolmaking and nut cracking, among chimpanzees residing in different locales in Africa) (Mercader, Panger, and Boesch 2002).

Combining Sounds to Produce Meanings

We have mentioned that various animals have sounds that indicate different meanings in specific contexts. Human languages, in addition, have units of sound that cannot be correlated with units of meaning. Every human language has between 12 and 60 of these sound units, called *phonemes*. A **phoneme** is a unit of sound that distinguishes meaning in a particular language. For example, in English, the difference between "dime" and "dine" is distinguished by the sound difference or phonemic difference between /m/ and /n/. English has 45 phonemes, Italian has 27, and Hawaiian has 13 (Farb 1974).

Nonhuman animals cannot combine their sound units to communicate new meanings; one vocalization is given to indicate a specific response. In contrast, in human languages, the same sounds can be combined and recombined to form different meanings. As an illustration, the sounds usually represented by the English letters *p, t, c,* and *a* (the vowel sound in the word *bat*) have no meaning on their own. But they can be used to form words like *pat, tap, cat, apt, act, tact, pact,* and so on, which do have meanings. The Hawaiian language, with only 13 sound units, has almost 3,000 words consisting of different combinations of three sounds and many thousands of words formed by combinations of six sounds. Phonemes that may have no meaning alone can be combined and recombined to form literally as many meaningful units (words) as people need or want. Primates and other animals do not have this ability.

Having defined these features of human language, we can discern fundamental differences between human and animal communication. However, some researchers working with chimpanzees in laboratories are still not willing to label human languages as "true languages," as distinguished from "animal communication systems." They criticize what they refer to as the "anthropocentric" view of language—the view that takes human language as its standard. Because chimpanzees do not have the physical ability to form the sounds made by humans, it may be unfair to compare their language strictly in terms of vocal communication.

The Evolution of Language

12.3 Describe what anthropologists conclude about the evolution of language.

Throughout the centuries, linguists, philosophers, and physical anthropologists have developed theories concerning the origins of human language. One early theory, known as the "bowwow" theory, maintains that language arose when humans imitated the sounds of nature by the use of onomatopoeic words, such as *cock-a-doodle-do*, or *sneeze*, or *mumble*. Another theory associated with the Greek philosopher Plato argues that language evolved as humans detected the natural sounds of objects in nature. Known as the "dingdong" theory, this argument assumed that a relationship exists between a word and its meaning because nature gives off a harmonic ring. For example, all of nature, including rocks, streams, plants, and animals, was thought to emit a ringing sound that could be detected by humans. The harmonic ring of a rock supposedly sounded like the word *rock*. Both theories have been discredited, replaced by other scientific and linguistic anthropological hypotheses concerning the evolution of language. When anthropologists study the evolution of language, they draw on evidence from all four fields of anthropology: physical anthropology, archaeology, linguistic anthropology, and cultural anthropology, studies in genetics and psycholinguistics, as well as experiments in communication with animals and humans.

In Chapter 7 (pp. 150–151), we discussed the contemporary evidence for the evolution of language among hominins focusing on the requisites for anatomical and internal brain changes that would be required for the linguistic capacities as well as the acquisition of the FOXP2 gene. In addition to these developments, a recent hypothesis regarding language evolution proposed by neuroscientist and anthropologist Michael A. Arbib and his colleagues Katja Liebal and Simone Pika suggests that human linguistic capacities may have evolved through the development of gestures rather than vocalization per se (2008). The data from current studies on primate vocalizations, facial expressions, and gestures used by primates and prelinguistic human children suggest that the use of gestures coupled with improved modes of imitation provided the foundations for the emergence of a protolanguage for ancestral creatures related to the human line. Prelingustic human children communicate with gestures prior to spoken language. Nonhuman primates also communicate with some basic gestures. Arbib et al. propose that the growth of neurology for imitation and improved forms of pantomime associated with gestures may have been the important keys for the development of linguistic abilities within the ancestral human lineage (2009). Obviously, gestural communication would be supplemented with vocalization in the full development of human language capacities, but these researchers emphasize that language is multimodal with both gestures and vocalization, and this research has helped illuminate what may have been initially important in providing the basics of human language.

Additionally, another aspect of language evolution appears to be related to the development of "mirror neurons" in humans. Mirror neurons were discovered through experiments with macaque monkeys. Gallese and colleagues found that when measuring the activity of neurons in one specific area of the brain, these neurons discharged along with specific goal-directed manual activities of these monkeys, and also when the monkeys observed humans doing the same manual activities (1996). These mirror neurons provide a mechanism for linking the intentions of a sender of a message to a receiver, a necessary component of language. Many experiments have indicated that mirror neurons exist in humans. The mirror neuron network has been correlated with complex learning. The network appears to be related to both imitation (not found in monkeys) and the ability to understand the intentions and emotions of others, usually referred to as "Theory of Mind" or TOM, also prerequisites for complex language capacities. Some researchers hypothesize that Broca's area of the brain evolved atop of the mirror neuron circuits to create the capacity for language development involving manual, (tool use), facial, and vocal behaviors (Arbib 2011).

Some linguists and primatologists believe that the emergence of human language suggests that at some point in the expansion of the brain, a rewiring of the human brain developed that allowed for what is known as *recursion*, the linguistic capacity to build an infinite number of sentences within sentences (Hauser, Chomsky, and Fitch 2002). Other models emphasize the evolution of words and sounds, as well as motor control and other features of the language capacity as important as recursion (Lieberman 2007; Pinker 1994; Jackendoff and Pinker 2005). Anthropologist Dan Sperber and his colleague Deirdre Wilson suggest that fully modern human language involves making inferences about what people are saying to one another in particular contexts (1996). They point out that compared with humans, chimpanzees have only a very rudimentary capacity to make inferences about the beliefs and intentions of another chimpanzee. Thus, communication capacities for humans are connected with our cognitive capacities for developing inferences in particular cultural contexts. Whatever the precise determinants of the evolution of language, it is difficult to identify the critical stage in the evolution from a simple, sign-based communication system to a more advanced, symbolic form of language. It is, however, recognized that this capacity broadly expanded human capabilities for adaptation and creativity.

As stated Chapter 7 in the discussion of hominin linguistic evolution, although anthropologists may disagree with one another regarding the actualities and purpose of language capacities in humans, this capacity for language was probably the last major step in our biological evolution. Since that time, human history has been dominated by *cultural* rather than *biological* evolution. This cultural evolution and the subsequent developments in adaptation and creativity could not have occurred before a fully evolved language capacity.

The Structure of Language

12.4 Discuss how linguistic anthropologists study language.

Linguistic anthropologists compare the structure of different languages. To do so, they study the sounds of a language (*phonology*), the words of a language (*morphology*), the *sentence structure* of a language (*syntax*), the meaning of a language (*semantics*), and the *rules* for the appropriate use of a language (*pragmatics*). More than 7,000 languages have existed throughout history, all of which have contained these five components, although the components vary considerably from one language to another.

Phonology

Phonology is the study of the sounds used in language. Although all human languages have both vowel and consonant sounds, no language makes use of all the sounds humans can make. The sounds of all languages are either oral or nasal. To study phonetic differences among languages, linguists have developed the International Phonetic Alphabet (IPA), which enables them to transcribe all the sounds produced in the world's languages. Each sound is used somewhere in the world, although no single language contains all of them. Each language has its own phonetic inventory, consisting of all the sounds normally produced by its speakers, and also its own phonemic inventory, consisting of the sound units that can produce word contrasts in the language. As we have already seen, human languages, which have only a limited number of sounds, can combine these sounds to produce complex meanings.

Linguists attempt to discover the phonemes, or contrasting sound-units, of a language by looking for what are called minimal pairs: words that are identical except for one difference in sound. For example, the English words *lot* and *rot* form a minimal pair; they are identical except for their beginning sounds, spelled *l* and *r*. The fact that English speakers recognize *lot* and *rot* as different words establishes that /l/ and /r/ are contrasting sound-units, or phonemes, in English. In contrast, when Japanese children acquire their native language, they do not make a sharp categorical distinction between the /l/ and /r/

sounds. Japanese adult speakers do not hear the distinction between /l/ and /r/, even when they listen very carefully to English speakers. Patricia Kuhl and her Japanese colleagues studied how Japanese infants attend to different sounds of their own language and why they do not make distinctions between /l/ and /r/ (1996). This research suggests that as we are exposed to our language environment, the initial sounds we detect as infants in our first language alter the neurological networks in our brains, resulting in enduring effects on our ability to distinguish particular sounds within a language.

When linguistic anthropologists analyze the phonological system of a language, they attempt to organize the sounds, or **phones**, of the language into a system of contrasting phonemes. For example, English speakers produce both a /p/ sound and the same sound accompanied by *aspiration*, a light puff of air, symbolized in the IPA as /ph/; compare the difference between the *p* sounds in *spy* and *pie*. Because in English the sounds /p/ and /ph/ never form a minimal pair and their pronunciation depends upon their position in a word, these sounds are allophones of the same phoneme. In other languages, such as Aymara (spoken in Bolivia, Peru, and Chile), the aspiration of consonants produces a phonemic contrast: Compare the Aymara words /hupa/, which means "they," and /hupha/, which is a kind of cereal. In Aymara, then, the sounds /p/ and /ph/ belong to separate phonemes, just as /l/ and /r/ do in English, as we saw before. This illustrates the fact that the "same" sounds may be contrastive in one language and not contrastive in another. Also, what sounds like a /b/ to a native Spanish speaker sounds like a /p/ to a native English speaker. Obviously, neurological changes are occurring within the brain as a child acquires his or her native language.

In addition to aspiration, sounds may be modified in other ways, including nasality, pitch, stress, and length of time the sound is held. Many Asian languages, such as Chinese and Thai, are *tonal*; that is, a word's meaning is affected by the tones (contrasting pitches) of the sounds that make up the word. Put another way, the tones of the language have phonemic value. To an English speaker's ear, a Chinese or Thai speaker sounds musical. For example, in Thai, *may* can mean "new," "to burn," or "silk," depending upon the tone used.

Pueblo Indians use many nasalized sounds to produce phonemic differences. Arab speakers use the back of the tongue and the throat muscles, whereas Spanish speakers use the tip of the tongue. The !Kung San or Ju/'hoansi of southern Africa have a unique manner of producing phonemic differences. They use a sharp intake of air to make clicks that shape meaning for them. Their language also requires more use of the lips to produce smacks than most other languages. The Ju/'hoansi language has been referred to as a "clicking language."

Most people are unaware of the complex physiological and mental processes required to pronounce the sounds of their native tongue. Only through extensive phonetic and phonological analysis by linguists and anthropologists is this component of language understood.

Morphology

To study the words of human languages, anthropologists isolate the **morphemes**, the smallest units of a language that convey meaning. The study of morphemes is called **morphology**. Morphemes may be short, containing only a single phoneme, or they may include a combination of phonemes. They are the minimal building blocks of meaning and cannot be reduced further. *Bound morphemes* are those morphemes that cannot stand alone, such as suffixes and prefixes. For example, in English, *s* is a bound morpheme that indicates the plural, and the prefix *un* is a bound morpheme meaning "not." *Free morphemes*, in contrast, are independent units of meaning; they can stand alone, for example, as nouns, verbs, adjectives, or adverbs. Words such as *boy*, *girl*, *happy*, and *close* are free morphemes.

In any language, morphemes are limited in number, and languages differ in how these morphemes are used and combined. In contrast to many languages, English has complex rules governing the formation of plurals of certain words (for example, *geese*, *mice*, *children*, and *shrimp*). Some languages, such as Chinese, generally use one morpheme for each word. Other languages, such as the Eskimo (Inuit) languages, combine a large number of affixes to form words.

An important way in which languages differ is the extent to which they use morphology to convey meaning. For example, in English, we can say, "The girl sees the dog," or, "The dog sees the girl." The nouns *girl* and *dog* do not change form, and only their position in the sentence indicates which is subject and which is object. But in Russian, *dyevushka videt sobaku* means, "The girl sees the dog." "The dog sees the girl," is *sobaka videt dyevushku*. Note that the endings on the nouns show which is subject and which is object, even if the word order is changed: *Sobaku videt dyevushka* still means, "The girl sees the dog."

Syntax

The **syntax** of a language is the collection of rules for the way phrases and sentences are made up out of words. For example, these rules determine whether a subject comes before or after a verb or whether an object follows a verb. Linguistic anthropologist Joseph Greenberg and colleagues (Greenberg, Denning, and Kemmer 1990) classified languages based on word order within sentences—that is, the location of the subject (S), the verb (V), and the object (O). They demonstrated that these components occur in six possible orders: VSO, SVO, SOV, VOS, OSV, and OVS. But, in fact, Greenberg and his colleagues found in their cross-linguistic comparison that usually just three patterns of word order occur: VSO, SVO, and SOV. Since their study, other languages have been discovered with the VOS, OSV, and OVS forms, though the last two are extremely rare (Smith 1999).

Although most languages permit variation in syntax to allow for emphasis in expression, most linguists suggest that some innate universal capacities may influence word order. For example, the expression for the English sentence, "The boy drank the water" can be found in all languages. Notice the variations in syntactical order among six different languages:

(Hausa is a West African language. Quechua is a language of the ancient Incas and their modern descendants.)

The syntax of a language also includes rules for trans-

	S	V	O
English:	the bóy	dránk	the wáter
	S	V	O
Russian:	mál'c_ik	vy'pil	vódu
	V	S	O
Arabic:	s_áraba	lwáladu	lma-a
	S	V	O
Hausa:	ya-ro-	yás_a-	ruwa-
	S	V	O
Thai:	dègchaaj	dyym	nàam
	S	O	V
Quechua:	wámbra	yakúta	upiárqan

forming one kind of sentence into another—for example, for forming questions from statements. To form questions from statements, English has a rule that moves the auxiliary verb from its normal position in the sentence to a position at the front of the sentence. This rule allows us to take the statement: "Mary will study for the exam." and, by moving *will* to the front, transform it into the question: "Will Mary study for the exam?"

Semantics

Semantics is the study of the meaning of the symbols, words, phrases, and sentences of a language. The field of semantics has led to important developments in linguistic anthropology. Linguistic anthropologists focus on the meaning of language as it relates to beliefs, concepts, and patterns of thought in different societies. A specialty has developed to account for the meaning of concepts and terms relating to kinship and other cultural phenomena. This specialty sometimes referred to as *ethnosemantics*, overlaps with the field of cognitive anthropology introduced in Chapter 11.

Kinship Terms   The goal of ethnosemantics is to understand the meanings of words, phrases, and sentences and how members of other societies use language to organize things, events, and behaviors. For example, this type of analysis has been applied to the kinship terminologies of many societies. It became increasingly clear to many anthropologists that they could not understand the kinship terms of other societies by simply translating them into English. English terms such as *mother, father, brother, brother-in-law, cousin, aunt,* and *uncle* treat the meaning of kinship differently than do the kinship terms of other societies.

Some groups classify their kin with very precise terms for individuals, no matter how distantly they are related. English kin terms are fairly precise and distinct with respect to genealogical relatedness, yet English does not specify every kin relationship precisely. For example, English speakers do not distinguish between maternal and paternal uncles or aunts. Chinese kinship terminology, on the other hand, includes different terms for one's mother's brother and one's father's brother. There are separate terms for every sibling, as well as for different cousins. This is an example of a highly descriptive kinship terminology. Other forms of kinship terminology are highly generalized. In the Hawaiian kinship system, there is no specific term to parallel the English term *father*. Instead, the Hawaiians use one general term to classify their father and all male relatives in their father's generation. Some kinship terminologies, such as those of the Iroquois Indians, are intermediate between the descriptive and the generalized forms. The Iroquois have one single term for one's father and one's father's brother, but two separate terms for one's mother and one's mother's brother.

Ethnosemanticists or cognitive anthropologists have worked out systematic methods to understand the kinship terminologies of many different societies by focusing on the distinctive common features of these terminologies (D'Andrade 1995). For example, in English, there is a male and female contrast with every kin term except cousin. In addition, the feature of generation is designated in terms such as *uncle* and *nephew, aunt* and *niece*, and in these same terms, we distinguish between ascending and descending generations. There is also a contrast between direct (same generation) and collateral (different generation) relatives. Great-uncles and great-aunts are collateral relatives, whereas brothers and sisters are direct relatives. Ethnosemanticists use these methods to analyze other forms of kinship terminology in various societies.

A fascinating study by Larry Hirschfeld suggests that there are some universal aspects regarding the meaning of kinship terminology (1986, 1989). Hirschfeld found that children and adults assume that kinship terms refer to a "natural affinity" for their own genealogical relatives and families. Children appear to have an intuitive understanding of the relationship between kinship terms and their relatives and family. Kinship terms are used to refer to people who share a common descent and an internal "essence." The family is based upon a particular group of people and is different from a group of students in a class or other types of groups. Anthropologist Doug Jones has followed this model of linguistic research on kinship terms and also suggests that there is a "universal" aspect to kinship terminology found among all societies (2000, 2003, 2004). Other cognitive anthropologists continue to investigate kinship terminologies and other cultural phenomena to seek out both similarities and differences among human groups (Bloch and Sperber 2002).

Language Acquisition

12.5 Explain how children acquire their languages.

Although human infants are born with the ability to speak a language, they are not born preprogrammed to speak a particular language such as English. Just as infants are exposed to enculturation to absorb and learn about their culture, they must be exposed to the phonemes, morphemes, syntax, and semantics of the language within their culture. Linguistic anthropologists have examined this process, drawing on different hypotheses regarding language acquisition.

One of the earliest discussions in Western society of how humans learn their language came in the late fourth-century writings of the Catholic theologian Augustine in his famous book *Confessions* (1995). Augustine believed that as we hear our parents speak words and point to objects, we associate the words with the objects. Later, the empiricist philosopher John Locke (1632–1704) maintained a similar belief and suggested that the human mind at birth is like a blank tablet, a *tabula rasa*, and that infants learn language through habit formation. This hypothesis was further developed by twentieth-century behavioral psychologists such as B. F. Skinner, who maintained that infants learn language through conditioned responses and feedback from their environment. This behaviorist approach to language became the dominant model of how language was acquired for many years. In the behaviorist view, an infant might babble a sound that resembles an acceptable word like *mama* or *daddy* and would then be rewarded for that response. Thus rewarded, the child would use the word *daddy* in certain contexts. According to Skinner, children learn their entire language through this type of social conditioning.

The Enlightenment philosopher René Descartes (1596–1650) advocated a contrasting view of language learning. He argued that innate ideas or structures in the human mind provide the basis for learning language. Until the late 1950s, most linguists and anthropologists working on language assumed that Locke's model—and, by extension, Skinner's—was correct. However, by about 1960, evidence began to accumulate that suggested that, in fact, humans come into the world especially equipped

A teacher and a young child.

not only to acquire their own native language but also to acquire any other human language.

Chomsky on Language Acquisition

The most influential modern proponent of a view that is somewhat similar to Descartes's hypothesis is linguist Noam Chomsky. Chomsky is interested in how people acquire *grammar*, the set of rules that determine how sentences are constructed to produce meaningful statements. Most people cannot actually state the rules of their grammar, but they do use the rules to form understandable sentences. For example, in English, young children can easily transform the active sentence, "Bill loves Mary," into a passive sentence, "Mary is loved by Bill." This change requires much grammatical knowledge, but most English speakers carry out this operation without consciously thinking about it.

According to Chomsky, all children acquire these complex rules readily and do not seem to have difficulty producing meaningful statements, even when they have not been exposed to linguistic data that illustrate the rules in question. In other words, children acquire these complex rules with minimal exposure to the language. Furthermore, children are able to both produce and understand novel sentences they have never heard before. All this would be impossible, Chomsky claims, if acquiring language depended on trial-and-error learning and reinforcement, as the behaviorist psychologists led by Skinner had thought. In other words, Chomsky suggests that we are born with a brain *prewired* to enable us to acquire language easily; Chomsky often refers to this prewiring as *universal grammar*.

Universal grammar serves as a template, or model, against which a child matches and sorts out the patterns of morphemes and phonemes and the subtle distinctions that are needed to communicate in any language. According to Chomsky, a behavioristic understanding of language learning is too simplistic to account for the creativity and productivity of any human language. In his view, the universal grammar of the human mind enables the child to acquire language and produce sentences never heard before. In addition, Chomsky and others who study language acquisition propose a *critical period*, beginning with infancy and lasting through about the age of five and the onset of puberty, during which language acquisition must take place. If children are not exposed to language during that period, they may never be able to acquire it, or they may learn it only in a very rudimentary fashion. Chomsky believes that the human brain contains genetically programmed blueprints or *modules* for language learning, and he often refers to language acquisition as a part of children's "growth," not something they do, but rather something that happens to them. In addition, Chomsky argues that there is a difference in *kind* between primate communication and human language capacities. He suggests in a well-known statement that "Olympic athlete broad-jumpers can *fly* some 30 feet in the air, but humans do not have the capacity to *fly* like chickens or other birds." The capacity for flying, like the "language capacity," has very different physical and anatomical requirements.

Another important contribution of Chomsky's is the realization that human languages, despite their apparently great diversity, are really more alike than they are different. Anthropologists had previously assumed that languages could vary infinitely and that there was no limit to what could be found in a human language. Chomsky and the researchers that followed him, in contrast, have cataloged many basic, underlying ways in which all languages are really the same. In this view, a hypothetical Martian linguist visiting Earth would probably decide that all humans speak dialects of one human language. Note that this is somewhat parallel to the search for *cultural universals* described in Chapter 10.

Creole and Pidgin Languages

One source of evidence for Chomsky's model of innate universal grammar is research on specific types of languages known as *creole* and *pidgin* languages. Linguist Derek Bickerton has compared these two types of languages from different areas of the world. Pidgin and creole languages develop from cross-cultural contact between speakers of mutually unintelligible languages. A *pidgin* form of communication emerges when people of different languages develop and use a simple grammatical structure and words to

Noam Chomsky

communicate with one another. For example, in the New Guinea highlands, where many different languages were spoken, a pidgin language developed between the indigenous peoples and the Westerners.

In some cases, the children of the pidgin speakers begin to speak a *creole* language. The vocabulary of the *creole* language is similar to that of the pidgin, but the grammar is much more complex. There are more than 100 known creole languages. Among them are the creole languages developed between African slaves and Europeans, leading to languages such as Haitian and Jamaican Creole. Hawaiian Creole emerged after contact between English-speaking Westerners and native Hawaiians.

What is remarkable, according to Bickerton, is that all these languages share similar grammatical patterns, despite the lack of contact among these diverse peoples. For example, Hawaiian Creole uses the English word *walk* in a different manner from standard English. The phrase *bin walk* means "had walked"; *stay walk* is continuing action, as in, "I am walking" or, "I was walking"; and *I bin stay walk* means, "I had been walking." Although this phrasing might sound unusual to a person from England or the United States, it does conform to a clear set of grammatical rules. Very similar tense systems are found in all other creole languages, whatever their vocabularies or geographic origins.

Bickerton suggests that the development of creole languages may parallel the evolution of early human languages. Because of an innate universal grammatical component of the human mind, languages emerged in uniform ways. The prehistoric languages would have had structures similar to those of the creole languages. As languages developed in various types of environments with different characteristics, different vocabularies and sentence structures evolved. Yet, when societies are uprooted by cultural contact, the innate rules for ordering language remain intact. Bickerton's thesis suggests that humans do have some sort of universal linguistic acquisition device, as hypothesized by Chomsky (Bickerton 1985, 1999, 2008).

Sign Language in Nicaragua: A Case for the Innateness of Language

An interesting study of deaf children in Nicaragua conducted by linguistic anthropologist Ann Senghas and her colleagues also supports the view that language has some innate characteristics, as Chomsky has indicated. This study demonstrates how language can develop from a gesture system to a full-fledged language with grammar, symbols, and meanings (Senghas, Kita, and Ozyurek 2004). Nicaragua's deaf schools were established in 1977 and had many hearing impaired children who interacted with one another. These children came from various backgrounds and regions of the country and had developed different means of communication with their parents. The school that was established focused on teaching the children to read lips and speak Spanish. Senghas and her colleagues studied three generations of deaf schoolchildren in Managua, Nicaragua, and found that they were actually constructing linguistic rules from various gestures that they were using with one another over the years. These gestures were different from any other communicative gestures found in other sign languages. The studies indicate that the preadolescent children are much more capable of learning the new deaf language than the older children, thus indicating that there is a "critical stage" in the capacity for learning grammar, syntax, and rules of language. This study demonstrated that this deaf language, invented by these Nicaraguan children, developed from a gestural sign system to a more structured linguistic system. This linguistic study provides more confirmation of Chomsky's views on language acquisition and also of the research on the transition from pidgin to creole languages previously described. It appears that children's brains are predisposed to learn the rules of complicated grammar and impose grammatical structure in innovative and productive ways. This study of deaf Nicaraguan children indicates that there is a biologically based language acquisition device that enables young children to learn and create extremely complex fundamental grammatical and linguistic systems with symbolic meanings understood by all of them.

It appears that language acquisition depends upon both biological readiness and learning. The ability to speak seems to be biologically programmed, whereas a specific language is learned from the society the child grows up

Children using sign language

in. Children who are not exposed to language during their "critical period" may not be able to learn to use language properly. Research such as Chomsky's provides for further advances in a biocultural or interactionist approach to test hypotheses regarding language, biology, mind, and thought. A recent book by linguist Andrea Moro discusses the use of new technologies in neuroimaging that has enabled a more comprehensive understanding of how language is integrated with our neurology (2008). The use of positron emission topography, or PET, and functional magnetic resonance imaging, or fMRI has led to a biolinguistic revolution that has resulted in an enhanced understanding of language acquisition, genetics, neuroscience, and the universal grammar that Chomsky has been discussing for the last 50 years. The future of this research is bound to unlock more crucial areas of knowledge about the biological aspect of language for anthropological research.

Language, Thought, and Culture

12.6 Discuss the relationship between language and culture.

In the early part of the twentieth century, Edward Sapir and Benjamin Whorf carried out studies of language and culture. Sapir was a prodigious fieldworker who described many Native American languages and provided the basis for the comparative method in anthropological linguistics. Whorf, an insurance inspector by profession and a linguist and anthropologist by calling, conducted comparative research on a wide variety of languages. The research of Sapir and Whorf led their students to formulate a highly controversial hypothesis that differs dramatically from the theories of Chomsky and the ethnosemantics of cognitive anthropologists and linguists.

Anthropologists At Work

Russell Bernard: Saving Languages

There are more than 7,000 languages distributed throughout a population of more than 7 billion people in the world. As many linguistic anthropologists have noted, however, tens of thousands of languages have become extinct through the years. In Western Europe, hundreds of languages disappeared with the expansion of agricultural empires that imposed their languages on conquered peoples. For example, during the expansion of the Roman Empire for approximately a thousand years, many tribal languages disappeared as they were replaced by Latin. Currently, only 45 native languages still exist in Western Europe.

When Columbus discovered the Americas, more than 2,000 languages existed among different Native American peoples. Yet, even in pre-Columbian America, before 1500 A.D., native languages were displaced by the expansion of peoples such as the Aztecs and Incas in Central and South America. As the Spanish and British empires expanded into these regions, the indigenous languages began to disappear even more rapidly. A similar process has been ongoing throughout Asia, Africa, and the Middle East.

The majority of people in the world speak one of the "large" groups of languages, such as Mandarin Chinese (with more than 1 billion speakers), Spanish, or English. Most of the more than 4,000 languages that exist are spoken in small-scale societies that have an average of 5,000 people or so. For example, Papua New Guinea alone has perhaps as many as a thousand different languages distributed among various ethnic groups (Diamond 1993). Other islands in countries such as Indonesia may have as many as 400 different languages. Yet, in all of the areas of the Pacific and Asia, the "large" languages are beginning to replace the "small" ones.

Some linguists estimate that if the present rate of the disappearance of languages remains constant, within a century or two our 4,000 languages could be reduced to just a few hundred. For example, as young people in the Pacific Islands begin to move from rural to urban regions, they usually abandon their traditional language and learn a majority tongue to be able to take advantage of educational and economic opportunities. As the media—television, radio, newspapers, and now the Internet—opt for a majority language, more people will elect to abandon their native languages. These are global processes that have resulted in linguistic homogeneity and the loss of traditional languages.

In North America and Alaska, there are some 200 languages, ranging from Inuit and Yupik among the native Alaskans to Navajo, Hopi, Choctaw, Creek, Seminole, Chickasaw, and Cherokee in other areas. However, many of these languages are now on the verge of extinction. As Europeans began to expand and control North America and Alaska, they forced Native American children to speak the English language as a means of "civilizing" them. In many cases, Native American children were removed from their families and were forbidden to speak their native languages. In addition, most Native American peoples have had to learn English to adjust to circumstances in an English-language-dominated society. Thus, very few of the Native American languages are actively spoken today.

Some people say that this process of global and linguistic homogenization and the loss of traditional languages is a positive development. As people begin to speak a common language, communication is increased, leading to improvements in societies that formerly could not unify through language. For example, in India, hundreds of languages existed before the British colonized the area. As the educated class in India (a small minority at the time) began to learn and speak English, it helped provide a means of unifying India as a country. Many people say that for the purpose of developing commerce and political relationships, the abandonment of native languages is a good

Native American children use computers to learn their native languages.

thing. Many businesspeople and politicians argue that multiple languages inhibit economic and political progress, and the elites of many countries have directly encouraged language loss.

A number of linguistic anthropologists, however, disagree with these policies. They may agree that people ought to have some common language to understand one another, to conduct business, and to pursue common political goals. But, they argue, this does not have to mean eliminating minority languages. It requires only that people become bilingual or multilingual. In most societies throughout the world, including Western Europe, people routinely learn two or more languages as children. The United States and Japan are exceptional in being monolingual societies. Linguistic anthropologists find from their studies that people who are forced to abandon their native languages and cultures begin to lose their self-esteem. Bilingualism would permit these people to retain their own language while simultaneously learning the majority language to be able to share in a common national culture.

The U.S. government is beginning to realize that bilingualism has a positive influence on community development among minority populations such as Native Americans. In the recent past, a number of educational programs were funded under the U.S. Bilingual Education Act. This act encouraged the development of English-speaking skills; however, it also offered instruction in the native languages. During the 1980s,

(continued)

there were more than 20 Title VII projects serving Native American students from 16 different language backgrounds. Through these government-sponsored programs, linguistic anthropologists have been actively engaged in both research and language renewal activities among the Native American population (Granadillo and Orcutt-Gachiri 2011). For example, the Cherokee communities of North Carolina have funded language revitalization through their casino revenue streams. They use toddler immersion programs, parent workshops, master-apprentice nests, emergent Cherokee literature, and online classes and podcasts. These kinds of activities have led many younger Native Americans to become interested in studying their traditional languages, which have improved classroom learning, thereby inhibiting high dropout rates among young students.

Anthropologist Russell Bernard has promoted the value of maintaining the native languages of people through the use of microcomputers (1992). Bernard received his Ph.D. from the University of Illinois and is professor emeritus of anthropology at the University of Florida. He has done research in Greece, Mexico, and the United States and has taught or done research at universities in the United States, Greece, Japan, and Germany. Bernard's areas of research include technology and social change, language death, and social network analysis. Since 1987, Bernard has participated in summer courses, sponsored by the U.S. National Science Foundation, on research methods and research design. Bernard co-authored *Native Ethnography* with Jesús Salinas Pedraza, emphasizing

collaboration between anthropologists and native peoples. Bernard was the 2003 recipient of the Franz Boas Award from the American Anthropological Association and is a member of the National Academy of Sciences.

Bernard assisted Native Americans with the development of writing systems and literature for native languages. Through computer technology, anthropologists can help native peoples produce literature in their own languages for future generations. Bernard emphasizes that this will enable all of humanity to profit from the ideas of these people. Bernard was able to establish a center in Mexico where the Indian population could learn to use computers to write in their native languages. Sixty Indian people have learned to write directly in languages such as Mixtec, Zapotec, Chatino, Amuzgo, Chinantec, and Mazatec. Since his pioneering innovations, people like the Cherokee have developed Tsalagi (Cherokee) computer keyboards to use in the modern classroom, which has enabled a vibrant Internet presence for the script as well as the spoken language (Granadillo and Orcutt-Gachiri 2011). Native authors will use these computers and texts to teach adults and children of their home regions to read. Projects such as these represent opportunities for anthropologists to apply their knowledge in solving important problems in U.S. society and beyond.

More recently, linguistic anthropologists have been contributing to the globally based Internet forum known as the Rosetta Project with a Web site http://rosettaproject.org. This Rosetta Project is a global collaboration between linguistic specialists and native speakers

of the world's languages, including endangered languages. The Rosetta Project has thousands of essays and blog posts, and reports on different endangered languages throughout the world. For example, one report discusses the 275 endangered Australian Aboriginal languages and how the Australian government has a new program to help support the translation, teaching, and saving of these Aboriginal languages. Another report by linguist Laura Welcher discusses the Navajo language, currently spoken by about 150,000 people who also speak English, and another several thousand who are monolingual and speak only Navajo (2009). However, many young Navajo are not learning the Navajo language, and English is supplanting the traditional language of the community. This endangered Navajo language was important as a code used by the U.S. military during World War II. The Navajo code talkers were recruited by the U.S. military to send verbal messages by radio to provide support troops in the field. At the time of World War II, there was not much knowledge of the Navajo language because their communities were physically and socially isolated. However, as Welcher suggests, linguistic anthropologists have learned much more about the grammatical structures and lexicon of most of the world's languages; therefore, it would be very difficult to have the "code talking" phenomena in this era. The Rosetta Project is being used as a heuristic tool to bring together native speakers of languages and linguists to establish a foundation to save the endangered languages throughout the world.

The Sapir–Whorf Hypothesis

The **Sapir–Whorf hypothesis** suggests that there is a close relationship between the properties or characteristics of a specific language and its associated culture, and that these features of specific languages define experiences for us. In other words, although humans everywhere have approximately the same set of physical organs for perceiving reality—eyes to see, ears to hear, noses to smell—the human nervous system is bombarded with sensations of all kinds, intensities, and durations. These sensations do not all reach our consciousness. Rather, humans have a

filtering device that classifies reality. This filtering device, according to the Sapir–Whorf hypothesis, is based on the characteristics of a specific language. In this view, certain features of language, in effect, provide us with a special pair of glasses that heightens certain perceptions and dims others, determining what we perceive as reality.

A Case Study: The Hopi Language
To understand this hypothesis, we look at some examples given by Whorf. He compared the grammar of English with that of the Native American Hopi language, spoken in the southwestern part of the United States. He found that the

verb forms indicating tense differ in these two languages. English contains past, present, and future verb forms; the Hopi language does not. In English, we can say, "I came home," "I am coming home," or, "I will come home." The Hopi do not have a verb corresponding to the use of *come* (Whorf 1956). From this type of example, Whorf inferred that Hopi and English speakers think about time in fundamentally different ways.

English speakers conceptualize time in a measurable, linear form, speaking of a length of time or a point in time. We say that time is short, long, or great. We can save time, squander it, or spend it. To the Hopi, in contrast, time is connected to the cycles of nature. Because they were farmers, their lives revolved around the different seasons for planting and harvesting. The Hopi, Whorf argued, saw time not as a motion in space (that is, as time passing) but as a "getting later" of everything that has ever been done. Whorf concluded that the Hopi did not share the Western emphasis on history, calendars, and clocks. From evidence such as this, Sapir and Whorf developed their hypothesis that the specific aspects of a language provide a grid, or structure that influences how humans categorize space, time, and other aspects of reality into a worldview. The Sapir–Whorf hypothesis is an example of *linguistic relativism* because it maintains that the world is experienced differently among different language communities.

Universals of Time Expression Linguistic anthropologist Ekkehart Malotki (1983) investigated the Sapir–Whorf hypothesis by reexamining the Hopi language. His research, based on many interviews with Hopi speakers, showed that, in fact, the Hopi calculate time in units very similar to those used by native English speakers. He concluded that Whorf had exaggerated the extent to which specific linguistic features influence a people's perceptions of time and demonstrated that the Hopi do make linguistic distinctions between the past and the present based on tense form. In the Hopi language, tense is distinguished between future and nonfuture instead of between past and future.

Anthropologist Hoyt Alverson (1994) investigated four different, unrelated languages to determine how time is conceptualized. Alverson studied the metaphors and symbolic usages of time in the Mandarin language of China, the Hindi language of India, the Sesotho language of Africa, and English. He looked at 150 different linguistic usages of time from native speakers and showed that there are basic metaphors that universally underlie the conceptualization of time in any language. However, in different languages, time may be conceptualized in one or more of five universal possibilities. For example, time is usually conceptualized as partible or divisible, or it can be expressed as being linear, circular, or oscillating, or

Hopi female child with traditional hairstyle

as being a causal force or is spatialized in relation to the human body. This study, along with that of Malotki (1983), suggested that all humans share a common cognitive framework when conceptualizing time. These findings undoubtedly have implications for humanity's biological heritage, a universal cognitive evolution, and a common identity as a species.

Weak Linguistic Relativity

Although these studies appear to have refuted the Sapir–Whorf hypothesis, most linguistic anthropologists agree that a relationship exists between language and thought. Rather than asserting that language determines thought, they maintain that language influences the speaker's thinking and concepts. Some experts refer to this approach as a "weak" version of the linguistic relativity hypothesis.

Some contemporary researchers have looked for ways to reformulate the Sapir–Whorf hypothesis in the form of a more precise, testable hypothesis about the relationship among language, thought, and behavior. For example, John Lucy (1992) compared speakers of English and Yucatec Maya to see if their languages led them to perform differently on tasks involving remembering and sorting objects. As predicted from the grammar of the languages, English speakers appeared to attend more closely to the number and also to the shape of the objects, while Mayan speakers paid less attention to the number and more attention to the material from which the objects were made.

It is also true that specific languages contain the vocabulary needed to cope in particular environments. The need for a specific vocabulary in a society does not necessarily mean that language determines our perception of reality. After all, when a need to express some unlabeled phenomenon arises, speakers easily manufacture new words. English-speaking skiers, like Eskimos (Inuit), distinguish among several types of snow, speaking of powder, corn, and so on.

Language may also influence social perception. For example, many people in English-speaking societies have long objected to the use of *man*, *men*, and *mankind* to refer to humanity and *he* to refer to any person, male or female. The word "man" developed in Old English to refer to "a human being," and there were several words for females, *wif*, and males *wer* or *carl* (Bonvillian 2010). "Man" was joined with these to designate genders, *wifman* and *werman* or *carlman*. Eventually *wifman* became "woman" and "man" referred to males. Contemporary experimental studies indicate that the use of the masculine terms such as man as in "Political Man," "Economic Man," or "Urban Man" reinforces the idea that humanity is male and women are outsiders, marginal, and the "second sex" (Bonvillian 2010). Other gender-biased language occurs when words such as *lady* and *girl* are used in a demeaning manner to refer to women. In addition, the tradition of addressing females by the title *Mrs.* or *Miss* reflects gender bias in English-speaking countries (Bonvillian 2010).

To help explain this presumed bias, another linguistic anthropologist, M. J. Hardman-de-Bautista (1978), has formulated the notion of linguistic postulates, distinctions that are made obligatorily in language and that also reflect distinctions central to culture. For example, in English, biological sex is marked on the third-person singular pronouns (*she*, *he*). This distinction between female and male permeates English-speaking culture in important ways—for example, in how children are socialized into appropriate behavior ("be a nice little girl," "act like a lady," "be a man," and the like). In the Aymara language of Peru and Bolivia, in contrast, the third-person pronoun is not marked for sex or number, so the Aymara word *jupa* means "she/he/they." For Aymara, the relevant contrast is human versus nonhuman, and *jupa* cannot be used to refer to an animal, such as a dog or llama; instead, a different pronoun must be used. Aymara children are not taught to behave like "nice girls" or "good boys," but to behave "like human beings, not like animals." Linguistic anthropologists who study Chinese or the Bantu languages of Africa find that despite the gender inequalities associated with these societies, the languages do not distinguish sex or gender in their pronoun usage. So, the features of specific languages do not always reflect the social conditions and values of a particular society. Linguistic anthropologists continue to investigate these issues of gender and language in different societies.

Historical Linguistics

12.7 Describe how anthropologists study the history of languages.

Historical linguistics is the study of language change and the historical relationships among different languages in an effort to discover what kinds of changes occur in languages and why. Research on this subject began in the late eighteenth century when Sir William Jones, a British legal scholar, suggested that the linguistic similarities of Sanskrit, an ancient Indian tongue, to ancient Greek, Latin, German, and English indicate that these languages were descended from a common ancestral language. It was discovered that these languages are part of one family, the Indo-European family, and share certain words and grammar. For example, the English word *three* is *trayas* in Sanskrit, *tres* in Latin, *treis* in Greek, and *drei* in German (see Table 12.1). The similarity in Indo-European languages led some early anthropologists to conclude that all current languages could be traced to a single language family.

The Family-Tree Model

Modern historical linguists agree that they probably can never reconstruct the original language, but they still may be able to reach far back into history to reconstruct an early **protolanguage**, a parent language for many ancient and modern languages. Many linguists hold the view that all languages change in a regular, recognizable way and that similarities among languages are due to a historical relationship among these languages. In other words, the languages of people living in adjacent areas of the world would tend to share similar phonological, syntactical, and semantic features. For example, the Romance languages of French, Spanish, Portuguese, Italian, and Romanian developed from Latin because of the historical relationship with one another through the influence of the Roman Empire. This view is known as the family-tree theory of language change (see Figure 12.1).

Most recently, historical linguists have been working with archaeologists to reconstruct the Proto-Indo-European language. They have found that the Indo-European languages did spread within distinctive regions for certain societies. British archaeologist Colin Renfrew (1989) hypothesizes that the spread of the Indo-European languages was linked to the spread of a particular technology and material culture. He suggests that the Indo-European languages spread throughout Europe from

Table 12.1 Comparative Word Chart of Indo-European Languages

English	Sanskrit	Latin	Greek	German	Old English
To bear	Bhar	Ferre	Fero	Gebären	Beran
Father	Pitar	Pater	Patir	Vater	Fæder
Mother	Matar	Mater	Mitir	Mutter	Modor
Brother	Bhratar	Frater	Frater	Bruder	Brodor
Three	Trayas	Tres	Treis	Drei	Brie
Hundred	Sata	Centum	Ekaton	Hundert	Hund
Night	Nisitha	Noctis	Nikta	Nacht	Niht
Red	Rudhira	Ruber	Erithros	Rot	Read
Foot	Pada	Pedis	Podos	Fuss	Fot
Fish	Piska	Piscis	Ikhthis	Fisch	Fisc
Goose	Hamsa	Anser	Khin	Gans	Gos
What	Kwo	Quod	Ti	Was	Hwæt
Where	Kva	Quo	Pou	Wo	Hwær

Source: Table from *The Way of Language: An Introduction* by Fred West. Copyright ©1975. Reproduced by permission of Heinle & Heinle, a division of Thomson Learning. Fax 800-730-2215.

Figure 12.1 This family-tree model shows the relationships among the various Indo-European languages.

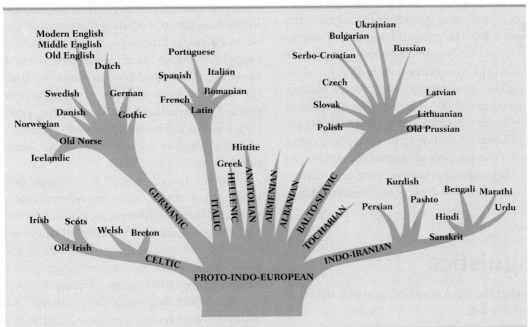

an original homeland in Anatolia, today part of Turkey, as early cultures adopted intensive agriculture. Similarly, English is currently promoted throughout the world as the language of television, computers, and other features of Western technology.

Assessing Language Change

To reconstruct a family tree of languages, the linguist compares the phonological characteristics (sounds) and morphological characteristics (words) of different languages. Linguistic anthropologist Morris Swadesh (1964) developed a systematic method of assessing historical language change. His goal was to date the separation of languages from one another using a statistical technique known as glottochronology (from the Greek *glotta*, meaning "tongue," and *chronos*, meaning "time"). Swadesh reasoned that the vocabulary of a language would remain stable at times, but would change rapidly at other times. Words for plants, animals, or technology would change quickly if the speakers migrated or came into contact with other groups. Swadesh thought, however, that a *core vocabulary* (pronouns and words for numbers or for the body, earth, wood, and stone) would remain immune to cultural change. He thought that if we could measure the rate of retention of this core vocabulary, then we could measure the separation of one language from another.

By comparing core vocabularies from different languages, linguists found that on average, 19 percent of this core vocabulary would change in a language in approximately 1,000 years. In other words, about 81 percent of the core vocabulary would be retained. From this formula, linguistic anthropologists have reconstructed languages and produced "family trees" of languages from around the world.

Through the study of language change, linguistic anthropologists have put to rest the idea that all current languages in the world can be traced to a single language family. Language change has been swift in some circumstances and gradual in others. Multiple borrowings, or the spread of vocabulary and grammar throughout the world, have affected most languages. Linguistic researchers Sarah Thomason and Terrence Kaufman emphasize that many of the world's languages, including Russian, French, and English, have undergone radical change through language mixing (1988). Thomason and Kaufman claim that in the same way that many creole languages have emerged (discussed earlier in this chapter), other languages have developed through intensive culture contact. Instead of language developing from one source, there apparently are different centers and regions of language change.

Sociolinguistics

12.8 Describe what the field of sociolinguistics tells us about language use.

Linguistic anthropologists have researched the use of language in different social contexts, a field known as *sociolinguistics*. The sociolinguist takes the speech community as the framework for understanding the variation of speech in different social contexts. In general, linguistic anthropologists refer to this as the study of **pragmatics**,

the rules for using language within a particular speech community.

The speech community is a social unit within which speakers share various ways of speaking. For example, in American society, certain patterns of English syntax and pronunciation are acceptable in specific contexts (American Standard English), whereas others are considered unacceptable. An American child may sometimes learn nonstandard words in the family environment, and if the family considers them cute, the child may continue to use them. Eventually, however, the child moves out of the family into the larger speech community, encountering speech habits that differ from those of the home. If the child uses those words in school or with others, he or she will be reprimanded or laughed at.

Through a process of enculturation and socialization into the speech community, the child learns the language used in a variety of social contexts. Language plays a prominent role in the process of enculturation. American children learn the regional pronunciation and grammatical usages within their speech community.

Dialectal Differences in Spoken Language

A speech community may consist of subgroups that share specific linguistic usages within a larger common language family. If the linguistic usages of these subgroups are different but mutually intelligible, their language variations are called dialects. **Dialects** are linguistic differences in pronunciation, vocabulary, or syntax that may differ within a single language. For example, dialectal differences in American Standard English exist in the Northeast, Midwest, South, and Southwest of the United States. In the southern United States, one might hear such grammatical constructions as, "It wan't [or weren't] me" and such pronunciations as *Miz* for *Mrs.* and the frequent loss of *r* except before vowels: *foah* for *four*, *heah* for *hear*, and *sulfuh* for *sulfur* (West 1975).

Certain dialects of English are looked on as more prestigious than others, reflecting educational, class, ethnic, race, and regional differences. When viewing language as a global phenomenon, however, all languages are dialects that have emerged in different locales and regions of the world. In actuality, the English language is not one standard language, but consists of many different dialects. To say that British English is more "correct" than American Standard English simply because England is the homeland of English does not make sense to a linguist. The forms of English spoken in England, Australia, Canada, the United States, India, South Africa, and the West Indies have distinctive differences in pronunciation and vocabulary. The same generalization can be applied to many languages and dialects (Pinker 1994).

Some linguists studying speech communities in the United States have concluded that specific regional dialects are gradually disappearing. As people move from one region to another for jobs and education and as television and movies influence speech patterns, Americans are beginning to sound more alike. Many of the same processes are influencing different dialects and languages the world over (Pinker 1994).

African-American Vernacular English (AAVE)

A number of linguists have been doing research on African-American Vernacular English (AAVE), a distinctive dialect of American English spoken by some African-Americans. Popularly, the term *Ebonics* is sometimes used for AAVE. Ebonics is derived from the words *ebony* and *phonics*, meaning "black sounds" (Rickford 1997, 1998). AAVE is also known as Black English Vernacular (BEV), Black English (BE), and African-American English (AAE). The majority of African-Americans do not speak AAVE or Ebonics; however, it is commonly spoken among working-class African-Americans and, in particular, among adolescent African-Americans. Linguistic anthropologists have suggested that Ebonics may have emerged as a creole language under the conditions of slavery in the United States. As slaves from Africa, captured from different areas and speaking an enormous variety of languages, were placed together on plantations in the American South, they developed a pidgin language to communicate. From this pidgin, the children may have created a systematic syntax and grammar, as they were at the critical stage of language learning. Just as Jamaican and Haitian Creole emerged in the Caribbean under the conditions of slavery, a variety of creole languages may have evolved in the United States.

One form of an early creole still exists among African-Americans on the Sea Islands off the coast of South Carolina and Georgia. This creole is known as Gullah, and it is spoken by about 300,000 people. Gullah has some grammatical characteristics that are similar to West African languages; today it has been influenced strongly by standard English and southern regional dialects (Bonvillian 2010). Other forms of creole speech may have been introduced by the large numbers of slaves coming from Jamaica or Barbados into the American South, or they could have emerged within early communities of slaves within the United States. Ebonics may very well be a product of this early creolization.

Linguist John Rickford (1997, 1998) notes that Ebonics or the contemporary dialect AAVE is not just the use of slang. There are some slang terms in AAVE, such as *chillin* ("relaxing") and *homey* ("close friend"), but there is a systematic grammar and pronunciation within the language. Sentences within AAVE have standard usages, such as *He runnin* ("He is running"), *He be running* ("He is usually running"), and *He bin runnin* ("He has been running for a long time and still is"). Other rules, such as dropping

consonants at the end of words such as *tes(t)* and *han(d)*, are evident in Ebonics. Rickford emphasizes that AAVE is not just a lazy form of English; AAVE is no more lazy English than Italian is a lazy form of Latin. These are different dialects within a language, just as Scottish is a dialect of English, with systematically ordered grammar and pronunciation usages.

A controversy regarding Ebonics or AAVE developed in Oakland, California, when the school board announced that it was going to recognize AAVE as a separate language. The school board was committed to teaching American Standard English to the African-American students. However, because of the prejudices and misunderstandings regarding AAVE as "a lazy form of English," the Oakland school board set off a controversy all over the United States. Linguistic anthropologist Ronald Kephart has commented on this Ebonics controversy based on his extensive research on the creoles in the Caribbean (Monaghan, Hinton, and Kephart 1997). Kephart studied creole English on the islands of Carriacou and Grenada. He did research on young students who were reading in the creole language as well as learning standard forms of English. The children who read in the creole language were able to learn the standard forms of English more readily, and they enjoyed the process. Kephart suggests that the recognition of AAVE by the school board in Oakland would help children learn American Standard English. These children would appreciate the fact that the language they brought with them into the school was to be respected as another form of English, and they would develop more positive attitudes about themselves and not be treated as "illiterate" or "lazy" children. This would help promote more effective learning strategies and enable these students to master American Standard English in a more humane manner.

The use of AAVE by some African-Americans also indicates what is referred to by linguistic anthropologists as "code-switching behavior." Some African-Americans use AAVE deliberately as a means of establishing rapport and solidarity with other African-Americans. They may switch to American Standard English in conversations with non-African-Americans, but move back to AAVE depending on the interactional context. This code switching has been documented by linguistic anthropologists in multiple studies (Bonvillian 2010).

Honorifics in Language

Sociolinguists have found that a number of languages contain honorific forms that determine the grammar, syntax, and word usage. Honorific forms of language are used to express differences in social levels among speakers and are common in societies that maintain social inequality and hierarchy. Honorific forms can apply to the interaction between males and females, kin and nonkin, and higher- and lower-status individuals. For example, in many of the Pacific island societies such as Hawaii, a completely separate honorific vocabulary was used when addressing a person who was part of the royal family. People of lower rank were not allowed to use these forms of language among themselves.

In the Thai language, a number of different types of honorific pronouns are used in various social contexts. Factors such as age, social rank, gender, education, officialdom, and royal title influence which pronouns are used. For example, the first-person pronoun *I* for a male is *phom*, a polite form of address between equals. The pronoun for *I* shifts to *kraphom* if a male is addressing a higher-ranking government official or a Buddhist monk. It shifts to *klaawkramom* when a male is addressing the prince of the royal family. All together, there are 13 different forms of the pronoun *I*. Similar differences exist for the other pronouns in Thai to express deference, politeness, and respect (Palakornkul 1972; Scupin 1988).

In the Japanese and Korean languages, honorific forms require speakers to distinguish among several different verb forms and address terms that indicate deference, politeness, or everyday speech. Different speech levels reflect age, gender, social position, and out-groupness (the degree to which a person is considered outside a particular social group) (Martin 1964; Sorensen 2006). Specifically, as discussed in Chapter 11, the Japanese distinguish between *tatemae* and *honne* in all of their linguistic expressions: *Tatemae* is a very polite form of expression used with strangers; *honne* is the expression of "real" feelings and can be used only with close friends and family. The Japanese use "respect markers" with nouns, verbs, and other modifiers to demonstrate deference, politeness, and also gender status differences (Bonvillian 2010).

Greeting Behaviors

The exchange of greetings is the most ordinary, everyday use of language and gesture found universally. Yet, sociolinguistic studies indicate that these routine greeting behaviors are considerably complex and produce different meanings in various social and cultural contexts. In many contexts, English speakers in the United States greet one another with the word *Hi* or *Hello*. (The word *hello* originated from the English phrase *healthy be thou*.) Members of U.S. society also greet one another with questions such as "How are you?" or "How's it going?" or "What do you know?" or the somewhat popular, but fading "Whassup?" In most contexts, these questions are not considered serious questions, and these exchanges of greetings are accompanied by a wave or a nod, a smile, or other gesture of recognition. They are familiar phrases that are used

as exchanges in greetings. These greetings require little thought and seem almost mechanical.

Among Muslim populations around the world, the typical greeting between two males is the shaking of hands accompanied by the Arab utterance *As-salam ale-kum*, "May the peace of [Allah] be with you." This is the phrase used by Muslims even in non-Arabic-speaking societies. The Qur'an, the sacred religious text of Muslims, has an explicit requirement regarding this mode of greeting for the male Muslim community (Caton 1986). A similar greeting of *Shalom aleichem*, "May peace be with you," is found among the Jewish populace throughout the world. In some Southeast Asian societies such as Vietnam, the typical greeting translates into English as, "Have you eaten rice?"

All these greetings express a concern for another person's well-being. Although the English and Vietnamese greetings appear to be concerned with the physical condition of the person, whereas the Arab and Jewish phrases have a more spiritual connotation, they all essentially serve the same social purpose: They enable humans to interact in harmonious ways.

Yet, there is a great deal more social information contained in these brief greeting exchanges than appears on the surface. For example, an English-speaking person in the United States can usually identify the different types of social contexts for the following greeting exchanges:

1. "Hi, Mr. Thomas!"
   "Hello, Johnny. How are you?"

2. "Good morning, Monica."
   "Good morning, sir."

3. "Sarah! How are you? You look great!"
   "Bill! It's so good to see you!"

4. "Good evening, Congressman."
   "Hello there. Nice to see you."

In greeting 1, the speakers are a child and an adult; in 2, there is a difference in status, and the speakers may be an employer and employee; in 3, these speakers are close acquaintances; in 4, the second speaker does not remember or know the other person very well (Hickerson 1980).

One of the authors of this text did a systematic sociolinguistic study of greeting behaviors found among different ethnic and religious groups in Thailand (Scupin 1988). Precise cultural norms determine the forms of greetings given to people of different status levels and ethnic groups. The traditional greeting of Thai Buddhists on meeting one another is expressed by each raising both hands, palm to palm, and lightly touching the body between the face and chest. Simultaneously, the person utters a polite verbal phrase. This salutation, known as the *waaj* (pronounced "why"), varies in different social contexts. The person who is inferior in social status (determined by age and social class) initiates the *waaj*, and the higher the hands are raised, the greater the deference and politeness expressed. For example, a young child will *waaj* a superior by placing the fingertips above the eyebrows, whereas a superior returning a *waaj* will raise the fingertips only to the chest. A superior seldom performs a *waaj* when greeting someone of an inferior status. Other ethnic and religious groups such as the Muslims in Thailand use the *waaj* in formal interactions with Thai Buddhists, but among themselves, they use the traditional Muslim greeting described previously.

Another form of Thai greeting found among Buddhists includes the *kraab*, which involves kneeling down and bowing to the floor in conjunction with the *waaj* in expressing respect to a superior political or religious official. The *kraab* is used to greet a high-ranking member of the royal family, a Buddhist monk, a respected official, and, traditionally, one's parents (Anuman-Rajadhon 1961; Scupin 1988). These deferential forms of greeting are found in other societies that maintain social hierarchies based on royal authority or political or religious principles.

Although greeting behaviors differ from one society to another, anthropologists find that all peoples throughout the world have a means to greet one another to establish a basis for social interaction and demonstrate their concern for one another's welfare.

A Cambodian woman greeting a Buddhist monk

Arab men kissing one another on the cheek as a greeting.

Nonverbal Communication

12.9 Discuss other forms of communication humans use besides language.

In interacting with other people, we use nonverbal cues, as well as speech. As with language, nonverbal communication varies in human populations, in contrast to the nonverbal communication of nonhuman animals. Dogs, cats, and other animals have no difficulty communicating with one another in nonverbal ways. Human nonverbal communication, however, is extremely varied. It is often said that humans are the only creatures who can misunderstand one another.

Kinesics

Some anthropological linguists study gestures and other forms of body language. The study of **kinesics** is concerned with body motion and gestures used in nonverbal communication. Researchers estimate that humans use more than 250,000 facial expressions. Many of these expressions have different meanings in various circumstances. For example, the smile indicates pleasure, happiness, or friendliness in all parts of the world. Yet in certain contexts, a smile may signify an insult (Birdwhistle 1970). Thus, the movement of the head, eyes, eyebrows, and hands or the posture of the body may be associated with specific symbolic meanings that are culturally defined.

Many types of nonverbal communication differ from society to society. Americans point to things with their fingers, whereas other peoples point with only their eyes, their chins, or their heads. Shaking our head up and down means "yes" and from side to side means "no," but in parts of India, Greece, and Turkey, the opposite is true. An "A–OK" sign in the United States or England means "you are all right," but it means "you are worth zero" in France or Belgium, and it is a very vulgar sign in Greece and Turkey (Ekman, Friesen, and Bear 1984). Pointing to your head means "he or she is smart" in the United States, whereas it means "stupid" in Europe. The "V" sign of the 1960s meant "peace"; in contrast, in World War II England, it meant "victory"; in Greece, it is an insult. Obviously, humans can easily misunderstand each other because of the specific cultural meanings of nonverbal gestures.

Despite all these differences, however, research has revealed certain universal features associated with some facial expressions. For example, research by psychologist Paul Ekman and his colleagues suggests that there are some basic uniformities regarding certain facial expressions. Peoples from various societies recognize facial expressions indicating emotional states such as happiness, grief, disgust, fear, surprise, and anger. Ekman studied peoples recently contacted by Western society, such as the Fore people of Papua New Guinea (Ekman 1973). When shown photos of facial expressions, the Fore had no difficulty determining the basic emotions that were being expressed. This research overlaps the psychological anthropology studies of emotions discussed in the previous chapter. Ekman has concluded that some universal emotional expressions are evident in certain facial displays of humans throughout the world.

Some human facial expressions are based on universally recognized emotions.

Proxemics

Another nonverbal aspect of communication involves the use of space. **Proxemics** is the study of how people in different societies perceive and use space. Studies by Edward T. Hall (1981), the pioneering anthropologist in this area, indicate that no universal rules apply to the use of space. In American society, people maintain a different amount of "personal space" in different situations: We communicate with intimate acquaintances at a range of about 18 inches; however, with nonintimates, our space expands according to how well we know the person. In some other societies, people communicate at very close distances irrespective of the relationship among them.

Nonverbal communication is an important aspect of social interaction. Obvious gestural movements, such as bowing in Japan and shaking hands in the United States, may have a deep symbolic significance in certain contexts. The study of nonverbal communication will enrich our understanding of human behavior and might even improve communication among different societies.

Summary and Review of Learning Objectives

12.1 Compare and contrast how the laboratory studies of nonhuman animal communication differs from what is found in the studies of nonhuman animals in the wild.

A number of researchers in laboratory studies were able to teach chimpanzees various signs through gesture use. In some cases, these chimpanzees were able to combine these signs to communicate. A later study indicated that researchers may have been cuing chimpanzees to elicit particular signs or gestures. Sue Savage-Rumbaugh has tried to eliminate the methodological problem of giving ambiguous hand signs to train chimpanzees in her laboratory studies. She taught a 10-year-old *bonobo*, or "pygmy" chimpanzee named Kanzi to communicate with lexigrams, the graphic, geometric word-symbols that act as substitutes for human speech; By age six, Kanzi had mastered a vocabulary of ninety symbols. However, the chimpanzees or gorillas in laboratory settings do not progress beyond that of a human child of two and a half. In contrast to the laboratory studies, the field studies of chimpanzees and gorillas in their native habitats demonstrated that they used calls and gestures that were directly tied to their emotional states, such as fear, annoyance, or sexual excitement.

12.2 Discuss what makes human languages unique in comparison with nonhuman animal communication.

Modern studies on animal communication suggest that the language gap separating humans from other animals is not as wide as it once appeared. These studies also indicate that fundamental differences exist between animal communication and human languages. The question is not whether animals can communicate; we know that almost every animal can. However, linguistic anthropologists have identified a number of distinctive characteristics of human languages that make it distinct from nonhuman animal communication. The four most important features are productivity, displacement, arbitrariness, and combining sounds. Productivity refers to how users of human languages, even small children, can create sentences never heard before by anyone. Displacement means that humans can discuss the past, present, future and many abstract phenomena. Arbitrariness refers to how the sounds of language and words rarely have a relationship or connection to the meaning of the objects or abstract notions they represent. And, combining sounds is also a unique feature of human languages. Nonhuman animals are not able to combine sounds to create new meanings.

12.3 Describe what anthropologists conclude about the evolution of language.

Anthropologists have concluded that the earliest hominins did not have the language capacities of modern humans. However, new research indicates that the FOXP2 gene found in the DNA of both Neandertals and modern *Homo sapiens* that are associated with language and speech may have evolved as early as 300,000 years ago. Other aspects of language may have developed in relationship to gestural abilities of early hominins. Some linguists and primatologists believe that the emergence of human language suggests that at some point in the expansion of the brain, a rewiring of the human brain developed that allowed for what is known as *recursion*, the linguistic capacity to build an infinite number of sentences within sentences.

12.4 Discuss how linguistic anthropologists study language.

Linguistic anthropologists study the structure of language by examining sound patterns (phonology), the meaning of words (morphology), and how these meaningful units are put together in phrases and sentences (syntax). They also focus on the meaning (semantics) of different terms used to classify reality. Although there are many differences in how people in various societies use terms to describe kinship relations and physical phenomena, cognitive anthropologists have found some universals, such as the way people classify relatives. This suggests that humans have common biological capacities that determine how they perceive certain aspects of reality.

12.5 Explain how children acquire their languages.

Current research on language acquisition indicates that children are born with a brain *prewired* to enable humans to acquire language easily. This prewiring is associated with what Noam Chomsky calls a *universal grammar*. Universal grammar serves as a template, or model, against which a child matches and sorts out the patterns of morphemes and phonemes and the subtle distinctions that are needed to communicate in any language. Thus, children are innately wired to be able to acquire any language that they are exposed to at an early age. The formation of creole languages found in many societies with multiple languages provides evidence for Chomsky's model of language acquisition.

12.6 Discuss the relationship between language and culture.

Early anthropologists such as Edward Sapir and Benjamin Whorf argued that the language that one acquires had a definitive influence on the perception of time, space, and other cultural phenomena. Current research indicates that the Sapir-Whorf hypothesis is limited in explaining how language determines culture; however, a weaker form of this hypothesis appears to be valid in demonstrating how language influences our perceptions and culture.

12.7 Describe how anthropologists study the history of languages.

Historical linguistics is the study of how languages are related to one another and how they have diverged from one another. Linguistic anthropologists have examined the historical relationships among languages by studying the phonology, words, syntax, and semantics through systematic methods such as glottochronology. This research has helped understand how languages change through time.

12.8 Describe what the field of sociolinguistics tells us about language use.

Sociolinguistics focuses on the relationship between language and society. It examines social interactions and the ways in which people use certain linguistic expressions that reflect the dialect patterns of their speech community. Researchers have found that many languages have nuances in linguistic usage such as greeting patterns or speech differences that vary according to age, gender, and status.

12.9 Discuss other forms of communication humans use beside language.

The study of nonverbal communication is also a rich field for linguistic anthropology. Although much nonverbal communication varies around the world, some forms can be understood universally. Anthropologists focus on the use of body language (kinesics) and the use of space (proxemics) to understand better how people supplement their spoken language skills with nonverbal communication.

Key Terms

communication, p. 270
dialects, p. 286
ethologists, p. 272
kinesics, p. 290
language, p. 270
morphemes, p. 276

morphology, p. 276
phoneme, p. 274
phones, p. 276
phonology, p. 275
pragmatics, p. 286
protolanguage, p. 284

proxemics, p. 291
Sapir–Whorf hypothesis, p. 282
semantics, p. 277
syntax, p. 276

Chapter 13
Anthropological Explanations

Learning Objectives

After reading this chapter you should be able to:

13.1 Explain the weaknesses of the nineteenth-century unilineal evolutionary approaches in anthropology.

13.2 Describe the basic strengths and weaknesses of the diffusionist approach in understanding different cultures.

13.3 Discuss historical particularism developed by Franz Boas.

13.4 Explain the differences between structural functionalism and psychological functionalism.

13.5 Discuss the twentieth-century neoevolutionary approaches, including cultural materialism.

13.6 Describe the Marxist approach in anthropology that emerged in the 1970s.

13.7 Discuss the symbolic anthropology approach as a humanist method.

13.8 Discuss the approach of feminist anthropologists.

13.9 Discuss the strengths and weaknesses of the postmodern approach in anthropology.

In his conclusion to an excellent book titled *Culture, Self, and Meaning* (2000), anthropologist Victor de Munck writes about how anthropology needs to engage itself in an interdisciplinary effort to understand human behavior and culture. He refers to the ancient Hindu-Buddhist story regarding the blind men and the elephant. This story was popularized by the nineteenth-century poet John Godfrey Saxe in 1900 and begins:

> It was six men of Indostan
>   To learning much inclined
> Who went to see the Elephant
>   (Though all of them were blind),
> That each by observation
>   Might satisfy his mind.
> The First approached the Elephant,
>   And happening to fall
> Against his broad and sturdy side,
>   At once began to bawl:
> "God bless me! but the Elephant
>   Is very like a wall!"

In the poem, each of the blind men steps forward to examine the elephant. One feels the tusk and says the elephant is like a spear. Another grabs the trunk and likens the elephant to a snake. The poet concludes:

> And so these men of Indostan
>   Disputed loud and long,
> Each in his own opinion
>   Exceeding stiff and strong,
> Though each was partly in the right
>   And all were in the wrong!

Thus, each of the blind men was mistaking his own limited understanding of the part of the elephant for the fuller reality of the whole. In this chapter on anthropological explanations, we need to keep this fable in mind. Anthropologists in every age have been attempting to understand humanity as a whole, but in reality, they had only partial understandings. Yet, each of these types of explanations has provided some limited perspectives on human behavior and culture. And, eventually, the knowledge accumulated from these partial perspectives has been probed and evaluated by anthropologists to offer a far more comprehensive picture of humanity in the twenty-first century than what we had in earlier centuries.

Another thing we need to keep in mind in this chapter is that anthropology consists of both the scientific and the humanistic orientations. In Chapter 1, we discussed the scientific method and its application to anthropology. In that discussion, we noted how anthropologists collect and classify data and then develop and test hypotheses. In the physical sciences, scientists use hypotheses to formulate theories from which they make predictions about natural phenomena. Chemists can rely on precise mathematical laws to help them deduce and predict what will happen

This photo of a Japanese woodblock print illustrates the story of the "Blind Men and the Elephant."

when two chemical elements interact with one another. Physicists can predict from laws of gravity and motion what will happen when a spherical object is dropped from a building at a certain speed. These types of predictions allow engineers to produce aircraft that use certain fuels and withstand various physical pressures, enabling them to fly long distances.

Although anthropology relies on the scientific method, its major objective is to provide explanations of human society and behavior. Human behavior is extremely complicated. The product of many different, interacting variables, it can seldom, if ever, be predicted. Anthropologists cannot predict the outcome of interactions between two individuals or among small groups, let alone among large groups at the societal level. Consequently, anthropology as a discipline does not have any specific theories and laws that can be used to predict human action or thought. For the most part, anthropologists restrict their efforts to testing hypotheses and improving their explanations of human society and behavior.

We need to remember that anthropology also employs methods in the humanities to interpret human endeavors in religion, art, folklore, oral and written poetry, and other complex symbolic activities. This chapter will examine both the scientific and the humanistic attempts to comprehend the differences and similarities of human behavior and cultures.

Nineteenth-Century Evolutionism

13.1 Explain the weaknesses of the nineteenth-century unilineal evolutionary approaches in anthropology.

Although many philosophers and historians in Western society, including Aristotle and Herodotus in Greek society and later Europeans such as John Locke, Immanuel Kant, and Johann Gottfried Herder, reflected on the concept of culture, it was nineteenth-century anthropologists who began to investigate the concept of "culture" as used today. Modern anthropology emerged from the intellectual atmosphere of the Enlightenment, an eighteenth- and nineteenth-century philosophical movement that stressed social progress based on human reason, and Darwin's theory of evolution based on naturalistic rather than supernatural explanations of humanity. The first professional anthropologist—that is, an individual appointed to an academic position in anthropology—was a nineteenth-century British scholar, Edward B. Tylor. In 1871, Tylor published a major work titled *Primitive Culture*. At that time, Great Britain was involved in imperialistic expansion all over the world. Tylor thus had access to descriptions of non-Western societies through his contacts with travelers, explorers, missionaries, traders, and government officials. He combined these descriptions with nineteenth-century philosophy and Charles Darwin's ideas to develop a theory of societal evolution.

Unilineal Evolution: Tylor

The major question addressed by early anthropologists was: Why are societies at similar or different levels of evolution and development? Many people ask the same kinds of questions today. Tylor tried to answer that question through an explanation known as unilineal evolution. **Unilineal evolution** is the view that societies evolve in a single direction toward complexity, progress, and civilization. Tylor's basic argument was that because all humans are bestowed with innate rational faculties, they are continuously improving their societies. Through this process of evolution, societies move toward "progress" and "civilization."

In arriving at this conclusion, Tylor used accounts from Western observers to compare certain cultural elements from different societies, including technology, family, economy, political organization, art, religion, and philosophy. He then organized this evidence into categories or stages, ranging from what he termed "savagery" to "barbarism" to "civilization" (see Figure 13.1). Theorists like Tylor assumed that hunter-gatherers and other non-Western societies were living at a lower level of existence than were the "civilized" societies of Europe. This was an ethnocentric view of societal development based on the belief that Western society is the center of the civilized world and that non-Western societies are inherently inferior.

Tylor and other nineteenth-century thinkers also claimed that "primitives" would eventually evolve through the stages of barbarism to become civilized like British gentlemen and ladies. However, Tylor believed that these societies would need some assistance from the civilized world to reach this stage.

Unilineal Evolution: Morgan

Another nineteenth-century anthropologist who developed a unilineal scheme of evolution was an American, Lewis Henry Morgan (1818–1881). Morgan was a lawyer and banker who became fascinated with Native American Indian societies. He gathered information on the customs, language, and other cultural aspects of the Iroquois-speaking peoples of upstate New York. Eventually, under the auspices of the Smithsonian Institution, he distributed questionnaires to missionaries and travelers to collect information about many other non-Western societies.

Edward B. Tylor (1832–1917)

Figure 13.1 Edward Tylor's view of unilineal evolution

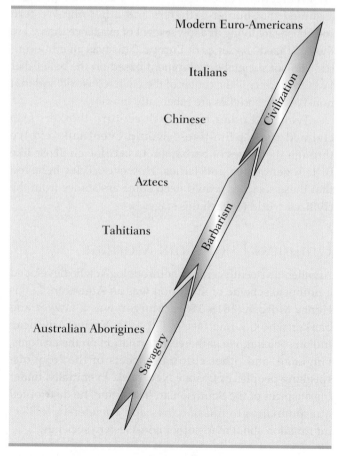

Morgan and Kinship Theories Morgan was particularly interested in kinship terms used in different parts of the world. He observed that the Iroquois kinship terms were very different from those of English, Roman, Greek, and other European societies. He also noticed that these kinship terms were similar to those of the Ojibwa Indians, a group living in the midwestern United States. This led him to explore the relationship between the Iroquois and other peoples. Using the aforementioned questionnaires, he requested specific information on kinship terms from people all over the world.

From these data, Morgan began to conceive of the evolution of the family in a worldwide sense. He speculated that humans originally lived in "primitive hordes," in which sexual behavior was not regulated and individuals did not know who their fathers were. He based this assumption on the discovery that certain peoples, such as Hawaiians, use one general term to classify their father and all male relatives in their father's generation (see Chapter 12). He postulated that brother-sister marriage then developed, followed by group marriage, and eventually by a matriarchal family structure in which women held economic and political power. Morgan believed that the final stage of the evolution of the family began when males took control of the economy and politics, instituting a patriarchal system.

In addition to exploring the evolution of the family, Morgan, like Tylor, surveyed technological, economic, political, and religious conditions throughout the world. He compiled this evidence in his book *Ancient Society* ([1877] 1964) which presented his overall scheme of the evolution of society. Paralleling Tylor's views, Morgan believed in a hierarchy of evolutionary development from "savagery" to "civilization."

According to Morgan, one crucial distinction between civilized society and earlier societies is private property. He described the "savage" societies as "communistic," in contrast to "civilized" societies, whose institutions are based on private property.

Unilineal Evolution: A Critique

Although these nineteenth-century thinkers shared the view that humanity was progressing through various stages of development, their views were ethnocentric, contradictory, and speculative and their evidence secondhand, based on the accounts of biased Europeans. The unilineal scheme of evolution was much too simplistic to account for the development of different societies.

In general, the unilineal evolutionists relied on nineteenth-century racist views of human development and misunderstandings of biological evolution to explain

Lewis Henry Morgan (1818–1881)

societal differences. For example, both Morgan and Tylor believed that people in various societies have different levels of intelligence. They believed that the people in so-called "savage societies" were less intelligent than those in "civilized societies." As will be discussed in Chapter 23, this view of different levels of intelligence among different groups is no longer accepted by the scientific community or modern anthropologists. Nevertheless, despite their inadequate theories and speculations regarding the evolution of society, these early anthropologists provided the first systematic methods for thinking about and explaining the similarities and diversity of human societies. Like the blind men and the elephant, these anthropologists had only a limited perception and understanding of human behavior and culture.

Diffusionism

13.2 Describe the basic strengths and weaknesses of the diffusionist approach in understanding different cultures.

Another school of thought that used the comparative method to explain why different societies are at different levels of development is diffusionism. **Diffusionism**, which developed in the early part of the twentieth century, maintains that societal change occurs when societies *borrow* cultural traits from one another. Cultural knowledge regarding technology, economic ideas, religious views, or art forms spreads, or diffuses, from one society to another. There were two major schools of diffusionism: the British version associated with G. Elliot Smith and William J. Perry and the German version associated with Father Wilhelm Schmidt.

British Diffusionism

The British school of diffusionism derived its theory from research on ancient Egypt. Smith and Perry were specialists in Egyptian culture and had carried out research in Egyptology for a number of years. From this experience, they concluded that all aspects of civilizations, from technology to religion, originated in Egypt and diffused to other cultural areas. To explain the fact that some cultures no longer had cultural traits from Egypt, they resorted to an ethnocentric view, maintaining that some cultures had simply become "degenerate." That is, in contrast to the civilized world, the less-developed peoples had simply forgotten the original ideas borrowed from Egypt.

German Diffusionism

The German school of diffusionism differed somewhat from the British school. Schmidt and his followers argued that several early centers of civilization had existed and that from these early centers cultural traits diffused outward in circles to other regions and peoples. In German, this view is referred to as the *Kulturkreise* (culture circles) school of thought. In explaining why some primitive societies did not have the characteristics of civilization, the German school, like that of the British diffusionists, argued that these peoples had simply degenerated. Thus, diffusionist views, like the unilineal evolutionary views,

The Great Giza pyramid of Egypt. Some early anthropologists believed that all civilizations stemmed from ancient Egypt.

represent ethnocentric perspectives of human societies outside the mainstream of Western civilization.

The Limitations and Strengths of Diffusionism

Early diffusionist views were based on erroneous assumptions regarding humankind's innovative capacities. Like the unilineal theorists, diffusionists maintained racist assumptions about the inherent inferiority of different non-Western peoples. They assumed that some people were not sufficiently innovative to develop their own cultural traits.

Another limitation of the diffusionist approach is its assumption that cultural traits in the same geographical vicinity will inevitably spread from one society to another. Anthropologists find that diffusion is not an inevitable process. Societies can adjoin one another without exchanging cultural traits. For example, as we saw in Chapter 10, generations of Amish people in the United States have deliberately maintained their traditional ways despite being part of a nation in which modern technology is predominant.

However, diffusionism as a means of understanding societal development does have some validity. For instance, diffusionism helps explain the emergence of the classical civilizations of Egypt, Greece, Phoenicia, and Rome. These peoples maintained continuous contact through trade and travel, borrowing many cultural traits from one another, such as writing systems. Thus, these anthropologists, again like the blind men and the elephant, had some partial explanations to offer on human behavior and society.

Historical Particularism

13.3 Discuss historical particularism developed by Franz Boas.

An early twentieth-century movement that developed in response to the unilineal evolutionary theory was led by the U.S. anthropologist Franz Boas. This movement proposed an alternative answer to why societal similarities and differences exist. Boas was educated in Germany as a natural scientist. Eventually, he conducted fieldwork among the Eskimo (Inuit) in northern Canada and a Native American tribe known as the Kwakiutl or *Kwakwaka'wakw*, who lived on the northwest coast. He later solidified his position as the nation's foremost leader in anthropology at Columbia University in New York, where he trained many pioneers in the field until his retirement in 1937. Boas had a tremendous impact on the development of anthropology in the United States and internationally.

Boas versus the Unilineal Evolutionists

Boas became a vigorous opponent of the unilineal evolutionists. He criticized their attempts to propose stages of evolution through which all societies pass. He also criticized their use of the comparative method and the haphazard manner in which they organized the data to fit their theories of evolutionary stages. He maintained that these nineteenth-century schemes of evolution were based on insufficient empirical evidence. Boas called for an end to "armchair anthropology," in which scholars took data from travelers, traders, and missionaries and plugged them into a speculative model of evolution. He proposed that all anthropologists do rigorous, scientifically based fieldwork to collect basic ethnographic data.

Boas's fieldwork experience and his intellectual training in Germany led him to conclude that each society has its own unique historical development. This theory, known as **historical particularism**, maintains that each society must be understood as a product of its own history. This view led Boas to adopt the notion of cultural relativism, the belief that each society should be understood in terms of its own cultural practices and values (see Chapter 10). One aspect of this view is that no society evolved to a level higher or lower than that of another. Thus, we cannot rank any particular society above another in terms of degree of savagery, barbarity, or civility. Boas called for an end to the use of derogatory ethnocentric terms.

The Boasian view became the dominant theoretical trend in anthropology during the first half of the twentieth century. Anthropologists began to do rigorous ethnographic fieldwork in different societies to gather sound empirical evidence. Boas instituted the *participant observation method* as a basic research strategy of ethnographic fieldwork (see Chapter 14). This strategy enabled ethnographers to gather valid empirical data to explain human behavior. Boas also encouraged his students to develop their linguistic skills so that they could learn the languages of the peoples they studied.

Boas worked in all four subfields of anthropology: physical anthropology, archaeology, ethnology, and linguistics. Some of his most important work involved taking precise assessments of the physical characteristics, including brain size and cranial capacity, of people in different societies. Boas was one of the first scientists in the United States to demonstrate that the brain size and cranial capacity of modern humans are not linked directly to intelligence. Prior to his studies many believed that different races had less intelligence than others based on brain size or cranial capacities. His research indicated that brain size and cranial capacity differ widely within all races.

Boas's findings challenged the racist assumptions put forward by the unilineal evolutionists. They also repudiated the type of racism that characterized black-white relations in the United States, as well as Nazi theories of racial superiority.

A direct outgrowth of the Boasian approach was the emergence of *culture-and-personality theory* in American anthropology. Boas trained two particularly noteworthy students, Ruth Benedict and Margaret Mead, pioneering anthropologists whose research was described in Chapter 11. The anthropological school represented by Benedict and Mead led to the development of more careful research regarding personality and culture. The methods used in this field have been refined and tested by many anthropologists. As a result, we now have a better understanding of enculturation and personality formation in human societies. Boas's efforts set the stage for a sound scientific approach in anthropology that led to definite progress in our comprehension of race and other issues in explaining human behavior and culture. Additionally, Boas pioneered the study of art, religion, folklore, music, dance, and oral literature, providing the humanistic aspect of the anthropological enterprise.

The contribution to anthropology of Boas and historical particularism was the recognition and importance of culture on the conscious and unconscious mind of individuals within specific regions of the world. Boas and his students emphasized the significance of cultural differences among peoples and criticized the earlier, racialistic explanations for behavior and culture. The

weakness of this historical particularism approach is that it tended to eschew any cross-cultural explanations for human behavior. Currently, most anthropologists agree that cross-cultural regularities, universals, and variations do exist.

Functionalism

13.4 **Explain the differences between structural functionalism and psychological functionalism.**

At approximately the same time that Boas and his U.S. students were questioning the claims of the unilineal evolutionists, British anthropologists were developing their own criticisms through the school of thought known as functionalism. **Functionalism** is the view that society consists of institutions that serve vital purposes for people. Instead of focusing on the origins and evolution of society, as the unilineal theorists did, the British functionalists explored the relationships among different institutions and how these institutions function to serve the society or the individual. The question of whether these institutions serve the interests of the society at large or the interests of the individual divided the school of functionalism into two camps, each associated with a prominent figure in British anthropology. These two figures were A. R. Radcliffe-Brown and Bronislaw Malinowski.

Structural Functionalism: Radcliffe-Brown

The type of functionalism associated with Radcliffe-Brown is sometimes referred to as *structural functionalism*. Radcliffe-Brown had done research in Africa and on the Andaman Islands in southeastern Asia. He focused on social structures as reflected in the differing institutions that function to perpetuate the survival of *society*. He argued that a society's economic, social, political, and religious institutions serve to integrate the society as a whole. For example, he studied the social institutions that function to enhance group solidarity in small-scale societies. In some of his research, he emphasized how males had to marry outside their particular clan into another clan. Once the male marries, he establishes an important relationship with his wife's kin. Because he is an outsider, he has to show extreme respect to his new in-laws so that he does not produce hostility. The male may also establish a "joking relationship" with them, whereby hostility is reduced by playful teasing. Radcliffe-Brown suggested that all norms for specific behaviors and obligations among different people in kinship relationships promote order and stability. Thus, to Radcliffe-Brown, these social institutions serve society's needs.

Franz Boas (1858–1942).

Psychological Functionalism: Malinowski

Malinowski's functionalism differed from that of Radcliffe-Brown in that it focused on how society functions to serve the *individual's* interests or needs. This view is known as *psychological functionalism*. Malinowski did his major ethnographic study in the Trobriand Islands off the coast of Papua New Guinea. He tried to demonstrate how individuals use cultural norms to satisfy certain needs.

Malinowski's analysis of magic among the Trobriand Islanders illustrates his psychological functionalism. He observed that when the islanders went fishing in enclosed lagoons where fishing was reliable and safe, they depended on their technical knowledge and skill alone. When they went fishing on the open sea, however, which was more dangerous and highly unpredictable, they employed extensive magical beliefs and techniques. Thus, Malinowski argued that the use of magic arises in situations in which humans have no control over circumstances, such as weather. Magical techniques are used to reduce internal anxieties and tensions for these individuals. In addition to magic, the Trobrianders have an elaborate system of beliefs concerning death, the afterlife, sickness, and health. These beliefs aid in serving the needs of individuals as they adapt to the circumstances and exigencies of life. In other words, the individual has needs, both physiological and psychological, and cultural institutions, customs, and traditions exist to satisfy them.

The Limitations of Functionalism

Like the other early developments in anthropology, functionalism has its theoretical weaknesses. It fails to explain why societies are different or similar. Why do some societies have different types of institutions, such as the extended family, when similar ones, such as the nuclear family, might be able to serve the same function? This weakness arose from the tendency of functionalists to ignore historical processes. They were not concerned with the historical development of differing institutions, but rather focused exclusively on how these institutions serve society and the individual. They could not explain, for example, why British society experienced rapid technological change, whereas other societies did not, when all of these societies had similar needs.

Functionalists were also unable to explain social and cultural change very well because they tended to view societies as static and unchanging. They could not explain why, if all institutions perform a particular function, these institutions would need to change.

Functionalism as a school of thought has influenced a great deal of research in anthropology. By focusing on the detailed, specific functions of institutions within existing societies, it encouraged the collection of valuable ethnographic data. As with Boas in U.S. anthropology, Radcliffe-Brown and Malinowski moved their field beyond the speculative theories of the "armchair anthropologists."

Twentieth-Century Evolutionism

13.5 Discuss the twentieth-century neoevolutionary approaches, including cultural materialism.

After World War II, some anthropologists renewed their interest in evolutionary explanations of societal and cultural phenomena. Up until that time, most anthropologists had devoted themselves to criticizing the unilineal evolutionists. But some anthropologists, led by Leslie White of the University of Michigan, suggested a new, twentieth-century perspective on the evolution of society, which is sometimes referred to as *neoevolutionism*.

Bronislaw Malinowski in the Trobriand Islands

White treated societies, or *sociocultural systems*, as entities that evolved in relation to the amount of energy captured and used by each member of society. This energy is directed toward the production of resources for their survival. In White's words, "Culture evolves as the amount of energy harnessed per capita per year is increased, or as the efficiency of the instrumental means of putting the energy to work is increased" ([1949] 1971, 368). In other words, the degree of societal development is measured by the amount of energy harnessed by these sociocultural systems. The greater energy resources available, the more highly evolved the sociocultural system.

White's hypothesis of cultural evolution explained the differences in levels of societal development by examining differences in technology and energy production. For example, he hypothesized that small-scale hunting-and-gathering societies had not developed complex sociocultural systems because they depended primarily on human energy for production. Because of a limited energy source for producing resources, their societies were simple, meager, and undeveloped. But following the agricultural revolution and the capture of energy through the domestication of plants and animals, sociocultural systems changed dramatically. The agricultural revolution represented an efficient use of human energy in harnessing new energy reserves, such as using draft animals to pull plows. In turn, these technological changes led to the emergence of cities, complex states, powerful political and religious elites, and new ideologies.

According to White, tracing the modern industrial age, as fossil-fuel technology developed, new forms of energy such as coal, oil, and natural gas were used, and sociocultural changes accelerated. Up until the Industrial Revolution, the changes in agricultural societies had been gradual, taking several thousand years. In contrast, the Industrial Revolution has taken less than 500 years to produce widespread global transformations. Because White focused on sociocultural change on the global level, rather than in particular societies, his approach has been called *general evolution*.

Steward and Cultural Ecology

At about the same period of time, anthropologist Julian Steward turned his attention to the evolution of society. Steward was instrumental in establishing the field of cultural ecology. Also called *ecological anthropology*, **cultural ecology** stresses the interrelationship among the natural conditions in the environment—rainfall, temperature, soils—and technology, social organization, and attitudes within a particular sociocultural system. Steward focused on how specific sociocultural systems adapt to environmental conditions.

Steward's cultural-ecology framework divides sociocultural systems into two different spheres: the culture core and secondary features. The *culture core* consists of those elements most closely related to subsistence: the environment, technology, and economic arrangements. The other characteristics, such as social organization, politics, and religion, constitute *secondary features* of society. Because Steward investigated the detailed characteristics of different environments, his approach is referred to as *specific evolution*, as opposed to White's general evolution. Steward emphasized that cultural evolution was not unilineal, but *multilineal*. **Multilineal evolution** is the view that societies and cultures have evolved and are evolving in many different directions. One of his most illustrative case studies involved the Shoshone Indians of the Great Basin of the western United States.

A Case Study: The Shoshone   The Shoshone were hunter-gatherer groups whose society revolved around gathering seeds, pine nuts, roots, and berries and hunting rabbits and antelopes. Steward discovered that these subsistence activities had definite effects on the organization of Shoshone kinship groups. Like all hunter-gatherer societies, the Shoshone were nomadic, moving from one location to another based on the availability of food. The Shoshone lived in a hot, dry desert environment that supported meager supplies of plants and animals. These people were forced to live in small, elementary family units and travel frequently in search of food. For a few months in the winter, however, they could live in larger social groups among interrelated family units because of the supply of pine nuts in the mountains. Thus, the environment and the availability of resources had a definite influence on the form of social organization during different seasons for these hunter-gatherer societies.

Through cases like this, Steward demonstrated how environmental influences (part of the culture core) affect the cultural developments in a sociocultural system. Steward used this approach to examine the agricultural civilizations of South America, Mesoamerica, the Near East, and the Far East. He found remarkable parallels in the evolution of these different civilizations. They all had irrigation systems, specialized occupations, centralized governments, and formalized state religions. Steward emphasized that many of these parallels were the result of similar environmental conditions, such as river valleys and alluvial plains that offered opportunities for the emergence of agricultural civilizations.

The Strengths of Neoevolutionism

The twentieth-century evolutionists differed from the nineteenth-century evolutionists in several ways. First, they did not assume a unilineal direction of society through formalized stages such as savagery, barbarism, and civilization. In later chapters, we will demonstrate how different forms of societies developed in relationship to variant geographical, prehistoric, and historical circumstances, a contribution that the neoevolutionists made to our current understanding of societal development. Second, they were not ethnocentrically biased or racist when it came to understanding why different societies are at various levels of development. They abandoned crude terms such as "savagery" and explored environment, technology, and energy resources in assessing levels of sociocultural development. Third, they did not assume that sociocultural evolution toward complexity (or "civilization") is always equated with "progress," as did the nineteenth-century theorists. The neoevolutionists held that some aspects of small-scale societies are, in fact, better than those of complex societies. For example, in some respects, family and social relationships tend to be more stable in small-scale societies than in large, complex societies.

Cultural ecology has become an extremely sophisticated area of research. It has been influenced by developments in biological ecology and theories derived from mathematics, computer modeling, and related sciences. Cultural ecologists do careful research on energy expenditures, use of resources, exchanges of nutrients, and population, as well as on the interrelations among these factors and with cultural values. As we shall see in later chapters, the research findings of ecological anthropology help to explain some basic sociocultural similarities and differences.

Criticisms of Cultural Ecology

A number of anthropologists have criticized the cultural-ecology approach for a variety of reasons. Early critics claimed that in emphasizing the role of the environment, cultural ecologists do not take into account historical or political factors (Geertz 1963a; Friedman 1974; Keesing 1981; Hefner 1983). Thus, for example, cultural ecologists can explain how Shoshone culture represents an adaptation to a desert environment, but they cannot explain how or why the Shoshone came to reside in an environment with scarce resources. An explanation of this kind would require detailed historical research, examining local and global political factors.

Another criticism is that cultural ecology reduces human behavior to simple adaptations to the external environment. Because of the emphasis on adaptation, cultural ecologists tend to view every cultural element as the best of all possible solutions to the problems of subsistence and energy requirements. In fact, many sociocultural adaptations may involve compromises at the time that turn out later to be maladaptations.

For example, a number of early cultural ecologists have used their models to explain the development of warfare in different societies. Some hypothesize that warfare is associated with land ownership, population size, and resource shortages (Vayda 1961; Sweet 1965; Meggitt 1977). As populations expand in areas with scarce resources, societies resort to warfare to secure additional resources and thereby restore stability to the sociocultural system. Critics suggest that this explanation ignores various historical, political, and cultural factors that contribute to warfare, such as conflicting political or religious ideologies. Furthermore, they suggest that this is an extreme form of adaptationism. In most cases, warfare is definitely maladaptive.

Cultural Materialism

The late anthropologist Marvin Harris refined the neoevolutionary approach of White and Steward as a perspective he called cultural materialism. **Cultural materialism** is a research strategy that focuses on technology, environment, and economic factors as key determinants in sociocultural evolution. Cultural materialists divide all sociocultural systems into infrastructure, structure, and superstructure. The *infrastructure* includes the technology and practices used for expanding or limiting the production of basic resources such as food, clothing, and shelter. The *structure* consists of the domestic economy (family structure, domestic division of labor, age, and gender roles) and the political economy (political organization, class, castes, police, and military). The *superstructure* includes philosophy, art, music, religion, ideas, literature, advertising, sports, games, science, and values (see Figure 13.2).

According to cultural-materialist theory, the infrastructure largely determines the structure and superstructure of sociocultural systems. As the infrastructure changes, the structure and superstructure may change accordingly. Technology, energy, and environmental factors are crucial to the development of all aspects of society. All societies must devise ways to obtain food and shelter, and they must possess an adequate technology and energy to provide for the survival and continuity of the population. Although cultural materialists do not deny that superstructural and structural components of society may influence cultural evolution, they see infrastructural factors as being far more important. This theoretical

Figure 13.2 The model for cultural materialism

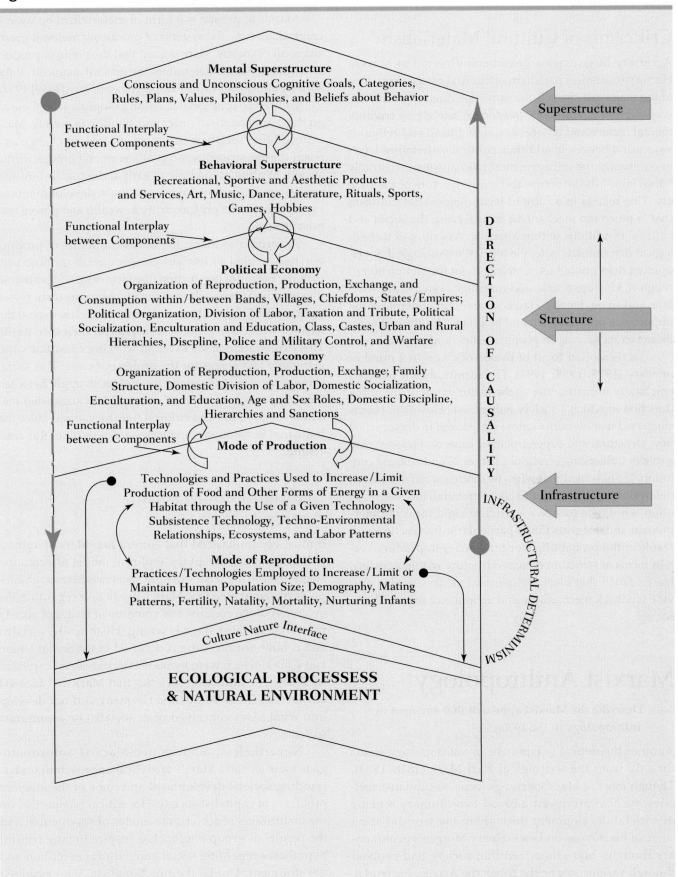

Mental Superstructure
Conscious and Unconscious Cognitive Goals, Categories,
Rules, Plans, Values, Philosophies, and Beliefs about Behavior

Functional Interplay
between Components

Behavioral Superstructure
Recreational, Sportive and Aesthetic Products
and Services, Art, Music, Dance, Literature, Rituals, Sports,
Games, Hobbies

Functional Interplay
between Components

Political Economy
Organization of Reproduction, Production, Exchange, and
Consumption within/between Bands, Villages, Chiefdoms, States/Empires;
Political Organization, Division of Labor, Taxation and Tribute, Political
Socialization, Enculturation and Education, Class, Castes, Urban and Rural
Hierachies, Discpline, Police and Military Control, and Warfare

Domestic Economy
Organization of Reproduction, Production, Exchange; Family
Structure, Domestic Division of Labor, Domestic Socialization,
Enculturation, and Education, Age and Sex Roles, Domestic Discipline,
Hierarchies and Sanctions

Functional Interplay
between Components

Mode of Production
Technologies and Practices Used to Increase/Limit
Production of Food and Other Forms of Energy in a Given
Habitat through the Use of a Given Technology;
Subsistence Technology, Techno-Environmental
Relationships, Ecosystems, and Labor Patterns

Mode of Reproduction
Practices/Technologies Employed to Increase/Limit or
Maintain Human Population Size; Demography, Mating
Patterns, Fertility, Natality, Mortality, Nurturing Infants

Culture Nature Interface

**ECOLOGICAL PROCESSESS
& NATURAL ENVIRONMENT**

Superstructure

Structure

Infrastructure

DIRECTION OF CAUSALITY

INFRASTRUCTURAL DETERMINISM

perspective represents an extension of the foundations laid down by White and Steward.

Criticisms of Cultural Materialism

A variety of criticisms have been directed at Marvin Harris's theoretical paradigm of cultural materialism. One of the major criticisms is the same one directed at cultural ecology; that is, Harris focuses too exclusively on environmental factors and ignores social, political, and religious values and beliefs. In addition, cultural materialism tends to emphasize the infrastructural mechanisms that strictly "determine" the structure and superstructure of the society. This results in a form of technological determinism that is much too mechanistic in analyzing the social and cultural conditions within a society. As critics of technological determinists note, the level of technological development does not tell us anything about the complexity of religion, kinship, family and marriage systems, art, folklore, and so on. Finally, Harris's paradigm underplays the importance of symbolism and language and the influence these factors have upon people's beliefs and motivations.

Harris replied to all of these criticisms in a number of texts (1979, 1988, 1999). He admitted that he does emphasize infrastructure as the major determinant of the direction in which a society will evolve. However, Harris suggested that his critics ignore his attempt to demonstrate how structural and superstructural aspects of society play a role in influencing conditions for social and cultural evolution. He indicated that when he discusses infrastructural determinism, he means this in a "probabilistic" sense. In other words, he eschews a strict or rigid form of determinism and suggests that a particular infrastructure will result in the probabilities or tendencies to produce certain forms of structure or superstructure within a society. Harris noted that ideas, beliefs, and values can also provide feedback mechanisms and generate change within a society.

Marxist Anthropology

13.6 Describe the Marxist approach that emerged in anthropology in the 1970s.

Another theoretical perspective in anthropology stems directly from the writings of Karl Marx (1818–1883). Though most of Marx's writings focus on capitalist societies, he also produced a broad evolutionary scheme of societal development throughout the world. Basing some of his notions on Lewis Henry Morgan's evolutionary thought, Marx theorized that society had evolved through various stages: the tribal, the Asiatic, the feudal, and, finally, the capitalist stage. Having advanced this far,

according to Marx, these societies would then proceed to the socialist and communist stages.

Marx's approach is a form of materialism because it emphasizes how the systems of producing material goods shape all of society. Marx argued that the mode of production in material life determines the general character of the social, political, and spiritual processes of life ([1859] 1959).

Unlike the functionalist anthropologists, who focused on the maintenance of order and stability in society, Marx believed that society is in a state of constant change as a result of class struggles and conflicts among groups within society. Writing at the time of early industrialization and capitalism in Europe, he viewed these developments as causes of exploitation, inequality in wealth and power, and class struggle.

According to Marx, the industrial mode of production had divided society into classes: *capitalists*, those who own the means of production (the factories), and *proletariat* (the workers), those who sell their labor to the owners as a commodity. The members of the capitalist class exploit the labor of workers to produce a surplus for their own profit. This exploitation leads to harsh working conditions and extremely low wages for the proletariat class. This social arrangement sets the stage for a class struggle between these opposing segments of society. Marx suggested that all the major social and cultural transformations since the Industrial Revolution could be seen as a result of this class conflict.

Evaluation of Marxist Anthropology

It must be emphasized that current neo-Marxist anthropologists do not accept the unilineal model of evolution suggested by Marx. For example, most neo-Marxist anthropologists recognize that Marx's prediction regarding the evolution of the socialist and communist stages of society from the capitalist stage is wrong. Historically, socialist and communist revolutions occurred in the Soviet Union and China, which were by no means industrial-capitalist societies. The industrial societies that Marx had focused on, such as Great Britain and Germany, did not develop into what Marx conceived of as socialist or communist societies.

Nevertheless, modern neo-Marxist anthropologists view as valid Marx's analytical approach to understanding societal development and some of the inherent problems of capitalist society. His critical perspective on the institutions of society, the modes of production, and the results of group conflict has inspired many fruitful hypotheses regarding social and cultural evolution and development. Unlike the functionalists, who assumed that society's institutions were balancing conflicting

An Indian farmer working in his fields. Marx believed that societies evolved through stages such as the Asiatic, in which land was cultivated by peasant farmers.

interests, the Marxist anthropologists have demonstrated that conflict is an inherent aspect of human behavior and culture. In later chapters dealing with globalization issues, we will discuss some of the neo-Marxist anthropological explanations.

Symbolic Anthropology: A Humanistic Method of Inquiry

13.7 Discuss the symbolic anthropology approach as a humanist method.

Another theoretical orientation in anthropology is **symbolic anthropology**, the study of culture through the interpretation of the meaning of the symbols, values, and beliefs of a society. This school of thought focuses on the symbolic rather than the material aspects of culture. Symbolic anthropologists suggest that many cultural symbols cannot be readily reduced to the material conditions and adaptive mechanisms of a society, as proposed by cultural materialists. Rather than viewing values, beliefs, and ideologies as a reflection only of environmental, technological, or economic conditions, symbolic anthropologists argue that these cultural symbols may be completely autonomous from material factors.

From this standpoint, symbolic anthropologists reject the use of the scientific method as applied to human behavior. The goal of their research is, instead, to interpret the meaning of symbols within the worldviews of a particular society. For example, recall that in Chapter 10 we discussed the hairstyles of the Rastafarians in Jamaican society. We also discussed Mary Douglas's interpretation of

the prohibition of different foods, including pork, among the ancient Israelites. The hairstyles of the Rastafarians in Jamaican society and the prohibition of eating certain foods such as pork among the ancient Israelites are examples of these symbols. The anthropologist Mary Douglas focused on the symbolic classification of various foods as being "clean" or "pure" and "unclean" or "polluted." The symbolic anthropologist tries to discern how such symbols help people produce meaning for themselves and their communities. A particular hairstyle or the classification of different foods may become a symbolic metaphor, communicating a message.

The methodology of symbolic anthropology focuses on the collection of data—especially data reflecting the point of view of the members of the society studied—on kinship, economy, ritual, myth, and values. Symbolic anthropologists describe this type of data collection as producing a *thick description*, the attempt to interpret the relationships among different symbols within a society. To do this, symbolic anthropologists must interpret the meanings of the symbolic beliefs and metaphors from the point of view of the people in a specific society. The aim of symbolic anthropologists is to show how other peoples' values, beliefs, and ideologies are meaningful and intelligible.

Criticisms of Symbolic Anthropology

A number of criticisms have been directed at symbolic anthropology. One major charge is that symbolic anthropologists focus exclusively upon cultural symbols at the expense of other variables that may influence human thought and behavior. Symbolic anthropologists may therefore neglect the conditions and processes that lead to the making of culture (Roseberry 1982; Fox 1985). For example, economic power and political power may be important factors in the development of cultural values and norms. Dominant groups may be responsible for the emergence of cultural hegemony in a society. Critics emphasize that culture cannot be treated as an autonomous phenomenon separate from historical, political, and economic processes and conditions that affect a society.

Another criticism is that symbolic anthropology substitutes one form of determinism for another. Instead of emphasizing technological or economic variables, symbolic anthropologists stress the meaning of cultural symbols. Despite their rejection of scientific causal explanations, they have been accused of reducing explanations of society and human activity to the "meanings" of cultural beliefs and symbols. Despite these criticisms, most anthropologists agree that symbolic anthropologists have contributed to our understanding of how humans have developed their symbolic cultures.

Materialism versus Culturalism

One major division in anthropology is between those anthropologists who prefer materialist explanations of society and those who prefer culturalist explanations. To some extent, this division reflects the differences between the scientific approach and the humanistic-interpretive perspective in anthropology (see Chapter 1). The scientists and materialists focus on technological, environmental, biological, and economic factors to explain human behavior and society. This group—which includes cultural materialists, some Marxist anthropologists, and evolutionary psychologists—views many aspects of culture as having a material purpose. Culturalists, including the structuralists and some psychological anthropologists such as Ruth Benedict and Margaret Mead (discussed in Chapter 11), and the symbolic anthropologists focus on the symbolic aspect of culture. Their aim is to interpret the meaning of symbols in a society. To the culturalists, symbols and culture may not have a material purpose at all, but rather establish meaningfulness for the people in a society.

Anthropologist Richard Barrett (1984) notes that the difference between the materialist and culturalist approaches is related to the nature of society and human existence itself. As Barrett emphasizes, every society must confront the problem of adjusting to the practical circumstances of life. People need food, shelter, clothing, and the necessary technology and energy for survival. This is the material component of culture; it is related to survival. But there is also the nonmaterial aspect of culture: norms, values, beliefs, ideologies, and symbols. These cultural norms and symbols have emotional significance. Symbols may not be related at all to the practical circumstances of life; instead, they may indicate some aesthetic or moral values that are not related to the material conditions of society.

Thus, the distinction between the material and non-material aspects of culture has led to different approaches to the analysis of human behavior and society. In later chapters, we learn how anthropologists have employed these approaches in explaining and interpreting human affairs.

Feminist Anthropology

13.8 Discuss the approach of feminist anthropologists.

One of the most important developments in anthropological theory was the emergence of a feminist orientation. After the beginning of the twentieth century, a number of female pioneers such as Ruth Benedict, Margaret Mead, Elsie Crews Parsons, Eleanor Leacock, and Phyllis Kaberry began to have a definite impact on the field of anthropology. Margaret Mead popularized the findings

of anthropology by writing a monthly article in *Redbook* magazine, which circulated widely among women in the United States. As we shall see in Chapter 16, Mead was also the first to focus on gender roles within different societies and question a rigid biological determinist view of male and female roles.

With the development of the feminist movement in U.S. society in the 1960s and 1970s (see Chapter 17), many female anthropologists initiated a *feminist perspective*. This feminist perspective challenged the tendency to concentrate on the male role and underestimate the position of women within different societies. Before the 1970s, most anthropologists were male, and for the most part, women were neglected in ethnographic research. And in some societies like the Middle East Islamic societies, it is very difficult for male anthropologists to interview women (see Chapter 22). As more women became involved in anthropology, they questioned the traditional emphasis on the male position and the invisibility of women in ethnographies. These feminist anthropologists emphasized that gender roles had to be taken into account in ethnographic research (Mascia-Lees and Black 2000). They also challenged essentialist or stereotypical portrayals of women. As we shall see in later chapters, these feminist anthropologists have produced enormous insights regarding the role of women in societies throughout the world.

Feminist anthropologists directed their criticisms at a variety of targets that had become prevalent in the discipline. For example, they questioned the underlying assumptions made by the sociobiologists regarding male and female behavioral tendencies. The feminist anthropologists argued that the view of men as sexually promiscuous and females as sexually conservative and desiring monogamy as a reproductive strategy was an overgeneralization and essentialist stereotype. They critiqued the view that males and females were radically different based on biological traits such as hormonal differences. In addition, they directed their criticisms at the physical anthropologists who argued that females had become dependent on males for food and other resources, whereas males were developing tools and other strategies for hunting purposes. They suggested that the female role in human evolution had been overlooked. And feminist anthropologists criticized ethnographic descriptions that presented the male as the more active, aggressive agent within the family and the female as passive and inactive in terms of her behavior. These types of descriptions appeared in the ethnographies of the functionalists during the 1930s and 1940s (Mascia-Lees and Black 2000). Thus, feminist anthropologists provided new, insightful hypotheses and created a more general awareness of gender and women's issues within the discipline.

One of the leading feminist anthropologists is Sherry Ortner, who wrote an important essay in 1974, "Is Female to Male as Nature Is to Culture?" In this essay, Ortner tackled the view regarding what appeared to be the universal subordination of women throughout the world. She tried to answer the question of why women were perceived and treated as inferior, second-class citizens in the vast majority of societies. In her analysis, Ortner drew on the structuralist approach in anthropology. Recall that the view of the founder of structuralism, Claude Lévi-Strauss (see Chapter 11), was that the fundamental structural binary oppositions of the human mind were "nature" and "culture." Within this structuralist format, Ortner argued that since women gave birth and cared for children, they were perceived as being "closer" to nature. In contrast, men were involved in political affairs and other, more symbolic activities and were perceived to be "closer" to the "creative aspect" of culture and, therefore, cognitively "superior." According to Ortner, this nature/culture opposition of males and females had structural consequences for the social position of men and women within all societies. Women were regarded as inferior beings and were subjugated in societies worldwide.

This essay was a landmark piece in early feminist anthropology. More recently, Ortner returned to this early essay, which had received a lot of critical attention from other women in anthropology. On the basis of this critical attention, she reexamined her original essay in "So, Is Female to Male as Nature Is to Culture?" in a chapter of her book *Making Gender: The Politics and Erotics of Culture* (1996). In this chapter, she grants that in some societies the appearance of male superiority and female inferiority is fragmentary and very difficult to determine. She also concurs with her critics that the structuralist explanation regarding the distinction between nature and culture that resulted in the universal subordination of women was not very useful. However, she does think that this nature/culture distinction is something that all of humanity faces. But in different societies and historical conditions, men and women may articulate and respond to these distinctions in enormously variant ways. In general, Ortner suggests that the universal or near-universal male dominance and subordination of women is caused by a complex interaction of functional arrangements in society, power dynamics, and also biological differences between males and females. Ortner has offered some insightful hypotheses for further research on gender and women's issues in anthropology.

Criticisms of Feminist Anthropology

Although feminist anthropology has contributed substantially to the discipline in providing a critical awareness for male anthropologists, some anthropologists argue that this perspective has become too extreme and exaggerated. For example, some feminist anthropologists have put forth the view that biological factors have absolutely nothing to do with male and female differences (Collier and Yanagisako 1987). An enormous amount of data from various scientifically evaluated fields has demonstrated that both nature and nurture are important in shaping gender and male and female differences. Thus, the view that nature does not have anything to do with gender seems to be too extreme (Stone 2010).

In addition, some feminist anthropologists have argued that all of the scientific hypotheses and most of science are based on a Western cultural framework and an *androcentric* (male-centered) perspective. Consequently, male anthropologists cannot do research on women in other societies because of their androcentric biases; only women can conduct research on women and gender issues. These views also appear to be extreme. At present, most male anthropologists have been attuned to the feminist critique of anthropology and have adjusted to a more sensitive understanding of gender and women's issues. Many male anthropologists today consider themselves to be feminist anthropologists.

Also, as we have emphasized in this book, scientifically based hypotheses are tested by many individuals in both Western and non-Western societies, and as more women come into the field of anthropology, they will become actively involved in this type of testing. Thus, science and scientific hypotheses are not just products of a Western cultural framework and an androcentric perspective. The scientific method used correctly and precisely will weed out any erroneous biases or data and will result in a more comprehensive and refined understanding of the social and cultural world.

Postmodernism and Anthropology

13.9 Discuss the strengths and weaknesses of the postmodern approach in anthropology.

Although ethnographic fieldwork has long been a fundamental aspect of anthropology, one current school, **postmodernism**, is challenging basic ethnographic assumptions and methodologies. This group, known as postmodernist anthropologists, includes such figures as James Clifford, George Marcus, and Michael Fischer. The postmodernists suggest that traditional ethnographic research is based on a number of unsound assumptions. One such assumption is that the ethnographer is a detached, scientifically objective observer who is not influenced by the premises and biases of her or his own society. Clifford characterizes one of the models maintained by ethnographers such as Malinowski as that of the "scientific participant-observer" (1983). In his ethnographies, Malinowski eliminated any reference to himself and recorded data that were then written as the documentation of an "objective scientist." Malinowski produced his descriptions as if he did not have any involvement with the Trobriand people. It was as if he were some sort of computing machine without feelings, biases, or emotions, who was simply recording everything about native life.

According to postmodernist critics, ethnographies such as those compiled by Malinowski were intended as a type of scientific study in which the subjects behaved and the ethnographer simply recorded this behavior. From this standpoint, the postmodernists complain that the ethnographers assume they have a thoroughly scientific and objective view of reality, whereas the native view is highly subjective, based on traditional beliefs and cosmologies.

Postmodernists and Contemporary Research

One of the basic reasons for the postmodernist critiques is that the situation for ethnographic studies has changed substantially. Until recently, most subjects of ethnographic studies were illiterate peoples adjusting to the impact of the West. But as more people throughout the world become educated and familiar with the field of anthropology, Western ethnographers could no longer claim to be the sole authorities regarding anthropological knowledge. Many people in Latin America, Africa, the Middle East, and Asia can, and do, speak and write about their own cultures (some have become anthropologists themselves), and they are disseminating knowledge about their own societies. The world is no longer dependent on Western anthropologists to gather ethnographic data. Indigenous people are beginning to represent themselves and their societies to the world.

Postmodernists have recommended that ethnographers today adopt a different way of researching and writing. Instead of trying to distance themselves from their subjects, ethnographers should present themselves in dialogue with their subjects. Clifford (1983) argues that an ethnography should consist of many voices from the native population, rather than just those of the ethnographer and a few of his or her informants.

Reaction to this postmodernist critique has varied within the discipline. On the one hand, some ethnographers have charged the postmodernists with characterizing traditional ethnographic methodologies unjustly. Many ethnographers, they contend, were engaged in a form of dialogue with their informants and other members of the societies being studied. On the other hand, the postmodernist debate has stirred many anthropologists to rethink their roles. Currently, more ethnographers are writing about their actual interactions and relationships with the people

they study. Ethnographers must take account of their own political position within the society under investigation. This type of data and personal reflection is no longer pushed into the background, but instead is presented as a vital ingredient of the ethnography. In the 1980s, a number of ethnographies appeared that reflected the postmodernist emphasis on interaction between ethnographers and their subjects. Some of these new ethnographies are based on the life histories of people within the studied population.

Following two periods of fieldwork among the !Kung San or Ju/'hoansi San, hunters and gatherers of the Kalahari Desert in southwestern Africa, the late Marjorie Shostak completed a life history, *Nisa: The Life and Words of A !Kung Woman* (1981). Shostak interviewed numerous !Kung women to gain a sense of their lives. She focused on the life history of Nisa, who discussed her family, sex life, marriage, pregnancies, experiences with !Kung men, and reaction to growing older. Shostak cautioned that Nisa does not represent a "typical" !Kung or Ju/'hoansi San female because her life experiences are unique (as are the experiences of all individuals in any society). In addition, Shostak exercised extreme care in discussing with Nisa the material that would go into the book to ensure a faithful representation of Nisa's life.

If we look back over years of ethnographic research, we find many accounts in which anthropologists were scrupulous in their representation of people in other societies. To this extent, the postmodernist critics have exaggerated the past mistakes of ethnographers. However, the postmodernists have alerted ethnographers to some unexamined assumptions concerning their work. Today, most anthropologists do not claim a completely "objective" viewpoint. Anthropologists generally want to maintain empathy with the people they study, yet they usually attempt some critical detachment as well. Otherwise, they could easily become merely the spokespersons for specific political interests and leaders in a community (Errington and Gewertz 1987).

Collaborative fieldwork, with teams of ethnographers and informants working together to understand a society, is most likely the future direction for ethnographic study. The image of a solitary ethnographer such as Malinowski or Margaret Mead isolated on a Pacific island is outmoded (Salzman 1989). Collaborative research will lead to more systematic data collection and will offer opportunities to examine hypotheses of both ethnographers and subjects from a variety of perspectives.

Shifts in Anthropological Explanations

We began this chapter with the Hindu legend of the blind men and the elephant. The moral of that story was that we all have partial understandings of the world. As we have sketched a number of different anthropological explanations and critiques in this chapter, it is obvious that no one explanation provides a full understanding of human behavior and culture. In a recent essay assessing anthropological theory, British anthropologist Roy F. Ellen proposes that explanation and interpretation must be what he terms "conjunctural" (2010). In other words, anthropological explanations provide a framework within which to pose both general and comparative questions about human diversity and origins, whether biological, social, cultural, or (indeed) biocultural or biosocial. In other words, anthropological explanations and interpretations must be carefully structured into different levels incorporating biological and ecological factors, individual decision making, and the historical, social and

cultural factors that influence individuals. Ellen views anthropological theories as a pyramid with nested levels of explanations with the most general types of questions at the top and more local-level cultural interpretations at the bottom. This theoretical framework enables anthropologists to produce more synthetic and holistic explanations of human behavior in the past and present. After more than a century of anthropological research, we do have an improved and more comprehensive understanding of culture, society, and the role of individual behavior than we did in the nineteenth century. Through constant critical evaluation, hypothesis testing, and refinement of explanations and interpretations by anthropologists, we ought to know even more about these phenomena in the future.

Summary and Review of Learning Objectives

13.1 Explain the weaknesses of the nineteenth-century unilineal evolutionary approaches in anthropology.

The first professional anthropologists, notably E. B. Tylor and Lewis Henry Morgan, proposed a theory known as unilineal evolution to explain the differences and similarities in societal evolution. The unilineal evolutionists maintained that societies evolve in one direction from a stage of savagery to one of civilization. These unilineal views of evolution were based on ethnocentric and racist views of the nineteenth century.

13.2 Describe the basic strengths and weaknesses of the diffusionist approach in understanding different cultures.

In the early twentieth century a theory of diffusionism was invoked as the best explanation of the differences and similarities among societies. The British diffusionists argued that all civilization emanated from Egypt, whereas the German diffusionists maintained that there were several original centers of civilization. Modern anthropologists have criticized these diffusionist approaches based on archaeological and cross-cultural research of many different societies. However, one strength of the diffusionist approach does remain, as it is well known that societies borrow ideas and technologies from one another.

13.3 Discuss historical particularism developed by Franz Boas.

Another early twentieth-century theory, historical particularism, was developed in the United States from the ideas of Franz Boas. Boas criticized the nineteenth-century unilineal view that societies could be ranked and compared

with one another as "savage," "barbaric," or "civilized." Instead, he argued that each society is a unique product of its geographical and historical circumstances. This view of historical particularism is still important in modern anthropological explanations.

13.4 Explain the differences between structural functionalism and psychological functionalism.

The functionalist approaches developed in early twentieth century British anthropology. Anthropologists such as A. R. Radcliffe-Brown were structural functionalists, viewing cultural institutions as satisfying societal needs such as maintaining order and stability. In contrast, Bronislaw Malinowski focused on cultural institutions as serving biological and psychological needs such as reducing anxiety. Although functionalist explanations proved limited in explaining such matters as cultural change, they did provide valuable ethnographic data.

13.5 Discuss the twentieth-century neoevolutionary approaches, including cultural ecology and cultural materialism.

Following World War II, some anthropologists turned to new evolutionary theories. Anthropologists such as Leslie White and Julian Steward began to analyze how environment, technology, and energy requirements led to the evolution of societies. This neoevolutionism avoided the ethnocentric ideas of nineteenth-century unilineal evolution. Also, as an outgrowth of neoevolutionism, a school of thought known as cultural materialism developed through the writings of Marvin Harris. Harris systematized the analysis of sociocultural systems and maintained that the key determinant of sociocultural evolution is the infrastructure, including technology, environment, and material conditions.

13.6   Describe the Marxist approach in anthropology that emerged in the 1970s.

Another anthropological school of thought evolved from the writings of Karl Marx. In the 1970s, a number of anthropologists applied Marxist ideas about the mode of production to the analysis of preindustrial and industrial societies. Marxist anthropologists introduced a global view of societal evolution.

13.7   Discuss the symbolic anthropology approach as a humanist method.

Symbolic anthropology focuses on the study of the cultural symbols, beliefs, and ethos of a society. Symbolic anthropologists treat cultural traditions as texts that need to be interpreted by the ethnographer in the same way that humanists interpret literary texts. Symbolic anthropology represents a method of interpreting cultural traditions without reducing them to material conditions.

13.8   Discuss the approach of feminist anthropologists.

Feminist anthropology emerged in the 1970s to challenge some of the explanations that males were expressing about gender and women's issues. These feminist anthropologists have made an enormous contribution to ethnographic studies by refocusing attention the significant role that women play in different societies.

13.8   Discuss the strengths and weaknesses of the postmodern approach in anthropology.

Postmodern anthropology developed as a critical program that suggested that traditional ethnographic research has a Western bias and was overly scientific. This postmodern program has produced a much more self-reflective type of ethnography that entails examining one's own political position within an ethnographic context. However, the postmodernists' tendency to reject the scientific method in anthropology has been a mistake that neglects a multiple array of data from biology and psychology that has contributed to better explanations of human similarities and differences throughout the world.

Key Terms

cultural ecology, p. 301
cultural materialism, p. 302
diffusionism, p. 297

functionalism, p. 299
historical particularism, p. 298
multilineal evolution, p. 301

postmodernism, p. 307
symbolic anthropology, p. 305
unilineal evolution, p. 295

Chapter 14
Analyzing Sociocultural Systems

Learning Objectives

After reading this chapter you should be able to:

14.1 Discuss how cultural anthropologists prepare to study society and culture.

14.2 Describe the actual research methods used for ethnographic studies.

14.3 Discuss some of the ethical dilemmas of ethnographic research.

14.4 How do cultural anthropologists analyze their ethnographic data?

14.5 Discuss the contemporary view of sociocultural evolution used by anthropologists.

14.6 Describe the types of sociocultural systems studied by anthropologists?

14.7 Describe the strengths and limitations of the cross-cultural approach.

As we discussed in Chapter 10, at times anthropologists use the term *sociocultural system* as a combination of the terms *society* and *culture* in analyzing their data. We also saw that there are some basic cultural universals that are found in all societies (Brown 1991). This chapter provides insight on how anthropologists do research on the universal characteristics of sociocultural systems. Anthropologists approach universal features of sociocultural systems as *variables*. Immediately, this terminology suggests that these universals can *vary* within different sociocultural systems, and this is exactly what anthropologists have discovered in their research. There are basic universal similarities among all humans, but within different societies, these universal features exhibit tremendous variations. To account for patterned relationships within a sociocultural system anthropologists use *both* scientific causal *and* humanistic interpretations of cultural beliefs.

Anthropologists use the *holistic approach* to analyze sociocultural systems, which means demonstrating how all of these universals and variables interact and influence one another. Although anthropologists refer to *sociocultural systems*, the word *system* is used in a metaphorical manner. It does not suggest that sociocultural systems are somehow running "above," like some computer system in human affairs. Humans are not just automatons driven by some mechanical cultural system. Rather, humans as individuals are actively involved in managing, shaping, and modifying their culture from within these so-called systems. In this chapter we discuss the research methods used in ethnographic research as well as the potential ethical dilemmas of this type of research.

In later chapters, we examine different types of universals and cultural variations found in different sociocultural systems to illustrate the interconnections of these variables.

Ethnographic Fieldwork

14.1 Discuss how cultural anthropologists prepare to study society and culture.

In Chapter 1, we introduced the subfield of anthropology known as cultural anthropology. This subfield focuses on the ethnographic study of contemporary societies all over the world. To prepare for ethnographic fieldwork, the anthropologist must be grounded in the different theoretical perspectives of anthropology that are discussed within different chapters of this text. This background knowledge is especially important for developing a research design for the fieldwork.

A *research design* is a strategy formulated to examine a particular topic that specifies the appropriate methods for gathering the richest possible data. The research design must take into account the types of data that will be collected

and how those data relate to existing anthropological knowledge. In the research design, the cultural anthropologist specifies the types of methods that will be used in the investigation. Typically, the cultural anthropologist develops the research design, which is then reviewed by other anthropologists who recommend it for funding by various government or private research foundations.

Before going into the field for direct research, the cultural anthropologist analyzes available *archival data*, including photos, films, missionary reports, business and government surveys, musical recordings, journalistic accounts, diaries, court documents, medical records, birth, landholding documents, and death, marriage, and tax records. These data help place the communities to be studied in a broad context. Historical material in the archives helps the cultural anthropologist evaluate the usefulness of the observations and interviews he or she will document. Archival data can enrich the sources of information that fieldworkers obtain once they get to the field. They must also read the published anthropological, historical, economic, sociological, and political science literature on the geographic region toward which they are heading.

Ethnographic Research and Strategies

14.2 Describe the actual research methods used for ethnographic studies.

After receiving funding and obtaining the proper research clearances from the country of destination, the cultural anthropologist takes up residence in that society to explore its institutions and values. This is the basis of the *participant observation* method, which involves learning the language and culture of the group being studied and participating in its daily activities. Language skills are the most important asset that a cultural anthropologist has in the field, and the ability to communicate in the local language makes participant observation much easier and more enlightening. Anthropologist Victor de Munck views participant observation as a very powerful method and the "jewel on the crown of methodology within cultural anthropology" (2009). It involves collecting data within a specific cultural context and evaluating that data with rigorous techniques.

Participant observation includes making accurate descriptions of the physical locale and the daily activities of people in the society. This involves creating maps or at least being able to read maps to place the society's physical location in perspective. It may also involve intensive investigation into soil conditions, rates of precipitation, surveys of crops and livestock, and other environmental factors. Most importantly, participant observation involves the maintenance of accurate and reliable records of the cultural anthropologist's direct observations of human social interaction and behavior.

Some cultural anthropologists use what is called *time-allocation analysis* to record how much time the people in the society spend in various activities: work, leisure, recreation, religious ceremonies, and so on. For example, in a classic study Allen Johnson (1975) did a systematic pioneering study of time allocation among the Machiguenga Indians, who live in the Andes Mountains of Peru. He found that men worked 4.6 hours per day, and women worked 4.2 hours per day in the production and preparation of food. Women spent 2.1 hours and men spent 1.4 hours per day in craft production. Men were involved in trade and wage work, and women did housework and cared for children. The total amount of labor time allocated for this work was 7.6 hours for men and 7.4 hours for women. Johnson and other anthropologists sponsored a 10-year time-allocation studies program based at UCLA that eventually compared data from 14 different lowland Indian Amazonian societies (1987–1997). This project measured time allocation for males, females, and youth in these societies. These types of time-allocation studies can be useful in assessing how different societies use their time in various activities.

Key Informants

Usually, cultural anthropologists learn about the society through trusted *key informants*, who offer insight into the culture's patterns (Powdermaker 1966; Wax 1971; Agar 1980). These informants become the initial source of information and help the cultural anthropologist identify major sources of data. Long-term collaboration with key informants is an integral part of quality ethnographic research.

The cultural anthropologist tries to choose key informants who have a deep knowledge of the community. These informants are usually "native cultural anthropologists" who are interested in their own society. They may serve as tutors or guides, answering general questions or identifying topics that could be of interest to the cultural

Cultural Anthropologist Sabah Rahmani interviewing a member of the Kayapo tribe in the Amazon.

anthropologist. They often help the cultural anthropologist establish rapport with the people in the community. In many situations, the people may not understand why the cultural anthropologist is interested in their society. The key informant can help explain the cultural anthropologist's role. In some cases, the key informant may become involved in interviewing other people in the community to assist the cultural anthropologist in collecting data. The relationship between the key informant and the cultural anthropologist is a close personal and professional one that often produces lifelong friendship and collaboration.

Interviews

Cultural anthropologists use a number of *unstructured interviews*, which involve open-ended conversations with informants, to gain insights into a culture. These unstructured interviews may include the collecting of life histories, narratives, myths, and tales. Through these interviews, the cultural anthropologist may also find out information on dispute settlements, legal transactions, political conflicts, and religious and public events. Unstructured interviews sometimes involves on-the-spot questioning of informants.

The strength of this type of interviewing is that it gives informants tremendous freedom of expression in attempting to explain their culture (Bernard et al. 1986). The informant is not confined to answering a specific question that is designed by the cultural anthropologist. The informant may, for example, elaborate on connections between certain beliefs and political power in the community. Fredrik Barth (1975, 2002) discovered through his informant among the Baktaman people of New Guinea that when young males go through their initiation ceremonies, they are introduced to the secret lore and sacred knowledge of the males who are in authority. Thus, cultural beliefs are transmitted along with political authority. Barth found that this secretive sacred knowledge was often arcane and ambiguous. As these young Baktaman males went through each stage of the ritual, the knowledge became much more mysterious and ambiguous. It appeared that the most important feature of the ritual was the reinforcement of elder authority and group bonding. Without his informant's help, Barth might not have paid attention to this relationship between belief and the transmission of authority.

Following an unstructured interview, the cultural anthropologist focuses upon specific topics of interest related to the research project. In some cases, the cultural anthropologist then begins to develop *structured interviews*. Structured interviews can involve asking the same questions of every individual in a given sample. The cultural anthropologist must phrase the questions in a meaningful and sensitive manner, a task that requires knowledge of both the language and the cultural lifestyle of the people being studied.

By asking the same questions of every individual in a sample, the cultural anthropologist is able to obtain more accurate data. If the cultural anthropologist receives uniform answers to a particular question, then the data are more likely to be reliable. If a great deal of variation in responses is evident, then the data will be more unreliable or may indicate a complex issue with many facets. The structured interview helps assess the validity of the collected data. By asking people the same type of question, the cultural anthropologist attempts to gain more quality control over his or her findings (de Munck 2009). This type of data quality control must be a constant aspect of the cultural anthropologist's research strategy. However, as we discussed in Chapter 10, contemporary anthropologists concur that there is always a great deal of variation in cultural beliefs, values, and norms in every society. Thus, one cannot offer a simplistic account of "a culture" in the same way that anthropologists did in the 1930s, 1940s, and 1950s. Anthropologists want to avoid what is referred to as the *reification* of a culture. In the past, anthropologists tended to portray cultures and societies as if all the people within a society were sharing a homogeneous culture. As indicated in Chapter 11, this was a typical problem with the early culture and personality studies.

To develop an effective questionnaire, the cultural anthropologist must collaborate with her or his informants (de Munck 2009). This is tedious and difficult methodological work, but it is necessary if the cultural anthropologist is to understand the workings of the society. If the society is large, the cultural anthropologist must distribute the questionnaire to a random sample of the society. A **random sample** is a representative sample of people of different ages, genders, economic and political statuses, and other characteristics within the society. In a random sample, all the individuals in the society have an equal chance of being selected for the survey. If the cultural anthropologist draws information from only one sector of the population—for example, males or young people—the data may be biased. This shortcoming would limit the ability of the cultural anthropologist to develop a well-rounded portrait of the society.

Quantitative and Qualitative Data Through the structured interviews, the cultural anthropologist gathers basic **quantitative data**: census materials, dietary information, income and household-composition data, and other data that can be expressed as numbers. This information can be used as a database for developing a description of the variations in economic, social, political, and other patterns in the society. For example, dietary information can inform the cultural anthropologist about the basic health and nutritional problems that the society may have. Quantitative data provide background for the cultural anthropologist's direct and participant observations and further open-ended interviews with the individuals in the society.

Sometimes, these objective quantitative data are referred to as an aspect of the *etic* perspective of the anthropologist. The **etic perspective** is the outsider's objective, quantifiable data that are used to scientifically analyze the culture of a society. *Etic* is derived from the term *phonetics* in linguistics, which are the sounds of a language.

Most of the data obtained through participant observation and interviewing are **qualitative data**, nonstatistical information that tends to be the most important aspect of ethnographic research. Qualitative data include descriptions of social organization, political activities, religious beliefs, and so on. These qualitative data are often referred to as part of the **emic perspective**, the insider's view of his or her own society and culture. The term *emic* is derived from the word *phonemics* in linguistics, which refers to the sound units of language that have "meaning" for the speakers of the language (see Chapter 12). For example, as we discussed in Chapter 10, the religious beliefs of some societies have influenced their cultural preferences for various foods. Islamic and Jewish cultural traditions prohibit the eating of pork, and orthodox Hindus encourage meatless vegetarian diets. The *emic* qualitative data gathered about a society help cultural anthropologists understand the *etic* quantitative data. Ordinarily, both the etic, quantitative and the emic, qualitative data are integral to ethnographic research. Although there are considerable philosophical differences among anthropologists over the precise criteria on which emic knowledge and etic knowledge differ, most agree that the insider's emic understandings and perceptions of his or her culture differ from the outsider's etic views to some degree. Cultural anthropologists strive to understand the culture from both the outsider's and the insider's perspectives in their ethnographic descriptions.

Cultural anthropologists have a number of different methods for recording qualitative data. The best-known method is *field notes*, systematic recordings of observations or interviews in a field notebook. Cultural anthropologists should have some training in how to take useful field notes and how to manage them for more effective coding and recording of data. An increasing number of cultural anthropologists now use laptop computers as a means of constructing databases to manage their field notes. They select appropriate categories for classifying the data. For example, a cultural anthropologist may set up specific categories for kinship terms, religious taboos, plants, animals, colors, foods, and so on. These data can then easily be retrieved for analysis. Some cultural anthropologists rely on tape recorders for interviews, although they recognize the problems such devices present for producing valid accounts. Some people may feel self-conscious about having their personal thoughts recorded. Most ethnographic fieldworkers utilize photography to record and help document their findings. Cultural anthropologists must use extreme caution when using these technologies, however, for in some cultures people are very sensitive about being recorded or photographed.

Today, many anthropologists use video cameras when gathering primary data. Video recording is one of the most exciting recent developments in anthropology and has stimulated a new area of anthropological research known as visual anthropology. The visual documentation of economic, social, political, and ritual behavior sometimes reveals intricate patterns of interaction in a society—interaction that cannot otherwise be described thoroughly. One drawback to video recording, however, is that people who know they are being filmed frequently behave differently from the way they would normally. This may distort the cultural anthropologist's conclusions. On the other hand, the video can be shown to informants so they comment on the recorded behaviors. William Rittenberg, who did studies of Buddhist rituals in villages in central Thailand, often played back his video recordings of rituals for members of the community. The informants, including the Buddhist monks, viewed the recordings and offered more elaborate explanations of the meanings of the ritual. These strategies frequently help the cultural anthropologist gain a more comprehensive understanding of the culture.

Culture Shock   Ethnographic fieldwork can be a very demanding task. Cultural anthropologists sometimes experience **culture shock**, a severe psychological reaction that results from adjusting to the realities of a society radically different from one's own. A cultural anthropologist enculturated in the United States could experience culture shock when having to eat unfamiliar foods such as reptiles or insects, reside in uncomfortable huts in a rain forest, or observe practices that may not occur within his or her own society. Of course, the actual degree of culture shock may vary, depending upon the differences and similarities between the society studied and the anthropologist's own society. The symptoms may range from mild irritation to surprise or disgust.

Usually, after the cultural anthropologist learns the norms, beliefs, and practices of the community, the psychological disorientation of culture shock begins to diminish. Part of the challenge for anthropologists is adjusting to a different society and gaining a much better perspective on one's own society. In fact, most anthropologists report considerable culture shock upon returning home from another society. They will never again view their own society and culture in the same light. The adjustment process of culture shock out in the field and upon returning from the field enables cultural anthropologists to better understand themselves and their own society.

Ethics in Anthropological Research

14.3 Discuss some of the ethical dilemmas of ethnographic research.

Cultural anthropologists must not only be trained in appropriate research and analytical techniques, but also abide by the ethical guidelines of their discipline. In many instances, cultural anthropologists conduct research on politically powerless groups dominated by more powerful groups. When cultural anthropologists engage in participant observation, they usually become familiar with information that might, if made public, be harmful to the community or to individuals. For example, when researching isolated or rural communities, cultural anthropologists might come across economic or political behavior and information that could be used by government authorities. This information might include the specific sources of income for people in the community or the participation by people in the community in political opposition to the government. Whenever possible, cultural anthropologists attempt to keep such information confidential so as not to compromise their informants or other sources of data.

Most ethnographic reports do not include the real identities of informants or other people. Cultural anthropologists usually ensure their informants' anonymity, if at all possible (de Munck 2009). Sometimes, cultural anthropologists use pseudonyms (fictional names) to make identification difficult. In addition, cultural anthropologists ensure the confidentiality regarding their research to make sure that no one knows the identity of the participants who provided data. The data should not be traceable to individuals through name, residential, e-mail, or IP addresses.

Cultural anthropologists also attempt to be frank and open with the population under study about the aims of the research. At times, this is difficult because the community does not understand the role of the cultural anthropologist. Out of courtesy, the cultural anthropologist should give the community a reasonable account of what he or she wants to do. The American Anthropological Association has developed a code of ethics that was last published in 2012 (American Anthropological Association 2012). The code provides anthropologists with ethical guidelines to help make decisions while in the field.

In general, cultural anthropologists do not accept research funding for projects that are supposed to be clandestine or secretive. This type of research was conducted by some anthropologists in the past during World War II and the Cold War (Wax 2008). There has been a recent attempt by the U.S. military to recruit anthropologists during the wars in Afghanistan and Iraq referred to as the Human Terrain System (HTS). Many contemporary anthropologists have grave reservations about undercover research in war zones (Price 2011). However, a recent discussion regarding the ethics for anthropologists considering participating in war zone research by Carolyn Fluehr-Lobban who describes how ethnographic knowledge can contribute towards "doing no harm" in the complex settings that exist since 9/11 (2013). "Doing no harm" is promoted as the principal ethical guideline by the American Anthropological Association statement on ethics and professional responsibility (2012). Fluehr-Lobban notes that the HTS mission statement focuses on the prevention of harm to U.S. troops and local communities in combat zones, where saving lives is the intention of the mission (2013). She argues that many anthropologists who criticize the HTS overlook the benefits that accrue from ethnographic research and advice given to the military. Robert Rubinstein, Kerry Fisher, and Clementine Fujimoro have also contributed a nuanced understanding of the role of anthropologists who consult with the military since 9/11 (2012). They suggest that anthropologists can contribute some useful advice and assistance to the military. Anthropologist David Edwards, an Afghanistan specialist, believes that ethnographers ought to be doing research on HTS itself (2010). This issue will likely remain a contested area of ethical responsibility among anthropologists for some time.

Analysis of Ethnographic Data

14.4 How do cultural anthropologists analyze their ethnographic data?

The results of ethnographic research are documented in a descriptive monograph referred to as an *ethnography*. In writing the ethnographic description, the cultural anthropologist must be extremely cautious. The accumulated field notes, photos, perhaps video or tape recordings, and quantitative data from survey sources must all be carefully managed to reduce bias, distortion, and error. The cultural anthropologist must analyze these data, making sure to cross-check the conclusions from a variety of sources, including informants, censuses, observations, and archival materials. In addition, the cultural anthropologist should plainly distinguish the views of the people being studied from his or her interpretation of those views.

Universals, Independent Variables, and Dependent Variables   Culture, society, and human behavior are not just a random array of occurrences that develop without rhyme or reason. They are the result of universal features and interacting variables that influence the human condition. In analyzing a sociocultural system, anthropologists frequently find that different universals and specific variables interact with one another. The interaction of two variables is

called a **correlation**. For example, a particular society may experience both population increases and a high incidence of warfare. This does not necessarily mean that the population growth causes the warfare or vice versa; it simply means that both conditions exist within the society. To determine whether a causal relationship exists between these variables would require further investigation, including, in many cases, comparisons with other societies. Further research may indicate that the relationship between population and warfare is a spurious correlation; that is, two variables occur together, but each is caused by some third variable.

Alternatively, research may indicate that in a certain society the rate of population growth does influence the frequency of warfare. In such cases, the anthropologist might hypothesize that population increases cause the high incidence of warfare. This hypothesis could then be tested and evaluated by other anthropologists.

In determining cause-and-effect relationships, anthropologists distinguish between independent and dependent variables. An **independent variable** is the causal variable that produces an effect on another variable, the **dependent variable**. That is, the dependent variable may *depend* upon or be explained at least in part, by the independent variable. In the previous example, population growth is the independent variable because it determines the incidence of warfare, which is the dependent variable.

In actuality, this example of determining causal relationships is far too simplistic. Anthropologists recognize that no aspect of culture and society can be completely explained by any single cause or independent variable. They rely instead on hypotheses that are *multivariate* or *multidimensional*, in which many variables interact with one another. This multidimensional approach must be kept in mind when considering the specific variables explored by cultural anthropologists in their study of different societies. The multidimensional approach is linked with the holistic perspective in anthropology—that is, the attempt to demonstrate how sociocultural systems must be understood through the interconnections among universals and specific variables.

Universals and Variables Studied by Cultural Anthropologists

The major variables and universal features of sociocultural systems include subsistence and the physical environment, demography, technology, the economy, the family, social structure, and gender, the political organization, law, and warfare, religion, art, and music. Although this is not a complete list of the universals and specific variables studied by cultural anthropologists, it provides the general framework for understanding different societies. In later chapters we will discuss these variables and universal characteristics of different sociocultural systems.

Sociocultural Evolution: A Contemporary Model

14.5 **Discuss the contemporary view of sociocultural evolution used by anthropologists.**

In the following sections of this chapter, we will be discussing different types of sociocultural systems described by anthropologists: bands, tribes, chiefdoms, agricultural states, industrial and postindustrial states. We want to emphasize that these typologies should not be used to endorse a unilineal view of evolution that nineteenth-century anthropologists proposed. Contemporary anthropologists are very aware of the considerable problems with a unilineal, ladder-like evolutionary perspective. As discussed in Chapter 13, contemporary anthropologists view cultural evolution as *multilineal* with tremendous variations within these different forms of societies depending on ecological, historical, economic, and political conditions as well as many other factors. Contemporary anthropologists are also cognizant of the manner in which different forms of societies may oscillate from one form to another during different periods of time. Although in later chapters we will be mentioning the cultural universals found among these sociocultural systems, we will also be highlighting the tremendous variation within these different forms of societies discussed. We will note how these categories such as tribe and chiefdom have been subject to much criticism by anthropologists. Additionally, as we mentioned earlier, we recognize that these categories of sociocultural systems must be viewed as "ideal types" that do not conform to the actual realities, complexities, diversity, and of people and "cultures." However, we do think that these categories are useful as ideal types or heuristic tools to begin to understand the similarities and different aspects of various societies and cultural evolution.

Types of Sociocultural Systems

14.6 **Describe the types of sociocultural systems studied by anthropologists.**

Foragers, Band, or Hunter-Gatherer Societies

In Chapter 7, we discussed the Paleolithic period (Old Stone Age) and the emergence of hunting and gathering, which as a means of subsistence goes back to at least one million years ago. A hunter-gatherer society depends on hunting animals and gathering vegetation for subsistence. These hunter-gatherer societies are also known as **foraging societies**. As the next chapter indicates, food production as a subsistence pattern developed relatively recently, about 12,000 to 10,000 years ago. Thus, for almost 99 percent of humanity's life span, humans lived as foragers. This lifestyle has been the most enduring and persistent adaptation humans have ever achieved. Therefore, band societies have been the basic type of sociocultural system for perhaps as long as one million years. When archaeologists do studies of the artifacts found during the Paleolithic to understand the human past, they often look to the ethnographic studies of modern hunter-gatherers. As we shall see in later chapters, most contemporary hunter-gatherer societies, with their relatively small groups, low population density, highly nomadic subsistence strategies, and loosely defined territorial boundaries, have social organizations that tie kin (related individuals) together and foster unity within and among groups. Constant circulation of material goods in such societies not only enhances and maintains kin ties through mutual obligations, but also inhibits the accumulation of wealth by any individuals in the society. This enables these societies to remain **egalitarian**—to have very small differences in wealth among individuals. There are no rich or poor in most of these societies.

Also, the most common form of political organization among ethnographically documented hunter-gatherer societies is the band, a fairly small group of people tied together by close kinship relations. A band is the least complex form of political system—and most likely the oldest. Typically, as we will see in Chapter 18, each band is politically independent of the others and has its own internal leadership. Most of the leaders in the bands are males, but females also take on some important leadership roles. Leaders are chosen because of their skills in hunting, food collecting, communication, decision making, or other personal abilities. Political leaders, however, generally do not control the group's economic resources or exercise political power as they do in other societies, and there is little, if any, social stratification between political leaders and others in the band. In other words, band societies are highly *egalitarian*, with no major differences between those with and those without wealth or political power. Thus, leaders of bands must lead by persuasion and personal influence, rather than by coercing or withholding resources. Leaders do not maintain a military or police force and thus have no definitive authority.

Although it is tempting to draw a similar picture of Paleolithic or Old Stone Age hunters, the analogy is not without limitations. The archaeological record of the Paleolithic is consistent with small kin-based groups. Yet, archaeological information on Paleolithic hunter-gatherers suggests that their subsistence strategies varied substantially and probably included the beginnings of some of the complexity, socioeconomic inequality, and the more sedentary lifestyle that characterize more recent periods (Price and Brown 1985; Jochim 1998; Boyd and Richerson 1992). In addition, anthropologists have found a vast range of different subsistence and technological developments among both past and contemporary hunter-gatherer societies throughout the world (Kelly 1995; Ames 2004). As we will see, there are some hunting-gathering societies that were *settled* and *not nomadic* that evolved a much more complex economic, social, and political culture, primarily because of the environmental and demographic conditions that existed in some areas of the world.

Most importantly, the contemporary hunting-gathering societies are not living "fossils" of the Old Stone Age, but *fully modern humans just like you and me*. In contrast to Paleolithic hunting-and-gathering societies that resided in nearly *all* the major biomes and environments of the world, contemporary band societies exist only in limited, marginal environments, those that are not suitable for intensive agriculture and tremendous population increases. In addition, these modern human band societies are enmeshed in the process of globalization, which has had dramatic consequences for their lifestyle. Contemporary hunter-gatherer societies have been in contact with outsiders such as the agricultural societies surrounding them for many years (Bailey et al. 1989; Ames 2004). Thus, what we learn from contemporary band societies does not inform us about the "pristine" Paleolithic societies.

Most nineteenth-century Western (and non-Western) scholars, scientists, politicians, and others, including anthropologists, had very racist and ethnocentric beliefs about "savages," "barbarians," and "culturally inferior peoples with low intelligence" throughout the world. Reflecting the views of the nineteenth century, Mark Twain considered the Shoshone Indians of the Great Basin in Nevada to be "the wretchedest type of mankind I have ever seen up to this writing" (Wright 2000).

Sometimes, these views are still perpetuated about contemporary hunting-and-gathering societies in Africa, Asia, and South America. However, in the twentieth century, cultural anthropologists began to conduct long-term ethnographic research among these people and discovered that the people within these societies have very complex beliefs and a tremendous amount of cultural knowledge about the plants, animals, medical techniques, and environments in which they have been living. Most importantly, contemporary hunters and gatherers are *modern peoples* who have adapted to more extreme, marginal environmental and ecological conditions than have modern societies. Further, some people from these band societies (such as the Shoshone Indians) are highly educated and working as computer scientists, engineers, and even anthropologists. Their intelligence or intellectual capacities allow them to learn new languages, mathematics,

and other modern technologies just as other modern peoples do.

However, the basic question still arises in many people's minds: If these hunting-and-gathering peoples are generally as intelligent and modern as we in the industrialized and more advanced societies of the world are, why did they not develop more complex technologies and subsistence strategies where they lived? In other words, from our contemporary perspective in our advanced high-tech world, why did these hunter-gatherers continue to rely on their "antiquated" techniques and social life for coping in their environments? Why didn't they develop computers and other high-tech accoutrements? As we shall see in later chapters, contemporary ethnographic research has demonstrated that part of the reason for the perceived lack of technological and cultural development is the geographical, environmental, ecological, and historical circumstances that have influenced the development of these societies and cultural traditions.

For example, with respect to the geographical and ecological factors that have had an influence on the development of certain technological and sociocultural conditions in sub-Saharan Africa, prehistoric North and South America, some areas of the Pacific Islands, and Asia, Jared Diamond's book *Guns, Germs, and Steel: The Fates of Human Societies* (1997) has been influenced by many anthropologists.

Drawing on ethnographic research about the plants, animals, and cultures of the Pacific Islands of Papua New Guinea as well as an enormous range of geographic, ecological, archaeological, and historical data, Diamond investigates why the Eurasian continent, including Europe, Russia, and China, had some definite geographical and ecological advantages—compared to sub-Saharan Africa, prehistoric North and South America, the Pacific Islands, and elsewhere—that resulted in the development of complex societies in that continental region. He notes that the Eurasian continent had early connections with the Near East or Fertile Crescent areas of the Nile and Tigris-Euphrates rivers, which contained species of plants and animals such as wheat, barley, oats, sheep, cattle, goats, pigs, and horses that were easily domesticated for the development of complex agricultural societies. These ideas spread rapidly across the Mediterranean areas of Greece and Rome to other areas of Europe and beyond.

In contrast, sub-Saharan Africa, the Pacific Island areas such as Australia, and the Americas had very *few species* of animals and plants that could be domesticated; they also had major geographical obstacles such as large tropical rain forests, deserts, and infertile land that inhibited the development of agriculture and the rapid diffusion or spread of technologies and ideas from one area to the next. These factors limited the technological and sociocultural developments of these areas of the world, whereas the ecological and geographical advantages enjoyed on the Eurasian continent fostered more complex technological and sociocultural developments. Although some archaeologists and anthropologists have refined Diamond's understanding of these developments in different areas of the world, they concur that these geographical and environmental factors did have an enormous influence on technological and sociocultural developments for preindustrial societies.

You will notice that in later chapters, we refer to hunter-gatherers in both the past and the present tenses. As a result of contacts with other peoples, many traditional practices and institutions of band societies have been transformed. The past tense is used to describe these traditional phenomena. Those traditions that have managed to persist into the present are discussed in the present tense.

The Concept of Tribe in Anthropology

The term *tribe* is used loosely to characterize *two* different types of subsistence systems: *horticulturalist* and *pastoralist*. Unlike hunting-and-gathering societies, tribal societies are *food-producing groups* that depend on the limited domestication of plants and animals. Politically, *tribes* are usually defined as noncentralized sociocultural systems in which authority is diffused among a number of kinship groups and associations.

Some anthropologists, most notably the late Morton Fried (1967, 1975), have objected to the use of the term *tribe* to characterize these societies. The word *tribe* is derived from the Latin term *tribus*, which was used by the Romans to refer to certain peoples who were not technologically advanced. Fried claimed that the term is often applied to a particular group by a more powerful group and usually has a pejorative connotation.

One aspect of Fried's criticism has created some theoretical controversy in anthropology. Fried argued that tribal organization is not an evolutionary stage, emerging from the simpler stage represented by the foraging society, as most anthropologists had maintained. He suggested that, for the most part, tribes are usually "secondary" developments that evolve through contacts with other societies. This contact occurs when large, complex state societies, both agricultural and industrial, create tribal groups through the process of subjugation and domination. In many cases, these tribal groups become subjugated ethnic minorities in state societies.

Fried's criticisms have sensitized most anthropologists to the vagueness of the term *tribe*. In the past and sometimes currently, the term has been used haphazardly to refer to an enormous range of societies that have almost nothing in common. As we see in later chapters, there is a tremendous range of environments and social structures, as well as political, religious, and other features that do not fit neatly into the concept of the *tribe*. Despite these reservations, the term *tribe* describes the many different types of horticulturalist and pastoralist societies that are not politically centralized that bridge the gap between bands and chiefdoms (Lewellen 1983).

Just as we saw in the prior discussion of band societies, since the twentieth century cultural anthropologists have done extensive ethnographic fieldwork among these tribal societies and have found that the people have a tremendous understanding of their environments and a normal range of intelligence that compares with that of other modern humans. Many of these people in tribal societies in North and South America, in Melanesia, and other regions of the world have been educated and have become physicians, attorneys, engineers, politicians, and also anthropologists. So, again, this question arises for many people in advanced industrial societies: Why did these tribal societies not develop more complex technologies and sociocultural systems? It is obvious that it does not have anything to do with "race," because the North American Indians in tribal societies had genetic and biological traits similar to those of other Asians (see Chapter 6), but they did not develop civilizations such as those in China or elsewhere in Asia. What, then, is the explanation for their perceived lack of technological and sociocultural complexity?

Geographical and ecological conditions gave enormous advantages to some areas of the world, such as the Eurasian continent, which had the package of domesticated animals and plants that diffused and spread across Europe and other areas very rapidly without major geographic boundaries such as mountains, tropical rain forests, and deserts (Diamond 1997). This resulted in tremendous advantages for Greece, Rome, and other complex

Bedouin tribal pastoralists who rely on camels in the Middle East.

societies in the development of agricultural civilizations. Archaeologists and other anthropologists have done extensive research on the lack of domesticated animals and plants, as well as geographical barriers that restricted the diffusion of technologies and ideas from one area to another in many regions of the world such as the Americas and the Pacific Islands.

For example, anthropologists have done extensive fieldwork in the Melanesian Islands of Papua New Guinea. The peoples in this region were fairly isolated from other societies until the 1930s, when Australians, as well as Germans and other Europeans, began to explore the islands. There are hundreds of different tribes and languages in this region because many of these people were separated by geographical boundaries in the mountain and highland areas and the lowland areas. In addition, just as in North, Central, and South America or Australia, these people of Papua New Guinea had very few domesticated plants and animals compared to the Near East or the Eurasian continent. In addition, there were no metals available in the region, unlike the Near East or Eurasia. These ecological, geographical, and historical circumstances give us a better understanding of why tribal peoples have not developed more complex sociocultural systems than any views about the lack of intelligence or racial inferiority.

The Concept of the Chiefdom

Like the term *tribe* or *band*, the term *chiefdom* has caused a certain amount of confusion outside anthropology. A major reason for this is that chiefdoms have little to do with what people commonly refer to as "chiefs." In the past, Western explorers, missionaries, and government officials used the label "chief" to describe any individual who held a leadership role in a non-Western, stateless society. In contrast to this common usage, anthropologists use *chiefdom* to refer to a form of complex society that is intermediate between the band and tribal societies and the formally organized bureaucratic state societies described later. A chiefdom is a political economy that organizes regional populations in the thousands or tens of thousands through a hierarchy of leaders, or chiefs. Typically, **chiefs** own, manage, and control the basic productive factors of the economy and have privileged access to strategic and luxury goods. These leaders are set off from the rest of society by various cultural practices and symbols, such as clothing, jewelry, specialized language, and social status. Thus, chiefdom societies are not *egalitarian* in the sense that band and tribal societies are.

Another reason that the term *chiefdom* is often unclear is that chiefdom societies vary greatly with respect to political, economic, and cultural forms. Hence, even anthropologists frequently disagree about which societies should be classified as chiefdoms. Some consider the chiefdom to be a subcategory of the tribe, whereas others view it as qualitatively different from tribes and bands (Service [1962] 1971; Sahlins 1968; Earle 1997). Anthropologists have designated two different forms of chiefdoms: One is a centralized political system with localized chiefs who control economic, social, political, and religious affairs; a second is more decentralized, with centers of political power and authority distributed throughout a region and with chiefs having control over different local arenas. Although most anthropologists now recognize the limitations of the term *chiefdom* as it is applied to a vast range of societies in different circumstances, most also consider it a valuable category for cross-cultural and comparative research.

As with tribal and foraging societies, hundreds of chiefdoms existed during at least the past 12,000 years of human history. Chiefdoms were widespread throughout Polynesia, including the islands of Hawaii, Tahiti, and Tonga. They also flourished in parts of North, Central, and South America; North Africa; the Middle East; sub-Saharan Africa; the Caribbean; and Southeast Asia; and in Europe during the days of the Roman Empire. Today, however, very few of these chiefdoms remain as autonomous societies. Therefore, the past tense is used to discuss most of these societies. Not surprisingly, a great deal of the research on chiefdoms is based upon archaeological and historical documentation.

The precise transition to a chiefdom society from a prior form of society is not well documented in any part of the world. But through comparisons with tribal and foraging societies, anthropologists have developed various hypotheses to explain this transition. The central question is: How did one particular descent group (or several descent groups) manage to gain advantages or monopolies of resources over other descent groups? In other words, how did social stratification and economic inequality emerge from the egalitarian economic and political processes found in tribal or foraging societies?

Up until the twentieth century, many people in both Western and non-Western regions of the world, including scientists, scholars, politicians, anthropologists, and others, had racist and ethnocentric views of people within these chiefdom societies and believed they had low intelligence and racial traits that kept them undeveloped compared with industrialized or more advanced societies. If many of the Native Hawaiians or other Polynesian peoples, Native Americans, or other people who were living in chiefdom societies have become doctors, lawyers, computer scientists, biologists, and anthropologists, as has happened today, why were those chiefdoms lacking in advanced technologies or more developed societies?

The different types of Pacific Islands have been studied by anthropologists for many years. In some Pacific island areas such as Australia, the people were organized as bands and lived as hunter-gatherers, whereas in Papua New Guinea, the people domesticated some plants such as yams, raised pigs, as we saw above, and became tribally organized societies. However, the people that eventually migrated to the islands of Polynesia, such as Tahiti, Samoa, Hawaii, and Easter Island, developed multifaceted sociocultural societies known as chiefdoms with extremely sophisticated monument and sculpture constructions, extensive centralized economic and political systems, and elaborate temples with full-time priests, musicians, and others who officiated at and performed highly complex rituals. Each one of these different island areas had plant and animal resources, ecological conditions, climate, and geographical conditions that either enabled complex sociocultural developments or inhibited the emergence of these developments. The island of Australia contained very few animals and plants that could be domesticated and had very few areas of arable land suitable for agricultural developments. Papua New Guinea had a little more, whereas the islands of Polynesia had an enormous array of rich and varied landscapes with ecological resources that offered much more potential for sociocultural complexity and the development of chiefdoms.

Agricultural States

As discussed earlier in Chapter 7, throughout much of their prehistory, humans have relied on hunting wild animals and gathering wild plants. During the Neolithic period, beginning about 12,000 years ago, new patterns of subsistence developed involving the domestication of plants and animals and the emergence of tribal societies: horticulturalists and pastoralists. About 5,000 years ago or so, as we discussed in Chapter 8, some peoples became settled in regions with abundant resources and developed complex chiefdom societies. Archaeologists and historians have discovered increasing technological capacities and more social complexity during this extended period of the Neolithic era. As a result, many peoples developed **intensive agriculture**, the cultivation of crops by preparing permanent fields year after year, often using irrigation and fertilizers. In contrast to horticulture, intensive agriculture enables a population to produce enormous food surpluses to sustain dense populations in large, permanent settlements.

In some regions, beginning as much as 5,500 years ago, the intensification of agriculture was accompanied by the appearance of complex agricultural states. Anthropologists use the term *state* to describe a wide range of societies that differ structurally from bands, tribes, and chiefdoms. As discussed in Chapter 9, the major difference between *state* and *prestate societies* is a bureaucratic organization (or government). A state is a political system with centralized bureaucratic institutions to establish power and authority over large populations in clearly defined territories.

Geographical and ecological advantages have played an important role in where agricultural civilizations have developed. For example, agriculture civilizations developed around the major river valleys of the Near East in Mesopotamia and Egypt, but there were no such areas in sub-Saharan Africa. In addition, some areas such as the Near East and Europe had domesticated animals such as sheep, cattle, goats, and horses, whereas neither sub-Saharan Africa nor the Americas had many domesticated animals. Also, some areas did not have geographical barriers such as mountains, rain forests, or deserts that inhibited the flow of agricultural patterns from one area to another. The Near East and Europe were contiguous, and technology and agricultural patterns diffused quickly throughout these regions. The Mediterranean Sea enabled the cultures of Greece and Rome to have considerable contact with the ideas and agricultural patterns of Egypt and the Near East. Other areas of the world were not as fortunately located.

Contemporary developments in specific world areas are explored in later chapters on globalization in Latin America, Africa, the Caribbean, the Middle East, and Asia where once traditional agricultural states existed; these regions are now undergoing significant change. As with bands, tribes, and chiefdoms, the agricultural states no longer exist in the same form as they did in the past. The political economy, social organization, and religious traditions that emerged, however, have had consequences that persist up to the present.

Industrial and Postindustrial States

The *Industrial Revolution* is the term used to describe the broad changes that occurred during the latter part of the eighteenth century in Europe. However, the roots of these dramatic changes in the structure and organization of society were there much earlier. Anthropologists consider the causes of the Industrial Revolution and its consequences for the states in which it occurred. This is an extremely important topic because it emphasizes how anthropologists interpret and explain the development of the Industrial Revolution in Europe, rather than in other regions of the world. Traditionally, most cultural anthropologists did research on preindustrial societies; however, many cultural anthropologists have turned their attention to doing ethnography in the industrial regions of the world, including Europe, Russia, the United States, Canada, Australia, and Japan. These cultural anthropologists have to take a very interdisciplinary approach, drawing on the work of historians, economists, political scientists, and sociologists.

An **industrial society** uses sophisticated technology based on machinery powered by advanced fuels to produce material goods. A primary feature of industrial societies in comparison with preindustrial societies is that most productive labor involves factory and office work, rather than agricultural or foraging activities. This pattern has produced new forms of economic organization and social-class arrangements. In terms of political organization, industrial societies became the first well-developed **nation-states**—political communities that have clearly defined territorial borders dividing them from one another. All modern industrial nation-states exercise extensive political authority over many aspects of the lives of their citizenry through the application of formalized laws and a centralized government.

One of the early explanations of why Europe succeeded in developing the Industrial Revolution and other societies did not is that Europeans were superior to other people mentally and intellectually. Anthropologists do not accept this claim of European mental and intellectual superiority. This idea has a long history that is connected with racist beliefs that go back deep into Western history (see Chapters 6 and 23 on race). According to this racist view, non-European races were cognitively deficient and incapable of developing advanced technology, and that is why Europe was the center of the rise of industrial society. Again, anthropologists have refuted the basis of these racist arguments through systematic biological, archaeological, and cultural research throughout the world (see Chapters 6 and 23).

An enormous amount of geographical, archaeological, and anthropological research demonstrates that the European Industrial Revolution developed not as the result of the "unique" genius, intelligence, or particular superior cultural values of Europeans, but as the result of an unpredictable sequence of prehistoric and historical processes (Diamond 1997). As mentioned before, most of the plants and large mammals that could be domesticated existed in the Near East, whereas Africa and the Americas lacked easily domesticated species of plants and animals for agriculture. The Near Eastern pattern of plant and animal domestication spread into the Eurasian continent, which included China and Europe, because Europe, the Near East, and Asia were contiguous. Further, this diffusion of agriculture and domesticated animals happened quickly in Europe and Asia because unlike in Africa and the Americas, there were no substantial geographic barriers such as oceans, deserts, and rain forests to inhibit the spread of this agricultural package across the Near East and Mediterranean areas to the Eurasian continent. The Near Easterners, Europeans, and Asians developed resistance to certain diseases as a result of living with domesticated animals such as cattle and pigs for many years, and these animals, along with abundant harvests, enabled the Near Easterners, Europeans, and Asians to develop cities with large populations, governments, specialized economic systems, and writing systems, as described

previously. Centuries later, the Europeans developed the technological knowledge and political power to conquer other areas of the world that did not have these agricultural resources.

The process of agricultural development just described led to further cultural and economic developments that gave Europe the edge in the beginnings of the Industrial Revolution. China was almost to the same point of development in the 1600s, but for historical and political reasons, China did not begin to expand beyond its boundaries. Consequently, Europe, not China, became the center of the Industrial Revolution during that period.

Anthropologists address the question of why Europe was the center of the Industrial Revolution by drawing on a wide range of historical sources from many regions of the world. Only by taking a global perspective can we answer this question. Anthropologists such as Jack Goody (1996) and Eric Wolf ([1982] 1997) have adopted this global perspective and have examined the interrelationships between the non-European world and Europe to shed light on this question.

A major factor leading to the emergence of industrial states in European society was the increased contact among different societies, primarily through trade. Although long-distance trade was present in agricultural states, the major regions of the world were relatively isolated from one another. Trade was conducted in Asia, the Near East, Europe, and Africa, and internally within the Americas before 1500 A.D., but the difficulties of transportation and communication inhibited the spread of ideas, values, and technology among these regions. Although Europeans had contact with non-Europeans through religious wars such as the Crusades and the travels of adventurers such as Marco Polo, they did not engage in systematic relations with non-Europeans until after the year 1500.

The upper class and royalty of agricultural European society encouraged long-distance trade as a means of accumulating wealth. Their principal motivation was to build a self-sufficient economy as a basis for extending their centralized government. This type of economic system is often referred to as *mercantilism*. **Mercantilism** is a system in which the government regulates the economy of a state to ensure economic growth, a positive balance of trade, and the accumulation of gold and silver. Eventually, European countries such as the Netherlands, Great Britain, France, and Russia became mercantile competitors with Spain and Portugal. They formed private trading companies such as the British East India Company, which were subsidized by the government. As economic wealth began to amass in Europe through the accumulation of gold, silver, and other commodities from the Americas, Asia, Africa, and the Middle East, the political center of power also shifted to Europe. These economic and political changes were accompanied by major transformations in non-Western societies. These changes in non-Western societies are discussed in later chapters.

The global diffusion of philosophical and practical knowledge provided the basis for the scientific revolution in the West. Ideas and technology that were developed in the civilizations of China, India, the Middle East, Africa, and the Americas provided the stimulus for the emergence of scientific enterprise in Europe. Eventually, scientific methods based on deductive and inductive logic (see Chapter 1) were allied with practical economic interests to provide the basis for the Industrial Revolution in Europe. But, again, many of the ideas and technological developments that gave rise to the Industrial Revolution in Europe had emerged earlier in agricultural civilizations in other regions of the world. The scientific revolution would not have developed in Europe without the knowledge of scientific and mathematical concepts previously developed in India, the Middle East, and Asia.

The notion that there was a unique European miracle associated with the so-called white race is a fallacy. The idea that Europeans were superior geniuses who were capable of developing the industrial civilization is also a fallacy. Without the diffusion of knowledge and technologies from other regions of the world, Europe would not have been able to develop the Industrial Revolution. Slowly and gradually, over a period of some 400 years, the combination of scientific and commercial alliances in Europe produced dramatic consequences that transformed economic, social, and political structures through the process of **industrialization**—the adoption of a mechanized

An industrial technology factory scene.

means of production to transform raw materials into manufactured goods.

The overall consequences of the Industrial Revolution are often referred to as **modernization**—the economic, social, political, and religious changes related to modern industrial and technological change. Modernization was not an overnight occurrence. It took more than 400 years, from 1600 on, to develop in the West, and modernity remains an ongoing process. It depended upon the commercial transformations brought about through years of mercantilism that led to the accumulation of capital for investment and the gradual diffusion of practical knowledge and scientific methods that engendered technological innovations.

Since the 1970s, in the most advanced industrial societies—such as the United States, the United Kingdom, Japan, Germany, Canada, and Australia—the largest and most rapidly expanding component of the economy is based on information technology such as the Internet, computers, and other related occupations. Some anthropologists refer to these societies as *postindustrial societies* because more people are employed in service and high-technology occupations than in manufacturing. A **postindustrial society** is based on information technology that is interconnected in a global network throughout the world. Information is the key component of a postindustrial society because people must acquire a great deal of technical knowledge to function effectively, and educational requirements for many jobs have increased substantially. Sometimes postindustrial societies are referred to as *postfordism*, the type of society that was manufacturing-based, like Henry Ford's auto company in the early twentieth century in the United States. To meet the demands of a postindustrial economy, an increasing percentage of the population attends college (and graduate and professional schools), and computer skills have been integrated into the educational curriculum. With their capacity to process and manipulate vast amounts of data, computers have become essential in these societies. Anthropologists are doing extensive ethnographic research on the development of this postindustrial society in numerous locations (McCreery 2000; McCreery and McCreery 2006; Denoon et al. 2001; Lewellen 2002; Harvey 1990). We will discuss the various characteristics of these postindustrial societies in later chapters.

Cross-Cultural Research

14.7 Describe the strengths and limitations of the cross-cultural approach.

This chapter has focused on the fieldwork by cultural anthropologists and the different types of sociocultural systems they study. Although the primary objective of ethnographic research is to improve our understanding of a particular sociocultural system, another aim is to provide a basis for comparing different societies and to offer general explanations for human behavior. Specific ethnographies provide the necessary data for this type of cross-cultural research, which is usually referred to as *ethnological* research. Anthropologists use ethnological research to further explore the universal and specific cultural conditions that influence the development of societies throughout the world.

Cross-cultural research has been an ongoing project in anthropology for the past hundred years or so. Recently, a great deal of ethnographic data has been computerized in the Human Relations Area Files, commonly known as the HRAF. The HRAF contains descriptive ethnographic data on more than 300 societies. Initiated by George P. Murdock of Yale University, it is made up of original ethnographic descriptions classified for cross-cultural research purposes. Murdock incorporated data on 862 societies in his *Ethnographic Atlas* (1981b) and on 563 societies that cover the major geographic regions of the world in his *Atlas of World Cultures* (1981a). These ethnographic databases enable scholars to retrieve information quickly and can be used for statistical and computerized cross-cultural research. They are extremely valuable sources for assessing the differences and similarities among cultures. Cross-cultural studies allow anthropologists to make distinctions between behaviors that are culture specific and those that are universal. These distinctions help anthropologists provide general explanations for human behavior. In doing so, these studies help fulfill the major goals of anthropological research.

Cross-cultural methods have some limitations, however. One major weakness is that some cultural anthropologists in the past may not have taken historical circumstances into account when describing the particular conditions in a society. This omission may have led to a static, unchanging portrait of the society studied. For example, the description of the economic practices of people in Africa, Asia, or the Pacific Islands may not make sense outside of a specific historical context. These societies had historical relationships with other societies outside of their own cultural boundaries, and these relationships resulted in changes in the particular economic practices observed by the cultural anthropologist. In later chapters of this text, we explore why cultural anthropologists must understand the historical context of the different societies that they study so that they can fully comprehend the behavior being observed.

Another problem with cross-cultural studies lies with faulty ethnographic reporting, which can produce unreliable data, contributing, in turn, to a distorted image of the society being studied. Consequently, anthropologists approach cross-cultural research with caution. Contemporary anthropologists who use these data must review the work of their predecessors who gathered the basic information to assess its validity. Through careful examination of the original data in the HRAF and other cross-cultural databases, modern anthropologists will make further progress toward formulating sound generalizations regarding the cultures of humankind.

Summary and Review of Learning Objectives

14.1 Discuss how cultural anthropologists prepare to study society and culture.

Cultural anthropologists conduct fieldwork in different societies to examine people's lifestyles and behavior. They have to develop a research design to examine a particular topic that specifies the appropriate methods for gathering the richest possible data. Before going into the field for direct research, the cultural anthropologist analyzes available archival data, including photos, films, missionary reports, business and government surveys, musical recordings, journalistic accounts, diaries, court documents, medical records, birth, landholding documents, and death, marriage, and tax records. Historical material in the archives helps the cultural anthropologist evaluate the usefulness of the observations and interviews he or she will document. They must also read the published anthropological, historical, economic, sociological, and political science literature on the geographic region toward which they are heading.

14.2 Describe the actual research methods used for ethnographic studies.

Cultural anthropologists conduct fieldwork in different societies to examine people's lifestyles and behavior. They describe societies in written studies called ethnographies, which focus upon behavior and thought among the people studied. Cultural anthropologists must use systematic research methods and strategies in their examination of society. Their basic research method is participant observation, which involves participating in the activities of the people they are studying. Ethnographic studies are based on participant observation, the use of key informants, extensive interviewing and the collection of both quantitative and qualitative data.

14.3 Discuss some of the ethical dilemmas of ethnographic research.

In conducting ethnographic research the cultural anthropologist may encounter some ethical dilemmas that may be harmful to the subjects of the studies. The American Anthropological Association has produced ethical guidelines that emphasize "doing no harm," among the people being studied. One recent ethical dilemma is whether anthropologists should participate in studies in war zones where they consult and advise the military.

14.4 How do cultural anthropologists analyze their ethnographic data?

In their analyses of sociocultural systems, anthropologists investigate cause-and-effect relationships among different independent and dependent variables. They use a multidimensional approach, examining the interaction among many variables to provide explanations for the similarities (universals) and differences among societies.

14.5 Discuss the contemporary view of sociocultural evolution used by anthropologists.

Contemporary anthropologists view sociocultural evolution as multilineal with tremendous variations within these different forms of societies depending on ecological, historical, economic, and political conditions and many other factors. Contemporary anthropologists are also cognizant of the manner in which different forms of societies may oscillate from one form to another during different periods of time.

14.6 Describe the types of sociocultural systems studied by anthropologists?

Anthropologists describe different sociocultural systems as bands, tribes, chiefdoms, agricultural states, and industrial and postindustrial states. This is not to endorse a unilineal type of sociocultural evolution, and anthropologists explore the specific geographical, ecological, economic, and historical factors that gave rise to these different sociocultural systems.

14.7 Describe the strengths and limitations of the cross-cultural approach.

Many ethnographic data have been coded for computer use in cross-cultural studies. These cross-cultural studies can be employed to develop general explanations regarding human behavior in specific societies and across cultural boundaries. Yet, a major weakness is that some cultural anthropologists in the past may not have taken historical circumstances into account when describing the particular conditions in a society. This omission may have led to a static, unchanging portrait of the society studied. Another problem with cross-cultural studies lies with faulty ethnographic reporting, which can produce unreliable data, contributing, in turn, to a distorted image of the society being studied. Consequently, anthropologists approach cross-cultural research with caution. Contemporary anthropologists who use these data must review the work of their predecessors who gathered the basic information to assess its validity.

Key Terms

chiefs, p. 320
correlation, p. 316
culture shock, p. 315
dependent variable, p. 316
egalitarian, p. 317
emic perspective, p. 314
etic perspective, p. 314

foraging societies, p. 317
independent variable, p. 316
industrial society, p. 321
industrialization, p. 323
intensive agriculture, p. 321
modernization, p. 323
nation-states, p. 322

mercantilism, p. 322
postindustrial society, p. 323
qualitative data, p. 314
quantitative data, p. 314
random sample, p. 314

Chapter 15
Environment, Subsistence, and Demography

Chapter Outline

 ## Learning Objectives

After reading this chapter you should be able to:

15.1 Discuss the relationship between subsistence and the physical environment (biomes).

15.2 Describe how anthropologists study population with reference to fertility, mortality, and migration.

15.3 Describe the different environments and subsistence activities of foragers.

15.4 Discuss the demographic conditions for foragers.

15.5 Describe the environments and subsistence for horticulturalists and pastoralists.

15.6 Describe how settling down influences population growth for horticulturalists and pastoralists.

15.7 Describe the environments and subsistence activities for chiefdoms.

15.8 Describe the changes for populations in agricultural states.

15.9 Discuss the development of energy sources in industrial and postindustrial societies.

15.10 Discuss the demographic transition for industrial and postindustrial societies.

Subsistence and the Physical Environment

15.1 Discuss the relationship between subsistence and the physical environment (biomes).

Living organisms, both plant and animal, do not live or evolve in a vacuum. The evolution and survival of a particular species is closely related to the type of physical environment in which it is located. The speed of a jackal has evolved in relationship to its predators and prey in East Africa, just as the arctic fox has evolved in relationship to the local ecology (the relationships between living things and their environment) of the Arctic. Of course, this relationship between organism and ecological context applies to plants as well as animals. For example, the physical characteristics of the orchid plant make it suited to a tropical environment. The environment affects organisms directly and, as Charles Darwin noted, affects the passing on the propagation of adaptive characteristics: those characteristics that enable individuals to survive and reproduce in their environment.

Biologists use the term *adaptation* to refer to the process in which an organism adjusts to environmental pressures. Organisms adapt to the environment through the physical traits that they inherit. Like other creatures, as we have seen in Chapter 6, humans have adapted to their respective environments through physical changes in body size and shape, blood groups, skin coloration, and biological traits. Humans, however, have adapted to their specific environments primarily through *culture*. By any measure, humans have been the most successful species in adapting to different types of environments. Like other species, humans exhibit physical and biological adaptation to the specific environments that they occupy. In addition, humans have the incredible capacity for symbolic and social learning, allowing for countless human cultural adaptations. Humans occupy an extraordinary range of environments, from the tropics to the Arctic, and have developed cultural solutions to the various challenges arising in these diverse regions. Anthropologists study these cultural solutions or adaptive strategies and to explain both the similarities and the differences exhibited among societies.

Modern Cultural Ecology

The term *ecology* was coined by German biologist Ernest Haeckel in the nineteenth century from two Greek words (οἶκος and -λογία) that mean "the study of the home." **Ecology** is the study of living organisms in relationship to their environment. Here we define environment broadly to include life-forms and the physical characteristics found in a particular geographical region. In biology, ecological studies focus on how plant and animal populations survive and reproduce in specific environmental niches. An **environmental niche** is a given set of ecological conditions that a life-form uses to make a living, survive, and adapt. From an anthropological perspective in particular, it is crucial to bear in mind that ecology encompasses all plants and animals in a given environment, *including humans*.

As discussed in Chapter 13, cultural ecology is the systematic study of the relationships between the environmental niche and culture. Anthropologists recognize that all humans can adjust in creative ways to different environments. Nevertheless, humans, like other organisms, are universally connected to the environment in a number of ways. Just as the environment has an impact on human behavior and society, humans have a major impact on their environment. Modern cultural ecologists examine these dynamic interrelationships as a means of understanding different societies.

Biomes

In their studies of different environments, cultural ecologists use the concept of a *biome*. A **biome** is an area distinguished by a particular climate and certain types of plants and animals. Biomes may be classified by certain attributes, such as mean rainfall, temperature, soil conditions, and vegetation that support certain forms of animal life (Campbell 1983). Cultural ecologists investigate the relationship between specific biomes and human sociocultural systems. Some of the different biomes that will be encountered in this text are listed in Table 15.1.

Table 15.1 Various Biomes Discussed in the Text, along with Their Major Characteristics

Biome	Principal Locations	Precipitation Range (mm/year)	Temperature Range (hr °C) (daily maximum and minimum)	Soils
Tropical rain forest	Central America (Atlantic coast) Amazon basin Brazilian coast West African coast Congo basin Malaya East Indies Philippines New Guinea Northeastern Australia Pacific islands	1,270–12,700 Equatorial type frequent torrential thunderstorms Tradewind type; steady, almost daily rains No dry period	Little annual variation Max. 29–35 Min. 18–27 No cold period	Mainly reddish laterites
Tropical savanna	Central America (Pacific coast) Orinoco basin Brazil, south of Amazon basin North Central Africa East Africa South Central Africa Madagascar India Southeast Asia Northern Australia	250–1,900 Warm-season thunderstorms Almost no rain in cool season Long dry period during low sun	Considerable annual variation; no really cold period *Rainy season (high sun)* Max. 24–32 Min. 18–27 *Dry season (low sun)* Max. 21–32 Min. 13–18 *Dry season (higher sun)* Max. 29–40 Min. 21–27	Some laterites; considerable variety
Temperate grasslands	Central North America Eastern Europe Central and Western Asia Argentina New Zealand	300–2,000; evenly distributed through the year or with a peak in summer; snow in winter	*Winter* Max. −18–29 Min. −28–10 *Summer* Max. −1–49 Min. −1–15	Black prairie soils Chestnut and brown soils almost all have a lime layer
Temperate deciduous forest	Eastern North America Western Europe Eastern Asia	630–2,300; evenly distributed through year; droughts rare; some snow	*Winter* Max. −12–21 Min. −29–7 *Summer* Max. 24–38 Min. 15–27	Gray-brown podzol Red and yellow podzols
Northern coniferous forest	Northern North America Northern Europe Northern Asia	400–1,000; evenly distributed; much snow	*Winter* Max. −37–1 Min. −54–9 *Summer* Max. 10–21 Min. 7–13	True podzols; bog soils; some permafrost at depth in places
Arctic tundra	Northern North America Greenland Northern Eurasia	250 -750; considerable snow	*Winter* Max. −37–7 Min. −57–8 *Summer* Max. 2–15 Min. −1–7	Rocky or boggy Much patterned ground permafrost

Source: Adapted from W. D. *Billings, Plants, Man, and the Ecosystem*, 2nd ed. ©1970. Reprinted by permission of Brooks/Cole, an imprint of the Wadsworth Group, a division of Thomson Learning.

Subsistence Patterns and Environments

In U.S. society, when we have the urge to satisfy our hunger drive, we have many options: We can go to a local fast-food restaurant, place money into a machine to select our choice of food, or obtain food for cooking from a grocery store or supermarket. These are just a handful of ways that humans obtain food. Cultural anthropologists study **subsistence patterns**—the means by which people in various societies acquire food. As we shall see, the amounts of sunlight and rainfall and the types of soil, forests, and mineral deposits all affect subsistence patterns. The specific biome and environmental conditions may limit the development of certain types of subsistence patterns. For example, Arctic conditions are not conducive to agricultural activities, nor are arid regions suitable for rice production. These are the obvious limitations of biomes and environmental conditions on subsistence patterns.

The earliest type of subsistence pattern—known as foraging or hunting and gathering—goes back among early hominins to perhaps two million years ago. This pattern of subsistence, along with others such as horticulture, pastoralism, various types of intensive agriculture, and developments in agribusiness in industrial societies, is introduced later. As we shall see, these subsistence patterns not only are influenced by the environment, but also directly affect the environment. In other words, as humans transform their subsistence pattern to adapt to the environment, the environment is also transformed to varying degrees, depending upon the type of subsistence pattern developed. All humans alter their environment in some way. The result is called an *anthropogenic landscape*; these landscapes are created by foragers and by industrialists alike, though the degree and intensity of alteration may vary. The interaction between subsistence pattern and environment is an extremely important topic in anthropology and has a direct bearing on the future of human-environment relationships.

One other aspect of subsistence and the environment relates to the use of energy in different societies. In Chapter 13, we discussed Leslie White's attempt to explain sociocultural evolution in terms of energy use. He suggested that sociocultural evolution progressed in relationship to the harnessing of energy. A number of anthropologists, including John Bodley (1985), attempted to quantify White's ideas. Bodley suggested that sociocultural systems can be divided into *high-energy cultures* and *low-energy cultures* and that these categories have implications for the evolution of society. More recently, archaeologist Ian Morris has systematically measured energy capture by prehistoric peoples compared with modern contemporary societies (2010, 2013). By energy capture Morris means that range of energy that includes food (whether consumed directly or fed to animals that are used for labor or consumption), fuel (whether for cooking, heating, cooling, firing kilns and furnaces, or powering machines, and including wind and water power, and wood, coal, oil, gas, and nuclear power), and raw materials (whether for construction, metalwork, pot making, or any other purpose) (2013: 53). Food energy and non-food energy, such as fuel, and raw materials can be measured in kilocalories per capita, per day. This is a broader measure of energy capture than expressed by White or Bodley, but Morris's model is more comprehensive and quantitatively more sophisticated. Morris is able to use archaeological evidence from different time periods, including the Paleolithic up to the present, to compare

energy capture among various types of societies. We shall refer to these measurements used by Morris later in our discussions.

Demography

15.2 Describe how anthropologists study population with reference to fertility, mortality, and migration.

Human use of natural resources and energy, and the subsistence strategies employed to "make a living" in a given environment, relate to variables such as population size and growth rates. These variables are the basis of the field of **demography**, the study of the quantitative and statistical aspects of a population. Demographers study changes in the size, composition, and distribution of human populations. They also study the consequences of population increases and decreases for human societies. Demographic anthropology is an important specialty in anthropology.

Much of the research in demographic anthropology is concerned with the quantitative description of population. Demographic anthropologists design censuses and surveys to collect population statistics on the size, age, and gender composition, and increasing or decreasing growth of the population of a society. After collecting these data, demographic anthropologists focus on three major variables in a population: fertility, mortality, and migration.

Fertility, Mortality, and Migration

To measure **fertility**—the number of births in a society—demographic anthropologists use the **crude birth rate**, that is, the number of live births in a given year for every thousand people in a population. They also measure **mortality**—the incidence of death in a society's population—by using the **crude death rate**, that is, the number of deaths in a given year for every thousand people in a population. In measuring the **migration rate**—the movement of people into and out of a specified territory—demographic anthropologists determine the number of in-migrants (people moving into the territory) and the number of out-migrants (people moving out of the territory). They then use these numbers to calculate the **net migration**, which indicates the general movement of the population in and out of the territory.

To assess overall population change, demographic anthropologists subtract the crude death rate from the crude birth rate to arrive at the *natural growth rate* of a population. The natural growth rate is usually the major indicator of population change in a society. Anthropologists calculate the total population change by adding the rate of migration to other measures of growth. A number of other variables also influence rates of fertility, mortality, and migration.

Fecundity—the potential number of children that women are capable of bearing—influences fertility rates. Fecundity varies, however, according to the age of females at puberty and menopause, nutrition, workload, and other conditions in the societies and individuals being studied.

Life expectancy is the number of years an average person can expect to live. A component of particular importance in determining the life expectancy of a given society is the **infant mortality rate**—the number of babies per thousand births in any year who die before reaching the age of one. When the infant mortality rate is high, the life expectancy—a statistical average—decreases. In many countries throughout the world, the **childhood mortality rate**—the number of children per thousand per year who die before reaching the age of five—is a major problem. Disease, nutrition, sanitation, warfare, the general standard of living, and medical care are some of the factors that influence mortality, life expectancy, and infant and child mortality rates.

Migration is related to a number of different factors. In many instances, migration is *involuntary*. For example, the Cajun people of Louisiana are descendants of French people who were forced out of Canada by the British in the 1700s. Migration can also be *voluntary*. This type of movement is influenced by what demographers refer to as *push-pull factors*. **Push factors** are those that lead people to leave specific territories; Examples are poverty, warfare, and political instability. **Pull factors**, such as economic opportunity, peace, and political freedom, are powerful incentives for people to move to other societies.

Population and Environment

Demographic anthropologists study the relationship between environments (specific biomes) and population. One variable they investigate is **carrying capacity**—the maximum population that a specific environment can support, as determined by the environment's potential energy and food resources. Some environments contain food and energy resources that allow for substantial population increases, whereas other environments contain only limited resources. For example, in the past, desert and Arctic biomes had carrying capacities that severely limited population increases. In contrast, various river valley regions containing water and fertile soils permitted opportunities for a larger population size. As we shall see in, the development of mechanized agriculture, fertilizers, and synthetic pesticides increases the carrying capacity in many different environments.

Population and Culture

Demographic anthropologists examine the relationship between environment and population, as well as the cultural values, beliefs, and practices that affect fertility,

mortality, and migration rates. In some societies, religious beliefs encourage high birth rates. In others, political authorities institute programs to increase or decrease population growth. Anthropologists gather data and develop hypotheses about individual and household decisions regarding the "costs and benefits" of having children as well as the fertility outcomes of these decisions. Anthropologists also investigate strategies of population regulation, such as birth control techniques. These and other research topics in demographic anthropology are introduced in the following discussions.

Modern Foraging Environments and Subsistence

15.3 Describe the different environments and subsistence activities of foragers.

During the last 10,000 years, hunting-gathering, band, or foraging societies have become fewer in number and are now restricted to marginal environments. Deserts, tropical rain forests, and Arctic areas are considered **marginal environments** because *until recently*, these areas needed huge investment in both labor and capital to irrigate deserts, slash down tropical forests for agriculture, or cultivate crops in the Arctic. Consequently, those few foraging or hunter-gatherer societies that adapted to these marginal environments managed to exist in relative isolation from surrounding groups. Figure 15.1 shows the locations of the major hunter-gatherer societies that are discussed in this textbook.

Marginal environments restrict the amount of energy capture for foraging societies. Recall that energy capture refers to calories measured in food and nonfood calories such as fuel and raw materials (see page above 329, Morris 2013). In marginal environments, nonfood energy is relatively restricted, and foragers have fewer material goods. Foragers depend on their own human energy for hunting game and collecting vegetation when available. For example, in some tropical forest environments the total (food and nonfood) energy capture can be as low as 4,000–5,000 kilocalories per capita per day. In comparison in the contemporary United States, energy capture is 230,000 kcal/cap/day (Morris 2013: 56).

Deserts

Various cultural-ecological studies focus on foragers surviving in desert environments. One long-term study focuses on the !Kung San or Ju/'hoansi San of the Kalahari Desert in southwestern Africa. The San have occupied

Figure 15.1 Hunter-gatherers discussed in this textbook

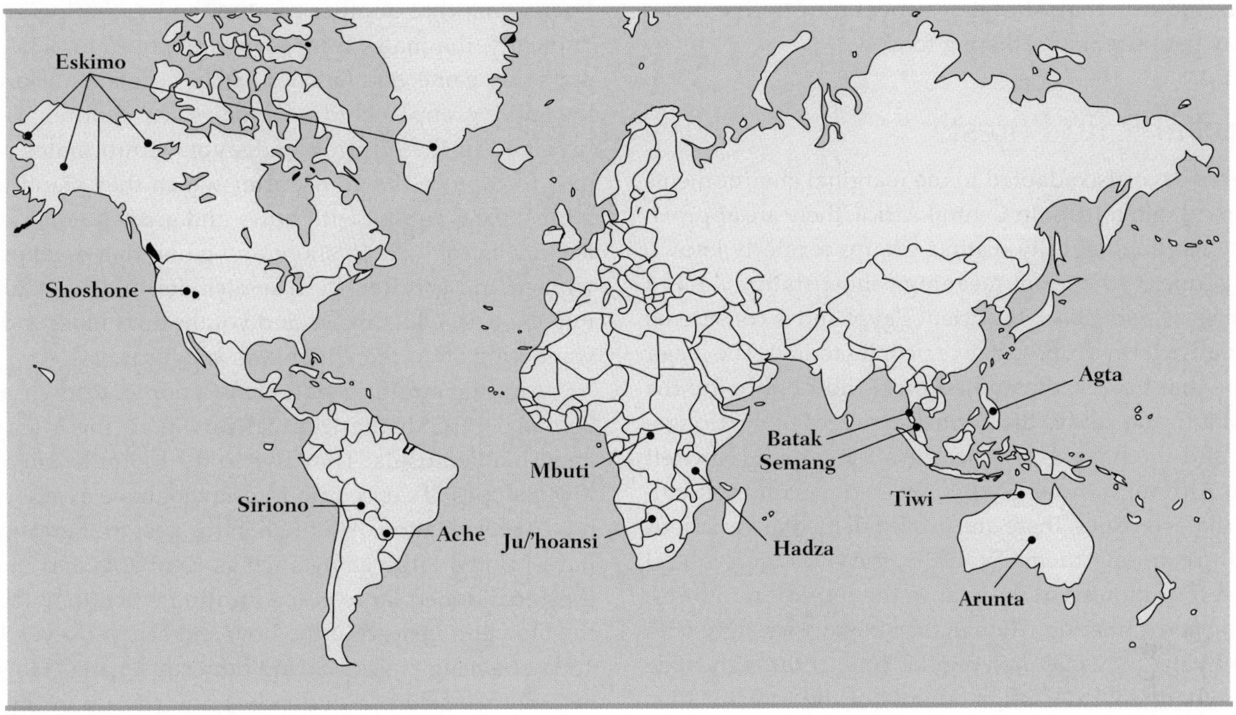

southern Africa for thousands of years along with another, biologically related population known popularly as the Hottentots, or Khoi. Archaeologist John Yellen (1985) located prehistoric sites in the Kalahari that have been dated to well over 11,000 years ago. This evidence suggests that the !Kung San were residing in the Kalahari desert before agriculture spread to the surrounding region.

Most historians and archaeologists agree that the processes of migration and culture contact with surrounding societies have affected the !Kung San and that the "modern" !Kung San do not represent a pure remnant of Paleolithic society. The frequency of interaction with other cultures accelerated for the San as Europeans settled throughout southern Africa in the eighteenth century (see Chapter 21). The San people (Bushmen) of southern Africa consist of close to 100,000 people who reside in six countries (Angola, Botswana, Namibia, South Africa, Zambia, and Zimbabwe). Most of the San people reside in the countries of Botswana and Namibia in the Kalahari Desert and consist of different populations such as the G/ui San, !Xo San, Kua, and Ju/'hoansi San (Hitchcock 2004a). The Ju/'hoansi San, who currently number approximately 7,000 and live in Botswana and Namibia, have been studied by anthropologists for almost 70 years.

Richard Lee, who has studied the Ju/'hoansi San from the 1960s until the present, provided a comprehensive picture of their traditional food-gathering and dietary practices. At the time he studied them in the 1960s and early 1970s, between 60 and 80 percent of the Ju/'hoansi San

diet consisted of nuts, roots, fruit, melons, and berries, which were gathered by the women. Meat from hunting was less common, providing only 20 to 30 percent of the diet. To procure this food, the Ju/'hoansi San did not need to expend enormous amounts of time and energy. In fact, Lee estimated that Ju/'hoansi San adults spent between two and three days each week finding food. Women often were able to gather enough in one or two days to feed their families for a week, leaving time for resting, visiting, embroidering, and entertaining visitors. Males spent much of their leisure time in ritual activities, including curing ceremonies (Lee 1972b, 1979, 1993, 2013).

Other foraging societies existed in various arid and semiarid desert biomes, an example being the Great Basin Shoshone, a Native American Indian group. Shoshone males hunted and trapped game, and Shoshone females gathered seeds, insects, and assorted vegetation. Both males and females harvested wild pinyon nuts, which the women mixed with seeds and insects and ground into flour for cooking.

Many of the Australian Aborigines were hunter-gatherers living in deserts that made up one-third of the continent. One group, known as the Arrernte, lived in the interior desert region. They subsisted on the various species of animals and plants found in their habitat. Women and children gathered seeds, roots, snails, insects, reptiles, burrowing rodents, and eggs of birds and reptiles.

Arrernte males specialized in hunting larger game such as the kangaroo, the wallaby, and the ostrich-like emu, as well as smaller birds and animals. Ethnographic studies indicate that Aborigines spent four to five hours per day per person in gathering food.

Tropical Rain Forests

Foragers have also adapted to the marginal environments of tropical rain forests. In Central Africa, there are approximately ten linguistically distinct groups formerly known as "Pygmies" (the term, meaning "short stature," has a long history going back to ancient Egypt and is considered a pejorative term by these native peoples today). The major groups that have been studied most thoroughly are the Efé, Mbuti, and Aka of the northeastern area of the Congo-Zaire and the Baka of southeastern Cameroon (Hewlett 1996). Although these groups have some common cultural characteristics, there are also fundamental variations in culture among them. Typically, these foragers spend at least four months of the year in the tropical rain forest hunting and gathering. Though they identify strongly with forest living, they maintain regular contact through trade and exchange with groups outside of the forest. Thus, none of these groups are completely isolated. Some of the groups such as the Efé have more sustained dependent relationships with outsiders than others, which influences their social organization and culture (Bailey 1991).

The group of foragers known as the Mbuti resides in the luxuriant Ituri rain forest. The first evidence of the Mbuti peoples came from early Egyptian accounts of an expedition into the Ituri forest. From other archaeological data, it appears that the Mbuti have inhabited this region for at least 5,000 years. Yet they, too, were in contact with people residing outside of the rain forest.

The late Colin Turnbull (1983) conducted in-depth ethnographic research among the Mbuti in the 1960s. He found that the division of labor among the Mbuti is different from that of other hunting-and-gathering groups. Typically, the males hunt elephants, buffalo, wild pigs, and other game, and females gather vegetation. However, the entire group, including females and children, is often involved in the hunting endeavor. Mbuti males set up nets to capture the game, after which they stand guard with spears. Youths with bows and arrows stand farther back from the nets to shoot any game that escapes, and women and children form semicircles to drive the game into the nets. Older males and youths hunt independently, wandering off to shoot monkeys and birds.

Another hunting-gathering people, known as the Semang, inhabit the tropical forests of the Malaysian and Thai Peninsula. They live in the foothills and on the lower slopes of dense rain forests that have exceptionally heavy precipitation. Although in the past the Semang may have hunted large game such as elephants and buffalo, they abandoned large-game hunting when they took up the blowgun instead of the bow and arrow (Keyes 1995). Today, Semang males fish and hunt small game. However, Semang subsistence depends primarily upon the wild fruits and vegetables, including yams, berries, nuts, and shoots, gathered by females.

Arctic Regions

Survival in Arctic conditions has inspired numerous creative adjustments by groups of foragers popularly known as the Eskimo. Eskimo used to be the common term for Arctic peoples around the globe. Today, these peoples in Canada and Greenland are usually designated *Inuit*, while in Alaska the term *Eskimo* is still used to distinguish this group from other Native populations. This population is further subdivided into two groups: the *Inupiat* (*Inupiaq*

A Baka couple in the West African rainforest

in the singular) for Native Alaskans from the north and northwest, and *Yupik* and Siberian *Yupik* for those in the southwest and St. Lawrence Island (Arctic Studies Center 2004). Early Inuit culture has been dated to at least 2500 B.C. Some Inuit live in northwestern Alaska near the Bering Sea, and others live in the Arctic regions of northern Canada, extending eastward all the way to Greenland. The Eskimo in northwestern Alaska hunt sea mammals such as bowhead whales, seals, and walruses. Interior groups such as the Netsilik in central Canada, who were studied by cultural anthropologist Asen Balikci and others, hunt caribou, musk oxen, an occasional polar bear, seals, and birds. They also fish in nearby bays.

Because vegetation historically was scarce in Arctic regions, it was a prized food. For example, after killing the caribou, male hunters ate the animal's stomach so as to obtain the valued undigested vegetation. Although their diet consisted primarily of meat, the Inuit generally satisfied their basic nutritional requirements of carbohydrates, proteins, and vitamins from eating berries, green roots, fish, and fish oil. They preferred cooked foods, but boiling food over fires fueled by blubber oil was slow and expensive; consequently, the Inuit ate most of their food raw.

The division of labor among the Inuit was unlike that of most other foraging societies. Because of the scarcity of vegetation, women were not specialized collectors. However, during the summer season, males and females gathered larvae, caribou flies, maggots, and deer droppings that contained vegetation.

Mobility and Subsistence

No matter what their particular environment, most band societies share one characteristic: mobility. As food and other resources become scarce in one site, the groups have to move on to another. The Mbuti, for example, reside in certain areas during the rainy season and other areas during other seasons, depending on the supply of game (Turnbull 1983). The Ju/'hoansi San moved frequently in pursuit of resources. During the winter dry season, they congregated in large groupings around several watering holes, but during the rainy season, the groups dispersed into small units. The Ju/'hoansi San moved when subsistence required it (Lee 1969). Most Inuit groups also have to move during different seasons to pursue game and other resources. For example, the Inuit of northwestern Alaska move from the coastal areas into the interior regions during the summer season to hunt herds of caribou.

Nomadic behaviors are not arbitrary or spontaneous. Rather, they are carefully planned to minimize labor while providing vital resources. These patterns of mobility represent an admirable appreciation and intimate knowledge of the environment in which these foragers reside.

Demographic Conditions for Foragers

15.4 Discuss the demographic conditions for foragers.

Many modern foragers live in marginal environments and travel from location to location. The requirement of mobility to procure resources has a major effect on demographic conditions in these societies. Unlike food producers, hunters and gatherers must depend on naturally occurring food resources in their territories, which limits excessive population growth. Generally, the population size of foragers is extremely low in accordance with the limited carrying capacity of their environments.

Inuit hunter

Demographic studies such as those done by cultural anthropologists Richard Lee, Nancy Howell, and Patricia Draper on the Ju/'hoansi San have enabled anthropologists to make certain generalizations concerning demographic conditions among modern foragers. Population size among the Ju/'hoansi San was carefully controlled in a number of ways. According to Lee (1979), the Ju/'hoansi San tried to control the number of people who could be supported in specific territories and provide sufficient resources. Having too many people leads to shortages of resources, whereas having too few people leads to ineffective foraging strategies. Despite their attempts to control their population in various ways at different times, like all people, the Ju/'hoansi San misjudged and sometimes paid the ultimate price for overpopulation.

Fissioning

One of the most important means of limiting population growth for foragers is *fissioning*. **Fissioning** is the moving of people from one group to another or the fragmenting of the group into smaller units when the population begins to increase and food or other material resources become scarce. Resource scarcity creates population pressure in the form of hardships and problems that emerge as the biome's resources become overtaxed. In such cases, the typical response is for a portion of the population to migrate to another geographic region. Fissioning was most likely the primary means of population control for Paleolithic foragers and to some extent, explains the worldwide expansion of the human species.

Modern foragers practice fissioning to a limited extent. Its success depends upon the presence of unoccupied land into which the excess population can expand. In situations where a growing population is surrounded by other populations and fissioning is not possible, conflict between groups becomes likely, although sometimes fusion, or the combining of groups, occurs (Hammel and Howell 1987).

Infanticide and Geronticide

Another means of population control in some foraging societies is **infanticide**, the deliberate abandonment or killing of infants, usually immediately after birth. Infanticide has been well documented in foraging societies. Physical anthropologist Joseph Birdsell (1968) hypothesized that infanticide is a way of birth spacing. He argued that because a woman can carry only one child in her arms at a time as a nomadic gatherer, there is a need to space childbirth. Yet, this did not account for other women than the mother who may have been carrying children or men who may be carrying children. When Nancy Howell (1979) did her ethnographic research among the San, she reported

six cases out of 500 births, and thus infanticide among the San was not as common as earlier anthropologists such as Birdsell believed it was. It was practiced only if the child was severely deformed or in some other way physically challenged or if a mother had a child that was being nursed and could not sustain an additional child.

Most cases of infanticide in these foraging societies appear to be decisions made by individuals in response to famine conditions or to anticipated food and material scarcities (Harris and Ross 1987). Infanticide in some of these societies is also associated with the birth of twins (supporting two children might be difficult or impossible) and of genetically abnormal infants.

One popular legend about the Inuit and other peoples in the Arctic suggested that **geronticide** (the killing of old people) was very frequent. However, more recent ethnographic research indicates that this practice was never universal among the Arctic peoples. It was common in some parts of their range, but more so among the Inuit (Greenland to northern Alaska) than the Yupik (western and southwestern Alaska). Even among the Inuit, some groups found the practice repugnant. Where it was practiced, geronticide was rare except during famines. As long as there was enough food to go around, everyone got their share, including the relatively unproductive members. Given that the usual diet consisted of caribou, fish, and sea mammals, the supplies of which were fairly dependable, many years could pass between episodes of scarcity. Considering the dangers of hunting, the old and infirm were not expected to hunt and could live a long life.

On the other hand, when food did run short among the Inuit, the old and sick may have been perceived as a drain on the community. They may have been abandoned to die. The victim might be taken out in the wilderness and left there, or the whole village might pick up and move away while the old person slept. However, if the villagers were unexpectedly restored to prosperity, they would return to welcome the abandoned person back into the community. Most of what has been called *geronticide* is better called *assisted suicide*. Assisted suicide was common throughout the range inhabited by Yupik and Inuit alike. In times of famine or hardship, older Inuit often believed they were a burden and asked their younger relatives to kill them. Similar requests could be made by any individual, young or old, for any number of reasons: pain, grief, or clinical depression. The person who was asked to help was obligated to comply even if he had misgivings (Oswalt 1999).

Fertility Rates for Foragers

Other lines of demographic research investigate the relatively slow rate of population growth for foraging societies. Some anthropologists are testing demographic hypotheses on the relationship among nutrition, physiological stress, breast feeding, and rates of fertility (Howell 2000; Lee 1979). The purpose of these studies is to determine whether biological factors, rather than cultural practices such as infanticide, may induce low fertility rates and thus, slow population growth for foragers.

For example, Nancy Howell's research on the Ju/'hoansi San indicates that a low-caloric diet and the high energy rate needed for female foraging activities may postpone the occurrence of menarche, the onset of menstruation at puberty, which does not appear in Ju/'hoansi San females until a mean age of 16.6 years (Howell 2000), compared with 12.9 years in the United States. The low body weight of Ju/'hoansi San females, which averages 90 pounds, also influences the late onset of menarche. This slower rate of maturation may be related to the low fertility of the Ju/'hoansi San.

Other studies have suggested that breast feeding contributes to low fertility rates. Breast feeding stimulates the production of prolactin, a hormone that inhibits ovulation and pregnancy (McKenna, Mosko, and Richard 1999). Ju/'hoansi San women breast-feed their infants for three to four years. Considering the workload and general ecological conditions Ju/'hoansi San women must deal with, this prolonged nursing may produce a natural, optimal birth interval, or spacing of children (Blurton Jones 1986, 1987). This factor, along with sexual abstinence, abortion, infanticide, and delayed marriage, may be evidence of early forms of fertility control in prehistoric foraging societies.

Environment and Subsistence for Horticulturalists and Pastoralists

15.5 Describe the environments and subsistence for horticulturalists and pastoralists.

Horticulture is a form of agriculture in which people use a limited, nonmechanized technology to cultivate plants. One major type of horticulture is known as *swidden agriculture*. This system was once widespread, but today is found primarily in tropical rain forests. Approximately 250 million people throughout the world currently engage in swidden agriculture (Moran 2007).

Swidden agriculture (sometimes known as slash-and-burn agriculture) involves the production of food without the intensive use of labor, but it does involve an extensive use of land. However, it does not involve a complex technology. As generally practiced, it is a cyclical process that begins with clearing a tract of land by cutting down the trees and then setting fire to the brush. The burned

vegetation and ashes remain, and the nutrients from them are unlocked and sink into the soil. After the land is cleared and burned, various crops are planted. In most cases, women and children spend a great deal of time weeding and tending the gardens. Typically, after the crops are planted and harvested for several years, the garden plot is left fallow (unplanted) for 3 to 15 years, and the cultivators must shift to a new location. The major reason for swidden agriculture in tropical rain forests is that the soils are poor in nitrogen. Swiddening enriches the soil and makes crop production more efficient. Thus, swidden agriculture, if done properly, can be regenerative and productive in tropical forest environments.

People who practice swidden agriculture must maintain a delicate balance with their environment. If the plot is not left fallow and is cultivated too often, grasses and weeds may colonize the area at the expense of forest regrowth. The land then becomes useless or overexploited. Some horticulturalists have recleared their land too often and have brought devastation to some forest environments; others have been able to reside in one location for almost a century (Carneiro 1961). In general, compared with foragers, swidden agriculturalists are less nomadic and more sedentary.

Amazon Horticulturalists: The Yanomamö

One South American tribe, the Yanomamö, practices swidden agriculture along with hunting and gathering in the tropical forests of the Amazon between the borders of Brazil and Venezuela. There are approximately 21,000 Yanomamö between Brazil and Venezuela (Hames 2004). Napoleon Chagnon studied the Yanomamö for more than 30 years. Approximately 80 to 90 percent of their diet comes from their gardens (Chagnon 2012). Yanomamö males clear the forest, burn the vegetation, and plant the crops; the females (and sometimes the children) weed the garden and eventually harvest the crops. Generally, the Yanomamö do not work on subsistence activities for food production more than three to four hours per day. A Yanomamö garden lasts for about three years from the time of the initial planting; after this period, the garden is overrun with scrub vegetation, and the soil becomes depleted.

Early cultural ecologists assumed that slash-and-burn cultivators are forced to relocate because the soil becomes exhausted. Chagnon, however, has shown that Yanomamö decisions to move are not based simply upon soil depletion. In fact, as the soil begins to lose its capacity to support crops, the Yanomamö make small adjustments, such as extending a previous garden or clearing a new tract of land near the old one. Chagnon discovered that major population movements of the Yanomamö are due instead to warfare and political conflict with neighboring groups. Thus, a sedentary life in these Amazonian societies is not simply a product of ecological conditions; it also involves strategic alliances and political maneuvers designed to deal with human populations in nearby communities (Chagnon 2012).

Although horticulture is the primary subsistence activity of many Amazonian tribes, hunting, fishing, and gathering typically supplement this activity (Chagnon 2012; Hames 2004). The Yanomamö gather wild foods, especially palm fruits and a variety of nuts, pods, tubers, mushrooms, and honey. They hunt game birds and a number of animals. In addition, they collect toads, frogs, and many varieties of insects.

New Guinea Horticulturalists: The Tsembaga

The Melanesian Islands of Papua New Guinea have many tribal horticulturalist populations, some of whom were not contacted by Western society until the 1930s. Archaeologists have traced early horticultural developments in highland New Guinea to 7000 B.C. (White and O'Connell 1982). One group, the Tsembaga Maring, has been studied thoroughly by the late anthropologist Roy Rappaport (1984).

The Tsembaga live in two river valley areas surrounded by mountains. They cultivate the mountain slopes with their subsistence gardens. Tsembaga males and females clear the undergrowth from the secondary forest, after which the men cut down the trees. When the cut vegetation dries out, it is stacked up and burned. The women then plant and harvest crops, especially sweet potatoes, taro, manioc, and yams; 99 percent of the Tsembaga diet by weight consisted of vegetables, particularly these root crops. The Tsembaga also domesticate pigs, but these animals are usually consumed only during certain ritual occasions.

Horticulturalists in Woodland Forest Areas: The Iroquois

In the past, many Native American groups such as the Iroquois, who resided in the eastern woodland region of North America, practiced horticulture. Actually, the term *Iroquois* was derived from a French use of a Basque term that translates as "killer people" because they were involved in much warfare with other tribes and then with the Europeans when they arrived. The people themselves use the native Seneca word *Haudenosaunee*, which means "the Longhouse people," because they lived in large longhouses described later (Sutton 2007). The *Haudenosaunee* included five major tribes: the Mohawk, Seneca, Onondaga, Oneida, and Cayuga. The first major ethnographic study of these people was conducted by the nineteenth-century anthropologist Lewis Henry Morgan, and he relied on his Seneca Indian informant Ely Parker. These tribes lived in the upper New York State region, where rivers such as the St. Lawrence and Hudson drain into the area, providing fertile ground for horticultural activities. These horticultural practices probably appeared between 2300 and 1000 B.C. and were adopted as a regular subsistence system around 400 A.D. (Fagan 2000). Eventually, the native peoples of this region began to raise maize and other crops along with local wild species. Most archaeologists have concluded that this horticultural pattern of maize, beans, and squash originated in Mesoamerica and then extended across the regions of North America, spreading out to the Ohio River Valley areas and eastward to Native American groups such as the Iroquois.

A tropical forest showing slash and burn technique

A depiction of an Iroquois male

Environment and Subsistence for Pastoralists

In Central Asia, the Middle East, North and East Africa, South America, northern and southern Europe, and highland Tibet, there were—and, in some cases, still are—**pastoralists**, groups whose subsistence activities are based on the care of domesticated animals. The use of herd animals differs from group to group, and again, as with foragers or bands, anthropologists find a great deal of variation among pastoralist tribes (Salzman 2004). The Bedouins (the Arabic term for "camel breeders") of Arabia and North Africa, for example, use the camel mainly for transportation; they use the hair for tents and other purposes and sometimes consume the meat. Other pastoralist groups, such as the Saami (Lapps) of Scandinavia and the Eveny of northeastern Siberia, have in the past completely depended upon reindeer, deriving most of their food and other vital resources from them. In South America, some tribal pastoralists in the Andes Mountains bred llamas and alpacas for transportation and wool for clothing. Other pastoralist tribes, such as the Basseri, Qashqai, and Bahktiari of Iran, have a complex of animals, including horses, donkeys, sheep, goats, and cattle, that they maintain and herd for their livelihood. Although some pastoralists may have small gardens, most of them have only their herd animals for subsistence purposes. These domesticated animals provide food such as milk, butter, blood, and meat; wool and hair for clothing; bone and horn for tools and weapons; skin for making leather; traction for loads and plows; and transportation for travel, warfare, recreation, and ritual (Salzman 2004).

The care of herd animals requires frequent moves from camp to camp and sometimes involves long migrations. Some groups, such as the Tungus of Siberia, who are reindeer pastoralists, trek more than 1,000 miles annually. The Basseri, Qashqai, and Bahktiari of Iran, with their complex of animals, migrate hundreds of miles seasonally through mountainous regions from winter pastures to highland pastures (Barth 1961; Beck 1991; Salzman 2004). These pastoralist migrations are not aimless; the groups know the layout of the land and move to territories that contain specific grazing pastures or waterholes during different seasons. Other pastoralist tribes, such as the Turkman of northeastern Iran, are more settled but migrate once in a while because of political conflict with the government (Salzman 2004).

East African Cattle Complex

In an area stretching from southern Sudan through Kenya, Uganda, Rwanda, Burundi, Tanzania, Mozambique, and into parts of South Africa, various pastoralists herd cattle

The Iroquois constructed their villages with *longhouses* in the center of the settlement. Longhouses were large, multifamily houses built with upright posts that supported horizontal poles for rafters. Large slabs of bark, laced together with cords of plant fiber, covered the framework of the longhouses. Iroquois males cleared the primary forest around the village and burned the cut litter. In the spring, the women planted 15 varieties of maize, beans, squash, and other crops, which they later harvested and processed. The Iroquois left part of the primary forest standing so that deer, squirrels, fox, and bear were available for hunting. The forest also provided nuts, berries, and many species of wild plants.

After harvesting the crops in the fall, the men would concentrate their subsistence activities on game such as deer and bear. In the spring, while the women planted crops, the men fished in the many lakes and rivers and also captured birds. Like many other slash-and-burn cultivators, the Iroquois farmed their fields until the fields were no longer fertile, after which they cleared new fields while the old ones lay fallow. After a generation or so, depending on local conditions, the fertile fields were located far enough away from the village that the entire community moved so that it could be closer to the gardens.

as their means of subsistence. Most of these groups do not depend entirely on their cattle for subsistence needs, as they plant gardens to supplement their food resources. These pastoralist groups include the Maasai, Nuer, Karimojong, Pokot, Sebei, Samburu, and the Dinka.

The Nuer Anthropologist E. E. Evans-Pritchard (1940, 1951, 1956) conducted a classic study of a pastoralist group called the Nuer. The Nuer reside along the upper Nile River and its tributaries in southern Sudan. Because of the flatness of this region, the annual flooding of the Nile during the rainy season, and the heavy clay soils, the Nuer spend the wet season on high, sandy ground, where they plant sorghum, a cereal grass used for grain. This horticulture is very limited, however, because strong rainfall, as well as elephants, birds, and insects, destroy the crops. Therefore, cattle are the most important subsistence resource for the Nuer.

The Nuer view cattle herding with a great deal of pride. In the dry season, they move with their cattle into the grassland areas. The cattle transform the energy stored in the grasses, herbs, and shrubs into valuable subsistence products. Yet, as is true of other herders in this area, the basis of the Nuer subsistence is not consumption of cattle. Rather, they depend heavily on the blood and milk of their animals. Every few months during the dry season, the cattle are bled by making small incisions that heal quickly. The Nuer boil the blood until it gets thick, roast it, and then eat it. The cows are milked morning and night; some of the milk is used to make butter. The Nuer slaughter their old cattle, which then calls for elaborate ceremonies or sacrifices.

Demographics and Settlement

15.6 Describe how settling down influences population growth for horticulturalists and pastoralists.

Generally, as humans developed the capacity to produce food through the domestication of animals and plants, the carrying capacity of particular territories increased to support a greater population density than had been possible for foraging societies. Whereas foraging populations lived in small bands, tribal societies became much more densely populated. According to Murdock's (1967) cross-cultural tabulations, the median size of horticulturalist societies ranges from 100 to more than 5,000 people in specific territories, and pastoralists have a median size of 2,000 people in particular niches. Some tribal populations have denser populations in large regions in which villages are connected through economic, social, and political relationships.

Compared with most foraging societies, tribal societies are relatively settled within fairly well-defined territories. As mentioned earlier, horticulturalists are somewhat

mobile, having to move to fertile lands every so often, but they generally settle in one locale for a number of years.

Of course, many pastoralist societies are nomadic, but their wanderings are limited to specific pastures and grasslands to care for their animals. Because pastoralists move seasonally from pasture to pasture, they place less intense population pressure on each area. Population densities for pastoralists range from one to five persons per square mile of land; however, in the richly endowed grassland environment of Central Asia, the Kalmuk Mongols maintain an average density of about eighteen people per square mile. In general, pastoralist populations are denser than are those of foragers, but in many cases, both are spread thinly over the land (Sahlins 1968; Salzman 2004; Gurven et al. 2010; Borgerhoff Mulder et al. 2010).

Like foraging societies, both horticulturalist and pastoralist societies experience slow population growth because of limited resources. To regulate their populations, tribal societies have adopted the same strategies as bands, especially fissioning. Other cultural practices designed to control population growth include sexual abstinence, infanticide, abortion, and a prolonged period of nursing.

Environment, Subsistence, and Demography for Chiefdoms

15.7 Describe the environments and subsistence activities for chiefdoms.

Most chiefdom societies have occupied ecological regions that contain abundant resources, usually more abundant than the resources in the areas inhabited by foraging and tribal societies.

Pacific Island Chiefdoms

In the area known as Polynesia, which extends westward from Hawaii to New Zealand and includes Samoa, Tahiti, and Tonga (see Figure 15.3), various chiefdoms existed. The arable land on these Pacific Islands is very fertile, and the soil is covered by a dense forest growth. Rainfall is plentiful, and the average temperature is 77° F year-round. Tahiti is a typical example of a Polynesian island on which most of the people resided on the coastal flatlands.

One important aspect of subsistence for the Tahitian people was the bountiful harvest from the sea. Fish and shellfish accounted for a substantial portion of their diet. The coconut palm, which grows abundantly even in poor soil, provided nourishment from its meat and milk, as well as oil for cooking. The breadfruit plant was another important foodstuff; if fermented, breadfruit can be stored in pits for long periods of time.

Figure 15.2 This map highlights many tribal societies including those discussed in this textbook.

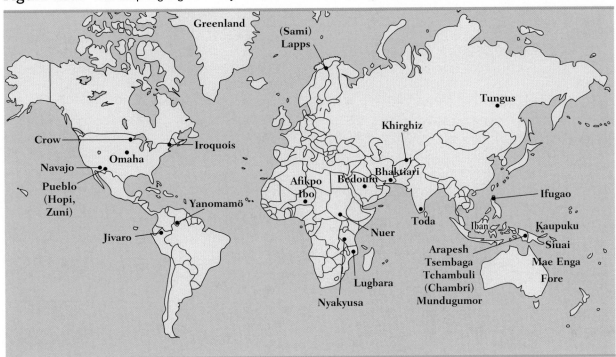

Like many other chiefdom societies, the Tahitians practiced intensive horticulture, in which one improves crop production by irrigating, fertilizing, hoeing, and terracing the land. Using intensive horticulture (and enjoying near-perfect weather conditions), the Tahitians were able to make efficient use of small parcels of arable land. Although this type of agriculture demanded labor, time, and energy, the agricultural yields it produced were much greater than those produced by tribal peoples who practiced slash-and-burn horticulture.

The Tahitians' most important crops were taro, yams, and sweet potatoes. Supplementing these crops were bananas, plantains, sugar cane, and gourds. Protein requirements were met by the consumption of seafood and such animals as domesticated pigs, chickens, and, on occasion, dogs. (The Polynesians did distinguish between dogs that were kept as pets and those that were used for food.) The native peoples of Hawaii, Samoa, Easter Island, and the Cook Islands had essentially the same ecological setting for the development of a highly productive subsistence strategy.

African Chiefdoms

Anthropologist Jacques Maquet (1972) suggested that a very high proportion of precolonial African societies were chiefdoms. These savanna chiefdom societies included peoples such as the Kpelle of Liberia, the Bemba of Zambia, and the Luba and Songhe of Central Africa. These chiefdoms developed in the dry forest, the woodland savanna, and the grassy savanna. In the savanna regions,

the use of intensive horticulture, including the use of hoes, produced a surplus of crops consisting of cereals such as sorghum, millet, cassava, and maize and legumes such as peas and beans. Archaeologists have determined that sorghum, rice, and millet were cultivated as far back as 1000 B.C. (McIntosh and McIntosh 1993; R. McIntosh 2005). Generally, these chiefdoms were more decentralized, and power was diffused throughout wide-ranging areas by localized leadership (McIntosh 1999; R. McIntosh 2005).

Native American Chiefdoms

The Mississippi Region One prehistoric ecological region in North America where various chiefdom societies flourished was the area along the Mississippi River extending from Louisiana northward to Illinois. One of the primary cultural centers of the North American chiefdoms was the Cahokian society, located near where the Mississippi and Missouri Rivers come together. This area contained extremely fertile soil and abundant resources of fish, shellfish, and game animals. The Cahokian people also practiced intensive horticulture, using hoes and fertilizers to produce their crops. The Cahokian chiefdom society emerged around 950 A.D. and reached its peak by about 1100. At that point, it had evolved into an urban center with a population of about 20,000 people.

The Northwest Coast Another region in North America that contains a vast wealth of natural resources is the area of the Northwest Coast. This area is bounded by the Pacific Ocean on the west and mountain ranges on the

Figure 15.3 The Pacific Islands, where many chiefdoms were located

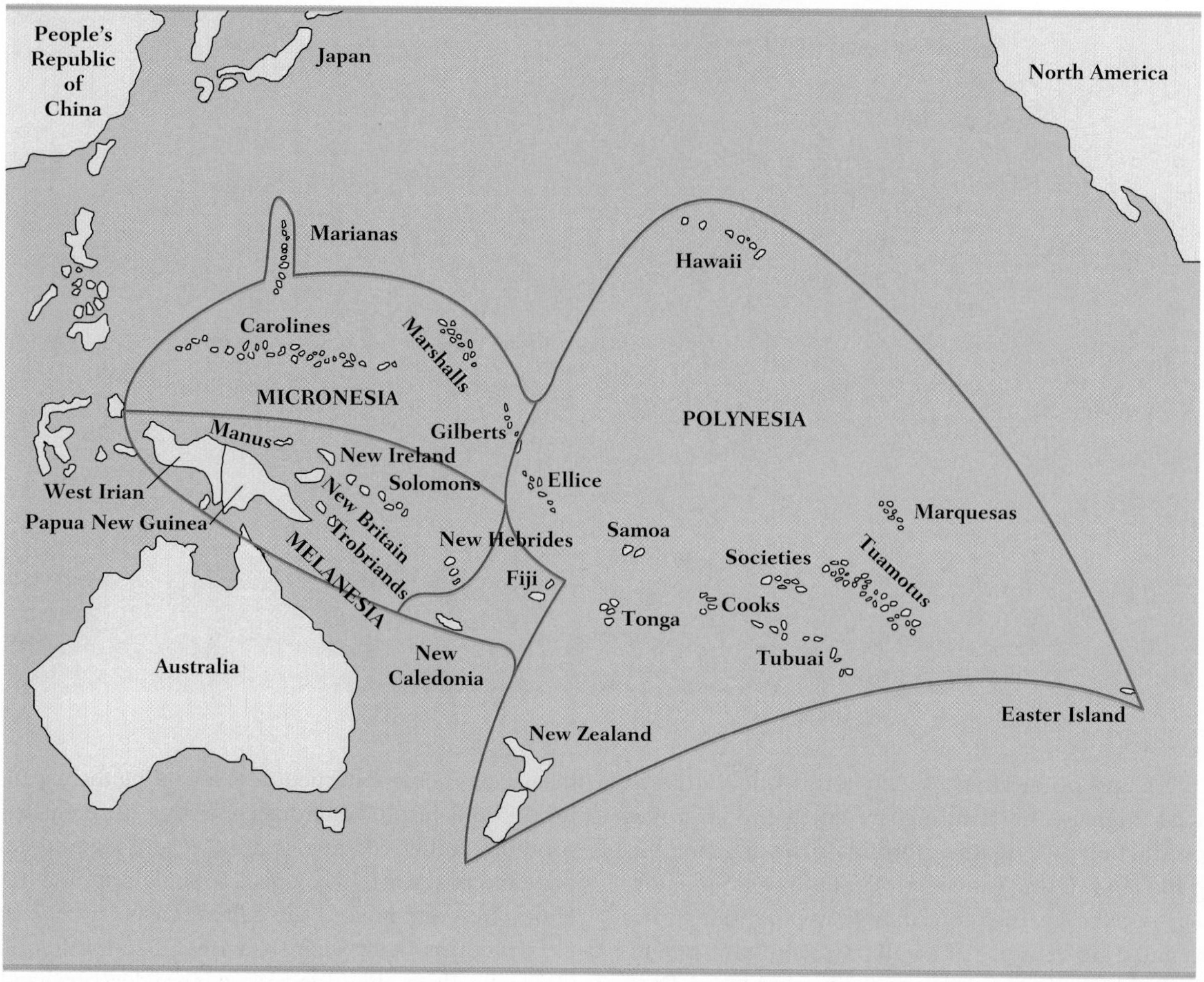

east. Numerous groups, such as the Haida, Tlingit, Tsimshian, Kwakiutl (Kwakwaka'wakw), Bella Coola, Bella Bella, Nootka, Makah, and Tillamook, lived in this region (see Figure 15.4 These societies are usually categorized as chiefdoms, although they do not fit the ideal pattern as neatly as do the Polynesian societies (Lewellen 1983). Although there were some differences in respect to subsistence and adaptation for each group, the patterns were very similar for the entire region.

One of the major reasons the Northwest Coast groups do not fit as well into the chiefdom category is that they were essentially hunters and gatherers and did not practice any horticulture or agriculture. Because of their economic, social, and political features, however, they have been traditionally characterized as chiefdoms. The unique ecological conditions of the region enabled these societies to develop patterns not usually associated with the hunters and gatherers discussed earlier. Instead of residing in marginal environments, as did many foragers, these peoples lived in environments rich with resources.

The ecological conditions on the Northwest Coast were as ideal as those of the Pacific Islands. The climate

was marked by heavy rainfall, and the mountain barrier to the east sheltered the region from cold winds from the continent. The region could, therefore, support rich forests of cedar, fir, and other trees. Game such as deer, bears, ducks, and geese were plentiful, and berries, roots, and other plants were easily harvested. The most important food resources, however, came from the coastal and inland waters. Streams and rivers were filled every fall with huge salmon, which were smoked and dried for storage, providing a year-round food source. The coastal waters supplied these groups with shellfish, fish, and sea mammals such as seals, sea otters, and porpoises.

The environments of the Pacific Islands, the Mississippi region, and the Northwest Coast of North America produced what is known as **regional symbiosis**. In regional symbiosis, a people reside in an ecological habitat divided into different resource areas; groups living in these different areas become interdependent. People in one region may subsist on fishing; in another region, on hunting; and in a third region, on cultivation. These groups exchange products, thus establishing mutual dependency.

Figure 15.4 The Northwest Coast, where various chiefdoms were located

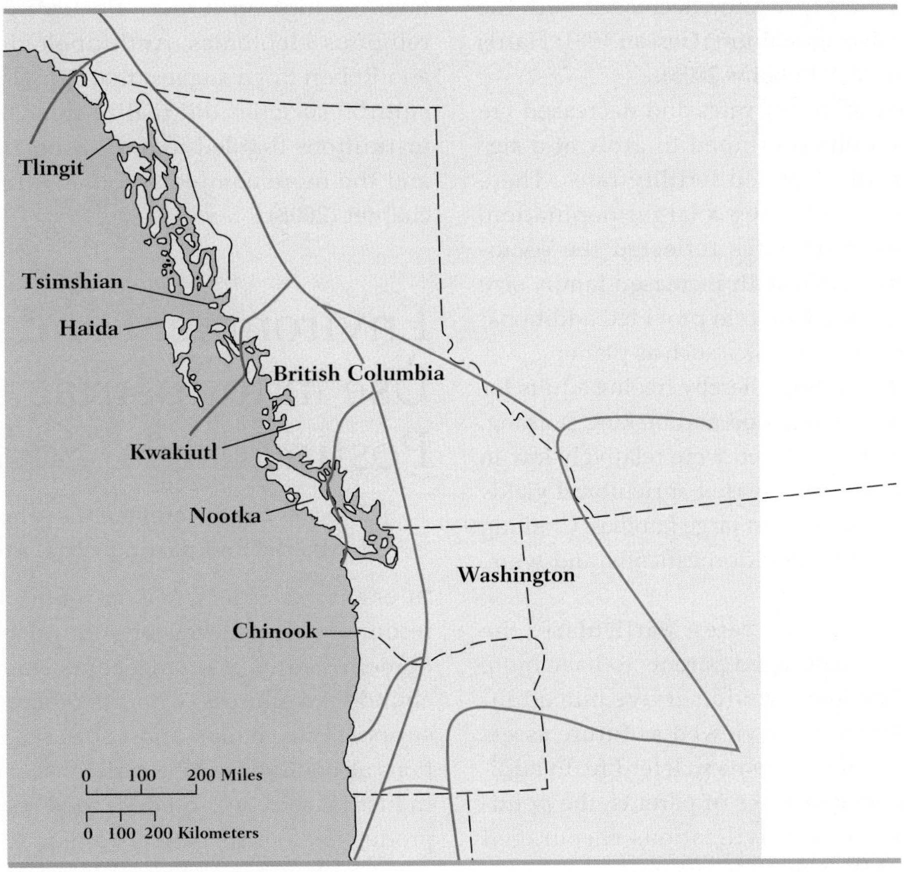

Demography

Anthropologists hypothesize that population growth is an important factor in the centralized administration and social complexity associated with chiefdoms (Carneiro 1967; Dumond 1972). Chiefdom populations, which range from 5,000 to 50,000 people, frequently exceed the carrying capacity of the region (Drennan 1987; Johnson and Earle 2000). Population growth leads to an increased risk of shortages of food and other resources. To maintain adequate resources, these societies give certain individuals the power and authority to organize systematically the production and accumulation of surplus resources (Sahlins 1958; Johnson and Earle 2000).

Environment and Demography in Agricultural States

15.8 Describe the changes for populations in agricultural states.

As discussed in Chapter 9, the development of agricultural states or civilizations based on intensive agriculture began as early as 8000 B.C. With the emergence of intensive agriculture the amount of food and nonfood energy capture (food and nonfood) increased substantially. Archaeologists such as Ian Morris rely on material artifacts, estimated crop yields, trade patterns, and other comparative evidence to measure energy capture in different agricultural civilizations (Morris 2013). From averages of 4,000–5,000 kilocalories per capita per day for foragers, some farmers increased their energy capture to as much as 25,000 kcal/cap/day (Morris 2013: 57). Agricultural states produce much more food calories and have a wider range of nonfood fuels and raw materials and other technologies to maximize energy capture.

After the transition to intensive agriculture, population began to increase dramatically along with an increase in agricultural production, enabling people to settle in large urban areas. These population increases produced conditions that led to higher mortality rates. Poor sanitation coupled with the domestication of confined animals led to frequent epidemics that affected both animals and humans. The overwhelming fossil and ethnographic evidence suggests that pre-Neolithic and Paleolithic peoples had fewer health problems and less disease than did Neolithic peoples. This debunks the notion that evolution always results in progress for humans, a nineteenth-century belief. Disease, warfare, and famines all contributed to higher mortality rates in agricultural societies than those found in bands, tribes, or chiefdoms. The majority of paleoanthropological and archaeological studies also suggest that life expectancy decreased with the development of intensive agriculture (Hassan 1981; Harris and Ross 1987; Cohen 1994; Robbins 2005).

Despite increased mortality rates and decreased life expectancies, populations continued to grow at a significant rate because of increased fertility rates. There were some advantages in having a larger population. Undoubtedly, higher birth rates reflected the socioeconomic benefits associated with increased family size in agricultural civilizations. Children provided additional labor for essential agricultural tasks, such as planting, caring for animals, and harvesting, thereby freeing adults for other labor, such as processing food and making clothing. The actual costs of rearing children were relatively low in agricultural states, in which increased agricultural yields produced surplus foods to support large families. Clothing and shelter were manufactured domestically and were, therefore, inexpensive.

In addition, the mortality rates, particularly the infant mortality rates, encouraged parents to have more children to ensure that some would survive into adulthood. Moreover, children were viewed as future assets who could take care of their parents in later life. In addition to the socioeconomic motives of parents, the political dynamics in agricultural civilizations encouraged high fertility rates. All of the agricultural states promoted the ideal of having large families (Harris and Ross 1987). These societies depended upon a large labor force to maintain their extensive agricultural production and

military operations. *Pronatalist* population policies, those favoring high birth rates, frequently were backed up by religious ideologies. Anthropologists Peter Richerson and Robert Boyd suggest that denser populations in agricultural societies did realize some benefits resulting in institutions that led to more cooperation, coordination, and the more complex economy discussed in the next chapter (2008).

Environment and Energy Use in Industrial and Postindustrial Societies

15.9 Discuss the development of energy sources in industrial and postindustrial societies.

In earlier chapters, we saw how the availability of resources affects levels of political and economic development. States and chiefdoms emerged in areas with abundant resources, whereas other environments could support only bands and tribes. Environmental conditions also influenced the early phases of industrialization. Industrial societies still depended heavily on agricultural production to meet basic food requirements, but industrialization transformed agricultural production itself. The major natural resource requirements for industrial societies are based on harnessing new sources of energy, especially fossil fuel energy.

Figure 15.5 Map of the major agricultural states

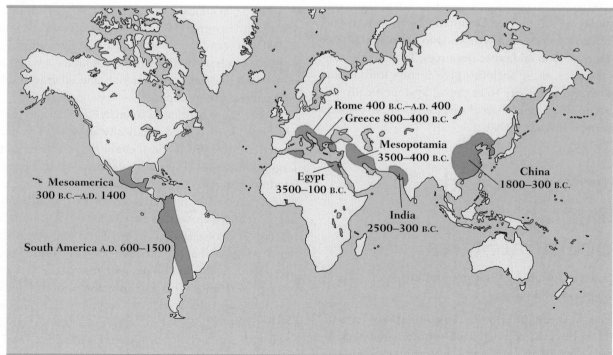

Figure 15.6 Energy consumption among the various types of societies. Note the dramatic increase in consumption in the modern industrial and postindustrial societies.

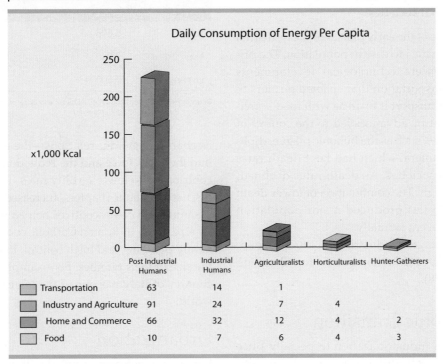

Daily Consumption of Energy Per Capita

	Post Industrial Humans	Industrial Humans	Agriculturalists	Horticulturalists	Hunter-Gatherers
Transportation	63	14	1		
Industry and Agriculture	91	24	7	4	
Home and Commerce	66	32	12	4	2
Food	10	7	6	4	3

Figure 15.7 U.S. energy consumption by energy resources, 1635-2000

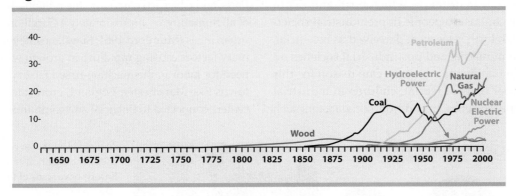

Before the Industrial Revolution, no state used more than 25,000 kilocalories per capita daily, and tribal horticulturalists and intensive agriculturalist farmers used between 4,000 and 25,000 kilocalories. These societies are classified as low-energy cultures. In contrast, early industrial societies using fossil fuels almost tripled their consumption of energy to 70,000 kilocalories. During the later phases of industrialization, energy consumption quadrupled in high-energy cultures such as the United States to as much as 230,000 kilocalories per day. Energy use and expenditures have risen dramatically in all industrial societies (see Figure 15.6).

In the low-energy preindustrial societies, human or animal labor was the chief source of energy, supplemented by firewood, wind, and sometimes water power. In contrast, in high-energy societies, fossil fuels such as coal, natural gas, and petroleum became the primary energy sources. During the early phases of the Industrial Revolution, societies in Europe and America relied upon fossil fuels found in their own territories, but they eventually began to exploit resources from other regions.

In later chapters, we examine the consequences of these patterns of high energy use on the different environments of the world.

Demographic Change

15.10 Discuss the demographic transition for industrial and postindustrial societies.

One major consequence of the early phases of the Industrial Revolution was a dramatic increase in population. The primary reasons for this were technological developments in agriculture and transportation that enabled farmers to grow more food and transport it to areas with food scarcities. In addition, scientific advances led to the control of some infectious diseases, such as the bubonic plague, diphtheria, typhus, and cholera, which had kept death rates high in preindustrial societies. As death rates declined, birth rates remained high. The combination of lower death rates and high birth rates produced major population increases of about 3 percent annually.

During this early stage of industrialism, Europe's population grew from about 140 million in 1750 to 463 million in 1914 (Staviranos 1998).

The Demographic Transition

During later phases of industrialization (especially since the development of postindustrial societies since the 1960s), population growth began to decline in societies like England, other countries in Western Europe, the United States, and Japan. Demographers refer to this change as the **demographic transition**, in which birth and death rates decline. In contrast to people in preindustrial societies, in which high birth rates were perceived as beneficial, many people in industrial and postindustrial societies no longer see large families as a benefit. One reason for this view is the higher costs of rearing children in industrial and postindustrial societies. In addition, social factors such

Table 15. 2 Population in Selected Industrial Cities

City	2007 (in thousands)	2015 (projected density in thousands)
Tokyo	35,676	36,371
New York	19,040	19,974
Los Angeles	12,500	13,160

Source: Reprinted from *The World Almanac and Book of Facts 2010*. Copyright © 2010 Infobase Publishing. All rights reserved.

as changing gender relations—the entry of more women into the work force and the reduction in family size—have contributed to lower fertility rates. These social factors are discussed in later chapters. Increased knowledge of family planning and contraceptives helped people to control family size. Even in Roman Catholic countries that discourage family planning and birth control, individuals are limiting the size of their families. For example, the Roman Catholic country of Italy has one of the lowest fertility rates in the world.

Urbanization

Population increases, coupled with the movement of workers from farms to factories, resulted in the unprecedented growth of urban centers (see Table 15.2). During the nineteenth century, the populations of cities such as London, Paris, and Chicago soared into the millions. By 1930, one-fifth of all humanity, or approximately 415 million people, lived in urban areas (Mumford 1961; Stavrianos 1998). One of the primary factors causing rapid urban growth was the increasing need for labor in the machine-based factory system. Factory towns like Manchester, England, grew into large industrial centers connected to financial and communications districts.

A photo of an Italian couple with one child. The postindustrial societies of Europe have some of the lowest fertility rates in the world.

Summary and Review of Learning Objectives

15.1 Discuss the relationship between subsistence and the physical environment (biomes).

A biome is an area distinguished by a particular climate and certain types of plants and animals. Biomes may be classified by certain attributes, such as mean rainfall, temperature, soil conditions, and vegetation that support certain forms of animal life. Cultural ecologists investigate the relationship between specific biomes and human sociocultural systems. Biomes influence the kind of subsistence patterns that humans develop primarily through cultural solutions. For example, deserts, tropical rain forests, or Arctic environments demand different subsistence patterns.

15.2 Describe how anthropologists study population with reference to fertility, mortality, and migration.

To measure fertility—the number of births in a society—demographic anthropologists use the crude birth rate, that is, the number of live births in a given year for every thousand people in a population. They also measure mortality—the incidence of death in a society's population—by using the crude death rate, that is, the number of deaths in a given year for every thousand people in a population. In measuring the migration rate—the movement of people into and out of a specified territory—demographic anthropologists determine the number of in-migrants (people moving into the territory) and the number of out-migrants (people moving out of the territory). They then use these numbers to calculate the net migration, which indicates the general movement of the population in and out of the territory.

15.3 Describe the different environments and subsistence activities of foragers.

Modern day foragers reside in marginal environments: deserts, tropical rain forests, and Arctic regions. The subsistence activities of contemporary foragers reflect the marginality of those environments. In the past, other people surrounding those marginal environments were not interested in those territories because of the expense of labor or shortage of resources such as water or the scarcity of arable land. Thus, foragers could maintain their subsistence in these marginal areas without too much interference from outsiders.

15.4 Discuss the demographic conditions for foragers.

Foragers had to limit the size of their population in specific regions according to resource availability. They limited their population through fissioning, sexual abstinence, abortion, infanticide, and delayed marriage may be evidence of early forms of fertility control in prehistoric foraging societies.

15.5 Describe the environments and subsistence for horticulturalists and pastoralists.

Horticulture is a form of agriculture in which people use a limited, nonmechanized technology to cultivate plants. One major type of horticulture is known as *swidden agriculture*. This system was once widespread, but today is found primarily in tropical rain forests. The land is burned, cleared, and cultivated in cycles where the land is left fallow for periods of time so that the forests can redevelop. Pastoralists are tribal groups whose subsistence activities are based on the care of domesticated animals. The use of herd animals differs from group to group, and some are more nomadic than others.

15.6 Describe how settling down influences population growth for horticulturalists and pastoralists.

Generally, as humans developed the capacity to produce food through the domestication of animals and plants, the carrying capacity of particular territories increased to support a greater population density than had been possible for foraging societies. The median size of horticulturalist societies ranges from 100 to more than 5,000 people in specific territories, and pastoralists have a median size of 2,000 people in particular niches. Some tribal populations have denser populations in large regions in which villages are connected through economic, social, and political relationships.

15.7 Describe the environments and subsistence activities for chiefdoms.

Most chiefdom societies have occupied ecological regions that contain abundant resources, usually more abundant than the resources in the areas inhabited by foraging and tribal societies. Chiefdoms developed in Polynesia in the Pacific Islands because of the rich resources in these islands. The biome of Polynesia enabled the people to have access to arable land, seafood, and other resources for producing foodstuffs. In the Northwest Coast of the Americas, chiefdoms developed as a result of the abundant supplies of salmon and other seafood, along with plenty of game in the forest areas. Despite the fact that Northwest Coast Native Americans were hunter-gatherers, the abundant resources enabled them to develop highly centralized chiefdom societies.

15.8 Describe the changes for populations in agricultural states.

After the transition to intensive agriculture, population began to increase dramatically along with an increase in agricultural production, enabling people to settle in large urban areas. These population increases produced conditions that led to higher mortality rates. Poor sanitation coupled with the domestication of confined animals led to frequent epidemics that affected both animals and humans. Despite increased mortality rates and decreased life expectancies, populations continued to grow at a significant rate because of increased fertility rates. There were some advantages in having a larger population. Undoubtedly, higher birth rates reflected the socioeconomic benefits associated with increased family size in agricultural civilizations. Children provided additional labor for essential agricultural tasks, such as planting, caring for animals, and harvesting, thereby freeing adults for other labor, such as processing food and making clothing. The actual costs of rearing children were relatively low in agricultural states, in which increased agricultural yields produced surplus foods to support large families. Additionally, the governments of these agricultural states promoted pronatalist policies that were intended to supply manpower for military purposes and agricultural production.

15.9 Discuss the development of energy sources in industrial and postindustrial societies.

Before the Industrial Revolution, no state used more than 25,000 kilocalories per capita daily, and tribal horticulturalists and intensive agriculturalist farmers used between 4,000 and 25,000 kilocalories. These societies are classified as low-energy cultures. In contrast, early industrial societies using fossil fuels almost tripled their consumption of energy to 70,000 kilocalories. During the later phases of industrialization, energy consumption quadrupled in high-energy cultures such as the United States to as much as 230,000 kilocalories per day.

15.10 Discuss the demographic transition for industrial and postindustrial societies.

The demographic transition has taken place with the development of industrial and postindustrial societies since the 1960s. In the demographic transition, population growth declines because both birth rates and death rates decline. In contrast to people in preindustrial societies, in which high birth rates were perceived as beneficial, many people in industrial and postindustrial societies no longer see large families as a benefit. One reason for this view is the higher costs of rearing children in industrial societies and postindustrial societies. In addition, social factors such as changing gender relations—the entry of more women into the work force and the reduction in family size—have contributed to lower fertility rates in postindustrial societies.

Key Terms

biome, p. 327
carrying capacity, p. 330
childhood mortality rate, p. 330
crude birth rate, p. 329
crude death rate, p. 329
demographic transition, p. 344
demography, p. 329
ecology, p. 327
environmental niche, p. 327

fecundity, p. 330
fertility, p. 329
fissioning, p. 334
geronticide, p. 334
horticulture, p. 335
infant mortality rate, p. 330
infanticide, p. 334
life expectancy, p. 330
marginal environments, p. 330

migration rate, p. 329
mortality, p. 329
net migration, p. 329
pastoralists, p. 337
pull factors, p. 330
push factors, p. 330
regional symbiosis, p. 340
subsistence patterns, p. 328

Chapter 16
Technology and Economies

Chapter Outline

 ## Learning Objectives

After reading this chapter you should be able to:

16.1 Discuss the anthropological explanations of technology.

16.2 Discuss how anthropologists study economics in different societies.

16.3 Describe the technologies of foraging societies.

16.4 Describe how the economy works in foraging societies.

Technology   The term *technology* is derived from the Greek word *techne*, which refers to "art" or "skill." When we hear this term, we usually think of tools, machines, clothing, shelter, and other such objects. As defined by modern anthropologists, however, **technology** consists of all the human techniques and methods of reaching a specific subsistence goal or of modifying or controlling the natural environment. Technology is cultural in that it includes methods for manipulating the environment. It consists of physical tools and of cultural knowledge that humans can apply in specific ways to help themselves survive and thrive in changing environments in which they live and work. In societies in which people use technologies, such as bows and arrows, canoes, plows, penicillin, or computers, the cultural knowledge needed to construct, design, and use these materials is extremely important.

To sustain life, human societies need to produce and allocate goods and services to provide food, clothing, shelter, tools, and transportation. **Goods** are elements of material culture produced from raw materials in the natural environment, ranging from the basic commodities for survival to luxury items. The commodities for survival may include axes and plows for clearing land and cultivating crops. Luxury commodities include such items as jewelry, decorative art, and musical instruments. **Services** are elements of nonmaterial culture in the form of specialized skills that benefit others, such as giving spiritual comfort or providing medical care. Goods and services are valued because they satisfy various human needs. To produce these goods and services, societies must have suitable technologies.

Anthropological Explanations of Technology

16.1 **Discuss the anthropological explanations of technology.**

As we saw in an earlier section of the text, in the nineteenth century, anthropologists such as E. B. Tylor and Lewis Morgan constructed a unilineal scheme of cultural evolution in which societies progressed from the simple, small-scale societies of "savages" to the more complex industrial technologies of modern civilizations. In the twentieth century, these simplistic views of technological evolution were rejected through detailed ethnographic research. Anthropologists in the 1950s and 1960s such as Leslie White and Julian Steward—who became known as *cultural materialists*—came to view technology as one of the primary factors of cultural evolution. White defined technology as an energy-capturing system made up of energy, tools, and products—that is, all the material means with which energy is harnessed, transformed, and expended (1959). These anthropologists viewed technology as a basic and primary source of sociocultural change. They argued that we cannot explain different technological developments in society with reference to "cultural values." Instead, technology must be viewed as a method designed to cope with a particular environment. Therefore, variations in environment, or habitat, could account for the differences between, say, the Inuit (Eskimo) and the Australian Aborigine societies.

White's views on technology, as well as the views of other cultural materialists, have been criticized as a rigid form of "technological determinism." Although the cultural materialists see sociological, ideological, or emotional factors as conditioning or limiting the use or development of technology, these factors exert little influence on sociocultural systems compared to technology's dominant role. Anthropologists are currently evaluating this cultural materialist hypothesis to determine whether technology is a primary variable in societal development, or a number of factors work in conjunction with technology to condition societal developments and evolution. So far, anthropologists have concluded that technology alone does not result in cultural change and transformation, but rather cultural values, beliefs, and practices interact with technology to create changes. For example, the Old Order Amish people reject modern technology because of their significant religious beliefs and cultural values. Technology has to be understood with respect to the cultural context in which it is accepted, rejected, or modified by human communities.

Anthropology and Economics

16.2 Discuss how anthropologists study economics in different societies.

Like other animals, humans universally require food and shelter. In addition, humans have special needs for other goods and services, ranging from hunting materials to spiritual guidance. As we have seen, these goods and services are produced through technology. The **economy** of a society consists of the social relationships that organize the production, exchange, and consumption of goods and services. **Production** is the organized system for the creation of goods and services. **Exchange** is the process whereby members of society transfer goods and services among themselves. **Consumption** is the use of goods and services to satisfy desires and needs. In this chapter, we are going to examine these three different components of the economy in various forms of society.

Anthropologists have found that the economy is closely connected with the environment, subsistence base, demographic conditions, technology, and division of labor of the society. The **division of labor** consists of specialized economic roles (occupations) and activities. In small-scale societies, the division of labor is typically simple, and in large-scale societies, it is extremely complex. In the twentieth century, ethnographic descriptions of different types of societies generated two perspectives on economic systems: the *formalist* and *substantivist* approaches.

The Formalist Approach

The formalist approach maintains that all economic systems are fundamentally similar and can be compared with one another. Formalists assume that all people try to act "rationally," maximizing their individual self-interests and gains. In other words, all humans have a psychological inclination to calculate carefully their self-interests. Formalists hypothesize that people do not always choose the cheapest and most efficient strategies to carry out their economic decisions, but they do tend to look for the best rational strategy for economic decision making.

Formalists hold that the best method for studying any economy is to employ the same general theories developed by economists. Formalists collect quantitative data and interpret these data using sophisticated mathematical models developed by economists. They focus on such economic variables as production and consumption patterns, supply and demand, exchange, and investment decisions. One classic formalist study, by anthropologist Sol Tax (1953), focused on economic decision making in Guatemalan Indian communities. Tax analyzed the economic transactions in the traditional markets of these communities. He concluded that although the economy was undeveloped, the people made the same types of economic decisions as people in the developed world. Tax referred to these Indians as "penny capitalists."

The Substantivist Approach

The substantivist approach draws its supporting hypotheses from twentieth-century ethnographic studies. Substantivists maintain that the ways of allocating goods and services in small-scale societies differ fundamentally from those in large-scale Western economic systems. Thus, the social institutions found in small-scale societies or larger agricultural societies produce economic systems that are fundamentally different from the market economies of Western societies. According to substantivists, preindustrial economies are not driven by the motive of individual material gain or profit, as are industrial economies. They argue that the economy is *embedded* in the sociocultural system, including the kinship systems, values, beliefs, and norms of the society. They also argue that modern capitalist societies are *embedded* within an economy based on market exchange. In general, substantivists emphasize that precapitalist societies have different forms of logic and processes from the market exchange economies of capitalist societies. These precapitalist societies also have other forms of exchange, such as reciprocity and redistribution. We focus on these other forms of exchange later.

Contemporary Economic Anthropology

Most anthropologists today do not identify exclusively with the formalist or the substantivist perspective; instead, they recognize the contributions of both perspectives to our knowledge of economic systems (Wilk 1996; Gudeman 1986; Bloch and Parry 1989). Modern anthropologists investigate the different patterns of production, ownership, distribution, exchange, and consumption in relationship to ecological, demographic, and cultural factors, which influence economic choices, risk, and consumption preferences. They collect quantitative economic data along with more qualitative cultural data (*emic* or insider's understandings) to explain the workings of economic choices and systems. As we shall see in later chapters, most economic anthropologists are not as concerned with how precapitalist societies organize their economies; rather, they are more concerned with how precapitalist economies change as they are influenced by globalization and contact with the global market economy. In addition, many anthropologists are using psychological experiments based on game theory or other models to assess how people make their economic decisions (Boyd and Richerson 2004; Henrich et al. 2004). These new psychological experiments tend to demonstrate that human economic decision making is not wholly based on rational calculations, but rather is influenced by "emotional" or "cultural" factors regarding choices and preferences. For example, Henrich et al. used economic games to collect data on exchange behaviors from 15 small-scale societies around the world, finding that in no society was behavior consistent with the "selfishness axiom" (that people seek to maximize their own gains and expect others to do the same), as predicted by the neoclassical economist perspective (e.g., "rational choice")(2004). In fact, the results of the study indicated that rather than focusing only on economic outcomes, people were also concerned with *how* a transaction took place, nonmaterial outcomes (e.g., reputation) and fairness. Research on these topics is important for understanding more than just behavior in economic games and experiments. This research is aimed at developing explanations for the origins of human cooperation. Humans rely on each other to survive, so explaining cooperation is of primary importance within anthropology.

One other area of new anthropological research on economic choices and preferences was inspired by anthropologist/sociologist Pierre Bourdieu. Bourdieu discussed three different forms of capital that individuals had in respect to their socioeconomic status or class background (1977, 1984). He distinguished *economic capital*, based on the wealth and assets of individuals, *social capital*, the social networks based on kinship, family ties, or political allies, and *cultural capital*, the tastes or aesthetic preferences for symbolic goods such as literature, art, foods, or music. These different forms of capital influenced economic choices and preferences for individuals within different socioeconomic strata or class background. Bourdieu argued that all three forms of capital gave individuals advantages or disadvantages for the accumulation of wealth, power, and status within different societies. Anthropologists have been investigating these different forms of capital in various societies and how they influence economic decisions regarding exchange and consumption.In later chapters, we discuss the empirical data gathered by anthropologists about different types of production, exchange, and consumption, and how they are affected and dramatically influenced by global change.

Technology in Foraging Societies

16.3 Describe the technologies of foraging societies.

In Chapter 7, we discussed the evolution of technology during the Paleolithic period. The crude stone tools of the Lower Paleolithic gave way to the more sophisticated stone tool complex of the Upper Paleolithic. As humans migrated across the continents, technology became specialized, enabling populations to adjust to different types of environments.

Until recently, anthropologists believed that many modern hunter-gatherers had limited technologies.

Nineteenth-century anthropologists thought that these limited technologies reflected simplicity of mind and lack of skill. Modern anthropologists, in contrast, regard these technologies as highly adaptive in particular ecological conditions. These band societies also enhanced their technologies with many clever techniques, indicating that these technologies were not completely "static." More importantly, remember that technology does not refer just to tools or artifacts; it also includes the cultural knowledge that has to be maintained by the society. All foraging peoples have an extensive knowledge of their environmental conditions and of technological means for adapting to the challenges in these environments.

Desert foragers such as the Ju/'hoansi San used small bows and arrows and spears. Australian Aborigines did not have the bow and arrow, but they used the well-known boomerang (which did not return to the thrower), spears, and spear-throwers (*atlatls*) for hunting in desert areas. Some of the Australian Aborigines developed fish hooks for harvesting eels in various streams and canals that increased their potential resources. In tropical rain forests, foragers make traps, snares, and sometimes nets such as those used by the Mbuti. The Mbuti also make fire-hardened wooden spears and arrow tips for hunting. Some foraging groups, like the Semang, use the blowgun for hunting game. Most of the desert and rain forest foragers use natural poisons to make their hunting more efficient. In some cases, the foragers place various types of poisons from plants in streams to kill fish. In other cases, they put poison on the tips of their arrows to kill game.

As we have seen, fruit and vegetable gathering is at least as important as hunting in foraging societies. In the desert and tropical rain forest, the implements for gathering are uncomplicated. The cultural knowledge needed for gathering, however, is profound. The people need to know where to find the plants, when to find them during different seasons, which plants are edible, which plants are scarce or plentiful, and so on. In most cases, gathering food is the responsibility of women and children. The typical tool is a simple sharpened stick for digging up tubers or getting honey out of hives. Sometimes foragers also use net bags, bark, wooden bowls, or other natural objects to carry nuts, seeds, water, or fruit. For example, Ju/'hoansi San women used large ostrich eggs to hold and carry water.

An extremely complex foraging technology was created by the Inuit (Eskimo) to procure animal food resources. The classic Inuit technology has evolved over the past 3,000 years and includes equipment made from bone, stone, skin, wood, and ice. Inuit technology also includes kayaks, dogsleds, lances, fish spears, bows and arrows, harpoons with detachable points, traps, fish hooks, and soapstone lamps used with whale and seal oil for heating and cooking. Unlike the desert and rain forest foragers, who wear very little clothing, the Eskimo people have developed sophisticated techniques for curing hides from caribou and seals to make boots, parkas, and other necessary Arctic gear. They make snow goggles out of baleen and ivory that have narrow slits for their eyes to prevent snow blindness. However, again, one cannot simply categorize all of these "Eskimo" hunting-gathering societies into one simple "band" form of society. As Allen Johnson and Timothy Earle indicate in their cross-cultural research, another group of "Eskimo," the Tareumiut, is closely related linguistically to other groups, but adopted a whale-hunting subsistence strategy with large *umiaks* or boats. This has enabled them to develop a much more complex sociocultural system that has allowed them to endure long, hard winters more comfortably than other Inuit (2000).

Economics in Foraging Societies

16.4 **Describe how the economy works in foraging societies.**

Despite the vast differences in physical environment, subsistence, and technology, most foraging societies have very similar economic systems. The major form of economic system identified with these societies is called the **reciprocal economic exchange system** (Sahlins 1972). A reciprocal economic system is based on exchanges among family groups as a means of distributing goods and services throughout the society. The basic principle underlying this system is **reciprocity**, the widespread sharing of goods and services in a society. One reason for this system of reciprocal exchange is that food and other resources must usually be consumed immediately. There is very little storage capacity for any surplus, so it makes sense to share what cannot be used anyway.

Reciprocity

The many descriptions of economic transactions and exchanges in foraging societies have led anthropologist Marshall Sahlins to distinguish three types of reciprocity: generalized, balanced, and negative (Sahlins 1965, 1972).

Generalized Reciprocity
Generalized reciprocity is based upon the assumptions that an immediate return is not expected and that the value of the exchanges will balance out in the long run. Sometimes anthropologists refer to this type of reciprocity as *delayed exchange*. The value of the return is not specified, and no running account of repayment of transactions is calculated. Although generalized reciprocity exists in all societies—for example, in the United States, parents pay for their offspring's food, clothing, and shelter—in foraging societies these transactions form the basis of the economic system.

Anthropologists used to refer to generalized reciprocity as a *gift* to distinguish it from trade or barter. Neither altruism nor charity, however, accurately describes these transactions. Rather, these exchanges are based on socially recognized family and kinship statuses. Because such behaviors are expected, gratitude or recognition is usually not required. In fact, in this form of reciprocity, it might be impolite or insulting to indicate that a return is expected. For example, among the Ju/'hoansi San and Eskimo foragers, a "thank you" for food or other services is interpreted as an insult (Freuchen 1961; Lee 1969). Generosity is required in these small-scale societies to reduce envy and social tensions, promote effective cooperation, distribute resources and services, and create obligations.

Examples of generalized reciprocity occur among foragers like the Ju/'hoansi San, Mbuti, and Inuit (Eskimo). Aside from food, which is shared with everyone in the group, the San have a generalized delayed exchange system known as *hxaro*, which not only circulates goods but also—and primarily—solidifies social relationships by creating mutual obligations among related kin (Lee 1993, 2013). Anthropologist Polly Weisner has been conducting a long-term study of the *hxaro* system which involves exchanging goods ranging from beads, arrows, tools, and clothing (2002). Exchange partners were said to "hold each other in their hearts" and they were willing to assist one another when they were in need (Weisner 2002). Constant circulation of these material goods not only enhances and maintains kin ties through mutual obligations, but also inhibits the accumulation of wealth by any individuals in the society (Smith et al. 2010). There is some variation in how goods are shared in these societies. Peter Gardner did ethnographic research on the Paliyan, a hunter-gatherer society in India, and found that the hunters each get an identical share of the meat with a double portion for the individual who struck the dangerous animal first (2013: 80). This sharing and cooperation enables these societies to remain egalitarian, meaning that there are very small differences in wealth among individuals.

Balanced Reciprocity
A more direct type of reciprocal exchange with an explicit expectation of immediate return is **balanced reciprocity**. This form of reciprocity is more utilitarian and more like trade and barter than is generalized reciprocity. The material aspect of the exchange is as important as the social aspect. People involved in these transactions calculate the value of the exchanges, which are expected to be equivalent. If an equal return is not given, the original donor may not continue the exchange relationship. Balanced reciprocity is usually found in the context of more distant kinship relations. Because most exchanges and transactions in modern foraging societies take place among close kin, balanced reciprocity is practiced less frequently than is generalized reciprocity.

Negative Reciprocity
Sahlins (1972) defined **negative reciprocity** as the attempt to get something for nothing. Negative reciprocity means no reciprocity at all. It may involve bargaining, haggling, gambling, cheating,

!Kung San or Ju/'hoansi foragers

theft, or the outright seizure of goods. This reflects mistrust between and among groups. In general, negative reciprocity is least common in small-scale foraging societies, in which kinship relations and trust predominate.

Exchange and Altruism   In foraging societies, where reciprocity reigns, people may appear to outsiders as naturally generous, altruistic, and magnanimous. But as Lee noted in reference to the economy of the !Kung San or Ju/'hoansi San:

> If I had to point to one single feature that makes this way
> of life possible, I would focus on sharing. Each Ju is not an
> island unto himself or herself; each is part of a collective.
> It is a small, rudimentary collective, and at times a fragile
> one, but it is a collective nonetheless. What I mean is that
> the living group pools the resources that are brought into
> camp so that everyone receives an equitable share. The !Kung
> and people like them don't do this out of nobility of soul or
> because they are made of better stuff than we are. In fact,
> they often gripe about sharing. They do it because it works
> for them and it enhances their survival. Without this core of
> sharing, life for the Ju/'hoansi would be harder and infinitely
> less pleasant. (1993:60)

It appears that these hunting-and-gathering peoples are no more "noble" or less "materialistic" than other people. Rather, the conditions of their existence have led them to develop economic practices that enable them to survive in their particular habitat. As humans, it appears that we reciprocate with one another in all societies. The strategy of "I'll scratch your back and you scratch mine" is found everywhere. This generalized reciprocity helps develop *prosocial norms*. **Prosocial norms** are cultural rules that promote cooperation, trust, and altruism within a society. And in a small-scale foraging society where trust can be generated among everyone, these prosocial norms are enforced through patterns of generalized reciprocity.

Collective Ownership of Property

In the nineteenth century, Lewis Morgan proposed that early economic systems associated with small-scale societies were communistic. In his book *Ancient Society* ([1877] 1964), Morgan claimed that during the early stages of cultural evolution, productive technology and economic resources were shared by all members of a society. As indicated earlier, Morgan's views shaped and influenced the ideas of Karl Marx in his vision of early communist and future communist societies. Today, Morgan's views appear too simplistic to account for the vast range of economic systems found in small-scale societies.

Ethnographic data indicate that hunting-and-gathering societies have differing forms of property relations, which reflect their particular ecological conditions. Among some groups, such as the Ju/'hoansi San, the Eskimo, and the Shoshone, where resources are widely distributed, cultural anthropologists report that there are no exclusive rights to territory (Durning 1992; Smith et al. 2010). Although specific families may be identified with a local camp area, territorial boundaries are extremely flexible, and exclusive ownership of resources within a territory is not well defined. For example, among the Ju/'hoansi San, land tenure was very complex. Areas of land rights were called *n!orse*, and *n!orse* varied in terms of water and nut resources (Lee 1979; Weisner 2002). Also, sacred sites were frequently associated with territories that contained various resources such as water, wild plants, shade trees, fuel wood, and other items for toolmaking and were said to be owned by individual families (Hitchcock 2004a). Yet, few restrictions were placed against other families or groups in using these resources (Weisner 2002; Lee 1979). Many foraging groups may have rights of temporary use or rights to claim resources if needed, but not the "once-and-for-all" abstract forms of property rights that exist in modern capitalist societies (Bloch 1983; Smith et al. 2010).

However, in other foraging societies, such as that of the Owens Valley Paiute Indians who resided near the edge of the Great Basin region in the American West, exclusive rights to territory were well defined and defended against outsiders. The Paiute were heavily dependent upon pinyon nuts, which were concentrated in one area and were a more predictable source of food than game animals. Specific territorial ties and exclusive rights to land containing these resources became important for bands and families. The defense of these resources was economically beneficial to the Paiute. In a comparison of territorial rights among different hunter-gatherers, anthropologists Rada Dyson-Hudson and Eric Smith (1978) found that the greater the predictability and concentration of resources within a particular region, the more pronounced the conceptions of private ownership and exclusive rights to territory among foragers.

Other forms of private property in foraging societies—pets, ornaments, clothing, and items of technology such as bows, knives, scrapers, and blowguns—are associated with individuals. Such items are usually regarded as a form of private personal property over which the person who owns them has certain rights.

The Original Affluent Society?

Until the 1960s, the traditional picture of foraging societies was that of people with limited technologies who were at the mercy of a harsh environment. It seemed that in these dire environmental circumstances, people had to work constantly to survive. In the 1960s, however, anthropologists began to draw on ethnographic studies to produce a much different image of hunter-gatherer societies. Modern cultural anthropologists gathered basic data on the types of production systems that hunter-gatherers use, the amount of time they spend in production and subsistence, the role of mobility in their adaptation, and how long they live.

The ethnographic data reported in Lee and DeVore's (1968) work indicates that contemporary foraging societies usually have an adequate and reliable food base. Lee (1972a, 1972b, 1979, 1993, 2013), for example, has argued that the Ju/'hoansi San diet was nutritionally adequate. The data also indicate that these foragers expended minimal labor to provide for their basic physical needs. Finally, the life expectancy in these societies turns out to be much greater than was once thought. These findings have led some anthropologists to refer to foragers as "original affluent societies" or "leisured societies" (Sahlins 1972). Sahlins, for example, argued that the worldview and cultural values of foragers differ radically from those of capitalist societies. He suggested that the sharing-oriented economy of people such as the Ju/'hoansi San demonstrates that the forager's needs are few and are easily satisfied by a relatively meager amount of labor time. In Sahlins's view, foragers take the "Zen road to affluence" —they do not value the accumulation of material goods in the same way that people in modern capitalist societies do.

For nomadic populations, the accumulation of excess resources would be unproductive. Material possessions would be burdensome when trekking across the ice of the Arctic or through the dense rain forests. Without a way to store large quantities of food, it would be irrational to accumulate food resources only to have them spoil.

Further evidence of the affluence of foragers is drawn from the demographic conditions for these groups. For example, Lee argued that the composition of the Ju'hoansi San population demonstrates that these people were not on the edge of starvation. Ten percent of the individuals surveyed by Lee were over 60 years of age, "a proportion that compares favorably to the percentage of elderly in industrialized populations" (Lee 1968:36). The blind, senile, or disabled continued to be supported by the Ju/'hoansi. The system of reciprocal exchanges thus ensures the survival of these individuals.

The Affluence Hypothesis Challenged

Some recent anthropological research, however, has challenged the notion of the original affluent societies. Although the San and similar groups may spend only a few hours each day and a few days each week bringing in basic food resources, they must also spend time making tools, weapons, and clothing; processing and cooking food; planning for future foraging activities; solving disputes; healing the sick; and raising children (Konner 2002). In other words, we can view the Ju/'hoansi San and other foragers as affluent only if we restrict our definition of work to the actual quest for food.

The study of the Ache, who live in the rain forest of eastern Paraguay, illustrates the shortcomings of the affluence hypothesis. A team of cultural anthropologists analyzed Ache subsistence activities (Hill et al. 1985; Hill and Hurtado 1996). They discovered that Ache males spend 40 to 50 hours a week in the quest for special kinds of food. Time-allocation studies such as this challenge the notion that all foragers spend minimal time in pursuit of food resources.

Furthermore, recent medical research has challenged Lee's arguments that the Ju/'hoansi San diet is nutritionally sound. Although the diet is well balanced in respect to carbohydrates, proteins, and fats, the overall caloric intake of the San appears to be inadequate. The small physical size of the San may be due to mothers usually not supplementing nursing with additional food intake for infants more than six months old. Moreover, the entire San population has suffered from seasonal food shortages and starvation (Konner 2002).

This recent research on the Ju/'hoansi San does not totally refute the overall hypothesis regarding the original affluent societies. In general, it appears that in some cases, especially in the tropical rain forest, groups like the Mbuti and the Semang have an abundance of vegetables and fruits. In contrast, groups such as the Shoshone and the Ache have to expend much more time in securing basic resources. When there is a ready presence of resources, relative affluence is possible. But when these items are absent or less plentiful, subsistence becomes much more demanding.

Another factor that influences the relative affluence of foraging societies is the ability to preserve resources over a period of time. Although most of these societies did not store food, groups such as the Inuit or other Arctic groups had limited storage capacities. Some Arctic foragers dug holes beneath the permafrost so that they could store meat. The storage of meat, berries, and greens enabled these groups to maintain a certain amount of affluence even in winter. Thus they had a steady, reliable source of meat and vegetation as a base for subsistence activities.

In a recent reassessment of wealth transmission among different hunter-gatherer societies, anthropologists Eric A. Smith and colleagues conclude that the portrait of these societies as purely communistic with pervasive equality is mistaken (2010a, 2010b). In addition to material wealth, these anthropologists add **embodied wealth**, the physical or bodily health of individuals and groups, and **relational wealth**, kinship networks and alliances that enhance an individual's or group's success. Their reassessment indicates that are some relational wealth inequalities that have to do with supportive exchange networks and kinship alliances which tend to favor some individuals within specific families over others. Although material wealth is minimal in these foraging societies, *embodied wealth* such as health conditions and *relational wealth* or social connections are extremely important. Overall, this reassessment indicates that inequality in wealth is very moderate in general, and to a great extent, reflects the pioneering ethnographic descriptions of the original affluent societies by anthropologist Richard Lee and others.

Technology among Horticulturalists and Pastoralists

16.5 Describe the technologies of horticulturalist and pastoralist societies.

The whole range of tribal technologies is extremely broad and varies among differing populations, depending on whether they are horticulturalists or pastoralists and on the types of environments to which they have had to adapt. Technological innovations found in tribal societies include woodworking, weaving, leatherworking, and the production of numerous copper ornaments, tools, and weapons.

Horticulturalist Technology

Horticulturalist groups used sharpened digging sticks and sometimes wooden hoes to plant small gardens. Up until the 1950s, the swidden horticulturalists such as the Yanomamö used crude stone or wooden axes to fell the primary forest. They would build their villages, called *shabono*, in a clearing surrounded by primary forests. It sometimes took weeks for a small group of males to cut down a wooded area for a garden. Today, they use machetes and steel axes to clear the primary forests (Chagnon 2012; Hames 2004).

Many horticultural societies have also developed technologies to aid in hunting and fishing to supplement their horticultural activities. For example, some Amazonian peoples, such as the Jivaro of Ecuador and Peru, often use blowguns, which propel poison darts up to 45 yards, to kill monkeys and birds deep in the forest (Harner 1972). The Yanomamö use large, powerful bows, sometimes five to five and half feet long, and long arrow shafts with a splintered point, dipped in *curare*, a deadly poison (Chagnon 2012; Hames 2004). Amazonian horticulturalists also mix poisons into local waters, causing the fish to rise to the surface in a stupefied condition; they are then gathered for food (Harner 1972; Chagnon 2012; Hames 2004).

The woodland Iroquois tribes used both the blowgun and the bow (called the self-bow) and arrow to hunt game in surrounding forests. The Iroquois carefully selected light wooden branches for arrow shafts, dried them to season the wood, and then smoothed them with stone and bone tools. To make the arrow twist in flight, they took feathers from eagles, turkeys, and hawks, which they then attached with a glue made from animal tissues, sinew, or horns. Arrowheads were made from wood, stone, horn, antler, shell, or raw copper (Garbarino 1988).

Horticulturalists such as the Pacific Islanders, who were not slash-and-burn farmers and who resided in more permanent locations, tended to have a more elaborate technology. In addition to the simple digging stick used to cultivate the irrigated gardens, they had many other sophisticated tools and utensils. Although the Pacific Islanders had no metals or clay for pottery, they had many specialized kinds of shell and woodworking tools for making jewelry, knives, rasps, and files.

Pastoralist Technology

The mobility required by the pastoralist lifestyle prevented these groups from using an elaborate technology. Pastoralists such as the Mongols and the Bedouins carried all of their belongings with them in their yearly migrations. Their technologies aided them in these mass movements; for example, they had saddles for their horses and camels, weapons for hunting, equipment for taking care of their livestock and processing food, and tents that could be moved during migrations. Other pastoralists such as the Nuer of East Africa constructed huts of thatch in permanent locations that served as home bases where a certain number of people remained during the migration season.

Economics in Horticulturalist and Pastoralist Societies

16.6 Discuss money and property ownership in horticulturalist and pastoralist economies.

As in hunting-and-gathering societies, *reciprocity* is the dominant form of exchange of economic resources in tribal economic systems. All three forms of reciprocity—generalized, balanced, and negative—are used by tribal societies. *Generalized reciprocity* tends to occur within close kinship groupings. Balanced and negative reciprocity occur among more distant kinship groupings. One example of balanced reciprocity occurs among the Yanomamö, who maintain a system of trade and feasting activities with other villages. One village will host a feast, inviting another village to attend. During the feast, the villagers exchange tools, pots, baskets, arrows, dogs, yarn, and hallucinogenic drugs. The feast activities sustain intervillage cooperation, marital exchanges, and political and military alliances (Chagnon 1997; Hames 2004). The villagers calculate these transactions and exchanges very carefully to determine exact equivalencies. If an equal return is not given, then the original donor village will discontinue the exchange relationship. This may lead to hostilities and, perhaps, warfare between the villages.

Money

Unlike foragers, some tribal societies engage in monetary exchange-- that is, transactions that involve money. **Money** is a medium of exchange based on a standard value. According to economists, money has four functions:

1. It enables people to pay for a good or service, and then it circulates to allow for subsequent purchases.
2. It serves as a uniform standard of value for goods and services within a society.
3. It has a store of value; that is, its standard of value does not fluctuate radically from one time to another.
4. It serves as a form of deferred payment; that is, it can express a promise to pay in the future with the same standard value. (Neale 1976)

Economic anthropologists classify money into two types: *general-purpose money* (or multipurpose money) and *limited-purpose money* (or special-purpose money). General-purpose money serves all four of the above functions. It can be used as a medium of exchange for most of the goods and services in society. Limited-purpose money, in contrast, is restricted to the purchase of specific goods and services. The paper currencies used in the United States and other industrial societies are examples of general-purpose money. In contrast, most tribal societies that practice monetary exchange use limited-purpose money.

Peoples in some of the Pacific Islands and other coastal areas have used a variety of shells to conduct trade relations. In other tribal societies, livestock, cloth, salt, feathers, animal teeth, and sometimes women functioned as money. This type of money was used for specialized exchange circumstances. For example, the Siane of New Guinea exchanged food for other subsistence goods, and they exchanged luxury items such as bird feathers only for other luxury items. Another separate level of exchange took place with respect to prestige items such as certain forms of shell necklaces (Salisbury 1962).

Property Ownership

Ownership of property, especially land for horticulturalists and animals for pastoralists, takes on significance in tribal societies that it does not have in band societies. The concept of property ownership becomes more clearly defined in tribal societies and is based on a web of social relations involving rights, privileges, and perhaps duties and obligations regarding the use of a particular piece of land, a herd of animals, or other objects. These horticultural and pastoralist societies do have demonstrable patterns of inequality among specific families in relationship to the transmission of land and animals from parents to offspring. However, in a recent overall assessment of wealth inequality, there tends to be more inequality in pastoralist societies than in the horticulturalist societies (Gurven et al. 2010; Borgerhoff Mulder et al. 2010). One of the reasons for more persistent inequality in wealth in pastoralist societies depends on the transmission of animals from parents to offspring (Borgerhoff Mulder et al. 2010).

In tribal societies, exclusive right to use property is rare. With some exceptions, property rights in tribal societies are generally vested in family and wider kinship groupings. Usually, specific tribal families have use rights to farmland, pastures, animals, and other items. The property of tribal societies is transferred to offspring through inheritance; individual access to property, however, in many cases is largely determined by status and kinship networks. In other words, in tribal societies, an individual gains certain rights, privileges, and obligations with respect to property through inheriting land and animals through kinship networks, or what is described as *relational wealth* (Gurven et al. 2010). Social status and wealth in tribal societies is usually determined by kinship, age, and gender.

Property rights in tribal societies are not completely static with respect to statuses. Rather, they may fluctuate according to the availability of basic resources. If land is plentiful in a specific tribe, for example, outsiders who need land may be granted rights to use the land. On the other hand, if there is a shortage of land, rights to that property may become more narrowly defined and may be defended if the land is intruded on. Grazing land for pastoralists or arable land for horticulturalists may become limited, and if this occurs, use rights may be defined more exclusively for particular family and kinship groupings. In contrast to foraging societies, in tribal societies warfare frequently results from encroachments on more narrowly defined property.

Tribal societies generally possess certain types of personal property. As seen in the discussion of subsistence activities, there are different forms of pastoralist societies that vary with respect to the amount of nomadic mobility and animals available (Salzmann 2004; Gurven et al. 2010). In some cases because of the demands of a nomadic life, pastoralist property tends to be portable (saddles, tents, and similar objects), whereas much horticultural property tends to be immovable, like housing structures and land. In other cases, individuals in pastoralist societies have the opportunity to amass concentrations of wealth compared to horticulturalists (Gurven et al. 2010).

Technology in Chiefdoms

16.7 Describe technology and housing in chiefdom societies.

Chiefdom societies developed technologies that reflected their abundant and varied natural resources. Although the Polynesians relied primarily on digging sticks for **intensive horticulture**, the method of crop production by irrigating, fertilizing, hoeing, and terracing hillsides, they also had many specialized tools—including implements to cut shells and stones—for making jewelry, knives, fish hooks, harpoons, nets, and large canoes. Likewise, the Cahokian society in prehistoric Illinois had an elaborate technology consisting of fish hooks, grinding stones, mortars and pestles, hoes, and many other tools. These more elaborate technologies resulted in many specialized occupations for the development of crafts, tools, and, as we will see, artists, musicians, and many other artisans. With these specialized occupations and the resulting complex division of labor, patterns of hierarchy and social stratification began to emerge in chiefdom societies.

Housing in Chiefdoms

The dwellings used in chiefdom societies varied over regions, depending on the materials available. The traditional Pacific island houses of Tahiti and Hawaii were built with poles and thatched with coconut leaves and other vegetation. The island houses needed repair from time to time, but generally were long-lasting dwellings.

Similarly, the Cahokian people built firm housing by plastering clay over a wood framework. In the Northwest Coast villages, people lived in houses made of cedar planks, which were some of the most solid houses constructed in all of America before European colonization. Recently, archaeologists have been excavating these cedar plank houses in the Northwest Coast to understand the characteristics of households. Dana Lepofsky and her colleagues have been comparing the cedar plank houses built in the coastal villages of the Northwest Coast with the inland houses in British Columbia and Washington (2009; Rodning 2010). They find that in the coastal villages the plank houses are arranged in rows facing the water. The houses in the interior regions are not arranged in rows or circles. In addition, they also find that the cedar plank houses become larger as more permanent types of settlements are developed.

In all these chiefdom societies, the housing structures of the chief's family were much more elaborate, spacious, and highly decorated than those of other people. Yet, archaeologists Gary Coupland and his colleagues find that in the Northwest Coast houses there are different types of households. In the larger structures associated with the chiefs, families of different status levels were living within the same house, whereas in smaller houses there were only low-status residents (2009). They interpret these findings to suggest that the multistatus large households functioned to maintain an enhanced communal and cooperative atmosphere as patterns of increased social hierarchy and ranking developed within these chiefdom societies. Chiefdom societies had to manage and balance the new patterns of inequality and stratification through political, economic, and religious strategies, but also through social integration.

Economy in Chiefdoms

16.8 Describe the unique type of economic exchange that emerged in chiefdom societies.

Food Storage

One aspect of the economy that often played a key role in chiefdom societies was the storage of food. For chiefdoms to exist, resources had to be abundant, and people needed a technology for storing and preserving these resources. Food storage was a key variable in the ability of a society to become economically productive, creating the potential for economic and political stratification. Although there were occasional instances of food storage in some nomadic hunter-gatherer societies in marginal environments, food storage was not common among foragers or tribal societies (Testart 1988). Archaeologist Brian Hayden has emphasized how the storage of food was a risk-reducing strategy and enabled chiefdoms to pool their resources to enhance a "social safety network" for many families (2009). In chiefdoms, families would store more food than was needed to reduce risk in the face of uncertainties in the future.

The Northwest Coast Native Americans provide an example of food storage methods practiced by chiefdoms. These societies experienced two different seasonal cycles: in the summer, the groups engaged in fishing, hunting, and gathering; in the winter, little subsistence activity occurred. During the winter, these peoples lived on stored food, particularly smoked and preserved salmon. In these circumstances, certain descent groups and individuals accumulated surpluses, thereby acquiring a higher position in the society.

Property Ownership

Property ownership developed when a powerful individual, a chief, who was the head of a lineage, a village, or a group of interrelated villages, claimed exclusive ownership of the territory within the region. To use the land, other people had to observe certain restrictions on their production and turn over some of their resources to the chiefs.

In chiefdom societies, property ownership tended to become more closely identified with particular descent groups and individuals. For example, on the Northwest Coast, fishing sites with large and predictable runs of salmon tended to be owned and inherited by particular corporate kin groups. As another example, specific chiefs among the Trobriand Islands owned and maintained more or less exclusive rights to large canoes that were important in regional trade.

Recently, D. Blair Gibson concludes from his examinations of early medieval Irish texts that land within Irish chiefdoms was regarded as a private commodity for chiefs (2008). The holding and transfer of land was restricted to the chiefs and their dependents, whereas the land held by commoners was held communally. These forms of private property for chiefs were widespread among chiefdom societies.

Political Aspects of Property Ownership

Anthropologists differ over how much exclusive ownership the chief had over his realm. As we shall see in a later chapter, the political authority of a chief did have some limitations. Accordingly, the claim to exclusive rights over the territories may, in some cases, have been restricted. For example, among the Kpelle of Liberia in West Africa, the land was said to be owned formally by the paramount chief (the highest-ranking chief), who divided it into portions for each village in the chiefdom. These portions were then distributed in parcels to families of various lineages. Once land was parceled out, it remained within the lineage until the lineage died out. In this sense, the paramount

chief was only a steward holding land for the group he represented (Gibbs 1965). Among the Trobriand Islands, in theory, a *dala*, a corporate matrilineal kin group comprised of some 65 persons, owned its own land for cultivating yams and other crops for exchange. However, a *dala* leader (a son within the matrilineage) had effective control over the access and allocation of crops from the land (Weiner 1976).

Economic Exchange in Chiefdoms

Chiefdom societies practiced a number of different types of economic exchange. Two basic types of exchange are reciprocal exchanges and redistributional exchanges.

Reciprocal Exchange   Like all societies, chiefdoms engaged in reciprocal exchanges. One classic case of balanced reciprocal exchange occurred among the Trobriand Islanders, as described by Bronislaw Malinowski ([1922] 1961). The Trobrianders, intensive horticulturalists who raised yams and depended heavily on fishing, maintained elaborate trading arrangements with other island groups. They had large sea canoes, or outriggers, and traveled hundreds of miles on sometime dangerous seas to conduct what was known as the *kula* exchange.

The Kula Exchange   The **kula** was the ceremonial trade of valued objects that took place among a number of the Trobriand Islands. In his book *Argonauts of the Western Pacific* ([1922] 1961), Malinowski described how red-shell necklaces and white-shell armbands were ritually exchanged from island to island through networks of male traders. The necklaces traditionally traveled clockwise, and the armbands traveled counterclockwise. These necklaces and armbands were constantly circulating, and the size and value of these items had to be perfectly matched (hence, balanced reciprocity). People did not keep these items very long; in fact, they were seldom worn. There was no haggling or discussion of price by any of the traders.

Trobriand males were inducted into the trading network through elaborate training regarding the proper etiquette and magical practices of the *kula*. The young men learned these practices through their fathers or mothers' brothers and eventually established trading connections with partners on other islands.

A more utilitarian trade accompanied the ceremonial trade. Goods such as tobacco, pottery, coconuts, fish, baskets, and mats were exchanged through the Trobriand trading partners. In these exchanges, the partners haggled and discussed price. Malinowski referred to this trade as secondary trade, or **barter**, the direct exchange of one commodity for another. He argued that the ceremonial *kula* trade created emotional ties among trading partners and that the utilitarian trade was secondary and incidental. Because of this argument, Malinowski is often referred to as one of the first substantivist economic anthropologists (see earlier). He hypothesized that the economic production and exchange of utilitarian goods were embedded in the social practices and cultural norms of the *kula* exchange, which was noneconomic.

Some anthropologists, however, hypothesized that the ceremonial trade was only the ritual means for conducting the more utilitarian transactions for material goods. Annette Weiner (1987) reanalyzed the *kula* trade and in her interviews with older informants found that Malinowski had overlooked the fact that certain armbands or necklaces, known as *kitomu*, were owned by the chiefs. The *kitomu* could be used to make bridewealth payments, to pay funeral expenses, or to build a canoe. In other words, they were more like money. At times, a chief would add some *kitomu* into the *kula* transactions to attract new partners and new wealth. These chiefs would take economic risks with their shells to accumulate valuable private profits. If a chief gained a new partner through these transactions, he would be able to gain more wealth. If he was not able to gain new partners, however, he could lose some of his investments.

Thus, Weiner viewed the *kula* not as a system of balanced reciprocity, but as a system of economic competition in which certain traders tried to maximize social and political status and to accumulate profits. Although the *kula* exchanges emphasized the notions of equality and reciprocity, this was, in fact, an illusion. In actuality, trading partners tried to achieve the opposite—ever-larger profits and status.

Malinowski overlooked the fact that the trade items of the *kula* exchange, referred to as "wealth finances," were critically important in establishing a chief's social status and personal prestige. For example, only the chiefs were able to control the extensive labor needed to construct outrigger canoes, the means by which the trade was conducted. Through the control of labor, the chiefs were able to dominate the production system and thus benefited politically from the *kula* exchange of luxury valuables (Earle 1987; Johnson and Earle 2000).

Redistributional Exchange

The predominant form of economic exchange in chiefdom societies, and one that is not usually found in hunter-gatherer and tribal societies, is **redistributional economic exchange**, which involves the exchange of goods and resources through a centralized organization. In the redistributional system, food and other staples, such as craft goods, are collected as a form of tax or rent. The chiefs (and subsidiary chiefs) then redistribute some of these goods and food staples back to the population at certain times of the year. This system thus assures the dispersal of food and resources throughout the community through a centralized agency. Archaeologist Brian Hayden emphasizes how these feasting activities and redistributional exchanges in chiefdoms provide for a "social safety network for families" (2009).

Potlatch

A classic example of a chiefdom redistributional system was found among the Native Americans of the Northwest Coast. Known as the *potlatch*, it was described at length among the Kwakiutl (Kwakwaka'wakw) by Franz Boas (1930) and was later interpreted by Ruth Benedict (1934).

The term **potlatch** is a Chinook word that is translated loosely as "giveaway." In a **potlatch** local leaders gave away large quantities of goods and resources in order to redistribute their wealth. Potlatches were held when young people were introduced into society or during marriage or funeral ceremonies. Families would prepare for these festive occasions by collecting food and other valuables such as fish, berries, blankets, and animal skins, which were then given to local leaders in many different villages. In these potlatch feasts, the leaders of different villages competed by attempting to give away or sometimes destroy more food than their competitors. Northwest Coast Indians believe that the more gifts that were bestowed on the people or destroyed by a chief, the higher the status of that chief.

Benedict found the potlatch feasts and rivalry among chiefs to be the result of their megalomaniacal personalities. To substantiate this view, she presented this formal speech made by a Kwakiutl (Kwakwaka'wakw) chief (1934:191):

> *I am the first of the tribes, I am the only one of the tribes. The chiefs of the tribes are only local chiefs. I am the only one among the tribes. I search among all the invited chiefs for greatness like mine. I cannot find one chief among the guests. They never return feasts. The orphans, poor people, chiefs of the tribes! They disgrace themselves. I am he who gives these sea otters to the chiefs, the guests, the chiefs of the tribes. I am he who gives canoes to the chiefs, the guests, the chiefs of the tribes.*

Despite the apparent wastefulness, status rivalry, and megalomaniacal personalities suggested by Benedict, contemporary anthropologists view the potlatch feasts as having served as a redistributional exchange process. For example, despite the abundance of resources in the Northwest Coast region, there were regional variations and periodic fluctuations in the supply of salmon and other products. In some areas, people had more than they needed, whereas in other regions, people suffered from frequent scarcities. Given these circumstances, the potlatch helped distribute surpluses and special local products to other villages in need (Piddocke 1965).

Marvin Harris (1977) argued that the potlatch also functioned to ensure the production and distribution of goods in societies that lacked ruling classes. Through the elaborate redistributive feasts and conspicuous consumption, the chiefs presented themselves as the providers of food and security to the population. The competition among the chiefs meant that both the "haves" and the

Northwest Coast chiefdom potlatch

"have-nots" benefited from this system. According to Harris, this form of competitive feasting enabled growing chiefdom populations to survive and prosper by encouraging people to work harder and accumulate resources. Feasting and exchanges provide for "social safety networks" and also build the reputation of chief's families who have more resources to provide others (Hayden 2009).

Redistribution in Polynesia Another classic example of redistribution appears in the historical records of native Polynesian societies. In societies such as Tahiti and Hawaii, people who were able to redistribute goods and resources among various villages and islands emerged as leaders. After crops were harvested, a certain portion (the "first fruits of the harvest") was directed to local village leaders and, then, given to higher-level subsidiary chiefs who were more centrally located. These goods were eventually directed toward the paramount chiefs, who redistributed some of them back to the population during different periods of the year (Sahlins 1958; Kirch 1984). Along with coordinating exchanges, the chiefs could also decree which crops were to be planted and how they were to be used.

Redistributional exchange economic systems are similar to reciprocal exchange economic systems in that they involve transfers of goods and other resources among related villagers. A major difference between the two systems is that the latter is predominant in societies that are highly egalitarian, whereas in the chiefdom societies that have redistributional exchange economic systems, rank and status are *unequal.*

Within a redistributional system, local leaders and related individuals not only have a higher status and rank, but are also able to siphon off some of the economic surplus for their own benefit. This inequality creates a **hierarchical society** in which some people have access to more wealth, rank, status, authority, and power than other people do. This redistributional exchange system among the Polynesian chiefdoms has been referred to as an early form of taxation (Johnson and Earle 2000). Thus, many anthropologists and other scholars have referred to these

societies as "kleptocracies," meaning that the chiefs at the top were draining off the resources from others to enhance their own economic and political power (Diamond 1997).

Technology in Agricultural States

16.9 Discuss agricultural state innovations in technology and diffusion.

One major factor that contributed to the evolution of agricultural states was the development of a more sophisticated technology. To some extent, this represented modifications of existing technologies. Stone tools such as axes, hammers, knives, and scrapers were refined for more prolonged use. Increased knowledge of metallurgy enabled some agricultural peoples to create more durable tools. For example, copper, tin, and iron ores were smelted and cast into weapons, armor, ornaments, and other tools. Many technological innovations were dramatically expressed in myriad artwork and monumental constructions, exemplified by such massive structures as the Pyramid of the Sun at Teotihuacán in Mexico, which rises more than 200 feet in the air and covers some 650 square feet.

Agricultural Innovations

Technological innovations were of key importance in increasing crop yields in agricultural states. Humans in various world areas developed specialized techniques to exploit local natural resources more efficiently. Initially, water had to be transported by hand, but later civilizations crafted devices such as the *shaduf*, a pole-and-lever device that is believed to have originated in Southwest Asia more than 4,000 years ago. Many of the "Old World" civilizations in Southwest Asia, the Nile Valley, and India and the "New World" civilizations in the Americas created complicated irrigation systems that extended the amount of land that could be cultivated.

Old World agricultural civilizations reached a pivotal point with the advent of the plow, with which farmers could turn soil to a much greater depth than had previously been possible, radically transforming it by reaching deeper into the soil to replenish it with nutrients. The plow thus enabled agricultural peoples to utilize fields on a more permanent basis and occupy the same land for many generations.

The first plows were modifications of the hoe and were probably pulled by the farmers themselves. Eventually, oxen were harnessed to the plows, and farmers gained the ability to cultivate large plots. Then, as people forged innovations in metallurgy, wooden-tipped plows were replaced by plows made first of bronze and then of iron.

Teotihuacàn pyramid in Central Mexico.

Oxen-drawn, iron-plowed agriculture spread widely, transforming civilizations throughout the Old World (Shenk et al. 2010).

Early New World civilizations never used the plow. Instead, they devised a wide variety of other agricultural innovations in response to particular environmental settings. For example, in the Oaxacan Valley in Mexico, the people practiced *pot irrigation*, in which farmers planted their crops near small, shallow wells and used pots to carry water to their fields (Flannery 1968). More complicated irrigation techniques undergirded agriculture in other American agricultural states. In both the highland and the lowland regions of Mesoamerica, the Mayan civilization (300 B.C.–1500 A.D.) created agricultural technology to support densely populated urban centers. Because no evidence of intensive agriculture had been discovered, archaeologists initially hypothesized that the Maya lived in widely dispersed villages with ritual centers consisting of relatively few inhabitants. However, using more careful study techniques, researchers have proved that the Maya devised sophisticated irrigation systems throughout lowland areas, which provided food for the large urban centers.

The Diffusion of Technology

In today's globally interconnected societies, we take the diffusion, or exchange, of technological innovations for granted, and indeed, archaeologists have uncovered evidence that certain ideas—such as iron technology and plow agriculture—diffused over large areas during ancient times. However, the fact remains that before 1500 A.D., most regions of the world were comparatively isolated, and technological innovations were not spread as readily as they are today. Also, changes in agriculture and the diffusion of ideas was small, gradual, and involved a complex of conditions involving social, economic, cultural, political, ideological, and possibly psychological factors

that influenced the rates of change and diffusion (van der Veen 2010).

Certain areas experienced greater technological advances than did others. For example, the Near East, China, and parts of India had made remarkable technological and scientific achievements compared with those of Europe before 1500 A.D. (Diamond 1997). Among the major innovations identified with China alone are paper-making, movable-type printing, paper money, guns and gunpowder, compasses, underwater mining, umbrellas, hot-air balloons, multistage rockets, and scientific ideas concerning the circulation of blood and the laws of motion (Frank 1998). Little was known of these technological and scientific developments in Western societies until much later.

Economics in Agricultural States

16.10 Describe the type of economies that developed in agricultural civilizations.

The creation of substantial food surpluses, along with better food-storing technologies, led to new forms of economic relations in agricultural states. Many people could be freed from working in the fields to pursue other specialized functions. Hundreds of new occupations developed in the urban centers of agricultural states. Craftsworkers produced tools, clothing, jewelry, pottery, and other accessories. Other workers engaged in commerce, government, religion, education, the military, and other sectors of the economy.

This new division of labor influenced both rural and urban areas. Farm laborers not only were involved in essential food production, but also turned to craft production to supplement their income. Over time, some agricultural villages began to produce crafts and commodities not just for their own consumption, but also for trade with other villages and with the urban centers. Through these activities, rural villages became involved in widespread trading alliances and marketing activities.

Property Rights

Despite the complex division of labor in agricultural states, the major source of wealth was arable land. In effect, the ownership of land became the primary basis for an individual's socioeconomic position. The governing elite in most of the agricultural states claimed ownership over large landholdings, which included both the land and the peasant or slave labor that went with it (Brumfiel 1994).

Two major forms of property ownership predominated in agricultural states, depending upon whether they were large-scale centralized states or decentralized feudal states. Eric Wolf (1966) identified one type of property ownership in which a powerful government claimed ownership of the land, appointed officials to supervise its cultivation, and collected the surplus agricultural production. In the other type of property ownership, a class of landlords who owned the land privately inherited it through family lines and oversaw its cultivation. In certain cases, peasants could own land directly and produce surpluses for the elites. Agricultural states thus developed major inequalities between those who owned land and those who did not. Bureaucratic and legal devices were developed by the elites to institute legal deeds and titles, and land became a resource that was bought, sold, and rented.

A new form of economic system known as the tributary form became predominant. **Tribute**, in the form of taxes, rent, or labor services, replaced economic exchanges based on kinship reciprocity or chiefdom redistribution. Wolf ([1982] 1997) referred to this as a **tributary mode of production**, in contrast to the *kin-ordered mode* of production of nonstate societies. Under these conditions, a hierarchy emerged in which the elite, who resided in the urban centers or on landed estates collected tribute, and the peasants, who cultivated the land, paid tribute to this elite (Wolf 1966, [1982] 1997). In some of the more centralized states such as Rome, systematic taxation systems were developed. In addition, Rome demanded tribute from outlying regions of its empire (M. E. Smith 2004).

The Command Economy versus the Entrepreneur

In the large-scale centralized states, a form of **command economy** emerged, wherein the political elite controlled production, prices, and trading. Some agricultural states became expansive world empires that extracted tribute and placed limits on people's economic activities. State authorities controlled the production, exchange, and consumption of goods within the economies of these bureaucratic empires. Although private trade and entrepreneurial activities did occur at times within these bureaucratic empires, it was rare (Brumfiel 1994; Chanda 2007). For example, China and Rome attempted to organize and control most aspects of their economy by monopolizing the production and sale of items like salt and iron. At the same time, Roman civilization had a tremendous amount of commercialization with extensive markets in goods and services, large-scale international trade, and entrepreneurial elites (M. E. Smith 2004).

In the less centrally organized agricultural states, more independent economic activity was evident. For example, during the feudal periods in Western Europe and Japan, the lack of a dominant elite that organized and managed the economic affairs of the society enabled more autonomous economic production and exchange to occur at the local level. Entrepreneurs had freedom to develop and innovate within the context of feudal political economies. This was a key factor in the later economic development of these regions.

The Peasantry

Peasants are people who cultivate land in rural areas for their basic subsistence and pay tribute to elite groups. The socioeconomic status of the peasantry, however, varied in agricultural societies. As we have seen, rights to land differed between the bureaucratic empires and the less centralized societies. In most agricultural states, elites claimed rights to most of the land, and the peasantry in the rural areas paid tribute or taxes as a type of rent (Wolf 1966, [1982]1997). In other cases, the peasants owned the land they cultivated; nevertheless, they still paid tribute from their labor surplus or production. In the case of feudal Europe, the peasants, or serfs, were bound to the estates owned by lords, or nobles.

Whatever their status, all peasants had to produce a surplus that flowed into the urban centers. It is estimated that this surplus, including fines, tithes, and obligatory gifts, represented at least half of the peasants' total output (Brumfiel 1994; Sanderson 1999). Also, in the bureaucratic civilizations such as Egypt and Teotihuacán, the peasantry provided much of the compulsory labor for large-scale government projects such as massive irrigation works and pyramids. Although research on peasants has demonstrated that they were often able to evade some of these obligations or to hide some of their surpluses, most were subject to burdensome demands from the elites.

The Moral Economy Despite the domination of the peasantry by the agricultural state or by landlords, at times and in different circumstances the peasantry developed norms that emphasized community cooperation in production, distribution, consumption, and exchange in the village. These norms led to what some anthropologists have referred to as a moral economy for the peasantry. This **moral economy** involved sharing food resources and labor with one another in a reciprocal manner to provide a form of social and economic insurance so that individual families would not fall into destitution (Scott 1976; Richerson and Boyd 2005). Peasant families would exchange labor with each other to aid in the production of crops. In addition, rituals and festivals occurred at which peasants were encouraged to donate and exchange food and goods to be distributed throughout the community. Although the moral economy of the peasantry was not always successful and individual families did become impoverished, in many cases it did help sustain the viability of the village community.

Trade and Monetary Exchange

As previously discussed, the production of agricultural surpluses and luxury items in agricultural states resulted in a great deal of internal and external trade. This trade included raw materials for production, such as copper, iron ore, obsidian, and salt. Long-distance trade routes over both land and sea spanned immense geographical areas. Through constant policing, governing elites enforced political order and military security over these trade routes. In turn, this protection led to the security and maintenance of extensive road networks that aided commercial pursuits. For example, the Romans constructed roads and bridges that are still in use today (Stavrianos 1995).

Extensive caravan routes developed in areas such as the Near East and North Africa. The Bedouins, Arabic-speaking pastoralists, used camels to conduct long-distance trade, carrying goods from port cities on the Arabian Peninsula across the desert to cities such as Damascus, Jerusalem, and Cairo. In Asia, other caravan routes crossed the whole of China and Central Asia, with connections to the Near East. In the Americas, long-distance trade developed between Teotihuacán and the Mayan regions.

In conjunction with long-distance trade, monetary exchange became more formalized. In the Near East (and probably elsewhere), foodstuffs such as grains originally could be used to pay taxes, wages, rents, and other obligations. Because grains are perishable and bulky, however, they were not ideal for carrying out exchanges. Thus, general-purpose money based on metals, especially silver and copper, came into use (M. E. Smith 2004). The sizes and weights of these metals became standardized and were circulated as stores of value. At first, bars of metal were used as money, but eventually smaller units of metal, or coins, were manufactured and regulated. After developing printing, the Chinese began to produce paper money as their medium of exchange.

The Rise of Merchants and Peripheral Markets

One result of the development of a formalized monetary system was the increased opportunity for merchants to purchase goods not for their own consumption, but to be sold to people who had money. Merchants made up a new status category of people who, although below the elites, often prospered by creating demands for luxury goods and organizing the transportation of those goods across long distances. Much of the trade of the Near Eastern empires, followed by the Greek, Roman, Byzantine, and Islamic Mediterranean commercial operations, was stimulated by merchants who furnished imported luxury goods from foreign lands for consumption by internal elites (Wolf [1982] 1997; M. E. Smith 2004). Sometimes, as in the case of the Aztecs, the merchants of these empires also doubled as spies and provided information to governing authorities regarding peoples in outlying regions.

With increasing long-distance trade and other commercial developments, regional and local marketplaces, as well as marketplaces in the urban areas, began to emerge. Foodstuffs and other commodities produced by peasants, artisans, and craftsworkers were bought and sold in these marketplaces. In early cities such as Ur, Memphis, Teotihuacán, and Tikal, markets were centrally located, offering both imported and domestically manufactured items, as well as food. In addition, marketplaces arose throughout the countryside. A steady flow of goods developed from villages to regional and national capitals.

Although many goods were bought and sold in these regional markets, the vast majority of people—that is, the peasantry—did not receive their subsistence items from these markets. Nor were people engaged full-time in producing or selling in these marketplaces (Bohannon and Dalton 1962). The regional and local markets existed only as a convenient location for the distribution of goods. In many cases, the activity was periodic. For example, in medieval Europe, traveling fairs that went from city to city enabled merchants to bring their local and imported goods to be bought and sold.

Most goods were bought and sold in markets through a system known as haggling. *Haggling* is a type of negotiation between buyer and seller that establishes the price of an item. The buyer asks a seller how much he or she wants for an item, the seller proposes a figure, and the buyer counters with a lower price, until a price is finally agreed upon. However, in some of the more centralized states, the government officials fixed prices of goods and services for the market, paralleling the types of command economies that would develop later in the industrial age (M. E. Smith 2004).

Technology and Economic Change in Industrial and Postindustrial Societies

16.11 Describe technology and economic changes for industrial and postindustrial societies.

Industrialization was fueled by a series of technological innovations that occurred after the middle of the eighteenth century. The major change was a movement from human and animal labor to mechanical, or machine, labor. More recently, through science, engineering, and commerce, technological innovations ranging from automobiles to electronics to computers have continued to transform industrial societies, many of which became **postindustrial societies**. These technologies have not only made communication and transportation more efficient, but have also contributed to a vast international global economic network in which all societies can interact. Through the Internet, the World Wide Web, e-mail, fax machines, cell phones, television, and satellite transmissions, societies are increasingly linked to a global economy.

Technology and Work

The technological revolution transformed basic work conditions in industrial societies. The factory system imposed a new work pace and led to a new form of discipline for laborers. Factory and mine workers were organized around the machine's schedule, and work became increasingly time oriented. Most work in the early factories was highly routinized and repetitious.

Preindustrial workers had some control over the quantity and quality of their products and the pace of their labor, but early industrial workers had little control over these matters. Karl Marx, a major critic of industrial capitalism, saw that industrial workers were estranged and alienated by their work conditions and that they viewed their labor as meaningless and beyond their control.

The Division of Labor

The division of labor in industrial economies is much more complex than it is in preindustrial economies. Industrial economies have three identifiable sectors, which correspond to the division of labor. The **primary sector** represents the part of the industrial economy devoted to the extraction of raw materials and energy; it includes agriculture, lumber, fishing, and mining. The **secondary sector** includes the factories that take the raw materials and process them for consumption. The **tertiary sector**, sometimes referred to as the *service sector*, includes the financial and banking industries and other businesses, such as automobile repair, communications, health care, computer services, government, and education.

In the first phases of industrialization, most of the labor force was engaged in the *primary sector*, extracting raw materials for industrial production. Further mechanization of industry led to an increase of the labor force in the *secondary*, or manufacturing, sector. These workers are the manual, or "blue-collar," workers in the secondary sector. Finally, in the advanced phases of industrialization, an increasing percentage of the labor force has become located in the *tertiary sector*, or various service industries.

Currently, in the most advanced industrial societies—such as the United States, the United Kingdom, Japan, Germany, Canada, and Australia—the *tertiary sector* is the largest and most rapidly expanding component of the economy. These societies are *postindustrial societies* because more people are employed in service and high-technology occupations than in manufacturing. Information is the key component of a postindustrial economy because people must acquire a great deal of technical knowledge to function effectively, and educational requirements for many jobs have increased substantially. Sometimes postindustrial societies are referred to as *postfordism*, to differentiate them from the type of society that was manufacturing based like Henry Ford's auto company in the early twentieth century in the United States. To meet the demands of a postindustrial economy, an increasing percentage of the population attends college (and graduate and professional schools), and computer skills have been integrated into the educational curriculum. With their capacity to process and manipulate vast amounts of data, computers have become essential in these societies. Anthropologists are doing extensive ethnographic research on the development of this postindustrial society in numerous locations (McCreery 2000; McCreery and McCreery 2006; Denoon et al. 2001; Lewellen 2002; Harvey 1990).

Anthropologist at Work

GABRIELLA COLEMAN: The Ethnographer of Geeks and Hackers

Many anthropologists have been exploring the information technology developments in postindustrial societies. One unique ethnographic research project on postindustrial computer technology was initiated by anthropologist Gabriella Coleman. Coleman completed her B.A. degree in religious studies at Columbia University. While at Columbia University in the early 90s she became interested in the free software available through an operating system developed by Linux that offered licensing enabling computer users to copy, modify, and share the source code. This was an alternative to the operating systems such as Microsoft or Apple that were costly and proprietary. Coleman went on to the University of Chicago for her M.A. and Ph.D. in sociocultural anthropology. Coleman planned to do ethnographic research on spiritual healing in Guyana.

However, an illness during graduate school kept her from pursuing that overseas research. Coleman began exploring the Internet, chat rooms, and online bulletin boards to learn about free software. She took classes in copyright law and system administration and began to make connections within geek and hacker communities in San Francisco and elsewhere. Later, Coleman volunteered at the Electronic Frontier Foundation (EFF) that was devoted to keeping the Internet free of government

(continued)

or corporate control. For her Ph.D. dissertation research, Coleman focused on the subculture of computer hackers and their ethics regarding free and open source software.

Following her graduate studies, Coleman was a postdoctoral fellow in the Center for Cultural Analysis at Rutgers University, a postdoctoral fellow in the Program of Science, Technology, and Society at Alberta University, a faculty fellow in the School of Social Science at Princeton University, and she taught at New York University. She is currently a faculty associate at the Berkman Center for Internet & Society at Harvard University, and an assistant professor and Wolfe Chair in Scientific and Technological Literacy, Department of Art History and Communication Studies, which is affiliated with the Department of Anthropology at McGill University in Quebec, Canada. Coleman's research led to her Princeton University Press book *Coding Freedom: The Ethics and Aesthetics of Hacking.* In this book she writes about the prototypical "hacker," which does not refer necessarily to illegal hacking. These hackers were primarily males who began tinkering with household appliances and then programming computers when they were very young. These hackers make connections with like-minded people through chat rooms, e-mail lists, and conferences to explore free and open software, but also to engage in political movements like the EFF that defend the freedom of the Internet from corporate and government control. The hackers become activists involved in legal battles and organizations such as the Debian Project. Coleman describes the Debian Project as an open-source organization that has its own "Social

Contract," "Constitution," and "Free Software Guidelines," and maintains a rigorous program that evaluates the competency of the programmers. Debian also ensures that the members of the community are versed in the legal and ethical codes of free software.

In January 2012, the U.S. Congress proposed bills that wanted to reinforce copyright laws, especially within the entertainment industry. The hacker community began to protest against these laws as did Google, Wikipedia, and Twitter. Coleman introduces the subculture of the hackers and their engagement with anticorporate and antigovernment. The values and ethos of these geeks include transparency, autonomy, and free inquiry, which are the center of democratic processes. While at New York University, one of Coleman's students began to participate in the Occupy Wall Street movement at Zuccotti Park in Manhattan. The student took her ideals of open-source and freedom of expression learned from Coleman into the Occupy Wall Street movement. The ethos of open-source and nonhierarchical democratic processes merged with the Occupy activists, and they tried to build a digital base for the movement (Schneider 2013). The open-source movement was also influential in youth movements in Spain where activists called for a 'Charter of the Commons,' referring to the preindustrial common land shared by villagers.

Currently Coleman has been engaged in ethnographic research through chat rooms and Twitter hashtags on the loosely organized, globally based group of hackers and activists known as "Anonymous." Anonymous has the same ethos of freedom of information and transparency of the

Gabriella Coleman

open-source hackers. The "Anons" were involved in destroying the dictators' Web sites during the Arab Spring and played key roles in the Occupy movement. Various media outlets such as CNN, the Huffington Post, and other news organizations draw on Coleman's expertise in their coverage of the Anonymous movement. Her next book will cover her research on Anonymous. Coleman emphasizes that the media and popular culture often misrepresents the hackers as irresponsible and as maintaining a deviant subculture. Yet, as her studies demonstrate, these hackers foster independent inquiry, freedom, and other cherished values of a truly democratic society. The hackers have bolstered our civil liberties, especially when it comes to free speech and privacy. Coleman's ethnographic research has been influential in the public conversations on the political, legal, and ethical dilemmas facing the rapid developments of information technology in postindustrial societies.

Economic Exchange

Like other types of societies, industrial states engage in reciprocal and redistributional economic exchanges. Reciprocal exchanges, such as Christmas gifts and gifts of funds for college tuition, frequently occur within the family. The graduated income tax in U.S. society represents one form of redistributional exchange in which income is collected from some people and flows back to society. Taxes also represent a form of tributary economic exchange, which is characteristic of agricultural states.

Market Economies　In addition to these activities, industrial states developed a new pattern of exchange based on a market economy. A **market economy** is a pattern of economic exchange based upon the value of goods and services determined by the supply and demand of items such as commodities, land, and also labor. The evolution of the market economy, linked with industrial technological developments, radically changed the way goods and services are produced and exchanged in industrial societies. Goods and services are assigned monetary value and are bought and sold with general-purpose money. The prices of these goods and services depend upon the supply and demand of these items on the world market.

Moreover, in the market economy, the basic factors of production—land, labor, and capital—are assigned monetary prices and are bought and sold freely in the marketplace. Thus, market forces, rather than kinship or prominent leaders, determine the general process of economic exchange.

In agricultural societies, goods and services were bought and sold in regional or local markets. These markets, however, were not based on market exchange; instead, buyers and sellers met and haggled over the price of goods. This is a type of non-market price determination. In contrast, in industrial societies, buyers and sellers do not have to meet face to face. Buyers can compare prices from different sellers, and the prices themselves are established according to supply and demand. Impersonality and lack of haggling between buyer and seller are the general patterns in market exchanges.

Perspectives on Market Economies

Market forces based on the supply and demand of land, labor, and capital began to drive economic production, exchange, and consumption in industrial societies. The market process, which determined the prices of these factors of production, exerted tremendous influence over all aspects of these industrializing societies. The new economic forces and processes were described by the "father of modern economics," Adam Smith. In his book, *An Inquiry into the Nature and Causes of the Wealth of Nations* (1776), Smith argued that both buyers and sellers would reap rewards from market exchange and competition because prices would be lower for consumers and profits higher for sellers. The result would be increased prosperity for all segments of society. Smith viewed the market economy as a mechanism for promoting progress.

In contrast, 100 years later, Karl Marx offered a gloomier picture of industrial societies. Marx focused on how the market economy determined the price and organization of human labor, bringing about misery for millions of people. Marx believed that industrial capitalist societies must be transformed to a new form of socialist society in which the factors of production would not be driven by the market, but would be controlled by the *state* to ensure an even division of profits among all classes.

Eventually, both capitalist and socialist forms of industrial societies developed in different regions of the world. To highlight some of the variations among industrial societies, we next examine the development of capitalism and socialism in some of these regions.

Capitalism   As is evident from the previous discussion, the Industrial Revolution was intricately connected with the emergence of capitalism in Western societies. **Capitalism** is an economic system in which natural resources, as well as the means of producing and distributing goods and services, are privately owned. Capitalist societies share three basic ideals: First, the factors of production are privately owned, and an emphasis on private property has become the standard incorporated into all economic, legal, and political documents of capitalist societies; second, companies are free to maximize profits and accumulate as much capital as they can; and third, free competition and consumer sovereignty are basic to all economic activities. Ideally, people are free to buy and sell at whatever prices they can to satisfy their own interests. Also, government regulation of economic affairs is usually discouraged.

Capitalism in the United States   Capitalism spread into North America after England and other European countries established colonies. The English incorporated major portions of North America as a colony during the mercantile period. But eventually the Americans, whose ancestors had originally been colonists, began to control their own economic and political destinies, which

Wall Street trading scene

led to the American Revolution of the late eighteenth century. Following independence, capitalist economic development and industrialization proceeded rapidly in the United States. Bountiful natural resources provided the raw materials for factory production, and millions of immigrants arrived from Europe, providing a source of cheap labor for factories. U.S. industry grew quickly, and by 1894, the nation had the world's fastest-growing economy.

Despite the ideals of pure capitalism, which discouraged government regulation of the economy, the U.S. government actively encouraged industrial economic expansion through state subsidies, protective tariffs, and other policies. For example, the government promoted the development of a nationwide railroad system by providing large financial incentives, rights to land, and subsidies to individual capitalists. In addition, through the Homestead Act of 1862, free land was given to people who wanted to settle frontier regions.

By the late nineteenth century, rapid economic expansion had produced a new moneyed class that held a great proportion of assets. A relatively small number of people controlled a large number of industries and other commercial enterprises in the areas of finance and capital. The wealthiest one percent of the population owned about one-third of all capital assets (wealth in land or other private property). Economic expansion also spurred the growth of a large middle class, which exerted a powerful influence on both the economic and the political structure of U.S. society.

Capitalism in Japan

Japan was an agricultural feudal society from the period of the first *shogunate* in the twelfth century until about 1870, after which it rapidly industrialized. Following a period of historical isolation from the West during the Tokugawa period (1600–1870), Japan was forced to open its doors to outside powers such as the United States. The Japanese recognized the technological advancements of the Western world, and to avoid being colonized like other Asian countries, they rapidly modified their society to accommodate industrial capitalism. But the socioeconomic and political conditions that made rapid capitalist development possible existed before Japan's intensive contact with the West.

For example, during the Tokugawa period, internal trade and entrepreneurial developments flourished in highly developed urban centers such as Tokyo and Kyoto. Moreover, Japan had a highly educated class of *samurai*, who were in a position to bring about innovations in society (Befu 1971; McCreery and McCreery 2006). Following the opening of Japan to the West, the Japanese abandoned the feudal system and centralized their government under the Meiji emperor. With help from Western advisors (1868–1912), the Meiji government introduced a mandatory education system and modern military technology.

The government also took concrete steps to help introduce capitalism (Geertz 1963b; McCreery and McCreery 2006). It taxed the peasants to raise money for industrialization and subsidized certain entrepreneurial families, the *zaibatsu*, who gained control of the major industrial technologies. Families such as the Mitsubishis were encouraged to invest in needed industries to compete with Western interests. Thus, the government developed key industries in Japan by cooperating with private interests and families.

Socialism

A different type of economic system developed in some industrial societies as a historical response to capitalism. **Socialism** is an economic system in which the state, ideally as the representative of the people, owns the basic means of production. Although individuals may own some consumer goods such as housing and automobiles, they are not allowed to own stock in corporations or wealth-generating property related to the production of capital goods. Socialism evolved as a response to the considerable economic inequalities that existed in capitalist societies. To create more economic equality and less exploitation of working people, socialist philosophers promoted ideals that contrasted with those of capitalism. According to socialist ideals, meeting the population's basic needs takes precedence over the enrichment of a small number of people.

Socialism in the Former Soviet Union

In contrast to Marx's predictions that socialist revolutions would occur in industrial societies, socialism initially developed in Russia, which was primarily agricultural and feudal. From about 1000 A.D., the basic form of land tenure in Russia was based on the *mir*, or peasant commune, which was linked to feudal estates for which the serfs or peasants provided labor (Dunn and Dunn 1988). During the nineteenth century, feudalism was abolished, and the serfs were freed from the estates. The Russian economy, however, remained largely dependent on wheat exports and Western capital (Chirot 1986; Gellner 1988; Ensminger 2002).

As in Japan, the Russian elites realized that they had to industrialize quickly if they were to survive. The central government subsidized industrialization by taxing the peasantry heavily and importing European industrial technology. As a result, Russia gradually began to industrialize. However, the new economic burdens on peasant society, a military defeat by the Japanese in 1905, and the widespread suffering produced by World War I severely weakened the government of the emperor, or czar. The result was the Russian Revolution of 1917.

Under the leadership of Vladimir Lenin, the new Soviet state implemented a number of policies designed to create a more egalitarian society that would meet the basic needs of all the people. All wealth-generating property (the means of production) was placed under government control. The government collectivized agriculture by taking land from landowners and distributing the peasant population on collective, state-controlled farms. State authorities systematically regulated all prices and wages. In addition, the government—through a centralized system of Five-Year Plans—initiated a policy of rapid industrialization to try to catch up with the West.

Hybrid Economic Systems To some extent, neither capitalism nor socialism exists in pure form according to the ideals espoused by their leading theorists. Government intervention in the economy exists in both types of economic systems. In some industrial societies such as Sweden, and to a lesser extent in Western European countries and England, a hybrid form of economic system referred to as democratic socialism developed. In these societies, the key strategic industries that produce basic capital goods and services are government owned, as are certain heavy industries such as steel and coal and utilities such as telephone companies. At the same time, much of the economy and technology is privately owned, and production takes place for private profit. Some politicians and citizens support this hybrid form of economy in the United States, whereas others resist it vehemently. On the other hand, some of the hybrid economic systems such as that of Sweden are beginning to move away from the mixed system and introduce more privatization to reduce economic, social, and medical costs for their governments.

The Evolution of Economic Organizations

As industrial and postindustrial economies developed in capitalist, socialist, and democratic-socialist societies, the major economic organizations increased in size and complexity. In capitalist societies, family businesses grew into corporations, which were established as legal

Soviet factory scene after the Russian Revolution of 1917.

entities to raise capital through the sale of stocks and bonds. Eventually, these corporations increased their economic holdings and were able to concentrate their ownership on the society's major technology and strategic commodities such as steel and oil. Through expansion and mergers, they came to dominate economic production and exchange. The result was **oligopoly**, in which a few giant corporations control production in major industries. For example, in the United States in the early 1900s, there were 35 domestic automobile companies, but by the 1950s, only three remained. This process of corporate expansion ushered in a phase of capitalism known as **monopoly capitalism**, a form of capitalism dominated by large corporations that can reduce free competition through the concentration of capital. This concentration of capital enables oligopolies to control prices and thereby, dominate the markets.

In socialist societies such as the former Soviet Union, in which private ownership of technology was prohibited, the government controlled and managed the major economic organizations. The equivalent of the large capitalist corporation is the state-owned enterprise, which has some degree of financial autonomy, although government authorities established production goals. The majority of state enterprises were still small or medium in size, but the enterprises of the Soviet state became more concentrated (Kerblay 1983; Ensminger 2002). These enterprises followed the production aims established by the various ministries, which were ultimately controlled by Communist Party officials.

Multinational Corporations In the capitalist, socialist, and hybrid economic systems, corporations increased in size to become large multinational corporations with enormous assets. **Multinational corporations** are economic organizations that operate in many different regions of the world. Multinational corporations are based in their home countries but own subsidiaries in many other countries. For example, American-based I.T.T., a multinational corporation with more than 400,000 employees, has offices in 68 different countries. Although approximately 300 of the 500 largest multinational corporations are based in the United States, others, such as Unilever, Shell, and Mitsubishi are based in England, Western Europe, and Japan, respectively. The socialist societies of the former Soviet Union and Eastern Europe had large state-owned multinational corporations that coordinated their activities through what was known as Comecon (a committee that coordinated multinational activities worldwide).

The evolution of the multinational corporation has had tremendous consequences for the global economy. Anthropologist Alvin Wolfe proposed that multinational corporations are beginning to evolve into supranational organizations that are stronger than the nation-state (1977, 1986, 2006). In addition, various multinational corporations are interconnected in the world global economy into large-scale oligopolies (Chandler and Maizlish 2005; Kapferer 2005). The top CEOs in the various multinational corporations sit on one another's boards of directors. In addition, the multinational corporations are increasingly involved in joint ventures, consolidating their capital assets and technologies to produce goods and services throughout the world. We consider the global effects of these multinational corporations in different societies in later chapters.

Capitalist Consumer Societies

Another major change in industrial capitalist societies and the development of multinational corporations is the extent of production and consumption of consumer goods (Wilk 1995). During the twentieth century, and especially after World War II, corporations in the United States and other capitalist countries began to engage in extensive marketing to create demand for a plethora of consumer goods, including automobiles, home appliances, televisions, and other products. Corporations launched advertising campaigns targeting people of all ages, especially children and young people, as potential consumers for these products. Major investments in advertising and marketing campaigns to create demand for consumer goods were promoted through the media, especially television. Eventually, cartoons and amusement parks such as Disneyland became vehicles for promoting toy products and other goods for young people. Television and media advertising, along with easy credit, created enormous demand for various consumer goods in these capitalist societies. These patterns of consumption have resulted in extensive global ecological, economic, and cultural changes. We discuss some of the global consequences of capitalist consumer societies in Chapter 24, on contemporary global changes.

Summary and Review of Learning Objectives

16.1 Discuss the anthropological explanations of technology.

Most anthropologists recognize that technology is one of the most important variables that impact a sociocultural system. However, anthropologists are cautious about technological determinism, the view that technology determines all aspects of society. Anthropologists have concluded that technology alone does not result in cultural change and transformation, but rather cultural values, beliefs, and practices interact with technology to create changes.

16.2 Discuss how anthropologists study economics in different societies.

Anthropologists have studied the economics of various societies by analysing the production, exchange, and consumption of goods and services. Contemporary anthropologists use both formalist and substantivist approaches in understanding different forms of economic systems.

16.3 Describe the technologies of foraging societies.

The technologies of foraging societies include many innovations for hunting and gathering including the bow and arrow, boomerang, and many other hunting devices. The Inuit technology included a vast collection of tools and clothing to adapt to the Arctic conditions. However, technology does not refer just to tools or artifacts; it also includes the cultural knowledge that has to be maintained by the society. All foraging peoples have an extensive knowledge of their environmental conditions and of the appropriate means of solving technological problems in these environments.

16.4 Describe how the economy works in foraging societies.

Foraging societies have an economic system based on reciprocity. A reciprocal economic system is based on exchanges among family groups as a means of distributing goods and services throughout the society. The basic principle underlying this system is reciprocity, the widespread sharing of goods and services in a society. One reason for this system of reciprocal exchange is that food and other resources must usually be consumed immediately. There is very little storage capacity for any surplus, so it makes sense to share what cannot be used anyway.

16.5 Describe the technologies of horticulturalist and pastoralists societies.

Horticulturalist groups used sharpened digging sticks and sometimes wooden hoes to plant small gardens. Today, they use machetes and steel axes to clear the primary forests .

Many horticultural societies have also developed technologies to aid in hunting and fishing to supplement their horticultural activities. For example, some Amazonian peoples, such as the Jivaro of Ecuador and Peru, often use blowguns and powerful bows combined with poisons. Pastoralists use saddles, weapons for hunting, and other equipment to care for their animals.

16.6 Discuss money and property ownership in horticulturalist and pastoralist economies.

Many horticultural and pastoralist tribal societies practice monetary exchange using limited-purpose money.

Some tribal people in the Pacific islands used a variety of shells to conduct trade relations. In other tribal societies, livestock, cloth, salt, feathers, animal teeth, and sometimes women functioned as money. The concept of property ownership becomes more clearly defined in tribal societies and is based on a web of social relations involving rights, privileges, and perhaps duties and obligations regarding the use of a particular piece of land, a herd of animals, or other objects. These horticultural and pastoralist societies do have demonstrable patterns of inequality among specific families in relationship to the transmission of land and animals from parents to offspring. However, in a recent overall assessment of wealth inequality, there tends to be more inequality in pastoralist societies than in the horticulturalist societies.

16.7 Describe technology and housing in chiefdom societies.

Some chiefdom societies in Polynesia used digging sticks for intensive horticulture, but they also had many specialized tools—including tools to cut shells and stones—for making jewelry, knives, fish hooks, harpoons, nets, and large canoes. Likewise, the Cahokian society had an elaborate technology consisting of fish hooks, grinding stones, mortars and pestles, hoes, and many other tools. The housing used in chiefdom societies varied over regions, depending on the materials available. The traditional Pacific island houses of Tahiti and Hawaii were built with poles and thatched with coconut leaves and other vegetation. The island houses needed repair from time to time, but generally were long-lasting dwellings. Similarly, the Cahokian people built firm housing by plastering clay over a wood framework. In the Northwest Coast villages, people lived in houses made of cedar planks, which were some of the most solid houses constructed in all of America before European colonization.

16.8 Describe the unique type of economic exchange that emerged in chiefdom societies

Some chiefdoms relied on reciprocal economic systems such as the famed *kula* exchange system of the Trobriand islands studied first by Bronislaw Malinowski. However, most chiefdom societies used a unique form of redistributional economic exchange, which involves the exchange of goods and resources through a centralized organization. In the redistributional system, food and other staples, such as craft goods, are collected as a form of tax or rent. The chiefs (and subsidiary chiefs) then redistribute some of these goods and food staples back to the population at

certain times of the year. One type of this redistributional exchange, developed among the Northwest Coast chiefdoms, is known as the "potlatch." These feasting activities and redistributional exchanges in chiefdoms provide for a social safety network for families.

16.9 Discuss agricultural state innovations in technology and diffusion.

In some areas of the Old World agricultural civilizations metallurgy was developed that made plows and weapons more powerful. Many other irrigation techniques were developed throughout the world that produced more efficient crop growing in agricultural civilizations. Archaeologists have uncovered evidence that certain ideas—such as iron technology and plow agriculture—diffused over large areas during ancient times. However, the fact remains that before 1500 A.D., most regions of the world were comparatively isolated, and technological innovations were not spread as readily as today. Certain areas experienced greater technological advances than did others. For example, the Near East, China, and parts of India had made remarkable technological and scientific achievements compared with those of Europe before 1500 A.D. Among the major innovations identified with China alone are papermaking, movable-type printing, paper money, guns and gunpowder, compasses, underwater mining, umbrellas, hot-air balloons, multistage rockets, and scientific ideas concerning the circulation of blood and the laws of motion. Little was known of these technological and scientific developments in Western societies until much later.

16.10 Describe the type of economies that developed in agricultural civilizations.

In agricultural civilizations, many people could be freed from working in the fields to pursue other specialized functions. Hundreds of new occupations developed in the urban centers of agricultural states.

Craftsworkers produced tools, clothing, jewelry, pottery, and other accessories. Other workers engaged in commerce, government, religion, education, the military, and other sectors of the economy. In some agricultural civilizations, a tributary mode of production, where the elite, who resided in the urban centers or on landed estates collected tribute, and the peasants, who cultivated the land, paid tribute to this elite In the large-scale centralized states, a form of command economy emerged, wherein the political elite controlled production, prices, and trading.

16.11 Describe technology and economic changes for industrial and postindustrial societies.

The major technological change for industrial societies was a movement from human and animal labor to mechanical, or machine, labor. More recently, through science, engineering, and commerce, technological innovations ranging from automobiles to electronics to computers have continued to transform industrial societies into postindustrial societies. The division of labor was transformed in industrial and postindustrial societies into different sectors. The primary sector represents the part of the industrial economy devoted to the extraction of raw materials and energy; it includes agriculture, lumber, fishing, and mining. The secondary sector includes the factories that take the raw materials and process them for consumption.

The tertiary sector, sometimes referred to as the *service sector*, includes the financial and banking industries and other industries, such as automobile repair, communications, health care, computer services, government, and education. The industrial economies led to the global market economy and the emergence of capitalism and socialism, with the more recent development of hybrid economic systems. With the expansion of the industrial and postindustrial economies, large multinational corporations expanded their activities throughout the world.

Key Terms

balanced reciprocity, p. 351
barter, p. 357
capitalism, p. 365
command economy, p. 361
consumption, p. 349
division of labor, p. 349
economy, p. 349
embodied wealth, p. 354
exchange, p. 349
generalized reciprocity, p. 351
goods, p. 348
hierarchical society, p. 359
intensive horticulture, p. 356
kula, p. 357

market economy, p. 364
money, p. 355
monopoly capitalism, p. 367
moral economy, p. 361
multinational corporations, p. 367
oligopoly, p. 367
negative reciprocity, p. 351
peasants, p. 361
postindustrial societies, p. 362
potlatch, p. 358
primary sector, p. 363
production, p. 349
prosocial norms, p. 352

reciprocal economic exchange system, p. 351
reciprocity, p. 351
redistributional economic exchange, p. 358
relational wealth, p. 354
secondary sector, p. 363
services, p. 348
socialism, p. 366
technology, p. 348
tertiary sector, p. 363
tributary mode of production, p. 361
tribute, p. 361

Chapter 17

Social Structure, the Family, Gender, and Age

 Learning Objectives

After reading this chapter you should be able to:

17.1 Discuss the general components of social structure, including status, the family, marriage, gender, and age.

17.2 Describe the social structure, family, marriage, gender, and age in foraging societies.

17.3 Describe the social structure, family, marriage, descent groups, gender, and age for tribal societies.

17.4 Discuss how status differences, the family, gender, and age are related in chiefdom societies.

Social Structure

17.1 Discuss the general components of social structure, including status, the family, marriage, gender, and age.

All inorganic and organic things, from planets to living cells, have a structure—they consist of interrelated parts in a particular arrangement. Anthropologists use the idea of structure when they analyze different societies. Societies are not just random, chaotic collections of people who interact with one another. Rather, social interaction in any society takes place in regular patterns. As we discussed in Chapter 11, people learn the norms, values, and behavioral patterns of their societies through enculturation. In the absence of social patterns, people would find social life confusing. Anthropologists refer to this pattern of relationships in society as the **social structure**. Social structure provides the framework for all human societies, but it does not determine decision making of individuals.

Components of Social Structure

One of the most important components of social structure is *status*. **Status** is a recognized position that a person occupies in society. A person's status determines where he or she fits in society in relationship to everyone else. Status may be based on or accompanied by wealth, power, prestige, or a combination of all of these. Many anthropologists use the term **socioeconomic status** (SES) to refer to how a specific position is related to the division of labor, the political system, and other cultural variables.

All societies recognize both *ascribed* and *achieved* statuses. An **ascribed status** is one that is attached to a person from birth or that a person assumes involuntarily later in life. The most prevalent ascribed statuses are based upon family and kinship relations (for example, daughter or son), sex (male or female), and age. In addition, in some societies, ascribed statuses are based on one's race or ethnicity. For example, as we shall see in a later chapter, skin color was used to designate ascribed status differences in South Africa under the system of apartheid.

In contrast, an **achieved status** is one based at least in part on a person's voluntary actions. Examples of achieved statuses in the United States are one's profession and level of education. Of course, one's family and kinship connections may influence one's profession and level of education. George W. Bush's and John Kerry's educational level and status are interrelated to their families of birth. However, these individuals had to act voluntarily to achieve their status.

Closely related to status is the concept of social *roles*. A **role** is a set of expected behavior patterns, obligations, and norms attached to a particular status. The distinction between status and role is a simple one: You "occupy" a certain status, but you "play" a role (Linton 1936). For example, as a student, you occupy a certain status that differs from those of your professors, administrators, and other staff. As you occupy that status, you perform by attending lectures, taking notes, participating in class, and studying for examinations. This concept of role is derived from the theater and refers to the parts played by actors on the stage. Whether you are a husband, mother, son, daughter, teacher, lawyer, judge, male, or female, you are expected to behave in certain ways because of the norms associated with that particular status.

As mentioned, a society's social statuses usually correspond to wealth, power, and prestige. Anthropologists find that all societies have inequality in statuses, which are arranged in a hierarchy. This inequality of statuses is known as **social stratification**. The degree of social stratification varies from one society to another, depending on technological, economic, and political variables. Small-scale societies tend to be less stratified than large-scale societies; that is, they have fewer categories of status and fewer degrees of difference regarding wealth, power, and prestige.

In some societies, wealth, power, and prestige are linked with ownership of land or the number of animals acquired. In U.S. society, high status is strongly correlated with income and property. Exploring the causes of differing patterns of social stratification and how stratification relates to other facets of society is an important objective in ethnographic research.

The social structure of any society has several major components that anthropologists study when analyzing a society. These components are discussed in the following sections on the family, marriage, gender, and age.

The Family

In a comprehensive cross-cultural study, George Murdock (1945) found that all societies recognize the family. Thus, the family is a *universal* feature of humans and may have its roots in our primate heritage (Chapais 2008). Anthropologists define the **family** as a social group of two or more people related by blood, marriage, or adoption who live or reside together for an extended period, sharing economic resources and caring for their young. Anthropologists differentiate between the *family of orientation*, the family into which people are born, and the *family of procreation*, the family within which people reproduce or adopt children of their own (Murdock 1949). The family is a social unit within a much wider group of relatives, or *kin*. Kinship relationships beyond the immediate nuclear family play a significant role in most societies throughout the world. Anthropologists study kinship relationships along with the family to fully comprehend how individual thought and behavior is influenced by these interacting aspects of human communities.

Although variations exist in types and forms, as mentioned before, George Murdock found that the family is a universal aspect of social organization. The reason for the universality of the family appears to be that it performs certain basic functions that serve human needs. The primary function of the family is the nurturing and enculturation of children. The basic norms, values, knowledge, and beliefs of the culture are transmitted to children through the family.

Another function of the family is the regulation of sexual activity. Every culture places some restrictions on sexual behavior. Sexual intercourse is the basis of human reproduction and inheritance; it is also a matter of considerable social importance. Regulating sexual behavior is, therefore, essential to the proper functioning of a society. The family prohibits sexual relations within the immediate family through the incest avoidance behaviors, as discussed in Chapter 11.

Families also serve to protect and support their members physically, emotionally, and often economically from birth to death. In all societies, people need warmth, food, shelter, and care. Families provide a social environment in which these needs can be met. Additionally, humans have emotional needs for affection and intimacy that are most easily fulfilled within the family.

The two major types of families found throughout the world are the *nuclear* and *extended* families. A typical **nuclear family** is composed of two parents and their immediate biological offspring or adopted children. George Murdock believed that the nuclear family is a universal feature of all societies (1949). What he meant by this was that all societies have a male and female who reproduce children and are the core of the kinship unit.

However, as we shall see later, the nuclear family is not the principal kinship unit in all societies. In many societies, the predominant form is the **extended family**, which is composed of parents, children, and other kin relations bound together as a social unit.

Marriage

In most societies, the family is a product of **marriage**, a social bond sanctioned by society between two or more people that involves economic cooperation, social obligations, rights, duties, and sometimes culturally approved sexual activity. Two general patterns of marriage exist: **endogamy**, which is marriage between people of the same social group or category, and **endogamy**, marriage between people of different social groups or categories.

A marriage may include two or more partners. **Monogamy** generally involves two individuals in the marriage. Though this is the most familiar form of marriage in Western industrial societies, it is not the only type of marriage practiced in the world. Many societies practice some form of **polygamy**, or *plural marriage*, which involves a spouse of one sex and two or more spouses of the opposite sex. There are two forms of polygamy: **polygyny**, marriage between one husband and two or more wives, and **polyandry**, marriage between one wife and two or more husbands. Although the majority of the world's population currently practices monogamy, polygyny is a common form of marriage and is permitted in 80 percent of human societies, many of which have relatively small populations (Murdock 1981a, 1981b). Although polyandry is the rarest form of marriage, a new survey of polyandry indicates that it occurs in 81 different societies (Starkweather and Hames 2012). Although marriages typically involve the uniting of males and females, a number of societies have homosexual marriages that are recognized socially and legally (L. Stone 2010). As we shall see, anthropologists have developed hypotheses regarding why certain forms of marriage develop within particular sociocultural systems.

Gender

Gender relationships are another important component of the social structure of a society. When anthropologists discuss relationships between males and females in a society, they distinguish between *sex* and *gender*. **sex** refers to the biological and anatomical differences between males and females. These differences include the primary sexual characteristics—the sex organs—and the secondary sexual characteristics, such as breasts and wider hips for females and more muscular development of the upper torso and extensive body hair for males. Note that these are general tendencies, to which many exceptions exist. That is, many males are smaller and lighter and have less body hair than many females. Nevertheless, in general, males and females are universally distinguished by physiological and anatomical differences (L. Stone 2010).

In contrast to sex, most anthropologists view *gender* as cultural rather than biological. **gender** refers to the specific human traits attached to each sex by a society. As members of a particular society, males and females occupy certain statuses, such as son, daughter, husband, wife, father, and mother. In assuming the gender roles that correspond to these different status positions, males are socialized to be "masculine" and females are socialized to be "feminine." Definitions of masculine and feminine vary among different societies (Yangisako and Collier 1990; L. Stone 2010).

Gender and Enculturation   One major issue regarding gender is the degree to which enculturation influences male and female behavior. To study this issue, anthropologists focus on the values, beliefs, and norms that may influence gender roles. They also observe the types of activities associated with young boys and girls. In many societies, boys and girls play different games as an aspect of enculturation. For example, in U.S. society, boys in comparison with girls are traditionally encouraged to participate in aggressive, competitive team sports. Cultural values and beliefs that affect gender roles are found in other societies as well.

Sex and the Division of Labor   A basic component of the division of labor in most societies is the assigning of different tasks to males and females. In studying this phenomenon, anthropologists focus on the issue of whether physical differences (sex differences) between males and females are responsible for these different roles. To address this issue, they ask a number of questions: Is there a universal division of labor based on sex? Does physical strength have anything to do with the work patterns associated with gender? Do childcare and pregnancy determine or influence economic specialization for females? To what degree do values and beliefs ascribed to masculine or feminine behavior affect work assignments?

Gender and Status   Another important issue investigated by anthropologists is the social and political status of males and females in society. As is discussed later, some early anthropologists such as Lewis Morgan believed that females at one time had a higher social and political status than males, but that through time this pattern was reversed. Anthropologists currently focus on how the status of males and females is related to biological factors, the division of labor, kinship relations, political systems, and values and beliefs.

Although sex characteristics are biologically determined, gender roles vary in accordance with the technological, economic, and sociocultural conditions of particular types of societies. In this and later chapters, we explore some recent studies by anthropologists who have broadened our understanding of the variation of gender roles among a wide range of societies.

Age

Like kinship and gender, age is a universal principle used to prescribe social status in sociocultural systems. The biological processes of aging are an inevitable aspect of human life; from birth to death, our bodies are constantly changing. Definite biological changes occur for humans in their progress from infancy to childhood to adolescence to adulthood to old age. Hormonal and other physiological changes lead to maturation and the onset of the aging process. For example, as we approach old age, our sensory abilities begin to change: Our capacities for taste, eyesight, touch, smell, and hearing begin to diminish. Gray hair and wrinkles appear, and we experience a loss of height and weight and an overall decline in strength and vitality. Although these physical changes vary greatly from individual to individual and to some extent are influenced by societal and environmental factors, these processes are universal.

The biology of aging, however, is only one dimension of how age is related to the social structure of any specific culture. The human life cycle is the basis of social statuses and roles that have both a physical and a cultural dimension. The cultural meanings of these categories in the life cycle vary among different societies, as do the criteria people use to define age-related statuses. The definitions of the statuses and roles for specific ages have wide-ranging implications for those in these status positions.

Age and Enculturation   As people move through the different phases of the human life cycle, they continually experience the process of enculturation. Because of the existence of different norms, values, and beliefs, people in various societies may be treated differently at each phase of the life cycle. For example, the period of enculturation during childhood varies among societies. In the United States and other postindustrial societies, childhood is associated with an extensive educational experience that continues for many years. In many preindustrial societies, however, childhood is a relatively short period, and children assume adult status and responsibilities at a fairly young age.

Another factor influenced by aging in a society is how individuals are viewed at different ages. How is *old age* defined? For example, in many societies, old age is not defined strictly in terms of the passage of time. More frequently, old age is defined in respect to changes in social status, work patterns, family status, or reproductive potential (Cowgill 1986). These factors influence how people are valued at different ages in a society.

Age and the Division of Labor   The economic roles assumed by a person at different stages of the life cycle may also depend on age. Children everywhere are exposed to the technological skills they will need to survive in their environment. As they mature, they assume specific positions in the division of labor. Just as male and female roles differ, the roles for the young and old differ. For example, in some preindustrial societies, older people occupy central roles, whereas in others, they play no important roles at all. In industrial and postindustrial societies, the elderly generally do not occupy important occupational roles.

Age and Status   Age is one of the key determinants of social status. People are usually assigned a particular status associated with a phase of the life cycle. The result is **age stratification**, the unequal allocation of wealth, power, and prestige among people of different ages. Anthropologists find that age stratification varies in accordance with the level of technological development. For example, in many preindustrial societies, the elderly have a relatively high social status, whereas in most industrial societies, the elderly experience a loss of status.

One of the most common ways of allocating the status of people at different ages is through *age grades*. **Age grades** are statuses defined by age through which a person moves as he or she ages. For example, the age grades in most industrial societies correspond to the periods of infancy, preschool, kindergarten, elementary school, intermediate school, high school, young adulthood, middle age, young old, and old old (Cowgill 1986). Each of these grades conveys a particular social status.

Social Structure in Hunter-Gatherer Societies

17.2 Describe the social structure, family, marriage, gender, and age in foraging societies.

The fundamental social organization in foraging societies is based upon family, marriage, kinship, gender, and age. The two basic elements of social organization for foraging populations are the nuclear family and the band. The nuclear family is the small family unit associated with procreation: parents and offspring. The nuclear family is most adaptive for hunting-gathering societies because it allows for the flexibility needed in a society that depends upon hunting and distribution of hunted game (Fox 1967; Pasternak 1976). Frequent nomadic mobility favors small nuclear family groupings for foraging tasks. Typically, hunting and gathering is conducted by small groups of nuclear families. For example, during certain seasons, the Baka forest people in Cameroon forage in the forest and build small huts made of bowed limbs covered with leaves for their nuclear families (Campagnoli 2005). Later during the season, these Baka nuclear families would settle in more permanent camps for several months with other relatives.

The most common type of band is made up of a related cluster of nuclear families ranging in size from 20 to 100 individuals. At times, in societies such as the desert-dwelling Shoshone Indians, the bands may break up into nuclear families to locate food and other resources. Under other circumstances, several families may cooperate in hunting and other foraging activities. In some instances, bands may contain up to four or five (sometimes more) extended families, in which married children and their offspring reside with their parents. These multifamily bands provide the webs of kinship for foraging societies, enabling them to cooperate in subsistence and economic exchanges.

The specific number of people in a band depends upon the carrying capacity of the natural environment. Most foraging groups had a range of 20 to 100 people. Foragers in the desert, the Arctic, and the tropical rain forest all lived in small multifamily bands residing in separate territories. Typically, band organization is extremely flexible, with members leaving and joining bands as circumstances demand. Personal conflicts and shortages of resources may encourage people to move into or out of bands. In some cases, when food or water resources are scarce, whole bands may move into the territories of other bands.

Marriage and Kinship

Although a number of foraging groups such as the Ache practice *polygyny*, marriage between one male and two or more females, the most common type of marriage found in foraging societies is monogamy (Hill and Hurtado 1996; Ember, Ember, and Low 2007). Marriages are an important means of cementing social relationships. In some cases, betrothals are arranged while the future spouses are still young children. Typically, the girl is much younger than the male. For example, Ju/'hoansi San girls are often married between the ages of 12 and 14, whereas males may be 18 to 25 or older.

Although these marital arrangements are regular features of foraging societies, it does not mean the couple easily accepts these arranged marriages. A San woman expressed herself on her first marriage:

When I married my husband Tsau I didn't fight too hard, but I cried a lot when I was taken to sleep in his hut. When the elders went away I listened carefully for their sleeping. Then, when my husband fell asleep and I heard his breathing, I very quietly sat up and eased my blanket away from his and stole away and slept by myself out in the bush.

In the morning the people came to Tsau's hut and asked, "Where is your wife?" He looked around and said, "I don't know where my wife has gone off to." Then they picked up my tracks and tracked me to where I was sitting out in the bush. They brought me back to my husband. They told me that this was the man they had given to me and that he wouldn't hurt me.

After that we just lived together all right. At first when we slept under the same blanket our bodies did not touch, but then after a while I slept at his front. Other girls don't like their husbands and keep struggling away until the husbands give up on them and their parents take them back. (Lee 1993:83)

Marriage Rules

Marital arrangements in foraging societies are intended to enhance economic, social, and political interdependence among bands and to foster appropriate band alliances. To do this, rules are established to determine who may marry whom. Many of these rules concern marriages among cousins. A common marriage rule found in foraging societies is referred to as *cross-cousin marriage*. A **cross-cousin** is the offspring of one's father's sister or one's mother's brother. In effect, a cross-cousin marriage means that a male marries a female who is his father's sister's daughter or his mother's brother's daughter.

In addition, foraging societies frequently have rules of residence that specify where the married couple must reside. Most band societies practice **patrilocal residence**, in which the newly married couple resides with the husband's father. Thus, if a man marries a woman from a different band, she must join her husband's band. In such societies, the patrilocal residence rule and cross-cousin marriage combine to create a system called *restricted marital exchange*, in which two groups exchange women

(Lévi-Strauss 1969). The purpose of this system is to foster group solidarity by encouraging kinship alliances.

The kinship diagram in Figure 17.1 gives a visual model of the social structure in some foraging societies. In the diagram, Ego is used as a point of reference, and kinship relationships are traced from Ego's offspring, parents, grandparents, and other relatives. Note that Ego has married his father's sister's daughter (his cross-cousin on his father's side). Because of the rule of patrilocal residence, Ego's father's sister had to move to another band with her husband. Therefore, Ego is marrying outside his own band.

Like Ego, Ego's wife's brother has married a woman outside his band. In keeping with the cross-cousin rule, their daughter has married Ego's son. Ego's daughter will eventually marry someone from another band. Through the rules of cross-cousin marriage and patrilocal residence, this restricted exchange develops strong networks of interfamily and interband kinship relations. These kin networks widen over the generations, expanding reciprocal economic, social, and political relationships.

Brideservice

Some foraging societies practice **brideservice**, in which a male resides for a specified amount of time with his wife's parents' band. The rule of residence that requires a man to reside with his wife's parents is called **matrilocal residence**. Among the Ju/'hoansi San, brideservice can last eight to ten years, and the husband and wife don't return to the husband's father's band for residence (the patrilocal rule) until after several children are born (Lee 1993). The husband will help his wife's band in its subsistence activities, which helps consolidate

Figure 17.1 Kinship and marriage patterns in hunting and gathering societies

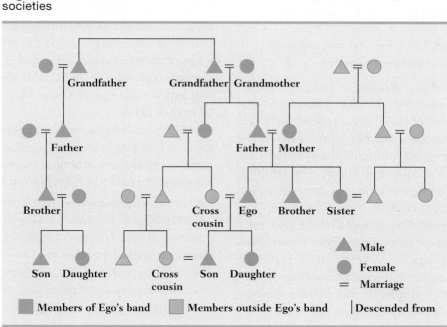

both economic and social ties between the two bands. Another reason the Ju/'hoansi San practice brideservice is that females are not sexually mature at the time of their marriage. San girls who marry before their menarche are not expected to have sexual intercourse with their husbands. Thus, the brideservice period coincides with female maturation. But brideservice also functions to reinforce the kinship and reciprocal ties between bands. Other foraging groups like the Ache of Paraguay practice matrilocal residence without brideservice (Hill and Hurtado 1996).

Other Marital Patterns among Foragers Not all foraging societies conform to the marital patterns just described. For example, in the past, most Eskimo (Inuit) marriage involved no preferred rules regarding cousin marriage or rituals and ceremonies sanctioning the new couple's relationship. Traditionally, the man and woman simply begin residing with each other. To some extent, the Inuit viewed this marriage arrangement as a pragmatic and utilitarian relationship for economic and reproductive purposes (Balikci 1970). In addition, polyandry (marriage between one woman and more and two or more men) has been a feature of Inuit culture (Starkweather and Hames 2012). Undoubtedly, polyandry was associated with the long absence of males on hunting trips and the fear of wife abduction or unfaithfulness. In addition, as men produce most of the food in Inuit society, women would benefit from having more than one male provider. In some cases, the Inuit would establish formal polyandrous relationships with other males, frequently brothers, in what is known as *fraternal polyandry.*

Divorce In most cases, divorce is easily accomplished in hunting-and-gathering societies. For example, Ju/'hoansi San divorces, which are most frequently initiated by the wife, are simple matters characterized by cordiality and cooperation. The divorced couple may even live next to one another with their new spouses. Because there are no rigid rules or complex kinship relations beyond the nuclear family to complicate divorce proceedings, the dissolution of a Ju/'hoansi San marriage is a relatively easy process (Lee 1993, 2013). As mentioned earlier, the Ache foragers of Paraguay practice polygyny, which is unusual for hunter-gatherers (Hill and Hurtado 1996). The Ache also practice a *serial monogamy* form of marriage with frequent divorces, and a woman may have 12 or more spouses during her lifetime. The Ache marriages endure from several hours to 47 years (Hill and Hurtado 1996).

Divorce was also frequent and easily obtained among the Inuit (Balikci 1970). As with the San, one reason for this was the lack of formal social groups beyond the nuclear family. Another reason was the absence of strict rules governing marriage and postmarital residence. Significantly, divorce did not necessarily lead to the cutting of kin ties. Even if an Inuit couple separated, and this happened for nearly 100 percent of the marriages studied, the kin ties

endured (Burch 1970). Sometimes the couple reunited, and the children of first and second marriages became a newly blended family. Thus, divorce actually created kin ties, an important aspect of sociocultural adaptation in severe Arctic conditions.

Gender

Gender as an aspect of social structure in foraging societies is an extremely important area of ethnographic research. Cultural anthropologists have been examining the interrelationships among patterns of gender, subsistence, economy, and political organization.

Gender and the Division of Labor Prior to recent ethnographic research on foraging societies, anthropologists believed that male subsistence activities, especially hunting and fishing, provided most of the food resources. In the traditional sex-based evolutionary perspective, males did the hunting and women gathered the vegetation and cooperated within a pair-bonded nuclear family (Lovejoy 1981, Washburn and Lancaster 1968). In some of the foraging societies such as the Ju/'hoansi San, Semang, and Mbuti, women provided most of the food by gathering plants (Martin and Voorhies 1975; Dahlberg 1981; Lee 1993, 2013; Weisner 2002). In addition, women also sometimes hunt or indirectly procure meat. Among the Batak foragers of the rain forests of Malaysia and the Agta in the Philippines, both men and women perform virtually every subsistence task (Estioko-Griffin and Griffin 1978; Endicott 1988). Women among the Agta go out into the forest to kill wild boars, just as the men do. The Tiwi of Australia and the Hadza foragers of East Africa demonstrate this same pattern (Goodale 1971; Woodburn 1982).

Carol Ember's cross-cultural study of foragers indicated that males have typically obtained meat by hunting and fishing (Ember 1978). However, as Nicole Waguespack's recent global study of both ethnographic and archaeological evidence indicates, even in societies dominated by meat procurement, women play important economic roles and are involved in many different types of activities such as leatherworking and building shelters (2005). The division of labor cannot be simply described as a sex-based division of labor with men hunting and women gathering vegetation.

Sex-Based Explanations of the Division of Labor One early question posed by cultural anthropologists was: Why is the division of labor in foraging societies so strongly related to a sex (i.e., men hunt, women gather)? There are several possible answers to this question. The first answer is that males tended to hunt and women tended to be engaged in gathering or other nonsubsistence activities because males are stronger and have more endurance in the pursuit of large game. Another answer is that because women bear and nurse children, they lack the freedom of mobility necessary to hunt (Friedl 1975). A third answer is that gathering, especially near a base camp, is a relatively safe activity that entails no potential dangers for women who are either pregnant or caring for children (Brown 1970b). Keeping their offspring alive and providing for them is a fundamental aspect of women's activities in foraging societies (Gurven and Hill 2009).

There is evidence for and against each of these theories. In some foraging societies, men and women are involved in both hunting and gathering. Further, women often perform tasks that require strength and stamina, such as carrying food, children, water, and firewood. Thus, gathering resources is not a sedentary or leisurely activity. Based on this evidence, anthropologist Linda Marie Fedigan proposed that heavy work and childcare activities are not mutually exclusive, as previously argued (1986).

In an essay entitled "Why do Men Hunt?: A Reevaluation of 'Man the Hunter' and the Sexual Division of Labor," Michael Gurven and Kim Hill assess some of the current explanations of male-female activities in foraging societies (2009). The traditional explanation for male hunting is to provision their families. However, hunting meat is less reliable and more costly than other means of foraging. One hypothesis suggested that males take on the high-cost and low-yield hunting in order to "show off" their status and physical abilities to attract females for mating opportunities (Hawkes and Bliege-Bird 2002; Hawkes et al. 2010). This is referred to as the "costly signaling model." Gurven and Hill provide a comprehensive, multidimensional model for why men hunt (2009). In their model, costly signaling is one factor that motivates male hunting activity, but it needs to be combined with other factors such as investing in children (parental investment), the social insurance provided with sharing and cooperation through coalition and alliance building, and assisting ill or incapacitated members of the foraging group. This model provides a fruitful avenue for further investigation of why men hunt in foraging societies.

Many research questions pertaining to gender roles and subsistence among foragers remain for future anthropologists. Much of the recent evidence suggests that gender roles and subsistence activities are not as rigid as formerly thought. In these cases, it appears that the subsistence strategies for both males and females are open and that behavior is flexible.

Female Status Closely related to gender roles and subsistence is the question of the social status of women. Empirical data suggest that gender relations tend to be more *egalitarian*—men and women have more or less equal status—in foraging societies than in other societies (Friedl 1975; Shostak 1981; Endicott 1988; Lepowsky 1993; Ward 2003).

This may reflect the substantial contributions women make in gathering food.

Richard Lee notes, for example, that as a result of their important role in economic activities, Ju/'hoansi San women participate equally with men in political decision making (1981, 2013). Ju/'hoansi San women are treated respectfully, and there is little evidence of male domination or the maltreatment of females. A similar generalization could be applied to the Mbuti, Semang, and Agta, as well as to most of the other foragers. This hypothesis suggests, however, that in societies in which female contributions to the food supply are less critical or less valued, female status is lower. For example, among some of the traditional Eskimo and other northern foraging groups for which hunting is the only subsistence activity, females do not gather much in the way of resources for the family. Consequently, those societies tended to be more patriarchal, or male dominated, in political and economic matters (Friedl 1975; Martin and Voorhies 1975; Lepowsky 1993; Ward 2003).

Clearly, equality between males and females in foraging societies is not universal. In some groups, such as the Ju/'hoansi San and Agta, women have more equality, whereas in others, such as the traditional Eskimo, females have a lower status. Even in the most egalitarian groups, males tend to have some inherent cultural advantages. In some cases, meat is viewed as a more luxurious and prestigious food and thus enhances the male status. In addition, males are more likely to become the political and spiritual leaders in foraging societies. When considering gender relations in a broad, cross-cultural perspective, however, foragers tend to have much more equality than do most other societies.

Age

Like kinship and gender, age is used in virtually all foraging societies as a basis for assigning individuals their particular status in the social hierarchy. Patterns of age stratification and hierarchy vary considerably from society to society, depending on environmental and cultural conditions. Age is also a primary aspect of the division of labor in foraging societies.

The Roles of the Elderly In foraging societies, old age tends to be defined less in terms of chronology and more in terms of some change in social status related to becoming less involved in subsistence or work patterns or to becoming grandparents (Glascock 1981). In all societies, however, the onset of old age is partially defined in terms of the average life span. The general demographic and ethnological data on foraging societies indicate that definitions of "old age" vary from 45 to 75 years old.

An early study of aging hypothesized that in hunting and gathering societies, older people wield little power and have low status (Simmons 1945). This argument was based on the assumption that because foraging societies had few material goods that older people controlled and could use as leverage with the younger generation, old age represented a loss of status. This hypothesis suggested that the status of older people is correlated with subsistence and economic activities. As foraging people age and decline in strength and energy, their subsistence contribution may be limited, thereby diminishing their status.

Most of the current ethnographic data, however, do not support this hypothesis. In an early account of foragers in the Andaman Islands off the coast of India, for example, A. R. Radcliffe-Brown ([1922] 1964) described the reverence and honor given to older males. Among the Mbuti in the Central Congo in Africa, age is a key factor in determining status, and the elders make the most important economic and political decisions for the group. Despite the fact that young people sometimes openly ridicule older people, the elders are able to dominate Mbuti society because of their cultural knowledge (Turnbull 1983).

Anthropologists who have studied the Ju/'hoansi San point out that though there was little material security at old age, the elderly were not abandoned and had a relatively high status (Thomas 1958; Lee 1979, 2013). Despite the fact that older people do not play a predominant productive role in subsistence activities, they are able to remain secure because of close kinship ties.

Anthropologists find that older people in foraging societies have a higher status than do younger people. Because of their accumulated knowledge, which is needed for subsistence activities, political decision making, and intellectual and spiritual guidance, older people tend to be respected. Human memory serves as the libraries of these societies and is important for the preservation of culture and the transmission of knowledge. Cultural traditions are memorized and handed down from generation to generation, and control of these traditions forms the basis of esteem.

In general, only in cases of extreme deprivation are the elderly in foraging societies maltreated. In their investigation of the treatment of the elderly in a wide variety of foraging societies, researchers concluded that practices directed against the elderly, such as abandonment, exposure, and killing, occur only under severe environmental circumstances, in which the elderly are viewed as burdens rather than assets (Glascock 1981). These practices have been documented for groups such as the Eskimo, but these cases appear to be exceptional. In most foraging societies, the young have moral obligations to take care of the elderly.

Childcare Activities Turnbull (1983) has remarked that one of the significant universal roles of elderly grandparents is babysitting. While the parents in foraging societies are involved in subsistence chores like hunting and collecting, grandparents often are engaged in childcare activities. Among the Ju/'hoansi San and the Mbuti, elderly grandparents care for small children while the children's mothers are away on gathering activities. The elderly teach the grandchildren the skills, norms, and values of the society. Reflecting on the Mbuti elders, who spend time telling stories and reciting myths and legends, Turnbull indicates that this role is the primary function of the Mbuti elderly in the maintenance of culture. In most foraging societies, this is the typical pattern for relationships between the young and the old. Recently, anthropologist Kristen Hawkes (2004) studied how the "Grandmother Effect" and the longer life span of women have had significant survival value in providing childcare for and nurturing the young children in foraging societies. She notes that in both historical and contemporary foraging societies, a third or more of women live beyond 45. The survival of these postmenopausal women would be extremely important for the welfare

An older !Kung San or Ju/'hoansi woman

and survival of these grandchildren in these foraging communities.

Social Structure in Tribes

17.3 Describe the social structure, family, marriage, descent groups, gender, and age for tribal societies.

Tribal societies differ from foraging societies in that tribal peoples produce most of their subsistence foods through small-scale cultivation (horticulture) and the domestication of animals (pastoralism). The evolution of food production corresponds to new forms of social organization. Like bands, social organization among tribes is largely based upon kinship. Rules concerning kinship, marriage, and other social systems, however, are much more elaborate in tribal societies, which have to resolve new types of problems, including denser populations, control of land or livestock, and sometimes warfare.

New and diverse forms of social organization have enabled tribal societies to adjust to the new conditions of food production. Unlike foragers, who sometimes have to remain separate from one another in small, flexibly organized bands, food producers have had to develop social relationships that are more fixed and permanent. Tribal social organization is based on family, the descent group, gender, and age. The social organization of tribal societies is much more complex than that of band societies.

Families

The most common social grouping among tribal societies is the *extended family*. Most extended families consist of three generations—grandparents, parents, and children—although they can also contain married siblings with their spouses and children. Compared with the nuclear family, the extended family is a larger and more stable social unit that is more effective in organizing and carrying out domestic economic and subsistence activities (Pasternak 1976; L. Stone 2010). Even the extended family, however, cannot satisfy the complex needs of tribal societies for cooperation, labor, and reciprocity. To meet these needs, tribal groups have developed even more "extended" types of social organization, based on both kinship and nonkinship principles.

Descent Groups

One of the more extended social groupings that exist in tribal societies is the descent group. A **descent group** is a social group identified by a person in order to trace actual or supposed kinship relationships. Descent groups are the predominant social units in tribal societies.

One major type of descent group is based on lineage. Anthropologists define **lineages** as descent groups composed of relatives, all of whom trace their relationship through *consanguineal* (blood) or *affinal* (marriage) relations to an actual, commonly known ancestor. Everyone in the lineage knows exactly how she or he is related to this ancestor.

Unilineal Descent Groups

Unilineal descent groups are lineage groups that trace their descent through only one side of the lineage or through only one sex. The most common type of unilineal descent group is a **patrilineal descent groups**, or *patrilineage*, composed of people who trace their descent through males from a common, known male ancestor (see Figure 17.2, top). Patrilineal descent groups are the predominant form of lineage in tribal societies (Pasternak 1976; L. Stone 2010).

Another form of unilineal descent group is the **matrilineal descent group**, or *matrilineage*, whose members calculate descent through the female line from a commonly known female ancestor (see Figure 17.2, bottom). Matrilineal descent groups occur most frequently in horticultural societies, although they are not the most common organizations. Matrilineal descent is found among a small number of North American tribal societies such as the Iroquois, Hopi, and Crow; among a number of tribes throughout Central and South Africa; and among a few peoples who live in the Pacific Islands (L. Stone 2010).

One very rare type of unilineal grouping is based on *double descent*, a combination of patrilineal and matrilineal principles. In this type of social organization, an individual belongs to both the father's and the mother's lineal descent groups. Several African tribal societies, such as the Afikpo Igbo in Nigeria, have a double-descent type of social organization (Ottenberg 1965).

Ambilineal Descent Groups One other type of descent group is known as ambilineal descent. An **ambilineal descent group** is formed by tracing an individual's descent relationships through either a male or a female line. The members of these groups are not all related to each other through a particular male or female. Therefore, technically, this form of descent group is not unilineal. Usually, once an individual chooses to affiliate with either the father's or the mother's descent group, he or she remains with that descent group. Because each individual may choose his or her descent group, the ambilineal system offers more opportunity for economic and political strategizing. This choice frequently takes into account the relative economic resources or political power of the two family groups.

Bilateral Descent A number of tribal societies practice **bilateral descent**, in which relatives are traced through

Figure 17.2 A patrilineal descent system; (top) a matrilineal descent system (bottom).

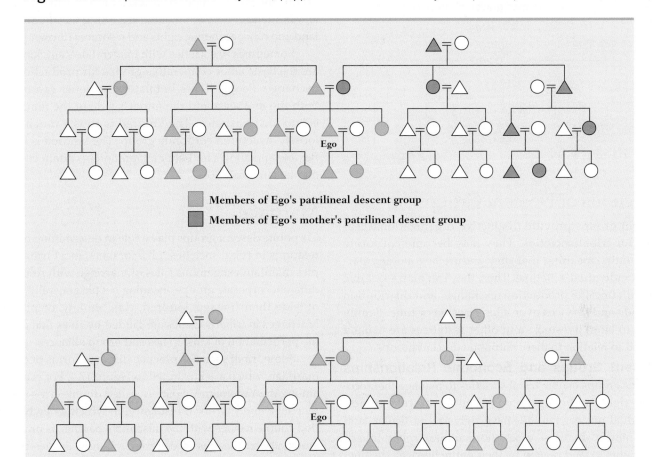

Members of Ego's patrilineal descent group

Members of Ego's mother's patrilineal descent group

Members of Ego's matrilineal descent group

Members of Ego's father's matrilineal descent group

both maternal and paternal sides of the family simultaneously. This type of descent system does not result in any particular lineal descent grouping. For that reason, it is not too common in tribal societies. In those cases in which bilateral descent is found among tribes, a loosely structured group known as a *kindred* is used to mobilize relatives for economic, social, or political purposes. **kindreds** are overlapping relatives from both the mother's and the father's side of a family that an individual recognizes as important kin relations (see Figure 17.3). In U.S. society, for example, when a person refers to all of his or her relatives, that person is designating a type of bilateral kindred. This bilateral kindred, however, has no functional significance in U.S. society compared to its role in a tribal society.

Clans A **clan** is a form of descent group whose members trace their descent to an unknown ancestor or, in some cases, to a sacred plant or animal spirit. Members of clans usually share a common name, but are not able to specify definitive links to an actual genealogical figure. Some clans are *patriclans*, groups distinguished by a male through whom

descent is traced. Other clan groupings are *matriclans*, in which descent is traced through a female. Some tribal societies have both clans and lineages. In many cases, clans are made up of lineages that link their descent to a mythical ancestor or sacred spirit. In such systems, clans are larger groupings, consisting of several different lineages.

Phratries and Moieties Among the more loosely structured groups found in tribal societies are phratries and moieties. **Phratries** are social groupings that consist of two or more clans combined. Members of phratries usually believe they have some loose genealogical relationship to one another. **Moieties** (derived from the French word meaning "half") are composed of clans or phratries that divide the entire society into two equal divisions. In some cases, such as among the North American Hopi, the moiety divisions divide the village in half. People have to marry outside their own moiety. In addition, each moiety has specific functions related to economic and political organization and religious activities. Wherever phratries and moieties are found in tribal societies, they provide models for organizing social relationships.

Figure 17.3 A kindred consists of relatives from both side of a family that Ego recognizes as important kin relations

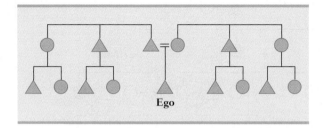

Functions of Descent Groups

Descent groups provide distinctive organizational features for tribal societies. They may become corporate social units, meaning that they endure beyond any particular individual's lifetime. Thus, they can play a key role in regulating the production, exchange, and distribution of goods and services over a long period of time. Family rights to land, livestock, and other resources are usually defined in relation to these corporate descent groups.

Descent Groups and Economic Relationships

Descent groups enable tribal societies to manage their economic rights and obligations. Within the descent groups, individual nuclear families have rights to particular land and animals. In most cases, horticultural tribes inherit their rights to land owned by their entire lineage. The lineage allocates the land to members of the lineage through what anthropologists (and attorneys) call *usufruct* rights or corporate rights to the land. Among some more advanced patrilineal horticulturalist peoples, land is sometimes transmitted from generation to generation through an eldest male, an inheritance pattern known as **primogeniture**. A less common pattern is **ultimogeniture**, in which property and land are passed to the youngest son.

In horticultural societies, separate families within patrilineages have joint rights to plots of land for gardening. For example, among the Yanomamö, villages are usually made up of two patrilineages; families within these lineages cultivate their own plots of land (Chagnon 2012). In this sense, the Yanomamö patrilineage is a like a corporate group. The transmission of status, rights, and obligations through these patrilineages occurs without constant disputes and conflicts. In these tribal societies, land is usually not partitioned into individual plots and cannot be sold to or exchanged with other descent groups.

Iroquois tribal society was based on matrilineal corporate groupings. Matrilineages among the Iroquois resided together in longhouses and had collective rights over tools and garden plots. These matrilineages were also the basic units of production in the slash-and-burn cultivation for maize and other crops. Property was inherited through matrilineal lines from the eldest woman in the corporate group. She had the highest social status in the matrilineage and influenced decision making regarding the allocation of land and other economic rights and resources (Brown 1970a).

Sometimes in societies with bilateral descent, kindreds are the basic labor-cooperative groups for production and exchange. People living in bilateral societies can turn to both the mother's and the father's side of the family for economic assistance. The kindred is thus a much more loosely structured corporate group. The kindred is highly flexible and allows for better adaptation in certain environmental circumstances.

Marriage

Corporate descent groups play a role in determining marital relations in tribal societies. Like foragers, most tribal peoples maintain exogamous rules of marriage with respect to different corporate groups, meaning people generally marry outside their lineage, kindred, clan, moiety, or phratry. Marriages in tribal societies are guided by rules that ensure the perpetuation of kinship ties and group alliances.

Some tribal societies practice different forms of cousin marriage, which are illustrated in Figure 17.4. For example, among the Yanomamö, a pattern called double cross-cousin marriage and patrilocal residence, in which a newly married couple resides with the husband's parents, is practiced among patrilineages in different villages. Males in one patrilineage, in effect, exchange sisters, whom they may not marry, with males of other patrilineages. When the sons of the next generation repeat this form of marriage, each is marrying a woman to whom he is already related by kinship. The woman whom the man marries is both his father's sister's daughter and his mother's brother's daughter. The woman is marrying a man who is both her mother's brother's son and her father's sister's son. This form of patrilineal exogamous marriage is common in many tribal societies. It is a type of restricted marriage exchange that helps provide for the formation of economic and political alliances among villages (Chagnon 2012; Hames 2004).

Some patrilineal tribal societies, including several in Southeast Asia, prefer a more specific rule of *matrilateral*

Figure 17.4 Different types of cousin marriage

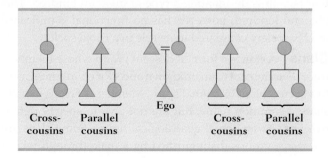

cross-cousin marriage. In this system, males consistently marry their mother's brothers' daughters. This produces a marital system in which females move from one patrilineage to another. More than two lineages are involved in this system. The patrilineages become specialized as either wife givers or wife takers. In an example with three lineages—A, B, and C—anthropologists have noted cycles of marital exchange. Lineage B always gives women to lineage A, but takes its wives from lineage C (see Figure 17.5). Claude Lévi-Strauss (1969) refers to this type of marital system as general exchange, in contrast to restricted exchange, which is practiced between two lineages.

Another form of cousin marriage found in some patrilineal societies is **parallel-cousin marriage**, in which a male marries his father's brother's daughter. Unlike the other forms of cousin marriage, parallel-cousin marriage results in endogamy—marriage within one's own descent group (see Figure 17.6). This form of marriage is found among the Bedouin and other tribes of the Middle East and North Africa.

Polygyny Cross-cultural research has demonstrated that *polygyny*, in which a male marries two or more females, occurs most frequently in tribal societies (Ember, Ember, and Low 2007). In a classic cross-cultural study, anthropologists Kay Martin and Barbara Voorhies (1975) emphasized that polygyny is an ecologically and economically adaptive strategy for tribal populations. The more wives an individual male has, the more land or livestock he will control for allocation and exchange. This leads to an increase in both the labor supply and the overall productive value of the household. In addition, wealth in many of these tribal societies is measured in the number of offspring. Reproducing children for one's descent group is viewed as prestigious, and the children also become productive members of the household.

Anthropologist Douglas White (1988) did extensive cross-cultural research on polygyny. He describes one widespread type of polygyny as a wealth-enhancing form of marriage in which elder males accumulate several wives for productive labor, which increases their wealth. Strongly correlated with this wealth-enhancing polygyny is the ability to acquire new land for expansion. As new land becomes available, the labor produced by co-wives is extremely valuable. According to White, this wealth-enhancing form of polygyny is also related to warfare and the capture of wives. In his research, he found that tribal warfare often involved the capture of women from other groups as a major means of recruiting new co-wives for elder males.

Recently, a carefully controlled statistical multiple regression analysis of a broad cross-cultural sample from the Human Relations Area Files has indicated that the prevalence of warfare and the loss of males from warfare is highly correlated with polygynous marriages in nonstate societies (Ember, Ember, and Low 2007). This research indicates that the frequency of warfare, which as we will see in the next chapter is a fundamental aspect of tribal societies, is associated with the shortage of males and an increase in polygyny.

In addition to increasing wealth, polygyny enables certain individuals and lineages to have a large number of children. For example, roughly 25 percent of Yanomamö marriages are polygynous. One sample group of 20 Yanomamö political leaders had 71 wives and 172 children among them (Chagnon and Irons 1979). One Yanomamö individual named Shinbone had 11 wives and 43 children (Chagnon 2012). The Yanomamö case tends to demonstrate that polygyny is associated with warfare, high male mortality, and other factors including reproductive fitness.

Bridewealth Exchange Among many tribal societies, marriages are accompanied by an exchange of wealth. The most common type of exchange, particularly among patrilineal societies, is called **bridewealth**, which involves the transfer of some form of wealth, sometimes limited-purpose money like shells or livestock, from the descent group of the groom to that of the bride. Bridewealth is not a commercial exchange that reduces a bride to a commodity; that is, the bride's family does not "sell" her to her husband's family. Bridewealth serves to symbolize and highlight the reciprocities and rights established between two descent groups through marriage. In a patrilineal society,

Figure 17.5 Matrilateral cross-cousin marriages among three lineages

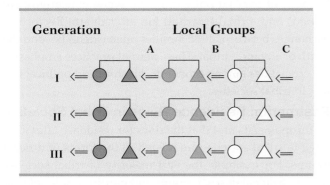

Figure 17.6 Patrilateral parallel-cousin marriage

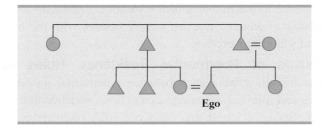

the bride becomes a member of a new corporate group that acquires access to her labor and eventually, to her offspring. In return, the husband's kin group has certain responsibilities toward the wife. The bridewealth reflects these mutual rights and obligations and compensates the bride's family for the loss of her labor and her reproductive potential. Once the bridewealth is paid, any children she has belong to the groom's family. It helps to forge an alliance between the two kin groups. One cross-cultural study of marriage transactions suggests that bridewealth exchanges in tribal societies relate to the need to introduce new female labor into the household, the transmission of property, and the enhancement of status for males (Schlegel and Eloul 1988). Failure to pay the bridewealth usually leads to family conflicts, including the possible dissolution of the marriage.

Polyandry Not all tribal societies are polygynous. Just as in some hunter-gatherer groups, polyandry exists in tribal societies (Starkweather and Hames 2012). *Polyandrous marriages* are between a woman and two or more men. Systematic formal patterns of polyandry are found in formerly tribal societies in the Himalayan regions of northern India, Sri Lanka, and Tibet and, until recently, among the Todas of southern India. The most common type of classical polyandry is fraternal polyandry, in which brothers share a wife.

The Toda were a buffalo-herding, pastoralist tribe of approximately 800 people. Traditionally, parents arranged the marriages when the partners were young children. When a Toda girl married a specific individual, she automatically became a wife of his brothers, including those who were not yet born. Through patrilocal residence rules, the wife joined the household of the husband. There was little evidence of sexual jealousy among the co-husbands. If the wife became pregnant, the oldest male claimed paternity rights over the child. The other co-husbands were "fathers" in a sociological sense and had certain rights regarding the child, such as labor for their households. Biological paternity was not considered important. The most prevalent explanation for the development of polyandry among the Toda was that female infanticide was practiced, leading to a scarcity of females (Rivers [1906] 1967; Oswalt 1972; Walker 1986).

Among other cases of formal polyandry, such as in the Himalayan areas, a lack of land and resources fostered this practice. Nancy Levine found that among the Nyinba of northwestern Nepal, the ideal form of marriage is a woman who marries *three brothers from another family* (1988; Boyd and Silk 2012). This enables one husband to farm the land, another to herd livestock, and a third to engage in trade. Levine discovered that the males in these polyandrous marriages were very concerned about the paternity of their own children and favored close relationships with their own offspring, just as would be predicted by an evolutionary psychology hypothesis (see Chapter 11).

Anthropologists indicate that nonclassical cases of polyandry are much more frequent than indicated within the ethnographic record (Borgerhoff Mulder 2009; Hrdy 2000; Starkweather and Hames 2012). In some cases, informal types of polyandry are usually recorded as *serial monogamy* and polygyny where females are married to different males at various periods during their lifetimes. Monique Borgerhoff Mulder's ethnographic research among the horticulturalist group known as the Pimbwe of Tanzania discovered many cases of women mating with multiple men during their lifetimes (2009). Informal polyandry is also found in many tribal societies such as the Yanomamö when there is a shortage of males due to warfare or diseases (Starkweather and Hames 2012).

The Levirate and Sororate The corporateness of descent groups in some tribal societies is exemplified by two rules of marriage designed to preserve kin ties and fulfill obligations following the death of a spouse. These rules are known as the levirate and the sororate. The **levirate** is the rule that a widow is expected to marry one of her deceased husband's brothers. In some societies, such as those of the ancient Israelites of biblical times and the contemporary Nuer or Tiv tribe, the levirate rule requires a man to cohabit with a dead brother's widow so that she can have children, who are then considered to be the deceased husband's. The essential feature of the levirate is that the corporate rights of the deceased husband and the lineage endure even after the husband's death. The **sororate** is a marriage rule that dictates that when a wife dies, her husband is expected to marry one of her sisters.

Both the levirate and the sororate provide for the fulfillment of mutual obligations between consanguineal (blood) and affinal (marital) kin after death. Reciprocal exchanges between allied families must extend beyond the death of any individual. These marital practices emphasize the crucial ties among economic, kinship, and political factors in tribal societies.

Postmarital Residence Rules in Tribal Societies

Anthropologists find that the rules for residence after marriage in tribal societies are related to the forms of descent groups. For example, the vast majority of tribal societies have patrilineal descent groups and patrilocal rules of residence. A less frequent pattern of postmarital residence is matrilocal residence, in which the newly wedded couple lives with or near the wife's parents. Yet, another rule of residence found in matrilineal societies is known as avunculocal, in which a married couple resides with the husband's mother's brother.

Causes of Postmarital Residence Rules By studying the relationships between postmarital residence rules and forms of descent groups in tribal societies, anthropologists have found that residence rules often represent adaptions to the practical conditions a society faces. The most widely accepted hypothesis states that rules of postmarital residence usually develop before the form of descent groups in a society (Fox 1967; Keesing and Strathern 1998; Martin and Voorhies 1975). For example, limited land and resources, frequent warfare with neighboring groups, population pressure, and the need for cooperative work may have been important factors in developing patrilocal residence and patrilineal descent groups. The purpose of these male-centered rules of residence and descent may have been to keep fathers, sons, and brothers together to pursue common interests in land, animals, and people.

What, then, creates matrilocal rules and matrilineal descent? One explanation, based on cross-cultural research by Melvin and Carol Ember (1971), proposed that matrilocal rules developed in response to patterns of warfare. The Embers suggested that societies that engage in internal warfare—warfare with neighboring societies close to home—have patrilocal rules of residence. In contrast, societies involved in external warfare—warfare a long distance from home—develop matrilocal residence rules. In societies in which external warfare takes males from the home territory for long periods of time, there is a strong need to keep the women of kin groups together. The classic example used by the Embers is the Iroquois, whose males traveled hundreds of miles away from home to engage in external wars, and this produced matrilocal residence and matrilineal descent.

Marvin Harris (1979) extended the Embers' hypothesis to suggest that matrilocal rules and matrilineal descent emerge in societies in which males are absent for long periods, for whatever reason. For example, among the Navajo, females tended sheep near their own households, and males raised horses and participated in labor that took them away from their homes. The Navajo had matrilocal residence and matrilineal descent.

Generalizations on Marriage in Tribal Societies

It must be emphasized that descent, marriage, and residence rules are *not static* in tribal societies. Rather, they are flexible and change as ecological, demographic, economic, and political circumstances change. For example, tribal groups with rules of preference for marriage partners make exceptions to those rules when the situation calls for it. If a tribal society has norms that prescribe cross-cousin or parallel-cousin marriage and an individual does not have a cousin in the particular category, various other options will be available for the individual.

There are usually many other candidates available for an arranged marriage. As anthropologist Ward Goodenough (1956) demonstrated long ago, much strategizing goes on in tribal societies in determining marital choice, residence locales, and descent. Factors such as property and the availability of land, animals, or other resources often influence decisions about marital arrangements.

Often tribal elders will be involved in lengthy negotiations regarding marital choices for their offspring. These people, like others throughout the world, are not automatons responding automatically to cultural norms. Kinship and marital rules are ideal norms, and these norms are often violated.

Divorce Among tribal peoples, especially those with patrilineal descent groups, divorce rates may be related to bridewealth exchanges. One traditional view suggested that in patrilineal descent societies with a high bridewealth amount, marriages tend to be stable. In Evans-Pritchard's (1951) account of Nuer marriage, he noted that one of the major reasons for bridewealth is to ensure marital stability. In lineage societies, the man's family pays a bridewealth in exchange for the rights to a woman's economic output and fertility. The greater the bridewealth, the more complete the transfer of rights over the woman from her own family to that of her husband. The dissolution of a marriage, which requires the return of bridewealth, is less likely to occur if the bridewealth is large and has been redistributed among many members of the wife's family (Gluckman 1953; Leach 1953, 1954; Schneider 1953). In contrast, when the bridewealth is low, marriages are unstable, and divorce is frequent.

As Roger Keesing (1981) has pointed out, however, this hypothesis raises a fundamental question: Is marriage stable because of high bridewealth costs, or can a society afford to have a norm of high bridewealth only if it has a stable form of marriage? Keesing's own theories concerning divorce focus on rules of descent. In general, societies with matrilineal descent rules have high divorce rates, whereas patrilineal societies have low rates. In matrilineal societies, a woman retains the rights to her children and so is more likely to divorce her husband if he misbehaves. Among the matrilineal Hopi and Zuni, for example, a woman has only to put a man's belongings outside her house door to secure a divorce. The husband then returns to his mother's household, and the wife and children remain in the wife's household (Garbarino 1988).

Marriages in matrilineal descent groups tend to be less enduring than those in patrilineal groups because of the clash of interests (or corporate rights) over children. When a woman's primary interests remain with her lineage at birth and the people of her descent group have control over her and her children, her bond to her husband and his lineage tends to be fragile and impermanent (Keesing 1975). In contrast, in patrilineal societies, the wife has been fully incorporated into the husband's lineage. This tends to solidify patrilineal rights over children, leading to more durable marital ties.

Gender

Gender is an extremely important element of social structure in tribal societies. Cross-cultural ethnographic research on tribal societies has contributed to a better understanding of male-female relations. Anthropologists are interested in the interrelationships among gender roles, subsistence practices, female status, patriarchy, and sexism in tribal societies.

Gender and Enculturation: Margaret Mead's Study

Although nineteenth-century anthropologists addressed the question of gender roles, their conclusions were largely speculative and were not based on firsthand ethnographic research. In the twentieth century, anthropologists went into the field to collect information concerning the roles of males and females. The first landmark ethnographic study of gender roles was carried out by Margaret Mead and involved three New Guinea societies: the Arapesh, the Mundugumor, and the Tchambuli. Mead's study was published in 1935 and was titled *Sex and Temperament in Three Primitive Societies*.

Mead described these three tribes as having totally different types of gender roles. Among the Arapesh, males and females had similar attitudes and behavior. Mead described both sexes as unaggressive, cooperative, passive, and sensitive to the needs of others. Based on U.S. standards of the time, Mead described the Arapesh as feminine. In contrast, Mead described Mundugumor males and females as aggressive, selfish, insensitive, and uncooperative, much like the U.S. stereotype of masculinity. The Tchambuli, according to Mead, represented a complete reversal of U.S. conceptions of gender roles. Tchambuli females were dominant politically and economically, whereas males were submissive, emotionally dependent, and less responsible. Females were the breadwinners and the political leaders; they also engaged in warfare. Males stayed near the domestic camp and cared for the children. One of their primary activities was artistic work such as dancing, painting, and jewelry making. Hence, by U.S. standards, Tchambuli women were masculine, and Tchambuli men were feminine.

Mead concluded that societies can both minimize and exaggerate social and cultural differences between males and females. She argued that gender differences are extremely variable from society to society. Mead's study challenged the status quo in U.S. society regarding gender-role stereotypes. It also appealed strongly to the emerging feminist movement because it asserted that culture, rather than biology, determines (and limits) gender roles. Tchambuli women became an important symbol for the feminist movement in the United States during the 1960s.

Mead's Study Reappraised

After restudying the Tchambuli (who actually call themselves the Chambri) during the 1970s, anthropologist Deborah Gewertz (1981) concluded that Mead's description of the reversal of gender roles was not a completely accurate hypothesis. Although Gewertz concludes that Mead was essentially valid in her descriptions and observations, she did not stay long enough

to see what was happening to the Chambri. According to Gewertz, Mead had viewed the Chambri at a time when they were going through a unique transition. For example, in the 1930s, the Chambri had been driven from their islands by an enemy tribe. All their physical structures and artwork had been burned. Consequently, the Chambri men were engaged full-time near the domestic camps in creating artwork and rebuilding at the time Mead conducted her study. Mead assumed that these were typical activities for males, when, in fact, they were atypical. After assessing her ethnographic data carefully, Gewertz concludes that the Chambri do not exhibit the complete reverse of traditional male and female gender roles that Mead had described. Gewertz found that the Chambri males allocate and control the distribution of goods and valuables and, hence, are dominant politically and economically, despite the fact that females produce most of the goods.

Gewertz's reevaluation of Chambri gender-role patterns challenges the hypothesis presented by Mead regarding the tremendous flexibility of gender roles in human societies. Although Gewertz notes that cultural values do influence gender roles, a complete reversal of the male and female roles was not evident in the Chambri case. Like many anthropologists of the era of the 1930s, Mead did not account for the complex regional histories that influenced gender roles in these New Guinea tribal societies.

Patriarchy Despite Mead's conclusions concerning gender roles among the Tchambuli, most modern anthropologists agree that a pattern of matriarchy, in which females regularly dominate males economically and politically, is not part of the archaeological, historical, and ethnographic record (Bamberger 1974; Friedl 1975; Ortner 1974, 1996; L. Stone 2010). (See "Critical Perspectives: Were There Matriarchal States?" pages 395–396.) With some exceptions, most tribal societies tend to be patriarchal. Anthropologists have offered many hypotheses to explain the prevalence of patriarchy.

Sociobiologists and evolutionary psychologists view patriarchy in tribal societies as a consequence of innate reproductive strategies, leading to enhanced reproductive fitness. In this view, males are unconsciously motivated to reproduce with as many females as possible to increase their chances of reproductive success. As we have seen, some tribal males have many more children than others. These reproductive strategies involve competition among males for females. According to this model, this male competition, in turn, leads to political conflict and increases in warfare. These factors produce the patterns of patrilocality, patrilineality, polygyny, and patriarchy in tribal societies (Van den Berghe and Barash 1977; Chagnon and Hames 1979; Chagnon 2000). Another biologically based view suggested by Steven Goldberg is that males are always dominant in society because male hormones cause them to compete more strongly than women for high status and dominance (1993).

Instead of referring to innate biological drives, cultural materialists such as William Divale and Marvin Harris (1976) maintained that patriarchy and gender hierarchy are caused by the scarcity of resources and recurring warfare in tribal societies. In general, when material resources are scarce, especially in horticultural societies, warfare between competitive tribes is prevalent. Because most warriors are male, both the status and the power of males in these societies become intensified. For these reasons, a male-supremacy complex develops. The Divale and Harris study was subject to extensive criticism based on methodological flaws and inadequate data (Hirschfeld et al. 1978). However, a cross-cultural study using the Human Relations Area Files indicates that the intensification of warfare is strongly associated with the decline of female status (Khalturina and Khorotayev 2006). This study found that societies that emphasize socialization for male aggression and an ideology of male toughness and superiority results in a higher frequency of wife beating and a higher level of separation between genders. In addition, confirming the earlier research discussed earlier, this cross-cultural analysis found that polygyny results from extensive warfare and increased male mortality, which decreases female power and enhances patriarchy. The relationship among tribal warfare, polygyny, and the development of patriarchal societies is a potential research project for future anthropologists.

Patriarchy and Sexism in Tribal Societies Other anthropologists emphasize that although biological or material considerations may contribute to male domination, the cultural values used to define *female* are extremely important in the maintenance of tribal patriarchies. In other words, in many tribal societies, female roles have much less prestige than male roles. Many tribal societies adhere to mythologies, beliefs, and ideologies that justify male domination and female subordination. These mythologies, beliefs, and ideologies reinforce **sexism**—prejudice and discrimination against people based on their sex. Many patrilineal horticultural societies of New Guinea, for example, separate females from males during menstruation because they believe that menstruating females are unclean and will harm the community. Menstrual blood was often associated with witchcraft or the production of harmful potions; therefore, regular contacts with women were prohibited. Women were often thought to be radically different physically and psychologically from males, and their bodily fluids and essences were dangerous and evil (Lindenbaum 1972). These male anxieties, mythical beliefs, and prejudices frequently led to discriminatory practices against females. For example, most tribes in New Guinea have rules of residence that separate husbands and wives

into different houses, and young boys are taken from their mothers and segregated into men's houses.

In many of these tribal societies, women are excluded from political and sacred ritual activities, as well as from military combat. This limitation results in the cultural definition of males as the primary gender that ensures the survival of the society. Because of these views, women in many of these tribal societies are often subjected to social subordination, sexual segregation, excessive domination, and systematic physical abuse (Lindenbaum 1972; Chagnon 1997). At times, they are deprived of material resources during pregnancy, denied the same access to food as males, and are physically mutilated. Sexist ideologies are often used to justify these practices.

Yet, there is variation among tribal societies. Based on ethnographic research among the Vanatinal tribal people of Papua New Guinea, Maria Lepowsky reports that there is very little ideology of male dominance and no prohibitions regarding contact with women who are menstruating (1993). Lepowsky argues that the women among the Vanatinal are respected and treated as equals with the men. Vanatinal women can gain prestige through trading and exchanging valuables. Nevertheless, these women are not allowed to hunt, fish, or make war. Vanatinal men control and retain power over the mobilization of warfare and threats of violence. Thus, Vanatinal society is not a perfectly gender-egalitarian society. Another factor that has played a role in understanding gender roles and taboos in Papua New Guinea is that, to some extent, the anthropologists overemphasized the male interpretations of these taboos against women without taking into consideration the voices of women. In some cases, the women viewed the men's semen just as polluting as the men considered their menstrual blood.

Gender, Subsistence, and Female Status A number of anthropologists propose that the status of women in tribal societies depends on their contributions to subsistence activities. As we have seen, both males and females are involved in horticultural production. Males usually clear the ground for the gardens, whereas women weed and harvest the crops. In cross-cultural surveys of tribal horticultural societies, women actually contribute more to cultivation activities in horticultural societies than do men (Martin and Voorhies 1975; Goody 1976). Nevertheless, patriarchy reigns in conjunction with a sexist ideology in most of these tribal groups. In some matrilineal horticultural societies, however, the status of females tends to be higher.

Female Status in Matrilineal Societies In matrilineally organized societies such as the Iroquois, Hopi, and Zuni of North America, women have considerable influence in economic and political decision making. Also, the mothers and sisters of the wives in matrilineages can often offer support in domestic disputes with males. In addition, rights to property—including land, technology, and livestock—are embodied in the matrilineages. In general, however, males in matrilineal societies hold the influential positions of political power and maintain control over economic resources. In most matrilineal societies, the mother's brother has political authority and economic control within the family. Thus, matrilineality does not translate into matriarchy.

The Iroquois: Women in a Matrilineal Society

The Iroquois offer a good example of the status of females in matrilineal societies. The families that occupied the Iroquois longhouses were related through matrilineages. The senior women, their daughters, the daughters' children, the brothers, and the unmarried sons built the longhouses. Although husbands lived in the longhouses, they were considered outsiders. The matrilineages of the longhouse maintained the garden plots and owned the tools in common. These matrilineages planted, weeded, and harvested the corn, beans, and squash. The Iroquois women processed, stored, and distributed all of the food and provisioned the men's war parties. The men were highly dependent on the food supplies of the women.

The elder matrons in these matrilineages had the power to appoint the sachem, a council leader of the Iroquois political system. A council of 50 sachems governed the five different tribes of the Iroquois confederacy. Often they appointed their younger sons to this position and would rule until their sons were of age. Women could also influence decisions about peace and warfare and determine whether prisoners of war should live or die (Brown 1970a).

Clearly, as the Iroquois case indicates, women influenced the political and economic dynamics in some matrilineal societies. In their cross-cultural survey, Martin and Voorhies (1975) found that the status of women is higher in horticultural societies that practice matrilineal descent. In many of these matrilineal societies, males developed political power only if they had strong support from the relatives of their wives. Nevertheless, these findings also indicate that in the matrilineal societies, males still exercise political authority and assume control over key economic resources. In these societies, women may be held in high regard, but they are still economically and politically subordinate to men.

Age

As mentioned above, all societies have *age grades*, groupings of people of the same age. Within an age grade, people learn specific norms and acquire cultural knowledge. In some tribal societies, age grades have become specialized as groupings that have many functions.

Age Sets

In certain tribal societies of East Africa, North America, Brazil, India, and New Guinea, specialized age groupings emerged as multifunctional institutions. In some tribal societies, age grades become much more formalized and institutionalized as age sets. **Age sets** are groups of people of about the same age who share specific rights, obligations, duties, and privileges within their community. Typically, people enter an age set when they are young and then progress through various life stages with other members of the set. The transition from one stage of life to the next within the age set is usually accompanied by a distinctive rite of passage.

Age Sets and Age Grades among the Tribal Pastoralists A number of tribal pastoralists of East Africa, such as the Karimojong, Masaai, Nuer, Pokot, Samburu, and Sebei, have specialized age-set and age-grade systems that structure social organization. The Sebei, for example, have eight age-set groups, each of which is divided into three subsets. The eight groups are given formal names, and the subsets have informal nicknames. Sebei males join an age set through initiation, in which they are circumcised and exposed to tribal secret lore and indoctrination.

The Sebei initiations are held approximately every six years and the initiation rituals extend over a period of six months. Those who are initiated together develop strong bonds. Newly initiated males enter the lowest level of this system, the junior warriors. As they grow older, they graduate into the next level, the senior warriors, while younger males enter the junior levels. Groups of males then progress from one level to the next throughout the course of their lifetimes (Goldschmidt 1986).

The Sebei age sets serve an important military function. The members of the age set are responsible for protecting livestock and for conducting raids against other camps. In addition, age sets are the primary basis of status in these societies. Among the most basic social rankings are junior and senior military men and junior and senior elders. All social interactions, political activities, and ceremonial events are influenced by the age-set system. The young males of other East African pastoralists, such as the Maasai and Nuer, go through similar painful initiation rites of passage at puberty that move them from the status of a child to that of a warrior adult male, and they live separately from other younger and older people (Evans-Pritchard 1951; Salzman 2004). The corporate units of age sets provide for permanent mutual obligations that continue through time. In the absence of a centralized government, these age sets play a vital role in maintaining social cohesion.

The Elderly Among tribal pastoralists and horticulturalists, older people make use of ownership or control of property to reinforce their status. Societies in which the elderly control extensive resources appear to show higher levels of deference toward the aged (Silverman and Maxwell 1983). The control of land, women, and livestock and their allocation among the younger generations are the primary means by which the older men (and sometimes older women, in matrilineal societies) exercise their power over the rest of society. In many cases, this dominance by the elderly leads to age stratification or inequalities.

The system in which older people exercise exceptional power is called **gerontocracy**—rule by elders (usually male) who control the material and reproductive resources of the community. In gerontocracies, elderly males tend to monopolize not only the property resources, but also the young women in the tribe. Access to human beings is the greatest source of wealth and power in these tribal societies. Additionally, older males benefit from the accumulation of bridewealth. Through these processes, older men tend to have more secure statuses and economic prerogatives. They retire from subsistence and economic activities and often assume political leadership in tribal affairs. In this capacity, they make important decisions regarding marriage ties, resource exchanges, and other issues.

Gerontocratic tribal societies continue to be prominent today. Among the ancient Israelites—once a pastoralist tribe—the elders controlled the disposition of property and marriages of their adult children, and the Bible mentions many examples of tribal patriarchs who were involved in polygynous marriages. In a modern pastoralist tribe—the Kirghiz of Afghanistan—the elderly enjoy extensive political power and status gained partially through the control of economic resources. In addition, the elders are thought to be wise, possessing extensive knowledge of history and local ecological conditions, as well as medical and veterinary skills crucial to the group's survival (Shahrani 1981). Thus, the possession of cultural knowledge may lead to the development of gerontocratic tendencies within tribal societies.

Social Structure in Chiefdoms

17.4 Discuss how status differences, the family, gender, and age are related in chiefdom societies.

In our earlier discussion of social structure, we introduced the concept of social stratification, the inequality among statuses within society. Chiefdom societies exhibit a great deal of stratification. They are divided into different **strata** (singular: stratum), groups of equivalent statuses based on ranked divisions in a society. Strata in chiefdom societies are not based solely on economic factors, but rather cut across society based on prestige, power, and religious beliefs and practices.

Rank and Sumptuary Rules

Chiefdom societies are **hierarchical societies** wherein some people have greater access than others to wealth, rank, status, authority, and power. The various families and descent groups—households, lineages, and clans in chiefdoms—have a specific ascribed rank in the society and are accorded certain rights, privileges, and obligations

based on that rank. Social interaction between lower and higher strata is governed by **sumptuary rules** or cultural norms and practices used to differentiate the higher-status groups from the rest of society. In general, the higher the status and rank, the more ornate the jewelry, costumes, and decorative symbols. For example, among the Natchez, Native Americans of the Mississippi region, the upper-ranking members were tattooed all over their bodies, whereas lower-ranking people were only partially tattooed (Schildkrout and Kaeppler 2004).

Some of the Pacific chiefdoms had sumptuary rules requiring that a special orator chief speak to the public instead of the paramount chief. The highest paramount chiefs spoke a noble language with an archaic vocabulary containing words that commoners could not use with one another. Other sumptuary rules involved taboos against touching or eating with higher-ranking people. Sumptuary rules also set standards regarding dress, marriage, exchanges, and other cultural practices. In many of the chiefdoms, social inferiors had to prostrate themselves and demonstrate other signs of deference in the presence of their "social superiors." Symbols of inequality and hierarchy were thoroughly ingrained in most of these societies.

A Case Study: Polynesia and Stratified Descent Groups The ethnohistoric data on the Polynesian islands contain some of the most detailed descriptions of social stratification within chiefdom societies. The ideal basis of social organization was the conical clan (see Figure 17.7), an extensive descent group having a common ancestor who was usually traced through a patrilineal line (Kirchoff 1955; Sahlins 1968; Goldman 1970). Rank and lineage were determined by a person's kinship distance to the founding ancestor, as illustrated in Figure 17.7. The closer a person was to the highest-ranking senior male in a direct line of descent to the ancestor, the higher his or her rank and status were. In fact, as Marshall Sahlins (1985) suggested, the Hawaiians did not trace *descent*, but rather *ascent* toward a connection with an ancient ruling line.

Although Polynesian societies reflected a patrilineal bias, most had ambilineal descent groups (Goodenough 1955; Firth 1957). Senior males headed local descent groups in the villages. These local groups were ranked in relation to larger, senior groups that were embedded in the conical clan. Because of ambilateral rules, people born into certain groups had the option of affiliating with either their paternal or their maternal linkages in choosing their rank and status. In general, beyond this genealogical reckoning, these chiefdom societies offered little in the way of upward social mobility for achieved statuses.

Marriage

As in tribal societies, most marriages in chiefdoms were carefully arranged affairs, sometimes involving cousin

Figure 17.7 Model of a conical clan

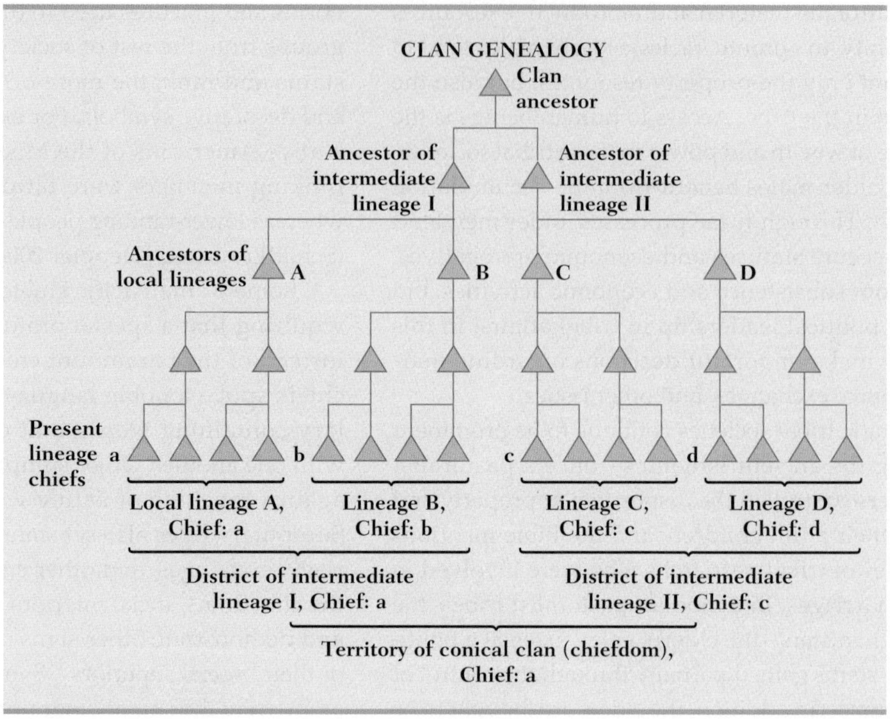

marriages from different descent groups. People who married outside of their descent group (exogamy) usually married within their social stratum (endogamy). In some chiefdom societies, however, marriages were sometimes arranged between higher-strata males and females of lower strata (a *hypergynous* marriage). Anthropologist Jane Collier (1988) noted that women in chiefdom societies that emphasized hereditary rank tended to avoid low-ranking males and tried to secure marriages with men who possessed more economic and political prerogatives.

One chiefdom in North America illustrates a situation in which marriage provided a systematic form of social mobility for the entire society. The Natchez Indians of the Mississippi region were a matrilineal society divided into four strata: the Great Sun chief (the eldest son of the top-ranking lineage) and his brothers, the noble lineages, the honored lineages, and the inferior "stinkards." All members of the three upper strata had to marry down (*hypogamy*) to a stinkard. This resulted in a regular form of social mobility from generation to generation. The children of the upper three ranks took the status of their mother unless she was a stinkard.

If a woman of the Great Sun married a stinkard, their children became members of the upper stratum, the Great Sun. If a noble woman married a stinkard, their children became nobles. However, if a noble man married a stinkard, their children would drop to the stratum of the honored lineage. Through marriage, all stinkard children moved up in the status hierarchy.

Although this system allowed for a degree of mobility, it required the perpetuation of the stinkard stratum so that members of the upper strata would have marriage partners. One way the stinkard stratum was maintained was through marriage between two stinkards; their children remained in the inferior stratum. In addition, the stinkard category was continually replenished with people captured in warfare.

Endogamy Marriages in chiefdom societies were both exogamous and endogamous. Although marriages might be exogamous among descent groupings, the spouses were usually from the same stratum (endogamy). These endogamous marriages were carefully arranged so as to maintain genealogically appropriate kinship bonds and descent relations in the top-ranking descent group. Frequently, this involved cousin marriage among descent groups of the same stratum. Among Hawaiian chiefs, rules of endogamy actually resulted in sibling marriages, sometimes referred to as royal-incest marriage. One anthropologist categorized these sibling marriages as attempts to create alliances between chiefly households among the various Hawaiian Islands (Valeri 1985).

Polygyny Many of the ruling families in chiefdom societies practiced polygyny. Among the Tsimshian of the Northwest Coast, chiefs could have as many as 20 wives, usually women from the high-ranking lineages of other groups. Lesser chiefs would marry several wives from lower-ranking lineages. In some cases, a Tsimshian woman from a lower-ranking lineage could marry up through the political strategies of her father. For example, a father might arrange a marriage between a high-ranking chief and his daughter. All these polygynous marriages were accompanied by exchanges of goods that passed to the top of the chiefly hierarchy, resulting in accumulations of surplus resources and wives (Rosman and Rubel 1986). Among the Trobriand Islanders, male chiefs traditionally had as many as 60 wives drawn from different lineages. Many chiefdom societies exhibited high rates of polygyny in the high-ranking strata.

General Social Principles in Chiefdoms

Among chiefdom societies, the typical family form was the extended family, with three generations living in a single household. In the Pacific region, for example, the basic domestic unit was usually a household made up of three generations; in some cases, two or three brothers with their offspring were permanent residents of the household. The households in a specific area of a village were usually part of one lineage. The extended family household was usually the basic economic unit for subsistence production and consumption in chiefdom societies.

Postmarital residence varied among chiefdoms. Patrilocal, matrilocal, and ambilocal types of residence rules were found in different areas. The ambilocal rule, found in many chiefdoms of the Pacific, enabled people to trace descent to ancestors (male or female) who had the highest rank in the society. This flexibility enabled some individuals to attain access to property, privileges, and authority in spite of the inherent restrictions on status mobility in chiefdom societies (Goodenough 1956).

Gender

Typically, gender relations were highly unequal in chiefdom societies, with males exercising economic and political dominance over females. Bridewealth payments, along with arranged marriages, enabled men to claim rights to the labor of children and women. This practice was particularly significant among the highest-status descent groups. A woman's chances of success depended entirely on the rank of her siblings and parents. Higher-ranking males who wanted to control and manage their marital relations, labor, and potential offspring frequently married women with low-ranking brothers.

If a woman was fortunate enough to be born or marry into a high-ranking descent group, her ascribed or achieved status was secured. Anthropologist Laura Klein described how some high-ranking women among the Tsimshian Indians were able to maintain very high status in their society (1980). According to Sahlins (1985), some wives of high-ranking chiefs in traditional Hawaiian society married as many as 40 males (a type of royal polyandry) to maintain their high status. Thus, the women of the ruling stratum had a higher status than men or women from other strata. In an interesting discussion of the different chiefdoms that existed in the area of Appalachia in North America, archaeologists Lynne Sullivan and Christopher Rodning indicate that

there was a complementary relationship between males and females, which involved different pathways to power among the ruling elite (2001). The males ruled over the towns and villages, whereas the women ruled over the kinship groupings. These distinctions were demonstrated in

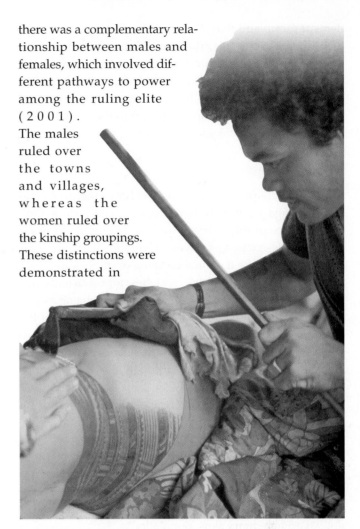

Tattooing in the Pacific Islands was used frequently to symbolize status relationships

the burials of the chiefly elite. The males were buried in the public architecture, while females were buried in the residential architecture.

Thus, among the ruling chiefly elite, women in chiefdoms had an important high status, but in general, men controlled and dominated economically and politically in chiefdom societies.

Age

In many chiefdom societies, senior males had much more authority, rank, and prestige than other people. As in some tribal societies, this form of inequality produced gerontocratic systems. As people—especially in the higher-ranking descent groups—aged, they received more in the way of status, privileges, and deference from younger people. Because senior males controlled production, marriages, labor, and other economic activities, they became the dominant political authorities. Senior males also possessed special knowledge and controlled sacred rituals, reinforcing their authority. One of their major responsibilities was to perpetuate the beliefs that rank depended on a person's descent group and that status was hereditary. As in some of the tribal societies, the combination of patriarchy and gerontocracy resulted in cultural hegemony—the imposition of norms, practices, beliefs, and values that reinforced the interests of the upper stratum. This cultural hegemony will become more apparent in the discussion of law and religion in chiefdom societies.

Slavery

In the next chapter, we will discuss how chiefdoms frequently engaged in systematic, organized warfare. One consequence of this warfare was the taking of captives, who were designated as slaves. Slavery in chiefdoms generally did not have the same meaning or implications that it did in more complex state societies, and it usually did not involve the actual ownership of a human being as private property. In this sense, it was very different from the plantation slavery that developed later in the Americas. With some exceptions, most of the slaves in chiefdoms were absorbed into kin groups through marriage or adoption and performed essentially the same type of labor that most other people did. Nevertheless, in contrast to the more egalitarian band and tribal societies, chiefdom societies did show the beginnings of a slave stratum.

We have already mentioned an example of a chiefdom slave system in our discussion of the Natchez. Recall, however, that upper-ranking members were obliged to marry members of the stinkard stratum; thus, the Natchez did not have a hereditary slave population.

One exception to these generalizations involves some of the Northwest Coast American Indians, who maintained a hereditary slave system. Because marrying a slave was considered debasing, slavery became an inherited status (Kehoe 1995). The children of slaves automatically became slaves, producing a permanent slave stratum. These slaves—most of them war captives—were excluded from ceremonies and on some occasions were killed in human sacrifices. In addition, they were sometimes exchanged, resulting in a kind of commercial traffic of humans. Even in this system, however, slaves who had been captured in warfare could be ransomed by their kinfolk or could purchase their own freedom (Garbarino 1988).

Social Structure in Agricultural States

17.5 Discuss the family, kinship, marriage, gender, and age patterns in agricultural states.

Because agricultural states were more complex and more highly organized than prestate societies, they could not rely solely on kinship for recruitment to different status positions. Land ownership and occupation became more important than kinship in organizing society. In centralized agricultural societies, the state itself replaced kin groups as the major integrating principle in society.

Kinship and Status

Nevertheless, as in all societies, family and kinship remained an important part of social organization. In elite and royal families, kinship was the basic determination of status. Royal incest in brother-sister marriages by both Egyptian and Incan royalty shows the importance of kinship as a distinctive means of maintaining status in agricultural societies. The typical means of achieving the highest statuses was through family patrimony, or the inheritance of status. Access to the highest ranks was generally closed to those who did not have the proper genealogical relationships with the elite or the nobility.

The Extended Family The extended family was the predominant family form in both urban and rural areas in most agricultural states. Family ties remained critical to most peasants; typically, the members of the peasant extended family held land in common and cooperated in farm labor. To some extent, intensive agricultural production required the presence of a large extended family to provide the necessary labor to plant, cultivate, and harvest crops (Wolf 1966; L. Stone 2005). Large domestic groups had to pool their resources and labor to maintain economic production. To encourage cooperation, generalized reciprocal economic exchanges of foodstuffs, goods, and labor were common in these families.

Other Kinship Principles In a cross-cultural survey of 53 agricultural civilizations, Kay Martin and Barbara Voorhies (1975) found that 45 percent had patrilineal kin groupings, another 45 percent had bilateral groupings, and 9 percent had matrilineal groupings. In some Southeast Asian societies, such as Myanmar (Burma), Thailand, and Cambodia, bilateral descent existed along with kindred groupings. In some circumstances, these kindreds provided domestic labor for agricultural production through reciprocal labor exchanges. Families connected through kindreds would regularly exchange labor for the transplanting or harvesting of rice crops.

Family Structure among the Nayar One matrilineal society, the Nayar in the state of Kerala in southern India, had unusual marriage practices that produced a remarkably different type of family structure. They practiced a visiting ritualized mating system called the *sambandham* (joining together) (Gough 1961; L. Stone 2005). Once every ten years or so, the Nayar would hold this ceremony to "marry" females of one matrilineage to males of another matrilineage. At the ceremony, the male would tie a gold ornament around the neck of his ritual bride. After seclusion for three days, sexual intercourse might or might not take place, depending on the girl's age. After this, the couple would take a ritual bath to purify themselves of the pollution of this cohabitation. After the ceremony, the male had no rights regarding the female. Later, the female could enter a number of marriages with males of her same caste or usually a higher caste, a marriage practice called *hypergamy*, and have children. Women could not marry men of a lower caste. The Nayar system was unusual because none of the husbands resided with his wife. A husband would visit his wife at night, but did not remain in the household. The matrilineal group assumed the rights over her and her children. Because the females could have more than one spouse, the society was polyandrous; however, because the males could also have more than one spouse, the Nayar were also polygynous. Thus, the household family unit consisted of brothers and sisters, a woman's daughters and granddaughters, and their children. The bride and her children were obliged to perform a ceremony at the death of her "ritual" husband.

From the Western viewpoint, the Nayar marital arrangement might not seem like a family because it does not tie two families together into joint bonds of kinship or even husband-wife bonds. In addition, males had very little biological connection to their children. This system, however, was a response to historical circumstances in southern India. Traditionally, most Nayar males joined the military. In addition, lands owned by the matrilineal groups were worked by lower-caste, landless peasants. Children did not work on their family land. Therefore, young Nayar males had no responsibilities to the matrilineal group and were free to become full-time warriors (L. Stone 2010). Recent ethnographic research on the Nayar has demonstrated that there is little remaining of this unusual marriage system and that the matrilineal system has become increasingly patrilineal, with a shift to a nuclear family and husband-wife monogamy (Menon 1996).

Marriage

Marriage practices, all of which have economic and political implications, reveal the significance of social ties in agricultural societies. Because marriage had far-reaching outcomes, the selection of marital partners was considered too important to be left to young people. Marriages were usually arranged by parents, sometimes with the aid of brokers, who assessed alliances between extended families with respect to land, wealth, or political connections. This was especially the case among the political elite, such as in Roman society (L. Stone 2005). In some cases (for example, China), arranged marriages were contracted when the children were young (see Chapter 11). As in chiefdom societies, elite marriages were frequently endogamous. Peasants, however, generally married outside their extended families and larger kin groups.

Dowry and Bridewealth   Most agricultural states practiced some form of marital exchange involving land, com-

modities, or foodstuffs. In Asia and some parts of Europe, the most common type of exchange was the **dowry**—goods and wealth paid by the bride's family to the groom's family. In this sense, the dowry appears to be the reverse of bridewealth, in which the groom's family exchanges wealth for the bride. The dowry was used as a social and economic exchange between families to arrange a marriage contract. Upon marriage, the bride in an Indian, European, or Chinese family was expected to bring material goods into her marriage.

In a cross-cultural comparison, Jack Goody (1976) found that bridewealth occurs more frequently in horticultural societies, whereas the dowry is found in complex agricultural societies. In Europe and Asia, intensive agriculture was associated with the use of plows and draft animals, high population densities, and a scarcity of land. Goody hypothesized that one result of the dowry system was to consolidate property in the hands of elite groups. As commercial and bureaucratic families expanded their wealth and increased their status, these groups began to move from bridewealth to dowry. As bridewealth was a means of circulating wealth among families by creating alliances between the groom's and bride's families, the dowry served to concentrate property and wealth within the patrilineal line of families. Elites in India, China, and Greece relied on this form of marital exchange.

Although dowry exchanges were most significant in the upper socioeconomic groups, in which wealth and status were of central significance, they were also supposed to be customary among the peasantry. Bridewealth was not unknown in peasant society. In both northern and southern India, bridewealth became more common among the lower socioeconomic classes. In the poorest families, there was little to be inherited anyway, and the actual exchanges were mainly for the costs of the wedding feast and for simple household furnishings.

Polygyny   In contrast to prestate societies, polygyny was rare in agricultural states, except among the elite. In some cases, the rulers of these state societies in Asia, the Middle East, Europe, and elsewhere had large harems, in which many different women were attached to one ruler. The royal households of many agricultural states had hundreds or even thousands of women at the disposal of the rulers. China, Japan, Korea, Nepalese, Vietnam, Thailand, Indonesia, Persia, Mongol Central Asia, Mughal India, Ottoman Turkey, Mayan and Aztec regimes, and the biblical kingdoms among others had royal families with many wives and concubines (Tambiah 1976; Bennett 1983). Many of the European kings had extensive polygynous households, even after Christianity had developed norms against such forms of marriage (Stone 2005). Elite males who were wealthy were able to keep mistresses or concubines in addition to their wives. For example, many elite Chinese males kept concubines or secondary wives, despite laws against this practice.

Other agricultural states had similar polygynous practices for individuals in high-ranking socioeconomic positions. In addition, many of the marriages were endogamous, that is, within the same high-caste or upper-class category, as were those of the chiefdom societies discussed earlier.

For most of the populace, however, monogamy was the primary form of marriage. Economist Ester Boserup (1970) argued that the general absence of polygyny in societies with plow agriculture is due to the lack of land that could be accumulated by adding wives to one's family. Similarly, Goody (1976) hypothesized that in agricultural societies where land is a scarce commodity, peasants could not afford the luxury of polygyny. Obviously, wealth and status influenced the marriage patterns found in agricultural civilizations.

Divorce
For the most part, divorce was rare in agricultural civilizations. The corporate nature of the extended family and the need for cooperative agricultural labor among family members usually led to normative constraints against divorce. In addition, marriage was the most important vehicle for the transfer of property and served as the basis for alliances between families and kin groups. Thus, families tended to stay together, and enormous moral, political, and social weight was attached to the marriage bond. In India, marriage was considered sacred, and therefore divorces were not legally permitted. Similar norms were evident in the feudal societies of Europe, where Christianity reinforced the sanctity of the family and the stability of marriage.

For women, however, marriage offered the only respectable career or means of subsistence. Most women faced destitution if a marriage was terminated. Thus, few women wanted to dissolve a marriage, regardless of the internal conflicts or problems. This pattern reflects the unequal status of males and females.

Gender, Subsistence, and Status
The transition to intensive agriculture affected the subsistence roles of both males and females. Martin and Voorhies (1975) noted that in agricultural systems, the amount of labor that women contributed to food production declined. For example, the adoption of plow agriculture greatly diminished the need for weeding, a task that was primarily taken care of by women. They hypothesized that as women's role in agriculture decreased, their social status decreased accordingly. Thus, agricultural civilizations were even more patriarchal than were tribes or chiefdoms. Women were viewed as useless in the agricultural economy, and for the most part, they were confined to cooking, raising children, and caring for the domestic animals. They had little contact outside their immediate families.

Martin and Voorhies (1975) emphasized that a definite distinction arose in agricultural states between men's and women's roles. Women were restricted to *inside* (domestic) activities, whereas males were allowed to participate in *outside* (public) activities. In general, women were not allowed to own property, engage in politics, pursue education, or participate in any activity that would take them outside the domestic sphere. Since Martin and Voorhies did their research, a number of feminist anthropologists have questioned the simplistic dichotomy between the domestic and public realms for gender roles. In some cases, the domestic domain encompassed some of the activities of the public sphere and vice versa. However, they have agreed that this distinction has helped analyze gender in most agricultural societies (Lamphere 1997; Ortner 1996). Generally, most studies concur that the female role was restricted in many of these societies.

Female Seclusion
The highly restricted female role in many agriculture societies was reflected in a number of cultural practices. For example, China adopted the tradition of foot binding, which involved binding a young female child's feet so her feet would not grow. Although this practice was supposed to produce beautiful feet (in the view of Chinese males), it had the effect of immobilizing women. Although less of a handicap for upper-class females, who did not have to participate in the daily labor requirements of most women and were carried around by servants, foot binding was also practiced by the peasantry during various periods, which meant that peasant women had to work with considerable disabilities.

Similarly, many areas of the Near East, North Africa, and South Asia practiced *purdah*, a system that restricted women to the household. **Purdah** is a Persian word that is translated as "curtain" or "barrier." In this system, women had to obtain permission from their husbands to leave the house to visit families and friends. In some of these regions, a woman had to cover her face with a veil when in public (Beck and Keddie 1978; Fernea and Fernea 1979). Female seclusion was one of the ways in which males tried to control the paternity of the children that they were raising. Segregating females from males was a means of ensuring that wives would not become sexually involved with other men.

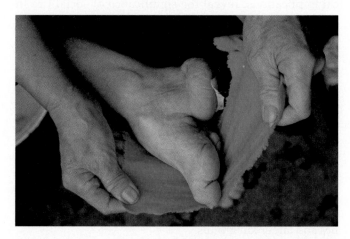

The binding of women's feet in traditional agricultural China led to results shown in this photo

Patriarchy and Sexism Sexist ideology developed in agricultural states as a means of reinforcing the seclusion of women. In many agricultural societies, females were viewed as inherently inferior and dependent on males. The so-called natural superiority of males was reinforced in most of the legal, moral, and religious traditions in agricultural states, including Confucianism, Islam, Hinduism, Judaism, and Christianity. In the Old Testament there are many references to women as considered the property of the husbands, equivalent to animals and other household property. In Leviticus 27:3–7, women are valued in currency (shekels) much less than males.

The New Testament also supported patriarchal attitudes toward women. In Ephesians (5:22–24), it states, "Wives, be subject to your husbands, as to the Lord. For the husband is the head of the wife as Christ is the head of the church. As the church is subject to Christ, so let wives also be subject in everything to their husbands."

Many passages from Islam's Qur'an endorsed patriarchal attitudes and cultural values (as we will see in Chapter 22), as did Hinduism, Buddhism, and other religions developing in the agricultural societies throughout the world. In many of these agricultural societies, males were viewed as more intelligent, stronger, and more emotionally mature. In addition, many of these societies viewed women as sexually dangerous; women caught having premarital or extramarital sex were punished severely. In some cases, they were executed by stoning, as mentioned in Leviticus in the Old Testament and in the Qur'an. In contrast, males were permitted to engage in extramarital affairs or have many wives or mistresses.

Variations in the Status of Women The role and status of women in agricultural civilizations varied by region. For example, in some areas where soil conditions were poor, both male and female peasants had to work together in the fields to produce for the household, which tended to create more gender equality. In most Southeast Asian countries, such as Thailand and Cambodia, both males and females worked together in rice cultivation. In some cases, land was divided equally among all children, regardless of gender, indicating that in these societies females had relative equality with males. Although in these countries women were mostly confined to the domestic sphere and to household tasks, they played an important role in decision making and financial matters within the rural communities (Keyes 1995; Van Esterik 1996; Winzeler 1996; Scupin 2006a).

Anthropologists have discovered other exceptions regarding the role and status of peasant women in public in some agricultural civilizations. In China, Mesoamerica, and West Africa, many women participated as sellers in the marketplaces, taking some of the surplus produce or crafts made in the villages. However, this activity was generally restricted to older women whose children were grown. In some cases, the role of a market woman did lead to higher status. Many of these women participated in the public sphere, but were still segregated from male political activities. Moreover, these women had to perform their domestic chores as well as their marketplace activities.

Women play an important role in markets in agricultural societies.

Critical Perspectives

Were There Matriarchal States?

Anthropologists have not found any substantive archaeological or ethnographic evidence for the existence of matriarchal societies. There are, of course, societies that have a matrilineal social organization, in which one traces descent through the mother's side of the family. But as we have discussed earlier, matriliny does not translate into a matriarchal society in which women would have economic and political dominance over males. Within societies organized by matrilineal descent, such as the Iroquois Indian peoples mentioned before, males tend to dominate in political and economic affairs. Women may have a more

The Greek goddess Artemis as expressed in this Roman copied sculpture of Diana of Versaille.

(*continued*)

active role in these areas, but patriarchy exists as the prevalent gender pattern in these matrilineal societies.

However, the belief that there were once matriarchal societies that were overcome by male-dominated, warlike societies has a long history in the West. For example, after examining Greek and Roman mythology, law, religion, and history, the German lawyer Johann Jacob Bachofen wrote an influential book called *Das Mutterrecht* (*The Mother-Right*), published in 1861. Bachofen suggested that matrilineal kinship combined with matriarchy was the first form of human evolutionary development. He reasoned that since no child could determine its paternity, kinship, descent, and inheritance could be recognized only through women. Bachofen argued that women dominated these early primitive societies both economically and politically. Anthropologist John MacLellan developed this same theme in his book *Primitive Marriage: An Inquiry into the Origin of the Form of Capture in Marriage Ceremonies* (1865). A number of other scenarios of this evolution from matriarchy to patriarchy were published in European books.

Using similar reasoning, Lewis Henry Morgan, an early American anthropologist (see Chapter 13), reinforced this Victorian view of ancient matriarchal societies. Based on his ethnographic study of Iroquois Indian society and other sources, Morgan argued in his famous book *Ancient Society* (1877) that there must have been an early stage of matriarchal society. He studied kinship terms from different areas of the world to substantiate this view. Morgan suggested that a patriarchal stage of evolution replaced an earlier form of matriarchy as more advanced forms of agriculture developed. In his understanding, matriarchal societies were based on the communal ownership of property and polyandry (females married to two or more males). He argued that patriarchy evolved along with the concept of private property and ownership. Morgan suggested that males invented the institution of monogamy in order to ensure the paternity of their children. This enabled them to pass their private property on to their male heirs.

Europeans Karl Marx and Friedrich Engels became enthusiastic about Morgan's ideas in *Ancient Society*. Engels wrote about the connection between the evolution of private property and the emergence of patriarchal societies in his book *The Origin of the Family, Private Property, and the State* in 1884. This book, along with other writings by Marx and Engels, provided the intellectual foundation of the socialist and communist movement in the nineteenth and twentieth centuries. Following Morgan, Marx and Engels believed that revolutionary change in the economy, caused by the evolution of advanced forms of agriculture, resulted in men taking control of the politics from women. As men gained control over herd animals and farmland, they also instituted the marriage pattern of monogamy, in which females pledged lifetime fidelity to one man. This institution assured males of the paternity of their own children. Engels referred to this commitment as "the world historical defeat of the female sex." He and Marx argued that the institution of the patriarchal family and monogamy became the basis for treating females as property and commodities, demonstrated in existing rituals such as the "giving away of the bride by the father to the groom" in Western wedding ceremonies. Women became servants of men and provided sustenance to support male authority and wealth accumulation in capitalist societies. Marx and Engels believed that Victorian sexist attitudes and male chauvinism had been developed to assure male authority and paternity. They believed that the global transformation from matrilineal and matriarchal societies into patrilineal and patriarchal societies established one of the integral components resulting in exploitative capitalist societies.

Other important thinkers of the twentieth century, such as Sigmund Freud (see Chapter 11), transmitted these ideas regarding early matriarchal societies. One European archaeologist, the late Maria Gimbutas, proposed that early "matristic" societies were once the predominant form of society in ancient Europe (1982, 1991). She argued that in the period she calls "Old

Europe" (between 6500 and 3500 B.C.), peaceful, sedentary villages existed where men and women formed equal partnerships with one another. Gimbutas drew on a number of types of artifacts to make her case. Based on art, architecture, figurines, ceramic pottery, marble, gold, grave goods, and other artifacts, she suggested that the culture of "Old Europe" was centered on the belief in a Great Mother Goddess and other goddesses. According to Gimbutas, a "queen-priestess" ruled and maintained control over this matrifocused religious tradition. She found no evidence of weapons or warfare from that time period, challenging the assumption that warfare is endemic and universal in human societies. In addition, Gimbutas argued that these societies were completely egalitarian, with no classes, castes, or slaves and, of course, no male rulers.

According to Gimbutas, "Old Europe" was invaded by tribal horse-riding pastoralists known as the Kurgan by 4400 B.C. These Kurgan pastoralists from the Eurasiatic steppes, who were male dominated, were associated with the earliest forms of Indo-European languages, and developed religious traditions and mythologies that reflected a warrior cult. They maintained a pantheon of male gods representing the sun, stars, thunder, and lightning, and they were associated with warrior-like artifacts such as daggers and axes. Eventually, the Kurgan introduced iron plows that were used to cultivate the land. This technological innovation altered forever the relationship between males and females in European society. Males with plows and draft animals supplanted the female-oriented forms of cultivation. As the Kurgan society replaced the "Old Europe," women were relegated to the domestic aspect of subsistence activities. According to Gimbutas, the mythical and ideological culture perpetuated by the Kurgans continued until the beginnings of Christianity in Europe and beyond.

Archaeologist Lynn Meskell (1995) has criticized the picture of Old Europe and the Kurgan culture presented by Maria Gimbutas. Meskell notes that since the nineteenth century, there has been a recurrent interest in the notion of original, matriarchal Mother Goddess societies. This view has been perpetuated in some of the ecofeminist and "New Age" religious literature. Meskell argues that these New Age feminists utilize Gimbutas to ground their movement in a utopian vision of the past. She suggests that these Mother Goddess "gynocentric" theories of prehistory serve as vehicles for attempting to overturn patriarchal institutions in today's societies. However, Meskell suggests that these gynocentric views are based on inadequate scholarship and actually damage the positive aspects of gender research in anthropology. She and many other archaeologists note that Gimbutas neglected a tremendous amount of data and artifacts that would demonstrate the fallibility of her thesis. Numerous artifacts such as artwork indicating the prevalence of male deity figurines were dismissed in Gimbutas's data collection. Artifacts indicating warfare, human sacrifice, and fortifications are abundant throughout the archaeological record dated within Gimbutas's Old Europe period. And the view of Kurgan patriarchal domination of this once-peaceful matristic society is too simplistic to explain the complexities of European archaeology. Meskell concludes that the belief that there were distinctive stages of matriarchal and patriarchal societies is a remnant of the Victorian past. She argues that these simplistic views do not do justice to interpretations in archaeology

or feminist anthropological and gender studies in the twenty-first century.

Of course, there were agricultural societies that worshipped female goddesses and maintained mythologies about matriarchal societies. In fact, there were agricultural societies that had females who held important leadership and political roles, such as the famed Cleopatra. Yet, the evidence from archaeology and ethnography suggests that female political supremacy and domination over the economy did not exist. Despite Cleopatra's political authority, a male elite clearly controlled the economy and politics in ancient Egypt.

As we have seen in this chapter, the status of women in most of the agricultural societies in the past, including the goddess-worshipping ones, was very low. Both males and females have used mythologies and beliefs about early matriarchies throughout history. Nineteenth-century males used these beliefs to justify the status and authority of what they believed to be more evolved and advanced "patriarchal" institutions. Today, some women in the ecofeminist and New Age movements use these myths to perpetuate their vision of a utopian society. Many contemporary anthropologists, both male and female, argue that the terms *patriarchy* and *matriarchy* are too limited as dichotomies to assess the position of women in many societies of the world. For example, in a recent ethnography, *Women at the Center: Life in a Modern Matriarchy* (2002), based on 18 years

of study in Minangkabau, Indonesia, anthropologist Peggy Reeves Sanday challenges the framework and stereotype of many Western peoples who believe that the religion of Islam consistently subordinates women with its patriarchal traditions. She finds that in Indonesia, the cultural beliefs about women have always been relatively egalitarian and that these beliefs have resisted any attempt at subordinating women in this society. Anthropologists are working all over the world to refine their approach to gender issues and are investigating various global changes influencing gender change. In addition, one of the major goals of anthropology is to enhance and improve the rights of women and men throughout the world (see Chapter 25). But to do so, we must have an accurate assessment of what the archaeological and ethnographic records tell us. Without this assessment, we can neither further our knowledge of humanity nor aid in the improvement of the human condition.

Points to Ponder

1. What kind of data would be needed to infer a true matriarchal society in the past?

2. What are the strengths and weaknesses of the belief in an early matriarchal society?

3. Could there ever be a truly matriarchal society? If so, how could one develop?

4. What has this Critical Perspectives box taught you about analyzing anthropological data?

Social Stratification in Agricultural States

17.6 Discuss the type of stratification characteristic of agricultural states.

As previously mentioned, agricultural civilizations were highly stratified, and social mobility was generally restricted to people with elite family or kinship backgrounds. Thus, sometimes anthropologists classify these societies as **closed societies**, in that social status was generally *ascribed*, rather than *achieved*. For example, in traditional Chinese society, people born outside the emperor's family had two paths to upward mobility. One route was

to be born into the gentry—the landowning class that made up about 2 percent of Chinese families. The second route was to become a mandarin—a Chinese bureaucrat and scholar—by becoming a student and passing rigorous examinations based on classical Confucian texts. Although in theory this option existed for all males, in fact it was restricted to families or clans that could afford to spend resources for educating a son (DeVoe 2006).

The Caste System

India and some areas connected with Hindu culture, such as Nepal, developed a much more restrictive form of social inequality known as the caste system. A **caste** is an endogamous social grouping into which a person is born and in which the person remains throughout his or her lifetime. Thus, an individual's status in a caste system is ascribed, and movement into a different caste is impossible. The Indian caste system evolved from four basic categories, or *varnas*, that were ranked in order from Brahmans (priests) to Ksaitryas (warriors) to Vaisyas (merchants) to Sudras (laborers). Hence, the caste into which a person was born determined that person's occupation. In addition, people were required to marry within their caste. Although contact among members of different castes was generally discouraged, the castes were interrelated through various mutual economic exchanges and obligations known as the *jajmani* system. We discuss how the process of globalization is influencing the caste structure found in India and elsewhere in Chapter 22. However, the process of globalization is influencing the caste structure in India and elsewhere.

Slavery   Another form of social inequality and ascribed status was slavery. Slavery tends to increase as a society increases its productive technology, as trade expands, and as states become more centrally organized (Goody 1980; Van den Berghe 1981). For example, the Mediterranean empires of the Greeks, Romans, Arabs, and Turks used vast numbers of slaves in galleys, monument construction, irrigation works, plantation agriculture, and major public works projects.

Slave systems differed from one society to another. The Greeks and Romans reduced the status of the slave to a subhuman "thing" that was considered an instrument or tool, differing from inanimate tools only by the faculty of speech (Worsley 1984). Indigenous African kingdoms practiced large-scale slavery in which nobles owned hundreds of slaves (Goody 1980). Most of these slaves worked on plantations or in households, although some became advisors to, and administrators for, nobles. While African slavery involved the capture and sale of human beings, eventually the slaves could be incorporated into the kinship groups.

In a comprehensive review of indigenous Asian and African slavery, anthropologist James Watson (1980) referred to *open* and *closed* forms of slavery. The indigenous African form of slavery was open in that slaves could be incorporated into domestic kinship groups and even become upwardly mobile. In contrast, the slave systems of China, India, Greece, and Rome were closed, with no opportunities for upward mobility or incorporation into kinship groups. The two different types of slavery were correlated with specific demographic conditions and political economies. In societies such as those in Africa or Thailand, where land was relatively abundant and less populated, more open forms of slavery developed (Goody 1971; Turton 1980). In these societies, the key to power and authority was control over people, rather than land. In political economies such as Greece, Rome, China, and India, where land was scarce and populations much more dense, closed forms of slavery emerged. The key to power and wealth in these societies was control over land and labor.

Social Structure in Industrial and Postindustrial States

17.7 **Discuss the social structure, family, marriage, gender, and age patterns in industrial and postindustrial societies.**

The impact of industrialization on kinship, family, gender, aging, and social status has been just as dramatic as its impact on demography, technology, and economic conditions.

Kinship

Kinship is less important in industrialized states than in preindustrial societies. New structures and organizations perform many of the functions associated with kinship in preindustrial societies. For example, occupational and economic factors in most cases replace kinship as the primary basis of social status; a person no longer has to be part of an aristocratic or elite family to have access to wealth and political power. Generally, as states industrialized, newly emerging middle-class families began to experience upward economic and social mobility, and economic performance, merit, and personal achievement, rather than *ascribed* kinship relationships or birthright, became the primary basis of social status.

Of course, kinship and family background still have a definite influence on social mobility. Families with wealth, political power, and high social status can ensure that their children will have the best education. In addition, *nepotism*, favoritism for their own kin in small-scale businesses and other enterprises, including the political system in industrial and postindustrial societies, still plays an important role. For example, members of the Roosevelt, Kennedy, and Bush families retain their roles in politics and positions of authority in U.S. society. These families provide their offspring with professional role models and values that emphasize success. They also maintain economic and political connections that enhance their offspring's future opportunities. Hence, their children have a head start over children from lower socioeconomic categories. However, kinship alone is not the fundamental determinant of social status and rank, as it was and still is in preindustrial societies.

Family

We have discussed the various functions of the family: socializing children, regulating sexual behavior, and providing emotional and economic security. In industrial societies, some of these functions have been transformed in important ways, as seen in the diminishing importance of the extended family and the emergence of the smaller nuclear family. Some basic functions, such as reproduction and the primary care and socialization of children, are still performed in the nuclear family.

The family's economic role has changed dramatically. In industrial and postindustrial societies, the family is no longer an economic unit linked to production. The prevalence of wage labor in industrial societies has been one of the principal factors leading to the breakdown of the extended family and the emergence of the nuclear family (Wolf 1966; Goody 1976). The extended family in peasant societies worked on the land as a cooperative economic unit. When employers began to hire individual workers for labor in mines, factories, and other industries, the extended family as a corporate unit no longer had any economically productive function.

Another factor leading to the diminishing importance of the extended family has been the high rate of geographical mobility induced by industrialization. Because much of the labor drawn into factories and mines initially came from rural areas, workers had to leave their families and establish their own nuclear families in the cities. Land tenure based on the extended family was no longer the driving force it had been in preindustrial societies. In addition, as manufacturing and service industries expanded, they frequently moved or opened new offices, requiring workers to relocate. The economic requirements of industrializing societies had the effect of dissolving extended family ties that were critical in preindustrial societies.

Historians, sociologists, and anthropologists have studied the disintegration of the extended family in industrial England, Europe, and North America for decades (e.g., Goode 1963, 1976, 1982, L. Stone 2010). Although the large, extended patrilineal group families gradually broke down during the medieval period in Europe, a pattern of smaller kin-group families and bilateral descent (tracing descent through both sides of the family) emerged throughout Europe (Goody 1983, 2000). Although a similar process occurred in Russia and Japan, to some extent it was delayed in those countries. For example, in Russia, the nuclear family began to replace the extended family following the emancipation of the serfs (Kerblay 1983). Yet, anthropologists note that the nuclear family is not the ideal norm in Russian society. Surveys indicate that Russians do not consider it proper for older parents to live alone and that many consider the grandfather to be the head of the family. These ideal norms reflect the older traditions of the extended peasant family in Russia (Dunn and Dunn 1988).

In Japanese society, the traditional family was based upon the *ie* (pronounced like the slang term "yeah" in American English). The *ie* is a patrilineal extended family that had kinship networks based upon blood relations, marriage, and adoption (Befu 1971; Shimizu 1987; McCreery and McCreery 2006; Hendry 2013). The *ie*, an indigenous term, is translated as "house," but more broadly suggests the idea of household continuity. Included in the *ie* are all living and deceased relatives, as well as those as yet unborn, and the relationships in the "house" are characterized by Confucian premises of loyalty and benevolence (Hendry 2013). The *ie* managed its land and property assets as a corporate group and was linked into a hierarchy of other branch *ie* families, forming a *dozoku*. The *dozoku* maintained functions similar to those of the peasant families of other agricultural societies. With industrialization and now postindustrialization in Japan, the rurally based *ie* and *dozoku* began to decline, and urban nuclear families called the *kazoku* began to develop (Befu 1971; Kerbo and McKinstry 1998; McCreery and McCreery 2006). However, Joy Hendry describes how the traditional *ie* continues to be honored in Japan (2013). Hendry indicates that there is some tension in keeping this tradition of *ie* alive, particularly because of the differences in expectations between the younger and older generations (2013). The older generations' focus is on devotion to the ancestors and the notion of being bound to a familial social identity, while the younger generations' focus is on individuality and the emphasis on individual prerogatives and rights. Despite such tension, the success of an individual is still often predicated upon the success of the group or family to which one belongs. Certainly, the principle of *ie*, with its emphasis on the responsibility of an individual to represent his or her family, sharply contrasts with the Western emphasis on the rights of the individual to do essentially as he or she pleases. The shift from the *ie* and *dozuku* to the *kazoku* has been very sudden and recent; many older people in Japan have not really adjusted to this change.

Despite the general tendency toward the breakup of the extended family in industrialized societies, specific groups in these societies may still retain extended family ties. For example, extended, peasant-type families exist in rural regions such as Uzbekistan, Azerbaijan, and Georgia, which were formerly part of the Soviet Union (Kerblay 1983). Similar tendencies can be found in rural British, European, and Japanese societies. Even in the urban areas of nations such as the United States and Great Britain, some ethnic groups maintain extended family ties. In the United States, some African-Americans, Hispanic Americans, Arab Americans, and Asian Americans enjoy the loyalty and support of extended family ties, enhancing their economic and social organization within the larger society (Stack 1975; Macionis 2014b; S. L. Brown 2012; Bigler 2012; Benson 2012).

Marriage

One of the major changes in marriage in industrialized societies is that it has become much more individualized; that is, the establishment of the union has come to involve personal considerations more than family arrangements. This individualistic form of marriage is usually based on *romantic love*, which entails a blend of emotional attachment and physical and strong sexual attraction. Some anthropologists have hypothesized that erotic attraction and romantic love existed in preindustrial societies and were universal (Fisher 1992; Jankowiak and Fischer 1992; Jankowiak 1995, 2008). There are many ethnographic descriptions of couples falling in love in both prestate and agricultural state societies. The classical literature of China, Arabia, India, Greece, and Rome, as well as various religious texts such as the Bible, is filled with stories about romantic love, as are the lore of preindustrial societies such as those of the Ojibway Indians of North America and the San hunting-gathering society discussed earlier. However, these anthropologists find that romantic love sometimes leads to marriage, but often results in premarital or extramarital sexual relationships, or resistance to an arranged marriage. Shakespeare's play *Romeo and Juliet* underscores the conflict between romantic love and the familistic and practical considerations of marriage in Western Europe during the Renaissance. Anthropologist Charles Lindholm did cross-cultural research on this topic and suggests that even though romantic love may have existed in many known cultures, it did not in many others, and that the correlation between romantic love and the reproduction of children is very weak. Lindholm asserts that societies that arrange marriages for economic and political benefit tend to have far higher birth rates than those that do not (2001). Lindholm traces the existence of the courtly ideals and poetic expressions of romantic love to the Islamic world in the medieval period, where it eventually percolated into Renaissance European culture (2001).

William Jankowiak did a much more extensive cross-cultural survey of romantic love, drawing on folklore and interviews with ethnographers from many different areas (2008). In the book *Intimacies: Between Love and Sex*, Jankowiak and Paladino (2008) discuss two distinct types of love—companionship or companionate love (sometimes called comfort love or attachment love) and passionate or romantic love. These two different forms of love have their own logic and endocrinology. Companionate or comfort love involves a deeply emotional affection felt toward those with whom we are intimately involved and whose lives are deeply intertwined with ours. "In contrast, passionate love involves the idealization of another, within an erotic setting, with the presumption that the feeling will last for some time into the future" (Jankowiak and Paladino 2008:5). Although romantic love tends to be more physical, companionate love is more spiritually based. Both kinds of love occur in all cultures.

However, most anthropologists concur that the ideals of romantic love did become more widespread in Europe, resulting in the diffusion of this form of marriage throughout Western culture. The ideals found within the biblical tradition of Jewish *nomos* and expressed later in the Christian concept of *agape* and its devaluation of sexuality

had some cultural effects on the concept of romantic love in marriage (Lindholm 1995; de Munck 1998). Eventually, the Roman Catholic Church in 1439 A.D. defined marriage as based upon the choice of the individuals, and decreed that it was the seventh sacrament and was spiritually based (L. Stone 2010).

Of course, many people within the upper classes persisted in arranged marriages (as described in the novels of the British author Jane Austen). The royal families of Europe arranged the marriages of their children for political alliances, as well as for economic consolidation of property rights. Cousin marriage, as described above, for many forms of society, was maintained in the European upper classes. Many nineteenth-century Victorians, including Charles Darwin and members of upper-class families, such as the famous wealthy banking Rothschild family of Europe, married their cousins on a regular basis, just as the people of the Old Testament and the early Christian and Roman era did in earlier agricultural societies. As mentioned earlier in the textbook, this "inbreeding" does not necessarily lead to harmful genetic results (Conniff 2003).

Anthropologist Jack Goody made a considerable contribution to the study of marriage and family in Europe that has led to a better understanding of the development of Western society (1983, 2000). Goody indicates that the Western European marriage pattern began to diverge from the Mediterranean pattern by the end of the Roman Empire in the 6th century A.D. The Mediterranean and Roman pattern of marriage was strongly patrilineal and usually involved cross-cousin marriage. Women were not allowed to own property or participate in the public sphere, with strong gender segregation. In contrast, the Western European pattern became more bilateral; cousin marriage was banned, exogamy was promoted, and women had greater rights to property. Goody notes that this shift was a result of Roman Catholic Church policies that opposed to cousin marriage, levirate marriages, the adoption of children, and divorce. Goody suggests that the material interests of the Church led to these policies. Cousin marriage, patrilineal descent inheritance, adoption, the levirate, and divorce ensured that property would be retained with families and households. The banning of cousin marriage and patrilineal inheritance practices would redirect wealth and property that widows and other relatives would donate to the Church. As a result of these changes in Church policy, Goody suggests that the social structure of Western Europe was dramatically transformed and influenced the economic and political developments of the Western world (2000).

As we will see in later chapters, cousin marriage is still a major way in which marriage is arranged in many non-Western societies throughout the world. However, the cultural tradition of free marital choice based upon romantic love, especially among the upwardly mobile middle and lower-middle classes in Europe following the Renaissance and the Industrial Revolution, began to spread throughout the region of Europe and into Western culture. It exists today in the United States and other regions of the world influenced by Western culture and Christianity. As many sociologists, anthropologists, and historians of Europe suggest, industrialization and modernization weakened agricultural-structured property arrangements and extended family and kinship relationships; families became smaller, and geographical mobility increased. This tended to foster more individualism, personal autonomy, choice, new forms of self-cultivation, and romantic love in European societies (L. Stone 2010).

Prior to the industrialization of Europe years ago, however, many families still persisted in trying to have their children married within the same class, ethnic, and religious categories, and children were often married through the intervention of parents, who arranged their relationships. Romantic love may have existed in preindustrial societies (and in many cases, it was the basis for extramarital relationships), but it did not usually become the primary basis of marriage until after the Industrial Revolution. As cultural values became more individualistic, along with the rise of new groups of middle-class families, many couples began to choose their own spouses. As the extended family declined in significance, important decisions such as selection of a marriage partner increasingly were made by individuals, rather than by families.

Although individuals select their own marriage partners in most industrialized societies, the parents within these societies often attempt to enhance marital choices in certain categories. For example, parents of the upper and upper-middle classes often choose certain colleges and universities for their children so that they will meet suitable marriage partners. Many parents sponsor social activities for their children to meet potential marriage partners of their own socioeconomic, ethnic, and religious affiliations. In some areas, such as the southern United States and Quebec, Canada cousin marriage was still practiced until recently to promote the consolidation of property rights and transmit wealth within the families. Nineteen U.S. states permit first-cousin marriage (Conniff 2003; Molloy 1990).

To some extent, even in industrialized societies, individual choice of marriage partners is circumscribed by parental guidance and other cultural norms. However, many people in an industrialized society such as the United States find that because of the breakdown in family and community ties, individuals find it more difficult to meet prospective spouses. Many individuals are from homes where their parents have been divorced at least once, and consequently this reduces the possibility of meeting someone through their family. For that reason, there has been an increase in dating and matchmaking services and computer dating services in postindustrialized societies such as the United States. Thousands of these dating and matchmaking services, along with Internet Web sites aimed at helping singles find a spouse, have developed within the past decade.

One exception needs to be noted with respect to the relationships between industrialization and commercialization and individualized decision making in the selection of marriage partners. The exception is Japanese marital practices. Courtly love, closely resembling romantic love, was discussed in classical literature such as Lady Murasaki's *Tale of Genji* in the Japanese court of the tenth century. In Japanese society, the most typical, traditional form of marriage was arranged through a go-between, a *nakoda*, who set up a meeting for a man and woman to get to know each other (Hendry 2013). The *nakoda* would establish an alliance between two extended households. This pattern is known as the *samurai* form of marriage because the warrior-scholars practiced it during the Tokugawa period.

With industrialization in Japanese society, romantic love has had an effect on the selection of marriage partners, and currently many Japanese individuals choose their own mates. But anthropologist Joy Hendry (2013) notes that "love marriages" are still suspect and go against the serious practical concerns of marital ties and the traditional obligations felt by people toward their parents. In many cases, *nakoda* are still used to arrange marriages in this highly modern society. Currently, there is a cultural struggle between generations of the young versus the old over what type of marriage and family relationships ought to be maintained in Japanese society (McCreery and McCreery 2006).

Approximately one-third of the marriages in Japan are arranged. A man and woman of marriageable age are brought together in a formal meeting called an *omiai*, arranged by the *nakoda*. "Love marriages" based on romantic love, called *renai kekkon*, may occur, but in most cases, parents still have veto power over their children's marital partners (Kerbo and McKinstry 1998). Marriage in Japan is still very much a family consideration, rather than just an individual's own choice or decision. Yet, some members of the younger generation in Japan are beginning to opt for "romantic love" and personal choice for their marital partners. And one of the signs of this new trend in marriage is that these young Japanese, especially among the middle and upper classes, will have a "Christian-style" wedding, rather than a typical Japanese wedding ceremony, with some of them going to Hawaii for their ceremonies.

Divorce All but a few industrialized societies have legalized divorce, and obtaining a divorce has become easier. In general, little social stigma is associated with divorce in industrialized societies (Quale 1988). Divorce rates tend to be higher in industrial societies than in preindustrial societies. Although historians and anthropologists find that marriages were very unstable even in medieval Europe, most marriages dissolved because of high death rates (L. Stone 2010). Beginning in the fourth century, the Roman Catholic Church in Europe banned divorce. As discussed previously, anthropologists such as Jack Goody attribute these changes in divorce and marriage to the Church's opposition to the breakup of property of the heirs that might have been appropriated by the Church (1983, 2000).

Among the many factors that contribute to high divorce rates in industrialized societies is the dissatisfaction that some people experience in their marital relationships. People who enter a marital bond with the ideals and expectations of romantic love may experience a conflict between those ideals and the actualities of marital life. Women who are more financially independent in industrialized societies are much less likely to remain in bad marriages. In preindustrial societies, in which marriages were actually alliances between corporate kin groups, individuals typically did not have the freedom to dissolve the marital bond. As individualistic decision making increased with the emergence of industrialization, however, partners in an unsatisfying relationship were more willing to consider divorce.

Divorce rates of most Western industrialized societies have ballooned during the last century. For example, the U.S. rate increased tenfold over the past century (Macionis 2014). The same pattern is evident in Russia, where traditional taboos regarding divorce have been replaced by more tolerant attitudes (Kerblay 1983).

In Japan, however, the divorce rate decreased after industrialization (Befu 1971). In contrast to most agricultural societies, Japan had a fairly high divorce rate prior to the Meiji period. This was not due to conflicts between husband and wife; instead, divorce resulted when elders in the husband's family rejected a young bride because she did not conform easily enough to family norms, did not bring enough of a dowry, or for other reasons. The traditional postmarital rule of residence was patrilocal, with the wife moving in with the husband's father's household (Goode 1982). With industrialization and the breakdown of these traditional patterns, the divorce rate began to fall. More recently, however, the divorce rate has begun to increase in Japan, as industrialization creates the tensions experienced in all industrial societies. Yet, the divorce rate in Japan is still only one-fifth that of the United States (Kerbo and McKinstry 1998; Hendry 2013). To some extent, the traditional norms and expectations regarding the female gender role in Japanese society have undoubtedly had an influence on this lower divorce rate. Traditionally, the Japanese woman is not supposed to threaten the primacy of the husband's role as head of the family. She is supposed to dedicate herself to her husband and children. Work outside of the home should be undertaken only to boost family income when it is necessary, and upon having children, the Japanese woman is expected to be a full-time homemaker (Kerbo

and McKinstry 1998). Consequently, many fewer Japanese women have the financial capability to sustain themselves outside of a marriage. Currently, many young people in Japan are contesting the issues of gender and individual choice (McCreery 2007; McCreery and McCreery 2006).

Gender

Industrialization had a profound impact upon gender relationships, particularly in England, Europe, and North America. The transition from an agricultural economy to an industrial wage economy drew many women from the domestic realm into the workplace. In general, women have become more economically self-sufficient and less dependent on men for support.

Gender and the Division of Labor Although women in Western industrial societies have entered the workforce in considerable numbers in the last several decades, most women work in a small number of occupations within the service economy, especially in underpaid clerical positions. In addition, women in industrial societies perform the majority of domestic tasks, such as household chores and childcare, which are still considered by many the primary responsibility of women. Male occupations and the husband's income are usually considered the primary source of family income. Consequently, women in these societies have a dual burden of combining their domestic role with employment outside the home (Bernard 1981, 1987; Bannister 1991). A similar pattern is seen in Japanese society (McCreery and McCreery 2006).

The gender wage gap highlighting the difference between women and men in U.S. society has been studied thoroughly by sociologists at the Institute for Women's Policy Research (IWPR). In a report issued by the IWPR in 2014, these sociologists found that during 2013, median weekly earnings for female full-time workers were $706, compared with $860 per week for men, a gender-wage ratio of 82.1 percent. In addition, there is a penalty for U.S. women working in predominantly female compared to predominantly male occupations. This penalty is highest for both women and men working in occupations that require at least a four-year college or university degree. Women in highly skilled, predominantly female occupations make only 71 percent of median hourly earnings of women who work in highly skilled, male-dominated occupations, almost $10 less per hour (and $12 less per hour than men working in highly skilled, male-dominated occupations). Lack of equal pay with men at the same general skill level and with the same gender composition of occupation costs women from $3,555 to $17,450 per year for full-time work. Women's median earnings are lower than men's in nearly all occupations, whether they work in occupations predominantly done by women, occupations predominantly done by men, or occupations with a more even mix of men and women. Also, nearly twice as many women are in poverty compared to men (Hegewisch and Hartmann 2014).

There was more wage disparity for both African-American and Hispanic women compared with white males. Hispanic women have the lowest median earnings at $541 per week (61.2 percent of the median weekly earnings of white men at $884). African-American women have median weekly earnings of $606, or 68.6 percent of the median weekly earnings of white men. (Hegewisch and Hartmann 2014).

Female Status in Industrial Societies   To some degree, industrialization undermined the traditional form of patriarchy. In most preindustrial societies, males held considerable authority and control over females. This authority diminished in industrial societies as women gained more independence and gender relations became more egalitarian. As we have seen, however, women are still restricted in the workplace and have a dual burden of outside work and domestic chores. This indicates that the cultural legacy of patriarchy still persists in most industrial societies.

As their economic role has changed, women have attempted to gain equal economic and political rights. The call for gender equality began with women from upper- and middle-class families. Unlike working-class women, these early women's rights advocates were financially secure and had much leisure time to devote to political activism. They eventually secured the right to vote in the United States and in other industrialized nations. In addition, with increasing educational levels and economic opportunities, more women entered the workforce. For example, by 1977, nearly 55 percent of all adult females in the United States were in the workforce; by 2012, that number was more than 75 percent, as illustrated in Figure 17.8.

Feminism   During the 1960s, a combination of economic and social forces fueled the feminist movement in many industrialized societies. During the 1950s, many U.S. women began to question their roles as solitary homemakers, especially after they participated heavily within the workforce during the World War II years. They were not

More than 75 percent of women are participating in the U.S. workforce.

Figure 17.8   U.S. Labor force participation by age and gender: women 25-54. (From Sullivan, David. "Trends in Labor Force Participation" Chicago: Federal Reserve Bank. June 2013.)

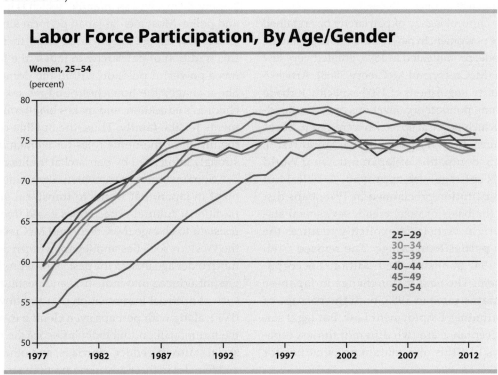

happy with their domestic roles as housewives serving their husbands, on whom they were dependent economically, and they wanted more direct participation in the outside world. **Feminism** is the belief that women are equal to men and should have equal rights and opportunities. The contemporary feminist movement has helped many women discover that they have been denied equal rights and dignity. This movement has a much broader base of support than the early women's rights movement. Among its supporters are career women, high school and college students, homemakers, senior citizens, and many men.

Feminists have secured some concrete gains and helped change certain attitudes in the United States. For example, in a landmark legal decision in 1972, the American Telephone and Telegraph Company (AT&T), the world's largest employer of women, was forced to pay $23 million in immediate pay increases and $15 million in back pay to employees who had suffered sex discrimination. In addition, women have been admitted to many formerly all-male institutions such as the U.S. Military Academy at West Point (Macionis 2014).

Despite these gains, many female workers continue to be segregated into low-paying service occupations. To resolve this and other problems, the feminist movement supported the Equal Rights Amendment (ERA) to the U.S. Constitution to prohibit discrimination because of gender. Although the ERA was supported by almost three-fourths of American adults and passed by Congress in 1972, it failed to win ratification by the states. Apparently, the idea of full equality and equivalent pay for equivalent work has not received the full endorsement of U.S. society. Even in an advanced industrial society, the cultural legacy of patriarchy remains a persistent force.

In Japan, the cultural legacy of patriarchy has retained its grip on the role of women. In newly industrializing Japan, the Meiji Civil Code, promulgated in 1898, granted very few rights to women (McCreery and McCreery 2006). Article 5 in the Police Security Regulations of 1900 explicitly forbade women from joining political organizations or even attending meetings at which political speeches were given. These laws would remain in force in Japan until after World War II.

After the U.S. occupation of Japan following World War II, women's suffrage was approved. Article 14 of the Japanese Constitution proclaimed in 1946, bans discrimination on the basis of race, creed, sex, social status, or family origin. Article 24 explicitly requires the consent of both parties to marriage. The revised Civil Code issued in 1947 abolishes the traditional *ie* corporate family system. The next major change in Japanese women's legal status came in 1985, with the passage of the Equal Opportunities Employment Law. But legal status and social acceptance are two different things, especially when laws like this one contain no penalties for violation.

However, during the 1970s, wives and mothers who moved to the suburbs were the daughters of women accustomed to being stay-at-home wives. Just as in the United States and Europe, more and more Japanese women were entering the workforce. As elsewhere in the industrial world, the cost of educating the children was rising. Some women always had to work simply to make ends meet. Now more looked for work to keep up with the neighbors or to be sure that their families could afford the new consumer goods that everyone wanted. Many young women typically took jobs that lasted only until they married. Then, returning to the labor force after their children started school, they could find only low-paying, part-time work. They could supplement their household's income, but rarely earned enough to be financially independent.

Japanese women were, however, becoming more highly educated. In 1955, only 5 percent of women received postsecondary education, and more than half of those went only to junior college. However, as of 2002, 48.5 percent of Japanese women received some form of postsecondary education, compared to 48.8 percent of men; 33.8 percent of women attended university. Higher education combined with still limited opportunities was a recipe for dissatisfaction—and provided at best temporary relief (McCreery and McCreery 2006).

Yet, even when women are in the workforce in Japanese society, up until recently, they tended to have a second-class status when compared to men. Many college-educated women in offices are expected to wear uniforms and to serve tea and coffee to the men, and they are treated as if they are office servants (Hendry 2013; Kerbo and McKinstry 1998). They are expected to defer to men in the office and present themselves as infantile, which is interpreted as cute and polite. Most men in Japan perform almost no domestic chores and expect to be waited on by their wives. Despite this tradition of patriarchy in Japan, the Japanese woman has a powerful position within the domestic household. She manages the household budget, takes charge of the children's education, and makes long-term financial investments for the family. Thus, the outside-of-the-home and the inside-of-the-home roles for women in Japan are still strongly influenced by patriarchal traditions.

Some women are active in a growing feminist movement in Japan that wants to transform gender roles, but traditional cultural expectations based upon patriarchy are resistant to change (McCreery and McCreery 2006). In both the Western societies and Japan, women are marrying at a much older age than in the past. New reproductive technologies introduced into industrial and postindustrial societies, such as artificial insemination (AI) and in vitro fertilization (IVF), along with perhaps even cloning in some societies in the future, will undoubtedly influence the moral, legal, and social status of gender, marriage, and other issues of males and females in these advanced postindustrial societies.

Age

Another social consequence of industrialization is the loss experienced by the elderly of traditional status and authority. This trend reflects the changes in the family structure and the nature of cultural knowledge in industrial and postindustrial societies. As the nuclear family replaced the extended family, older people no longer lived with their adult children. Pension plans and government support programs such as Social Security replaced the family as the source of economic support for the elderly. At the same time, exchanges of resources between elders and offspring became less important in industrial societies (Halperin 1987). Thus, elderly family members lost a major source of economic power.

The traditional role of the elderly in retaining and disseminating useful knowledge has also diminished. Sociologist Donald O. Cowgill (1986) hypothesizes that as the rate of technological change accelerates in industrial societies, knowledge quickly becomes obsolete, which has an effect on the status of elderly people. Industrialization promotes expanding profits through new products and innovative services, all of which favor the young, who, through formal education and training, have greater access to technological knowledge. In addition, the amount of cultural and technical information has increased to the point where the elderly can no longer store all of it. Instead, libraries, databases, and formalized educational institutions have become the storehouses of cultural knowledge.

The result of these changes, according to Cowgill, has been the rapid disengagement of the elderly from their roles in industrial societies. Although many elderly people remain active and productive, they no longer possess the economic, political, and social status they did in preindustrial societies. In some cases, the elderly are forced to retire from their jobs in industrial societies to make way for the younger generation. For example, up until recently in industrial Japan, the elderly were forced to retire at the age of 55 and often had difficulties adjusting to their senior years.

The status and roles of the elderly have changed much more dramatically in the West than in Japan. In Japanese society, the tradition of family obligations influenced by Confucian values and ethos serves to foster the veneration of the elderly. In addition, about three-fourths of the elderly reside with their children, which encourages a greater sense of responsibility on the part of children toward their parents. In 2002, official estimates put Japan's total population at 127,435,000. Of that total, 23,628,000 (18.5 percent) were age 65 or older. Only 18,102,000 (14.2 percent) were 14 or younger. In 2001, the life expectancy for Japanese men had risen to 78.07 years. The life expectancy for Japanese women was 84.83 years (McCreery and McCreery 2006).

Theorists such as Cowgill suggest that because Japan or the former Soviet Union had industrialized much later than Western societies, there has been less time to transform family structures and the status of the elderly. This view is supported by a comparison between the most modern industrialized urban sectors of these societies and the rural regions. For example, in the more rural regions in Russia and, until recently, in Japan, the extended family or *ie* was still the norm, and the elderly remained influential and esteemed. Thus, the high status of the aged in Japan and Russia may represent delayed responses to industrialization (Cowgill 1986). However, presently, Japan is undergoing a rapid transformation in these patterns, and as in the United States and Western Europe, older people are becoming much more independent and are enjoying their privacy and lack of dependence on their natal families (McCreery and McCreery 2006; Hendry 2013).

Social Stratification in Industrial and Postindustrial Societies

17.8 Compare the class structures of Britain, the United States, Japan, and the former Soviet Union.

We have discussed the type of social stratification that existed in preindustrial societies. Bands and tribes were largely egalitarian, whereas chiefdoms and agricultural states had increased social inequality based on ascribed statuses. Chiefdoms and agricultural states are classified as closed societies because they offer little, if any, opportunity for social mobility. In contrast, industrial states are classified as **open societies** in which social status can be achieved through individual efforts. The achievement of social status is related to the complex division of labor, which is based on specialized occupational differences. Occupation became the most important determinant of status in industrial states. Societal rewards such as income, political power, and prestige all depend on a person's occupation.

This is not to say that industrial states are egalitarian. Rather, like some agricultural states, they have distinctive classes based upon somewhat equivalent social statuses. The gaps among these classes in terms of wealth, power, and status are actually greater in industrial than in preindustrial societies. Thus, although people in industrial states have the opportunity to move into a different class from that into which they were born, the degree of stratification in these societies is much more extreme than it is in preindustrial societies. Let's examine the types of stratification systems found in some industrial states.

The British Class System

Some industrial states continue to reflect their agricultural past. Great Britain, for example, has a class system that retains some of its feudal-like social patterns. It has a symbolic monarchy and nobility based on ascribed statuses passed down from generation to generation. The monarchy and nobility have titles such as prince, princess, knight, peer, and earl. These individuals have to be addressed with the appropriate form: your royal highness, sir, lord, lady. The British political system reflects its feudal past in the structure of the House of Lords, in which up until 2001 membership was traditionally inherited through family. This contrasts with the House of Commons, to which individuals are freely elected. Although the monarchy and the House of Lords have relatively little power today, they play an important symbolic role in British politics.

Class divisions in modern Britain are similar to those in many other European societies. They include a small upper class, which maintains its position through inheritance laws and the education of children in elite private schools; a larger middle class, which includes physicians, attorneys, businesspeople, and other occupations in the service sector; and a large working class employed in the primary and secondary sectors of the economy. Yet, social mobility in Great Britain is open, and people can move from one class to another.

The degree of social mobility in Great Britain, as well as in other industrial states, is to some extent a result of recent changes in the industrial economy. With advanced industrialization, an increasing percentage of jobs are found in the tertiary (service) sector, whereas the primary and secondary sectors have declined. Therefore, the number of white-collar workers has grown, and the number of blue-collar workers has decreased. Consequently, many of the sons and daughters of blue-collar workers have a higher social status than do their parents. For example, in Great Britain, approximately 40 percent of the sons of manual workers have moved into the middle class since the 1950s (Robertson 1990; Macionis 2014). Sociologists refer to this as *structural mobility*, a type of social mobility resulting from the restructuring of the postindustrial economy, producing new occupational opportunities. Technological innovations, economic booms or busts, wars, and increasing numbers of jobs in the service-sector, white-collar occupations can affect this mobility from working class to middle class or upper class.

Class in the United States

Most research demonstrates that the rate of social mobility in the United States is about the same as in other industrial states. Approximately one-third of the children within the working class stay within the same class background during their lives (Macionis 2014). Although the United States differs from Great Britain in that it has never had an official class system with a titled aristocracy, it is not a classless society. The class structure of the United States consists of five categories based upon equivalent social statuses, which are largely determined by occupation, income, and education (see Table 17.1). Although these class boundaries are very "fuzzy" and are not rigid, they continue to influence whether an individual can achieve social mobility.

One of the principal cultural ideals of the United States is that any person can move up the social ladder through effort and motivation. For this reason, upper-class and upper-middle-class Americans tend to believe that economic and social inequalities arise primarily from differences in individual abilities and work habits. Additionally, most individuals in the United States claim that they belong to the middle class in U.S. society, despite the fact that they might not fall into the economic category of that class (Wolfe 1999). Most Americans believe that equal opportunities are available to all individuals based upon personal responsibility, ingenuity, and work habits. These cultural beliefs, therefore, help justify social inequity.

In fact, many factors besides individual efforts—such as family background, race, ethnicity, gender, wealth, property, and assets and the state of the national and world economies—affect a person's location and mobility on the socioeconomic ladder. For example, African-Americans, Native Americans, and Hispanics historically have lower rates of mobility than do Asian-Americans and white, middle-class Americans.

Some postindustrial societies in Europe maintain the vestiges of feudal-like social patterns such as symbolic monarchies. This is a recent photo of Queen Elizabeth of the United Kingdom.

Table 17. 1 The American Class System in the Twenty-First Century: A Composite Estimate

Class and Percentage of Total Population	Income	Property	Occupation	Education	Personal and Family Life	Education of Children
Upper class (1–3%)	Very high income, most of it from wealth	Great wealth Old wealth, control over investment	Managers, professionals, high civil and military officials	Liberal arts education at elite schools	Stable family life Autonomous personality	College education by right for both sexes
Upper-middle class (10–15%)	High income	Accumulation of property through Savings	Lowest unemployment	Graduate training	Better physical and mental health and health care	Educational system biased in their favor
Lower-middle class (30–35%)	Modest income	Few assets Some savings	Small-business people and farmers, lower professionals, semiprofessionals, sales and clerical workers	Some college High school Some high school	Longer life expectancy Unstable family life	Greater chance of college than working-class children Educational system biased against them
Working class (40–45%)	Low income	Few to no assets No savings No assets	Skilled labor Unskilled labor	Grade school	One-parent homes Conformist personality	Tendency toward vocational programs
Lower class (20–25%)	Poverty income	No savings	Highest unemployment Surplus labor	Illiteracy, especially functional illiteracy	Poorer physical and mental health Lower life expectancy	Little interest in education, high dropout rates

SOURCE: Adapted from *Social Stratification: The Interplay of Class, Race, and Gender*, 2nd ed., by Daniel W. Rossides, © 1997. Adapted by permission of Pearson Education, Inc., Upper Saddle River, NJ.

Class in Japan and the Former Soviet Union

Most research indicates that despite the cultural emphasis on group harmony, class divisions and conflicts exist in Japan. Sociologist Rob Steven (1983) has identified five major classes in Japanese society: the bourgeoisie or capitalist class (owners of the major industries), the petty bourgeoisie (small-business owners), the middle class (professional and other service workers), the peasantry (rural farmers), and the working class (industrial laborers). The primary means of social mobility in Japanese society is the educational system, which is highly regimented and rigorous from the elementary years through high school. Higher education is limited to those students who excel on various achievement exams, a system that to some extent reflects class background. As in other industrial societies, middle- and upper-class students have better opportunities. The rate of social mobility in Japan is similar to that of other industrial states (Lipset and Bendix 1967). However, the most current anthropological research demonstrates that a rigid class structure does not dominate Japanese society and that most people believe that through education and their own personal efforts, they can rise to more economically and socially viable positions. Some individuals from lower-class categories, just as in the United States, have risen to the top as celebrities, artists, and CEOs. Thus, the ideal of moving ahead in an increasingly affluent society such as Japan tends to promote more optimism about one's prospects (McCreery and McCreery 2006).

Ever since the Russian Revolution in 1917, the former Soviet Union claimed to be a classless society because its system was not based upon the private ownership of the means of production. In fact, however, it had a stratified class system based upon occupation. Occupations were hierarchically ranked into four major status groups based on income, power, and prestige. The highest-ranking statuses consisted of upper-level government officials, Politburo members who were recruited from the Communist Party. The second tier consisted of professional workers such as engineers, professors, physicians, and scientists, as well as lower-level government workers. The third tier was made up of the manual workers in the industrial economy, and the bottom rung was composed of the rural peasantry (Kerblay 1983; Dunn and Dunn 1988). Most sociologists agree that this hierarchy of statuses reflects a class-based society.

Summary and Review of Learning Objectives

17.1 Discuss the general components of social structure, including status, the family, marriage, gender, and age.

Status is a recognized position that a person occupies in society. A person's status determines where he or she fits into society in relationship to everyone else. Status may be based on or accompanied by wealth, power, prestige, or a combination of all of these. All societies recognize both *ascribed* and *achieved* statuses. When an individual occupies a particular status, he or she plays a role based on the norms associated with the status. Anthropologists define the family as a social group of two or more people related by blood, marriage, or adoption who live or reside together for an extended period, sharing economic resources and caring for their young. The two main types of family found throughout the world are the nuclear family and the extended family. Marriage is a social bond sanctioned by society between two or more people that involves economic cooperation, social obligations, rights, duties, and sometimes culturally approved sexual activity. Anthropologists find different patterns of marriage including monogamy and polygamy. Forms of polygamy include polygyny and polyandry. Gender is the culturally based human traits that are assigned to individuals based on their sex (biological traits). Although sex characteristics are biologically determined, gender roles vary in accordance with the technological, economic, and sociocultural conditions of particular types of societies. Age is a universal principle used to prescribe social status in sociocultural systems.

17.2 Describe the social structure, family, marriage, gender, and age in foraging societies.

The two basic elements of social organization for foraging populations are the nuclear family and the band. The nuclear family is the small family unit associated with procreation: parents and offspring. The nuclear family appears to be most adaptive for hunting-gathering societies because of the flexibility needed for the location and easy distribution and exchange of food resources and the other exigencies of hunting. The most common type of band is made up of a related cluster of nuclear families ranging in size from 20 to 100 individuals.

The most common type of marriage found in foraging societies is monogamy. A common marriage rule found in foraging societies is referred to as *cross-cousin marriage*. A cross-cousin is the offspring of one's father's sister or one's mother's brother. In effect, a cross-cousin marriage means that a male marries a female who is his father's sister's daughter or his mother's brother's daughter.

Cross-cousin marriage creates interband alliances and kin networks for reciprocal exchanges.

Contrary to most stereotypes about the gender-based division of labor in foraging societies with male hunting providing most of the meat and protein for the group, in many cases females provide most of the foodstuffs involving the collection of vegetation. The status of women within band societies is usually fairly equal to men, primarily because males and females both contribute toward provisioning for the families. The elderly have a high status in band societies because of their accumulated store of knowledge and the assistance in childcare and other family responsibilities.

17.3 Describe the social structure, family, marriage, descent groups, gender, and age for tribal societies.

The most common social grouping among tribal societies is the extended family. Most extended families consist of three generations—grandparents, parents, and children—although they can also contain married siblings with their spouses and children. Aside from extended families, tribes also maintain descent groups in order to trace actual or supposed kinship relationships. One major type of descent group is based on lineage. Anthropologists define lineages as descent groups composed of relatives, all of whom trace their relationship through *consanguineal* (blood) or *affinal* (marriage) relations to an actual, commonly known ancestor. The most common type of descent group is a patrilineal descent group, composed of people who trace their descent through males from a common, known male ancestor. Another form of descent group is the matrilineal descent group, or *matrilineage*, whose members calculate descent through the female line from a commonly known female ancestor. Some tribes have ambilineal descent groups, formed by tracing an individual's choice of descent relationships through either a male or a female line. In other cases, tribes have kindreds based on bilateral descent and consist of relatives on both the father's and mother's lines. Other types of descent groups for tribes include clans, phratries, and moeities that are based on more fictional or spiritual relationships to ancestors or family members.

Marriage in tribal societies involves exogamy, meaning marriage outside of one's family, and descent group or lineage, clan, phratry or moiety. Many tribes practice cross-cousin marriage, but a few have rules of parallel-cousin marriage, where a male marries a female, his father's brother's daughter within his own patrilineal descent group. The most common form of marriage among tribes is polygyny, where a man has more than one wife. Along with polygyny, a husband's family has to contribute bridewealth, animals or other resources for the bride's family. A few tribes in the Himalayan mountains and South India practice polyandry, where women have more than one husband. Some tribes have the rules of levirate (a widow marries her dead husband's brother) or the sororate (a widower marries his dead sister's sister).

With some exceptions, gender inequality and patriarchy and sexist views towards women are prevalent in tribal societies. However, in matrilineal societies, women have a higher status than men, despite the fact that men still control the political sphere. Respect for the elderly sometime results in gerontocratic rule, where the elderly, mostly males, maintain authority over tribal politics.

17.4 Discuss how status differences, the family, gender, and age are related in chiefdom societies.

In contrast to band and tribal societies, chiefdoms have ranked extended families and descent groups in hierarchies within different strata. The various families and descent groups—households, lineages, and clans—have a specific ascribed rank in the society and are accorded certain rights, privileges, and obligations based on that rank. Marriage is usually endogamous in chiefdoms, which entails marriage among people of the same strata. Polygynous marriages were often associated with chiefs who may have many wives. Gender relationships were usually unequal in chiefdoms, with women ranked below men, except for women who were in the chiefly stratum, whose status was very high. The elderly had a relatively high status within chiefdom societies.

17.5 Discuss the family, kinship, marriage, gender, and age patterns in agricultural states.

Like tribes and chiefdoms, agricultural state societies maintained the extended family. Extended families were prevalent in both urban and rural areas and had wealth, power, and prestige based on land ownership and their relationship to the elite class. Agricultural societies had descent groups based on patrilineages, matrilineages, or bilateral descent with kindreds. Arranged marriages and cousin marriages prevailed in agricultural societies, with frequent polygyny found among the male elite. Most agricultural societies had dowry rules where the bride's family had to contribute wealth to the husband's family.

With some exceptions in Southeast Asia where bilateral descent was important, patriarchy and excessive sexism was prevalent in agricultural societies resulting in female seclusion and veiling. Patriarchy was the common practices of all of the religious traditions that developed in agricultural states, including Confucianism, Hinduism, Judaism, Christianity, and Islam.

17.6 Discuss the type of stratification characteristic of agricultural states.

Agricultural civilizations were highly stratified and social mobility was generally restricted to people with elite family or kinship backgrounds. Thus these societies were closed societies in that social status was generally *ascribed*, rather than *achieved*. In some cases, this resulted in caste systems in India or Nepal. In other cases, slavery became prevalent. Slave systems varied in agricultural societies dependent on local economic and political conditions. The indigenous African form of slavery was open in that slaves could be incorporated into domestic kinship groups and even become upwardly mobile where land was relatively abundant and less populated. In contrast, the slave systems of China, India, Greece, and Rome were closed, with no opportunities for upward mobility or incorporation into kinship groups where land was scarce and populations much more dense, and social mobility was limited for slaves.

17.7 Discuss the social structure, family, marriage, gender, and age patterns in industrial and postindustrial societies.

Kinship is less important in industrialized and postindustrial states than in preindustrial societies. New structures and organizations perform many of the functions associated with kinship in preindustrial societies. Occupational and economic factors in most cases replace kinship as the primary basis of social status; a person no longer has to be part of an aristocratic or elite family to have access to wealth and political power. Of course, kinship and family background still have a definite influence on social mobility. Families with wealth, political power, and high social status can ensure that their children will have the best education. The nuclear family becomes the predominant form of family structure in industrial and postindustrial societies. Instead of arranged marriages, marriage in Western industrial and postindustrial societies were based on choice and romantic love, but in Japan the parents are still often involved in marriage choice. Gender relations have become more equal in industrial and postindustrial societies; however, feminist movements have emerged that critique the remaining aspects of patriarchy that still prevail.

Respect for the elderly has declined in most industrial and postindustrial societies as a result of the rapid changes in technology. However, in Japan respect for the elderly has been maintained as an aspect of the Confucian tradition.

17.8 Compare the class structures of Britain, the United States, Japan, and the former Soviet Union.

In contrast to the closed societies of chiefdoms or agricultural societies, industrial and postindustrial states are classified as open societies, in which social status can be achieved through individual efforts. Occupation became the most important determinant of status in industrial and postindustrial states. This is not to say that industrial or postindustrial states are egalitarian. Class structures develop in industrial and postindustrial societies. The British class structure retains some aspects of an agrarian society with a monarchical royal family, and aristocratic titles and statuses for some upper class members. The class structure of the United States consists of categories based upon equivalent social statuses, which are largely determined by occupation, income, and education. Although these class boundaries are very "fuzzy" and are not rigid, they continue to have an influence on whether an individual can achieve social mobility. Recently social mobility has increased in both Britain and the United States because of the rapid transformation of the postindustrial information-based technology and economy.

Although Japan has a class structure similar to that of the United States, most people believe that through education and their own personal efforts, they can rise to more economically and socially viable positions. Ever since the Russian Revolution in 1917, the former Soviet Union claimed to be a classless society, because its system was not based upon the private ownership of the means of production. In fact, however, it had a stratified class system based upon occupation, income, power, and privileges.

Key Terms

achieved status, p. 372
age grades, p. 375
age sets, p. 388
age stratification, p. 375
ambilineal descent group, p. 380
ascribed status, p. 372
bilateral descent, p. 380
brideservice, p. 376
bridewealth, p. 383
caste, p. 397
clan, p. 381
closed societies, p. 397
cross-cousin, p. 376
descent group, p. 380
dowry, p. 393
endogamy, p. 373
exogamy, p. 373
extended family, p. 373

family, p. 373
feminism, p. 404
gender, p. 374
gerontocracy, p. 389
hierarchical societies, p. 389
kindreds, p. 381
levirate, p. 384
lineages, p. 380
marriage, p. 373
matrilineal descent groups, p. 380
matrilocal residence, p. 376
moieties, p. 381
monogamy, p. 373
nuclear family, p. 373
open societies, p. 405
parallel-cousin marriage, p. 383
patrilineal descent groups, p. 380
patrilocal residence, p. 376

phratries, p. 381
polyandry, p. 373
polygamy, p. 373
polygyny, p. 373
primogeniture, p. 382
purdah, p. 394
role, p. 372
sex, p. 373
sexism, p. 387
social stratification, p. 372
social structure, p.372
socioeconomic status, p. 372
sororate, p. 384
status, p. 372
strata, p. 389
sumptuary rules, p. 389
ultimogeniture, p. 382
unilineal descent groups, p. 380

Chapter 18
Politics, Warfare, ar

 ## Learning Objectives

After reading this chapter you should be able to:

18.1 Discuss how anthropologists understand politics, warfare, and law.

18.2 Discuss the characteristics of politics in foraging societies.

18.3 Describe the features of violence and warfare in foraging societies.

18.4 Discuss the characteristics of politics in tribal societies.

18.5 Discuss how anthropologists explain tribal warfare.

18.6 Describe political authority in chiefdoms.

ow anthropologists explain the
n and origins of chiefdoms.

the features of politics in
ltural civilizations.

18.9 Discuss the characteristics of politics in
industrial and postindustrial societies.

18.10 Discuss how warfare changes in industrial
and postindustrial states.

Politics, Warfare, and Law

18.1 **Discuss how anthropologists understand politics,
warfare, and law.**

In the early twentieth century, German sociologist Max
Weber introduced definitions of political power and
authority that have since been adopted and modified by
cultural anthropologists. Weber defined **political power**
as the ability to achieve personal ends despite opposition.
In this sense, political power can be based on physical or
psychological *coercion*. Weber perceived this type of political power as *illegitimate*, in that it is unacceptable to most
members of a society. According to Weber, the most effective and enduring form of political power is based on
authority, power generally perceived by members of society as legitimate, rather than coercive.

A brief example will illustrate the difference between
illegitimate and legitimate power. If a large country
invades and conquers a smaller one, the occupied people
generally will not consider their new rulers to be legitimate. Thus, the rulers must rely on coercion to enforce
their laws and to collect payments in the form of taxes or
tributes. In contrast, most U.S. citizens voluntarily comply with the tax laws. Although they may complain, they
perceive their government as representing legitimate
authority. Although physical coercion and force might be
used to arrest some people who refuse to pay their taxes,
in the majority of cases such actions are not necessary.

The general categories used by anthropologists to
describe political systems are *band*, *tribe*, *chiefdom*, and
state. A band is the least complex—and most likely the
oldest—form of political system. Political institutions in
band societies are based on close kinship relations within a
fairly small group of people. Tribes are more complex societies with political institutions that unite larger groupings
of people into a political system. Generally, tribal societies
developed alongside food production. Tribes do not have
centralized, formal political institutions, but they do have
sodalities, groups based upon kinship, age, or gender that
provide for political organization. For example, in some
tribal societies of Papua New Guinea, secret male societies
function as political institutions.

Chiefdoms are more complex than tribal societies
because they are formalized and centralized. Chiefdoms
establish centralized, legitimate authority over many communities exercised through various complex economic,

social, and religious institutions. However, despite their
size and complexity, chiefdoms are still fundamentally
organized by kinship principles. Although chiefdoms have
different levels of status and political authority, people
within these levels are related to one another through
kinship ties.

States are political systems with centralized bureaucratic institutions to establish power and authority over
large populations in defined territories. State systems are
not based on kinship. Instead, state bureaucracies govern society on behalf of ruling authorities through procedures that plan, direct, and coordinate complex political
processes. State political systems range from the early
bureaucratic political units of agricultural societies such
as ancient Egypt and China to the modern industrial and
postindustrial societies of the United States, Japan, and
numerous European nations.

Nevertheless, it must be emphasized here that this
classification does not represent a single scheme of political
evolution for the entire world. Again, we must stress that
political evolution did not develop in a one-directional,
unilineal type of evolution. The archaeological and ethnographic data demonstrate again and again that a stage-
by-stage development or evolution from band to tribe to
chiefdom to state did not occur in all areas. Contemporary
anthropologists have demonstrated that political evolution
is multilineal. These classifications of band, tribe, chiefdom, and state are to be used only as categories to organize
the vast amounts of data accumulated by anthropologists.
As with all models, the boundaries separating the various
categories are somewhat arbitrary and fuzzy.

Decision Making in a Political System

An important topic in the study of a society is the day-
to-day, individual decision making and competition for
power and authority. In studying this topic, anthropologists may focus on *fields* or *arenas* within a society. A field
is an area in which political interaction and competition
take place (Bourdieu 1977). It may involve a part of a society, or it may extend beyond the boundaries of a society.
For example, a field could be a whole tribe, a chiefdom, a
state, or several of these units. A political arena is a more
local network specific in which individual actors or small
groups compete for power and authority. An arena may be

made up of factions, elites, or political parties in a society. Another aspect of political anthropology is the focus on how political succession occurs within different societies— in other words, who is appointed or elected to a position of political authority or who inherits such a position in a society. As we shall see, there are various ways of determining who gains political power and authority.

Warfare and Feuds

The study of politics involves an understanding of political conflicts within and among societies. Two major forms of conflicts are warfare and feuds. Anthropologists define **warfare** as armed combat among territorial or political communities. They distinguish between *internal warfare*, which involves political communities within the same society and *external warfare*, which occurs among different societal groups. A **feud** is a type of armed combat occurring within a political community, revenge seeking among kinship groups (Otterbein 1974; Kelly 2003). Anthropologists examine the different biological, environmental, demographic, economic, social, political, and other cultural variables that influence warfare and feuds.

Law and Social Control

Another aspect of political anthropology is the study of law and social control. As discussed in Chapter 10, one aspect of nonmaterial culture is the normative dimension, sometimes referred to as an *ethos*. All societies maintain an ethos that encourages certain behaviors and prohibits others. This ethos, along with the society's values, makes up the moral code that shapes human behavior. The particular ethos of a society represents an attempt to establish social control through various internal and external mechanisms. The internal mechanisms of social control are built into the enculturation process itself. Through enculturation, people learn the specific norms that make up society's expectations. Thereafter, those who violate these norms frequently experience emotional and cognitive discomfort in the form of guilt. Thus, internalized norms can shape and influence people's behavior, even in the absence of constraints from other people.

Despite these internal mechanisms, however, individuals frequently violate norms. For a variety of reasons, including biological influences on behavior, enculturation does not bring about perfect social control in a society. Hence, in addition to internal mechanisms, societies use external mechanisms to enforce norms. External mechanisms take the form of sanctions: rewards (positive sanctions) for appropriate behaviors and punishments (negative sanctions) for inappropriate behaviors.

Societies vary with respect to both the nature of their moral code and the types of external sanctions used to enforce the moral code. What one societal group considers deviant or unethical may be acceptable to another group. For example, divorce is an acceptable solution for severe marital conflicts in the United States. In Italy and Ireland, however, despite recent legislation that allows divorce, many still view it as an unethical pattern of behavior.

In large, complex social groups, sanctions are usually highly formalized. Rewards can take the form of public awards, parades, educational or professional degrees, and banquets. Negative sanctions include fines, imprisonment, expulsion, and sometimes death. In small-scale societies, sanctions tend to be informal. Examples of positive sanctions are smiles, handshakes, pats on the back, hugs, and compliments. Negative sanctions include restricted access to certain goods and services, gossip, frowns, impolite treatment, and ostracism.

Law as Formalized Norms and Sanctions

Anthropologists describe *laws* as clearly defined norms, violations of which are punished through the application of formal sanctions by ruling authorities. In the 1960s, cultural anthropologist Leopold J. Pospisil attempted to distinguish law from other social norms, based on his research among the Kapaukan tribe of New Guinea. He specified four criteria that must be present for a norm to be considered a law: (1) authority, (2) intention of universal application, (3) obligation, and (4) sanction (1967). To institutionalize legal decisions, a society must have members who possess recognized authority and can, therefore, intervene to settle disputes. These authorities must be able to enforce a verdict by either persuasion or force. Their verdicts must have universal application; that is, these decisions must be applied in the same manner if a similar situation arises in the future. This distinguishes legal decisions from those based purely on political expediency.

Obligation refers to the status relationships among the people involved in the conflict. If status relationships are unequal, the rights, duties, and obligations of the different parties can vary. Legal decisions must attempt to define the rights and obligations of everyone involved and to restore or create an equitable solution for the community. Finally, punitive sanctions must be applied to carry out the legal decision. More recently in ethnographic studies, anthropologists have abandoned any simplistic, universalistic aspect that separates law from norms. Presently, anthropologists study the language, symbolism, and discourse used in society to distinguish legal sanctions along with historical and global developments that have an influence on legal processes. *PoLAR: The Political and Legal Anthropology Review* features many articles by anthropologists as they study legal processes in many different countries of the world.

Political Organization in Foraging Societies

18.2 Discuss the characteristics of politics in foraging societies.

Just as the band is the fundamental element of social organization in most hunting-and-gathering societies, it is also the basic political unit. As we saw in the last chapter in the discussion of social organization, bands are tied together through kinship and marriage, creating reciprocal economic exchange and social relationships throughout the community. Each band, however, is politically independent of the others and has its own internal leadership. Most of the leaders in the bands are males, but females also take on some important leadership roles. Leaders are chosen because of their skills in hunting, food collecting, communication, decision making, or other personal abilities.

Political leaders generally do not control the group's economic resources or exercise political power as they do in other societies, and there is little, if any, social stratification between political leaders and others in the band. In other words, typically band societies are highly egalitarian, with no fundamental differences between those with and those without wealth or political power. Thus, leaders of bands must lead by persuasion and personal influence rather than by coercion or the withholding of resources. Leaders do not maintain a military or police force and thus have no definitive authority.

In extensive cross-cultural studies of the political processes of hunting-gathering societies, Christopher Boehm (1993, 1999) developed an imaginative hypothesis to explain the lack of political power and domination in these egalitarian societies. Boehm suggested that there is a pattern of *reverse dominance* in these societies, which keeps anyone from becoming coercive or politically dominating the group in any manner. Reverse dominance ensures that the whole group will have control over anybody who tries to assert political power or authority over them. Reverse dominance is practiced through criticism and ridicule, disobedience, strong disapproval, the execution of offenders or extremely aggressive males, the deposing of leaders, or outright desertion (an entire group leaving a particularly dominant leader). Boehm finds that reverse dominance and related political processes are widespread in band societies, reinforcing patterns of egalitarianism.

In a related hypothesis, Peter Gardner (1991) suggests that foraging societies tend to have strong cultural values that emphasize individual autonomy. Like Boehm, Gardner suggests that hunter-gatherers dislike being dominated and disdain conforming to norms that restrict their individual freedom. From reviewing many cases of band societies, Gardner has found that the cultural values promoting individual autonomy enable these people to sustain their egalitarian way of life while promoting flexibility in their behavior, a distinguishing feature of foraging societies.

Characteristics of Leadership

In most cases, individuals in hunting-and-gathering societies do not seek out leadership roles because there are few benefits or advantages in becoming a leader. Leaders do not accrue power or economic resources in these egalitarian societies. They do, however, have a tremendous responsibility for the management of the band. In a classic essay in political anthropology, Claude Lévi-Strauss (1944) described the band leader of the Nambikuara of South America as entirely responsible for selecting the territories for procuring game; ordering and organizing hunting, fishing, and collecting activities; and determining the conduct of the band in relation to other groups in the region. Yet, Lévi-Strauss emphasized the consensual aspect of this leadership pattern. The leader has no coercive power and must continuously display skill in building consensus within the band to provide political order. On the other hand, Lévi-Strauss did report that the leaders of the Nambikuara did have more wives than other individuals.

A quotation from a Ju/'hoansi San leader sums up the pattern of leadership among hunter-gatherer societies: "All you get is the blame if things go wrong." Another remark recorded by Richard Lee to a question about who was the leader of the local band, "Of course we have headman! In fact, we are all headman. . . . Each one of us is headman over himself" (1979:348). Morton Fried (1967) notes a remark frequently heard from band leaders: "If this is done it will be good." These remarks indicate the lack of authority that leaders of bands have in these societies. Lévi-Strauss (1944), however, states that some people in all societies desire the nonmaterial benefits such as prestige that can be gained through assuming leadership responsibilities. Therefore, despite the lack of political power or material benefits, foraging leaders may be motivated by other cultural concerns.

Another characteristic of band political leadership is that it is transient; leaders of bands do not hold permanent positions or offices. Informal leadership is somewhat situational in that it varies according to circumstances; the band will call on the appropriate type of leader when dealing with a specific type of activity. In some bands, for example, certain individuals may be good at solving disputes within the band or between bands. These individuals may be chosen to deal with such problems when they arise. In general, then, band leadership is diffuse and decentralized.

This minimal pattern of leadership also involves an informal type of political succession. Most hunting-and-gathering societies have no definitive rules for passing leadership from one individual to another. Rather, leadership is based on personal characteristics. It may also be based on supernatural powers that the individual is believed to possess. When an individual dies, his or her influence and authority also die. This lack of rules for succession emphasizes the decentralization of political power and authority in band societies.

Warfare and Violence in Foraging Societies

18.3 Describe the features of violence and warfare in foraging societies.

Contemporary foraging societies generally engage in very limited warfare. However, Carol and Melvin Ember's cross-cultural research indicates that foragers were engaged in frequent warfare in the past (1992). Some archaeological evidence suggests that early foragers may have been involved in extensive warfare (Keeley 1996; LeBlanc 2003; Walker 2001). However, since most foraging societies were limited in population size, the archaeological evidence for violence and warfare is not abundant (Fry 2013; Ferguson 2013). Most of the evidence drawn from ethnographic research in marginal environments suggests that warfare among contemporary foragers take the form of sporadic violence, rather than continual fighting (Kelly 2003). With almost the entire population engaged in the day-to-day hunting and collecting of food, no long-term fighting can be sustained. Also, the lack of centralized political institutions to implement large-scale military mobilization inhibits the development of intense or frequent warfare; no standing armies with specialized warriors can be organized for continual warfare (Roscoe 2013).

The Tiwi of Australia provide a classic case of "restrained" warfare among contemporary foraging populations (Hart, Pilling, and Goodale 1988). War parties of 30 men from two different bands, each armed with spears and wearing white paint symbolizing anger and hostility, met in an adjoining territory. The dispute had originated because some of the males from one band had apparently seduced females from the opposing band. In addition, the senior males of one band had not delivered on their promise to bestow daughters to the other band—a deliberate violation of the norms of reciprocal marital exchange. Both sides first exchanged insults and then agreed to meet with one another on the following day to renew old acquaintances and to socialize. On the third day, the duel resumed, with males throwing spears in all directions, resulting in a chaotic episode in which some people, including spectators, were wounded. Most of the battle however, involved violent talk and verbal, rather than physical abuse. Although variations on this type of warfare existed among the Tiwi, warfare generally did not result in great deal of bloodshed.

Richard Lee described conflict among the Ju/'hoansi San, which involves fights and homicides. Lee (1993) found 22 cases of homicide by males and other periodic violence, usually related to internal disputes over women. As Eric Wolf (1987:130) commented: "Clearly the !Kung are not the 'Harmless People' that some have thought them to be: They fight and sometimes injure other individual !Kung." Raymond Kelly did a broad cross-cultural survey of warfare and violence in band societies and concluded that although violence did occur, it did not involve sustained vengeance and enduring warfare between family band groupings; rather, it involved individual cases of revenge that were brief (2003).

Anthropologist Bruce Knauft (1988) has offered several generalizations concerning violence in foraging societies, which coincide with Kelly's hypothesis. First, these societies lack a competitive male-status hierarchy; in fact, there is a strong tendency to discourage this type of interpersonal competition. Status competition among males is a major source of violent conflict in other types of societies. Second, in contrast to many other societies, public displays of interpersonal violence are not culturally valued among foragers. Instead, these societies seek to minimize animosities. Finally, because of the emphasis on sharing food and other resources, rights to property are not restricted. All these factors serve to reduce the amount of violence in these societies.

Conflict Resolution

Because of the lack of formal government institutions and political authority, social control in foraging societies is based on informal sanctions. One basic mode of conflict resolution that occurs frequently among groups such as the Ju/'hoansi San is for the people involved to move to another band. Thus, the flexibility of band organization itself is an effective means of reducing conflict. Furthermore, the economic and social reciprocities and the frequent exchanges among bands serve to reduce conflicts. These reciprocal ties create mutual obligations and interdependencies that promote cooperative relationships.

Nevertheless, violations of norms do lead to more structured or more ritualized means of conflict resolution in foraging societies. Among the Mbuti, for example, age groups play specific roles in the conflict resolution process. Children play an essential role in resolving conflicts involving misbehavior such as laziness, quarreling, or selfishness. Children ridicule people who engage in these behaviors, even if these people are adults. Young children excel at this form of ridicule, which usually is sufficient to resolve the conflict.

When these measures do not succeed, the elders in the group assert their authority. They try to evaluate the dispute carefully and show why things went wrong. If necessary, they walk to the center of the camp and criticize individuals by name, although they frequently use humor to soften their criticism. Through this process, elders reinforce the norms and values of Mbuti society (Turnbull 1983).

The Eskimo Song Duel Another example of dispute resolution is the Eskimo (Inuit) song duel. The song duel was often used to resolve conflicts between males over a particular female. Because Eskimo society lacks specific rules of marriage, males would sometimes accuse others of wife stealing. In these types of conflicts, the two males encountered each other in front of a large public meeting. They then insulted each other through improvised songs, and the crowd resolved the conflict by selecting a winner. With the declaration of a winner, the dispute was resolved without the use of any formal court system or coercion (Hoebel [1954] 1968). Other methods of conflict resolution among the Eskimo included wrestling and punching matches. (An excellent recent film made by the Canadian Inuit people called *Atanarjuat: The Fast Runner* shows some of the punching and wrestling matches among the Inuit.)

Political Organization in Horticultural and Pastoralist Tribes

18.4 Discuss the characteristics of politics in tribal societies.

Like band societies, tribal societies have *decentralized political systems*, in which authority is distributed among a number of individuals, groups, and associations. Political leadership is open to any male (especially older males) in the society and is usually based on personal abilities and qualities.

Sodalities

Although anthropologists recognize that tribes are the most varied of all small-scale societies, Elman Service ([1962] 1971) attempted to distinguish the tribe from the band by referring to the existence of sodalities (associations). In tribal societies, two types of sodalities exist: kinship sodalities, including lineages and clans, and nonkin sodalities, voluntary and involuntary associations. Kinship sodalities

are the primary basis for political organization in tribal societies. Nonkin sodalities, such as age sets, village councils of elders, male secret societies, and military societies, also have political functions and are mostly voluntary associations that cut across kinship ties by creating alliances outside the immediate kin groups.

In both horticulturalist and pastoralist societies, descent groups such as lineages and clans are the most common political sodalities. Intravillage and intervillage politics are based on these groups, through which alliances are created that assist in maintaining peaceful and harmonious relationships within the tribe. As we have seen, these descent groups are instrumental in carrying out reciprocal exchanges involving bridewealth, women, and other goods, and they are often the only basis for maintaining order. Kinship is the primary basis for political activities and processes in tribal societies.

How Leaders are Chosen

In horticulturalist and pastoralist societies, political leaders are recruited from within descent groups. As in band societies, however, these leaders do not have much coercive power and formal authority. Although many tribes engage in warfare, political leadership tends to be almost as weak and diffuse as it is in band societies. A number of anthropologists hypothesize that this decentralized and limited form of political leadership is due to the constant movement involved in swidden (or slash-and-burn) agriculture and to the nomadism associated with pastoralism (Evans-Pritchard 1940; Vayda 1961; Sahlins 1968; Lindholm 2002; Salzman 2004). They suggest that permanent, long-term settlement in one locale is needed for the development of an effective, centralized form of political authority. In addition, population density and size are relatively small in scale in most tribal societies, which tends to result in decentralized political units (Roscoe 2013).

Village Headman Some horticultural groups like the Yanomamö select a village headman. To become an effective leader, this individual must be "generous" and be able to motivate feasting and exchange activities among different lineages in the village. To become generous, the individual must cultivate more land, which requires more productive labor. These headmen have larger gardens than the average family and can offer feasts and food to villagers to demonstrate their generosity. One way to be more productive is to have more wives. As we have seen in the last chapter, the Yanomamö leaders are polygynous. Thus, polygynous marital relations enable a Yanomamö headman to sustain his generosity and political status.

The Yanomamö headman has no recognized authority to enforce political decisions in the group; he has to lead more by example than by coercion (Chagnon 2012; Hames 2004). He must persuade people to obey the norms of the village, and he gives advice and suggestions on subsistence, economic, and ritual matters. Among the Ndembu horticulturalist tribe studied by Victor Turner, a village headman has to be aggressive, but this has to be balanced by tact, generosity, and the ability to serve as a mediator of conflicts (1957).

Big Man   Another style of political leadership and organization found among some horticultural groups, particularly in Melanesia, is the *big-man* system. One of the most detailed classic descriptions of this system was compiled by anthropologist Douglas Oliver (1955), who did fieldwork in the Solomon Islands among the Siuai tribe. According to Oliver, the aspiring Siuai big man has to collect as many wives as possible to form kinship alliances with other descent groups. In addition, he must accumulate a large number of pigs and grow taro (an edible root crop) to feed them. Most of this productive labor is carried out by the man's wives. When a man has enough pigs, he has a pig feast, in which he attracts followers while humiliating rival big men. If the leader is able to recruit a few hundred men through the "generosity" demonstrated by the feast, these followers may begin to build a "clubhouse" to demonstrate their political commitment to the big man.

The big-man political organization of the Siuai is both formidable and fragile. It is formidable in that the pig feasts can enable a man to attract more and more followers and thus, more power. This system provides the basis for political and war-making alliances. The big man is also able to command and sometimes coerce other people. At the same time, the political loyalties of the followers of the big man are not long-lasting; the lineage of the big man does not assume any of his political power or authority. With the death of the big man, the entire political organization collapses, and loyalties and allegiances shift to another or several other big men, who compete through pig feasts for political alliances. Hence, the big man, like the hunter-gatherer leader, cannot pass on power or build permanent structures of authority.

There has been much more recent extensive ethnographic research on the big-man systems of Papua New Guinea that suggests that it is very diverse in different regions (Roscoe 2013). This system of tribal politics cannot be reduced to a simplistic model. In some regions, the big man can consolidate alliances through the exchange of surplus crops and pigs (maintained by the labor of women) at feasts with many individuals; in other regions, the resources available to sustain these alliances may be more limited. Big men gained their status as warriors, hunters, or ritual experts and leadership was based on political entrepreneurship, oratory skills, skills in mediation and conflict resolution, diplomacy, and other organizational talents (Roscoe 2013). Additionally, "big men" political systems are dependent on population size. If the population

A "Big man" of a tribe in Papua New Guinea

is small and based on face-to-face communication, "big men" politics was limited. However, denser populations resulted in "great men," rather than "big men," who were more powerful (Roscoe 2013).

Pastoralist Tribal Politics

Pastoralist tribal groups tend to have similar political organizations, depending upon the degree of their nomadic lifestyle. Some pastoralist societies depend upon the agricultural societies within their region and are not completely self-sufficient. In these groups, leadership tends to become more permanent and centralized. For example, among the Basseri, a nomadic pastoralist group in Iran, leadership was vested in the *khan*, who was a strong force in decision making within the tribe (Barth 1961). Yet, in reality, the power and authority of the khan were extremely limited, and he had to rule from consensus (Salzman 2000, 2004). It appears that in tribal pastoralist societies, the greater the degree of nomadic independence, isolation, and self-sufficiency of a group, the more diffuse and egalitarian its political leadership (Lindholm 2002).

Segmentary Lineage Systems   One traditional form of political organization found among such groups as the Nuer of East Africa and the Bedouins of Arabia is the **segmentary lineage system.** A segmentary lineage system is a type of political organization in which multiple descent groups (usually patrilineages) form at different levels and serve political functions. This system reflects a complex, yet flexible, arrangement of lineage groups. Among the Nuer, for example, the patrilineages are identified with particular territories in the tribal area. These patrilineages have both maximal lineages, which include descendants who trace their ancestors back through many generations, and minimal lineages, segments of the maximal lineage whose descendants trace their ancestry back only one or two generations. Minimal lineages are nested within the maximal lineage, and all members of the lineage can link themselves directly to the same maximal blood ancestor.

Complementary Opposition   The segmentary lineage system is composed of the various patrilineages, both maximal and minimal, that can be united for military or political purposes. The process by which alliances are formed and conflicts are resolved in this system is referred to as complementary opposition. **Complementary opposition** is the formation of groups that parallel one another as political antagonists. To understand this process, imagine a village with two different maximal lineages. We will call the maximal lineages A and B, the minimal lineages within A we will call A1 and A2, and the minimal lineages within B we will call B1 and B2 (see Figure 18.1).

Now imagine that a member of B2 commits an offense against a member of B1. A feud may erupt, but it will usually be settled within the maximal lineage (B) to which both minimal lineages belong. However, should B2 commit an offense against A2, a different process unfolds. Both A2 and A1 will unite in opposition to B2, which, in turn, will join with B1. The result is a large-scale feud between maximal lineages A and B. This process can extend beyond the lineages to an entire population. For example, in the event of an outside attack, all of the maximal lineages will unite to defend the tribe.

Figure 18.1 A model of a segmentary lineage system

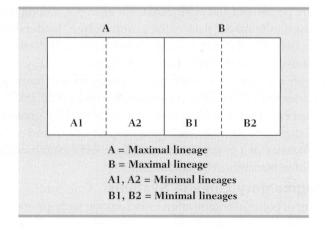

A = Maximal lineage
B = Maximal lineage
A1, A2 = Minimal lineages
B1, B2 = Minimal lineages

In the process of complementary opposition, then, kinspeople may be allies under one set of circumstances and enemies under another. Through this process, the segmentary lineage system can achieve political goals without any definitive type of centralized leadership, such as kings, chiefs, or headmen. The philosophy behind complementary opposition is summarized in an old Bedouin proverb:

> Me against my brother
> I and my brother against our cousins
> I and my brother and my cousins against non-relatives
> I and my brother and my cousins and friends against
>   the enemies in our village
> All of these and the whole village against another
>   village. (Murphy and Kasdan 1959:26)

Many other pastoralist societies have maintained segmentary lineage systems. For example, during their nomadic pastoralist existence prior to the establishment of the kingdom of Israel, the ancient Israelites appear to have been organized on the basis of segmentary lineages without any centralized political institutions. (In the Bible, patrilineal groups are referred to in English as *families*.)

Among segmentary lineage societies, feuds frequently erupt between lineages and result in retaliation or compensation without the imposition of force by a centralized authority. If a member of a particular lineage kills a member of another lineage, the victim's lineage may seek blood revenge. The Nuer attempted to prevent this type of blood revenge by reducing the tension between the victim's and the murderer's lineages. In Nuer society, an individual known as the *leopard skin chief* sometimes provides sanctuary for a murderer and attempts to negotiate compensation with the victim's lineage. In some instances, compensation takes the form of cattle, a desired possession that can be used as bridewealth.

Again, contemporary anthropologists demonstrate that the segmentary lineage system is not a static or fixed structure or cultural belief system that determines political alliances and consolidation. Instead, it needs to be seen as a structure that is often drawn on by individuals to produce political coalitions and negotiations for compensation in varying ecological, economic, and social circumstances (Salzman 2004; Lindholm 2002).

Explaining Tribal Warfare

18.5 Discuss how anthropologists explain tribal warfare.

Both internal and external warfare is far more common among tribes than among contemporary foragers. This does not suggest that all tribal societies were engaged in warfare, and there very well may have been long interludes in which tribes did not engage in warfare (Otterbein 2000). At least in some cases, tribal warfare was exacerbated by political processes resulting from external global developments (Ferguson and Whitehead 1999, Ferguson 2013). Generally, anthropologists reject the notion that humans are by nature aggressive and warlike, possessing a definitive "biological instinct for violence" (See Critical Perspectives Box, Human Aggression: Biological or Cultural?). However, it is clear that humans in the past and present have the potential for warfare. As humans we have a wide behavioral repertoire, a set of potentials that can be triggered by specific environmental factors. Therefore, most discussions of tribal warfare focus on environmental, demographic, and other external political and cultural factors that may result in warfare.

Among horticulturalist societies, members of one village frequently raid other villages for territory, women, or, occasionally, head-hunting (removing the head of a slain enemy and preserving it as a trophy). In a detailed analysis of warfare among the Mae Enga of highland New Guinea, anthropologist Mervyn Meggitt (1977) noted that land shortages and ecological conditions are the most important causes of warfare. The Mae Enga, numbering more than 30,000, are organized into phratries (two or more clans), clans, and localized patrilineal groups. Meggitt distinguishes among different types of warfare involving phratries, clans, and patrilineages.

Phratry warfare involving the entire Mae Enga tribe is mostly ceremonial and serves to display status and prestige between big men and males. Phratry warfare is extremely limited. Interclan and interlineage internal warfare, however, is vicious and ongoing, with conquering kin groups seizing the land of the conquered patrilineages. Meggitt noted that 58 percent of cases of internal warfare were over land, and in 74 percent of the cases, the victors incorporated some or all of the land of the victims. The Mae Enga themselves interpret their internal warfare as a consequence of population growth in relation to the scarcity of land for cultivation.

The Yanomamö and Protein Shortages
Cultural materialists Divale and Harris (1976) explained warfare among the tribal Yanomamö of the Amazon in terms of ecological factors. They viewed the internal warfare of the Yanomamö as an indirect means of regulating population growth. Divale and Harris suggested that the Yanomamö institutions and values that relate to intervillage warfare emerge from the group's cultivation practices and nutritional deficiencies. They hypothesized that the Yanomamö expand their cultivation because they experience protein shortages. Thus, the intensification of warfare in which villages raid one another's game reserves is an adaptive Yanomamö response or mechanism that indirectly and unintentionally serves to inhibit population growth. The limited protein supplies are inadequate to support larger populations.

Other anthropologists have rejected the protein-shortage explanation of Yanomamö warfare. Napoleon Chagnon and Raymond Hames (1979) measured the amount of protein consumed in different Yanomamö villages and encountered no clinical signs of shortages. Furthermore, they discovered that some villages that consumed high amounts of protein engaged in warfare as frequently as villages that consumed low amounts.

Biological Hypotheses of Tribal Warfare
Anthropologist William Durham (1976) offered an evolutionary biological hypothesis of tribal warfare. An example of his model is his study of the Mundurucu of the Amazon, who had a reputation for continual warfare and head hunting against other tribes. Although Durham did not rule out competition for resources and land as an explanation for warfare, he hypothesized that, ultimately, warfare is an adaptive reproductive strategy. In Durham's view, tribal warfare is a means of increasing *inclusive fitness* or reproductive success for related kin-groups on a tribal level in competition with other tribal populations in the region. In other words, if the population of a rival tribe is reduced, one's own tribe may increase its rate of survival and reproduction. Durham believed that increasing the number and survival of offspring (one's own genes) into the next generation is the underlying motivation for tribal warfare. He is not suggesting that this was a conscious evolutionary process, but rather that this was an underlying strategy that resulted in reproductive success for various tribal populations.

Multidimensional Explanations of Tribal Warfare
All the preceding hypotheses view tribal warfare as having in some way an adaptive function for society or individuals within society. But many critics say that although population pressure, competition for land and livestock, and reproductive success may help explain tribal warfare, these variables need to be combined with cultural factors such as honor, prestige, and the enhancement of male status.

Anthropologist Walter Goldschmidt (1989) noted that males in tribal societies are induced to go to war against other groups through institutionalized religious and cultural indoctrination. Although in some tribal societies warriors are given material rewards such as women or land, in most cases nonmaterial rewards such as prestige, honor, and spiritual incentives are just as important. More recently, anthropologist Scott Atran and his colleagues have been emphasizing the religious and sacred imperatives for warfare and human conflict (Atran and Ginges 2012, Atran and Henrich 2010). They note that humans will kill and die not only to protect their kin and kith, but for religious and moral convictions that bind their groups together. Most likely, this generalization applies to all societies that engage in warfare.

Critical Perspectives

Human Aggression: Biological or Cultural?

In Chapter 8 (page 194) we discussed the topic of "Warfare Before Civilization." Throughout history, humans have been confronted with questions about violence and aggression. Enlightenment philosophers such as Thomas Hobbes and Jean-Jacques Rousseau wrote about primitive societies in the state of nature, which they believed revealed the "natural" inclinations of humans. In *Leviathan* (1651) by Hobbes, humans were characterized as naturally violent, and life in primitive societies was described as "nasty, brutish, and short." Hobbes believed that the cultural lifestyle of primitives was devoted to a "war of all men against all men." He argued that only a strong state could coerce people to be peaceful. In contrast, Rousseau, in *The Social Contract* (1762), argued that primitive societies were peaceful, harmonious communities. He classified these people as "Noble Savages." He claimed that the onset of civilization was the corrupting force that resulted in warfare and conflict within these societies.

One of the problems with both of these competing frameworks for understanding human nature is that they were based on superficial, fragmentary, and stereotypical depictions of small-scale societies. They drew upon the stories, myths, and legends of explorers, missionaries, and government officials of that time to describe the native peoples of America and elsewhere. During the twentieth century, with the development of systematic ethnographic studies of indigenous societies, anthropologists began to build a better understanding of violence, aggression, and warfare in these societies.

In today's world of mass media, we are constantly confronted with accounts of violence and aggression, ranging from sports brawls to assaults and murders to revolutions and wars. The seeming universality of aggression has led some people to conclude with Hobbes that humans are "naturally" violent and innately depraved. Or is Rousseau more correct in his view that the development of civilization and its various corruptions caused once-peaceful societies to become warlike and aggressive? What are the causes of human aggression? Is violence inbred, or is it learned? Not surprisingly, anthropologists and other social scientists have been examining these questions for decades, often arriving at conflicting conclusions. Some tend to be more Hobbesian, whereas others are more Rousseauian. To some extent, these disputes concerning the origins of violence reflect the biology-versus-culture debate.

Sigmund Freud, in a famous letter to Albert Einstein, indicated that he believed that humans were innately vicious with a lethal streak ([1933] 1964). Freud attributed this inhumane behavior to the unconscious operation of *Thanatos* or the "death instinct," which he opposed to the "life instinct" or *Eros*. He believed that *Thanatos* functioned in every living human to reduce life to its original primal state of inert matter. When *Thanatos* is blocked by *Eros*, its energy is displaced outward to subjects other than the self, resulting in aggression towards individuals and groups. Freud believed that civilization and culture, or the super ego of the mind, (see Chapter 11, pp. 252-253) demanded that humans repress these primitive tendencies toward destruction and aggressive behavior if they were going to live in peace.

Some psychologists and ethologists attribute warfare and violence to humans' psychobiological genetic heritage. For example, ethologist Konrad Lorenz developed an elaborate biological hypothesis based on comparisons of human and nonhuman animal behaviors. In his widely read book *On Aggression* (1966), Lorenz proposed that during humanity's long period of physical evolution, certain genes were selected that provide humans with an aggressive instinct, which has survival value for the species. He argued that this instinct evolved through natural selection because of intergroup warfare and competition. Lorenz noted that nonhuman animals usually do not kill within their species and that aggression among males within species is highly ritualized and rarely leads to death. Male deer, wolves, and other social animals fight each other, but this fighting establishes a hierarchy of dominant and submissive males and, therefore, helps to ensure order within the group. Thus, nonhuman animals have an instinct for inhibiting aggression that is activated by ritualized fighting behavior.

According to Lorenz, humans, in contrast, have evolved as physically weak creatures without sharp teeth, claws, beaks, or tremendous strength. Therefore, the instinct for inhibiting violence was not selected for the human species. According to Lorenz, this accounts for the prevalence of warfare in human societies and makes humans highly dangerous animals. Compounding this loss of instinctual inhibitions against violence is the human technological capacity to produce deadly weapons. Many anthropologists challenged this concept of a universal instinct for aggression. Citing ethnographic evidence from sociocultural systems that experienced little violence, Ashley Montagu, and, most recently, Douglas Fry and Leslie Sponsel propose that cultural factors are more important than biological factors in determining or influencing aggression (Montagu 1968; Sponsel 1998, Fry 2006, 2013). These anthropologists argue that human behavior can be shaped and influenced in many ways. Humans can be extremely violent or extremely peaceful, depending on the prevailing cultural values and norms. In general, these anthropologists were more Rousseauian in their approach, arguing that external forces such as industrial societies and globalization had an effect on tribal or small-scale societies.

The anthropologist Napoleon Chagnon hypothesized that aggression is related to strategies that have to do with reproduction and increasing one's ability to have more children (2000). This sociobiological view of warfare and aggression has been challenged by other anthropologists (Thorpe 2003; Ferguson 1995, 2013, Fry 2006, 2013). Though anthropologists such as Chagnon, influenced by evolutionary psychology, denied the existence of an aggressive instinct, they agreed that humans possess an innate capacity or potential for violence. Violent behavior can be triggered by a number of factors that threaten humans' capacity to survive and reproduce, including scarcities of resources, excessive population densities, and significant ecological developments. Sociobiologists and evolutionary psychologists do, however, acknowledge that the norms and values of a particular sociocultural system can either inhibit or enhance aggressive tendencies. Thus, the same pressures that would lead to warfare in one society might be resolved without violence in a society with a different set of values.

In a book entitled *The Human Potential for Peace: An Anthropological Challenge to Assumptions about War and Violence*, Douglas Fry provides discussions of some prehistoric and contemporary societies that managed to be peaceful including the Semai of Malaysia, the Ifaluk of Micronesia, and some Inuit (2006). Though the prehistory and history of humanity has demonstrated that people are capable of the most heinous acts of violence and brutality, Fry emphasizes that peace-making strategies and the absence of warfare is also evident in some societies.

In this chapter, we see that warfare is much more prevalent in tribal societies than in the contemporary hunting-gathering bands. Tribal societies such as the horticulturalist Yanomamö, some North American Indian tribes, and the pastoralist Nuer were more frequently involved in violence and aggression. This violence and warfare appear to have developed prior to the influence of colonialism and outside global pressures, suggesting that the cultivation of crops and the domestication of animals as food sources by these tribal societies are related to the origins of warfare, as well as to the cultural norms and values (Ember and Ember 1992; LeBlanc 2003). Territories, ecological competition, socialization for male aggression, and land become more important within these tribal societies. Yanomamö lineages are important as social units that defend territories against raids and thefts of crops. Likewise, Nuer lineages defend their cattle against thefts or raids. Most of the tribal societies are engaged in these defensive strategies involving warfare. Yet as we saw above, contemporary band or hunter-gatherer societies have very limited warfare (though they do have homicide and violence).

Currently, most anthropologists concur that human aggression and violence result "partially" from both biological and cultural factors, although they continue to disagree about the relative importance of the two. There is an ongoing debate among primatologists about the level of violence and aggression in chimpanzee and gorilla societies. Contrary to Lorenz's theories about nonhuman animals having no incidence of violence, primatologists have much more evidence of some violence and aggression from their ongoing studies (Goodall 1986; Wilson and Wrangham 2003). Anthropological research on the origins of combativeness and hostility has raised some basic questions concerning human nature and behavior and continues to be an important area of research on this topic.

Points to Ponder

1. If cultural norms and values can promote violence, can they also eliminate or sharply reduce it?

2. Can you foresee a society (or a world) in which conflicts and problems are resolved peacefully? Or will violence always be with us?

3. Given the complex relationships among various cultural and biological factors, what concrete steps can a society take to reduce the level of aggressive behavior?

Law and Conflict Resolution among Tribes

Tribal societies that have no centralized political institutions for addressing internal conflicts must, for the most part, rely primarily on informal and formal sanctions to resolve conflicts. Because tribes have larger, more settled populations and more complex kinship networks than do bands, they cannot resolve disputes merely by having people move to another location. Thus, many tribal groups have developed more formalized legal techniques and methods of conflict resolution.

In general, tribal societies have no formal courts and no lawyers. However, ethnographers have found in such societies some individuals, usually older males, who are highly skilled in negotiation and conflict resolution. These individuals may become mediators who help resolve disputes among clans, lineages, and other descent groups.

JOCTIAN, CHIEF OF THE NUEHR TRIBE (AFTER BAKER).

Leopard Skin Chief of the Nuer

One example of a mediator is the Nuer leopard skin chief, who attempts to restore amicable relations between Nuer patrilineages after a homicide. It is important to note that the chief has no authority to enforce legal decisions, a pattern typical of mediators in tribal societies. These mediators preside over the litigation procedures, but the final decision can be reached only when a consensus is achieved among the different descent groups.

Ordeals   Another, more formalized legal mechanism found in some tribal societies is known as the *ordeal*. Anthropologist R. F. Barton described a classic case of an ordeal among the Ifugao, a horticulturalist tribe of the Philippines (1919). An Ifugao individual accused of a transgression who wanted to claim innocence might submit to an ordeal. Barton described several types of ordeals found among the Ifugao. In one type, referred to as the hot-water ordeal, a person had to reach into a pot of boiling water to pull out a pebble and then replace it. In another, a red-hot knife was lowered onto a person's hand. If the party was guilty, his or her hand would be burned badly; if innocent, it would not be. If there were two disputants, they both had the hot knife lowered onto their hands. The one burned more severely was judged to be the guilty party. A third type of ordeal among the Ifugao involved duels or wrestling matches between the disputants.

A *monkalun*, or arbiter, supervised all of these ordeals. The Ifugao assumed, however, that spiritual or supernatural intervention was the ultimate arbiter in these cases and that moral transgressions would be punished not by the *monkalun*, but by cosmic religious forces and beings who oversee the social and moral order of Ifugaoan life. The *monkalun* interpreted the evidence and acted as an umpire in deciding the guilt or innocence of an individual.

Oaths and Oracles   Some tribal societies use oaths and oracles to arrive at legal decisions. An **oath** is an attempt to call on a supernatural source of power to sanction and bear witness to the truth or falsity of an individual's testimony. Some tribal groups rely on **oracles**, individuals or sacred objects believed to have special prophetic abilities, to help resolve legal matters. Individuals who are believed to have oracular or prophetic powers are empowered to make legal decisions. One example is the Azande, a tribal group in East Africa described by Evans-Pritchard (1937). The Azande used oracles to help decide criminal cases.

In general, ordeals, oaths, and oracles are more common among tribal societies with weak authority structures, in which power is widely diffused throughout the society. Individuals in these societies lack the authority to enforce judicial rulings and, therefore, do not want to accept the full responsibility for making life-and-death decisions that would make them politically vulnerable (Roberts 1967).

Political Authority in Chiefdoms

18.6   Describe political authority in chiefdoms.

Whereas the political structures of bands and tribes were impermanent and indefinite, chiefdom political structures were well defined, permanent, and corporate. In chiefdoms, the leadership functions were formalized in the institutionalized office of chief, with the personal qualities of the chief being unrelated to the responsibilities and prerogatives of the office. (An **office** refers to the position of authority assigned to a person.) In most cases, the chief's office had clearly defined rules of succession. The office of the chief existed apart from the man who occupied it, and upon his death, the office had to be filled by a man from a similar chiefly family. This system differed markedly from the big-man system found in some tribes, in which leadership positions were attached to particular individuals based on personal characteristics. Tribal societies had no hereditary rules of succession; the big man's authority could not be passed on to his sons or to other kin.

In many of the Polynesian chiefdoms, the rule of succession was based upon primogeniture, in which the eldest son assumed the status (and realm) of the father. This form of political succession is prevalent in other chiefdom societies as well. The rule of primogeniture helped to avoid a power struggle when the chief died, and it provided for continuity for the overall political (and economic) system (Service 1975).

As is evident from our previous discussions, the chiefs had a great deal of control over both surplus prestige goods and strategic resources, including food and water. This control enhanced chiefly status, rank, and authority, ensuring both loyalty and deference on the part of those from lower descent groups. In addition, it enabled the chiefs to exercise a certain amount of coercion. They could recruit armies, distribute land and water rights to families, and sentence someone to death for violating certain societal norms.

Limits on Chiefly Power   Nevertheless, chiefs did not maintain absolute power over their subjects. They ruled with minimal coercion based on their control over economic production and redistribution, rather than on fear or repression. This political legitimacy was buttressed by religious beliefs and rituals, which are discussed in the next chapter.

A Case Study: The Trobriand Islands   The political systems of the Pacific island societies had varying degrees of chiefly authority. Chiefly authority was more limited among the Trobrianders than among the Hawaiians and Tahitians. The Trobriand chief had to work to expand his arena of power and status and to prevent other chiefs from destroying or diminishing his ancestral rights (Weiner 1987). Much economic and political competition existed among the chiefs of matrilineal descent groups. A Trobriand chief gained rights, legitimacy, and authority through descent. That authority, however, also depended upon what the chief accomplished in terms of redistributing food and other resources by giving feasts. Generosity was, therefore, one of the most important aspects of Trobriand chieftaincy. If generosity was not demonstrated, the chief's power, authority, and legitimacy diminished. Chiefs were frequently replaced by other, more generous, people within the chiefly family.

A Case Study: Hawaii and Tahiti The indigenous Hawaiian and Tahitian chiefdoms tended to be more fully developed than those of the Trobrianders. For example, Hawaiian society was divided into various social strata composed of descent groups. The highest-ranking noble stratum, known as *ali'i*, was made up of district chiefs and their families. Within the highest-ranking descent groups, the eldest son or daughter inherited the political and social status of the father. Above the *ali'i* were the paramount chiefs, or *ali'inui*, who ruled over the islands.

The paramount chiefs and district chiefs were treated with reverence and extreme deference. They were carried around on litters, and the "commoners"—farmers, fishermen, craftsworkers, and "inferiors"—had to prostrate themselves before the nobles. Political legitimacy and authority were much more encompassing than in the Trobriand case.

This does not mean, however, that the Hawaiian or Tahitian chiefs had absolute or despotic power. In fact, most of the evidence indicates that the political stability of Tahitian and Hawaiian chiefdoms was somewhat delicate. There were constant challenges to the paramount and district chiefs by rival leaders who made genealogical claims to rights of succession. In addition to manipulating genealogical status, these rivals would marry women of chiefly families in order to be able to challenge a paramount chief's leadership. In many cases, paramount chiefs had to demonstrate their authority and power not only through the redistribution of land, food, and prestige goods, but also through warfare against rival claimants. If a paramount chief was unable to hold his territorial area, challengers could increase their political power, and the political legitimacy of the paramount chief might diminish substantially. Permanent conquest by rival chiefs over a paramount chief resulted in a new ranking system in which the lineage of the conquering group supplanted that of the paramount chief. When this occurred in Hawaii, the paramount chief's descent group was sacrificed to the new ruler's deities (Valeri 1985). Thus, conquest did not result in the complete overthrow of the society's political structure. Rather, it consisted of revolts that minimally reordered social and political rankings. The basic fabric of the chiefdoms was not transformed; one noble lineage simply replaced another.

In some cases, the chiefs tried to establish a more permanent basis of power and authority. For example, chiefs occasionally meted out a death sentence for those accused of committing treason or of plotting to overthrow a chief. Yet this use of force was rarely displayed. Despite the fact that authority was centralized, political legitimacy was based ultimately upon consensus and the goodwill of the populace, rather upon than military coercion. Polynesian chiefs could normally expect to command a majority of the labor and military needed in their domains simply by occupying their political office. However, if things were going badly or if the chief was not fair and generous in redistributing food and resources or in settling disputes, armed revolts could begin, or political struggles could erupt—not to overthrow the political or social order, but to substitute one chief for another.

The Evolution of Chiefdoms

18.7 Discuss how anthropologists explain the evolution and origins of chiefdoms.

A number of anthropologists, including the late Elman Service ([1962] 1971), hypothesized that in some cases chiefdom societies emerged because of *regional symbiosis*. Because particular descent groups were strategically located among territories with different resources, these groups played a key role in the exchange and allocation of resources throughout the population. Eventually, some of the leaders of these descent groups became identified as the chiefs or centralized leaders. In other words, by regulating the exchange of resources, the chiefs held these formerly autonomous regions together under a centralized administration. In a detailed account of the evolution of chiefdoms, Service (1975) referred to *cultural ideology*, as well as ecological variables, to identify certain individuals and descent groups as chiefs. He argued that particular individuals and their descent group were recognized as having more prestige and status than others. A consensus thus emerged within the society regarding who became chiefs.

Based on his research of Polynesian chiefdoms, archaeologist Timothy Earle (1977, 1997) challenged the hypothesis that chiefdoms emerged through regional symbiosis. By analyzing the ecological conditions and reconstructing exchange networks in Hawaii and other Polynesian locations, Earle found that commodity exchanges were much more limited and did not involve large-scale exchanges among specialized ecological regions, as had been described by Service and others. Exchanges were localized, and most households appear to have had access to all critical resources.

Earle (1987, 1997) suggested that the key factor in the evolution of chiefdoms was the degree of control over vital productive resources and labor. In the case of Hawaii, with population growth, land became a scarce commodity, and competition for the limited fertile land developed. Chiefs conquered certain agricultural lands over which they claimed exclusive rights. Other people received use rights to small subsistence plots in return for their work on the chief's lands. This system permitted the chiefs to exercise much more extensive control over resources and labor. According to Earle, in contrast to the paramount chief as the steward of the land, these chiefs not only had "title" to the land, but also effectively controlled the labor on it. Thus, the chiefly families had a great deal of power and authority over other people.

Archaeologists have emphasized that chiefdoms are varied around the world (Kowalewski 2008). Most archaeological studies indicate that there was not a simple unilineal evolution from hunter-gatherer to tribes to chiefdoms. In many areas, chiefdoms were unstable political systems that oscillated back and forth through decentralized forms to centralized forms. The late Edmund Leach's classic ethnographic research emphasized the cycling and oscillation from egalitarian tribal societies to hierarchical chiefdoms and back to egalitarian forms of unstable political systems among the Kachin peoples of highland Burma (1954). In addition, sometimes chiefdoms emerged when large agricultural states disintegrated. In his analysis of chiefdoms in Tanzania, Thomas Hakånsson draws attention to how chiefdoms are also sometimes embedded in larger networks with agricultural societies through trade, exchange, and political processes (1998, 2007, 2010). Thus, again, there was no simple unilineal evolution from egalitarian tribes to chiefdoms; there were different trajectories of evolution in various areas and periods of time. Archaeologists find this pattern of cycling among chiefdoms in many areas of the world (Kowalewski 2008; S. McIntosh 1999; R. McIntosh 2005).

Warfare Warfare among chiefdom societies was more organized than among bands or tribes, primarily because the political and economic mechanisms in chiefdoms were more centralized and formalized. In many cases, chiefs were able to recruit armies and conduct warfare in a systematic manner.

Anthropologist Robert Carneiro (1970) views warfare as one of the decisive factors in the evolution of chiefdoms. The objective of many chiefs was to extend their chiefdom regionally so as to dominate the populations of surrounding communities and, thereby, control those communities' surplus production. As chiefdoms expanded through warfare and conquest, many of the people in the conquered territories were absorbed into these chiefdoms. In certain cases, these chiefdoms succeeded because of their technological superiority. In many other cases, such as in Polynesia, they succeeded because the surrounding communities were circumscribed by oceans and had no choice but to be absorbed by the conquering chiefdoms.

Law in Chiefdoms

Legal and religious institutions and concepts were inextricably connected in chiefdom societies. These institutions existed to sanction and legitimize the political economy and social structure of chiefdoms. They played a critical role in maintaining the cultural hegemony discussed earlier. As with the political economy, mechanisms of law and social control were more institutionalized and centralized in chiefdom societies., In bands and tribes social norms were unwritten, and social conflicts were resolved through kinship groups, often with the intervention of a leader who was respected but lacked political authority. In contrast, the authority structure in chiefdoms enabled political leaders to act as third-party judges above the interests of specific kin groupings and to make definitive decisions without fear of vengeance. Chiefs had the power to sanction certain behaviors by imposing economic fines or damages, by withholding goods and services, and by publicly reprimanding or ridiculing the offending parties. Chiefs could use their economic and political power to induce compliance. They were not just mediators; rather, they engaged in **adjudication**, the settling of legal disputes through centralized authority.

Within chiefdoms, a dispute between kin groups was handled in the same way it was handled in band and tribal societies—through mediation by the groups. Chiefdoms differed substantially from these other societies, however, in their treatment of crimes against authority. These crimes were of two general types: direct violations against a high-ranking chief, and violations of traditional customs, norms, or beliefs, injuring the chief's authority (Service 1975). Such crimes carried severe punishments, including death. The reason for such severe punishments is that these crimes were perceived as threatening the basis of authority in the chiefdom system.

Politics in Agricultural States

18.8 Discuss the features of politics in agricultural civilizations.

The scale of state organization varied in agricultural civilizations. In some areas, there existed large-scale bureaucratic empires that organized and controlled wide-ranging territories. Examples are centralized governments in the Near Eastern empires of Mesopotamia and Egypt; Rome, which controlled an empire that incorporated more than 70 million people throughout its long period of domination; China, in which a large centralized bureaucracy managed by government officials ruled over perhaps as many as 100 million people; and American empires like the Aztecs, which ruled over millions of people.

In contrast, state societies in Africa, India, and Southeast Asia were much less centralized and had less authority over adjacent regions. Anthropologist Aidan Southall (1956) applied the term *segmentary states* to African states in which the ruler was recognized as belonging to an appropriate royal segmentary lineage, but had only symbolic and ritual authority over outlying regions. Centralized bureaucratic structures in such states did not effectively control outlying peripheral areas. Anthropologist Clifford Geertz (1980) used the term **theater state** to refer to the limited form of state society in Southeast Asia. The power of the theater state was mostly symbolic and theatrical, with many ceremonies to demonstrate the political legitimacy of the regime. The power and authority of the theater state have been compared with the light of a torch, radiating outward from the center and gradually fading into the distance, merging imperceptibly with the ascending power of a neighboring sovereign (Geertz 1980; Hauser-Schäublin 2003). Another anthropologist, the late Stanley Tambiah, used a model to characterize two different forms of state societies: *galactic polity* and *radial polity* (1976). A **galactic polity** is a type of state that rules primarily through religious authority and cosmologies, whereas a **radial polity** is a state that rules more directly through government and military officials that have more centralized control over various provinces and regions. Although Tambiah initially applied this model to explain states and kingdoms in South and Southeast Asia, it is now widely used by archaeologists and others to interpret and explain various regions such as the Mayan civilizations in Mesoamerica (Lucero 2003; Takashi 2006).

Feudalism, a decentralized form of political economy based on landed estates, existed in agricultural civilizations during different historical periods. Although anthropologists and historians have indicated that there are tremendous differences among the forms of feudalism in various societies, there are some similarities. To some extent, some of these feudal regimes were very similar to the chiefdom societies discussed earlier. Usually, as in Western history, feudal regimes resulted from the breakdown of large-scale centralized states. Feudal political economies emerged at various times in Western Europe and Japan. In these systems, lords, like chiefs, were autonomous patrons who owned land, maintained control over their own military (knights and *samurai*), and demanded labor and tribute from their serfs. Political power varied from a highly decentralized form of authority (the nobles) to a more centralized form (a king or emperor). For example, during the Tokugawa period in Japan (1600–1868), the *daimyo* (lords) had to reside in the central capital, Edo (present-day Tokyo) for a year to demonstrate loyalty to the ruler, or *shogun*. This represented a more centralized form of feudalism.

Law in Agricultural States

Agricultural states formalized legal decisions and punishments not only through laws, but also through court systems, police, and legal specialists such as judges. In many of these societies, law became highly differentiated from customs, norms, traditions, and religious dogma (Vago 1995). Writing systems enabled many of these societies to keep records of court proceedings.

The first recognized codified laws originated in the Near Eastern civilization of Babylon. The Babylonian code of law, known as the Code of Hammurabi, was based on standardized procedures and precedents for dealing with civil and criminal offenses. Other agricultural states, such as China, Rome, and India, developed formalized legal systems, including court systems. Morton Fried (1978) used evidence from the Code of Hammurabi to demonstrate that these laws reinforced a system of inequality by protecting the rights of the governing class, while keeping the peasants in a subordinate status. In other words, the Code of Hammurabi was designed to allow those in authority to have access to scarce resources.

In contrast, some anthropologists emphasized the benefits of codified laws for the maintenance of society (Service 1978b). They argued that the maintenance of social and political order was crucial for agricultural states. Serious disruptions would have led to the neglect of agricultural production, which would have had devastating consequences for all members of society. Thus, legal codes such as the Code of Hammurabi, the Biblical laws of the Israelites, the laws of Manu of India, the Confucianist codes of China, and the Roman imperial laws benefited everyone by maintaining social and political order.

Obviously, both of these perspectives provide useful insights into the role of law in agricultural states. Ruling elites developed these codified legal systems to their advantage, but these systems also functioned to control crime and institute political order.

Mediation and Self-Help

Despite the emergence of codified systems, the practice of mediation and self-help in the redress of criminal offenses did not completely disappear. For example, these practices continued centuries after the development of the

Greek state (Claessen, Van De Velde, and Smith 1985). In addition, oaths, oracles, and ordeals remained as methods for determining legal decisions in many agricultural civilizations.

A Case Study: Law in China The legal system of China evolved through various dynasties, culminating in the complex legal codes of the Han dynasty (206 B.C.–220 A.D.). Chinese criminal codes specified punishments for each offense, ranging from blows with a cane to execution by strangulation, by decapitation, or even by slow slicing. Punishments also included hard labor and exile. Chinese civil law included rules on agricultural property, family, and inheritance.

Decisions involving civil law frequently were left to arbitration between the disputants in the local community. In this sense, many legal decisions depended upon self-regulation of small groups. Use of written laws and the court system was generally restricted to cases that affected society as a whole. County magistrates familiar with the legal codes administered the law and recorded the decisions, which served as precedents for future cases. A hierarchy of judicial bodies from the county magistrates to the imperial court served as courts of appeal for serious cases. Despite the existence of a highly formalized court system, however, most scholars concur that Chinese law was weak. Because local magistrates had hundreds of thousands of people under their jurisdiction and the police force was relatively powerless, law enforcement was ineffective at the local level. Basic law enforcement relied instead on informal processes and sanctions administered by community leaders (Clayre 1985).

Warfare Warfare, especially defensive warfare, was an integral aspect of agricultural state development (Roscoe 2013). The state emerged, in most cases, as a result of conflict and competition among groups that eventually led to domination by a ruling group (Carneiro 1970, Cohen 1984; Roscoe 2013). Thus, with the emergence of state societies, warfare increased in scale and became much more organized. As governing elites accumulated more wealth and power, warfare became one of the major means of increasing their surpluses. Archaeologist V. Gordon Childe (1950), a conflict theorist, maintained that the ruling class in agricultural societies turned its energies from the conquest of nature to the conquest of people.

A cross-cultural study of external warfare by Keith Otterbein found that the capacity for organized warfare is much greater in agricultural state societies than in band, tribal, and chiefdom societies. State societies usually have a centralized political and military leadership, as well as professional armies and military training. In addition, surpluses of foodstuffs and luxury items frequently attract outside invaders, particularly nomadic pastoralists. Otterbein (1994) concluded that the primary motivation for warfare in state systems was to gain political control over other people. In the feudal societies of Western Europe and Japan, professional classes of knights and samurai protected the interests and resources of nobles. In addition, these warrior classes were used to wage offensive warfare against neighboring estates to increase landholdings and the supply of manpower.

Political Organization in Industrial and Postindustrial States

18.9 **Discuss the characteristics of politics in industrial and postindustrial societies.**

As European and American societies began to industrialize, the nature of their political organization was transformed. Members of the middle class grew economically powerful and were drawn to the idea of popular sovereignty—that is, that the people, rather than the rulers, were the ultimate source of political authority. In addition, because the middle classes (particularly the upper-middle class) were the primary beneficiaries of industrial capitalism, they favored a type of government that would allow them economic freedom to pursue profits without state interference. The American and French revolutions of the eighteenth century that inspired other revolutionary movements in Europe and elsewhere reflected these new socioeconomic and political trends. The feudal aristocratic patterns were thus eventually replaced with representative, constitutional governments. The overriding ideal in these democratic states is freedom or personal liberty, which includes freedom of expression, the right to vote, and the right to be represented in the government. Representation is based on the election of political leaders selected from various political parties that engage in competition for offices.

Although representative governments emerged in earlier centuries, their political ideals were not immediately realized. For example, in the United States, political rights, including the right to vote, were not extended to women and other minorities until the twentieth century.

Another aspect of political change was the growth of **nationalism**, a strong sense of loyalty to the nation-state based upon shared language, values, and culture. Before the development of nationalism, the primary focus of loyalty was the local community, religion, and the family (Anderson 1991; Eriksen 2010; Scupin 2012b). For example, in agricultural states, peasants rarely identified with the interests of the ruling elites. In industrial states, however, with the increase in literacy and the development of a print technology, nationalism became a unifying force. Print technology was used to create what political scientist Benedict Anderson (1991) refers to as "imagined communities," an allegiance to a nation-state that is often far removed from everyday family or local concerns. As a literate populace began to read about its history and culture in its own language, its members developed a new type of self-identification, and eventually people began to express pride in and loyalty to these newly defined countries.

Anderson, though, is not suggesting that nationalism is just "invented"; rather, he argues that people who begin to define themselves as members of a nation will never know, meet, or even hear of most of their fellow members (1983). He notes that the fact that people are willing to give up their lives for their nation or country means that nationalism has a powerful influence on people's emotions and sentiments. This loyalty to a nation is a byproduct of literacy and the proliferation of the media in promoting specific ideas regarding one's nation.

Michael Herzfeld, an anthropologist who has written extensively about nationalism, notes that nationalism parallels religious cosmologies in that it creates distinctive differences between the believers and nonbelievers, the insiders and outsiders, and it reaffirms that the world is meaningful and sacred to people (1992). Herzfeld did ethnographic research in Greece, and in his book *Ours Once More: Folklore, Ideology, and the Making of Modern Greece* (1986), he focused on how Greek nationalism was created and managed by state authorities. One of the themes in his book is how nineteenth- and twentieth-century Greek intellectuals drew on folklore from rural areas to present an image of modern Greece as a continuation of its traditional classical past. The Greek state has drawn on a classical past that has been imagined as the root of all Western civilization to produce a contemporary source of nationalism for its citizens. This classical image of Greece as the mythical foundation of Western society and democratic institutions was reemphasized in the 2004 Olympics in Athens, Greece. A variety of symbols and motifs from ancient Greek culture and myth was projected internationally to promote Greece's unique national identity and culture, as well as its role as the foundation of Western civilization. Herzfeld's historical and cultural treatment indicates that the bureaucrats and intellectuals selected certain images and neglected other aspects of the past to develop this sense of nationalism for Greek citizens. For example, they selectively underplayed the role of the Ottoman Empire and the Turkish influence on Greek society for centuries. The Turks were considered outsiders and not an integral part of Greek national culture. The manufacture of nationalism by state authorities and intellectuals who romanticized the classical past and rural villages produced a culture of loyalty to, and a sense of, the sacredness of Greek national culture. Many other industrialized societies, such as England, France, Japan, and Russia, could be used to illustrate this same pattern in the production of nationalism, a contemporary trait of modern nation-states.

Deutscher Tag in Nürnberg, 1923.
Die SA ist angetreten

This Nazi rally in Nuremburg, Germany in 1923 demonstrates an extreme form of nationalism in an industrial society.

Political Organization in Socialist States

The former Soviet Union was the first nation to declare that it had a socialist government that would be dominated by the working class—the proletariat—rather than the upper class or middle class. According to Marxist theory, this socialist government was to be only a transitional stage of state development, to be followed by a true form of communism in which the state would wither away. In Marx's view, in the communist stage there would be no need for the state, or government, because everyone's needs would be completely taken care of through people who would be free to produce and create for the community.

In the ensuing years, the ideals of the socialist state ruled by the proletariat and the movement toward an egalitarian communism were not realized in the Soviet Union. Instead, the Communist Party of the Soviet Union, with about 18 million members out of a total population of about 300 million, dominated the government, selecting about 1 million bureaucratic elite (the *apparatchiki*) to rule over the society. The Soviet Union became a totalitarian state that controlled the economy, the political process, the media, the educational system, and other social institutions. During certain periods of extreme repression, as under Joseph Stalin in the 1930s, millions of people were killed or exiled to forced labor camps. Citizens were prohibited from organizing politically, and official opposition to state policies was not tolerated. This form of totalitarian government also existed in the socialist countries of Eastern Europe that were dominated by the Soviet Union.

Industrialism and State Bureaucracy

One similarity among the governments of the West, Japan, and the former Soviet Union is the degree to which the state has become a highly developed bureaucracy. It appears that when an industrial economy becomes highly specialized and complex, a strong, centralized government develops to help coordinate and integrate the society's complicated political and economic affairs. Of course, as previously discussed, in socialist societies such as the Soviet Union, this growth and centralization of the state are more extreme.

Law

Legal institutions are more formalized in industrial states. In general, the more complex the society, the more specialized the legal system (Schwartz and Miller 1975). As discussed earlier, legal institutions became formalized in some of the intensive agricultural states with the emergence of codified written law, records of cases and precedents, courts and government officials such as judges, procedures for deciding cases, and a police force to enforce legal decisions. These innovations in legal systems have been expanded in modern industrial societies.

In industrial states, laws become more complex and bureaucratically formalized with the development of national and local statutes, the compilation of private and public codes, the differentiation between criminal and civil laws, and the creation of more specialized law-enforcement agencies. With the development of centralized national governments, hierarchies of legal codes were formulated that ranged from national constitutions to regional and local codes. One of the most distinctive features of law in industrial societies is the proliferation of public and procedural law, referred to as *administrative law* (Vago 1995).

Administrative law reflects the emerging bureaucratic rules and technical requirements in the various legal institutions and agencies in industrial states. Courts in modern industrial states play an important role not only in adjudication, but also in mediation and other methods of conflict resolution. In addition, the legal system is the most important means of inducing social change in complex industrial societies. For example, during the 1960s legislation was used to gain civil rights for ethnic minorities such as African-Americans in the United States.

Japanese Law

The unique configuration of Japanese values and norms, in comparison with those of Western or Soviet society, has produced a different form of legal system in Japan. The Confucian ethos and traditional Japanese norms emphasizing group harmony have deeply influenced legal processes and institutions. The Japanese generally adopt extrajudicial, informal means of resolving disputes and prefer reaching legal compromises as opposed to assigning moral blame or deciding on the rightness or wrongness of an action. When a dispute arises, a mediator is usually employed to bring about harmony and reconciliation. The Japanese prefer the mediator to a lawyer, who is less likely to know the parties or to have a personal relationship with them. In this sense, the Japanese mediation system resembles those of small-scale tribal societies (Hendry 2013).

In Japanese society, there tends to be no legal or societal pressure for absolute justice. The proper, moral action is to accept blame for a wrongdoing and resign oneself to the consequences. Conflict resolution outside the court system and codified law tends to be the rule with respect to civil law. Obviously, one of the differences between Japan and the United States is the overwhelming cultural homogeneity of Japan. In contrast, the United States is a highly heterogeneous society with many different ethnic groups and cultural backgrounds. The relative homogeneity of Japanese society facilitates the resolution of conflicts through informal means, rather than through the legal system, as in the United States. However, it appears that Japan's rate of litigation is beginning to increase (Vago 1995).

Warfare and Technology in Industrial and Postindustrial States

18.10 Discuss how warfare changes in industrial and postindustrial states.

We noted already that warfare increased with the territorial expansion of agricultural empires such as the Chinese, Roman, Aztec, and Indian Empires. To some extent, this increase in warfare was linked to technological developments such as the invention of iron weapons. In addition, the nature of warfare began to change with the development of centralized state systems that competed with rival territories. These general tendencies were accelerated with the evolution of industrial states.

Industrial states began to develop military technologies that enabled them to carry on fierce nationalistic wars in distant regions. One of the prime motivations for these wars was the desire to establish economic and political hegemony over foreign peoples. The industrial nation-states became much more involved in economic rivalry over profits, markets, and natural resources in other territories. Most historians conclude that these imperialist rivalries were among the principal reasons for World War I.

World War I marked a watershed in the evolution of military warfare. It was a global war in which nation-states mobilized a high proportion of their male populations and reoriented their economic systems toward military production and support. The numbers of combatants and noncombatants killed far outnumbered those of any previous war in any type of society.

The combination of technological advances and centralized military organizations dramatically changed the nature of warfare. Tanks, airplanes, and other modern weapons enabled industrial states to wage tremendously destructive global warfare, as witnessed by World War II. This expanding military technology was inextricably linked to industrial technology. The rise of industries such as the airlines, automobiles, petroleum and plastics, and electronics and computers was related to the development of war technology. And, of course, the atomic era began in 1945 when the United States dropped atomic bombs on the Japanese cities of Hiroshima and Nagasaki. Since that time period, the proliferation of nuclear weapons in many countries of the world has concerned many citizens in industrial and postindustrial societies.

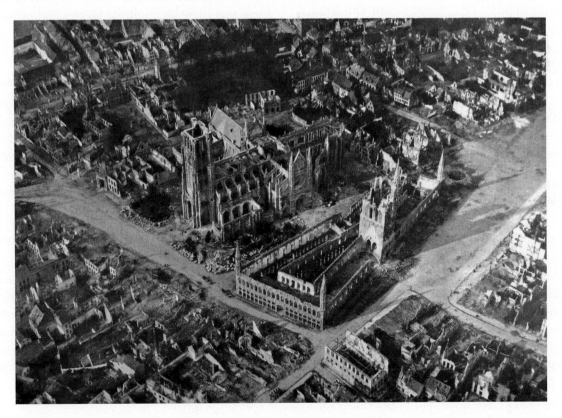

This shows the World War I destruction of the city of Ypres in Belgium in 1915.

Summary and Review of Learning Objectives

18.1 Discuss how anthropologists understand politics, warfare, and law.

Anthropologists have been influenced by Max Weber's understanding of politics. Weber defined political power as the ability to achieve personal ends despite opposition. In this sense, political power can be based on physical or psychological *coercion*. Weber perceived this type of political power as *illegitimate*, in that it is unacceptable to most members of a society. Anthropologists analyze the basis of political power, authority, and decision making in different forms of sociocultural systems, bands, tribes, chiefdoms, and states. Anthropologists define warfare as armed combat among territorial or political communities. They distinguish between *internal warfare*, which involves political communities within the same society or culture, and *external warfare*, which occurs among different societal groups. A feud is a type of armed combat occurring within a political community and usually involving one kin group taking revenge against another kin group. Laws are understood as formalized norms with sanctions found in different societies. Four criteria that must be present for a norm to be considered a law: (1) authority, (2) intention of universal application, (3) obligation, and (4) sanction.

18.2 Discuss the characteristics of politics in foraging societies.

The basic political unit of foraging societies is the band, which is politically independent of other bands and has its own internal leadership. Leaders are chosen because of their skills in hunting, food collecting, communication, decision making, or other personal abilities. There is minimal stratification between the leaders and other members of the band. Typically, leaders do not aspire to become political leaders with authority over others in band societies.

18.3 Describe the features of violence and warfare in foraging societies.

There is a minimal amount of violence and warfare in contemporary foraging societies. Sometimes as among the Tiwi aboriginals of Australia, symbolic forms of warfare are found. Although violence and homicide are found in foraging societies, various means of conflict resolution are based on the mobility of band members to join other bands, the lack of interpersonal status competition among males, or institutional mechanisms such as song duels found among the Inuit.

18.4 Discuss the characteristics of politics in tribal societies.

Tribal societies have *decentralized political systems*, in which authority is distributed among a number of individuals, groups, and associations. Political leadership is open to any male (especially older males) in the society and is usually based on personal abilities and qualities. In tribal societies, two types of sodalities exist: kinship sodalities, including lineages and clans, and nonkin sodalities, such as age sets, village councils of elders, male secret societies, and military societies. These nonkin sodalities also have political functions and are mostly voluntary associations that cut across kinship ties by creating alliances outside the immediate kin groups. In horticultural tribes village headman or "big men" as found in Papua New Guinea become political leaders. Many pastoralist tribes have segmentary lineage systems as political units that form oppositional kin groups when resolving political disputes.

18.5 Discuss how anthropologists explain tribal warfare.

Warfare is much more prevalent in tribal societies than band societies. Some anthropologists have offered cultural materialist hypotheses focusing on nutritional deficiencies for explaining tribal warfare, while others have promoted sociobiological models. Currently most anthropologists agree that there are multiple factors that influence tribal warfare including prestige for warriors, and morality and religion that bind tribes together.

18.6 Describe political authority in chiefdoms.

Unlike bands or tribes, chiefdoms were centrally organized with permanent political offices and rules of succession for establishing political authority. There were limits to chiefly power based on the generosity of chiefs, and how the legitimacy of authority was perceived by the populace. Legal authority in chiefdoms is based on adjudication of cases ruled over by chiefs.

18.7 Discuss how anthropologists explain the evolution and origins of chiefdoms.

In explaining the origin of chiefdoms, some anthropologists emphasized regional symbiosis among different areas that exchanged food and resources with a redistributional center. Other archaeologists have focused on the ability of chiefs to manage control over vital resource areas to establish political authority. In any case, anthropologists do not accept a unilineal view of the evolution of chiefdoms from tribes; there was often an oscillation or cycling from tribes to chiefdoms and back again, or the economic dependence of chiefdoms on agricultural states in some regions.

18.8 Discuss the features of politics in agricultural civilizations.

A diversity of forms of political organization developed in agricultural states, ranging from large-scale centralized governments with bureaucracies, to different states based on kinship in some areas of Africa, to theater states in areas of Southeast Asia or India. One influential anthropological classification used is the distinction between radial and galactic models of state authority. Legal authority for agricultural states is usually based on written criminal and civil laws.

18.9 Discuss the characteristics of politics in industrial and postindustrial societies.

Generally, in the case of European and American industrial societies, more representative democratic governments begin to develop based on popular sovereignty. In addition, nationalism emerges as a strong sense of loyalty to the nation-state based upon shared language, values, and culture. Before the development of nationalism, the primary focus of loyalty was the local community, religion, and the family. These industrial and postindustrial societies developed strong, centralized governments to help coordinate and integrate the society's complicated political and economic affairs. Legal developments become more complex and involved the development of national and local statutes, the compilation of private and public codes, the differentiation between criminal and civil laws, and the creation of more specialized law enforcement agencies.

18.10 Discuss how warfare changes in industrial and postindustrial states.

Warfare has become more lethal in industrial and postindustrial societies, along with technological developments ushering in global wars such as World Wars I and II. The dangers of lethal warfare are increasingly widespread as more nations attempt to develop nuclear weapons.

Key Terms

adjudication, p. 424
authority, p. 412
complementary opposition, p. 418
feud, p. 413
feudalism, p. 425
galactic polity, p. 425

nationalism, p. 426
oath, p. 422
office, p. 422
oracles, p. 422
political power, p. 412
radial polity, p. 425

segmentary lineage system, p. 418
sodalities, p. 412
theater state, p. 425
warfare, p. 413

Chapter 19
Religion and Aesthetics

 Learning Objectives

After reading this chapter you should be able to:

19.1 Discuss how anthropologists such as Clifford Geertz define religion.

19.2 Discuss how anthropologists define myth and ritual.

19.3 Describe the stages of rites of passage as discussed by anthropologists.

19.4 Discuss the new developments by cognitive anthropologists and their understanding of religion.

19.5 Discuss how anthropologists study art and music in different societies.

19.6 Describe examples of religion found in foraging societies.

19.7 Describe examples of art and music found in foraging societies.

19.8 Describe examples of religion found in horticulturalist and pastoralist societies.

19.9 Discuss how religion is interrelated with politics in chiefdom societies.

19.10 Describe examples of art, architecture, and music in chiefdom societies.

19.11 Describe some examples of ecclesiastical and universalistic religions found in agricultural societies.

19.12 Describe some examples of art, architecture, and music in agricultural societies.

19.13 Discuss religion and secularization in industrial and postindustrial societies.

19.14 Discuss some developments in art and music in industrial and postindustrial societies.

Religion

19.1 **Discuss how anthropologists such as Clifford Geertz define religion.**

As we saw in Chapter 7, archaeologists have discovered some limited evidence of religious beliefs and practices associated with archaic *Homo sapiens neanderthalensis*, or Neandertals, that date back to 100,000 years ago. Religion is a cultural universal, although specific beliefs and practices vary significantly from one society to another. For example, some religions are based on the worship of an all-knowing, all-powerful supreme being, whereas others have many deities, and some may have no deities at all. The term *religion* is derived from the Latin term *religio*, which has had different meanings in Western history. In some cases, it referred to a "transcendent" experience that individuals had beyond normal, everyday social life, but at other times, it referred to "superstition" or "piety" (Salver 1993). It has been extremely difficult for anthropologists to define religion with a simple formula because it varies so much from one region and culture to another (Scupin 2008; Saler 1993; Boyer 2001).

Humans learn their religious traditions through the process of enculturation. Religious convictions are, therefore, shaped by the historical and social situations in which a person lives. For example, a person enculturated in ancient Greece would most likely have believed in many deities, among whom Zeus was the most powerful.

In studying the anthropology of religion, a critical point must be understood: Anthropologists are not concerned with the "truth" or "falsity" of any particular religious belief. As anthropology is partially based on the scientific method, the field of anthropology is not competent or able to investigate supernatural or metaphysical questions that go beyond empirical data. Rather, anthropological research on religion focuses on the relationship of doctrines, beliefs, and other religious questions to aspects of cognition, emotions, and society. Most anthropologists recognize that religious faith is not a testable proposition that can be analyzed by science or logic. Faith is beyond empirical findings that can be uncovered by scientific investigation. The major questions posed by anthropologists are these: How do religious beliefs become established within a society? How do religious beliefs affect, relate to, and reflect the cognitive, emotional, and sociocultural conditions and concerns of a group of people?

In addition, anthropologists often use the humanistic-interpretive approach when analyzing religious beliefs, symbols, and myths. Clifford Geertz offered a definition of religion to use as a tool in this humanistic-interpretive mode of understanding religion:

A religion is a system of symbols which acts to establish powerful, pervasive, and long-lasting moods and motivations in men by formulating conceptions of a general order of existence and clothing these conceptions with such an aura of factuality that the moods and motivations seem uniquely realistic. (197:90)

Let us examine this definition more closely. Central to any religion is a "system of symbols," which includes all sacred objects, ranging from Christian crucifixes, Native American "medicine pouches," and Buddhist relics to sacred myths such as Genesis or the Ramayana of Hinduism. These symbols produce "moods," such as happiness and sadness, and "motivations" that provide direction or ethical goals in a person's life. Hence, religious symbols enhance particular feelings and dispositions, creating an intense 'sense of awe' in individuals. This awe is induced through the use of sacred symbols in rituals and other religious performances to create an atmosphere of mystery going beyond everyday experience. But religious symbols also create and reaffirm a worldview by "formulating conceptions of a general order of existence." This worldview provides meaning or purpose to life and the universe. A religious worldview helps people discern the meaning of pain and suffering in the world. Sacred myths help people make sense of the world and also explain and justify cultural values and social rules. One problem with Geertz's definition of religion is that it does not recognize the diversity of cultural beliefs, conceptions, and symbolic meanings and the multiplicity of practices and variation within any religious tradition. In other words, as we emphasized in earlier chapters, presently anthropologists are more aware that the concept of a homogeneous culture as used in the past is not useful in understanding different religions or civilizations.

More recently, anthropologist David Parkin has reconstructed Geertz's definition of religion and combined it with a more current anthropological understanding of emotions and cognition in his studies of Muslims in Zanzibar, East Africa (2007). Parkin suggests that Geertz's definition tended to separate emotions and cognition in categorical ways, but today anthropologists recognize that these two factors are inextricably combined. The ethnographic study of the Islamic tradition in Zanzibar by Parkin indicates that these people learn their religion through formal modes of cognition, but unconscious cognitive and emotional processes influence what they learn.

Myth and Ritual

19.2 Discuss how anthropologists define myth and ritual.

The study of religious traditions includes the analysis and interpretation of myths. **Myths** consist of a people's assumed knowledge about the universe and the natural and supernatural worlds and about humanity's place in these worlds. In Chapter 3, we presented some basic myths or cosmologies regarding the creation of the universe. All societies have such sacred myths. Anthropologists focus on a number of questions regarding myths: Why do myths of a particular type exist in different societies? What is the relationship between myths and other aspects of sociocultural systems? Are myths distortions of historical events? Or as Geertz suggested, do myths provide a blueprint for comprehending the natural and social world for a society? What are the functions of myths? How are myths interpreted and reinterpreted by different people within the society?

Rituals

The final portion of Geertz's definition—that these systems of symbols act to clothe those conceptions in "such an aura of factuality that the moods and motivations seem uniquely realistic"—attempts to deal with the question often asked about religious belief: How do humans come to believe in ideas about spirits, souls, revelations, and many unsupportable or untestable conceptions? Geertz's answer to this question is that religious rituals in which

humans participate create an "aura of factuality." It is through ritual that deeper realities are reached. Religion is nonempirical and nonrational in its search for truth. It is not based on conclusions from scientific experience, but is "prior" to experience. Religious truth is not "inductive," providing evidence for metaphysical explanations. It symbolically and abstractly evokes the ultimate concerns of humans. Through ritual activities, these symbolic and abstract nonempirical truths are given meaning.

Religious **rituals** consist of repetitive behaviors that communicate sacred symbols to members of society. Examples of religious rituals are the Catholic Mass, Jewish Passover rites, and Native American sweat lodge rites, which include prayer, meditation, and other spiritual communication. Anthropologist Edmund Leach (1966) emphasized that religious rituals communicate these sacred symbols and information in a condensed manner. He noted that the verbal part of a ritual is not separable from the behavioral part and that rituals can have different symbolic meanings for people in a society. In other words, religious rituals convey a unique, personal, psychological experience for every individual who participates.

Recently, the anthropologist Harvey Whitehouse, using a cognitive-evolutionary approach, suggests that there are two different modes of religiosity: the doctrinal and the imagistic (Whitehouse 2004). The doctrinal mode is the formal scriptural or oral traditions that are associated with what children and adults learn from constant repetition within their religious tradition. In contrast, the imagistic mode is deeply emotional and results from an intense personal experience that an individual has with his or her religious tradition. In many cases, Whitehouse suggests, the imagistic mode of religiosity results from what he calls "flashbulb memories" from singular incidents that an individual has in ritual experiences. He did ethnographic research on traumatic puberty life cycle initiation rituals in Melanesia and describes how these rituals create flashbulb memories that result in an imagistic mode of religiosity for these males. These flashbulb memories highlight the "trauma" of these ritual experiences and induce images that remain with individuals throughout their lives. This distinction between doctrinal and imagistic modes of religiosity has been an important means of understanding religious rituals for contemporary anthropologists.

Rites of Passage

19.3 Describe the stages of rites of passage as discussed by anthropologists.

Anthropologists have done considerable research on the **rites of passage**, rituals associated with the life cycle and the movement of people between different age-status levels. Almost all cultures have rites of passage to demarcate these different stages of the life cycle. Arnold Van Gennep (1960), a Belgian anthropologist, wrote a classic study of different rites of passage throughout the world. He noted similarities among various rites connected with birth, puberty, marriage, and funerals. According to Van Gennep, these rites of passage are characterized by three interconnected stages: *separation*, *marginality*, and *aggregation*.

The first phase, *separation*, transforms people from one age status to another. In this phase, people leave behind the symbols, roles, and norms associated with their former position. The second phase, referred to as *marginality*, places people in a state of transition or a temporary period of ambiguity. This stage often involves separating individuals from the larger society to undergo traditional ordeals or indoctrination. The final phase is *aggregation*, or incorporation, when individuals assume their new status. Later, the anthropologist Victor Turner refined the

model of Van Gennep and referred to the three stages as *structure*, *antistructure* or *liminality*, and *communitas* (1969). *Structure* is the initial status of the individual. The period of *liminality* is the temporary period of ambiguity, marginality, and antistructural. Turner defined *communitas*, as also part of the antistructural phase where the individual felt a strong bond and a sense of equality with others. The final phase of the rite of passage is reincorporation, marking a return to, and reunion with, society with a wholly new status.

The best-known examples of these rites of passage are various religious rituals associated with adolescence, such as the confirmation rituals associated with Catholicism and the *bar mitzvah* and *bat mitzvah* rituals in Judaism. However, college and university graduation ceremonies are a more secular form of a rite of passage for U.S. students.

CRITICAL PERSPECTIVES: GRADUATION: A Rite of Passage in U.S. Society

As the United States continues to change from an industrial to a postindustrial society, more people are attending college to gain the skills and knowledge necessary to prepare them for careers. Consequently, one rite of passage that people increasingly look forward to is graduation from college. This rite of passage is similar to those in many other societies. Rites of passage, as mentioned above, are described by anthropologists as rituals that change the status of an individual within society. The late Victor Turner divided rites of passage into three distinctive stages: an initial structured phase (the original status of the individual); a liminal phase, wherein the individual is in a highly ambigu-

ous and antistructured status called "communitas," where the student feels a strong emotional bond with others of equal status. In the final stage, the individual is reincorporated back into society with a new status (1969).

For most students, their undergraduate university or college education is a time of "liminality" or an ambiguous, transitional period of life. This liminal period is marked by an extensive four or five years of study, examinations, and research papers, as well as social activities. During this liminal phase, students are neither children nor adults. If they reside on campus in dormitories or residence halls, they live separate from society. Like the initiates in rites of passage in small-scale societies, the students are exposed to former types of "secret knowledge," such as evolution or more controversial views of sexuality, gender, and religion. Students are often taken away from their local neighborhoods and locales and placed with other students from ethnic and class backgrounds different from their own. This liminal period is often a time of stress and uncertainty. The commencement ceremony marks the final stage of the rite of passage, as the graduates reenter society with a wholly new status.

The commencement ceremony dates back to the 12th century at the University of Bologna in what is now

Italy. Shortly thereafter, it spread to other European universities. The first U.S. graduates went through their commencement in 1642 at Harvard College. These first commencement ceremonies lasted several days and were accompanied by entertainment, wrestling matches, banquets, and dances.

The academic costumes worn by graduates come directly from the late Middle Ages and the Renaissance. The black gowns and square caps, called mortarboards, were donned to celebrate the change in status. A precise ritual dictates that the tassel that hangs off the cap should be moved from the right side to the left side when the degree is conferred.

Like rites of passage in other societies, graduation from college represents a transition in status. In Latin, *gradus* means "a step," and *degradus* means "a rung on a ladder." From the first, we get the word *graduation*; from the second, *degree*. Both words are connected to a stage in life, the end of one period of life and the beginning of another. To graduate means to change by degrees.

Typically, college graduates move from the status of a receiver to that of a giver. During the liminal period, many students are subsidized and nurtured by society and especially by parents. However, after graduation and reincorporation back into society, they become givers in all sorts of ways. A degree qualifies graduates for jobs and careers to which they would not otherwise have access. Upon getting their jobs, former students will be givers and contribute to the workplace. In addition, degree holders will begin to subsidize others through taxes. Many will marry and accept such responsibilities as raising children and paying mortgages. This movement from receiver to giver represents a fundamental life-cycle transition for many U.S. students.

Points to Ponder

1. As you move toward your degree in college, do you believe that what you are learning has any relationship to what you will need after your change in status?
2. In what ways would you change the educational process so that it would help you develop your potential?
3. Do you think the grading system used by most colleges and universities is a fair means of assessing your acquisition of knowledge and skills?
4. What would you suggest as a better means of evaluating students?
5. What kinds of expectations do you have about your change in status after you receive your degree?

Religious Specialists

One important area of research in the anthropology of religion is the study of religious specialists in different societies. Every society has certain individuals who possess specialized sacred knowledge. Such individuals officiate over rituals and interpret myths. The type of religious specialist varies with the form of sociocultural system. **Shamans** are usually part-time religious practitioners who are believed to have contact with supernatural beings and powers. They do not have a formalized official status as religious practitioners in their respective societies. Shamans are involved in various types of healing activities, treating both physical and psychological illnesses. Aside from their religious functions, they participate in the same subsistence activities and functions as anyone else in their society. Anthropologists also use terms such as *native healer, medicine man,* and *medicine woman* to refer to these practitioners.

The terms **priest** and **priestess** refer to full-time religious specialists who serve in an official capacity as a custodian of sacred knowledge. In contrast to shamans, priests and priestesses are usually trained through formal educational processes to maintain religious traditions and rituals. Priests and priestesses are usually associated with more complex sociocultural systems.

Religious Movements

Another topic of interest in the anthropology of religion is the analysis of religious movements. In early approaches of the social sciences, religion was viewed simply as an outcome of certain economic or political conditions in society. It was assumed that as society developed modern economic and political institutions, religious traditions would disappear. Religion was viewed as a peripheral element that served only to conserve society as a static system. Today, however, some anthropologists have begun to analyze religious beliefs and worldviews as major variables that induce societal change. For example,

cultural anthropologists studying Islamic fundamentalist movements have concluded that, in the Middle East, religion is a major force for social change. These new modes of understanding and explaining religious movements are analyzed in later chapters.

Cognition and Religion

19.4 Discuss the new developments by cognitive anthropologists and their understanding of religion.

In Chapter 11, we introduced the fields of cognitive anthropology and evolutionary psychology. A number of cognitive anthropologists such as Pascal Boyer, Scott Atran, Harvey Whitehouse, Stewart Guthrie, and Joseph Henrich, have drawn on these two fields in order to explore religion. In Boyer's *Religion Explained: The Evolutionary Origins of Religious Thought* (2001) and Atran's *In Gods We Trust: The Evolutionary Landscape of Religion* (2002), these anthropologists recognize the importance of the humanistic-interpretive approach in understanding religion, but they also want to explore the scientific-causal aspects of religion and the universal aspects of religion everywhere. These anthropologists investigate questions such as these: Why does religion matter so much in people's lives everywhere? Are there any common features of religion? Why do certain types of religious beliefs develop, rather than other types? Drawing upon a vast range of cross-cultural data, these anthropologists suggest that evolution and natural selection have designed the human mind to be "religious." Although there is a tremendous diversity of religious traditions throughout the world, some types of religious beliefs have more resilience and are retained and culturally transmitted by humans more than others. In all societies, children are exposed to various religious beliefs and practices. But as Atran and Boyer emphasize, because of specific predispositions and intuitions within our evolutionary-designed mind, certain forms of religious beliefs and concepts have exceptional relevance and meaning for humans.

In a related discussion regarding some of the most common features of religion, cognitive anthropologist Stewart Guthrie argues that human religious beliefs and concepts are based on the cognitive phenomena of anthropomorphism. **Anthropomorphism** is the psychological disposition to project and perceive human characteristics in nonhuman phenomena. In his book *Faces in the Clouds: A New Theory of Religion*, Guthrie suggests that anthropomorphism is an inherent aspect of our cognitive and thinking processes (1993). As humans perceive the world, they tend to project human agency-like characteristics into the world. For example, when we look at clouds we tend to perceive human "faces in the cloud." Guthrie draws on worldwide ethnographic data to indicate many similar phenomena reported by people. When humans project these human agency-like characteristics in many cases they are attributed to unseen agents such as deities, spirits, or supernatural forces. Humans attribute agency to many types of nonhuman entities, including clouds, computers, wind, or other phenomena. Guthrie asserts that as we grapple with complex phenomena, our cognitive processes use our understanding of persons and humans to interpret these complex phenomena. These cognitive processes are unconscious, but they have consequences for the emergence of religious thinking in all humans.

In contrast to the intuitive knowledge and inferences that become a reliable basis for comprehending the natural and social world, both Atran and Boyer emphasize that religious beliefs and knowledge are mostly counterintuitive (Boyer 2001; Atran 2002). Religious spirits and gods have properties that normal people do not have. Although most humans treat religious spirits and gods as persons, they are radically different from what our intuitions tell us about persons. For the most part, they do not eat, grow old, or die; they can even fly through space, become invisible, change shape, and perceive our innermost thoughts. Gods and spirits become invisible partners and friends of people, but these spiritual beings are unlike normal persons. These spiritual agents can be at several places at one time and have full access to our innermost thoughts and specific behaviors and actions. Some societies have a concept of a god that knows everything. Adults and children at an early age understand that normal people do not have these capacities for knowledge.

These counterintuitive abilities of spirits and gods, including their full access to our thoughts and specific behaviors, are "attention grabbing" for humans throughout the world. Spiritual agents who have this full access to knowledge become extremely relevant in understanding human social and moral conditions. Beings that can know our innermost thoughts and all of our behaviors resonate

with our social and moral intuitions. Thus, religious beliefs and concepts become widespread and plausible in all societies because of the way human cognition is organized and designed. Beliefs in witches, ancestral spirits, and angry or beneficent gods become easily represented in all cultures because they are dependent on our human cognitive capacities and intuitive understanding of the natural and social worlds. These religious phenomena activate and trigger our human cognitive capacities and intuitive abilities, which results in the universal distribution of certain types of spiritual beliefs and concepts.

These cognitive anthropologists explain why religious beliefs have become so powerful throughout human prehistory and history. They do not suggest that there is a specialized area of the brain or "religious instinct" that is a religious center that handles god- or spiritual-related thoughts. In addition, they do not suggest that there are specific people who have exceptional religious abilities and were responsible for establishing religious beliefs and practices. Religion, like other everyday matters in our natural and social circumstances, does not require special capacities. Rather, religious beliefs and concepts become relevant to humans everywhere because they readily coincide with our cognitive capacities and our intuitive and inferential abilities. These beliefs and teachings are likely to have a direct effect on people's thoughts, emotions, and morality.

Additionally, many religious beliefs are different from our everyday common-sense beliefs and intuitions. Religious beliefs have commonalities such as spiritual agents that have full access to our innermost thoughts, concepts of life after death, and concepts of morality all over the world; most likely they have a long evolutionary history. Other religious beliefs may have developed in the past, but they did not have the sustaining power of the ones known today, and they disappeared. The religious beliefs that still exist have a central relevance to many people, are extremely powerful, and converge with their cognitive capacities and abilities. In some cases, people may give up their lives or kill others based on their particular religious beliefs. These cognitive anthropological explorations of the interconnection between human cognition and religious expression have contributed to anthropological hypotheses about our cognitive capacities and about links between biological and psychological developments and our religious life.

Recently, a number of cognitive anthropologists have combined the cognitive approach to religion described above with an understanding of how religious beliefs and rituals induce both cooperation within groups and enmity between different groups (Atran 2010; Atran and Henrich 2010; Whitehouse 2004). As we have seen in earlier chapters, reciprocity and exchange through economics, kinship, and marriage maintain "prosocial" norms for altruistic cooperation in small-scale societies. However, how are prosocial norms for cooperation among people maintained in large-scale societies and interrelationships that are no longer based directly on reciprocity and kinship relations? Cognitive anthropologists suggest that as large-scale agricultural civilizations develop, major religious traditions and shared sacred values, beliefs, and rituals become the stabilizing prosocial norms for cooperation among people who no longer share kinship connections (Atran 2010; Atran and Henrich 2010; Whitehouse 2004; Whitehouse and Martin 2004). Building large-scale monuments (e.g., temples and pyramids) involved increasing commitments of labor to sustain particular religious beliefs and sacred values. These activities were costly to the individuals. The people who did not participate in these costly projects tended to be punished by other members of their societies. Thus, most people tended to cooperate and participate, regardless of cost. These shared initiatives produced cooperation and collective action among people of different family and socioeconomic backgrounds.

However, as these complex religious traditions and sacred values that reinforced group solidarity and cooperation, economic and demographic expansion frequently resulted in conflict and warfare between different agricultural civilizations. This competition and conflict among civilizations led people to become more deeply committed to particular religious beliefs and practices within their own groups. Cooperation to defend one's own civilization and religious tradition became essential (Atran 2010; Atran and Henrich 2010; Whitehouse 2004; Whitehouse and Martin 2004). According to these cognitive anthropologists, this competition among agricultural civilizations and their religious traditions expanded the sphere of cooperation and solidarity *within* groups, but often created the potential for enmity and conflict *between* different groups. This hypothesis is supported by evidence presented in the last chapter—that agricultural civilizations were often engaged in warfare and territorial expansion.

Aesthetics: Art and Music

19.5 Discuss how anthropologists study art and music in different societies.

As described in Chapter 1, many anthropologists study the art and music of different societies throughout the world. They define **art** as a diverse range of activities and skills, and the products of those activities that are used as expressions and representations of human emotions, intellect, and creativity. Art includes different modes of painting, sculpture, printmaking, photography, and other visual media. *Architecture* is also an art form that involves the practical applications of creative expression in its buildings

and structures. **Music** is an art form based on the organization of sounds in combination and in temporal relationships to produce audible works for performance in various communities. The field of ethnomusicology is the study of music as it is connected with the cultural traditions in different societies. Ethnomusicologists study songs, dances, musical instruments and compositions, and other dramatic performances that accompany music.

Anthropologists and ethnomusicologists discuss how art and music have distinct functions for societies and individuals. Art and music help create social bonds through shared creative experiences and expressions of group identity. In addition, art and music enhance cognitive flexibility and reduce emotional anxiety for individuals. Art assists individuals and groups in extending their daily sensory and imaginary experiences outside of the present, into the future and back into the past. Art and music can aid the construction of beliefs and patterns of morality as these creative processes interconnect with myths, legends, and collective narratives of their particular group. In all societies, exposure to art and music enter into childhood enculturation and help situate individuals within their environments. Often the major rites of passage and ceremonies regarding birth, initiation, coming of age, marriage, and death are accompanied by art and music. The symbolic imagery of the arts produces an imaginary world that assists in the cognitive and emotional development indispensable for human adaptations and becomes an important source of a meaningful life.

In Western societies both art and music are historically associated with the fine arts or "high culture." Recall our discussion of anthropologist/sociologist Pierre Bourdieu's views of different forms of capital: economic capital, social capital, and cultural capital (see Chapter 16, p. 350). Bourdieu described cultural capital as based on the *aesthetic* tastes and preferences for certain symbolic forms of literature, art, music, or foods that distinguished people with respect to their socioeconomic background. (1984). For many centuries, the upper-class elites of Western societies determined and established the criteria for *aesthetic* tastes, or preferences for what was beautiful or inspirational in fine art and music. Elite expressions of Western culture fine art were usually contrasted with popular, folk, or "primitive" art or music, which was characterized as less refined or backward and less sophisticated than fine art. However, anthropologists take a much broader cross-cultural view of art and music than the Western elite. Although Franz Boas discussed the art in Northwest Coast American Indian cultures and entitled his book *Primitive Art* (1927), this work challenged the assumptions of the earlier elite understandings of art. Boas stressed the principle of cultural relativism and debunked the categories of "savages," or "primitive," versus civilized peoples (see Chapter 13). Anthropologists emphasize that art and musical expression are universal and found in all societies (Brown 1991). Ethnomusicologists and anthropologists who study music and art find that what is considered beautiful or refined is dependent on the complex cultural context in different societies. Thus, they challenge the Western elite views of *aesthetics* regarding perceptions of beauty and taste. This anthropological perspective entails a framework that includes the entire world's catalog of art and music that express and represent human emotions, intellect, and creativity. This anthropological perspective will become apparent in the later consideration of arts in different societies.

Religion among Foragers

19.6 Describe examples of religion found in foraging societies.

The religions associated with modern foragers are based on oral traditions referred to by the religious studies scholar Mircea Eliade (1959) as "cosmic religions." These religions are intimately associated with nature. The natural cycle of seasons; inorganic matter such as rocks, water, and mountains; and other features of the natural environment are invested with sacred significance. All foraging societies have sacred places associated with the landscape where they live. These sacred spots are often marked or painted with petroglyphs (rock paintings) that identify the spiritual significance of the territories of these peoples. Spirit and matter are inseparable. In addition, cosmic religions are not identified with any particular historical events or individuals, as are the "literate" religious traditions of Judaism, Islam, Christianity, Buddhism, and Hinduism.

The sacredness of the natural environment is sometimes expressed in a form of **animism**, the belief that spirits reside within all inorganic and organic substances. The nineteenth-century anthropologist Edward Tylor used the term *animism* in reference to the earliest religious traditions (see Chapter 13). However, a number of current anthropologists are using the term *animism* to refer to the very respectful relationship between humans and others, including animals, plants, and inorganic objects in their cultural environment (Harvey 2006; Bird David 1999; Sponsel 2012). Anthropologist Nurit Bird David describes how the hunter-gatherer Nayaka peoples of South India perceive themselves as fully integrated with their ecological and social environment, which includes other organic and inorganic beings (1999). This Nayaka animistic view contrasts with the basic scientific cosmologies that predominate in Western culture that tend to conceptualize individual humans as separate from nature and material substances. The metaphysical conceptions in the

Ju/'hoansi San, Australian Aborigine, or Mbuti cultural tradition tend to be similar to this new conception of animism currently adopted by anthropologists.

The Dreamtime

An illuminating example of a cosmic religion among foragers is the Australian Aborigine notion of dreamtime (Stanner 1979). The dreamtime exists in the "other world," the world associated with the time of creation, where a person goes in dreams and visions and after death. It is believed that at the time of creation, the ancestors deposited souls of all living forms near watering holes, and eventually these souls or spirits were embedded in all matter, from rocks and water to trees and humans. The unification of all substance and spirit was a byproduct of the work of these ancestral beings. All of these spirits come to the world from the dreamtime; the birth of the universe is like a fall from the dreamtime. The Aborigines had symbolic representations of their ancestral beings that anthropologists referred to as *totems*. A **totem** is a mythical ancestor, usually a plant or an animal, that symbolizes a particular group. **Totemism** is a religious belief that associates a particular group with a symbolic and spiritual connection with specific natural species, objects, or other phenomena. The Aborigines had totemic symbols such as kangaroos or wallabies or plants that symbolized their ancestral beings.

The Aborigines believe that the ancestral beings still exist in the dreamtime, where they act as intermediaries between that world and the profane, everyday world of human affairs. The ancestral beings intervene in life, controlling plant, animal, and human life and death. This fundamental belief provides explanations for pain, joy, chaos, and order in human life. The dreamtime is a fundamental and complex conception that embraces the creative past and has particular significance for the present and future.

The dreamtime also conveys certain notions of morality. According to Aborigine traditions, the ancestral beings originally lived like other humans and had the capacity for being both moral and immoral, both good and evil (Stanner 1979). The immoral behavior of the dreamtime beings is highlighted to accentuate what is proper and moral in human affairs. Thus, this religion creates a moral order, which functions to sustain social control in the physical world. Although the dreamtime ancestors do not directly punish human wrongdoers, they have provided a blueprint for proper behavior with respect to obligations, reciprocities, and social behavior in general.

Inuit Religion

The Inuit (Eskimo) maintain a traditional religious belief system that involves curers or healers who control and manipulate the supernatural world. In contrast to some of the "literate" religious traditions, Inuit religion did not assume the existence of an omnipotent supreme being. The Inuit did believe that every living creature possesses a soul or spirit that is reincarnated after death. The Inuit did not maintain a belief in an afterworld, or heaven, in which these souls congregate after death. Instead, they believed that the souls of the deceased remain near the living. The spirits of animals allow themselves to be hunted and are constantly reincarnated in other animal forms, to be hunted again to ensure the Inuit way of life.

Within these general conceptions of spirituality, the Inuit believe in *soul loss*, in which a person's soul is taken from the body as a result of unforeseen circumstances. Soul loss causes mental and physical illness for the individual. It is often believed that the soul has been stolen by another spirit. The Inuit coped with these situations through shamanism.

Two major forms of shamanism are found in Inuit culture. One form is hereditary, passed on through either parent. The more common variety involves people who receive shamanistic powers through direct contact with the supernatural, usually through dreams, visions, or hallucinations. In most cases, the shamans are male; however, some Inuit females also become shamans. In the Bering Straits area, Inuit male and female shamans are believed to be able to own dead souls and spiritual beings called *tunghat*. Typically, the more spirits and souls these shamans own, the more they increase their spiritual status. The shamans are believed to be able to journey to the realm of the dead souls and spiritual beings to induce changes in the weather or cure the sick or ensure the prosperity and reincarnation of animals (Lowenstein 1993).

People usually go through an extensive training period before they can begin practicing as a shaman. Eskimo shamans learn various relaxation and meditation techniques to induce trance states. They also learn methods of healing, curing, and exorcism. These techniques are used to produce group emotional experiences to enhance spiritual growth. In many cases, the shamanistic performances work effectively in curing illnesses or resolving emotional problems. Undoubtedly, in certain instances, the Eskimo beliefs and cultural conceptions surrounding shamanism trigger certain states of mind that produce positive psychological and even physical consequences, such as overcoming illness and injuries.

Rites of Passage among Foragers
The Australian aborigine rites of passage were connected to the beliefs of dreamtime described above. According to Aborigine conceptions, life without the dreamtime is extremely unsatisfactory. The invisible side of life becomes visible through rituals, ceremonies, myths, art, and dreams. Aborigines believe that through these activities they communicate with their ancestral beings. This belief is reflected in Aborigine rites of passage. In initiation rite of passage

An Inuit shaman with tambourine-like drum

ceremonies at puberty, it is believed that the individual moves farther and farther back into the dreamtime. In puberty rituals, which for males included circumcision, *subincision* (the cutting of the penis lengthwise to the urethra), and other bloodletting actions, the individual is dramatically moved from one status to another through contact with the dreamtime. The rite of passage at death moves the individual into the invisibility of the dreamtime.

The period of childhood among foragers is a time of playful activity and excitement. But it is also a time when children learn their basic subsistence activities, economic responsibilities, and political roles. In his studies of the Mbuti of the African Congo, Turnbull (1963, 1983) has provided us with a thorough account of childhood in a foraging society.

At the age of three, the Mbuti child enters the *bopi*, a tiny camp about a hundred yards away from the main camp, which might be considered a playground. Older children and adults do not enter the bopi. Within the bopi, all the children are part of an age grade and are equal to one another and remain so throughout the rest of their lives. It is the area in which children become enculturated and learn the importance of age, kinship, and gender and of the activities associated with these statuses.

Within the bopi are noncompetitive play activities for boys and girls. Many of these activities reinforce the rules of hunting and gathering. The elders bring the children out of the bopi to show them how to use nets to hunt animals. Children also play house to learn how to take care of their households later in life. Before the age of puberty, boys and girls quit going into the bopi and join the main camp with older youths. When they reach puberty, Mbuti males and females have separate, informal rites of passage. The puberty ritual, known as the Elima for Mbuti females, occurs at the first menstruation, which is an occasion for great rejoicing because it is a sign that the girl is ready for marriage and motherhood. For a month, the girl resides in a special hut with her age-mates, and she is watched over by an older female. The girl learns the special songs of the Elima and occasionally appears in front of the hut while young men sit outside to admire the girls. At this time, the females sing the Elima songs, and the boys sing in response in a form of flirtation. Through their participation in the Elima ritual, the Mbuti males demonstrate their readiness for adulthood and marriage.

Among the Ju/'hoansi or !Kung San, young teenage males had to kill their first antelope and were tattooed on their foreheads, but also went through a rigorous rite of passage called *choma* in which they had to experience hunger, cold, thirst, and extreme fatigue from continuous dancing over a six-week period while learning much cultural knowledge (Shostak 1981). The Baka foragers of the Cameroon also had dramatic rite of passage rituals. They would have their teeth filed and chipped, proving their courage and endurance. During the ritual, the initiates would be surrounded and teased by other children (Higgens 1985).

Art, Music, and Religion

19.7 **Describe examples of art and music found in foraging societies.**

The art of foraging societies is intimately related to nature. Animals, plants, humans, and other components of the natural environment are the major subjects. This naturalistic art also has a religious significance, as nature and spirit are viewed as inseparable. Rock paintings with highly symbolic images of natural phenomena are found in most foraging societies. It is believed that this art is sacred and can be used to make contact with supernatural sources.

Traditional Inuit (Eskimo) art products include many items made from ivory, one of the few rigid materials available in the Arctic. Human and animal figurines, which were worn as amulets to enhance supernatural powers and practices, dominate Eskimo artistic output. The Eskimo also carve masks in ivory (or sometimes wood) for use by their shamans.

The music of foraging societies is generally divided into recreational (folk or popular) and religious music. The Mbuti, for example, have no instrumental music, but they have many songs and dances. In their vocal music, they have a precise sense of harmony, giving each singer one note to produce at a given moment. This leads to a harmonic pattern that is passed around a circle of people. This technique is often used in Mbuti recreational music.

The sacred music of the Mbuti is believed to be much more important than their recreational music, and much of it is linked to the *Elima* rites of passage discussed earlier. In the *Elima*, young girls and boys sing back and forth to one another in harmony. There are also other sacred songs that only men sing. The intensity of the singing builds so as to reach the spirit of the rain forest. One of the hunters goes off into the forest to echo the song of his fellows so that the spirit may be sure to hear it. As in most societies, Mbuti ritual music usually has a standardized form, with little improvisation allowed. Ritual music helps sustain the cultural and spiritual traditions of the people. The lyrics of the music emphasize the sacred symbols that are maintained in Mbuti society. As the group chants the music together, a sense of sacredness is created in the community.

Music and religion are inextricably bound within the shamanistic rituals of the Inuit (Eskimo). In the shamanistic performances, a drum is used to enhance the rhythmic songs. The shaman's songs are simple, chantlike recitations that have no actual words. Short phrases are repeated again and again. The drumming and song chants are used to establish contact with the spirits. Anthropologist Rodney Needham (1967) suggested that the use of instruments such as the drum in shamanistic rituals not only heightens the spiritual atmosphere of the ceremony, but also affects psychological (and neurological) processes that produce altered states of consciousness in individuals.

A contemporary indigenous painting entitled "Honey Ant Dreaming" by Australian aborigine artist Marion Swift.

Religion Among Horticulturalists and Pastoralists

19.8 Describe examples of religion found in horticulturalist and pastoralist societies.

Given the immense diversity from tribe to tribe, it is very difficult to generalize about tribal religions. Like hunter-gatherer religions, tribal religions tend to be *cosmic religions*; that is, the concepts, beliefs, and rituals of these religions are integrated with the natural environment, seasonal cycles, and all living organisms (Sponsel 2012). Animism and shamanism are common religious traditions.

Animism and Shamanism in South America

The mingling of animism and shamanism as discussed earlier for foragers is also evident among some tribes. Some of these Amazonian tribes of South America use the extracts of certain plants for shamanistic practices. The Yanomamö, for example, use a hallucinogenic snuff called *ebene* to induce visual and auditory hallucinations during which it is believed an individual will have direct contact with the spirit world. The *ebene* powder is blown through a bamboo tube into the nostrils to gain contact with the *hekura* spirits. These spirits, numbering in the thousands, are believed to reside in trees, in rocks, and even within people's chests. Through the use of *ebene*, Yanomamö shamans fall into trances, enabling them to attract and control the *hekura* for various purposes (Chagnon 2012).

The Jivaro of Ecuador use a tea-like drink, *natema*, which enables almost anyone to achieve a trance state. *Natema* is concocted by boiling vines to produce a hallucinogenic drink containing alkaloids, which are somewhat similar to LSD and mescaline. Among the Jivaro, approximately one out of every four males is a shaman. Any adult, male or female, who desires to become such a practitioner simply gives a gift to an experienced shaman, who, in turn, gives the apprentices a drink of *natema*, as well as some of his own supernatural power in the form of spirit helpers. The spirit helpers, or darts, are believed to be the major causes of illness and death. Some Jivaro shamans send these spirit helpers to infect enemies. Others gain the ability to cure illnesses through the use of their clairvoyant powers (Harner 1972).

The animistic spiritual beliefs of the Yanomamö are demonstrated in the funerary rituals. After death the Yanomamö cremate the body and place the burned bones and ashes of the dead in a pot, mixed with a banana mush; this mixture is then eaten by the relatives of the deceased (Chagnon 2012). They believe that the soul of the individual needs to be protected by family members after death. Members of the family consume the ashes and burned

The Yanomamö preparing ashes of their dead before drinking them in their funerary rituals.

bones to absorb and free the soul of the individual for salvation. They believe that if this funerary ritual is not done properly, the soul of the deceased may be trapped in the world between life and death.

Witchcraft and Sorcery

Many tribal societies practice witchcraft and sorcery. Evans-Pritchard, in a classic ethnographic study of the Azande tribe of East Africa, referred to **witchcraft** as a belief in an innate, psychic ability of some people to harm others, whereas **sorcery** is a magical strategy in which practitioners manipulate objects to bring about either harmful or beneficial effects (1937). Contemporary anthropologists regard this distinction as too clear-cut and view the belief in occult powers to be much more culturally variant, ambivalent, and diffuse in meaning to be subject to this type of precise definition.

Anthropologists perceive witchcraft and sorcery as strategies for people to understand bad luck, illness, injustice, and other misfortunes that they cannot otherwise explain. Sorcerers and witches in tribal societies of Africa and Melanesia are often described as insatiably hungry individuals who eat others by absorbing their reproductive powers, children, sexual fluids, and flesh (Patterson 2008). These conjurers are usually connected with kinship and descent because these are all-important aspects of tribal society. In many cases, families direct supernatural assaults at one another. Witches and sorcerers may manipulate spirits to inflict diseases or use poisons on others. Many tribal peoples perceive the cosmos as composed of various spirits that can affect human lives. Although these peoples accept cause-and-effect explanations for most occurrences, certain phenomena such as pain and suffering do not seem to have "natural" causes and are instead, explained in terms of witchcraft and sorcery.

The Role of Witchcraft In Evans-Pritchard's study of the Azande, witchcraft played a role in all aspects of life. Any misfortunes that could not be explained by known causes, such as a lack of game or fish or a crop failure, were attributed to witchcraft. The Azande believed that a person became a witch because of an inherited bodily organ or blackish substance known as *mangu*. The identity of a witch was even unknown to the individual who had this *mangu*. A male could inherit it only from another male, a female only from another female. The identity of a witch was determined by a "poison oracle." A carefully prepared substance called *benge* was fed to a bird, and a yes-or-no question was put to the oracle. Whether the bird survived or died constituted the answer to whether someone was a witch. After a witch died, the Azande performed autopsies to determine whether witchcraft was carried in a family line.

Anthropologist Clyde Kluckhohn (1967) analyzed witchcraft beliefs among the Navajo Indians of the southwestern United States. Navajo witches were considered despicable monsters. The Navajo believed that the witches could transform themselves into animals. In these werewolf-like transformations, they ate the meat of corpses and made poisons from dried and ground human flesh, especially that of children. These poisons were thrown into houses of enemies, buried in cornfields, or placed on victims. Fatal diseases were believed to result from the poisons. The Navajo had antidotes (the gall bladders of an eagle, bear, mountain lion, or skunk) to forestall witchcraft activity, and they usually carried these antidotes with them into public situations.

Kluckhohn learned that the Navajo believed witchcraft was related to economic differences. The Navajo thought that those who had more wealth had gained it through witchcraft activities such as robbing graves and stealing jewelry from the dead. The only way a person could refute such an accusation was to share his or her wealth with friends and relatives. Thus, Kluckhohn hypothesized that the belief in witchcraft had the effect of equalizing the distribution of wealth and promoting harmony in the community.

The Role of Sorcery In tribal groups in Africa, New Guinea, and North America, sorcery is also used to influence social relationships. Among many tribes, one form of sorcery is used to promote fertility and good health and to avert evil spells. Another type is used to harm people whom the sorcerer hates and resents. In some cases, sorcery is used to reinforce informal sanctions.

One example of how societies use sorcery to explain misfortunes is provided by Shirley Lindenbaum's (1972) study of various New Guinea tribes. Among the Fore people, sorcery is often used to explain severe illnesses and death, whereas in other tribal groups, such as the Mae Enga, sorcery is not important. In particular, the Fore accuse sorcerers of trying to eliminate all women in their society, thereby threatening the group's survival. At the time of Lindenbaum's fieldwork, the Fore were faced with an epidemic disease that was devastating their population. This epidemic disease was found to be a variant of Creutzfeldt–Jakob disease (mad cow disease), with which the Fore were infected as a result of eating human brains (Diamond 1997). In this traumatic situation, Lindenbaum found that sorcery aided in explaining fundamental survival questions.

Totemism

In addition to animism, shamanism, witchcraft, and sorcery, tribal religions are intertwined with corporate descent groupings, particularly clans and lineages that are linked with totemic spirits believed to assist and watch over the group. Recall that clans are descent groups with fictive ancestors. Many of these clan ancestors are totemic spiritual beings, symbolically personified by a deceased ancestor, animal, or plant found in specific environments. For example, among many Native American tribes, lineage groupings such as clans, moieties, and phratries divide the society into different groupings. Each group is symbolized by a particular animal spirit, or totem, which the group recognizes as its ancestor. Among the various totems are eagles, bears, ravens, coyotes, and snakes. There are as many tribal spirits or deities as there are constituent kin groupings. Although each grouping recognizes the existence of all the deities in the entire tribe, the religious activities of each group are devoted to that group's particular spirit.

Ghost Lineage Members among the Lugbara

The Lugbara of Uganda, Africa, illustrate the familial aspect of tribal religion (Middleton 1960). The Lugbara believe that the dead remain an integral part of the lineage structure of their society. Ancestors include all the dead and living forebears of a person's lineage. The spirits of the dead regularly commune with the elders of the lineages. Shrines are erected to the dead, and sacrifices are offered to ensure that the ancestors will not harm people. It is believed that people have direct contact with their ancestors at these shrines, especially during the sacrifices.

A Lugbara elder explained the relationship between the dead and the living:

> *A ghost watches a man giving food at a sacrifice to him. A brother of that ghost begs food of him. The other will laugh and say "Have you no son?" Then he thinks, "Why does my child not give me food? If he does not give me food soon I shall send sickness to him." Then later that man is seized by sickness, or his wife and his children. The sickness is that of the ghosts, to grow thin and to ache throughout the body; these are the sicknesses of the dead.* (Middleton 1960:46)

Art and Music in Tribal Societies

Art in tribal societies has both utilitarian and ceremonial functions. The expressive art of the tribes of Papua New Guinea and of the U.S. Southwest is used to decorate utensils such as baskets, bowls, and other tools. It is also deeply connected with religious and sacred phenomena. Various tribes in the interior highlands of Papua New Guinea use body decorations as their principal art form, whereas the tribal peoples in the coastal regions make large, impressive masks that symbolize male power. These tribes also use various geometric designs to decorate their ceremonial war shields and other paraphernalia.

The Pueblo Indians of the U.S. Southwest, such as the Hopi and Zuni, use distinctive designs in their artworks to represent a harmonious balance among humans, nature, and the supernatural. The groups create colorful sand paintings that are erased after the ceremony is completed. In addition, they make masks and dolls to be used in the *katchina* cult activities. *Katchinas* are spiritual figures that exercise control over the weather, especially rainfall, which is particularly important in this arid region. *Katchina* art is used in various dance ceremonies and is believed to help produce beneficial weather conditions. Because clay is abundant in the Southwest, the Pueblo Indians developed elaborate pottery with complex geometric motifs and animal figures representing different tribal groups in the area.

Musical Traditions

Music and musical instruments vary from one region to another. For example, various tribes in sub-Saharan Africa produce a vast range of musical instruments, including drums, bells, shells, rattles, and hand pianos. The musical

A Katchina doll associated with the Native American Hopi of the Southwest U.S.

instruments are heard solo and in ensembles. The hand piano, or *mbira*, is a small wooden board to which a number of metal keys are attached. The keys are arranged to produce staggered tones so that certain melodic patterns can be improvised. Along with the instrumentation, singing is used in many cases to invoke specific moods: sadness, happiness, or a sense of spirituality (Mensah 1983).

Native American tribal musical traditions also vary from region to region. The musical instruments consist primarily of percussive rattles and drums. The drumming is done with a single drumstick, although several drum players may accompany the drummer. The traditional tribal music includes spiritual hymns, game songs, recreational dance music, war dance music, and shamanistic chanting. Most of the songs, even the game and recreational songs, are inseparable from sacred rituals related to crop fertility, healing, and other life crises. Nearly all of the music is vocal, sung by choruses. Many of the song texts contain extensive use of syllables such as "yu-waw, yu-waw, hi hi hi, yu-wah hi." These songs help to create a hypnotic spiritual consciousness that produces an appropriate sacred atmosphere (McAllester 1983, 1984).

Religion in Chiefdoms

19.9 Discuss how religion is interrelated with politics in chiefdom societies.

Religious traditions in chiefdom societies were in some respects similar to the cosmic religions described for the band and tribal societies. That is, they reflected the belief that the spiritual and material aspects of nature could not be separated from one another. Religious worldviews were oriented to the cyclical pattern of the seasons and all other aspects of nature. The natural order was also the moral and spiritual order. The religious concepts in chiefdom societies were based upon oral traditions perpetuated from generation to generation through elaborate cosmological myths. The most dramatic difference between chiefdom religions and band and tribal religions is the degree to which chiefdom religions legitimized the social, political, and moral status of the chiefs.

A Case Study: Law and Religion in Polynesia
Nowhere was the relationship between law and religion clearer than among the Polynesian Island chiefdoms. Hawaiian chiefs, for example, were believed to be either gods or sacred intermediaries between human societies and the divine world. Hawaiian chiefdoms have been referred to as **theocracies**, societies in which people rule not because of their worldly wealth and power, but because of their place in the moral and sacred order. The political and legal authority of Hawaiian, Tongan, and Tahitian chiefs was reinforced by a religious and ideological system known as the *tabu* system, which was based

on social inequalities. **Tabu** (or tapu) was a Polynesian term for a variety of social restrictions or prohibitions that had spiritual connotations. There were tabus in respect to planting certain crops, eating specific foods, and other cultural matters. Social interaction in these societies was carefully regulated through a variety of tabus. Elaborate forms of deference and expressions of humility distinguished various strata, especially those of commoners and chiefs.

Religious beliefs buttressed the tabu system. The Polynesians believed that people are imbued with cosmic forces referred to as **mana**. These spiritual forces were powerful and sometimes dangerous. They were inherited and distributed according to a person's status and rank. Paramount chiefs had a great deal of mana, subsidiary chiefs had less, and commoners had very little. Violations of certain tabus—for example, touching a member of a chiefly family—could bring the offender into contact with the chief's mana, which was believed to cause death.

These magical forces could also be gained and lost through a person's moral actions. Thus, the success or failure of a chief was attributed to the amount of mana he controlled. This was also reflected in the economic and political spheres. On the one hand, a chief who was a good redistributor and maintained order was believed to possess a great amount of mana. On the other hand, if things went badly, this reflected a loss of magical powers. When one chief replaced another, the deposed chief was believed to have lost his powers.

Shamanism in Chiefdoms

Shamanism was practiced in many chiefdoms and has been thoroughly described among the Native American Indian groups of the Northwest Coast. Like other social institutions, shamanism reflected the hierarchical structure of these societies. The shamans became the personal spiritual guides and doctors of the chiefs and used their knowledge to enhance the power and status of high-ranking chiefs. For example, it was believed that the shamans had the ability to send diseases into enemies and, conversely, to cure and give spiritual power to the chief's allies.

In addition, shamans danced and participated in the potlatch ceremonies on behalf of the chiefs (Garbarino 1988). Widespread throughout the chiefdoms of the Northwest Coast was the belief in a "man-eating spirit." These groups believed that an animal spirit could possess a man, which transformed him into a cannibal. During the potlatch ceremonies, shamans would dance, chant, and sing, using masks to enact the transformation from human to animal form to ward off the power of the man-eating spirit. Through these kinds of practices, shamans could help sanction the power and authority of the high-ranking chiefs. The chiefs demonstrated their generosity through the potlatch, whereas the shamanistic ceremonies

exhibited the supernatural powers that were under the control of the chiefs.

By associating closely with a chief, a shaman could elevate both his own status and that of the chief. The shaman collected fees from his chiefly clients, which enabled him to accumulate wealth. In some cases, low-ranking individuals became shamans by finding more potent spirits for a chief. No shaman, however, could accumulate enough wealth to rival a high-ranking chief (Garbarino 1988).

Human Sacrifice

Another practice that reflected the relationships among religion, hierarchy, rank, and the legitimacy of chiefly rule was human sacrifice, which existed in some—but not all—chiefdoms. Among the Natchez Indians, for example, spectacular funerary rites were held when the Great Sun chief died. During these rites, the chief's wives, guards, and attendants were expected to sacrifice their lives, feeling privileged to follow the Great Sun into the afterworld. Parents also offered their children for sacrifice, which, they believed, would raise their own rank. The sacrificial victims were strangled, but they were first given a strong concoction of tobacco, which made them unconscious. They were then buried alongside the Great Sun chief in an elaborate burial mound.

Human sacrifice was also practiced in the Polynesian region. In native Hawaii, there were two major rituals: the *Makahiki*, or so-called New Year's festival, and the annual rededication of the *Luakini* temple, at which human sacrifices were offered (Valeri 1985). Some of the sacrificial victims had transgressed or violated the sacred tabus. These victims frequently were brothers or cousins of the chiefs who were their political rivals. It was believed that these human sacrifices would help perpetuate the fertility of the land and the people. Human sacrifice was the prerogative of these chiefs and was a symbolic means of distinguishing these divine rulers from the rest of the human population. Such rituals effectively sanctioned the sacred authority of the chiefs.

Art, Architecture, and Music

19.10 Describe examples of art, architecture, and music in chiefdom societies.

Compared with band and tribal societies, chiefdom societies had more extensive artwork, which reflected two different tendencies in chiefdom societies: a high degree of labor organization and the status symbols associated with high-ranking chiefs. One of the most profound examples of the artwork of a chiefdom society is found on Easter

Island. Between 800 and 1,000 monumental stone figures, known as *moai*, have been discovered there. (See Chapter 7 page 166). These figures vary in height from less than two meters to almost ten meters (about 30 feet) and weigh up to 59 metric tons. After sculpting these figures in quarries, laborers dragged them over specially constructed transport roads and erected them on platforms. This project called for an extensive, regionwide labor organization. The symbolic design of these statuaries evokes the power, status, and high rank of the chiefs of Easter Island (Kirch 1984).

The large mounds associated with the Cahokian chiefdom complex near the Mississippi and Illinois Rivers also represented extensive labor projects and a hierarchical society. Different types of earthen mounds surrounded the city of Cahokia. In the center of the city is a large, truncated, flat-topped mound. This mound is 100 feet high, covers 16 acres, and is built of earth, clay, silt, and sand. It took perhaps 200 years to construct. This flat-topped mound is surrounded by hundreds of smaller mounds, some conical in shape, others flat-topped. Although the Cahokian society collapsed around 1450 A.D. (before European contact), archaeologists know from other remaining Mississippian chiefdom societies such as the Natchez Indians that the flat-topped mounds were used chiefly for residences and religious structures, whereas the conical mounds were used for burials.

Another example of the labor and status associated with chiefdom art forms comes from the Native Americans of the Northwest Coast. These groups produced totem poles, along with decorated house posts and wooden dance masks. The carved wooden totem poles and house posts were the ultimate status and religious symbols, indicating high social standing and linkages between the chiefs and the ancestral deities. Typically, a totem pole was erected on the beach in front of a new chief's house, which had decorated house posts. The symbolic messages transmitted through these poles expressed the status hierarchies in these societies (Marshall 1998).

An artist's recreation of Cahokia, a large native American site of some 20,000 people that constructed large-scale mounds.

Music

We have already mentioned the important shamanistic dances that accompanied the potlatch activities of the Northwest Coast chiefdoms. Most of the traditional music of chiefdom societies exemplified the interconnections among sociopolitical structure, religion, and art. The traditional music of Polynesia is a good example of these interconnections. Although work songs, recreational songs, and mourning songs were part of everyday life, formal music was usually used to honor the deities and chiefs (Kaeppler 1980). In western Polynesia, on the islands of Tonga, Tikopia, and Samoa, much of the traditional music consisted of stylized poetry accompanied by bodily movements and percussion instruments such as drums.

In some ceremonies, formal poetic chants were sung in verses. In other contexts, people sang narrative songs, or *fakaniua*, describing famous places, past events, and legends, accompanied by hand clapping in a syncopated, complex rhythmic pattern.

The traditional formal musical style of eastern Polynesia, including the Hawaiian Islands, also consisted of complex, integrated systems of poetry, rhythm, melody, and movement that were multifunctional, but were usually related to chiefly authority. The Hawaiians had a variety of musical instruments, including membranophones made of hollow wooden cylinders covered with sharkskin, mouth flutes, rhythm sticks, and bamboo tubes. In contrast to performers of the other islands, traditional Hawaiian musical performers and dancers were highly organized and trained in specially built schools under the high priests. The major function of the Hawaiian performers was to pay homage to the chiefs and their ancestral deities through religious chants and narrative songs.

Religion in Agricultural States

19.11 Describe some examples of ecclesiastical and universalistic religions found in agricultural societies.

As state societies emerged, cultural elements such as political power, authority, and religion became much more closely intertwined. The religious traditions that developed in most of the agricultural states are referred to as ecclesiastical religions, in which there is no separation between state and religious authority. Generally, all people in the political jurisdiction are required to belong to the ecclesiastical religion; however, there may be other rituals and beliefs from other religious traditions found in these agricultural states.

Ecclesiastical Religions

Major ecclesiastical religious traditions emerged in agricultural civilizations around the world. Mesopotamia, Egypt, China, Greece, Rome, Mesoamerica, and South America developed some of the earliest **ecclesiastical religions**. These religious traditions were limited to the specific territory of these societies and were intimately tied to their particular state organization. The Mesopotamian, Egyptian, Confucian (Chinese), Greek, Roman, Mayan, Aztec, and Incan religious traditions integrated both political and religious functions for their own people. The Aztec religion emerged between the fourteenth and sixteenth centuries A.D. in the city they called Tenochtitlán, in the central valley region of present-day Mexico (Carrasco 2002; Fagan 1998). The Aztecs had moved from the northern regions of Mesoamerica and conquered this region. They called the ancient city of Teotihuacán, which had been built centuries earlier (100 B.C.), the "Abode of the Gods." Tenochtitlán was divided into four major quarters that had extensive pyramids, courtyards, residences, and craft industry factories producing pottery, weapons, and other goods. In the center of the city stood the Temple of Quetzacoatl, the most important temple for the Aztecs. Aztec rituals were led by the temple priests and included fasting and the offering of flowers, foods, and cloth for sacrifices, as well as a variety of types of human sacrifices. The Mayan and other Mesoamerican states had similar religions and rituals. In the ecclesiastical religions of many agricultural states, such as those of the Egyptians, Aztecs, Maya, Chinese, Greeks, and Romans, the government officials were often the priests who managed the rituals and maintained the textual traditions for these people.

Divine Rulers, Priests, and Religious Texts

Most of the early ecclesiastical religions taught that their rulers had divine authority. For example, the rulers of Mesopotamia and the pharaohs of Egypt were believed to be divine rulers upholding the moral and spiritual universe. Various Greek and Roman rulers attempted to have themselves deified during different historical periods. In South and Southeast Asia, political rulers known as *rajahs* were thought to have a semidivine status that was an aspect of their religious traditions. Even during later times in agricultural Europe, kings were believed to inherit their rule from God and sanctioned their rule through Christian traditions of "divine right."

Ecclesiastical religious traditions are based on written texts interpreted by professionally trained, full-time priests, who became the official custodians of the religious cosmologies and had official roles in the political hierarchy. They presided over state-organized rituals called **rites of legitimation**, which reinforced the divine authority of the ruler. In these rituals, the priests led prayers, chants, and hymns addressed to the kings and the various deities (Parrinder 1983; Fagan 1998). As in chiefdom societies, religion sanctified and legitimized the authority of political leaders.

One of the major functions of the priests was to standardize religious beliefs and practices for the society. Individualistic religious practices and beliefs were viewed as threatening to state authorities. For example, among the Maya, state authorities perceived the shamanistic practice of taking hallucinogens to control spirits as too individualistic. As the ecclesiastical religion developed, only the Mayan priests were allowed to take mind-altering drugs. Priests managed the use of these hallucinogens on behalf of state-organized ritual activities (Dobkin de Rios 1984).

In the ecclesiastical religions of the Mayan and Aztec civilizations of Mesoamerica, human sacrifices and blood offerings were often part of the state rituals and managed by the priests. Pictorial and inscriptional evidence indicates that blood sacrifices were required for many, if not the majority, of rituals involving the priestly elite. Often, this was accomplished with the blood of captives. However, the blood of the elite themselves was required for some specific rituals. The location for these elite sacrifices was in the temples atop the major pyramids and in the royal palaces (Fuller and Fuller 2008).

Human sacrifice and blood offerings among the Aztec religion have to be understood in the context of the Aztec creation story. The Aztecs believed that they were created during the time of the fifth sun when the god Quetzalcoatl journeyed to the underworld and received from Mictlantecuhtli (god of death, darkness, and underworld) the bones and ashes of the humans who died during the time of the fourth sun. The god Quetzalcoatl grinds the bones and ashes of the fourth sun humans. He then adds his own blood to the mixture by performing an autosacrifice (spilling his own blood as Maya kings were required to do in certain rituals). Quetzalcoatl mixes the blood from his penis into the ground ash and bone. The first male child and first female child emerge from the mixture; they are the ancestors to all Aztecs. Quetzalcoatl gave his own blood to make humans. Thus humans must repay a "blood debt" to the gods. Human sacrifice is the means of this repayment.

There were many cosmological components in the explanation of human sacrifice and the spilling of blood by the Aztecs. The cosmological explanation was related to the Aztec calendar. The Aztec calendar was based on a cycle of five ages or "suns" and four destructions. The First Age or Sun began some 3,000 years ago and was called 4-Jaguar. This age lasted 676 years and was marked by battles among various deities. This First Sun was destroyed, and the cosmos was in darkness. The Second Sun, called

4-Wind, was created and lasted 364 years. Deities battled, and eventually the winds came and destroyed the universe including the Sun. The Third Sun, called 4-Rain, was created, which really meant rain of fire. Ultimately, the gods destroyed the people, the sun, and the universe once more. The Fourth Sun, called 4-Water, was created and lasted 52 years before the heavens collapsed and water swallowed up everything. Finally, the Fifth Sun was the period in which the Aztecs lived; it was named the 4-Movement. This period involved the movement of the sun in an orderly fashion across the heavens. The Aztecs believed that this age would end with a major catastrophe. Some of the sources of the Aztec tradition suggest that human sacrifice was necessary to nourish the sun and keep the universe intact.

Offerings of human blood nourished the Aztec deities, and they reciprocated by providing regular rains and fertile soil, as well as keeping the sun on its daily cycle. The Aztecs believed that the gods would go hungry and the world would come to an end without human sacrifice. The Aztecs had references to mystical forces, expressed in the Nahualt word *teotl* that signified a sacred power that was manifested in nature and in mysterious sacred places. The Aztecs believed that this mystical force could be harnessed by the spilling of blood and human sacrifice.

There were different forms of human sacrifice ranging from decapitation, shooting with darts or arrows, drowning, burning, hurling from heights, strangulations, entombments, starvation, and gladiatorial combat. However, the major sacrificial rituals came with the capture of various peoples from outlying regions of the Aztec empire. These rituals took place mostly in the 80 different temples in Tenochtitlán that had skull racks, along with other ceremonial structures. This ritual began with a four-day preparatory period of holy fasting involving vigils, offerings of flowers, food, and cloth. The actual sacrificial rituals lasted around 20 days and were marked by the sacrificial victims singing hymns as they were marched to the temple. The victims were placed on a sacrificial stone as a priest cut open the chest to offer the beating heart to the sun for vitality and nourishment. The body was rolled down the steps of the temple where it was dismembered and then cooked. Squash blossoms were mixed with the flesh. The nobles and other elite, but not the commoners, consumed the bodies (Fuller and Fuller 2008).

Universalistic Religions

Other religious traditions that developed in early agricultural societies became **universalistic religions**, consisting of spiritual messages that were believed to apply to all of humanity, rather than just to their own cultural heritage. There are two major branches of universalistic religions:

One emerged in southern Asia and resulted in Hinduism and Buddhism; the other developed in the Near East and led to the formation of the historically related religions of Judaism, Christianity, and Islam.

Hinduism

The term "Hinduism" does not come into use until the 1820s, when British colonial rulers added the suffix "ism" to conform to European nomenclature for religious traditions. It was only in the nineteenth century that the many indigenous Indian religious formations were collectively named "Hinduism." Before this, the people of India did not have a term for the various collections of beliefs, practices, and rituals associated with multifarious religious groups. However, today, Indians have accepted the term Hinduism as a collective term for their religious tradition (Weisgrau 2008). The early origins of Hinduism are associated with the Indo-Aryans, a group speaking Sanskrit who arrived and settled in northern India about 1800 B.C. The most enduring contribution of the Indo-Aryans is a massive collection of texts and sacred scriptures composed and orally transmitted in an early form of Sanskrit known collectively as the Vedas. The four Vedas appearing in chronological order are *Rig Veda*, *Sama Veda*, *YajurVeda*, and *Athara Veda*. Later expository prose texts associated with the Vedas are collectively called *Brahmanas*. Later texts known as the *Upanishads* were compiled beginning in about 800 B.C. The Vedas are concerned with prayer, ritual, and sacrifice; the *Sanskrit* term *brahman* has many meanings, including the prayers themselves and the power inherent in their recitation. The same term denotes the priests (alternatively Anglicized as "Brahmin"), who had exclusive access to the language and content of the Vedas.

Three major deities mentioned in the Vedas are Brahma, Vishnu, and Shiva, and are associated with the cyclic creation, protection, and destruction of the universe consisting of millions of years. This three-part pantheon remains as the preeminent figures of divine power in the Hindu religious tradition. The Upanishad texts develop the major religious doctrines of Hinduism. The major doctrines include the processes of transmigration of the soul (*atman*) and rebirth or **samsara**, the perpetual wandering of the soul through a cycle of birth and rebirth, associated with pain and suffering of mortal cycles of life and death. The principle of **karma** suggests that the conditions of each rebirth are directly dependent upon an individual's actions in previous lives. **Moksha**, or release of the soul from mortal pain and the cycle of birth, death, and rebirth, is the ultimate goal of Hinduism and is achieved through an individual's withdrawal from preoccupation with the material world.

Hindu temples become the major ritual sites for worship in India. In addition to the tripartite pantheon of

Brahman, Vishnu, and Shiva, a multiplicity of deities and multiple interpretations resulted in what is termed *Bhakti*, or devotional movements, which stress personal devotion through songs and prayers in local languages, usually expressed through group following of a particular saintly prophet or poet. These developments have made Hinduism one of the most complex and rich religious universalistic religions of the world.

Buddhism

The Buddhist tradition emerged from the teachings of Siddharta Gautama, later known as Buddha ("the enlightened one") or Lord Buddha. Siddharta Gautama was born about 560 B.C. in Lumbini, north of Nepal's southern border with India and about 100 miles from the Indian city of Benares. He was born into a Hindu royal family and had a life of privilege and luxury. His mother, Maya, was known as a woman of exceptional virtue who dreamed auspiciously that a white elephant had entered her womb. Maya died seven days after giving birth, which was later interpreted by Buddhist sages as signifying that as she had fulfilled her great purpose in life, to give birth to a Buddha, she could fulfill no other (Calkowski 2008).

Siddharta was educated in the arts, sciences, and athletics. As his father, the rajah (Hindu king), had been given a prophecy that his son was destined to be a great ruler, he wanted to shelter him from the harsher realities of life. For example, whenever Siddharta ventured outside these palaces, his father made certain that the sick and elderly were out of sight. In his adolescence, Siddharta married a princess called Yashodara, who gave birth to a son named Rahula. In his twenties, Siddharta undertook four journeys outside of the palace walls which would transform his perception of the world. During his first journey, Siddharta noticed a feeble old man and learned that aging was the future of every being. On his second journey, he encountered a man wasting away from an illness and became aware that illness was an ever-present possibility of existence. The third journey exposed Siddharta to the cremation of a corpse, acquainting him with the fate of all humans. On his fourth journey, Siddharta encountered a wandering holy man who traveled with his begging bowl and radiated contentment.

These four signs resulted in Siddharta leaving his family and material attachments to follow the example of the holy man who felt contentment. Siddharta shaved his head and shed his princely garments for a simple yellow robe, took up yoga exercises, followed a rigorous diet, and trained with Hindu religious teachers in an attempt to unite his self with the origin and meaning of the universe. However, after maintaining this ascetic life for five years, Siddharta concluded that he was no nearer to enlightenment than he had been before beginning

these practices. His body was failing to sustain his intellect. Thus, Siddharta resolved to restore his bodily health and again took up the path of a homeless wanderer with his begging bowl. Eventually, Siddharta seated himself beneath a fig tree, which came to be known as the Bodhi tree or the "tree of knowledge," and he began to meditate on the nature of his failure to achieve salvation. It is under this tree that he finally attained **nirvana** or spiritual enlightenment and witnessed his previous lives, and perceived the cycle of birth, death, and rebirth or *samsara*. After achieving enlightenment or *nirvana*, he realized the four noble truths, which account for suffering in the world, the cause of this suffering, the possibility of release from suffering, and how to attain that release. Upon completing these meditations, Siddharta was the Buddha, which meant that as an enlightened one, he could escape at once from the cycle of existence, *samsara*, and attain *nirvana*.

Following his enlightenment the Buddha founded an order of monks known as the *sangha* to implement his teachings. He did subscribe to two major tenets of Hinduism, *karma* and *samsara*, the cycle of rebirth, but envisioned a far greater flexibility for *karma* than Hindu doctrine permitted. The Buddha held that if an individual attained proper mindfulness in one's present lifetime, one could transcend the negative consequences of one's previous life and escape what was considered one's fate according to *karma*. The Four Noble Truths taught in Buddhism are:

1. All existence is suffering: birth, aging, illness, anxiety, misery, pain, despair, and the inability to satisfy one's desires.
2. The source of suffering is desire and ignorance.
3. Suffering must be eliminated. One must escape the cycle of rebirth and enter *nirvana*, the blessed state of nonexistence.
4. The way to eliminate suffering is to follow the Eightfold Path.

The Eightfold Path, the Buddha's prescription for a proper orientation towards life, constitutes a middle path to the attainment of enlightenment. It requires the acceptance and practice of the following:

1. Right knowledge – referring to the understanding of the Four Noble Truths.
2. Right attitude – cultivating an attitude of peacefulness and goodwill as opposed to that of sensual desire and malice.
3. Right speech – not lying or gossiping, but directing one's speech towards harmonious interaction with others.
4. Right action – adhering to moral actions.
5. Right occupation – not injuring others through one's occupation.

6. Right effort – eliminating evil impulses and nurturing good ones.
7. Right mindfulness – avoiding the dictates of desire in one's speech, deeds, and emotional state.
8. Right composure – attaining the intense level of concentration that enables the practitioner to resist what would distract him or her from the goal of attaining salvation.

The Buddhist tradition expanded through missionaries outside of India, north to Tibet, China, Korea, Japan, and Vietnam. It also traveled south and southeast to Sri Lanka, Myanmar (Burma), Thailand, Laos, and Cambodia. As Buddhism spread to these different regions it developed into two major divisions: Theravada Buddhism and Mahayana Buddhism, with many sectarian differences found within various countries. Buddhism has developed a very complex and diverse universalistic religious tradition.

Judaism

Judaism, the religious observances and beliefs of the Jewish people, comprises an ancient, ordered set of rituals, symbols, tenets, and practices (Glazier 2008). Judaism begins with the Biblical patriarch Abraham when, according to Jewish belief, God established a covenant with him. The Jewish tradition regards the covenant as a divine promise to Abraham and his descendants that they would enjoy the special blessing of God. Emphasizing monotheism and ethical behavior, Judaism was embraced by the ancient Hebrews, yet their practices also differed in important ways from the modern Jewish traditions. For example, the sacrifice of livestock to God, so ubiquitous in the Old Testament, ceased to be a part of Jewish observance more than 2,000 years ago. The religion of Abraham also evolved with the first five books of the Hebrew Bible, or *Torah*, received by Moses. It constitutes the core sacred text of Judaism from that time (approximately 3,500 years ago) to the present and makes clear the way the covenant changed from the era of Abraham to that of Moses.

The central tenets and religious values of Judaism focus on God, the Land of Israel, and the *Torah*. However, Judaism is characterized by flexibility in belief, partly because no centralized hierarchical religious authority codifies and enforces religious precepts. While rabbis offered interpretations of the sacred texts, their variant understandings emerged throughout time. Judaism tends to value ethical practice and moral action above letter-perfect conformity to abstract theological or ritual rules.

Judaism emphasizes that human beings are uniquely capable of performing good deeds over the course of their lives. The Hebrew term for such righteous acts (*mitzvot*, sing; *mitzvah*) provides insight into a person's connection to God, for the term also means a divine command. Thus one who acts with kindness and compassion to help a fellow human being is literally carrying out God's will. Every good deed performed is, in effect, a religious act. Although God remains unknowable, the observance of commandments makes God manifest in the world as people find ways of helping others. Thus, God's creation is an unending process, continuing to unfold in the virtuous actions of people. The Jewish tradition believes that God is revealed in history—that is, through the action of people within a community.

Judaism is also inseparably bound to the land of Israel. Even through the 20 centuries of exile between the Roman conquest and the establishment of the modern state of Israel in 1948, Jewish prayers and liturgy focused on a return of its people. Returning to the land of Israel depended on the coming of the messiah who would deliver them to their promised sacred homeland, ending 2,000 years of exile. The covenant between the Jewish people and God raises the question of "the chosen people," a concept referred to in the *Torah*. The idea of a chosen people is not exclusionary, for all people are entitled to the rewards of the divine plan, according to Judaism. Instead, the Jews were chosen to serve God in particular ways that would guide others in living morally and ethically. "Chosenness" means that the covenant placed particular responsibilities on the Jewish people to demonstrate by their own actions the universal truth of God's commandments. Thus there is in the concept of the "chosen" a tension between the very particular and specific relationship of one nation to God and more general meanings that encompass all of humankind. Thus, Judaism is very much a universalistic religious tradition.

Judaism is a religion focused on this world. Accordingly, the concept of heaven is little developed, and hell hardly at all. While the Bible refers to a place where the soul goes after death, it is at best a vague conception. In the Jewish tradition, heaven and hell are experienced in this life as the rewards and punishments for human actions. Upright and honest living provides its own satisfactions. Despite references to Satan in the Hebrew Bible, there is minimal development of a personified evil. Moreover, the Jewish value on free will and the human power to make decisive choices for good or ill leaves no room for a concept of Satanic temptation or spiritual evil. Judaism takes a critical view of beliefs that absolve people of responsibility.

The preeminent text of Judaism is the *Torah*, the first five books of the Hebrew Bible. The *Torah* also refers to other writings, particularly the rabbinical commentaries contained in the *Talmud*, consisting of more than 60 books. The *Talmud* records the thinking and decisions of rabbis during various periods. The study of the *Talmud* is taken up by relatively few people, mainly rabbis and religious scholars. Another principal text of Judaism is the *Midrash*, which dates from the same period as the *Talmud*.

Christianity

Christianity, another universalistic religion, arose out of the Jewish tradition. Christianity originated in Roman Palestine—that is to say, with the life and teachings of the Jewish religious innovator Jesus Christ (circa 3 B.C. to 30 A.D.). Jesus led an exemplary life, teaching and attempting to reform the Jewish religious traditions. As a result of his critical views of the establishment in Roman Palestine, Jesus was arrested and crucified by Roman authorities. Christians believe that he arose from the dead and appeared to many of his disciples and followers. Through the evangelical work of his original apostles and other early followers, the Christian message was retained and transmitted widely throughout the Middle East and later in Rome. The earliest form of organized Christianity was the Roman Catholic Church, which claims that it is the original church founded by Christ and that it enjoys an unbroken chain of priestly ordination known as "apostolic succession" from the first communities of early Christianity (Murphy 2008).

The gradual process of centralization and cultural standardization of Roman Catholicism was greatly advanced by the Emperor Constantine's conversion to Christianity in 312 A.D. Christianity had suffered varying degrees of official persecution, but by the close of its fourth century, the religion had been elevated to the status of the official religion of the Roman Empire. When the western regions of the Roman Empire crumbled in the fifth century under the assault of the so-called "barbarians," the Roman Church pursued the religious conversion of the invading (principally Germanic) peoples. During the Middle Ages, the Church not only succeeded in converting most Europeans to Christianity; it also served as a formidable force for the integration of cultural and social forms in the continent. By 1000 A.D. Roman Catholicism was the official religion of every Western European state.

The central religious doctrine of Roman Catholicism begins with the simple conviction that Jesus is both fully human and fully divine. Jesus is the incarnation on earth of God (the Supreme Being) for the purpose of securing the redemption of humankind. Christians believe that the sins of the first humans, Adam and Eve, caused them to be cast from an earthly paradise, the Garden of Eden, and removed them from full communion with God. This *original sin* is the inheritance of all human beings, a condition that alienates them from God. The Old Testament texts are believed to be accounts of God's direct intervention in the efforts of the Jews, the Chosen People, to reestablish their communion with God. The New Testament

of Christianity records the life and teachings of Jesus, who while miraculously born of a human mother, the Virgin Mary, is the Son of God. As God's embodiment on earth, Jesus opened the gates of heaven through his life, suffering, death, and resurrection, providing redemption for all human beings with the means for their salvation. Catholics believe that at the end of this earthly life, the souls of all human beings will enter into one of three realms or states of being. Those who have been absolved of their sins will go to *heaven* which is paradisiacal principally because the souls admitted there, or *saints*, enjoy the beatific presence of God. The souls of those people who must still pay for sins that are not of such a magnitude as to condemn them definitively go to *purgatory* until such time as they are prepared to enter heaven. Finally, those who die without repenting and being absolved of mortal (very serious) sins are condemned to an eternity of punishment in *hell*.

Roman Catholicism is monotheistic, but complexly so. One of its most distinctive doctrines is that of the *Holy Trinity*. According to this belief, God is unitary, but expressed in three distinct persons: the Father, the Son (Jesus Christ), and the Holy Spirit. The basis of belief in the Trinity, as in other Catholic doctrines, is faith rather than human reason. The Virgin Mary, while herself entirely human, is the only saint entitled to special veneration, known as *hyperdulia*. Fundamental to the Catholic understanding of Mary is her perpetual virginity. The Catholic Church is also characterized by an elaborately developed *cult of the saints*. Saints are exemplary Catholics who are certified as having attained salvation, who are considered to be worthy of veneration, and who can be called upon to intercede with God on behalf of the faithful. Catholics also believe in *angels*, both good and evil, who are spiritual beings, neither human nor divine. *Satan* (from a Hebrew word meaning "adversary"), sometimes referred to as *Lucifer* ("light bearer"), is a member of the lowest choir of the lowest hierarchy of angels. Over time he became transformed by tradition into the opponent of God and the leader of all evil angels and demons.

Protestantism

Protestant Christianity began as a reform movement in the Catholic Church in the early sixteenth century. A German theologian named Martin Luther publicly objected to the Roman Catholic practice known as the sale of indulgences. Indulgences, which allowed the wealthy essentially to buy forgiveness from their sins, were already a focus of criticism throughout Europe. In his complaint, however, Luther also questioned some of the Catholic theology, including the celibacy of priests and a variety of other basic points of Church belief and practice. The Church reacted harshly, excommunicating Luther in 1521 and declaring him a political outlaw. However, because of political and economic factors, the "Reformation," as it is known, began to percolate through Europe with other leaders such as John Calvin (Buckser 2008).

Like Roman Catholics, most Protestants contend that these three entities—Father, Son, and Holy Spirit—comprise a single supreme being, the doctrine of the Trinity. Many Protestants also posit the existence of another supernatural being: Satan, a fallen angel who rules over Hell and tempts human beings into sin. God and Satan may be served in their kingdoms by angels and devils. Protestantism traces these beliefs almost exclusively to the Old Testament of Judaism. The other part, the New Testament, contains several accounts of Jesus's life as well as letters and histories from his early followers. Protestantism takes the Bible as its ultimate source of legitimacy; all rules, rituals, and beliefs are valid only insofar as they have grounding in scripture. One of the first acts of the early Protestants, for example, was the abolition of such Catholic traditions as confession and clerical celibacy, neither of which were called for in the scriptures.

Protestantism focuses on individual belief that tends to produce individualism and a level of antiauthoritarianism throughout the Protestant world. At the same time, these beliefs allow considerable room for disagreements, and they provide little institutional structure for resolving them. These differences affect their ritual and liturgical structures, leading to striking diversity among the various denominations and sects of Protestantism. Unlike Catholicism, Protestantism had no uniform creed or centralized organization and hierarchy. Most Protestant churches agreed with Luther's central theses: that sinners could achieve salvation only by faith, not by good works, and that the Bible, not any church organization, held the final authority on Christian doctrine. But beyond that there was little to hold these Protestant denominations and sects together. These different churches varied greatly in their connection to political authorities. Although Protestantism began as universalistic tradition, in some cases it evolved into ecclesiastical religions identified with specific political regions. Some Protestant denominations became integral parts of the state, with the ruler serving as head of the church. Monarchs headed up national churches in England and Scandinavia, for example, while small-scale theocracies existed in various European cities. John Calvin achieved near dictatorial control for the Reform movement in Geneva. However, others, like the Anabaptists, that eventually evolved into the Mennonites, Amish, and other Protestant religious groups, shunned worldly politics.

Islam

The Islamic faith developed with the life of Muhammad ibn Abdullah (ca. 570-632), who was born in the city of Mecca, in what is now Saudi Arabia. He was born as a member of the Querysh ethnic group, which maintained political and economic control over Mecca. At that time Mecca was an important trading post and spiritual center for animistic and polytheistic traditions. The Querysh were originally a nomadic group in the desert, but became involved in organizing trading caravans across the Arabian desert to cities such as Damascus and Jerusalem. Up until the age of 40, Muhammad was a successful trader within the Querysh group. He had married a woman named Khadijah, who was the head of a wealthy trading family, and had four daughters, including Fatima. Muhammad had gained a reputation of being a businessman known as *al-Amin*, the trusted one (Scupin 2008b; Sidky and Akers 2006).

At about the age of 40 Muhammad began to seek out more spiritual satisfaction and went to a serene cave on Mt. Hira, an area near Mecca, where he fasted and began to meditate. Muslims believe that it was at Mt. Hira that Muhammad began to receive revelations from God, *Allah* (the Arabic term for God), through the intermediary of the angel Gabriel, *Jibral*. After consulting his wife and other family members, Muhammad realized, and others began to believe, that he was indeed receiving revelations from God. These revelations continued for some 23 years. According to the Islamic tradition, the most important of the revelations was that there was only one God, *Allah*, and that Muhammad was the prophet of God. Muslims believe that Muhammad is the final prophet in a long line, including Noah, Moses, and Jesus, who are referred to in the Bible. Muslims share with Christians and Jews the faith that Abraham was the founder and first Prophet of their tradition. However, Muslims believe that Jews and Christians had strayed from the faith, and that before Muhammad's revelations, people were living in an age of religious ignorance, known as the *Jahilliyah*. In fact, Muslims do not believe that Muhammad founded a new religion, but instead was a religious reformer who was trying to restore the faith for all people, including Jews and Christians.

After receiving his initial revelations, Muhammad began to preach in Mecca of the universalistic, transcendent deity—*Allah*. These teachings are believed to have threatened the economic and political interests and religious beliefs of the Querysh families. Consequently, Muhammad was shunned and persecuted and had to move to the city of Yathrib, (later called *Medina*, the "City of the Prophet"), a city about 200 miles north of Mecca, with some of his followers. This move to Medina took place in the year 622 A.D. and is known as the *Hijra* (the emigration), and it marks the first year in the Islamic calendar. In Medina, Muhammad continued as religious leader but also ruled as supreme judge and political ruler of the earliest Islamic state and society, which incorporated many of the Bedouin groups in the Arabian peninsula. Following the consolidation of his authority, he returned to take control of Mecca, which became the center of a vast Islamic empire. Muhammad died in 632 A.D., at the age of 72 and is believed by all Muslims to have led an exemplary life, and through his revelations and activities left behind a rich cultural and religious tradition, which would have an enormous influence on the world.

Several bodies of texts have become important within the Islamic tradition. The central text of Islam is the Qur'an ("recitation"), which consists of the revelations received for 23 years by Muhammad. In the Qur'an the term *al-Islam* means "submission and peace," and Muslim refers to "one who submits." The Qur'an is considered the supreme glory of the Arabic language, which is divided into 114 chapters (*surahs*) with some 6,000 verses (*ayahs*). A Jew or Christian reading the Qur'an will recognize various religious teachings, such as the narratives of the spiritual covenant established with the Prophet Abraham, the Garden of Eden with Adam and Eve, Noah and the flood, the various names of the prophets such as Moses, and references to Jesus and his mother Mary; she is the only woman called by name in the Qur'an, and she is mentioned more times than in the New Testament. The Qur'anic conception of the universe includes a heaven, an earth, and a hell, with humans as God's representatives on earth who are ultimately going to be measured and judged according to their deeds. There are also angels such as *Jibril* and an evil adversary of the prophets and Allah, known as *Iblis*, or *Shaytan*. The root of Islamic ethics is that God ordains humans to implement his will, leaving individuals completely responsible to follow the path of righteousness or evil. Humans are depicted as limited, weak, and subject to temptation, but through repentance humans can return to the path of righteousness. The term "Islam" refers to "submission to the will of Allah" and "Muslims" are those who "submit to Allah's will." The Qur'an refers to a day of reckoning, where all humans will be judged according to their deeds, and the righteous will go to heaven, while the evil ones will be condemned to eternal fires.

Another set of texts within Islam are known as the *hadith*, which are composed of the words and deeds of the prophet Muhammad as reported by his early followers. After his death, his companions collected reports of what he had said or done and preserved them for subsequent generations. One other body of religious texts that developed in the Islamic world is known as the *Sharia*, or Islamic law. The *Sharia* texts evolved gradually from the foundations of the Qur'an and *hadith*. The *Sharia* became the basis of political rule for the various Islamic states as well as a normative code defining criminal laws, and family and marital relationships. As Islam spread beyond Mecca and the Arabian peninsula, the Qur'an and *hadith* were often vague or silent about new circumstances and differing cultural conditions. Consequently, the *Sharia* was developed to deal with these new conditions. Because of poor transportation and

transcultural communications among different regions, four different schools of Islamic law emerged within a period of some two centuries. These schools, named after Muslim theologians, are known as the Maliki, Hanifa, Al-Shafi, and Hanbali. These schools of Islamic law reflected more conservative or liberal legal traditions, depending on the political and cultural context of different countries. Eventually religious judges, *qadi* and *mufti* (one who issues *fatwa*, or religious rulings) came to oversee the various forms of *Sharia* in different civilizations of the Islamic world.

After Muhammad's death in 632 A.D., rivalries developed within the Islamic community, ultimately leading to a schism. The immediate cause of this schism was a dispute over the choice of a *Caliph* or Islamic ruler. Muhammad did not have a son to become the *Caliph*. Consequently, one faction of the Islamic community believed that the *Caliph* should be the closest male relative of the prophet. This was the husband of the prophet's daughter Fatima, a man named Ali. However, other people within the Islamic community believed that the *Caliph* should be Abu Bakr, a very close disciple of the prophet. Eventually, the majority within the community selected Abu Bakr. The result was a conflict between the majority group, the *Sunni*, and a minority sect known as the *Shia Ali* (the partisans of Ali), which persists to this day.

Although there are minor differences with respect to ritual practices, the major doctrinal difference between the Sunni and Shia has to do with religious leadership. The Shia believe that the earthly Islamic community needs to be led by a charismatic, religious leader, and ideally a direct lineal male descendant of Ali, who acts as an intermediary between the human and the divine world. These Shia religious leaders, or Imams, were believed to have a spiritual power, *baraka*, which enabled them to lead the Islamic community. Ali did become the *Caliph* for a brief period of time (656–661 A.D.), but was not able to sustain leadership for the Muslim majority. Ali had two sons, Hasan and Husayn, who became religious martyrs, dying in a battle with the Sunni majority to establish the Shia.

The major rituals of Islam stated in the Qur'an are known as the "Five Pillars of Islam," or *ibadat* ("acts of service"). The Qur'an's first pillar specifies that all Muslims must profess faith in Allah, and Muhammad as Allah's prophet. This is known as the *shahada*, or confession of faith. Secondly, Muslims must pray five times a day (*salat*), facing the sacred city of Mecca. Third, they must fast (*sawm*) during the month of Ramadan, the ninth month of the Islamic calendar. During Ramadan Muslims cannot eat or drink between sunrise and sunset, must refrain from smoking and sexual intercourse, and maintain a spiritual state of mind. Fourth, they must give alms (*zakat*) to support the poor, orphans, and handicapped within their communities. And finally, they are obliged to make a pilgrimage *hajj* to Mecca at least once in their lifetimes (if they are financially and physically able). The *hajj* takes place in the twelfth month of the Islamic calendar. During the *hajj*, pilgrims participate in various rituals such as circumambulating the *Kaaba* ("cube"), the site of the earliest mosque believed to be built by the Prophet Abraham. As Muslim converts became more familiar with these rituals and prayers, they gradually learned more about the *Sharia* and other complex theological matters.

Art, Architecture, and Music

19.12 Describe some examples of art, architecture, and music in agricultural societies.

Unlike the art and music of bands, tribes, or chiefdoms, in agricultural civilizations, there were full-time artists, architects, and musicians supported by wealthy elites. However, outside of royal or elite circles, other folk or popular art and music emerged as expressions of peasant or local cultural traditions.

Each of the centers of civilizations in Mesopotamia, Egypt, India, China, Ancient Greece, Rome, as well as the Olmec, Mayan, and Incan cultures of the Americas, developed a unique, characteristic style of art and architecture. Much of this was reflected in the particular religions of these civilizations. For example, the paintings found on pottery or in other locations and sculpture of Mesopotamia and Egypt expressed the tradition of the semidivine rulers, priests, and various deities. Much of the ancient Greek and Roman architecture, paintings, pottery, and sculpture also focused on the spiritual deities. However, these classical artists paid particular attention to the beauty and form of the anatomy and muscles of the human body, as is evident in their paintings and sculpture.

In the Chinese and Indian civilizations, many art styles flourished in pottery, carving, calligraphy, and paintings. The art styles vary greatly from era to era, and each one is traditionally named after the ruling dynasty. For example, in China, the Tang Dynasty (618–907 A.D.) paintings emphasize idealized landscapes, whereas Ming Dynasty (1368–1644 A.D.) paintings, which are busy and colorful, focus on narrative storytelling. In the medieval period in Western and Byzantine civilizations, the focus of art was to glorify the biblical and religious themes of the Christian tradition with the use of glass mosaics, vivid colors, and gold in the backgrounds of paintings. In much of the Islamic world, there was a prohibition on using human images in sculpture or painting, which resulted in an emphasis on using calligraphy representing verses of the Qur'an and geometric patterns in paintings and architecture.

The Kamamkara Buddhist sculpture in Japan.

Various styles of music unique to each agricultural civilization flourished during different periods. In Mesopotamia and Egypt, harps, flutes, lyres, lutes, and cymbals have been represented in paintings and sculptures and discovered as artifacts by archaeologists. Indian classical music is one of the oldest musical traditions in the world, extending back to the Vedic religious tradition. In the Vedic tradition, forms of chanting were developed that are still present in the Hindu ritual tradition today. Indian classical music evolved what is known as *raga* rhythms and tones played with sitars, drums, and flutes; it is often accompanied by classical dancers. Indian classical dance emerged within the *Bhakti* tradition, where young females learned dances devoted to specific Hindu deities. Chinese royal court musicians developed their own musical notation and styles of musical genres accompanied by string and wind instruments. The royal courts of Korea, Central, and Southeast Asia had musical traditions based on religious themes.

In Western cultures, music was derived from the classical traditions of ancient Greece. The Greek theater had mixed male and female choruses for both secular entertainment and spiritual ceremonies. Various string instruments such as the lyre as well as wind instruments were developed, and musical literacy was an important part of education for elite males. During the medieval period of Western culture, the Catholic Church initiated a form of chanting in Latin, which eventually developed into the monophonic sacred liturgy known as the Gregorian chant. Although much of the music of the Western medieval period was based on sacred church music, there also existed a vibrant tradition of folk secular songs and dances that emerged in the rural communities of serfs and peasants.

Religion and Secularization in Industrial and Postindustrial Societies

19.13 Discuss religion and secularization in industrial and postindustrial societies.

Ever since the Renaissance and Enlightenment periods, Western industrial states have experienced extensive **secularization**, the historical decline in the influence of religion in society. Scientists such as Galileo and Charles Darwin developed ideas that challenged theological doctrines. European secular philosophers such as the Renaissance political writer Nicolo Machiavelli and the Enlightenment philosophers Thomas Hobbes, John Locke, Jean-Jacques Rousseau, and Voltaire increasingly proposed naturalistic (nonsupernatural) scientific explanations of both the natural and the social worlds. Secularization has influenced all industrialized states. For example, most people in these societies do not perceive illness as the result of supernatural forces; rather, they rely upon physicians trained in scientific medical practices to diagnose and cure diseases. However, secularization has developed much deeper roots in European culture than in that of the United States. One of the major reasons for the difference is that European society had experienced deadly, genocidal religious wars for generations, and political leaders and intellectuals were anxious to escape from them. In contrast, in U.S. society, which had religious freedom and little religious warfare, this extreme secular trend was not as apparent. Most people in the United States still participate in religious activity, much more than Europeans do. Yet, there are differences among various class and education groups in both Europe and the United States.

Despite the increase of secularization in the West, religion has not completely disappeared from industrial states. For example, the United States has experienced a great deal of secularization, and yet it remains one of the most religious societies in the world. Polls indicate that almost 81 percent of all Americans profess a belief in some sort of divine power (National Opinion Research Center 2012). Most anthropologists who have studied the question of how religious Americans are have concluded that the answer is extremely complex, because it relates to ethnic, political, and social-class issues. Many Americans claim religious affiliation in relationship to their communal or ethnic identity; others may belong to religious organizations to gain a sense of identity and belonging or to gain social prestige. Whatever the reasons, secularization has not substantially eroded religious beliefs and institutions in the United States.

Religion in Socialist States

In the former Soviet Union, secularization had been an aspect of the ideological apparatus of the state. According to Marxist views, religion is a set of beliefs and institutions used by the upper classes to control and regulate the lower classes. The ultimate aim of socialist societies is to eradicate religion, thereby removing a major obstacle to equality. For this reason, the Soviet Union and socialist Eastern European nations repressed religious organizations and officially endorsed atheism.

Despite these policies, 15 percent of the urban population and 30 percent of the rural population practiced religion in the Soviet Union. There were about 40 million Russian Orthodox Catholics, 600,000 Protestants, and up to 45 million Muslims in a country that proclaimed itself as atheistic for five decades (Kerblay 1983; Eickelman 1993). Thus, religious beliefs appear to have been a continuing source of inspiration and spiritual comfort for many citizens of the Soviet state.

Religion in Japan

Japan has also experienced a great deal of secularization as it has industrialized. Traditional Japanese religion was an amalgamation of beliefs based on an indigenous animistic form of worship referred to as Shintoism, combined with Confucianism, Taoism, and Buddhism, which spread from China. Most Japanese and Western observers agree that secularization has diminished the influence of these traditional faiths. Although the majority of Japanese still turn to Shinto shrines and Buddhist ceremonies for life-cycle rituals or personal crises and the temples teem with people during the various holidays, most modern Japanese confess that they are not deeply religious (Befu 1971; Hendry 1987; McCreery and McCreery 2006).

However, most anthropologists concur that religious beliefs and practices are so thoroughly embedded in Japanese culture that religion cannot easily be separated from the national identity and way of life. In fact, the term "religion" was not part of the Japanese lexicon until after Western missionaries introduced Christianity into Japan. After Westerners brought the term "religion" into Japan, Japanese scholars and intellectuals began to use this concept of religion as a separate domain (Thomas 2013). Many Japanese refer to *nihondo* ("the Japanese way") as the basis of their national, ethnic, and cultural identity. *Nihondo* refers to Japanese cultural and spiritual beliefs and practices, including those influenced by traditional Shinto,

Confucianist, Taoist, and Buddhist religions. It appears that the beliefs and customs associated with these traditions are intimately bound up with Japanese identity.

Art and Music

19.14 Discuss some developments in art and music in industrial and postindustrial societies.

After the industrial and scientific revolutions, Western artistic developments reflected these technological, economic, social, and cultural trends. Artistic paintings, sculptures, and printmaking became more secular in content and theme than in previous eras. However, in the eighteenth and nineteenth centuries, some Western artists began to reject these secular and scientific developments, resulting in what is known as the Romantic period that focused on the emotions and passions of individuals. Later artistic movements derived from the Romantic period were symbolism and impressionism, as developed by painters such as Claude Monet and Vincent Van Gogh. Western artistic movements in the twentieth century led to cubism, dadaism, surrealism, and a variety of styles including abstract impressionism, abstract expressionism, symbolism, and modernism, each attempting to innovate beyond the other. Some of these developments were initiated by the increasing global connections of the twentieth- and twenty-first-century artists, as Pablo Picasso, Henri Matisse, and Paul Gauguin incorporated indigenous art forms of Africa, Asia, Native America, the Pacific Islands, and elsewhere. During the Cold War, the Soviet Union and Eastern European socialist countries had their own artistic developments emphasizing social realism and depictions of ideal worker conditions. Throughout the industrial world in

architecture, the skyscraper became the symbolic form associated with the power of modern progress.

A postmodern artistic movement that influenced painting, sculpture, and architecture emerged with the age of postindustrialism in the 1960s and 70s that recycled and mixed classical art forms from the past with novel expressions of twentieth- and twenty-first-century art. In addition, this postmodern artistic movement was influenced by the anthropological perspective and cultural relativism that questioned the aesthetic barriers between so-called "high culture" or the "fine arts" and popular or folk art. Contemporary painting, sculpture, printmaking, film, or other visual media are significantly shaped by global interconnections that highlight the hybridity among different styles that create a global artistic culture. Ongoing anthropological research on this hybridity of art styles and movements continues to contribute towards a broad cross-cultural and intercultural interpretation of global artistic developments.

Music

The music of industrial and postindustrial societies also reflected the new socioeconomic, political, and secular trends. In the musical tradition of Europe, public concerts and operas featured singers, strings, brass, woodwinds, pipe organs, harpsichords, and other instruments that had both religious and secular elements. Although these early classical music traditions were associated with the aristocracy, the ideals of the French Revolution that emphasized universal human rights and the breakdown of the feudal aristocratic order influenced composers such as Ludwig Beethoven to produce major symphonic works that reflected

Pablo Picasso's painting Guernica brings together modern and indigenous forms of art to express the destructiveness of modern warfare of World War II.

Famed jazz musician Wynton Marsalis.

the ideals of rights for everyone. Beethoven represents the composer who merged the classical and Romantic trends in the music of Europe. Later Romantic composers such as the German Richard Wagner drew on the folk religions of Europe to write operas to express the new nationalistic political trends in Germany and elsewhere. This Romantic musical movement attempted to express the emotional and passionate aspects of the new nationalism emerging in Europe.

In the twentieth century, with the development of the phonograph and radio, all types of music began to be distributed and listened to throughout the world. With the expansion of these media, the U.S. blues and jazz that developed from the slavery experience of African-Americans became an extremely important genre of global music. These forms of African-American musical styles were adopted by white American composers and big bands, thus becoming the mainstream popular music of the 1920s, 30s, and 40s. Similarly, in the mid-twentieth century, rock and roll music, derived from blues, jazz, and country music using electric or acoustic guitars, piano keyboards, saxophones, harmonicas, and other instruments, became an influential popular music trend. After the 1960s, in the postindustrial societies of the United States, Europe, and Japan, different subgenres of rock and roll, such as rockabilly, jazz-rock fusion, blues rock, heavy metal, punk rock, and rap and hip-hop music initiated by African-Americans influenced global musical developments. Since

that time, like in other art forms, with increasing interconnections among societies, hybridity among different musical forms has been expanding the range of a global music culture. For example, a 2014 music and art exhibition in Canada called *Beat Nation: Hip Hop as Indigenous* combines the indigenous music and art from the Native Americans of Canada with the beats and graffiti of hip-hop music and art to challenge stereotypes.

Ethnomusicologists have been engaged in recording music and describing how the music is integrated with culture contexts of various societies around the world. Mickey Hart, the drummer for the Grateful Dead, a popular rock and roll group, has been interested in ethnomusicology for many years. In a book sponsored by National Geographic called *Songcatchers: In Search of the World's Music* (2003), Hart explores how ethnomusicologists have been attempting to record and preserve music in different areas of the world. He traces the very first recordings of ethnomusicologist and songcatcher, Jesse Walter Fewkes, who conserved the singing of a Passamaquoddy Indian in 1890. Since that first recording, Hart describes the various ethnomusicologists who have taken their equipment to every remote corner of the world to help preserve the musical expressions of humanity. Ethnomusicologists continue to expand our musical horizons by recording and conserving the world's musical styles and developments.

Summary and Review of Learning Objectives

19.1 Discuss how anthropologists such as Clifford Geertz define religion.

Clifford Geertz's definition of religion as *"a system of symbols which acts to establish powerful, pervasive, and long-lasting moods and motivations in men by formulating conceptions of a general order of existence and clothing these conceptions with such an aura of factuality that the moods and motivations seem uniquely realistic"* has been very influential in the interpretative-humanistic understanding of religion in different societies. Central to any religion is a "system of symbols," which includes all sacred objects from Christian crucifixes, Islamic crescents, or Buddhist relics to sacred myths such as Genesis or the Ramayana of Hinduism. These symbols produce "moods," such as happiness and sadness, and "motivations" that provide direction or ethical goals in a person's life. Religious symbols enhance particular feelings and dispositions, creating an intense sense of awe in individuals. This sense of awe is induced through the use of sacred symbols in rituals and other religious performances to create an atmosphere of mystery going beyond everyday experience. But religious symbols also create and reaffirm a worldview by "formulating conceptions of a general order of existence." This worldview provides meaning or purpose to life and the universe. A religious worldview helps people discern the meaning of pain and suffering in the world. Sacred myths help people make sense of the world and also explain and justify cultural values and social rules. Despite some modern criticisms, this definition provided a means of studying religions with a humanistic-interpretive framework.

19.2 Discuss how anthropologists define myth and ritual.

Myths consist of a people's assumed knowledge about the universe and the natural and supernatural worlds and about humanity's place in these worlds. Religious rituals consist of repetitive behaviors that communicate sacred symbols to members of a society. Anthropologists investigate and describe rituals of many different cultures.

19.3 Describe the stages of rites of passage as discussed by anthropologists.

Anthropologists discuss three stages of rites of passage as 1) *structure*, 2) *antistructure* (or *liminality*, and *communitas*), and 3) *reincorporation*. *Structure* is the initial status of the individual. The period of *liminality* is the temporary phase of ambiguity, marginality, and antistructure. *Communitas* is also part of the antistructural phase where the individual felt a strong bond and a sense of equality with others. The final phase of the rite of passage is reincorporation, marking a return to, and reunion with, society with a wholly new status.

19.4 Discuss the new developments by cognitive anthropologists and their understanding of religion.

Cognitive anthropologists assess the evidence from psychologists on how children learn their religious beliefs and concepts based upon some innate predispositions and "intuitive knowledge" that are an aspect of human nature. Anthropomorphism, the psychological disposition to project and perceive human characteristics in nonhuman phenomena, is found in all societies. Children and adults attribute human agency-like characteristics into the world, which appears to be an inherent aspect of our cognitive and thinking processes. Many of the beliefs about gods and spirits are counterintuitive, but many of them coincide with our cognitive capacities, intuitive knowledge, and human emotions. Cognitive anthropologists also explore how religion produces prosocial norms, group stability, and cooperation within groups, but simultaneously increases the possibility of conflict with external groups.

19.5 Discuss how anthropologists study art and music in different societies.

Ethnomusicologists and anthropologists who study music and art find that what is considered beautiful or refined is dependent on the complex cultural context in different societies. Thus, they challenge the Western elite views of *aesthetics* regarding perceptions of beauty and tastes in art and music.

The elite views were based on distinctions between "high culture," or "fine art," versus "folk," or "primitive art." Anthropologists introduced the concept of cultural relativism into the study of art and music to critique these elite views.

19.6 Describe examples of religion found in foraging societies.

Foraging religions, often referred to as cosmic religions, are intimately associated with nature. The sacredness of the natural environment is sometimes expressed in a form of animism, the belief that spirits reside within all inorganic and organic substances. Current anthropologists are using the term "animism" to refer to the very respectful relationship between humans and others, including animals, plants, and inorganic objects in their cultural environment. Examples of foraging religions include the "Dreamtime" religion of the Australian Aborigines, or the spiritual beliefs about souls of animals and humans maintained by the Inuit (Eskimo) peoples of the Arctic.

19.7 Describe examples of art and music found in foraging societies.

Rock paintings with highly symbolic images of natural phenomena are found in most foraging societies. It is believed that this art is sacred and can be used to make contact with supernatural sources. Traditional Inuit (Eskimo) art products include many items made from ivory, one of the few rigid materials available in the Arctic. Human and animal figurines, which were worn as amulets to enhance supernatural powers and practices, dominate Eskimo artistic output. The Eskimo also carve masks in ivory (or sometimes wood) for use by their shamans. The music of foraging societies is generally divided into recreational (folk or popular) and religious music. Some foraging groups like the Mbuti have no instrumental music, but they have many songs and dances. Music and religion are inextricably bound within the shamanistic rituals of the Inuit (Eskimo). In the shamanistic performances, a drum is used to enhance the rhythmic songs. The shaman's songs are simple, chant-like recitations that have no actual words. Short phrases are repeated again and again. The drumming and song chants are used to establish contact with the spirits.

19.8 Describe examples of religion found in horticultural and pastoralist societies.

In addition to animism, shamanism, witchcraft, and sorcery, tribal religions are intertwined with descent groupings, particularly clans and lineages that are linked with totemic spirits believed to assist and watch over the group. Thus, tribal religions are very familistic.

19.9 Discuss how religion is interrelated with politics in chiefdom societies.

The most dramatic difference between chiefdom religions and band and tribal religions is the degree to which chiefdom religions legitimized the social, political, and moral status of the chiefs. For example, Hawaiian chiefs were believed to be either gods or sacred intermediaries between human societies and the divine world. Hawaiian chiefdoms have been referred to as theocracies, societies in which people rule not because of their worldly wealth and power, but because of their place in the moral and sacred order. The political and legal authority of chiefdoms was reinforced by norms and rules based on social inequalities. Wherever shamanism existed among chiefdoms, the shamans reinforced the authority of the chiefs.

19.10 Describe examples of art, architecture, and music in chiefdom societies.

Chiefdom art and music reflected a high degree of labor organization and the status symbols associated with high-ranking chiefs. One of the most profound examples of the artwork of a chiefdom society is found on Easter Island, where there are large stone figures known as *moai*. The symbolic design of these statuaries evokes the power, status, and high rank of the chiefs of Easter Island. Likewise, the large mounds associated with the Cahokian chiefdom complex represented extensive labor projects and a hierarchical society. Different types of earthen mounds surrounded the city of Cahokia.

19.11 Describe some examples of ecclesiastical and universalistic religions found in agricultural societies.

Major ecclesiastical religious traditions emerged in agricultural civilizations around the world. Mesopotamia, Egypt, China, Greece, Rome, Mesoamerica, and South America developed some of the earliest ecclesiastical religions. These religious traditions were limited to the specific territory of these societies and were intimately tied to their particular state organization. Other agricultural civilizations developed what is known as universalistic religions that consisted of beliefs and rituals applying to all of humanity. Hinduism, Buddhism, Judaism, Christianity (Catholic and Protestant) and Islam are the major universalistic religions that are studied by anthropologists.

19.12 Describe some examples of art, architecture, and music in agricultural societies.

In agricultural civilizations, full-time artists, architects, and musicians supported by royal families and elites, produced a great deal of the art, architecture, and music. This art and music was largely based on religious themes. However, outside of royal or elite circles, more folk or popular art and music emerged as expressions of peasant or local cultural traditions. Each of the centers of civilizations in Mesopotamia, Egypt, India, China, Ancient Greece, Rome, as well as the Olmec, Mayan, and Incan cultures of the Americas developed a unique, characteristic style of art. Much of the art and architecture reflected the particular religions found in these civilizations. Various styles of music unique to each agricultural civilization flourished during different periods. In Mesopotamia and Egypt, harps, flutes, lyres, lutes, and cymbals have been represented in paintings and sculptures; these have been discovered as artifacts by archaeologists. Indian classical music and dance represent one of the oldest musical traditions in the world, extending back to the Vedic religious tradition. Medieval Western music was associated with the liturgy of the Roman Catholic Church.

19.13 Discuss religion and secularization in industrial and postindustrial societies.

Ever since the Renaissance and Enlightenment periods, Western industrial and postindustrial states have experienced extensive secularization, the historical decline in the influence of religion in society. However, despite the trend for secularization, religion continues to thrive in the United States in contrast to some European societies based on their different historical circumstances. Genocidal religious wars developed in Europe compared to the freedom and tolerance for most religious traditions in the United States. Religion was repressed in the former Soviet Union, but various religious traditions continued to exist. Although Japan has been described as a highly secular country, the religious traditions of Shintoism, Buddhism, and Confucianism are incorporated into modern Japanese culture.

19.14 Discuss some developments in art and music in industrial and postindustrial societies.

Following the industrial revolution, artistic paintings, sculptures, and printmaking became more secular in content and theme than in previous eras. However, in the eighteenth and nineteenth centuries, some Western artists began to reject these secular and scientific developments. resulting in what is known as the Romantic period. Later artistic movements were symbolism, impressionism, cubism, dadaism, surrealism, and a variety of abstract impressionism, abstract expressionism, symbolism, and modernism. Some of these developments were initiated by the increasing global connections of the twentieth and twenty-first century artists as they incorporated indigenous art forms of Africa, Asia, Native America, the Pacific Islands and elsewhere. A postmodern artistic movement developed in the 1960s and 70s that recycled and mixed classical art forms from the past with novel expressions of twentieth and twenty-first century art. It was influenced by the anthropological perspective and cultural relativism that questioned the aesthetic barriers between so-called "high culture" or the "fine arts" and popular or folk art. Contemporary painting, sculpture, printmaking, film, or other visual media are significantly shaped by global interconnections that highlight the hybridity among different styles that create a global artistic culture.

The music of industrial and postindustrial societies also reflected the new socioeconomic, political, and secular trends. In the musical tradition of Europe, public concerts and operas were associated with the aristocratic elite. However, some composers such as Beethoven were influenced by the new socioeconomic and political trends of the French Revolution. Later, Romantic composers such as Richard Wagner drew on the folk religions of Europe to write operas that expressed the new nationalistic trends in Germany.

In the twentieth century, with the development of the phonograph and radio, all types of music began to be distributed and listened to throughout the world. With the expansion of these media, the U.S. blues and jazz that developed from the slavery experience of African-Americans became an extremely important genre of global music. After the 1960s, in the postindustrial societies of the United States, Europe, and Japan, different subgenres of rock and roll, rap, and hip hop music initiated by African-Americans influenced global musical developments. Since that time, as in other art forms, with increasing interconnections among societies, hybridity among different musical forms has been expanding the range of a global music culture.

Key Terms

animism, p. 439

anthropomorphism, p. 437

art, p. 438

ecclesiastical religions, p. 447

karma, p. 448

mana, p. 445

moksha, p. 448

music, p. 438

myths, p. 434

nirvana, p. 449

priest, p. 436

priestess, p. 436

rites of passage, p. 434

rites of legitimation, p. 447

rituals, p. 434

samsara, p. 436

secularization, p. 455

shamans, p. 436

sorcery, p. 442

tabu, p. 445

theocracies, p. 439

totemism, p. 439

totem, p. 439

universalistic religions, p. 448

witchcraft, p. 442

Chapter 20

Globalization, Culture, and Indigenous Societies

Learning Objectives

After reading this chapter you should be able to:

20.1 Discuss how anthropologists define globalization.

20.2 Describe some of the technological and economic trends resulting in globalization.

20.3 Compare the three theoretical approaches to analyzing globalization.

20.4 Discuss how anthropologists analyze globalization.

20.5 Discuss how anthropologists criticize some of the approaches to understanding politics, culture, and globalization.

20.6 Discuss the consequences of globalization on indigenous peoples.

20.7 Describe the different forms of resistance to globalization by indigenous peoples.

20.8 Discuss how anthropologists contribute to the understanding of globalization.

Globalization: A Contested Term

20.1 Discuss how anthropologists define globalization.

Anthropologist Richard Wilk has described on his Web site what he terms the *Globobabble* that has infected the discussions of contemporary trends. These terms include *Globalacious*, *Globalasia*, *Globalatio*, *Globalemic*, and *Globaloney*. He introduces his Web site on globalization at Indiana University with his statement that "[i]n this globalized global age, when everything has globated to the point where it is completely globulous, we obviously need some new vocabulary to describe the globish trends that are englobing us all" (http://www.indiana.edu/~wanthro/babble.htm 2000).

We are only at the early stages of developing a concept of globalization that could be shared by all anthropologists. Anthropologists have discovered that not all people share exactly the same form of culture or patterns of culture within the same society, and the same is true today with respect to the anthropological community with respect to agreement on a precise concept of globalization. Just as the meanings of cultural values, beliefs, values, and norms are often the subject of conflict among groups and individuals within a society, the term *globalization* is often contested and argued about by anthropologists. It is at best an imprecise "narrative" or "metaphor" for understanding what is occurring presently in the world within and among different societies. Generally speaking, anthropologists usually refer to **globalization** as the broad-scale changes and transformations that have resulted from the impact of industrialization and the emergence of an interconnected global economy, with the spread of capital, labor (migration), and technology across national borders. Globalization continues to occur today through the increasing spread of industrial technology—including electronic communications, television, and the Internet—and the expansion of multinational corporations into the non-Western world.

However, despite this general consensus, there has been an ongoing debate within anthropological circles as to when globalization actually began. Most anthropologists connected this process with the developments following the Industrial Revolution in Western Europe and the spread of these developments throughout many societies in the world. However, some

anthropologists refer to globalization as developing during the 1500s, within the period of Western European exploration and early colonization, whereas others link it to earlier time periods in East Asia, especially Chinese technological and economic developments prior to 1500 A.D. (Frank 1998). Other anthropologists identify some elements of globalization in various areas in early history and prehistory and even among "tribal cultures" (Friedman 1998).

Despite these differences among anthropologists, we all can recognize various elements of globalization within our everyday lives in the United States or any other society in the world. We recognize a remarkable acceleration in computer technological developments, migration trends, and changing communications with the Internet, e-mail, fax, television, and other media that have brought the societies in the world into what is sometimes referred to as a "global village" or "spaceship Earth" or a "world without walls." The journalist Thomas Friedman has been writing about global trends since the publication of his book called *The Lexus and the Olive Tree: Understanding Globalization* (2000). Friedman emphasized the positive aspects of globalization: the integration of the world economy and financial markets and the pervasive development of international political coalitions and cooperation, replacing the archaic processes that dominated the world during the Cold War years. In that book, Friedman made the famous statement that whenever two societies share a McDonald's, they will not go to war against one another. However, Friedman's book was written prior to September 11, 2001, and the attacks on the World Trade Center and the Pentagon. This tragic episode caused many Americans and Westerners to reflect upon how globalization may not

The September 11, 2001 tragedy in New York City

always bring the world closer together, but rather may result in severe political and cultural conflict.

In our everyday life, we recognize globalization in our educational settings because there are many students from every area of the world in our universities and colleges. We see globalization with our professional athletic teams: Russians and East Europeans play on professional hockey teams; Latin Americans, Caribbean peoples, and Asians from Japan and Korea are on professional baseball teams; Chinese players such as Yao Ming are joining athletes from the Dinka and Nuer groups of East Africa on professional basketball teams; and Tiger Woods, who is part Thai, part Chinese, part African American, and part American Indian, represents a truly multicultural individual who has excelled in international golf tournaments. When tourists travel to Asia, they can turn on the television in their hotels and view not only CNN and the BBC, but also versions of MTV with their own traditions of music and dance, including hip-hop and rap music in India. So these elements of globalization surround us in the United States and other areas of the world. Despite the differences and disagreements among social scientists and anthropologists over the precise meaning of the term *globalization*, we surely are aware of these globalization processes around us.

Globalization: Technological and Economic Trends

20.2 **Describe some of the technological and economic trends resulting in globalization.**

In 1980, fewer than two million computers existed in the world, and nearly all of them took up a great deal of space. As of 2014 there were an estimated two billion computers in the world. Although most of these computers are personal desktop or laptop computers, there are an increasing number of tablet computers such as iPads or Kindle Fire, and even more smartphones that can connect to the Internet. Major companies such as Microsoft and Intel are producing computer technology so rapidly that when an individual or company purchases a computer off the shelf, the technology is already obsolete. No one can keep pace with these rapid developments in computer chips and software. Trends in technology trends are transforming industrial societies, as we discussed in Chapter 16, into what social scientists call *postindustrial societies*. Postindustrial economies have smaller manufacturing sectors and have developed high-tech computer hardware and software capacities. Work in information rather than "manual labor," has transformed the global economy. As a result

of this trend, Bill Gates of Microsoft is one of the richest billionaires in the world.

The Internet was developed by the U.S. Department of Defense in the 1960s. At first, the Internet was developed to help scientists and engineers working together on defense-related projects communicate research findings more easily to one another. However, the Internet today is used not just by scientists and academics to conduct research or to download music, but also by multinational corporations that have integrated the global economic developments among many societies.

Economic aspects of globalization are also visible to most people today. When consumers buy their clothing in the United States from the Gap, Walmart, Banana Republic, or other retailers, they find that most of it is produced in Asia, the Caribbean, Latin America, or islands in the Pacific. Automobile manufacturers such as Ford, Chrysler, and GM have plants all over the world, including China, Mexico, and Europe. Auto companies are now transnational corporations; Ford and GM have joint production programs with Japanese and South Korean auto manufacturers such as Honda, Toyota, Mitsubishi, and Hyundai and have manufacturing plants in the United States, Europe, Latin America, and Asia. The Honda Accord is produced in Ohio, but Dodge vehicles are produced outside the United States. As we shall discuss further in Chapter 24 on contemporary global trends, multinational corporations are continually merging into large conglomerates and oligopolies to promote more economic efficiency and international manufacturing and marketing to enhance their revenues (Kapferer 2005).

As we saw in Chapter 16, economic anthropologists study the production, distribution, and consumption of goods and services in different societies. Today, economic anthropologists focus on how the economies of different societies are transformed by these globalization factors. One important topic now being studied by anthropologists is what has been termed *outsourcing*. In Chapter 24,

Bill Gates

we discuss the consequences of the relocation of manufacturing plants such as Nike to regions in Asia to enhance revenues and reduce the costs of labor for multinational corporations. Most recently, one of the consequences of postindustrial developments is a new trend in the relocation of white-collar information technology (IT) jobs from the United States, Japan, and Europe to areas such as India and China. Many Americans and other Westerners are alarmed by the fact that many engineering, computer-related service, chip design, tax form service, and telecommunications jobs are now transferred to India or China. When Americans have a problem with their Microsoft Word documents, they call an 800 number for Microsoft and often talk to someone in China or India about how to solve these problems. Economists predict that by 2015, the United States will shift some 3.3 million IT jobs to India. India is adding some two million college graduates a year, most of them with degrees in engineering and IT. As of 2010, the cost for hiring an engineer in the United States is approximately $50–$60 an hour compared to $25–$30 an hour in India or China (Cherian 2010).

Globalization: General Theoretical Approaches

20.3 Compare the three theoretical approaches to analyzing globalization.

Social scientists have used three major theoretical approaches to examine globalization: modernization theory, dependency theory, and world-systems theory. Each has provided a model for analyzing the impact of globalization on industrial and nonindustrial societies.

Modernization Theory

The historical intellectual heritage of what is called modernization theory is associated with the prolific German scholar and sociologist Max Weber (1864–1920). To some extent, Weber was reacting to the earlier ideas of Karl Marx (discussion to follow), who argued that the "material conditions," including technology, environment, and the economy, determined or influenced the cultural beliefs and values of different people within a society. In contrast, Weber recognized that cultural values and beliefs had a very significant influence on the development of particular technological and economic conditions in a society. He focused on the relationship of cultural values to economic action and behavior. Weber's views on the modernization of society have influenced many economic, historical, sociological, and anthropological interpretations. He noted that all humans provided significance and meaning to their orientations, practical actions, and behavior in the world (Keyes 2002). Modernization theory absorbed Weber's view and emphasized how ideas, beliefs, and values have transforming effects on practical activity within society. Societies are products not just of technology and a particular mode of production or economy, but also of *culture*, which shapes and influences the modes of thinking and significance for action within a society.

Using a broad cross-cultural and global approach, modernization theorists relying on Weber's model maintain that premodern and preindustrial societies were *traditional* in their values, whereas people in *modern industrial capitalist societies* endorsed rationality. While traditional societies were guided by sentiments and beliefs passed from generation to generation, modern societies embraced rationality and used deliberate strategies, including

This photo shows an office scene in India with workers employed to assist people with computer problems all over the world. Many companies such as Microsoft and Apple outsource many aspects of their businesses overseas.

scientific methods, to pursue efficient means to obtain particular goals. Like Weber, the modernization theorists argued that traditional cultural beliefs are swept away by the process of rationalization as a society modernizes. They view the rationalization of society as the historical change from a traditional worldview to scientific rationality as the dominant mode of human thought and action.

One of Weber's most influential books, which later influenced the modernization approach to globalization, was *The Protestant Ethic and the Spirit of Capitalism* (1904). In that work, Weber sought to understand the values that influenced the emergence of industrial capitalist society. Through a historical analysis, he theorized that the specific values of hard work, thrift, and discipline as exhibited within the Calvinist religious tradition in Europe in the seventeenth century resulted in more rational, scientific, and efficient technological and economic conditions, ushering in the development of industrial capitalism, or modernity.

Modernization Theory and the Cold War

Although modernization theory had its roots in nineteenth-century Enlightenment ideas, as espoused by Max Weber and other social scientists, it became the leading model for understanding globalization in the 1950s in the context of the Cold War between the United States and the Soviet Union. During that period, these two superpowers were competing for economic resources and the political allegiance of different nations. Modernization theory provided a model to explain how social and cultural change could occur in all societies through industrial capitalism.

Max Weber (1864–1920).

One of the most influential proponents of modernization is the American economist W. W. Rostow, who was an advisor to presidents during the Cold War years. Rostow argued that although modernization occurred first in the West, it could develop in all societies provided that those societies meet certain preconditions. According to Rostow (1978), evolution from a traditional preindustrial society to a modern industrial society takes place through five general stages:

1. *Traditional stage.* Premodern societies are unlikely to become modernized because of *traditionalism*— persisting values and attitudes that represent obstacles to economic and political development. According to modernization theorists, traditionalism creates a form of "cultural inertia" that keeps premodern societies backward and underdeveloped. Traditionalism places great significance on maintaining family and community relationships and sentiments, which inhibit individual freedom, individual achievement, and entrepreneurial initiative. For example, many traditional societies have values that emphasize an allegiance to the family and clan, rather than individual achievement.

2. *Culture-change stage.* One of the preconditions for modernization involves *cultural and value changes*. People must accept the belief that progress is both necessary and beneficial to society and to the individual. Belief in progress is linked to an emphasis on individual achievement, which leads to the emergence of individual entrepreneurs who will take the necessary risks for economic progress. Modernization theorists insist that these changes in values are brought about through education and will result in the erosion of traditionalism.

3. *Takeoff stage.* As traditionalism begins to weaken, rates of investment and savings will begin to rise. Economic changes provide the context for the development of industrial capitalist society. England reached this stage by about 1783, and the United States by about 1840. Modernization theorists believed that this stage is reached only through foreign aid to support the diffusion of education, which reduces traditionalism and encourages the transfer of industrial technology from capitalist societies to premodern societies.

4. *Self-sustained growth stage.* At this stage, the members of the society intensify economic progress through the implementation of industrial technology. This process involves a consistent reinvestment of savings and capital in modern technology. It also includes a commitment to mass education to promote advanced skills and modern attitudes. As the population becomes more educated, traditionalism continues to erode.

5. *High economic growth stage.* This last stage involves the achievement of a high standard of living, characterized by mass production and consumption of material goods and services. Western Europe and the United States achieved this stage in the 1920s, and Japan reached it in the 1950s.

The modernization model includes both noneconomic factors, such as cultural values including individualism, and economic behavior such as entrepreneurship as pre-conditions for modernization. In fact, in stage two, the changes in cultural values are the most important pre-requisites for eliminating traditionalism and generating patterns of achievement. Modernization theorists view cultural values and traditionalism as the *primary* reasons for the lack of economic development. The practical impli-cation that derives from this model is that before a country should receive foreign aid, traditionalism and the values that support it must be transformed.

Like Rostow, who drew on Max Weber, psychologist David McClelland (1973) maintained that a *need for achieve-ment* represents the most important variable in producing the process of modernization. McClelland argued that a need for achievement is not just a desire for more mate-rial goods, but rather an intrinsic need for satisfaction in achieving success. He believed that desire for achievement leads to increased savings and accumulation of capital. McClelland claimed to have found evidence for this need in some non-Western countries such as Japan, Taiwan, and Korea, as well as in Western countries.

First, Second, and Third Worlds

The moderni-zation model of the Cold War led to the categorization of societies into three "worlds": the First, Second, and Third Worlds. According to the modernization theorists, the **First World** is composed of modern industrial states with predominantly capitalist economic systems. These socie-ties became industrialized "first." Included in this group are Great Britain, Western Europe, Australia, Canada, New Zealand, Japan, and the United States. The **Second World** consisted of industrial states that had predominantly socialist economies. It included the former Soviet Union countries and many of the former socialist countries of Eastern Europe—for example, Poland and Hungary. The **Third World** referred to premodern agricultural states that maintain traditionalism. The Third World encompassed the vast majority of the people in the world, including most of Latin America, Africa, the Middle East, and Asia.

Criticisms of Modernization Theory

Moderniza-tion theory enabled social scientists to identify various aspects of social and cultural change that accompany glo-balization. By the 1960s, however, modernization theory came under attack by a number of critics. One of the major criticisms is that the applied model of modernization has failed to produce technological and economic development in the so-called Third World countries. Despite massive injections of foreign aid and education projects sponsored by wealthy First World countries, most Third World coun-tries remained underdeveloped. An *underdeveloped society* has a low gross national product (GNP), the total value of goods and services produced by a country. Anthropologists emphasize that one cannot understand or explain the evo-lution of society through the precise ladder-like stages postulated by the modernization theorists. Most societies throughout the world exhibit "hybridity" or a complex combination of economic, social, political, and cultural beliefs and values.

Some critics view modernization theory as ethnocen-tric, or "Westerncentric." They believe that this theory pro-motes Western industrial capitalist society as an ideal that ought to be encouraged universally. These critics argue that Western capitalist societies have many problems, such as extreme economic inequality and the dislocation of community and family ties, and they question whether a Western model of modernization is suitable or beneficial for all societies. They do not agree that all societies must emulate the West to progress economically. In addition, they do not want this model of modernity imposed on them from outside countries.

Modernization theorists have also been criticized for citing traditional values as obstacles to technological and economic development in the Third World. Critics consider this an example of "blaming the victim." They charge that this argument oversimplifies both the conditions in Third World countries and the process of industrialization as it occurred in the West. For example, anthropologists and historians have recognized that individual entrepreneurs in the West and in Japan had a great deal of economic free-dom, which encouraged independent initiative. As dis-cussed in Chapter 18, both Europe and Japan experienced historical periods of feudalism when their governments did not have systematic control over independent economic activities in local regions. Consequently, entrepreneurs had freedom to develop their technologies and trading oppor-tunities. In contrast, many Third World people have a so-called need to achieve, but lack the necessary economic and political institutions and opportunities for achievement.

Another criticism of modernization theory is that it neglects the factors of global economic and political power, conflict, and competition within and among societies. For example, the wealthier classes in Third World countries that have benefited from the new technology and other assets from the First World often exploit the labor of the lower classes. This conflict and division between classes may inhibit economic development. Modernization theo-rists also tend to view First, Second, and Third World countries as existing in isolation from one another.

One other major problem with the modernization theorists is that the terms *First*, *Second*, and *Third World countries* are too simplistic today to account for the great diversity that anthropologists actually discover in these societies. Modernization theory was a product of Cold War politics, in which the capitalist West (the First World) was in global competition with the socialist East (the Second World), and the rest of the world (the Third World) was influenced by Cold War politics. However, as we shall see in Chapter 24, sweeping changes have been transforming the Eastern-bloc countries, including former members of the Soviet Union, resulting in the dissipation of most Second World socialist societies. In addition, the phrase *Third World societies* tends to lump together many societies that are at different levels of socioeconomic development. For example, Saudi Arabia, rich in oil resources, cannot be compared with Bangladesh, which has very little natural resource wealth upon which to draw. Some countries in the so-called Third World are much better off economically, with ten to twenty times the national wealth of other countries. Although the terms *First*, *Second*, and *Third Worlds* are still used in the media and elsewhere, we should be aware that this terminology is a legacy of the Cold War and is no longer relevant to an understanding of present-day societies.

Dependency Theory

Criticism of modernization theory led to another general model and approach that emerged primarily from the underdeveloped world. Known as **dependency theory**, this approach is a model of socioeconomic development that explains globalization and the inequality among different societies as resulting from the historical exploitation of poor, underdeveloped societies by rich, developed societies.

The historical roots of the dependency view of globalization are connected with the well-known German social philosopher Karl Marx (1818–1883). As mentioned previously in Chapter 13, Marx had argued that the *material things* of life were primary and that cultural beliefs and values were secondary. Later, Marx wrote many tracts such as *Economic and Philosophic Manuscripts* (1844) and *Das Kapital* (in English, *Capital*) (1867), which emphasized his philosophy of materialism, sometimes referred to as historical materialism.

According to Marx's historical materialist thesis, economic realities, or what Marx termed the *mode of production* which included the way a society organizes its economy and technology, were the primary determinants of human behavior and thought. A second ingredient in Marx's historical materialist thesis was the proposition that all human history was driven by *class struggle*, perpetual conflicts between the groups that owned resources and had political power and those who owned very little

and had almost no political power. Marx and his close collaborator Friedrich Engels developed a sweeping *unilineal and global evolutionary scheme* (see Chapter 13) based upon the different modes of production that societies had developed since early prehistory. The earliest mode of production was hunting and gathering, followed by the development of agriculture, succeeded by feudalism, which evolved into industrial capitalism. Each of these different modes of production was transformed by class conflicts and struggles, resulting in the successive stages of societal evolution.

Writing at the time of early industrialization and capitalism in Europe in the nineteenth century, Marx and Engels viewed these developments as causes of exploitation, inequality in wealth and power, and class struggle. They believed that a struggle was emerging between the bourgeoisie (the owners of factories, mines, and other industries) and the proletariat (the working class) in industrial capitalist societies such as England, Germany, and the United States. They maintained that through this class conflict, new modes of production would develop—first socialism and eventually communism, which represented the end of class conflict, private property, poverty, economic exploitation, warfare, and power struggles.

Dependency theory was influenced by Marxism and is associated with theorists such as Andre Gunder Frank, who denied that underdevelopment is the product of the persistence of traditionalism in preindustrial societies, as the modernization theorists maintained. Dependency theorists contend instead that wealthy industrialized capitalist countries exploit underdeveloped precapitalist societies for the cheap labor and raw materials needed to maintain their own industrial technologies. Through this process, impoverished underdeveloped countries became economic and political dependencies of wealthy industrialized capitalist countries.

Dependency theorists suggest that capitalism increased the prosperity and the power of Western nations at the expense of poor nations. Especially after 1870, following the early phases of industrialism, a new type of relationship developed between industrialized and nonindustrialized societies. As manufacturing expanded, the industrial nations' needs for raw materials and markets for their manufactured goods increased. Also, changing patterns of consumption created more demands for new foodstuffs and goods such as tea, coffee, sugar, and tobacco from nonindustrialized regions. The availability of cheap labor in underdeveloped countries contributed to increasing wealth and profits in industrial nations. Thus, according to dependency theorists, the wealth and prosperity of the industrial capitalist countries was due largely to the exploitation of the underdeveloped world.

The need for raw materials, consumer goods, cheap labor, and markets led to increasing **imperialism**, the economic and political control of a particular nation or territory by an external nation. Although imperialism had developed among preindustrial agricultural states, it did not involve the whole world. In contrast, industrial countries such as Great Britain, the United States, France, Germany, the Netherlands, Belgium, Russia, and Japan divided the nonindustrialized areas into "spheres of economic and political influence." Most of the nonindustrialized regions became *colonies* that exported raw materials and provided labor and other commodities for the industrialized nations.

Dependency theorists categorize the industrial capitalist countries as the *metropole* societies that maintain dependent *satellite countries* in the underdeveloped world. Through the organization of the world economy by the industrial capitalist societies, the surpluses of commodities produced by cheap labor flow from the satellites to the metropole. The satellites remain underdeveloped because of economic and political domination by the metropole. Despite the fact that many satellite countries have become politically independent from their former colonial rulers, the emergence of multinational corporations based in the industrialized capitalist societies has produced a new form of imperialism, *neoimperialism*. The industrial capitalist societies control foreign aid, international financial institutions such as the World Bank and the International Monetary Fund (IMF), and international political institutions such as the United Nations, all of which function to maintain their dominant position.

Criticisms of Dependency Theory Unlike modernization theory, the dependency approach demonstrates that no society evolves and develops in isolation. By examining the interrelationships between the political economies of industrial capitalist and precapitalist countries, theorists showed conclusively that some aspects of underdevelopment are related to the dynamics of power, conflict, class relations, and exploitation.

Critics, however, have noted a number of flaws in the dependency approach. Generally, dependency theory tends to be overly pessimistic. It suggests that dependency and impoverishment can be undone only by a radical restructuring of the world economy to reallocate wealth and resources from wealthy industrial capitalist countries to impoverished precapitalist countries. Economic development, however, has occurred in some countries that have had extensive contact with industrial capitalist societies. Notably, Japan moved from an underdeveloped society to a wealthy industrial capitalist position after the 1950s. Other countries such as Taiwan and

South Korea have also developed in a similar manner. In contrast, some poor societies that have had less contact with the industrial capitalist societies remain highly undeveloped.

Critics also point out that dependency theorists neglect the internal conditions of underdeveloped countries that may inhibit economic development. Rapid population growth, famine and hunger, the excessive control of the economy by centralized governments, and, in some instances, traditional cultural values may inhibit economic development.

World-Systems Theory

Another general model that tried to explain global trends is known as **world-systems theory**. World-systems theorists maintain that the socioeconomic differences and inequalities among various societies are a result of an interlocking global political economy. The world-systems model represents a response to both modernization and dependency theories. Sociologist Immanuel Wallerstein, who developed the world-systems approach, agrees with the dependency theorists that the industrial nations prosper through the economic domination and exploitation of nonindustrial peoples. His world-systems model (1974, 1979, 1980) places all countries in one of three general categories: *core, peripheral*, and *semiperipheral*. **Core societies** are the powerful industrial nations that exercise economic domination over other regions. Most nonindustrialized countries are classified as **peripheral societies**, which have very little control over their own economies and are dominated by the core societies. Wallerstein notes that between the core and peripheral countries are the **semiperipheral societies**, which are somewhat industrialized and have some economic autonomy, but are not as advanced as the core societies (see Figures 20.1a and 20.1b). In the world-systems model, the core, periphery, and semiperiphery are inextricably connected, forming a global economic and political network. No societies are isolated from this global web of connections.

Unlike dependency theorists, Wallerstein believes that under specific historical circumstances a peripheral society can develop economically. For example, during the worldwide depression of the 1930s, some peripheral Latin American countries, such as Brazil and Mexico, advanced to a semiperipheral position. Wallerstein also explains the recent rapid economic development of countries such as Taiwan and South Korea in terms of their favored status by core societies. Because the United States was in competition with the Soviet Union and feared the emergence of communism in Asia, it invested huge amounts of technology and capital in Taiwan and South Korea.

Figure 20.1a The world system around 1900.

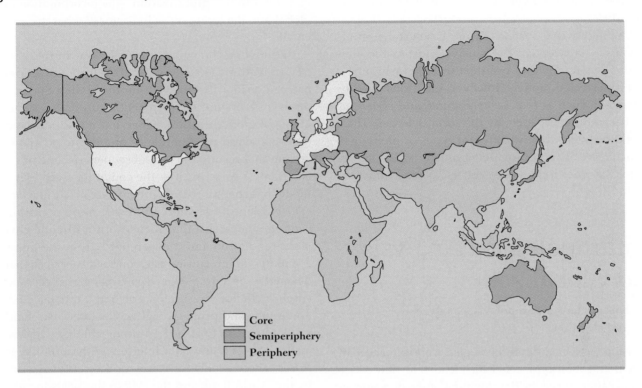

Figure 20.1b The world system, 2000.

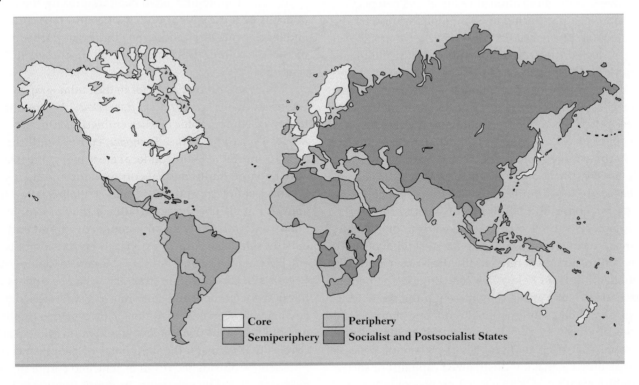

Criticisms of World-Systems Theory Although Wallerstein's world-systems theory has some advantages over modernization and dependency theories, critics note some weaknesses (Shannon 1988). One criticism is that the theory focuses exclusively on economic factors at the expense of noneconomic factors such as politics and cultural traditions. In addition, it fails to address the question of why trade between industrial and nonindustrial nations must always be exploitative. Some theorists have noted that in certain cases peripheral societies benefit from the trade with core societies in that, for example, they may need Western technology to develop their economies (Chirot 1986).

Although world-systems theory has been helpful in allowing for a more comprehensive and flexible view of global economic and political interconnections, it is not a perfected model. However, the terms used by Wallerstein, such as *core*, *semiperipheral*, and *peripheral*, have been adopted widely by the social sciences. These terms did illustrate how different types of global networks interrelate and provided a much-needed substitute for the older terminology of *First*, *Second*, and *Third Worlds*.

Anthropological Analysis and Globalization

20.4 Discuss how anthropologists analyze globalization.

Before the 1960s, many anthropologists were influenced by the modernization approach, which tended to view societies in isolation. Since the development of the dependency and world-systems perspectives, however, anthropologists have become more attuned to the global perspective. For example, a pioneering book on globalization by the late Eric Wolf, *Europe and the People without History* ([1982] 1997), reflected these developments in anthropological thought. Wolf espoused a global perspective by drawing on modernization, dependency, and world-systems approaches, while criticizing all of them for their weaknesses. Yet, as more in-depth ethnographic research has been conducted throughout the world, anthropologists have become more skeptical of these general approaches. Such labels as *traditional*, *modern*, *metropole-satellite*, and *peripheral* are too simplistic to classify realistically the diverse economic and cultural traditions in the world. Anthropologists discovered that there are no predictable, unilineal, or unalterable patterns of societal evolution. Many anthropologists refer to themselves as studying "globalization from below" by focusing on the people in local areas being affected by these multinational technological as well as international economic and political policies produced by globalization. Additionally, cultural anthropologists find that globalization is not a process dominated by the major industrialized capitalist or socialist countries; rather, it is a nuanced process of interactive relations between the local and global levels. As Wolf emphasized in *his works*, ethnographers must attend to the study of local-level processes, as well as integrating an empirical understanding of the global trends that are incorporated at the local level. Sometimes anthropologists refer to this **glocalization**—the incorporation of the global into the local—as an indicator of what this process entails.

Following the end of the Cold War in the 1990s, a new paradigm of economic development began to emerge, primarily from within the United States. This model of economic development incorporated some elements of modernization theory, but it also reflected the expansion and predominance of a capitalist economic system that resulted in the subsequent decline of socialism in most societies after the end of the Cold War. This model of economic development is referred to as *neoliberalism*. **Neoliberalism** is a philosophical, political, and economic strategy that focuses on reducing government regulation and interference within the domestic economy and on cutting back on social services that are deemed to be a drag on a free market global economy. It emphasizes fewer restrictions on both capitalist business operations and property rights. Neoliberalism tends to reject unionism for labor, environmentalism, and social justice causes that would interfere with capitalist enterprises. These neoliberal economic projects were adopted by the World Bank and the IMF in the 1990s to enhance the expansion of capitalism after the Cold War. Since the 1990s, anthropologists have been describing the consequences of these global policies for different countries and local levels throughout the world. The consequences of these neoliberal policies will be discussed in later chapters.

Many anthropologists refer to their ethnographic projects as studying *"globalization from below."* In a recent collection of ethnographic studies entitled *Globalization from Below: The World's Other Economy*, cultural anthropologists focus on the people in local areas being affected not only by large multinational corporations and their capital and technology and governments (globalization from above), but also by the transnational flow of people and goods with relatively small amounts of capital and illegal and semilegal forms of transactions outside of bankers, bureaucracies, and lawyers (Mathews, Ribeiro, Alba Vega 2012). Globalization from above can be understood through government and corporate statistics, sales figures, and national economic indicators. However, this "bottoms-up" globalization from below is reliant on ethnographic studies that focus on the daily lives of people and their transactions outside the realm of state and corporate business statistics. The extensive, in-depth fieldwork based primarily on qualitative data collected by ethnographers can often challenge some of the statistical generalizations and abstract models of mainstream political science and economics.

Anthropologists at Work

ERIC WOLF: A Global Anthropologist

Eric Wolf was born in Vienna, Austria, in 1923. After elementary school, he went to *gymnasium*, a combined middle school and high school, in Czechoslovakia. At an early age, he was exposed to many diverse ethnic groups and nationalistic movements. His parents later sent him to England, where he first discovered the natural sciences. In 1940, Wolf came to the United States to attend Queens College. He majored in a variety of subjects until he finally settled on anthropology. In 1943, he joined the U.S. Army and saw combat in Italy, returning with a Silver Star and a Purple Heart. After World War II, Wolf completed his studies at Queens College and then went on to graduate from Columbia University, where he had studied with Ruth Benedict and Julian Steward. He did ethnographic fieldwork in Puerto Rico, Mexico, and the Italian Alps.

Having been exposed to peasant groups during his childhood in Europe, Wolf focused his studies on the peasantry in different parts of the world. Through his fieldwork in areas such as Puerto Rico and Mexico, he became interested in how peasants adjust to global change. In a number of essays, he refined the analytical approach to understanding the peasantry. His early books include *Sons of the Shaking Earth* (1959), an overview of the historical transformations in Mesoamerica caused by Spanish colonialism; *Peasants* (1966), an analytic treatment of peasants throughout the world; and *Peasant Wars of the Twentieth Century* (1969), an examination of peasant revolutions.

Because of the success of his early books and his global perspective in his comprehensive *Europe and the People without History* ([1982] 1997), Wolf has had a tremendous influence upon many anthropologists and other social scientists. *Europe and the People without History* won several awards and Wolf was awarded a grant from the MacArthur Foundation, frequently called the "genius" award. Candidates are recommended by 100 anonymous nominators and reviewed by panels of experts.

Eric Wolf (1923–1999).

Recipients can spend the grant money as they wish on their own research projects. Wolf wrote another influential text called *Envisioning Power* (1999) about ideology and its relationship to political economy, global developments, and culture.

Eric Wolf died in March 1999, but his contributions to anthropological thought and his emphasis on the global perspective will endure forever within the profession.

Globalization, Politics, and Culture

20.5 Discuss how anthropologists criticize some of the approaches to understanding politics, culture, and globalization.

Aside from economic developments, some recent globalization models that focus on political interrelationships and culture have been associated with particular political scientists. In one major book, *Jihad vs. McWorld: Terrorism's Challenge to Democracy* (2001), political scientist Benjamin Barber argues that globalization represented by the spread of McWorld (McDonald's, Macintosh computers, and Mickey Mouse) through many societies has resulted in *jihad* (the Arabic term for "Holy War" and defense of the Islamic faith) by those who resist these global trends and, therefore, react in antagonistic ways, including supporting terrorism of the sort that led to 9/11. Barber emphasizes how the proliferation of McDonald's restaurants and the expansion of other related cultural trends have imposed cultural homogeneity or domination in the media, individual consumption preferences, politics, religion, and other institutions in the world. The *jihad* reaction (which is not limited to the Islamic world) includes many other local-level political and religious responses to McWorld's cultural uniformity. For example, the country of France has mounted protests against McDonald's "fast food" as representing an assault on the "slow food" of French cooking. In addition, France has tried to limit the amount of English vocabulary that penetrates the media through films and television programs from America. Barber gives many other examples of *jihad* that represent a defense of an indigenous culture from the McWorld global tendency, some of which have become extremely violent and dangerous.

Harvard political scientist Samuel Huntington wrote *The Clash of Civilizations and the Remaking of the World Order* (1996), another well-known analysis of globalization that continues to resonate with many people in the West and other regions of the world. In this influential book, Huntington argues that a unitary "Western civilization and culture" is at odds with "Islamic civilization and culture," "Hindu civilization and culture," and "Confucian civilization and culture." Huntington argues that these Islamic and Asian cultures do not have the institutions for developing civil democratic societies, individualism, free markets, or other elements that will enable them to coexist peacefully with Western culture. He envisions these cultural and regional blocs as fragmenting the world order and resulting in more conflict and instability throughout the world. Huntington's perspective has perpetuated a view that has been widely accepted within both the West and the Islamic world, especially after the tragedy of 9/11 and the aftermath of the United States-led invasions of Afghanistan and Iraq. Huntington has been an influential political advisor to the U.S. government, including the State Department. His clash-of-civilizations thesis has been used to develop foreign policy strategies in the Islamic world and in Asia since its initial publication.

Cultural anthropologists who do current ethnographic research in the Islamic world or Asia are critical of the sweeping generalizations perpetuated by Barber and Huntington. In contrast to these political scientists, who generally interview the political elites of these different countries and read the religious doctrines of these people, ethnographers live among these people on a day-to-day basis for years and observe and interview them. Cultural anthropologists do not just interview the political elites; they also interview and observe the middle class, working class, peasants and rural villagers, religious clerics of all levels, and other indigenous people. They find tremendous diversity in terms of religions, ethnic groups, and politics, as well as in terms of aspects of civil society, within these regions. The views of Huntington and Barber are also based on antiquated understandings of "culture" as forms of fixed beliefs and values shared within a "homogeneous civilization." This understanding of fixed and widely shared "culture" is not found in non-Western societies (or any society) by cultural anthropologists. People in both non-Western Islamic and Asian (and Western) societies are constantly reinterpreting and transforming their cultural conceptions as they are exposed to rapid changes through the Internet, the media, consumption patterns, and other results on globalization processes. Cultural anthropologists find that there is no uniform "Islamic culture or civilization," "Confucian culture or civilization," "Asian culture or civilization," or "Western culture or civilization," despite the rhetoric that political and religious leaders espouse in these respective regions (Eickelman and Piscatori 2004; Scupin 2003c, 2006a, 2007a, 2008). There are considerable variations in culture among the peoples in all these regions of the world. These so-called civilizations and cultures have been cross-fertilizing one another for generations, and simplistic stereotypes cannot summarize the enormous diversity in culture that exists in these societies.

Globalization and Indigenous Peoples

20.6 **Discuss the consequences of globalization on indigenous peoples.**

We discussed how the modernization theorists during the Cold War years divided the world into three major types of societies: the First, Second, and Third Worlds. However, as we have seen, anthropologists have done much research on band, tribal, and chiefdom societies. Sometimes these societies are referred to as the *indigenous* or *aboriginal*, or *first nation* societies indicating the fact that these societies were the initial native peoples in a particular region. Another phrase used for these peoples is *Fourth World* societies, adding another classification to the First, Second, and Third World categories. However, as we have already discussed the limitations of the "Three Worlds" modernization approach associated with the Cold War, we will not use this phrase.

The expansion of globalization often produced traumatic and violent changes in many of these indigenous societies. These peoples were absorbed as subordinate ethnic groups in larger nation-states or in some cases became extinct. When absorbed, they usually were forced to abandon their traditional language and culture, a process anthropologists refer to as **ethnocide**. In other situations, aboriginal peoples faced **genocide**, the physical extermination of a particular group of people. The Tasmanians of Australia and some Native American groups were deliberately killed so that colonists could take their lands and resources. The attitudes of the Europeans toward these indigenous peoples reflected racism and ethnocentrism, which resulted in many massacres of these aboriginal peoples.

Vanishing Foragers

As seen in Chapter 15, most contemporary bands, or foraging societies, have survived in marginal environments: deserts, tropical rain forests, and Arctic regions. Because these lands are not suitable for agriculture, foragers lived in relative isolation from surrounding populations. Following the emergence of industrial states and the extensive globalization induced by industrialism, these former marginal areas became attractive as unsettled frontiers with low population densities and bountiful, valuable natural resources such as land, timber, energy resources, and minerals. Industrial states have expanded into these regions, searching for energy supplies and resources such as oil and minerals in the deserts and Arctic areas, and land and timber from the tropical rain forests. One result of this process has been increased contact between globalization processes and foraging societies, often with tragic results such as *ethnocide*, and sometimes even *genocide*.

The Ju/'hoansi San

The bands of the African deserts and tropical rain forests have been devastated by confrontations with expanding industrial states and globalization. The Ju/'hoansi San people of the Kalahari Desert, who, before the 1950s, had little contact with industrialized nations, are now caught in the midst of forced change. Many of the Ju/'hoansi San live in Botswana and Namibia, which for many years were controlled by the more industrialized country of South Africa. Currently, the Ju/'hoansi San population in Botswana and Namibia is about 11,000 people (Biesele and Hitchcock 2013). Beginning in the 1960s, the South African government began to expand into the Kalahari Desert. In the process, it restricted the Ju/'hoansi San hunting territories and attempted to resettle them in a confined reservation at Tjum!kui, which represented only 11 percent of their ancestral land (Hitchcock et al. 1996; Hitchcock 2004a). It further attempted to introduce the Ju/'hoansi San to agriculture—the cultivation of maize, melons, sorghum, and tobacco—and cattle raising. However, because of the unsuitability of the land and inadequate water supplies these activities have not succeeded. Consequently, the Ju/'hoansi San have become increasingly dependent on government rations of corn, salt, sugar, and tobacco.

In both Botswana and Namibia, the only economic opportunities for Ju/'hoansi San males lie in doing menial chores, clearing fields, and building roads. The government initially paid Ju/'hoansi San laborers with mealie (ground corn), sugar, or tobacco but eventually switched to money. The introduction of this cash economy transformed traditional relationships in Ju/'hoansi San society. People who previously had embraced a reciprocal exchange system that enhanced their kinship and social ties now had to adjust to a system in which resources were managed for one's own family. Conflicts arose between those who wanted to share and others who were forced to become self-interested and hide resources even from their own kin.

In some of the areas where the Ju/'hoansi San were settled, population began to increase. This is a typical consequence of a shift from a foraging to a settled life. With increased crowding came epidemics, particularly tuberculosis, that have claimed many lives. Moreover, in response to the rapid transformation of their lifestyle, many Ju/'hoansi San resorted to frequent drinking, and much of their wage labor earnings went into alcohol consumption. As a consequence, alcoholism is a common problem.

Other Ju/'hoansi San males at the Tjum!kui reservation were recruited by the South African military to engage in campaigns during the 1960s and 1970s against the South-West African People's Organization (SWAPO), guerrilla insurgents who opposed the South African regime. The Ju/'hoansi San were valued as soldiers because they were good trackers and courageous fighters. Most of them, however, were unaware of the geopolitical strategies and racist policies of the South African government. They were simply attracted to military service by the promise of high wages.

Richard Lee believed that this involvement in the South African military increased the amount of violence in Ju/'hoansi San society. Lee documented only 22 cases of homicide among all the Ju/'hoansi between 1922 and 1955. In contrast, seven murders were recorded in a single village known as Chum!kwe during the brief period from 1978 to 1980, a major increase (Lee 1993). According to Lee, the aggressive values and norms associated with militarism increased the tendency toward violence in Ju/'hoansi San society.

The confinement to the reservation and the restriction from hunting-and-gathering subsistence resulted in reduced access to protein, foods, and other items for reciprocal exchanges; a decline in handicraft production; and rising dissatisfaction and frustration by the Ju/'hoansi San people toward the outsiders and the government that controlled their land (Biesele 2000; Biesele and Hitchcock 2013). In addition, increasing health and social problems, including higher suicide and murder rates, alcoholism, more patriarchal control and abuse of women, and increases in sexually transmitted diseases, including HIV/AIDS infections, have resulted in higher mortality rates (Hitchcock 2004b; Biesele and Hitchcock 2013).

Since the 1990s, many of these San people have been involved in legal battles with their governments over land and hunting rights. In Botswana, the government has been trying to relocate the San from their ancestral land in the Central Kalahari Desert to other locations. The Botswana government has claimed that these San people needed to take up an agricultural lifestyle and abandon their traditional hunting-gathering way of life. In three different relocation events, San homes, health centers, schools, and water supplies were destroyed and shut down by the government. The San were placed in resettlement camps outside of the Kalahari and had no access to hunting or their traditional lands. Although the government has denied that they were forcing the San off their ancestral land, the Botswana courts ruled that the attempt at relocation was unconstitutional. Opponents of the relocation have said that the real motivation for these government actions was because diamonds were discovered in the 1980s, and the government wants to use the Kalahari as a tourist attraction. In 2006, the Botswana courts ruled that the San could go back to their ancestral land to continue their traditional lifestyle; however, the government has tried to prevent them from resettling by blocking their access to water supplies and denying them hunting permits (Survival International 2010). In April 2008, the Human Rights Council of the United Nations criticized the Botswana government for not allowing the San to return to their ancestral land.

In Namibia, the Ju/'hoansi San established what is known as a conservancy to oversee the wildlife resources in the region. It is a block of communal land of about 9,000 square kilometers on which people can utilize the wildlife resources and make decisions about land use. A number of game animals such as the springbok and eland were imported into the area to promote tourism in the area. This conservancy, called Nyae Nyae, has been successful in producing income for the group and giving assistance for conservation projects. However, a number of refugees have flooded into Namibia, which has created problems for resettling these populations in the Kalahari region. To some degree, these refugees threatened the conservancy projects in Namibia (Hitchcock and Biesele 2002; Biesele and Hitchcock 2013). The Nyae Nyae conservancy has established successful literacy and education programs among the Ju/'hoansi San, and they are recording their history and cultural heritage. Yet, the resource base in Nyae Nyae is threatened by increased numbers of livestock, firewood gathering, illegal hunting, and illegal fencing (Biesele and Hitchcock 2013). Although the Namibian government has supported the land rights of the Ju/'hoansi San, there is pressure from multinationals who want to exploit the mineral resources of the Kalahari. Though the Nyae Nyae conservancy in Namibia has been more successful for the Ju/'hoansi San than in Botswana, there are many challenges for these indigenous people as they adapt to globalization.

The Mbuti The late Colin Turnbull examined cases of African foragers who have faced decimation through forced cultural change. Turnbull did the major ethnographic study, discussed in Chapter 15, of the Mbuti, who live in the Ituri rain forest of the Congo, formerly Zaire. He noted (1963, 1983) that the Mbuti had been in contact with outsiders for centuries, but had chosen to retain their traditional hunting-and-gathering way of life. During the colonial period in what was then the Belgian Congo, however, government officials tried to resettle the Mbuti on plantations outside the forest.

Following the colonial period, the newly independent government of Zaire continued the same policies of forced resettlement. In the government's view, this move would "emancipate" the Mbuti, enabling them to contribute to the economy and to participate in the national political process (Turnbull 1983). The Mbuti would become national citizens and would also be subject to taxation. Model villages were built outside the forest with Mbuti labor. Convinced by government officials that they would benefit, many Mbuti at first supported these relocation projects.

The immediate results of this resettlement, however, were disastrous. Turnbull visited the model villages and found many of the Mbuti suffering from various diseases.

Because the Mbuti were unaccustomed to living a sedentary life, they lacked knowledge of proper sanitation. Turnbull found that the Mbuti water had become contaminated and that the change of diet from forest products to cultivated crops had created nutritional problems.

More recently, globalization has had other effects on many of the Mbuti people. In 1992, as a result of international pressure, the government created an area called the Okapi Faunal Reserve or "green zone" to conserve the rain forest and indirectly to preserve the Mbuti way of life. The law protecting the reserve decreed that poaching protected animals such as elephants, leopards, chimpanzees, and gorillas was forbidden (Tshombe 2001). However, the "green zone" has not been protected due to the extreme political, institutional, and horrifying genocidal warfare and conflict crises faced by the Democratic Republic of the Congo. The region is besieged by civil wars, and political stability is eroding. Almost six million people have been killed since 1998. Some of the children in the region are also being forced to become soldiers. Because of the weakened state and the impossibility of monitoring and regulation, immigrants to the Ituri forest cleared the land for agriculture, resulting in the rapid deterioration of the soil: Multinational companies continued logging throughout the forest area, and elephant poaching increased, with the killing of about 100 elephants between 1998 and 2000.

One of the most devastating consequences in the Ituri forest came from the introduction of coltan mining (Harden 2001). Coltan is a mineral found in the forests of the Congo near where the Mbuti live. The Democratic Republic of the Congo has 70 percent of the world's coltan. Coltan is refined in the United States and Europe into tantalum, a metallic element used in capacitors and other electronic components for computers, cell phones, and pagers. The electronics and computer industries are heavily dependent on coltan. Many of the Mbuti have been recruited by the mining industry to dig for coltan. They chop down great swaths of the rain forest and dig large holes in the forest floor to obtain this vital mineral, which is used in electronic equipment far away from the Ituri forest. The Mbuti use picks and shovels to dig out this mineral, which was worth $80 a kilogram in the early part of 2001. They could earn as much as $2,000 a month, which represented more cash wages than the Mbuti had ever seen. Thousands of other immigrants began to pour into the area to take advantage of this new, profitable mineral needed by the high-tech businesses of the postindustrial societies.

This encounter between the high-tech world and the Ituri forest resulted in painful circumstances for the Mbuti. First, the mining created major environmental damage to the rain forest, which these people depended on in their hunting and gathering. The streams of the forest were polluted, trees were cut down, and the large holes in the ground ruined the environment. A health problem brought about by resource extraction is the effect of coltan mining on women and children who work in the mines. As more women and children pound the stone which contains coltan, it releases fibers that get into their lungs, causing respiratory problems.

The growing migrant population began to poach and kill the lowland gorillas and other animals for food. Lowland gorillas have been reduced to fewer than 1,000, and other forest animals were overhunted. Along with the increase of the population in the mining camps came prostitution, the abuse of alcohol, conflict, exploitation by outside groups, and the spread of diseases such as gonorrhea.

Additionally, by the spring of 2001, the price of coltan fell from $80 to $8 a kilogram. A slump in cell phone sales and the decrease in the high-tech economy created a glut of coltan on the global market, which had consequences for the people of the rain forest. Mining camps that had ravaged the rain forest were still filled with migrants, prostitutes, and some of the Mbuti people, but many people abandoned these camps. However, some Mbuti have not returned to their traditional hunting-and-gathering way of life. Many of them lost the land that sustained their way of life. The weakness of the state, civil wars, and ethnic conflict surrounding the Mbuti enabled outsiders to take over their forest land. Globalization resulted in ecological damage and social and cultural dislocations for the Mbuti people in a very short time.

Despite the consequences of globalization and its impact on these foragers of the rain forest, some of these people have been adapting more successfully to their new circumstances. Some of the Baka foragers of Cameroon have established themselves outside of the rainforest with schools, hospitals, and other modern facilities. Some of the Baka even travel to Europe to perform their traditional music and dance. Despite the fact that the

A Mbuti family in the Ituri forest

Baka are a very small minority in Cameroon, they have established themselves as very effective administrators throughout the country. Success among the Baka debunks the simplistic stereotype of "pygmies" in Africa as being "undeveloped" and "unintelligent." At the same time, globalization and its subsequent developments have led to rising rates of epidemic diseases including the HIV-AIDS problem among the former foraging populations (Froment 2004).

Tribes in Transition

The process of globalization that began with increased contact between societies throughout the world has dramatically affected many horticulturalist and pastoralist tribes. For example, many Native American societies suffered serious disruptions as a result of European colonization of the Americas. The Spanish, French, Dutch, and British came to the Americas in search of precious metals, furs, and land for settlement. Each of these countries had different experiences with the indigenous peoples of North America. But wherever the Europeans settled, indigenous tribes were usually devastated through depopulation, deculturation, and, in many cases, physical extinction.

North American Horticulturalists The collision of cultures and political economies between Native Americans and Europeans can be illustrated by the experiences of the Iroquois of New York State. The traditional horticulturalist system of the Iroquois was described in Chapter 15. British and French settlers established a fur trade with the Iroquois and nearby peoples during the late 1600s. French traders offered weapons, glass beads, liquor, and ammunition to the Iroquois in exchange for beaver skins. Eventually, the Iroquois abandoned their traditional economy of horticulture supplemented by limited hunting to supply the French with fur pelts. The French appointed various *capitans* among the Iroquois to manage the fur trade. This resulted in the decline of the tribe's traditional social and political order (Kehoe 1995; Sutton 2011).

Meanwhile, the intensive hunting of beaver led to a scarcity of fur in the region, which occurred just as the Iroquois were becoming more dependent on European goods. The result was increased competition between European traders and various Native Americans who were linked to the fur trade. The Iroquois began to raid other tribal groups, such as the Algonquins, who traded with the British. Increasing numbers of Iroquois males were drawn into more extensive warfare. Many other Native American tribal peoples also became entangled in the economic, political, and military conflicts between the British and French over land and resources in North America.

The Relocation of Native Americans Beginning in the colonial period, many Native American tribes were introduced to the European form of intensive agriculture, with plows, new types of grains, domesticated cattle and sheep, fences, and individual plots of land. The white settlers rationalized this process as a means of introducing Western civilization to indigenous peoples. However, whenever Native Americans became proficient in intensive agriculture, many white farmers viewed them as a threat. Eventually, following the American Revolution, the government initiated a policy of removing Native Americans from their lands to open the frontier for white settlers. A process developed in which Native Americans were drawn into debt for goods and then pressured to cede their lands as payment for these debts (Sutton 2011).

Ultimately, the U.S. government developed the system of reservations for resettling the Native American population. Under Andrew Jackson in the 1830s, many southeastern tribal groups were resettled into western regions such as Oklahoma. In many cases, Native Americans were forcibly removed from their land, actions that colonists justified as a way of bringing Western civilization and Christianity to these peoples. The removal policies led to brutal circumstances such as the Trail of Tears, when thousands of Shawnees and Cherokees living in Georgia and North Carolina were forced to travel hundreds of miles westward to be resettled. Many died of starvation and other physical deprivations on this forced march.

The patterns of land cession were repeated as white settlers moved westward. European Americans justified these behaviors through the concept of Manifest Destiny, the belief that they were responsible for extending the benefits of Western civilization throughout the continent. Military force frequently was used to overcome Indian resistance.

In 1890, Native Americans held title to 137 million acres of land. By 1934, these holdings had been reduced to 56 million acres. After suffering the dispossession of most of their lands, the majority of Native Americans were forced to live on reservations, most of which were unsuitable for agriculture. Lack of employment opportunities led to increased impoverishment for many of these people. The Bureau of Indian Affairs (BIA) oversees the reservations. Before 1934, Native Americans were viewed as wards of the state, and the BIA established Indian schools to introduce "civilization" to Native American children. The BIA was empowered to decide whether Native Americans could sell or lease their land, send their children to boarding schools, or practice their traditional religion.

Native North American Indians in the Twentieth-First Century Based upon a survey of archaeological materials and fossil evidence, anthropologists have assessed and estimated how dramatic the population decline precipitated by colonization and settlement was. Estimates based on these studies indicate that there were from 8 to 18 million Native Americans in North America prior to European contact (Sutton 2011). But by 1890, when Native Americans made their last stand at Wounded Knee, South Dakota, their population had declined to under 400,000, a reduction of about 95 percent. This trend reflects the effects of warfare, forced marches, loss of traditional lands, and diseases such as smallpox, measles, influenza, and tuberculosis, to which Native Americans lacked immunity.

In the twenty-first century, the Native American population has increased to about 4 million. Approximately two-thirds of Native Americans live on reservations, and most of the remaining one-third reside in major metropolitan areas. Native Americans are far below the average American in terms of income and education.

Today, multinational corporations want to develop the reserves of coal, oil, natural gas, and uranium on Native American reservation lands, such as the Hopi and Navajo territories. Other companies have been making lucrative offers to lease Native American lands to be used as garbage landfills and toxic waste dumps. These monetary offers have produced splits within Native American communities; some favor the offers as a means of combating poverty, whereas others condemn mining or any other commercial activity as a desecration of their sacred land. Many other Native American Indian communities have developed casinos as a source of income for their people. These issues have caused splits in the communities and present difficult decisions for Native Americans regarding how much they want to participate in the gambling industries.

South American Horticulturalists In the Amazon rain forests, tribal peoples such as the Yanomamö, the Jivaro, and the Mundurucu are facing dramatic changes as a result of globalization. Beginning in the 1950s, European and American missionaries representing different Christian denominations began to settle in the Amazon region and competed to "civilize" peoples such as the Yanomamö. In Venezuela, the major missionary group is the Salesians, a Catholic missionary order. The missionaries attempted to persuade Yanomamö communities to reside in their mission stations. The Yanomamö who have settled near the missions have increased the population density in the region, and this has led to a shortage of vital resources (Hames 2004). The missionaries set up schools and teach the Yanomamö new methods of agriculture and train them to spread these ideas among others. However, most of the Yanomamö have not adopted Christianity and have tremendous pride in their own native traditions (Hames 2004). With the building of highways and increased settlement in the Amazon rain forest—developments sponsored by the Brazilian government—the Yanomamö became increasingly exposed to influenza, dysentery, measles, and common colds. In some regions, almost 50 percent of the population has fallen victim to these diseases (Kellman 1982; Hames 2004).

One consequence of contact with the outside world was the Yanomamö's adoption of the shotgun for hunting in the forest. The Yanomamö originally obtained shotguns from the missionaries or other employees at the missions. Initially, Yanomamö hunters who knew the forest very well became proficient in obtaining more game. In time, however, the game in the rain forest grew more scarce. Consequently, the Yanomamö had to hunt deeper and deeper into the rain forest to maintain their diet. In addition, as indicated by anthropologist Raymond Hames (1979a), the Yanomamö had to expend much more labor in the cash economy to be able to purchase shotguns and shells to continue hunting. Additionally, some Yanomamö began to use the shotgun as a weapon in waging warfare and political intimidation and raiding others.

Recent Developments among the Yanomamö   The Amazon rain forest is experiencing new pressures. Prospectors, mining companies, energy companies, and government officials interested in industrial development are eager to obtain the gold, oil, tin, uranium, and other minerals in the 60,000 square miles of forest straddling the Brazilian-Venezuelan border, where the Yanomamö live. A 1987 gold rush led to the settlement of at least 40,000 prospectors in Yanomamö territory. The prospectors hunt game in the forest, causing scarcities and increased malnutrition among the Yanomamö. Clashes between prospectors and the Yanomamö have led to many deaths. In August 1993, gold miners massacred Yanomamö men, women, and children in Venezuela. After the attack, a Yanomamö leader described the massacre: "Many miners surrounded the lodge and started to kill Yanomamö. The women were cut in the belly, the breasts and the neck. I saw many bodies piled up" (Brooke 1993:A9). This is similar to what happened in the United States when gold miners came into Native American territories in the 1800s. The miners bring epidemic diseases and violence that result in high mortality rates for the Yanomamö (Hames 2004). Although the Venezuelan government has made some efforts such as training some Yanomamö as paramedics and health workers, they remain susceptible to respiratory diseases and drug resistant forms of malaria (Romero 2008).

Alarmed by these developments, concerned anthropologists, missionaries, and Brazilians have formed a committee to reserve an area for the Yanomamö to practice their traditional way of life. The Brazilian government and business leaders opposed this proposal, but eventually the government allotted 8,000 square miles of land, which became known as Yanomamö Park. The land, however, was subdivided into small parcels that were impossible to defend against outsiders. In 1995, officials of the National Brazilian Indian Foundation (FUNAI) assured anthropologist Napoleon Chagnon that there were no more than a few hundred illegal miners in the Yanomamö area and that they were systematically trying to find and expel them (Chagnon 2012). However, there are still news reports from Brazil indicating that more gold miners are infiltrating the area.

In Brazil, the drive toward economic development and industrialization has stimulated the rapid and tragic changes affecting the Yanomamö. The survival of the 9,000 Yanomamö in Brazil is in question. Their population has declined by one-sixth since the gold rush began in 1987. In contrast to Brazil, the Venezuelan government has been developing more humane and effective policies toward the Yanomamö natives. In 1991, then Venezuelan President Carlos Andrés Pérez took action to develop a reserve for the Yanomamö, a "special biosphere" or national park of some 32,000 square miles of rain forest that would be closed to mining and other development (Chagnon 2012). Then, in 1992, the Venezuelan government designated the Venezuelan Amazonas as a new state in its national political structure. State governments are being given more control over their own populations and resources. The resources of the new Amazonas state will probably include mineral wealth and tourism. Thus, the Yanomamö of Venezuela will become increasingly drawn into contact with outsiders. Whether this will mean more tragedy and epidemic diseases and economic problems for these natives is a question that can be answered only in the future. (See "Critical Perspectives: Ethical Controversies in El Dorado" in Chapter 25.)

Pastoralist Tribes   Pastoralists have also been subjected to expanding industrial societies. The adaptive objectives of pastoralists tend to be at odds with the primary aims of state societies. Because of their nomadic way of life, pastoralists cannot be easily incorporated into and controlled by state societies. They are not usually subject to the same processes of enculturation as settled peoples. They do not attend schools, and they may place their tribal loyalties above their loyalties to the state. Rapid change among pastoralist societies is evident in some Middle Eastern countries.

Middle Eastern Pastoralists: The Bedouins   Anthropologist Donald Cole (1984) conducted research on the Bedouins of Saudi Arabia, groups of nomadic pastoralists. Cole focused on one particular group, the Al-Murrah, a tribe of 15,000 who live in the extreme desert conditions of Rub al-Khali. Traditionally, Al-Murrah subsistence was based on caravan trade, which depended on the care of camels and other animals. The Al-Murrah traded commodities with oasis centers for dates, rice, and bread. On average, they traveled about 1,200 miles annually during their migrations across the desert. They were also an autonomous military force, conducting raids and warfare.

The attempt to incorporate the Bedouin population into the Saudi state has been an ongoing process, going back to the early phases of state formation in the Arabian peninsula during the age of Muhammad (622–632 A.D.). As Cole indicates, this process of settling and controlling the Bedouins accelerated following the emergence of the modern petroleum industry. To facilitate this process, the Saudi government drafted Al-Murrah males into their national guard. The principal leader of the Al-Murrah, the emir, has been recognized by the Saudi government as the commander of this national guard unit. The government gives the emir a share of the national budget, and he distributes salaries to the tribespeople. Thus, the emir has become a dependent government official of the Saudi state.

The traditional subsistence economy based on nomadism and the care of herds of animals appears to be at an end. Camels are being replaced by pickup trucks. Bedouins are settling in cities and participating in the urban economy. All of the formerly self-sufficient Bedouin communities are being absorbed into nation-states throughout the Arabian Peninsula.

The Qashqa'i Cultural anthropologist Lois Beck (1986, 1991, 2014) has written in-depth ethnographic accounts of how globalization has influenced the Qashqa'i pastoralist tribe of Iran. The Qashqa'i reside in the southern part of the Zagros Mountains. Beck emphasized that the Qashqa'i "tribe" was to some degree a creation of state processes within Iran. In other words, the Qashqa'i tribe was not a self-contained entity, but rather was formed through the long-term process of incorporating tribal leaders into the Iranian nation-state. During different historical periods, the state offered land and political protection to the Qashqa'i in exchange for taxes. Through that process, the Qashqa'i leadership was able to maintain some autonomy. Eventually, the Qashqa'i political system became increasingly centralized around an economic and political elite. This is an example of how tribes may be formed as a result of an expansionist state political system.

As with other pastoralist societies, the Qashqa'i relationship with the central government in Iran was not always beneficial. During the 1960s, the Iranian government under Shah Pahlavi wanted to modernize and industrialize Iran rapidly with Western support (see Chapter 22). The government viewed the Qashqa'i as resisting modernization and used military force to incorporate them. This policy resulted in the establishment of strong ethnic boundaries between the Iranians and the Qashqa'i. The

Qashqa'i began to emphasize their own ethnic identity and to demand more autonomy.

In the initial stages of the Iranian Revolution led by Ayatollah Khomeini, the Qashqa'i joined demonstrations against the shah. Following the revolution, however, the Qashqa'i found themselves subject to patterns of discrimination and repression similar to those they had endured under the shah. Because they never accepted the revolutionary doctrines of the Khomeini regime, they were considered a threat to the ideals of the state. Consequently, Khomeini's Revolutionary Guards harassed the Qashqa'i. Thus, Qashqa'i autonomy and local authority continued to erode under the pressures of the nation-state of Iran. Since that time the Qashqa'i people have had difficulties in adapting to the political atmosphere in postrevolutionary Iranian society (Beck 2014).

East African Pastoralists and Globalization

Earlier, we discussed pastoralists of East Africa such as the Nuer, Maasai, Dinka, and others who maintain cattle-keeping on the savannah. Many of these East African tribes are now caught within the interregional net of globalization and disaster. A series of regional wars have broken out in East Africa as a byproduct of colonialism, ethnic rivalry, and political competition within the last decade. For example, during the 1990s in the Republic of Sudan, a war between the Muslim north and the Christian south had affected the Nuer and Dinka tribes that reside in the southern area. Nuer tribal peoples had been recruited into the Sudanese People's Liberation Army to fight against the north. Weapons have flowed into their society and have become new luxury items. Instead of cows being exchanged through reciprocal ties between kinsmen, weapons are now used as a source of wealth and money. The Nuer and other groups were using their cattle to obtain guns and ammunition from different military factions, and these guns have begun to displace the traditional power relationships within the communities (Hutchinson 1996). In 2011, following 20 years of civil war, South Sudan became an independent country from Sudan based on a referendum. However, warfare between the Nuer and Dinka fueled by ethnic political conflict and the international importation of weapons has continued. If these tribal people do survive in the warfare, many of them become displaced migrants living in poverty in urban areas and refugee camps. Globalization has brought tragedy to most of these once self-sufficient autonomous tribal pastoralists.

Chiefdoms in Transition

Chiefdom societies were economically and politically centralized societies existing in different regions of the world (Chapter 18). Some chiefdoms experienced a fate similar to that of many of the other indigenous societies. For example, when the Canadian European settlers, followed by their military and political apparatus, confronted the Northwest Coast Native American chiefdom societies such as the Nootka and the Kwakiutl (Kwakwaka'wakw), they did not have any understanding of the functions and uses of the redistributional exchange system known as the potlatch. The European Canadians viewed these practices as wasteful, destructive, and anticapitalistic. The custom of chiefs giving away large amounts of resources at large potlatch feasts was perceived as extremely dysfunctional. The Canadian government banned these practices in the 1880s and used military force against the Indian groups that were not cooperative. Eventually, the traditional salmon-fishing activities of these native chiefdoms were made obsolete by the more industrialized forms of fishing and the canning factories introduced through the American and Canadian multinational firms. This, along with the epidemics introduced by Europeans, resulted in both depopulation and economic decline. Common problems such as malnutrition and alcoholism found among many societies disrupted by rapid global transitions remain systemic among these Native American chiefdoms (Sutton 2011). Yet, many of these people of the Northwest Coast chiefdoms have restored their traditional potlatch feasting activities and are becoming more educated and adept at dealing with the new global trends. They are constructing new, beautiful museums and relearning their traditional art forms, including the building of the totem poles and other artistic works. This represents a new cultural and religious revitalization among these people.

The Hawaiian Islands Anthropological and historical research demonstrates that centrally organized chiefdoms, such as those of Tahiti and Hawaii in Polynesia, developed complex *state* organizations themselves following Western contact. Before contact with the West, Hawaii contained eight inhabited islands with a population of about 600,000. Paramount chiefs who maintained a redistributional exchange economy ruled through divine authority. The Hawaiian Islands were contacted by the English expedition of Captain Cook in 1778, and the islands were eventually penetrated by traders, whalers, missionaries, and other outsiders. The impact of the Western encounter resulted in a unique religious "revolution" when compared with the experiences of other aboriginal societies we have discussed.

Cook's expedition on behalf of the British, which began in the 1760s, set the stage for the colonization of the Pacific. At the time of Captain Cook's discovery of Hawaii, the paramount chief on the island of Hawaii was engaged in warfare with the chief of the island of Maui, who had already incorporated the islands of Oahu and Molokai under his chieftaincy. The reaction to Cook's arrival during this period was shaped by the aboriginal religious culture. He appeared during the time of Makahiki, a time of

religious-based human sacrifices, and he was perceived as someone extremely powerful, perhaps a *god* or at the least an important foreign chief. There is a heated debate among anthropologists who have investigated the historical records of Cook and other British explorers along with ethnohistorical accounts from native Hawaiians today about whether Cook was perceived as a god, and whether the natives killed him for religious or cosmological reasons or for political purposes (Sahlins 1985, 1995; Obeyesekere 1992). Anthropologists do concur that both the native accounts and the British historical records indicate that the distribution of Cook's bones supports the theory that he was being treated as a sacrificial victim (Sahlins 1995).

Later, Kamehameha, a nephew of the Hawaiian chief, built his reputation as a fearless warrior in the Maui campaign. When the chief of Hawaii died, Kamehameha became his successor. Because the island of Hawaii offered good anchorage and became a vital strategic point of contact with Europeans, Kamehameha had an advantage over any other rivals in trading with European ships. The Hawaiians began to trade products such as sandalwood with Europeans, and in exchange, Kamehameha received guns and light cannon. Eventually, he was able to employ European help in conquering most of the other islands of Hawaii and transformed the Hawaiian chiefdoms into a unified, centralized military kingdom or state.

Kamehameha died in 1819 and was succeeded by his son Liholiho, later known as Kamehameha II. Since Western contact, Hawaii continued to be heavily influenced by Western culture. A number of traditional taboos of the Hawaiian culture were violated on a regular basis. Some of the Hawaiian women became involved in sexual and romantic relationships with Westerners and openly ate with men, violating traditional taboos (Ortner 1996; Sahlins 1995). Some of the commoner people traded openly with Europeans, which also violated traditional norms and taboos, causing tension between the rulers and commoners. Seeing practical advantages in trading with the Europeans and enhancing their power over their kingdom, in 1819 Liholiho, the new ruler, and other members of the royal family began to deliberately flout the most sacred traditional taboos of their ancient religion. The royal family began to systematically dismantle the aboriginal religious traditions and practices, which represented a revolutionary transformation in religious thought and culture for Hawaiian society. This transformation of religion was accomplished prior to the coming of Christian missionaries to Hawaii. This religious revolution was resisted by some of the conservative people of Hawaii, and Liholiho had to arm his forces to defeat the more conservative faction within the kingdom. This Hawaiian revolution appeared to be an intentional strategy on the part of the ruling family to enhance its political control over the military kingdom.

The sandalwood trade declined in the 1830s and was replaced by the whaling industry, which began to dominate commerce in Hawaii. Because the island was located in the vicinity of a major whaling area of the Pacific, New England whalers used Hawaii as an important base for provisioning and relaxation. However, during the 1830s, various companies began to develop sugar plantations in Hawaii, which eventually became successful, resulting in the influx of more Europeans, including various Christian missionaries from the United States. Many of the missionaries were themselves sugar planters or were connected with sugar planters. Private property was introduced, and land was bought and sold. As the sugar plantations were developed, substantial native Hawaiian land was lost to the planters.

Additionally, the native Hawaiians were subjected to devastating epidemics introduced by the Westerners. Whooping cough, measles, influenza, and other diseases led to rapid depopulation among the native peoples. As Hawaii became increasingly incorporated into the U.S. political economy during the nineteenth and twentieth centuries, the native population dwindled to about 40,000 people. Depopulation resulted in a labor shortage for the sugar planters, who began to import labor from the Philippines, Japan, and China. In 1893, the United States, backed by American Marines, who represented the families of the missionaries and plantation owners such as Sanford Dole (the cousin of the founder of Dole pineapples), overthrew the Hawaiian monarchy. Five years later, Hawaii was annexed as a colony of the United States.

Following U.S. colonization, the Hawaiian Islands were dominated by U.S. global, political, and economic interests, and the native Hawaiians became a marginal group in their own islands. Eventually, through more contact with Western societies, the Pacific islands such as Hawaii and Tahiti experienced depopulation, deculturation, forced labor, and increased dependency on the global economy. The American and European settlers imported labor from Asia, introduced the system of private property, abolished the traditional patterns of authority, and incorporated the islands into colonial empires. As these islands were integrated into colonial systems, the people were forced to adjust to the conditions of the global economy.

Through missionary schooling and activities, the native Hawaiian people were forbidden to speak their native language or practice any of their traditional religious or cultural activities, which were deemed barbaric and uncivilized. These policies led to societal and cultural disintegration for the native population. Combined with the growing Asian population, with new settlers from North America who were rapidly developing the sugar economy, and with the expansion of mass tourism to Hawaii from the mainland United States, the small Hawaiian population began to lose not only its native lands, but also its cultural and ethnic identity (Friedman 1992).

Forms of Resistance among Indigenous Peoples

20.7 Describe the different forms of resistance to globalization by indigenous peoples.

Globalization processes have dramatic consequences for these different indigenous societies. In most cases, they have resulted in depopulation, epidemic diseases, increased warfare, loss of political autonomy, and loss of control over their future. In some cases, indigenous societies responded with resistance movements to try to stem the tide of globalization. At times, these resistance movements involved *revitalization movements* that attempted to restore some traditional aspects of native culture.

Revitalization among Native Americans

Native American societies developed a number of revitalization movements as a defensive strategy in their confrontation with European colonialism and increasing globalization. One type of movement was associated with a particular prophet who was able to mobilize the population both politically and spiritually. In the Pueblo groups of the Southwest, a prophet leader known as Popé organized a rebellion against the Spanish rulers in 1680. The Pueblo tribes attacked the Spanish, killed the Catholic priests in the missions, and attempted to reinstitute Pueblo traditions. Twenty years later, Spanish troops based in Mexico defeated this movement and reasserted their authority over the region.

Other Native American prophets such as Handsome Lake, Pontiac, Tecumseh, and Chief Joseph combined traditional religious values with military activities to resist European and American expansion into their territories. Eventually the U.S. military defeated all of these leaders (Sutton 2011).

The Ghost Dance   One of the best-known revitalization movements was the Ghost Dance movement of the late 1800s. The Ghost Dance spread through the region of Nevada and California and across the Rocky Mountains to Plains groups such as the Cheyenne, Arapaho, and Sioux. The movement became associated with the prophet Wovoka, a Paiute who was believed to have received spiritual visions of the future during an eclipse of the Sun. Wovoka taught that if the Native American people did the Ghost Dance, a hypnotic dance with spiritual meanings, the whites would disappear, and a train would come from the East with the ghosts of recently deceased Native Americans, signaling the restoration of Native American autonomy and traditions. Wovoka stressed nonviolent resistance and nonaccommodation to white domination (Kehoe 1989; Scupin 2008a).

Among the groups influenced by the Ghost Dance was the Lakota Sioux, who were forced to reside on five reservations in South Dakota. In 1890, the Lakota Sioux leader, Kicking Bear, introduced a special shirt, called a "ghost shirt," that he claimed would protect the Sioux from the bullets of the white soldiers. The wearing of the ghost shirts precipitated conflicts between the U.S. military and the Sioux, culminating in a massacre of almost 200 Sioux at Wounded Knee, South Dakota, on December 29, 1890. Following that confrontation, Sioux leaders such as Kicking Bear surrendered to the U.S. military.

The following are among the most common refrains of the Ghost Dance songs:

> My children,/When at first I liked the whites,/
> I gave them fruits,/I gave them fruits. (Southern Arapaho)
> The father will descend/The earth will tremble/
> Everybody will arise,/Stretch out your hands. (Kiowa)
> We shall live again./We shall live again. (Apache)
> (Rothenberg 1985:109–110)

These Ghost Dance songs and dances are heard among the Native Americans up to the present. For example, in February 1973, Wounded Knee once again became the site for a violent confrontation between the Plains Indians and U.S. military forces. Led by Russell Means and spiritual leader Leonard Crow Dog, who were Lakota Indians, the organization known as AIM, the American Indian Movement, took over the Pine Ridge Indian reservation at Wounded Knee. AIM accused the tribal government leaders of political and economic corruption and demanded justice and civil rights for all Native Americans. Leonard Crow Dog led a Ghost Dance ritual during the 70- day occupation to create solidarity and spiritual renewal among the Sioux at Wounded Knee. In addition, the Sun Dance ritual was conducted at Pine Ridge in 1973. Firefights between AIM and the FBI and U.S. forces were common throughout the longest siege in American history since the Civil War. The events of 1973 at Wounded Knee represented the frustration and resentment of many Native Americans regarding their conditions after a century of subordination by the U.S. government. The Ghost Dance led by Leonard Crow Dog symbolized the spiritual resurgence and religious renewal of contemporary Native Americans on the Plains.

More recently, since 1986, an annual Chief Big Foot Memorial Ride, a 191-mile horseback ride by the Lakota

Big Foot's frozen body after the massacre of Wounded Knee in 1890.

and others through the Badlands of South Dakota in the middle of the winter, is held in remembrance of Sitting Bull, who was killed by agents of the U.S. Army, and commemorates Chief Big Foot's band of Minneconjou Lakota and the painful history of Native Americans. Beginning at the Standing Rock Reservation on December 14th, the riders begin their journey to Chief Sitting Bull's camp on December 15th, the place where he was assassinated on that day in 1890. There, the riders offer prayers and remembrance as they continue their journey to Wounded Knee Creek, which ends on December 29th, on the Pine Ridge Reservation, where hundreds of Lakota were massacred by the 7th Cavalry. This use of history is an illustration of the ongoing revitalization movement related to the Ghost Dance that anthropologists and Native American activists and scholars are describing as a means of understanding how globalization continues to have an impact on these indigenous societies.

The Peyote Cult Another form of revitalization movement developed among Native Americans on one Oklahoma reservation in the 1880s. It was also a nonviolent form of resistance, based on a combination of Christian and Native American religious beliefs. The movement is referred to as the peyote cult. Peyote (*Lophophora williamsii*) is a mild hallucinogenic but nonaddictive drug contained in the bud of a cactus, which is either chewed or drunk as tea. For thousands of years peyote was used in some Native American rituals for inducing spiritual visions, especially in the Southwestern desert areas around the Rio Grande in both Mexico and the United States. A number of Navajo Indians in the Southwest became involved in the ritual use of peyote (Aberle 1966). During their incarceration on the Oklahoma reservation, some of the Comanche, Kiowa, and other Plains Indians began to combine biblical teachings with the peyote ritual (Steinmetz 1980). During the ritual, which took place in a tepee, the participants surrounded a fire and low altar and took peyote as a form of communal sacrament to partake of the "Holy Spirit." Eventually, the peyote cult grew in membership and was legalized on the Oklahoma reservation as the Native American Church (NAC) in 1914. It has spread throughout at least 50 other Native American tribes, and approximately 250,000 Indians are associated with the NAC (Sutton 2011).

Melanesia and New Guinea: The Cargo Cults

As various Europeans colonized the islands of Melanesia, the native peoples' lives were forever transformed. The Dutch, French, British, and Germans claimed different areas as colonies. The Dutch, from their colonial base in Indonesia, took over the western half of New Guinea. It is now known as Irian Jaya and is a province of the country of Indonesia. In the 1880s, German settlers occupied the northeastern part of New Guinea. In the 1890s, gold was discovered in New Guinea, and many prospectors from Australia and other places began to explore the region. At the beginning of World War I in 1914, the Australians conquered the German areas. During World War II, the Japanese, Australians, and U.S. troops fought bitter battles in New Guinea. After the war, Australia resumed administrative control over the eastern half of the island until 1975, when Papua New Guinea was granted political independence. Today, the country of Papua New Guinea occupies the eastern half of the island of New Guinea and has about 4 million people.

The colonization of Melanesia and Papua New Guinea was both a dramatic and a traumatic experience for native peoples as they faced new economic systems with the introduction of cash wages, indentured labor, plantations, taxation, new forms of political control, and the unfathomable technologies and apparently fabulous riches of the Europeans. Prospectors, traders, and soldiers during the world wars created a highly unstable and unpredictable environment for Melanesian natives. Among the Melanesian religious reactions to this rapid change, often loosely labeled revitalization movements, were the "cargo cults," a form of millenarian religious movement.

Beginning in the nineteenth century and continuing up to the present, millenarian cult movements spread throughout many areas of Melanesia. Generally, in New Guinea, the coastal or seaboard peoples were contacted first by Europeans, and by the end of the nineteenth century, they were subjected to intensive pressures from the outside world. The highland peoples were contacted much later and were not fully penetrated by the Europeans and Australians until after the 1930s. Many native peoples referred to the European or Australian goods that were loaded off ships or aircraft as *kago*, translated by anthropologists as "cargo." The native peoples became aware of a dazzling array of goods, such as steel axes, matches, medicines, soft drinks, umbrellas, and, eventually, jet planes and helicopters. Because native peoples had no exposure to industrial production, they did not see how these Western goods were manufactured. Many, therefore, believed that these goods were generated through spiritual forces, which delivered cargo to humans through spiritual means. Many tribal groups of this region attempted to discover the identity of the cargo spirits and the magical-ritual techniques used by Westerners to induce the spirits to deliver the particular commodities.

One New Guinean man who led a millenarian cult movement is known as Yali. Yali had lived in the coastal area of New Guinea, and in the 1950s, the Australians recognized him as an important future leader of his people. He had been a World War II war hero, fighting with the Allies against the Japanese. The Australians took Yali to Australia to show him how the industrial goods were produced. Nevertheless, Yali maintained the belief that there must be a supernatural cause or divine intervention for the ability of Westerners to be able to produce cargo. He originated a millenarian cult movement known as Wok bilong Yali (Lawrence 1964) and began to preach in hundreds of villages throughout New Guinea about the need to develop spiritual techniques to duplicate the white man's delivery of cargo. Over the years of this movement, Yali's teaching ranged from recommending close imitation of the Europeans to opposing white culture and returning to traditional rituals to help deliver the cargo. Although later Yali openly rejected the millenarian cult movements' beliefs, after his death in 1973 many of his followers began to teach that Yali was a messiah, equivalent to the white man's Jesus. In their religious literature, they propagated these ideas of messiahship by using Yali's sayings to help develop a religious movement that was an alternative to Christianity.

However, some of the millenarian cult movements combined traditional rituals with Christian beliefs in the hope of receiving the material benefits they associated with the white settlers. One movement, described by anthropologist Paul Roscoe (1993), developed among the Yangoru Boiken of Papua New Guinea. It merged some of the millennial teachings of Canadian missionaries from the Switzerland-based New Apostolic Church (NAC). Roscoe describes how those in the movement believed that on Sunday, February 15, 1981, Yaliwan, a leading spiritual and political leader, was going to be crucified, ushering in the millennium. The villagers believed that the Earth would rumble, hurricanes would arrive, the mountains would flash with lightning and thunder, and a dense fog would cover the Earth. Afterward, Yaliwan would be resurrected as the native counterpart of Jesus, and the two Jesuses would judge the living and the dead. They believed that the whites and native members of the NAC would usher in a new "Kingdom of Rest," described as an earthly utopian paradise with an abundance of material goods and peaceful harmony between native peoples and whites. The millennial teachings of the NAC were interpreted and integrated with traditional Yangoru beliefs in spirits of the dead and other magical practices. Some of the traditional aboriginal beliefs had millenarian aspects, promising the Yangoru economic prosperity and political autonomy. Therefore, the NAC missionary teachings based on millenarian views were easily integrated with the traditional beliefs of the Yangoru. Though the crucifixion did not take place, millenarian movements continue to have some influence on religious and political affairs in Papua New Guinea.

Various anthropologists have attempted to explain the development of the millenarian cult movements of Melanesia. One early explanation by anthropologist Peter Worsley (1957) viewed these millenarian cults as rational attempts at explaining unknown processes that appeared chaotic to the natives. The myths and religious beliefs of the cults also helped mobilize political resistance against colonialism. The cults provided an organizational basis for political action for the various Melanesian tribes. Groups who spoke different languages and maintained separate cultures joined the same religious cult, which enabled them to form political organizations to challenge European and Australian colonial rule. Other explanations rely on more spiritually based phenomena, emphasizing how the cargo cults represent the resurgence of aboriginal religious thought, which is more creative and authentic than that of the newer missionary religions that came to Melanesia.

Today, most anthropologists recognize that these millenarian cults are extremely varied. As they learn more about cult movements in different regions of Melanesia, they discover that some have millenarian aspects, while others do not. Some integrate aboriginal beliefs and practices with the teachings of Christianity, a form of *syncretism*, while others feature a revival of the aboriginal elements and a rejection of the Christian teachings. A few of the movements developed into vital political movements and even violent rebellions, whereas others tend to have a purely spiritual influence. Anthropologists agree that the analysis of these cults is a fruitful area of investigation, and much more needs to be documented through interviews, historical examination, and intensive ethnographic research.

A Hawaiian Religious Renaissance

As U.S. corporate capitalism and tourism came to dominate the economy in Hawaii, every aspect of the traditional Hawaiian culture was affected. At present, the tourist industry generates close to 40 percent of Hawaii's income. Tourists crowd the hotels, restaurants, streets, highways, beaches, golf courses, and parks throughout Hawaii. The advertising industry attempts to promote the image of Hawaii as a romantic and exotic paradise setting where tourists can enjoy the traditional dancing, music, and culture of "primitive" peoples. Ads show skimpily clad women and men dancing before fires on near-deserted beaches. The tourist industry is trying to preserve the traditional culture of Hawaii because it is "good for business."

However, native Hawaiians resist the marketing of their culture. Beginning in the 1970s, with a growing awareness of their marginal status in the U.S. political economy and with more familiarity with the civil rights movement in the mainland United States led by various minorities, many Hawaiians have launched a movement known as the Hawaiian Renaissance. The Hawaiian Renaissance was a resurgence of interest in aboriginal Hawaiian culture, including the traditional language and religious beliefs. The movement is fundamentally antitourist. Many contemporary native Hawaiians who are part of the new movement understand that their traditional culture has been mass marketed and mass consumed. They feel that their traditional culture has been overly commercialized, and they resent the tourist industry for selling the Hawaiian tradition.

Some of the spiritual elements of the native religious beliefs have been reintroduced and revitalized in the context of the Hawaiian Renaissance movement. For example, a number of native Hawaiians have become involved in environmental activism. In doing so, they draw on traditional religious beliefs. They are attempting to prohibit the destruction of the rain forests and other natural settings by developers. The native peoples emphasize a spiritual renewal and refer to traditional Hawaiian gods and goddesses that are associated with the natural areas in order to protect these areas from destructive tourist and commercial forces. In some areas, the native Hawaiians are restoring some of the ancient temples, or *heiaus*. Up until recently native Hawaiians have been seen making offerings to the god Pele at the rim of Halemaumau Crater in the Hawaii Volcanoes National Park. Some aboriginal young people complain about their parents' conversion to Christianity and the negative views expressed by Westerners about their traditional culture and religion. However, most important, the revitalization of their religious culture is part of an overall attempt to preserve their heritage and reclaim their cultural identity and selfhood. As native peoples of Hawaii were subjected to overwhelming and traumatic cultural change, they found that they were marginalized in their own land. After losing their land, their autonomy, and their culture, these

Native Hawaiians march in a demonstration in 2002. Many Native Hawaiians are reclaiming their traditional cultural traditions and resisting U.S. and Western culture.

native Hawaiians have been involved in reconstructing and reinvigorating some of their aboriginal spiritual beliefs as a means of repossessing their cultural identity (Friedman 1995).

A Lost Opportunity?

As Brian Fagan noted in his book *Clash of Cultures* (1984b), which surveys the disappearance of many indigenous societies, the same confrontations between incompatible cultural systems were played out in many parts of the world during the late nineteenth century and continue to this day in the Amazon rain forests and other remote areas such as the Pacific Islands. Some government officials and businesspeople in industrial countries view the drastic modifications that took place and are taking place among prestate societies as necessary for the achievement of progress. This view is, of course, a continuation of the nineteenth-century unilineal view of cultural evolution, which overestimates the beneficial aspects of industrial societies. Depopulation, deculturation, fragmentation of the social community, increasingly destructive warfare, unemployment, and increases in crime, alcoholism, and degradation of the environment are only some of the consequences of this so-called progress. As Fagan (1984b:278) emphasized:

Progress has brought many things: penicillin, the tractor, the airplane, the refrigerator, radio, and television. It has also brought the gun, nuclear weapons, toxic chemicals, traffic deaths, and environmental pollution, to say nothing of powerful nationalisms and other political passions that pit

human being against human being, society against society. Many of these innovations are even more destructive to non-Western societies than the land grabbing and forced conversion of a century and a half ago.

As we discussed in previous chapters and this one, these prestate societies were not idyllic, moral communities in which people lived in perfect harmony with one another and their environment. Warfare, sexism, infanticide, slavery, stratification, and other harmful practices existed in some of these societies. Nonstate societies are not inherently *good*, and industrial societies are not inherently *evil*. Both types of societies have advantages and disadvantages, strengths and weaknesses. There are benefits associated with industrial societies, such as hospitals, better sanitation, and consumer goods, that bring comfort and enjoyment, but nonstate societies also have benefits to offer to industrial societies.

Anthropological research has begun to alert the modern industrial world to the negative implications of the rapid disappearance of first nation peoples—specifically, the loss of extensive practical knowledge that exists in these populations. In the nineteenth-century view (and sometimes even in twenty-first-century discourse), nonstate societies were described as backward, ignorant, and nonscientific. Ethnographic research, however, demonstrates that these peoples have developed a collective wisdom that has contributed practical benefits for all of humankind.

Native American Knowledge

In a book titled *Indian Givers*, anthropologist Jack Weatherford (1988) summarized the basic knowledge, labor, and experience of Native American peoples that have contributed to humankind's collective wisdom. Native Americans introduced 300 food crops to the world, including potatoes and corn. Their experiments with horticultural diversity generated knowledge regarding the survival of crops in different types of environments. They recognized that planting a diversity of seeds would protect the seeds from pests and diseases. Only recently have farmers in the industrialized world begun to discover the ecological lessons developed by Native Americans.

The medical knowledge of Native Americans, which is based on experience with various plants and trees, has benefited people throughout the world. Weatherford uses the example of quinine, derived from the bark of the South American cinchona tree, which is used to treat malaria. Ipecac was made from the roots of an Amazonian tree as a cure for amoebic dysentery. Native Americans treated scurvy with massive doses of Vitamin C, using a tonic made from the bark and needles of an evergreen tree. They also developed treatments for goiter, intestinal worms, headaches (with a medication similar to aspirin), and skin problems.

The lesson from Weatherford's book is that without the contributions of Native American societies, humankind may not have acquired this knowledge for years. As globalization results in the disappearance of many of these indigenous societies and peoples, we risk losing a great deal of knowledge. For example, as the Amazon rain forests are invaded and destroyed by governments and multinational interests, not only do we lose hundreds of species of plants and animals, but we also lose the indigenous societies with their incalculable knowledge of those species. Thus, it is in humanity's best interests to abandon the view that deculturation, subjugation, and—sometimes—the extinction of nonstate societies represent a form of progress.

The most difficult issue that faces anthropologists, government officials, and aboriginal peoples is how best to fit traditional patterns in with the modern, industrial world. The fact that these nonstate societies were, and are, almost powerless to resist the pressures from global economic and political forces creates enormous problems. Multinational corporations, national governments, missionaries, prospectors, and other powerful groups and institutions place these indigenous societies in vulnerable circumstances. How will nonstate societies withstand these pressures and continue to contribute to humankind?

Preserving Indigenous Societies

Most anthropologists argue that indigenous peoples should be able to make free and informed choices regarding their destiny, instead of being coerced into assimilating (Hitchcock 1988, 2004b; Biesele and Hitchcock 2013; Bodley 1990). As previously discussed, many nonstate societies have tried to resist domination by outside powers, but generally have lacked the power to do so successfully. In some cases, anthropologists assisted these peoples in their struggles. Many anthropologists such as Megan Biesele and Robert Hitchcock who do ethnographic research among the Ju/'hoansi San are not only engaged in ethnographic studies of these populations, but also are supporting human rights efforts and economic and educational projects to enhance the ability of these people to become more informed about what comes along with globalization and increasing contact with the outside world (Biesele and Hitchcock 2013). Many anthropologists are active in Cultural Survival, an organization devoted to assisting indigenous peoples and their struggles with governments and multinational corporations.

Also, since the 1970s, many indigenous peoples themselves have become active in preserving their way of life. For example, at a 1975 assembly on the Nootka, a Northwest Coast American Indian chiefdom on Vancouver Island, the World Council of Indigenous Peoples was founded. Fifty-two delegates representing indigenous peoples from 19 countries established this council, which has become a nongovernmental organization of the United Nations (Fagan 1984b). The council endorsed the right of indigenous peoples to maintain their traditional economic and cultural structures. It emphasized that native populations have a special relationship to their languages and should not be forced to abandon them. It further stressed that land and natural resources should not be taken from native populations. However, as we have seen above, at times governments and multinational corporations are oblivious to the rights of indigenous peoples and their rights to their ancestral lands. As these peoples have become more educated, they have been involved in employing the Internet resources and other communications technologies to unify different indigenous groups throughout the world. In 2007, after many years of negotiations, the United Nations adopted the Declaration on the Rights of Indigenous Peoples. Hopefully, this resolution will enable the indigenous people to improve their economic, social, health, and educational conditions in the global arena.

Pro- and Anti-globalization: An Anthropological Contribution

20.8 Discuss how anthropologists contribute to the understanding of globalization.

Throughout the world, there are both positive and negative appraisals of the process of globalization and its impact on different types of societies. In his book, *In Defense of Globalization* (2004), international economist Jagdish Bhagwati notes that politicians and movements in the United States on the right and the left have mounted political arguments against globalization. The politicians on the right emphasize the negative effects of globalization on the U.S. economy, whereas some on the left argue that globalization serves only the capitalist interests of multinational corporations and results in harmful and negative consequences for the environment and in economic exploitation in underdeveloped societies. After many years of economic research on the developing global trends in Asia and elsewhere, Bhagwati suggests that both sides of this anti-globalization political crusade are extreme and that we need to empirically evaluate the realities of both positive and negative consequences of globalization. He urges a middle-of-the-road approach based on a pragmatic solution to deal with the impact of globalization.

Bhagwati suggests that globalization trends need to be studied to comprehend their effects not only on economic and environmental developments, but also on pro- and antiglobalization ideologies across the political spectrum. Areas that need to be examined include migration and immigration policies, the role of NGOs (nongovernment organizations), increasing inequality both within societies and between societies, workers' wages, child labor, prostitution, gender inequities, childcare and work issues, and constraints on the emergence of democratic institutions and civil society that can sustain positive and inhibit negative trends in globalization.

Cultural anthropologists and their research projects all around the world are perfectly situated to understand globalization at the local level through their ethnographic findings. As we shall see in Chapter 24, many ethnographic research projects are aimed at assessing both the positive and the negative aspects of globalization through empirical investigation of current environmental, demographic, and technological trends, as well as economic, political, and religious developments that have emerged in many regions of the world. Obviously, during this historical time period, globalization has produced some high-stakes

An anti-globalization protest by union workers in 2007.

winners and losers among different countries and groups within countries. For example, everyone in the pro- and anti-globalization factions concurs that there has been a widening of the wealth gap both within and among different societies. In Chapter 24, we shall see how anthropologists are evaluating this issue, as well as others, through their extensive ethnographic research.

CRITICAL PERSPECTIVES: Globalization and Mcdonald's

When many people around the world think of globalization, the McDonald's fast-food restaurants come to mind. McDonald's (serving 20 million people a day around the world) represents to many people the cultural hegemony or dominance of U.S. capitalism around the world. As mentioned in this chapter, the political scientist Benjamin Barber views McDonald's as an aspect of the McWorld (including Macintosh computers and Mickey Mouse) that signals the cultural spread of globalization stemming from U.S. society. The triumph of the Big Mac and Hollywood films is viewed by some people as a negative sign that a country has been penetrated by the imperial domination of U.S. culture. However, when cultural anthropologists study the cultural spread and diffusion of McDonald's into the different societies of the world, they find that

globalization is not a one-sided process and that like other external cultural elements, McDonald's restaurants are transformed and localized by the people within these societies.

This process of "glocalization" of McDonald's occurs throughout the world. Harvard anthropologist James Watson edited a volume called *Golden Arches East: McDonald's in East Asia* that contains essays by cultural anthropologists who have studied how the "globalization" of McDonald's takes place in China, Japan, Korea, and Taiwan (2006). In this book, UCLA anthropologist Yunxiang Yan describes how this globalization of McDonald's has emerged in China. Since McDonald's moved in as the iconic symbol of American culture and globalization in Beijing during the 1990s, it has been attractive to Chinese citizens not only because of its food, but also because of the ability of the citizens to consume popular cultural values stemming from the United States. Following the decline of the rigid Maoist orthodoxy and Communist ideology prior to the 1990s, McDonald's

McDonalds in the People's Republic of China.

was perceived as a means of expressing freedom of choice in taste and lifestyle to many Chinese. Yunxiang Yan noted that other cultural values associated with American traditions also diffused into China, along with the popular culture associated with the Big Mac, and that these values were also absorbed and localized into Chinese society. For example, despite some resistance to American cultural hegemony by some of the Chinese, Yunxiang interviewed others who said that NBA games,

Coca-Cola, Hollywood movies, and the Declaration of Independence all belong to the shared culture of all human societies (2006:34).

The sociologist Peter Berger refers to this process observed by Yunxiang as the "sacramental consumption" of food that carries the cultural freight of individual freedom, democracy, and human rights, which he also links with the eating of a Big Mac in the former Soviet Union (2002). Similarly, anthropologist Conrad Kottak refers to McDonaldization as a secular religion with a sacred text called an "Operations Manual" that has strong cultural resonance for many (2003). Anthropologists who study McDonald's in Japan, such as Tamotsu Aoki and Emiko Ohnuki-Tierney, find similar glocalization processes at work. According to Ohnuki-Tierney (2006), meat had been available since the 1920s, but prior to World War II, most Japanese did not eat much of it. They ate primarily vegetables and seafood. However, after the U.S. occupation of Japan following the war, gradually some of the wealthier Japanese began to consume meat products, including beef. Following the period of postwar affluence in Japan, they began to eat meat with gusto because it was associated with the Western civilization, science, technology, and culture being integrated into Japanese culture. Eventually, McDonald's came to Japan in the 1970s. By 1982, McDonald's was the most profitable fast-food company in Japan. McDonald's began a marketing campaign to target higher-income middle-class people who were benefiting from the growth of the Japanese economy by establishing its restaurants in areas where real estate was expensive, such as on the Ginza in Tokyo and near train stations. With the introduction of McDonald's into Japan, eating habits were changed radically, as described by these anthropologists. The traditional form of lunch for most Japanese was the box lunch called *obento*. However, as Japanese customers came to eat lunch in McDonald's, they learned to hold the bread and meat in their hands, munching on their favorite teriyaki burger or *McChao* (chicken-fried rice), while standing (to appear more American) at the counters during their lunch breaks. Although other Japanese restaurants adopted the fast-food program for traditional dishes such as *ramen* Chinese noodles, take-out *sushi*, or *gyudon* (a bowl of rice topped with beef), McDonald's remained a very popular feature of Japanese cuisine.

Anthropologist Tulasi Srinivas has studied the "McDonaldization" process of globalization in India (2002). The major marketing obstacle that faced McDonald's in India was the image of a beef patty on a bun in the eyes of the majority of Hindu peoples, who maintain beliefs regarding the sacredness of cows. Srinivas noted that McDonald's invested a great deal of time and money to build appropriate kitchens in their restaurants that prevented the mixing of vegetarian foods with meat products. Eventually, McDonald's began to localize its foods by developing the Maharajah Mac, a type of Indian spiced hamburger, along with a vegetarian menu. However, this was not appealing to the majority of Indian consumers. Srinivas concludes that companies such as McDonald's, Pizza Hut, and KFC, which represent the standardization and cultural homogenization of food, do not become profitable in the multiethnic, pluralistic consumer atmosphere in India. Sociologist George Ritzer, in his provocative book *The McDonaldization of Society*, describes the standardized and homogenized commercialization of U.S. popular culture as lowering the level of sophistication wherever its long tentacles reach (2010). In contrast to the change reflected in Peter Berger's phrase "sacramental consumption" for the former Soviet Union and China, Srinivas emphasizes that this aspect of the Big Mac does not apply to India because the Indian population resides in a pluralistic democratic nation. Thus, glocalization of McDonald's takes a much different form in India.

Finally, in a broad, comprehensive essay accompanying his study of McDonald's in Indonesia, anthropologist Ronald Lukens-Bull demonstrates the process of glocalization, which has taken a different form in that country (2003). The Big Mac came to Jakarta, Indonesia, in 1990, and by 2003, there were 108 stores employing about 800 people. Lukens-Bull indicates that McDonald's is a prestigious and expensive form of dining for the vast majority of Indonesians. It is identified with an upwardly mobile middle class of consumers—young teens who wear jeans and watch a version of MTV Asia. In central Jakarta, the major McDonald's—near the Hard Rock Café, Chili's, movie theaters, and department stores—has a 40-foot inflatable Ronald McDonald in a Buddhist– or Sufi Islamic–like meditative position. Local Indonesians refer to him as "Ronald Bertapa," or the Meditating Ronald. Thus, Ronald Bertapa is a powerful syncretic symbol in Indonesia associated with the original Hindu-Buddhist traditions of Indonesia blended with the legends of the nine original Sufi saints who brought Islam to Indonesia. Another Ronald McDonald statue in Bali appears to co-opt art and culture in order to market hamburgers to Western tourists. And one other Ronald McDonald figure in East Java was referred to as the "freedom fighter." This "freedom-fighting" Ronald McDonald was pictured riding on a tank with friends waving the Indonesian flag to celebrate independence from the Dutch. The multiplicity of symbols associated with McDonald's and its particular glocalization in Indonesia represents a cultural accommodation to external sources and also the ambivalence that those external sources reflect in various modes of discourse about modernity, Western influence, and its impact on Islamic culture in Indonesia.

Points to Ponder

1. What do you see as the negative and positive aspects of McDonald's restaurants moving into different societies of the world?
2. What does the adaptation of the new forms of McDonald's in different societies suggest about culture change?
3. If you were traveling outside of the United States, would you eat in a McDonald's restaurant and why?

Summary and Review of Learning Objectives

20.1 Discuss how anthropologists define globalization.

There is no widespread consensus within anthropology on what the definitive aspects of globalization are. However, globalization is usually referred to as the broad-scale changes and transformations that have resulted from the impact of industrializaion and the emergence of an interconnected global economy, with the spread of capital, labor (migration), and technology across national borders. Globalization continues to occur today through the increasing spread of postindustrial technology—including electronic communications, television, and the Internet—and the expansion of multinational corporations into the non-Western world.

20.2 Describe some of the technological and economic trends resulting in globalization.

Globalization is occurring rapidly through the development of a high-tech computer- and Internet- based technology and the expansion of global capitalism throughout the world.

20.3 Compare the three theoretical approaches for analyzing globalization.

Various theories that developed from early ideas of Max Weber and Karl Marx to explain the process of globalization have led to models such as modernization, dependency, and world-systems theory. Weber investigated the cultural and religious beliefs of Western societies that resulted in capitalism, which inspired the modernization theories of the 1950s and 60s during the Cold War. This modernization approach developed the model of the First, Second, and Third Worlds. Karl Marx focused on the material factors such as technology and the economy that led to capitalism, which influenced the dependency approaches to globalization from the time of the 1970s. World Systems theories were also inspired by the Marxist approaches to how global capitalism had created interconnections among different types of societies throughout the world.

20.4 Discuss how anthropologists analyze globalization.

Anthropologists have drawn from different models of globalization to explore glocalization, an understanding of global trends as they interconnect with the local cultures understood through ethnographic studies. Anthropologists often describe their research as "globalization from below," as they focus on qualitative and quantitative data that are beyond the statistics of government or corporate reports analyzed by most political scientists and economists.

20.5 Discuss how anthropologists criticize some of the approaches to understanding politics, culture, and globalization.

Some of the approaches used by political scientists such as Benjamin Barber and Samuel Huntington have resulted in stereotypical notions of Asian, Islamic, and Western civilizations and conflict based on simplistic concepts of culture and history. Ethnographic studies of Asian, Islamic, or Western societies have revealed a great deal of diversity among ethnic groups, socioeconomic classes, and political views within those societies that cannot be reduced to monolithic stereotypes regarding a "clash of civilizations."

20.6 Discuss the consequences of globalization on indigenous peoples.

Anthropologists have found that globalization often results in ethnocide and sometimes genocide as globalization reaches indigenous peoples who have lived in various marginal environments or are small-scale ethnic minorities. As these small-scale indigenous societies are drawn into the world economy, they face new diseases, depopulation, forced settlement, and sometimes genocidal policies, warfare, and other negative consequences that result from globalization.

20.7 Describe the different forms of resistance to globalization by indigenous peoples.

Following their military defeat in the nineteenth century, many Native Americans developed revitalization movements such as the Ghost Dance tradition or the Peyote Cult as attempts to restore their native cultural and spiritual beliefs. Other revitalization or millenarian movements such as the cargo cults of Melanesia in New Guinea were forms of resistance to globalization. Native Hawaiians are involved in restoring their temples and religious traditions. They demonstrate to resist the tourism and commodification of their spiritual and cultural beliefs.

20.8 Discuss how anthropologists contribute to the understanding of globalization.

Through rigorous ethnographic studies, anthropologists investigate and assess both the positive and negative consequences resulting from globalization in different societies throughout the world.

Key Terms

core societies, p. 468
dependency theory, p. 467
ethnocide, p. 472
First World, p. 466
genocide, p. 472

globalization, p. 462
glocalization, p. 470
imperialism, p. 468
neoliberalism, p. 470
peripheral societies, p. 468

Second World, p. 466
semiperipheral societies, p. 468
Third World, p. 466
world-systems theory, p. 468

Chapter 21
Globalization in Latin America, Africa, and the Caribbean

Learning Objectives

After reading this chapter you should be able to:

21.1 Discuss the early phases of Western colonialism in Latin America, Africa, and the Caribbean.

21.2 Describe the demographic, economic, and religious changes associated with globalization in Latin America, Africa, and the Caribbean.

21.3 Discuss why independence, nationalist, and revolutionary movements developed in Latin America, Africa, and the Caribbean.

21.4 Describe how Latin America, Africa, and the Caribbean countries are situated in the global economy today.

21.5 Discuss what anthropologists have learned about the peasantry in Latin America, Africa, and the Caribbean.

21.6 Describe the characteristics of family and gender relationships in Latin America, Africa, and the Caribbean.

21.7 Discuss the issues related to ethnicity in Latin America, Africa, and the Caribbean.

21.8 Discuss how urbanization has influenced Latin America, Africa, and the Caribbean.

Most anthropologists have focused on non-Western countries for their ethnographic research. To understand how globalization processes have influenced local conditions and cultures, they have had to adopt a broad global perspective in their research. The non-Western countries of Latin America, Africa, and the Caribbean comprise a complex of diversified regions and cultures that cannot be easily characterized. The various countries in these regions are located in different types of environmental zones, ranging from highland mountain areas to lowland river valleys and from small island regions to complex urban centers. Each country is made up of various ethnic groups in different proportions. As a result of globalization, all these countries are at different stages of political and economic development. In Chapters 16, 18, and 20 we discussed various band, tribal, and chiefdom societies (that are very diverse) that exist in these different regions, as well as the impact of globalization on their development. This chapter begins with an overview of the spread of globalization and colonialism in Latin America, Africa, and the Caribbean. We then examine some consequences of globalization processes for these regions. Finally, we discuss a number of ethnographic studies that have illuminated the effects of globalization on various institutions in these countries.

One of the points that we want to stress is that globalization is always a painful process for any society. When Europe, the United States, and Japan went through industrialization, as discussed in Chapters 16 and 17, families were dislocated and disrupted by rapid urbanization and other changes. People were torn away from their traditional communities of support, and ethnic and religious communities no longer provided the source of security they once did. Extensive migration, urban congestion, increases in deviance and crime, political corruption, population growth, pollution, and other social problems accompanied industrialization in these so-called First World countries.

But the countries that we discuss in this chapter and the next are facing these globalization processes in a much different way from the early industrialized countries. The industrialized nations, such as the United States and the countries of Europe had *centuries* to adjust to these processes, whereas other areas of the world have been experiencing aspects of globalization for a short period of time. Although these processes began during the time of colonization for most of these countries, it is only within the past few decades that globalization has penetrated deeply within the fabric of these societies.

Globalization and Colonialism

21.1 Discuss the early phases of Western colonialism in Latin America, Africa, and the Caribbean.

Latin America

Following Columbus's explorations in the 1400s, Spanish and Portuguese *conquistadores* led expeditions to the Americas. As discussed in Chapter 14, this was the period of *mercantilism*, a system in which the government regulates the economy of a state to ensure economic growth, a positive balance of trade, and the accumulation of wealth, usually gold and silver. These European states were competing to accrue wealth to build their national treasuries. The Portuguese and Spanish were the first Europeans to engage in this mercantilist competition. Columbus believed that he had reached islands off Asia, and the Spanish and Portuguese were anxious to acquire access to this new trade route, in part to cut off the Muslim monopoly on trade in the Mediterranean and Asia. Thus, the primary objectives of the conquistadores were to find wealth and to conquer the Americas.

The indigenous societies of Latin America consisted of four major types of sociocultural systems: small-scale hunting-gathering bands; horticulturalist tribes, who lived in permanent or semipermanent villages and supplemented their diet by hunting, fishing, and gathering; and chiefdoms and agricultural empires, such as the those of the Aztecs and Incas, which had made complex achievements in technology, architecture, economic organization, and statecraft.

In 1494, the Spanish and Portuguese governments agreed to the Treaty of Tordesillas, which divided the world into two major mercantilist spheres of influence. As a result, in the Americas the Portuguese took control of what is now Brazil, and the Spanish gained access to most of the remainder of Latin America.

Cortés and the Aztec Empire The first major collision between the Spanish and the indigenous peoples occurred in 1519, when Hernando Cortés confronted the Aztec Empire in Mexico. After landing at Veracruz, Cortés encouraged many native groups who had been conquered and subjugated by the Aztecs to revolt against the Aztecs and their ruler, Montezuma. Besieged by these rebellious peoples and the superior weaponry of the Spaniards—especially guns and cannons—the Aztec state quickly crumbled. In 1521, Cortés and his Native American allies captured Tenochtitlán, establishing Spanish domination over the entire empire.

The Spanish then went on to conquer Mesoamerica, including Mexico, Honduras, and Guatemala, as well as areas in southeastern and southwestern North America. Similar conquests occurred in various regions of South America, such as Francisco Pizarro's conquest of the Incas. The Spanish ransacked these civilizations, taking the gold, silver, precious stones, and other valuables these people had accumulated. After this first phase of conquest and occupation, the Spanish began to exploit this wealth for the benefit of their home country. They developed systems of mining, commercial agriculture, livestock raising, and trading. These new forms of economic organization drastically transformed the sociocultural systems of the Americas.

The region of Brazil in South America contained no productive agricultural states such as those of the Aztecs and Incas, and the native population consisted of only about one million people. Therefore, instead of searching for wealth in the form of gold, silver, and other precious goods, the Portuguese turned immediately to developing commercial agriculture and introduced sugar plantations. The plantation system initially relied on local labor, but because there were few natives in this area, the Portuguese also imported African slaves.

The Spanish and Portuguese established an elaborate bureaucracy to manage control over their colonies. They set up viceroyalties to administer political power that would serve the royal interests in the home countries. All of the modern borders and national identities of Latin America today are derived from the lines drawn by the viceroyalties representing the royal families in Spain and

Figure 21.1 A map of contemporary Latin America and the Caribbean

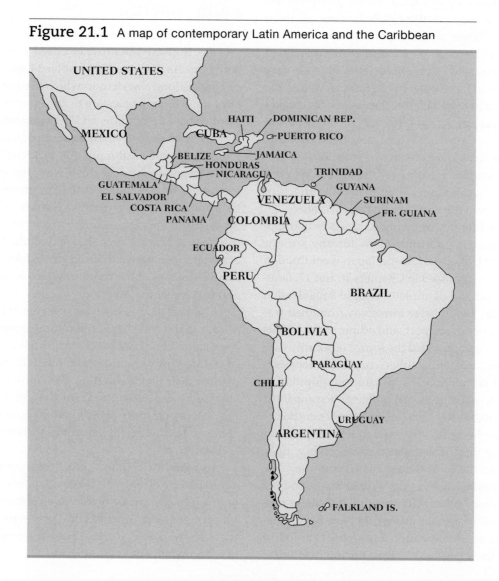

Portugal. In addition, the Spanish established a policy known as *reducciones de Indios* (reductions of the Indians) to assimilate the indigenous Indians into European culture and religion. The indigenous Indians were relocated and concentrated into garrison towns or *pueblos* supervised by the Spanish military and priests.

Africa

European expansion into Africa began with the Portuguese, who came seeking gold; their explorers reached the West African coast in the second half of the fifteenth century. Although they did not find in Africa the vast amounts of gold that the Americas had yielded, they discovered another source of wealth: slaves.

Slave Trade   In earlier chapters, we noted that slavery was an accepted institution in some chiefdoms and agricultural states around the world. Slavery existed throughout much of the ancient agricultural world, including Egypt, Greece, Rome, the Middle East, and parts of Africa. Until the twentieth century, various Middle Eastern empires maintained an extensive slave trade based on African labor (Hourani 1991). In Africa, agricultural states such as the Asante kingdom kept war captives and criminals as slaves. This slavery, however, was much different from that of later Western societies (Davidson 1961; Goody 1980). In Chapter 17, we discussed the "open" forms of slavery associated with societies with abundant land and low populations. In Africa, this open system included slaves who were attached to extended families and became part of the domestic social unit. They could own property and marry, and they were protected from mutilation and murder by formalized norms or legal institutions.

The Portuguese initiated the major European slave trade around 1440. They took slaves from coastal areas of West Africa to Portugal and to some islands in the Mediterranean. African slaves became the major source of labor for the expanding plantation systems in North and South America, Portugal, and Holland. By the 1700s, England and France became the dominant slave-trading nations.

Unlike the open forms of slavery found in Africa, these Western countries classified slaves as property; they had no personal rights and could never be incorporated into the owner's domestic family or social system. These countries traded goods and weapons with certain African groups, who, in turn, supplied the Europeans with slaves. Sometimes, African leaders simply relied upon the local institutions of slavery to sell their own slaves to the Europeans. In many cases, however, coastal Africans raided inland villages for slaves. These practices had emerged in the earlier slave trade with the Islamic empires to the north.

Millions of slaves were taken from Africa and transported to Latin America and the Caribbean. The Atlantic slave trade declined in the early nineteenth century, when antislavery movements in Britain and France led to the prohibition of slave trading. British ships patrolled the coasts of Africa to capture slave traders, although many ships eluded this blockade. The slave trade through Britain ended in 1808, but the complete abolition of this trade was not possible until countries such as Brazil and the United States abandoned their plantation systems. The United States made slavery illegal in 1865, and Brazil did so in 1888. The devastating effect of the slave trade, however, has continued to plague Africa to the present.

Colonization in Africa   Europeans generally did not venture into the interior of Africa for colonization during the mercantilist phase from 1500 to 1600. The threat of malaria and military resistance kept them in the coastal regions. During the late nineteenth century, however, European nations began to compete vigorously for African territories. To serve their needs for raw materials and overseas markets, the British, French, Dutch, Belgians, and Germans partitioned different areas of Africa into colonies, as reflected in the boundaries of present-day countries.

In West Africa, the difficult climate and the presence of diseases such as malaria discouraged large-scale European settlement. The British, French, and Germans, however, established commercial enterprises to control the production and exportation of products such as palm oil (used in soap making) and cocoa (Wolf [1982] 1997, 2001).

In Central Africa, King Leopold of Belgium incorporated the 900,000 acres of the Congo as a private preserve. He controlled the basic economic assets of the region through stock ownership in companies that were allowed to develop the rubber and ivory trade. In doing so, the king used brutal methods of forced labor that caused the population to decline by one-half (from 20 million to 10 million) during his reign, from 1885 to 1908 (Miller 1988).

In East Africa during the 1880s, the Germans and the British competed for various territories to develop plantations and other enterprises. This rivalry eventually resulted in treaties that gave the British the colony of Kenya and the Germans a large territory known as Tanganyika. British and German settlers flocked to these countries and took possession of lands from the native peoples.

The colonization of southern Africa began in the late seventeenth century, when Dutch explorers built a refueling station for their ships at Cape Town. From that site, Dutch settlers, first called Boers and later Afrikaners, penetrated into the region. The Boers displaced, and often enslaved, the native peoples, including foragers such as the Ju/'hoansi San and tribal peoples such as the Hottentots. They eventually adopted a racially based, hierarchical system in which the Boers occupied the highest ranks, followed by the coloreds (people of mixed parentage), the Bantu-speaking agriculturalists, and people like the Ju/'hoansi San and Hottentots. Each group was segregated from the others and treated differently. The Boers eventually decimated most of the Hottentots through genocidal policies.

As the Dutch were settling these lands, the British were also penetrating into southern Africa. They incorporated several kingdoms, which they transformed into native reservations under British control. Fearful of British expansion, the Boers migrated north into lands that had long been inhabited by the Bantu-speaking Zulus. This migration became known as the Great Trek. Although the Zulus fought bitterly against this encroachment, they were defeated in 1838 by the superior military technology of the Boers (Service 1975).

As the Boers moved north, they established the republics of Natal, the Orange Free State, and the Transvaal. In the meantime, gold and diamonds had been discovered in these areas, leading to intense competition between the British and the Boers. In the Boer War of 1899–1902, the British defeated the Boers and annexed all their republics. In 1910, the British established the Union of South Africa.

The Caribbean

The Caribbean islands consist of four distinct geographical regions: The first contains the Bahamas, nearest to the coast of North America; the second, called the Greater Antilles, consists of Cuba and Hispaniola (Haiti and the Dominican Republic), Jamaica, the Cayman Islands, Puerto Rico, and the Virgin Islands; the third, the Lesser Antilles, includes Antigua, Barbuda, Dominica, St. Lucia, St. Vincent, the Grenadines, Grenada, and St. Christopher-Nevis (St. Kitts); the fourth, off the coast of South America, includes Trinidad, Tobago, Barbados, Aruba, Curacao, and Bonaire. Some of the islands, such as Cuba, Haiti,

Figure 21.2 A map of sub-Saharan Africa, highlighting some of the peoples discussed in the chapter

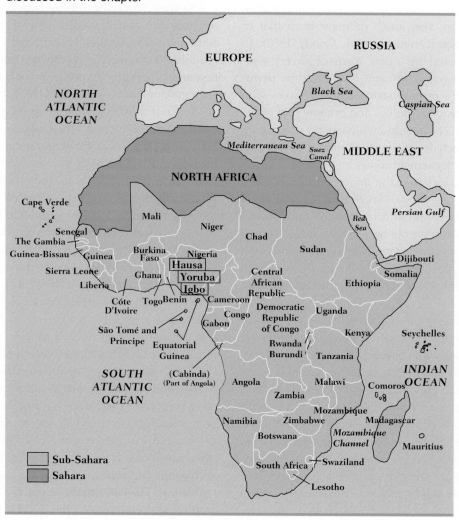

and Puerto Rico, came under Spanish rule by 1500. Others were divided up by other European powers, such as the British, French, and Dutch.

Unlike the mainland regions, these islands did not have large, complex agricultural states with accumulated treasures. Therefore, the colonial powers introduced commercialized agriculture, usually in the form of sugar plantations, an agricultural system that had been developing in the Mediterranean region (Mintz 1985; Kephart 2012). As these sugar plantations were developed, large numbers of African slaves were imported by the Europeans to labor on these plantations. When the African slave trade began to decline, the British replaced slave labor with East Indian workers on some of the islands. Thus, the islands of the Caribbean are an extremely diverse region, with Hispanic, French, Dutch, African, and East Indian cultural influences.

Consequences of Globalization and Colonialism

21.2 Describe the demographic, economic, and religious changes associated with globalization in Latin America, Africa, and the Caribbean.

Demographic Change

The immediate impact of the West on Mesoamerica, South America, Africa, and the Caribbean was disastrous for local populations. In Mesoamerica, South America, and the Caribbean, the native population began to decline drastically. One of the major reasons for this decline was the introduction of diseases—smallpox, typhoid fever, measles, influenza, the mumps—to which the Indians had no resistance because they had never been exposed to them. In Brazil and the Caribbean, the importation of African slaves led to the introduction of diseases such as malaria and yellow fever. Although the numbers vary, archaeologists estimate that at least 25 million people lived in Mesoamerica when the Europeans arrived; by 1650, only 1.5 million remained (Wolf [1982] 1997). In some areas, 95 percent of the indigenous population was wiped out by disease (Skidmore and Smith 2005).

Rapid depopulation was also due to the stresses induced by the new forms of labor to which these peoples were subjected. Large-scale slave raiding decimated native populations. Rigorous forms of enforced labor—including slavery—in mining, on plantations, and in livestock raising created serious health problems and caused numerous deaths. In addition, the collapse of the indigenous patterns of intensive agriculture brought about famines and food shortages. All of these factors increased the social and biological stresses that aided the spread of disease in these populations (Wolf [1982] 1997).

The demographic consequences of the slave trade in Africa were also immense. Historians estimate that as many as 40 million Africans were captured from the interior between 1440 and 1870 (Davis 1984, 2006; Miller 1988). During this period, about 30 million Africans perished on their march from the inland regions or during the voyage to the New World. Approximately 12 million Africans were imported forcibly to the Americas. Many of them were in their prime reproductive years, which, in conjunction with the wars between the coastal and interior regions, may account for the slow growth of Africa's population during this period (Wolf [1982] 1997).

In the long run, however, Western expansion and colonialism in non-Western countries brought unprecedented demographic growth to the populations of these agricultural states. For example, the population of Mexico tripled in the nineteenth century from 2.5 million to 9 million, and Cuba's population increased from 550,000 in the nineteenth century to 5.8 million in 1953. Apparently, as Europeans began to change the indigenous population from traditional subsistence peasant farming to the production of cash crops, fertility rates began to rise in the traditional villages. There were labor shortages in the villages, and peasants responded by having larger extended families to try to maintain their subsistence peasant farming (Robbins 2013). And generally, fertility rates continue to remain high in most of the countries of Latin America, Africa, and the Caribbean.

Eventually, new medical and sanitation practices introduced by modernization led to a tremendous reduction in death rates through the control of smallpox, plague, yellow fever, and malaria. Meanwhile, birth rates remained high. The combination of reduced death rates and high birth rates led to dramatic population increases. In Chapter 24, we discuss some of the global effects of these population trends.

Economic Change

The economic changes that occurred with globalization in Latin America, Africa, and the Caribbean wrought a dramatic transformation in these societies. In Latin America, the Spanish developed large-scale mining operations that used forced labor. In addition to gold, the Spanish discovered vast supplies of silver in Mexico and Bolivia. The American mines eventually became the major source of bullion accumulated by mercantile Spain. For example, of the 7 million pounds of silver extracted from these mines, the Spanish Crown collected 40 percent.

New patterns of economic organization were introduced in Latin America and the Caribbean after the

Iberian (Portuguese and Spanish) conquest. In the Spanish areas, the Crown rewarded the *conquistadores* with the *encomienda*, or grants of Indian land, tribute, and labor, which reduced the Indians to dependents because it was based upon forced labor.

Eventually, the *encomienda* system was superseded by the *hacienda* (in Brazil, *fazenda*), or large-scale plantation. Established during the colonial period, *haciendas* and *fazendas* remained the major economic institutions in Latin America until the mid–twentieth century. The owners, called *hacendados* or *fazendieros*, acquired status, wealth, and power by owning the land and subjugating the tenants, or peons, who were tied to the *haciendas* through indebtedness and lived in shacks. In certain respects, the *haciendas* and *fazendas* were similar to the feudalistic manors of European societies described in Chapter 18.

Although the *haciendas* and *fazendas* were self-sufficient economic units providing the essential resources for the owners and tenants, they were not efficient (Wolf 1969, [1982] 1997). The *hacendados* tended to be preoccupied with their social prestige and comfortable lifestyle and did not attempt to produce cash crops for the world market or use their land productively. This pattern of inefficient, localized production and marketing of the *haciendas* is still visible in much of Latin America.

After three centuries of Iberian rule, much of Latin America consisted of these inefficient *haciendas*, economically deprived Indian communities with limited land, and a native population that was undernourished, maltreated, overworked, and reduced to bondage. An enormous social gap developed between the Indian peons and a class of individuals who identified with Iberian political and economic interests.

The wealthy *hacendados* were also the most important political leaders or *caudillos* who held political power over many peasants and Indians in the different regions of Latin America. They were the unelected sheriffs and judges who administered their own law with armed private militias. This form of leadership in Latin America is referred to as *caudillismo*, which laid the foundation for the pattern of postcolonial military-based dictatorships that emerged throughout much of Latin America.

In Africa during the first phase of colonialism, the different European powers attempted to make their colonies economically self-sufficient. African labor was recruited for work on the commercialized plantations and in the gold and diamond mines. Native workers received substandard wages and were forced to pay head taxes to the colonial regimes. Head taxes were assessed for each individual and had to be paid in cash. By requiring cash payments, the colonial governments forced villagers to abandon subsistence agriculture and become wage laborers. In eastern and southern Africa, many choice agricultural lands were taken from the native peoples and given to British and Dutch settlers. As the demand for exports from Africa increased in the world-market system, the colonial powers began to develop transportation and communication systems, linking coastal cities with inland regions. The purpose of these systems was to secure supplies of natural resources and human labor.

These colonial processes completely disrupted the indigenous production and exchange systems. Africans were drawn into the wage economy. Monetary systems based on European coinage were introduced, displacing former systems of exchange. The price of African labor and goods came to be determined by the world market. Global economic conditions began to shape the sociocultural systems and strategies of native peoples throughout Africa.

One major consequence of Western colonialism was the integration of many agricultural village communities into wider regional and global economic patterns. Although the precolonial traditional villages were probably never entirely self-sufficient and were tied to regional and national trading networks, through Western colonialism, the village peasantry was no longer isolated from

A Mayan corn farmer of Guatemala

cities, and the global market determined the prices for agricultural goods. The transformation of agricultural economies triggered dramatic changes in traditional rural communities. Because few peasants had enough capital to own and manage land, much of the land fell into the hands of colonial settlers, large landowners, and moneylenders. In many cases, these changes encouraged absentee land ownership and temporary tenancy. Long-term care of the land by the peasantry was sacrificed for immediate profits. Land, labor, and capital were thus disconnected from the village kinship structures of reciprocity and redistribution, or what has been referred to as the *moral economy* (see Chapter 16). Peasants were incorporated into the global capitalist cash economy.

Religious Change

Numerous religious changes occurred with globalization. The Roman Catholic Church played a major role in Latin American society during the colonial period. Initially, the *conquistadores* were not sure whether the native peoples were fully human; that is, they were not certain that the natives had souls. After the Spanish authorities, backed by the Pope, ruled that the Indians did indeed have souls and could be saved, various missionaries began to convert the Indians to Catholicism. Through the *reducciones de Indios* policies, the Spanish missionaries established the garrison towns, *pueblos*, and villages where the Indians were relocated and forced to assimilate to European culture and Catholicism. However, as the Indian population converted and died off, the Catholic Church began

to become more self-interested. During the sixteenth century, the Catholic Church became the largest landholder in Latin America, earning huge sums from rents on its property.

In general, the Spanish missionaries repressed the indigenous religious traditions of the native peoples and forced them to convert to Catholicism. However, the indigenous religions of Mesoamerica, for example, were able to absorb the foreign Catholic beliefs and practices without giving up their own (Berdan 1982). Many local religious conceptions were somewhat analogous to Catholic beliefs. A process of religious **syncretism** developed, in which indigenous beliefs and practices blended with those of Christianity. For example, the central theological tenet of Christianity, that Jesus sacrificed his life for the salvation of humanity, was acceptable to people whose religious traditions included human sacrifices for the salvation of Mesoamerican peoples (see Chapter 19). The Indians were also attracted to the elaborate rituals and colorful practices associated with the Virgin Mary and the saints. Catholic beliefs and practices were assimilated into traditional indigenous cosmologies, creating powerful symbolic images and rituals.

One well-known tradition that has endured in Mexico, representing a combination of pre-Hispanic and Spanish Catholic religious beliefs and practices, is the *Día de los Muertos* (the Day of the Dead). The *Día de los Muertos* takes place on November 2nd, the day after All Saints' Day (*Todos los Santos*). This is the time when the souls of the dead return to Earth to visit their living relatives. *Día de los Muertos* is a time when families get together

This photo shows the candy skulls, called *calaveras*, for the Day of the Dead in Mexico

for feasting. They construct altars to the dead and offer food, drink, and prayers to the souls of their dead relatives. The altar usually has a photograph of the dead person, along with an image of Jesus or the Virgin Mary. For those who died as children,the altar may have toys or sugar treats made in the shape of animals. Mexicans prepare for this day many months before. They prepare candy skulls, *calaveras*, which are given out to everyone in the family and to friends. The families incur a substantial expense for the foods, chocolate sauces (*mole*), and drinks, along with flowers, candles, and incense, for the festivities. Food, drinks, and gifts of the *calaveras* are exchanged to symbolize strong linkages among family members, both living and dead. It is the most important ritual in Mexico, exemplifying the crucial links between the past pre-Hispanic symbolic culture and the present. The *Día de los Muertos* represents the persistence of cultural traditions despite the globalizing processes and religious traditions that came with European colonialism (Norget 1996, 2006; Garciagodoy 1998).

Despite the official position of the Catholic Church in Latin America and the Caribbean, indigenous religious traditions have survived for centuries, partly because Catholicism had evolved over a long period in Europe, during which it absorbed a number of indigenous "pagan" traditions. Thus, Catholicism was predisposed to accommodate the indigenous religious traditions in the Americas (Ingham 1986).

In addition, the slaves that were imported from Africa to Latin America and the Caribbean brought traditional African religious beliefs and practices that were also absorbed into Catholicism. In Brazil, these religious traditions are referred to as *Umbanda* and *Macumba*; in northeast Brazil, they are known as *Candomble*. In Cuba, these syncretic traditions are called *Santería*, which involves the sacrifice of animals such as goats and chickens in various rituals (Bowen 2005).

On the island of Haiti, many of the people believe in the tradition known as *Vodoun*. *Vodoun* is a similar combination of African and other traditions. *Vodounists* believe that they communicate directly with spirits. *Vodoun* traditions have evolved into a code of ethics, education, and a system of politics that are evident throughout Haitian society. Secret *vodoun*-based practices are highly complex spiritual cosmologies and communities that control much of everyday life in Haiti. These secret societies trace their origins to escaped slaves that organized revolts against the French colonizers. They meet at night and use traditional African drumming and celebrations. The *vodounists'* complex belief system involves practices of priests or priestesses that can do harm to people. One practice is known as *zombification*. Using the poison of a puffer fish, they can cause an individual to appear to die and then recover several days later. The victims of the poisoning remain conscious but are not able to speak or move. Zombification and the threat of zombification were used by the secret societies to police the

A *voudon* altar in Haiti

Haitian rural communities and maintain order (Metraux, Charters, and Mintz 1989; W. Davis 1997). All these syncretic traditions combining traditional African religions and Catholicism are sometimes called *spiritism* and are evident in many parts of Latin America and the Caribbean.

With European colonization in Africa came missionaries who established schools to spread Christianity. As in Latin America, many of the missionaries in Africa were paternalistic toward the native peoples and tried to protect them from the worst abuses of colonialism. Mission schools served as both hospitals and education centers. Many people sent their children to the Christian schools because this education offered opportunities for better jobs and higher social status, and many people educated in the mission schools became part of the elite.

At the same time, however, the missionaries attempted to repress traditional religious beliefs and practices. The missionaries believed that to be "saved," the Africans had to abandon their customary practices and embrace the Christian faith. To some extent, the ethnocentrism and sometimes racism of the missionaries in Africa had tragic consequences for many native peoples. Through the educational system, Africans were taught that their traditional culture was shameful, something to be despised. In many cases, this led to a loss of ethnic and cultural identity and sometimes induced feelings of self-hatred.

As various Christian denominations missionized throughout Africa, a number of syncretistic movements began to emerge among the indigenous peoples. They became known as Independent African Church denominations referred to as "Zionist," "Spiritual," or "Prophet." The leaders of these churches are often called prophets and are known for their charismatic powers of healing. Facing the crisis created by colonialism and the loss of their traditional culture, many indigenous Africans turned to these traditions for relief. In some cases, these syncretic traditions combining traditional spiritual beliefs and Christianity have played a pivotal role in political movements throughout Africa (Comaroff 1985).

Political Changes: Independence and Nationalist Movements

21.3 **Discuss why independence, nationalist, and revolutionary movements developed in Latin America, Africa, and the Caribbean.**

One important consequence of globalization and colonialism in various Latin American, African, and Caribbean areas was the development of political movements that emphasized independence and nationalistic ideas. Some of the indigenous peoples became educated under the colonial regime and began to assert their independence. After approximately 300 years of European domination, the various regions of Latin America and the Caribbean began to demand their political autonomy from the colonial regimes. An educated descendant of the ancient Incans, Tupac Amaru, led a rebellion in Peru against the Spanish rulers. Simón Bolívar (1783–1830), a national hero among both Venezuelans and Colombians, led a broad-based independence/nationalist movement. In the French colony of Saint Domingue (modern-day Haiti), a major uprising by educated slaves influenced by the ideas that motivated the French Revolution overthrew the French regime and beat back Napoleon's armies; this action became a warning for all the various colonial regimes in the region (Mintz 1985).

During the decades following World War II, European colonial rule ended in Africa; by the 1970s, no fewer than 31 former colonies had won their independence. The first country to do so, the West African nation of Ghana, became independent of Britain in 1957. Kwame Nkrumah, a charismatic leader who mobilized workers, youths, professionals, and farmers to speed up the pace of decolonization, led the Ghanian independence movement. Ghana's success intensified independence movements elsewhere. By the early 1960s, all of the West African countries, including the French colonies of Niger, Mali, Senegal, and Dahomey, had gained their independence, making a fairly smooth transition to independent political control.

In the Congo region, however, because of the Belgians' rigid exploitative political and economic policies, the independence movement was much more difficult. Belgian colonial policies had brutalized the native population, and the inadequate educational system had failed to produce an educated elite, affording Africans in the Belgian colonies little opportunity to gain political training for self-rule or nation building. When Belgium finally granted independence to the Congo in 1960, it was due more to international pressure than to nationalist movements.

In East Africa, the large numbers of white settlers vigorously resisted nationalist movements. In Kenya, for example, hostility between the majority Kikuyu tribe and white settlers who had appropriated much of the best farmland contributed to the Mau Mau uprisings, which resulted in thousands of deaths and the imprisonment of thousands of Kikuyu in detention camps. Jomo Kenyatta, a British-educated leader who was trained as an anthropologist and who had completed an anthropological study of the Kikuyu, led Kenya to independence in 1963 with his call for *Uhuru* ("freedom" in Swahili). In the colony of

Tanganyika, nationalist leader Julius Nyerere organized a mass political party insisting on self-rule. Tanganyika achieved independence in 1961 and in 1964 merged with Zanzibar to form the nation of Tanzania.

In South Africa, colonization eventually produced a system of racial stratification known as **apartheid**, in which different populations were assigned different statuses with varying social and political rights based on racial criteria. Dutch settlers, or Afrikaners, inaugurated the apartheid system when they came to power after World War II, and apartheid was the official policy of South Africa until the early 1990s.

Apartheid was based on white supremacy and assumed that the culture and values of nonwhite Africans rendered them incapable of social, political, and economic equality with whites. The government enforced this system through legal policies designed to bring about strict segregation among populations that were classified into different "races." The population was stratified into a hierarchy with whites, who numbered about 4.5 million, at the top. Approximately 60 percent of the whites were Afrikaners, and the rest were English-speaking. An intermediate category consisted of coloreds—the 2.6 million people of mixed European and African ancestry—and Asians, primarily immigrants from India and Malaysia, who numbered about 800,000.

At the bottom of the hierarchy were the approximately 21 million black South Africans, who were divided into four major ethnic groups: the Nguni, which includes the Xhosa, Zulu, Swazi, and Ndebele; the Sotho; the Venda; and the Tsonga (Crapanzano 1986). Important cultural and linguistic differences exist among these groups.

The policies of apartheid affected every aspect of life in South Africa. Blacks were segregated socially and forced into lower-paying—and frequently hazardous—occupations. They could not vote or take part in strikes, and they had to carry passes and observe curfews. In 1963, the South African government created a series of black states called Bantustan homelands, to which millions of black South Africans were forcibly removed.

Opposition to apartheid led to the emergence of various resistance and liberation movements, including the major resistance group, the African National Congress (ANC), formed in 1912. Although the ANC began as a moderate political organization calling for a unified South Africa representing all races in the government, it turned to armed struggle in response to ruthless suppression by the government. Many people were killed, and resistance leaders such as the late Nelson Mandela were imprisoned for many years.

Forced by international pressures, the government implemented some reforms in the 1980s and early 1990s,

abolishing laws that had once confined blacks to the rural homelands, forbade them to join legal trade unions, reserved skilled jobs for whites, and prohibited interracial marriages. Black nationalist groups and the clergy, led by Archbishop Desmond Tutu, negotiated with the government for other political reforms.

In April 1994, all South Africans participated in a national election for the first time, electing Nelson Mandela's ANC with a solid majority. Mandela, who became president, agreed to share power with whites during a five-year transitional period and tried to implement an economic blueprint for South Africa that included building new homes, electrification projects, free and mandatory education, and millions of new jobs. In June 1999, South Africa's parliament chose Thabo Mbeki and in 2009 Jacob Zuma as freely elected presidents. Zuma, also a member of the ANC, is striving to carry out some of Nelson Mandela's programs to develop a multiracial and multicultural democratic society (Clarke-Ekong 2012).

Nelson Mandela (1918–2013).

Explaining Revolution

In some of the countries of Latin America, Africa, and the Caribbean, revolutionary movements emerged as a response to the consequences of globalization and colonialism. Anthropologists have been examining the causes of revolution in Latin America and other non-Western countries. A **revolution** is a dramatic, fundamental change in a society's political economy brought about by the overthrow of the government and the restructuring of the economy. The classical understanding of revolution is derived from the writings of Karl Marx, who explained revolutions as the product of the struggle between the propertied and nonpropertied classes. For example, Marx predicted that the discontented proletariat would rise up against their bourgeois masters and overthrow capitalism (see Chapter 13). The revolutions in most non-Western countries, however, have not followed the Marxist model. Most countries in Latin America, Africa, and the Caribbean did not have a substantial proletariat and bourgeoisie. Rather, their revolutions were identified with the peasants.

Social scientists have found, however, that the poorest peasants did not organize and participate in peasant revolutions. People living in extreme poverty were too preoccupied with everyday subsistence to become politically active. Severe poverty tends to generate feelings of fatalism and political apathy. Generally, it is the middle class that leads and organizes revolutionary activity. The emerging middle class, which consisted of intellectuals and businesspeople, as well as some peasants, began to organize against the *hacendados* and the governing elite. For example, the Indians and peasants played a vital role in the Mexican Revolution of 1910–1920. At that time, 1 percent of the Mexican population owned 85 percent of the land, whereas 95 percent owned no land at all (Wolf 1969; Chirot 1986). Peasant leaders such as Emiliano Zapata, who called for the redistribution of land, carried out guerrilla campaigns against the *hacendados*. Although the revolution did not establish an egalitarian state, it did bring about the redistribution of land to many of the Indian communities.

In Latin American and Caribbean countries where power remained in the hands of the elites, revolutionary movements continued to develop throughout the twentieth century. From the Cuban Revolution of the 1950s through the Nicaraguan Revolution of the 1980s, peasants joined with other dissatisfied elements in overthrowing elite families. Countries such as El Salvador continue to experience peasant revolutions. The *hacienda* system produced tenant farmers, sharecroppers, and day laborers on large estates, a situation that will inevitably make peasant guerrillas a continuing presence in some Latin American nations.

Uneven Economic Development

21.4 Describe how Latin America, Africa, and the Caribbean countries are situated in the global economy today.

Throughout the twentieth and twenty-first centuries, the countries of Latin America, Africa, and the Caribbean have increasingly been incorporated into the global economy. These countries, however, differ in their degree of integration into this global economy. The legacy of colonialism stifled economic development by creating what is sometimes referred to as **monocultural dependency**, the reliance on a single major economic resource for the global economy. For example, in Latin America until recently, Brazil and Colombia depended on coffee exports, Bolivia on tin, Chile on copper, Peru on guano fertilizer, and Ecuador and the Central American Republics on bananas. In the Caribbean, Cuba and the Dominican Republic depended on sugar. African economies were subject to the same kinds of monocultural dependencies, producing cocoa, sugar, tea, coffee, or palm oil for the wealthy colonial powers. These nations found it difficult to break out of this monocultural dependency and develop more diversified resources for the international market. Other countries, such as Mexico, Venezuela, and Nigeria, have substantial oil resources, which has resulted in a more prominent position in the global economy. In some regions, small-scale industrialists produce manufactured goods alongside the crops and cattle of the plantations. In many cases, however, these industrialists have to depend on Europe and North America for their machinery. They are also discovering that the internal market for their products is extremely limited because their own societies lacked a consuming middle class. These economic conditions have resulted in peripheral and semiperipheral economies in Latin America, Africa, and the Caribbean.

Peripheral Societies

Anthropologists find that some countries in Latin America, Africa, and the Caribbean remain peripheral societies. The core societies developed these countries as export platforms—that is, nations whose economies concentrate almost exclusively on the export of raw materials and agricultural goods to the core nations. Most recently, through economic strategies dominated by the global neoliberalism policies (see Chapter 20) of the United States and other core countries, the World Bank, and the International Monetary Fund, elite families and local sponsors of capitalist developments have been favored in these peripheral countries. The elites have minimized restrictions on foreign investments and encouraged the production of cash crops for the export economy. The entire economy in these peripheral societies has been reorganized to produce profits and commodities for the core societies.

A Case Study: The United Fruit Company An example of the development of a peripheral country by a multinational corporation involves the U.S.-based United Fruit Company in Central America (Bucheli 2003). United Fruit obtained rights to thousands of acres of empty tropical lowlands in Central America for banana plantations. It enlisted local Indians, *mestizos*, and blacks from the Caribbean islands to work the plantations. Anthropologist Philippe Bourgois (1989b, 2003) studied one of the plantations operated by United Fruit, which expanded in 1987 to become the multinational Chiquita Brands. He investigated the archival records of United Fruit to determine how the North Americans managed the plantations.

Focusing on the Bocas Del Toro plantation in Panama, Bourgois observed the interactions among the various ethnic groups on the plantation. He discovered that the North Americans used race and ethnicity as a form of manipulation. He described the relationship between management and labor as based on a hierarchy in which each of the four ethnic groups—blacks, *mestizos*, Indians, and white North Americans—worked at different tasks. Indian workers were used to spread corrosive fertilizers and dangerous pesticides. The management rationale for this practice was that "the Indian skin is thicker, and they don't get sick." Indians were not paid a full wage because, according to superiors, "the Indian has low physiological needs…. The Indian only thinks of food; he has no other aspirations. He works to eat" (1989b:x).

Blacks worked in the maintenance department's repair shops and electrical division because, Bourgois was told, they are "crafty and don't like to sweat." The *mestizo* immigrants from Nicaragua were worked as hard as the Indians because they "are tough, have leathery skin [*cueron*], and aren't afraid of sweating under the hot sun" (1989b:xi). The white North Americans were the top management because "they are the smartest race on earth" (1989b:xi). Management used these stereotypes to classify the multiethnic workers, thereby segregating each ethnic group in a separate occupation and preventing the workers from uniting to organize labor unions. Bourgois found that racism, ethnicity, inequality, exploitation, and class conflict were all interrelated in a continuing process in the day-to-day realities of a banana plantation economy. In addition, as these people were drawn into this global economy to produce bananas for the export market, they abandoned their traditional peasant agriculture that had sustained them for many centuries. These United Fruit Company policies resulted in the underdevelopment of this Central

Photo of banana plantation workers for the United Fruit Company

American region into a peripheral monocultural dependent economy.

Semiperipheral Societies

A number of countries in Latin America and Africa, because of their valuable strategic resources, have emerged as semiperipheral societies. Two examples of peripheral societies that have become semiperipheral are Mexico and Nigeria.

Mexico Following a political revolution, Mexico gradually achieved stability under the control of a single political party, the Party of the Institutionalized Revolution (PRI). One-party rule, however, fostered corruption and inefficiency, resulting in personal enrichment for political officials. The government nationalized the key industries, including the important oil industry, which had been developed by foreign multinational corporations. Despite political authoritarianism and corruption, the Mexican economy continued to grow with gradual industrialization.

During the 1970s, as the industrial world experienced major oil shortages, the Mexican government implemented a policy of economic growth through expanded oil exports. International lending agencies and financial institutions in the core countries offered low-interest loans to stimulate industrial investment in Mexico. As a result, Mexico initially experienced an impressive growth rate of eight percent annually and moved from a peripheral to a semiperipheral nation.

This progress was short-lived, however. Surpluses on the petroleum market in the early 1980s led to falling prices for Mexican oil. Suddenly, Mexico faced difficulties in paying the interest on the loans that came due. The government had to borrow more money, at higher interest rates, to cover its international debt, which exceeded $100 billion. This excessive debt began to undermine government-sponsored development projects. Through neo-liberal economic policies foreign banks and lending organizations such as the International Monetary Fund demanded that the government limit its subsidies for social services, food, gasoline, and electricity. These policies led to inflation and a new austerity that adversely affected the standard of living of the poor and the middle classes of Mexico.

Another development influencing Mexico's economic status is the expansion of U.S. multinational corporations into Mexico. Since the 1980s, thousands of U.S. companies have established plants inside Mexico to take advantage of the low wage rates, lax environmental standards, and favorable tax rates there. These plants, known as *maquiladoras*, have drawn hundreds of thousands of peasants and workers, primarily women from rural communities, to expanding cities such as Juárez, a border city (Cravey 1998; Prieto 1997). This was partially a result of the North American Free Trade Agreement (NAFTA), which, in 1994, linked the economies of the United States, Canada, and Mexico to form a free trade zone and stimulate economic growth throughout the region. Among the companies that have established plants in Mexico are Fisher-Price, Ford, Emerson Electric, Zenith, Sara Lee, and General Electric.

Faced with mounting debts and unemployment and with pressures from the neoliberal global policies of the World Bank and the International Monetary Fund, the Mexican government did everything possible to attract multinational corporations. This was also seen as a solution to the problem of the migration of Mexican workers to the United States as illegal aliens. Until recently, the *maquiladoras* employed approximately 500,000 people and accounted for 17 percent of the Mexican economy. Although many *maquiladora* workers appeared satisfied with their jobs, the *maquiladoras* have created a number of problems for Mexico. Because they pay such low wages, they have not transformed workers into consumers, which has restricted their consumer and economic expansion. Other problems include occupational health hazards, the taxing of sewer systems and water supplies, and high turnover rates among workers. Currently, many of the multinationals based in Mexico are moving their companies to China, where low wages and attractive opportunities exist for corporations to lower their labor costs further and maximize their profits. This globalization process has been identified by ethnographers who do research in the area (Friedman 2006; Heyman 2001; Smart and Smart 2003).

Nigeria Under British rule, Nigeria developed an export economy centered on palm oil and peanut oil, lumber, cocoa, and metal ores. As in Mexico, after independence, a new commodity was discovered that had major consequences for Nigerian society—petroleum. The discovery of oil appeared to be an economic windfall for Nigeria, and the government saw it as the foundation for rapid economic growth. Many Africans from other nations immigrated to Nigeria in search of opportunity.

By the 1980s, more than 90 percent of Nigeria's revenues came from the sale of petroleum. These monies were used to fuel ambitious economic development schemes. As in Mexico, the Nigerian economy fell into disarray when oil prices dropped during the first half of the 1980s. This resulted in massive foreign debt and despite tremendous economic expansion during the 1970s, unemployment rose, and the Nigerian government expelled virtually all non-Nigerian workers and their families, forcing millions of Africans to return to their homelands, where the local economies could not absorb them.

By the late 1980s, cocoa was the only important Nigerian agricultural export. Oil production and the vast wealth that it represented for Nigeria had actually contributed to the decline of agriculture because the government invested heavily in the petroleum industry, neglecting the agricultural sector (Rossides 1990a). For some time, Nigeria was dependent on the core countries for imported foods. Following 1999, Nigeria has developed a democratic representative government that has tried to reform the political and economic system that was plagued with corruption. The new democratic system has brought about a turnaround in its economy. The gross domestic product (GDP) in Nigeria doubled between 2005 and 2007. In addition, while much of its oil wealth was spent on imported goods such as automobiles, motorcycles, and televisions, which fueled inflation and did not benefit an underdeveloped industrial sector, the agricultural sector is beginning to come back. The agricultural sector accounts for some 41 percent of the GDP. In 2004, Nigeria's annual per capita income was $1,000 and as of 2009, it grew to over $2,400, one of the highest figures of any African country, but far below that of many other semiperipheral societies (Infoplease.com 2010).

South Africa: An Economy in Transition

The country of South Africa, as described above, is going through a painful transition, following the abolition of apartheid, to a democratic society in which every citizen has equal voting rights. However, the legacy of apartheid is still apparent, with inequalities among the various groups that were classified as races within South Africa. The official black unemployment rate is more than six times that of the white minority population. More than 50 percent of the black population under 30 is unemployed. Black education, housing, and other material conditions are far behind those of the white population in South Africa. With the rise of the ANC and the election of Nelson Mandela, Thabo

Mbeki, and as of 2009, Jacob Zuma as presidents, a new direction is being forged to stimulate the South African economy.

The ANC is trying to develop opportunities to close the gap between the black and white populations in education, health, and economic prospects. The South African economy was in recession prior to the abolition of apartheid due to the international economic boycott and withdrawal of investments from its major corporations, which imposed a burden on the new leaders in their attempt to develop economic opportunities. The white population still holds the dominant positions within the South African economy, but a number of government policies are being enacted to further the education of black entrepreneurs so they can develop greater incentives for participation in economic ventures. In addition, the South African government since the end of apartheid has developed a policy to redistribute 30 percent of the land to the native black population over the next 10 years. However, many white farmers are resisting this land redistribution and only about eight percent of the land has been redistributed. The government is also publicizing its stability in order to attract foreign investment and venture capital into South Africa.

High crime rates, high unemployment rates, and the low educational levels of the black population continue to be the most pressing problems for the government in its efforts to maintain stability and economic growth in South Africa. The ANC government can take pride in accelerating the rate of education among the black population. It knows that more educated and literate South Africans mean more trained, skilled workers to take advantage of—and create—new economic opportunities for its future.

Ethnographic Studies

21.5 Discuss what anthropologists have learned about the peasantry in Latin America, Africa, and the Caribbean.

As Latin American, African, and Caribbean countries were drawn increasingly into the global economy, the status and lifestyles of the group called the peasantry were transformed. Anthropologists have been studying this transformation of the peasantry for many decades. For example, cultural anthropologists such as Robert Redfield (1930), Alfonso Villa Rojas (Redfield and Villa Rojas 1934), Oscar Lewis (1951), and Victor Goldkind (1965) had been studying peasant communities in Latin America and the Caribbean since the 1920s.

A problem in generalizing about behavior in rural communities of non-Western countries is the tremendous variation from one community to another, and as these countries became integrated into the global economy, the peasantry became more heterogeneous. This variation is due to the different historical processes that have influenced these communities. For example, research by Eric Wolf (1955b, 1959) led to some important insights regarding the different types of peasant communities in some regions of Latin America and Asia. Wolf distinguished between *closed peasant communities* and *open peasant communities*. The **closed peasant community** is made up of peasants who lived in the highland regions of Mexico and Guatemala or in more isolated areas. In these communities, a person had ascribed economic and social status, and there was a great deal of internal solidarity and homogeneity. The peasants produced primarily for subsistence, rather than for the world market. Many closed peasant communities in Central America, consisted of Indian refugees who attempted to isolate themselves from the disruptive effects of Spanish colonial policies. They held their land in common, but much of this land was marginal.

An **open peasant community** consisted primarily of peasants who were directly drawn into the world market. These communities were located in the lowland areas of Latin America. Land was owned individually, rather than being held in common. The open peasant community evolved in response to the intrusion of colonialism, which brought about the development of plantations and the production of commodities for the core societies. In open communities, some peasants sold as much as 90 to 100 percent of their produce to outside markets, which enabled them to achieve some economic stability; however, they were subject to the fluctuations in the global economy.

Most recently, because of the global consequences of the neoliberalist projects, including NAFTA, discussed earlier, peasant lives are being transformed. Responding to the demands of NAFTA, the Mexican government has been trying to reform the agricultural system. Mexico is flooded with imported crops such as corn from the United States. The peasants who own and farm small parcels of land cannot compete with the prices of U.S.-produced corn. In addition, the peasants who produce sugar cane cannot export to the United States because of a clause in the NAFTA agreement that protects the U.S. sugar industry. And the less costly U.S.-produced fructose corn syrup preferred by the soft-drink industry is also affecting the sugar cane producers in Mexico.

Anthropologist James McDonald has been studying small farmers in different areas of Mexico to determine the consequences of NAFTA and neoliberalist global policies (1997, 1999, 2001). Since the 1990s, after years of neglect, the Mexican government, influenced by NAFTA, has been attempting to privatize and introduce the "free market" into the agricultural economy. Small farmers were encouraged to reorganize and form larger producer groups to take advantage of the newer, high-tech agricultural methods and make their farms more competitive, productive, and efficient. McDonald focused upon a study of dairy farmers in Guanajuato and Michoacán, Mexico, who managed cows in the production of milk.

In Guanajuato, the size of the dairy ranches ranged from under 20 cows to as many as 200. Guanajuato has been successful in integrating its dairy farmers into the global economy. This region is close to the U.S. border and has a more open political system, and its economy is also dependent on remittances from migrants to the United States.

In Michoacán, the dairy farms were smaller, with an average of only 20 cows. Following NAFTA, large, private commercial dairies supported by state and federal governments reorganized these dairy farmers and gave them limited training to enhance productivity and efficiency. The result of these new organizations was to create alliances between private businesspeople and politicians, who began to displace the older rural elites. These new elites concentrated their wealth and authority and dictated the policies and economic conditions for the rural farmers. In some cases, even when these new entrepreneurs had failing businesses, they managed to maintain their rewards and privileges. Politicians benefited from these arrangements and supported policies and legislation that profited the entrepreneurs. McDonald concludes that with further privatization and the new free-market policies in Mexico, extensive economic inequalities, political corruption, and continuing dislocations of the small independent farmer are bound to occur.

As a result of his ethnographic research on neoliberalist policies in rural Mexico, McDonald began to notice the cultural effects of the drug-trade and the narco-economy and its consequences in this region (2009). In using an approach to "globalization from below," he began to observe the effects of the narco-economy and new patterns of economic, social, and political developments in the rural communities. McDonald investigated these trends in one small agricultural town of about 10,000 with the pseudonym Buenavista where extraordinary forms of urban-oriented consumer culture had developed, characterized by large ostentatious houses sometimes costing $300,000 or more, new massive warehouses, upscale apartment buildings, high-stakes gambling in cockfights, new malls, spas, cybercafés, and the emergence of new forms of social and capital privileges that challenged and subverted older hierarchies of status and power. Local farmers and others in the community began to notice how narco-money fueled new developments and provided a huge effect, directly and indirectly, on jobs and the economy in transportation, banking, communications, construction, and other services. These new forms of consumption were not for the dairy farmer clientele, but were clearly aimed at those with new disposable income and new urban-oriented tastes and preferences.

McDonald observed how the narco-economy penetrated the local rural economy through repatriation of young male migrants who participated in the drug-trafficking networks across the U.S. border and then returned to buy farmland in Buenavista and become farmers, which was the traditional means of acquiring status and legitimacy in the rural communities. These farmers tapped into the traditional networks of *caciques* (political bosses) or patronage systems to take advantage of resources that helped develop their investments. McDonald placed these local developments in the context of the increasing violence and death tolls associated with the drug cartels such as *La Familia* that have established parallel political systems in Mexico, eroding state legitimacy, and the global processes influencing these conditions, such as the tremendous demand for illegal drugs based in the United States, rises in rates of local drug addiction, and NAFTA neoliberal policies. McDonald's ethnographic studies indicate that the local, rural, communities and towns of border regions have developed problematic economic and political conditions in relationship to neoliberal projects and global processes that have resulted in major transformations for rural Mexico.

African Peasants: A Unique Phenomenon?

Anthropologists David Brokensha and Charles Erasmus (1969) maintained that rural Africans were not typical peasants because of the distinctive nature of precolonial African states. They suggested that most precolonial states had very limited control over their populations and that Africans were able to retain control over their land and their economic production. Other anthropologists suggested that sub-Saharan Africans could not be characterized as peasants because in many cases they were still horticulturalists (Goldschmidt and Kunkel 1971).

Anthropologists Godfrey Wilson and Max Gluckman of the Rhodes-Livingstone Institute in southern Africa engaged in detailed studies of African society. They distinguished six types of regions based upon an array of factors, such as degree of urbanization and industrialization, relative importance of subsistence and cash cropping, and nature of the work force. They also examined such related phenomena as rural-to-urban migration, depopulation, unionization, and prevailing political issues. These and other studies helped produce an improved understanding of how the global economy directly affected the African people (Vincent 2002).

Most anthropologists now agree that the general term *peasant* does not apply to the diverse peoples found in the African agricultural or rural countryside. In some regions, there were rural peoples who could be designated "peasants," whereas in other regions the term was not applicable. The historical experience of Africa was much different from that of medieval Europe, Latin America, or Asia. Environmental, economic, and political circumstances varied from region to region, involving different types of societal adaptations. In addition, the presence of so many colonial powers in Africa created greater diversity than was the case in Latin America, which was colonized almost exclusively by the Spanish and Portuguese. Thus, the current political economy of Africa is more heterogeneous than that of many other regions.

Social Structure

21.6 Describe the characteristics of family and gender relationships in Latin America, Africa, and the Caribbean.

Ethnographic studies have illuminated aspects of the social structure, including family and gender relations, of various countries of Latin America, Africa, and the Caribbean. As in most rural agricultural societies, the traditional family unit was an extended family that provided aid for people living in marginal subsistence conditions. But with the growth of industry and wage labor and with the redistribution of land from communities to individuals, many large extended families were forced to break up. Thus, the typical family in many urban areas today is the nuclear family. Ethnographers, however, have found some unique features of kinship and social structure in these countries.

Latin American Social Relationships

Many traditional peasant communities maintain **fictive kinship ties**—that is, *extrafamilial* social ties that provide mutual-aid work groups for the planting and harvesting of crops and for other economic and political activities. George Foster described one type of fictive kinship tie in Mexican peasant communities known as the **dyadic contract**, a reciprocal exchange arrangement between two individuals (a dyad). According to Foster (1967), to compensate for the lack of voluntary organizations or corporate groups beyond the nuclear family in these communities, males and females establish dyadic contracts to exchange labor, goods, and other needed services. These extra-kin social ties help sustain peasants who are vulnerable to the new demands of the unpredictable global market economy. Dyadic contracts can be established with people of equal or different status or with supernatural beings such as Jesus, the Virgin Mary, and the saints. People develop dyadic contracts with these supernatural sources in hopes of inducing specific spiritual and material benefits. They care for the shrines of Jesus, the Virgin Mary, and the saints to demonstrate their loyalty and obedience.

Dyadic contracts between individuals of equal status are based on generalized reciprocal exchanges: continuing exchanges that are not short-term, but rather bind two people in cooperative relationships for many years. This is an attempt to develop the older forms of the moral economy that existed prior to globalization.

The dyadic contracts between people of unequal status, known as **patron-client ties**, are informal contracts between peasant villagers and nonvillagers (including supernatural beings). The patron is an individual who combines status, power, influence, and authority over the client. Patrons include politicians, government employees, town or city friends, and local priests.

One type of dyadic contract found in Latin America is known as the *compadrazgo*, associated with the rite of passage of baptism and Catholicism. Cultural anthropologists have investigated *compadrazgo* relationships extensively (Redfield 1930; Wolf and Mintz 1950; Foster 1967). This institution, brought to the Americas with Catholicism, has become an integral aspect of Latin American social relationships. During the colonial period, the *hacendado* often served as godparent to the children of peons. The result was a network of patron-client ties involving mutual obligations and responsibilities. The godparent had to furnish aid in times of distress such as illness or famine. In return, the peon had to be absolutely loyal and obedient to the *hacendado*.

The *compadrazgo* system eventually spread throughout rural and urban areas. Every individual has a *padrino* (godfather) and *madrina* (godmother) who are sponsors at baptismal rituals. The sponsors become the co-parents (*compadres, comadres*) of the child (Davila 1971; Romanucci-Ross 1973). The most important social relationship is the one between the *compadres* and the parents, who ideally will assist one another in any way possible. The contemporary *compadrazgo* is a remarkably flexible extra-kin relationship that sometimes reaches across class lines to help rural peoples cope with the tensions and anxieties of globalization and modern life in Latin America.

Machismo Gender relationships in Latin America have been strongly influenced by the Spanish and Portuguese colonial experience. The basic traditional values affecting gender relations are known as *machismo*, the explicit code for the behavior of Latin American males. As a part of this code, the "true man" (*macho*) is supposed to be courageous, sexually virile, aggressive, and superior to women. A woman, in contrast, is supposed to be passive, sexually conservative and faithful, obedient, and completely devoted to her mate. These ideals and values have affected gender relations throughout Latin America.

Yet, many cultural anthropologists who have done research in Latin American peasant communities have observed that the actual behaviors of males and females do not conform completely to the ideals of *machismo*. In an early study Oscar Lewis observed that in Tepoztlán,

The baptism of a child in Mexico (Catholic)

husbands were not the dominant authoritarian figures in the family that they wanted to be, and wives were not completely submissive (1951). Instead, in many families, he found conflict between the spouses over authority. Most families tended to follow a middle course. The wife did little to challenge the authority of her husband, and the husband was not too overbearing toward his wife. In a recent study, anthropologists Adriana Manago and Patricia Greenfield found that rural Mayan women in Chiapas, Mexico were promoting gender equality and developing an indigenous form of feminism while taking a critical stance towards traditional patriarchy (2011). It appears that challenges to patriarchy are trends that are influencing gender relations throughout Latin America.

African Social Relationships

Because many African societies are composed of horticulturalist or pastoralist peoples in transition to different forms of socioeconomic status, their social organization largely centers on lineages and extended families. But as in other regions of the world, as globalization, industrialization, and the commercialization of agriculture develop, social organization inevitably changes, and lineages and extended families are being transformed.

As seen in Chapter 17, the anthropologist George Murdock suggested that all families worldwide can be reduced to the nuclear family. Murdock (1949) had argued that the extended family, or polygynous African family, really consists of multiple nuclear families with a common husband and father. However, some cultural anthropologists have challenged Murdock with respect to the African family. Niara Sudarkasa (1989), an anthropologist who

did ethnographic research on the Yoruba and other West African groups, saw this Murdockian hypothesis as a distortion of the basic elements of the African family. She argued that the male-female dyad and offspring do not perform the basic functions of the family in African society. That is, the nuclear family is not the unit of economic production or consumption, not the unit of socialization, and is not the unit that provides emotional support. A typical African family, such as that of the Yoruba, consists of a group of brothers, their wives, their adult sons and grandsons and their wives, and any unmarried children. Marriages usually are polygynous, and the husband has a room separate from his wives. Every wife has a separate domain, with her own cooking utensils and other furnishings. Co-wives depend on the senior wife to be a companion and confidante. Sudarkasa concluded that the nuclear family is not the basic "building block" of the African family. She further maintained that Western cultural anthropologists misunderstand and distort the practice of polygyny in African society. She noted that most of the anthropological literature emphasizes the negative characteristics of polygyny, such as rivalry and discord among co-wives. Her research demonstrated that co-wives develop important emotional and social bonds that create a nurturing environment for both co-wives and children.

Although not all anthropologists have accepted Sudarkasa's views, most concur that there are many variations of the African family, depending on sociocultural conditions. In the urban areas of Africa, the extended family and polygyny are declining in influence. Several factors are responsible for these changes. As employment opportunities develop outside

A Yoruban man and family members

agriculture, prompting migration from rural to urban areas, extended family ties break down. Wage employment in mines and industrial firms tends to disrupt extended families that are tied to agricultural land. In addition, many African governments often promote "modern" family and marriage practices to alter traditional ways of behavior, which they perceive as impeding economic development. To some extent, the elites of these societies accept Western conceptions of the family, romantic love, and monogamy.

Gender in Africa   Most African societies tend to be patriarchal, placing women in a subordinate status. In 1988, for example, women provided approximately 60 to 80 percent of the household food needs in many parts of Africa (Smith-Ivan 1988). They often worked 10 to 12 hours a day, and in many instances, their workload increased after colonization and independence. As colonial regimes forced males to migrate to mines for employment, women were forced to assume the major subsistence roles for the family. Because their husbands' wages were meager, women had to grow and collect food for their families. In most cases, the lack of formal education prevented females from entering the wage-labor economy, so they were unable to buy property and send their children to school.

Despite providing much of the agricultural labor and household food needs, women in rural Africa tend to be the poorest people on the world's poorest continent. The European colonial powers often allocated land to males, but African women were given rights to land only through their relationship to males (Henn 1984; Tandon 1988). This tended to decrease the status of females in African society. Males were considered the head of the household and earned income, whereas females were viewed as the providers of the family's social needs (such as childcare) and the producers of the future labor force. Following independence, males were given access to credit, training, and new skills to improve agricultural production. Because females did not have collateral through landownership, they were denied the credit and training needed for commercialized agriculture.

The globalization of the economy and rural villages has also influenced the emergence of the major AIDS crisis in Africa. For example, this deadly disease is spread as African males migrate long distances from their rural communities in search of job opportunities in trucking. These men have contact with women prostitutes, who are also drawn into these jobs to support new lifestyles and care for their families. The males return to their communities infected with the HIV virus and infect their wives, resulting in more health problems for women throughout Africa. The cost of drugs to contain this heterosexual spread of HIV appears to be prohibitive in these developing rural communities (Robbins 2013).

Urban Women   African women in the urban regions often receive a formal education and tend to have more independence than do rural women. In West Africa, where females have traditionally been employed in urban markets, some educated women have become prominent self-employed entrepreneurs. In general, however, even highly educated women are confined to the service sector of the urban economy, working in clerical or secretarial occupations (Robertson 1984; Smith-Ivan 1988). Urban women who are without formal education and who lack the support of extended families and village communities are especially vulnerable to exploitation and alienation. Without extended family members to assist with childcare, women often are restricted to unskilled, low-wage occupations, such as making clothing, that require them to remain at home.

Because South Africa was largely a settler colony and possesses a strong economy, the role of women there is somewhat different from that in other parts of Africa. Some African women are employed as domestics in white homes or as clerical and textile workers in the industrial sector. Despite their valuable contribution to these sectors of the economy, however, they earn 20 percent less than the minimum wage (Smith-Ivan 1988; Ramsey 2010).

A rural African woman with child in Burkina Faso.

One positive development in many African countries is the increasing attention given to women. The pivotal role of women in agriculture and the urban areas is increasingly being recognized and supported by various governments. Prenatal and health care for mothers and babies has improved. New cooperatives for women in rural agriculture and improvements for women working in factories have been established by government policies. Women are also beginning to play a more important role in politics. Yet, these advances could be subject to economic declines and political instability (Ramsey 2010). Thus, the role of women in both rural and urban Africa depends on the adjustment to the new demands and opportunities of globalization.

Patterns of Ethnicity

21.7 Discuss the issues related to ethnicity in Latin America, Africa, and the Caribbean.

As a result of European conquest and colonization, the ethnicity of Latin America, Africa, and the Caribbean became increasingly diverse and heterogeneous.

Ethnicity in Latin America

In Latin America, a small minority of Spanish and Portuguese rulers, never exceeding five percent of the total population, dominated the native population. During the colonial period, these Europeans established a racially based hierarchy that emphasized "the whiter, the better." Following the conquest, people born in Spain and Portugal went to Latin America to improve their social status. The Europeans eventually intermarried or had illicit relationships with native Indian women. The offspring of these interrelationships were called *mestizos*, a new social class in Latin America. After three centuries, the *mestizo* population grew to become the majority in Latin America, representing approximately 60 percent of the population. In addition, in Brazil and the Caribbean, the intermarriages of Africans and Europeans produced a group known as *mulattos*.

Gradually, in certain regions of Latin America and the Caribbean, the new populations of *mestizos* and *mulattos* began to outnumber the indigenous peoples. The relative populations of these different groups vary from region to region. For example, only about 10 percent of the Mexican population speaks an Indian language, as opposed to about 50 percent in Guatemala, which is more geographically isolated. Brazil's population is about 11 percent black and 33 percent *mulatto*. Areas in Bolivia, Peru, and Ecuador that are farther from the commercial coastal regions are primarily *mestizo* and Indian; only 10 percent of their populations are European or white. In contrast, in the coastal areas of Argentina and Uruguay, the European component of the population is more prominent.

In countries such as Mexico and Guatemala, the Indian population as a minority has faced obstacles in attaining economic and political opportunities. The *indios* (Indian) population is the most likely to live in poverty, have poor educational opportunities, work menial jobs, and suffer from poor health conditions. Ethnographers have found that one of the only routes to upward social and economic mobility for the Indian population was **assimilation**, the adoption of the culture and language of the dominant group in society (Nash 1989). Some Indians did assimilate by adopting the language, clothing, and culture of the dominant Spanish majority and thereby becoming *ladino*. The ethnic distinction between a *ladino* and an Indian was based on a cultural boundary. However, currently many Indians have tried to maintain their ethnic distinctiveness and have recently been involved in asserting their Indian ethnic identity in an attempt to attain economic and political rights.

For example, in the rain forest of southern Mexico, especially in the province of Chiapas, the Mayan Indians have been mobilized politically into what is referred to as the Zapatista movement. In 1994, after NAFTA was signed by the United States, Mexico, and Canada, the Zapatista movement, named after Emiliano Zapata (the famous Mexican revolutionary of 1910), began using guerilla warfare tactics against Mexican government forces to attain political and economic rights or autonomy from the government. In this area, the Mayan Indian population is dominated economically and politically by a wealthy group of landowners and ranchers. Traditionally, the Mayan Indians had a certain amount of communal land, or *ejidos*, that they could share. In the 1980s, in order to encourage private enterprise and capitalism in agriculture, the Mexican government declared that *ejido* land could be sold. The Maya lost their communal land, which they had been using for their basic subsistence. In addition, the Maya viewed NAFTA as a threat to their local corn economy because the North American U.S. corporate agricultural system would flood the market with cheap corn. For these various reasons, the Zapatistas, led by a mysterious charismatic figure known as Subcomandante Marcos, declared war on the Mexican government. This movement has drawn on the traditional ethnic roots of the Maya as a means of mobilizing a political struggle against a dominant majority in the midst of globalization (Nash 1997). A Mayan woman leader, Major Ana Maria, led an assault on the capital of San Cristobol de la Casas. The Mexican government and military responded with 15,000 troops to mercilessly hunt down the Zapatistas in the rain forest. However, many citizens of Mexico began to express sympathy with the Zapatistas, so the Mexican government called off its troops.

Although most of the violence erupted during the early phase of this Zapatista movement, the ethnic resistance of these Mayan people persists, creating tensions between them and the Mexican government. The Zapatista movement was not based on traditional Marxist or Maoist revolutionary ideology, but on a desire to get land back that had been taken from them by the government. Subcomandante Marcos, an educated man who was not indigenous to the area, used the Internet and global media to spread highly poetic and literary narratives to convince the international community that the Maya were not out to grab power, but rather to gain their rights back from the Mexican government. In 2003, the Zapatistas created a number of autonomous municipalities with indigenous representatives who feature a moral and ethical government without corruption and exploitation. Through these institutions, they have developed elementary schools to increase literacy, healthcare facilities, shoe and textile businesses, and transportation and consumer cooperatives. Although this was a local indigenous political movement, it had a global impact, as protestors against some of the negative aspects of globalization wore signs that said, "We are all Zapatistas" in Seattle, Prague, Quebec, and Cancun, Mexico. Indigenous movements can be transformed by global developments, but they can also result in new forms of globalization through the international media available today.

The Zapatista movement is one aspect of the process of *indigenization* that is transforming many Latin American countries. Most of the Indian groups have adopted the term *indigena* rather than *indios*, which was a Spanish colonial term. This process of *indigenization* refers to how the native *indigena* populations of countries like Guatemala, Ecuador, Peru, Venezuela, Brazil, Argentina, Mexico, Nicaragua, and Colombia are mobilizing politically and dramatically influencing the politics and culture of these regions (Jackson and Warren 2005). Indigenous groups that were previously viewed as *mestizo* or mixed have begun to emphasize their *indigena* ethnic identity and have mobilized political movements in these different countries. The country of Brazil has recognized more than 30 different indigenous groups in Northeast Brazil, which formerly was viewed as a mixed ethnic region. Andean communities in Ecuador and Peru have asserted their Amerindian ethnic identity to organize political movements.

Anthropologist Livia Stone has been following a recent development of political activism growing out of the *indigena* movements in Chiapas, Mexico (2013). This transnational activist movement is known as *compañerismo*, a general term of solidarity used to address audiences in Mexico and Latin America. This *compañerismo* movement is devoted to developing autonomous self-governing political communities for people outside the control of the Mexican government and multinational corporations. The *compañerismo* movement draws on the Zapatista model of self-government and antiglobalization to criticize the corruption of politicians who pass legislation to enable multinational corporations to take advantage of rural peoples. This movement has been attracting more middle class and environmentalist groups, feminists, and other activists in Latin America. Unlike earlier revolutionary movements in Latin America, these *compañerismo* activists are not organizing to take over the state, but rather want to build communities that are outside of both the state and multinational corporations. This movement will undoubtedly influence the political landscape in Latin America in the future.

Various transnational and global movements such as NGO and United Nations multicultural policies that emphasized the political rights of these indigenous Amerindian communities and criticized older forms of assimilation have stimulated and transformed the politics in these Latin American countries. For example, Evos Morales, who is an indigenous Aymara Amerindian of Bolivia, was elected president of Bolivia in 2006 as a result of the grass-roots indigenous movements. The late Hugo Chavez of Venezuela drew on his partial Amerindian ethnic identity to gain political support. Both of these leaders emphasized their Amerindian identity to strengthen their political movements against the perceived "white" (European) establishment. However, the opposition leaders in some of these countries criticize the indigenous political movements of promoting racism and class/ethnic conflict (Jackson and Warren 2005). Although these indigenous movements have tended to foster a more democratic, grass-roots orientation in Latin America, it remains to be seen whether they will promote more political divisiveness and ethnic fragmentation.

Ethnicity in Africa

In Africa, the term *tribe* has negative connotations and is seldom used. Consequently, peoples of different language groups and cultures refer to themselves as "ethnic groups." Anthropologist Herbert Lewis (1992) estimated that there are no fewer than 1,000 distinct ethnic groups among the more than 50 countries in Africa. As independence movements spread, many people hoped that the new African nations would develop as plural societies in which diverse ethnic groups would share power and tolerate cultural differences. These plural societies, however, generally have not developed. Anthropologists find that political parties are linked with specific ethnic groups. As one ethnic group assumes power, it usually forms a one-party state and establishes a military government that dominates other groups. This has become one of the major problems in African societies.

One country that has been the subject of much ethnographic research on ethnic relationships is Nigeria. The resolution of ethnic problems in Nigeria may provide a model for other African countries. Nigeria is the most populous nation of Africa, with about 150 million people, consisting of many different ethnic groups. Approximately 300 different languages are recognized by the Nigerian government. The three major ethnic divisions, which make up two-thirds of the Nigerian population, are the Yoruba, the Hausa, and the Igbo (Ibo).

More than 12 million Yoruba live in the southwest region of Nigeria and across its borders in neighboring Benin. The Yoruba were the most highly organized precolonial urban people in West Africa. The majority of the Yoruba were subsistence farmers. The men traditionally supplemented their diet through hunting and fishing.

British colonialism changed the political economy of Nigeria. As a result of colonization commercialized agriculture that emphasized cocoa production, railroads, automobiles, new manufactured goods, Christian churches and schools, and industry entered Yoruban society. One-fifth of the people live in the urban areas of Nigeria such as Lagos and Ibadan. Wage employment and industrialization are rapidly transforming the society of the Yoruba, creating new class structures and integrating

their traditional kingdom into the Nigerian nation and the global economy.

To the north of the Yoruba live the Hausa, who number about 20 million. Like the Yoruba, the Hausa had developed large urban areas with extensive trade routes. Hausa cities had elaborate markets that offered different types of foodstuffs and crafts produced by farmers and craftspeople. British anthropologist M. G. Smith (1965) pioneered extensive ethnographic and historical research on Hausa society.

The Hausa made their home in a savanna where the farmers cultivated various crops and maintained cattle for trade and consumption. Hausa craftspeople smelted iron and crafted iron tools for farming, sewing, working leather, and hunting. As with the Yoruba, most Hausa peasants were engaged in subsistence agriculture, but cash crops such as cotton and peanuts were introduced by the British and changed the nature of economic production and consumption.

The third major ethnic group in Nigeria is the Igbo people of the southeastern region. Igbo anthropologist Victor Uchendu (1965) completed a major ethnographic study of the Igbo. His descriptions of Igbo society are extremely insightful because he blends an anthropological focus with an insider's perspective.

Most of the Igbo were primarily root-crop subsistence farmers who grew yams, cassava, and taro. Unlike some of the other West African peoples in the area, both Igbo males and females were engaged in agricultural production. Like most other traditional West African societies, the Igbo used some of their agricultural production for exchanges within the villages and trade outside the region. Women dominated trade in the rural village markets, whereas men dominated trade with other regions.

Uchendu described the traditional political system of the Igbo as unique. Igbo villages were essentially autonomous. At the village level, a form of direct democracy operated in which all adult males participated in decision making. Leadership was exercised by male and female officeholders who had developed power and influence gradually. Executive, legislative, and judicial functions were divided among leaders, lineages, and age-grade associations.

After Nigeria became independent in 1960, it was confronted with the types of ethnic problems that beset many other African nations. The British had drawn political boundaries without respect to the traditional territorial areas of indigenous kingdoms or ethnic groups. For example, the Yoruba live in both Benin and Nigeria, and the Hausa reside in both Niger and Nigeria. Consequently, when Nigeria achieved independence, the presence of various ethnic groups inhibited the political unification of the new nation. Most of the Hausa, Igbo, and Yoruba identified with their own ethnic groups and territories.

Anthropologist Abner Cohen, who examined the role of ethnicity and political conflict in Nigeria, focused on Hausa traders in the Yoruban city of Ibadan. Cohen (1969, 1974) described how ethnic distinctions between the Hausa and Yoruba became the basis of political and economic competition. Cohen used the term *retribalization* to refer to the Hausa strategy of using ethnic affiliations as an informal network for economic and political purposes. These networks were, in turn, used to extend and coordinate Hausa cattle-trading activities in Ibadan. Cohen's ethnographic research in Ibadan has become a model for analyzing ethnic trends in urban areas throughout the world. Cohen demonstrated how ethnic processes and the meaningful cultural symbols used by ethnic groups can mobilize political and economic behavior. These cultural symbols aided ethnic groups in Nigeria in their struggle to attain a decent livelihood and political power in the urban communities. This process, however, generated tensions among the various groups.

Nigeria's multicultural society was racked by interethnic, religious, and political competition and conflict. In the mid-1960s, these conflicts erupted into civil war. Because the Igbo people had had no historical experience with a centralized state, they resented the imposition of political authority over them. This led to conflict among the Igbo, the Yoruba, and the Hausa. Following the collapse of a civilian government in the 1960s, the Igbo were attacked and massacred in northern Nigeria. The Igbo fled as refugees from the north and called for secession from Nigeria. In 1967, under Igbo leadership, eastern Nigeria seceded and proclaimed itself the independent Republic of Biafra. The result was a civil war in which non-African powers assisted both sides. After three years of bitter fighting and a loss of about two million people, Biafra was defeated, and the Igbo were reincorporated into Nigeria.

Under a series of military-dominated regimes, Nigeria has succeeded in healing the worst wounds of its civil war. One strategy was to incorporate all ethnic and religious groups into the military leadership. In addition, the country was carved into 19 states, the boundaries of which cut through Yoruba, Hausa, and Igbo territories. This encouraged the development of multiethnic coalitions and a federalist political system (Krabacher, Kalipeni, Layachi 2011).

However, presently Nigeria faces new forms of political terrorism and violence perpetuated by groups such as Boko Haram that continue to be problematic. Anthropologist Conerly Casey has been doing ethnographic research for eight years among doctors and healers in ethnically and religiously diverse communities in northern Nigeria, including interviews with young people who had experienced and participated in various forms of violence (2014). She indicates that Muslim youth gangs that participate in movements to enforce *shari'a* criminal codes in northern Nigeria have tribal warrior traditions that influence their behavior. These youth face high rates of inflation and political instability. Frequently, they are mobilized by political and religious leaders to participate in movements framed as "ethnic," "religious," or "regional" conflicts, and to steal or traffic drugs, women, and arms. She indicates that the Boko Haram terrorist group that recently kidnapped more than 300 young girls and used extreme violence in northern Nigeria needs to be understood within this context of these movements and the various Muslim youth gangs.

Currently, ethnic loyalties and religious identities appear to be very powerful bases for social and political life in Africa. This has produced the potential for political disintegration in many African states. Like other African countries, Nigerians hope that when ethnic and religious factions develop new social ties based on education, class backgrounds, and new forms of nationalism, older forms of association will weaken. Nation-building projects that unify different ethnic groups remain the most formidable challenge facing Nigeria and other African countries.

More recently, Rwanda, another African country, has experienced Africa's worst attempted genocide in modern times and is still recovering from the shock. The Rwandan case is particularly alarming because the groups in conflict speak the same language and share national territory and traditions. The country has been beset by ethnic tension associated with the traditionally unequal relationship between the dominant Tutsi minority and the majority Hutus. Major conflicts began when Belgian colonial rulers gave the Tutsi a monopoly of state power (Middleton 2000). As we have seen elsewhere in the world, using ethnicity as a political weapon is a product of modern politics that often reflects a real or imagined inequity of resource distribution and allocation (Bowen 2001; Clarke-Ekong 2012; Middleton 2000).

Before the modern era, some Africans did consider themselves Hutu or Tutsi, Nuer or Zande, but these labels were not the characteristic of everyday identity. A woman living in Rwanda drew her identity from where she was born, from her lineage and in-laws, and from her wealth. Tribal or ethnic identity was rarely important in everyday life and could change as people moved over vast areas in pursuit of trade or new lands. Conflicts were more often within tribal categories than between them, as people fought over sources of water, farmland, or grazing rights.

In Rwanda and Burundi, German and Belgian colonizers admired the taller people called Tutsis, who formed a small minority in both colonies. The Belgians gave the Tutsis, the minority group, privileged access to education and jobs and even instituted a minimum height requirement for entrance to college. To enable colonial officials to distinguish Tutsi from non-Tutsi, everyone was required to carry identity cards with tribal labels. Fortunately, people cannot be forced "racially" into the neat compartments that this requirement suggests. Many Hutus are tall and many Tutsis are short; furthermore, many Hutus and Tutsis had intermarried to such an extent that they were not easily distinguished physically (nor are they today). They spoke the same language and carried out the same religious practices. In most regions of the colonies, the categories became economic labels: Poor Tutsis became Hutus, and economically successful Hutus became Tutsis. Where the labels *Hutu* and *Tutsi* had not been much used, patrilineal descent groups with lots of cattle were simply labeled *Tutsi*, and the poorer lineages were labeled *Hutu*. Colonial discrimination against Hutus created what had never existed before: a sense of collective Hutu identity, a Hutu cause. In the late 1950s, Hutus began to rebel against Tutsi rule (encouraged by Europeans on their way out) and then created an independent, Hutu-dominated state in Rwanda; this state then gave rise to Tutsi resentments and to the creation of a Tutsi rebel army, the Rwandan Patriotic Front.

In Rwanda, the continuing slaughter stemmed from efforts by the dictator-president Juvenal Habyarimana to wipe out his political opposition, Hutu as well as Tutsi. In 1990–1991, Habyarimana began to assemble armed gangs into a militia called Interahamwe. The militia carried out its first massacre of a village in March 1992, and in 1993, it systematically began to kill Hutu moderates and Tutsis (Bowen 2001; Clarke-Ekong 2012).

Paul Kagame, the current president of Rwanda, grew up in Uganda, where his Tutsi parents fled to escape Hutu violence. He has attempted to play down any ethnic agenda in Rwanda, presenting himself as a Rwandan and not a Tutsi. Like other African countries, Rwanda is attempting to forge a national identity that will supersede any ethnic identity (Clarke-Ekong 2012). Anthropologist Jennie Burnet has been doing current ethnographic work on women and other communities in Rwanda to gain an understanding of the traumatic consequences of the genocide and ethnic tensions within this African country (2006, 2008). It is hoped that her ethnographic work will help provide insight into the dilemmas so that these women and other ethnic groups will resolve their ethnic tensions in the future.

Ethnicity in the Caribbean

Ethnicity in the Caribbean is a complex, diverse mixture of imported African slaves, East Indian laborers, and various Europeans. One conventional ethnic classification is based upon skin color, especially on the distinction between black and brown. Beginning with the illicit offspring of European whites and slave women, a category of *mulattoes* began to gain certain advantages. At present, "brown" on

many Caribbean islands such as Jamaica is synonymous with middle class, and these people are associated with the professional occupations (Eriksen 1993; Yelvington 2001; Kephart 2012).

After the arrival of East Indians in the Caribbean, new ethnic relations began to develop. In contrast to the blacks, East Indians were free to develop their own ethnic communities. Thus, in the Caribbean, the East Indian descendants are divided among different linguistic and cultural groups. There are Hindu and Muslim ethnic communities, as well as Tamil and other language communities. Many of the Indians have used these ethnic ties to form effective networks to enhance their professional careers. In response to the large Indian communities on islands such as Trinidad, the black community has begun to strengthen its own ethnic identity. The blacks have begun to develop stereotypes, such as the "backward" Indian communities and the "progressive" Europeanized black communities. Many of the black, brown, and Indian communities have been revitalizing their own ethnic identities in the context of globalization within the Caribbean region.

Urban Anthropology

21.8 Discuss how urbanization has influenced Latin America, Africa, and the Caribbean.

Urban anthropologists who have done research on the globalizing and transnational changes occurring in Latin America, Africa, and the Caribbean have helped improve our understanding of issues such as poverty and rural-to-urban migration (Smart and Smart 2003; Hannerz 1992). These topics are of vital interest to government officials and urban planners, economists and development technicians, and international agencies. Population growth and urbanization in underdeveloped non-Western nations have posed global problems that urgently need to be resolved. Urban anthropologists working in these regions are providing data that can be used to help alleviate these global problems.

The mass movement of people from rural areas to the cities is a major trend in these regions. Between 1950 and 1980, the proportion of the population living in urban areas increased from 41 to 65 percent. Cities such as Mexico City, Rio de Janeiro (Brazil), Buenos Aires (Argentina), San Juan (Puerto Rico), and Lagos (Nigeria) are among the largest metropolitan areas in the world. For example, it is predicted that by 2015, the population of Mexico City will exceed 20 million (World Book Online Infofinder 2014). The rate of population growth and urbanization in these societies is much higher than in the postindustrial societies discussed in Chapter 15.

Much of this urban growth is due to internal migration. Migrants are pushed away from the countryside by population growth, poverty, lack of opportunity, and the absence of land reform. They are pulled to the city by the prospects of regular employment, education and medical care for their children, and the excitement of urban life. Rapid urbanization has led to the development of illegal squatter settlements, or high-density shantytowns, in and just outside urban areas. Shantytowns provide homes for the impoverished and unskilled migrants. Anthropologists have found that in some of these settlements, some people are optimistic about finding work and improving their living conditions. In the shantytowns, the new migrants take advantage of city services such as running water, transportation, and electricity. However, in the worst slums in non-Western cities, many of these new migrants are so poor that they are forced to live in the streets.

Some anthropologists have focused their research on the poverty conditions of many of the non-Western urban centers. One well-known pioneer is Oscar Lewis, who studied families of slum dwellers in Mexico City (1961) and in San Juan and New York (1966). From these studies and from other evidence collected by urban anthropologists, Lewis concluded that the cultural values of the slum dwellers inhibited them from pursuing economic opportunities. He referred to these values as the **culture of poverty**.

Lewis described the people who maintained this culture of poverty as having a sense of fatalism, apathy, and hopelessness with respect to aspirations for economic or social mobility. They tended to be suspicious and fearful, disdained authority, and did not plan for the future. Alcoholism, violence, and unstable marriages were common. According to Lewis, these values were passed on to children through the enculturation process. Thus, poverty and hopelessness were perpetuated from generation to generation.

To be fair, Lewis stressed that the culture of poverty was a result of the lack of economic opportunities in the slum neighborhoods. Moreover, he carefully noted that these attitudes affected only about 20 percent of the people living in these areas. Nevertheless, many critics have charged that Lewis's hypothesis is an example of "blaming the victim"; that is, it attributes poverty to the negative attitudes of poor people themselves, rather than to the economic and social stratification of their society. Some anthropologists have challenged the assertion that these attitudes are widespread among slum residents. For example, Helen Safa (1974) conducted research on a shantytown in San Juan Puerto Rico and did not find the hopelessness and apathy that were portrayed in Lewis's studies. Safa found that the poor in the shantytowns have values emphasizing hard work, thrift, and determination. Her data contained little to confirm Lewis's characterization of the poor as having a pathological culture.

Safa and other anthropologists emphasize that these culture of poverty values are not perpetuated from

A *favela* or slum area in Guatemala city.

generation to generation, as Lewis suggested. Rather, each individual develops attitudes and strategies toward achievement depending on the availability of *real* economic opportunities. She observed that because of rapid economic growth in Puerto Rico, a few privileged people were able to attain upward mobility. This limited mobility led poor people to believe that economic and social advancement was due to individual and personal initiative, rather than socioeconomic factors. In fact, Safa contends, socioeconomic conditions in Puerto Rico are, to a great extent, a consequence of global economic processes beyond the control of individuals in the shantytowns.

Another aspect of globalization in Latin America is related to how international tourism has an influence on urban migration and traditional rural culture. Alicia Re Cruz has been doing research on the rural to urban migration of Mayan peoples in the Yucatan region of Mexico to the major tourist destination of Cancún, Mexico (2003). Re Cruz found that migrants from the rural villages to Cancún were stigmatized by people in their villages as "less Mayan" and "de-Mayanized." The urban Mayan migrants go to Cancún to participate in the wage-labor sector and to provide more opportunities for their families. The traditional Maya fear that this urban migration will be destructive to their cultural identity. They see their cultural heritage and ethnic identity reduced to commodities in the tourist atmosphere of the Cancún area. In Cancún, the local government and businesses attempt to market and commodify the traditional culture heritage of the Maya for the international tourist industry. The traditional Mayans in the rural areas view this appropriation and commodification of their cultural heritage as dangerous and a threat to their Maya identity. The international tourism industries of Cancún have incorporated many of the Maya towns and villages within its vicinity. The Maya in these towns and villages are aware of their subordinate role in the global economy of Cancún, but the handicraft artists and other workers continue to produce what the tourists want to perceive as the "authentic" Maya cultural heritage. International tourism has produced this commodification of the indigenous cultural heritages in many locales and regions of Latin America and other areas of the world.

As we have seen, globalization has proceeded rapidly throughout the regions of Latin America, Africa, and the Caribbean. Walmart, McDonald's, and other multinational entities are growing everywhere throughout these regions. Sometimes this phenomenon has created rapid, unequal social and economic developments in various regions of these countries, as discussed previously. As the people are adjusting to these new processes—including population growth, urbanization, and industrial and rural agricultural developments, as well as the accompanying social, structural, political, religious, and ethnic change and tensions—the short-term result has been new problems and new challenges for them. We return to a discussion of some of the contemporary global trends that are influencing societies throughout the world in Chapter 24. As mentioned at the beginning of this chapter discussion, these societies are coping with these new developments in a much more concentrated time period than the Western, industrial, European-influenced societies of the global economy. It is hoped that anthropologists can help these societies provide solutions to overcome some of their difficulties, a topic addressed in our last chapter.

Summary and Review of Learning Objectives

21. 1 Discuss the early phases of Western colonialism in Latin America, Africa, and the Caribbean.

Following Columbus's explorations in the 1400s, Spanish and Portuguese *conquistadores* led expeditions to the Americas. This was the period of mercantilism when European states were competing to accumulate wealth to build their national treasuries. The conquistadores conquered the Native American civilizations and began the process of colonization. In Africa, various European powers beginning with the Portuguese developed the slave trade between Africa, and the Caribbean, and the Americas. Later, in the nineteenth century, to serve their needs for raw materials and overseas markets, the British, French, Dutch, Belgians, and Germans partitioned different areas of Africa into colonies, as reflected in the boundaries of present-day countries. The Spanish, British, French, and Dutch created colonies in the Caribbean islands and established sugar plantations based on African slavery.

21. 2 Describe the demographic, economic, and religious changes associated with globalization in Latin America, Africa, and the Caribbean.

Demographically, Latin America, Africa, and the Caribbean were devastated by diseases or slavery. However, over time, all these countries experienced declining death rates brought about by Western colonialism, and populations began to increase rapidly because of high birth rates. Economically, these societies were drawn into the global economy and were transformed by producing commodities that were demanded by the wealthier core societies. Patterns of land ownership were reordered, and many peasants were producing for economic elites. Religious changes and patterns of syncretism, the combination of indigenous religious traditions with Christianity, occurred in all these countries because of Western expansion and missionary influence.

21. 3 Discuss why independence, nationalist, and revolutionary movements developed in Latin America, Africa, and the Caribbean.

One important consequence of globalization and colonialism in various Latin American, African, and Caribbean areas was the development of political movements that emphasized independence and nationalistic ideas. Some of the indigenous peoples became educated under the colonial regime and began to assert their independence and national identities. Several countries of Latin America and the Caribbean developed revolutionary movements directed at the redistribution of land and wealth from the elite. These movements represented anticolonial sentiments and resulted in many new countries in Latin America, Africa, and the Caribbean.

21. 4 Describe how Latin America, Africa, and the Caribbean countries are situated in the global economy today.

The countries of Latin America, Africa, and the Caribbean have been absorbed into the global economy at different levels, depending on the resources that are available in their regions. Some countries remain poor and underdeveloped because their economies are heavily dependent on the wealthy core countries. Other countries, including Mexico and Nigeria, have oil resources that could be used to help develop their economies. However, despite oil resources, these non-Western countries still find themselves with various obstacles to developing their economies.

21. 5 Discuss what anthropologists have learned about the peasantry in Latin America, Africa, and the Caribbean.

The peasantry differs in various countries, based on the peoples' traditional agricultural activities and new global relationships to the world economy. Because of the predominance of horticulture in African society, in many regions, a peasantry like that of Latin America did not develop.

21. 6 Describe the characteristics of family and gender relationships in Latin America, Africa, and the Caribbean.

Most of rural Latin America, Africa, and the Caribbean have patriarchal extended families. In some cases, such as in Latin America, people developed fictive kin ties beyond the extended family to support their economic and political activities. Patriarchy was reinforced by Western colonial attitudes and resulted in gender inequality. Although gender inequality is a problem throughout Latin America, Africa, and the Caribbean, some indigenous feminist movements have developed to challenge patriarchy.

21. 7 Discuss the issues related to ethnicity in Latin America, Africa, and the Caribbean.

As a result of European conquest and colonization, the ethnicity of Latin America, Africa, and the Caribbean became increasingly diverse and heterogeneous. In Latin America, a small minority of Spanish and Portuguese rulers, never exceeding five percent of the total population, dominated the native population. During the colonial period, these Europeans established a racially-based hierarchy that emphasized "the whiter, the better." The Europeans eventually intermarried or had illicit relationships with native Indian women. The offspring of these interrelationships were called *mestizos*, a new social class in Latin America. After three centuries, the *mestizo* population grew to become the majority in Latin America. In addition, in Brazil and the Caribbean, the intermarriages of Africans and Europeans produced a group known as *mulattos*. The Indian population of Latin America who refer to themselves as *indigena* are developing economic and political movements to improve their status.

In Africa there are over a thousand ethnic groups. Although most African countries are attempting to build their nations, ethnic and religious ties are sometimes obstacles for political developments. Nigeria continues to confront problems with political terrorism and violence from groups such as Boko Haram. The country of Rwanda faced the most difficult genocidal tragedy as a result of the mobilization of ethnic ties among the Tutsi and Hutu. Ethnicity in the Caribbean is a complex, diverse mixture of imported African slaves, East Indian laborers, and various Europeans. Currently, the ethnic descendants of the African population have mobilized to compete with the East Indian and European communities.

21. 8 Discuss how urbanization has influenced Latin America, Africa, and the Caribbean.

Rapid population growth and shortages of land have led to mass migrations of people in Latin America, Africa, and the Caribbean from rural to urban areas. This has resulted in squatter settlements, poverty, and inequality in these rapidly growing cities. The migrants frequently find adaptive ways to adjust to the urban settlements through their family and ethnic ties.

Key Terms

apartheid, p. 500
assimilation, p. 509
closed peasant community, p. 504
culture of poverty, p. 514

dyadic contract, p. 506
fictive kinship ties, p. 506
monocultural dependency, p. 501
open peasant community, p. 504

patron-client ties, p. 506
revolution, p. 501
syncretism, p. 497

Chapter 22
Globalization in the Middle East and Asia

Chapter Outline

 ## Learning Objectives

After reading this chapter you should be able to:

22.1 Discuss the anthropological contributions to understanding the Middle East and Asia since 9/11/01.

22.2 Describe the early colonization of the Middle East and Asia.

22.3 Discuss the demographic, economic, and religious consequences of globalization in the Middle East and Asia.

22.4 Discuss the political consequences of globalization and colonialism in the Middle East and Asia.

22.5 Discuss what has created uneven development in the Middle East and Asia.

22.6 Discuss the major features of family and gender relations in the Middle East and Asia.

22.7 Discuss the factors that influence ethnic tensions in the Middle East and Asia.

22.8 Discuss the links between globalization and Islamic movements.

Anthropology Following 9/11

22.1 Discuss the anthropological contributions to understanding the Middle East and Asia since 9/11/01.

Following the tragic events of 9/11, when the suicidal attacks on the World Trade Center and the Pentagon destroyed thousands of human lives, an enormous number of books about the Islamic world, the Middle East, and Asia have been written. Many of these were written by religious studies specialists who examine the religious texts of Islam, Buddhism, and Hinduism and then interpret the cultures, values, and behaviors of these Asian and Middle Eastern peoples as "radically different" from those of peoples in Western society. Other writers are political scientists who interview the political elites in these regions; they also tend to portray these societies as not having the same kinds of democratic or other institutions that Western societies or cultures have. Even before 9/11, they predicted a "clash of civilizations" (Huntington 1996). Since that date, these views have become more dominant in the Western media and in government circles.

Anthropologists have been doing ethnographic research in these areas of the Middle East and Asia for decades. Some of the earlier ethnographic research drew on simplistic understandings of "culture"as discussed in Chapter 10. One assumption put forth by these earlier anthropologists was that a "culture" or "civilization" could be summed up within a portrait based on sometimes superficial understandings of how that "culture" (values, beliefs, worldviews, norms, and behavior) was *shared by everyone within the society in the same manner.* For example, anthropologist Raphael Patai wrote a book called *The Arab Mind* in the 1950s—based upon a simplified view of culture and language, along with some brief observations—in which he discussed the millions of people within the Arab world as supposedly sharing the same culture. Patai's book was used by the U.S. military to train U.S. soldiers engaged in Iraq to understand Arab culture and behavior with disastrous results (Starrett 2004).

Earlier, we discussed how contemporary anthropologists have refined this understanding of "culture" or "civilization" to emphasize how varied the values, beliefs, norms, and behaviors are among men, women, young, and old and how the culture is constantly in dynamic interaction with historical, economic, political, ethnic, and religious developments. Especially with recent globalization trends, when different regions of the world are experiencing more contact with the outside world through print, the Internet, television, films, fax, e-mail, and other global media, the "culture" of these groups is in a continuing dynamic interaction with the factors stemming from these trends. Anthropologists who do ethnographic research in these regions today find a tremendous variety of political and religious beliefs within any of the Middle Eastern or Asian societies. These anthropologists reside among the people in these areas for an extensive period and interview not just political elites, but also peasants, farmworkers, urban working-class people, religious clerics of many different traditions, and others. They find the simplistic portraits of "Islamic culture," "Jewish culture," "Buddhist or Hindu culture," and "Middle Eastern or Asian civilizations" provided by many of these specialists are too static, and they contain "stereotypical" images that do not do justice to the tremendous variety of values, beliefs, norms, institutions, and behaviors of the billions of people in these regions. Since the 9/11 tragedy, many anthropologists consult with and advise Western governments and also work with people in the Middle East and Asia to help provide more insight into these regions, which are changing very rapidly. In this way, anthropologists hope to improve intercultural and interfaith dialogue on these issues to help reduce tensions and violence within and among these various societies (Scupin 2003c).

As in Latin America, Africa, and the Caribbean, the process of globalization has been going on in the Middle East and Asia since the exploration of these regions by Europeans. These are vast heterogeneous regions with different ethnic groups and cultures that have had contact with each other through trade and exploration since the first millennium. For the purposes of this chapter, the Middle East includes the areas of both North Africa and Southwest Asia (see Figure 22.1). Many of the countries in these regions were influenced by the development of Islamic culture and the Arabic language. Traditionally, this area was referred to as the "Near East" to distinguish it from the "Far East." At other times, it has been mistakenly labeled the "Arab world." The term *Arab* refers to

Figure 22.1 Map of the Middle East

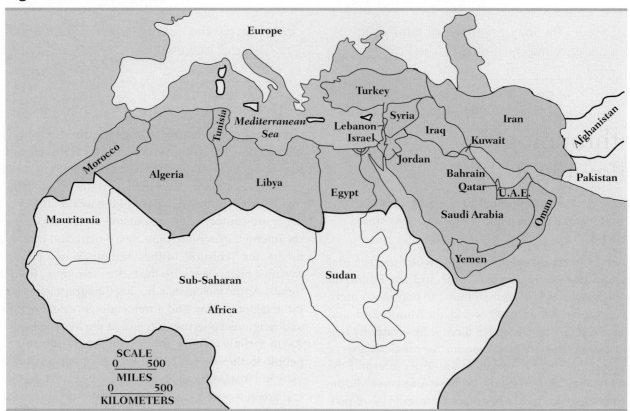

people who speak the Arabic language; included within this category of Arabic-speaking regions are the countries of Jordan, Syria, Iraq, Saudi Arabia, Yemen, Oman, and the Persian Gulf states such as Kuwait, Bahrain, Qatar, and the United Arab Emirates. The Middle East, however, also contains non-Arabic-speaking countries such as Israel, Turkey, and Iran. Thus, the Middle East as described in this chapter comprises peoples with different histories, languages, ethnicities, and religions.

Asia is also a culturally diverse continent with a wide variety of sociocultural systems. This chapter focuses on three regions: South Asia, East Asia, and Southeast Asia (see Figure 22.2).

These regions of Asia contain most of the world's population, more than three billion people. Different forms of societies have developed in these areas, ranging from the hunter-gatherer and horticultural societies of the tropical rain forests, to the pastoral nomads of northern China, to the advanced industrial society of Japan. (We have already discussed Japanese society in our earlier chapters on industrial and postindustrial societies.) This chapter focuses primarily on the agricultural or rural societies in Asia that have been recently transformed by globalization processes. It discusses the findings of anthropologists who use a global perspective that reflects the ongoing changes and transitions in the societies of the Middle East and Asia.

Early Colonialism and Globalization

22.2 Describe the early colonization of the Middle East and Asia.

The Middle East

Aside from the Portuguese, most Europeans did not have much direct contact with the Middle East until the 1800s. As European countries industrialized, however, they came to view the Middle East as an area ripe for imperial control. In the European view, the Middle East could supply raw materials and provide markets for manufactured goods. Napoleon Bonaparte led an expedition to Egypt in 1798, bringing it under French rule for a brief period. He planned to incorporate Egypt as a colony that would complement French economic interests. Because of British rivalry following the Napoleonic Wars, the French had to evacuate Egypt; nevertheless, Europeans gradually attained more influence in the region.

Although the British did not directly colonize Egypt until 1882, various European advisors influenced Egyptian rulers to develop specific commodities for the world market. Egypt's rulers and upper classes cooperated with Western interests in these activities to induce economic growth. Factories were built for processing sugar, and

Figure 22.2 Map of contemporary Asia

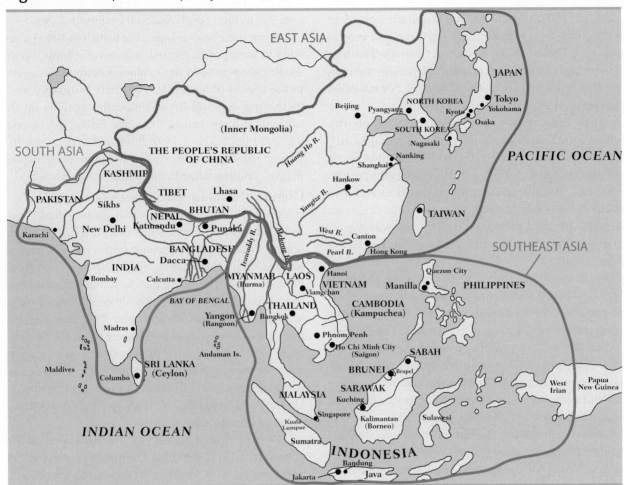

cotton became the most important agricultural commodity in the country. The most important development project that affected ties between the Middle East and the West was the Suez Canal, which connects the Mediterranean Sea with the Gulf of Suez. Completed in 1869, the Suez Canal was financed through capital supplied by French and British interests. The canal shortened the distance between East and West, thereby drawing the Middle East into the orbit of the core nations.

To offset British expansion in the Middle East, the French began to build a North African empire, taking control of Algeria, Tunisia, and Morocco. Morocco was considered the most "perfect" French colony, in which, through indirect rule, the French devised a "scientific colony" that required only a small number of French officials to supervise a vast territory. Thus, the French ruled through urban elites, rural leaders, and Moroccan religious officials. They developed large commercial enterprises such as railroads and mining, as well as various agricultural operations. These commercial enterprises enabled the colony to pay for itself, a definite asset for the French.

European expansion in the Middle East continued throughout the nineteenth and early twentieth centuries.

Although not directly colonized, Turkey, which was then the center of the Ottoman Empire, came under the economic control of Western interests. To reduce the disparity in economic development between their country and Europe, Turkish rulers gave concessions to French and British interests to develop industries and services in Turkey. These enterprises produced cheap goods that undermined native Turkish businesses. By the end of the nineteenth century, Turkey had become a peripheral society, exporting raw materials, providing cheap labor, and depending on core societies for manufactured goods. This led to the end of the Ottoman Empire.

Although not as industrialized as many other European countries, Russia began to expand toward the Middle East during the mid-1800s and eventually assumed control over various regions of Central Asia, absorbing the Muslim populations of Samarkand, Tashkent, and Turkestan. To secure access to the warm waters of the Persian Gulf, Russia also moved into Iran (formerly Persia), taking control of the northern half of the country. The British, who maintained control of commerce in the Persian Gulf through their naval fleet, were thus threatened by this Russian expansion. As a countermeasure, they moved into southern

Iran and funneled capital into the region by developing a tobacco monopoly and financing other economic projects. Eventually, in 1907, the British and Russians agreed to divide Iran into three spheres, with northern and central Iran, including Tehran, in the Russian sphere; southeastern Iran in the British sphere; and an area between in the neutral zone. The Iranians were neither consulted nor informed about the terms of this agreement (Keddie 1981).

Another area that was contested between the Russians and the British was Afghanistan. Geographically, Afghanistan is situated between the Middle East and South Asia. It is a country made up of various ethnic groups who were Muslims involved in agricultural practices and also nomadic pastoralism in the rugged mountains, deep valleys, deserts, and arid plateaus. Afghanistan was a remnant of one of the major Muslim empires founded in the seventeenth century.

In the nineteenth century, the Russians tried to colonize Afghanistan by completing a railroad to the Afghan border, and the British countered by building a railway from their colonized portion of South Asia northward. This "Great Game," played out between the British and Russians, left Afghanistan as a buffer state between these colonial powers. Various Afghan leaders had to negotiate between and give concessions to these authorities to maintain their independence (Sidky and Akers 2006).

Following World War I, the European powers divided the Middle East into different spheres of influence. In addition to their North African empire, the French gained the countries of Lebanon and Syria as direct colonies. Other areas such as Turkey and the Arabian Peninsula remained politically independent but became peripheral states. The British took Egypt, Iraq, and Palestine as direct colonies. Jewish leaders in Europe were calling for the resettlement of Jews in their original homeland in Palestine because Jewish communities had faced discrimination and persecution for centuries in Europe. Influenced by this movement, known as Zionism, the British eventually agreed to allow the immigration of thousands of European Jews to Palestine, with dramatic consequences for the Middle East.

Asia   Intensive economic and political contact between Asia and the West began during the period of European mercantilism. The first phase of Western expansion into Asia began with the Portuguese trade in India, China, and Southeast Asia. The next phase involved the Dutch, French, and British, who established private trading companies in Asia to secure access to exportable goods.

India, Myanmar (Burma), and Malaysia   Western nations resorted to direct colonization in Asia following the Industrial Revolution. For example, Britain colonized India, gaining control over the production of export cash crops such as jute, oil seeds, cotton, and wheat. Because India did not have a strong centralized state, it could not resist British colonization. The opening of the Suez Canal facilitated

Britain's management of its Asian colonies, and by 1900, the British had established direct economic and political control over 300 million South Asians (Hardgrove 2006).

From their base in India, the British initiated a series of wars to incorporate Burma as a direct colony. Eventually, the British expanded their colonial domination southward to the region of Malaysia. To satisfy industrial societies' increasing demand for commodities such as tin (for the canning industry) and rubber, the British developed mining and plantations in both Burma and Malaysia. In addition, as the demand for rice grew in the world market, the British commercialized rice production for export.

China   The industrial nations also attempted to carve out colonies in China. Although that country had been open to European trade ever since the Portuguese established ports in Macao in the sixteenth century, China successfully resisted direct colonization by the West for several reasons. First, it was farther from the West than other Asian countries. Second, China had a highly centralized state empire in which mandarin officials controlled local regions and, thus, was a more formidable empire than other Asian countries. Third, the Chinese government was not impressed with Western goods and technology. Chinese officials had been familiar with Western products from the time of Marco Polo in the fifteenth century and forbade the importation of Western commodities.

Despite this resistance, the British eventually gained access to China through the introduction of opium. Attempts by the Chinese government to prohibit the illegal smuggling of this drug into the country led to the Opium Wars of 1839–1842 between Great Britain and China. Britain defeated China, subsequently acquiring Hong Kong as a colony and securing other business concessions. Eventually, international settlements were established in cities such as Shanghai, which became sovereign city-states outside the Chinese government's control (DeVoe 2006).

The Dutch Empire   The Dutch expanded into the East Indies, eventually incorporating the region—now known as Indonesia—into their colonial empire. By the nineteenth century, the Dutch had developed what they referred to as the Kultur-System, which lasted until 1917. Through this system, Indonesian peasants were allowed to grow only certain cash crops, such as sugar, coffee, tobacco, and indigo, for the world market. These crops were developed at the expense of subsistence crops such as rice. The policy of coerced labor and exploitation of the peasantry held back the economic development of the Indonesian islands (Geertz 1963a; Hefner 2000; Lukens-Bull 2006).

French Indochina   French imperial rivalry with Britain had direct consequences for Southeast Asia. By 1893, the French conquered and established direct colonial rule over Cambodia, Vietnam, and Laos—a region that became known as Indochina. In northern Vietnam, French settlers directed the production of coal, zinc, and tin; in the southern areas near the Mekong River, they developed the land to produce rubber and rice exports (Scupin 2006a).

Thailand: An Independent Country One country in Southeast Asia that did not become directly colonized was Thailand. The Thai monarchy, which had some experience with Western interests, developed economic and political strategies to play European rivals against one another, while adopting Western innovations. European business interests were allowed to aid in the development of some goods, but not to exercise direct political control. To some extent, this suited the geopolitical strategies of both the British and the French, who preferred Thailand as a buffer state between their colonial domains (Slagter and Kerbo 2000; Scupin 2006b).

The Philippines The Philippines were directly colonized first by Spain and then by the United States. Spain took control of most of the Philippine Islands during the sixteenth century. As in Latin America, the Spanish established *pueblos* (towns) in which colonial officials directed Filipino peasant labor and collected tribute. Eventually, *encomiendas*—land grants to Spanish settlers—developed into *haciendas*, on which tobacco, sugar, and indigo were planted for export to the world market. Aside from these agricultural enterprises, the Spanish encouraged few commercial developments. During the Spanish-American War of 1898, the United States defeated Spanish forces in both the Philippines and the Caribbean. Many Filipinos sided with the United States in hopes of achieving independence from Spain. When the United States refused to recognize Philippine independence, numerous Filipinos redirected their resistance efforts against the United States. After a protracted war in which 600,000 Filipinos lost their lives and many more were placed in concentration camps, the Philippines were directly colonized by the United States. The United States continued to organize native Filipino labor to produce cash crops such as tobacco, sugar, and indigo as export commodities for the world market (Lukens-Bull 2006).

Consequences of Colonialism

22.3 Discuss the demographic, economic, and religious consequences of globalization in the Middle East and Asia.

Demographic Change

Western expansion and colonialism in non-Western countries brought unprecedented demographic growth to the populations of these agricultural states. As in Latin America, Africa, and the Caribbean, the development of

intensive cash-crop cultivation often resulted in rapid population growth. As labor shortages developed in subsistence agriculture as a result of moving labor into cash-cropping agriculture for the European market, peasant farmers began to increase their family size (Robbins 2013). This increase in fertility led to rapid population growth in many of the Middle Eastern and Asian societies. Eventually, Europeans introduced new medical and sanitation practices that led to a tremendous reduction in death rates through the control of smallpox, plague, yellow fever, and malaria. Meanwhile, birth rates remained high. The combination of reduced death rates and high birth rates led to dramatic population increases. For example, the population of India increased by one-third between 1881 and 1931 and then doubled between 1931 and 1971. In Chapter 24, we shall discuss some of the global effects of these population trends.

Unlike the situation in the West, population growth in colonized non-Western countries was not coupled with sustained and rapid industrialization. The expanding Middle Eastern and Asian populations, therefore, had to be absorbed by the intensification of agricultural production. For example, population growth in Indonesia under the Dutch led to what Clifford Geertz referred to as "agricultural involution" (1963a). The commercialization of agriculture and the use of coerced labor increased production somewhat, but the rates of increase could not keep pace with population growth. Agricultural yields per day of labor actually decreased. In addition, as the population grew, land became scarcer. Thus, the system of intensified agriculture was increasingly unable to feed the growing population.

As a result of colonialism, major urban centers grew quickly in the Middle East and Asia. For example, the cities of Cairo in Egypt and Tehran in Iran began to grow at tremendous rates. In India, the British created port cities such as Calcutta, Bombay, and Madras that became international trading and financial centers. In China, Shanghai and Nanking developed into major urban centers as a result of the expansion of Western businesses. Southeast Asian cities such as Rangoon, Bangkok, Saigon, Jakarta, Kuala Lumpur, Singapore, and Manila expanded rapidly. These cities attracted rural migrants, who crowded into squatter settlements and slums.

Economic Change

The economies of the countries of the Middle East and Asia during the nineteenth century were directed toward the production of agricultural goods such as tea, sugar, tobacco, cotton, rice, tin, and rubber for export. Prices of these goods were subject to fluctuations in the world market. Land that had been converted to growing these export crops could no longer support peasant villages. Native handicrafts declined dramatically in importance in comparison with export-oriented commodity production. In addition, as in other colonized areas of the world, imported Western-manufactured goods flowed into Middle Eastern and Asian nations. Thus, these societies became more dependent on core industrial societies.

As in Latin America, Africa, and the Caribbean, one major consequence of Western colonialism and globalization was the integration of many agricultural village communities into wider regional and global economic patterns. The *precolonial* traditional villages were never entirely self-sufficient and were tied to regional and national trading networks. However, under Western colonialism, the village peasantry in the Middle East and Asia was no longer isolated from cities, and the global market determined the prices for agricultural goods. This global transformation of agricultural economies triggered dramatic changes in non-Western rural communities. Because few peasants had enough capital to own and manage land, much of the land fell into the hands of colonial settlers, large landowners, and money lenders. In many cases, these changes encouraged absentee landownership and temporary tenancy. Long-term care of the land by the peasantry was sacrificed for immediate profits. As in the case of the peasants of Latin America, Africa, and the Caribbean, land, labor, and capital were thus disconnected from the village kinship structures of reciprocity and redistribution, or what has been referred to as the *moral economy* (see Chapter 16). As globalization occurred, these peasants were incorporated into the global cash economy. Their lives were now dependent on the fluctuations of a global economy that determined their success or failure as farmers.

In a recent study of how the moral economy is changing with respect to recent globalization, Christina Dames did ethnographic research in the rugged mountain region of West Kalimantan in Indonesian Borneo (2012). This is a multiethnic area with Dayak, Melayu, Chinese, and other, smaller, ethnic groups. Since Indonesia became independent of Dutch colonial rule, extensive globalization has influenced this region. Dames observed the rapid spread of globally based financial banking institutions into the area. Banks such as the *Bank Rakyat Indonesia* (The Indonesian People's Bank, BRI) are becoming increasingly available to people who, until recently, had few alternatives to being "unbanked." The growing accessibility of these financial institutions has had far-reaching effects. However, Dames found that the spread of these formal financial institutions did not signal the decline of informal aspects of a moral economy. In Kalimantan Barat, a traditional rotating savings and credit association (ROSCA), *arisan*, remains an important economic and social tool for people from all walks of life. People also often organize themselves in financial cooperatives, or *koperasi*, the epitome of the Indonesian ideology promoted widely known as *gotong royong*—mutual aid and assistance or reciprocity.

When Dames studied the use of these financial institutions, she focused on issues such as trust and monitoring of reputation of people, especially in respect to *arisan* and local cooperatives. Membership in these organizations is dependent on the intimate knowledge of other member's lives based on kinship and neighborhood ties, their financial circumstances, their activities, and their trustworthiness. The perceived risks of saving money in an informal financial institution such as *arisan* and local cooperatives was much lower than formal banking. Dames observed how new economic developments and globalization are changing the ways in which people use money and credit, and how they manage debts. As cash and third-party credit (i.e., credit not offered from one individual to another, but rather from a financial intermediary such as a bank or a credit union) become available in even extremely

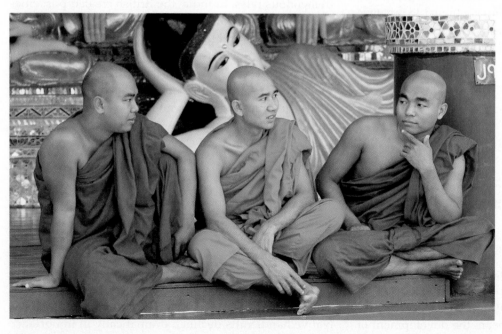

Buddhist monks in Myanmar (Burma)

remote locations, social and exchange relationships are bound to change. Yet, informal relationships based on kinship or ethnicity, and trust and monitoring play a role in the economic decision making and the willingness of these people to cooperate or not in these new global banking institutions.

Religious Change

The major religious traditions of most of the societies in the Middle East and Asia are Islam, Hinduism, and Buddhism. The Islamic tradition dates to the life of Muhammad, who was born in 570 A.D. in the city of Mecca, which is now in Saudi Arabia (see Chapter 19). Two other South Asian religions—Hinduism and Buddhism—have influenced civilizations throughout the region (see Chapter 19). Since the Middle East and Asia had the highly literate religious traditions of Islam, Hinduism, and Buddhism, Western Christian missionaries had a much more difficult time trying to convert native populations in these regions. The religious traditions in these regions provided basic spiritual cosmologies, beliefs, and meanings that satisfied vast numbers of these people in their coping with universal needs and questions. However, in many cases, the Western missionaries in these Middle Eastern and Asian countries were instrumental in teaching some of the basic cultural values of the Western world, including political ideas regarding democratic institutions, civil liberties, and individual freedom.

Political Change: Independence and Nationalism

22.4 Discuss the political consequences of globalization and colonialism in the Middle East and Asia.

During the nineteenth and twentieth centuries, the extension of Western power into the Middle East and Asia elicited responses ranging from native reformist activities to nationalist independence movements. Because most people in these regions were Muslims, Hindus, or Buddhists, many of the anticolonial responses reflected a religious orientation. In response to Western colonialism, Muslim, Hindu, and Buddhist leaders called for a rethinking of their religious traditions to accommodate pressures from the West. Reformers such as Muhammad Abduh in Egypt and Rabinda Tagore in India argued that the sources of Western strength developed in part from early Middle Eastern and Asian contributions to science, medicine, and scholarship (see Chapter 16). Thus, the reformists exhorted believers to look to their own indigenous

religious traditions as a source of inspiration to overcome Western economic and political domination. Reformist movements spread throughout the Muslim, Hindu, and Buddhist areas, especially among the urban, educated classes, paving the way for later nationalist and independence movements across the regions (Scupin 2008b; Weisgrau 2008).

Similarly, most of the anticolonial, nationalist, and independence movements that emerged in Asia were linked to local religious or political developments. They were also associated with the rise of Western-educated groups that articulated nationalist demands.

A Nationalist and Independence Movement in India

As in other colonies, the British desired an educated class of Indians to serve as government clerks and cultural intermediaries between the British and the colonized people. The British sponsored a national system that included universities and training colleges, which educated thousands of Indians. These people became part of a literate middle class, familiar with Western liberal thought regarding human rights and self-determination. A small, powerful merchant class that benefited from British economic policies also emerged.

Whereas India formerly had been fragmented into separate language groups, the colonial educational system provided the cultivated middle classes with a common language, English. Improved transportation and communication media such as railroads, print technology, and the telegraph accelerated the movement for national unity. In addition, the educated classes became increasingly aware of the hypocrisy of British "values" such as equality and democracy when they were exposed to racism and discrimination in the form of exclusion from British private hotels, clubs, and parks.

The majority of the Indian population, however, was not middle class, but was made up of peasants who lived in rural village communities and did not speak English. Thus, the middle-class nationalist movement did not directly appeal to them. This gulf between the middle class and the peasants was bridged by a remarkable individual, Mohandas Gandhi, later called the Mahatma, or "great soul." Although from the middle class, Gandhi fused Hindu religious sentiments with Western political thought to mobilize the peasantry against British domination. Anthropologist Richard Fox contributed an extensive analysis of Gandhi's role in the anticolonial struggle (1989). In his study, Fox emphasized the role of an individual with charismatic abilities in bringing about major social and cultural change within a society.

Hindu traditions provided the model for Gandhi's strategies of nonviolent resistance. He called for the

Mohandas Gandhi (1869–1948).

peaceful boycott of British-produced goods, telling the villagers to maintain their traditional weaving industries to spin their own cloth. Through his protests and boycotts, he rallied millions of Indians in a mass movement that eventually could not be resisted. In 1947, two years after the end of World War II, the British were forced to relinquish their empire in South Asia (Hardgrove 2006; Weiss 2008).

Revolutionary Movements in Asia

As in Latin America, Africa, and the Caribbean, a number of revolutionary movements developed in the Middle East and Asia as a result of globalization and contact with Western colonialism and power. The revolutions that developed in Asia had worldwide repercussions. In China, a grassroots revolutionary movement developed out of anti-Western, nationalistic movements. In the early twentieth century, Sun Yat-Sen, a doctor educated in Hawaii and Hong Kong, championed the formation of a democratic republic in China, gaining support among the peasants by calling for the redistribution of land. The movement

toward democracy failed, however. Instead, the military under Chiang Kai-Shek, who did not sympathize with peasant resistance movements or democratic reforms, assumed control of China. These developments encouraged the growth of the Chinese Communist Party under Mao Zedong. Mao's guerrillas engaged in a protracted struggle against Chiang Kai-Shek's forces in the 1940s.

Mao Zedong was familiar with Karl Marx's prediction that the urban *proletariat* or working class would direct revolutions toward socialism and communism. Mao, in contrast, believed that the rural peasantry could become the backbone of a communist revolution (Wolf 1969; DeVoe 2006). Through the Chinese Communist Party, Mao began to mobilize the peasantry and combine traditional notions of Confucianism with his brand of Marxism, sometimes called *Maoism*. Calling for the overthrow of the landlords and Western forms of capitalism that he blamed for social and economic inequality, Mao made Marxism comprehensible to Chinese peasants. By 1949, after two decades of struggle, Mao and his peasant-based armies gained control of the country, renaming it the People's Republic of China.

Vietnam experienced the most dramatic nationalist and revolutionary movement of any of the French colonies of Southeast Asia. After World War II, the French attempted to reestablish their colonial regime in Indochina. Leading the opposition was Ho Chi Minh, who, like many other Vietnamese, was frustrated by French colonialism and its negative impact on his society. Ho Chi Minh believed in the communist ideal but, like Mao Zedong, adapted Marxist ideology to the particular concerns of his nationalist struggle (Wolf 1969; Scupin 2006b). His well-organized peasant army, the Vietminh, defeated the French forces at Dien Bien Phu in 1954. This defeat led to the withdrawal of the French from Vietnam.

Following Dien Bien Phu, the French and the Vietminh agreed to a temporary division of the country into North Vietnam under Ho Chi Minh and South Vietnam under Ngo Dinh Diem. The nation was to be unified through elections in 1956, but the elections were never held. As a Cold War strategy, the United States, meanwhile, committed itself to the survival of an independent, non-communist South Vietnam, supplying Diem with massive economic, political, and military support. Diem lacked widespread support among the South Vietnamese population, however, and he brutally repressed dissent against his regime. He was overthrown in a military coup in 1963.

As communist opposition, supported by North Vietnam, escalated in the South, the United States dramatically increased its level of military involvement. By 1967, more than 500,000 U.S. troops were stationed in Vietnam. Unable to defeat the Vietnamese guerrillas, the United States entered into a long period of negotiation with the Vietnamese communists, finally signing a peace treaty in

Mao Zedong (1893–1976).

Ho Chi Minh (1890–1969).

January 1973. Two years later, North Vietnam overran the South, thereby unifying the nation (Scupin 2006b).

Uneven Economic Development

22.5 Discuss what has created uneven development in the Middle East and Asia.

By redirecting economic development toward an export-oriented global economy, Western colonialism and globalization transformed many of the formerly agricultural countries into *peripheral*, dependent economies. The wealthy *core* industrial societies of the West provided economic and political support to those elites who instituted policies to promote economic growth. Many of these elites in the Middle East and Asia minimized restrictions on foreign investment and opened their borders to multinational corporations. In addition, some of these societies had vital resources that enabled them to develop a special type of relationship with the wealthy industrialized core societies. However, a number of these societies, especially in Asia, began to attempt to withdraw from globalization and capitalism and to develop self-sufficient economies.

Oil and the Middle East

The discovery of vast sources of oil in the Middle East has revolutionized trade and politics and brought tremendous social change to the region. Oil became the major energy source for the industrial world. Multinational corporations based in the core societies developed these resources, controlling both oil production and prices, to maintain economic growth in their home countries. As nationalist independence movements spread, however, many countries demanded control over their oil. Nations such as Libya, Iran, Saudi Arabia, Iraq, and Kuwait began to *nationalize* their oil industries, and the multinational corporations eventually lost most of their controlling interests in the region.

Political conflicts between the Arabs and Israel in the 1970s resulted in a boycott of the sale of oil to the global economy by the Islamic countries and other oil-producing countries known collectively as the Organization of Petroleum Exporting Countries (OPEC). This resulted in a rapid increase of the price of oil around the world, compared to the prices of the 1950s and 1960s. The continued rise in the cost of oil since the 1970s has enabled the oil-producing countries of the region to accumulate vast wealth and has fueled worldwide inflation, raising the costs of all goods and raw materials. The per capita incomes of some Middle Eastern countries with smaller populations eventually surpassed those of many *core* countries. Realizing that they were dependent on a single export commodity, however, Middle Eastern countries took certain steps to diversify their economies. Smaller countries, such as Saudi Arabia, with a population of about 27 million people, and Kuwait, with only 3.5 million—both ruled by royal dynastic families—financed some capital-intensive industries such as cement and detergent manufacturing and food processing. In doing so, these small Arab countries ensured high incomes for most of their population, which tended to enhance their political legitimacy and stability.

Larger oil-rich countries such as Iran and Iraq pursued rapid economic development to increase national wealth and legitimize their political regimes. Shah Muhammad Reza Pahlavi of Iran and Saddam Hussein of Iraq invited multinational corporations and consultants from core countries to help diversify their industries and develop their military technology. In contrast to the smaller countries, however, Iraq and Iran, with their larger populations (26 million and 68 million, respectively), had more difficulty raising economic standards for everyone immediately.

The vast majority of the people of the Middle East, however, *do not live* in oil-rich countries. These nations include Egypt, Syria, Jordan, Lebanon, and Morocco; although they have developed some industries to diversify their economies, they remain to some extent peripheral societies dependent on the wealthier industrial core societies.

Withdrawal from the Global Economy

Some countries, by adopting a socialist form of economic system, tried to develop economically outside of the capitalist global economy. In China, following his victory in 1949, Mao Zedong implemented an economic development plan modeled on that of the Soviet Union. He

Saudi Arabia became a wealthy state based on oil following the OPEC oil boycott of the 1970s.

collectivized agriculture by appropriating the land owned by the elite and gave it to the peasants. Mao established cooperatives in which a number of villages owned agricultural land in common, and he also sponsored the development of heavy industries to stimulate economic growth. Communist Party officials, known as cadres, managed both the agricultural cooperatives and the industrial firms.

When these policies failed to generate economic growth, Mao launched a radically different effort in 1958 favoring a decentralized economy. This plan, known as the "Great Leap Forward," established locally based rural and urban communes that organized the production and distribution of goods and services. Each commune, consisting of 12,000 to 60,000 people, was subdivided into brigades of 100 to 700 households, production teams of about 35 households, and work teams of 8 to 10 households. Each commune was supposed to be self-sufficient, containing a banking system, police force, schools, day-care centers, mess halls, hospitals, and old-age centers. The communes established their own production goals and reinvested their profits in the commune.

Although some aspects of the Great Leap Forward were successful, especially those involving health care and literacy, the program failed to promote agricultural and industrial development. In fact, it was marked by famine, political corruption, and economic retardation. Mao then initiated an ideological campaign to eliminate corruption and political "deviance," while restoring revolutionary consciousness. This campaign, known as the "Cultural Revolution" lasted from 1966 to 1976. Mao organized young people into groups called the Red Guards to purify China of any capitalist, traditional Confucianist, or Western tendencies. Millions of people, primarily the educated classes, were arrested and forced to work on rural communes as punishment for their deviance from the communist path. By 1976, at the time of Mao's death, the Cultural Revolution had paralyzed economic development by eliminating the most skilled and educated classes, those who could have contributed to the nation's growth (DeVoe 2006).

Vietnam also tried to withdraw from the world capitalist system, implementing a socialist government based upon Marxist-Leninist principles. After the end of the Vietnam War, the government instituted a five-year plan that collectivized agriculture and relocated people from urban to rural communities. By 1978, 137 collective farms had been established; 4 million people, including half the population of Ho Chi Minh City (formerly Saigon), were resettled in what were called "new economic zones." These zones were organized to produce crops and operate light industry as a means of encouraging economic self-sufficiency. They were managed by Communist Party officials, many of whom had no direct experience in agriculture or industry (Scupin 2006b).

By 1981, Vietnam had become one of the poorest peripheral nations in the world. While food production and labor productivity decreased, inflation and unemployment rose. Military expenditures drained the economy of needed funds for capital development. Part of the reason that Vietnam was underdeveloped was the war itself. For example, the defoliation of forests as a result of U.S. bombing and the use of Agent Orange impeded the growth of timber. At the same time, however, many of the problems were a direct result of inflexible ideological commitments and lack of expertise on the part of Communist Party bureaucrats (Pike 1990; Scupin 2006b).

Ethnographic Studies
A Middle Eastern Village and Globalization

Ethnographic studies of rural villages in the Middle East have contributed to a more comprehensive understanding of globalization and the interconnections between peripheral and core nations. One early study of global transition was conducted by Hani Fakhouri (1972), who studied the Egyptian village of Kafr El-Elow, which at the time of Fakhouri's study (1966–1968) was undergoing substantial changes. About 80 percent of the Egyptian population lived in about 4,000 rural villages, many of which were being drawn into the global economy through rapid industrialization and the commercialization of agriculture.

Kafr El-Elow is located 18 miles south of Cairo. Before the 1920s, it was a relatively small farming community in which the *fellaheen* (peasants) practiced small-scale subsistence agriculture. After British colonization in the nineteenth century, the *fellaheen* began to grow cotton as an export commodity. By the 1920s, water pumps had been introduced into the village, and several industries had begun to develop. Roads were constructed, linking Kafr El-Elow with nearby industrializing communities. After the 1950s, industrialization accelerated, and subsistence farming was no longer the primary aspect of the Kafr El-Elow economy. Instead, many nearby industries related to steel, natural gas, cement, textiles, railroads, aircraft, and other products drew increasing numbers of *fellaheen* into the industrial work force; however, many villagers continued cultivating their crops after factory hours and on weekends to supplement their incomes.

By the 1960s, only about ten percent of the community was made up of peasants. Although the remaining *fellaheen* continued to plow their fields with draft animals, they also used some modern machinery such as crop sprayers and irrigation pumps. At the time of Fakhouri's study, agricultural productivity was very high, and the *fellaheen* were able to harvest three or four crops a year. Wheat and corn were cultivated for domestic consumption, primarily for making bread, and vegetables were grown for cash crops and home consumption. Cash crops became important enough that the Egyptian government built refrigerated bins to store the farmers' seeds and cuttings for replanting.

Industrialization brought to Kafr El-Elow new patterns of social mobility, an influx of migrants for urban labor, and rising incomes, which created new socioeconomic classes. These new classes demanded a variety of consumer goods and services not familiar to the traditional population. Bicycles, wristwatches, radios, and electricity for households became increasingly common. Preferences for Western clothing, housing, entertainment, and other commodities contributed to the decline of traditional handicraft industries and the rise of new businesses. Six businesses existed in 1930; in 1966, Fakhouri counted 78.

Egyptian peasant (*fellaheen*) life has been transformed by global changes.

Middle Eastern Family, Marriage, and Gender

22.6 Discuss the major features of family and gender relations in the Middle East and Asia.

An enormous amount of ethnographic research is available on family, marriage, and gender in Arab, Turkish, and Iranian societies. In all these societies, the ideal form of the family has been patrilineal, endogamous, polygynous, and patriarchal. The primary sources for the ideals of the Muslim family are Islamic religious texts, principally the Qur'an and the Sharia. Cultural anthropologists have discovered, however, that the ideals of the Muslim family do not always coincide with the realities of social life in the Middle East and North Africa.

In some parts of the Arab world, such as among the Palestinian communities, the term *hamula* is used to refer to an idealized descent group (a patrilineage or patriclan) that members view as a kinship group. The *hamula* is associated with a *patronym*, the name of a particular male who is thought to be a paternal ancestor. In rural areas, the typical *hamula* is a clan that embraces various patrilineages. The head of the clan is referred to as a sheik, a hereditary position. He resolves disputes and encourages cooperation among members of the clan. The *hamula* has always been a source of pride and loyalty in rural Arab communities.

Despite the description of the *hamula* as a patrilineal descent grouping associated with a particular patronym, cultural anthropologists find that it is frequently a loosely structured group combining patrilineal, affinal, matrilineal, and neighborhood relations (Eickelman 1998). Nevertheless, under different circumstances, it may serve to coordinate economic, political, and ceremonial affairs. Research on urban and rural communities in Lebanon, Kuwait, and other Arab countries suggests that loyalty to the *hamula* remains a component of social organization throughout the Muslim world (Al-Thakeb 1985; Eickelman 1998).

The Family As in most other agricultural societies, the extended family is the ideal in the Middle East. The traditional household espoused by Arabs, Turks, and Iranians is made up of the patriarch, his wife, one or more married sons and their families, and unmarried daughters and sons. Yet, as in the case of the *hamula*, these ideals are often not realized (Bates and Rassam 2000). Economic and demographic conditions such as landlessness, poverty, and geographical mobility frequently influence the size and dimension of the Muslim family.

As industrialization and consequent urbanization influence the Middle East, the nuclear family is becoming the normative pattern. Survey research on the Muslim family from Egypt, Syria, Libya, Jordan, Lebanon, Iraq, Bahrain, and Kuwait suggests that the nuclear family has become the predominant form in both rural and urban areas (Al-Thakeb 1981, 1985). Variability in family type is often related to socioeconomic status. The ideal of the nuclear family appears to be most prevalent among the middle and upper classes, which are most influenced by globalization. Among the lower socioeconomic classes, especially families involved in agriculture, the extended family retains its importance. Yet, even when the nuclear family predominates, wider kinship relations, including the *hamula*, sometimes remain important (Al-Thakeb 1985; Eickelman 1998).

Marriage Marriage is a fundamental obligation in the Islamic tradition. Unless financially or physically unable, every Muslim male and female is required to be married. Marriage is regarded as a sacred contract between two families that legalizes sexual relations and the procreation of children. In the Islamic tradition, there are no cultural beliefs or practices such as monasticism that sanction any form of life outside of marriage.

Islamic societies are known for endorsing the marriage practices of polygyny. Polygyny is mentioned once in the Qur'an (iv:3):

Marry of the women, who seem good to you, two, three, or four, and if ye fear that ye cannot do justice [to so many] the one [only].

Although polygynous marriage is permitted and to some extent represents an ideal norm from the early religious tradition within the Qur'an in Muslim societies, anthropologists find that most marriages are monogamous. For example, fewer than ten percent of married Kuwaiti males and about one percent of married Egyptian males are involved in polygynous marriages (Al-Thakeb 1985; Eickelman 1998). In Kafr El-Elow, Fakhouri (1972) found that only a few males had multiple wives. In questioning males involved in polygynous marriages, Fakhouri noted that the major rationales for taking a second wife were the first wife's infertility or poor health and the desire of wealthy males to demonstrate their high status.

Wealthy males in both urban and rural areas contract polygynous marriages. In the traditional pattern found in rural communities, a wealthy male from the landed elite contracts a *parallel-cousin marriage* and then takes a wife from another family (Bates and Rassam 2000). Polygyny is also found among the new elite in some of the wealthy oil-producing countries. However, economic limitations and the fact that the Islamic tradition prescribes equal justice for all wives encourage *monogamous* marriages among the majority of Muslims.

Arranged marriage based on parental decision making still predominates in most Islamic societies. Until recently, for example, Saudi Arabian males did not even view their wives until their wedding day. Some indicators suggest, however, that a degree of individual choice in marriage may become more prevalent. Anthropological research from Kuwait in the mid-1980s indicates that an individual's freedom to select a spouse varies according to education, socioeconomic status, age, and sex (Al-Thakeb 1985). As both males and females become more educated and achieve greater economic independence from their parents, they enjoy more freedom in mate selection, though typically in many communities, females have much less choice.

Divorce Like polygyny, divorce in traditional Islamic societies is a male prerogative. To obtain a divorce, a male does not need much justification; Islamic law specifies several means whereby a male can easily repudiate his wife. It also empowers a husband to reclaim his wife without her consent within a four-month period after the divorce. Traditionally, a Muslim wife did not have the same rights to obtain a divorce. A woman could, however, divorce her husband for reasons such as impotence, insanity, and lack of economic support—but to prove these accusations, she would need a very sympathetic judge (Esposito 2010).

Cultural anthropologists find it difficult to generalize about divorce and marriage in the Muslim world. In countries such as Egypt, Turkey, and Morocco, which have greater exposure to outside global influences, divorce laws for women have become liberalized. These countries have educated middle classes that support reform. In conjunction with these Islamic reform movements, along with the modification of divorce laws, some Muslim feminists have called for the abolition of polygyny. Certain countries—for example, Tunisia and Turkey—have prohibited this practice, and others have restricted it (Eickelman 1998).

Gender The Western image of the Arab or Muslim woman is frequently that of a female hidden behind a veil and completely dominated by the demands of a patriarchal society. Early Western scholars painted a grim and unwholesome portrait of the female in the Muslim household. Cultural anthropologists find that this image obscures the complexity of gender relations in the Middle East.

The patriarchal ideal and the status of the female in the Muslim world cannot be understood without reference to two views in the Islamic perspective. First, according to the Islamic tradition, before the origins of Islam, females were treated negatively. For example, in the pre-Islamic period, the Bedouins regularly practiced female infanticide by burying the unwanted child in sand. The Qur'an explicitly forbids this practice. Thus, Islam was viewed as having had a progressive influence on the role of women. Second, Islam condemns all sexual immorality, prescribing severe penalties for adultery. The Qur'an enjoins both males and females to be chaste and modest.

Islamic religious texts prescribe a specific set of statuses and corresponding roles for females to play in the Muslim family as daughter, sister, wife, and mother. Each of these statuses carries certain obligations, rights, privileges, and duties. These statuses are influenced by the patriarchal ideals of the Islamic texts. One passage of the Qur'an (iv:34) is often cited when referring to the role of women:

Men are in charge of women, because God (Allah) hath made the one of them to excel the other, and because they spend of their property (for the support of women). So good women are the obedient.

This passage provides the context for the development of various laws that have influenced the status of Muslim women. For example, traditionally a woman could inherit only a one-half share of her parents' estate, whereas her brothers could inherit full shares. This law assumed that a woman is fully cared for by her family and that when she marries, her husband's family will provide for her material needs. Thus, a Muslim woman does not need the full share of inheritance.

Another traditional code in Islamic law illustrates the patriarchal attitudes toward women with respect to political and legal issues. In legal cases, a woman is granted half the legal status of a man. For example, if a crime is committed, two women as opposed to one man are needed as legal witnesses for testimony. This legal equation of "two females equal one male" reflects the traditional Islamic image of women as less experienced and less capable than men in political and legal affairs.

Ethnographic research since the 1970s has demonstrated that male-female relations in these societies are far more complex than the religious texts might imply. By focusing exclusively on Islamic texts and laws, early researchers distorted and misunderstood actual practices and relations between males and females. Moreover, before the 1970s, much of the ethnographic research in Muslim societies was done by males, resulting in a skewed understanding of the position of women because male cultural anthropologists did not have the same access to female informants as did female cultural anthropologists. Eventually, female cultural anthropologists such as Lois Beck, Lila Abu Lughod, Soraya Altorki, and Elizabeth Fernea began to study the Muslim female world.

Female cultural anthropologists discovered that the position of Muslim women cannot be categorized uniformly. One major reason for variation is the extent to which Islamic countries have been exposed to the West. Some, like Tunisia, Egypt, and Turkey, have adopted legal reforms that have improved the status of women. For example, Egyptian women have had access to secondary education since the early 1900s and have had career opportunities in medicine, law, engineering, management, and government. The Egyptian constitution accords women full equality with men and—ideally—prohibits sexual discrimination in career opportunities. Muslim feminist movements dedicated to improving the status of women have emerged in those countries most affected by the West.

In contrast to Egypt, religiously conservative Saudi Arabia has highly restrictive cultural norms regarding women. Saudi Arabia was not colonized and thus was more isolated, and the religious and political authorities actively opposed Western values and culture within their society. The Saudi Arabian government, which has a constitution based on Sharia law, has interpreted Islamic law to declare that any mingling of the sexes is morally wrong. Saudi women are segregated from men; they attend separate schools and upon finishing their education, can seek employment only in exclusively female institutions such as women's hospitals, schools, and banks. Saudi women are forbidden by law to drive cars, and when riding on public buses, they have to sit in special closed sections. All Saudi public buildings must have separate entrances and elevators for men and women (Altorki 1986; Badran 1998).

Despite legal reforms and women's access to education in some Muslim societies, the notion that women are subordinate to men to some extent remains firmly entrenched. For example, in Egypt, a woman trained in law cannot become a judge or hold any position with legislative authority. Also, in Egypt, polygyny remains legal, and men can obtain divorces with minimal justification. In many respects, the patriarchal family remains the center of Islamic social organization. Hence, in some cases, attempts to reform women's status have been perceived as heretical assaults on the Islamic family and morality. Some of the recent Islamic revival movements have reactivated conservative, patriarchal cultural norms.

The Veil and Seclusion To many Westerners, the patriarchal order of the Islamic societies is most conspicuously symbolized by the veil and the other shapeless garments worn by Muslim women. As a female approaches puberty, she is supposed to be restricted and kept from contact with males. The veil is an outward manifestation of a long, extensive historical and cultural pattern (Beck and Keddie 1978; Fernea and Fernea 1979). The wearing of the veil and the enforced seclusion of the Muslim woman are known as *purdah*. These practices reinforce a separation between the domestic, private sphere of women and the male-dominated public sphere.

Veiling and *purdah* tend to be associated with urban Muslim women. Most scholars believe that the tradition of veiling originated in urban areas among upper-class women prior to the emergence of Islamic religious developments (Beck and Keddie 1978). Traditionally, many peasant and Bedouin women in the Middle East and North Africa do not wear the veil and generally have more

freedom to associate with men than do Muslim women who live in towns and cities. Many urban Muslim women report that the veil and accompanying garments offer practical protection from strangers and that when in public they would feel naked and self-conscious without these garments (Fernea and Fernea 1979).

In countries such as Egypt, Turkey, and Iran that had formerly abandoned traditional dress codes, some educated middle-class women have opted to wear the veil and the all-enveloping garments. However, most of them wear the *hijab* or headscarf. To some extent, this return to traditional dress reflects the revival movements now occurring throughout the Islamic world. For many Muslim women, returning to the veil is one way in which they can affirm their Islamic religious and cultural identity and make a political statement of resistance to Western power and influence (Hanson 2004).

Despite the gender segregation that exists within some Muslim communities, some anthropological studies indicate that many young Muslim women are beginning to challenge these patterns. In one illuminating study in the Middle Eastern country of Jordan, anthropologist

Many Muslim women have adopted the *hijab* or headscarf to symbolize their Islamic identity.

Laura Kaya discovered that young Muslim women find ways around gender segregation through Internet chat (2009). Kaya did ethnographic research in the Internet cafés that were used by young Muslim women and men to build romantic relationships. Despite the cultural norms against female and male direct interaction in the gender segregated world of Jordan, these young people often contacted one another in modest forms of romantic discourse through Internet chat. The Internet cafés are modern developments, and young men and women who were strangers often sit next to one another, something that would violate the cultural norms in other segregated settings. At times, the men would send the women in the same Internet café scanned photos of themselves or romantic e-cards. This might result in a meeting between a male and female who were not introduced by someone in their family, something that is prohibited by cultural norms. Kaya discovered that this form of Internet communication was a new mode of online dating that challenged the cultural norms of the Middle Eastern lifestyle. Although this new development of Internet café chatting opened up new opportunities for overcoming gender segregation, Kaya mentions that the women who were seen as active in these cafés were often stigmatized as having violated the honor of the family. Thus, the cultural norms that influence gender segregation are still very powerful in the context of Middle Eastern societies.

Social Structure, Family, and Gender in India and South Asia

In the aftermath of independence and the retreat of Western colonial authority in South Asia, cultural anthropologists began to explore the various societies of the region. Much of the early ethnographic research centered on rural communities of India, with cultural anthropologists such as McKim Marriott, Oscar Lewis, Milton Singer, and Alan Beals investigating the caste system of the Indian rural communities.

Origins of the Caste System The caste system of India was briefly introduced in Chapter 17. First, the caste system is a continuously evolving system. It has changed with respect to its early origins, during the British colonial experience in India, and up until contemporary times. It is not an essential or static feature of Indian society (Mines 2009). Most scholars associate the origins of the caste system with the Aryan peoples who settled in northern India after 1500 B.C. Various social divisions in Aryan society developed into broad ideological categories known as *varnas*. The term *varna* is associated with particular colors, although this did not entail a notion of skin color for different groups. At the top were the *brahmans* (priests), followed by the *kshatriyas* (warriors), the *vaisyas* (merchants), and the

sudras (commoners). This fourfold scheme provided the ideological cultural framework for organizing thousands of diverse groups.

The most important aspect of social life in India is not the *varna*, but what is known by people who speak Hindi, the language of North India, as **jatis**, of which there are several thousand, hierarchically ranked. *Jatis* are based on one's birth group or "kind" (Mines 2009). However, one's *jati* is also going to relate to marriage, economic, and ritual relations. Marriages are endogamous (marriage within a group) with respect to *jati*; *jatis* are thus ranked endogamous descent groups. Although ideally, each *jati* or caste was based upon a specific hereditary occupational group, in reality there were thousands of *jatis* and only a small number of occupations (Mines 2009). Nevertheless, a person's *jati* places him or her within a fairly rigid form of social stratification.

India is a country of tremendous variation from village to village and region to region. The caste system is very different from locale to locale (Mines 2009). Early cultural anthropologists found that *jati* relationships are intimately linked with what is known as the **jajmani economy** of most rural Indian villages. The typical Indian rural village consists of many different service castes, with one caste dominating the village both economically and politically. Traditionally, it was believed that all these castes were interconnected through mutual and reciprocal economic exchanges within the *jajmani* economy. The dominant caste controlled the land and exchanged hereditary land-use rights for other goods and services. For example, members of the dominant caste would have their hair cut and fingernails trimmed by a barber. Then, at harvest time, the barber would get a stipulated amount of grain from his client. In addition, the barber, carpenter, potter, and water carrier would exchange their goods and services with one another in a type of barter system. Every caste, even the lowest-ranking, had some access to housing, furniture, food, credit, and other items through these exchanges (Quigley 1999). Also, when the British colonized India, they did an extensive census and categorized various "caste" groups according to Western categories; sometimes these misunderstandings have persisted until the present (Dirks 2001; Scupin 2012d; Mines 2009).

More recent ethnographic studies have concluded that the *jajmani* system is collapsing because of globalization, beginning with British colonialism and the introduction of new consumer goods and technology into Indian villages. When people can use safety razors to shave, buy imported dishware and glasses, and use electric pumps to obtain water, many of the old occupations become superfluous. Consequently, many artisans and service workers leave their villages to market their skills elsewhere or, in many cases, to join the increasing number of unskilled migrants flooding the cities.

Although the *jajmani* system is disappearing and the Indian government has outlawed the most reprehensible aspects of the caste system, such as "untouchability" and discrimination, in its constitution, cultural anthropologists find that the caste system still persists (Scupin 2012d; Hardgrove 2006; Mines 2009). Contemporary India has caste hotels, banks, hospitals, and co-ops. Caste organization continues to delineate political factions in India. Most elections are decided by caste voting blocs, and politicians must, therefore, appeal to caste allegiances for support. Thus, caste remains one of the most divisive factors facing the democratic process in India.

Cultural anthropologists find that the caste system is reinforced to some extent by the religious beliefs of Hinduism. The doctrines of *karma* and reincarnation reinforce concepts of purity and pollution that correlate with caste hierarchy. An individual's *karma* is believed to determine his or her status and ritual state. It is believed that individuals born into low castes are inherently polluted, whereas higher-caste individuals such as Brahmans are ritually pure. This state of purity or pollution is permanent.

The late French anthropologist Louis Dumont (1970) argued that from the Hindu viewpoint humans have to be ranked in a hierarchy; egalitarian relationships are inconceivable. Dumont asserted that in this worldview, caste relations produce interdependency and reciprocity through exchanges and ritual relationships. He concluded that the cultural understandings of caste rules and of ritual purity and pollution have created a system of stratification based on widespread consensus.

In contrast, other anthropologists influenced by more materialist orientations argue that Hindu beliefs about caste were primarily ideological justifications for a system that emerged from long-standing inequalities in which a dominant group accumulated most of the land and other resources. They deny that a consensus exists concerning the appropriateness of caste relationships, citing as evidence the situation of the *harijans* (Children of God, a name given to them by Mahatma Gandhi to help alleviate discrimination against them), or *untouchables*, at the bottom of the caste hierarchy, who daily face discrimination and exploitation. Based upon their research in India, anthropologists Joan Mencher and Pauline Kolenda reported that the *harijans* resent, rather than accept, this treatment (Kolenda 1978; Mencher 1974).

Other anthropologists have refined their analyses of caste relations by combining both material and cultural variables. For example, contemporary ethnographers have described the complex interplay of material interests and cultural meanings of exchanges among castes in the *jajmani* system. They note how upper-caste Brahmans accept gifts and other material items from lower-caste members, but in this exchange, they ritually absorb the sins of the donors (Parry 1980; Raheja 1988; Quigley 1999; Mines 2009). For example, Raheja emphasizes that in these *jajmani* exchanges the lower- and upper-caste groups become equal and that strict hierarchy is undermined. She found that the land-owning dominant caste were not just distributing grains and other foods with other castes, but also their "inauspiciousness" (their sins, faults, and impurities) to other castes such as the barbers, sweepers, and Brahmans who were able to digest these sins and impurities and produce ritual purity. Thus, in many cases the caste exchanges are based on material factors and on the symbolic conceptions of Hinduism.

As a result of globalization and improvements in education in India, many low-caste "untouchables" have become educated and have been involved in political movements that resulted in affirmative action policies. There are quotas in the educational and other institutions in Indian society in order to help improve the status of the lower caste individuals. Many people in India have rejected the notion of caste and rank in Indian society, just as many Americans have rejected racism. However, caste discrimination in India and racism in the United States, as we will see in Chapter 23, are still enduring facts of life.

Family and Marriage in South Asia The most typical form of family in South Asia is the extended also known as joint family, which consists of three generations: grandparents, parents, and children. It may also include brothers and their wives and children within the same household. The extended family is the ideal norm for South Asian rural villages because it provides a corporate structure for landowning, labor, and other functions. Cultural anthropologists find, however, that families actually go through development cycles—an extended family at one point, a large extended family at another time, and a nuclear family at still other times. But despite modernizing influences, the cultural ideal of the joint family persists, even in most urban areas (Maloney 1974; Tyler 1986; Hardgrove 2006).

Parents arrange the marriages in South Asia. As noted, in northern India, people marry outside their patrilineage and village but inside their caste grouping. A married woman must switch allegiance from her father's descent group to that of her husband. After marriage, a woman moves into her husband's joint family household and must adjust to the demands of her mother-in-law. Currently, anthropologists find that the idea of arranged marriage is often the center of debate among young people in India (Mines 2009). The emerging middle class of young professionals involved in the booming Indian economy want more choice regarding their marriage partners, despite the fact that most marriages are still within one's caste group.

In Pakistan and Bangladesh, parallel-cousin marriage is often preferred, and polygynous marriages, in accordance with Muslim practices, are sometimes found.

However, again, a tremendously varied pattern is actually observed by anthropologists (Weiss 2006).

The Dowry   Another marital practice, found especially in northern India, is the dowry. The Indian bride brings to the marriage an amount of wealth that to some extent represents her share of the household inheritance. Typically, the dowry includes clothing and jewelry that the bride retains for her personal property, household furnishings, and prestige goods (Tambiah 1989). Upper-caste families try to raise a large dowry payment as a sign of their elevated status. In these cases, the dowry creates alliances between elite families.

Gender and Status in South Asia   The status of women in South Asia varies from one cultural area to another, especially in respect to urban versus rural communities. In Pakistan and Bangladesh, which are influenced by the Islamic tradition, many women are secluded according to the prescriptions of *purdah*. Until recently, Hindu women of northern India were subject to similar norms. Today, however, many Hindu women do not wear the veil and accompanying clothing, thereby distinguishing themselves from Muslims. Traditionally, in both Islamic and Hindu regions, a woman was expected to obey her father, her husband, and, eventually, her sons. Women ate after the men were finished and walked several paces behind them.

In the rural communities, older women, particularly mothers-in-law, gain more respect and status in the family. In certain cases, older women became dominant figures in the extended family, controlling the household budget. As some urban South Asian women have become educated, they have begun to resist the patriarchal tendencies of their societies. Some have even participated in emerging feminist political activities. As industrialization and urbanization continue, an increase in feminist activity would be expected. However, because about 80 percent of the population still resides in rural communities, patriarchal tendencies remain pervasive (Hardgrove 2006; Weiss 2006).

Family and Gender in China

Prior to the 1970s ethnographic research in China was severely restricted by the Chinese Communist government. During the 1970s, the United States and China developed a more formal cooperative relationship, and China began to allow some cultural anthropologists to conduct research within its borders. In the 1970s, Norman Chance became the first American cultural anthropologist allowed to conduct fieldwork in both rural and urban communes. His detailed ethnography of Half Moon Village in Red Flag Commune, near Beijing, offers important insights into the economic, social, political, and cultural developments of that period. Half Moon Village was one sector of the Red Flag Commune, which was one of the largest communes in China when it was formed in 1958. Red Flag occupied 62 square miles and contained 85,000 inhabitants in 17,000 households, organized into production brigades and work teams. The state owned the land and the sideline industries associated with the commune. The commune workforce consisted of more than 40,000 people, most of whom did agricultural work. Many of the commune's crops were sent to Beijing markets, providing a steady income for the villagers. Approximately 15 percent of the labor force worked in the commune's industrial sector.

The Family, Marriage, and Kinship in Red Flag Commune   Following the Chinese Revolution, the government initiated a campaign to eradicate the patriarchal nature of the Chinese family and clan. The Communist leadership viewed the traditional family, clan, and male dominance as remnants of precommunist "feudal" China, as well as major sources of inequality. The Chinese Communist Party passed legislation such as the marriage laws of 1950 to destroy the traditional clan and extended-family ties and create more equal relationships between males and females. The marriage laws required free choice in marriage by both partners, guaranteed monogamy, and established a woman's right to work and obtain a divorce without losing her children (DeVoe 2006; Brownell and Wasserstrom 2002).

Norman Chance's (1984) research indicated, however, that despite government attempts to alter family and kinship relations, Half Moon Village residents sought to maintain strong kinship ties for economic security. Chance discovered that many decisions concerning access to various jobs in the commune were based on kinship relationships. To ensure kinship ties, families maneuvered around government officials and decisions. In addition, younger family members looked to their elders for knowledge and advice. Chance found that harmonious relationships within the family were emphasized according to the centuries-old Confucianist traditions.

The role and the status of women have been strongly influenced by the ideals of the Chinese Communist Party leadership. Based on his study of Half Moon Village, Chance (1984) concluded that the status of women had improved under the Communist regime and that, in general, the new marriage laws had disrupted the Confucian pattern of rigid patriarchy. Young girls were no longer married off or sold. Women were no longer confined to the home; rather, they were encouraged to work along with the men in agriculture and industry.

Chance noted some other changes in the status of women. He regularly observed young men taking care of their children and doing tasks such as cooking, chores that were previously performed only by women. In addition, women had assumed decision-making roles in certain areas, especially in respect to family planning—a high priority for the Chinese government after 1976. After China adopted the well-known one-child policy, the Communist Party paid bonuses to families that had only one child (see Chapter 24). Families had to return the bonus to the government if they had a second child. Women were responsible for administering and monitoring this policy.

Despite these changes, however, Chance found that some remnants of the older patriarchal norms were still evident. For example, peasant women engaged in agricultural labor were unable to develop skills that would lead to better job opportunities in the factories and other sideline occupations of the commune. In contrast to men, women were restricted to unskilled jobs. In addition, women did not hold administrative positions on commune committees.

Chance also found that women's role in the family did not change dramatically. Typically, patrilocal residence rules prevailed at Half Moon Village. Chance noted that this often led to conflicts between the mother-in-law and daughter-in-law in the modern Chinese family, just as it had for centuries in the traditional Chinese family. In addition, despite the passage of the marriage laws, matchmaking and arranged marriages remained the norm, and villagers strongly disapproved of divorce. Couples still preferred male over female children to perpetuate family interests. Party officials frequently postponed efforts to alter these patriarchal patterns because such changes might cause stress and conflicts in the family unit.

Following globalization trends and the decline and collapse of rigid Maoist policies in the People's Republic of China since the 1980s, ethnographic research has found that an enormous change has influenced family and gender issues in this society (DeVoe 2006; Brownell and Wasserstrom 2002). Marriage rules are tending to become more flexible, based upon individual choice, rather than family arrangements, and women are becoming more independent and educated as they encounter the global economy, new technologies introduced by outsourcing (see Chapter 20), and the new global media, including the Internet, which are influencing cultural and social change (Appadurai 1996; Scupin 2006a). We shall return to this topic when we discuss the contemporary global trends in Chapter 24.

Ethnic Tensions

22.7 Discuss the factors that influence ethnic tensions in the Middle East and Asia.

As in most other societies, globalization has induced ethnic tensions that have divided many Middle Eastern and Asian countries. Anthropologist Dale Eickelman notes how difficult it is to maintain a simplistic perspective of ethnicity when viewing the population known as the Kurds (1995). Kurdish ethnic identity is constructed and shifted to adjust to many different circumstances and conditions. The Kurdish minority crosses several international borders. About 20 percent (about 14 million) live in Turkey, 7 million live in Iran and 6 million in Iraq, and another 2 million live in Syria. Their Kurdish identity is constructed and treated differently within these various countries of the Middle East. In general, the Kurds view themselves as an oppressed ethnic minority wherever they live, and they have faced considerable persecution and discrimination by all of these countries. They have struggled within all these different countries to form an autonomous country called Kurdistan, but thus far they have not succeeded. Following the U.S. invasion of Iraq in 2003, the Kurds found themselves no longer subject to the severe persecution and genocidal policies directed at them by Saddam Hussein; however, currently, they face hostility from the Sunni and Shi'a ethnic sectors of Iraqi society. These tensions may either impact negatively on civil unity and the stability of the government in Iraq or engender more ethnic and sectarian conflict.

China and Ethnic Minorities

The People's Republic of China, with over 1.3 billion people, includes approximately 104 million people (9.1 percent of the population) who are referred to as "national minorities." These minorities are ethnically distinct from the Han majority population, which make up 92 percent of the population. These official national minorities consist of 55 groups, 18 of which have more than one million members. China appeared to have "folk" concepts of group membership that were equivalent to the pseudoscientific concept of "race" that was developed in European society in the eighteenth and nineteenth centuries (see Chapter 23). In China, these folk notions of race were related to family, blood relationships, and descent. From the earliest centuries of Chinese civilization, one's social identity revolved around membership within a particular family and patrilineal group or clan known as *zu*, a group of people who could demonstrate through written records or oral history that they were part of the same descent group.

In China, the term *zu* for patrilineage was eventually redefined as *minzu*, which integrated people (*min*) and descent (*zu*) to refer to the people, "race," or nation of China. In a broad sense, it means the whole Chinese nation, that is, *zhonghuaminzu*. Officially, it includes all people who live within China's territory, which is comprised of 56 officially recognized *minzus*. In a narrow sense, *minzu* refers to a subgroup of the Chinese nation, for example, the Han, Mongols (Mengguzu), Tibetans (Zangzu), Muslims (Huizu), and so on. (Dikötter 1992, 2008; Gladney 1991, 1998, 2004).

One of the most ethnically complex areas of China is Yunnan province in the southwest region bordering Vietnam. In this area, there are 25 ethnic groups or *minzu*, many of whom have a different language and culture than the Han majority. Currently, the non-Han ethnic minorities in Yunnan account for about 34 percent of its total population. These groups include the Yi, Bai, Hani, Zhuang, Dai (Tai), Miao (Hmong), Jingpo, Lisu, Hui (Muslim), Lahu, Va (Wa), Naxi, Yao, Zang (Tibetan), Bulang (Blang), Primi (Pumi), Nu, Achang, Deang, Jino (Jinuo), Shui, Man (Manchus), Menggu (Mongolian), Buyi, and Dulong. Anthropologist Susan Blum did an extensive ethnographic study of many of these different ethnic groups in Yunnan (2001). She focused on how the Han majority classifies and treats the ethnic minorities of Yunnan and concludes that they are treated as ethnic inferiors (as the title of her study, *Portraits of "Primitives,"* suggests). Although the Chinese authorities have attempted to incorporate the different ethnic minorities in Yunnan as equal citizens as part of the Chinese nation and family, these minorities are considered backward and undeveloped in comparison with the Han majority population. At the same time, the Chinese government has been marketing the colorful costumes, music, and dance of these ethnic minorities in Yunnan as a cultural heritage area in order to increase its tourism to this region.

Anthropologist Dru Gladney has been conducting ethnographic research on the Muslim minority in China, illustrating how ethnic relations between the national minorities and Han majority have evolved and persisted (1991, 1998, 2004). There are ten Muslim ethnic nationalities or *minzu*: the Hui, Uyghur, Kazak, Dongxiang, Kirghiz, Salar, Tadjik, Uzbek, Baonan, and Tatar—consisting of over 20 million people. The earliest Muslim groups in China were descended from Arab, Persian, Central Asian, and Turkish peoples who migrated into China and settled in the northwest and southeast coastal regions. The Hui, who are the largest Muslim group, have a population of over nine million people and are widely distributed throughout China. They did not have a separate language, and spoke the language (mostly Chinese Mandarin) where they lived. The Hui reside in most of the counties and cities throughout China, including the large cities of Beijing and Shanghai. Unlike the other Muslim nationalities in China, the Hui speak the dialects of the other ethnic groups among whom they live, primarily the Han. Some of the Hui, however, reside in areas such as Tibet or Mongolia, where they speak the Tibetan or Mongolian language.

The Uyghur Muslims of China are a Turkic ethnic group of about eight million people, most of whom reside in Xinjiang, a southwestern region of China. During the period 744–840 A.D., the Uyghurs had an extensive empire stretching across Central Asia, extending from the Caspian Sea to the northeast area of Manchuria. The Uyghur maintain their own distinct language and culture and have extensive contacts with the Middle East and other Islamic regions (Gladney 2004). Most recently, the Uyghurs have been involved in massive demonstrations against the Han majority government based in Beijing. They have been asserting their ethnic and religious identity and believe that they have been treated as an inferior group in China. In July 2009, there was a major Uyghur demonstration against the Han-based Beijing government which resulted in almost 200 Uyghur deaths and thousands of injuries. The Chinese government has characterized these protests and demonstrations as part of a terrorist campaign and arrested over 1,000 Uyghur in order to repress this threat to its political control of this region. Thus, China continues to face a challenge within its borders from non-Han minorities.

Another example of ethnic and political tensions in the People's Republic of China has emerged since the 1950s between its Maoist government and the region once known as Tibet. Tibet was a traditional region in the eastern Himalayan Mountains that had tributary and political relationships with the government of China for many centuries. In Tibet, the indigenous people maintained a different form of Buddhism, language, and culture than did the Han majority in most of China. Traditionally, Tibet was ruled by the highest-ranking Tibetan Buddhist monk, known as the Dalai Lama, and one of five males in the region became a Buddhist monk. Following the establishment of the People's Republic of China, the Maoist government sent its military into Tibet during the 1950s to absorb this region. In 1959, the Dalai Lama, the fourteenth sacred ruling monk, and thousands of his followers fled Tibet and the Maoist regime, seeking safety as political and religious refugees in the area of Dharmsala in north India.

After Tibet's absorption into China in the 1950s, the Maoist Red Guards were sent to destroy Buddhist temples, burn religious texts, and purge the "backward feudal theocratic regime and superstitious religious culture" of the region. The Maoist government recruited many Han people to move to Tibet (under the People's Republic of China, the area of Tibet is known as Xizang) to foster the cultural assimilation of this region into the mainstream culture of the Han. Many Tibetans resisted this domination by the Han and were supported by the Dalai Lama's worldwide campaign to help restore Tibetan culture, ethnicity, and religion. Over the years, recognizing the political difficulties in pushing China for independence for Tibet, the Dalai Lama has campaigned only for some cultural and religious autonomy for this region. However, in 2008, hundreds of Tibetan monks led a massive protest demonstration in the capital city of Lhasa and other regions against the Han-based Beijing government. Some of the Tibetans attacked non-Tibetan ethnic groups including the Han majority. There were over 100 casualties and thousands of arrested Tibetans. A number of anthropologists, including Melvyn Goldstein and Marcia Calkowski, have been doing ethnographic work in this region for many years and have been consulting with the governments there and elsewhere on the ethnic, religious, and political tensions between the Tibetans and China (Goldstein 1997; Calkowski 2008).

As is obvious, in the Middle East and Asia many different ethnic and cultural traditions are colliding as a result of the process of globalization. This development is disrupting the traditional values and practices within the region, and in some cases, the overall reaction to this rapid process of change is to revert to a nostalgic past in which the traditional rural communities maintained the moral economy, the extended family, and other communal practices. However, this reaction to the process of rapid globalization has at times led to tensions among political, religious, and ethnic groups throughout these regions. Continuing ethnographic research is needed to help people understand each other's traditions as one possible major step in helping to reduce these regional tensions.

A Mosuo minority woman in Yunnan province in the Peoples Republic of China.

Anthropologists at Work

SUSAN BROWNELL, Ethnography and Sports in China

Susan Brownell traces her interest in China back to the stories told by her grandmother. Her grandmother's father, Earl Leroy Brewer, was governor of Mississippi, as well as a civil rights proponent and lawyer for the Mississippi Chinese Association in the 1910s and 1920s. Brownell's love of anthropology began when, as an undergraduate at the University of Virginia, she took Victor Turner's famous seminar, in which the participants reenacted different rituals from around the world. She wrote her first paper on sports for Turner's seminar in 1981, and his ideas continued to inspire her over the years. She was also a nationally ranked track-and-field athlete (in the pentathlon and heptathlon) from 1978 to 1990. She was a six-time collegiate All-American while at Virginia and competed in the 1980 and 1984 U.S. Olympic trials. In 1980, she worked for six weeks as a stunt double for the feature film *Personal Best*,

which depicted four years in the life of a young pentathlete played by Mariel Hemingway.

After starting the Ph.D. program at the University of California, Santa Barbara, she decided to try to combine her various interests in a dissertation on Chinese sports. While at Beijing University in 1985–1986 for a year of Chinese language studies, she joined the track team. She was chosen to represent Beijing in the 1986 Chinese National College Games, where she won a gold medal and set a national record in the heptathlon, earning fame throughout China as "the American girl who won glory for Beijing." She returned to China to study sport theory at the Beijing University of Physical Education (1987–1988). She was awarded her Ph.D. in 1990. After teaching at Middlebury College, the University of Washington, and Yale University, she joined the Department of Anthropology at the University of Missouri, St. Louis, in the fall of 1994. She has served as department chair, a member of the Postgraduate Grant Selection

Susan Brownell

Committee of the Olympic Studies Centre in Lausanne, and a member of the advisory council of the Wenner-Gren Foundation for Anthropological Research.

Brownell drew on her direct experience with Chinese athletics in *Training the Body for China: Sports in the Moral Order of the People's Republic* (1995), an insightful look at the culture of sports and the body in China. This was the first

(continued)

book on Chinese sports based on field-work in China by a Westerner. Brownell and Jeffrey N. Wasserstrom edited a volume entitled *Chinese Femininities/ Chinese Masculinities: A Reader* (2002). She is also the author of *Beijing's Games: What the Olympics Mean to China* (2008) and editor of *From Athens to Beijing: East Meets West in the Olympic Games* (2013) and *The 1904 Anthropology Days and Olympic Games: Race, Sport, and American Imperialism* (2008), which won the 2009 Anthology Award from the North American Society for Sport History. Together with William W. Kelly, she also edited *The Olympics in East Asia: Nationalism, Regionalism, and Globalism on the Center Stage of World Sports* (2011).

In the year leading up to and including the 2008 Beijing Olympic Games, Brownell was a Fulbright senior researcher affiliated with the Beijing Sport University. As one of the world's few experts on the Chinese sports world, with over two decades of engagement in it, she was in a position to act as a cultural bridge between China and the outside world. She provided information and advice on an informal basis to the Beijing Olympic Organizing Committee and the International Olympic Committee (IOC), and contributed to a report that was submitted to the Chinese government about the feasibility of establishing "protest zones" during the Olympics. The zones were announced, but none of the applications to use them were approved. However, many regarded it as a positive step toward greater tolerance of public protests in China, and once the precedent was set, it was repeated for the 2010 Asian Games in Guangzhou. Brownell was added to the academic expert team that was working with the Beijing municipal government on the "Olympic education" programs in the schools, and she translated their final report into English. She gave interviews to 100 journalists from over 20 countries, including NPR, CNN, the *Jim Lehrer News Hour* on PBS, BBC, Al Jazeera TV, *The Wall Street Journal*, AP, and others, and during the Olympic Games was a guest expert for the pre-view program "17 Days" on China Central Television's English-language international channel. She wrote essays for the Web site of the U.S. Embassy in Beijing and for the official magazine of the International Olympic Committee, *The Olympic Review*. Two years later, she become one of the few people to play a role in both of China's first mega-events, when she was a member of the academic experts' team that helped organize the forums held during the Shanghai World Expo 2010. She was the only non-Chinese person to provide input into the drafting of the "Shanghai Declaration," a document announced at the closing ceremony of the six-month exposition that summarized the vision of the future of globalization that had been expressed at the Expo.

While many politicians, advocacy groups, and intellectuals took advantage of the international media scrutiny brought on by these two mega-events to draw attention to China's human rights record, Brownell argued that the process of organizing these expositions would intensify China's engagement in the global community. She stated that it was necessary to view them from a social scientific point of view as part of a slow process that would play out over time, and would not satisfy the needs of politicians and journalists for headline-making, immediate results.

Her experience in the middle of the ideologically motivated debates that accompanied China's emergence as a superpower convinced Brownell of the importance of the discipline of anthropology for the twenty-first century. Cultural anthropology is the only academic discipline for which the primary research method is talking with living people face-to-face. This implies respect for the local knowledge possessed by everyday people—a respect that is not found in other disciplines. As the digital age enables the collection of ever bigger "big data," it is even more important to pay attention to what is going on in the lives of real people. Otherwise we run the risk of repeating grand miscalculations such as characterized the U.S. invasion of Afghanistan in 2001 or the global financial collapse of 2008, which were partly caused by a failure to collect information at the grassroots level and by overconfidence in abstractions.

Islamic Revitalization

22.8 Discuss the links between globalization and Islamic movements.

One pervasive trend throughout the Muslim world since the 1970s has been Islamic revivalism, sometimes known as fundamentalism. Contemporary revivalist movements have their roots in earlier reformist movements that sought to combine Islam with Western values as a means of coping with colonialism and industrialism. In countries such as Egypt, however, some members of fundamentalist groups such as the Muslim Brotherhood rejected reform in favor of the elimination of secular Western influences (Scupin 2008b; Sidky and Akers 2006; Starrett 1998). These movements encouraged the reestablishment of an Islamic society based on the Qur'an and Sharia (Islamic law). Some groups sought to bring about these changes peacefully, whereas others believed that an Islamic state could be established only through violent revolution.

Ethnographic studies have contributed to a better understanding of the sources of Islamic revival movements. One critical factor was the 1967 Arab–Israeli War, which resulted in the crushing defeat of the Arab states and the loss of Arab territories to Israel. This event symbolized the economic and political weakness of the Islamic nations and inspired many Muslims to turn to their faith as a source of communal bonds and political strength.

Another significant factor was the oil boom. Many fundamentalists believed that by bestowing rich oil reserves on these societies, Allah (God) was shifting power from the materialist and secular civilizations of the West to the Islamic world (Esposito 2010). The oil revenues of countries such as Libya, Iran, Saudi Arabia, and Kuwait have been used to support fundamentalist movements throughout the Muslim world.

Islamic Revolution in Iran

Islamic revivalistic movements in the Middle East surprised many Western social scientists. They assumed that with modernization and globalization these societies would become increasingly secularized and that the role of religion in economic, social, and political affairs would be reduced. Instead, most Muslim countries experienced Islamic movements that were linked to national, political, and economic issues.

One of the regions of the Middle East most affected by Islamic fundamentalist tendencies has been Iran. Through ethnographic, historical, and comparative research, anthropologists have contributed to an understanding of the Islamic revival in Iran. They cite a number of factors that converged to produce this revival.

Iran is predominantly a Shi'a Islamic society. As explained in Chapter 19, after the death of the Prophet Muhammad, the Islamic community was divided into the Sunni and the Shi'a sects. In the sixteenth century, Shah Ismail of the Safavid dynasty proclaimed Shi'ism the official religion of Iran. From that time, many Shi'a migrated to Iran for protection from the dominant Sunni rulers elsewhere. Traditional Shi'a theology does not distinguish between religion and politics; instead, based on the doctrine of the imamate, the Shi'a maintain that their religious leaders have both theological and political authority. The Shi'a clergy was organized into a religious hierarchy with a supreme Ayatollah (Sign of God), lesser Ayatollahs, and mullahs or local Islamic clergy at the mosque level. The clergy emphasize that Islamic beliefs and doctrine show no separation between religion and politics and that they ought to be the political as well as the religious rulers in Iran.

During the nineteenth century, the British and Russians were competing with one another in the so-called "Great Game" to control regions of the Middle East including Iran. The Iranian rulers, or shahs, offered a large number of concessions to British and Russian bankers and private companies and also attempted to modernize Iran's military and educational systems along Western lines. These policies generated internal opposition. The newly educated classes, who had acquired Western ideals of democracy and representative government, opposed the shahs' absolute power. In addition, the Shi'a clergy opposed the shah's political policies and secularization and Western education, which interfered with traditional education, which they controlled.

In 1925, the Pahlavi dynasty came to power in Iran. Reza Shah Pahlavi viewed the Shi'a religious leaders as obstacles to his plans for rapid modernization. He attempted to reduce their power by appropriating their lands, thus depriving them of income. Reza Shah decreed that secular laws would replace the Sharia laws and that women would no longer have to wear the veil.

During World War II, Muhammad Reza Pahlavi, supported by Russian and Western interests, replaced his father as ruler. The new shah continued the modernization and secularization policies of his father. By the 1960s, he had centralized all political authority in his hands. Many Western multinational corporations were attracted to Iran because of its vast oil reserves and growing gross national product. By the 1970s, about 43,000 Americans were living in Iran. The Iranian economy became increasingly dependent on Western imported goods, while internally, aside from oil production, few native industries were developed.

In 1963, the shah announced the White Revolution, which included the commercialization of agriculture through land reforms and the expansion of capitalism. It also included public ownership of companies and voting rights for women. The land reforms disrupted the traditional peasant economy, creating a class of landless peasants, who flocked to Iranian cities in search of scarce opportunities. The White Revolution further mobilized the opposition of the religious clergy, who saw the plight of the peasants. The shah was perceived as a puppet of the United States (the Great Satan) and Western imperialism. One of the major critics was the Ayatollah Khomeini, who was arrested and exiled in 1963.

The shah's policies alienated many other sectors of Iranian society. To buttress his power, the shah—along with his secret police, the SAVAK—brutally crushed any opposition to his regime. The Westernized middle class, university students, merchants in the bazaars, and the urban poor began to sympathize with any opposition to the shah's regime. These groups allied themselves with the Shi'a clergy and heeded the clergy's call for an Islamic revolution. For 15 years, Khomeini continued to attack the shah in pamphlets and taped sermons smuggled into Iran.

Although united in their opposition to the shah, various segments of Iranian society viewed the Islamic revolution in different terms. The rural migrants who flooded into the Iranian cities steadfastly supported the Shi'a clergy. The Westernized middle class viewed the Shi'a revolution in terms of its own democratic aspirations, believing that the religious leaders would play a secondary role in the actual administration of the Iranian state. Many university students had been influenced by the writings of Ali

Shariati, who interpreted Shi'a Islam as a form of liberation theology that would free their society from foreign domination. These elements in Iranian society formed a coalition that encouraged the social and political revolution led by Khomeini and the religious clerics. A cycle of demonstrations, violent protests, and religious fervor led to the downfall of the shah, and in 1979, Khomeini returned to Iran to lead the revolution.

Ever since the overthrow of the shah, the religious clerics have assumed nearly all of the important political positions. Khomeini announced the establishment of the Islamic Republic of Iran, a theocratic state ruled by the Shi'a clergy, who used the mosques as the basic building blocks of political power. All Iranians were forced to register at a mosque, which functioned as an amalgam of government office, place of worship, and local police force. A systematic campaign was waged to purge Iranian society of its Western influences. Alcohol, gambling, prostitution, and pornography were strictly forbidden; women were required to wear head scarves, and those who refused were sent to "reeducation centers." The Shi'a regime believed it had a religious duty to export its revolution to other areas of the Islamic world.

Since the Islamic revolution, most ethnographic research has been forbidden in Iran, so collecting data on recent trends has been difficult. From press reports, it is clear that the revolution has radically changed the nature of Iranian society. The revolution was not only a political revolution but also a total social and cultural transformation. Iran is, however, racked with internal conflicts among different classes, religious factions, and political groups. Economic problems exacerbated by the reduction in oil prices and a ten-year war against Iraq led to infighting among radical militants, conservative fundamentalists, and moderates.

In May 1997, Mohammad Khatami, a moderate Muslim cleric, won Iran's presidential election in a landslide victory over more conservative candidates. Khatami attracted a broad coalition of centrists, women, youth of both genders, and middle-class intellectuals to his cause. He is believed to be a direct descendant of the Prophet Muhammad, which helped him consolidate support. Although Khatami's victory did not result in immediate changes in the country's Islamic fundamentalist path, he tried to restrain the more conservative faction of the clergy that has ruled the country since 1979. The reform movement within Iran was trying to overcome the more conservative factions associated with the Islamic revolution. Even though the conservative political factions retained the controlling political force in Iran, Khatami and the reformists inspired many of the young people, especially women; democratic media; and other elements. Increases in education and the transnational flow of information, people, and cultures accompanying globalization fostered the development of a more democratically oriented populace.

However, the moderate reformers boycotted the Iranian election in 2004 because of the conservative opposition to criticisms of the government and a free press. This enabled the conservative clergy to obtain more control over the political economy in Iran, and a more conservative and nationalistic Iranian, Mahmoud Ahmadinejad, was elected. In 2009, Iran had another election that was marked by major street demonstrations on the part of the moderate reformers who wanted to develop more democratic policies. In addition to massive street demonstrations, the moderates utilized the Internet and Twitter to report on the government suppression of their movement. Despite international criticism of irregularities in the election process, the conservative Ahmadinejad was reelected.

Recently, in 2013, a vast majority of Iranians, including the young and women supporters, elected another moderate Muslim cleric, Hassan Rouhani, as president he has promoted strengthening ties with the West and the United States. However, since the death of Khomeini in 1989, the major political authority continues to reside with the Grand Ayatollah, Ali Khamanei, who represents the more conservative elements within Iranian society.

It appears that in Iran, as in many Islamic countries today, there is a severe political struggle between those who are more moderate, secular, and democratic in their orientation and those who are more conservative, fundamentalist, and anti-Western (Antoun 2001; Scupin 2008b). Recently, under the control of the conservative fundamentalist clergy, high unemployment rates, double-digit inflation, government control of industry, attempts to block any free trade and multinational enterprises in Iran, and international sanctions have created enormous economic problems for the country. Only time will tell whether Iran will be able to overcome factionalism and resolve its political and economic problems; however, these conflicts and developments may usher in more troubling concerns regarding the proliferation of nuclear weapons in the region.

Islamic Revitalization in Afghanistan

Another region where Islamic revitalization is playing a profound role is Afghanistan, which has had a very troubled history. As we have seen, the British and Russians tried to colonize the area during the nineteenth century in the so-called Great Game between these powers (Monsutti 2013). During this time, with British support, Afghan leaders such as Abdul Rahman attempted to modernize and unify its many ethnic groups by building roads and pacifying fractious tribes throughout the country. In the 1920s and 1930s, with increased education, many Afghan intellectuals were exposed to ideas based on constitutional democracy and nationalism. Some of these leaders tried to institute democratic processes; however, economic development programs were failing. Consequently, class-based Marxist movements began to emerge in Afghanistan, with the support of the Soviet Union. In 1973, a pro-Soviet Marxist leader staged a military coup and proclaimed himself president of the Republic of Afghanistan. Five years later, another military coup installed a communist government with the patronage of the Soviet Union.

The communist leadership and the Soviet Union underestimated the strength of the Islamic traditions and multiethnic assertiveness of Afghanistan. The ethnic groups of Afghanistan include the Pashtuns (the largest group, with about 47 percent of the population), Tajiks, Uzbeks, Turkmen, Kirghiz, Hazara, Baluchis, and others. The Sunni Muslims constitute about 88 percent of the population and the Shi'a Muslims, about 12 percent (Dupree 1980; Shahrani and Canfield 1984; Sidky and Akers 2006). These ethnic and religious coalitions began to resist the Soviet Union and the Marxist communist government. A nationwide Islamic struggle was launched, referred to as a *jihad*, or"holy struggle," by a group of "holy warriors" called the *Mujahidin* (Edwards 2002).

The Soviet Union invaded Afghanistan in 1979 to repress this Islamic resistance led by the exiled *Mujahidin* parties based in Iran and Pakistan. Cold War politics began to influence this struggle against the Russians, with several Western governments offering financial and military assistance to the *Mujahidin*. Many Afghans were driven out of their country into neighboring Pakistan. However, with increasing internal weaknesses within the U.S.S.R. and the fierce resistance of the *Mujahidin*, the Soviets withdrew from Afghanistan in 1989.

Following the withdrawal of the Soviet Union, ethnic differences and varying Islamic traditions and movements presented obstacles to the unification of the Afghans. Local Islamic and ethnic factions that had developed during the Soviet occupation began to fight for power, resulting in years of warfare in Afghanistan during the 1980s and 1990s. The Western governments that patronized the *Mujahidin* during the Cold War withdrew support, fearing an Islamic revolution similar to the one in Iran. Consequently, the factional fighting among ethnic and religious groups brought about political disorder and chaos in Afghanistan.

One Islamic faction that emerged in Afghanistan in 1994 was known as the Taliban. Anthropologists have described the social and religious background of the Taliban (Edwards 1996, 1998, 2002; Sidky and Akers 2006). The majority of the Taliban members are Afghan students recruited from Islamic religious schools in Pakistan. (The term *Taliban* refers to religious students.) The Taliban served as a militia that scored a series of victories over other ethnic and religious factions, thus consolidating control over most of the regions in Afghanistan.

The Taliban received a great deal of international attention because of its stringent Islamic guidelines and norms. Afghan men were forbidden to trim their beards. Afghan women were strictly secluded from any contact with men, were not allowed to work outside of the home, and had to wear the traditional covering known as the *burqa*. Ethnographers emphasize that many members of the Taliban were socialized and trained in Pakistan, outside the confines of traditional ethnic and tribal affinities within Afghanistan. Therefore, young men from different backgrounds were able to unify an Islamic revitalization movement based on a sense of frustration over 20 years of conflict, factionalism, and political disorder. The Taliban received support from many Afghans despite its attempt to impose a purified Islamic culture on the country. However, the Taliban also got backing from terrorist organizations such as al-Qaeda, which was headed by Osama bin Laden, the Saudi multimillionaire who directed terrorist activities against the United States.

In 2001, following the September 11 attack on the World Trade Center and the Pentagon, the U.S. military began a campaign to subvert the political control of the Taliban and root out al-Qaeda and other terrorists in Afghanistan. Most of the international community supported this effort to dethrone the Taliban and provide a more effective and humane political order in Afghanistan (Sidky and Akers 2006). However, even today, the Taliban has much support from different sectors of the rural and urban communities in Afghanistan that want more political order and stability within their regions.

The elections in Afghanistan in November 2004 resulted in a government led by Hamed Karzai, a Pashtun leader who actively opposed the communist regime in the 1980s and early 1990s. Although Karzai was initially supportive of the Taliban, he realized that its members were working on behalf of the radical Islamic fundamentalists. His father was murdered by the Taliban in 1999. By then, he had become an important figure and was selected as a provisional leader of Afghanistan by the Afghan leaders. Eventually, Karzai directed an opposition movement against the Taliban that was supported by the United States, Britain, and international organizations (Canfield 2004). In 2010, the United States increased the number of troops in Afghanistan in order to provide some political stability for the Karzai regime. Recently, the United States has been withdrawing troops from Afghanistan and developing policies to support elections and democratic institutions along with domestic and national security. Western analysts

The Taliban in Afghanistan.

continue to be concerned that Afghanistan could become a failed state that would be a haven for extremist elements like the Taliban and al-Qaeda to foment terrorist attacks.

Islam Interpreted One conclusion resulting from the many ethnographic studies of Islam in the Middle East and Asia is that this religious tradition, like all religious traditions, can have different interpretations, depending on the context. The Islamic religion can be combined with diverse types of political activity. It can provide ideological support for revolutionary change, as the case of Iran suggests, or it can help sustain a specific socioeconomic and political order, as in contemporary Saudi Arabia, where some 2,000 princes control the entire political economy and resources. Thus, political and religious leaders can use Islam to advance social justice, justify political oppression, or further the goals of one particular political group. Anthropologists find that a one-dimensional understanding of Islamic culture or civilization based on a simplistic stereotype or image of a static culture or civilization does not help explain the rapid cultural changes and movements emerging in these Middle Eastern and Asian regions of the world. The Islamic religious tradition is not monolithic and takes many different forms in various societies. Anthropologists are studying these trends all over the Islamic world.

For example, anthropologist Scott Atran, who did extensive research in the Middle East, has been analyzing the recent phenomenon of suicide bombing in the Middle East (2003, 2010). Most explanations of these violent expressions of groups like al-Qaeda and the so-called Islamic culture rely on simplistic accounts of cultural norms, "evil" religious beliefs that reflect traditions in the Qur'an regarding the sacredness of martyrdom, poor education, or socioeconomic conditions. Atran's analysis is based on a comprehensive, holistic account that draws on a multiplicity of factors, including the manipulation of kinship and group loyalty among young people, who are viewed as expendable by their political elites, as well as global economic, political, and military strategies perceived and interpreted as hostile to their religious and political interests. In his recent book *Talking to the Enemy: Faith, Brotherhood, and the (Un) Making of Terrorists* (2010), Atran draws on extensive interviews to detail the organization, norms, and practices of al-Qaeda and other terrorist networks to determine how religion and secularist notions influence terrorist activities. He describes how al-Qaeda has charismatic leaders, such as the late Osama bin Laden, and tightly knit networks based on kinship, clan, nepotism and the Islamic concepts of brotherhood, which invoke the ideals of martyrhood for their groups. As Atran indicates, there are millions of people who may express sympathy for al-Qaeda and its terrorism; however, there are only thousands who actually commit to violence. The individuals that do make this commitment to violence begin as small groups of volunteers consisting of friends and kin within specific neighborhoods, schools, workplaces, leisure activities such as soccer, cafés, and online chat rooms to become "bands of brothers." Atran discusses how emotional and moral commitments are nurtured within these small, jihadist terrorist networks. Additionally, most of these Muslim terrorists suffer from feelings of relative deprivation, viewing their own Islamic brethren as losing honor and respect in comparison with other groups in society.

Atran calls on governments to fund more anthropological research on these topics in order to comprehend and understand these violent developments (see Chapter 1, page 10). Many other anthropologists doing research in the Islamic world have developed more nuanced understandings of the emergence of Islamic militancy and the struggle against it by many Muslims in these societies; militancy cannot be summed up with a simplistic "clash of civilizations."

Anthropologists at Work

AKBAR AHMED, Islam and the "War on Terrorism"

Akbar Ahmed is the Ibn Khaldun Chair of Islamic Studies at American University in Washington, DC; a nonresident senior fellow at the Brookings Institution; and a visiting professor at the U.S. Naval Academy in Annapolis, MD, where he held the First Distinguished Chair of Middle East and Islamic Studies. Ahmed belonged to the senior Civil Service of Pakistan and was the Pakistan High Commissioner and Ambassador to the U.K. and Ireland. He earned his B.A. in English and history at Forman Christian College in Lahore, Pakistan, his M.A. at the University of Cambridge, and his Ph.D. in anthropology from the University of London, School of Oriental and African Studies. Ahmed has taught at Princeton, Harvard, and Cambridge universities.

Ahmed is the author of over a dozen award-winning books, including *Discovering Islam*, which was the basis of a six-part BBC TV series called *Living Islam*; the critically acclaimed *Journey into Islam: The Crisis of Globalization*; and *Journey into America: The Challenge of Islam*. Ahmed's most recent publication is *The Thistle and the Drone: How America's War on Terror Became a Global War on Tribal Islam* (2013). His forthcoming study, *Journey into Europe: the Spectre of Islam, Immigration and Empire* will be his fourth book examining the relationship between the West and Islam. In these books, Ahmed has been critical of the simplistic "clash of civilizations" thesis perpetuated by Samuel Huntington that became the dominant narrative of the U.S. government following the tragedy of 9/11/01. As an anthropologist, Ahmed is aware of the complexity and diversity within the so-called

Islamic civilization (see Chapter 20, pages 471–472). Regularly interviewed by CNN, NPR, BBC, and Al-Jazeera, he has appeared several times on *Oprah*, and has also been a guest of Nickelodeon and *The Daily Show* with Jon Stewart. Ahmed has been called the "world's leading authority on Islam and globalization."

Ahmed's recent book *The Thistle and the Drone: How America's War on Terror Became a Global War on Tribal Islam* is partially based on his experience as a civil service official for the Pakistan government prior to earning his degrees in anthropology. He was located in the tribal zone of Waziristan in Northwest Pakistan. Ahmed studied the tribal cultures and became familiar with many of the political leaders and elders in this zone. Waziristan is the region that was believed to be where the Taliban, al-Qaeda, and the late Osama bin Laden were hiding. The U.S. military has been using drones to kill targeted "Islamic terrorists" in Waziristan. Ahmed describes how these drones often kill innocent civilians, including women and children in this area. Ahmed demonstrates that this U.S. drone warfare has become one of the principal causes of more active terrorism in Pakistan, resulting in more recruits for the Taliban and al-Qaeda. His book discusses many other tribal regions of the Islamic world including Yemen, Somalia, and Kurdish areas where the "War on Terrorism" has increased conflict and violence directed at the central governments, the United States, and the West within Muslim communities.

Ahmed discusses how the West ought to win the "War on Terror" in the last chapter of his book. First, the United States and Western governments should learn from the research of anthropologists who have been

Akbar Ahmed

engaged in in-depth ethnographic studies of Muslim societies instead of relying on "instant terror experts," who have very little training and rely on the "clash of civilizations thesis." These instant experts tend to distort the history and religious culture of Muslims and perceive jihadists in every corner producing global terrorism. Ahmed notes that the former commander of coalition forces in Afghanistan, General Stanley McChrystal, admitted that the U.S. military had a very superficial understanding of Afghanistan and its tribal peoples. However, Ahmed describes how the U.S. military, based on its long wars in Iraq and Afghanistan, did gain a much greater understanding of tribal cultures and encouraged commanders to interact with tribal elders. Second, rather than focusing on a "clash of civilizations," Ahmed recommends fostering better relationships between central governments and tribal or minority Muslim ethnic peripheries. As these central governments recognize more autonomy, full political participation, and human rights for the tribal or ethnic Muslim communities, the less reason there will be for resistance, violence, and conflict, and fewer recruits for terrorist groups such as the Taliban and al-Qaeda.

Summary and Review of Learning Objectives

22.1 Discuss the anthropological contributions to understanding the Middle East and Asia since 9/11/01.

Anthropologists reside among the people in the Middle East and Asia for an extensive period and interview not just political elites, but also peasants, farm workers, urban working-class people, religious clerics of many different traditions, and others. Anthropologists find that the simplistic portraits of "Islamic culture," "Middle Eastern," or "Asian civilizations" provided by some nonanthroplogical specialists are too static and contain "stereotypical" images that do not do justice to the tremendous variety of values, beliefs, norms, institutions, and behaviors of the billions of people in these regions. Since the 9/11 tragedy, many anthropologists consult with and advise Western governments and also work with people in the Middle East and Asia to help provide more insight into these regions, which are changing very rapidly. In this way, anthropologists hope to improve intercultural and interfaith dialogue on these issues to help reduce tensions and violence within, and between, these various societies in the Middle East and Asia.

22.2 Describe the early colonization of the Middle East and Asia.

Aside from the Portuguese and Spanish, most Europeans did not have much direct contact with the Middle East or Asia until the late eighteenth and nineteenth centuries. As European countries industrialized, however, they came to view the Middle East and Asia as areas ripe for imperial control. The British, French, Dutch, and Russians began to colonize, directly and indirectly, throughout the regions of the Middle East and Asia. Although some countries retained their independence such as Turkey, China, and Thailand, these countries were still influenced by the global consequences of European colonization.

22.3 Discuss the demographic, economic, and religious consequences of globalization in the Middle East and Asia.

Demographically, in the long run, all these countries experienced declining death rates brought about by Western colonialism, and populations began to increase rapidly because of economic circumstances and the maintenance of high birth rates. Economically, these societies were drawn into the global economy and were transformed by producing commodities that were demanded by the wealthier core societies. Patterns of land ownership were reordered, and many peasants were producing for economic elites. Religious changes occurred; however, since most of the population in the Middle East and Asia was committed to the tradition of Islam, Hinduism, or Buddhism, Christianity did not make significant inroads into these colonized areas.

22.4 Discuss the political consequences of globalization and colonialism in the Middle East and Asia.

Western colonialism eventually gave way to political movements based on nationalism, independence, and sometimes revolutionary tendencies. These movements represented anticolonial sentiments and resulted in many new countries in the Middle East and Asia. Countries such as India were led by charismatic leaders such as Mahatma Gandhi, who mobilized millions of people to develop a national identity and notions of self-determination. In China and Vietnam, revolutionary leaders such as Mao Zedong and Ho Chi Minh organized millions of peasants to bring about new social and political orders based on Marxist ideals mixed with indigenous cultural ideals.

22.5 Discuss what has created uneven development in the Middle East and Asia.

These countries were absorbed into the global economy at different levels, depending on the resources that were available in their regions. Some countries remain poor and underdeveloped because their economies are heavily dependent on the wealthy core countries. In the Middle East, some countries have tremendous oil resources that could be used to help develop their economies. Despite oil resources, these Middle Eastern countries still find themselves dependent on the wealthy, industrialized core nations. Many of the countries in both the Middle East and Asia face internal population problems and under-developed economic systems that tend to make them marginal to the global economy. Countries such as China and Vietnam tried to withdraw from the global economy through a commitment to a socialist program.

22.6 Discuss the major features of family and gender relations in the Middle East and Asia.

In the Middle East, Islamic tradition and Arab cultural practices influence the patterns of family life and gender. Patterns of patriarchy and polygyny are found in some of these areas. However, ethnographers find a great deal of variation within these Islamic societies based on the contact they have had with Western countries. Ethnographic research on the caste system of India has revealed that this social structure of inequality is interconnected with both material economic conditions and Hindu religious beliefs. South Asian family, marriage, and gender patterns vary with respect to urban and rural differences.

Although during the Maoist period, the government tried to change the patterns of patriarchy and family in China, some traditional patterns were retained. Following globalization trends and the decline and collapse of rigid Maoist policies in the People's Republic of China since the 1980s, ethnographic research has found that an enormous change has influenced family and gender issues in this country. Marriage rules are tending to become more flexible, based upon individual choice, rather than family arrangements, and women are becoming more independent and educated as they encounter the global economy, new technologies introduced by outsourcing, and the new global media, including the Internet, which are influencing cultural and social change in both India and China.

22.7 Discuss the factors that influence ethnic tensions in the Middle East and Asia.

Globalization has induced ethnic tensions that have divided many Middle Eastern and Asian countries. Ethnic groups such as the Kurds of the Middle East have been subject to discrimination by the Arab, Iranian, or Turkish majorities where they live. New global trends create ethnic tensions for the Kurds in these different countries. China has 56 official ethnic groups, including the Tibetans, Ugyhurs, and others. Historically, the majority Han ethnic group has tended to treat the different ethnic minorities as backward and inferior peoples. Many of the Tibetans and Uyghurs are resisting Han ethnic and political dominance and want more political rights and autonomy.

22.8 Discuss the links between globalization and Islamic movements.

One of the consequences of globalization is the resurgence of Islamic movements in countries such as Iran and Afghanistan. Ethnographers have used their analytical skills to try to comprehend and explain Islamic revitalization movements in these countries of the Middle East and Asia. Anthropologists find that in the Muslim world of some 1.5 billion people, a very small minority are involved in violence. This finding has become more important following the tragedy of 9/11 in the United States.

Key Terms

hamula, p. 530
jajmani economy, p. 533
jatis, p. 533

jihad, p. 542
Mujahidin, p. 542

Chapter 23
Ethnicity

Chapter Outline

 ## Learning Objectives

After reading this chapter you should be able to:

23.1 Discuss the basic criticisms of scientific racism by anthropologists.

23.2 Discuss how race is understood in different societies.

23.3 Discuss the basis of ethnicity as understood by contemporary anthropologists.

23.4 Compare the difference between the primordialist and circumstantial perspectives on ethnicity.

23.5 Compare the different patterns of ethnic relations described by anthropologists.

23.6 Discuss the historical and contemporary conditions of race and ethnic groups in the United States.

23.7 Discuss why ethnonationalist movements have developed in relationship to globalization.

Race, Racism, and Culture

23.1 Discuss the basic criticisms of scientific racism by anthropologists.

As we saw in Chapter 6, physical characteristics such as skin pigmentation, nose shape, and hair texture have prompted people throughout history to classify humans into different "races." The word *race* is a loaded term in part because people use the word differently in different contexts to mean different things (MacEachern 2012; Keita et al. 2004). It can be used in census data or in other areas to refer to certain styles of music, dance, or literature. Biologists may employ the term *race* to refer to different species of plants and animals. The term *race* appears to have been derived from the Latin root *ratio,* with a meaning similar to species or kind (or thing). However, as seen in Chapter 6, attempts to employ racial classifications for humans based upon "scientific criteria" have foundered because they were too rigid to account for the tremendous variation within different so-called races. The vast majority of anthropologists today find dividing different populations into distinctive racial categories or classifications extremely problematic. Clearly, bounded, racially distinct populations are not found in the real world (MacEachern 2012; Keita et al. 2004; Brown and Armelagos 2001; Hartigan 2013a; Templeton 2013). However, it cannot be denied that humans in both the past and the present have used various racial classifications to categorize people and develop stereotypes about the behavior and mental abilities of different "racial categories." These categories have often been used throughout human history as the basis and justification of **racism**, the belief that some races are superior to others. Racism can often result in discrimination and hostile acts toward different peoples and societies (Fredrickson 2002).

Critiques of Scientific Racism

Prior to the Holocaust in Germany, a number of scholars within the field of anthropology were subjecting racialistic beliefs to rigorous testing and evaluation. In the United States, anthropologist Franz Boas (1858–1943), who had migrated from Germany, led a concerted effort to assess these racist ideas (Pierpont 2004; Degler 1991; Baker 2004). Boas and his students took precise assessments of the physical characteristics of different populations, including cranial capacity and brain size. His research began to challenge the racist views, demonstrating conclusively that the brain sizes and cranial capacities of modern humans differ widely within all so-called races. This anthropological research resulted in irrefutable findings that there were no "superior" or "inferior" races. Boas's research also confirmed that there were no direct links among race, brain size, cranial capacity, and intelligence levels.

This pioneering work initiated a program of research among the four fields of anthropology, which has continued over the past century to challenge racist beliefs wherever they appear. This research has demonstrated time and time again that racist beliefs have no basis in fact. Human groups never fit into such neat categories. For example, many Jewish people living in Europe during the Holocaust possessed the same physical features as those associated with the so-called Aryans. The Nazi physical anthropologists who advocated Aryan racist ideology found it difficult to define precisely which physical characteristics supposedly distinguished one race from another (Schafft 1999). Nevertheless, at present, a number of groups such as the Pioneer Fund persist in supporting research that purports to demonstrate scientifically that races differ in their brain size, mental abilities, and intelligence. Anthropologists are actively criticizing these erroneous racist views with sound, scientifically based research (Lieberman 2001; Lieberman and Scupin 2012).

Neo-Nazi groups in the U.S. persist in using unscientific racist beliefs to perpetuate racism.

The Cultural and Social Significance of Race

23.2 Discuss how race is understood in different societies.

Despite a century of anthropological research in genetics and DNA, physical measurements of crania, skin color, and other population data that demonstrate that "race" does not have any precise scientific validity, that term persists as a very powerful cultural and social construct to classify people in the United States and other areas of the world. The U.S. folk model of race is derived from early European classifications of "whites," "blacks," and "Asians." Other societies have similar folk classifications. For example, in Puerto Rico, an island colonized by Spain and later by the United States, racial classifications are used to categorize people by skin color. Puerto Ricans use *blanco* to refer to whites, *prieto* to refer to blacks, and *trigueño* to refer to tan-skinned people. In Brazil, a complex racial classification uses different criteria to categorize people. Brazilians do not see or define races in the same way as people in the United States. In Brazil, race is inextricably connected with one's socioeconomic status. An individual categorized as "black" in the United States might be categorized as "white" in Brazil based on his or her socioeconomic status (Harris 1964). However, in Brazil, as well as most other societies across the world, racial categories based on skin color are still maintained as the basis of discrimination and prejudice (Telles 2004; Kephart 2012; Scupin 2012a).

A recent study of the science of genomics in Mexico by anthropologist John Hartigan demonstrates that the folk model of race in Mexico differs substantially from the folk model of race in the United States (2013b). He observed and analyzed how the Mexican scientists classified the various populations in Mexico based on their genomes. Whereas the folk model of race in the United States is primarily based on skin color, Mexican biologists and scientists designated distinctive "genetically mixed populations" of *mestizos* and *indios* or Amerindian groups. These Mexican scientists deny that these groupings are based on "racial" categories because they did not involve discrimination practices. However, they emphasized that these populations in Mexico were "genetically unique" compared with European, Asian, and African populations. Hartigan indicates that these distinctive "genetically mixed" groups were designated because of the nationalist traditions in Mexico that focus on the mixed *mestizo* and *indigenismo* movements (See Chapter 21). Hartigan concludes that culture plays a powerful and fundamental role in how race is constructed in different societies.

Since the nineteenth century, the United States had what has been termed the **hypodescent concept** of racial classification. This means that in cases of racial mixture, the offspring had the race of the parent with the lower racial status. Because black Americans were considered to be of a lower racial status, a person was considered black if he or she had a black ancestor anywhere in the family history. This is known as the **one-drop rule** of racial classification because it was based on the myth that one drop of "black blood" was sufficient to determine racial blackness. Thus, Americans with both white and black ancestry were usually classified as black and were often encouraged to identify as black in personal and social contexts. In contrast, traditionally, a person was classified as white if he or she had no black ancestry anywhere in his or her family history. This means that in order to be white, a person had to prove a negative, the absence of black ancestors.

Other racial categories such as *mulatto* (one-half black and one-half white), *quadroon* (one-quarter black and three-quarters white), and *octoroon* (one-eighth black and seven-eighths white) were developed to go along with this one-drop rule. Until the 1950s, in Louisiana it was illegal for a doctor to give a blood transfusion from a black person to a white person. Despite the fact that this notion of the one-drop rule is mythical and is based upon false notions of "racial essences," these ideas still persist in some circles (Fluer-Lobban 2006).

In contrast to the one-drop rule, Native Americans Indians are treated differently in the United States. Because they have entitlements based on treaties and legislation, the U.S. government has sometimes imposed *blood quanta* rules of at least 50 percent ancestry from a particular tribe in order to be classified as a Native American. This rule has created considerable confusion both legally and socially for many Native American peoples. The one-drop and blood quanta rules emphasize that the mythical ideas of *racial essences* are deeply embedded within the folk culture of U.S. society. Anthropologists have long recognized that although these folk conceptions of race are obviously based on arbitrary categories, they have a profound social and cultural significance in many societies.

Ethnicity

23.3 Discuss the basis of ethnicity as understood by contemporary anthropologists.

In Chapter 10, we discussed the concept of an *ethnic group*, which is a collectivity of people who believe they share a common history, culture, or ancestry. As is evident in the discussion above, one of the fundamental misconceptions in early Western perspectives on race and culture, and in later racist views, was the confusion between "race" and "culture." Purported racial characteristics, such as skin color or nose shape, were associated with particular "essences" that determined behavior and cultural attributes. These misunderstandings were also prevalent in the early usages of the word *ethnicity*. The Greek term *ethnos* (derived from *ethnikos* and *heathenic*) was used to refer to non-Greeks, or to *other* peoples who shared some biological and cultural characteristics and a common way of life. The Greeks tended to refer to non-Greeks as peripheral, foreign barbarians, or *ethnea*, and referred to themselves as civilized peoples, *genos Hellenon* (Hutchinson and Smith 1996). Later, the word *ethnos*, as used in the Greek New Testament, was associated with non-Jewish and non-Christian peoples and nations that were referred to as pagans, heathens, and idolaters (Simpson and Weiner 1989). Eventually, in various European languages, the terms *ethnic, ethnical, ethnicity, ethnique*, and *ethnie* corresponded to an association with "race" (Simpson and Weiner 1989). Race, language, and religion were perceived as a fusion of physical and cultural traits by the Western scientists and anthropologists of the nineteenth century.

However, as emphasized previously and in earlier chapters of this textbook, one of the basic findings of the research of Franz Boas and later anthropologists is that the physical characteristics of a specific group of people are not associated with any particular behavior or culture or language. In other words, one's language or culture is not inherited through biological transmission or genetics. Boas stressed that culture was far more involved in explaining how people in different ethnic groups behaved than any biological factors. One acquires his or her language and culture through *enculturation*, by learning the language and various symbols, values, norms, and beliefs in the environment to which one is exposed.

Since the 1960s, anthropologists and other social scientists have generally used the term *ethnicity* or *ethnic group* to refer to an individual's cultural heritage, which is separate from one's physical characteristics. In the modern definition, we emphasize both the objective and subjective aspects of ethnicity. The *objective aspect* of ethnicity is the observable culture and shared symbols of a particular group. It may involve a specific language or religious tradition that is maintained by the group, or it may involve particular clothing, hairstyles, preferences in food, or other conspicuous characteristics. The *subjective aspect* of ethnicity involves the internal beliefs of the people regarding their shared ancestry. They may believe that their ethnic group has a shared origin, family ancestry, or common homeland. In some cases, they may believe that people of their ethnicity have specific physical characteristics in common. This subjective aspect of ethnicity entails a "we-feeling," a sense of community or oneness within one's own in-group versus other out-groups. It does not matter whether these beliefs are historically or scientifically accurate, genuine, or fictional. This subjective identification of individuals with an ideology of an (at least imagined) shared history, unique past, and symbolic attachment with a homeland is often the most important expression of ethnicity (Smith 1986, 2009).

Thus, one's ethnicity is not innately determined by biology or purported racial characteristics. Despite early classifications of the "European race" or the "English, German, French, and Polish races," these differences among Europeans were based not on physical differences but on linguistic and cultural variations. Likewise, there is no "African race." Rather, Africa is a continent where hundreds of distinct ethnic groups reside that vary from region to region. The descendants of African slaves living in the United States have a very different ethnicity from descendants of African slaves who live in the Caribbean islands. In Asia, the differences among the Chinese, Japanese, Koreans, Thais, Indonesians, Vietnamese, Cambodians, and Laotians are based not upon racial differences, but upon ethnic differences. Although there may be some minor genetic differences among these populations, they are slight and do not result in distinctive races (Keita et al. 2004). These ethnic groups have different languages, histories, and cultural traditions that create variations among them. Because ethnicity is based upon cultural characteristics, it is much more variable, modifiable, and changeable—and as we shall see, more situational—than an identity based upon physical characteristics.

Anthropological Perspectives on Ethnicity

23.4 Compare the difference between the primordialist and circumstantial perspectives on ethnicity.

The Primordialist Model

Anthropologists have employed a number of different theoretical strategies to study ethnic groups and processes of ethnicity. One early model of ethnicity that developed in the 1960s is known as the *primordialist model* and is associated with anthropologist Clifford Geertz. Geertz attempted to describe how many Third World countries were trying to build nations and integrate their political institutions based upon a "civil order"—a political system based on democratic representation processes, rather than traditional ties of kinship or religion. However, this new civil order clashed with older traditional or "primordial" aspects of kinship, race, ethnicity, language, and religion (Geertz 1963a).

Geertz suggested that ethnic attachments based upon assumed kinship and other social ties and on religious traditions are deeply rooted within the individual through the enculturation process. He maintained that ethnic affiliation persists because it is fundamental to a person's identity. In this view, as people are enculturated into a particular ethnic group, they form deep emotional attachments to it. These emotional sentiments are sometimes evident through **ethnic boundary markers**, such as religion, dress, language or dialect, and other visible symbols, which distinguish one ethnic group from another. But Geertz tended to focus on the intense internal aspects of ethnicity and the deep, subjective "feeling of belonging" to a particular ethnic group. This is one of the strengths of the primordialist perspective on ethnicity. It emphasizes the meaning and significance that people invest in their ethnic attachments. Geertz emphasized how the "assumed givens" are subjective perceptions of attributes such as blood ties and ancestry, which may or may not coincide with the actual circumstances of one's birth. Geertz went on to write that primordial ties are experienced by the people of these new Third World nations, and that despite the introduction of new forms of civil political institutions and ideologies, these ethnic attachments endure; at times they are obstacles as young nations attempt to integrate their societies based upon a new political civil order. He suggested that there is a basic conflict between the modern state and one's personal identity based upon these primordial ties.

The Circumstantialist Model Another model of ethnicity began to surface within anthropology during the 1960s, based upon research on multiethnic societies. In *Ethnic Groups and Boundaries*, anthropologist Fredrik Barth described a new approach to ethnicity (1969). In a number of case studies in his book, Barth noted the fluidity of ethnic relations in different types of multiethnic societies. Although ethnic groups maintain boundaries such as language to mark their identity, people may modify and shift their language and ethnic identity in different types of social interaction. He criticized a view of culture based on earlier anthropological research in small-scale societies that tended to treat ethnic groups as having discrete, impermeable boundaries. Barth emphasized the interaction between ethnic groups and how people identify with different elements of their own ethnicity, while expressing or repressing these elements and characteristics in different circumstances for economic, political, or other practical reasons. This approach is sometimes referred to as the *instrumentalist approach* to ethnicity, but it has become known widely in anthropology as the *circumstantialist model* of ethnicity.

In the circumstantialist approach, Barth emphasized how ethnic boundary markers such as language, clothing, and other cultural traits are not based on deeply rooted, enduring aspects of ethnicity. Instead, boundaries are constantly being revised, negotiated, and redefined according to the practical interests of people. Ethnic boundaries are generated by the varying contexts and circumstances that influence a particular individual. For example, in the United States, people of German descent may refer to themselves as German Americans to distinguish themselves from Irish Americans or Italian Americans. Should they happen to be among Europeans, however, these same people might refer to themselves simply as Americans. The circumstantialist model explains how people draw on their ethnic identity for specific economic, social, and political purposes. People strategically use their ethnic affiliations to serve as the basis of collective political mobilization or to enhance their economic interests. Barth demonstrated how some people modify and change their ethnic identity when it is perceived to be advantageous for their own interests. They may emphasize the ethnic or racial identities of others or establish boundaries between themselves and others in order to define themselves differently and interact with others for political or economic purposes. Thus, in Barth's view, ethnicity is not fixed and unchanging but instead fluid and contingent as people strategically use, define, and redefine their ethnicity to respond to their immediate basic needs.

Barth's analysis of ethnicity illustrates how individuals within ethnic groups that adapt to specific types of economic and political circumstances in a multiethnic society may emphasize their shared identity as a means of enhancing cooperation with other members of the group. Throughout the world, individuals migrating to different areas often use ethnic ties as a means of social adjustment. Individuals may pursue political interests through ethnic allegiances. In numerous situations, people may manipulate ethnic traditions and symbols to their advantage.

This circumstantialist view of ethnicity also asserts that ethnicity is displayed in varying degrees by different ethnic groups. Ethnic traits vary from one historical time to another, and group identity may shift from one generation to another. Ethnic groups are not stable collective entities. They may appear and vanish within a generation or less than a generation and may come into being during different historical periods. In order to discuss how these ethnic groups emerge, anthropologists use the term *ethnogenesis*. **Ethnogenesis** refers to the origins of an ethnic group. Ethnogenesis has taken place throughout the world in many different historical circumstances. For example, the English, Germans, French, and other major ethnic groups went through this process in Europe. Ethnogenesis is a continual, ongoing sociocultural and political process that began in prehistory and continues today for many people.

Over the years, most contemporary anthropologists have drawn from both the primordialist and the circumstantialist models to explain or interpret ethnicity. Both models have clarified the nuances of ethnic identity throughout the world. The primordialist model has been extremely useful in substantiating the persistence of ethnicity, whereas the circumstantialist model has helped demonstrate how ethnic identity can be altered and constructed in various economic and political conditions. Today, many contemporary anthropologists occupy a middle ground between these positions because they pay close attention to the detailed manner in which ethnicity may be both primordial and circumstantial.

Anthropologists today investigate how societal conditions may impinge upon how people define themselves ethnically. What are the ethnic categories that have enduring meaningfulness and purpose for people, and under what circumstances are those categories asserted, negotiated, reaffirmed, or repressed? Also, to what extent and to what ends are the elements of ethnicity "invented" and "imagined" by ethnic groups? Anthropologists have to provide a detailed understanding of the ethnogenesis of a particular ethnic group. How does an ethnic group come to construct a shared sense of identity? What are the particulars of this ethnic identity? Is most ethnicity tied to religion? Or is it based on common ancestors or shared myths of common history and territory? Furthermore, anthropologists find it necessary to understand the global and local economic and political dynamics and processes that affect ethnic relations in continually changing societies. Globalization, government policies, the labor market, urbanization, and other aspects of the political economy have a profound influence on how ethnicity is expressed in different societies.

Patterns of Ethnic Relations

23.5 **Compare the different patterns of ethnic relations described by anthropologists.**

Pluralism

In the book *Pluralism in Africa*, a number of anthropologists described a **plural society** as one where different groups are internally distinguished from each other by institutional and cultural differences (Kuper and Smith 1969). Instead of one identical system of institutions shared within a society, a plural society consists of ethnic groups that differ in social organization, beliefs, norms, and ideals. Building on this framework, anthropologists use the phrase *cultural pluralism* to describe how various ethnic groups maintain diverse cultures within one society. For example, the Amish in U.S. society exemplify cultural pluralism.

Different forms of plural societies are based on the political order and legal institutions. In some forms of plural societies, ethnic groups not only are divided culturally and structurally, but also are organized in highly unequal political relationships. Some of these societies evolved in ancient agricultural civilizations. However,

various forms of plural societies developed in more recent times under European colonialism in many parts of Latin America, the Caribbean, Africa, the Middle East, and Asia as we have seen in earlier chapters. These plural societies had a European elite that ruled through control of the political economies and the legal institutions of these colonized regions. Typically, these types of plural societies resulted in divisive ethnic conflict and strained ethnic relationships.

Other forms of plural societies are based upon more egalitarian relationships among ethnic groups. In these societies, the government protects the structural and cultural differences among the ethnic groups. Ethnic groups are formally recognized by the state and legal institutions in order to allocate political rights and economic opportunities proportionally. Each ethnic group has a great deal of political autonomy, and in theory, there is no politically dominant ethnic group. In Europe, Switzerland is often used as an example of a plural society, where different ethnic groups have distinctive cultures, but they also have parity or equality with each other. Switzerland consists of French, Italian, German, and Romansh ethnic groups, and they all have relatively similar political and economic opportunities. Another European country, Belgium, is also known as an egalitarian plural society, in which the population is divided into two major ethnic groups: the Dutch-speaking Flemish and the French-speaking Walloons. In such plural societies, ethnic groups have the legal and political right to maintain their own languages, educational systems, and cultures. A balance of power is often reached among the different ethnic groups according to a political formula that grants each group a proportional representation of the multiethnic population. As expected, cultural pluralism endures and remains stable in these ethnically egalitarian societies, resulting in relatively amicable relationships.

Many plural societies today fall between the inegalitarian and egalitarian forms. Following decolonization in most of the countries of Latin America, Africa, the Middle East, and Asia, the inegalitarian plural forms of society were dislodged. The European elites were replaced by indigenous elites in these postcolonial societies. However, as we saw in Chapter 21 and 22, these societies remained pluralistic because they comprised many different ethnic groups. In some cases, the indigenous elites represented one particular ethnic group and perpetuated a continuation of radically plural politics. In other situations, new indigenous-based governments developed policies to manage competition and rivalry among different ethnic groups. This resulted, under some conditions, in another form and pattern of interethnic relations known as assimilation.

Guatemalan Mayan women wear particular types of clothing to express their unique ethnic identities.

Assimilation

Assimilation is a process of ethnic boundary reduction that may come about when two or more ethnic groups come into contact with each other. One or more ethnic groups adopt the culture, values, beliefs, and norms of another ethnic group. The process of assimilation results in similarity of culture and homogeneity among ethnic groups. As would be expected, assimilation occurs more easily when the physical and cultural characteristics of the different ethnic groups are more similar from the beginning of contact. Anthropologists have been engaged in research to determine whether these general factors are valid in different societal and cultural contexts. But in order to refine their research, anthropologists distinguish different forms of assimilation: *cultural assimilation* and *biological assimilation*.

Cultural assimilation involves one ethnic group's adoption of the culture traits, including language, religion, clothing style, diet, and other norms, values, and beliefs, of another group. Sometimes anthropologists use the term *acculturation* to refer to the tendency of distinct cultural groups to borrow words, technology, clothing styles, foods, values, norms, and behaviors from each other. As groups come in contact with one another, they borrow from each other's cultures. Anthropologists, however, find

that cultural assimilation or acculturation can be a very complex process for many ethnic groups. These processes may vary, depending on government policies and other societal conditions. For example, some cultural assimilation may be voluntary, wherein a particular ethnic group may choose to embrace the culture of another. Many ethnic groups that immigrate into a particular society adopt the culture of the ethnically dominant faction to secure their political rights and economic prospects. In some societies, government and educational policies may encourage newcomers to assimilate the culture of the dominant ethnic group. During different historical periods, the policies of many governments such as the United States, France, Mexico, Nigeria, Israel, and China have promoted cultural assimilation on a voluntary basis within their societies.

Conversely, under some historical conditions, governments may require nonvoluntary, or *forced cultural assimilation*. This is where the government forces ethnic peoples to take on the culture of the dominant ethnic group of the society. Anthropologists sometimes refer to forced cultural assimilation as *ethnocide*, which implies the killing of the culture of a particular ethnic group (see Chapter 20). Ethnocide demands that an ethnic group abandon its language, religion, or other cultural norms, values, and beliefs and adopt the culture of the dominant group. This process of ethnocide occurred in various ancient agricultural civilizations such as Egypt, India, China, Rome, and the Aztecs. As these agricultural civilizations expanded and conquered territories and other populations, at times they forced these other peoples to assimilate and adopt the culture of the dominant ethnic group.

This pattern of induced ethnocide was also prevalent during more modern forms of colonialism. For example, as Europeans colonized areas of Latin America, the Japanese colonized areas in Asia such as Taiwan, and the United States colonized the region of North America, indigenous peoples were often forced to assimilate. This type of forced assimilation is usually extremely difficult for individuals. They have to forsake their own language and cultural traits to become a part of a group with a different, often antagonistic, set of values and beliefs. As was seen in earlier chapters, forced cultural assimilation and ethnocide continue to influence many contemporary patterns of ethnic relations.

Biological assimilation refers to the process of intermarriage and reproduction among different ethnic groups, resulting in the development of a new ethnic group. The process of biological assimilation has been taking place for thousands of years as different groups have been intermarrying and reproducing with each other. Usually, intermarriage among ethnic groups occurs after extensive interethnic contact, followed by a great deal of cultural and structural assimilation. Thus, ethnic boundaries have usually been extensively reduced, if not eliminated, when intermarriage takes place. The degree of biological assimilation may range from a society where there are no longer any cultural and biological distinctions among the population to a society where new forms of ethnicity have developed. Historically, in the United States, intermarriage among different European Americans (e.g., descendants of English, Irish, German, Italian, and Polish immigrants) has reduced most traditional ethnic boundaries. This process has created the development of a new ethnicity, *white Americans*. On the other hand, as is seen in Chapter 21 on Latin America and the Caribbean, new forms of ethnicity emerged as intermarriage took place among Europeans, native populations, and African slaves.

Ethnic Violence

Anthropologists have identified three other patterns of ethnic interaction. One is **segregation**, or the physical and social separation of categories of people. Segregation was the policy of many Southern states in the United States during the period from the abolition of slavery until the civil rights movement of the 1950s and 1960s. **Jim Crow laws** were developed, which resulted in the creation of separate facilities and institutions for African-Americans and white Americans. There were segregated schools, restaurants, drinking fountains, restrooms, parks, neighborhoods, and other public areas. As discussed in Chapter 21, until recently, the South African government had similar laws to segregate the races and ethnic groups within its legal constitution under *apartheid.*

Another pattern of ethnic interaction is *ethnic cleansing*, the attempt to remove an ethnic group from its location and territory within a society. Recently, the Serbs attempted to bring about ethnic cleansing and displace ethnic groups such as the Bosnians from different regions of Yugoslavia. In East Africa, former ruler Idi Amin expelled East Indian immigrants from Uganda for economic and political reasons. Following the Vietnam War, in 1975, the Vietnamese government encouraged the migration of more than one million ethnic Chinese from the country. These people were abruptly eliminated as an ethnic minority, despite the fact that many had assimilated into Vietnamese society. In the past, the U.S. government removed Native Americans from their territories, a process of ethnic cleansing that resulted in reservation life for these ethnic groups.

The final pattern of ethnic interaction is known as *genocide*, the systematic attempt to kill and totally eliminate a particular ethnic group. Genocide may overlap with ethnic cleansing. In the cases of both the U.S. government and Native Americans and the Serbs and Bosnians, removal policies were often combined with more deadly policies of genocide. When the British colonized Australia, native populations such as the Tasmanians were exterminated. There were 5,000 Tasmanians in 1800, but as a result of being attacked by the British, the last full-blooded Tasmanian died in 1876. In the settling of South Africa by the Dutch, indigenous populations such as the Hottentots were systematically killed off. In the twentieth century, the most horrific forms of genocide befell European Jews and other ethnic groups under Adolf Hitler's reign of terror in Germany and territories which his armies had occupied. The Nazi Party murdered about six million Jews and millions of other ethnic groups, including six million Poles and many European gypsies. In Cambodia, the communist ruler Pol Pot killed as many as two million people (one-fourth of the population) in what have become known as the "killing fields." Ethnic minorities, such as people with Chinese ancestry or Muslims, were favored targets in this genocidal campaign (Kiernan 1988). And as discussed in Chapter 21, in 1994, in the country of Rwanda in Central Africa, the majority ethnic group (the Hutus) slaughtered some half a million ethnic Tutsis within a few weeks. Although genocidal policies have been condemned under moral standards recognized throughout the world, they have appeared time and again in human history.

Racial and Ethnic Stratification

Racial and ethnic differences were often used as a basis of stratification within different societies. In the past, as agricultural states expanded into surrounding environments, a variety of perceived "racially" and ethnically different peoples were incorporated into the growing empires (see Chapter 18). Some of these groups were band, tribal, or chiefdom societies that spoke different languages and maintained different cultural or ethnic traditions. Once conquered or absorbed, they frequently found themselves under the rule of a particular dominant ethnic group. In many cases, the dominant group ascribed subordinate social and cultural statuses to them. Sometimes the conquered groups became slaves. In other cases, their members were viewed as "racially" or ethnically inferior and were given only limited opportunities for upward mobility. Thus, many ethnic and racial minorities were identified as subordinate classes and stigmatized as inherently inferior.

With the intensification of social stratification in agricultural states, social distance between the ruling elite and the rest of the population was accentuated not only by rights to land, wealth, and power, but also by restrictive laws. For example, among the Aztecs, patterns of deference and demeanor between the rulers and the ruled were highly formalized. The Aztec nobility were distinguished by clothing and jewelry, and they were believed to be vested with divine status (Berdan 1982). Aztec commoners were required to prostrate themselves before the emperor and were not permitted to speak to him or look at him. Similar patterns of deference and social etiquette developed throughout the agricultural societies in the Old and New Worlds.

In addition to social stratification based on occupation, many industrial and postindustrial societies have a system of stratification based upon ethnic or racial descent. For example, in the United States, various ethnic and racial groups such as African-Americans, Native American Indians, and Hispanics have traditionally occupied a subordinate status and have experienced a more restricted type of social mobility. In contrast, most Western European countries traditionally have been culturally homogeneous, without many minority ethnic groups. Recently, however, this situation has started to change, as many formerly colonized peoples, such as Indians, Pakistanis, and Africans, have moved to Great Britain, and other non-Western peoples have migrated to other European nations where migration has caused patterns of ethnic and racial stratification and discrimination.

In the former Soviet Union, many ethnic minorities resided in Estonia, Lithuania, the Ukraine, and Turko-Mongol areas such as Azerbaijan and Uzbekistan. Ethnic minorities lived outside the central Soviet territory, the heartland of the dominant Russian majority. Historically, the Soviet state had attempted to assimilate these national minorities by making the Russian language a compulsory subject in the educational system (Eickelman 1993; Maybury-Lewis 1997; Scupin 2012a). Although the Soviet state prided itself on the principles of equality and autonomy it applied to its national minorities, the outbreak of ethnic unrest and rebellion in these non-Russian territories in the mid-1990s demonstrated that these ethnic minority populations viewed themselves as victimized by the dominant ethnic Russian populace. Thus, ethnic stratification has been a component of industrial Russian society.

Japan appears to have even more ethnic homogeneity. The Japanese make up 99.4 percent of the population of 128 million people, with only 0.6 percent of the population being ethnic minorities (mostly Korean). Although the Japanese, like all other peoples, are the outcome of a long evolutionary history of mixture with different groups, a racialized notion of ethnic identity remains as a myth of cultural identity for the Japanese (Diamond 1998; Yoshino 1997, 1998; Scupin 2012c). Cultural anthropologists note that this tendency of the Japanese to view themselves as a "unique" race creates some distinctive patterns of ethnic stratification. For example, the small minority of Japanese of Korean ancestry have experienced widespread discrimination, even though they have adopted the Japanese language, most of the country's norms, and its cultural values.

In addition, a native-born Japanese population known as the *eta,* or *burakumin,* consisting of about three million people, occupies a lower status. Despite the fact that the *burakumin* are physically indistinguishable from most other Japanese, they reside in separated ghetto areas in Japan. They are descendants of peoples who worked in the leather-tanning industries, traditionally considered low-status professions. Most of the *burakumin* still work primarily in the shoe shops and other leather-related industries. Marriages between *burakumin* and other Japanese are still restricted, and other patterns of ethnic discrimination against this group continue (Befu 1971; Hendry 1987; Ohnuki-Tierney 1998; Scupin 2012c). In a recent ethnography the anthropologist Joseph Doyle Hankins has studied how the Japanese associate the smell of leather with the *burakumin,* signifying contagion and disgust (2013). Through hearsay and gossip, the notion that Japanese people can detect a *burakumin* person by smell has brought about stigmatization and ethnic discrimination. This prejudice has resulted in poverty, lower education attainment, delinquency, and other social problems for the *burakumin,* just as it has for some ethnic minorities in the United States.

Recently, the *burakumin* have mobilized politically and organized an internationally recognized Buraku Liberation and Human Rights research group in order to struggle against the ethnic stratification and discrimination they encounter in Japanese society. The Japanese government has recognized this ethnic discrimination and has taken legal action to improve the status of the *burakumin.* In addition, many of the traditional leather industries have been relocated to China and India, where labor costs and environmental standards are lower, eliminating part of the problem (Hankins 2013). However, the Buraku Liberation and Human Rights organization is still actively combating stratification and discrimination in Japan.

Ethnic Relations in the United States

23.6 Discuss the historical and contemporary conditions of race and ethnic groups in the United States.

To illustrate the dynamics of ethnic relations, we focus on U.S. society. We begin with an overview of the early English settlers to America, or the so-called WASP ethnic group, which provided the basic cultural heritage for U.S. society. In addition, we examine the patterns of non-WASP immigration from Europe in the nineteenth century and the consequences of this immigration for U.S. society.

WASP Dominance

The European colonization of what was to become the United States begins with the so-called WASPs, or white Anglo-Saxon Protestants. The term *WASP* has come to refer to the ethnic group with a particular cultural and institutional complex that dominated U.S. society for generations. The British settlers were able to overcome their rivals—the French, Spanish, and Dutch in colonial America—and were free to develop their own form of culture. With the exception of the Native Americans and enslaved African-Americans, four out of five colonial settlers in America were British Protestants. Smaller groups of settlers included Scots and Welsh, as well as Scotch-Irish (Protestants from Northern Ireland), Dutch, Germans, and Scandinavians. Although Anglo-American leaders such as Benjamin Franklin expressed fears that these non-English-speaking people with different cultures, such as the Germans, would take over Anglo-American culture, by the end of the seventeenth century these early non-Anglo settlers assimilated, culturally and structurally, becoming a part of the core WASP ethnic group that became dominant.

WASP ethnicity became preeminent in the United States through the establishment of its language, symbols, and culture. The English language was the fundamental underpinning of the cultural legacy that was bestowed by the WASPs on American society. It became the acceptable written and spoken language for the building of the nation-state and country, and it represented the standard for creating ethnic identity in colonial America. English was the institutional language of education, politics, and religion among the WASPs. From the early establishment of WASP culture, the expectation held that any subsequent ethnic groups that came to America would have to learn the English language. This was the first stage of what has sometimes been referred to as *Anglo-conformity*.

Along with the English language, the WASPs brought the basic economic, legal, and political institutional framework for U.S. society. One of the primary reasons for colonization of North America by the British settlers was to extract raw materials and to produce new markets for England. Commercial capitalism, including the right to own private property, was brought to America by the English settlers. The initiatives for taking land from Native Americans, for developing European forms of agriculture—including the importation of slaves—and for sending raw materials across the Atlantic were all aspects of the market-oriented capitalism that was transported from England to America. Following the American Revolution, this market-oriented capitalism became the cornerstone of the expansion of the Industrial Revolution in the United States. As the principal ethnic group engaged in the development of commercial capitalism and the Industrial Revolution, the WASPs were able to dominate the major economic capitalist institutions in U.S. society. At present, over 30 million people trace their descent to these English settlers (U.S. Census Bureau 2010).

New Ethnic Challenges for U.S. Society

The nineteenth century saw an enormous number of non-Anglos flowing in from other areas of the world that would begin to challenge the Anglo dominance of U.S. society. More than 30 million non-Anglo European immigrants came to the United States in the nineteenth century. Many were non-Protestants, maintaining either Catholic or Jewish religious traditions. In addition, especially with respect to those ethnic groups from Southern and Eastern Europe, these people spoke different languages that were historically far removed from the English language. As we saw in Chapter 6, many of these people were viewed as inferior, and there were exclusive immigration policies to keep them out of the United States.

German and Irish Americans

During the seventeenth century, approximately 7 million people born in the area now known as Germany settled in North America. Currently, more Americans trace their ancestry to Germany than any other country. Although it is difficult to assess these numbers precisely, some 46 to 50 million Americans are descendants of Germans (U.S. Census Bureau 2010) out of approximately 314 million people. Many of the German migrants entering the United States were urban-based people skilled in crafts, trades, or the professions. Some of these immigrants were German Jewish migrants who were adapting, along with other Germans, to the booming cities of New York, Cincinnati, St. Louis, Chicago, Pittsburgh, Milwaukee, Indianapolis, and Louisville. Located along waterways or railroads, these were attractive sites for urban skills (Glazier 2012). Breweries, bakeries, distilleries, flour mills, tailor shops, print shops, surveying businesses, and plumbing stores were established by these immigrants. A number of well-educated immigrants who had fled Germany for political reasons became important political activists and officials of the U.S. government. Thus, nineteenth-century German-American ethnic communities included both skilled and unskilled laborers (Scupin 2012c). Because of their numbers and the occupational diversity of their population, German Americans could develop extremely self-sufficient communities.

As the numbers of immigrants from Germany increased, rather than assimilating quickly into American society, many attempted to retain their ethnic identity, including their language, culture, and religious traditions. Many German immigrants wanted to conserve their ethnic and nationalist identity within the United States. Aside from German-language schools and churches, they began to establish ethnically based organizations such as music societies, theater clubs, beer halls, lodges, and political clubs. Through such organizations and institutions, as well as the private schools and churches in specific neighborhoods, various "Little Germanys" emerged in major cities such as St. Louis, Cincinnati, and Milwaukee. The endeavor to preserve German culture in the United States even led to a proposal to establish an exclusive German state in the Union (Cornell and Hartmann 1998).

The major influx of Irish immigrants into the United States came during the nineteenth century. Today, some 30 million persons in the United States trace their ancestry to the Irish (U.S. Census Bureau 2010). As the Irish Catholics settled in the United States, they adapted within many different types of occupations, skilled and professional. But because many of the Irish arrived with little education and capital, they were forced to take the lowest-wage jobs in factories, mines, and mills, in the construction of railways and canals, and in other unskilled occupations. For example, large numbers of Irish workers were employed in the construction of the Erie Canal in New York State. Later, Irish labor was used to build the intercontinental railroad across the United States. Others worked in foundries, railroad locomotive factories and repair shops, furniture factories, boat-building shops, breweries, and other industries using unskilled labor. Many Irish women began to work as domestic servants for WASP households or in the textile mills and factories in eastern cities such as New York and Boston.

As Irish and German immigration increased in the nineteenth century, xenophobic sentiments (fear of foreigners) helped usher in nativistic movements among WASPs. In particular, Roman Catholicism associated with the Irish was perceived to be untrustworthy. A political party known as the Know-Nothings developed. (They were labeled Know-Nothings because party members were instructed to divulge nothing about their political program and to say they knew nothing about it.) Much of the Know-Nothing Party activity was aimed at the Irish, who were unwelcome because they were Roman Catholic and, therefore, non-WASP. The Know-Nothing program aimed to elect only WASPs to political office, to fight against Roman Catholicism, and to restrict citizenship and voting rights to immigrants who had resided in the United States 21 years instead of the 5 years required by law. The Irish Catholics were perceived to be a "separate race" and were purported to have a distinctive biology that made them different from the WASPs. Members of the "Irish race" were perceived by the WASPs as undesirables who were immoral, unintelligent, uncouth, dirty, lazy, ignorant, temperamental, hostile, and addicted to alcohol. In cities such as Boston and New York, there were signs in storefronts, housing complexes, and factories saying "No Irish Need Apply" (Scupin 2012c).

During World Wars I and II, extensive anti-German prejudice and discrimination emerged within American society. As a reaction to these anti-German sentiments, rapid cultural assimilation began to dominate the German-American communities. German surnames and German business names were Anglicized. For example, the German surname Eisenhauer became Eisenhower, the surname of an important U.S. President.

Italian and Polish Americans

Many Southern and Eastern European ethnic groups—Greeks, Italians, Serbians, Hungarians, Bulgarians, Russians, Ukrainians, and Poles—began to immigrate to the United States between 1880 and 1915. The United States was undergoing an unprecedented economic and industrial transformation that demanded large reserves of labor. Expansion in the garment industry, food processing, mining, construction, and other manufacturing and service operations offered opportunities for people from Southern and Eastern Europe. Approximately two-thirds of the foreign-born population that came into the United States during this period was from these regions.

Unlike the Northern European groups such as the Germans and Irish, these new immigrants had languages and cultures that were extremely different from those of prior immigrants. Today, more than 15 million Americans trace their ancestry to Italy (U.S. Census Bureau 2010). Many of the early Italian immigrants had come through a form of indentured labor known as the *padrone system*. A *padrone*, or boss, would recruit laborers in Italy, pay for their passage to the United States, and arrange work for them, mostly in construction. Other Italian immigrants came through "chain-migration," one migrant following another through kinship networks. As Roman Catholics, they used the church organizations and other voluntary mutual aid societies to help them adapt to the new conditions in America. Because of such ties, eventually these immigrants began to perceive themselves as having a common identity as Italian Americans (Alba 1985). This new identity created the foundation for "Little Italys" in different urban areas such as New York, Boston, Chicago, and St. Louis.

Like many others from Europe, people from Poland were pushed and pulled by economic, political, and religious factors that influenced their decision to immigrate to America. Polish peasants (together with some members of the Polish middle class and intelligentsia) began to seek a new way of life in the United States. Letters from relatives and friends in America advertised high wages and employment opportunities in America. In addition, class, political, and religious oppression from occupying ruling empires propelled Polish immigration to America. Poles with sufficient funds could buy transatlantic tickets, whereas others depended on their relatives to provide kinship connections through the process of chain migration for their resettlement in America.

Although about three of every ten migrants returned to Poland, today about 9 million Americans trace their ancestry to Poland (U.S. Census Bureau 2010). Many of the Polish immigrants were taken to coal-mining towns like Scranton, Wilkes-Barre, Windber, and Hazleton in Pennsylvania or to the steel manufacturing cities of Pittsburgh and Cleveland. Other midwestern cities, such as Toledo, Milwaukee, Minneapolis, St. Louis, Chicago, and Detroit, attracted Poles who were seeking work in the mills, slaughterhouses, foundries, refineries, and factories. In 1920, Chicago had 400,000 Poles; New York, 200,000; Pittsburgh, 200,000; Buffalo, 100,000; Milwaukee, 100,000; and Detroit, 100,000 (Greene 1980). In these towns and cities, Polish immigrants founded neighborhoods and communities known individually and collectively as *Polonia* (Latin for "Poland").

With the unprecedented immigration into the United States from Southern and Eastern Europe in the first two decades of the twentieth century, Italians and Poles were subjected to severe discrimination and prejudice by many Americans. As we saw before, nativistic movements, beliefs in the superiority of the Anglo-Saxons, and anti-Catholicism were developing at this time. Like the Irish, the Italians and Poles were categorized by many WASPs as different "races" that were inferior intellectually and morally to the Anglo-Saxons. But this construction of an "Italian race" or a "Polish race" was even more severely restrictive than that applied to the Irish. An Anglo-Saxon-based racialism, which was linked to "scientific racism" in the 1880s and 1890s, grew in the United States as a reaction to the immigration of Southern and Eastern European peoples. The "Italian race" and the "Polish race," as well as other Southern and Eastern European "races," such as Jews, were classified as inferior in contrast to the Northern European "races."

Early Italian and Polish immigrants were also subjected to IQ and literacy tests; as expected, they scored lower than the "average" American. These tests were used as purported scientific proof of these new immigrants' inferior intellect (Kamin 1974). Racist beliefs were promoted by the media and other "scientific" works of the time. Anglo-Saxon Americans were warned not to intermarry with Italians and Poles because it would cause the degeneration of the "race." The "Italian race" and the "Polish race" were identified with correlates of behavior such as being jealous, overly emotional, rough, mean, dirty, and lazy, and with other negative characteristics.

Despite the racial prejudice and discrimination they faced, the German-, Irish-, Italian-, and Polish-American communities were able to adjust to their circumstances through organized efforts in economic and political activities. They joined unions and organized political parties to cope with discrimination and prejudice, and the second and third generations of these non-Anglo immigrants began to assimilate culturally into U.S. society (Scupin 2012b).

The Melting Pot: Assimilation or Pluralism?

As we saw earlier, U.S. society was challenged dramatically by the massive immigration of non-Anglo populations in the nineteenth and early twentieth centuries.

An Italian American family.

Questions were raised about whether German, Jewish, Irish, Italian, and Polish immigrants could really become "Americans." Nativistic groups such as the Know-Nothings and the American Protective Association directed prejudice and discrimination at these immigrants. This prejudice against Catholicism and other ethnic traits, including language and purported race, eventually resulted in restrictive immigration policies. During this same period, state and local authorities began to restrict the use of languages other than English in schools and to require all teachers to be U.S. citizens. Government policies promoted the use of the public school system to "Americanize" and assimilate the various non-Anglo immigrants.

One of the popular manifestations of these policies of assimilation evolving in U.S. society was the concept of the "melting pot." This became the popular symbol of ethnic interaction in the United States during the early twentieth century. The melting pot ideal implied that the new "American ethnicity" would represent only the best qualities and attributes of the different cultures contributing to U.S. society. It became a plea for toleration of the different immigrants as they poured into American society. It assumed that the American ideals of equality and opportunity for material improvement would automatically transform foreigners into Americans. It also suggested that the Anglo or WASP ethnicity was itself being transformed into a more comprehensive, global type of an American ethnic identity.

Despite the tolerant tone, universal appeal, and openness of the metaphor of the melting pot, it still emphasized assimilation. The belief that immigrants must shed their European ethnic identity and adopt a "Yankee" ethnic identity was at the heart of this concept. The second generation of Germans, Jews, Irish, Italians, and Poles thus tended to assimilate into the Anglo-American culture of the majority. Economic, social, and political benefits accrued to these "white ethnics" upon assimilation. To pursue the American Dream, the white ethnics assimilated culturally and structurally into the fabric of American society. The metaphor of the melting pot appeared to have some validity, at least for many of these white ethnics. As older ethnic neighborhoods and communities declined, most white ethnics abandoned their traditional languages and their ethnic traditions in order to adapt to American society. For example, many Jewish celebrities changed their names, including Tony Curtis (Bernie Schwartz), Doris Day (Doris Kapplehoff), and Kirk Douglas (Issur Danielovitch) (Glazier 2012).

Along with the assimilationist trend in U.S. society, the crystallization of the race concept of "whiteness" was reinforced. Eventually, the people who came from Ireland, Germany, Italy, Poland, and other European countries became "white Caucasians," or "white Americans" in contrast to other ethnic minorities (Jacobson 1998). For many Americans, "whiteness" became a new socially constructed category of race and ethnicity that differentiated these Europeans from non-Europeans in the United States. Native Americans, African-Americans, Hispanic Americans, and Asian Americans were nonwhites and thereby were excluded from the institutional benefits and privileges of people with white identities. Although there were some who still referred to the Anglo-WASP racial category, the enlarged category of a "white identity" assigned to Europeans tended to become part of the racial consciousness of U.S. society.

African-Americans

Although people of African descent have been involved in peopling and building civilization in the United States for as long as Europeans, there are various misrepresentations and stereotypes about African-Americans that have been perpetuated by the media and held by many U.S. citizens. For example, contrary to these stereotypes, two-thirds of African-Americans are working class, middle class, and above, and are not living in poverty conditions. Today, African-Americans constitute about 13.5 percent of the population, or about 40.7 million people (U.S. Census Bureau 2010; S. Brown 2012).

The majority of African-Americans trace their ethnic history to the slave-trading activities that brought approximately 500,000 Africans to the United States beginning in the seventeenth century. As discussed in Chapter 21, millions more were brought to Latin America and the Caribbean. Slaves were chained together for the trip across the Atlantic Ocean, and many of them were killed by disease and filthy conditions aboard the European sailing ships. The first U.S. slaves were auctioned off in 1619 in Jamestown, Virginia. Slavery was the foundation of the plantation system. Slavery was used in both the northern and the southern United States prior to the American Revolution due to labor shortages. In 1641, Massachusetts became the first colony to legalize slavery. The people of West and Central Africa were experienced farmers, skilled at iron smelting, cattle herding, and textile manufacture, and thus were viewed as valuable "commodities" by plantation owners (S. Brown 2012). Slaves labored for the benefit of the white plantation owners, planting and harvesting their crops from daybreak to sunset and even longer. Slave families were often divided when these humans were bought and sold in public auctions. Despite this attack against the family unit, most slaves married and attempted to maintain the family as much as possible (S. Brown 2012). The Southern laws enabled owners to treat their slaves as property and to discipline them in any way they desired to produce obedience and productivity. Although some slaves managed to resist and rebel against their oppression, the military and political power mustered by their owners denied the slaves any real control over their destinies.

Anthropologist Melville Herskovits did extensive studies of African-Americans in the United States. As a student of Franz Boas, he debunked many racist notions that maintained that African-Americans were an inferior race (S. Brown 2012). Herskovits, who had a deep knowledge of African cultures and societies, demonstrated that African-Americans were neither inferior nor a people without a past. He and other anthropologists provided a foundation for understanding the unique and substantial contributions that African-Americans have made to U.S. society.

Not all African-Americans were slaves. Some were "free blacks" who had earned their freedom by working in nonagricultural professions in the urban areas, primarily in the North. Many free blacks were descendants of runaway slaves or had purchased their freedom through their own labor. African-Americans frequently managed to adapt to their condition in the United States by maintaining their own Christian churches, which became the center of social life in their communities. Thus, the culture of African-Americans was forged in both slave and free conditions (S. Brown 2012). They developed their own unique music and gospel singing, which is still practiced, and they introduced many foods and agricultural and skilled techniques such as cattle herding that they brought from Africa.

Postslavery and Segregation In 1865, following the Civil War, the Thirteenth Amendment to the U.S. Constitution outlawed slavery. The Fourteenth Amendment granted citizenship to all people born in the United States. The Fifteenth Amendment, ratified in 1870, stated that neither race nor previous condition of slavery should deprive anyone of the right to vote. Despite these amendments to the Constitution, African-Americans found that obstacles were created to prevent them from becoming equal citizens under the law. In particular, Southern states began to disenfranchise blacks legally by passing state laws denying them access to equal education. Legislation that segregated U.S. society into two "racial castes" were referred to as *Jim Crow laws*.

If African-Americans resisted segregation laws that upheld separate schools, restaurants, drinking fountains, restrooms, parks, churches, and other institutions, they were beaten and sometimes lynched. Between 1882 and 1927, almost 3,500 African-Americans were lynched. Southern whites justified these lynchings as a form of social control. Organizations such as the Ku Klux Klan and the White Citizens Councils conducted lynchings, other violence, and intimidation against African-Americans (S. Brown 2012). Tired of suffering these deprivations in the southern areas, many African-Americans began to move to northern cities for jobs in newly developing industries and other enterprises. However, even in northern cities,

African-Americans often found that prejudice and discrimination awaited them.

The Civil Rights Movement Following World War II, many African-American males who had served in segregated divisions of the U.S. military recognized that they did not have the individual freedoms and equal opportunities for which they had fought. In the 1950s and 1960s, many African-Americans, sometimes assisted by white Americans, began to participate in a massive civil rights movement for individual freedoms and equal opportunities, as idealized within the American Constitution. In southern towns and cities, African-Americans began to organize what were called "sit-ins" in segregated restaurants, bus boycotts against segregated buses, and other protests led by leaders such as the Reverend Martin Luther King, Jr. The participants in the civil rights movement often faced brutal violence, bombings of black churches, arrests, and intimidation. Some African-American leaders such as Malcolm X of the Nation of Islam and Eldridge Cleaver of the Black Panthers called for armed defense against police brutality and violence aimed at their communities. As a result of the civil rights movement and other protests, the U.S. Congress passed a number of civil rights bills that provided for more individual rights, equal opportunity, and the breakdown of the Jim Crow laws.

African-Americans Today Despite the considerable gains of African-Americans following the civil rights movement, a disproportionate number of their communities are in poverty when compared to those of white U.S. citizens. During the 1980s, earnings declined for many African-Americans as industries in the United States closed and factory jobs were lost (Wilson 1980, 1997). Thus, African-American unemployment, especially among young black teenagers, rose considerably. Although African-Americans have made tremendous strides in educational achievement since the 1960s, black college students still graduate at only half of the average national rate in the United States. These factors have left many young African-Americans in inner cities susceptible to crime, drug addiction, and other dysfunctional behaviors. Twenty-four and one-half percent of African-Americans live in poverty (S. Brown 2012). The destiny of the African-American community in the twenty-first century will inevitably be influenced by a continued struggle for equality and individual rights, against racism.

Hispanic Americans

The U.S. Census reported that the Hispanic/Latino population has had the largest demographic increase in the last couple of decades compared with any other ethnic group in the United States. The Hispanic/Latino population is approximately 52 million people, or more than 15 percent

An African-American family.

of the U.S. population, making it larger than the African-American population (U.S. Census Bureau 2012).

The terms *Hispanic* and *Latino* are umbrella terms that include many diverse people (Bigler 2012). They include descendants of Mexicans, Puerto Ricans, Cubans, and smaller groups of Dominicans, Mayan Indians, Peruvians, and other Central and South American immigrants and their descendants. These Hispanics or Latinos comprise a cluster of distinct populations, each of which identifies with groups that are associated with different countries or regions of origin. Hispanics or Latinos do not constitute a particular "racial" group. Skin coloration, hair texture, facial features, and physical appearance vary considerably among and within these different populations.

Most of the U.S. Hispanic and Latino population lives in the Southwest. Following the Mexican War (1846–1848), the U.S. government annexed the areas now known as California, Colorado, New Mexico, Nevada, Utah, Texas, and most of Arizona. This area was known as *Aztlan* (home of the original Aztecs) to the Mexican population and represented half of Mexican territory. The influx of Anglos into these regions following the gold rush and the development of ranching, mining, and other activities rapidly made the Mexicans minorities within these new states of the United States. Although these Mexican minorities were promised equal rights if they chose to become American citizens, they were discriminated against by laws enacted by Anglo-dominated legislatures (Takaki 1990a). They also faced assaults and lynchings similar to those faced by African-Americans. Many Mexican Americans lost their lands and found themselves surrounded by Anglo-Americans who maintained racist and ethnocentric views about the superiority of their own race and culture.

Eventually, as ranching and industrial development expanded in the Southwest, many Mexican nationals were encouraged to immigrate to these U.S. regions to work as low-wage laborers. Mexicans were paid much lower wages than Anglos to work in the mines or to plant and harvest the various crops of the region. The industries and ranches became dependent on this Mexican labor, and people moved back and forth across the border very easily. The unstated policy of the U.S. ranchers and industrialists was to have the Mexicans fulfill the demands of the labor market, but to return to Mexico when the economy went sour. Thus, during the Great Depression of the 1930s, many Mexicans were rounded up and deported back to Mexico so that Euro-Americans could have their jobs. However, following World War II, Mexican labor was again in demand. This shortage resulted in what is known as the *Bracero* program, which allowed the United States to import Mexican labor to meet the demands of the economy (Bigler 2012).

Following the war, the U.S. government organized "Operation Wetback," which captured and deported to Mexico some 3.8 million people who looked Mexican. This was done without any formal legal procedures. Yet, many U.S. ranchers and industrialists continued to encourage the movement of Mexican labor back and forth across the border. As a result of the *Bracero* program and the importation of temporary workers, the Mexican-American population, both legal and illegal, has continued to increase to the present.

Puerto Rican Americans In contrast to Mexican Americans in the Southwest, New York City and the Northeast became the center for the Puerto Rican-American community. Puerto Rico came under U.S. control following the Spanish-American War of 1898. In 1917, Puerto Ricans became U.S. citizens, and as such, they were eligible to migrate to the United States without any restrictions. Following World War II, as industrial expansion increased, many Puerto Ricans were recruited and enticed to work in the low-wage sector vacated by Euro-Americans who were moving to the suburbs. Most of them settled in New York, and the people sometimes referred to themselves as "Nuyoricans," many of whom reside in "Spanish Harlem." They believed that they were going to participate in the American Dream of upward mobility. Manufacturing jobs and related industries, however, were declining in the 1970s and 1980s in New York and other regions. Like many African-Americans, Puerto Rican Americans were caught in the industrial and urban decline of this period. Better-paying unionized manufacturing jobs were disappearing, and this, combined with racism and discrimination, made it difficult for the Puerto Rican community to achieve the American Dream of upward mobility (Bigler 2012).

Cuban Americans   Prior to the Cuban Revolution in 1959 led by Fidel Castro, a relatively small number of Cubans had migrated to the United States for economic opportunities. However, following the revolution, some 400,000 Cubans immigrated to the United States. The first wave of the Cubans after the revolution comprised middle- and upper-class families who were threatened by the Castro government. These people were highly educated professionals, government officials, and businesspeople who brought capital and skills with them. Most of them settled in Miami, Florida, and were extremely successful in their adjustment to U.S. society. Many of them thought that they would return to Cuba to reestablish themselves after Castro was defeated (Bigler 2012).

During the Cold War, the U.S. government welcomed Cuban immigrants as political refugees fleeing a communist regime. A second wave of Cuban refugees came during the 1980s, when Castro allowed people to freely leave Cuba for the United States. About 10 percent of these refugees were ex-convicts and mental patients, and they have had a much more difficult time adapting to conditions in U.S. society. Overall, although many Cuban Americans speak both English and Spanish, they have maintained the Spanish language and Cuban culture within the boundaries of U.S. society.

Hispanic Americans Today   As indicated earlier, aside from the Mexican, Puerto Rican, and Cuban Americans, many other individuals are included within the terms *Hispanic* and *Latino*. These Hispanic/Latino people were influenced by the civil rights movement of the 1960s. Although African-Americans were at the center of the civil rights struggle, many Hispanic/Latino populations became involved in what some called the "Brown Power Movement." Civil rights activists such as Cesar Chavez, who led the United Farm Workers (UFW) struggle for Mexican-American workers, began to challenge the inherent racism, prejudice, and discrimination against Hispanic/Latino Americans. Some Mexican Americans began to call themselves "Chicanos" as a means of challenging the hyphenated-American ethnic policies of assimilation and the melting pot orientation of U.S. society. Mexican-American activists began to refer to *Aztlan* as their original homeland. Puerto Rican-American political activists also joined in many of the civil rights struggles against the assimilationist policies of the United States.

Today, the three largest Hispanic/Latino populations are concentrated in the Southwest, Northeast, and in Miami, Florida. Four out of five Mexican Americans reside in

A Hispanic American family.

the Southwest, one-third of Puerto Rican Americans live in New York City, and two-thirds of Cuban Americans live in the Miami area. But many others from the Dominican Republic, Nicaragua, El Salvador, Guatemala, Colombia, and other areas of the Caribbean and Central and South America are arriving in U.S. cities. Since many of these migrants are poor and unskilled, they have taken low-wage jobs in the informal labor sector of the economy. Over one-quarter of all Hispanic/Latino Americans live below the poverty level, and the median family income of Hispanics is roughly half that of Euro-Americans (Bigler 2012). Thus, the Hispanic/Latino communities face challenges as they confront this twenty-first century in the United States.

Asian and Arab Americans

Asian and Arab Americans represent highly diverse populations that arrived in the United States during the nineteenth and twentieth centuries. Asian Americans include people from China, Japan, Korea, the Philippines, Vietnam, India, Pakistan, and other countries. Arab Americans include people from Lebanon, Syria, Iraq, Egypt, Jordan, Yemen, and other Middle Eastern countries. The U.S. Census reports that there are approximately 17.3 million Asian Americans and about 2 million Arab Americans in the United States (U.S. Census Bureau 2012).

Chinese immigrants came during the mid-nineteenth-century gold-rush economic boom in California. Many of the Chinese worked as "coolie labor," building railways and taking other lower-status jobs shunned by whites. Japanese immigrants followed in the 1880s and found jobs as agricultural laborers, first in Hawaii and then in California (Benson 2012). Nativist white Americans viewed the Chinese as "The Yellow Peril" and their immigration as a threat, resulting in mob violence against them. Eventually, the Chinese Exclusion Act was passed, the first federal law ever enacted solely on the basis of race or nationality. Although the numbers of Japanese immigrants were smaller and did not engender similar hostile legislation, in 1913 laws were passed in California restricting the amount of land that could be purchased by the Japanese.

Japanese Americans faced their greatest challenge after December 7, 1941, when Japan bombed Pearl Harbor. President Franklin D. Roosevelt signed laws that resulted in the internment of 110,000 Japanese Americans in military detention camps. This relocation meant selling their homes, furniture, and businesses on very short notice, and much of their property was confiscated. They were placed in crowded, dirty military prisons surrounded by barbed wire and armed guards. Not one of the Japanese Americans had been accused of any disloyal act, and two-thirds of the population were *Nisei*—U.S. citizens by birth. Very little action was taken against German or Italian citizens at this time. Thus, this legislation and its implementation were based partially on the racist views held by many white Americans.

Koreans and Filipinos came to Hawaii to work on the sugar and pineapple plantations. Following World War II and the Korean War of the 1950s, Koreans came as wives of U.S. military personnel and as independent business people. Because the Philippines were acquired as a colony by the United States following the Spanish-American War of 1898, Filipinos were not subject to the same discriminatory anti-immigrant laws faced by Chinese and Japanese populations. Thus, many Filipinos came to work in the agricultural fields in California and other West Coast states. Despite the lack of discriminatory legislation, a number of race riots directed at Filipinos broke out during the Great Depression of the 1920s and 1930s. Several states also passed legislation against Filipino-white intermarriages (Benson 2012).

South Asians from India, Pakistan, and Bangladesh migrated to the United States during the twentieth century. In the early 1900s, Punjabi Sikhs migrated to northern and central California to work as agricultural laborers. Anthropologist Karen Leonard studied these Sikh migrants and found that many Sikh men intermarried with Mexican-American women (1997). It was next to impossible to get a white justice of the peace to recognize a Sikh and white marriage. The first generation of children of these Sikh–Mexican-American marriages learned Spanish and identified with their mother's cultural heritage. In the second generation, however, many of these children are beginning to identify with their father's Sikh traditions.

Following passage of the Immigration and Nationality Act of 1965, which opened the doors for Asian immigration, Chinese, Korean, Filipino, Vietnamese (after 1975, following the Vietnam War), and South Asian and Southeast Asian peoples arrived on U.S. shores. Aside from the Vietnamese, who arrived as political refugees, these Asian immigrants were seeking opportunities in the booming U.S. economy. Some were working-class people who did not know English and encountered problems in adjusting to their new homes. Others were highly skilled professionals or independent businesspeople who were very successful in their adaptation to the U.S. way of life. Because of the success and higher incomes of this latter group compared to most other immigrants, Asian Americans have been labeled a "model minority." Many Asian Americans, however, resent this stereotype because it tends to neglect the hard work and determination of these families despite racist attitudes and discrimination against them. This stereotype also neglects the problems and difficulties faced by working-class Asian Americans in U.S. society.

The Arab American communities are smaller than those of other nonwhite minorities and are often marginalized in discussions of ethnicity in the United States. The major problem encountered by Arab Americans is a monolithic negative stereotype of Arabs and the Islamic tradition. Despite the tremendous diversity within this population of two million people, many of whom are Christians, the prevalent stereotype of Arab Americans is based on fears of international terrorism. This stereotype was reinforced as a result of the September 11, 2001, attack on the World Trade Center and the Pentagon. Following that event, many Arab Americans became alarmed that they would all be lumped together as threats to U.S. society. There was some violence directed at Arab Americans and Islamic mosques. Many Arab Americans were arrested following 9/11 and were detained and released without substantial evidence of any links with terrorist networks. The negative stereotype of Arabs and the misunderstanding of their religion and history, as depicted in textbooks and the Western media, are the major problems that affect the Arab-American communities in the United States (Aswad and Abowd 2012).

An Arab American family

Cultural Pluralism

Beginning in the late 1950s and 1960s, the melting pot metaphor was challenged by many non-European ethnic groups. African-Americans, Hispanic Americans, Native Americans, Asian Americans, and other non-European ethnic groups demanded equal rights and opportunities for their respective communities. Non-European ethnic groups asserted that because of their skin color and other cultural elements, they were not as "meltable" as European ethnic groups. Some civil rights leaders, such as Martin Luther King, Jr., rejected the assimilationist policies of U.S. society and called for a plural society, where different ethnic groups could retain their culture and heritage, but have equal rights and opportunities with other Americans.

Three generations of an Asian American family.

The demand for cultural pluralism became a dominant trend in ethnic relations in the 1960s in U.S. society. Various non-European ethnic groups emphasized a pride in their own unique history, experience, and culture. "Black Power" among African-Americans, "Brown Power" among Hispanic Americans, and "Red Power" among Native Americans became the rallying anthems for cultural pluralism in America. Rather than emphasizing the melting pot as an ideal, non-European groups suggested that America should be a "salad bowl" or, better yet, a "stir fry," which implied that everyone could maintain his or her distinctive culture and ethnicity and still contribute to American society.

Multiculturalism in the United States

In the 1950s, during the Cold War, the United States opened its doors for political refugees from communist countries such as Hungary and Cuba. Later, in 1965, during the civil rights movement and amidst demands for more cultural pluralism in the United States, a new immigration law opened the doors again for immigration into the United States from different areas of the world. Since that time, there has been a significant growth in the population of peoples of non-European ancestry. A decline in the birth rate of the majority white population of European descent, coupled with new trends in immigration and higher birth rates of ethnic minorities, is changing the ethnic landscape of U.S. society.

As indicated by Figure 23.1, recent immigration from Europe to the United States represents a tiny fraction compared with immigration from Latin America and Asia. The ethnic diversity of non-European immigrants to the United States is remarkable. Among the Asians are Filipinos, Koreans, Chinese, Japanese, Vietnamese, Laotians, Cambodians, Thais, Indians, and Pakistanis. From Latin America come Mexicans, Central Americans from El Salvador and Guatemala, and people from various countries of South America. And from the Middle East and Africa come Palestinians, Iraqis, Iranians, Lebanese, Syrians, Israelis, Nigerians, and Egyptians.

Like the nineteenth-century immigrants from Europe, the majority of these immigrants have come to the United States seeking economic opportunities, political freedom, and improved social conditions. The United States has truly become much more of a multicultural society. A movement known as **multiculturalism** developed as an extension of the demand for cultural pluralism in U.S. society. As a result of this multiculturalist movement, federal, state, and local governments in the United States have encouraged the development of educational programs to prepare people to live in this new type of society.

Multiculturalism has led to revision of the curricula in educational programs throughout the United States. Instead of focusing narrowly on a Eurocentric or an Anglocentric version of history, texts were revised to include discussions of non-European ethnic groups and their contributions to U.S. history. Bilingual education was developed to extend equal education for students who were not proficient in English. The ongoing multicultural

Figure 23.1 Legal immigrants admitted to the United States by region of birth

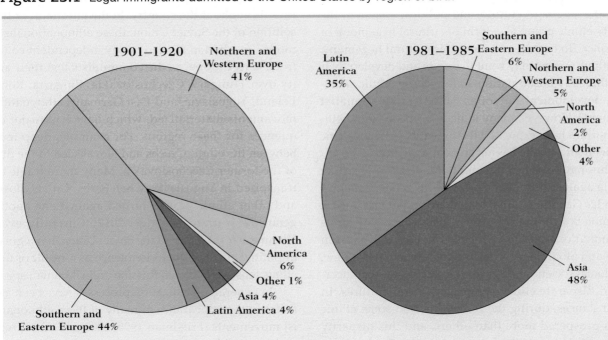

movement emphasizes that there is no single model type of "American." Cultural pluralism is endorsed fully, and the multiculturalist movement tends to suggest that there are no significant costs for retaining one's ethnic heritage.

The movement for multiculturalism views cultural and ethnic differences as positive. It downplays any kind of competition or conflict among ethnic groups. Rather, the emphasis is on encouraging tolerance and cooperation among different ethnic groups. The hope is that as students become more ethnically literate and more educated about ethnic groups, they will be able to appreciate and tolerate people from different ethnic backgrounds. In addition, they will be prepared to make personal decisions that will affect public policy, promoting a more harmonious form of ethnic and race relations in the United States.

Ethnonationalism

23.7 Discuss why ethnonationalist movements have developed in relationship to globalization.

In Chapter 20, we discussed how globalization has had an impact on culture, language, and national identity for many people throughout the world. One significant factor that influences ethnic groups and globalization is nationalism. In addition, as we saw in Chapter 18, *nationalism*—a set of symbols and beliefs providing the sense of belonging to a single political community—developed along with industrialism in Europe and elsewhere. Before the development of nationalism, the primary focus of loyalty was the local community; a particular ruler, ethnicity, or religion; or the family (Gellner 1983; Anderson 1991; A. Smith 2009). However, as nationalism has emerged in these societies, minority ethnic groups sometimes view the imposition of the language, culture, and political system of the majority ethnic group as a form of cultural hegemony or dominance. To contest and resist this cultural hegemony, these ethnic groups may want to secede and develop their own ethnically based nation-states. These ethnic secessionist developments are often called **ethnonationalist movements**. However, many indigenous peoples and ethnic minorities have expressed their identity in nationalistic terms without actually having an existing nation-state.

Ethnonationalist movements played a role in the struggle against European colonialism. Leaders such as Mohandas Gandhi in India, Jomo Kenyatta in East Africa, and Simón Bolívar in Latin America mobilized new forms of ethnonationalism in order to free themselves from European colonialism. After independence, these new, postcolonial societies had to form nation-states that incorporated disparate ethnic communities and cultures. In some instances, during the colonial period some ethnic groups prospered more than others, and this disparity often resulted in postcolonial states in which the dominant

ethnic group imposed its particular culture and language. Many of these postcolonial states still have a very weakly developed sense of nationalism because ethnic minorities perceive their own local interests and culture as being undermined by the dominant ethnic group. Many ethnonationalist movements emerged in areas of the world that were once colonized by Europeans and now play a role in the struggle against globalization.

Another variation of the postcolonial ethnonationalist movement occurred with the downfall of the Soviet Union and its satellite countries in Eastern Europe. Various ethnic minorities—Latvians, Estonians, Lithuanians, Belarusians, Ukrainians, Georgians, Azeris, Turkmens, Uzbeks, Tajiks, and others—began to accentuate their ethnic identities and regional nationalism as the Soviet empire began to collapse in the late 1980s. Historically, the Soviet Union comprised 15 autonomous Soviet Socialist Republics defined by ethnic groups or nationalities. However, under the orthodox Marxist ideology that provided the foundation for Soviet political policies, ethnic groups were supposed to "wither away" and be replaced by a Soviet "superethnicity." This was an attempt by the Soviet political elite to use their own version of nationalism, based upon a political creed, to produce a civil polity (Banks 1996; Gellner [1977] 1988). In reality, none of these autonomous regions were allowed political rights; all were strictly controlled by Soviet authorities in Moscow. Members of ethnic groups were subject to deportation or exile, and their boundaries were manipulated by the Soviet state.

In most cases, contrary to Marxist dogma, the various ethnic minorities did not abandon their cultural, linguistic, and religious traditions as expected. As the Soviet system began to disintegrate, a variety of ethnonationalist movements developed among these various ethnic minorities throughout the country. In the aftermath of the dissolution of the Soviet Union, these ethnonationalist aspirations resulted in myriad newly independent countries. In Eastern Europe, as the communists lost their authority over Hungary, Czechoslovakia, Bulgaria, Romania, Poland, Yugoslavia, and East Germany, ethnonationalist movements materialized, which have had major consequences for these regions. For example, deep tensions between the ethnic Czechs and Slovaks led to the division of the former Czechoslovakia. Many more tragic events transpired in Yugoslavia, when Serbs, Croats, Bosnians, and other ethnic groups turned against one another in genocidal warfare (Ballinger 2012). Currently, events in Ukraine, a former part of the Soviet Union, has a great deal of political instability and violence as a result of internal ethnic tensions between Russian and Ukrainian speakers.

In general, globalization processes have been a major factor in the appearance of many of these ethnonationalist movements (Friedman 1995, 2003). At times, regional and ethnic identities are accentuated in a response to, and as a defense against, the growing impact of the wider world on their lives. As we saw in our discussion of globalization processes in Chapter 20, this process is sometimes perceived as a "McWorld" tendency that stems from the United States. The communications media—including television, film, and the Internet—are diffusing particular forms of culture as the globalization process that has had an impact on all areas of the world. One of the responses to these globalizing trends is the reassertion and revitalization of people's own ethnic and local identity leading to ethnonationalist movements. Many ethnic groups view these globalizing trends as a menacing process that tends to obliterate their own cultural traditions. Today, as we saw in earlier chapters, there are various ethnonationalist movements among the Maya in Mexico; the Igbo, Yoruba, and Hausa in Nigeria; the Kurds in Iraq; and native Hawaiians in the United States. These ethnonationalist movements have become a prevalent aspect of social and political life in the twenty-first century.

Summary and Review of Learning Objectives

23.1 Discuss the basic criticisms of racism by anthropologists.

Anthropological research initiated by Franz Boas began to challenge racist views, demonstrating conclusively that the brain sizes and cranial capacities of modern humans differ widely within all so-called races. This anthropological research resulted in irrefutable findings that there were no "superior" or "inferior" races. Boas's research also confirmed that there were no direct links among race, brain size, cranial capacity, and intelligence levels. This pioneering work initiated a program of research among the four fields of anthropology, which has continued over the past century to challenge racist beliefs wherever they appear. This research has demonstrated time and time again that racist beliefs have no basis in fact.

23.2 Discuss how race is understood in different societies.

Despite the useless scientific enterprise of classifying races throughout the world, societies continue to use folk taxonomies of race to distinguish different people. These folk taxonomies have profound social and cultural meaning for societies around the world. Folk models of race differ widely in various societies. Puerto Rico, Brazil, and Mexico have folk models of race that are different than in the United States. In the United States, hypodescent notions of race based on the one-drop rule were used to classify racial groups. These cultural models have a powerful influence on how people perceive and view various populations in their countries.

23.3 Describe the basis of ethnicity as studied by contemporary anthropologists.

Since the 1960s, anthropologists and other social scientists have generally used the term *ethnicity* or *ethnic group* to refer to an individual's cultural heritage, which is separate from one's physical characteristics. Anthropologists emphasize both the objective and the subjective aspects of ethnicity. The *objective aspect* of ethnicity is the observable culture and shared symbols of a particular group. It may involve a specific language or religious tradition that is maintained by the group, or particular clothing, hairstyles, preferences in food, or other conspicuous characteristics. The *subjective aspect* of ethnicity involves the internal beliefs of the people regarding their shared ancestry.

23.4 Compare the difference between the primordialist and circumstantial perspectives on ethnicity.

The primordialist perspective on ethnicity emphasizes the meaning and significance that people invest in their ethnic attachments. These ethnic attachments are subjective perceptions of attributes such as blood ties and ancestry, which may or may not coincide with the actual circumstances of one's birth. The circumstantialist approach emphasizes how ethnic boundary markers such as language, clothing, and other cultural traits are not based on deeply rooted, enduring aspects of ethnicity. In the circumstantialist model, ethnic boundaries are continually being revised, negotiated, and redefined according to the practical interests of people.

23.5 Compare the different patterns of ethnic relations described by anthropologists.

Pluralism is a form of society based on autonomous ethnic groups residing together in one country. This pluralism can be inegalitarian or egalitarian. An inegalitarian plural society has one dominant ethnic group that holds sway over other ethnic groups. An egalitarian plural society has ethnic groups that are equal to one another. Another pattern of ethnic relations is based on cultural or biological assimilation. Cultural assimilation entails the adoption of the culture of the dominant ethnic groups by other ethnic groups. Biological assimilation occurs when different ethnic groups intermarry and reproduce with one another, creating yet another ethnic group. Other patterns of ethnic relations are segregation, ethnic cleansing, and genocide. Segregation was a feature of the United States during the

Jim Crow era and in South Africa during the apartheid period. Ethnic cleansing is the removal of an ethnic group from its territory, which occurred for most Native American Indian populations in the United States or more recently in the former Yugoslavia. Genocide, the most deadly form of ethnic violence has occurred in Nazi Germany, Rwanda, Cambodia, and other regions of the world.

23.6 Discuss the historical and contemporary conditions of race and ethnic groups in the United States.

The history of U.S. race and ethnic relations was defined by the white Anglo-Saxon Protestants (WASPs), who established the language, the political culture, and the religious culture in American society. Other Europeans who immigrated to the United States included the Irish, German, Italian, and Polish ethnic groups; these groups became known as the "white ethnics." All of these white ethnics encountered discrimination from the WASPs, but eventually assimilated, intermarried and became "white Americans." African-Americans arrived in the United States as slaves and have struggled for their political rights for centuries. After achieving their freedom from slavery following the U.S. Civil War, they faced years of discrimination under the segregation of the Jim Crow laws. Eventually, after World War II and the 1950s and 60s, African-Americans organized a major civil rights campaign that involved leaders such as Dr. Martin Luther King Jr. that offered the ideals of integration into U.S. society as equals. Although there has been considerable progress for African-Americans, because of historical disadvantages, there are still some major challenges that confront this population with respect to economic and political opportunities.

Hispanic Americans are a diverse group that includes Mexican, Cuban, and Puerto Rican Americans, along with smaller communities from Central and South America and the Caribbean, all of whom maintain distinctive cultural traditions in the United States. Like the African-Americans, these Hispanic groups encountered prejudice and discrimination and became involved in the civil rights struggles of the 1960s to improve their socioeconomic and political status. Currently, the Hispanic/Latino population is growing more rapidly than other nonwhite ethnic groups in the United States. Asian and Arab Americans are also represented in multiethnic America. Like the other nonwhite ethnic populations, the Asian and Arab Americans faced prejudice and discrimination and became involved in the civil rights struggles of the 1960s. The Asian communities are diverse with Chinese, Japanese, Korean, East Indian, Pakistani, and other South and Southeast Asian groups with their own distinctive ethnic traditions. The Asian Americans have moved ahead economically and politically in U.S. society, and are sometimes known as the "model minority." However, this "model minority" stereotype neglects the historical struggles of these groups and the continuation of poverty within some of the Asian communities. Since the tragedy of 9/11/01, the Arab Americans have encountered new forms of prejudice and discrimination and are stereotyped as "terrorists," in some books and other media.

23.7 Discuss why ethnonationalist movements have developed in relationship to globalization.

Various ethnonationalist movements developed in response to Western colonialism and globalization. In India and other colonized areas of the world, ethnic sentiments were mobilized as the basis for independence and nationalist movements. Later, under the Soviet Union, various ethnonationalist movements among the Latvians, Georgians, Ukrainians, or Azeris formed as secessionist movements that desired political autonomy and their own national and ethnic identity. At times, regional and ethnic identities are accentuated in a response to, and as a defense against, the growing impact of the wider world on their lives. The communications media—including television, film, and the Internet—are diffusing particular forms of culture as the globalization process has had an impact on all areas of the world. One of the responses to these globalizing trends is the reassertion and revitalization of people's own ethnic and local identity, leading to ethnonationalist movements. These movements among native American Indian and Hawaiian groups as well as Mayan, Kurds, and others are a feature of twenty-first century globalization.

Key Terms

biological assimilation, p. 553
cultural assimilation, p. 553
ethnic boundary markers, p. 551
ethnogenesis, p. 551

ethnonationalist movements, p. 566
hypodescent concept, p. 549
Jim Crow laws, p. 554
multiculturalism, p. 565

one-drop rule, p. 549
plural society, p. 552
racism, p. 548
segregation, p. 554

Chapter 24
Contemporary Global Trends

Learning Objectives

After reading this chapter you should be able to:

24.1 Compare the logic-of-growth model with the pessimistic model of global technological, environmental, and demographic developments.

24.2 Discuss the results of globalization for technology and energy use.

24.3 Discuss how globalization has had an impact on the environment.

24.4 Discuss globalization and demographic trends.

24.5 Discuss globalization and economic trends.

24.6 Discuss the political, ethnic, and religious trends resulting from globalization.

24.7 Discuss the role of anthropology as it studies current political, ethnic, and religious trends.

As we have seen throughout this textbook, especially in Chapter 20, global interdependence, or what we have called globalization, has become an undeniable fact in the contemporary world. This process began after the Neolithic revolution, when small-scale societies either were absorbed into larger states or became dependent on those states. Following the Industrial Revolution, the trend toward global interdependence escalated, especially through the process of European colonialism. As the world shrinks and industrial societies continue to expand, interconnections develop among different societies, creating a global village. The global village has been described as a world in which all regions are in contact with one another through the mass media, instantaneous communication, and highly integrated economic and political networks. This chapter reviews some of the recent trends associated with the development of this global village.

Pessimists versus Optimists on Globalization Issues

24.1 Compare the logic-of-growth model with the pessimistic model of global technological, environmental, and demographic developments.

Two basic perspectives—one negative, one positive—have influenced the analyses of global trends affecting the technological, environmental, and demographic developments that result from globalization.

The Doomsday Model

The negative perspective is sometimes referred to as the doomsday model, or the neo-Malthusian approach. This model predicts that if current population, environmental, and technological trends continue, they will produce a series of ecological disasters that will threaten human existence. In the 1970s, a group of scientists and academics known as the Club of Rome assessed these global trends and predicted worldwide scarcities and a global economic collapse. Using elaborate computer models developed at the Massachusetts Institute of Technology, these scientists concluded that current global trends in population growth, energy consumption, and environmental pollution will exhaust the world's natural resources within the next 100 years.

The Optimists: The Logic-of-Growth Model

Optimists such as Julian Simon (1981) foresee a more promising future for humankind. Simon noted that health improvements, including a decrease in infant mortality and an increase in life expectancy, are a global trend. Simon also argued that pollution has abated in most societies that have experienced economic growth. Simon believed that as development and economic improvements continue in different societies, people will provide funds to solve pollution problems.

Sometimes this perspective is referred to as the **logic-of-growth model**, which assumes that natural resources are infinite and that economic growth can continue indefinitely without long-term harm to the environment. For example, this model notes that Malthus had not foreseen the biotechnological revolution in agriculture that made land much more productive than was true in eighteenth-century England. Economists, including Simon, believe

that the food production problem in regions such as Africa can be attributed to farm collectivization, government attempts to control the prices of agricultural commodities, and other institutional problems. Simon cited statistics indicating that on a worldwide level food prices per person are decreasing, and food production per person is increasing.

The logic-of-growth theorists cite evidence showing that the costs of energy and other natural resources have actually fallen over time because humans have found creative technological solutions for producing and extracting these resources. For example, Simon argued that the increase in the price of oil in the 1970s was purely political. The cost of producing a barrel of oil is still about 15 to 25 cents. He noted how people in the past responded to shortages of firewood used for heating by turning to coal and from coal shortages by using oil. Simon believed that this ongoing process of creative innovation will continue.

Simon and other logic-of-growth theorists further suggest that population growth is a stimulus for, rather than a deterrent to, economic progress. The title of Simon's major book is *The Ultimate Resource* (1981), which he considers to be the human mind. Productivity and solutions for economic and environmental problems come directly from the human mind. In the long run, therefore, population growth helps to raise the standard of living in society by utilizing creative ideas and technologies to extract solutions. Another, more recent, book by British biologist Matt Ridley entitled *The Rational Optimist: How Prosperity Evolves* continues the themes that Simon endorsed (2010). Ridley emphasizes that rapid technological changes, economic growth, and modernity have produced a plethora of goods and services and has eliminated poverty, reduced pollution, and decreased worldwide population growth. Although Ridley and other logic-of-growth theorists admit that in the short term population growth may inhibit economic development, they conclude that countries ought not to restrict population growth forcibly and that eventually technological innovations and human creativity will solve our problems, just as they have in the past.

The Pessimists and the Optimists: An Anthropological Assessment

Most likely, both the pessimistic and the optimistic predictions regarding global problems are to some extent exaggerated. Predicting the future is risky for any social scientist, and to project complex global trends regarding population growth, environmental destruction, and technological change over many decades is highly problematic. The optimists believe that ever since the beginnings of civilization, humanity has benefited from technological progress. A comprehensive view of the past, however, challenges this assumption. For example, we saw in Chapter 15 that the emergence of intensive agriculture—one of the major developments in human history—produced benefits for small segments of the population, but adversely affected the majority of people by contributing to higher disease rates, increased inequality, and other problems. Conversely, the pessimists tend to underestimate the human capacity to devise technological solutions to global problems.

Anthropological research may help assess these global issues in a more cautious and analytic manner. With its holistic approach, anthropology has always been concerned with precisely those aspects of human interaction with the environment that are now being recognized widely by scientists studying global environmental change. The U.S. Committee on Global Change (1988) called for the development of an interdisciplinary science for understanding global change. The discipline of anthropology represents a prototype or model for the interdisciplinary science that would be needed to understand these changes (Rayner 1989). Anthropological data can help assess the causes of such phenomena as the greenhouse effect by examining land use choices and the impacts of economic activities and may assist in the development of policies on matters such as agriculture, biotechnology, pollution, and population growth by providing information on the links between local practices and global processes.

Technological Trends

24.2 Discuss the results of globalization for technology and energy use.

Ever since the Industrial Revolution, the scale of technological change has been global, rather than local. Industrial technology and electronics associated with advances in global communications spread from the core nations to the developing countries. Technical information about agricultural production is spread through television, the Internet, and satellites to villages in countries like India and Pakistan.

Energy Consumption Patterns

High energy consumption is not only creating environmental hazards, but also causes rapid depletion of resources. High-energy, industrialized societies such as the United States consume a major portion of the world's nonrenewable energy and resources. For example, in 2011, the United States used about 18,840,000 barrels of oil per day. The entire European Union used 13,250,000 barrels of oil per day, China used 9,790,000 barrels, and Japan used 4,464,000 barrels per day (*World Factbook* 2012). In contrast, the Central African Republic used 3,175 barrels per day; Afghanistan, 4,229 barrels; Bangladesh, 108,900 barrels; and Egypt, 816,300 barrels (*World Factbook* 2012).

The United States, containing 5 percent of the world's population, is the country that consumes the largest amount of the world's oil—almost 26 percent. The U.S. Geological Survey estimates that there are about three trillion barrels of proven reserves of oil worldwide. The entire world should reach its peak level of oil production in 2037, after which time output is expected to fall precipitously. The 23 percent of the world's population residing in industrial and postindustrial countries is consuming about 58 percent of the energy reserves that the planet is capable of producing. Yet there is the possibility of new technologies on the horizon that may mitigate these high energy consumption trends. Recently, the United States has increased its reserves of natural gas from the process of hydraulic fracking, using pressurized water and sand mixed with chemicals to produce shale gas and petroleum. Yet, this process may result in environmental problems such as groundwater pollution. More environmental research needs to be done on this new technology. Higher prices for energy also drives greater demand for safe nuclear power, large solar farms, automobiles that need less petroleum, and other alternative energy sources that may enhance the possibilities of reducing the demand for nonrenewable energy production throughout the world.

Were semiperipheral and peripheral countries, with 77 percent of the world's population, to adopt the same consumption patterns as the core nations, nonrenewable energy supplies and resources might not be sufficient to support global economic development. For example, as peripheral countries adopted mechanized farming, they increased their consumption of fossil fuels, leading to a worldwide jump in energy use (Schusky 1990). Lester Brown of the Earth Policy Institute reflects on this trend in respect to China: "If we assume that in 2030 there are three cars for every four people in China, as there now are in the United States, China will have 1.1 billion cars. The world currently has 860 million cars. To provide the needed roads, highways, and parking lots, China would have to pave an area comparable to what it now plants in rice. By 2030 China would need 98 million barrels of oil a day. The world is currently producing 85 million barrels a day and may never produce much more than that." (2008: 13–14). On the other hand, the United States has become more energy efficient in terms of agricultural production. The use of gasoline and diesel fuel per ton of grain has dropped by 64 percent since 1973 due to better agricultural practices (Brown 2008:34). Yet, energy costs to transport food over great distances by air and refrigerated trucks are rising. The U.S. energy costs in the food economy to transport, process, can, freeze, market, and package is greater than the entire economy of the United Kingdom (Brown 2008:35). As many developing countries shift from draft animals to tractors, nonrenewable energy use continues to rise in much of the world.

Traffic congestion has become a severe problem in countries such as India.

Environmental Trends

24.3 Discuss how globalization has had an impact on the environment.

As we saw in earlier chapters, hunting-gathering, horticulturalist, pastoralist, and intensive agriculturalist societies survived by extracting natural resources from a particular biome or environment. In these societies, people were directly linked with nature and the environment, and they lived in relative harmony with the natural environment. This is not to suggest that humans in preindustrial societies did not harm their environments in any manner. Slash-and-burn horticulture, intensive agriculture, pastoralism, and, sometimes, even foraging caused some environmental damage. Overgrazing, soil erosion, and the depletion of certain species have always been part of humankind's evolutionary development. The concept of the "ecological noble savage" that tended to describe indigenous peoples as living in complete harmony within their environments is largely mythical (Hames 2007; Nadasay 2005). There are some cases where indigenous peoples were practicing conservation, but in other circumstances there is evidence of ecological destruction. For example, birds and various species of animals were hunted to extinction by the peoples on some of the Pacific islands and in prehistoric America (Diamond 1997).

With the development of globalization, however, the negative consequences for the environment have multiplied rapidly. Ironically, many people in industrial societies came to believe that they had gained mastery over the natural environment and were, therefore, free from its constraints. But in recent decades, people have become more aware that they are as dependent on the natural environment as were preindustrial peoples. It has become evident that the pollution created by global industrialization is threatening the ecological balance of the planet and the health of plant and animal species, including humans.

Mechanized Agriculture and Pollution

One major source of pollution is commercialized, mechanized agriculture, known as agribusiness. **Agribusiness**, depends on the use of fossil fuels, chemical fertilizers, large tracts of land, and toxic chemicals such as herbicides and pesticides to increase agricultural yields. This form of agriculture is not only prevalent in the industrialized world, but also becoming common in developing countries. For example, some farmers in societies such as Mexico, India, and Indonesia have adopted mechanized agriculture. The spread of mechanized, high-tech agriculture has been labeled the **Green Revolution** (Schusky 1990). Through biotechnological research, sometimes known as genetic engineering, and other methods, scientists have produced hybrid species of wheat and rice seeds that generate higher agricultural yields. To take advantage of these yields, however, farmers must use expensive, capital-intensive technology for irrigation and cultivation; nonrenewable fossil fuels such as gasoline and oil; synthetic chemical fertilizers; and toxic weed killers, or herbicides, and pesticides.

The use of capital-intensive agriculture, however, can have negative consequences for the global environment. One of the most tragic cases resulting from the Green Revolution occurred in 1984 in Bhopal, India, where toxic fumes leaking from a chemical fertilizer plant killed or injured thousands of people. Many of the consequences of mechanized agriculture are much less dramatic (and, therefore, less publicized), although perhaps just as dangerous. For example, research has shown that much of the foods produced in both industrialized and developing countries contain traces of pesticides and other poisons. Even when governments ban the use of chemicals, the residues may remain in the food chain for many years. Because many new synthetic chemicals are being produced for agribusiness every year, the danger to the environment continues to increase.

Air Pollution

Air pollution, especially from the emissions of motor vehicles, power generators, and waste incinerators, continues to be a major problem for industrializing societies. As less developed countries industrialize, the degree of global air pollution steadily increases. Atmospheric pollution is depleting the Earth's ozone layer, which absorbs 99 percent of the ultraviolet radiation from the Sun. These pollutants could irreversibly alter the Earth's ability to support life. Satellite data show that during the period from 1978 to 1984, the ozone layer eroded at an average annual rate of 0.5 percent.

Scientific data suggest that the increased levels of carbon dioxide produced primarily by the burning of fossil fuels and tropical rain forests, methane, and nitrous oxide will create a **greenhouse effect**, or global warming. According to these studies, after solar rays reach the Earth's surface, the carbon dioxide (CO_2) in the atmosphere traps the heat and prevents it from radiating back into space. This process is melting the polar ice caps, which will raise sea levels, flood major coastal cities, create and intensify violent weather patterns such as the cyclical El Niño Southern Oscillation (ENSO), and turn the tropics into deserts. An enormous amount of scientific data has accumulated that confirms the greenhouse effect hypothesis and global warming. Emissions of these greenhouse gases are likely to increase in the future. Predictions based on present-day estimates suggest that by 2020, CO_2 emissions from industrialized countries will be 50 to 70 percent above 1990 levels.

Sufficient quantities of air pollutants such as NOx (oxides of nitrogen), SOx (oxides of sulfur), and carbon monoxide (CO) harm human health, causing pulmonary problems, asthma, allergies, and eye damage in the short term and cancer and neurological, reproductive, respiratory, and psychological disorders in the long term. Anthropologists who follow the studies of these air pollutants coupled with increased lead in blood levels, noise from manufacturing in urban areas, and new psychosocial stresses recognize that urban living is having an influence on health conditions throughout the world (Schell and Denham 2003).

However, as more countries such as China begin to emit more greenhouse gases, global warming and other pollution problems will proceed more quickly. Air pollution is a major concern for developing countries such as China and Mexico and for other areas of the world. Sixteen of the world's most air polluted cities are in China. These cities are facing an ecological and health crisis as a result of the industrial pollution created by rapid globalization. In China, 300,000 people a year face respiratory illnesses as a result of this pollution. China accounts for over 23 percent of the CO_2 emissions today. At this level, it has become the country with the largest emissions of CO_2 followed by the United States, which generates over 19 percent (*World Factbook* 2012). Stabilizing atmospheric concentrations of greenhouse gases will require reversing current emission trends. In addition, anthropologists find that the economic and social inequality that results from globalization has resulted in more health problems for peoples without basic resources (Nguyen and Peschard 2003).

Population Trends

24.4 Discuss globalization and demographic trends.

As discussed in Chapter 15, with industrialization, new demographic trends have arisen. A recent model used to measure population trends is based on the **demographic-transition theory**, which assumes a close connection between fertility and mortality rates and socioeconomic development (see Figure 24.1). According to the demographic-transition model, societies pass through three major phases of population change. During Phase 1, a high fertility rate is counterbalanced by a high mortality rate, resulting in minimal population growth. Phase 1 describes preindustrial societies. At first, societies used various methods of population regulation, such as self-induced abortions, postpartum abstinence, infanticide, and migration. As preindustrial societies developed intensive agriculture, populations began to increase, but disease, famine, and natural disasters kept mortality rates fairly high, thus limiting growth.

In Phase 2, population tends to increase rapidly because of continued high fertility rates coupled with lower mortality rates. Mortality rates decline because of increases in the food supply, the development of scientifically based medical practices, and improved public sanitation and health care. Improvements in nutrition and health care enable people to control certain diseases, thus diminishing infant mortality rates and increasing life expectancy. Consequently, during Phase 2, population growth is dramatic. Growth of this magnitude was associated with the

Figure 24.1 The demographic-transition model

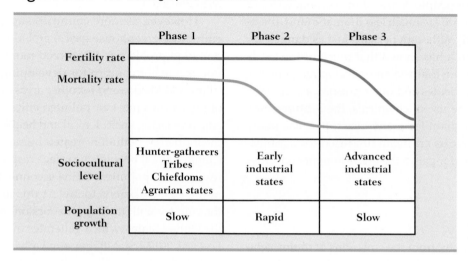

early phases of industrialization in Western Europe and North America, but it is also visible in many developing societies that are now in the early stages of industrialization. In particular, in many developing countries there is a "youth bulge," with larger populations of young people below the age of 25. It is expected that this youth bulge will result in higher populations in the near future.

Phase 3 of the demographic-transition model represents the stage in which fertility rates begin to fall, along with mortality rates. According to the model, as industrialization proceeds, family planning is introduced, and traditional institutions and religious beliefs supporting high birth rates are undermined. Values stressing individualism and upward mobility lead couples to reduce the size of their families. Phase 3 describes the stage of advanced postindustrial societies such as Western Europe, the United States, and Japan. Other trends, such as geographic mobility and the increased expense of rearing children, also affect reproductive decisions in industrial societies. Hence, in these societies, as the birth rate, or fertility rate, falls, population growth begins to decline.

The Demographic-Transition Model Applied

The demographic-transition model seems to have some validity when applied to global population trends. World population during the Paleolithic period (Phase 1) is estimated to have been about 10 million (Hassan 1981). Following the agricultural revolution, around the year 1 A.D., the global population was approximately 300 million. But after the early stages of industrialization (Phase 2), from 1650 to 1900, the world population tripled from 510 million to 1.6 billion. By 1950, the global population had risen to 2.5 billion, and by 1970, another billion people had been added. By 1990, the world population

was approximately 5.4 billion, with 150 babies being born every minute (see Figure 24.2). By 2011, the world population exceeded 7 billion.

Thomas Robert Malthus (1766–1834), a British clergyman and economist, is known as the father of demography. Malthus predicted that human populations would increase at a rapid, or exponential rate, but that the production of food and other vital resources would increase at a lower rate. Thus, populations would always grow more quickly than the food supply to support them. As a result, human societies would constantly experience hunger, increases in warfare, scarcity of resources, and poverty.

To measure the exponential growth rate, demographers use the concept of **doubling time**, the period it takes for a population to double. For example, a population growing at 1 percent will double in 70 years, one growing at 2 percent will take 35 years to double, and one growing at 3 percent will double in 23 years.

Figure 24.2 Global population growth from about 10 million people to 7 billion people.

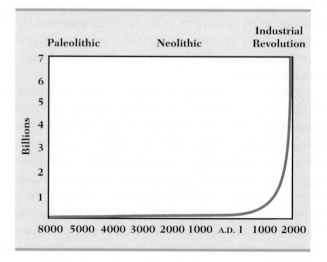

The industrial nations of Western Europe, the United States, and Japan have reached Phase 3 of the demographic-transition model. The U.S. population is growing at only 0.7 percent. Countries such as Germany, Hungary, Japan, and even Roman Catholic Italy actually have negative growth rates, meaning that they are not replacing the number of people dying with new births. For a society to maintain a given level of population, each woman must give birth to an average of 2.1 children. At this point, the society has achieved **zero population growth (ZPG)**, meaning that the population is simply replacing itself. When the average number of births falls below 2.1, a society experiences negative growth. Thus, Japan, with an average of 1.8 births, is actually experiencing a population decline of -0.2 percent, as is other Western European nations. Decreased growth rates in industrialized nations have helped lower the global growth rate from 2 to 1.7 percent.

The demographic-transition model provides a conceptual scheme for evaluating global population trends, especially for the core industrial societies, yet it must be used carefully as a hypothesis (Johnson-Hanks 2008). Although the industrial societies of North America, Western Europe, and Japan have reached Phase 3, the vast majority of the world's people reside in societies that are in Phase 2, with exponential growth rates. Population growth in African countries such as Kenya is almost 4 percent (doubling every 15 years), and Mexico's growth rate is 2.6 percent (doubling every 27 years). Thus, the demographic-transition hypothesis explains population trends in advanced industrial societies, but it may not accurately predict population growth elsewhere for Phase 3. Suggesting that all societies will follow the path of development of the advanced industrial societies is somewhat naïve. As we have seen from our discussion of industrial societies in Chapter 15, it took at least 500 years of historical experience for these countries to become fully industrialized and to reach Phase 3 of the demographic model.

Most rurally based peripheral societies maintain high birth rates related to their agricultural lifestyles. In rural agricultural societies, high death rates lead to higher birth rates so that some children survive to provide assets to the family. As these societies become industrialized, however, death rates tend to fall, leading to dramatic population increases. These societies have not had an extended time period to adjust to the demographic trends related to industrialization. Consequently, predicting a movement to Phase 3 is problematic. Most economically underdeveloped countries can attain population decline only through changes in technology, political economy, and social and cultural practices.

Yet, new demographic studies indicate that the population problems that were predicted in pessimistic terms in the recent past have been reevaluated. Anthropologists and demographers have discovered that as public health measures have improved with vaccinations, vitamins for pregnant women, and antibiotics. And the incentives and need for large rural families and children, previously encouraged in their traditional rural communities, has been reduced. In addition, women's living standards have improved as they take jobs in various occupations and in new factories that have moved to these regions from the postindustrial world (see Chapter 20); as a result, rates of population growth in rural areas in India, Pakistan, Africa, the Middle East, and other developing countries have decreased. For example in 1955, Bangladesh had a birth rate of 6.8 children, but in 2010 that ratio is less than half what it was, 2.6 children per woman. Neighboring India has seen a similar decline in birth rate from 5.9 to 2.6 children, and Pakistan has halved its birth rate in 20 years to 3.2 children per woman. Whereas the world population was predicted to grow to 12 billion in 2050, that number has been revised to 10 billion. Thus, as societies grow wealthier, better educated, more urbanized, and more emancipated, world population rates are predicted to continue to decline.

Anthropologists Rebecca Sear and David Coall have been assessing the results of the demographic transition for broad human evolutionary and reproductive trends (2011). Using cross-cultural and historical demographic research, they indicate that in preindustrial, predemographic transition societies, kinship was extremely important for ensuring the survival and nurturing of offspring. In particular, maternal and paternal grandmothers were vital for child survival in preindustrial societies. A rural community in the African country of Senegal reported that "A home without a grandmother is like a house without a roof" (Sear and Coall 2011:90). Grandmothers were also important for prenatal care for the mothers. Along with grandmothers, older siblings and sometimes fathers played a role in childcare and nurturing the children. In postdemographic transition societies, grandparents were found to have positive benefits for child development. In fact, in contrast to preindustrial societies, grandfathers in postdemographic transition societies were equally as important as grandmothers for child development and nurturing. However, as expected, along with the shift from preindustrial to industrial and postindustrial societies, families became more dependent on non-kin sources of childcare and nurturing. Sear and Coall conclude their essay based on Sarah Hrdy's book *Mothers and Others: The Evolutionary Origins of Mutual Understandings* (2009). Hrdy notes that our cognitive capacities for empathy and cooperation evolved within closely knit kinship groups in preindustrial societies. However, in industrial and postindustrial societies with loose kinship and family ties, our cognitive capacities for empathy and cooperation with others may deteriorate.

The One-Child Policy in China One developing country that has taken steps to drastically reduce its population growth is China. In the 1950s, Mao Zedong perceived China's revolution as being based on peasant production and small-scale, labor-intensive technology. For this reason, he encouraged population growth among the peasantry. After Mao's death, however, a new leadership group emerged that reversed his policies regarding population growth.

In 1979, a demographic study was presented at the Second Session of the Fifth National People's Congress that indicated that if the existing average of three children per couple was maintained, China's population would reach 1.4 billion by the year 2000 and 4.3 billion by the year 2080. Alarmed by the implications of these statistics, the government introduced a one-child policy designed to achieve zero population growth (ZPG), with a target of 1.6 children per couple by the year 2000. Families that restricted their family size to one child were given free health care and free plots of land. In addition, their children would receive free education and preferential employment treatment. Families that had more than one child would be penalized through higher taxes and nonpreferential treatment. The one-child policy was enforced by neighborhood committees at the local level, and contraceptives, sterilization, and abortion services were provided free of charge. Neighborhood committees monitored every woman's reproductive cycle to determine when she was eligible to have her one child.

With some exceptions, the one-child policy has been remarkably effective. Between 1980 and 1990, the birth rate in China was reduced, and the annual growth rate fell from 2.0 percent to 1.4 percent, a record unmatched by any developing nation. This rate is similar to those of the most advanced industrial societies (Fong 2004). Incentives, propaganda campaigns, and government enforcement combined to produce a new image of the Chinese family, one that had only a single child. Billboards and TV ads throughout China showed radiant mothers nurturing their one child.

Because the one-child policy is an attempt to reverse Chinese family patterns that have existed for thousands of years, it created controversies and problems. In the agricultural areas, it generated a great deal of resentment. Many Chinese prefer sons to daughters—a long-established Confucian tradition. In some cases, couples that have a daughter may practice female infanticide so that they may have a son to assume family responsibilities. Although infanticide is a criminal offense in China, it appears to be increasing in rural areas. Moreover, anthropologist Steven Mosher (1983) reported that government officials sometimes forced women to undergo abortions to maintain the one-child policy. More recently, anthropologist Susan Greenhalgh, a Chinese population policy expert, reported that one out of every eight Chinese women married in the 1970s had suffered the trauma of a second- or third-term abortion (2008). There were many reports of full-term abortions, involuntary sterilization, forcible insertion of IUDs, the abandonment of female children, and female infanticide.

In response to some of these conflicts, the Chinese government relaxed the one-child policy in 1989. Some rural parents could have two children; however, urban families were still restricted to one. This policy, known colloquially as "the one-son or two-child policy," placed a burden on second children who were females. Second-born daughters were subject to being placed in orphanages so that a family might have a son. China's orphanages were struggling to keep up with the number of female children. Additionally, the various ethnic minority groups have no restrictions on the number of children they can have. The minorities argued that through the one-child policy, the majority Han population would quickly become the dominant group in their regions. They viewed the policy as an attempt to reduce their population and pressured the government to relax restrictions on their population growth, which it did.

Demographer Vanessa Fong has investigated the unintended results of the one-child policy in China (2004). She found that many of the only children (sometimes called the "Little Emperors") are expected to be the primary providers for their elderly parents, grandparents, and parents-in-law. This results in considerable competition in the education system for these only children to aspire to elite status and gain economic opportunities to support their family networks, which sometimes results in stress because very few can obtain these elite positions. On the other hand, anthropologist Lihong Shi discovered that the rural people of northeast China have reduced their family size and recognized that the quality of parental investment in education for one child offers more opportunities than having more children (2013). In addition, she found that daughters also were beginning to get more parental support and investment compared to the past. Lihong Shi recorded a demographic shift from an emphasis on the quantity of children to a focus on quality of parental investment in children for their future opportunities.

In November 2013, the Chinese government announced that it would further relax the one-child policy by allowing families to have two children if one of the parents is an only child. But the government still offers higher rewards to those couples that have only one child.

Loss of Biodiversity

One of the major concerns regarding the consequences of globalization for the planet is the loss of biodiversity. **Biodiversity** is the genetic and biological variation within and among different species of plants and animals.

Biologists are not certain exactly how many species exist; new species are discovered every day. Biologists have described about 1.7 million species of animals, plants, and algae. They estimate that there may be over seven million species that have yet to be identified (Chapman 2009). About 50 percent of these species live in tropical rain forests. As humans, we are dependent on these living organisms for survival; in both preindustrial and industrial societies, people rely on plant and animal species for basic foodstuffs and medicinal applications.

Many plant and animal species are threatened with extinction, causing a loss of biodiversity. Biologists estimate that at least one species becomes extinct each day. And as globalization continues, it is estimated that perhaps as many as a dozen species will be lost per day. Back in 1996, biologist E. O. Wilson wrote in *In Search of Nature* (Wilson and Southworth 1996) that each year an area of rain forest half the size of Florida is cut down. If that continues, by 2020 the world will have lost 20 percent of its existing plant species forever. That is a loss of 30,000 species per year, 74 per day, 3 per hour. Wilson went on to write that we know almost nothing about the majority of plants and animals of the rain forests. We have not even named 90 percent of them, much less studied their properties or tapped their potential value. Wilson suggested that it is likely that a substantial portion of the planet's biodiversity will be eliminated within the next few decades. With the increase of industrialism, mechanized agriculture, and deforestation, as many as one-fourth of the world's higher plant families may become extinct by the end of this century.

Wilson believes that we are entering the greatest period of mass extinction in the planet's history. We have very limited knowledge of the world's plant and animal species. One out of every four prescription drugs comes from flowering plants. Yet, less than one percent has been studied for pharmacological potential. Many of these plants could be exploited as new food crops, pharmaceuticals, fibers, or petroleum substitutes (Joppa, Roberts, and Pimm 2010). Thousands of species of birds and fish are threatened by extinction; 1,217 birds, or 70 percent of all birds identified are in imminent danger of extinction, and 65 percent of freshwater fish in North America are either extinct or are endangered (Brown 2008:104–105). Groups such as the International Union for Conservation of Nature (IUCN), made up of over 11,000 volunteer scientists around the world, have organized to prevent the loss of biodiversity (www.iucn.org). As long as biodiversity can be preserved, it represents a wealth of information and potential resources that can be extremely beneficial for humanity. In addition, with the new developments in genetic engineering, which depends on biodiversity (genetic variation), humanity may be able to find new resources that provide solutions for food and health problems.

Ethnographic Research on the Green Revolution

An example of how ethnographic research can illuminate global problems involves studies of the Green Revolution in underdeveloped countries. Optimists such as Julian Simon (1981) and Matt Ridley (2010) cite the Green Revolution as one of the advancements made through technology and human creativity. In their view, the Green Revolution contradicts the basic assumptions made by the neo-Malthusians that population will outgrow the finite resources (food) of a particular area of land. Use of biotechnology and genetically modified (GM) hybrid species of high-yield wheat and rice and highly mechanized agricultural techniques has increased food production to a degree that could not have been anticipated by Malthusians of past ages.

However, many cultural anthropologists who have studied the adoption of mechanized agriculture in developing countries have found that these innovations have created unintended economic and social problems. In most cases, only wealthy farmers have the capital to invest in irrigation equipment, chemical fertilizers, and large tracts of land. To extend their landholdings, wealthy farmers buy out smaller farmers, creating a new class of landless peasants and a small group of wealthy farmers, which intensifies patterns of inequality and related economic and social problems (Schusky 1990).

Case Study: The Green Revolution in Shahidpur

One classic ethnographic study has shown that when the Green Revolution is carried out under the right conditions, it can be successful. Cultural anthropologist Murray Leaf (1984) studied the effects of the Green Revolution in the Punjab region of northern India. Leaf conducted research in a Sikh village called Shahidpur from 1964 to 1966 and then returned in 1978. The years 1965 and 1978 mark the onset and the complete adoption, respectively, of the Green Revolution in Shahidpur. Thus, Leaf was able to view the beginning and end of the process. During this period, the village switched from subsistence to mechanized agriculture.

The villagers adopted new strains of wheat, tractors, insecticides, and an irrigation technology on an experimental basis to determine whether this would increase their yields. Wealthy farmers adopted the technology readily, investing their capital in equipment and land. Poor peasants, however, also took the needed capital investment risks (with the support of government development agencies), and the risks paid off. Leaf's research demonstrated that in contrast to modernization theory, poor peasants are not constrained by traditional cultural patterns that might inhibit rational strategies of investment and savings. When these peasants saw they would directly benefit from these investments, they were willing to accept the economic risks.

More important, the villagers were willing to acquire the knowledge and technical skills needed to manage and ensure the continuity of their agricultural production.

Through a university extension center, new plant varieties and technologies were adopted on an experimental basis. The people could directly see the results of their agricultural experiments and respond appropriately to various conditions. The education was a low-cost investment, even with government-subsidized tuition for the poorest families. Furthermore, the university center provided training in the maintenance and repair of farm equipment and in other nonagricultural employment fields.

Leaf suggested that a key to the success of the Green Revolution in this region (in contrast to many other rural areas) is that government officials were more interested in development than in control. Government advice was always linked to the actual reactions among the villagers. Channels of communication were open between local and regional levels. Leaf's valuable ethnographic study offers some insights for those interested in furthering the Green Revolution in undeveloped peripheral societies.

GM Crops Ecological anthropologist Glen Stone follows the spread of genetically modified (GM) crops and related biotechnology in various areas of the world (2002, 2005). Stone studies GM crops, as well as other biotechnological strategies such as "tissue culture." He finds that many scientists, agricultural specialists, and economists either oppose or are proponents of these GM crops in different regions of India, Africa, and elsewhere. Stone follows the proposals of Monsanto, based in St. Louis, Missouri, which is the global leader in promoting biotechnology and GM products to replace current practices. It targets practices such as plowing, weeding, and seed-saving for traditional crop replacement in Africa and elsewhere. For example, Monsanto suggests that traditional indigenous African hoe cultivation should be replaced by "sustainable" biotechnology. In other words, Monsanto promotes this technology as a means of increasing crop growth and modernizing agriculture everywhere. Some of those skeptical about the use of GM for small-scale farmers have been accused of advocating a museum-like preservation of indigenous practices.

One of the problems identified by Stone in the adoption of these new GM biotechnology agricultural practices is what is referred to as "deskilling." In other words, the small farmers are replaced by machines and more high-tech agricultural developments. Farmers in the more industrialized and postindustrial countries may have access to education and information through government agencies and other institutions that may be lacking in some of the more rural peripheral countries of the world. Stone consults with many other anthropologists and investigates corporations such as Monsanto regarding the impact of these new biotechnologies and GM foods on agricultural developments in many regions in the world.

In a recent ethnographic study in rural Mexico in the state of Puebla, Elizabeth Fitting focuses on how farmers make decisions regarding GM maize or corn (2011). Corn was first domesticated in Mexico; thus, corn products such as tortillas continue to be important national symbols and metaphors for Mexican culture. Neoliberal policies linked with the NAFTA treaty among the United States, Canada, and Mexico since the 1990s have promoted transnational capital intensive agriculture, large-scale farms, and greater importation of GM fruits and vegetables, including corn from the United States and Canada into Mexico. Such neoliberal policies undermined small-scale corn agriculture in Mexico, and have caused increased inflation, rural unemployment, and migration from rural areas to urban areas like the maquiladoras near the U.S. border (see Chapter 21), or to the United States. Fitting found that the flood of GM corn imported from the United States and Canada into Mexico is perceived by many of the small-scale farmers as a threat to their livelihoods and to their traditional corn crops. Many of the farmers consider their local corn seeds better than the newer GM seeds introduced by Monsanto and other transnational corporations. Also, because of the contracts established between Monsanto and the farmers, they cannot save GM seeds and therefore have to pay for new seeds for every planting cycle. In addition, the farmers consider the local corn seeds as more suited to the soil conditions and climate in the region. These GM seeds are viewed as a threat to the environment and to the sustainability of corn agriculture in Mexico. The area of genetically modified crops and the "Green Revolution" has created controversies throughout the world, resulting in both positive and negative consequences (Stone 2010).

A Global Solution for Global Problems

In June 1992, in Rio de Janeiro, Brazil, representatives of 178 nations gathered at the Earth Summit. These representatives tried to set the stage for managing the planet Earth through global cooperation. The issues were the environment, climate change and global warming, population growth, deforestation, the loss of biodiversity, air and water pollution, and the threats of globalization throughout the world. Although the Earth Summit was successful because it received so much international attention and created worldwide awareness of global issues, the specifics of how soon problems were going to be solved, how much it would cost, and who was going to pay became extremely complicated.

A follow-up summit on climate change was held in Kyoto, Japan, in December 1997. The Kyoto Summit was organized by the Organization for Economic Co-operation and Development (OECD), which represents most industrialized countries of the world. The OECD is committed to helping its member countries move toward sustainable development for the planet's life-support system. The Kyoto Summit resulted in a protocol agreement endorsed by 110 countries to try to reduce greenhouse gases and stabilize atmospheric changes that would mitigate increasing global warming.

The Kyoto Protocol established targets and set the stage for international monitoring of greenhouse gas emissions from various countries. Part of the agreement encouraged the industrial countries to become partners with the developing countries to help curb greenhouse gas emissions throughout the world.

Not surprisingly, many leaders of developing countries blamed the industrialized countries for the problems. Heads of developing countries view themselves as victims of industrialized countries. For example, the Rio Declaration was going to contain a statement of principles on deforestation that would legally prohibit developing countries from burning their tropical rain forests. The developing countries objected to this statement because it was unfairly focused on the tropical rain forests and included nothing regarding the deforestation of the old-growth forests in the United States, Canada, and Europe. When a compromise could not be reached, the legally binding statement was scrapped for a weaker statement with no legal implications.

In addition, the industrialized countries, including the United States, were very reluctant to participate in some issues. For example, with respect to global warming, Japan and the European community had established limits on carbon dioxide emissions. In 2001, the United States dropped out of the Kyoto Summit agreement. The U.S. government claimed that the treaty was unacceptable because it would harm the U.S. economy. It contended that the cost of curbing greenhouse emissions from coal-burning power plants and automobiles was too great a burden on the U.S. economy and would result in the loss of jobs and profits. The U.S. administration argued that the Kyoto agreement made exceptions for countries such as China and India, which did not have to reduce their emissions, although these countries were emitting substantial amounts of greenhouse gases. In 2009, a new Climate Change Summit based in Copenhagen met to agree on a new treaty to replace the Kyoto Protocol agreement. Though a document called the Copenhagen Accord that recognized climate change as one of the greatest challenges facing the planet was drafted, the document was not legally binding and had no enforcement mechanisms to reduce emissions worldwide.

In November 2013, 189 countries were represented at another climate change summit in Warsaw, Poland. Again, no universal agreements regarding funding from the advanced industrial countries to support reductions in carbon dioxide emissions were established during the conference. China and 132 developing countries walked out of the summit to protest the lack of support from the industrialized country funding for controlling gas emissions in undeveloped countries. In the midst of the Warsaw summit, the Philippine government testified about the devastation and over 6,000 deaths from Typhoon Haiyan that resulted from warming temperatures of the ocean produced by climate change. Although the United States has reduced its CO_2 emissions by 11 percent since 2005, many other industrialized countries have not done as well.

Many of the developing countries at the climate change summits saw their number-one priority was economic survival, rather than saving the environment. Developing countries wanted to adopt industrialization as rapidly as possible to induce economic development. Although they agreed to some of the environmental mandates of industrialized countries, they did so only after requiring the industrialized countries to contribute large sums of money toward economic development. This continued to result in conflicts between the "have" and "have-not" countries.

Anthropological Research on Climate Change

Anthropologists Donald Nelson and Timothy Finan have been doing ethnographic research on climate change and its consequences for a rural population in the state of Ceará in Northeast Brazil (2009a, 2009b). This region of Brazil has been subject to droughts and climate variability for many years. Nelson and Finan studied how rural populations in Ceará were adapting to the dramatic environmental and severe economic changes resulting from climate variability and drought conditions, as well as to the social, political factors and inequalities in the region. Drought conditions have been a constant feature of this semiarid region for thousands of years. The anthropologists discovered that the government did provide some relief from drought conditions; however, for most of the time these rural farmers were in a condition they refer to as "persistent vulnerability." The farmers actually preferred the periods of drought because the government did provide some relief from poverty and suffering. During the droughts, inadequate rain results in poor agricultural prospects and scarcities of water for drinking. Until the mid-twentieth century, the droughts led to massive starvation, epidemic diseases, and very high rates of mortality. The periods of drought became embedded within the cultural memories of these farmers of Ceará.

The political dynamics in Ceará had developed as a long-term result of Portuguese colonialism and the pattern of inequality of land patterns from the *fazendas* (plantations) that were developed throughout different areas of Brazil. This pattern produced a system of patron-client relationships that were discussed in relation with Latin

America in Chapter 21. This patronage system has existed for hundreds of years and has inhibited the manner in which local and national governments plan for drought conditions and provide assistance during periods of climate change for these farmers. Approximately 2.5 million people are dependent on agriculture in the Ceará region, but only 15 percent of the agricultural land is irrigated, so climate change has a dramatic influence on the livelihood of the people. Unemployment, out-migration, and a lack of adequate education and health care are constant features of these people's lives. At the same time, population tends to increase in this area. Climate change produced by El Niño in 1997–1998 had severe consequences for the farmers of Ceará. Current patterns in climate change, the variability of rainfall, and higher temperatures indicate that there will be more droughts in the future for the region. Due to population increases, each drought period brings about the need for more resources and relief from local and national government sources. Nelson and Finan suggest that as future climate changes occur, the patronage system will have to give way to a more decentralized and democratic structure in which farmers will have much more decisive authority in making decisions about their circumstances and adaptations. This will hopefully lead to expanded educational and nonagricultural opportunities and better health care (2009a, 2009b).

In another ethnographic study, David McDermott Hughes investigates how the Caribbean island nations of Trinidad and Tobago have responded to climate change (2013). These low-lying island nations are very vulnerable to climate change, which has resulted in recent hurricanes, droughts, and fires. Rising sea levels are a concern for these people. Yet, Trinidad and Tobago have offshore oil rigs and are ranked thirty-eighth in the world in oil production. Trinidad and Tobago have tripled their CO_2 emissions since the 1990s, and are the fourth worst offenders in the world. Hughes conducted extensive interviews among the professional classes of Trinidad, who debated with him about climate change issues (2013). He found that educated professionals recognized the vulnerability of Trinidad and the impact of climate change, but they usually denied the industrial impact of their own oil industry and the emissions of CO_2. They tended to blame China and other larger industrial nations for CO_2 emissions and did not want to support policies to reduce their own island nation's emissions. These Trinidad professionals idealized their island nation as an "innocent victim" of climate change and defended their own oil industry pollution and emissions as a major source of economic development. Although Hughes found that some environmental activists were calling for a postcarbon society, many government officials and energy sector CEOs continued to deny the link between CO_2 emissions and climate change problems for Trinidad (2013). This sense of "victimhood" regarding responsibility for carbon emissions is indicative of many developing countries when they compare themselves to the wealthier industrial nations of the world.

In an essay entitled "Anthropology and Global Warming," Simon Batterbury indicates that many anthropologists are becoming more engaged in local research on rainfall patterns and other related phenomena regarding climate change (2008). He notes that anthropologists have organized international sessions on using indigenous knowledge from different areas of the world to account for patterns of climate change. Anthropologists such as A. Peter Castro (introduced in Chapter 1 as an applied anthropologist), David Brokensha, Dan Taylor, and Carla Roncoli have conducted ethnographic research on climate change in 15 different areas of the world (2012). Climate change is acknowledged as a major threat to the economic, political, and cultural life of people throughout the world. Anthropological research is necessary to help develop solutions for peoples in vulnerable communities who are impacted by climate variation. Anthropologists study the indigenous knowledge that local people maintain within their culture; this information often assists local and national governments in providing solutions for problems resulting from global climatic change.

In a recent article "A Changing Climate for Anthropological and Archaeological Research? Improving the Climate-Change Models," Paul Roscoe suggests that anthropologists can go beyond assisting local and national governments regarding climate change (2014). He indicates that archaeological and anthropological research can assist the modelling and predictions made by the Intergovernmental Panel on Climate Change (IPCC) in providing details on past and current sociocultural evolution and development. The IPCC produces the international reports on climate change. Normally, the IPCC relies on "explorative" scenarios that combine economic, statistical, and quantitative models along with qualitative narratives in order to forecast the future of greenhouse gas emissions (GGEs) and global temperatures. The archaeological and anthropological data has demonstrated that since the end of the Pleistocene about 10,000 years ago, thousands of small egalitarian foraging societies have since consolidated into about 200 politically centralized nations (Roscoe 2014:4). Although there have been collapses of agricultural civilizations in the past, overall sociocultural evolution has exhibited global technological, economic and political convergence with higher GGEs. In addition, cross-cultural research by anthropologists have demonstrated that patterns of status competition and the conspicuous consumption that has emerged in the highly industrialized and postindustrial societies are responsible for higher rates of GGEs. As Roscoe emphasizes absent a global catastrophe such as an asteroid strike, a thermonuclear war, or abrupt climatic change, these patterns of consumerism with higher rates of GGEs are likely to become widely influential throughout the world.

In order to reduce some of the uncertainties regarding climate change, Roscoe suggests that the integrative, cross-cultural, and transtemporal approaches of anthropological studies need to be incorporated into future IPCC reports. Anthropologists and archaeologists can specify long-term urbanization, population, technological, economic, and evolutionary trends that contribute to higher rates of GGEs. In addition, anthropologists may be able to mitigate some of these trends by promoting alternative models of global sustainability.

The Sustainability Model

Obviously, the problems resulting from globalization are extremely complex and are not going to be resolved without some sort of global unity. Anthropological research in countries throughout the world has resulted in a perspective sometimes known as the sustainability model. The **sustainability model** suggests that societies the world over need environments and technologies that provide sustenance not only for the present generation, but also for future generations. This model encourages resource management that does not degrade the environment for future generations. The sustainability model is opposed to the logic-of-growth model, which assumes that economic and technological growth will inevitably bring progress. The sustainability model is more realistic in assessing environmental and technological change and recommends policy changes to inhibit problems that are induced by globalization. Some countries are beginning to adopt this sustainability model of development by limiting their emissions, curbing population growth, and cleaning up pollution.

It must be recognized that the expansion of global multinational capitalism is not the only source of environmental problems in the world. The former U.S.S.R. had far worse environmental pollution than the advanced capitalist industrialized societies of Europe, the United States, and elsewhere. However, anthropologists fully understand that these global problems cannot be solved by country-by-country solutions. The challenge for this generation is to provide a global, internationally based organizational context and sound scientific research for the resolution of these problems. Neglecting these global problems is bound to result in massive difficulties for the future of humanity. Anthropological research can help in assessing these problems and thereby promoting the model of sustainability.

Economic Trends

24.5 Discuss globalization and economic trends.

As indicated in earlier chapters of this textbook, the contemporary global economy began with European expansion in the mercantile and colonial periods. Since World War II, participants in this world economic system have been classified (sometimes too simplistically) as core, semiperipheral, and peripheral countries, with the United States the leading core country. Trading and financial institutions in the capitalist countries controlled the international organizations such as the World Bank and the International Monetary Fund. The industrial-socialist countries of Eastern Europe and the former Soviet Union tried not to participate directly in the capitalist world economic system and also tried to create their own client states in areas such as Cuba, Angola, and Afghanistan. By the 1980s, however, new economic developments were radically restructuring the world economic system.

Multinational Corporations

One of the major factors behind the emergence of the global economic network is the multinational corporation. In Chapter 16, we discussed multinational corporations as they evolved in both the capitalist and socialist worlds. In many ways, multinational corporations opened the door for globalization by promoting the spread of technical and cultural knowledge to non-Western societies. In the modern era, these corporations expanded to the point that some anthropologists consider them a new societal institution beyond the state. For example, anthropologist Alvin Wolfe (1977, 1986, 2006) discussed how multinational corporations have integrated the manufacturing processes at a *supranational* level. They reorganized the electronics, garment manufacturing, and automobile industries. Today, products might be manufactured in several different countries, with the financing and organization of labor and also the outsourcing carried out by the multinational corporation. Wolfe suggested that this process will continue.

Jobs and Growth: A Positive Assessment   Given their power and influence, multinational corporations are highly controversial. With their tremendous capital assets, they can radically alter a society. The neoliberal global policies of the 1990s assumed that multinational corporations could enhance global economic development, thereby reducing poverty and hunger. The World Bank and International Monetary Fund sought to expand these multinational corporations into Latin America, Africa, the Middle East, and Asia, in order to bring capital and technology and to provide employment. From this vantage point, they create jobs and spur both short- and long-term economic growth.

Neocolonialism: A Negative Assessment   Dependency theorists, as discussed in Chapter 20 on globalization, suggest that multinational corporations actually intensified the problems of developing countries. They contend that such corporations create benefits for a wealthy elite and a small, upwardly mobile middle class, while the vast majority of the population remains in desperate poverty. Because the multinational corporations tend to invest in capital-intensive commodities, the majority of the population does not participate in the modernization of the economy. Furthermore, the entire society becomes dependent on corporations that are based outside the region, which inhibits the development of self-sufficiency and a more diversified economy.

According to this view, multinational corporations are simply the forerunners of a new form of neocolonialism, aimed at supplying the industrial world with natural resources and cheap labor. Multinational corporations based in core societies encourage peripheral societies to incur loans to produce a limited number of export-oriented commodities, a process that creates a cycle of economic indebtedness and increased dependency. In contrast to the older forms of colonialism, the core countries do not incur the expenses of maintaining direct political control over these societies; rather, they keep the peripheral nations in a state of dependency and maintain indirect political control by making contributions and paying bribes to politicians. In certain cases, however, when core countries feel threatened by political developments in peripheral nations, they resort to direct military intervention.

In a recent essay, anthropologist Ismael Vaccaro describes how the development of "hypermodernity and global capitalism" devastated many landscapes and communities throughout the world (2010). Vaccaro discusses how the managerial elites focus on reducing costs of labor and avoiding environmental regulations in order to increase profits; this involves multinational corporations moving rapidly from one country to another and creating negative consequences for the environment and various communities. He refers to the collapse of mining complexes, deforestation, depleted fishing stocks, and crumbling industrial sites in the core and peripheral countries as consequences of these new developments in the postmodern global economy. According to Vaccaro, these multinational corporate strategies disrupt the moral economies within the peripheral areas and ultimately result in dislocation, deindustrialization, and decay within the core countries.

Case Study: The Potlatch Corporation An example of what Vaccaro (2010) discusses in respect to the process of global economic expansion, hypermodernity and its consequences for peripheral countries can be seen in the case of the Potlatch Corporation, based in Western Samoa, studied by anthropologist Paul Shankman (1975, 1978, 1999). The corporation that Shankman studied was a large wood product firm called the Potlatch Corporation, based in the northwest coast region of the United States and named after the famed redistributional exchanges of Native Americans in that region (see Chapter 16). The

Potlatch Corporation surveyed the tropical hardwood trees in a portion of Western Samoa and found a dozen species that could be used for furniture and veneers. To facilitate the leasing of large amounts of land in Western Samoa (bypassing traditional landholding arrangements), the Potlatch Corporation requested that the Samoan government set up an agency to act as a broker on behalf of the corporation. Potlatch eventually won a number of concessions from the Samoan parliament.

Although Potlatch claimed to be committed to the economic development of Western Samoa, Shankman found that the monetary rewards from leasing the land did not prove to be as great as the people had expected. For example, Potlatch leased 28,000 acres of land for $1.40 an acre. In one project, in which it leased land from a group of seven villages, the average yearly income from leasing amounted to less than $11 per person. Royalties paid on cut timber were also low, amounting to 4 cents per cubic foot, part of which was to go back to the government for reforestation.

The Potlatch Corporation did provide jobs for 300 people in Western Samoa, making it one of the island's largest employers. Shankman discovered, however, that most of these people were formerly employed in agriculture, civil service, and light industry. Through the Potlatch projects, labor was simply shifted from other sectors of the economy to forestry. Thus, Potlatch did not really create jobs; rather, it simply shifted them to new sectors.

Shankman believed that Potlatch's leasing policies would ultimately create a scarcity of land, forcing more peasants to produce on marginal land. Moreover, Shankman suggested that the inflated cost of living generated by the company through higher wages, in addition to the negative consequences such as erosion of the rain forest caused by rapid lumbering, would result in long-term negative costs to the people of Samoa.

Shankman also noted that the risks assumed by the people of Western Samoa were much greater than those assumed by the multinational corporation. If Potlatch was successful, it could recoup its initial investments very quickly. If it lost revenue, it could simply leave the area. In contrast, the peasants did not have any capital to fall back on if they lost their land. Moreover, they had to live permanently with the economic, social, and ecological changes brought about by Potlatch's policies. Eventually, the Potlatch Corporation pulled out of the region. As Shankman (1990, 2000) concluded, this rapid pullout of Potlatch demonstrated a limited commitment to the people of Samoa.

Other anthropologists are conducting research similar to Shankman's. The consensus at this point appears to confirm his charges that the expansion of multinational corporations has created new forms of economic dependency and neocolonialism. Thus, in the short run, the global changes wrought by multinational corporations appear to have had negative consequences for developing societies. Whether this will be true over the long run remains to be seen.

In the case of the *maquiladoras* (multinational corporations that moved into the border regions of Mexico, as described in Chapter 21), many of these companies have folded up production there as labor and environmental costs have risen and have relocated in China and India. Mexico has lost some 500,000 manufacturing jobs to other lower-wage countries in just a few years. As China and India, through telecommunication and developing global media and technology, can produce at lower wages, many multinationals have moved and outsourced their manufacturing to those regions (Friedman 2006). Thus, multinational corporations continue to look for means of reducing labor costs and enhancing profits, which, at least in the short term, sometimes produces negative consequences for some of the developing countries of the world.

Emerging Global Economic Trends

Driven by new technological and scientific developments in areas such as biotechnology, telecommunications, microprocessor information systems, and other high-tech industrialization, the world economy continues to undergo rapid changes. The globalization of the world economy has produced a vast array of products and services in interlocking markets. World trade has accelerated over the last few decades, stimulating greater economic interdependency. These trends have resulted in a restructuring of the world economic system.

Changes in Socialist Countries The globalization of the economy has had traumatic consequences for the industrial, socialist-based economies of the countries of the former Soviet Union and Eastern Europe and for other peripheral socialist economies such as China and Vietnam. These state-administered economies did not produce the extensive economic development that they had promised. Government officials in these countries promoted five-year plans for economic development, but the plans did not lead to the production of prized consumer goods or a higher standard of living.

The late anthropologist Marvin Harris (1992) focused on the infrastructural problems in explaining the downfall of the socialist regimes of the Soviet Union and Eastern Europe. Harris suggested that the infrastructure, which encompasses the technological, economic, demographic, and environmental activities directed at sustaining health and well-being, always has a primary, determinant role in the functioning of a sociocultural system. The serious deficiencies and weaknesses in the infrastructure of the Soviet Union and the countries of Eastern Europe undermined the entire fabric of society. For example, the basic energy supply, based on coal and oil production, became stagnant,

and the generating plants for electricity were antiquated, leading to periodic blackouts and frequent breakdowns.

Harris described how the agricultural and marketing system for the production and distribution of food resulted in severe shortages, delays in delivery, hoarding, and rationing. In addition, increasing problems with, and costs incurred by, industrial pollution led to the deterioration of the socialist economies. According to Harris, the infrastructural deficiencies of these socialist systems had fundamental consequences for the basic health, safety, and ultimate survival of the people in these societies. These deficiencies eventually led to the societies' systemic breakdown.

The industrial-socialist societies faced major economic crises. Repeated failures in agriculture and industry led to frustration and unrest among the populace. Global communications with other societies, particularly those with much greater access to consumer goods, caused many people in socialist states to become frustrated with the inadequacy of their systems. People began to question the aims and policies of their leaders.

The Former Soviet Union: *Perestroika* **and** *Glasnost* In the former Soviet Union, Communist Party leader Mikhail Gorbachev responded to the people's criticisms and the economic crisis facing the country by instituting a series of reforms and economic restructuring known as *perestroika*. In effect, this policy involved the reintegration of the Soviet Union into the world-capitalist system. New joint ventures with capitalist firms were undertaken; McDonald's and other multinational corporations from the West and Japan were invited to participate in the Soviet economy. Soviet industrial corporations were reorganized to emphasize competition and the maximization of private profits for individual firms. Wages and salaries in Soviet industries were no longer controlled by the government; rather, they reflected market conditions and individual productivity.

To carry out *perestroika*, Gorbachev had to confront the bureaucratic elite that dominated the Soviet political economy (see Chapter 16). Because the reforms directly threatened the bureaucratic control of the political economy, he faced much resistance from government officials. Some of these bureaucrats were ideologically committed to the Marxist–Leninist model of communism and did not want the Soviet Union integrated into the world-capitalist economy. Others believed that tinkering with the economy with these reforms would induce more hardship for the Soviet people. For example, after the introduction of *perestroika* and the removal of government-controlled price restraints, the costs of food and other basic commodities skyrocketed.

As a means of implementing his economic reforms, Gorbachev also called for *glasnost*, usually translated as "openness," which involved the freedom to criticize government policies and officials. Newspapers and other media were allowed to express views that were in opposition to Communist Party dictates. *Glasnost* also permitted greater political freedom of expression, as well as democratic elections and a multiparty political system. The policy of *glasnost* led to mass demonstrations against the Soviet government and eventually to criticism and the downfall of Gorbachev himself.

As a result of the severe economic difficulties and subsequent political crises in the Soviet Union, many of the non-Russian republics began to declare sovereignty and independence. Regions such as Estonia, Lithuania, the Ukraine, Kazakhstan, Uzbekistan, Turkmenistan, and Azerbaijan cut their political ties with the Soviet Union. Although Gorbachev attempted to curtail these developments, sometimes with a show of military force, the Soviet empire began to collapse. Eventually, all of the non-Russian regions formed their own independent republics. The independent republics not only cut political ties, leaving the Russian republic by itself, but also began to restrict the export of their domestic commodities into Russia. This exacerbated the difficult economic conditions within the Russian state itself.

The successor to Mikhail Gorbachev, Boris Yeltsin, attempted to further the *perestroika* and *glasnost* policies of his predecessor. Yeltsin's primary goal was to transform the remains of the state-managed centralized economy of Russia into an economy in which managerial and consumer decisions are based upon market forces and the economy is in private hands. The Yeltsin government tried to radically restructure the political economy by ending price and wage controls, reducing or eliminating subsidies to factories and farms, slashing military expenditures, introducing new taxes, and balancing the national budget.

The United States and European economic leaders supported these policies, which became known as "shock therapy." This economic shock therapy had some positive consequences, but most economists agree that the peculiarities of the Soviet system were bound to prolong the process of economic reform. In the meantime, many Russians, who were accustomed to subsidies and government benefits, had to endure substantial hardships. A number of Russian bureaucrats began to use their positions to acquire economic assets through illegal maneuvers. Ponzi schemes, which used fake banks and financial institutions to gain large sums of capital from government organizations and the general population, were prevalent during this "shock therapy" period. This resulted in the rise of a capitalist oligarchy or elite in the major industrial and media sectors of the economy (Titma and Tuma 2001; Chua 2003). In addition, a lack of knowledge of how capitalism, free labor, and the market economy operate has resulted in major economic declines in agriculture and industry.

Mikhail Gorbachev

In 2000, Vladimir Putin, Yeltsin's prime minister, was elected president of Russia, promising to continue the economic reforms and democratization of Russian society. In 2008, Dmitry Medvedev was elected president while Putin remained as prime minister. In 2012 Medvedev and Putin changed positions with one another. Unfortunately, currently the Russian government under Putin has become more authoritarian, stifling some of the democratic tendencies. The question now is whether the people of Russia can be patient enough to endure these political and economic difficulties and enable the economy to grow at a pace that will enhance the overall socioeconomic conditions for the majority of people, which might become the basis for more democratic developments. Anthropologists who are actively engaged in ethnographic research in Russia advocate more qualitative research, in addition to the quantitative statistical research that is often the primary method used by economists, as they advise and consult with the Russian government and companies to enhance development.

Eastern Europe Stimulated by the policies of *perestroika* and *glasnost*, the Eastern European nations of East Germany, Poland, Czechoslovakia, Hungary, Romania, Bulgaria, and Yugoslavia began reforms of their socialist political economies. These countries had been restricted to trading primarily with the former Soviet Union and with one another. In the German Democratic Republic (East Germany), mass demonstrations and migrations of people to West Germany led to the fall of the communist government and the destruction of the Berlin Wall. Solidarity, a popular outlawed labor union led by Lech Walesa, toppled the government of Poland. Polish workers demanded economic reforms and a better standard of living than that offered by the socialist model. Democratic elections led to Walesa becoming prime minister. Walesa subsequently visited the United States and other Western countries in search of foreign investment. Many of the Eastern European socialist-bloc societies actively sought reintegration into the world-capitalist economy as a means of stimulating both economic growth and democratic freedom.

In a pioneering book entitled *What Was Socialism, and What Comes Next* (1996), anthropologist Katherine Verdery, who did most of her ethnographic work in the Eastern European country of Romania, summarized some of the problems and dilemmas facing this region. She wrote about how a different sense of time prevailed during the socialist period in Eastern Europe and how the new forms of capitalism and their industrial work rhythms, based upon progress and linear models, were disrupting these societies. Verdery noted that patterns of gender inequality based upon older patriarchal forms were reemerging in these postsocialist Eastern European countries. During the socialist period, gender relations were supposed to have been equalized. However, Verdery described how the socialist government in Romania reconfigured gender roles, making women dependent on a patrilineal-paternalistic state. After the downfall of socialism, Romania, Poland, Hungary, and other postsocialist countries have been emphasizing a return to "traditional values" regarding gender, which positions the woman once again in the home and doing household chores. To some extent, this gender organization of postsocialist society defines housework as "nonwork." As these Eastern European economies become more capitalistic, women will probably be drawn into the work force, but in the meantime, these women are returning to the older, patriarchal forms of family life.

In the final chapter of her book, Verdery commented on how the transformation of Eastern European and Russian societies may take a much different path toward capitalism than that of Western European and U.S. societies. The privatization of property there is likely to involve very different processes than in Western societies. Former socialist leaders will undoubtedly use the legal and political process to develop economic opportunities for themselves as they transfer the state enterprises into private hands. Verdery suggested that black markets, organized crime, and the manipulation of the legal and state apparatus by former socialist bureaucrats have had consequences for these postsocialist societies.

Following this pioneering study, a number of East European anthropologists have been doing ethnographic research in their own societies (Kürti and Skalník 2009). Their ethnographic studies provide details regarding the evolution of these postsocialist societies and their ongoing economic and political processes. Michał Buchowski has been doing research on the transition of postsocialist rural Poland (2009). He describes how many Western economists believe that the privatization of property is the central key in restoring East European postsocialist economies back to the road to capitalism. Poland, unlike most of the Eastern European or former USSR socialist societies did not experience the collectivization of land. For years the ideals of individual farming on privately owned land represented the symbolic resistance of Polish farmers to the USSR model of collectivization. From 1944-48 under Soviet supervision, 13,000 large landed estates were confiscated and redistributed to the peasants. Later, there were central government attempts at collectivization, but by 1989, 76 percent of arable land was retained as private land by farmers. Thus, less than one-quarter of the land was actually collectivized by state authorities. Since the 1990s neoliberal capitalist policies in Poland have resulted in larger land holdings by entrepreneurial farmers. Buchowski's research in the small community of Dziekanowice demonstrated that local ideals of land ownership coincided with the new neoliberal capitalist ideas of the "naturalness" of private property. Yet, many rural farmers who have lost their land or were former state workers have become unemployed. Buchowski concludes that this process of neoliberalism has resulted in increasing inequalities that define group and individual identities in rural Poland.

China Since Mao Zedong's death, China, under leaders such as Deng Xiaoping, has introduced many tenets of state capitalism. **State capitalism** is an economic system that directs and manages for-profit economic and commercial activity through a centralized bureaucratic government. Instead of relying on Communist Party cadre who wanted to instill egalitarian ideals, the new leadership sought to develop leaders with technical, agricultural, and scientific expertise. They encouraged students to obtain an education in the United States and other Western nations. They abolished the commune system and reorganized agricultural and industrial production based upon individual profits and wages for farmers and workers. The Chinese government called for modernization in agriculture, industry, science, and defense. In order to spur economic growth, they created four special economic zones (SEZs) in southern China near Hong Kong, Taiwan, and Southeast Asia (Zhu 2009). The SEZs were very successful in expanding economic growth, and the Chinese government expanded these trade zones to other areas. The People's Republic of China (PRC) had seen rapid growth of approximately 10 percent GDP (Gross Domestic Product) per year for over 30 years (Zhu 2009). The PRC is the second largest economy in the world, overcoming the economy of Japan and just behind that of the United States. However, uneven development and economic stratification between a new rich elite based in the urban areas and a rural population that makes up 60 percent of the Chinese population are major challenges for the PRC (Zhu 2009).

Although promoting economic change, the Chinese government has not endorsed much political reform. This has been referred to as the "Beijing Consensus," a model of state capitalist economic development under tight political control of the Communist Party (Zhu 2009). Party bureaucrats remain entrenched in power and resist all pressure to relinquish their authority. The absence of political freedom resulted in mass demonstrations by students and others in Tiananmen Square in Beijing in 1989. The Chinese government crushed this freedom movement with military force and has continued to repress any form of political dissent that threatens its authority. Beginning in 2010, the Chinese economic growth began to slow because of internal credit problems and less demand for exports. Since 2010, the Chinese government has been trying to transform the economy from an export-oriented form of state capitalism to a more consumer-driven economy. Whether these economic developments and further reintegration into the world economic system can work in China without corresponding political freedom is a question that remains to be answered.

Vietnam Confronted with leading one of the poorest countries in the world, the Vietnamese government in 1981 introduced a series of economic reforms called *doi moi* ("renovation") (Pike 1990). Some of the younger politicians in Vietnam are calling for greater participation in the world economic system, the introduction of private enterprise, and individual material benefits in the form of wages and salaries. The Vietnamese reformers face the same problems as those in China and Russia. With their memories of their colonial experience and wars against the capitalist nations, conservative bureaucrats who are committed to Marxist–Leninist ideology oppose reintegration into the world economic system. Reformers, in contrast, actively seek support from capitalist countries and the international community to pursue their economic liberalization policies and democratization. Recently, it appears that reformers have stronger influence regarding state policies. For example, they were instrumental in the negotiations that resulted in the United States lifting its trade embargo against Vietnam in January 1994. This shift in U.S. policy has led to increasing trade and capitalist economic activity in Vietnam. Since then, some progress in industrialization and agricultural development has been significant; however, many of the conservative bureaucrats have resisted these reforms, which may threaten their bureaucratic power and authority (Scupin 2006b).

Changes in the Core Societies: The United States and Japan
The globalization of the world economy has also had dramatic effects on the core industrial societies, such

as the United States and Japan. The United States currently exports about one-fifth of its industrial production. This is double what it was exporting in the 1950s, and that proportion is rapidly increasing. About 70 percent of those exported goods compete directly with goods produced by other nations. Some U.S. states depend heavily on the international economy. For example, approximately one-half of the workers in Ohio work directly on exports such as tires and automobiles. Honda, the major automobile company in Japan, has a large plant in Marion, Ohio. Most American corporations now conduct business on a global level. Although the United States remains the world's largest economy, with a gross national product twice the size of that of its nearest competitor, it no longer dominates as it did in the past. In fact, at the beginning of the twenty-first century, the United States had one of the largest trade deficits and the largest foreign debt of any nation.

In contrast, Japan has maintained a trade surplus. During the past several decades, the United States and Japan have engaged in global economic competition. This competition needs to be considered in the context of the world economic system. Anthropologists have long recognized that capitalism takes different forms in various areas of the world (Geertz 1963b; Ong 2006). The development of Japanese capitalism is very different from the growth of capitalism of the United States.

In the 1920s, in the early phases of Japanese industrialization, Japan's population began to expand. Lacking adequate natural resources such as fertile land, raw materials, and energy supplies, Japan became increasingly dependent on imported food and other raw materials. To secure a food supply to support its growing population, the Japanese began to act as an imperial power in Asia, colonizing Korea and Taiwan and expanding into China. Japanese imperialism in Asia was one of the direct causes of World War II.

During its occupation of Japan following World War II, the United States encouraged the development of corporate capitalism. The U.S. government viewed Japan as a capitalist center that could be used to forestall the spread of communism in Asia. Some of Japan's *zaibatsu*, wealthy family conglomerates, were broken up into smaller concerns. Others, such as the Mitsui and Mitsubishi families, were encouraged to invest in new equipment and technologies to induce rapid capitalist growth (Zhu 2009). Large sums of U.S. capital were funneled into the Japanese government and corporations such as Sony to stimulate corporate capitalism. These policies led to the "economic miracle" in Japan that occurred in the 1960s. By the end of that decade, Japan had become one of the world's leading exporters.

The Japanese government, however, realized that it was still dependent on energy and food from other regions of the world. The government constantly reminded its population that Japan must "develop exports or die." The government organized the Ministry of International Trade and Industry (M.I.T.I.) to mobilize industrial firms to export products such as automobiles and electronics; this would ensure a balance of funds to pay for the large quantities of food and energy that Japan imports. The M.I.T.I. helped finance Japan's huge exporting corporations so that it could maintain a favorable balance of trade. By the late 1980s, Japan had a large trade surplus. However, it imported approximately eight tons of fuel, food, wood, and other raw materials for every ton of goods it exported. Beginning in the late 1990s, the Asian fiscal and monetary crisis had major devastating consequences for the Japanese economy, which are only recently being corrected. Japan lost nearly half of its wealth and assets during the period from 1997 to 2001. Undertaking major reforms in its corporate-style economy and in its banking and financial practices, as well as reducing bureaucratic corruption, has helped Japan recover to some degree (McCreery and McCreery 2006).

Japan and the United States, as well as other core capitalist countries, are postindustrial societies, with a large component of their economy devoted to the service sector (see Chapter 16). At the same time, many of the basic manufacturing plants of these industrial economies are relocating into developing countries to exploit the cheaper labor supply. Thus, both Japan and the United States have been going through a deindustrializing process. Japanese multinational corporations have relocated auto factories and other industries to developing Asian countries such as Indonesia and Thailand. Ford Motor Company has relocated an engine manufacturing plant in Mexico. As the core countries have become increasingly internationalized, economic interdependency accelerates. Some theorists believe that this interdependency may become a key component in resolving conflict among nations in the global village as the globalization of trade and the media continues (Wright 2000; Friedman 2006).

The Semiperipheral NICs Another result of the globalization of the economy is the rise of the newly industrializing countries (NICs) from a peripheral to a semiperipheral status in the world economic system. Included here are the nations of South Korea, Hong Kong, Singapore, and Taiwan. Popularly known as the "Little Dragons of Asia," they compete with the economic might of Japan. Both Taiwan and Korea were colonies of Japan, whereas Hong Kong and Singapore were colonies of Great Britain. As with other colonized nations, they became peripheral dependencies. These countries, however, are rapidly industrializing and have broken their bonds of dependency. In some industries, such as electronics, these nations have manufactured products that compete with those of core countries like Japan.

The success of the NICs reflects the changing division of labor in the world economic system. As the multinationals relocated some of their labor-intensive industries to low-wage regions, the NICs were able to absorb some of these jobs. Like Japan, their success is partially due to U.S. economic support. In particular, during the 1950s and 1960s, the United States viewed South Korea and Taiwan as part of the capitalist bloc in Asia. The United States invested large sums of capital and foreign aid in these countries, thereby enabling them to develop as capitalist centers. South Korea was heavily subsidized by United States capital in both industry and agriculture to enhance its rapid growth in the 1960s and 1970s (Sorensen 2006; Zhu 2009). In addition, as in Japan, the governments in these countries directed the modernization of the economy through massive investment into export industries. The NICs have changed the context of the world economy through low-cost production methods and aggressive marketing. They have created a unique niche in the world economic system by exporting products that compete directly with those produced by the core countries. In many cases, they have expanded their overseas markets through joint ventures with multinational firms based in core countries. In other cases, they have created their own multinational corporations. For example, NIC multinational corporations have become global competitors as producers of semiconductors for electronic and computer equipment. The world's largest plastics firm is Formosa Plastics, based in Taiwan. The best-selling imported car in Canada is made by Hyundai in South Korea. However, as in Japan, these countries went through major economic declines following the Asian fiscal crisis of the late 1990s and are only recently recovering from those trends.

Global Economic Development and World Poverty One overall result of the global developments in the world economy is that despite economic inequalities that have continued to increase within and among countries, rates of global poverty are in decline. In 1990, 43 percent of the population in developing countries was subsisting on one dollar a day. The absolute number of people in

The Korean-made Hyundai has become a popular automobile throughout the world.

poverty was near 2 billion. By 2010, the percent of people living on one dollar a day was 21 percent or 1.2 billion people. Thus, the global poverty rate has been cut in half in just 20 years. A global think tank, the Brookings Institution, has stated in a recent report that by 2030, extreme poverty can be eliminated (Chandy, Ledlie, and Penciakova 2013). Developing countries have increased their GDP about 6 percent per year, 8 percent in East Asia, 7 percent in South Asia, and 5 percent in Africa. For every 1 percent increase in GDP, per capita poverty is reduced by approximately 1.7 percent. China and India, with their large populations but fairly rapid economic growth, have lifted many millions of people out of poverty. By 2030 many of the other developing countries should become semiperipheral rather than peripheral. However, in the politically unstable and fragile sub-Saharan African countries such as Democratic Republic of the Congo or Somalia, poverty rates will continue to be problematic.

Despite the positive report on the decline of global poverty, the *Global Risks 2014 Report* published by the World Economic Forum states that the increasing wealth gap between the rich and the poor, structural unemployment and underemployment, and environmental problems created by climate change will continue to create social and political instability (2014). Anthropologists continue to examine conditions at the local level to determine what consequences globalization has had for economic developments in different regions. Through this ethnographic research, anthropologists can better evaluate what kinds of policies work more effectively in enhancing the living standards of everyone.

Political, Ethnic, and Religious Trends

24.6 Discuss the political, ethnic, and religious trends resulting from globalization.

As the world economy becomes more integrated, major political changes are taking place in the global network. During the 1950s, some modernization theorists (Chapter 20) predicted that the various nations would become very similar as they were brought closer together in the global economy. People everywhere would share the same goods and services and, eventually, the same cultural values. This similarity would set the stage for a unified world government. Current trends indicate that such a movement may be taking place; for example, in 1999, 15 European countries agreed to accept the Euro as the form of currency in order to facilitate trade and to help develop a unified European economy. More countries have been added to the European Union (EU) since that time. The EU covers some 1.2 million square miles and contains 375 million people speaking 11 different languages.

It is currently the largest market in the world, and its gross domestic product (GDP) rivals that of the United States.

In addition, a unified European Parliament has been established, and Europeans no longer need passports to travel among the various countries. Some Europeans are beginning to think of themselves as "Europeans," rather than Italians, Greeks, Germans, Irish, or British. Is the nation-state giving way to larger political organizations and processes in future political evolution? Yet other political tendencies seem to indicate movement in the opposite direction, as many of the European nations such as the United Kingdom have not accepted the Euro. National identity and nationalism in Europe are still incredibly vibrant. And, in many areas, the nation-state appears to be fragmenting along linguistic, ethnic, and religious lines.

In considering these global political trends, many anthropologists find that the nation-state is too small to handle the immense problems in the world political economy: capital flows, economic development, management of technology, environmental and demographic trends, production of commodities, and labor problems. Organizations such as the United Nations, the International Monetary Fund, the World Bank, the World Trade Organization (WTO), the North American Free Trade Agreement (NAFTA), the European Union (EU), and the multinational corporations appear to be in the process of displacing the nation-state in the management of the global economy. Although the United Nations has not been effective in producing an international consensus on global problems, it may become more important in the future.

At the same time, the nation-state may be too large to care for the different needs of people at the local level. Government officials representing the nation-state may not have enough contact with the populace in local areas to respond to their needs, which can range from housing and food to the opportunity to express their cultural values. One sign of the fragmentation of the nation-state into smaller components is the increase of ethnic and religious tensions at the local level.

Ethnic Trends

Ethnic unrest and tension are prevalent in today's world. Newspapers, Internet, and television news are rife with stories about ethnic violence among the peoples of the former Soviet Union and Eastern Europe, Africa, Sri Lanka, India, Ireland, the Middle East, and the United States.

Anthropologists have been systematically examining ethnicity since the 1960s. As discussed in Chapters 10 and 23, an ethnic group is a collectivity of people who believe they share a common history and origins. Members of ethnic groups often share cultural traits such as language, religion, dress, and food. Today, as we saw in Chapters 21,

22, and 23, the countries of Latin America, Africa, the Caribbean, the Middle East, and Asia are plural societies that contain many ethnic groups.

As globalization occurs, with its rapid integration of nation-states, markets, and information technology, and as the management of economic and political development goes to the World Bank, the International Monetary Fund, the EU, the United Nations, and large multinational corporations, many people at the local level feel threatened by these global processes. Citizens of various countries lose faith in their government's abilities to represent their interests in these pluralistic societies. These globalization processes often exacerbate ethnic tensions and conflicts.

In previous chapters, we looked at the development of ethnonationalist movements in Latin America, the Caribbean, Africa, the Middle East, and Asia. As we saw, these ethnonationalist movements, such as the Zapatista movement in southern Mexico, were to some extent a result of earlier colonial policies as well as new trends in globalization such as NAFTA and new trade agreements between nation-states. Many ethnic groups express a desire to return to a simpler way of life with traditional culture and behavior. They distrust the new global managers and nation-state bureaucrats, whom they perceive as not having their local interests in mind, and these ethnonationalist movements are a reaction to these globalization tendencies. Restoring ethnic autonomy is sometimes seen as a strategy to rectify the globalization process.

The revival of local ethnic tendencies and identities is developing in the West, as well as in non-Western countries. Anthropologists are studying the ethnic resurgence of the Scots and why they want more independence in the United Kingdom, as well as why Quebec wants to separate from the rest of Canada (Handler 1988; Cohen 1996; Buchignani 2012; Ballinger 2012). These local ethnic movements for autonomy and separatism are a response to the weakening of older nation-state loyalties, induced by globalization. As globalization is fraught with anxieties and produces uncertainties in structures and institutions and as it develops in anarchic, haphazard fashion, carried along by economic, technological, and cultural imperatives, the ethnic group becomes the refuge for people who feel as if they have no control over these new forces.

Religion and Secularization

Just as ethnic trends create contradictory political trends, there are ongoing contradictory religious trends in the context of globalization. In Chapter 19, on religion and aesthetics in industrial and postindustrial societies, we discussed the process of secularization. Generally, traditional religious beliefs and rituals become separated from economic, social, and political institutions in industrial societies, and religion becomes a private affair for many people.

After the Enlightenment, social thinkers such as Auguste Comte and Karl Marx, as well as early anthropologists, predicted that as societies became increasingly industrialized and modernized, secularization would eradicate religious institutions and beliefs. They believed that this was an inevitable development. However, contemporary anthropologists doing research on this phenomena find that the terms "secular" and "religious" do not do justice to the variety of possible developments and the surprising combinations and configurations evident in different national settings (Cannell 2010; Asad 2003, 2011). Though secular/religious trends can result in polarizing tendencies such as in the Arab Spring or elsewhere, at times ethnographers find that the secular can become "sacred" and the religious secularized.

John Bowen has been engaged in ethnographic research in France on secular policies known as *laïcité*, that divide the country, especially with respect to the Muslim minority (2008, 2010). In what he refers to as an "anthropology of reasoning," Bowen investigated the public discourse, norms, and social contexts of how French politicians, intellectuals, the media, and Muslims reason and debate issues regarding the secular or *laïcité* and how secularity is implemented in cases such as the banning of the Islamic headscarf among women. *Laïcité* is interpreted by most French public figures as the basis of the Republican values that involved the removal of any "ostentatious" religious symbols from the public sphere. Historically, *laïcité* developed from the religious wars of Catholics and Protestants prior to the French revolution and through the proclerical and anticlerical struggles of revolutionary and postrevolutionary France. Unlike the United States, the French government subsidizes some religious schools within the Catholic, Protestant, and Jewish traditions, but enforces a policy that they have to accept students with different beliefs or origins and make religious courses optional. However, different interpretations among the French about the meaning of *laïcité* and what the "public sphere" entails are widely debated. Bowen describes *laïcité* as a highly contested concept, which has created difficulties for the Muslim minority.

The Muslims in France (approximately five million) include migrants from former French colonies such as Algeria, Morocco, Tunisia, Senegal, and Mali, along with Turkish immigrants who live primarily in city centers or peripheral rings around major cities such as Paris, Marseille, and Roubaix. Bowen did extensive field research in these sensitive Muslim areas. He found that since the 1980s, the children of Muslim immigrants initiated a movement for equal rights as citizens or residents of France. Many of them became more "Muslim" than their parent's generation with new opportunities to study Arabic and Islamic culture in France. Following 9/11 and other Muslim terrorist activities, Islam remains a security problem in the eyes of many within the French government and among non-Muslim citizens. Bowen explicates the subtle complexities and various interpretations of *laïcité* as it is debated among Muslim and non-Muslim citizens in respect to issues such as gender rights, the expansion of mosques and Islamic schools, and the perceived communalism among Muslims.

Bowen found that the debates and reasoning regarding these issues were often exaggerated and inflammatory; they were also promoted by extreme factions among Muslims and non-Muslims. Yet, what he demonstrates from his research is that there are historic parallels of how *laïcité* was implemented with respect to the Catholic, Protestant, and Jewish communities in France. Many wanted to maintain their faith communities while conforming to the norms of *laïcité* within Republican France. Similarly, the Muslims in France are asserting their identity and religious faith while developing new, reformist, and pragmatic ways of reasoning as well as Islamic institutions with commitments to the French norms and laws of *laïcité*. Although non-Muslims and Muslims continue to debate these issues, Bowen concludes that a path towards a gradual conciliation and accommodation has been opened for a more pluralistic atmosphere in France.

To some extent, religious institutions have survived in industrial societies because religious leaders have emphasized many of the cultural values—for example, nationalism—endorsed by other institutions. In addition, the persistence of religion may be a product of the secularization process itself. Many recent religious revivals have occurred in those societies that have been most affected by modernization. We saw this in Chapter 22, in the case of the Iranian Islamic revolution. As globalization introduces sweeping political, social, and ideological changes, many traditional beliefs and values are challenged. To cope with these destabilizing transformations, many people are reemphasizing traditional cultural values, including religion. For example, the fundamentalist movements in North America, whether Catholic, Jewish, or Protestant, can be partially understood as a reaction against secularization and modernization. Anthropologists Kathleen Stewart and Susan Harding address the emergence of Christian fundamentalist movements that have arisen in the United States (1999). Other anthropologists study Buddhist, Hindu, and Islamic fundamentalism in other parts of the world (Scupin 2003, 2008b; Weisgrau 2008; Antoun 2000; Munson 2008).

As people recognize that globalization is not incidental to their lives, but rather is a recognizable transformation in their everyday circumstances, they draw on religious traditions as a means of restoring power over their lives. The reconstruction and reinvigoration of their religious identity give some people a sense of greater control in what appears to be a "runaway" world. Fundamentalist religious movements articulate the uncertainties and distress brought about by expanding globalization and advocate alternative ways of organizing life on a more localized level.

The Role of Anthropology

24.7 Discuss the role of anthropology as it studies current political, ethnic, and religious trends.

Although the political, ethnic, and religious trends discussed in this chapter are essentially global, they also obviously affect people on the local level. Not surprisingly, therefore, cultural anthropologists are actively documenting local responses to global political and religious trends of people in the agricultural regions of Latin America, Africa, the Middle East, Asia, and nonstate societies, as well as in industrialized and postindustrialized societies. Cultural anthropologists record the various dislocations of global political and religious processes in these societies and the ways people attempt to cope with these global changes. The continuing agony of separatist, ethnic, and religious conflicts in Bosnia, Kosovo, Sri Lanka, and elsewhere is a politically destabilizing force. In addition, many cultural anthropologists conduct ethnographic research on recent religious trends among Christian charismatic and millennial fundamentalist movements in Latin America and elsewhere that have resulted from globalization. As we have seen in earlier chapters, anthropologists are conducting extensive ethnographic research in Latin America and the Caribbean, Africa, the Middle East, and Asia on recent religious developments.

The tragedy of 9/11 in the United States reflected partially the most violent, disruptive expression of the reaction to global trends within the Islamic world. Of course, the causes of these violent expressions such as 9/11 and other terrorist developments throughout the world can never be justified. In the post–September 11th United States, the terms apocalyptic and millennial are often invoked in the context of terrorist threats from the "outside." Numerous media discussions have employed these terms, already made familiar to Americans, to explain the attacks on the World Trade Center and the Pentagon. Unfortunately, explanation too often goes no further than a facile application of long-misunderstood labels and stereotypes. Media characterizations are often too simplified to add to our understanding of these global and religious trends and conflicts. For example, as noted in Chapter 20, Samuel Huntington, a political scientist at Harvard University, wrote the influential book entitled *The Clash of Civilizations and the Remaking of the World Order* (1996) that continues to resonate with many people in the West and other regions of the world. Huntington argued that a unitary "Western civilization and culture" is at odds with "Islamic civilization and culture," "Hindu civilization and culture," and "Confucian civilization and culture." He envisions these primordial ethnic and regional blocs as fragmenting the world order and resulting in more conflict and instability throughout the world. Huntington's views were reinforced in many Western and American minds, as well as in Muslim and Asian societies, as the tragedy of 9/11 unfolded.

However, as discussed in Chapter 20, the anthropologists who have conducted research in the regions discussed by Huntington have produced a much different picture of ethnic relations and civilizations. Each of these regions contains tremendous internal ethnic diversity, and these multiple groups are pursuing a wide range of economic-, political-, and religious-based goals and aspirations. As emphasized earlier in our discussions of culture and ethnicity (Chapters 10 and 23), these supposedly fixed "real" ethnic cultures and civilizations are in flux, producing plural, diverse, and continual dynamic change. Ethnic identities and civilizations are not static and stable. Processes of globalization and local-level political and economic processes are reproducing a constant tug of ethnic and national identity, along with the weakening of those identities and commitments among many different people within societies. Terrorist-minded and reform-minded peaceful groups are constantly in competition with one another in these different regions. Anthropologists also find many bases for pluralistic, democratic institutions within these different areas of the world that could sustain more democratic and pluralistic tendencies (Hefner 2000; Eickelman and Piscatori 2004; Scupin 2006, 2008b).

As cultural anthropologists continue to develop a more comprehensive understanding and explanation of these ethnic and global processes through intensive research, the "clash of civilizations" thesis appears as a caricatured and stereotypical image that produces more distortion and simplification than what more informed, on-the-ground ethnographic research indicates. In many societies influenced by global trends, existing institutions such as the nation-state have not been able to manage these new ethnic and religious conflicts and developments. Perhaps by understanding the specific aspirations of different peoples through ethnographic research, national governments and the international community will be more responsive to the local and diverse needs and interests of these peoples.

As anthropologists identify the cultural variations that hamper international coordination, they may help to contribute to the reduction of ethnic and religious tensions worldwide. Back in the 1980s, anthropologist John Bennett recommended that anthropologists synthesize their local studies (the micro level) with studies of global conditions (the macro level) to identify trends that militate against international cooperation and peaceful harmony (1987). As we will see in the following chapter, many anthropologists are trying to apply the findings of their ethnographic research to help improve human rights, promote economic and educational developments, and enhance other political reforms to produce more stable and harmonious communities both locally and globally.

Anthropologists make a concerted effort to understand the underlying historical and cultural motivations that contribute to ethnic and religious conflicts. In doing so, they may aid in humankind's understanding of its existence and the need for future cooperation, interfaith dialogue, and peace within the expanding global village.

Summary and Review of Learning Objectives

24.1 Compare the logic-of-growth model with the pessimistic model of global technological, environmental, and demographic developments.

The pessimistic model of global development is sometimes referred to as the doomsday model, or the neo-Malthusian approach. This model predicts that if current population, environmental, and technological trends continue, they will produce a series of ecological disasters that will threaten human existence. Using elaborate computer models developed at the Massachusetts Institute of Technology, these scientists concluded that current global trends in population growth, energy consumption, and environmental pollution will exhaust the world's natural resources within the next 100 years. The doomsday model has been challenged by a more optimistic model sometimes known as the logic-of-growth model that foresees a more promising future for humankind. This logic-of-growth model predicts that health improvements, including a decrease in infant mortality and an increase in life expectancy, are a global trend. This model says that pollution has abated in most societies that have experienced economic growth, and that population will level off as economic growth and education for women develops. Ethnographic research lends insight into how these different models apply in different societies.

24.2 Discuss the results of globalization for technology and energy use.

Technological changes resulting from industrialism have increased the consumption of energy and other raw materials. Higher energy costs have led to new technologies such as hydraulic fracking for natural gas supplies and new hybrid vehicles that will reduce reliance on these scarce energies.

24.3 **Discuss how globalization has impacted the environment.**

Environmental changes and globalization have had major consequences on agricultural development, air and water pollution, biodiversity, and climate change. Ethnographic research is helpful in illuminating these trends in specific societies.

24.4 **Discuss globalization and demographic trends.**

The demographic transition that developed along with industrialization had dramatic influences on population. Population growth declined in the core countries and rose in many peripheral underdeveloped societies because of a combination of reduced mortality rates and continued high birth rates. However, with improved health conditions and new opportunities for women, it appears that the population trends are slowing globally. Ethnographers are doing research on different aspects of demographic change such as the one-child policies of China.

24.5 **Discuss globalization and economic trends.**

Global capitalism, accompanied by multinational corporate expansion into different areas of the world, is creating both negative and positive developments. Neoliberal policies since the 1980s accelerated these economic trends. Multinational corporations create more economic interdependency among nations. While ethnographic research indicates that the changes introduced by these multinational corporations may not always generate economic advancement immediately in developing societies, perhaps in the long term, economic growth may be positive. Other global economic trends include the reintegration of socialist societies into the world-capitalist system. Russia, Eastern Europe, China, and Vietnam are abandoning orthodox forms of socialism to join the global market system. Ethnographers are involved in the study of these transitions to determine how this transformation changed postsocialist societies in different areas. China has adopted a form of state capitalism incorporating aspects of the free market directed by the central government. The Communist Party of China is managing and directing a transition from an export-led economy to a more consumer-demand economy. The core countries such as the United States and Japan compete with one another in the global economy. This competition has resulted in the expansion of multinational corporations into various areas of developing countries, leading to a new global division of labor. The Newly Industrialized Economies Countries (NICs) such as South Korea and Taiwan have been moving from peripheral to semiperipheral status in the world-market system. In general, global economic trends have resulted in the decline of global poverty, but with increased economic inequalities within and among different societies.

24.6 **Discuss the political, ethnic, and religious trends resulting from globalization.**

In contrast to global economic and political interdependency as exhibited by the European Union, local political, ethnic, and religious trends often move in the opposite direction. Ethnic separatist and ethnonationalist movements often divide people, making the promotion of national goals difficult. Religious fundamentalist movements often result from the rapid global processes and secularist developments that are perceived as eroding traditional cultural and religious beliefs, sometimes resulting in terrorism that partially explains the 9/11 tragedy in the United States (but does not justify it in any way). Anthropological studies of these trends may help improve our understanding of both local aspirations and global processes.

24.7 **Discuss the role of anthropology as it studies current political, ethnic, and religious trends.**

Cultural anthropologists record the various dislocations of global political, ethnic, and religious processes in various societies and the ways people attempt to cope with these global changes. The continuing agony of separatist, ethnic, and religious conflicts threatens people throughout the world. In addition, many cultural anthropologists conduct ethnographic research on recent religious fundamentalist and secularist trends that have resulted from globalization. By understanding the specific aspirations of different peoples through ethnographic research, national governments and the international community will be more responsive to the local and diverse needs and interests of these peoples. As anthropologists identify the cultural variations that hamper national and international coordination, they may help to contribute to the reduction of political, ethnic, and religious tensions worldwide.

Key Terms

agribusiness, p. 572
biodiversity, p. 576
demographic-transition theory, p. 573
doubling time, p. 574

greenhouse effect, p. 573
Green Revolution, p. 572
logic-of-growth model, p. 570
state capitalism, p. 585

sustainability model, p. 581
zero population growth (ZPG), p. 575

Learning Objectives

After reading this chapter you should be able to:

25.1 Describe the different roles of applied anthropologists.

25.2 Discuss the applied aspects of biological anthropology.

25.3 Define medical anthropology and discuss some of the research undertaken.

25.4 Define cultural resource management and discuss the role of archaeologists in the field.

25.5 Discuss the meaning of "cultural patrimony" and the role of NAGPRA legislation in the United States.

25.6 Discuss the applied aspects of cultural anthropology.

25.7 Discuss how applied anthropologists are engaged in human rights research.

Anthropologists undertake wide-ranging research in the discipline's four basic subfields: biological anthropology, archaeology, linguistics, and cultural anthropology. Within these subfields, there are diverse specializations that focus on the spectrum of human societies and their behaviors in the past and present, as well as human origins and modern human variation. As mentioned in Chapter 1, however, one of the most important areas of the discipline is **applied anthropology**, the use of anthropological research to provide practical solutions to problems faced by modern societies. Applied anthropology embraces each of the discipline's four basic fields. Indeed, some anthropologists have suggested that *all* anthropological research has the potential of practical application: It may be "applied." This chapter examines the varied roles that applied anthropologist play and some of the areas of biological anthropology, archaeology, linguistics, and cultural anthropology that deal with the application of anthropological information in solving practical problems in the modern world.

The Roles of the Applied Anthropologist

25.1 Describe the different roles of applied anthropologists.

The popular, if not accurate, images of anthropologists vary from the adventurous explorer in search of lost treasure to the absent-minded professor working away in the dusty halls of a museum. These perspectives, however entertaining, do not represent the modern anthropologist. Anthropologists are increasingly engaged in activities that have direct relevance to the modern world. Rather than being confined to the halls of the university, an increasing number of anthropologists have become practitioners of anthropology, actively engaging with the communities that they study and solving problems. These concerns range from assisting in murder investigations and protecting cultural resources, to assisting in development projects and medical treatment in various cultural settings.

In many respects, distinguishing applied anthropology from the other subdisciplines of anthropology presents a false dichotomy. All anthropologists share methodological, as well as theoretical, concerns; the difference lies in perceptions of the anthropologists' objectives, an arbitrary division based on the practicality of the intended outcomes. As the renowned cultural anthropologist Bronislaw Malinowski observed more than 70 years ago: "Unfortunately, there is still a strong but erroneous opinion in some circles that practical anthropology is fundamentally different from theoretical or academic anthropology. The truth is that science begins with application. . . .

What is application in science and when does 'theory' become practical? When it first allows us a definite grip on empirical reality" (1945:5).

Much of anthropological research can be seen as applied in some sense. Reviewing applied anthropology, Erve Chambers (1985) classified the different roles of applied anthropologists. Although he was primarily concerned with the applied aspects of cultural anthropology, his observations are equally relevant to the field's other subdisciplines. Chambers considered the varied roles of the anthropologist as: representative, facilitator, informant, analyst, and mediator. As a *representative*, the anthropologist becomes the spokesperson for the particular group being studied. Anthropologists have, for example, represented Native American communities in negotiations with state and federal authorities, mining companies, and development organizations. Anthropologists can also be seen as *facilitators*. In this capacity, anthropologists actively help bring about change or development in the community being researched. They may take a proactive, participatory role in economic or social change to improve medical care, education, or public facilities.

An alternative position is the *informant role*, in which the applied anthropologist transfers cultural knowledge obtained from anthropological research to federal, state, or international agencies that are working to promote change in particular areas. The U.S. government, for example, has long employed anthropologists as on-site researchers to provide data on how local-level service clients and delivery agencies respond to government policy. Informally, many archaeologists and anthropologists become involved in local activities and educational programs that present anthropological findings to the public.

Yet another role of applied anthropologists is that of *analyst*. Rather than being just a provider of data, the practicing anthropologist sometimes becomes engaged in the actual formulation of policy. In the United States, this has become an important area for archaeologists with the passage of the National Historic Preservation Act in 1966, the Native American Graves Repatriation Act of 1990, and other related cultural resources legislation. These laws provide increased protection for some archaeological resources by mandating the consideration of these resources in planning development, and also insuring the recognition of Native American concerns. Archaeologists have increasingly found employment in federal, state, or local governments reviewing proposals for development and construction projects that impact cultural resources and archaeological sites.

Another role Chambers identified is that of *mediator*, which involves the anthropologist as an intermediary among different interest groups that are participating in a development project. This may include private developers, government officials, and the people who will be affected by the project. As mediator, the anthropologist must try to reconcile differences among these groups, facilitating compromises that ideally will benefit all parties involved in the project. The following discussions highlight some of the applied work that biological anthropologists, archaeologists, and cultural anthropologists are engaged in. In Chapter 12 we mentioned the work of applied linguistic anthropologists as they are engaged in saving languages among indigenous peoples including Native Americans. See the box "Applying Anthropology: Saving Languages" in Chapter 12 on pages 281–282 to learn how applied linguistic anthropologists strive to save endangered languages that are rapidly disappearing.

Biological Anthropology

25.2 Discuss the applied aspects of biological anthropology.

As seen in the preceding chapters, biological anthropologists study humans as a natural species, studying humans in both the past and the present. Some of the basic information they gather focuses on human variation and includes the measurement, observation, and explanation of various physical characteristics. Anthropometry, for example, concerns the measurement of human body parts, while osteometry is the measurement of skeletal elements. This information is basic to the interpretation of fossil hominins, as well as human remains recovered from archaeological sites. However, some of this information also has immediate relevance to the present. Such knowledge may be used in combination with engineering data to design ergonomically efficient airplane cockpits, work environments, or equipment. Such data may also provide crucial assistance to the police in murder investigations or the identification of disaster victims. Physical anthropological study of the causes of diseases, when combined with knowledge of cultural anthropology, offers important insight into perceptions of medical treatment in different cultural settings. Some examples of anthropologists' practices are considered in this section.

Forensic Anthropology

A fragmentary skeleton is accidentally found in a desolate part of the desert. Through a series of twists and turns, an enterprising detective pieces together clues to a 20-year-old murder and brings a fugitive to justice. Such a scenario is the stuff of mystery novels, but real-life criminal investigations often do depend upon the identification of fragmentary skeletal remains. **Forensic anthropology** can be defined as the application of biological anthropological

data to law (Byers 2008). Biological anthropologists in this area of specialization are often called to assist police when unidentified human remains are found. Whereas human biologists and medical doctors focus on the body's soft tissues, forensic anthropologists study the hard tissues—the skeletal remains (Reichs 1998; Steadman 2009). Analysis of such material begins by reconstructing the skeleton and joining the often fragmentary and broken remains. Missing pieces might be reconstructed or estimated. The materials are then carefully measured and compared to anthropological data. This information may yield clues regarding the sex, approximate age, height, and physical characteristics of an individual.

Skeletal remains also provide a record of medical problems, illnesses, and the overall health of a person. The bones may preserve information about a person's physical state at the time of death, as well as the living conditions and health problems the individual faced during his or her lifetime. For example, broken bones, although healed, still leave a trace on the skeleton. Arthritis, certain infections, dietary stress, and nutritional deficiencies may also be in evidence. This kind of information may provide insight into living conditions in the distant human past, as, for example, when considering the consequences of domestication (see Chapter 8), but it also provides details that may be very helpful to the police in identifying victims. Unidentified skeletal remains from a white female, 5'4" to 5'6", 40 to 45 years of age, with a healed fracture of the left leg and traces of arthritis in the hands, would dramatically reduce the number of potential fits with reported missing person files.

Forensic Facial Reconstruction   A very specialized area within forensic anthropology deals with the reconstruction of faces (Prag and Neave 1997; Wilkinson 2004). Using average skin depths, muscle patterns, and knowledge derived from the skull, the researcher creates an image of what a person looked like when alive. This interdisciplinary work draws on information from anatomy, facial surgery, pathology, dentistry, and biological anthropology, as well as the skills of the artist.

A variety of different approaches have been used, including two-dimensional sketches by artists, computer reconstructions, or even detailed models based on reconstructed skulls. In the latter case, underlying muscles of clay are sculpted over the skull, or a model of it, and then covered with additional clay that represents the overlying tissues. The thickness of the skin is based on average thickness at different points of the skull, estimated for individuals of different ages, sexes, body builds, and ethnic groups—information that is inferred from the skeletal remains. A final model is prepared using plaster of Paris, which is colored, and given hair and eyes.

Forensic facial reconstruction is not without its limitations. As discussed in Chapter 6, humans vary tremendously in terms of their physical attributes, even within populations. While average tissue thicknesses may be calculated, there is not unanimous agreement on the most appropriate methods to use, and the characteristics present in specific individuals may vary widely (Iscan and Helmer 1993). In many instances, researchers may also have very limited information to infer attributes such as hair or skin color. Interpretations can, therefore, be quite subjective. Nevertheless, techniques such as these, whether using a pen and ink, a computer, or plaster models, help police put flesh on the bones and can be invaluable in investigations. Although the final products may not always be exact portraits, in some instances the resemblance to the living individual has proven remarkable.

Determining the Cause of Death   Forensic anthropology may also offer important clues about the actual circumstances of a person's demise, as well as the treatment of the body after death (Byers 2008; Haglund and Sorg 1997; Steadman 2009). Damage or trauma to the bones may provide a primary indicator of the cause of death. For example, bullet wounds, stabbings, and blunt-force trauma may be identified in skeletal remains. Careful study of the skeleton may also indicate whether an individual was killed where the body was found, or at another location and then transported to the site where the body was found. Forensic anthropologists may also be able to determine whether the body was disturbed or moved after burial. Such information may be extremely important in determining the cause of death. However, it may be equally important in reconstructing the events surrounding it. As in the case of archaeological and paleontological investigations, the *context* of the findings is very important. Hence, biological anthropologists with archaeological training can help ensure that all of the remains are recovered.

Because the cause of death may be central to a murder investigation and trial, the forensic anthropologist is often called upon to testify as an expert witness. In such cases, the researcher impartially presents his or her findings that may prove or disprove the identity or cause of death of the victim. The ultimate concern of the forensic anthropologist is not the outcome of the trial, but the evidence provided by the skeletal remains.

The amount of information extracted from skeletal remains can be surprising. For example, fractures of the hyoid bone, a small bone attached to the thyroid cartilage of the throat, may indicate strangulation. The location and kind of breaks may offer clues to the type of weapon used, as well as the position of the attacker relative to the victim. In the vein of a Sherlock Holmes novel, it may actually be possible to determine that a fatal blow was struck from behind by a right-handed assailant. Many illustrations from actual criminal cases can be recounted (Rathbun and Buikstra 1984; Sauer et al. 2003; Steadman 2009; 2013).

The key roles of both archaeology and forensic anthropology in determining the cause of death are illustrated by the John McRae murder case (Sauer et al. 2003). In 1997, police in northern Michigan were called when a farmworker uncovered human skeletal remains while excavating a refuse pit with a backhoe. On the basis of dental records, the police identified the victim as Randy Laufer, a 15-year-old boy who had disappeared 11 years previously. The principal suspect in the case was John McRae, who had previously owned the land where the bones were recovered. At the time of their discovery, the bones were fragmentary and devoid of flesh. More significantly, they had not been recovered under ideal conditions; structures formerly on the property had been removed and the remains disturbed by a backhoe. However, the archaeological and physical anthropological evidence proved crucial in bringing McRae to justice. Archaeologists were able to recover the remaining bones, locate the original burial pit, and reconstruct the placement of structures on the property when McRae owned it. The archaeological information established that the body had likely been buried no

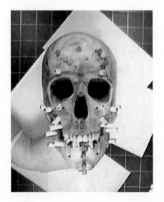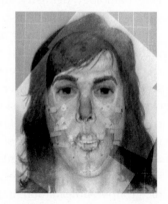

A specialized area of forensic anthropology deals with the reconstruction of facial features. The photographs illustrate (from left) the victim's skull, a reconstruction of the face, a sketch based on the reconstruction, and a photograph of how the victim actually appeared in life.
Source: Courtesy of Gene O'Donnell, FBI.

more than 15 feet from the front door of McRae's trailer, beneath a gravel driveway or just inside an adjacent barn. The skeletal evidence established Laufer's identity and also that he had been mutilated at the time of death. Study of the cut marks on the bones indicated that the boy had been stabbed or hacked in the left shoulder and his body cut in half.

Identifying Victims of War and Genocide   Forensic anthropologists have also played important roles in the identification of victims of natural disasters, airplane crashes, bombings, war, and genocide (Stewart 1970; Stover 1981, 1992; Snow et al. 1989; Snow and Bihurriet 1992; Steadman 2003). Forensic anthropologists and archaeologists have assisted in the documentation of human rights abuses and the recovery of victims from mass graves in Argentina, Brazil, Croatia, El Salvador, Haiti, Iraq, Poland, Rwanda, and many other world areas. For example, the *Polish Genetic Base of Totalitarianism Victims* has undertaken the excavation of mass graves and burials of individuals executed in Poland during the country's authoritarian regime between 1944 and 1956. Researchers draw on DNA recovered from the remains, as well as material culture and forensic data, to identify the victims.

Excavations of mass graves at Warszawa, Poland. Research by Marek E. Jasinski has focused on the victims of totalitarian regimes. Forensic anthropologists often play an important role in the identification of victims of natural disasters, airplane crashes, wars, and genocide. *Source*: Courtesy of Marek E. Jasinski, Institute of Historical Studies; Archaeology Programme Norwegian University of Science and Technology.

Anthropologists at Work

CLYDE COLLINS SNOW: Forensic Anthropologist

Clyde Collins Snow obtained a master's degree in zoology from Texas Tech University and planned to pursue a Ph.D. in physiology, but his career plans were interrupted by military service. While stationed at Lackland Air Force Base near San Antonio, he was introduced to the field of archaeology and became fascinated with the ancient artifacts discovered in the surrounding area.

After leaving the military, Snow attended the University of Arizona, where his zoological training and archaeology interests led him to a Ph.D. in physical anthropology. He became skilled at identifying old bones, as well as artifacts. With his doctoral degree completed, he joined the Federal Aviation Administration as a consulting forensic anthropologist, providing technical assistance in the identification of

victims of aircraft accidents. Snow also lent his expertise to the design of safety equipment to prevent injuries in aircraft accidents.

As word of Snow's extraordinary skill in forensic anthropology spread, he was called to consult on and provide expert testimony in many criminal cases. His testimony was crucial at the sensational murder trial of John Wayne Gacy, accused of murdering more than 30 teenagers in the Chicago area. Snow also collaborated with experts in the reinvestigation of President John F. Kennedy's assassination. These experts built a full-scale model of Kennedy's head to determine whether Lee Harvey Oswald alone could have inflicted all of Kennedy's wounds. They did not uncover any scientific evidence to contradict the Warren Commission's conclusion that Oswald was the sole assassin.

More recently, Snow and his team have been recognized for their contributions to human rights issues. Snow

Clyde Collins Snow

served as a consultant to the Argentine government's National Commission on Disappeared Persons in its efforts to determine the fate of thousands of Argentineans who were abducted and murdered by military death squads between 1976 and 1983, when the country was under the rule of a military dictatorship. As a result of his investigations, Snow was asked to testify as an expert witness in the trial of the nine junta members who ruled Argentina during the period of military repression. He also assisted people in locating their dead relatives.

Snow stressed that in his human rights investigative work he is

(continued)

functioning as an expert, not necessarily as an advocate. He must maintain an objective viewpoint in interpreting his findings. The evidence he finds may then be presented by lawyers (as advocates) in the interests of justice. Snow's and other forensic anthropological human rights work was supported by various agencies, such as the American Association for the Advancement of Science, the Ford Foundation, the J. Roderick MacArthur Foundation, Amnesty International, Physicians for Human Rights, and Human Rights Watch (Mann and Holland 2004). Clyde Collins Snow died on May 16, 2014. His applied research in forensic anthropology has been foundational in this field.

Many of the methods and techniques used by modern forensic anthropologists were needed during and after World War II to assist with the identification and repatriation of the remains of soldiers killed in battle. This remained an important role for forensic anthropologists during the Korean and Vietnam wars (Stewart 1970; Mann et al. 2003). Identification of the remains has often been dependent on matching the physical remains recovered with life histories provided by medical and dental records. In such cases, positive identification may be dependent on relatively minor variation in bony structures.

Today, biological anthropologists and forensic archaeologists continue to play important roles in locating and identifying American soldiers killed or missing in past conflicts (Mather 1994). The Joint POW/MIA Accounting Command (referred to as JPAC) is a United States Department of Defense task force whose mission is to account for all Americans who are listed as prisoners of war, or missing in action, from all past wars and conflicts. JPAC's missions span the globe, and the recovery of a single individual's remains, involving both documentary research and fieldwork, may take years. Researchers are now able to bring much more sophisticated techniques to the identifying of human remains. These methods include the extraction of DNA from small fragments of bone, which may be matched with the DNA of the soldier's surviving relatives.

Medical Anthropology

25.3 Define medical anthropology and discuss some of the research undertaken.

Another subfield of applied anthropology, medical anthropology, represents the intersection of cultural anthropology and the other four fields of anthropology, including biological anthropology (Brown and Barrett 2010; McElroy and Townsend 2009). **Medical anthropology** is the study of disease, health-care systems, medical practices, curing, and mental illness with a cross-cultural perspective. Medical anthropologists work with physicians, nurses, and other public health-care workers to apply their knowledge about cultural practices in different settings to provide more effective treatment. One of the key issues that medical anthropologists focus on is the comparison between Western-based biomedical scientific techniques and theories and other, nonscientific beliefs and models of disease, illness, and medicine. From a Western biomedical perspective, disease is the result of natural causes, including genetic disabilities, autoimmune factors, or external sources such as infectious microbes, injuries, or syndromes that impair the normal function of the body. Illness is the feeling of pain or sickness by individuals or populations. Health care provided by the Western biomedical model to diagnose and treat disease or illness involves physicians and nurses equipped with advanced technologies such as X-rays, MRIs, CT scans, surgery, and pharmaceutical medicines that are tested and developed through scientific methods.

Ethnomedicine

In other cultural settings, disease, illness, or injuries may be attributed to a variety of other reasons, including religious or spiritual beliefs. The beliefs may dramatically influence how medical treatment is viewed. Medical anthropologists developed the field of **ethnomedicine**, the study and comparison of traditional, spiritually based medical practices by different ethnic groups. Ethnomedicine reveals that concepts of disease and illness are not universally defined. The local culture deeply influences the understanding and meaning of physical impairment and the techniques used for healing. For example, medical anthropologists investigate the practices of acupuncture as developed in traditional Chinese medicine and the Ayurvedic beliefs about disease, illness, and healing maintained in the Hindu religious tradition. Both the Chinese and Ayurvedic Hindu medical beliefs are based on restoring balance and equilibrium within the body that might be lost as a result of injuries or illnesses, induced by the ingestion of inappropriate foods or exposure to climate changes or diseases.

Ethnomedicine in Thailand A classic example of medical anthropology and ethnomedicine is the work of Louis Golomb (1985), who conducted ethnographic research on curing practices in Thailand. Golomb did research on Buddhist and Muslim medical practitioners who rely on native spiritualistic beliefs to diagnose and cure diseases. These practices are based on earlier Hindu, magical, and animistic beliefs that had been syncretized with Buddhist and Muslim traditions. Practitioners draw on astrology, faith healing, massage, folk psychotherapy, exorcism, herbs, and charms and amulets to treat patients. The most traditional practitioners are curer-magicians, or shamans, who diagnose and treat every illness as an instance of spirit possession or spirit attack. Other practitioners are more skeptical of the supernatural causation of illness and diagnose health problems in reference to natural or organic causes. They frequently use herbal medicines to treat illnesses.

Golomb discovered that although Western-based scientific forms of medicine may be available, many Thais still relied on traditional practitioners. He found that even urban-educated elite, including those who had studied in the United States and other Western countries, adhered to both supernatural and scientific views. Golomb referred to this as *therapeutic pluralism*. He observed that patients do not rely on any single therapeutic approach, but rather use a combination of therapies that include elements of ritual, magic, and modern scientific medications. Parasites or germs are rarely seen as the only explanations of disease; a sick person may consult a clinic to receive medication to relieve symptoms, but may then seek out a traditional curer for a more complete treatment. Golomb emphasized that the multiplicity of alternative therapies encourages people to play an active role in preserving their health, something that has therapeutic benefits.

In Thailand, as in many other countries undergoing modernization and globalization, up-to-date medical facilities have been established, based on the scientific treatment of disease. Golomb found that personnel in these facilities are critical of traditional medical practices. He also discovered that while the people in the villages often respected the modern doctor's ability to diagnose diseases and prescribe medications to relieve symptoms, in most cases they do not accept the scientific explanation of the disease. In addition, villagers felt that modern medical methods are brusque and impersonal because doctors did not offer any psychological or spiritual consolation. Doctors also do not make house calls and rarely spend much time with patients. This impersonality in the doctor–patient relationship was also due to social status differences based on wealth, education, and power. Golomb found that many public health personnel expected deference from their rural clientele. For these reasons, many people preferred to rely upon traditional curers.

Through his study of traditional medical techniques and beliefs, Golomb isolated some of the strengths and weaknesses of modern medical treatment in Thailand. His work contributed to a better understanding of how to deliver health-care services to rural and urban Thais. For example, the Thai Ministry of Public Health began to experiment with ways of coordinating the efforts of modern and traditional medical practitioners. Village midwives and traditional herbalists were called on to dispense modern medications and distribute information about nutrition and hygiene. Some Thai hospitals have established training sessions for traditional practitioners to learn

modern medical techniques. Golomb's studies in medical anthropology offer a model for practical applications in the health field for other developing societies to follow.

Chinese Acupuncture Another example of the intersection of local cultural knowledge and Western medical practices is provided by Chinese medicine and the practice of acupuncture, which are based on cosmological beliefs derived from Daoist, Confucianist, and Buddhist beliefs. According to these beliefs, spiritual forces and energy known as *qi*, usually translated as "air" or "breath," inhabit all living things. As in other living things, *qi* flows through the human body along various channels or meridians. Injuries, illness, or disease are claimed to obstruct the flow of *qi* creating dysfunctions within the body. The acupuncturist attempts to control the flow of *qi* that might be obstructed by inserting needles to harmonize and restore equilibrium to bodily functions.

The Western model of biomedicine does not recognize the spiritual energy force *qi* or meridian channels within a scientific framework. However, Chinese acupuncture treatment has been accepted by many patients with illnesses as an alternative therapy within the United States. Medical anthropologist Linda Barnes has been studying Chinese acupuncture as it exists in the very cosmopolitan city of Boston, Massachusetts (2005). Through extensive interviewing of acupuncturists and patients as well as observing acupuncture treatment sessions for over two years, Barnes examined how patients and practitioners understand the effectiveness of acupuncture treatment. She notes that acupuncture derived from traditional Chinese medicine has been the basis of licensure and government regulations of the practice in the United States. Barnes describes five different forms of acupuncture traditions in the Boston area: the Worsley Five Elements school, Japanese acupuncture, and limited instances of the Korean, Vietnamese, and French schools. Some practitioners within different schools have trained with Chinese Daoist priests to learn how to harmonize the flow of *qi*. Some of the practitioners are Chinese Americans or Asian Americans, but many are Americans of European descent.

Barnes describes the variation of practices and beliefs about the efficacy of acupuncture within the different schools. Many patients select acupuncture as only one of many nonscientific therapies in tandem with other, Western biomedical scientific therapies. Some of the practitioners view their acupuncture treatments as a form of religious healing, whereas others, mainly European American practitioners, view it as embedded with "spirit." Some of the practitioners view the efficacy of acupuncture as "empowerment" for the individual. Barnes discusses how acupuncture has crossed the boundaries of Western biomedical practices, as it is accepted and regulated by the National Institutes of Health (NIH) as a Complementary and

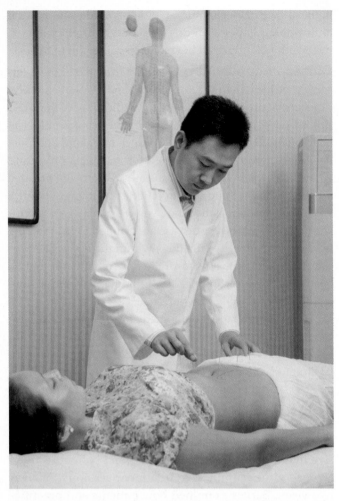

Chinese acupuncture treatments are readily available in U.S. society.

Alternative Medicine (CAM). In 1997, NIH has accepted the efficacy of acupuncture as an adjunct treatment for postoperative and chemotherapy induced nausea and vomiting, stroke rehabilitation, headache, low back pain, asthma, and other injuries or illnesses. Barnes describes how some practitioners agree that a patient's symptoms of illness may not always change, but nevertheless healing does occur. Some patients who use acupuncture for drug addiction withdrawal or chronic pain feel that it reduces their anxiety. Barnes concludes her essay by discussing therapeutic pluralism and the multiple meanings of the effectiveness of acupuncture by practitioners and patients and how this is embedded within the culture and values of U.S. society.

Tanya Luhrmann provides insight into the dynamics of religious healing and prayer that has a bearing on what medical anthropologists discover in their research on therapeutic pluralism (2013). In her studies of prayer and religious experience among Christians in Chicago and San Francisco, Luhrmann found that some individuals experienced prayer and healing differently than others. As part of her ethnographic research, Luhrmann used a survey instrument that measured the degree of "absorption," or hypnotic susceptibility and imaginative involvement in

narratives, myths, or other sensations. Absorption is the capacity to focus one's attention on the mind's object while neglecting the distractions of everyday life. The degree of absorption varies between individuals and at different times of the day for individuals. Through extensive interviews, meditation and prayer experiments, and surveys, Luhrmann found that those individuals who were more susceptible to prayer and healing experienced mystical states, out-of-body feelings, and lucid visions. She suggests that absorption is central to spirituality and religious experience. Universally, medical anthropologists find that some individuals experience religious and spiritual healing in different degrees based on this capacity for absorption.

Cultural Patterns and Epidemiology Other medical anthropologists focus specifically on **epidemiology**, which examines the spread and distribution of diseases and how they are influenced by cultural patterns. For example, these anthropologists may be able to determine whether coronary (heart) disease or cancer is related to particular cultural or social dietary habits, such as the consumption of foods high in sodium or saturated fats. These studies can often help health providers design more effective means for delivering health care and formulating healthcare policies (Schell and Denham 2003). Thus, applied medical anthropology deals with intervention, prevention, and policy issues in public health care. In addition, medical anthropologists also demonstrate the linkages between socioeconomic status, illness, and access to health care.

Medical anthropologist Caroline Wilson has been doing research on cardiac disease in the state of Kerala in South India (2010). Globalization has increased heart disease in India with diets richer in fats and sugar, reduced physical activity, increases in smoking, alcohol use, stress, and inequality. Kerala has high rates of cardiac disease, type 2 diabetes, high blood pressure, cholesterol, and obesity for both men and women from their late twenties onward. Thus, these medical problems are not due to aging. Wilson studied consumer practices, specifically eating and feasting activities, levels of physical activity, and the lifestyle among Hindus and Muslims in the city of Malabar in Kerala. She observed medical practices in outpatient clinics that were staffed by cardiologists and general physicians where patients were treated for hypertension, high cholesterol, and diabetes. Wilson participated in the social and cultural practices in various settings, in particular those practices that involved feasting and eating such as weddings, cooking classes, and many other rituals and events. As in many other societies, food becomes a means of establishing and maintaining social networks among these Hindu and Muslim families in Kerala, where a "good appetite" indicates both emotional and physical health, vitality, and well-being.

Wilson found that in the middle-class Hindu households, home cooking used less meat and oil. Affluent

Muslim households served meat-based curries three times a day, while some households added fish on a regular basis. However, outside of the home, both Hindu and Muslim men and women consumed more meat and fried foods. Fast-food restaurants and bakeries that serve fried chicken or biscuits, sweet cakes, and milkshakes have developed with increasing globalization in Kerala. At ritual functions such as wedding feasts, both Hindus and Muslims serve abundant portions of a spicy chicken cooked with oil and rice, *biriyani*. In these communities concerns are expressed regarding the increase of heart attacks and its relationship to nutrition. Yet, pressures to consume large amounts of food at feasting rituals are prevalent. Refusing to accept food is a sign of anger or annoyance. As Wilson says, "Breaking out of the culture of eating and feasting requires cognitive intent, to resist the flow of food and love in everyday life" (2010: 270). Dietary restrictions that inhibit participation in new forms of consumption among the affluent people of Kerala are signs of emotional ill-being. Wilson has identified this culture of overeating and feasting that relates to increases in cardiac disease in order to assist public health authorities in preventing these problems in Kerala.

Ethnographic studies such as these that combine a knowledge of the scientific understanding of disease and medicine, with in-depth local cultural knowledge have proven to be an effective combination in many other settings. They provide an excellent illustration of the relevance of anthropological research in solving important social and medical problems.

Medical Anthropology and Mental Illness

Another area of interest for medical anthropology is the study of mental illness in different societies. The major concerns of these studies revolve around two questions: Is there a universal concept of "normal" and "abnormal" behavior? Do mental illnesses differ in their symptoms or patterns in different societies? These questions serve as the basis for many medical anthropology projects in different societies.

What is Abnormal? In the early twentieth century, one of the assumptions in the fields of psychiatry and psychology was that mental illness and abnormal behavior are universal. In other words, depression, schizophrenia, psychoses, and other mental disorders are essentially the same for all humans. For example, in the field of psychiatry, particular types of mental disorders were classified by specific symptoms. Thus, a *psychosis* was classified as a type of mental disturbance characterized by personality disorganization, disturbed emotional responses, and a loss of contact with reality. A *neurosis* was characterized as a nonpsychotic disorder marked by considerable anxiety for individuals, especially when they are involved in social interaction.

Anthropologists such as Ruth Benedict challenged these classifications of mental illness in the 1930s. Benedict argued that all criteria of abnormality reflect the particular culture of the individual and must be understood within the context of that culture. In her classic book *Patterns of Culture* (1934), Benedict remarked:

> It does not matter what kind of "abnormality" we choose for illustration, those which indicate extreme instability, or those which are more in the nature of character traits like sadism or delusions of grandeur or of persecution, there are well-described cultures in which these abnormals function with ease and with honor and apparently without danger or difficulty to the society. (1934:263)

In other words, Benedict questioned whether any type of absolute standards of "normalcy" as defined by Western preoccupations and categories were satisfactory criteria for mental health. Benedict described a situation in which an individual heard very loud voices, was plagued by dreams of falling off cliffs, and feared being devoured by swarms of yellowjackets. This individual went into a trance state, lay rigid on the ground, and shortly thereafter recovered and danced for three nights in a row. Although in Western society this individual would be treated as "abnormal," Benedict suggested that this behavior and thought were not unusual in some societies. The individual described was a type of medicine man or woman and was not only accorded respect, but also enjoyed tremendous prestige within the particular Native American tribe to which he or she belonged.

Ethnographic descriptions such as these demonstrate the difficulties of classifying mental illness across cultural boundaries. When the concept of abnormality is applied cross-culturally, it becomes an extremely vague concept. Behavior that is considered deviant in one society may represent a culturally acceptable form of behavior in another. The fields of modern psychiatry and psychology have been attempting to revise their classification of mental illnesses and often work with anthropologists on joint research projects to refine understandings of psychological disorders.

Culture-Specific Disorders A number of ethnographic studies have focused on mental disorders that are unique to certain cultural settings. These culture-specific disorders include *latah*, *amok*, *windigo*, and *pibloktoq*. *Latah* has been described as a mental disorder in areas of Southeast and East Asia. In Southeast Asia, *latah* appears as a type of hysteria or fear reaction that afflicts women. They become easily startled and compulsively imitate behaviors or shout repetitive phrases that they have heard (echolalia). Sometimes, this disorder is triggered by the woman hearing the word *snake* or being tickled. In Mongolia, however, David Aberle (1961) described a form of *latah* that affects men. These men may be startled suddenly and put their hands into a fire, jump into a river, or begin to scream obscenities wildly.

Amok is a culture-specific disorder that is described in Malaysia, Indonesia, and parts of the Philippines. It is a disorder of middle-aged males that follows a period of withdrawal marked by brooding over a perceived insult. During this time, in which the individual loses contact with reality, he may suffer from stress and sleep deprivation and consume large quantities of alcohol. Then, a wild outburst marked by rage occurs, with the individual attempting a violent series of murderous attacks. The man may pick up a weapon such as a machete and attack any person or animal in his path. These aggressive, homicidal attacks will be followed by prolonged exhaustion and amnesia (Bourguignon 1979). *Amok* appears to be a culturally sanctioned form of violent behavior viewed as an appropriate response to a specific situation in these regions of Southeast Asia. (The Malay term *amok* has entered the English language, referring to wild, aggressive behavior, as in someone running *amok*.)

Another culture-specific disorder, formerly found among the males of the Chippewa, Cree, and Montagnais-Naskapi Indians in Canada, is referred to as the *windigo* psychosis. It is described as a disorder in which the affected individual becomes deeply depressed and begins to believe that he has been possessed or bewitched by the spirit of a *windigo*, a cannibal giant with a heart or entrails of ice. The individual may have symptoms of nausea, anorexia, and insomnia and may see other humans being transformed into beavers or other animals. As these hallucinations occur, the individual begins to have an overwhelming desire to kill and eat these humans (Barnouw 1985). This insatiable craving for human flesh has resulted in documented cases of homicide and cannibalism among some of these people (Marano 1982; Barnouw 1985).

The disorder *pibloktoq*, also referred to as Arctic hysteria, was found among Eskimo adults in Greenland and other Arctic regions. It may affect both men and women, but has been described more frequently among women. The subject is initially irritable or withdrawn and then becomes violently emotional. The victim may scream as if terrified, tear off her clothes, run out into the snow, jump into fire, throw things around, and begin to "speak in tongues." After this period of excitement, the woman sometimes has convulsive seizures and then might fall asleep. Upon awakening, she might be perfectly calm and have no memory of the incident. *Pibloktoq* usually had a high frequency in the winter, and a number of persons living in a small community may have been afflicted with it during the cold months (Wallace 1972). Thus, it may be a more extreme form of what Americans sometimes call "cabin fever."

A number of explanations have been put forth for these culture-specific mental disorders. For example, the *windigo* disorder has been attributed to the experience of starvation and famine conditions that can occur in the wintertime. Anthropologist Anthony Wallace (1972) suggested that a lack of calcium in the diet of Eskimos may partially explain the occurrence of *pibloktoq*. In these areas, the drastic annual variation in daylight may also be a cause of these behavioral and emotional disturbances (Bourguignon 1979).

Some critics believe that these culture-specific disorders may just be different expressions of certain illnesses such as paranoid schizophrenia or other types of psychoses. Persecution ideas, hysteria, panic disorders, and other bizarre behaviors occur in all societies to one degree or another. There is a substantial body of evidence from various sources that certain types of depression and schizophrenia are caused by biochemical disorders that are genetically inherited (Myers 2012). International surveys by the World Health Organization have examined disorders such as schizophrenia around the world and have found some basic similarities in the symptom profiles (Marsella 1979). Medical anthropologists have found, however, that the cultural beliefs and worldviews, family communication patterns, early childhood training, and particular life stresses of certain societies influence the content of these mental disorders (Goodman and Leatherman 1986). Conditions resulting in stress—including homelessness, war, living in refugee camps, and other anxiety-producing or depression-inducing conditions—can influence biological tendencies that may not appear in normal circumstances (Dressler 1991).

A study revealed that Nepalese children who had been child soldiers in the recent civil wars had higher levels of depression and (for females) posttraumatic stress disorder (PTSD) than did other children (Kuwert, Spitzer, et al. 2008). In some cases, symptoms of psychological disorders such as depression may be diagnosed differently within various societies. For example, medical anthropologist and psychiatrist Arthur Kleinman describes how the Chinese report the symptoms of depression differently from Americans (2004). Depression is a complex group of symptoms, including negative cognitions, psychomotor retardation, sleep disturbance, fatigue, and loss of energy. However, when Chinese report their symptoms of depression, they tend to focus on the physiological and bodily factors, rather than any psychological or mental disturbance. This difference in how symptoms are diagnosed and reported may be due to how the Chinese culture has been influenced by their traditional religious beliefs from Daoism and the concepts of *yin/yang*, which claims a complementary and interpenetrating equilibrium between these two forces or energies of the universe. The Chinese are socialized to maintain a dynamic balance between these *yin/yang* spiritual forces. This phenomenon involves beliefs about the inextricable linkage between body and mind. This cultural and religious tradition may influence why the Chinese emphasize the external causes of their depression, attributing their mental illness to somatic disorders or a loss of equilibrium.

Globalization and Mental Illness Globalization has had an influence on the prevalence of mental illness in different countries throughout the world. In a book entitled *Crazy Like Us: The Globalization of the American Psyche*, anthropologist Ethan Watters uses case studies from various regions such as Hong Kong in China, Sri Lanka, Zanzibar, and Japan to demonstrate how America and the Western biomedical models have dominated the understandings of mental problems such as anorexia and bulimia, posttraumatic stress disorder (PTSD), schizophrenia, and depression (2010). He indicates how there are multiple interpretations and constructions of these mental illnesses in these regions of the world. However, as American and Western biomedical, individualistic psychological care, and pharmaceutical-based models have penetrated these areas, the indigenous interpretations of mental illnesses are challenged and repressed. At times this results in dysfunctional psychological problems that interfere with the delivery of more communal mental health care.

In respect to American psychiatric and psychotherapy, anthropologist Tanya Luhrmann has conducted ethnographic research among American psychiatrists to determine how they diagnose and treat mental illness (Luhrmann 2000). She did four years of ethnographic fieldwork, including 16 months in clinical settings with psychiatric residents in training who were treating different kinds of mental illness. She also spent time in the classroom with students in psychiatric training to determine what basic ideas and beliefs they were learning. Luhrmann discovered that there were two different major paradigms or views of diagnosing patients with various mental illnesses as reflected in the title of her book *Of Two Minds: The Growing Disorder in American Psychiatry* (2000). The two competing models of mental illness that influenced psychiatric diagnosis and treatment were the biomedical and the psychodynamic. The biomedical model, which has become dominant within contemporary American psychiatry, involves treating mental illnesses such as depression with psychopharmacological drugs such as Zoloft, Cymbalta, or Prozac. The psychodynamic model in contrast suggests that patients ought to be treated with extensive psychotherapy. These two different models of mental illness have created strains within the psychiatric profession. The models have different moral sensibilities and have guided strategies in treating patients in distinctive ways. In some cases, the biomedical model has led to a type of "fast-food-psychiatry," which treats patients as victims without choices, whereas the psychodynamic model emphasizes a complex empathetic relationship with patients. Luhrmann indicates that both models are effective, and sometimes patients need both types of treatment; however, there is concern that the pharmaceutical industry

Tanya Luhrmann

through its extensive advertising may be creating a culture that has a negative influence on the treatment and diagnosis of mental illness in America.

Cultural Resource Management: Applied Archaeology

25.4 Define cultural resource management and discuss the role of archaeologists in the field.

Is the past worth preserving? One of the problems that humanity faces is how to safeguard the cultural heritage preserved in the archaeological record. Although archaeology may address questions of general interest to all of humanity, it is also important in promoting national heritage, cultural identity, and ethnic pride. Museums the world over offer displays documenting diverse local populations, regional histories, significant events, and cultural traditions. There are ever more specialized museums focusing on particular peoples, regions, or historic periods. Archaeologists must be concerned with the preservation of archaeological sites and the recovery of information from sites threatened with destruction, in addition to the interpretation and presentation of their findings to the more general public (Jameson 2004; Little 2007). As a result of these concerns, a very important area of specialization, within archaeology is **cultural resource management**. Cultural resource management (often referred to as CRM) focuses on the evaluation, protection, and supervision of cultural resources, including the archaeological record, as well as the arts, historic sites, and cultural property. Many archaeologists now find employment as applied archaeologists doing CRM, evaluating, salvaging, and protecting archaeological resources that are threatened with destruction.

Preservation of the past and effective cultural resource management are challenges to archaeologists, government officials, and the concerned public alike, as archaeological sites are being destroyed at an alarming rate. Archaeological materials naturally decay in the ground, and sites are constantly destroyed through geological processes, erosion, and animal burrowing (see Chapter 2). Yet, while natural processes contribute to the disappearance of archaeological sites, by far the greatest threat to the archaeological record is human activity. Construction projects such as dams, roads, buildings, and pipelines all disturb the ground and can destroy archaeological sites in the process. In many instances, archaeologists work only a few feet ahead of construction equipment, trying to salvage any information they can before a site disappears forever.

Some archaeological sites are intentionally destroyed by collectors searching for artifacts that have value in the antiquities market, such as arrowheads and pottery. Statues from ancient Egypt, Mayan terra cotta figurines, and Native American pottery may be worth thousands of dollars to antique dealers. To fulfill the demands, archaeological sites in many world areas are looted by pot hunters, who dig to retrieve artifacts for collectors, ignoring the traces of ancient housing, burials, and cooking hearths. Removed from their context, with no record of where they came from, such artifacts are of limited value to archaeologists. The rate of destruction of North American archaeological sites is such that some researchers have estimated that 98 percent of sites predating the year 2000 will be destroyed by the middle of the twenty-first century (Herscher 1989; Knudson 1989).

The rate at which archaeological sites are being destroyed is particularly distressing because the archaeological record is an irreplaceable, *nonrenewable* resource. That is, after sites are destroyed, they are gone forever, along with the unique information about the past that they contained. In many parts of the world, recognition of this fact has led to legislation aimed at protecting

archaeological sites (see Table 25.1). The rational for this legislation is that the past has value to the present; hence, it should be protected and interpreted for the benefit of the public.

Preserving the Past

Recognition of the value and nonrenewable nature of archaeological resources is the first step in the planning process. Archaeological resources can then be systematically identified and evaluated. Steps can be taken to preserve them by limiting development or designing projects in a way that will preserve the resource. For example, the projected path of a new road might be moved to avoid an archaeological site, or a building might be planned so that the foundations do not extend into a historic burial ground (see the photos of the African burial ground in New York City, page 605). Alternatively, if a site must be destroyed, effective planning can ensure that information about the site is recovered by archaeologists prior to its destruction.

One of the most spectacular examples of salvage archaeology arose as a result of the construction of a dam across the Nile River at Aswan, Egypt, in the 1960s (Abu-Zeid and El-Shibini 1997; Stock 1993). The project offered many benefits, including water for irrigation and the generation of electricity. However, the rising water behind the dam threatened thousands of archaeological sites that had lain undisturbed and safely buried by desert sand for thousands of years. The Egyptian government appealed to the international community and archaeologists from around the world to mount projects to locate and excavate the threatened sites.

Among the sites that were to be flooded by the dam was the temple of Pharaoh Ramses II at Abu Simbel, a huge monument consisting of four colossal figures carved from a cliff face on the banks of the Nile River. With help from the United Nations Educational, Scientific, and Cultural Organization (UNESCO), the Egyptian government was able to cut the monument into more than a thousand pieces, some weighing as much as 33 tons, and reassemble them above the floodwaters. Today, the temple of Ramses can be seen completely restored only a few hundred feet from its original location. Numerous other archaeological sites threatened by the flooding of the Nile were partly salvaged or recorded. Unfortunately, countless other sites could not be recorded or even identified before they were flooded.

Cultural Resource Management in the United States The first legislation in the United States designed to protect historic sites was the Antiquities Act of 1906, which safeguarded archaeological sites on federal lands (see Table 25.1). Other, more recent legislation, such as the National Historic Preservation Act passed in

Located just blocks from Wall Street in New York City, an eighteenth-century African burial ground was accidentally uncovered during construction of a federal office building in 1991. The 427 burials excavated at the site are testament to the enslaved Africans that made up the second largest slave population in colonial America. As many as 20,000 individuals may have been buried at the site. Following discovery, local community protests over the treatment and interpretation of the remains led to a delay in construction, modification of the construction plan, and the increased involvement of African-American researchers in the analysis of the finds.
Source: Courtesy of the General Services Administration.

1966, has extended protection to sites threatened by projects that are funded or regulated by the government. The federal Abandoned Shipwreck Act of 1988 gives states jurisdiction over shipwreck sites (King 2000, 2007, 2013). This legislation has had a dramatic impact on the number of archaeologists in the United States. Whereas most archaeologists had traditionally found employment teaching or working in museums, today a large proportion find employment in cultural resource management and are employed by federal, state, and local agencies, and private companies. Applied archaeologists conduct surveys before construction begins to determine if any sites will be affected. Government agencies such as the United States Forest Service have developed comprehensive programs to discover, record, protect, and interpret archaeological resources on their lands (Johnson and Schene 1987).

Unfortunately, current legislation in the United States leaves many archaeological resources unprotected. In many countries, excavated artifacts, even those located on privately owned land, become the property of the government. This is not the case in the United States. One example of the limitations of the existing legislation is provided by the case of Slack Farm, located near Uniontown, Kentucky (Arden 1989). Archaeologists had long known that an undisturbed Native American site of the Late Mississippian period was located on the property. Dating

roughly to between 1450 and 1650, the site was particularly important because it was the only surviving Mississippian site from the period of first contact with Europeans. The Slack family, who had owned the land for many years, protected the site and prevented people from digging (Arden 1989). When the property was sold in 1988, however, conditions changed. Anthropologist Brian Fagan described the results:

> *Ten pot hunters from Kentucky, Indiana, and Illinois paid the new owner of the land $10,000 for the right to "excavate" the site. They rented a tractor and began bulldozing their way through the village midden to reach graves. They pushed heaps of bones aside and dug through dwellings and potsherds, hearths, and stone tools associated with them. Along the way, they left detritus of their own—empty pop-top beer and soda cans—scattered on the ground alongside Late Mississippian pottery fragments. Today Slack Farm looks like a battlefield—a morass of crude shovel holes and gaping trenches. Broken human bones litter the ground, and fractured artifacts crunch underfoot. (1988:15)*

The looting at the site was eventually stopped by the Kentucky State Police, using a state law that prohibits the desecration of human graves. Archaeologists attempted to salvage what information was left, but there is no way of knowing how many artifacts were removed. The record of America's prehistoric past was irrevocably damaged.

Table 25.1 Major Federal Legislation for the Protection of Archaeological Resources in the United States

Antiquities Act of 1906	Protects sites on federal lands
Historic Sites Act of 1935	Provides authority for designating National Historic Landmarks and for conducting archaeological surveys before destruction by development programs
National Historic Preservation Act of 1966 (amended 1976 and 1980)	Strengthens protection of sites via the National Register and integrates state and local agencies into a national program for site preservation
National Environmental Policy Act of 1969	Requires all federal agencies to specify the impact of development programs on cultural resources
Archaeological Resources Protection Act of 1979	Provides criminal and civil penalties for looting or damaging sites on public and Native American lands
Convention on Cultural Property of 1982	Authorizes U.S. participation in the 1970 UNESCO conventions to prevent illegal international trade in cultural property
Cultural Property Act of 1983	Provides sanctions against the U.S. import or export of illicit antiquities
National Museum of the American Indian Act of 1989	Established the National Museum of the American Indian as part of the Smithsonian Institution; required the Smithsonian to inventory Indian and Native Hawaiian human remains and funerary objects in its collections, and to consider the repatriation of these items
Native American Graves Protection and Repatriation Act (NAGPRA) of 1990	Requires federal agencies and institutions that receive federal funding to return Native American cultural items to lineal descendants and culturally affiliated Indian tribes and Native Hawaiian organizations

Source: From *Discovering Our Past: A Brief Introduction to Archaeology* by Wendy Ashmore and Robert J. Sharer. Copyright ©1988 by Mayfield Publishing Company. Reprinted by permission of the publisher.

Regrettably, the events at Slack Farm are not unique. Many states lack adequate legislation to protect archaeological sites on private land. For example, Arkansas had no laws protecting unmarked burial sites until 1991. As a result, Native American burial grounds were systematically mined for artifacts. In fact, one article written about the problem was titled "The Looting of Arkansas" (Harrington 1991a). Although Arkansas now has legislation prohibiting the unauthorized excavation of burial grounds, the professional archaeologists of the Arkansas Archaeological Survey face the impossible job of trying to locate and monitor all of the state's archaeological sites. This problem is not unique. On federal lands, the protection of sites is dependent on a relatively small number of park rangers and personnel to police large areas. Even in national parks, such as Mesa Verde or Yellowstone, archaeological sites are sometimes vandalized or looted for artifacts. Much of the success in protecting sites is largely due to the active involvement of amateur archaeologists and concerned citizens who bring archaeological remains to the attention of professionals.

The preservation of the past needs to be everyone's concern. Unfortunately, however well-intentioned the legislation and efforts to provide protection for archaeological sites may be, they are rarely integrated into comprehensive management plans. For example, a particular county or city area might have a variety of sites and resources of

historic significance identified using a variety of different criteria and presented in various lists and directories. These might include National Historic sites designated through the National Historic Preservation office; state files of archaeological sites; data held by avocational archaeological organizations and clubs; and a variety of locations of historical importance identified by county or city historical societies. Other sites of potential historical significance might be identified through documentary research or oral traditions. Ideally, all of these sources of information should be integrated and used to plan development. Unfortunately, such comprehensive approaches to cultural resource management plans are rare rather than the norm.

Important strides have been taken in planning and coordinating efforts to identify and manage archaeological resources. Government agencies, including the National Park Service, the military, and various state agencies, have initiated plans to systematically identify and report sites on their properties. There have also been notable efforts to compile information at the county, state, and district levels. Such efforts are faced with imposing logistical concerns. For example, by the mid-1990s, over 180,000 historic and prehistoric archaeological sites had been identified in the American Southeast (including the states of Alabama, Arkansas, Florida, Georgia, Kentucky, Louisiana, Mississippi, North Carolina, South Carolina, and Tennessee). In addition, an estimated 10,000 new sites are discovered each year (Anderson and Horak 1995). A map of these resources reveals a great deal of variation in their concentration. On one hand, this diversity reflects the actual distribution of sites; on the other, it reflects the areas where archaeological research has and has not been undertaken. Incorporating the thousands of new site reports into the database requires substantial commitment of staff resources. What information should be recorded for each site? What computer resources are needed? The volume of information is difficult to process with available staff, and massive backlogs of reports waiting to be incorporated into the files often exist. Nevertheless, this kind of holistic perspective is needed to ensure effective site management and the compliance of developers with laws protecting archaeological sites. It also provides a holistic view of past land use that is of great use to archaeologists.

Cultural Resource Management in Global Perspective

Cultural resource management is a worldwide concern, particularly in developing countries that often lack legislation and resources to protect archaeological sites, but industrialized countries are faced with similar problems (Serageldin and Taboroff 1994; Schmidt and McIntosh 1996; Kankpeyeng and DeCorse 2004). On one hand, archaeological sites are looted for artifacts to be sold on the antiquities market. On the other hand, the priority given to development—including the construction of new housing, roads, and dams—often results in the destruction of archaeological sites. These facts are all the more troubling because some countries lack well-developed archaeological traditions, and the archaeological past will be gone before anyone has the opportunity to study it. To address these concerns, UNESCO launched the "World Decade for Cultural Development" in 1988, which emphasized the need to consider cultural resources planning in development (Serageldin and Taboroff 1994).

Development and the management of archaeological resources can go hand in hand. While the material traces of the past—including archaeological resources, historic buildings, and cultural sites—may be important in promoting cultural heritage and national identity, many governments have also started to realize the potential economic worth of effective cultural resource management. Cultural tourism, arising out of the human fascination with the past, has become a major revenue source for some nations. The treatment of cultural heritage as a commodity is most obvious in Western Europe and the United States, but many countries in Asia, South America, and Mesoamerica have also capitalized on their cultural patrimony (Layton 1989; Ekechukwu 1990; Bruner 1996a, b).

A number of archaeologists throughout the world are using their skills to both preserve archaeological sites and improve the lives of modern inhabitants of the communities where the sites are located. In countries such as Guatemala, the location of a number of spectacular Mayan ruins, archaeologists are increasingly integrating economic development and environmental preservation into their research programs. The ancient Mayan sites pose special conservation concerns because of their size. For example, Chocolá, the focus of research by American archaeologist Jonathan Kaplan, has more than 60 mounds, large irrigation systems, and numerous monuments (Bawaya 2005). Information from the site has shed insight into the origins of Mayan civilization. Yet the farmers of modern Chocolá, descendants of the ancient Maya, face poverty and disease. In the face of such modern needs, the preservation of ancient monuments and the surrounding environment is of limited concern.

The past cannot be preserved without addressing the concerns of the present. To address these problems, Kaplan has established a trash removal service, worked with an environmental scientist to improve drinking water, and developed plans for museums that might attract tourists and so stimulate economic development. He is also working with the local government officials on a plan that would allow farmers to swap land that includes important Mayan ruins for agricultural lands with no archaeological value. At El Pilar, another Mayan site, archaeologist Anabel Ford not only does archaeological excavations, but also directs efforts to help conserve the archaeological sites and the surrounding forest. Straddling the Belize and Guatemalan border, the site of El Pilar is also one of the richest forest areas in the world. Ford hopes the archaeological field research and the data recorded on the tropical forest will heighten the awareness of local officials, tourism directors, and others in the region to improve conservation methods.

Another important series of archaeological projects in the Amazon area in South America has studied human impact on the environment. Archaeologists Thomas Neumann, Anna C. Roosevelt, Clark Erickson, and Peter Stahl, as well as anthropological botanist Charles R. Clement, discovered that the early Native American societies in this region not only had very large settlements—overturning earlier archaeological assessments that the Amazon did not support large civilizations—but also contributed new methods that may help conserve this fragile environment (Mann 2002). These early civilizations had extensive agricultural systems that were crippled with the advent of European colonialism. Research provides insight into how to restore the productivity of the land and enable more efficient land use in the future. Thus, applied archaeology can provide new knowledge that will enhance the conservation and preservation of different environments throughout the world. A broad holistic perspective involving teams of archaeologists and other scientists is needed to ensure effective site management and the compliance of developers with laws protecting archaeological sites. It also provides a holistic view of past land use that is of great use to archaeologists. Called "community" or "action" archaeology by some, engagement with local peoples' needs has become an increasing concern of archaeologists worldwide.

The Study of Garbage

The majority of archaeological research deals with the interpretation of past societies. Whether the focus is on the Stone Age inhabitants of Australia or the archaeology of nineteenth-century mining communities in the American West, the people being examined lived at a time somewhat removed from the present. There are, however, some archaeologists who are concerned with the study of the refuse of modern society and the application of archaeological methods and techniques to concerns of the present—and the future. The focus for these researchers is not the interpretation of past societies, but the immediate application of archaeological methods and techniques to the modern world. The topics examined range from the use of archaeological data in marketing strategies to the best methods for marking nuclear waste sites. Archaeologists who routinely examine artifacts thousands of years old can, for example, provide important perspectives of the suitability of different materials and strategies that can be used to bury nuclear waste (Kaplan and Mendel 1982).

One of the more interesting examples of this kind of applied archaeology is *Le Projet du Garbage*, or the Garbage Project, that grew out of an archaeological method and theory class at the University of Arizona in 1971 (Rathje and Ritenbaugh 1984; Rathje 1992). Archaeologists William L. Rathje and Fred Gorman were so intrigued by the results of the student projects that they established the Garbage Project the following year, and the project is still going. The researchers gather trash from households with the help of the city of Tucson sanitation foremen, who tag the waste with numbers that allow the trash bags to be identified with specific census tracts within the city. The trash bags are not associated with particular households, and personal items and photographs are not examined. Over the years, research has been broadened to the study of trash from other communities, including Milwaukee, Marin County, and Mexico City, and also to the excavation of modern landfills in Chicago, San Francisco, and Phoenix, using archaeological methods.

Archaeological study of modern garbage has provided important insights into waste management procedures, marketing, food wastage, and recycling.

The Garbage Project has provided a surprising amount of information on a diversity of topics. On one hand, the study provides data that are extremely useful in monitoring trash disposal programs. As Rathje observed, study of waste allows the effective evaluation of current conditions, the anticipation of changing directions in waste disposal, and, therefore, more effective planning and policy making (1984:10). Reviewing data on the project, Rathje noted a number of areas in which this archaeological research dispelled some common notions about trash disposal and landfills. Despite common perceptions, items such as fast-food packaging, polystyrene foam, and disposable diapers do not account for a substantial percentage of the content of landfills. Rathje observed:

> Of the 14 tons of garbage from nine municipal landfills that the Garbage Project has excavated and sorted in the past five years, there was less than a hundred pounds of fast-food packaging—that is, containers or wrappers for hamburgers, pizzas, chicken, fish and convenience-store sandwiches, as well as the accessories most of us deplore, such as cups, lids, straws, sauce containers, and so on. (Rathje 1992:115)

Hence, fast-food packaging makes up less than one-half of one percent of the weight of landfills. The percentage by volume is even lower. Rathje further noted that despite the burgeoning of materials made from plastic, the amount of plastic in landfills has remained fairly constant since the 1960s, or even decreased. The reason for this, he believes, is that while more things are made of plastic, many objects are now made with less plastic. A plastic milk bottle that weighed 120 grams in the 1960s weighs 65 grams today.

Rathje found that the real culprit in landfills remains plain old paper. A year's subscription to *The New York Times* is roughly equivalent to the volume of 18,660 crushed aluminum cans or 14,969 flattened Big Mac containers. While some predicted that computers would bring about a paperless office, the photocopier and millions of personal printers ensure that millions of pounds of paper are discarded each year: "Where the creation of paper waste is concerned, technology is proving to be not so much a contraceptive as a fertility drug" (Rathje 1992:116). He also observed that despite popular perception, much of the paper in landfills is not biodegrading. Because of the limited amount of moisture, air, and biological activity in the middle of a landfill, much of the nation's newsprint is being needlessly preserved for posterity. Recycling paper products is a simple and cost effective alternative.

The Garbage Project has also provided information on a diversity of issues connected with food waste, marketing, and the disposal of hazardous materials. In these studies, archaeology has provided a unique perspective. Much of the available data on such topics has typically been provided by questionnaires, interviews, and data collection methods that rely on the cooperation of informants. The problem is that informants often present biased responses, consistently providing lower estimates of the alcohol, snack food, or hazardous waste that they dispose of than is actually the case. Archaeology, on the other hand, presents a fairly impartial material record. While there are sampling problems in archaeological data—some material may be sent down the garbage disposal and not preserved in a landfill—the material record can provide a fairly unambiguous record of some activities.

The Garbage Project has examined the discarding of food and food waste for the U.S. Department of Agriculture; the recycling of paper and aluminum cans for the Environmental Protection Agency; studies of candy and snack food consumption for dental associations and manufacturers; and the impact of a new liquor store on alcohol consumption in a Los Angeles neighborhood. In the latter case, researchers conducted both interviews and garbage analysis before and after the liquor store opened. The interview data suggested no change in consumption patterns before and after the store's opening. Study of the trash, however, showed a marked increase in the discard of beer, wine, and liquor cans and bottles. Studies such as these have wide applications for both marketers and policy makers.

Who Owns the Past?

25.5 Discuss the meaning of "cultural patrimony" and the role of NAGPRA legislation in the United States.

A critical issue for modern archaeologists and physical anthropologists is **cultural patrimony**—that is, who owns the human remains, artifacts, and associated cultural materials that are recovered in the course of research projects. Are they the property of the scientists who collected or excavated them? The descendants of the peoples discovered archaeologically? The owners of the land on which the materials were recovered? Or the public as a whole? Resolution of this issue has at times been contentious, and the position taken by anthropologists has not always been the best. Prior to the twentieth century, laws governing the deposition of antiquities were nonexistent or unclear, and the "owner" often became the person, institution, or country with the most money or the strongest political clout. Colonial governments amassed tremendous collections from their territories throughout the world; the spoils of war belonged to the victors. Such a position remained the norm until after the turn of the century. Rights of conquest were only outlawed by the Hague Convention of 1907 (Shaw 1986; Fagan 1992).

Prior to the twentieth century, there was also little or no legislation governing human remains. Researchers appropriated excavated skeletal material, medical samples, and even cadavers of the recently deceased (Blakely and Harrington 1997). Native American remains from archaeological sites were displayed to the public, despite the fact that some of the descendant communities found such displays inappropriate or sacrilegious. Scientific value was the underlying rational for ownership, though until the latter half of the twentieth century there was little discussion of this issue. As in the case of antiquities, value and ownership were vested in the politically stronger, whether a colonial government or the politically enfranchised within a country. Such remains had scientific value, and this was viewed as more important than the interests of other groups or cultural values.

Ironically, such views would seem to fly in the face of some of the basic tenets of modern anthropology, which underscore sensitivity and openness to other cultural perspectives and beliefs. In fact, archaeological resources and human remains at times do provide unique, irreplaceable information that cannot be obtained through any other source. Archaeologists and physical anthropologists have provided information extremely important in documenting the past of Native Americans and indigenous peoples throughout the world, at times serving to underscore their ties to the land and revealing forgotten cultural practices. But what is the cost of such information if the treatment and methods of obtaining the artifacts and remains are abhorrent to the populations whose history is represented? Researchers of the present cannot afford to ignore the views and concerns of the focus of their research.

Recognition of the validity of different concerns and perspectives of cultural patrimony has not made resolution of debate easier. Artifacts now in museums were, in some instances, obtained hundreds of years ago in ways that were consistent with the moral and legal norms of that time (see the box "The Elgin Marbles"). Many antiquities have legitimately changed ownership numerous times. Not infrequently, information about the original origins may be unclear, and there are differences of opinion or uncertainty about the cultural associations of some artifacts or cultural remains. These issues aside, there remain fundamentally different perspectives about the role of the descendant population.

Critical Perspectives

The Elgin Marbles

The story of the Parthenon sculptures—or Elgin Marbles as they came to be called—is a twisted tale of the nineteenth-century quest for antiquities, international politics, and the complexities of cultural heritage. The Parthenon, perched on a hilltop overlooking Athens, is a striking symbol of both ancient Greece and the modern Greek nation-state. It was built by the Greek ruler Pericles to commemorate the Greek victory over the Persians at Plataea in 479 B.C. A temple to Athena, the patron goddess of Athens, the Parthenon was deemed by Pericles to be one of the most striking edifices in the city. The Parthenon is clearly the most impressive of the buildings in the Acropolis, the cluster of classical structures that cover Mount Athena. It is regarded by some to be one of the world's most perfect buildings. The Parthenon was distinguished by a full surrounding colonnade, and the exterior walls were decorated with a processional frieze. The pediments, or peaked eaves, in the east and west also had exquisitely detailed sculptures.

The structure has endured for millennia, and it has come to embody classical civilization to the world. In recent years, the Parthenon has been the focus of several restoration efforts that have stabilized the structure, removed more recent additions, and replaced some of the fallen masonry.

The Parthenon still overlooks Athens, and hopefully it will for years to come. But while the Parthenon is

Two young horsemen join a procession of sculpted figures on the Parthenon frieze. The marbles were taken from Greece in the early nineteenth century and are now on display in the British Museum, London

an architectural treasure, today only traces of the magnificent art that once adorned it remain. Fragments of its frieze and sculptures are scattered in museums around the world. The largest collection is in the British Museum in London, where large portions of the Parthenon's frieze are displayed in a specially designed room. To understand why statuary of such clear cultural significance to Greece is to be found in England, one has to go back to the early nineteenth century and the exploits of Thomas Bruce, the seventh Earl of Elgin (Jackson 1992).

By the early nineteenth century, Britain was in the midst of a classical revival. The country's well-to-do traveled to Europe to visit the historic ruins of ancient Greece and Rome. The wealthier purchased statuary and antiquities for their estates. Patterns and illustrations from classical Greek and Roman motifs were reproduced and incorporated into architectural features, jewelry, and ceramic designs. Within this setting, Lord Elgin, a Scottish nobleman, set out to obtain sketches and casts of classical sculptures that might be used at his estate, then being built near the Firth of Forth.

In 1799, Elgin was appointed British ambassador to the Ottoman Empire, which extended over much of the eastern Mediterranean from Western Europe to Egypt. By the late eighteenth century, the Ottomans had ruled Greece for 350 years. A major military power and one-time master of the Mediterranean, the Ottomans have been viewed by historians in a variety of ways, but one thing is certain: They were not overly concerned with the glories of ancient Greece. During their rule the Parthenon was used as a mosque, then as an ammunition dump; also, various Turkish structures were built on the site. Much of the north colonnade was destroyed in the Venetian bombardment of 1687. Some of the Parthenon marble was ground to make lime, and bits of statuary were broken off (Jackson 1992). In 1800, one of the world's most perfect buildings was in a sorry state.

Elgin initially proposed that the British government finance a survey of the art of the Acropolis as a resource for British art. When this initiative was turned down, Elgin made his own plans and contracted laborers. Initially, his workers were to make copies of the Parthenon sculptures. In 1801, however, Britain defeated Napoleon's forces in Egypt, saving the Ottoman Empire. Coincidentally, Elgin soon obtained a permit from the Ottomans not only to copy and make molds of the Parthenon art, but also to "take away any pieces of stone with old inscriptions or sculptures thereon" (Jackson 1992:137). During 1801 and 1802, scaffolding was erected, and hundreds of laborers went to work on the Parthenon with blocks and tackles and marble saws. Some sculptures broke or crashed to the ground. Twenty-two ships conveyed the marbles, loaded in hundreds of crates, back to England.

The marbles hardly proved to be good fortune for Elgin. The expense of obtaining them ruined his credit, and he discarded the idea of installing them at his estate. Totaling all of his expenses, Elgin estimated that he had spent over £60,000. To recoup his costs, he began negotiations for sale of the marbles to the government for display in the British Museum. After long parliamentary debate, they were sold for £35,000 in 1816. More than half of this amount went to clear Elgin's debt.

Elgin's treatment of the Parthenon's marbles had its contemporary critics. Among the most vocal opponents was none other than the Romantic poet and celebrator of Greek art and culture, Lord Byron, who immortalized the story of the Elgin marbles in the poems "Childe Harold's Pilgrimage" and "Curse of Minerva." Disgusted by what he saw as the desecration of the Parthenon, Byron asked by what right Elgin had removed these treasures of national cultural significance.

Greece gained independence from Turkey in 1830, and the Parthenon became integrally tied to the new nation's identity. The first restoration efforts began soon after independence. In the years since their installation in the British Museum, the ownership of the Parthenon's marbles and demands for their return have periodically been raised by Greeks and Britons alike, but to no avail. In the 1980s, then Greek Minister of Culture Melina Mercouri charged the British with vandalism and argued that the continued possession of the marbles by the British Museum was provocative. Although garnering substantial support from ministers of culture from around the world, these efforts also proved unsuccessful.

In his defense of his actions, Elgin pointed to the poor conditions of the Parthenon and the ill treatment that the sculptures had received. If left in place they would surely have continued to deteriorate. Why not remove them and have them cared for and appreciated by those who could afford to preserve them? Despite criticism, Elgin believed he was saving the sculptures from the ravages of time and neglect. Time has proven Elgin at least somewhat correct. The Parthenon continues to present a complex and continuous preservation problem. Time has ravaged the remains of the sculptures that were not removed, and deterioration of the monument accelerated rather than diminished throughout the twentieth century. Stonework and architectural detail have been eaten away by erosion, pollution, and acid rain, as well as by early and poorly conceived restoration efforts. As recently as 1971, a UNESCO report stated that the building itself was so weakened that it was in danger of collapse. Recent supporters of retaining the Elgin Marbles argue that they were obtained honestly with the permission of the government then in power. Other ancient Greek treasures, such as the Venus de Milo (currently on display in the Louvre in Paris), have also been removed from the country. Are these to be returned as well? For the time being it seems that the Elgin Marbles will remain in London.

Points to Ponder

1. Do you feel Elgin was right or wrong to remove the marbles?
2. Should the Elgin Marbles be returned to Greece? On what basis did you make your decision?
3. The conservation of the Parthenon and the preservation of the sculptures are valid concerns. How can these concerns be reconciled with the question of ownership?

Native American Graves Protection and Repatriation Act

The most important legislation affecting the treatment and protection of archaeological and physical anthropological resources in the United States is the Native American Graves Protection and Repatriation Act (NAGPRA), passed on November 16, 1990 (McKeown 1998). This legislation is the most comprehensive of a series of laws dealing with the deposition of Native American burials and cultural properties. NAGPRA and related legislation require that federal institutions consult with the lineal descendants of Native American groups and Native Hawaiians prior to the initial excavation of Native American human remains and associated artifacts on federal or tribal lands. Under this legislation, federal agencies and institutions receiving federal funding are also required to **repatriate**—or return—human remains and cultural items in their collections at the request of the descendant populations of the relevant Native American group. NAGPRA also dictates criminal penalties for trade in Native American human remains and cultural properties.

The impact of NAGPRA has been profound, not only on the way many archaeological projects are conducted, but also on the way in which museums and institutions inventory, curate, and manage their collections. The law has, at times, placed very different worldviews in opposition. For many Native Americans, the past is intricately connected to the present, and the natural world—animals, rocks, and trees, as well as cultural objects—may have spiritual meaning (Bataille et al. 2000; Rose et al. 1996). This perspective is fundamentally different from that of most museums, where both human remains and cultural artifacts are treated as nonliving entities, and the continuing spiritual links with the present are, at least at times, unrecognized. Museums are traditionally concerned with the collection and exhibition of objects. Reburial or repatriation of collections is the antithesis of their mission. As one scholar noted: "No museum curator will gladly and happily relinquish anything which he has enjoyed having in his museum, of which he is proud, which he has developed an affection for, and which is one of the principal attractions of his museum" (Shaw 1986:46). In a similar vein, reburial and repatriation may conflict with researchers' desire for complete analysis and study. The intersection of these varied interests is highlighted by ongoing debate about the treatment of skeletal remains (Bruning 2006).

NAGPRA and repatriation also raise pragmatic concerns. Return of objects or remains is dependent on a complete and accurate inventory of all of a museum's holdings. Yet, often museums have amassed collections over many decades, and detailed information on all of their collections may not exist or be readily accessible. A case in point is the collection of the Peabody Museum of Archaeology and Ethnology at Harvard University. Founded in 1866, the Peabody has a massive collection from all over the world, including substantial Native American and ancient Mesoamerican holdings. In the 1970s and 1980s, before the passage of NAGPRA, the museum repatriated several burials, collections, and objects at the request of various constituencies. NAGPRA spurred the museum to complete a detailed inventory. They found that the estimated 7,000 human remains in the collections grew to an inventory of about 10,000, while the number of archaeological objects grew from 800,000 to 8 million (Isaac 1995). Following NAGPRA guidelines, the Peabody sent out summaries of collections to the 756 recognized tribal groups in the United States. Determining the cultural affiliations, the relevant descendant communities, and

the need for repatriation of all of these items is a daunting task.

Many museums have undertaken major inventories, revamped storage facilities, and hired additional staff specifically to deal with the issue of repatriation. Impending repatriation of collections and human remains has also spurred many institutions and researchers to reexamine old collections. Such study is necessary to ensure that the presumed age and cultural attribution of individual remains are correct. Of course, all of these concerns have serious budgetary considerations.

While NAGPRA has produced conflicts, it has also both vastly increased the tempo of work on skeletal collections and provided an avenue for new cooperation between Native Americans and researchers. Many of the collections now analyzed would not have been examined if not for NAGPRA. Native claims will, in some instances, necessitate additional research on poorly documented groups. Indeed, anthropological or archaeological research may be critical to assessing the association and ownership of cultural materials and human remains. On the other hand, anthropologists are given the opportunity to share their discoveries with those populations for whom the knowledge is most relevant.

Applied Cultural Anthropology

25.6 **Discuss the applied aspects of cultural anthropology.**

Planning Change

Over the years, many applied cultural anthropologists have worked in helping to improve societies through planned change. To assist governments, private developers, or other agencies, applied anthropologists are hired because of their ethnographic studies of particular societies. Government and private agencies often employ applied anthropologists to prepare **social impact studies**, research on the possible consequences that change will have for a community. Social-impact studies involve in-depth interviews and ethnological studies in local communities to determine how various policies and developments will affect social life in those communities.

Thayer Scudder and Elizabeth Colson (1979) carried out a classic social-impact study in the African country of Zambia. Scudder and Colson had conducted long-term ethnographic research for about 30 years in the Gwembe Valley in Zambia. In the mid-1950s, the Zambian government subsidized the development of a large-scale dam, which would provide for more efficient agricultural activities and electrification. Because of the location of the dam, however, the people in the Gwembe Valley would be forced to relocate. Scudder and Colson used the knowledge from their long-term research and subsequent interviews to study the potential impact of this project on the community.

From their social-impact study, Scudder and Colson concluded that the forced relocation of this rural community would create extreme stresses that would result in people clinging to familiar traditions and institutions during the period of relocation. Scudder did social-impact studies of various societies in Africa experiencing forced relocation due to dams, highways, and other developments. These studies enabled Scudder and Colson to offer advice to the various African government officials, who could then assess the costs and benefits of resettling these populations and could plan their development projects, taking into consideration the impact on the people involved.

Applied anthropologists often serve as consultants to government organizations, such as the U.S. Agency for International Development (USAID), that formulate policies involving foreign aid. For example, anthropologist Patrick Fleuret (1988), a full-time employee of USAID, studied the problems of farmers in Uganda after the downfall of Idi Amin in 1979. Fleuret and other USAID anthropologists discovered that on the heels of the political turmoil in Uganda, many of the peasants retreated into subsistence production, rather than participating in the market economy. They also found that subsistence production was affected by a technological problem—a scarcity of hoes for preparing the land for cultivation. In response, USAID anthropologists helped design and implement a system to distribute hoes through local cooperative organizations.

The plan for the distribution of hoes reflected the development of new strategies on the part of USAID and the facilitator role for applied anthropologists. Most of the development work sponsored by USAID and applied anthropology in the 1950s and 1960s was aimed at large-scale development projects such as hydroelectric dams and other forms of mechanized agriculture and industrialism. Often these huge projects were devised in terms of the modernization views proposed by economists such as Walt Rostow (see Chapter 20) and were designed to shift an underdeveloped country to industrialism very rapidly. However, many of these large-scale projects have resulted in unintended negative consequences. These projects often resulted in large public debt, economic inefficiencies, costly pollution, the erosion of sustainable agricultural production, and the massive disruption of local communities.

Most recently, USAID and applied anthropologists have modified their policies on development projects in many less-developed countries. They now focus on projects that involve small-scale economic change with an emphasis on the development of appropriate technologies. Rather than relying upon large-scale projects to have "trickle-down" influences on local populations, applied anthropologists have begun to focus more realistically on determining where basic needs must be fulfilled. After assessing the needs of the local population, the applied anthropologist can help facilitate change by helping people learn new skills.

The Vicos Project One early project that placed applied anthropologists in decision-making and analytical roles was run by Allan Holmberg of Cornell University. In the 1950s and 1960s, Holmberg and Mario Vásquez, a Peruvian anthropologist, developed what is known as the Vicos Project in the Andean highlands. Vicos is the name of a *hacienda* that was leased by Cornell in 1952 as part of a program to increase education and literacy, improve sanitation and health care, and teach new agricultural methods to the Andean Indians. Prior to the Vicos Project, the 1,700 Quechua-speaking Indians were peasant farmers who were not able to feed themselves. Their land on the *hacienda* was broken into small plots that were insufficient to raise potato crops. The Indians were indebted to the *hacendado* and were required to work on the *hacendado's* fields without pay to service their debts.

The anthropologists paid Indians for their labor and introduced new varieties of potatoes, fertilizers, and pesticides. New crops such as leafy vegetables and foods such as eggs and fruit were also introduced into their diet. Although the anthropologists took on the role of a new patron to the Indians, the overall aim was to dissolve historical patterns of exploitation and to guide the Indians toward self-sufficiency (Holmberg 1962; Chambers 1985, Isbell 2013). Through an educational program, the Indians became acquainted with forms of representative democratic organization. Developing more independence, they eventually overturned the traditional authority structure of the *hacienda*. In 1962, the Indians purchased the land of the *hacienda* from its former owners, which gave the Indians a measure of self-sufficiency. Overall, the Vicos Project led to basic improvements in housing, nutrition, clothing, and health conditions for the Indians. The most significant achievement of the project was to improve the education of the Indian peasants. Currently over 30 percent of the Vicos people are studying in postsecondary institutions (Isbell 2013). This educational background enabled the Vicos people to negotiate with outside agencies and to articulate their needs and demands clearly. It has enhanced their sense of empowerment and self-sufficiency. One of the other major contributions of the Vicos project was to make the subjugation of the Indian peasants by the *hacienda* system widely known (Isbell 2013).

Anthropologists at Work

JOHN MCCREERY: Applying Anthropology in Japan

This chapter has some examples of anthropologists who work outside the academic setting. John McCreery is an anthropologist who has lived in Japan since 1980 and has developed a productive and fruitful career in the area of advertising. For a number of years, he worked as a copywriter and creative director for Hakuhodo Incorporated, Japan's second largest advertising agency. In 1984, he and his wife and business partner, Ruth McCreery, founded The Word Works, a supplier of translation, copywriting, and presentation support services to Japanese and other clients with operations in Japan. While earning his living as vice president and managing director of The Word Works, he is also a lecturer in the Graduate Program in Comparative Culture at Sophia University in Tokyo. There, he teaches seminars on "The Making and Meaning of Advertising" and "Marketing in Japan." When asked, "How did an anthropologist get into advertising?" he replies, "In Taiwan I studied magicians. In Japan I joined the guild."

As an undergraduate in the honors college at Michigan State University, McCreery studied philosophy and medieval history. In the summer after his junior year, a friend recommended that he take a course in East African

ethnography taught by anthropologist Marc Swartz. The course and the thought of doing research that involved travel to exotic places were fascinating to McCreery. Another friend was studying Chinese, and noting that an anthropologist should have some experience with a non-Indo-European language, McCreery decided to study Chinese as well. As a result, he attended graduate school at Cornell University, doing a Ph.D. in anthropology and preparing to do research in Chinese anthropology. McCreery's first field research was in Puli, a market town in central Taiwan, where he and Ruth McCreery lived and worked from September 1969 to August 1971. He returned to Taiwan in 1976–1977, the summer of 1978, and again in 1983.

At Cornell, McCreery studied with Victor Turner. In Taiwan, McCreery focused his ethnographic study on religious traditions and worked with a Daoist master, Tio Se-lian. Both Victor Turner and Tio Se-lian were teachers with a willingness to listen, a flair for the dramatic, a passion for detail, and a breadth of humanity that moved all those with whom they came in contact. They, and senior creative director Kimoto Kazuhiko, who shared these earlier mentors' traits and gave McCreery his job at Hakuhodo, are the models he tries to emulate in his work.

McCreery's essays on Chinese religion and ritual have appeared in *The Journal of Chinese Religions* and the *American Ethnologist*. He is also the

John McCreery

author of a book, *Japanese Consumer Behavior: From Worker Bees to Wary Shoppers* (2000), which follows the trends in postindustrial Japan that have resulted in new consumption preferences and behaviors for Japanese men, women, and young people. Currently, he is involved in a long-term study combining social network analysis (SNA) with historical and ethnographic research (HER), exploring the world of top Japanese advertising creators. McCreery and his wife, Ruth, have completed a major comprehensive chapter evaluating the prehistory, language, history, and current cultural changes in Japan based on state-of-the-art anthropological research in a textbook on the *Peoples and Cultures of Asia* (Scupin 2006a). McCreery maintains his contact with other anthropologists through an Internet listserve, Anthro-list, the Savage Minds and PopAnth blogs, and the Open Anthropology Cooperative online forum. As a student you may want to check out these online opportunities.

Engaged Anthropology Problems sometimes arise between applied anthropologists and private developers or government officials, many of whom want to induce modernization and social change as rapidly as possible with capital-intensive projects, hydroelectric dams, and manufacturing facilities. In many cases, anthropologists recommend against these innovations because of their expense and inefficient use of labor resources and the heavy cost to communities.

In Chapter 20, we discussed the tragic consequences of globalization for many indigenous societies. In 1972,

the late David Maybury-Lewis established an advocacy organization called Cultural Survival, which is actively engaged in trying to reduce the costs imposed by globalization on small-scale societies. Driven by trade deficits and gigantic foreign debts, many governments in developing countries want to extract as much wealth as possible from their national territories. Highway expansion, mining operations, giant hydroelectric projects, lumbering, mechanized agriculture, and other industrial developments all intrude on the traditional lifestyle and territory of small-scale societies. Applied anthropologists

Many cultural anthropologists are applying their knowledge of culture to assist people and solve problems throughout the world.

connected with groups such as Cultural Survival try to obtain input from the people themselves and help them represent their interests to the government or private developers.

Maybury-Lewis (1985) admitted that the advocacy role in anthropology was extremely difficult and requires great sensitivity and complex moral and political judgments. Most recently, many small-scale societies and minority groups in developing countries are organizing themselves to represent their own interests. This diminished the role of the applied anthropologist as advocate or representative. Generally, anthropologists are pleased when their role as advocate or representative is diminished because this role is called for only when native people are dominated by forces from globalization that are beyond their control.

In a new volume titled *Toward Engaged Anthropology*, a number of anthropologists advocate applied approaches that involve using the theories and methods within anthropology to partner with the people studied to reduce inequities and other injustices (Beck and Maida 2013). The authors of this book promote "a kind of anthropology . . . in which partnerships, collaborations, and mutuality are central to the work, and local stake holders co-produce knowledge by providing their wisdom and expertise, even in co-authorship" (Beck and Maida 2013:8). In the volume, Thomas Hylland Eriksen describes how Norwegian anthropologists have done studies on the ethnic minority, the Sami. Their efforts with these nomadic pastoralists who herd reindeer have resulted in an indigenous rights movement, legislation on land tenure, and the formation of a Sami parliament with some political autonomy in their regions (2013). Partnerships among anthropologists and the people studied in order to improve environmental, economic, social, and political conditions is the major goal of applied anthropology.

Applied Anthropology and Human Rights

25.7 Discuss how applied anthropologists are engaged in human rights research.

Cultural Relativism and Human Rights

A recent development that has had wide-ranging consequences for applied anthropology and ethnographic research involves the ways in which anthropologists assess and respond to the values and norms of other societies. Recall our discussion of *cultural relativism*, the method used by anthropologists to understand another society through their own cultural values, beliefs, norms, and behaviors. In order to understand an indigenous culture, the anthropologist must strive to temporarily suspend judgment of that culture's practices (Maybury-Lewis 2002). Anthropologists refer to this as *methodological relativism* (Brown 2008). While difficult, this procedure does help the anthropologist gain insights into that culture. However, some critics have charged that anthropologists (and other people) who adopt this position cannot (or will not) make value judgments concerning the values, norms, and practices of any society. If this is the case, then how can anthropologists encourage any conception of human rights that would be valid for all of humanity? Must anthropologists accept such practices as infanticide, caste and class inequalities, slavery, torture, and female subordination out of fear of forcing their own values on other people?

Relativism Reconsidered These criticisms have led some anthropologists to reevaluate the basic assumptions regarding cultural relativism. In his 1983 book *Culture and Morality: The Relativity of Values in Anthropology*, Elvin Hatch recounted the historical acceptance of the cultural-relativist view. As we saw in Chapter 13, this was the approach of Franz Boas, who challenged the unilineal-evolutionary models of nineteenth-century anthropologists like E. B. Tylor, with their underlying assumptions of Western cultural superiority. Boas's approach, with its emphasis on tolerance and equality, appealed to many liberal-minded Western scholars. For example, the earlier nineteenth-century ethnocentric and racist assumptions held within anthropology were used at the 1904 World's Fair in St. Louis to display other peoples as barbaric, uncivilized, and savage people to the "civilized" citizens who viewed them. These "pygmies" from Central Africa were given machetes to show how they "beheaded" one another in their local regions, and the Igorot tribal people of the Philippines were given a dog to cook and eat daily in front of the "civilized" citizens of the United States in order to portray them as inferior races and cultures (Breitbart 1997). Such displays of these peoples during that period both distorted their

1904 World's Fair in St. Louis showing "pygmies" beheading one another. This was never an aspect of "pygmy" culture.

cultural practices and allowed *anthropologists* of the time to treat them in an inhumane and unethical manner; they also resulted in harmful practices toward these native peoples in different regions. Thus, the criticisms of these racist and ethnocentric views and the endorsement of cultural relativism were important human rights innovations by twentieth-century anthropologists. In addition, many Westerners were stunned by the horrific events of World War I and the devastation and massive casualties for people within Western societies that were supposedly morally and culturally superior to other, non-Western societies. Cultural relativism appealed to many people in the West as a corrective to the earlier racist and ethnocentric views (Hatch 1983; Brown 2008).

Ethical Relativism However, belief in cultural relativism led to the acceptance by some early-twentieth-century anthropologists of moral or **ethical relativism**, the notion that we cannot impose the values or morality of one society on other societies. Ethical relativists argued that because anthropologists had not discovered any universal moral values, each society's values were valid with respect to that society's circumstances and conditions. No society could claim any superior position over another regarding ethics and morality.

As many philosophers and anthropologists have noted, the argument of ethical relativism is a circular one that itself assumes a particular moral position. It is, in fact, a moral theory that encourages people to be tolerant toward all cultural values, norms, and practices. Hatch notes that in the history of anthropology many who accepted the premises of ethical relativism could not maintain these assumptions in light of their data. Ethical relativists would have to tolerate practices such as homicide, child abuse, human sacrifice, torture, warfare, racial discrimination, and even genocide. In fact, even anthropologists who held the ethical relativist position in the early period of the twentieth century condemned many cultural practices. For example, Ruth Benedict condemned the practice of

the Plains Indians to cut off the nose of an adulterous wife. Boas himself condemned racism, anti-Semitism, and other forms of bigotry. Thus, these anthropologists did not consistently adhere to the ethical relativist paradigm.

The horrors associated with World War II eventually led most scholars to reject ethical relativism. The argument that Nazi Germany could not be condemned because of its unique moral and ethical standards appeared ludicrous to most people. In the 1950s, some anthropologists such as Robert Redfield suggested that general standards of judgment could be applied to most societies. However, these anthropologists were reluctant to impose Western standards on pre-state indigenous societies. In essence, they suggested a *double standard* in which they could criticize large-scale, industrial state societies but not pre-state indigenous societies.

This double standard of morality poses problems, however. Can anthropologists make value judgments about homicide, child abuse, warfare, torture, rape, and other acts of violence in a small-scale society? Why should they adopt different standards in evaluating such behaviors in pre-state indigenous societies as compared with industrial state societies? In both types of societies, human beings are harmed. Do not all humans in all societies have equal value?

A Resolution to the Problem of Relativism Is there a resolution to these philosophical and moral dilemmas? First, we need to distinguish between *cultural relativism* (or *methodological relativism)* and *ethical relativism*. In other words, to understand the values, the reasoning and logic, and the worldviews of another people does not mean to accept all of their practices and standards (Salmon 1997). Second, we need to realize that the culture of a society is not completely homogeneous or unified. In Chapter 10, we noted how culture was distributed differentially within any society. All people do not share the same culture within any society. For example, men and women do not share exactly the same "culture" in a society. Ethnographic experience tells anthropologists that there are always people who may not agree with the content of the moral and ethical values of a society. Treating cultures as "uniform united wholes" is a conceptual mistake. For one thing, it ignores the *power relationships* within a society. Elites within a society can maintain cultural hegemony or dominance and can use harmful practices against their own members to produce conformity. In some cases, governments use the concept of relativism to justify their repressive policies and deflect criticism of these practices by the international community. In Asia, many political leaders argue that their specific culture does not have the same notion of human rights that is accepted in Western society. Therefore, in China or Singapore, human rights may be restricted by political rulers who draw on their cultural tradition to maintain repressive and totalitarian political policies (Ong 2006; Brown 2008). Those who impose these harmful practices upon others may be the beneficiaries of those practices.

To get beyond the problem of ethical relativism, we ought to adopt a humanitarian standard that would be recognized by all people throughout the world. This standard would not be derived from any particular cultural values—such as the U.S. Declaration of Independence—but rather would involve the basic principle that every individual is entitled to a certain standard of "well-being." No individual ought to be subjected to bodily harm through violence or starvation.

Of course, we recognize certain problems with this solution. Perhaps, the key problem is that people in many societies accept—or at least appear to accept—behaviors that Westerners would condemn as inhumane. For example, what about the Aztec practice of human sacrifice? The Aztecs firmly believed that they would be destroyed if they did not sacrifice victims to the Sun deity. Would an outside group have been justified in condemning and abolishing this practice? A more recent case involves the West Irian tribe known as the Dani, who engaged in constant warfare with neighboring tribes. They believed that through revenge they had to placate the ghosts of their kin who had been killed in warfare because unavenged ghosts bring sickness and disaster to the tribe. Another way of placating the ghosts was to bring two or three young girls related to the deceased victim to the funeral site and chop two fingers off their hands. Until recently, all Dani women lost from two to six fingers in this way (Heider 1979; Bagish 1981). Apparently, these practices were accepted by many Dani males and females.

In some Islamic countries, women have been accused of sexual misconduct and then executed by male members in what are called "honor killings." The practice of honor killings, which victimizes women, has been defended in some of these groups as a means to restore harmony to the society. The males argue that the shedding of blood washes away the shame of sexual dishonor. There have been a number of "honor killings" among immigrant Middle Eastern families within the United States. In both Africa and the Middle East, young girls are subjected to female circumcision, a polite term for the removal of the clitoris and other areas of the vagina. These practices, referred to by most human rights advocates as female genital mutilation/cutting (FGM or FGC), range from the cutting out of the clitoris to a more severe practice known as pharaonic infibulation, which involves stitching the cut labia to cover the vagina of the woman. One of the purposes of these procedures is to reduce the pleasure related to sexual intercourse and thereby induce more fidelity from women in marriage. Chronic infections are a common result of this practice. Sexual intercourse is painful, and childbirth is much more difficult for many of these women. However, the cultural ideology may maintain that an uncircumcised woman is not respectable, and few families want to risk their daughter's chances of marriage by not having her circumcised (Fluehr-Lobban 2003, 2013).

The right of males to discipline, hit, or beat their wives is often maintained in a male-dominated culture (Tapper and Tapper 1992–1993). Other examples of these types of practices, such as head-hunting, slavery, female subordination, torture, and unnecessarily dangerous child labor, also fall into this category. According to a universal humanitarian standard suggested here, all of these practices could be condemned as harmful behaviors.

The Problem of Intervention

The condemnation of harmful cultural practices with reference to a universal standard is fairly easy. The abolition of such practices, however, is not. Anthropologists recommend that one should take a pragmatic approach in reducing these practices. Sometimes intervention in the cultures in which practices such as genocide are occurring would be a moral imperative. This intervention would proceed not from the standpoint of specific Western values, but from the commonly recognized universal standards of humanitarianism.

Such intervention, however, must proceed cautiously and be based on a thorough knowledge of the society. Ethnographers must gather empirical knowledge, studying the history, local conditions, social life, and various institutions, and assess carefully whether the cultural practice is shown to clearly create pain and suffering for people. For example, in Thailand, many young women are incorporated into the prostitution and sex tourist industry to help increase their parents' income (Barmé 2002). This prostitution and sex tourist industry must be thoroughly understood within the historical, economic, and cultural context of Thai society prior to endorsing a human rights intervention that would abolish these practices. When such understanding is present, intervention should take place by engaging in a form of dialogue, rather than by preaching human rights in a monolithic manner to various people in the community.

In a recent ethnographic study of the attempt to abolish FGM in the Darfur region of the Sudan, anthropologist Ellen Gruenbaum focused on seven different communities to investigate how the UN agencies, the nongovernment organizations, and other human rights agencies are influencing these practices (2004). Gruenbaum found that at times women were participating in the FGM practices such as the pharaonic infibulation because they "perceived" them as a means of protection against rape and illicit premarital intercourse within their communities. Rape is often used in these communities as a means of warfare. Thus, the historical and cultural context of these practices needs to be investigated cautiously by anthropologists prior to advocating a rapid enforcement of human rights that may result in outright rejection of the dedicated human rights workers (Shweder 2003, 2013).

As is obvious, these suggestions are based on the highly idealistic standards of a universal humanitarianism. In many cases, intervention to stamp out a particular cultural practice may not be possible, and in some cases, it may cause even greater problems. In Chapter 20, we saw how outside global intervention adversely affected such peoples as the Ju/'hoansi, Mbuti, Yanomamö, and Native Hawaiians. Communal riots, group violence, or social chaos may result from the dislocation of certain cultural practices. Thus, caution, understanding, and dialogue are critical to successful intervention. Anthropologists need to be sensitive to cultural differences but not allow them to produce severe harm to individuals within a society.

Universal Human Rights

The espousal of universally recognized standards to eradicate harmful practices is a worthwhile, albeit idealistic goal. Since the time of the Enlightenment, Western societies have prided themselves on extending human rights. Many Western theorists emphasize that human rights have spread to other parts of the world through globalization, thus providing the catalyst for social change, reform, and political liberation. At the same time, as people from non-Western societies can testify, the West has also promoted intolerance, racism, and genocide. Western society has not always lived up to the ideals of its own tradition.

The Role of Applied Anthropology in Human Rights   Cultural anthropologists and applied anthropologists have a role in helping to define the universal standards for human rights in all societies. By systematically studying community standards, applied anthropologists can determine whether practices are harmful and then help provide solutions for reducing these practices. This may involve consultation with local government officials and dialogue with members of the community to resolve the complex issues surrounding the identified harmful customs. The exchange of ideas across cultures through anthropological research is beginning to foster acceptance of the universal nature of some human rights regardless of cultural differences.

A good illustration of this type of research and effort by applied anthropologists is the work of John Van Willigen and V. C. Channa (1991), who have done research on the harmful consequences of the dowry in India. As discussed in Chapter 22, India, like some other primarily agricultural societies, has the cultural institution known as the *dowry*, in which the bride's family gives a certain amount of cash or other goods to the groom's family upon marriage. Recently, the traditions of the dowry have led to increasing cases of what has been referred to as "dowry death" or "bride burning." Some husbands or their families have been dissatisfied with the amount of the dowry

that the new wife brings into the family. Following marriage, the family of the groom begins to make additional demands for more money and goods from the wife's family. These demands result in harassment and abuse of the wife, culminating in her murder. The woman is typically doused with kerosene and burned to death, hence the use of the term *bride burning*.

Dowry deaths have increased in recent years. In 1986, 1,319 cases were reported nationally in India. There are many other cases in which the evidence is more ambiguous, however, and the deaths of these women might be reported as kitchen accidents or suicides (Van Willigen and Channa 1991). In addition, the burdens imposed by the dowry tradition have led many pregnant women to pay for amniocentesis (a medical procedure to determine the health status of the fetus) as a means to determine the sex of the fetus. If the fetus is female, in many cases Indians have an abortion, partly because of the increasing burden and expense of raising a daughter and developing a substantial dowry for her marriage. Thus, male children are preferred, and female fetuses are selectively aborted.

Van Willigen, an American anthropologist, and Channa, an Indian anthropologist, studied the dowry problem together. They found that the national law established against the institution of the dowry (the Dowry Prohibition Act of 1961, amended in 1984 and 1986) is very tough. The law makes it illegal to give or take a dowry, but the law is ineffective in restraining the practice. In addition, a number of public education groups have been organized in India. Using slogans such as "Say No to Dowry," they have been advertising and campaigning against the dowry practices. Yet, the problem continues to plague India.

After carefully studying the dowry practices of different regions and local areas of India, Van Willigen and Channa concluded that the increase in dowry deaths was partially the result of the rapid inflationary pressures of the Indian economy, as well as the demands of a consumer-oriented economy. Consumer price increases have resulted in increasing demands for more dowry money to buy consumer goods. It has become more and more difficult to save resources for a dowry for a daughter or sister that is substantial enough to satisfy the groom's family. Van Willigen and Channa found that aside from wealth, family "prestige" that comes with wealth expenditures is sought by the groom's family.

From the perspective of the bride's family, dowry payments provide for present consumption and future earning power for their daughter through acquiring a husband with better connections and future earning potential. In a developing society such as India, with extremely high unemployment rates and rapid inflation, the importance of investing in a husband with high future earning potential is emphasized. When asked why they give a dowry when their daughters are being married, people respond, "Because we love them." The decision by the groom's family to forgo the dowry would also be very difficult.

There appears to be a very positive commitment to the institution of the dowry in India. Most people have given and received a dowry. Thus, declaring dowry a crime technically makes many people criminals. Van Willigen and Channa recommended that to be effective, the antidowry practices must be displaced by other, less problematic practices and that the apparent causes of the practice must be attacked. Women's property rights must be examined so as to increase their economic access. Traditional Hindu cultural norms regarding inheritance, which give sons the right from birth to claim the so-called ancestral properties, must be reformed. At present, male descendants inherit property, but females must pay for marriage expenses and dowry gifts. Van Willigen and Channa assert that a gender-neutral inheritance law in which women and men receive equal shares ought to be established to help reduce the discrepancy between males and females in India.

In addition, Van Willigen and Channa recommended the establishment of universal marriage registration and licensing throughout India. This may enable the government to monitor dowry abuses so that antidowry legislation could be more effective. These anthropologists concluded that a broad program to increase the social and economic status of women, along with more rigorous control of marriage registration and licensing, would be more effective in solving the dowry death problem in Indian society.

The use of applied anthropology, based on collaboration among Western and non-Western anthropologists, government and military officials, economic consultants and advisors, and local and national government leaders, to help solve fundamental human rights issues represents a commendable strategy for applied anthropologists in the future. It is hoped that through better cross-cultural understanding aided by ethnographic research, and through applied anthropology, universally recognized humanitarian standards will be widely adopted throughout the world. Many anthropologists are promoting advocacy anthropology, the use of anthropological knowledge to further human rights. Universal human rights would include the right to life and freedom from physical and psychological abuse, including torture; freedom from arbitrary arrest and imprisonment; freedom from slavery and genocide; the right to nationality; freedom of movement and departure from one's country; the right to seek asylum in other countries because of persecution in one's own country; the rights to privacy, ownership of property, and freedom of speech, religion, and assembly; the right of self-determination; and the right to adequate food, shelter, health care, and education (Sponsel 1996). Obviously, not all these rights exist in any society at present. However, most people will probably agree that these rights ought to be part of any society's obligations to its people.

As the expansion of the global village brings people everywhere together different societies experience greater pressures to treat one another in sensitive and humane ways. We live in a world in which our destinies are intertwined more closely than they have ever been. Yet, it is a world containing many different societies with varied norms and practices. Sometimes, this leads to mutual distrust and dangerous confrontations, such as the 9/11 tragedy in the United States.

Anthropologists may be able to play a role in bringing about mutual understanding of others' rights to existence. Perhaps through this understanding, we may be able to develop a worldwide, pluralistic **metaculture**, a global system emphasizing fundamental human rights, with a sense of political and global responsibility. This cross-cultural understanding and mutual respect for human rights may be the most important aspect of anthropological research today.

Some rural East Indian women face human rights problems.

Critical Perspectives

Ethical Controversies in El Dorado

In earlier chapters, we discussed the ethnographic research conducted by Napoleon Chagnon on the Yanomamö tribe in the Amazon. In 2000, Patrick Tierney, an investigative journalist, published a book titled *Darkness in El Dorado: How Scientists and Journalists Devastated the Amazon*, in which he alleged that Chagnon and other anthropologists and scientists working among the Yanomamö had destroyed their communities. Tierney's book accused Chagnon and geneticist James Neel of seriously disrupting the Yanomamö society and in some cases, increasing death rates among these people. Tierney alleged that Neel improperly used a measles vaccine among the Yanomamö, resulting in a measles epidemic that caused "hundreds, perhaps thousands of deaths." Tierney suggested that Neel did this in order to experiment in a natural laboratory, the isolated Yanomamö, and to observe an epidemic for scientific reasons. In other words, Tierney accused Neel and his accomplice Chagnon of carrying out a dangerous campaign among these people. He also claimed that Neel was conducting secret radiation experiments among the Yanomamö.

Darkness in El Dorado also indicted Chagnon for nefarious misdeeds in his role as an anthropologist. Tierney argued that Chagnon staged warfare and violence among the Yanomamö for filmmaker Timothy Asch in order to project an image of a warlike, violent people. In addition, Tierney argued that Chagnon fraudulently manipulated his analysis of warfare and violence among the Yanomamö to support his sociobiological views about how violence and aggression are adaptively advantageous for males. Tierney went on to allege that Chagnon himself is directly or indirectly responsible for the endemic warfare found among the Yanomamö. Tierney suggested that by introducing trade items such as machetes, metal goods,

Napoleon Chagnon with a Yanomamö male.

and imported foods to these tribal people, Chagnon created conditions for competition among villages for these goods, and consequently this competition resulted in intergroup warfare and violence. Tierney argued that Chagnon perpetuated an image of the Yanomamö as a naturally violent and warlike people, and as a result of this stereotype, 40,000 gold miners invaded Yanomamö territory between 1980 and 1987. Additionally, he said that the military and government officials used violence against the Yanomamö to remove them from their land. Tierney also alleged that Chagnon colluded with some Venezuelan politicians to help them gain control of Yanomamö land in return for illegal gold mining concessions to benefit himself and some other wealthy interests.

Napoleon Chagnon earned his B.A., M.A., and Ph.D. degrees in anthro-

pology at the University of Michigan. After completing his Ph.D. in 1966, he joined the Department of Human Genetics at the University of Michigan Medical School and participated in a multidisciplinary study of the Yanomamö Indians of Venezuela and Brazil along with the geneticist James Neel. Chagnon returned to do fieldwork among the Yanomamö almost every year for 30 years beginning in 1964, enabling him to conduct a long-term, systematic study of change within this population. Chagnon's ethnographic studies and the many educational films that he and his colleague Timothy Asch have produced have made the Yanomamö well known around the world.

In a book about his fieldwork, *Studying the Yanomamö* (1974), Chagnon describes both his analytical techniques and his immersion into

Yanomamö society. Over the years, he has written dozens of books and hundreds of articles about Yanomamö society and culture. These books made him one of the most well-known anthropologists in the world. The books sold in the millions to anthropologists who used them in their courses.

Tierney's allegations about Chagnon and Neel created a well-publicized controversy that was carried internationally in leading newspapers, the Internet, and other media. The book led to a number of investigations and soul-searching among anthropologists. Many began to ask themselves if this book was going to unhinge their whole discipline. Immediately, the University of Michigan and the University of California at Santa Barbara (both of which helped sponsor Chagnon's research), as well as the National Academy of Sciences and the American Anthropological Association launched investigations into the possible malfeasance of Neel and Chagnon. Teams of researchers began to assess every one of the allegations that Tierney made and to follow up every claim and every footnote in his book.

The most serious allegation—that Neel had improperly introduced a measles vaccine that resulted in loss of life among the Yanomamö—has been thoroughly refuted by leading scientists who investigated Neel's medical documents concerning the vaccination process (Dreger 2011; Lancaster and Hames 2011). The co-developer of the actual measles vaccine, Dr. Samuel Katz, has stated that the vaccine was not virulent and, thus, could not cause measles and that it had never done so in millions of applications. In addition, researchers found medical reports stating that Brazilian missionaries had caused the initial measles outbreak among the Yanomamö in November 1967, prior to the Chagnon–Neel expedition in 1968. Chagnon, Neel, and the medical team were actively trying to vaccinate the population to reduce the incidence of measles. Through investigation of Neel's field journals and daily logs, the allegation that he was using radiation experiments among the Yanomamö was refuted as well.

Researchers also investigated Tierney's claims regarding Chagnon's misdeeds in his role as an anthropologist. Although Timothy Asch, the filmmaker, had died before the publication of Tierney's book, many of his assistants who had done research for and helped edit the films on the Yanomamö insist that the films were not staged productions, but rather were authentic portrayals of the life of these people.

Tierney's claim that Chagnon was directly or indirectly responsible for the endemic warfare among these people has also been examined carefully. Archaeologists have exhumed an enormous amount of evidence of warfare in this region of the Amazon, going back at least 3,500 years. They have found that missionaries and other explorers had been publishing accounts of warfare among the Yanomamö since the sixteenth century. The Yanomamö describe themselves as *waitiri*, which Chagnon translated as "fierce and valiant." Chagnon changed the title of later editions of *The Yanomamö: The Fierce People* to *The Yanomamö*, saying that sometimes this word for "fierce" in Portuguese and Spanish may have resulted in some erroneous stereotypes.

Tierney's thesis that Chagnon's characterization of these people as fierce and violent resulted in the gold miners' attacks and invasions is not valid when examined historically. The treatment of indigenous Native American peoples by gold miners during the gold rushes in California and in the Black Hills of the Dakota region parallels the behavior of the gold miners in the Amazon. These gold miners often brutalized Native Americans. It did not take an anthropological description to motivate these misbehaviors, just as it did not take Chagnon's depictions to motivate gold miners, the military, and government officials to invade, attack, and attempt to take over Yanomamö land (Dreger 2011; Lancaster and Hames 2011).

One of the negative consequences of the publication of Tierney's book is that politicians, scholars, and journalists in various countries have been calling for a boycott of further anthropological and medical research on populations in their regions. Without assessing Tierney's claims, many countries have declared their populations "off limits" to anthropological research or medical care from outsiders (Gregor and Gross 2004). Surely, this will have negative effects on the indigenous peoples who may be invaded by gold miners, be infected by diseases from the outside, and experience the downside of globalization, without having their conditions ameliorated or improved by research and medical care.

The allegations in Tierney's book have been completely refuted with the completion of the final report of the American Anthropological Association (AAA) in 2001. As anthropologists were shaken worldwide by Tierney's allegations, the AAA appointed a task force that assessed the ethics of anthropological research in light of these claims. The AAA emphasized that it was not condemning or finding fault with or defending the past actions of Chagnon or others; rather, it was providing opportunities for all anthropologists to consider the ethics of several dimensions of the anthropological enterprise.

This controversy has caused anthropologists to reflect deeply on the ways in which they conduct research. However, as the various investigations of the scientific and ethical controversy indicate, Tierney's book contains many unfounded, misrepresented, and sensationalistic accusations about the conduct of anthropology among the Yanomamö. These misrepresentations fail to live up to the ethics of responsible journalism even as they pretend to question the ethical conduct of anthropology.

Most contemporary cultural anthropologists have modified their research strategies. Chastened by some of the postmodern critiques about fieldwork in anthropology (see Chapter 13), anthropologists today are much more sensitive to their own political position and activities among the people they are studying. Presently, many of the native peoples have become educated, and some of them are actively engaged in ethnographic

(continued)

research themselves. Anthropologists today are active in obtaining informed consent from the people they are studying to avoid harmful research activity. In other words, the population being studied must have the right to approve the research project and withdraw from it if it is harmful to their interests (Couzin-Frankel 2010). Sometimes, this creates complications as anthropologists come across difficult ethical and political problems in their research locations. However, ethnographic research ought to be practiced in accord with the ethical principles espoused by the medical oath of the Hippocratic creed: "Do No Harm," as discussed in Chapter 14.

To be fair to Chagnon, over the years he developed many close ties and friendships among the Yanomamö and organized a Yanomamö survival fund to try to help protect these people from external forces that wanted to take their land (Dreger 2011; Lancaster and

Hames 2011). Chagnon has written a recent book *Noble Savages: My Life among Two Dangerous Tribes, the Yanomamö and the Anthropologists* (2013) defending his research and intended as a critique of those anthropologists who made invalid allegations against him. As this book indicates, if it were not for the thorough ethnographic research on the Yanomamö by Chagnon, we would probably not be aware of the conditions and problems that these people face today. Ethnographic research and anthropological explanations and interpretations have to proceed, despite the negative publicity that they sometimes entail. On the other hand, anthropologists must be aware of some of the unintended results of their research that can result in harm to the populations among whom they reside. Without anthropologists, we are not going to be able to gain a comprehensive picture of humanity's diversity throughout the world. But obtaining

that portrait inevitably offers ethical and political challenges for anthropologists who want to contribute towards science and the humanities, but also to help improve conditions for humanity across the world.

Points to Ponder

1. Can you think of any cases where popular portrayals of scientific research proved to be dramatically wrong?
2. Can ethnographic research be conducted without changing the circumstances of the people being studied?
3. How should contemporary anthropologists conduct their ethnographic fieldwork?
4. How do you weigh the moral claims versus the scientific research in this controversy?

Summary and Review of Learning Objectives

25.1 Describe the different roles of applied anthropologists.

Rather than being confined to the halls of a university, an increasing number of anthropologists have become practitioners of anthropology, actively engaging with the communities that they study and solving problems in the modern world. Applied anthropologists may be in a *representative* role in which the anthropologist becomes the spokesperson for the particular group being studied. They can also be seen as *facilitators*. In this capacity, anthropologists actively help bring about change or development in the community being researched. An alternative position is the *informant role*, in which the applied anthropologist transfers cultural knowledge obtained from anthropological research to the government or other agency that wants to promote change in a particular area. Another role of applied anthropologists is that of *analyst*. Rather than being just a provider of data, the practicing anthropologist sometimes becomes engaged in the actual formulation of policy. Applied anthropologists may serve as *mediators* as well, which involves the anthropologist as an intermediary among different interest groups that are participating in a development project.

25.2 Discuss the applied aspects of biological anthropology.

Biological anthropologists study the biological aspects of humans in the past and the present. This includes the measurement, observation, and explanation of various physical characteristics. Anthropometry, for example, concerns the measurement of human body parts, while osteometry is the measurement of skeletal elements. This information is important in studying human evolution and modern human variation. However, some of this research also has immediate relevance to the present. For example, biological anthropological data may be used by engineers to design ergonomically efficient work environments, airplane cockpits, or equipment. A specialized field within biological anthropology is forensic anthropology, which can be defined as the application of biological anthropological data to law. Researchers in this area of specialization assist police when unidentified human remains are found, including murder investigations and the identification of disaster victims. Biological anthropological study of the causes of diseases, when combined with knowledge of cultural anthropology, offers important insight into perceptions of medical treatment in different cultural settings.

25.3 Define medical anthropology and discuss some of the research undertaken.

The field of medical anthropology draws on cultural and biological anthropology, as well as the other subfields of anthropology and other disciplines. Medical anthropologists study disease, health-care systems, medical practices, curing, and mental illness with a cross-cultural perspective. They often work with physicians and other public health care workers to apply their knowledge about cultural practices in different setting to provide more effective health care. Medical anthropologists study ethnomedicine, which examines traditionally based medical practices of different ethnic groups. These studies reveal that beliefs about disease and illness and medical treatment vary in different societies throughout the world. The study of these beliefs and medical approaches can enable medical anthropologists to help deliver more effective health care. Medical anthropologists also do epidemiological studies to determine the links between social and cultural factors and specific diseases such as cardiovascular problems, diabetes, AIDS, and other illnesses. In addition, medical anthropologists study cultural aspects of mental illnesses. Though certain forms of mental illness such as schizophrenia and depression are universal, the cultural understandings and treatments of these mental illnesses vary.

25.4 Define cultural resource management and discuss the role of archaeologists in the field.

Cultural resource management (often referred to as CRM) focuses on the evaluation, protection, and supervision of cultural resources, including the archaeological record, as well as the arts, historic sites and cultural property. One of the problems that humanity faces is how to safeguard the cultural heritage preserved in the archaeological record. Although archaeology may address questions of general interest to all of humanity, it is also important in promoting national heritage, cultural identity, and ethnic pride. Museums the world over offer displays documenting diverse local populations, regional histories, important events, and cultural traditions. The number of specialized museums focusing on particular peoples, regions, or historic periods has become increasingly important. Yet, the archaeological record is being destroyed at an alarming rate. In many parts of the world, recognition of this fact has led to legislation aimed at protecting archaeological sites. Archaeologists must be concerned with the preservation of archaeological sites and the recovery of information from sites threatened with destruction, as well as the interpretation and presentation of their findings to the more general public. Many archaeologists now find employment as applied archaeologists, doing CRM evaluating, salvaging, and protecting archaeological resources that are threatened with destruction.

25.5 Discuss the meaning of "cultural patrimony" and the role of NAGPRA legislation in the United States.

The most important legislation affecting the treatment and protection of archaeological and physical anthropological resources in the United States is the Native American Graves Protection and Repatriation Act (NAGPRA), passed on November 16, 1990. This legislation is the most comprehensive of a series of laws dealing with the deposition of Native American burials and cultural properties. NAGPRA and related legislation require that federal institutions consult with the lineal descendants of Native American groups and Native Hawaiians prior to the initial excavation of Native American human remains and associated artifacts on federal or tribal lands. Under this legislation, federal agencies and institutions receiving federal funding are also required to repatriate—or return—human remains and cultural items in their collections at the request of the descendant populations of the relevant Native American group. NAGPRA also dictates criminal penalties for trade in Native American human remains and cultural properties.

25.6 Discuss the applied aspects of cultural anthropology.

To assist governments, private developers, or other agencies, applied anthropologists are hired because of their ethnographic studies of particular societies. Government and private agencies often employ applied anthropologists to prepare social-impact studies, research on the possible consequences that change will have for a community. Rather than relying upon large-scale projects to have "trickledown" influences on local populations, applied anthropologists have begun to focus more realistically on determining where basic needs must be fulfilled. After assessing the needs of the local population, the applied anthropologist can help facilitate change by helping people learn new skills. Partnerships among anthropologists and the people studied to improve environmental, economic, social, and political conditions is the major goal of applied anthropology

25.7 Discuss how applied anthropologists are engaged in human rights research.

Early cultural anthropologists who accepted the tenets of cultural relativism sometimes also embraced ethical relativism, the idea that a person could not make value judgments about other societies. Although most anthropologists reject ethical relativism, the issue of universal standards to evaluate values and harmful cultural practices is still problematic. Many applied anthropologists are engaged in research on harmful practices in order to help promote their prevention. Proposing universal standards by which to make value judgments and help reduce harmful cultural practices remains one of the most important tasks for applied anthropology and future ethnographic research.

Key Terms

applied anthropology, p. 594

cultural patrimony, p. 609

cultural resource management, p. 604

epidemiology, p. 600

ethical relativism, p. 616

ethnomedicine, p. 598

forensic anthropology, p. 595

medical anthropology, p. 598

metaculture, p. 619

repatriate, p. 611

social impact studies, p. 612

Glossary

acclimatization   The physiological process of being or becoming accustomed to a new physical environment.

Acheulean   One of the major stone tool traditions of the Lower Paleolithic (the Early Stone Age). The stone tool technology generally associated with *Homo erectus*.

achieved status   A status that results, at least in part, from a person's voluntary actions.

adaptation   The process in which an organism makes a successful adjustment to a specific environment.

adaptive radiation   The relatively rapid evolution of a species in a new environmental niche.

adjudication   The settling of legal disputes through a formal, centralized authority.

aerial photography   Photographs taken from the air of archaeological sites and the landscape. Helpful to archaeologists in mapping and locating sites.

age grades   Statuses defined by age through which a person moves in the course of his or her lifetime.

age sets   Corporate groups of people of about the same age who share specific rights, obligations, duties, and privileges in their community.

age stratification   The unequal allocation of wealth, power, and prestige among people of different ages.

agency   The process of intentional conscious (self-aware) choices that humans make that may alter their social or cultural world.

agribusiness   Commercialized, mechanized agriculture.

agricultural states   States in which the power of the ruling elite was vested in the control of agricultural surpluses. This type of control typifies early states.

alleles   The alternate forms of a gene.

ambilineal descent group   A social kinship group formed by choosing to trace relationships through either a male or a female line.

analogy   Similarities in organisms that have no genetic relatedness resulting from convergent evolution.

anatomically modern *Homo sapiens*   The most recent form of human, distinguished by a unique anatomy that differs from that of earlier, archaic *Homo sapiens*.

animism   The belief that the world is populated by spiritual beings such as ghosts, souls, and demons.

antiquaries   Collectors whose interest lies in the object itself, not in where the fossils might have come from or what the artifact and associated materials might tell about the people that produced them. Collectors of this kind characterized the early history of archaeology.

anthropology   The systematic study of humankind.

anthropomorphism   A psychological disposition to project and attribute human characteristics to nonhuman phenomena.

apartheid   A political, legal, and social system developed in South Africa in which the rights of different population groups were based on racial criteria.

applied anthropology   The use of data gathered from the other subfields of anthropology to find practical solutions to problems in a society.

arboreal   Living in trees.

archaeology   The subfield of anthropology that focuses on the study of the material remains past societies to determine the lifestyles, history, and evolution of those societies.

archaeological sites   Places of past human activity that are preserved in the ground.

archaic   A post-Pleistocene hunting-and-gathering adaptation in the Americas characterized by tools suitable for broad-spectrum collecting and more intensive exploitation of localized resources. Corresponds in terms of general trends with the Mesolithic of Europe.

archaic *Homo sapiens*   The earliest form of *Homo sapiens*, dating back more than 200,000 years.

art   A diverse range of activities and skills and the products of those activities that are used as expressions and representations of human emotions, intellect, and creativity.

artifacts   The material products of past societies.

artificial selection   The process in which people select certain plants and animals for breeding.

ascribed status   A status that is attached to a person from birth—for example, sex, caste, and race.

assimilation   The adoption of the language, culture, and ethnic identity of the dominant group in a society by other groups.

authority   Power generally perceived by members of society as legitimate, rather than coercive.

balanced polymorphism   The mixture of homozygous and heterozygous genes of a population in a state of equilibrium.

balanced reciprocity   A direct type of reciprocal exchange with an explicit expectation of immediate return.

band   The least complex and, most likely, the oldest form of a political system.

barter   The direct exchange of one commodity for another; it does not involve the use of money.

beliefs   Specific cultural conventions concerning true or false assumptions shared by a particular group.

bilateral descent   A descent system that traces relatives through both maternal and paternal sides of the family simultaneously.

biodiversity   The genetic and biological variation within and among different species of plants and animals.

biological assimilation   The process by which formerly distinct groups merge through marriage and reproduction.

biome   An area distinguished by a particular climate and certain types of plants and animals.

bipedalism   The ability to walk erect on two hind legs.

brideservice   A situation in which a male resides with his wife's family for a specified amount of time.

bridewealth   The transfer of some form of wealth from the descent group of the groom to that of the bride.

broad-spectrum collecting   The exploitation of varied food resources in local environments.

capitalism   An economic system in which natural resources, as well as the means of producing and distributing goods and services, are privately owned.

carrying capacity   The maximum population that a specific environment can support.

caste   An endogamous social grouping into which a person is born and in which the person remains throughout his or her lifetime.

catastrophism   A theory proposed by the French naturalist Georges Chrétien Léopold Frédéric Dagobert Cuvier (1769–1832) that suggests that the extinct species seen in the fossil record represent different episodes of divine creation and destruction.

central place theory   A theory developed by the German geographer Walter Christaller in the 1930s that suggests that, given uniform topography, resources and opportunities, the distribution of settlements within a region should be perfectly regular. Political and economic centers would be located an equal distance from one another, and each in turn would be surrounded by a hierarchical arrangement of smaller settlements, all evenly spaced. This theory has been used by archaeologists investigating the origins and development of early states.

chief   A person who owns, manages, and controls the basic productive factors of the economy and has privileged access to strategic and luxury goods.

chiefdom   A political system based on kinship that has a formalized and centralized leadership, headed by a chief.

childhood mortality rate   The number of children who die before reaching the age of five.

civilization   In anthropological literature, civilization is a term generally used to refer to a complex society associated with the origins of urbanization and state formation. However, various features have been used as defining characteristics, including some or all of the following: urban centers; food surpluses; specialized division of labor; sociopolitical stratification; monumental architecture; record-keeping systems; developments in arithmetic, geometry, and astronomy; sophisticated art; long-distance trade; and state level political organization. There is, however, no agreed-upon list of which of these features are the key defining characteristics of a civilization. For this reason, the term *civilization* is only used in a general way to indicate a complex society with some of the preceding features.

clan   A form of descent group in some societies whose members trace their descent to an unknown ancestor or, in some cases, to a sacred plant or animal.

clinal distribution   The distribution of a physical trait in a population, often plotted on maps by clines, or zones.

clines   The zones on a map used to plot physical traits of populations.

closed peasant communities   Indian communities in highland areas of Latin America that were isolated from colonialism and the market economy.

closed society   A society in which social status is generally ascribed, rather than achieved.

Clovis-first hypothesis   A theory that maintains that the Clovis culture represents the initial human settlement of the Americas.

cognitive anthropology   The study of human psychological thought processes based on computer modeling.

command economy   An economic system in which the political elite makes the decisions concerning production, prices, and trade.

communication   The act of transferring information.

complementary opposition   The formation of groups that parallel one another as political antagonists.

composite tools   Tools, such as harpoons or spears, made from several components.

conflict theories   Theories that argue that state-level organization is beneficial only to the ruling elite and is generally costly to subordinate groups such as the peasantry.

consumption   The use of goods and services to satisfy desires and needs.

context   The specific location in the ground of an artifact or fossil and all associated materials.

continental drift   The separation of continents that occurred over millions of years as a result of the geological process of plate tectonics.

continuous variation   A phenomenon whereby variation in a particular trait or characteristic cannot be divided into discrete, readily definable groups, but varies continuously from one end of the spectrum to the other.

cosmologies   Ideas that present the universe as an orderly system, including answers to basic questions about the place of humankind.

core societies   Powerful industrial nations that exercise economic hegemony over other regions.

correlation   The simultaneous occurrence of two variables.

cross-cousin   The offspring of one's father's sister or one's mother's brother.

crude birth rate   The number of live births in a given year for every 1,000 people in a population.

crude death rate   The number of deaths in a given year for every 1,000 people in a population.

cultivation   The systematic planting and harvesting of plants to support the subsistence activities of a population.

culture   A shared way of life that includes the material products and nonmaterial products (values, beliefs, and norms) that are transmitted within a particular society from generation to generation.

cultural anthropology   The subfield of anthropology that focuses on the study of contemporary societies.

cultural assimilation   The process by which an ethnic group adopts the culture of another ethnic group.

cultural ecology   The systematic study of the relationships between the environment and society.

cultural hegemony   The control over beliefs, values, and norms exercised by the dominant group in a society.

cultural materialism   A research strategy that focuses on technology, environment, and economic factors as key determinants in sociocultural evolution.

culture of poverty   The hypothesis that sets of values sustaining poverty are perpetuated generation after generation within a community.

cultural patrimony   The ownership of cultural properties such as human remains, artifacts, monuments, sacred sites, and associated cultural materials.

cultural relativism   The view that cultural traditions must be understood within the context of a particular society's responses to problems, cultural practices, and values.

culture shock   A severe psychological reaction that results from adjusting to the realities of a society radically different from one's own.

cultural universals   Essential behavioral characteristics of humans found in all societies.

cultural resource management   The attempt to protect and conserve artifacts and archaeological resources for the future.

culture   A shared way of life that includes material products, values, beliefs, and norms that are transmitted within a particular society from generation to generation.

cut marks   Marks left on bones as a consequence of stone tool use, distinct from marks that might be left by a predator's teeth or natural weathering.

datum point   A reference point in an archaeological excavation, often some permanent feature or marker, from which all measurements of contour, level, and location are taken.

deductive method   A method of investigation in which a scientist begins with a general theory, develops specific hypotheses, and tests them.

dendrochronology   A numerical dating technique based on the varying pattern of environmental conditions preserved in the annual growth rings of trees.

dentition   The number, form, and arrangement of teeth.

demographic transition   The decline of birth rates and death rates during later phases of industrialization.

demographic-transition theory   A model used to measure population trends within a society that assumes a close connection between fertility and mortality rates and socioeconomic development.

demography   The study of population and its relationship to society.

Denisovans, or the Denisova hominins   A previously unknown species or subspecies of hominin identified on the basis of genetic material recovered from hominin bones discovered in Denisova cave in Siberia, Russia. Mitochondrial DNA and genomic data from bones dating between 30,000 to 48,000 years ago revealed a genetic pattern unlike that found in either modern humans or Neandertals. Additional study of the nuclear genome suggests that the Denisovans share a common origin with Neanderthals, and that they interbred with the ancestors of modern-day Melanesians and Australian Aborigines. Additional study of the genomic data suggests interbreeding with another, unknown human lineage distinct from the Neandertals and modern humans.

deoxyribonucleic acid (DNA)   A chain of chemicals contained in each chromosome that produces physical traits that are transmitted to the offspring during reproduction.

dexterity   The flexibility and efficient use of the digits (fingers and toes) of the feet and hands. This is a key characteristic of the primates that allows them to grasp and manipulate objects.

dependency theory   The theory that underdevelopment in Third World societies is the result of domination by industrial capitalist societies.

dependent variable   A variable whose value changes in response to changes in the independent variable.

descent group   A social group identified by a person in order to trace his or her real or fictive kinship relationships.

developmental acclimatization   Permanent or nonreversible adaptation to specialized environmental conditions such as high altitude.

dialect   A linguistic pattern involving differences in pronunciation, vocabulary, or syntax that occurs within a common language family.

diffusionism   The spread of cultural traits from one society to another.

diurnal   Active during the day.

division of labor   The specialized economic roles and activities within a society.

domestication   The systematic, artificial selection of traits in plants or animals to make them more useful to human beings.

dominance hierarchy   The relative social status or ranking order found in some primate social groups.

dominant   The form of a gene that is expressed in a heterozygous pair.

doubling time   The period of time required for a population to double.

dowry   Goods and wealth paid by the bride's family to the groom's family.

drives   Basic, inborn biological urges that motivate human behavior.

dyadic contract   A reciprocal exchange arrangement between two individuals.

ecclesiastical religions   Religious traditions that develop in state societies and combine governmental and religious authority.

ecofacts   Archaeological finds that have cultural significance but that are not artifacts manufactured or produced by humans. Examples of ecofacts would be botanical, faunal, and shell remains recovered from an archaeological site.

ecology   The study of living organisms in relationship to their environment.

ecological niche   The specific environmental setting to which an organism is adapted.

economy   The social relationships that organize the production, exchange, and consumption of goods and services.

egalitarian   A type of social structure that emphasizes equality among different statuses.

ego   Freud's term to refer to the aspect of the personality that is displayed to other individuals.

emic perspective   The study of a culture from an insider's point of view.

embodied wealth   The physical or bodily health of individuals or groups.

enculturation   The process of social interaction through which people learn their culture.

endocast   The casts of the interior of the cranium, either natural or manmade, that provide a replica of the surface of the brain.

endogamy   Marriage between people of the same social group or category.

environmental niche   A locale that contains various plants, animals, and other ecological conditions to which a species must adjust.

epigenetic   Modifications that affect the expression of genes that are external to the DNA sequence.

epidemiology   The study of disease patterns in a society.

Epipaleolithic   The time period of about 14,000 years ago in the Near East when people begin to subsist on resources such as fish, small game, and wild plants, and become more sedentary and less nomadic.

ethical relativism   The belief that the values of one society should never be imposed on another society.

ethnic boundary marker   The distinctions of language, clothing, or other aspects of culture that emphasize ethnicity.

ethnic group   A group that shares a culture.

ethnicity   Cultural differences among populations, usually based upon attributes such as language, religion, lifestyle, and cultural ideas about common descent or specific territory.

ethnoarchaeology   The study of material artifacts of the past along with the observation of modern peoples who have knowledge of the use and symbolic meaning of those artifacts.

ethnocentrism   The practice of judging another society by the values and standards of one's own.

ethnocide   A process in which a dominant group or society forces other groups to abandon their traditional language and culture.

ethnogenesis   The emergence of a new ethnic group.

ethnography   A description of a society written by an anthropologist who conducted field research in that society.

ethnohistory   The study of the history of a particular ethnic group based on written documents or oral narratives.

ethnologist   An anthropologist who focuses on the cross-cultural aspects of ethnographic studies.

ethnology   The subfield of anthropology that focuses on the cross-cultural aspects of ethnographic studies.

ethnomedicine   The study and comparison of traditional spiritually based medical practices by different ethnic groups.

ethnomusicology   The study of musical traditions in different societies.

ethnonationalist movements   The process of emphasizing the cultural distinctions of a particular group for political purposes.

ethnopoetics   The study of the poetry traditions and practices in different societies.

ethologist   A scientist who studies the behaviors of animals in their natural setting.

etic perspective   The study of a culture from an outsider's point of view.

evolution   Process of change within the genetic makeup of a species over time.

evolutionary psychology   The study of the human mind using evolutionary findings.

exchange   The transfer of goods and services from one member of society to another.

exogamy   Marriage between people of different social groups or categories.

experimental studies   Studies involving the replication of tools or activities to infer how ancient tools may have been made and used.

extended family   A family that is made up of parents, children, and other kin relations bound together as a social unit.

family   A social group of two or more people related by blood, marriage, or adoption who live or reside together for an extended period, sharing economic resources and caring for their young.

faunal correlation   The dating of fossils through the comparison of similar fossils from better-dated sequences.

faunal succession   Literally, "animal" succession; recognizes that life-forms change through time. First noted by the English geologist William Smith.

features   Nonmovable artifacts or traces of past human activity such as an ancient fire hearth, a pit dug in the ground, or a wall.

fecundity   The potential number of children that women in a society are capable of bearing.

feminism   The belief that women are equal to men and should have equal rights and opportunities.

fertility   The number of births in a society.

feud   A type of armed combat within a political community.

feudalism   A decentralized form of political economy based on landed estates, which existed during different historical periods in agrarian societies.

fictive kinship ties   Extrafamilial social ties that provide mutual-aid work groups.

fission-track dating   A numerical dating method based on the decay of an unstable isotope of uranium. Used to date volcanic rocks.

First World   The sector of the global economy that is composed of modern industrialized capitalist societies.

fissioning   The moving of people from one group to another area when their population begins to increase and food or other resources become scarce.

flotation   A specialized recovery technique in archaeology in which material from an excavation is placed in water to separate soil from organic remains such as plants, seeds, and charcoal.

folkways   Norms guiding ordinary usages and conventions of everyday life.

foraging society   Another classification used for a hunting-and-gathering society.

foramen magnum   The opening in the base of the skull through which the spinal cord passes.

forensic anthropology   The identification of human skeletal remains for legal purposes.

fossil The remains of bones and living materials preserved from earlier periods.

fossil localities Places where fossils are found. These may be locations where predators dropped animals they killed, places where creatures were naturally covered by sediments, or sites where early humans or primates actually lived.

founder effect A type of genetic drift resulting from the randomly determined genetic complement present in the founders of an isolated population.

Fourth World Indigenous, native, or aboriginal societies.

functionalism An anthropological perspective based upon the assumption that society consists of institutions that serve vital purposes for people.

galactic polity A type of state that rules primarily through religious authorities and cosmologies.

gametes Sex cells (such as egg and sperm in humans). They contain only half of the chromosomes found in ordinary body, or somatic, cells.

gene flow The exchange of genes between populations as a result of interbreeding.

gene pool The total collection of all the alleles within a particular population.

generalized reciprocity A type of reciprocal exchange based upon the assumption that an immediate return is not expected and that the value of the exchange will balance out in the long run.

genes Discrete units of hereditary information that determine specific physical characteristics of organisms.

genetic drift Change in allele frequencies within a population as a result of random processes of selection.

gender Specific human traits defined by culture and attached to each sex by a society.

genocide The physical extermination of a particular ethnic group in a society.

genotype The specific genetic constitution of an organism.

geronticide The killing of old people.

gerontocracy Rule by elders (usually male) who control the material and reproductive resources of the community.

globalization The worldwide impact of industrialization and its socioeconomic, political, and cultural consequences on the world.

glocalization The incorporation of global factors into the local culture.

goods Elements of material culture produced from raw materials in the natural environment, ranging from the basic commodities for survival to luxury items.

greenhouse effect Global warming caused when carbon dioxide traps heat from solar rays, preventing it from radiating back into space.

Green Revolution The use of bioengineering and industrial technology for agricultural purposes.

hamula The Arabic term for a clanlike organization.

Hardy-Weinberg theory of genetic equilibrium An idealized mathematical model that sets hypothetical conditions under which no evolution is taking place. Developed independently by G. H. Hardy and W. Weinberg, the model is used to evaluate evolutionary processes operating on a population.

heterozygous Having two different alleles in a gene pair.

hierarchical society A society in which some people have greater access than others to wealth, rank, status, authority, and power.

hieroglyphic writing An early pictographic writing system in which symbols denoted the ideas and concepts. People in different parts of the world developed hieroglyphic systems independently of one another.

historical linguistics The comparison and classification of different languages to discern the historical links among them.

historical particularism An approach to studying human societies in which each society has to be understood as a unique product of its own history.

holistic A broad, comprehensive approach to the study of humankind drawing on the four subfields of anthropology and integrating both biological and cultural phenomena.

hominids In taxonomic classification, hominids (members of family Hominidae), is a term that was traditionally used to refer to bipedal apes, a group that represents humans and their immediate ancestors. This classification was revised on the basis of the genetic study of modern primates. Family *Hominidae* now includes subfamilies *Ponginae* and *Homininae*, while hominins (members of the tribe *Homininae*) is used to refer to humans and their immediate ancestors.

hominins In taxonomic classification, hominins refers to members of the Hominini tribe of subfamily *Homininae*, which includes humans and their immediate ancestors. Hominins share a number of distinctive characteristics, particularly bipedalism.

homology Traits that have a common genetic origin, but may differ in form and function.

homozygous Having the same alleles in a gene pair.

horticulture A form of agriculture in which people use a limited, nonmechanized technology to cultivate plants.

hunter-gatherer society A society that depends on hunting animals and gathering vegetation for subsistence.

hybridization and assimilation models Models of the evolution of anatomically modern humans that allow for varying degrees of gene flow between *Homo sapiens* and earlier populations of archaic *H. sapiens* via gene flow or genetic admixture.

hypodescent concept A system of racial classification in which children of mixed parentage acquire the social and racial status of the parent whose social and racial status is lower.

hypothesis A testable proposition concerning the relationship between different sets of variables within the collected data.

id Freud's term to refer to the unconscious, innate drives such as sex and aggression found in all humans.

ideal culture What people say they do or should do.

ideographic writing systems An early form of writing in which simple pictures are used to communicate ideas, an individual picture expressing each idea. In actuality, this system involves neither language nor writing.

ideology Cultural symbols and beliefs that reflect and support the interests of specific groups within a society.

imperialism The economic and political domination and control of other societies.

incest Sexual relations or marriage between certain relatives.

incest avoidance Avoidance of sexual relations and marriage with members of one's own family.

incest taboo Strong cultural norms that prohibit sexual relations or marriage with members of one's own family.

independent variable A causal variable that produces an effect on another variable, the dependent variable.

inductive method A method of investigation in which a scientist first makes observations and collects data and then formulates a hypothesis.

industrialization The use of machines and other sophisticated technology to satisfy the needs of society by transforming raw materials into manufactured goods.

industrial society A society that uses sophisticated technology based upon machinery powered by advanced fuels to produce material goods.

infanticide The deliberate abandonment or killing of infants one year of age or younger.

infant mortality rate The number of babies per thousand births in any year who die before reaching the age of one.

instincts Genetically-based innate behaviors that allow animals to take advantage of specific environments.

integrationist theories A variety of theories that argue that state organization is, on the whole, advantageous and beneficial to all members of a society.

intelligence The capacity to process information and adapt to the world.

intensive agriculture The cultivation of crops by preparing permanent fields year after year, often using irrigation and fertilizers.

intensive horticulture A method of crop production by irrigating, fertilizing, hoeing, and terracing hillsides.

jajmani **economy** The Hindi term for the traditional caste-based economy in India.

jati The Hindi term for *caste*.

jihad The Arabic term that refers to a "holy struggle" against the destroyer of one's own religion and culture.

Jim Crow laws The laws that were used to segregate African

Americans from white Americans in the southern United States prior to the civil rights era.

karma   The Hindu belief that the conditions of one's life are directly dependent upon an individual's actions in previous lives as a result of reincarnation.

kindred   Overlapping relatives from both sides of a family that an individual recognizes as being part of his or her descent group.

kinesics   The study of body motion and gestures used in nonverbal communication.

knowledge   The storage and recall of learned information based on experience.

knuckle walking   A distinctive type of quadrupedal locomotion. Knuckle walkers, such as the gorilla, rest their hands on the ground in a curled position, with the tops of their curled middle and index fingers bearing their weight.

kula   A form of reciprocal exchange involving ceremonial items in the Trobriand Islands.

lactase deficiency   The inability to digest lactose, the sugar found in milk.

language   A system of symbols with standard meanings through which members of a society communicate with one another.

law of supraposition   States that in any succession of rock layers, the lowest rocks were deposited first and the upper rocks have been in place for progressively shorter periods. This assumption forms the basis of stratigraphic dating.

Levalloisian technique   A refined type of percussion flaking used during the Middle Paleolithic.

levirate   The rule that a widow is expected to marry one of her deceased husband's brothers.

life expectancy   The number of years an average person can expect to live.

lineages   Descent groups composed of relatives, all of whom trace their relationship through consanguineal or affinal relations to an actual, commonly known ancestor.

linguistic anthropology   The subfield of anthropology that focuses on the study of language.

linguistics   The study of language.

logic-of-growth model   The model and set of values that suggest that economic growth and technological developments will always represent progress for society.

logographic writing systems   Writing systems that use pictures or symbols to represent individual words or concepts, also sometimes referred to as ideographic writing systems. These systems can be contrasted with other writing systems that represent sounds, which are then used in combinations to construct words.

Lower Paleolithic   The earliest stage of the Stone Age characterized by the Oldowan and Acheulean stone tool industries, roughly spanning the period between 2.4 million and 200,000 years ago and including the tools produced by pre-*Homo sapiens* hominins.

mana   The Polynesian term referring to supernaturally significant powers.

marginal environment   An environment that is not suitable for intensive agriculture.

market economy   A pattern of economic exchange based on the value of goods and services determined by the supply and demand of these items.

marriage   A social bond sanctioned by society between two or more people that involves economic cooperation, social obligations, and culturally approved sexual activity.

material culture   Tangible products of human society.

matrilineal descent group   A social descent group whose members calculate descent through the female line from a commonly known female ancestor.

matrilocal residence   A rule of postmarital residence under which a man resides with his wife's parents.

medical anthropology   The study of disease, health care systems, and theories of disease and curing in different societies.

megaliths   Large stone complexes such as those found at Stonehenge that were used for burial chambers or astronomical observations. Such structures are the principal defining characteristic of the Megalithic, a Neolithic tradition found in Western Europe and Britain.

meiosis   The process by which gametes, which contain only half the number of chromosomes present in the original cell, are formed.

mercantilism   A system in which the government regulates the economy of a state to ensure economic growth, a positive balance of trade, and the accumulation of wealth, usually gold and silver.

Mesolithic   A post-Pleistocene hunting-and-gathering adaptation following the Paleolithic characterized by tools suitable for broad-spectrum collecting and more intensive exploitation of localized resources. Corresponds in terms of general trends with the Archaic of the Americas.

metaculture   A global system of values that transcends any particular culture.

microliths   Small flakes of stone probably used for harpoon barbs and specialized cutting tools during the Mesolithic.

middens   Ancient dumps or trash heaps.

Middle Paleolithic   The Middle Stone Age of the Paleolithic, characterized by innovations in tool technology, particularly the Levalloisian technique. Dated to approximately 200,000 to 40,000 years ago and associated with archaic *Homo sapiens*.

migration rate   The rate at which people move into and out of a specific territory.

mitosis   The process by which somatic cells divide to produce new cells with the full number of chromosomes present in the original cell.

modernization   Economic, social, political, and religious changes related to modern industrial and technological developments.

moieties   Descent groups made up of clans or phratries that divide the entire society into two equal divisions.

moksha   The release of one's soul from the cycles of birth, death, and rebirth or reincarnation, the ultimate goal of Hindus.

money   A durable medium of exchange, based upon a standard value that is used to purchase goods and services.

monocultural dependency   A form of political economy that depends on one major resource or crop for export to the world market.

monogamy   A form of marriage that involves two individuals.

monopoly capitalism   A form of capitalism dominated by oligopolies that can reduce free competition through the concentration of capital.

moral economy   An economy that involves reciprocity and redistribution among close kin and other villagers in a society.

mores   Stronger norms than folkways; violators are usually punished severely.

morphemes   The smallest units of a language that convey meaning.

morphology   The study of morphemes.

mortality   The incidence of death in a society's population.

Mousterian tradition   A Middle Paleolithic stone tool tradition associated with Neandertals in Europe.

mujahidin   The Arabic term for *holy warrior*.

multiculturalism   Policies adopted by governments to be inclusive to multiple ethnic groups within a society.

multilineal evolution   The view that societies and cultures have evolved and are evolving in many different directions.

multinational corporation   A transnational economic organization that operates in many different regions and is not necessarily associated with any one country.

multiregional evolutionary model   The view that *Homo sapiens* evolved from *Homo erectus* concurrently in different regions of the world.

multivariate analysis   A complex form of analysis that examines the distributions and interrelations among multiple variables or characteristics as, for example, patterns of disease, blood groups, and demographics in human populations.

music   An art form that is based on the organization of sounds in combination and in temporal relationships to produce audible works for performance in various communities.

mutations   A change in the genotype of an individual through the alteration of the chromosomes or DNA.

myth   Assumed knowledge about the universe and the natural and supernatural worlds and about humanity's place therein.

narrative   The oral or written representation of an event or a story.

nationalism   A strong sense of loyalty to the nation-state based on shared language, values, and culture.

nation-states Political communities that have clearly defined territorial borders with centralized authority.

natural selection A theory presented by Darwin and Wallace that nature or environmental circumstances determine which characteristics are essential for survival. Individuals with these characteristics survive and pass them on to their offspring.

negative reciprocity The opposite of reciprocity, involving getting something for nothing.

neoliberalism A post-Cold War philosophical and political theory that emphasizes the development of capitalist, nongovernmental, market-based strategies for economic development throughout the world.

Neolithic Literally the "New Stone Age," it was first categorized by polished stone tools. Later, it came to refer to the shift from food gathering to food production, as well as a suite of other characteristics and cultural features such as sedentary village life, animal husbandry, and pottery production. Though the term is still used, this package of characteristics is clearly not associated in many cultural settings.

net migration The total movement of a population into and out of a territory.

nirvana The Buddhist term for spiritual enlightenment and awareness.

nocturnal Active during the night.

nonmaterial culture Intangible products of human society, including values, beliefs, and norms.

norms Shared rules that define how people are supposed to behave under certain circumstances.

nuclear family A family that is composed of two parents and their immediate biological offspring or adopted children.

oath An attempt to call on a supernatural source of power to sanction and bear witness to the truth or falsity of an individual's testimony.

office A formal position of authority in a group or society.

Oldowan Industry The oldest stone tool industry and one of the major industries of the Lower Paleolithic (the Old Stone Age). It includes simple choppers and utilized flakes.

oligopoly The result when economic organizations merge and dominate within an economy.

one-drop rule The American social and legal custom of classifying anyone with one black ancestor, regardless of how far back, as black.

omnivorous Possessing a diverse, generalized diet consisting of plants, fruits, nuts, seeds, insects, and animals.

open peasant communities Communities in which peasants are involved in producing some of their crops for the world market.

open society A society in which social status can be achieved through individual efforts.

opposable thumb A highly flexible thumb that can touch the tips of the fingers; it is characteristic of the human primate.

oracle A person, sacred object, or shrine believed to have special or supernatural abilities.

paleoanthropology The study of human evolution through the analysis of fossil remains.

paleoecology *Paleo*, meaning "old," and *ecology*, meaning "study of environment." The area of research focusing on the reconstruction and interpretation of ancient environments.

paleoethnobotany The field of study that specializes in the interpretation of the relationship between plants and ancient human populations.

Paleolithic Literally meaning the "Old Stone Age," the Paleolithic refers to the archaeological periods principally represented by stone tools. It is generally divided into the Lower, Middle, and Upper Paleolithic, based on innovations in methods of stone tool manufacture and the appearance of new tool types. These periods are also referred to as the Early, Middle, and Late Stone Age in some world areas.

palynology The study of pollen grains, the minute male reproductive part of plants. It may provide a means of reconstructing past environments and of relative dating.

parallel-cousin marriage A system in which a person marries the offspring of a parental sibling of the same sex; for example, a male marries his father's brother's daughter.

participant observation The method used by the ethnographer who learns the culture of the group being studied by participating in the group's daily activities.

pastoralists Groups whose subsistence activities are based on the care of domesticated animals.

patriarchal Male-dominated.

patrilineal descent group A social group made up of people who trace their descent through males from a common, known male ancestor.

patrilocal residence A postmarital residence rule under which a newly married couple must reside with the husband's father.

patron-client ties Informal contracts between people of unequal status.

peasants People who cultivate land in rural areas for their basic subsistence and pay tribute to elite groups.

peripheral societies Societies that have very little control over their own economies and are dominated by the core industrial societies.

percussion flaking The production of tools by striking a stone with a hammerstone or other strong object to remove chips or flakes.

personality Stable patterns of thought, feeling, and action associated with a specific person.

phenotype The external, observable physical characteristics of an organism that result from the interaction of the organism's genetic makeup (the genotype) and its distinctive life history.

phoneme A basic unit of sound that distinguishes meaning in a language.

phones Units of sound in a language.

phonology The study of the sounds made in speech.

phratries Umbrella-like social groupings that consist of two or more clans.

phyletic gradualism The theory that speciation is a gradual process of evolution that occurs very slowly as different populations become isolated. It was originally proposed by Charles Darwin.

plate tectonics The gradual movement of plates on the Earth's surface as a result of geological processes, one consequence of which is the movement of continents or continental drift.

plural society A society made up of different ethnic groups.

political power The ability to achieve personal ends despite opposition.

polyandry Marriage between one wife and two or more husbands.

polygamy Marriage involving a spouse of one sex and two or more spouses of the opposite sex.

polygyny Marriage between one husband and two or more wives.

polymorphism A trait that exhibits variation within a species.

polytypic A species exhibiting physical variation in different regional populations.

population A group of organisms that interbreeds and occupies a given territory at the same time.

postindustrial society A society in which the tertiary or service sector of the economy predominates.

postmodernism A viewpoint that is critical of modern scientific and philosophical perspectives.

postorbital constriction A feature of *Homo erectus* in which the front portion of the skull is narrow and the forehead is low.

potassium-argon dating A numerical dating method based on the decay of an unstable isotope of potassium into the inert gas argon. It is used by paleoanthropologists to date volcanic rocks.

potlatch A form of redistributional exchange found among many Northwest Native American groups.

pragmatics The rules for using language within a particular speech community.

pre-Clovis hypothesis The hypothesis that the initial settlement of the Americas took place prior to the arrival of the populations represented by Clovis spear points and associated artifacts.

priest A full-time, formally trained, male religious specialist.

priestess A full-time, formally trained, female religious specialist.

primary sector The sector of an industrial economy that is devoted to the extraction of natural resources.

primates A diverse order of mammals, including humans, monkeys, and apes, that share similar characteristics.

primatology The study of primates.

primogeniture An inheritance pattern in which land or other wealth is transmitted from generation to generation through the eldest male.

production The organized system for the creation of goods and services.

prosocial norms   Cultural rules that promote cooperation, trust, and altruism within societies.

protolanguage   The parent language for many ancient and modern languages.

proton magnetometer   A sensor that can detect differences in the soil's magnetic field caused by buried features and artifacts.

prototypes   Initial classifications of the world that help the human mind organize external reality.

proxemics   The study of how people in different societies perceive and use space.

psychological anthropologist   An anthropologist who studies the interrelationship between the individual and culture, or the process of enculturation.

pull factors   The incentives that lead people to move to other societies.

punctuated equilibrium   The theory of evolution that species remain relatively stable for long periods, with major changes (punctuations) and new species arising very rapidly as a result of mutations or changes in selective pressures.

purdah   The Arabic term for the seclusion of women from men.

push factors   The conditions that lead people to leave specific territories.

quadruped   An animal, especially a mammal, that walks on all fours.

qualitative data   Nonstatistical information that tends to be the most important aspect of ethnographic research.

quantitative data   Data that can be expressed as numbers, including census materials, dietary information, and income and household-composition data.

racism   Beliefs and practices that advocate the superiority of certain races and the inferiority of others.

radial polity   A state that rules more directly through government and military officials that have more centralized control over various provinces and regions.

radiocarbon dating   A numerical dating technique based on the decay of the unstable isotope carbon-14. Can be used to date organic material such as charcoal, wood fragments, or skeletal material as much as 80,000 years old.

random sample   A representative sample of people of various ages or statuses in a society.

real culture   People's actual behaviors, as opposed to ideal culture.

recessive   Designating a gene that is unexpressed when occurring in a heterozygous pair with a dominant form.

reciprocal economic system   A system based upon transactional exchanges among family groups that allocate goods and services throughout the community.

reciprocity   The sharing of goods and services among people.

redistributional economic exchange   A system that involves the exchange of goods and resources through a centralized organization.

regional symbiosis   The pattern in which a particular society resides in an ecological habitat divided into different resource areas that become interdependent.

relational wealth   Kinship networks and alliances that can provide success for individuals or groups.

relative dating   A variety of dating methods that can be used to establish the age of a fossil, artifact, or geological feature relative to another.

relative deprivation   A group's awareness that it lacks economic opportunities and political rights for its members in contrast to other groups.

repatriation   The return of human remains or cultural property to a descendant community or interest group.

replacement model   The paleoanthropological theory that *Homo sapiens* evolved in one world area and then expanded, replacing regional populations of earlier hominids.

research design   A proposal in which the objectives of a project are set out and the strategy for recovering the relevant data is outlined.

resistivity   A subsurface detection method that identifies buried archaeological features. Measurement of variation in the electrical current passing between electrodes placed in the ground indicates variation in conductivity, which in turn is an indication of buried ditches, foundations, or walls that retain moisture to varying degrees and have varying degrees of conductivity.

revolution   A sudden, dramatic, fundamental change that usually involves the overthrow of a government.

rising expectations   The process in which a particular group begins to experience improvements in living conditions, stimulating the desire for further improvements.

rites of legitimation   Rituals that reinforce the divine authority of a ruler.

rites of passage   Rituals associated with the life cycle and the movement of people between different age-status levels.

rituals   Repetitive behaviors that communicate sacred symbols to members of a society.

role   A set of expected behavior patterns, obligations, and norms attached to a particular status.

sagittal crest   A bony ridge along the top of the skull.

samsara   The Hindu belief in birth, death, and rebirth or reincarnation of the soul.

Sapir–Whorf hypothesis   A hypothesis that assumes a close relationship between language and culture, claiming that language defines people's experiences.

schema   The mental codification of experience that includes a particular organized way of perceiving cognitively and responding to a complex situation or set of stimuli.

scientific method   A method used to investigate the natural and social world involving critical thinking, logical reasoning, and skeptical thought.

secondary sector   The sector of an industrial economy that is devoted to processing raw materials into manufactured goods.

Second World   In the terminology of the Cold War, the industrial socialist societies in the global economy.

secularization   The decline in the influence of religion in a society.

segmentary lineage system   A type of political organization in which multiple descent groups form at different levels and serve political functions.

segregation   The institutional separation of human populations or ethnic groups from one another.

semantics   The meaning of words, phrases, and sentences.

semiperipheral societies   Societies that have some degree of industrialization and some economic autonomy in the world economy, but are not as advanced as core societies.

seriation   A relative dating method based on the assumption that any particular artifact, attribute, or style will appear, gradually increase in popularity until it reaches a peak, and then progressively decrease.

services   Elements of nonmaterial culture derived from cultural knowledge in the form of specialized skills that benefit others, such as giving spiritual comfort or providing medical care.

sex   Biological differences between males and females.

sexism   Prejudice and discrimination against people based on their sex.

sexual dimorphism   The presence of different characteristics in males and females of the same species.

shamans   Part-time religious specialists who are believed to be linked with supernatural beings and powers.

signs   Units of meaning that are directly associated with concrete physical phenomena.

silica gloss   A distinctive residue left on stone blades used by people to harvest plants.

situational learning   A type of learning in which an organism adjusts its behavior in response to direct experience.

socialism   An economic system in which the state owns the basic means of production.

social grooming   A social activity of many primates that involves removing ticks, fleas, dirt, and debris from one another. It may serve as an important means of maintaining sociality.

social learning   A type of learning in which an organism observes another organism's response to a stimulus and then adds that response to its own collection of behaviors.

social stratification   The inequality of statuses in a society.

social structure   The pattern of relationships in a society.

social-impact studies   Research on the possible consequences of change in a society.

society A group of people who reside within a specific territory and share a common culture.

socioeconomic status A specific position determined by economic circumstances and other cultural variables within a society.

sociolinguistics The systematic study of language use in various social settings to discern the links between language and social behavior.

sodalities Groups based on kinship, age, gender, or other principles that provide for political organization.

somatic cells Body cells; unlike gametes (sex cells), they have the full number of chromosomes.

sorcery A magical strategy, often using various objects, that is believed to bring about either harmful or beneficial results.

sororate The marriage rule requiring a widower to marry one of his deceased wife's sisters.

speciation The development of new species.

species Groups of organisms with similar physical characteristics that can potentially interbreed successfully.

state A form of political system with centralized bureaucratic institutions to establish power and authority over large populations in clearly defined territories.

state capitalism An economic system that directs and manages for-profit economic and commercial activity through a centralized bureaucratic government.

status A recognized position that a person occupies in a society.

strata Groups of equivalent statuses based on ranked divisions within a society.

stratigraphic dating A relative dating method based on the supposition that the stratigraphic layers in an excavation or different rock strata are successively younger than the layers beneath them.

structural linguistics An area of research that investigates the structure of language patterns as they presently exist.

subsistence patterns The means by which people obtain their food supply.

sumptuary rules Cultural norms and practices used to differentiate the higher-status groups from the lower-status groups.

superego Freud's term to refer to the component of the personality that is formed through the individual's learning cultural norms.

survey An examination of a particular area, region, or country to locate archaeological sites or fossil localities.

sustainability model A model that emphasizes the conservation and preservation of environmental resources for future generations.

symbolic anthropology The study of culture through the interpretation of a society's symbols, values, beliefs, and ethos.

symbolic learning The ability to use and understand symbols.

symbols Arbitrary units of meaning that can stand for different concrete or abstract phenomena.

syncretism The blending of indigenous religious beliefs and practices with those introduced by outside groups.

syntax Rules for phrase and sentence construction in a language.

tabu The Polynesian term for a prohibition of specific behaviors.

taphonomy The study of the variety of natural and behavioral processes that led to the formation of a fossil locality. This may include traces of the activities of early human ancestors, as well as natural agencies such as erosion, decay, and animal activities.

taxonomy The science of classification that provides scientists a convenient way of referring to, and comparing, living and extinct organisms.

technology All the human techniques and methods of reaching a specific subsistence goal or of modifying or controlling the natural environment.

tertiary sector The sector of an industrial economy devoted to services.

theater state A limited form of state society in Southeast Asia.

theocracy A society in which people rule not because of their worldly wealth and power, but because of their place in the moral and sacred order.

theories Interconnected hypotheses that offer general explanations of natural or social phenomena.

thermoluminescence dating Dating method based on the amount of electrons trapped in crystalline minerals as a consequence of radioactive decay.

Third World In the terminology of the Cold War, premodern, nonindustrialized societies in the global economy.

totem A mythical ancestor, usually a plant or an animal, that symbolizes a particular group.

trace element analysis The study of elements in artifacts that may provide a distinctive signature of the artifacts' origin.

transitional forms The hominid fossils that are either advanced *Homo erectus* or early *Homo sapiens*.

tribes Complex societies having political institutions that unite horticulturalist or pastoralist groups into a political system.

tributary mode The economic system of an agricultural society that uses tribute to extract labor, taxes, or other services from peasants.

tribute The payment of labor, taxes, or other services from one group to another.

ultimogeniture An inheritance pattern in which property and land are passed to the youngest son.

uniformitarianism The view that the Earth's geological features are the result of gradual, natural processes that can still be observed.

unilineal descent group A lineage group that traces its descent through only one side of the lineage or through only one sex.

unilineal evolution The belief, widespread during the nineteenth, century that societies were evolving in a single direction toward complexity and industrial progress.

universalistic religions Religions whose spiritual messages apply to all of humanity.

Upper Paleolithic The most recent period of the Paleolithic, also referred to the Late Stone Age, defined by archaeologists on the basis of changes in stone tool technology, as well as other technological innovations.

use-wear and residue studies Studies of the damage or traces of use present on tools. Such traces may provide indications of how a tool was used.

values Standards by which a society defines what is desirable and undesirable.

variable A datum that varies from case to case.

vegiculture The propagation of plants by selectively dividing and replanting living plants.

warfare Armed combat among territorial or political communities.

witchcraft The innate psychic ability of some people that is believed to bring about harmful effects.

world-systems theory The view that core societies dominate peripheral and semiperipheral societies to create a global economic system.

zero population growth The level of reproduction that maintains population at a steady state.

zygote A cell formed by the combination of a male and female sex cell that has the potential of developing into a new organism.

References

Aberle, David F. 1961. "Arctic Hysteria and Latah in Mongolia." In Yehudi Cohen (Ed.), *Social Structure and Personality: A Casebook*. New York: Holt, Rinehart & Winston.

———. 1966. *The Peyote Religion among the Navajo*. New York: Wenner-Gren Foundation for Anthropological Research, Inc.

Abu-Lughod, Janet. 1961. "Migrant Adjustment to City Life: The Egyptian Case." *The American Journal of Sociology* 62: 22–32.

Abu-Lughod, Lila. 1987. *Veiled Sentiments: Honor and Poetry in a Bedouin Society*. Berkeley: University of California Press.

Abu-Zeid, M.A., and F. Z. El-Shibini. 1997. " Egypt's High Aswan Dam." *Water Resources Development*, 13, (2):, 209–217.

Adams, Robert McCormick. 1966. *The Evolution of Urban Society*. Chicago: Aldine.

———. 1981. *Heartland of Cities*. Chicago: Aldine.

Adams, Willi Paul. 1993. *The German Americans: An Ethnic Experience*, L. J. Rippley and Eberhard Reichmann (Trans.), Indianapolis: Indiana University–Purdue University at Indianapolis.

Adovasio, James M., and Jake Page. 2002. *The First Americans: In Pursuit of Archaeology's Greatest Mystery*. New York: Random House.

Agar, Michael. 1980. *The Professional Stranger: An Informal Introduction to Ethnography*. New York: Academic Press.

Ahmed, Akbar. 2013. The Thistle and the Drone: How America's War on Terror Became a Global War on Tribal Islam. Washington D.C.: Brookings Institution Press.

Aiello, Leslie, and Mark Collard. 2001. "Our Newest Oldest Ancestor?" *Nature* 410: 526–527.

Aiken, M. J. 1990. *Science Based Dating in Archaeology*. New York: Longman.

Aiken, M. J., C.B. Stringer, and P.A. Mellars. 1993. *The Origins of Modern Humans and the Impact of Chronometric Dating*. Princeton: Princeton University Press.

Aikens, C. Melvin, and Takayasu Higuchi. 1981. *Prehistory of Japan*. New York: Academic Press.

Alba, Richard. 1985. *Italian Americans: Into the Twilight of Ethnicity*. Englewood Cliffs, NJ: Prentice Hall.

Alemseged, Zeresenay, Fred Spoor, William H. Kimbel, René Bobe, Denis Geraads, Denné Reed, and Jonathan G. Wynn. 2006. "A Juvenile Early Hominin Skeleton from Dikika, Ethiopia." *Nature* 443: 296–301.

Algaze, Guillermo. 1993. "Expansionary Dynamics of Some Early Pristine States." *American Anthropologist* 95(2): 304–333.

Allardt, Erik. 1968. "Theories about Social Stratification." In *Social Stratification*, John A. Jackson (Ed.), New York: Cambridge University Press, pp. 14–24.

Allen, James P. 2000. *Middle Egyptian: An Introduction to the Language and Culture of Hieroglyphs*. Cambridge: Cambridge University Press.

Al-Thakeb, Fahad. 1981. "Size and Composition of the Arab Family: Census and Survey Data." *International Journal of Sociology of the Family* 2: 171–178.

———. 1985. "The Arab Family and Modernity: Evidence from Kuwait." *Current Anthropology* 25 (5): 575–580.

Altorki, Soraya. 1986. *Women in Saudi Arabia: Ideology and Behavior among the Elite*. New York: Columbia University Press.

Alverson, Hoyt. 1994. *Semantics and Experience: Universal Metaphors of Time in English, Mandarin, Hindi, and Sesotho*. Baltimore, MD: Johns Hopkins University Press.

American Anthropological Association 2012. *Statement-on-Ethics-Principles-of-Professional-Responsibility*. pdf. http://www.aaanet.org/profdev/ethics/upload/. Washington, DC: American Anthropological Association.

Ames, Kenneth. 2004. "Supposing Hunter-Gatherer Variability." Book Review Essay *American Antiquity* 69 (2): 364–374.

Anastasio, Thomas J., Kristen Ann Ehrenberger, Patrick Watson and Wenyi Zhang. (2012). *Individual and Collective Memory Consolidation: Analogous Processes on Different Levels*. Cambridge, MA: The MIT Press.

Anderson, Benedict. 1991. *Imagined Communities: Reflections on the Origin and Spread of Nationalism*. London: Verso.

Anderson, David G., and Virginia Horak (Eds.) 1995. *Archaeological Site File Management: A Southeastern Perspective*. Readings in Archaeological Resource Protection Series No. 3. Atlanta, GA: Interagency Archaeological Service Division.

Anderson, Richard L. 1989. *Art in Small-Scale Societies*. Upper Saddle River, NJ: Prentice Hall.

Andresen, John M., Brian F. Byrd, Mark D. Elson, Randall H. McGuire, Ruben G. Mendoza, Edward Staski, and J. Peter White. 1981. "The Deer Hunters: Star Carr Reconsidered." *World Archaeology* 13 (1): 31–46.

Andrews, Peter, and Lawrence Martin. 1987. "Cladistic Relationships of Extant and Fossil Hominoid Primates." *Journal of Human Evolution* 16: 101–118.

Antoun, Richard T. 2000. *Understanding Fundamentalism: Christian, Islamic, and Jewish Movements*. Walnut Creek, CA: AltaMira Press.

Anuman-Rajadhon, Phya. 1961. "Thai Traditional Salutation." *Journal of the Siam Society* 49 (2): 161–171.

Aoki, Tamotsu. 2002. "Aspects of Globalization in Japan." In Peter Berger and Samuel Huntington (Eds) *Many Globalizations: Cultural Diversity in the Contemporary World*. pp. 68–88. Oxford: Oxford University Press.

Appadurai, Arjun. 1996. *Modernity at Large, Cultural Dimensions of Globalization*. Minneapolis, London: University of Minnesota Press.

Arbib, Michael A. 2011. "From Mirror Neurons to Complex Imitation in the Evolution of Language and Tool Use." *Annual Review of Anthropology* 40, 257–273.

Arbib, Michael A., Katja Liebal, and Simone Pika. 2008. "Primate Vocalization, Gesture, and the Evolution of Human Language." *Current Anthropology* 49 (6): 1053–1076.

Arden, Harvey. 1989. "Who Owns Our Past?" *National Geographic* 75 (3): 378.

Ardener, Edwin. 2004. *Social Anthropology and Language (Anthropology and Ethnography)*. London: Routledge .

Armelagous, George, and Dennis van Gerven. 2003. "A Century of Skeletal Biology and Paleopathology: Contrasts, Contradictions, and Conflicts."*American Anthropologist* 105: 53–64.

Asad, Talal. 2003. *Formations of the Secular: Christianity, Islam, and Modernity*. Palo Alto: Stanford University Press.

———. 2011. "Freedom of Speech and Religious Limitations." In Craig Calhoun, Mark Juergensmeyer, and Jonathan VanAntwerpen (Eds.), *Rethinking Secularism*. Oxford: Oxford University Press. pp. 282–297.

Aswad, Barbara, and Thomas Abowd. 2012. "Arab Americans." In Raymond Scupin (Ed.), *Race and Ethnicity: The United States and the World* (2nd ed.). pp. 272–298. Upper Saddle River, NJ: Pearson Prentice Hall.

Atran, Scott. 1990. *Cognitive Foundations of Natural History*. Cambridge: Cambridge University Press.

———. 1998. "Folk Biology and the Anthropology of Science: Cognitive Universals and Cultural Particulars." *Behavioral and Brain Sciences* 21 (4): 547–609.

———. 2002. *In Gods We Trust: The Evolutionary Landscape of Religion*. Oxford, England: Oxford University Press.

———. 2003. "Genesis of Suicide Terrorism." *Science* 299 (5612): 1534–1539.

———. 2010. *Talking to the Enemy: Faith, Brotherhood, and the (Un)Making of Terrorists*. New York: Ecco, HarperCollins.

Atran, Scott, and Jeremy Ginges. 2012. "Religious and Sacred Imperatives in Human Conflict." *Science* 336, 855–857.

Atran, Scott, and Joseph Henrich. 2010. "The Evolution of Religion: How Cognitive By-Products, Adaptive Learning Heuristics, Ritual Displays, and Group Competition Generate Deep Commitments to Prosocial Religions." *Biological Theory* 5 (1): 18–30.

Atran, Scott, and Douglas Medin. 2008. *The Native Mind and the Cultural Construction of Nature*. Cambridge, MA: MIT Press.

Atran, S. D., D. Medin, N. Ross, E. Lynch, V. Vapnarsky, E. Ucan Ek, J. Coley, C. Timura, and M. Baran. 2002. "Folkecology, Cultural Epidemiology and the Spirit of the Commons." *Current Anthropology*, 43(3): 421–450.

Atran, Scott, Douglas Medin, and Norbert Ross. 2004. "Evolution and Devolution of Knowledge: A Tale of Two Biologies." *Journal of the Royal Anthropological Institute* 10 (2): 395–420.

Auel, Jean M. 1981. *The Clan of the Cave Bear*. New York: Bantam.

Augustine, Saint. [400] 1995. *Confessions*. G. Clark. (Trans.). Cambridge: Cambridge University Press.

Ayala, F. J. 1995. "The Myth of Eve: Molecular Biology and Human Origins." *Science* 270: 1930–1936.

Bachofen, Johann Jakob. [1861] 1992. *Das Mutterecht*. In Ralph Manheim (Trans.), *Myth, Religion and Mother Right: Selected Writings of J. J. Bachofen*. pp.3–21. Princeton: Princeton University Press.

Badran, Margot. 1998. "Gender, Islam and the State: Kuwaiti Women in Struggle, Preinvasion to Postliberation." In Yvonne Y. Haddad and John Esposito, (Eds.), *Islam, Gender, and Social Change*. Oxford: Oxford University Press.

Bagish, Henry H. 1981. *Confessions of a Former Cultural Relativist*. Santa Barbara, CA: Santa Barbara City College Publications.

Bailey, R. C., G. Head, M. Jenike, B. Own, T. Rechtman, and E. Zechenter. 1989. "Hunting and Gathering in Tropical Rain Forests: Is It Possible?" *American Anthropologist* 91 (1): 59–82.

Baker, Lee D. 2004. "Franz Boas out of the Ivory Tower." *Anthropological Theory* 4 (1): 29–52.

Baker, Leslie. 1989. "Cultural Survival Imports: Marketing the Rain Forest." *Cultural Survival Quarterly* 13 (3): 64–67.

Balikci, Asen. 1970. *The Netsilik Eskimo*. Garden City, NY: Natural History Press.

Ballinger, Pamela. 2012. "Europe." In Raymond Scupin (Ed.). *Race and Ethnicity: The United States and the World* (2nd ed.). pp. 387–416 Upper Saddle River, NJ: Pearson Prentice Hall.

Balter, Michael, and Ann Gibbons. 2000. "A Glimpse of Humans' First Journey Out of Africa." *Science* 288: 948–950.

Bamberger, Joan. 1974. "The Myth of Matriarchy: Why Men Rule in Primitive Society." In Michelle Zimbalist Rosaldo and Louise Lamphere, (Eds.). *Women, Culture, and Society*. pp.263–280. Stanford, CA: Stanford University Press.

Banks, Marcus. 1996. *Ethnicity: Anthropological Constructions*. London: Routledge.

Bannister, Robert C. 1991. *Jessie Bernard: The Making of a Feminist*. Bloomington: Indiana University Press.

Banton, Michael. 1998. *Racial Theories*. Cambridge: Cambridge University Press.

Bar-Yosef, O. 2011. "Climate Fluctuations and Early Farming in West and East Asia." *Current Anthropology* 52(4): 175–193.

Barash, David P. 1987. *The Hare and the Tortoise: Culture, Biology, and Human Nature*. New York: Penguin.

Barber, Benjamin R. 2001. *Jihad vs. McWorld: Terrorism's Challenge to Democracy*. New York: Ballantine Books.

Barker, G. 2006. *The Agricultural Revolution in Prehistory*. Oxford: Oxford University Press.

Barkow, Jerome H., Leda Cosmides, and John Tooby (Eds.). 1992. *The Adapted Mind: Evolutionary Psychology and the Generation of Culture*. New York: Oxford University Press.

Barmè, Scott. 2002. *Woman, Man, Bangkok: Love, Sex and Popular Culture in Thailand*. Lanham, MD: Rowman and Littlefield.

Barnes, Gina L. 1995. *An Introduction to Buddhist Archaeology*. World Archaeology 27(2): 165–182.

Barnes, Linda L. 2005. "American Acupuncture and Efficacy: Meanings and Their Points of Insertion." *Medical Anthropology Quarterly* 19 (3): 239–266.

Barnet, A. B., and R. J. Barnet. 1998. *The Youngest Minds*. New York: Simon & Schuster.

Barnouw, Victor. 1985. *Culture and Personality* (4th ed.). Homewood, IL: Dorsey Press.

Barret, Richard E., and Fang Li. 1999. *Modern China*. New York: McGraw-Hill.

Barrett, Leonard E. 1977. *Rastafarians: Sounds of Cultural Dissonance*. Boston: Beacon Press.

Barrett, Richard A. 1984. *Culture and Conduct: An Excursion in Anthropology*. Belmont, CA: Wadsworth.

Barth, Frederick. 1961. *Nomads of South Persia: The Basseri Tribe of the Khamseh Confederacy*. Boston: Little, Brown.

———. 1969. *Ethnic Groups and Boundaries*. Boston: Little, Brown.

———. 1975. *Ritual and Knowledge among the Baktaman of New Guinea*. Oslo: Universitets Forlaget; New Haven, CT: Yale University Press.

———. 2002. "Toward a Richer Description and Analysis of Cultural Phenomena." In Richard Fox and Barbara J. King. (Eds.), *Anthropology beyond Culture*. pp. 23–36. Oxford, England: Berg.

Barton, R. F. 1919. "Ifugao Law." *Publications in American Archeology and Ethnology* 15 (1): 92–109. Berkeley: University of California Press.

Bascom, William. 1969. *The Yoruba of Southwestern Nigeria*. New York: Holt, Rinehart and Winston.

Basi, Tina. 2004. "Faces and Places: Contested Spaces and Identity Construction of Women Working in the Delhi Call Centre Industry." Paper read at the British Association of South Asian Studies, London.

Bass, George Fletcher. 1963. "Underwater Archaeology: Key to History's Warehouse." *National Geographic* 124 (1): 138–156.

———. 1973. *Archaeology Beneath the Sea.* New York: Harper & Row.

Bass, George (ed). 2005. *Beneath the Seven Seas: Adventures with the Institute of Nautical Archaeology.* New York: Thames and Hudson.

Bass, George, Sheila D. Matthews, J. Richard Steffy, and Frederick H. van Doornink, Jr. (Eds.) 2004. *Serce Limani: An Eleventh-Century Shipwreck, Vol. 1, The Ship and Its Anchorage, Crew, and Passengers.* College Station: Texas A&M University.

Bassis, Michael S., Richard J. Gelles, and Ann Levine. 1991. *Sociology: An Introduction* (4th ed),. New York: McGraw-Hill.

Bataille, Gretchen, David M. Gradwohl, and Charles L. P. Silet. 2000. *The Worlds between Two Rivers: Perspectives on American Indians in Iowa.* Iowa City: University of Iowa Press.

Bates, Daniel G., and Amal Rassam. 2000. *Peoples and Cultures of the Middle East* (2nd ed.). Upper Saddle River, NJ: Prentice Hall.

Batterbury, Simon. 2008. "Anthropology and Global Warming." *The Australian Journal of Anthropology* 19 (1): 62–65.

Baugh, T. G., and J. E. Ericson (Eds.). 1994. *Prehistoric Exchange Systems in North America.* New York: Plenum.

Bawaya, Michael. 2005. "Maya Archaeologists Turn to the Living to Help Save the Dead." *Science* 309: 1317–1318.

Beall, Cynthia M. 2001. "Adaptations to Altitude: A Current Assessment." *Annual Review of Anthropology* 16: 423–455.

———. 2007. "Two Routes to Functional Adaptation: Tibetan and Andean High-altitude Natives." *Proceedings of the National Academy of Sciences*, U S A. 104, Supplement 1: 8655–8660.

Beall, C., K. Song, R. Elston, and M. Goldstein. 2004. "Higher Offspring Survival among Tibetan Women with High Oxygen Saturation Genotypes Residing at 4,000 m." PDF. *Proceedings of National Academy of Sciences*, PNAS, September 7, 10.1073/pnas 0405949101 (Anthropology-Social Sciences).

Beals, Kenneth L., Courtland L. Smith, and Stephen M. Dodd. 1984. "Brain Size, Cranial Morphology, Climate, and Time Machines." *Current Anthropology* 25 (3): 301–330.

Beard, K. C., M. F. Teaford, and A. Walker. 1986. "New Wrist Bones of *Proconsul africanus* and *P. nyanzae* from Rusinga Island, Kenya." *Folia Primatology* 47: 97–118.

Beatty, Andrew. 2006. "The Pope in Mexico: Syncretism in Public Ritual." *American Anthropologist* 108 (2): 324–335.

Beck, Lois. 1986. *The Qashqa'i of Iran.* New Haven, CT: Yale University Press.

———. 1991. *Nomad: A Year in the Life of a Qashqa'i Tribesman in Iran.* Berkeley: University of California Press.

———. 2014. *Local Political and Social Change in Iran: The Qashqa'i and the Post-Revolutionary Era.* New York: Routledge.

Beck, Lois, and Nikki Keddie (Eds.). 1978. *Women in the Muslim World.* Cambridge, MA: Harvard University Press.

Beck, Sam and Carl Maida (Eds.). 2013. *Toward Engaged Anthropology.* New York and Oxford: Berghahn Books.

Bednarik, R. G. 2011. *The Human Condition.* New York: Springer.

Beeman, William O. 1986. *Language, Status, and Power in Iran.* Bloomington: Indiana University Press.

Befu, Harumi. 1971. *Japan: An Anthropological Introduction.* San Francisco: Chandler.

———. 2009. "Concepts of Japan, Japanese culture, and Japanese" In Sugimoto, Yoshio (Ed.), *The Cambridge Companion to Modern Japanese Culture.* New York: Cambridge University Press.

———. 1993. *Cultural Nationalism in East Asia.* Berkeley: Institute of East Asian Studies, University of California.

Begun, David R. 2010. "Miocene Hominids and the Origins of the African Apes and Humans." *Annual Review of Anthropology* 39: 67–84

———. (Ed.). 2012. "The African Origin of Homo Sapiens." *Companion to Paleoanthropology.* London: John Wiley & Sons.

Behe, Michael J. 1996. *Darwin's Black Box: The Biochemical Challenge to Evolution.* New York: Free Press.

Beja-Pereira, Albano, Gordon Luikart, Phillip R. England, Daniel G. Bradley, Oliver C. Jann, Giorgio Bertorelle, Andrew T. Chamberlain, Telmo P. Nunes, Stoitcho Metodiev, Nuno Ferrand, and Georg Erhardt. 2003. "Gene-culture Coevolution between Cattle Milk Protein Genes and Human Lactase Genes." *Nature Genetics* 35 (4): 311–312.

Bell, Daniel. 1973. *The Coming of the Post-Industrial Society: A Venture into Social Forecasting.* New York: Basic Books.

Bell, James A. 1994. *Reconstructing Prehistory: Scientific Method in Archaeology.* Philadelphia: Temple University Press.

Bellah, Robert, Richard Madsen, William Sullivan, Ann Swidler, and Steven M. Tipton. 1985. *Habits of the Heart: Individualism and Commitment in American Life.* New York: Harper & Row.

———. 1998. "Is There a Common American Culture?" *Journal of the American Academy of Religion* 66 (3): 613–626. Reprinted in Barbara Mori (Ed.), 2000. *Stand! Contending Ideas and Opinions: Race and Ethnicity.* Bellevue, WA: Coursewise Publishing.

Bellwood, Peter. 2005. *First Farmers.* Oxford: Blackwell.

Benedict, Ruth. 1928. "Psychological Types in the Cultures of the Southwest." Reprinted in Margaret Mead (Ed.), *An Anthropologist at Work: Writings of Ruth Benedict.* Boston: Houghton Mifflin.

———. 1934. *Patterns of Culture.* Boston: Houghton Mifflin.

———. 1946. *The Chrysanthemum and the Sword.* Boston: Houghton Mifflin.

Benedict, Ruth, and Gene Weltfish. 1943. "The Races of Mankind," Public Affairs Pamphlet No. 85. New York: Public Affairs Committee, Inc.

Bennett, John W. 1987. "Anthropology and the Emerging World Order: The Paradigm of Culture in an Age of Interdependence." In Kenneth Moore (Ed.), *Waymarks: The Notre Dame Inaugural Lectures in Anthropology.* Notre Dame, IN: University of Notre Dame Press.

Bennett, Lynn. 1983. *Dangerous Wives and Sacred Sisters: Social and Symbolic Roles of High Caste Women in Nepal.* New York: Columbia University Press.

Benokraitis, Nijole V. 2005. *Marriage and Families: Changes, Choices, and Constraints* (5th ed.). Upper Saddle River, NJ: Prentice Hall.

Benson, Janet. 2012. "Asian Americans." In Raymond Scupin (Ed.), *Race and Ethnicity: The United States and the World* (2nd ed.). pp. 247–270. Upper Saddle River, NJ: Pearson Prentice Hall.

Bentley, A., N. Tayles, C. Higham, C. Macpherson, and T. C. Atkinson. 2007. "Shifting Gender Relations at Khok Phanom Di, Thailand: Isotopic Evidence from the Skeletons." *Current Anthropology* 48 (2): 301–314.

Bentley, Jeffery W., and Gonzalo Rodríguez. 2001. "Honduran Folk Entomology." *Current Anthropology* 42 (2): 285–300.

Benton, M. J. 2003. *When Life Nearly Died: The Greatest Mass Extinction All Time.* London: Thames and Hudson Ltd.

Berdan, Frances F. 1982. *The Aztecs of Central Mexico: An Imperial Society.* New York: Holt, Rinehart and Winston.

Berger, Peter L. 2002. "Introduction." In Peter L. Berger and Samuel P. Huntington, (Eds.), *Many Globalizations: Cultural Diversity in the Contemporary World.* Oxford: Oxford University Press.

Berger, T. D., and E. Trinkaus. 1995. "Patterns of Trauma among the Neanderthals." *Journal of Archaeological Science* 22: 841–852.

Berlin, Brent, and Paul Kay. 1969. *Basic Color Terms: Their Universality and Evolution.* Berkeley: University of California Press.

Bermúdez de Castro, J. M., M. Matinón-Torres, E. Carbonell, S. Sarmiento, A. Rosas, J. Van der Made, and M. Lozano. 2004. "The Atapuerca Sites and Their Contribution to the Knowledge of Human Evolution in Europe." *Evolutionary Anthropology* 13 (1): 25–41.

Bernard, Jessie. 1981. *The Female World.* New York: Free Press.
———. 1987. *The Female World from a Global Perspective.* Bloomington: Indiana University Press.

Bernard, R. H., Pertti Pelto, O. Werner, J. Boster, K. A. Romney, A. Johnson, C. Ember, and A. Kasakott. 1986. "The Construction of Primary Data in Cultural Anthropology." *Current Anthropology* 27 (4): 382–396.

Bernard, Russell H. 1992. "Preserving Language Diversity." *Human Organization* 51 (1): 82–89.

Bernard, Russell H., and Jesús Salinas Pedraza. 1989. *Native Ethnography: A Mexican Indian Describes His Culture.* Newbury Park, CA: Sage.

Bernasconi, Robert (Ed.). 2001. *Race.* Malden, MA: Blackwell Publishers.

Berns, Gregory S. and Scott Atran (2012). The Biology of Cultural Conflict. *Philosophical Transactions of the Royal Society, Biological Sciences.* 367: 633–639.

Berns, Gregory S., Emily Bell, C. Monica Capra, Michael J. Prietula, Sara Moore, Jeremy Ginges, and Scott Atran. (2012)." The Price of Your Soul: Neural Evidence for the Non-utilitarian Representation of Sacred Values." *Philosophical Transactions of the Royal Society, Biological Sciences.* 367: 754–762.

Berrin, K., and E. Pasztory (Eds.). 1993. *Teotihuacan: Art from the City of the Gods.* New York: Thames and Hudson.

Bhagwati, Jagdish. 2004. *In Defense of Globalization.* Oxford: Oxford University Press.

Bickerton, Derek. 1985. *Roots of Language.* Ann Arbor, MI: Karoma Publishing.
———. 1999. *Language and Human Behavior.* Seattle: University of Washington Press.
———. 2008. *Bastard Tongue: A Trailblazing Linguist Finds Clues to Our Common Humanity in the World's Lowliest Languages.* New York: Hill and Wang.

Bienkowski, Piotr and Alan Millard (Eds.). 2010. *Dictionary of the Ancient Near East.* Philadelphia: University of Pennsylvania Press.

Biesele, Megan. 2000. "The Ju/'hoansi San under Two States: Impacts of the South West African Administration and the Government of the Republic of Namibia." In Peter Schweitzer, Megan Biesele, and Robert Hitchcock (Eds.), *Hunters and Gatherers in the Modern World: Conflict, Resistance, and Self-Determination.* pp. 305–326. Oxford, England: Berghahn Books.

Biesele, Megan and Robert Hitchcock. 2011. *The Ju/'hoan San of Nyae Nyae and Namibian Independence: Development, Democracy, and Indigenous Voices in Southern Africa.* New York and Oxford: Berghahn Books.

Bigler, Ellen. 2012. "Hispanic Americans/Latinos." In Raymond Scupin (Ed.), *Race and Ethnicity: The United States and the World* (2nd ed.). pp. 203–237. Upper Saddle River, NJ: Pearson Prentice Hall.

Binford, Lewis. 1968. "Post-Pleistocene Adaptations." In Lewis R. Binford and Sally Binford (Eds.). *New Perspectives in Archaeology*, pp. 313–341. New York: Academic Press.
———. 1985. "Human Ancestors: Changing Views of Their Behavior." *Journal of Anthropological Archaeology* 1: 5–31.

Binford, Lewis R., and Sally Binford. 1966. "A Preliminary Analysis of Functional Variability in the Mousterian of Levallois Facies." *American Anthropologist* 68 (2): 238–295.

Binford, Lewis R., and Chuan Kun Ho. 1985. "Taphonomy at a Distance: Zhoukoudian, the Cave Home of Beijing Man?" *Current Anthropology* 26: 413–442.

Bird David, Nurit. 1999. "Animism Revisited: Personhood, Environment, and Relational Epistemology." *Current Anthropology* 40 (Special Issue, Culture. A Second Chance?): S67–S91.

Birdsell, Joseph B. 1968. "Some Predictions for the Pleistocene Based on Equilibrium Systems among Recent Hunter-Gatherers." In Richard B. Lee and Irven Devore (Eds.), *Man the Hunter.* pp. 229–240. Chicago: Aldine.
———. 1981. *Human Evolution* (3rd ed.). Boston: Houghton Mifflin.

Birdwhistle, Ray. 1970. *Kinesics and Context.* Philadelphia: University of Pennsylvania Press.

Bischof, N. 1972. "The Biological Foundations of the Incest Taboo." *Social Science Information* 2: 7–36.

Black, Edwin. 2004. *War Against the Weak: Eugenics and America's Campaign to Create a Master Race.* New York: Thunder's Mouth Press.

Blake, E. and A. B. Knapp. 2005. *The Archaeology of Mediterranean Prehistory.* John Wiley & Sons.

Blakely, Robert L., and Judith M. Harrington. 1997. *Bones in the Basement: Postmortem Racism in Nineteenth-Century Medical Training.* Washington, DC: Smithsonian Institution Press.

Blench, R. M. and K. MacDonald. 2000. *The Origins and Development of African Livestock: Archaeology, Genetics, Linguistics, and Ethnography.* London: University College London Press.

Blick, Jeffrey P. 1988. "Genocidal Warfare in Tribal Societies as a Result of European-Induced Culture Conflict." *Man* 23: 654–670.

Blim, Michael. 2005. *Equality and Economy: The Global Challenge.* Walnut Creek, CA: Altamira Press.

Blinderman, C. 1986. *The Piltdown Inquest.* Buffalo, NY: Prometheus Books.

Bloch, Maurice, and Jonathan Parry. 1989. *Money and the Morality of Exchange.* Cambridge: Cambridge University Press.

Bloch, Maurice. 1977. "The Past and the Present." *Man* 12: 278–292.
———. 1983. *Marxism and Anthropology.* Oxford: Oxford University Press.
———. 1985. "From Cognition to Ideology." In R. Fardon (Ed.), *Power and Knowledge: Anthropological and Sociological Approaches.* Edinburgh: Scottish Academic Press.
———. 2012. *Anthropology and the Cognitive Challenge.* Cambridge: Cambridge University Press.

Bloch, Maurice, and Dan Sperber. 2002. "Kinship and Evolved Psychological Dispositions: The Mother's Brother Controversy Reconsidered." *Current Anthropology* 43 (5): 723–748.

Blum, Susan D. 2001. *Portraits of "Primitives": Ordering Human Kinds in the Chinese Nation*. Lanham, MD: Rowman and Littlefield.

Blumenschine, Robert J. 1995. "Percussion Marks, Tooth Marks, and Experimental Determinations of the Timing of Hominid and Carnivore Access to Long Bones at FLK Zinjanthropus, Olduvai Gorge, Tanzania." *Journal of Human Evolution* 29: 21–51.

Blurton Jones, Nicholas. 1986. "Bushman Birth Spacing: A Test for Optimal Intervals." *Ethology and Sociobiology* 7 (2): 91–106.

———. 1987. "Bushman Birth Spacing: Direct Tests of Some Simple Predictions." *Ethology and Sociobiology* 8 (3): 183–204.

Boaretto E, X. Wu, J. Yuan, O. Bar-Yosef, V. Chu, Y. Pan, K. Liu, D. Cohen, T. Jiao, S. Li. 2009. Radiocarbon Dating of Charcoal and Bone Collagen Associated with Early Pottery at Yuchanyan Cave, Hunan Province, China. *Proceedings of the National Academy of Sciences* 106(24): 9595–9600.

Boas, Franz. 1927. *Primitive Art*. New York: Dover.

———. 1930. *The Religion of the Kwakiutl*, Vol. 10, Part II. Contributions to Anthropology. New York: Columbia University.

———. [1940] 1966. *Race, Language, and Culture*. New York: Free Press.

Boaz, Noel T., and Alan J. Almquist. 1997. *Biological Anthropology: A Synthetic Approach to Human Evolution*. Upper Saddle River, NJ: Prentice Hall.

Bocquet-Appel, Jean-Pierre. 2011. When the World's Population Took Off: The Springboard of the Neolithic Demographic Transition. *Science* 333 (6042): 560–561.

Bodley, John H. 1985. *Anthropology and Contemporary Human Problems* (2nd ed.). Mountain View, CA: Mayfield.

———. 1990. *Victims of Progress* (3rd ed.). Mountain View, CA: Mayfield.

Boehm, Christopher. 1993. "Egalitarian Behavior and Reverse Dominance Hierarchy." *Current Anthropology* 34 (3): 227–254.

———. 1999. *Hierarchy in the Forest: The Evolution of Egalitarian Behavior*. Cambridge, MA: Harvard University Press.

Bogin, B. A. 1978. "Seasonal Pattern in the Rate of Growth in Height of Children Living in Guatemala." *American Journal of Physical Anthropology* 49: 205–210.

Bohannon, Paul, and George Dalton. 1962. *Markets in Africa*. Evanston, IL: Northwestern University Press.

Bonvillian, Nancy. 2010. *Language, Culture, and Communication: The Meaning of Messages* (6th ed.). Upper Saddle River, NJ: Pearson Prentice Hall.

Bordes, François. 1968. *The Old Stone Age*. New York: McGraw-Hill.

Borgerhoff Mulder, Monique. 2009. "Serial Monogamy as Polygyny or Polyandry? Marriage in the Tanzanian Pimbwe." *Human Nature* 20: 130–150.

Borgerhoff Mulder, Monique, Ila Fazzio,William Irons, Richard L. Mcelreath, Samuel Bowles, Adrian Bell, Tom Hertz, and Leela Hazzah. 2010. "Pastoralism and Wealth Inequality: Revisiting an Old Question." *Current Anthropology* 51 (1): 35–48.

Borofsky, Robert. 2005. *Yanomami: The Fierce Controversy and What We Can Learn from It*. Berkeley: University of California Press.

Boserup, Ester. 1965. *The Conditions of Agricultural Growth: The Economics of Agrarian Change under Population Pressure*. Chicago: Aldine.

———. 1970. *Women's Role in Economic Development*. London: Allen & Unwin.

Boster, James. 1987. "Agreement Between Biological Classification Systems Is Not Dependent on Cultural Transmission." *American Anthropologist* 89 (4): 914–919.

Bourdieu, Pierre. 1977. *Outline of a Theory of Practice*. Cambridge: Cambridge University Press.

———.1984. *Distinction: A Social Critique of the Judgement of Taste*. London: Routledge.

Bourgois, Philippe. 1989. *Ethnicity at Work: Divided Labor on a Central American Banana Plantation*. Baltimore: Johns Hopkins University Press.

———. 2003. "One Hundred Years of United Fruit Company Letters." In Steve Striffler and Mark Moberg (Eds)., *Banana Wars: Power, Production, and History in the Americas*. Durham: Duke University Press.

Bourguignon, Erika. 1979. *Psychological Anthropology: An Introduction to Human Nature and Cultural Differences*. New York: Holt, Rinehart and Winston.

Bowen, John. 2001. "The Myth of Global Ethnic Conflict." In James E. Harf and Mark Owen Lombardi (Eds.), *Taking Sides: Clashing Views on Controversial Global Issues*. Guilford, CT: McGraw-Hill/Dushkin.

———. 2005. *Religions in Practice: An Approach to the Anthropology of Religion*, 3rd ed. Boston: Pearson Education, Inc.

———. 2008. *Why the French Don't Like Headscarves: Islam, the State and Public Space*. NJ: Princeton University Press.

———. 2009. *Can Islam Be French? Pluralism and Pragmatism in a Secularist State*. NJ: Princeton University Press.

Bower, Bruce. 1990. "Biographies Etched in Bone." *Science News* 138: 106–108.

———. 1991. "Fossil Finds Expand Early Hominid Anatomy." *Science News* 139: 182.

Boyd, Robert, and Pete Richerson. 1992. "How Microevolutionary Processes Give Rise to History." In Nitecki, Matthew H. and Doris V. Nitecki (Eds.), *History and Evolution* pp. 179–210. Albany: State University of New York Press.

Boyd, Robert, and Joan Silk. 2012. *How Humans Evolved* (6th ed.). New York: W. W. Norton.

Boyer, Pascal. 1994a. "Cognitive Constraints on Cultural Representations: Natural Ontologies and Religious Ideas." In L. A. Hirschfeld and S. Gelman (Eds.), *Mapping the Mind: Domain-Specificity in Culture and Cognition*. pp. 391–411. New York: Cambridge University Press.

———.1994b. *The Naturalness of Religious Ideas: A Cognitive Theory of Religion*, Berkeley, CA: University of California Press.

———. 1998. "Cognitive Tracks of Cultural Inheritance: How Evolved Intuitive Ontology Governs Cultural Transmission." *American Anthropologist* 100: 876–889.

———. 2001. *Religion Explained: The Evolutionary Origins of Religious Thought*. New York: Basic Books.

Boyer, Pascal and James V. Wertsch (Eds.) 2009. *Memory in Mind and Culture*. Cambridge: Cambridge University Press.

Brace, C. L. 1964. "The Fate of the 'Classic' Neanderthals: A Consideration of Hominid Catastrophism." *Current Anthropology* 5: 3–43.

———. 1967. *The Stages of Human Evolution: Human and Cultural Origins*. Englewood Cliffs, NJ: Prentice Hall.

———. 1989. "Medieval Thinking and the Paradigms of Paleoanthropology." *American Anthropologist* 91 (2): 442–446.

Brace, C. L., and M. F. A. Montagu. 1965. *Man's Evolution: An Introduction to Physical Evolution*. New York: Macmillan.

Braidwood, Robert J. 1960. "The Agricultural Revolution." *Scientific American* 203: 130–141.

Brain, C. K. 1981. *The Hunters or the Hunted?* Chicago: University of Chicago Press.

Bramble, D.M. and D. E. Lieberman. 2004. "Endurance Running and the Evolution of *Homo*." *Nature* 432: 345–352.

Braude, Benjamin. 1997. "The Sons of Noah and the Construction of Ethnic and Geographical Identities in the Medieval and Early Modern Periods."*The William and Mary Quarterly: A Magazine of Early American History and Culture* 54 (1): 103–142.

Breitbart, Eric. 1997. *A World on Display: Photographs from the St. Louis World's Fair, 1904.* Albuquerque: University of New Mexico Press.

Brill, R. H. 1964. "Applications of Fission-Track Dating to Historic and Prehistoric Glasses." *Archaeometry* 7: 51–57.

Briller, Sheryln H. and Amy Goldmacher. 2008. *Designing an Anthropology Career: Professional Development Exercises.* Walnut Creek, CA: AltaMira Press.

Britten, Roy J. 2002. "Divergence between Samples of Chimpanzee and Human DNA Sequences is 5%, Counting Indels," *Proceedings of the National Academy of Science* 99 (21): 13633–13635.

Brokensha, David, and Charles Erasmus. 1969. "African 'Peasants' and Community Development." In David Brokensha and Marion Pearsall (Eds.), *The Anthropology of Development in Sub-Saharan Africa.* Society for Applied Anthropology Monograph No. 10, pp. 85–100.

Brooke, James. 1993. "Brazil's Outrage Intensifies as Toll in Massacre Hits 73." *The New York Times*, August 23, p. A6.

Brooks, Alison, Fatimah L. C. Jackson, and Roy Richard Grinker. 2004. "Race and Ethnicity." In Ruth Osterweiss Selig, Marilyn R. London, and P. Ann Kaupp, (Eds.), *Anthropology Explored: Revised and Expanded: The Best of Smithsonian Anthronotes.* Washington, DC: Smithsonian Books.

Broom, Robert. 1938. "The Pleistocene Anthropoid Apes of South Africa." *Nature* 142: 377–379.

———. 1949. "Another New Type of Fossil Ape Man." *Nature* 163: 57.

Brophy, K. and Cowley, D. (Eds.), 2005. *From the Air: Understanding Aerial Archaeology.* London: The History Press Ltd.

Brothwell, D. R. and A. M. Pollard. 2001. *A Handbook of Archaeological Science.* Chicester: Willey.

Brown, Cecil H. 1984. *Language and Living Things: Uniformities in Classification and Naming.* New Brunswick, NJ: Rutgers University Press.

Brown, Donald E. 1976. *Principles of Social Structure: Southeast Asia.* London: Duckworth Press.

———. 1991. *Human Universals.* New York: McGraw-Hill.

———. 2012. "Ethnicity and Ethnocentrism: Are They Natural?" In Raymond Scupin (Ed.), *Race and Ethnicity: The United States and the World* (2nd ed.). pp. 81–92. Upper Saddle River, NJ: Prentice Hall.

Brown, James A. (Ed.), 1971. "Approaches to the Social Dimensions of Mortuary Practices." *Memoirs of the Society for American Archaeology* No. 25.

Brown, Judith K. 1970a. "Economic Organization and the Position of Women among the Iroquois." *Ethnohistory* 17: 151–167.

———. 1970b. "A Note on the Division of Labor by Sex." *American Anthropologist* 72: 1073–1078.

Brown, Karen McCarthy. 1992. *Mama Lola:A Voodoo Priestess in Brooklyn.* Comparative Studies in Religion and Society, No. 4. Berkeley: University of California Press.

Brown, Lester R. 1988. "The Vulnerability of Oil-Based Farming." *World Watch*, March/April. Reprinted in Robert Jackson (Ed.), *Global Issues 90/91.* Sluice Dock, Guilford, CT: Dushkin Publishing Group, 1990.

Brown, Michael F. 2008. "Cultural Relativism 2.0." *Current Anthropology* 49 (3): 363–383.

Brown, Peter, and Ron Barrett (Eds.), 2010. *Understanding and Applying Medical Anthropology* (2nd ed.). New York: McGraw-Hill.

Brown, Penelope. 2002. "Language as a Model for Culture: Lessons from the Cognitive Sciences." In Richard Fox and Barbara J. King (Eds.), *Anthropology beyond Culture.* pp. 169–192. . Oxford, England: Berg.

Brown, Susan Love. 2012. "African Americans." In Raymond Scupin (Ed.), *Race and Ethnicity: The United States and the World* (2nd ed.). pp. 171–200. Upper Saddle River, NJ: Pearson Prentice Hall.

Brown, T. M., and K. D. Rose. 1987. *"Patterns of Dental Evolution in Early Eocene Anaptomorphine Commomyodael from the Bighorn Basin, Wyoming." Journal of Paleontology* 61: 1–62.

Brownell, Susan, and Jeffrey N. Wasserstrom (Eds.), 2002. *Chinese Femininities: Chinese Masculinities.* Berkeley: University of California Press.

Brownell, Susan. 1995. *Training the Body for China: Sports in the Moral Order of the People's Republic.* Chicago, IL: University of Chicago Press.

Brues, A. M. 1977. *People and Races.* New York: Macmillan.

Brumfiel, E. O., and T. K. Earle. 1987. *Specialization, Exchange, and Complex Societies.* Cambridge: Cambridge University Press.

Brumfiel, Elizabeth. 1991. "Weaving and Cooking: Women's Production in Aztec Mexico." In Joan M. Gero and Margaret Conkey (Eds.), *Engendering Archaeology: Women and Prehistory*, pp. 224–251. Cambridge: Blackwell.

———.(Ed.), 2005. "Production and Power at Postclassic Xaltocan." *Arqueología de México*, No. 6, published by University of Pittsburgh Latin American Archaeology Publications and Instituto Nacional de Antropología e Historia (México, D.F.).

Bruner, Edward M. 1996a. "Tourism in the Balinese Borderzone." In Smadar Lavie and Ted Swedenburg, (Eds.), *Displacement, Diaspora, and Geographic Identity*, pp. 157–179. Durham: Duke University Press.

———. 1996b. "Tourism in Ghana: The Representation of Slavery and the Return of the Black Diaspora." *American Anthropologist* 98 (2): 290–304.

Brunet, Michel, Franck Guy, David Pilbeam, Hassane Taisso Mackaye, Andossa Likius, Djimdoumalbaye Ahounta, Alain Beauvilain, Cécile Blondel et al. 2002. "A New Hominid from the Upper Miocene of Chad, Central Africa." *Nature* 418: 145–151.

Bucheli, Marcelo. 2003. "United Fruit Company in Latin America." In Steve Striffler and Mark Moberg, (Eds.), *Banana Wars: Power, Production, and History in the Americas.* pp. 94–110. Durham: Duke University Press.

Buchignani, Norman. 2011. "Canada." In Raymond Scupin (Ed.), *Race and Ethnicity: The United States and the World,* (2nd ed.), pp. 420–429. Upper Saddle River, NJ: Prentice Hall.

Buchowski, Michał. 2009. "Property Relations, Class, and Labour in Rural Poland." In Kürti, László and Peter Skalník (Eds.), *Postsocialist Europe: Anthropological Perspectives from Home*. pp. 51–75. New York and Oxford: Berghahn Books.

Buckser, Andrew. 2008. "Protestantism." In Scupin, Raymond,, *Religion and Culture: An Anthropological Focus* (2nd ed.). pp. 402–429. Upper Saddle River, NJ: Pearson Prentice Hall Press.

Budge, E. A. Wallis. 1895. *The Book of the Dead*. London: Longmans.

———. 1900. *Egyptian Religion*. London.

Bulbeck, David. 2007. "Where the River Meets the Sea: A Parsimonious Model for Homo sapiens Colonization of the Indian Ocean Rim and Sahul." *Current Anthropology* 48 (2): 315–321.

Burch, Ernest J., Jr. 1970. "Marriage and Divorce among the North Alaskan Eskimos." In Paul Bohannon, (Ed.), *Divorce and After*, pp. 152–181. Garden City, NY: Doubleday.

Burnet, Jennie E. 2006. "Conceiving Unity: Coexistence and Reconciliation at the Micro-level in the New Rwanda." In Peter Uvin, Catherine Newbury, Alison Des Forges, and Timothy Longman, (Eds.), *A River of Death: Variations, Similarities, and Consequences of the Rwanda Genocide*. pp. 140–177. Unpublished ms.

———. 2008. "The Injustice of Local Justice: Truth, Reconciliation, and Revenge in Rwanda." *Genocide Studies and Prevention* 3 (2): 173–193.

Butzer, Karl W. 1984. "Long-Term Nile Flood Variation and Political Discontinuities in Pharaonic Egypt." In J. Desmond Clark and Steven A. Brandt (Eds.), *From Hunters to Farmers: The Causes and Consequences of Food Production in Egypt*, pp. 102–112. Berkeley: University of California Press.

Byers, S. N. 2008. *Forensic Anthropology*. Boston: Pearson Education.

Calkowski, Marcia. 2008. "Buddhism" In Scupin, Raymond., *Religion and Culture: An Anthropological Focus* (2nd ed.). pp. 273–302. Upper Saddle River, NJ: Pearson Prentice Hall Press.

Callender, Charles, and L. Kochems. 1983. "The North-American Berdache." *Current Anthropology* 24: 443–470.

Calloway, Colin G. 2003. *First Peoples: A Documentary Survey of American Indian History* (2nd ed.). New York: Bedford Books.

Campagnoli, Mauro. 2005. *Baka Pygmies*. http://www.maurocampagnoli.com.

Campbell, Anne, and Patricia C. Rice. 2004. "Why Do Anthropological Experts Disagree?" In Philip Carl Salzman and Patricia Rice, (Eds.), *Thinking Anthropologically: A Practical Guide for Students*. pp. 59–70. Upper Saddle River, NJ: Prentice Hall.

Campbell, Bernard G. 1983. *Human Ecology: The Story of Our Place in Nature from Prehistory to the Present*. Chicago: Aldine.

———. 1987. *Humankind Emerging* (5th ed.). Glenview, IL: Scott, Foresman.

Campbell, Christina J., Agustin Fuentes, Katherine MacKinnon, and Simon Bearder. 2007. *Primates in Perspective*. New York: Oxford University Press.

Canfield, Robert. 2004. "Karzai, Hamed." In Philip Mattar, (Ed.), *Encyclopedia of the Modern Middle East and North Africa* (2nd ed.). pp. 107–109. Chicago: Gale, MacMillan.

Cann, R. L., W. M. Brown, and A. C. Wilson. 1987. "Mitochondrial DNA and Human Evolution." *Nature* 325: 31–36.

Cannell, Fenella. 2010. "The Anthropology of Secularism." *Annual Review of Anthropology* 39: 85–100.

Carballo, David M. 2011. Obsidian and the Teotihuacan State: Weaponry and Ritual Production at the Moon Pyramid. *University of Pittsburgh Memoirs in Latin American Archaeology*, No. 21.

Carlisle, R. (Ed.), 1988. *Americans before Columbus: Perspectives on the Archaeology of the First Americans*. Pittsburgh: University of Pittsburgh Press.

Carlisle, R. C., and J. M. Adavasio. 1982. *Collected Papers on the Archaeology of Meadowcroft Rockshelter and the Cross Creek Drainage*. Pittsburgh: University of Pittsburgh.

Carneiro, Robert. 1961. "Slash and Burn Cultivation among the Kuikura and Its Implications for Cultural Development in the Amazon Basin." In Johannes Wilbert (Ed.), *The Evolution of Horticultural Systems in Native South America, Causes and Consequences: A Symposium. Anthropologica*, Supplement Publication No. 2, pp. 47–67.

———. 1967. "On the Relationship between Size of Population and Complexity of Social Organization." *Southwestern Journal of Anthropology* 23: 234–243.

———. 1970. "A Theory of the Origin of the 'State.'" *Science* 169: 733–738.

———. 1988. "Indians of the Amazonian Forest." In Julie Sloan Denslow and Christine Padoch, (Eds.), *People of the Tropical Rain Forests*. pp. 73–86. Berkeley: University of California Press.

Carr, C. 1995. "Mortuary Practices." *Journal of Archaeological Method and Theory* 2(2):105–200.

Carr, K. W., J. M. Adovasio, and D. R. Pedler. 1996. "Paleoindian Populations in Trans-Applachia: The View from Pennsylvania." Paper presented at the Integrating Appalachian Archaeology Conference. Albany: New York State Museum.

Carrasco, David. 2002. "Aztec Religion: Sacred Cities, Sacred Actions." In Lawrence E. Sullivan (Ed.), *Native Religions and Cultures of Central and South America: Anthropology of the Sacred*. pp. 330–392. . New York: Continuum International Publishing Group, Inc.

Carter, George F. 1988. "Cultural Historical Diffusion." In Peter J. Hugill and Bruce D. Dickson (Eds.), *The Transfer and Transformation of Ideas and Material Culture*. pp. 3–22. College Station: Texas A&M University Press.

Cartmill, Matt. 1997. "Predation, Feeding Strategies, and Primate Origins." In N. Boaz and A. J. Almquist (Eds.), *Biological Anthropology: A Synthetic Approach to Human Evolution*, pp. 192–93. Upper Saddle River, NJ: Prentice-Hall.

Castro, Bermúdez De J. M., J. L. Arsuaga, E. Carbonell, A. Rosas, I. Martinez, and M. Mosquera. 1997. "A Hominid from the Lower Pleistocene of Atapuerca, Spain: Possible Ancestor to Neanderthals and Modern Humans." *Science* 276: 1392–1395.

Castro, A. Peter. 1995. *Facing Kirinyaga: A Social History of Forest Commons in Southern Mount Kenya*. Indigenous Knowledge Series. London: Intermediate Technology Publications.

———, **(Ed.)** 1998a. "Special Section on Historical Consciousness and Development Planning." *World Development* 26 (9): 1695–1784.

———. 1998b. "Sustainable Agriculture or Sustained Error? The Case of Cotton in Kirinyaga, Kenya." *World Development* 26 (9): 1719–1731.

Castro, A. Peter (Ed.), 1998. "Special Section on Historical Consciousness and Development Planning." *World Development* 26 (9): 1695–1784.

Castro, A. Peter, and Erik Nielsen. 2001. "Indigenous People and Co-Management: Implications for Conflict Management." *Environmental Science and Policy* 4 (4–5): 229–239.

Castro, A. Peter, and Erik Nielson (Eds.), 2003. *Natural Resource Conflict Management Case Studies: An Analysis of Power, Participation and Protected Areas*. Rome: Food and Agricultural Organization of the United Nations.

Castro, A. Peter, Dan Taylor, and David Brokensha (Eds.), 2012. *Climate Change and Threatened Communities: Vulnerability, Capacity and Action*. London: Practical Action Publishing.

Catchpole, C. K., and P. J. B. Slater. 1995. *Bird Song: Biological Themes and Variations*. Cambridge: Cambridge University Press.

Caton, Steven C. 1986. "Salam Tahiyah: Greetings from the Highlands of Yemen." *American Ethnologist* 13 (2): 290–308.

Cauvin, J. 2000. *The Birth of the Gods and the Origins of Agriculture*. Cambridge: Cambridge University Press.

Cavalli-Sforza, L.Luca, Paolo Menozzi, and Alberto Piazza. 1994. *The History and Geography of Human Genes*. Princeton: Princeton University Press.

Chagnon, Napoleon A. 1974. *Studying the Yanomamö*. New York: Holt, Rinehart and Winston.

———. 2000. "Manipulating Kinship Rules: A Form of Male Yanomamö Reproductive Competition." In Lee Cronk, Napoleon Chagnon, and William Irons, (Eds.), *Adaptation and Human Behavior: An Anthropological Perspective*. pp. 115–129. New York: Aldine De Gruyter.

———. 2012. *Yanomamö* (6th ed.). Belmont, CA: Wadsworth CENGAGE Learning.

———.2013. *Noble Savages: My Life among Two Dangerous Tribes--the Yanomamö and the Anthropologists*. New York: Simon and Schuster.

Chagnon, Napoleon, and Raymond Hames. 1979. "Protein Deficiency and Tribal Warfare in Amazonia: New Data." *Science* 20 (3): 910–913.

Chagnon, Napoleon, and William Irons. 1979. *Evolutionary Biology and Human Social Behavior*. North Scituate, MA: Duxbury Press.

Chakrabarti, D. K. 1999. *India: An Archaeological History*. Oxford: Oxford University Press.

Chambers, Erve. 1985. *Applied Anthropology:A Practical Guide*. Englewood Cliffs, NJ: Prentice Hall.

Chance, Norman. 1984. *China's Urban Villagers: Life in a Beijing Commune*. New York: Holt, Rinehart and Winston.

Chanda, N. 2007. *Bound Together: How Traders, Preachers, Adventurers, and Warriors Shaped Globalization*. New Haven: Yale University Press.

Chandler, Alfred G., and Bruce Maizlish. 2005. *Leviathans: Multinational Corporations and the New Global History*. Cambridge: Cambridge University Press.

Chandy, Laurence, Natasha Ledlie, and Veronika Penciakova. 2013. "The Final Countdown: Prospects for Ending Extreme Poverty by 2030." Policy Paper 2013–2014. The Brookings Institution.

Chang, Kwang-Chih. 1970. "The Beginnings of Agriculture in the Far East." *Antiquity* 44 (175): 175–185.

———. 1975. "From Archaeology to Hostoy: The Neolithic Foundations of Chinese Civilization." In Chang Chunshu, (Ed.), *The Making of China: Main Themes in Premodern Chinese History*, pp. 38–45. Englewood Cliffs, NJ: Prentice Hall.

———. 1986. *The Archaeology of Ancient China* (4th ed.). New Haven, CT: Yale University Press.

Chang, Te-Tzu and Bor S. Luh. 1991. *Rice Production* (2nd ed.). New York: Springer.

Chapais, Bernard. 2008. *Primeval Kinship: How Pair-Bonding Gave Birth to Human Society*. Cambridge, MA: Harvard University Press.

Chapman, Arthur. 2009. *Numbers of Living Species in Australia and the World*. 2nd ed. Canberra: Australian Government, Department of the Environment, Water, Heritage, and the Arts.

Chapman, Robert, Ian Kinnes, and Klavs Randsborg (Eds.), 1981. *The Archaeology of Death*. Cambridge: Cambridge University Press.

Charvát, Petr; Zainab Bahrani and Marc Van de Mieroop. 2002. *Mesopotamia Before History*. London: Routledge.

Chase, P. G., and H. L. Dibble. 1987. "Middle Paleolithic Symbolism: A Review of Current Evidence and Interpretations." *Journal of Anthropological Archaeology* 6: 263–293.

Cherian, Jacob. 2010. "Outsourcing to India, China Cost Effective Despite Pres. Obama's Move to Revoke Tax Breaks" *Ground Report*. http://www.groundreport.com/Business/Offshoring-to-India-China-Cost-Effective-Despite-P/2917155.

Childe, V. Gordon. 1936. *Man Makes Himself*. London: Watts.

———. 1950. "The Urban Revolution." *Town Planning Review* 21: 3–17.

———. 1952. *New Light on the Most Ancient East*. London: Routledge.

Chirot, Daniel. 1986. *Social Change in the Modern Era*. San Diego, CA: Harcourt Brace Jovanovich.

Chomsky, Noam. 1980. *Rules and Representation*. New York: Columbia University Press.

———. 1986. *Knowledge of Language: Its Nature, Origin, and Use*. New York: Praeger.

———. 1995. *The Minimalist Program*. Cambridge, MA: MIT Press.

———. 2002. *On Nature and Language*. A. Belletti and Luigi Rizzi. (Eds.), Cambridge: Cambridge University Press.

Chouin, G. L. and C. R. DeCorse. 2010. "Prelude to the Atlantic Trade: New Perspectives on Southern Ghana's pre-Atlantic History (800–1500)." *Journal of African History* 51:123–145.

Chua, Amy. 2003. *World on Fire: How Exporting Free Market Democracy Breeds Ethnic Hatred and Global Instability*. New York: Doubleday.

Christaller, Walter. 1933. *Die Zentralen Orte in Süddeutschland*. Jena, Germany: Karl Zeiss.

Ciochon, R. L., and R. Corruccini (Eds.), 1983. *New Interpretations of Ape and Human Ancestry*. New York: Plenum Press.

Ciochon, R. L., J. Olsen, and J. James. 1990. *Other Origins: The Search for the Giant Ape in Human Prehistory*. New York: Bantam Books.

Claessen, Henri J. M., and Peter Skalnik. 1978. "The Early State: Theories and Hypotheses." In Claessen, Henri J. M. and Peter Skalnik. *The Early State*, pp. 3–29. New York: Mouton Publishers.

Claesson, H. J. M., P. Van De Velde, and E. M. Smith. 1985. *Development and Decline: The Evolution of Sociopolitical Organization*. South Hadley, MA: Bergin & Garvey.

Clapp, Nicholas. 1999. *The Road to Ubar: Finding the Atlantis of the Sands*. NY: Houghton Mifflin.

Clark, Grahame, and Stuart Piggott. 1965. *Prehistoric Societies*. New York: Knopf.

Clark, J. Desmond. 1970. *The Prehistory of Africa*. New York: Praeger.

———. 1979. *Mesolithic Prelude*. Edinburgh: Edinburgh University Press.

Clark, J. Desmond, and Steven A. Brandt. 1984. *From Hunters to Farmers: The Causes and Consequences of Food Production in Africa*. Berkeley: University of California Press.

Clark, J. Desmond, and J. W. K. Harris. 1985. "Fire and Its Roles in Early Hominid Lifeways." *African Archaeological Review* 3: 3–27.

Clarke-Ekong, Sheilah 2012. "Africa" in *Race and Ethnicity: The United States and the World* (2nd ed.). Raymond Scupin, (Ed.)., pp. 324–341. Upper Saddle River, NJ: Pearson, Prentice Hall.

Clayre, Alasdair. 1985. *The Heart of the Dragon*. Boston: Houghton Mifflin.

Clegg, Margaret. 2004. "Modern Approaches to the Evolution of Speech and Language." *General Anthropology* 10 (2): 8–12.

Clegg, Margaret, and L. C. Aiello. 2002a. "Paying the Price of Speech? An Analysis of Mortality Statistics for Choking on Food." *American Journal of Physical Anthropology* (Supplement 30): 126.

———. 2002b. "Estimating Hyoid Bone Morphology in Earlier Hominine Species." *American Journal of Physical Anthropology* (Supplement 34).

Clemens, W. A. 1974. "Purgatorius, an Early Paromomyid Primate Mammalia." *Science* 184: 903–906.

Clifford, James. 1983. "On Ethnographic Authority." *Representations* 1: 118–146.

Coe, Kathryn., Nancy Aiken, and Craig Palmer. 2006. Once Upon a Time: Ancestors and the Evolutionary Significance of Stories. *Anthropological Forum*, 16(10): 21–40.

Coe, Michael. 1977. *Mexico* (2nd ed.). New York: Praeger.

——— .2011. *The Maya*. New York: Thames & Hudson.

Coe, Michael, Dean Snow, and Elizabeth Benson. 1986. *Atlas of Ancient America*. New York: Facts on File.

Coe, Michael D., and Mark Van Stone. 2005. *Reading the Maya Glyphs*. London: Thames & Hudson

Cohen, Abner. 1969. *Custom and Politics in Urban Africa*. Berkeley: University of California Press.

———. 1974. *Urban Ethnicity*. London: Tavistock.

Cohen, Anthony. 1996. "Personal Nationalism: A Scottish View of Some Rites, Rights, and Wrongs." *American Ethnologist* 23 (4): 802–815.

Cohen, Mark Nathan. 1977. *The Food Crisis in Prehistory*. New Haven, CT: Yale University Press.

———. 1994. "Demographic Expansion: Causes and Consequences." In Tim Ingold (Ed.) ., *Companion Encyclopedia of Anthropology*, pp. 265–296. New York: Routledge.

Cohen, Mark Nathan, and George J. Armelagos. 1984. *Paleopathology at the Origins of Agriculture*. New York: Academic Press.

Cohen, Ronald. 1978. "Introduction." In R. Cohen and E. Service (Eds.), *Origins of the State: The Anthropology of Political Evolution, pp. 1–20*. Philadelphia: Institute for the Study of Human Issues.

Cohen, Ronald, and Elman Service (Eds.), 1978. *Origins of the State: The Anthropology of Political Evolution*. Philadelphia: Institute for the Study of Human Issues.

Cole, Donald Powell. 1984. *Nomads of the Nomads: The Al-Murrah Bedouin of the Empty Quarter*. Prospect Heights, IL: Waveland Press.

Cole, Michael, and Sylvia Scribner. 1974. *Culture and Thought: A Psychological Introduction*. New York: Wiley.

Collier, Jane Fishburne. 1988. *Marriage and Inequality in Classless Societies*. Stanford, CA: Stanford University Press.

Collier, Jane Fishburne, and Sylvia Junko Yanagisako (Eds.), 1987. *Gender and Kinship: Towards a Unified Analysis*. Stanford: Stanford University Press.

Colson, Elizabeth. 2003. "Forced Migration and the Anthropological Response." *Journal of Refugee Studies* 16 (1): 1–18.

Comaroff, Jean. 1985. *Body of Power, Spirit of Resistance*. Chicago: University of Chicago Press.

Comaroff, Jean, and John L. Comaroff. 1991. *Of Revelation and Revolution: Christianity, Colonialism, and Consciousness in South Africa*. Vol. 1. Chicago: University of Chicago Press.

Connah, Graham. 2001. *African Civilizations: Precolonial Cities and States in Tropical Africa: An Archaeological Perspective*. Cambridge: Cambridge University Press.

Connell, Dan. 1987. "The Next African Famine." *Dollars and Sense*. Reprinted in Robert Jackson (1990) *Global Issues 90/91*(6th ed). Sluice Dock, Guilford, CT: Dushkin Publishing Group.

———. 1997. *Reconstructing Human Origins: A Modern Synthesis*. New York: Norton Press.

Conniff, Richard. 2003. "Go Ahead, Kiss Your Cousin." *Discover* 24 (8): 1–6.

Cooney, G. 2000. *Landscapes of Neolithic Ireland*. London: Routledge.

Conroy, Glenn C. 1990. *Primate Evolution*. New York: W. W. Norton.

Conroy, Glenn C., and Michael Vanier. 1990. "Endocranial Features of *Australopithecus africanus* Revealed by 2- and 3-D Computer Tomography." *Science* 247: 839–841.

Conversi, Daniele (Ed.), 2002. *Ethnonationalism in the Contemporary World: Walker Connor and the Study of Nationalism*. London: Routledge .

Coolidge, Frederick L., and Thomas Wynn. 2009. *The Rise of Homo sapiens*. Chichester: Wiley.

Cornell, Stephan, and Douglas Hartmann. 1998. *Ethnicity and Race: Making Identities in a Changing World*. Thousand Oaks, CA: Pine Forge Press.

Coupland, Gary, Terence Clark, and Amanda Palmer. 2009. "Hierarchy, Communalism and the Spatial Order of Northwest Coast Plank Houses: A Comparative Study." *American Antiquity* 74 (1): 77–106.

Couzin-Frankel, Jennifer. 2010. "Researchers to Return Blood Samples to the Yanomamö." *Science* 328: 1218.

Cowan, C. Wesley, and Patty Jo Watson (Eds.). 1992. *The Origins of Agriculture: An International Perspective*. Washington, DC: Smithsonian Institution Press.

Cowgill, Donald O. 1986. *Aging around the World*. Belmont, CA: Wadsworth.

Crapanzano, Vincent. 1986. *Waiting: The Whites of South Africa*. New York: Random House.

Cravey, A. J. 1998. *Women and Work in Mexico's Maquiladoras*. Lanham, MD: Rowman and Littlefield.

Crawford, G. W. 1992. "Prehistoric Plant Domestication in East Asia." In C. Wesley Cowan and Patty Jo Watson, (Eds)., *The Origins of Agriculture: An International Perspective*, pp. 7–38. Washington, DC: Smithsonian Institution Press.

Crawford, Harriet. 1993. *Sumer and the Sumerians*. New York: Cambridge University Press.

Crockford, C. and C. Boesch. 2003. "Context-specific calls in Wild Chimpanzees, *Pan troglodytes verus*: Analysis of Barks. *Animal Behaviour* 66: 115–125.

———. 2005. Call Combinations in Wild Chimpanzees. *Behaviour* 142: 397–421.

Cronk, Lee. 1999. *That Complex Whole: Culture and the Evolution of Human Behavior.* Boulder, CO: Westview Press.

———. 2003. "Reciprocity and the Power of Giving." In James Spradley and David McCurdy (Eds.), *Conformity and Conflict: Readings in Cultural Anthropology.* pp. 139–145. Boston: Allyn & Bacon.

Crumley, Carole L. 1976. "Toward a Locational Definition of State Systems of Settlement." *American Anthropologist* 78: 59–73.

Cyran K. A., and M. Kimmel. 2010. "Alternatives to the Wright-Fisher Model: The Robustness of Mitochondrial Eve Dating." *Theoretical Population Biology* 78 (3): 165–172.

Dagosto, M. 1988. "Implications of Postcranial Evidence for the Origin of Euprimates." *Journal of Human Evolution* 17: 35–56.

Dahlberg, Frances (Ed.). 1981. *Woman the Gatherer.* New Haven, CT: Yale University Press.

Dalley, S. (Ed.). 1998. *The Legacy of Mesopotamia.* Oxford: Oxford University Press.

Dames, Christina. 2012. *Gender, Ethnicity, Infrastructure, and the Use of Financial Institutions in Kalimantan Barat, Indonesia.* Ph.D. dissertation, Anthropology Department. Columbia: University of Missouri.

D'Andrade, Roy G. 1989. "Cultural Cognition." In M. Posner (Ed.), *Foundations of Cognitive Science.* Cambridge, MA: MIT Press.

———. 1995. *The Development of Cognitive Anthropology.* Cambridge: Cambridge University Press.

D'Andrea, A. C. and J. Casey. 2002. "Pearl Millet and Kintampo Subsistence." *African Archaeological Review* 19(3): 147–173.

Dalton, Rex. 2010. "Fossil Finger Points to New Human Species. DNA Analysis Reveals Lost Relative from 40,000 Years Ago." *Nature* 464: 472–473.

Daniel, Glyn. 1981. *A Short History of Archaeology.* New York: Thames and Hudson.

Daniels, Peter T., and William Bright (Eds.). 1995. *The World's Writing Systems.* New York: Oxford University Press.

Darnell, Regna. 1998. *And Along Came Boas: Continuity and Evolution in Americanist Anthropology.* Studies in the History of Language Sciences. Amsterdam: John Benjamins Publishing Co.

Dart, Raymond A. 1925. "*Australopithecus africanus*: The Man-Ape of South Africa." *Nature* 115: 195–199.

———. 1967. *Adventures with the Missing Link.* Philadelphia: Institutes Press.

Darwin, Charles. 1979. *The Illustrated Origin of Species.* New York: Hill & Wang.

Darwin, Charles, and E. Mayr. [1859] 1966. *The Origin of Species* (Facsimile of the 1st ed.). Cambridge, MA: Harvard University Press.

Davidson, Basil. 1961. *The African Slave Trade.* Boston: Atlantic; Little, Brown.

Davies, Paul. 2000. *The Fifth Miracle: The Search for the Origin and Meaning of Life.* New York: Simon and Schuster.

Davila, Mario. 1971. "Compadrazgo: Fictive Kinship in Latin America." In Nelson Graburn, (Ed.), *Readings in Kinship and Social Structure.* pp.396–405. New York: Harper & Row.

Davis, David Brion. 1997. "Constructing Race: A Reflection." *The William and Mary Quarterly: A Magazine of Early American History and Culture.* 54 (1): 7–18.

———. 2006. *Inhuman Bondage. The Rise and Fall of Slavery in the New World.* Oxford: Oxford University Press.

Davis, Wade. 1997. *The Serpent and the Rainbow.* New York: Touchstone Books.

Dawkins, Richard. 1976. *The Selfish Gene.* Oxford, England: Oxford University Press.

Day, Michael H. 1986. *Guide to Fossil Man*, 4th ed. Chicago: University of Chicago Press.

Deacon, Terrence. 1997. *The Symbolic Species: The Co-evolution of Language and the Brain.* New York: W.W. Norton.

Deblij, Harm J., and Peter O. Muller. 1985. *Geography: Regions and Concepts* (4th ed.). New York: John Wiley.

DeCorse, Christopher. 1996. "Documents, Oral Histories, and the Material Record: Historical Archaeology in West Africa." *World Archaeological Bulletin* 7:40–50.

———. 2001. *An Archaeology of Elmina: Africans and Europeans on the Gold Coast, 1400–1900.* Washington, DC: Smithsonian Institution Press.

Deetz, James. 1996. *In Small Things Forgotten: An Archaeology of Early American Life.* New York: Anchor Books.

DeFrancis, John. 1984. *The Chinese Language: Fact and Fantasy.* Honolulu: University of Hawaii Press.

Degler, Carl N. 1991. *In Search of Human Nature: The Decline and Revival of Darwinism in American Social Thought.* New York: Oxford University Press.

de Heinzelin J, J. D. Clark, T. White, W. Hart, P. Renne, G. WoldeGabriel, Y. Beyene, and E. Vrba. 1999. "Environment and Behavior of 2.5-Million-Year-Old Bouri Hominids." *Science* 284 (5414): 625–629.

De La Torre, Ignacio. 2004. "Omo Revisited." *Current Anthropology* 45 (4): 439–453.

deLumley, H. 1969. "A Paleolithic Camp at Nice." *Scientific American* 220: 42–59.

Demarest, William J., and Benjamin D. Paul. 1981. "Mayan Migrants in Guatemala City." *Anthropology, UCLA* 11 (12): 43–73.

Dematte, P. 1999. "Longshan-era Urbanism: The Role of Cities in Predynastic China." *Asian Perspectives* 38: 119–153.

Dembski, William A. 1999. *Intelligent Design: The Bridge between Science and Theology.* Dallas: Intervarsity Press.

D'Emilio, John. 1988. *Intimate Matters: A History of Sexuality in America.* New York: Harper & Row.

de Munck, Victor (Ed.), 1998. *Love and Culture.* New York: Columbia University Press.

———. 2000. *Culture, Self, and Meaning.* Prospect Heights, IL: Waveland Press.

———. 2009. *Research Design and Methods for Studying Cultures.* Lanham, MD: AltaMira Press.

Denham, T. P. 2005. "Envisaging Early Agriculture in the Highlands of New Guinea: Landscapes, Plants and Practices." *World Archaeology* 37: 290–306.

Denham, T. P., J. Iriarte, and L. Vrydaghs (Eds.), 2007. *Rethinking Agriculture: Archaeological and Ethnoarchaeological Perspectives.* Walnut Creek, CA: Left Coast.

Dennell, Robin W. 1992. "The Origins of Crop Agriculture in Europe." In C. Wesley Cowan and Patty Jo Watson, (Eds.), *The Origins of Agriculture: An International Perspective,* pp. 71–100. Washington, DC: Smithsonian Institution Press.

Denoon, D., M. Hudson, G. McCormack, and Morris Suzuki (Eds.), 2001. *Multicultural Japan: Paleolithic to Postmodern.* Cambridge: Cambridge University Press.

Desmond, Adrian, and James Moore. 1991. *Darwin: The Life of a Tormented Evolutionist.* New York: Warner Books, Inc.

Deshpande, Omkar, Serafim Batzoglou, Marcus W. Feldman, and L. Luca Cavalli-Sforza, 2009. "A Serial Founder Effect Model for Human Settlement Out of Africa." *Proceedings of the Royal Society B276,* 291–300.

Devoe, Pamela. 2006. "China." In Raymond Scupin (Ed.),*Peoples and Cultures of Asia.* pp. 185–225. Upper Saddle River, NJ: Prentice Hall.

de Waal, Frans (Ed.), 2001. *Tree of Origin: What Primate Behavior Can Tell Us about Human Social Evolution.* Cambridge: Harvard University Press.

Diamond, Jared. 1987. "The Worst Mistake in the History of the Human Race." *Discover* (May): 64–66.

———. 1993. "Speaking with a Single Tongue." *Discover* (February): 78–85.

———. 1997. *Guns, Germs, and Steel: The Fates of Human Societies.* New York: W. W. Norton & Co.

———. 1998. "Japanese Roots." *Discover* 19 (June: 86–94).

———. 2005. *Collapse: How Societies Choose to Fail or Succeed.* New York: Penguin Books.

Diaz, May N. 1966. *Tonala: Conservatism, Responsibility and Authority in a Mexican Town.* Berkeley: University of California Press.

Dickemann, Mildred. 1979. "Female Infanticide, Reproductive Strategies, and Social Stratification." In N. Chagnon and W. Irons, (Eds.), *Evolutionary Biology and Human Social Behavior: An Anthropological Perspective,* pp. 321–367. North Scituate, MA: Duxbury Press.

Diehl, Michael W. (Ed.), 2000. *Hierarchies in Action: Cui Bono?* Southern Illinois University, Carbondale, Center for Archaeological Investigations, Occasional paper no. 27.

Dikötter, Frank. 1992. *The Discourse of Race in Modern China.* Stanford: Stanford University Press.

——— (Ed.), 1997. *The Construction of Racial Identities in China and Japan: Historical and Contemporary Perspectives.* Honolulu: University of Hawaii Press.

———. 2008. "The Racialization of the Globe: An Interactive Interpretation." *Ethnic and Racial Studies* 28 (4): 1–19.

Dillehay, Thomas D. 1989. *Monte Verde: A Late Pleistocene Settlement in Chile,* Vol. 1. Washington, DC: Smithsonian Institution Press.

———. 1997a. "The Battle of Monte Verde." *The Sciences* (January/February): 28–33.

———. 1997b. *Monte Verde: A Late Pleistocene Settlement in Chile,* Vol. 2. Washington, DC: Smithsonian Institution Press.

———. 2000. *The Settlement of the Americas.* New York: Basic Books.

Dillehay, Thomas D., and David J. Meltzer. 1991. *The First Americans: Search and Research.* Boca Raton, FL: CRC Press.

Dirks, Nicholas B. 2001. *Castes of Mind: Colonialism and the Making of Modern India.* Princeton: Princeton University Press.

Divale, William, and Marvin Harris. 1976. "Population, Warfare, and the Male Supremacist Complex." *American Anthropologist* 78: 521–538.

Dobkin de Rios, Marlene. 1984. *Hallucinogens: Cross-Cultural Perspectives.* Albuquerque: University of New Mexico Press.

Donnan, Christopher B., and Donna McClelland. 1979. *The Burial Theme in Moche Iconography.* Washington, DC: Dunbarton Oaks.

Donnan, Christopher, and Luis Jaime Castillo. 1992. "Finding the Tomb of a Moche Priestess." *Archaeology* 45 (6): 38–42.

Donnelly, Nancy D. 1992. "The Impossible Situation of Vietnamese in Hong Kong's Detention Centers." In Pamela DeVoe (Ed.), *Selected Papers on Refugee Issues.* pp. 120–132. Arlington, VA: American Anthropological Association.

Dorn, R., et al. 1986. "Cation Ratio and Accelerator Radiocarbon Dating of Rock Varnish on Archaeological Artifacts and Land Forms in the Mojave Desert." *Science* 213: 830–833.

Dorn, R., and D. Whitley. 1988. "Cation-Ratio Dating of Petroglyphs Using PIXE." *Nuclear Instruments and Methods in Physics Research* 35: 410–414.

Douglas, Mary. 1966. *Purity and Danger: An Analysis of the Concepts of Pollution and Taboo.* London: Routledge and Kegan Paul.

Dowie, Mark. 2009. *Conservation Refugees: The Hundred Year Conflict between Global Conservation and Native Peoples.* Cambridge, MA: MIT Press.

Dreger, Alice. 2011. "Darkness's Descent in the American Anthropological Association: A Cautionary Tale." *Human Nature.* DOI 10.1007/s12110-011-9103-y.

Drennan, Robert D. 1987. "Regional Demography in Chiefdoms." In Robert D. Drennan and Carlos A. Uribe, (Eds.), *Chiefdoms in the Americas.* pp. 307–324. New York: University Press of America.

Dressler, William. 1991. "Social Class, Skin Color, and Arterial Blood Pressure in Two Societies." *Ethnicity and Disease* 1: 60–77.

Drinnon, Richard. 1980. *Facing West: The Metaphysics of Indian-Hating and Empire Building.* Minneapolis: University of Minnesota Press.

Druzhkova AS, O. Thalmann, V.A.Trifonov, J.A.Leonard, N.V. Vorobieva, et al. 2013. "Ancient DNA Analysis Affirms the Canid from Altai as a Primitive Dog." *PLoS ONE* 8(3): 57754.

Duarte C., Maurício J., Pettitt P. B., Souto P., Trinkaus E., van der Plicht H., and J. Zilhão. 1999. "The Early Upper Paleolithic Human Skeleton from the Abrigo do Lagar Velho (Portugal) and Modern Human Emergence in Iberia." *Proceedings of the National Academy of Sciences* 96 (13): 7604–7609.

Dubois, E. 1894. "*Pithecanthropus erectus,* Transitional Form between Man and the Apes." *Scientific Transactions of the Royal Dublin Society* 6: 1–18.

Dumond, Don E. 1972. "Population Growth and Political Centralization." In Brian Spooner, (Ed.), *Population Growth: Anthropological Implications,* pp. 286–310. Cambridge, MA: MIT Press.

Dumont, Louis. 1970. *Homo Hierarchicus: An Essay on the Caste System,* Mark Sainsburg (Trans.). Chicago: University of Chicago Press.

Dunand, Françoise, and Christiane Zivie-Coche. 2005. *Gods and Men in Egypt: 3000 BCE to 395 CE.* David Lorton (Trans.). Cornell: Cornell University Press.

Dunn, Stephen P., and Ethel Dunn. 1988. *The Peasants of Central Russia.* Prospect Heights, IL: Waveland Press.

Dupree, Louis. 1980. *Afghanistan.* Princeton: Princeton University Press.

Durham, William H. 1976. "Resource Competition and Human Aggression. Part I: A Review of Primitive War." *Quarterly Review of Biology* 51: 385–415.

———. 2002. "Cultural Variation in Time and Space: The Case for a Population Theory of Culture." In Richard Fox and Barbara J. King (Eds.), *Anthropology beyond Culture*. Oxford, England: Berg.

Durning, A. 1992. *Guardians of the Land: Indigenous Peoples and the Health of the Earth*. Worldwatch Paper No. 112. Washington, DC: Worldwatch Institute.

Dye, David H. 2009. *War Paths, Peace Paths: An Archaeology of Cooperation and Conflict in Native Eastern North America*. Lanham, MD: AltaMira Press.

Dyson-Hudson, Rada, and Eric Alden Smith. 1978. "Human Territoriality: An Ecological Reassessment." *American Anthropologist* 80 (1): 21–41.

Earle, Timothy. 1977. "A Reappraisal of Redistribution: Complex Hawaiian Chiefdoms." In T. Earle and J. Ericson (Eds.), *Exchange Systems in Prehistory*. pp.213–229. New York: Academic Press.

———. 1987. "Chiefdoms in Archaeological and Ethnohistorical Perspective." *Annual Review of Anthropology* 16: 299–308.

———. 1997. *How Chiefs Come to Power: The Political Economy in Prehistory*. Stanford, CA: Stanford University Press.

Earle, T., and J. Ericson (Eds.), 1977. *Exchange Systems in Prehistory*. New York: Academic Press.

Edwards, David. 1996. *Heroes of the Age: Moral Fault Lines on the Afghan Frontier*. Berkeley: University of California Press.

———. 1998. "Learning from the Swat Pathans: Political Leadership in Afghanistan, 1978–97." *American Ethnologist* 25 (4): 712–728.

———. 2002. *Before Taliban: Genealogies of the Afghan Jihad*. Berkeley: University of California Press.

———. 2010. "Counterinsurgency as a Cultural System." *Small Wars Journal*. December 27.

Eerkens, J. W., K. J. Vaughn, M. Linares-Grados, C. A. Conlee, K. Schreiber, M. D. Glascock, and N. Tripcevich. 2010. "Spatio-temporal Patterns in Obsidian Consumption in the Southern Nasca Region, Peru." *Journal of Archaeological Science* 37 (4): 825–832.

Ehret, Christopher. 1980. "On the Antiquity of Agriculture in Ethiopia." *Journal of African History* 20:161–177.

Ehret, Christopher, and Merrick Posnansky. 1982. *The Archaeological and Linguistic Reconstruction of African History*. Berkeley: University of California Press.

Eickelman, Dale F. 1976. *Moroccan Islam: Tradition and Society in a Pilgrimage Center*. Modern Middle East Series, Vol. 1. Austin and London: University of Texas Press.

———. 1982. "The Study of Islam in Local Contexts." *Contributions to Asian Studies* 17: 1–16.

———, (Ed.), 1993. *Russia's Muslim Frontiers: New Directions in Cross-Cultural Analysis*. Bloomington and Indianapolis: Indiana University Press.

———. 1995. "Ethnicity." In John L. Esposito (Ed.), *The Oxford Encyclopedia of the Modern Islamic World*, Vol. 1. pp. 449–452. New York: Oxford University Press.

———. 1998. *The Middle East and Central Asia: An Anthropological Approach*. Upper Saddle River, NJ: Prentice Hall.

Eickelman, Dale F., and James Piscatori. 2004. *Muslim Politics* (2nd ed.). Princeton: Princeton University Press.

Ekechukwu, L. C. 1990. "Encouraging National Development through the Promotion of Tourism: The Place of Archaeology." *Cultural Resource Management* 20: 120–125.

Ekman, Paul. 1973. "Cross-Cultural Studies of Facial Expressions." In P. Ekman (Ed.), *Darwin and Facial Expression:*

A Century of Research in Review. pp. 169–220. New York: Academic Press.

Ekman, Paul, Wallace V. Friesen, and John Bear. 1984. "The International Language of Gestures." *Psychology Today*, May:. 64–69.

Eliade, Mircea. 1959. *The Sacred and the Profane: The Nature of Religion*. New York: Harper & Row.

Ellen, Roy F. 2010. "Theories in Anthropology and Anthropological Theory." *Journal of the Royal Anthropological Institute (N.S.)* 16: 387–404.

Elson, Christina M. and Michael E. Smith. 2001. "Archaeological Deposits from the Aztec New Fire Ceremony." *Ancient Mesoamerica* 12(2): 157–174.

Ember, Carol. 1978. "Myths about Hunter-Gatherers." *Ethnology* 17: 439–448.

Ember, Carol, and Melvin Ember. 1992. "Warfare, Aggression, and Resource Problems: Cross-Cultural Codes." *Cross-Cultural Research* 26 (1–4): 169–226.

Ember, Melvin. 1975. "On the Origin and Extension of the Incest Taboo." *Behavior Science Research* 10: 249–281.

Ember, Melvin, and Carol Ember. 1971. "The Conditions Favoring Matrilocal versus Patrilocal Residence." *American Anthropologist* 73: 571–594.

———. 1979. "Male-Female Bonding: A Cross-Species Study of Mammals and Birds." *Behavior Science Research* 14: 37–56.

Ember, Melvin, Carol Ember, and Bobbi Low. 2007. "Comparing Explanations of Polygyny." *Cross-Cultural Research* 41 (4): 428–440.

Endicott, Kirk. 1988. "The Basis of Egalitarian Social Relations among the Batak Foragers of Malaysia." Paper presented at the Eighty-Seventh Annual Meeting of the American Anthropological Association, Phoenix, AZ.

Endicott, P., S. Y. Ho, and C. Stringer. 2010. "Using Genetic Evidence to Evaluate Four Palaeoanthropological Hypotheses for the Timing of Neanderthal and Modern Human Origins." *Journal of Human Evolution* 59: 87–95.

Engels, Frederick. [1884] 1972. *The Origin of the Family, Private Property, and the State*. New York: Pathfinder Press.

England, Nora. 2003. "Mayan Language Revival and Revitalization Politics: Linguists and Linguistic Ideologies." *American Anthropologist* 105 (4): 733–743.

Englund, R. K. 1998. "Texts from the Late Uruk Period." In J. Bauer, R. K. Englund, and M. Kreernik (Eds)., *Mesopotamien: Späturuk-Zeit und Frühdynastische zeit*, pp. 15–233. Freiburg: Universitätsverlag Freiburg Schweiz.

Ensminger, Jean (Ed.), 2002. "Experimental Economics: A Powerful New Method for Theory Testing in Anthropology." In Jean Ensminger (Ed.)., *Theory in Economic Anthropology*. pp. 59–78. Walnut Creek: CA: AltaMira Press.

Erickson, Mark T. 1999. "Incest Avoidance: Clinical Implications of the Evolutionary Perspective." In Wenda R. Trevathan, E. O. Smith, and James J. McKenna, (Eds). pp. 165–182. *Evolutionary Medicine*. New York and Oxford: Oxford University Press.

Eriksen, Thomas Hylland. 2010. *Ethnicity and Nationalism: Anthropological Perspectives* (3rd ed.). London: Pluto Press.

———. 2013. "Norwegian Anthropologists Study Minorities at Home: Political and Academic Agendas" In Sam Beck and Carl Maida (Eds.). pp. 35–49. New York and Oxford: Berghahn Books.

Errington, Frederick, and Deborah Gewertz. 1987. "Of Unfinished Dialogues and Paper Pigs." *American Ethnologist* 14 (2): 367–376.

Errington, Joseph. 2003. "Getting Language Rights: The Rhetorics of Language Endangerment and Loss." *American Anthropologist* 105 (4): 723–732.

Esposito, John. 2002. *Unholy War: Terror in the Name of Islam.* Oxford: Oxford University Press.

———. 2010. *Islam: The Straight Path* (4th ed.). Oxford: Oxford University Press.

Estioko-Griffin, Agnes, and Bion P. Griffin. 1978. "Woman the Hunter: The Agta." In Frances Dahlberg (Ed.), *Woman the Gatherer*, pp. 121–152. New Haven, CT: Yale University Press.

Evans, Karin. 2000. "The One-Child, Maybe-One-More Policy." In Elvio Angeloni,(Ed.), *Anthropology 2001/2002.* pp. 96–100. New York: McGraw-Hill, Dushkin.

Evans, Robert K., and Judith A. Rasson. 1984. "Ex Balkanis Lux? Recent Developments in Neolithic and Chalcolithic Research in Southeastern Europe." *American Antiquity* 49: 713–741.

Evans, Susan, and Peter Gould. 1982. "Settlement Models in Archaeology." *Journal of Anthropological Archaeology* 1: 275–304.

Evans-Pritchard, E. E. 1937. *Witchcraft, Oracles and Magic among the Azande.* Oxford: Clarendon Press.

———. 1940. *The Nuer.* Oxford: Clarendon Press.

———. 1951. *Kinship and Marriage among the Nuer.* Oxford: Clarendon Press.

———. 1956. *Nuer Religion.* New York: Oxford University Press.

Fagan, Brian. 1984a. *The Aztecs.* New York: W. H. Freeman.

———. 1984b. *Clash of Cultures.* New York: W. H. Freeman.

———. 1988. "Black Day at Slack Farm." *Archaeology* 41 (4): 15–16, 73.

———. 1992. *Rape of the Nile.* Providence, RI: Moyer-Bell.

———. 2001. *Grahame Clark: An Intellectual Life of an Archaeologist.* Cambridge, MA: Westview.

Fakhouri, Hani. 1972. *Kafr El-Elow: An Egyptian Village in Transition.* New York: Holt, Rinehart & Winston.

Farb, Peter. 1974. *Word Play: What Happens When People Talk.* New York: Knopf/Bantam.

Farley, John E. 1990. *Sociology.* Upper Saddle River, NJ: Prentice Hall.

Farr, Grant M. 1999. *Modern Iran.* New York: McGraw-Hill.

Fathi, Nazila. 2004. "Conservatives in Iran Battle the Spread of Foreign Investment." *New York Times International*, 10 October, p.16.

Fedarko, Kevin. 2004. "This Ride Is About Our Future." *Parade Magazine*, May 16, pp. 4–5.

Feder, Kenneth L. 2014. *Frauds, Myths, and Mysteries: Science and Pseudoscience in Archaeology.* New York: McGraw-Hill.

Fedigan, Linda M. 1983. "Dominance and Reproductive Success in Primates." *Yearbook of Physical Anthropology* 26: 91–129.

———. 1986. "The Changing Role of Women in Models of Human Evolution." *Annual Review of Anthropology* 15: 25–66.

Fell, Barry. 1980. *Saga America.* New York: Times Mirror.

Feng-Chi, Chen and Wen-Hsiung Li. 2001 "Genomic Divergences between Humans and Other Hominoids and the Effective Population Size of the Common Ancestor of Humans and Chimpanzees." *American Journal of Human Genetics*, 68(2): 444–456.

Ferguson, R. Brian. 1995. *Yanomamö Warfare: A Political History.* Santa Fe, NM: School of American Research Press.

———. 1997. "Review of War before Civilization: The Myth of the Peaceful Savage." *American Anthropologist* 99: 424–425.

———. 2013. "Pinker's List: Exaggerating Prehistoric War Mortality" In Douglas P. Fry (Ed.), *War, Peace and Human Nature: The Convergence of Evolutionary and Cultural Views.* pp. 112–131. Oxford: Oxford University Press.

Ferguson, R. Brian, and Neil L. Whitehead (Eds.), 1999. *War in the Tribal Zone: Expanding States and Indigenous Warfare* (2nd ed.). Santa Fe, NM: School of American Research Press.

Ferguson, Leland G. 1992. *Uncommon Ground: Archaeology and Colonial African America 1650–1800.*Washington, DC: Smithsonian Institution Press.

Fernea, Elizabeth W., and Robert A. Fernea. 1979. "A Look behind the Veil." *Human Nature.* 2: 68–78.

Fessler, Daniel M. T. 1999. "Toward an Understanding of the Universality of Second Order Emotions." In Alexander Laban Hinton, (Ed.), *Biocultural Approaches to the Emotions.* pp. 75–116. Cambridge: Cambridge University Press.

Fessler, Daniel M. T., and C. D. Naverette. 2003. "Meat is Good to Taboo: Dietary Proscriptions as a Product of the Interaction of Psychological Mechanisms and Social Processes." *Journal of Cognition and Culture* 3: 1–40.

Firth, Raymond. 1957. "A Note on Descent Groups in Polynesia." *Man* 57: 4–8.

Fisher, Helen E. 1992. *Anatomy of Love: The Natural History of Monogamy, Adultery, and Divorce.* New York: W. W. Norton.

Fitch, W. T. 2000. "The Phonetic Potential of Nonhuman Vocal Tracts: Comparative Cineradiographic Observations of Vocalizing Animals."*Phonetica* 57 (2–4): 205–218.

Fitch, W. T., and J. Giedd. 1999. "Morphology and Development of the Human Vocal Tract: A Study Using Magnetic Resonance Imaging." *Journal of the Acoustical Society of America* 106 (3, pt. 1): 1511–1522.

Fitting, Elizabeth. 2011. *The Struggle for Maize: Campesinos, Workers, and Transgenic Corn in the Mexican Countryside.* Durham and London: Duke University Press.

Flannery, Kent. 1965. "The Ecology of Early Food Production in Mesopotamia." *Science* 147: 1247–1256.

———. 1968. "Archaeological Systems Theory and Early Mesoamerica." In Betty Jane Meggers,(Ed.), *Anthropological Archaeology in the Americas*, pp. 67–87. Washington, DC: Anthropological Society of Washington.

———. 1972. "The Cultural Evolution of Civilizations." *Annual Review of Ecology and Systematics* 4: 399–426.

———. 1973. "The Origins of Agriculture." *Annual Review of Anthropology* 2: 271–310.

———. 1985. "Los Origenes de la Agricultura en México: Las Teorías y la Evidencia." In T. Rojas-Rabiela and W. T. Sanders (Eds.), *Historia de la Agricultura: Epoca Prehispánica-Siglo XVI*, pp. 237–265. Colección Biblioteca del INAH, Instituto Nacional de Antropología e Historia.

Fleagle, John G. 1983. "Locomotor Adaptations of Oligocene and Miocene Hominoids and Their Phyletic Implications." In R. Ciochon and R. Corruccini (Eds.), *New Interpretations of Ape and Human Ancestry*, pp. 301–324. New York: Plenum Press.

———. 2013. *Primate Adaptation and Evolution*, 3rd ed. San Diego: Academic Press.

Fleagle, J. G., T. M. Bown, J. O. Obradovich, and E. L. Simons. 1986. "How Old Are the Fayum Primates?" In J. G. Else and P. C. Lee (Eds.), *Primate Evolution*, pp. 133–142. Cambridge: Cambridge University Press.

Fleagle, J. G., and R. F. Kay. 1987. "The Phyletic Position of the *Parapithecidae*." *Journal of Human Evolution* 16: 483–531.

Fleagle, John G., and Christopher C. Gilbert (Eds.), 2008. *Elwyn Simons: A Search for Origins.* New York: Springer.

Fleuret, Patrick. 1988. "Farmers, Cooperatives, and Development Assistance in Uganda: An Anthropological Perspective." In David Brokensha and Peter D. Little (Eds.), *Anthropology of Development and Change in East Africa.* pp. 59–76. Boulder, CO: Westview Press.

Flinn, Mark. V., and B. G. England. 1997. "Childhood Stress and Family Environment." *Current Anthropology* 36: 854–866.

Fluehr-Lobban, Carolyn. 1998. "Cultural Relativism and Universal Rights." http://www.cs.org/publications/featuredarticles/1998/fluehrlobban.htm.

———. 2000. "How Anthropology Should Respond to an Ethical Crisis." *Chronicle of Higher Education, Point of View,* 6 October, B-24.

———,(Ed.), 2003. *Ethics and the Profession of Anthropology: Dialogue for Ethically Conscious Practice.* Walnut Creek, CA: AltaMira Press.

———. 2004a. "Cultural Relativism and Universal Human Rights." In Ruth Osterweiss Selig, Marilyn R. London, and P. Ann Kaupp (Eds.), *Anthropology Explored: Revised and Expanded: The Best of Smithsonian Anthronotes.* pp. 102–115. Washington, DC: Smithsonian Books.

———. 2004b. "Challenges of Providing Anthropological Expertise: On the 'Arab-Black Conflict' in Darfur." *Anthropology News,* 7–8 October.

———. 2006. *Race and Racism: An Introduction.* Lanham, MD: AltaMira Press.

———. 2013. *Ethics and Anthropology: Ideas and Practices.* Lanham, MD: AltaMira Press.

Fong, Vanessa. 2004. *Only Hope: Coming of Age under China's One-Child Policy.* Stanford: Stanford University Press.

Ford, Richard I. 1985. "Prehistoric Food Production in North America." University of Michigan, Museum of Anthropology, Paper 75.

Fossey, Dian. 1983. *Gorillas in the Mist.* Boston: Houghton Mifflin.

Foster, George M. 1967. *Tzintzuntzan: Mexican Peasants in a Changing World.* Boston: Little, Brown.

Fouts, R. S. 1997. *Next of Kin: What Chimpanzees Have Taught Me about Who We Are.* New York: William Morrow and Company.

Fouts, R. S., and R. L. Budd. 1979. "Artificial and Human Language Acquisition in the Chimpanzee." In D. A. Hamburg and E. R. McCown (Eds.), *The Great Apes,* pp. 374–392. Menlo Park, CA: Benjamin/Cummings.

Fowler, Brenda. 2000. *Iceman: Uncovering the Life and Times of a Prehistoric Man Found in an Alpine Glacier.* Chicago: Chicago University Press.

Fox, Richard G. 1985. *Lions of the Punjab: Culture in the Making.* Berkeley: University of California Press.

———. 1989. *Gandhian Utopia: Experiments with Culture.* Boston: Beacon Press.

Fox, Richard G., and Barbara King (Eds.). 2002. *Anthropology beyond Culture.* Oxford, England: Berg.

Fox, Robin. 1967. *Kinship and Marriage: An Anthropological Perspective.* Baltimore: Penguin.

Frahm, Ellery. 2012. "Fifty Years of Obsidian Sourcing in the Near East: Considering the Archaeological *Zeitgeist* and Legacies of Renfrew, Dixon, and Cann." *International Association for Obsidian Studies Bulletin* 47 (Summer): 7–18

———. 2014. "Buying Local or Ancient Outsourcing? Locating Production of Prismatic Obsidian Blades in Bronze-Age Northern Mesopotamia." *Journal of Archaeological Science* 41(1): 605–621.

Frank, Andre Gunner. 1993. "Bronze Age World System Cycles." *Current Anthropology* 34 (4): 383–429.

———. 1998. *Reorient: Global Economy in the Asian Age.* Berkeley: University of California Press.

Franklin, A. Clifford, E. Williamson, and I. R. L. Davies. 2005. "The Nature of Infant Color Categorization: Evidence from Eye Movements on a Target Detection Task." *Journal of Experimental Child Psychology.* 91: 227–248.

Frayer, David W., Milford H. Wolposs, Alan G.Thorne, Fred H. Smith, and Geoffrey G. Pope. 1993. "Theories of Modern Human Origins: The Paleontological Test." *American Anthropologist* 95 (1): 14–50.

Fredrickson, George M. 2002. *Racism: A Short History.* Princeton, NJ: Princeton University Press.

Freeman, Derek. 1983. *Margaret Mead and Samoa: The Making and Unmaking of an Anthropological Myth.* Cambridge, MA: Harvard University Press.

———. 1997. *Margaret Mead and the Heretic: The Making and Unmaking of an Anthropological Myth.* New York: Penguin.

———. 1999. *The Fateful Hoaxing of Margaret Mead* (2nd ed.). Boulder, CO: Westview.

Freuchen, Peter. 1961. *Book of the Eskimos.* Cleveland: World Publishing Co.

Freud, Sigmund. 1891. "Hypnosis." Reprinted in A. A. Roback. 1957. *Freudiana: Including Unpublished Letters from Freud, Havelock Ellis, Pavlov, Bernard Shaw, Romain Rolland, et al.* P. ii. Cambridge, MA: Science-Art Publishers.

———. 1913. *Totem and Taboo: Some Points of Agreement between the Mental Lives of Savages and Neurotics.* James Strachey (Trans). New York: W. W. Norton.

———.[1933] 1964. "Why War" Reprinted in Strachey, J. (Ed. and Trans.) *The Standard Edition of the Complete Psychological Works of Sigmund Freud.* London: Hogarth.

Fried, Morton. 1953. *Fabric of Chinese Society: A Study of the Social Life of a Chinese County Seat.* New York: Praeger.

———. 1967. *The Evolution of Political Society: An Essay in Political Anthropology.* New York: Random House.

———. 1975. *The Notion of Tribe.* Menlo Park, CA: Cummings.

———. 1977. "First Contact and Political Theory." In Ronald K. Wetherington, (Ed.), *Colloquia in Anthropology,* Vol. 1. pp. 17–33. Taos, NM: Fort Burgwin Research Center, Southern Methodist University.

———. 1978. "The State, the Chicken and the Egg: Or What Came First?" In R. Cohen and E. R. Service (Eds.), *Origins of the State: The Anthropology of Political Evolution,* pp. 35–48. Philadelphia: Institute for the Study of Human Issues.

Friedl, Ernestine. 1975. *Women and Men: An Anthropologist's View.* New York: Holt, Rinehart & Winston.

Friedman, Jonathan. 1974. "Marxism, Structuralism, and Vulgar Materialism." *Man* 9: 444–469.

———. 1992. "Narcissism, Roots, and Postmodernity: The Constitution of Selfhood in the Global Crisis." In Scott Lash and Jonathan Friedman, (Eds.), *Modernity and Identity.* pp. 167–194. Oxford: Basil Blackwell.

———. 1995. *Culture Identity and Global Process.* London: Sage Publications.

———. 1998. *System, Structure, and Contradiction: The Evolution of Asiatic Social Formations* (2nd ed.). Walnut Creek, CA: AltaMira Press.

———, Ed. 2003. *Globalization, the State, and Violence.* Walnut Creek, CA: AltaMira Press.

Friedman, Thomas. 1999. *The Lexus and the Olive Tree: Understanding Globalization.* New York: Farrar, Straus, and Giroux.

———. 2006. *The World Is Flat: A Brief History of the Twenty-First Century.* New York: Farrar, Straus, and Giroux.

Frisancho, A. R. 1979. *Human Adaptation: A Functional Interpretation.* St. Louis, MO: C. V. Mosby.

Froment, Alain. 2004. "Worlds Transformed: Indigenous People's Health in Changing Rainforests." *Cultural Survival* 28 (2) Online at http://www.culturalsurvival. org/publications/cultural-survival-quarterly/none/ do-people-belong-forest.

Fry, Douglas. 2006. *The Human Potential for Peace: An Anthropological Challenge to Assumptions about War and Violence.* Oxford: Oxford University Press.

———. 2013. (Ed.), *War, Peace, and Human Nature: The Convergence of Evolutionary and Cultural Views.* Oxford: Oxford University Press.

Fuller, Dorian Q. 2011. Finding Plant Domestication in the Indian Subcontinent. *Current Anthropology* 52(4): 347–362.

Fuller, Michael, and Neathery Fuller. 2008. "Agricultural State Religions." In Raymond Scupin (Ed.), *Religion and Culture: An Anthropological Focus.* 2nd ed. pp. 226–248. Upper Saddle River, NJ: Pearson Prentice Hall.

Futuyma, D. J. 1995. *Science on Trial: The Case for Evolution.* New York: Pantheon Books.

Gallese, Vittorio, Luciano Fadiga, Leonardo Fogassi, Giacomo Rizzolatti. 1996. "Action Recognition in the Premotor Cortex." *Brain* 119, 593–609.

Gannon, J., R. L. Holloway, D. C. Broadfield, and A. R. Braun. 1998. "Asymmetry of Chimpanzee Planum Temporale: Humanlike Pattern of Wernicke's Brain Language Area Homolog." *Science* 279: 220–222.

Garbarino, Merwyn. 1988. *Native American Heritage* (2nd ed.). Prospect Heights, IL: Waveland Press.

Garciagodoy, Juanita. 1998. *Digging the Days of the Dead: A Reading of Mexico's Dias de Muertos.* Niwot: University Press of Colorado.

Gardner, Howard. 1983. *Frames of Mind: The Theory of Multiple Intelligences.* New York: Basic Books.

Gardner, Peter. 1991. "Foragers Pursuit of Individual Autonomy." *Current Anthropology* 32: 543–558.

———.2013. "Meat distribution, game, and spirits: a response to Knight" *Current Anthropology* 54 (1): 80.

Gardner, Robert A., and Beatrice T. Gardner. 1969. "Teaching Sign Language to a Chimpanzee." *Science* 16: 664–672.

Garn, Stanley. 1971. *Human Races* (3rd ed.). Springfield, IL: Chas. C Thomas.

Garza, Christina Elnora. 1991. "Studying the Natives on the Shop Floor." *Business Week,* September 30, pp. 74–78.

Gay, Phillip T. 2001. *Modern South Africa.* Boston: McGraw-Hill.

Geertz, Clifford. 1960. *The Religion of Java.* Glencoe, IL: Free Press.

———. 1963a. *Agricultural Involution: The Processes of Ecological Change in Indonesia.* Berkeley and Los Angeles: University of California Press.

———. 1963b. *Peddlars and Princes: Social Change and Modernization in Two Indonesian Towns.* Chicago: University of Chicago Press.

———. 1963c. *Old Societies and New States: The Quest for Modernity in Asia and Africa.* New York: Free Press.

———. 1966. "Religion as a Cultural System." In Michael Banton, (Ed.), *Anthropological Approaches to the Study of Religion.* Association of Social Anthropologists Monographs, No. 3.

———. 1973. *The Interpretation of Cultures: Selected Essays by Clifford Geertz.* New York: Basic Books.

———. 1980. *Negara: The Theatre State in Nineteenth-Century Bali.* Princeton, NJ: Princeton University Press.

———. 1983. "Common Sense as a Cultural System." In Clifford Geertz (Ed.), *Local Knowledge: Further Essays in Interpretive Anthropology.* pp. 19–35. New York: Basic Books.

———. 2000. *Available Light: Anthropological Reflections on Philosophical Topics.* Princeton, NJ: Princeton University Press.

Gellner, David. 2004. *The Anthropology of Buddhism and Hinduism: Weberian Themes.* Oxford: Oxford University Press.

Gellner, Ernest. 1983. *Nations and Nationalism.* Oxford: Oxford University Press.

———. Ed. [1977] 1988. *State and Society in Soviet Thought.* Oxford: Basil Blackwell.

Gelman, Susan. A., and James. P. Byrnes (Eds.). 1991. *Perspectives on Language and Thought: Interrelations in Development.* New York: Cambridge University Press.

Genographic Project. www.nationalgeographic.com/ Genographic.

Gewertz, Deborah. 1981. "A Historical Reconsideration of Female Dominance among the Chambri of Papua New Guinea." *American Ethnologist* 8 (1): 94–106.

Gibbons, A. 2011. "A New View of the Birth of *Homo sapiens.*" *Science* **331,** 392–394.

Gibbs, James L. 1965. "The Kpelle of Liberia." In James L. Gibbs (Ed.), *Peoples of Africa.* pp.197–240. New York: Holt, Rinehart & Winston.

Gibson, Blair D. 2008. "Chiefdoms and the Emergence of Private Property in Land." *Journal of Anthropological Archaeology* 27 (1): 46–62.

Gibson, Jon L. 2000. *The Ancient Mounds of Poverty Point: Place of Rings.* Gainesville, Florida: University Press of Florida.

Giddens, Anthony. 1992. *The Transformation of Intimacy: Sexuality, Love and Eroticism in Modern Societies.* Stanford, CA: Stanford University Press.

Gilkey, Langdon. 1983. "The Creationism Issue: A Theologian's View." *Cosmology and Theology Concilium* 166 (1983), 55–69.

Gil-White, Francisco. 2001. "Are Ethnic Groups Biological 'Species' to the Human Brain?" *Current Anthropology* 42 (4): 515–554.

Gimbutas, Marija. 1982. "Old Europe in The Fifth Millenium B.C.: The European Situation on The Arrival of Indo-Europeans." In Edgar C. Polome,(Ed.), pp. 1–60. . *The Indo-Europeans in the Fourth and Third Millennia.* New York: Karoma Press.

———. 1991. *The Civilization of the Goddess: The World of Old Europe.* San Francisco: Harper Collins.

Gingerich, P. D. 1984. "Punctuated Equilibrium—Where is the Evidence?" *Systematic Zoology,* 33 (3): 335–338.

———. 1986. "Plesiadapis and the Delineation of the Order Primates." In B. Wood, L. Martin, and P. Andrews, (Eds.), *Major Topics in Primates and Human Evolution,* pp. 32–46. Cambridge: Cambridge University Press.

———. 1990. "African Dawn for Primates." *Nature* 346: 411.

Gish, Duane. 1995. *Evolution: The Fossils Still Say No.* Green Forest, AR: Master Books.

Gishlik, Alan D. 2004a. "Darwin's Finches: The Story of Darwin's Finches." In *Icons of Evolution? Why Much of What Jonathan Wells Writes about Evolution Is Wrong.* pp. 159–178. Washington, DC: National Center for Science Education.

———. 2004b. "Evolutionary Paths to Irreducible Systems: The Avian Flight Apparatus." In M. Young , and T. Edis (Eds.), *Why Intelligent Design Fails: A Scientific Critique of the New Creationism*, pp. 58–71. Brunswick, NJ: Rutgers University Press.

Gladkih, M. I., N. Korneitz, and O. Seffer. 1984. "Mammoth-Bone Dwelling on the Russian Plain." *Scientific American* 251 (5): 164–175.

Gladney, Dru C. 1991. *Muslim Chinese: Ethnic Nationalism in the People's Republic.* Cambridge, MA: Harvard University Press.

———. 1998. *Ethnic Identity in China: The Making of a Muslim Minority Nationality.* Orlando, FL: Harcourt Brace.

———. 2004. *Dislocating China: Muslims, Minorities, and Other Subaltern Subjects.* Chicago: University of Chicago Press.

Glascock, Anthony P. 1981. "Social Assets or Social Burden: Treatment of the Aged in Nonindustrial Societies." In C. L. Fry (Ed.), *Dimensions: Aging, Culture and Health.* pp. 13–31. New York: Praeger.

Glazier, Jack. 2008. "Judaism" In *Religion and Culture: An Anthropological Focus* (2nd ed.) Raymond Scupin (Ed.), pp.350–359. Upper Saddle River, NJ: Pearson Prentice Hall Press.

——— 2012. "Jewish Americans." In Raymond Scupin (Ed.), *Race and Ethnicity: The United States and the World* (2nd ed.). pp. 153–169. Upper Saddle River, NJ: Pearson, Prentice Hall.

Gleason, Philip. 1980. "American Identity and Americanization." In Stephan Thernstrom, (Ed.), *Harvard Encyclopedia of American Ethnic Groups*, pp. 31–59. Cambridge, MA: Harvard University Press.

Gluckman, Max. 1953. "Bridewealth and the Stability of Marriage." *Man* 53: 141–142.

Gmelch, George, and G. Zenner (Eds.). 2002. *Urban Life: Readings in Urban Anthropology.* Prospect Heights: IL: Waveland Press.

Gobineau, Joseph-Arthur. [1966] 1854. *Essays on the Inequality of Human Races.* Adrian Collins (Trans.). Los Angeles: Noontide Press.

Godard, Victoria, Joseph Llobera, and Chris Shore (Eds.). 1994. *The Anthropology of Europe: Identities and Boundaries in Conflict.* Oxford, England: Berg.

Goldberg, Steve. 1993. *Why Men Rule: A Theory of Male Dominance.* London: Open Court.

Golding, William G. 1981. *The Inheritors.* New York: Harcourt Brace Jovanovich.

Goldkind, Victor. 1965. "Social Stratification in a Peasant Community: Redfield's Chan Kom Reinterpreted." *American Anthropologist* 67: 863–884.

Goldman, Irving. 1970. *Ancient Polynesian Society.* Chicago: University of Chicago Press.

Goldschmidt, Walter. 1986. *The Sebei: A Study in Adaptation.* New York: Holt, Rinehart & Winston.

———. 1989. "Inducement to Military Participation in Tribal Societies." In Paul R. Turner, David Pitt (Eds.), *The Anthropology of War and Peace: Perspectives on the Nuclear Age*, pp. 15–29. Granby, MA: Bergin & Garvey.

Goldschmidt, Walter, and Evelyn J. Kunkel. 1971. "The Structure of the Peasant Family." *American Anthropologist* 73: 1058–1076.

Goldstein, Melvyn C. 1997. *The Snow Lion and the Dragon: China, Tibet, and the Dalai Lama.* Berkeley: University of California Press.

Golomb, Louis. 1985. *An Anthropology of Curing in Multiethnic Thailand.* Urbana: University of Illinois Press.

Goodale, Jane. 1971. *Tiwi Wives: A Study of the Women of Melville Island, North Australia.* Seattle: University of Washington Press.

Goodall, Jane Van Lawick. 1971. *In the Shadow of Man.* New York: Dell.

———. 1986. *The Chimpanzees of Gombe.* Cambridge, MA: Harvard University Press.

———. 1990. *Through a Window: Thirty Years Observing the Chimpanzees of Gombe.* Boston: Houghton Mifflin.

Goode, William J. 1963. *World Revolution and Family Patterns.* New York: Free Press.

———. 1982. *The Family* (2nd ed.). Englewood Cliffs, NJ: Prentice Hall.

Goodenough, Ward H. 1955. "A Problem in Malayo-Polynesian Social Organization." *American Anthropologist* 57: 71–83.

———. 1956. "Residence Rules." *Southwestern Journal of Anthropology* 12: 22–37.

Goodluck, Helen. 1991. *Language Acquisition: A Linguistic Introduction.* Oxford: Blackwell.

Goodman, Alan H., John Lallo, George J. Armelagos and Jerome C. Rose. 1984. "Health Changes at Dickson Mounds (A.D. 950–1300)." In Mark Cohen and George Armelagos (Eds.), *Paleopathology at the Origins of Agriculture*, pp. 271–305. Orlando, Florida: Academic Press.

Goodman, Jeffrey. 1981. *American Genesis.* New York: Berkley.

Goodman, M., M. L. Baba, and L. L. Darga. 1983. "The Bearings of Molecular Data on the Cladogenesis and Times of Divergence of Hominoid Lineages." In R. L. Ciochon and R. Corruccini, (Eds.), *New Interpretations of Ape and Human Ancestry*, pp. 67–86. New York: Plenum Press.

Goodman, A., and T. Leatherman (Eds.). 1986. *Building a New Biocultural Synthesis.* Ann Arbor: University of Michigan Press.

Goody, Jack. 1971. *Technology, Tradition, and the State in Africa.* London: Oxford University Press.

———. 1976. *Production and Reproduction: A Comparative Study of the Domestic Domain.* Cambridge: Cambridge University Press.

———. 1980. "Slavery in Time and Space." In James L. Watson, (Ed.), *Asian and African Systems of Slavery*, pp. 17–42. Berkeley and Los Angeles: University of California Press.

——— 1983. *The Development of the Family and Marriage in Europe.* New York: Cambridge University Press.

———. 1987. *The Interface between the Written and the Oral.* Cambridge: Cambridge University Press.

———. 1996. *The East in the West.* Cambridge: Cambridge University Press.

———. 2000. *The European Family: A Historico-Anthropological Essay.* Malden, MA: Blackwell.

Goody, Jack, and Stanley J. Tambiah. 1973. *Bridewealth and Dowry.* Cambridge: Cambridge University Press.

Goodyear, Albert C. 1999. "Results of the 1999 Allendale Paleoindian Expedition." *Legacy* 4 (1–3): 8–13.

Gopnik, Alison, Andrew N. Meltzoff, and Patricia Kuhl. 2001. *The Scientist in the Crib: What Early Learning Tells Us about the Mind.* New York: HarperCollins.

Gordon, Alison. 2004. "Ape-ing Language: Communicating with Our Closest Relatives." In *Anthropology Explored: The Best of Smithsonian Anthronotes.* pp. 9–11. Washington, DC: Smithsonian Books.

Gorman, Chester A. 1969. "Hoabhinian: A Pebble-Tool Complex with Early Plant Associations in Southeast Asia." *Science* 163: 671–673.

———. 1977. "A Priori Models and Thai Prehistory: A Reconsideration of the Beginning of Agriculture in Southeast Asia." In Charles A. Reed, (Ed.), *Origins of Agriculture*, pp. 321–355. The Hague: Mouton.

Gossett, Thomas F. 1963. *Race: The History of an Idea in America*. Dallas: Southern Methodist University Press.

Goucher, Candice L. 1981. "Iron Is Iron 'til It Is Rust!: Trade and Ecology in the Decline of West African Iron Smelting." *Journal of African History* 22 (1): 179–184.

Gough, Kathleen. 1975. "The Origin of the Family." In Rayna Reiter (Ed)., *Towards an Anthropology of Women*. pp. 51–76. New York: Monthly Review.

Gould, James L. 1986. "The Locale Map of Honey Bees: Do Insects Have Cognitive Maps?" *Science* 232: 861–863.

Gould, James L., and Peter Marler. 1987. "Learning by Instinct." *Scientific American* 256: 74–85.

Gould, R. A. 1980. *Living Archaeology*. Cambridge: Cambridge University Press.

Gould, Stephen. J. 1977. *Ever Since Darwin*. New York: W. W. Norton.

———. 1985. *The Flamingo's Smile*. New York: W. W. Norton.

———. 1987. "Bushes All the Way Down." *Natural History* 87 (6): 12–19.

Gould, Stephen. J., and Niles Eldredge. 1972. "Punctuated Equilibrium: The Tempo and Mode of Evolution Reconsidered." *Paleobiology* 3: 115–151.

Graber, Robert B., and Paul B. Roscoe. 1988. "Introduction: Circumscription and the Evolution of Society." *American Behavioral Scientist* 31: 405–415.

Granadillo, Tania and Heidi A. Orcutt-Gachiri (Eds.). 2011. *Ethnographic Contributions to the Study of Endangered Languages*. Tucson: University of Arizona Press.

Grant, P. R. 1999. *Ecology and Evolution of Darwin's Finches*. Princeton, NJ: Princeton University Press.

Green, Ernestine (Ed.). 1984. *Ethics and Values in Archaeology*. New York: Free Press.

Green, Richard E., Johannes Krause, Adrian W. Briggs, Tomislav Maricic, Udo Stenzel, Martin Kircher, Nick Patterson, et al. 2010. "A Draft Sequence of the Neandertal Genome." *Science* 328 (5979): 710–722.

Greenberg, Joseph H. 1986. "The Settlement of the Americas." *Current Anthropology* 27: 477–497.

Greenberg, Joseph H., Keith Denning, and Suzanne Kemmer (Eds.) 1990. *On Language: Selected Writings of Joseph H. Greenberg*. Palo Alto, CA: Stanford University Press.

Greene, Brian. 1999. *The Elegant Universe:Superstrings, Hidden Dimensions, and the Quest for the Ultimate Theory*. New York: Vintage Books.

Greene, Victor. 1980. "Poles." In Stephan Thernstrom (Ed.), *Harvard Encyclopedia of American Ethnic Groups*, pp. 787–803. Cambridge, MA: Harvard University Press.

Greenhalgh, Susan. 2008. *Just One Child: Science and Policy in Deng's China*. Berkeley: University of California Press.

Gregor, Thomas, and Daniel Gross. 2004. "Guilt by Association: The Culture of Accusation and the American Anthropological Association's Investigation of *Darkness in El Dorado*." *American Anthropologist* 106 (4): 687–698.

Griffin, Donald. 1985. *Animal Thinking*. Cambridge, MA: Harvard University Press.

Gross, Paul and Barbara Forest. 2004. Creationism's *Trojan Horse: The Wedge of Intelligent Design*. New York: Oxford University Press.

Groves, Colin, and Catharine Fitzgerald. 2010. "Healthy Hobbits or Victims of Sauron," *HOMO-Journal of Human Comparative Biology* 61: 211.

Gruenbaum, Ellen. 2004. "Humanitarian Aid to Women and the Children of Darfur." *Anthropology News*, October: 8–11.

Guha, Ashok S. 1981. *An Evolutionary View of Economic Growth*. Oxford: Clarendon Press.

Gunz, Philip, Fred L. Bookstein, Philipp Mitteroecker, Andrea Stadlmayr, Horst Seidler and Gerhard W. Weber. 2009. "Early Modern Human Diversity Suggests Subdivided Population Structure and a Complex Out-of-Africa Scenario." *Proceedings of the National Academy of Sciences of the United States of America* 106 (15): 6094–6098.

Gurven, Michael, Monique Borgerhoff Mulder, Paul L. Hooper, Hillard Kaplan, Robert Quinlan, Rebecca Sear, Eric Schniter et al. 2010. "Domestication Alone Does Not Lead to Inequality: Intergenerational Wealth Transmission among Horticulturalists. *Current Anthropology* 51 (1): 49–64.

Guthrie, Stewart. 1993. *Faces in the Clouds: A New Theory of Religion*. New York: Oxford University Press.

Haas, Jonathan. 1982. *The Evolution of the Prehistoric State*. New York: Columbia University Press.

Habgood, Phillip. 1985. "The Origin of the Australian Aborigines." In Phillip Tobias, (Ed.), *Hominid Evolution: Past, Present, and Future*, pp. 367–380. New York: Alan R. Liss.

Haglund, K., and M. H. Sorg. 1997. *Forensic Taphonomy: The Postmortem Fate of Human Remains*. Boca Raton, FL: CRC Press.

Haile-Selassie, Yohannes; Gen Suwa, Tim D. White. 2004. "Late Miocene Teeth from Middle Awash, Ethiopia, and Early Hominid Dental Evolution". *Science* 303 (5663): 1503–1505.

Hakånsson, Thomas N. 1998. Rulers and Rainmakers in Pre-colonial South Pare, Tanzania: The Role of Exchange and Ritual Experts in Political Fragmentation. *Ethnology* 37: 263–283.

———. 2004. The Human Ecology of World Systems in East Africa: The Impact of the Ivory Trade. *Human Ecology* 32: 561–591.

———. 2007. The Decentralized Landscape: Regional Wealth and the Expansion of Production in Northern Tanzania before the Eve of Colonialism. In L. Cligget and C. Pool (Eds.), *Economies and the Transformation of Landscape.*, pp. 239–266. Walnut Creek, CA: AltaMira Press.

———. 2010. "Comment" on "Intergenerational Wealth Transmission and Inequality in Premodern Societies: History and the Problem of Synchronic Models." *Current Anthropology* 51 (1): 105–107.

Hale, Kenneth, Michael Krauss, Lucille Watahomigie, Akira Yamamoto, Colette Craig, Laverne Jeanne, and Nora England. "Endangered Languages." *Language* 68 (1): 1–43.

Hall, Edward T. 1969. *The Hidden Dimension*. New York: Anchor Press.

———. 1981. *The Silent Language*. New York: Anchor Press.

Hall, Martin. 1988. "Archaeology under Apartheid." *Archaeology* 41 (6): 62–64.

Halperin, Rhoda. 1987. "Age in Cross-Cultural Perspective: An Evolutionary Approach." In Philip Silverman, (Ed.), *The Elderly as Modern Pioneers*. pp. 283–311. Bloomington: Indiana University Press.

Halverson, John. 1987. "Art for Art's Sake in the Paleolithic." *Current Anthropology* 28: 63–89.

Hames, Raymond B. 1979a. "A Comparison of the Efficiencies of the Shotgun and the Bow in Neotropical Forest Hunting." *Human Ecology* 7 (3): 219–252.

———. 1979b. "Relatedness and Interaction among the Ye'Kwana: A Preliminary Analysis." In N. Chagnon and W. Irons (Eds.), *Evolutionary Biology and Human Social Behavior: An Anthropological Perspective*, pp. 238–251. North Scituate, MA: Duxbury Press.

———. 2004. "Yanomamö: Varying Adaptations of Foraging Horticulturalists." In Ember, Carol, Melvin Ember, and Peter Peregrine (Eds.) *New Directions in Anthropology*. Electronic Resource CD. Upper Saddle River, NJ: Prentice Hall Press.

Hamilton, D. L., and Robyn Woodward. 1984. "A Sunken 17th Century City: Port Royal, Jamaica." *Archaeology* 37 (1): 38–45.

Hammel, E. A., and Nancy Howell. 1987. "Research in Population and Culture: An Evolutionary Framework." *Current Anthropology* 28 (2): 141–160.

Hammer, M. F., T. Karafet, A. Rasnayagam, E. T. Wood, T. K. Alteide, T. Jenkins, R. C. Griffiths, A. R. Templeton, and S. L. Zegura. 1998. "Out of Africa and Back Again: Nested Cladistic Analysis of Human Y Chromosome Variation." *Molecular Biology and Evolution* 15: 427–441.

Hammer, Michael F., and Stephen L. Zegura. 2002. "The Human Y Chromosome Haplogroup Tree." *Annual Review of Anthropology* 31: 303–321.

Handler, Richard. 1988. *Nationalism and the Politics of Culture in Quebec.* Madison: Wisconsin University Press.

Hankins, Joseph Doyle. 2013. "An Ecology of Sensibility: The Politics of Scents and Stigma in Japan." *Anthropological Theory* 13 (1/2): 49–66.

Hannerz, Ulf. 1992. *Cultural Complexity: Studies in the Social Organization of Meaning.* New York: Columbia University Press.

Hansen, Karen T. 2004. "The World in Dress: Anthropological Perspectives on Clothing, Fashion, and Culture." *Annual Review of Anthropology* 33: 369–392.

Harden, Blaine. 2001. "The Dirt in the New Machine." *The New York Times Magazine*, August 12, pp. 35–39.

Hardgrove, Anne. 2006. "India." In Raymond Scupin (Ed.), *Peoples and Cultures of Asia.* pp. 103–141. Upper Saddle River, NJ: Prentice Hall.

Harding, R. M., S. M. Fullerton, R. C. Griffiths, J. Bond, M. J. Cox, J. A. Schneider, D. S. Moulin, and J. B. Clegg. 1997. "Archaic African and Asian Lineages in the Genetic Ancestry of Modern Humans." *American Journal of Human Genetics* 60: 772–789.

Hardman-de-Bautista, M. 1978. "Linguistic Postulates and Applied Anthropological Linguistics." In V. Honsa and M. Hardmande-Bautista (Eds.), *Papers on Linguistics and Child Language.* pp. 117–136. The Hague: Mouton.

Harlan, J. R. 1971. "Agricultural Origins: Centers and Noncenters." *Science* 174: 468–474.

———. 1992. "Indigenous African Agriculture." In C. Wesley Cowan and Patty Jo Watson, (Eds.), *The Origins of Agriculture: An International Perspective*, pp. 59–70. Washington, DC: Smithsonian Institution Press.

Harlow, Harry F., and Margaret K. Harlow. 1961. "A Study of Animal Affection." *Natural History* 70: 48–55.

Harner, Michael J. 1972. *The Jivaro: People of the Sacred Waterfalls.* Garden City, NY: Natural History Press.

———. 1977. "The Ecological Basis for Aztec Sacrifice." *American Ethnologist* 4: 117–135.

Harrington, Spencer P. M. 1991a. "The Looting of Arkansas." *Archaeology* 44 (3): 22–30.

———. 1991b. "Shoring Up the Temple of Athena." *Archaeology* 45 (1): 30–43.

Harris, E. E., and J. Hey. 1999. "X Chromosome Evidence for Ancient Human Histories." *Proceedings of the National Academy of Sciences, USA* 96: 3320–3324.

Harris, Marvin. 1964. *Patterns of Race in the Americas.* New York: Norton Press.

———. 1977. *Cannibals and Kings: The Origins of Cultures.* New York: Random House.

———. 1979. *Cultural Materialism: The Struggle for a Science of Culture.* New York: Random House.

———. 1985. *The Sacred Cow and the Abominable Pig: Riddles of Food and Culture.* New York: Simon & Schuster.

———. 1988. *Culture, People, Nature: An Introduction to General Anthropology* (5th ed.). New York: Harper & Row.

———. 1992. "Distinguished Lecture: Anthropology and the Theoretical and Paradigmatic Significance of the Collapse of Soviet and East European Communism." *American Anthropology* 94 (2): 295–305.

———. 1999. *Theories of Culture in Postmodern Times.* Walnut Creek, CA: AltaMira Press.

Harris, Marvin, and Eric Ross. 1987. *Death, Sex, and Fertility: Population Regulation in Preindustrial and Developing Societies.* New York: Columbia University Press.

Harrison, D. F. N. 1995. *The Anatomy and Physiology of the Mammalian Larynx.* Cambridge: Cambridge University Press.

Harrold, Francis B., and Raymond A. Eve. 1987. *Cult Archaeology and Creationism: Understanding Pseudoscientific Beliefs about the Past.* Iowa City: University of Iowa Press.

Hart C. W. M., Arnold Pilling, and Jane Goodale. 1988. *The Tiwi of North Australia* (3rd. ed). New York: Holt, Rinehart & Winston.

Hart, Donna, and Robert S. Sussman. 2005. *Man the Hunted: Primates, Predators, and Human Evolution.* Boulder: Westview Press.

Hart, Mickey (with K. M. Kostyal). 2003. *Songcatchers: In Search of the World's Music.* Washington, DC: National Geographic.

Hartigan, John (Ed.). 2013a. *Anthropology of Race: Genes, Biology, and Culture.* Santa Fe: School for Advanced Research Press.

———. 2013b "Looking for Race in the Mexican "Book of Life": INMEGEN and the Mexican Genome Project" In John Hartigan (Ed.), *Anthropology of Race: Genes, Biology, and Culture.* Santa Fe: School for Advanced Research Press.

Hartwig, Walter Carl (Ed.). 2002. *The Primate Fossil Record.* Cambridge NY: Cambridge University Press.

Harvey, David. 1990. *The Conditions of Postmodernity.* Cambridge, MA: Blackwell Publishers.

Harvey, Graham. 2006. "Animals, Animists, and Academics." *Zygon* 41 (1): 9–20.

Hassan, Fekri A. 1981. *Demographic Archaeology.* New York: Academic Press.

Hatch, Elvin. 1973. *Theories of Man and Culture.* New York: Columbia University Press.

———. 1983. *Culture and Morality: The Relativity of Values in Anthropology.* New York: Columbia University Press.

Hauser, M. D., Chomsky, N., and W. T. Fitch. 2002. "The Faculty of Language: What is It, Who Has It, and How Did It Evolve?" *Science* 298: 1569–1579.

Hauser-Schäublin, Brigitta. 2003. "The Precolonial Balinese State Reconsidered: A Critical Evaluation of Theory Construction on the Relationship between Irrigation, the State, and Ritual." *Current Anthropology* 44 (2): 153–181.

Hawks, John. 2013. "Significance of Neandertal and Denisovan Genomes in Human Evolution." *Annual Review of Anthropology* 42: 433–449.

Hawks, John, Eric T. Wang, Gregory M. Cochran, Henry C. Harpending, and Robert C. Moyzis. 2007. "Recent Acceleration of Human Adaptive Evolution." *Proceedings of the National Science Academy* 26; 104 (52): 20753–20758.

Hawkes, Kristen. 2004. "The Grandmother Effect." *Nature* 428: 128–129.

Hawkes, Kristen, and R. L. Bliege Bird. 2002. "Showing Off, Handicap Signaling, and the Evolution of Men's Work." *Evolutionary Anthropology* 11: 58–67.

Hawkes, K., O'Connell, J. F., and Coxworth, J. E. 2010. "Family Provisioning is Not the Only Reason Men Hunt." *Current Anthropology* 51(2): 259–264.

Hawkes, K., K. Hill, and J. F. O'Connell. 1982. "Why Hunters Gather: Optimal Foraging and the Ache of Eastern Paraguay." *American Ethnologist* 9: 379–398.

Hawkins, Gerald S. 1965. *Stonehenge Decoded*. New York: Doubleday.

Hayashida, Frances. 2008. "Ancient Beer and Modern Brewers: Ethnoarchaeological Observations of *chichi* Production in Two Regions of North Coast of Peru." *Journal of Anthropological Archaeology* 27 (2): 161–174.

Hayden, Brian. 1993. "The Cultural Capacities of Neandertals." *Journal of Human Evolution* 24: 113–146.

———. 2009. "The Proof is in the Pudding: Feasting and the Origins of Domestication." *Current Anthropology* 50 (5): 597–601.

Haynes, C. V., Jr. 1991. "Geoarchaeological and Paleohydrological Evidence for a Clovis-Age Drought in North America and Its Bearing on Extinction." *Quartinary Research* 35: 438–450.

Hays-Gilpin, Kelley. 2004. *Ambiguous Images: Gender and Rock Art*. Lanham, Maryland: AltaMira Press.

Hays-Gilpin, Kelley, Ann Cordy Deegan, and Elizabeth Ann Morris. 1998. *Prehistoric Sandals from Northeastern Arizona: The Earl H. and Ann Axtell Morris Research*. Tucson: University of Arizona Papers in Anthropology 62.

Hays-Gilpin, Kelley, and David S. Whitley (Eds), 1998. *Reader in Gender Archaeology*. London: Routledge.

Hefner, Robert W. 1983. "The Culture Problem in Human Ecology: A Review Article." *Comparative Studies in Society and History* 25 (3): 547–556.

——— **(Ed.)** 1998. *Democratic Civility: The History and Cross-Cultural Possibility of a Modern Political Ideal*. New Brunswick, NJ: Transaction.

———. 2000. *Civil Islam: Muslims and Democratization in Indonesia*. Princeton, NJ: Princeton University Press.

Heider, Karl. 1979. *Grand Valley Dani: Peaceful Warriors*. New York: Holt, Rinehart & Winston.

———. 1991. *Landscapes of Emotion: Mapping Three Cultures of Emotion in Indonesia*. Cambridge: Cambridge University Press.

Heitzman, James. 2004. *Network City: Planning the Information Society in Bangalore*. New Delhi: Oxford University Press.

Hellenthal, Garrett, George B. J. Busby, Gavin Band, James F. Wilson, Cristian Capelli, Daniel Falush, Simon Myers. 2014. "A Genetic Atlas of Human Admixture History." *Science* 343 (6172): 747–751.

Hendry, Joy. 1987. *Understanding Japanese Society*. London: Croom Helm.

———. 2013. *Understanding Japanese Society* (4th ed). New York: Routledge.

———. 1992. "Introduction and Individuality: Entry into a Social World." In Roger Goodman and Kirsten Refsing (Eds.), *Ideology and Practice in Modern Japan*. London: Routledge.

Henn, B. M., C. R. Gignoux, M. W. Feldman, J. L. Mountain. 2009. "Characterizing the Time Dependency of Human Mitochondrial DNA Mutation Rate Estimates,", *Molecular Biology and Evolution* 26 (1): 217–230.

Henn, Jeanne K. 1984. "Women in the Rural Economy: Past, Present, and Future." In Margaret Jean Hay and Sharon Stichter (Eds.), *African Women South of the Sahara*, pp. 1–19. London: Longman.

Henrich, Joseph, Steven Heine, and Ara Norenzayan. 2010. "The Weirdest People in the World." *Behavioral and Brain Sciences* 33 (2/3): 1–75.

Henrich, Joseph, Robert Boyd, Samuel Bowles, Colin Camerer, Ernst Fehr, and Herbert Gintis (Eds.). 2004. *Foundations of Human Sociality: Economic Experiments and Ethnographic Evidence from Fifteen Small-Scale Societies*. Oxford: Oxford University Press.

Henry, Donald O. 1984. "Preagricultural Sedentism: The Natufian Example." In Douglas T. Price and James A. Brown, (Eds)., *Prehistoric Hunter-Gatherers: The Emergence of Cultural Complexity*, pp. 365–84. New York: Academic Press.

———. 1989. *From Foraging to Agriculture*. Philadelphia: University of Pennsylvania Press.

Henry, John. 2002. *The Scientific Revolution and the Origins of Modern Science*. New York: Palgrave.

Herdt, Gilbert. 1987. *The Sambia: Ritual and Custom in New Guinea*. New York: Holt, Rinehart & Winston.

Herdt, Gilbert, and Robert J. Stoller. 1990. *Intimate Communications: Erotica and the Study of Culture*. New York: Columbia University Press.

Herring, George C. 1979. *America's Longest War: The United States and Vietnam*. New York: John Wiley.

Herrnstein, Richard J., and Charles Murray. 1994. *The Bell Curve: Intelligence and Class Structure in American Life*. New York: Free Press.

Herscher, Ellen. 1989. "A Future in Ruins." *Archaeology* 42 (1): 67–70.

Herzfeld, Michael. 1986. *Ours Once More: Folklore, Ideology, and the Making of Modern Greece*. New York: Pella Publishing Co.

———. 1992. *The Social Production of Indifference: Exploring the Symbolic Roots of Western Bureaucracy*. Chicago: University of Chicago Press.

Hewlett, Barry S. 1996. "Cultural Diversity among African Pygmies." In S. Kent (Ed)., *Cultural Diversity among Twentieth-Century Foragers: An African Perspective*. Cambridge: Cambridge University Press.

Hewes, Gordon W., 1961. "Food Transport and the Origin of Hominid Bipedalism." *American Anthropologist*, 63, 687–710, (1961).

Heyman, Josiah. 2001. "On U.S.–Mexico Border Culture." *Journal of the West* 40 (2): 50–59.

Hickerson, Nancy Parrott. 1980. *Linguistic Anthropology*. New York: Harper & Row.

Higgins, K. 1985. "Ritual and symbol in Baka life history." *Anthropology and Humanism Quarterly* 10 (4): 100–106.

Higham, Charles. 2005. "Complex Societies of East and Southeast Asia." In Chris Scarre (Ed.), *The Human Past: World*

Prehistory and the Development of Human Societies, pp.552–593. New York: Thames and Hudson. .

Hijab, Nadia. 1998. "Islam, Social Change, and the Reality of Arab Women's Lives." In Yvonne Haddad and John Esposito (Eds.), *Islam, Gender, and Social Change,*, pp. 45–55. Oxford, England: Oxford University Press.

Hill, D. 1977. *The Impact of Migration on the Metropolitan and Folk Society of Carriacou, Grenada.* New York: American Museum of Natural History.

Hill, K., H. Kaplan, K. Hawkes, and A. M. Hurtado. 1985. "Men's Time Allocation to Subsistence Work among the Ache of Eastern Paraguay." *Human Ecology* 13: 29–47.

Hill, K., and A. M. Hurtado. 1996. *Ache life history: The Ecology and Demography of a Foraging People.* New York: Aldine de Gruyter.

Hinde, Robert A., and Joan Stevenson-Hinde. 1987. *Instinct and Intelligence* (3rd ed.). Burlington, NC: Scientific Publications Department, Carolina Biological Supply Company.

Hinton, Alexander Laban (Ed.) 1999. *Biocultural Approaches to the Emotions.* Cambridge: Cambridge University Press.

Hirschfeld, Lawrence. 1986. "Kinship and Cognition: Geneaology and the Meaning of Kinship Terms." *Current Anthropology* 27: 217–242.

———. 1989. "Rethinking the Acquisition of Kinship Terms." *International Journal of Behavioral Development* 12: 541–568.

———. 1996. *Race in the Making: Cognition, Culture, and the Child's Construction of Human Kinds.* Cambridge, MA: MIT Press.

Hirschfeld, Lawrence, James Howe, and Bruce Levin. 1978. "Warfare, Infanticide, and Statistical Inference: A Comment on Divale and Harris." *American Anthropologist* 80: 110–115.

Hitchcock, Robert. 1988. *Monitoring Research and Development in the Remote Areas of Botswana.* Gaborone: Government Printer.

———. 2001. "'Hunting is Our Heritage': The Struggle for Hunting and Gathering Rights among the San of Southern Africa." *Parks, Property, and Power: Senri Ethnological Studies, 59.* Osaka, Japan: National Museum of Ethnology.

———. 2003a. "Land, Livestock and Leadership among the Ju/'hoansi San of North Western Botswana." *Anthropologica* 45: 89–94.

———. 2003b. "Human Rights and Indigenous Peoples in Africa and Asia." In David P. Forsythe and Patrice C. McMahon, (Eds.) *Human Rights and Diversity: Area Studies Revisited.* pp. 205–228. Lincoln and London: University of Nebraska Press.

———. 2004a. "Sharing the Land: Kalahari San Property Rights and Resource Management." In Thomas Widlock and Wolde Gossa Tadesse (Eds.), *Property and Equality, Vol. 2: Encapsulation, Commercialization, Discrimination*, pp. 191–207. New York: Berghahn Books.

———. 2004b. "Human Rights and Anthropological Activism among the San." In Carole Nagengast and Carlos G. Velez-Ibanez (Eds.),*Human Rights: The Scholar as Activist.* Oklahoma City: Society for Applied Anthropology.

Hitchcock, Robert K., and Megan. Biesele. 2002. "Controlling Their Destiny: Ju'hoansi of Nyae Nyae." *Cultural Survival Quarterly* 26, (2): 13.

Hitchcock, Robert K., John E. Yellen, Diane J. Gelburd, Alan J. Osborn, and Aron L. Crowell. 1996. "Subsistence Hunting and Resource Management among the Ju/'hoansi of Northwestern Botswana." *African Study Monographs* 17 (4): 153–208.

Ho, S. Y., M. J. Phillips, A. Cooper, and A. J. Drummond,. 2005. "Time Dependency of Molecular Rate Estimates and Systematic Overestimation of Recent Divergence Times," *Molecular Biology and Evolution* 22 (7): 1561–1568.

Hobbes, Thomas. [1651] 1958. *Leviathan.* New York: Liberal Arts Press.

Hockett, Charles F., and R. Ascher. 1964. "The Human Revolution." *Current Anthropology* 5: 135–168.

Hodgson, J. A., C. M. Bergey, and T. R. Disotell. 2010. "Neanderthal Genome: The Ins and Outs of African Genetic Diversity." *Current Biology* 20, R517–R519.

Hoebel, E. Adamson. [1954] 1968. *The Law of Primitive Man.* New York: Atheneum.

Hoffecker, John F., Scott A. Elias, and Dennis H. O'Rourke. 2014. "Out of Beringia?" *Science* 343 (6174): 979–980.

Holden, Constance. 2000. "Selective Power of UV." *Science* 289: 1461.

Hole, F., J. McCorriston,. 2009. "The Ecology of Seasonal Stress and the Origins of Agriculture in the Near East." *American Anthropologist* 93(1): 46–69.

Holl, A. F. C. 2009. "Coping with Uncertainty: Neolithic Life in the Dhar Tichitt-Walata, Mauritania, (ca. 4000–2300 BP)." *C. R. Geoscience* 341: 703–712.

Holloway, R. L. 1985. "The Poor Brain of *Homo sapiens neanderthalensis*: See What You Please." In E. Delson (Ed.), *Ancestors: The Hard Evidence*, pp. 319–24. New York: Alan R. Liss.

Hollox, Edward. 2005. "Evolutionary Genetics: Genetics of Lactase Persistence – Fresh Lessons in the History of Milk Drinking." *European Journal of Human Genetics,* 13, 267–269.

Holmberg, Allan R. [1950] 1969. *Nomads of the Long Bow: Siriono of Eastern Bolivia.* Garden City, NY: Natural History Press.

———. 1962. "Community and Regional Development: The Joint Cornell-Peru Experiment." *Human Organization* 17: 12–16.

Holmes, Lowell D. 1987. *Quest for the Real Samoa: The Mead/ Freeman Controversy and Beyond.* South Hadley, MA: Bergin & Garvey.

Hooker, J. T. (Ed.) 1990. *Reading the Past: Ancient Writing from Cuneiform to the Alphabet.* London: British Museum Press.

Hopkins, Keith. 1982. "Aspects of the Paleogeography of Beringia During the Late Pleistocene." In D. M. Hopkins, J. Matthews, C. Schweger, and S. Young, (Eds.), *The Paleoecology of Beringia*, pp. 3–28. New York: Academic Press.

Hostetler, John A. 1980. *Amish Society* (3rd ed.). Baltimore, MD: Johns Hopkins University.

Hourani, Albert. 1991. *A History of the Arab Peoples.* Cambridge: Cambridge University Press.

Howell, N., C. B.Smejkal, D.A. MacKey, P.F. Chinnery, D.M. Turnbull, and C. Herrnstadt."The Pedigree Rate of Sequence Divergence in the Human Mitochondrial Genome: There Is a Difference between Phylogenetic and Pedigree Rates." *American Journal of Human Genetics* 72 (3): 659–670.

Howell, Nancy. 1976. "The Population of the Dobe Area !Kung." In Richard B. Lee and Irven DeVore, (Eds.), *Kalahari Hunter-Gatherers.* Cambridge, MA: Harvard University Press.

———. 1979. *Demography of the Dobe !Kung.* New York: Academic Press.

Howells, W. W. 1976. "Explaining Modern Man: Evolutionists versus Migrationists." *Journal of Human Evolution* 5: 477–496.

Hoyle, Fred. 1977. *On Stonehenge.* San Francisco: W. H. Freeman.

Hrdy, Sarah. 2000. The Optimal Number of Fathers: Evolution, Demography, and History in the Shaping of Female Mate Preferences. In D. LeCroy and P. Moller (Eds.), *Evolutionary Perspectives on Human Reproductive Behavior* (pp. 75–96). Annals of the New York Academy of Sciences.

———. 2009. *Mothers and Others: The Evolutionary Origins of Mutual Understandings.* Cambridge, MA: Belknap Press.

Hsu, Francis. 1948. *Under the Ancestor's Shadow: Chinese Culture and Personality.* New York: Columbia University Press.

———. 1981. *Americans and Chinese: Passage to Differences* (3rd ed.). Honolulu: University of Hawaii Press.

Hughes, David McDermott. 2013. "Climate Change and the Victim Slot: From Oil to Innocence." *American Anthropologist* 115 (4): 570–581.

Huntington, Elsworth. 1924. *Civilization and Climate.* New Haven, CT: Yale University Press.

Huntington, Samuel P. 1996. *The Clash of Civilizations and the Remaking of the World Order.* New York: Simon & Schuster.

Hutchinson, John, and Anthony D. Smith (Eds.). 1996. *Ethnicity.* Oxford: Oxford: University Press.

Hutchinson, Sharon. 1996. *Nuer Dilemmas: Coping with Money, War, and the State.* Berkeley: University of California Press.

Hutton, James. 1785. *Theory of the Earth: Or an Investigation of the Laws Observable in the Composition, Dissolution and Restoration of Land Upon the Globe.* London.

Inden, Ronald D. 2000. *Imagining India.* Bloomington: Indiana University Press.

Information Please Almanac. 1991. "Energy, Petroleum, and Coal, by Country," pp. 146–47. Boston: Houghton Mifflin.

Infoplease.com. 2010. "Nigeria" Country Report, United States State Department Report."

Ingham, John. M. 1986. *Mary, Michael, and Lucifer: Folk Catholicism in Central Mexico.* Austin: University of Texas Press.

Inman, Mason. 2008. "China CO2 Emissions Growing Faster than Anticipated." *National Geographic News.* http://news.nationalgeographic.com/news/2008/03/080318-china-warming.html.

Ingstad, Helge and Anne Stine Ingstad. 2001. *The Viking Discovery of America: The Excavation of a Norse Settlement in L'Anse Aux Meadows, Newfoundland.* Checkmark Books. New York.

Insoll, Timothy. 2004. *Archaeology, Ritual, Religion.* London: Routledge.

———. ed. 2011. *Oxford Handbook of the Archaeology of Ritual and Religion.* Oxford: Oxford University Press.

Institute for Women's Policy Research. 2010. "Fact Sheet, The Gender Wage Gap: 2009." www.iwpr.org.

Irwin, G. 1993. *Prehistoric Exploration and Colonization of the Pacific.* Cambridge: Cambridge University Press.

Isaac, Barbara. 1995. "An Epimethean View of the Future at the Peabody Museum of Archaeology and Ethnology at Harvard University." *Federal Archaeology.* Offprint Series, Fall/Winter, pp. 18–22.

Isaac, Barry L. 1977. "The Siriono of Eastern Bolivia: A Reexamination." *Human Ecology* 5: 137–154.

Isaac, G. L. 1978a. "The Food-Sharing Behavior of Protohuman Hominids." *Scientific American* 238 (4): 90–108.

———. 1978b. "The Archeological Evidence for the Activities of Early African Hominids." In C. J. Jolly (Ed.), *Early Hominids of Africa,* pp. 219–254. London: Duckworth.

Isbell, Billie Jean. 2013. "Lessons from Vicos." In Sam Beck and Carl Maida (Eds.), *Toward Engaged Anthropology.* pp. 45–89. New York and Oxford: Berghahn Books.

Iscan, Mehmet Yasar, and Richard Helmer (Eds.). 1993. *Forensic Analysis of the Skull: Craniofacial Analysis, Reconstruction, and Identification.* New York: Wiley-Liss.

Issak, Mark. 2005. *The Counter-Creationism Handbook.* Westport: Greenwood Press.

Isçan, M. Y. S., and K. A. R. Kennedy. 1989. *Reconstruction of Life from the Skeleton.* New York: Alan R. Liss.

Jablonka, E. and M. J. Lamb. 2006. *Evolution in Four Dimensions: Genetic, Epigenetic, Behavioral, and Symbolic in the History of Life.* Cambridge: MIT Press.

Jablonski, Nina. 2004. "The Evolution of Human Skin and Skin Color." *Annual Review of Anthropology* 33: 585–623.

———. 2012. *Living color: The biological and social meaning of skin color.* Berkeley: University of California Press.

Jablonski, Nina G., and Leslie Aiello. 1998. *The Origin and Diversification of Language.* Berkeley: University of California Press.

Jablonski, Nina, and George Chaplin. 2000. "The Evolution of Skin Color." *Journal of Human Evolution* 39 (1): 57–106.

———. 2010. "Colloquium Paper: Human Skin Pigmentation as an Adaptation to UV radiation." *Proceedings of the National Academy of Sciences of the United States of America* 107, Supplement 2: 8962–8968.

Jackendoff, Ray, and Steven Pinker. 2005. "The Nature of the Language Faculty and Its Implications for Evolution of Language" (reply to Fitch, Hauser, and Chomsky). *Cognition 9* (7): 211–225.

Jackson, Donald Dale. 1992. "How Lord Elgin First Won—and Lost—His Marbles." *Smithsonian* 23 (9): 135–146.

Jackson, Jean E., and Kay Warren. 2005. "Indigenous Movements in Latin America, 1992–2004: Controversies, Ironies, New Directions."*Annual Review of Anthropology* 34: 549–573.

Jackson, Peter. 1995. *Dear Uncle Go: Male Homosexuality in Thailand.* Bangkok: Bua Luang Books.

Jacobson, Matthew Frye. 1998. *Whiteness of Different Color: European Immigrants and the Alchemy of Race.* Cambridge, MA: Harvard University Press.

Jameson, John H. 2004. *Reconstructed past: Reconstructions in the Public Interpretation of Archaeology and History.* Walnut Creek, CA: AltaMira Press.

Jankowiak, William (Ed.). 1995. *Romantic Love: A Universal Experience?* New York: Columbia University Press.

——— **(Ed.)** 2008. *Intimacies: Between Love and Sex.* New York: Columbia University Press.

Jankowiak, William R., and Edward F. Fischer. 1992. "A Cross-Cultural Perspective on Romantic Love." *Ethnology 3* (2): 149–155.

Jensen, Arthur. 1980. *Bias in Mental Testing.* New York: Free Press.

Jeong, Choongwon, Gorka Alkorta-Aranburu, Buddha Basnyat, Maniraj Neupane, David B. Witonsky, Jonathan K. Pritchard, Cynthia M. Beall, and Anna Di Rienzo. 2013. "Admixture Facilitates Genetic Adaptations to High Altitude in Tibet." *Nature Communications* 5 (3281).

Jett, Stephen C. 1978. "Precolumbian Transoceanic Contacts." In Jesse D. Jennings (Ed.), *Ancient North Americans.* pp. 557–613. San Francisco: W. H. Freeman.

Jochim, Michael. 1998. *A Hunter-Gatherer Landscape.* New York: Plenum.

Johanson, D. C., T. D. White, and Y. Coppens. 1978. "A New Species of the Genus *Australopithecus* (Primates: Hominidae) from the Pliocene of Eastern Africa." *Kirtlandia* 28: 1–14.

Johanson, Donald, and Maitland Edey. 1981. *Lucy: The Beginnings of Humankind*. New York: Simon & Schuster.

Johanson, Donald C., and James Shreeve. 1989. *Lucy's Child: The Discovery of a Human Ancestor*. New York: Avon Books.

Johanson, Donald, and Timothy White. 1979. "A Systematic Assessment of Early African Hominids." *Science* 203: 321–330.

Johanson, Donald C., M. Taieb, and Y. Coppens. 1982. "Pliocene Hominid Fossils from Hadar, Ethiopia. *American Journal of Physical Anthropology* 57 (4): 1973–1977.

John Paul II. 1996. "Truth Cannot Contradict Truth." Encyclical Address to the Pontifical Academy of Sciences, October, Vatican City.

Johnson, Allen W. 1975. "Time Allocation in a Machiguenga Community." *Ethnology* 14: 301–310.

Johnson, Allen, and Timothy Earle. 2000. *The Evolution of Human Societies: From Foraging Group to Agrarian State* (2nd ed.). Stanford, CA: Stanford University Press.

Johnson, Ronald W., and Michael G. Schene. 1987. *Cultural Resources Management*. Malabar, FL: Robert E. Krieger.

Johnson-Hanks, Jennifer. 2008. "Demographic Transitions and Modernity." *Annual Reviews of Anthropology* 37: 301–315.

Jolly, Alison. 1985. *The Evolution of Primate Behavior*, 2nd ed. New York: Macmillan.

Jones, Doug. 2000. "Group Nepotism and Human Kinship." *Current Anthropology* 41 (5): 779–809.

———. 2003. "Kinship and Deep History: Exploring Connections between Culture Areas, Genes, and Language." *American Anthropologist* 105 (3): 501–514.

———. 2004. "The Universal Psychology of Kinship: Evidence from Language." *Trends in Cognitive Sciences* 8 (5): 211–215.

Jones, M. K. 2002. *The Molecule Hunt*. New York: Arcade Publishing.

Jones, Steve, Robert Martin, and David Pilbeam (Eds.). 1992. *The Cambridge Encyclopedia of Human Evolution*. New York: Cambridge University Press.

Joppa, Lucas N., David L. Roberts, and Stuart L. Pimm. 2010. "How Many Species of Flowering Plants are There?" *Proceedings of the Royal Society B* doi: 10.1098rspb 2010.1004.

Jorde, Lynn B. and Stephen P. Wooding. 2004. "Genetic Variation, Classification and 'Race'." *Nature Genetics* 36 (11): S28–S33.

Jurmain, Robert, L. Kilgore, W. Trevathan, and R.L Ciochon. 2014. *Introduction to Physical Anthropology*. (2013–2014 ed.). Belmont, CA: Wadsworth. Cengage Learning.

Kaeppler, Adrienne L. 1980. "Polynesian Music and Dance." In Elizabeth May (Ed.), *Musics of Many Cultures*. Berkeley: University of California Press.

Kamin, Leon. 1974. *The Science and Politics of I.Q.* New York: Wiley.

Kankpeyeng, B. W., and C. R. DeCorse. 2004. "Ghana's Vanishing Past: Development, Antiquities and the Destruction of the Archaeological Record." *African Archaeological Review* 21 (2): 89–128.

Kapferer, Bruce. 2005. *Oligarchs and Oligopolies: New Formations of Global Power*. New York and Oxford: Berghahn Books

Kaplan, Maureen F., and John E. Mendel. 1982. "Ancient Glass and the Disposal of Nuclear Waste." *Archaeology* 35 (4): 22–29.

Karnow, Stanley. 1984. *Vietnam: A History*. New York: Penguin.

Katz, Solomon (Ed.). 2003. *The Encyclopedia of Food and Culture*. New York: Charles Scribner's Sons.

Kay, Paul. 2005. "Color Categories are Not Arbitrary." *Cross Cultural Research* 39: 72–78.

Kay, R. F., M. Plaukin, P. C. Wright, K. Glander, and G. H. Albrecht. 1988. "Behavioral and Size Correlates of Canine Dimorphism in Platyrrhine Primates." *American Journal of Physical Anthropology* 88: 385–397.

Kay, Richard. 2000. "Parathecidae." In E. Delson Tattersall, and J. van Couvering, (Eds)., *Encyclopedia of Human Evolution and Prehistory*. New York: Garland.

Kaya, Laura Pearl. 2009. "Dating in a Sexually Segregated Society: Embodied Practices of Online Romance in Irbid, Jordan."*Anthropological Quarterly* 82 (1): 251–278.

Keddie, Nikki R. 1981. *Roots of Revolution: An Interpretive History of Modern Iran*. New Haven, CT: Yale University Press.

Keegan, William F. (Ed.). 1987. *Emergent Horticultural Economies of the Eastern Woodlands*. Occasional Publications No. 7. Carbondale: Southern Illinois University, Center for Archaeological Investigations.

Keeley, Lawrence. H., and Nicholas. Toth. 1981. "Microwear Polishes on Early Stone Tools from Koobi Fora, Kenya." *Nature* 293: 4644–65.

Keeley, Lawrence H. 1996. *War before Civilization*. New York: Oxford University Press.

Keesing, Roger M. 1975. *Kin Groups and Social Structure*. New York: Holt, Rinehart & Winston.

———. 1981. *Cultural Anthropology: A Contemporary Perspective*. New York: Holt, Rinehart & Winston.

Keesing, R. M., and A. J. Strathern. 1998. *Cultural Anthropology: A Contemporary Perspective* (3rd ed.). Fort Worth: Harcourt Brace Jovanovich.

Kehoe, Alice Beck. 1989. *The Ghost Dance: Ethnohistory and Revitalization*. New York: Holt, Rinehart & Winston.

———. 1995. *North American Indians: A Comprehensive Account* (2nd ed.). Upper Saddle River, NJ: Prentice Hall.

Keita, S. O. Y., R. A. Kittles, C. D. M. Royal, G. E. Bonney, P. Furbert Harris, G. M. Dustin, and C. N. Rotimi. 2004. "Conceptualizing Human Variation." *Nature Genetics* 36 (11): 17–20.

Kellman, Shelly. 1982. "The Yanomamös: Portrait of a People in Crisis." *New Age Journal*, May. Reprinted in *Anthropology 88/89*. 1988. Sluice Dock, Guilford, CT: Dushkin Publishing Group.

Kelly, Raymond C. 2003. *Warless Societies and the Origin of War*. Ann Arbor: University of Michigan Press.

Kelly, Robert L. 1995. *The Foraging Spectrum: Diversity in Hunter-Gatherer Lifeways*. Washington, DC: Smithsonian Institution Press.

Kenyon, Kathleen M. 1972. "Ancient Jericho." In *Old World Archaeology: Foundations of Civilization, Readings from Scientific American*. San Francisco: W. H. Freeman.

Kephart, Ronald. 2012. "Latin America and the Caribbean." In Raymond Scupin (Ed.), *Race and Ethnicity: The United States and the World*, (2nd ed.). pp. 302–322. Upper Saddle River, NJ: Pearson Prentice Hall.

Kephart, William M., and William Zellner. 1994. *Extraordinary Groups: The Sociology of Unconventional Life Styles* (4th ed.). New York: St. Martin's Press.

Kerblay, Basile. 1983. *Modern Soviet Society*. New York: Pantheon.

Kerbo, Harold R., and John A. McKinstry. 1998. *Modern Japan*. New York: McGraw-Hill.

Keyes, Charles F. 1995. *The Golden Peninsula: Culture and Adaptation in Mainland Southeast Asia*. Honolulu: University of Hawaii Press.

———. 2002. "Weber and Anthropology." *Annual Review of Anthropology* 31: 233–255.

Khalturina, Darya, and Andrey Khorotayev. 2006. "Women's Status and War in Cross-Cultural Perspective: A Reconsideration." *World Cultures*. 15 (2): 209–257.

Kiernan, Ben. 1988. "Orphans of Genocide: The Cham Muslims of Kampuchea under Pol Pot." *Bulletin of Concerned Asian Scholars* 20 (4): 2–33.

King, Thomas F. 2000. *Federal Planning and Historic Places: The Section 106 Process*. Walnut Creek, CA: AltaMira Press.

———. 2007. *Saving Places that Matter: A Citizen's Guide to the National Historic Preservation Act*. Walnut Creek, CA: LeftCoast Press.

———. 2013. *Cultural Resource Laws and Practice*. Walnut Creek, CA: AltaMira Press.

Kinsey, Warren G. (Ed.). 1987. *The Evolution of Human Behavior: Primate Models*. Albany: State University of New York Press.

Kirch, Patrick V. 1984. *The Evolution of the Polynesian Chiefdoms*. Cambridge: Cambridge University Press.

Kirchoff, Paul. 1955. "The Principles of Clanship in Human Society." *Davidson Anthropological Journal* 1:1. Reprinted in Morton H. Fried (Ed.). 1958. *Readings in Anthropology*, 2 vols. New York: Thomas Y. Crowell.

Kitcher, Phillip. 1982. *Abusing Science: The Case against Creationism*. Cambridge, MA: MIT Press.

Klein, Laura. 1980. "Contending with Colonization: Tlingit Men and Women in Charge." In Mona Etienne and Eleanor Leacock, (Eds.), *Women and Colonization*. pp. 88–108. New York: Praeger.

Kleinman, Arthur. 2004. "Culture and Depression." *New England Journal of Medicine, 351*: 951–953.

Kluckhorn, Clyde. 1967. *Navajo Witchcraft*. Boston: Beacon Press.

Knauft, Bruce 1985. *Good Company and Violence: Sorcery and Social Action in Lowland New Guinea Society*. Berkeley: University of California Press.

———. 1988. "Reply to Betzig, Laura. On Reconsidering Violence in Simple Human Societies." *Current Anthropology* 29 (4): 629–633.

———. 1993. *South Coast New Guinea Cultures: History, Comparison, Dialectic*. Cambridge: Cambridge University Press.

———. 1996. *Genealogies for the Present in Cultural Anthropology*. London and New York: Routledge Press.

———. 1999. *From Primitive to Postcolonial in Melanesia and Anthropology*. Ann Arbor: University of Michigan Press.

———. 2002. *Exchanging the Past: A Rainforest World of Before and After*. Chicago: University of Chicago Press.

———. (Ed.). 2002. *Critically Modern: Alternatives, Alterities, Anthropologies*. Bloomington: Indiana University Press.

Knudson, Ruthann. 1989. "North America's Threatened Heritage." *Archaeology* 42 (1): 71–75.

Kobayashi-Hillary, Mark. 2004. *Outsourcing to India: The Offshore Advantage*. Berlin: Springer Verlag.

Kolenda, Pauline. 1978. *Caste in Contemporary India: Beyond Organic Solidarity*. Menlo Park: Benjamin/Cumming Publishing Co.

Kondo, Dorinne. 1990. *Crafting Selves: Power, Gender, and Discourses of Identity in a Japanese Workplace*. Chicago: University of Chicago Press.

Konner, Melvin. 2002. *The Tangled Wing: Biological Constraints on the Human Spirit* (2nd ed.). New York: Holt, Rinehart & Winston.

———. 2010. *The Evolution of Childhood: Relationships, Emotion, Mind*. Cambridge, MA: Belknap Press of Harvard University Press.

Korbin, Jill E. 2003. "Children, Childhoods, and Violence." *Annual Review of Anthropology* 32: 431–446.

Kottak, Conrad P. 2003. *Mirror for Humanity: A Concise Introduction to Cultural Anthropology* (3rd ed.). New York: McGraw-Hill.

Kowalewski, Stephen A. 2008. "Regional Settlement Pattern Studies." *Journal of Archaeological Research* 16: 225–285.

Krabacher, Thomas, Exekiel Kalipeni, and Azzedine, Layachi (Eds.). 2011. *Africa* (13th ed.). New York: McGraw-Hill.

Krause, Johannes, Carles Lalueza-Fox, Ludovic Orlando, Wolfgang Enard, Richard E. Green, Hernán A. Burbano, Jean-Jacques Hublin, et al. 2007. "The Derived *FOXP2* Variant of Modern Humans Was Shared with Neandertals" *Current Biology* 17(21): 1908–1912.

Krause, Johannes; Fu, Qiaomei; Good, Jeffrey M.; Viola, Bence; Shunkov, Michael V.; Derevianko, Anatoli P. & Pääbo, Svante. 2010. "The complete mitochondrial DNA genome of an unknown hominin from southern Siberia", *Nature* 464 (7290): 894–897'

Kraybill, Donald. 2001. *The Riddle of Amish Culture*. Baltimore: Johns Hopkins University Press.

Krings, M., A. Stone, R. W. Schmitz, H. Krainitski, M. Stoneking, and S. Paabo. 1997. "Neandertal DNA Sequences and the Origins of Modern Humans." *Cell* 90: 19–30.

Kromkowski, John A. 2003. "2000 Census Ethnicity Data." In *Race and Ethnicity 04/05*. 14th ed. Guilford, CT: McGraw-Hill.

Kronenfeld, David B. Giovanni Bennardo, Victor C. de Munck, and Michael D. Fischer (Eds.). 2011. *A Companion to Cognitive Anthropology*. Malden, Mass: Wiley-Blackwell

Kruckman, L. 1987. "The Role of Remote Sensing in Ethnohistorical Research." *Journal of Field Archaeology* 14: 343–51.

Kuhl, P. K., and P. Iverson. 1995. "Linguistic Experience and the 'Perceptual Magnet Effect'." In W. Strange, ed., *Speech Perception and Linguistic Experience: Issues in Cross-Language Research*. Timonium, MD: York Press.

Kuhl, P. K., and A. N. Meltzoff. 1996. "Infant vocalizations in response to speech: Vocal imitation and developmental change." *Journal of the Acoustical Society of America*. 100: 2425–38.

Kuijt, I. 2000. *Life in Neolithic Farming Communities: Social Organization, Identity, and Differentiation*. New York: Kluwer Academic.

Kumar, S., A. Filipski, V. Swarna, A. Walker, and S. B. Hedges. 2005. "Placing confidence limits on the molecular age of the human-chimpanzee divergence." *Proceedings of the National Academy of Sciences*, 102: 18842–18847.

Kuper, Adam. 1988. *The Invention of Primitive Society*. London: Routledge Press.

Kuper, Leo, and M. G. Smith. 1969. *Pluralism in Africa*. Berkeley and Los Angeles: University of California Press.

Kurin, Richard. 1980. "Doctor, Lawyer, Indian Chief." *Natural History* 89 (11): 6–24.

Kürti, László and Peter Skalník (Eds.). 2009. *Postsocialist Europe: Anthropological Perspectives from Home*. New York and Oxford: Berghahn Books.

Kurtz, Donald V. 1982. "The Virgin of Guadalupe and the Politics of Becoming Human." *Journal of Anthropological Research* 38: 194–210.

Kusimba, Chapurukha M. 1999. *The Rise and Fall of the Swahili States*. Walnut Creek, CA: AltaMira Press.

Kuwert, P., C. Spitzer, et al. 2008. "Trauma and Post-traumatic stress symptoms in former German child soldiers of World War II." *International Psychogeriatrics* 20 (5): 1014–18.

Laitman, Jeffrey T. 1984. "The Anatomy of Human Speech." *Natural History* 93 (8): 20–27.

Lahr, Marta Mirazon, and Robert Foley. 1994. "Multiple Dispersals and Modern Human Origins." *Evolutionary Anthropology* 3 (2): 48–60.

Laitman, Jeffrey T. 1984. "The Anatomy of Human Speech." *Natural History* 93 (8): 20–27.

Lakoff, George. 1987. *Women, Fire, and Dangerous Things*. Chicago: University of Chicago Press.

Lakoff, George, and Mark Johnson. 2000. *Philosophy in the Flesh: The Embodied Mind and Its Challenge to Western Thought*. New York: Basic Books.

Laland, Kevin N., and Bennett G. Galef. 2009. *The Question of Animal Culture*. Cambridge: Harvard University Press.

Lamason, Rebecca L., Manzoor-Ali P. K. Mohideen, Jason R. Mest, Andrew C. Wong, Heather L. Norton, Michele C. Aros, Michael J. Jurynec, Xianyun Mao, Vanessa R. Humphreville, Jasper E. Humbert, Soniya Sinha, Jessica L. Moore, Pudur Jagadeeswaran, Wei Zhao, Gang Ning, Izabela Makalowska, Paul M. McKeigue, David O'Donnell, Rick Kittles, Esteban J. Parra, Nancy J. Mangini, David J. Grunwald, Mark D. Shriver, Victor A. Canfield, and Keith C. Cheng. 2005. "SLC24A5, a Putative Cation Exchanger, Affects Pigmentation in Zebrafish and Humans." *Science* 310 (5755): 1782–1786.

Lamberg-Karlovsky, C. C. 1989. *Archaeological Thought in America*. Cambridge: Cambridge University Press.

Lamphere, Louise. 1997. "The Domestic Sphere of Women and the Public World of Men: The Strengths and Limitations of an Anthropological Dichotomy." In C. Brettel and C. Sargent (Eds)., *Gender in Cross-Cultural Perspective*, 2nd ed. Upper Saddle River, NJ: Prentice Hall.

Lancaster, Jane B. and Raymond Hames. 2011. "Statement on the Publication of Alice Dreger's Investigation, *Darkness's Descent in the American Anthropological Association: A Cautionary Tale*. DOI: 10.1007/s12110–01–9106–8.

Landes, David S. 1998. *The Wealth and Poverty of Nations: Why Some Are So Rich and Some So Poor*. New York: W. W. Norton.

Langergraber, Kevin E., Kay Prüfer, Carolyn Rowney, Christophe Boesch, Catherine Crockford, Katie Fawcett, Eiji Inoue, et al. 2012. "Generation times in wild chimpanzees and gorillas suggest earlier divergence times in great ape and human evolution." *Proceedings of the National Academy of the United States of America* 109 (39): 15716–15721.

Larsen, Clark Spencer. 1995. "Biological Changes in Human Populations with Agriculture." *Annual Review of Anthropology* 24: 185–213.

Laughlin, Robert M. 2004. "Linguistic Survival among the Maya." In Ruth Osterweiss Selig, Marilyn R. London, and P. Ann Kaupp (Eds.), *Anthropology Explored: Revised and Expanded: The Best of Smithsonian Anthronotes*, . P. 31. Washington, DC: Smithsonian Books.

Lavallée, D. 1990. "La Domestication Animale en Amérique du Sud: le Point des Connaissances." *Bulletin de l'Institut Francais d'Etudes Andines* 19(1): 25–44.

Laville, H., J. Riguad, and J. Sackett. 1980. *Rock Shelters of the Perigord*. New York: Academic Press.

Lawrence, Peter. 1964. *Road Belong Cargo: A Study of the Cargo Movement in the Southern Madang District, New Guinea*. Manchester: Manchester University Press.

Layton, R., ed. 1989. *Who Needs the Past? Indigenous Values and Archaeology*. London: Unwin Hyman Ltd.

Leach, Edmund. [1953] 1954. "Bridewealth and the Stability of Marriage." *Man* 53:179–80; *Man* 54: 173.

———. 1966. "Ritualization in Man in Relation to Conceptual and Social Development." *Philosophical Transactions of the Royal Society of London*, Series B 251 (772): 403–8.

———. 1988. "Noah's Second Son." *Anthropology Today* 4 (4): 2–5.

Leaf, Murray J. 1984. *Song of Hope: The Green Revolution in a Punjab Village*. New Brunswick, NJ: Rutgers University Press.

Leakey, L. S. B. 1959. "A New Fossil Skull from Olduvai." *Nature* 201: 967–70.

———. 1961. "Exploring 1,750,000 Years into Man's Past." *National Geographic* 120 (4): 564–89.

Leakey, M. D. 1971. *Olduvai Gorge*, Vol. 3. Cambridge: Cambridge University Press.

Leakey, M. D., and R. L. Hay. 1979. "Pliocene Footprints in Laetoli Beds at Laetoli, Northern Tanzania." *Nature* 278: 317–23.

Leakey, M. G., F. Spoor, F. H. Brown, P. N. Gathogo, and C. Kiarie. 2001. "New Hominin Genus from Eastern Africa Shows Diverse Middle Pliocene Lineages." *Nature* 410: 433–40.

Leakey, Meave G., C. S. Feibel, I. McDougall, and A. Walker. 1995. "New Four-Million-Year-Old Hominid Species from Kanapoi and Allia Bay, Kenya." *Nature* 376: 565–71.

Leakey, Meave; Spoor, Fred; Dean, M. Christopher; Feibel, Craig S., Antón, Susan C.; Kiarie, Christopher; Leakey, Louise N. 2012 "New fossils from Koobi Fora in northern Kenya confirm taxonomic diversity in early Homo". *Nature* 488 (7410): 201–4.

Leap, William. 1988. "Indian Language Renewal." *Human Organization* 47 (4): 283–91.

LeBlanc, Steven A., with Katherine E. Register. 2003. *Constant Battles: The Myth of the Peaceful, Noble Savage*. New York: St. Martin's Press.

Lechner, Frank L., and John Boli(Eds.). 2000. *The Globalization Reader*. Malden, MA: Blackwell Publishers.

Lee, Richard B. 1968. "What Do Hunters Do for a Living, Or How to Make Out on Scarce Resources." In R. B. Lee and Irven DeVore, (Eds.), *Man the Hunter*, pp. 30–43. Chicago: Aldine.

———. 1969. "Kung Bushman Subsistence: An Input-Output Analysis." In A. P. Vayda, ed., *Environment and Cultural Behavior: Ecological Studies in Cultural Anthropology*. Garden City, NY: Natural History Press.

———. 1972a. "The Intensification of Social Life among the !Kung Bushmen." In Brian Spooner, ed., *Population Growth: Anthropological Implications*, pp. 343–50. Cambridge, MA: MIT Press.

———. 1972b. "Population Growth and the Beginning of Sedentary Life among the !Kung Bushmen." In Brian Spooner, ed., *Population Growth: Anthropological Implications*, pp. 330–42. Cambridge, MA: MIT Press.

———. 1979. *The !Kung San: Men, Women, and Work in a Foraging Society.* Cambridge: Cambridge University Press.

———. 1981. "Politics, Sexual and Nonsexual in an Egalitarian Society: The !Kung San." In Gerald Berreman, ed., *Social Inequality: Comparative and Developmental Approaches*, pp. 83–101. New York: Academic Press.

———. 2013. *The Dobe Ju/'hoansi.* 4th ed. Belmont, CA: Wadsworth Cengage Learning.

Lee, Richard B., and Irven DeVore (Eds.). 1968. *Man the Hunter.* Chicago: Aldine.

Lende, Daniel L. and Greg Downey. (2012). *The Encultured Brain: An Introduction to Neuroanthropology.* Cambridge, MASS: The MIT Press.

Lenski, Gerhard E. 1966. *Power and Privilege: A Theory of Social Stratification.* New York: McGraw-Hill.

Leonard, Karen Isaksen. 1997. *The South Asian Americans.* Westport, CT: Greenwood Press.

Leone, Mark P., and Parker B. Potter. 1988. *The Recovery of Meaning: Historical Archaeology in the Eastern United States.* Washington, DC: Smithsonian Institution Press.

Lepowsky, Maria. 1993. *Fruit of the Motherland: Gender in an Egalitarian Society.* New York: Columbia University Press.

Levine, Nancy. 1988. *The Dynamics of Polyandry.* Chicago: University of Chicago Press.

Levinton, Jeffrey. 1988. *Genetics, Paleontology, and Macroevolution.* New York: Cambridge University Press.

Lévi-Strauss, Claude. 1944. "The Social and Psychological Aspects of Chieftainship in a Primitive Tribe: The Nambikuara of Northwestern Matto Grosso." *Transactions of the New York Academy of Sciences* 7: 16–32.

———. 1966. *The Savage Mind*, trans. George Weidenfeld and Nicholson, Ltd. Chicago: University of Chicago Press.

———. 1969. *The Elementary Structures of Kinship*, rev. ed., trans. J. H. Bell. Boston: Beacon Press.

Lewellen, Ted C. 1983. *Political Anthropology: An Introduction.* South Hadley, MA: Bergin & Garvey.

———. 2002. *The Anthropology of Globalization: Cultural Anthropology Enters the 21st Century.* Westport, CT: Bergin & Garvey.

Lewin, Tamar. 1986. "Profile of an Anthropologist Casting an Anthropological Eye on American Consumers." *The New York Times*, May 11.

Lewis, Herbert. 1992. "Ethnic Loyalties Are on the Rise Globally." *Christian Science Monitor*, December 28. Reprinted in Jeffress Ramsay, ed. 1993. *Africa*, 5th ed. Guilford, CT: Dushkin Publishing Group.

Lewis, Oscar. 1951. *Life in a Mexican Village: Tepotzlan Restudied.* Urbana: University of Illinois Press.

———. 1961. *The Children of Sanchez: Autobiography of a Mexican Family.* New York: Random House.

———. 1966. *La Vida: A Puerto Rican Family in the Culture of Poverty—San Juan and New York.* New York: Random House.

Lewontin, R. 1972. "The Apportionment of Human Diversity." In Theodore Dobzhansky and William C. Steere (Eds.), *Evolutionary Biology*, Vol. 6, pp. 381–98. New York: Plenum Press.

Li, Wen-Hsiung, and Masako Tanimura. 1987. "The Molecular Clock Runs More Slowly in Man Than in Apes and Monkeys." *Nature* 326: 93–96.

Liebenberg, L. 2006. "Persistence hunting by Modern Hunter-Gatherers", *Current Anthropology* 47(6): 1017–1025.

Lieberman, Daniel E., Dennis M. Bramble, David A. Raichlen, and John J. Shea. 2007. "The evolution of endurance running and the tyranny of ethnography: A reply to Pickering and Bunn (2007)". *Journal of Human Evolution* 53: 434–437.

Lieberman, Leonard. 2001. "How Caucasoids Got Such Big Crania and Why They Shrank: From Morton to Rushton." *Current Anthropology* 42: 69–95.

Lieberman, Leonard, and Scupin, Raymond. 2011. "A History of 'Scientific' Racialism." In *Race and Ethnicity: The United States and the World*, Raymond Scupin. 2nd ed. pp. 11–31. Upper Saddle River, NJ: Pearson, Prentice Hall.

Lieberman, Philip. 1984. *The Biology and Evolution of Language.* Cambridge, MA: Harvard University Press.

———. 1991. *Uniquely Human: The Evolution of Speech, Thought, and Selfless Behavior.* Cambridge: Harvard University Press.

———. 2007. "The Evolution of Human Speech: Its Anatomical and Neural Basis." *Current Anthropology* 48 (1): 39–66.

Lieberman, Philip, and R. C. McCarthy. 1999. "The Ontogeny of Cranial Base Angulation in Humans and Chimpanzees and Its Implications for Reconstruction Pharyngeal Dimensions." *Journal of Human Evolution* 36 (5): 487–517.

Lightfoot, K. G. 2005. *Indians, Missionaries, and Merchants: The Legacy of Colonial Encounters on the Colonial Frontiers.* Berkeley: University of California Press.

Lindenbaum, Shirley. 1972. "Sorcerers, Ghosts, and Polluting Women: An Analysis of Religious Belief and Population Control." *Ethnology* 2 (3): 241–253.

Lindholm, Charles. 1986. "Kinship Structure and Political Authority: The Middle East and Central Asia." *Comparative Study of Society and History* 28 (2): 334–355.

———. 1995. "Love as an Experience of Transcendence." In William. Jankowiak, (Ed.), *Romantic Love: A Universal Experience?* pp.57–71. New York: Columbia University Press.

———. 1996. *The Islamic Middle East: An Historical Anthropology.* Oxford: Blackwell Publishers.

———. 1998. "The Future of Love." In V. de Munck, ed., *Romantic Love and Sexual Behavior: Perspectives from the Social Sciences.* Westport, CT: Praeger Press.

———. 2001. *Culture Identity: The History, Theory, and Practice of Psychological Anthropology.* Boston: McGraw-Hill.

———. 2002. *The Islamic Middle East: Tradition and Change*, rev. ed. Malden, MA: Blackwell Publishers.

Lindholm, Charles, and Cherry Lindholm. 1980. "What Price Freedom?" *Science Digest* (November–December): 50–55.

Linton, Ralph. 1936. *The Study of Man.* New York: Appleton-Century-Crofts.

———. 1942. "Age and Sex Categories." *American Sociological Review* 7: 589–603.

Lipset, Seymour Martin, and Reinhard Bendix. 1967. *Social Mobility in Industrial Society.* Berkeley: University of California Press.

Little, Barbara J. 2007. *Historical Archaeology: Why the Past Matters.* Walnut Creek, CA: LeftCoast Press.

Liu, Hua, Franck Prugnolle, Andrea Manica, and François Balloux, 2006. "A Geographically Explicit Genetic Model of Worldwide Human-Settlement History." *American Journal of Human Genetics* 79(2), 230–237.

Liu, Li. 2009. "State Emergence in Early China." *Annual Review of Anthropology* 38: 217–232.

Lizardo, Omar. 2004. "The cognitive origins of Bourdieu's Habitus." *Journal for the Theory of Social Behaviour*, 34(4): 375–401.

Lockwood, Victoria S. 2003. *Globalization and Culture Change in the Pacific.* Upper Saddle River, NJ: Prentice Hall.

Loprieno, Antonio. 1995. *Ancient Egyptian, A Linguistic Introduction,* New York: Cambridge University Press

Lorenz, Konrad. 1966. *On Aggression.* New York: Harcourt, Brace & World.

Lovejoy, Owen C. 1981. "The Origin of Man." *Science* 211: 341–350.

———. 1984. "The Natural Detective." *Natural History* 93 (10): 24–28.

———. 1988. "Evolution of Human Walking." *Scientific American* 259 (5): 118–125.

Lovejoy, Owen C., Gen Suwa, Scott W. Simpson, Jay H. Matternes, and Tim D. White. 2009. "The Great Divides: *Ardipithecus ramidus* Reveals the Postcrania of Our Last Common Ancestors with African Apes." *Science* Vol. 326 (5949): 73, 100–106.

Lovejoy, Owen C., and R. S. Meindl. 1972. "Eukaryote Mutation and the Protein Clock." *Yearbook of Physical Anthropology* 16: 18–30.

Lowe, John W. G. 1985. *The Dynamics of Apocalypse: Systems Simulation of the Classic Maya Collapse.* Albuquerque: University of New Mexico Press.

Lowenstein, Tom. 1993. *Ancient Land, Sacred Whale: The Inuit Hunt and Its Rituals.* New York: Farrar, Straus, & Giroux.

Lucas, Gavin. 2012. *Understanding the Archaeological Record.* New York: Cambridge University Press.

Lucy, J., and R. Shweder. 1979. "Whorf and His Critics: Linguistic and Nonlinguistic Influences on Color Memory." *American Anthropologist* 81: 581–615.

Lucy, John. 1992. *Grammatical Categories and Cognition: A Case Study of the Linguistic Relativity Hypothesis.* Cambridge: Cambridge University Press.

Luhrmann, Tanya. 2000. *Of Two Minds: The Growing Disorder in American Psychiatry.* New York: Alfred A. Knopf.

———. 2013. "Building on William James: The Role of Learning in Religious Experience." In Dimitris Xygalatas and William W. McCorkle, Jr. (Eds.), *Mental Culture: Classical Social Theory and the Cognitive Science of Religion.* Bristol, CT: Acumen Publishing Limited.

Lukens-Bull, Ronald A. 2003. "Ronald McDonald as a Javanese Saint and an Indonesian Freedom Fighter: Reflections on the Global and the Local."*Crossroads: An Interdisciplinary Journal of Southeast Asian Studies* 17 (1): 108–128.

———. 2006. "Island Southeast Asia." In Raymond Scupin (Ed.), *Peoples and Cultures of Asia.* pp. 384–419. Upper Saddle River, NJ: Prentice Hall.

Lutz, Catherine. 1988. *Unnatural Emotions: Everyday Sentiments on a Micronesian Atoll and Their Challenge to Western Theory.* Chicago: University of Chicago Press.

Lyell, Charles. 1830–1833. *Principles of Geology* (3 vols). London.

Lyman, R. Lee. 2010. "What Taphonomy Is, What it Isn't, and Why Taphonomists Should Care about the Difference." *Journal of Taphonomy* 8(1):1–16.

MacDonald, Sharon (Ed.), 1993. *Inside European Identities: Ethnography in Western Europe.* Oxford, England: Berg.

MacEachern, Scott. 2012. "Race." In Raymond Scupin (Ed.), *Race and Ethnicity: The United States and the World* (2nd ed.). pp. 34–55. Upper Saddle River, NJ: Pearson Prentice Hall.

MacGrew, William C. 1992. *Chimpanzee Material Culture: Implications for Human Evolution.* Cambridge: Cambridge University Press.

Macionis, John. 2004a. *Cities and Urban Life* (3rd ed.). Upper Saddle River, NJ: Prentice Hall.

———. 2014. *Sociology.* (15th ed.). Upper Saddle River, NJ: Prentice Hall.

MacLennan, John Ferguson. 1865. *Primitive Marriage: An Inquiry into the Origin of the Form of Capture in Marriage Ceremonies.* Edinburgh: A. and C. Black.

MacNeish, Richard. 1970. *The Prehistory of the Tehuacan Valley.* Austin: University of Texas Press.

Madry, Scott. 2003. "Introduction to Remote Sensing. " In A. Houston and M. Rycroft (Eds.), *Keys to Space, An Interdisciplinary Approach to Space Studies,* pp. 15–3 to 15–14, New York: McGraw-Hill.

———. 2007. "An Evaluation of Google Earth for Archaeological Aerial Prospection and Site Survey." In J. T. Clark and Emily Hagemeister (Eds.), *Digital Discovery: Exploring New Frontiers in Human Heritage. CAA 2006—Computer Applications and Quantitative Methods in Archaeology,* Proceedings of the 34th Conference, Fargo, United States, April 2006. Budapest: Archaeolingua.

Madry, Scott., J. Sellers, and M. Rycroft. 2003. "Space in Our Lives." In A. Houston and M. (Eds.), *Keys to Space, An Interdisciplinary Approach to Space Studies,* pp. 1–1 to 1–9, New York: McGraw-Hill.

Madry, Scott and Elizabeth A. Madry. 2010. *Interdisciplinary Research and Method in Historical Ecology: A Burgundian Landscape.* Walnut Creek, CA: Left Coast Press.

Malinowski, Bronislaw. [1922] 1961. *Argonauts of the Western Pacific.* New York: Dutton.

———. 1927. *Sex and Repression in Savage Society.* New York: Meridian Books.

———. 1945. Introduction. In P. Kaberry (Ed.), *The Dynamics of Culture Change: An Inquiry into Race Relations in Africa.* pp. 1–13. New Haven, CT: Yale University Press.

Maloney, Clarence. 1974. *Peoples of South Asia.* New York: Holt, Rinehart and Winston.

Malotki, Ekkehart. 1983. *Hopi Time: A Linguistic Analysis of the Temporal Concepts in the Hopi Language.* Berlin: Mouton.

Manago, Adriana and Patricia Greenfield. 2011. "The Construction of Independent Values among Mayan Women at the Forefront of Social Change: Four Case Studies." *Ethos* 39 (1): 1–29.

Manhein, Mary H. 2013. *Bone Remains: Cold Cases in Forensic Anthropology.* Baton Rouge: Louisiana State University Press.

Mann, Charles. 2002. "1491." *Atlantic Monthly,* March.

Mann, Robert W., Bruce E. Anderson, Thomas Holland, David R. Rankin, and Johnny E. Webb, Jr. 2003. "Unusual 'Crime' Scenes: The Role of Forensic Anthropology in Recovering and Identifying American MIAs." In Dawnie Wolfe Steadman, (Ed.), *Hard Evidence: Case Studies in Forensic Anthropology,* pp, 108–116. Upper Saddle River, NJ: Prentice Hall.

Mann, Robert W., and Thomas D. Holland. 2004. "America's MIAs: Forensic Anthropology in Action." In Ruth Osterweiss Selig, Marilyn R. London, and P. Ann Kaupp, (Eds)., *Anthropology Explored: Revised and Expanded: The Best of Smithsonian Anthronotes.* Washington, DC: Smithsonian Books.

Maquet, Jacques. 1972. *Civilizations of Black Africa.* London: Oxford University Press.

Maricic, Tomislav, Viola Günther, Oleg Georgiev, Sabine Gehre, Marija Ćurlin, Christiane Schreiweis, Ronald

Naumann, et al. 2012. A Recent Evolutionary Change Affects a Regulatory Element in the Human FOXP2 Gene. *Molecular Biology and Evolution* 30 (4): 844–852.

Marano, Lou. 1982. "Windigo Psychosis: The Anatomy of an Emic-Etic Confusion." *Current Anthropology* 23: 385–412.

Marinatos, Spiridon. 1939. "The Volcanic Destruction of Minoan Crete." *Antiquity* 13: 425–439.

Marler, Peter., and Hans Slabbekoorn. 2004. *Nature's Music: The Science of Birdsong.* San Diego: Elsevier Scientific.

Marsden, Peter. 2003. *Sealed by Time: The Loss and Recovery of the* Mary Rose. Portsmouth: The Mary Rose Trust Ltd.

———. 2009. *Your Noblest Shippe: Anatomy of a Tudor Warship.* Portsmouth: The Mary Rose Trust Ltd.

Marsella, Anthony J. 1979. "Cross-Cultural Studies of Mental Disorders." In Anthony J. Marsella, Ronald G. Tharp, and Thomas J. Cibrowski, (Eds.),*Perspectives on Cross-Cultural Psychology.* pp. 107–115. New York: Academic Press.

Marshall, Yvonne. 1998. "By Way of Introduction from the Pacific Northwest Coast." *World Archaeology* 29 (3): 311–316.

Martin, Kay, and Barbara Voorhies. 1975. *Female of the Species.* New York: Columbia University Press.

Martin, Linda G. 1989. "The Graying of Japan." Population Reference Bureau, *Population Bulletin* 44 (July): 1–43. Washington, DC: U.S. Government Printing Office.

Martin, R. D. 1990. *Primate Origins and Evolution: A Phylogenetic Reconstruction.* Princeton, NJ: Princeton University Press.

Martin, Samuel. 1964. "Speech Levels in Japan and Korea." In Dell Hymes, (Ed.), *Language in Culture and Society: A Reader in Linguistics and Anthropology.* pp.407–413. New York: Harper & Row.

Marx, Karl. [1859] 1959. *A Contribution of the Critique of Political Economy.* New York: International Publishers.

Mascia-Lees, Frances, and Nancy Johnson Black. 2000. *Gender and Anthropology.* Prospect Heights, IL: Waveland Press.

Mathews, Gordon, Gustavo Lins Ribeiro, and Carlos Alba Vega (Eds). 2012. *Globalization from Below: The World's Other Economy.* Oxon and New York: Routledge.

Mather, Paul D. 1994. *M.I.A.: Accounting for the Missing in Southeast Asia.* National Defense University Press.

Matsuoka, Y., Y. Vigouroux, M. M. Goodman, G. J. Sanchez, E. Buckler, and J. Doebley. 2002. "A Single Domestication for Maize Shown by Multilocus Microsatellite Genotyping." *Proceedings of the National Academy of Sciences* 99 (9): 6080.

Mauss, Marcel. 1985. "A Category of the Human Mind: The Notion of Person; the Notion of Self," (Trans.) W. D. Halls. In Michael Carrithers, Steven Collins, and Steven Lukes (Eds.), *The Category of the Person: Anthropology, Philosophy, History.* pp.1–25. Cambridge: Cambridge University Press.

May, Darlene. 1980. "Women in Islam: Yesterday and Today." In Cyriac Pullapilly (Ed.), *Islam in the Contemporary World.* Notre Dame, IN: Cross Roads Books.

Maybury-Lewis, David. 1985. "A Special Sort of Pleading: Anthropology at the Service of Ethnic Groups." In R. Paine (Ed.), *Advocacy and Anthropology.* St. John's: Institute of Social and Economic Research, Memorial University of Newfoundland.

———. 1997. *Indigenous Peoples, Ethnic Groups, and the State.* Needham Heights, MA: Allyn & Bacon.

———. 2002. *Indigenous Peoples, Ethnic Groups, and the State* (2nd ed.). Boston: Pearson Education, Allyn & Bacon.

Mayr, E. 1982. *The Growth of Biological Thought: Diversity, Evolution, and Inheritance.* Cambridge, MA: Belnap Press.

McAllester, David P. 1983. "North American Native Music." In Elizabeth May (Ed.), *Music of Many Cultures: An Introduction.* Berkeley: University of California Press.

———. 1984. "North America/Native America." In Jeff Todd Titon (Ed.), *Worlds of Music: An Introduction to the Music of the World's Peoples.* New York: Schirmer Books.

McClelland, David. 1973. "Business Drive and National Achievement." In A. Etzioni and E. Etzioni-Halevy (Eds.), *Social Change.* Chapter 18. New York: Basic Books.

McClung de Tapia, Emily. 1992. "The Origins of Agriculture in Mesoamerica and Central America." In C. Wesley Cowan and Patty Jo Watson(Eds.), *The Origins of Agriculture: An International Perspective*, pp. 143–72. Washington, DC: Smithsonian Institution Press.

McCreery, John. 2000. *Japanese Consumer Behavior: From Worker Bees to Wary Shoppers.* Honolulu: University of Hawaii Press.

McCreery, John, and Ruth McCreery. 2006. "Japan." In Raymond Scupin (Ed.), *Peoples and Cultures of Asia.* pp. 230–275. Upper Saddle River, NJ: Prentice Hall.

McDaniel, L. 1998. *The Big Drum Ritual of Carriacou: Praise Songs in Memory of Flight.* Gainesville: University Press of Florida.

McDonald, James H. 1997. "Privatizing the Private Family Farmer: NAFTA and the Transformation of the Mexican Dairy Sector." *Human Organization* 56 (1): 321–332.

———. 1999. "The Neoliberal Project and Governmentality in Rural Mexico: Emergent Farmer Organization in the Michoacan Highlands."*Human Organization* 58 (3): 274–284.

———. 2001. "Reconfiguring the Countryside: Power, Control, and the (Re)Organization of Farmers in West Mexico." *Human Organization* 60 (3): 247–258.

———. 2009. "The Cultural Effects of the Narcoeconomy in Rural Mexico." *Journal of International and Global Studies* 1 (1): 1–29.

McDougall, Ian and T. Mark Harrison, 1999, *Geochronology and thermochronology by the* $^{40}Ar/^{39}Ar$ *method*, Oxford: Oxford University Press.

McDougall, Ian, Francis H. Brown, and John G. Fleagle. 2005. "Stratigraphic placement and age of modern humans from Kibish, Ethiopia". *Nature* 433 (7027): 733–736.

McElroy, A. and P. Townsend. 2009. *Medical Anthropology in Ecological Perspective* (5th ed.). Philadelphia: Westview.

McHenry, Henry M. 1982. "The Pattern of Human Evolution Studies on Bipedalism, Mastication, and Encephalization." *Annual Review of Anthropology* 11: 151–173.

———. 1988. "New Estimates of Body Weight in Early Hominids and Their Significance to Encephalization and Megadentia in Robust Australopithecines." In F. E. Grine, (Ed.), *Evolutionary History of the Robust Australopithecines*, pp. 133–148. Hawthorne, NJ: Aldine.

McIntosh, Rob. J. 2005. *Ancient Middle Niger: Urbanism and the Self-Organizing Landscape.* Cambridge: Cambridge University Press.

McIntosh, Susan Keech and Roderick J. McIntosh. 1993. "Current Directions in West African Prehistory." *Annual Review of Anthropology* 12: 215–258.

———. 2013. *Seeking the Origins of Takrur: Archaeological Excavations and Survey in the Middle Senegal Valley*. New Haven: Yale University Publications in Anthropology.

McIntosh, Susan. 1999. *Beyond Chiefdoms: Pathways to Complexity in Africa*. Cambridge: Cambridge University Press.

McKenna, James, Sarah Mosko, and Chris Richard. 1999. "Breastfeeding and Mother-Infant Cosleeping in Relation to SIDS Prevention." In Wenda R. Trevathan, E. O. Smith, and James J. McKenna (Eds.), *Evolutionary Medicine*. pp. 53–74. New York and Oxford: Oxford University Press.

McKeown, C. Timothy. 1998. "Ethical and Legal Issues, Complying with NAGPRA." In Rebecca A. Buck, Amanda Murphy, and Jennifer Schansberg, (Eds.), *The New Museums Registration Methods*. Washington, .DC.: American Association of Museums.

McPherron, Shannon P., Zeresenay Alemseged, Curtis W. Marean, Jonathan G. Wynn, Denné Reed, Denis Geraads, René Bobe, and Hamdallah A. Béarat, 2010. "Evidence for Stone-Tool-Assisted Consumption of Animal Tissues Before 3.39 Million Years Ago at Dikika, Ethiopia." *Nature* 466: 857–860.

Mead, Margaret. 1928. *Coming of Age in Samoa*. New York: Morrow.

Mead, Margaret. 1930. *Social Organization of Manu'a*. Bernice P. Bishop Museum, Bulletin No. 76. Honolulu: Museum Press.

———. 1935. *Sex and Temperament in Three Primitive Societies*. New York: Mentor.

Meadow, Richard H. 1996. "The Origins and Spread of Agriculture and Pastoralism in Northwestern South Asia." In D. R. Harris (Ed.), *The Origins and Spread of Agriculture and Pastoralism in Eurasia*, pp. 390–412. . London: UCL Press.

Meggers, Betty J. 1992. "Jomon-Valdivia: Similarities, Convergence, or Contact?" *NEARA Journal* 27: 23–32.

———. 1980. "Did Japanese Fishermen Really Reach Ecuador 5000 Years Ago?." *Early Man*, 2:4 (Winter 1980), 15–19.

Meggitt, Mervyn. 1977. *Blood Is Their Argument: Warfare among the Mae Enga Tribesmen of the New Guinea Highlands*. Palo Alto, CA: Mayfield.

Mellaart, James. 1975. *The Earliest Civilizations of the Near East*. London: Thames and Hudson.

Mellars, P. A. 1988. "The Origin and Dispersal of Modern Humans." *Current Anthropology* 29: 186–188.

Meltzer, D. J. 1993. "Pleistocene Peopling of the Americas." *Evolutionary Anthropology* 1 (5): 157–169.

Mencher, Joan P. 1965. "The Nayars of South Malabar." In M. F. Nimkorr, (Ed.), *Comparative Family Systems*, pp. 162–191. Boston: Houghton Mifflin.

———. 1974. "The Caste System Upside Down: Or the Not-So-Mysterious East." *Current Anthropology* 15: 469–494.

Menon, Shanti. 1996. "Male Authority and Female Autonomy: A Study of the Nayars in South India." In M. J. Maynes, A. Waltner, B. Stroland, and U. Strasser (Eds.), *Gender, Kinship, Power: A Comparative Interdisciplinary History*. New York: Routledge.

Menotti, Francesco. 2004. *Living on the Lake in Prehistoric Europe: 150 Years of Lake-Dwelling Research*. New York: Routledge.

Mensah, Atta Annam. 1983. "Music South of the Sahara." In Elizabeth May, (Ed.), *Music of Many Cultures: An Introduction*. Berkeley: University of California Press.

Menze, Bjoern and Jason A. Ur. 2011. "Mapping Patterns of Long-Term Settlement in Northern Mesopotamia at a Large Scale." *Proceedings of the National Academy of Sciences of the United States of America* 109(14): 5146.

Mercader, Julio, Melissa Panger, and Christophe Boesch. 2002. "Excavation of a Chimpanzee Stone Tool Site in the African Rainforest." *Science* 296: 1452–1455.

Mernissi, Fatima. 1975. *Beyond the Veil: Male-Female Dynamics in a Modern Muslim Society*. Cambridge, MA: Schenkman.

Merrill, William L. 2004. "Identity in Colonial Northern Mexico." In Ruth Osterweiss Selig, Marilyn R. London, and P. Ann Kaupp (Eds,), *Anthropology Explored: Revised and Expanded: The Best of Smithsonian Anthronotes*. Washington, DC: Smithsonian Books.

Meskell, Lynn. 1995. "Goddesses, Gimbutas and 'New Age Archaeology'." *Antiquity* 69 (262), May.

Messenger, John. 1971. "Sex and Repression in an Irish Folk Community." In Donald S. Marshall and Robert C. Suggs (Eds.), *Human Sexual Behavior: Variations in the Ethnographic Spectrum*. New York: Basic Books.

Metraux, Afred, Hugo Charteris, and Sidney Mintz. 1989. *Voodoo in Haiti*. New York: Schocken Books.

Middleton, John. 1960. *Lugbara Religion*. London: Oxford University Press.

———. 1978. *Peoples of Africa*. New York: Arco.

———, (Ed.). 2000. *Encyclopedia of Africa: South of the Sahara*, Vol. 2. New York: Simon and Schuster/MacMillan.

Miller, Duncan E. and N. J. Van Der Merwe. 1994. "Early Metal Working in South of the Saharan Africa." *Journal of African History* 35: 1–36.

Miller, Kenneth R. 2000. *Finding Darwin's God: A Scientist's Search for Common Ground Between God and Evolution*. New York: HarperCollins.

Miller, N. F. 1992. "The Origins of Plant Cultivation in the Near East." In C. Wesley Cowan and Patty Jo Watson (Eds.), *The Origins of Agriculture: An International Perspective*, pp. 39–58. Washington, DC: Smithsonian Institution Press.

Millon, René. 1976. "Social Relations in Ancient Teotihuacán." In Eric R. Wolf, (Ed.), *The Valley of Mexico: Studies in Prehispanic Ecology and Society*. Albuquerque: University of New Mexico Press.

———. 1993. "The Place Where Time Began: An Archaeologist's Interpretation of What Happened in Teotihuacan History". In Berrin, Kathleen and Esther Pasztory (Eds.), *Teotihuacan: Art from the City of the Gods*. New York: Thames and Hudson. pp. 16–43.

Milner, Nicky. 2006. "Subsistence". In Chantal Conneller, *Mesolithic Britain and Ireland: New Approaches*. Warren, Graeme. Stroud: Tempus.

Mines, Diane P. 2009. *Caste in India*. Key Studies in Asian Studies No. 4. Ann Arbor: Association for Asian Studies.

Mintz, Sidney W. 1985b. *Sweetness and Power: The Place of Sugar in Modern History*. New York: Viking.

Mintz, Sidney, and Christine M. Dubois. 2002. "The Anthropology of Food and Eating." *Annual Reviews in Anthropology*. 31: 99–119.

Mithen, Steven. 1996. *The Prehistory of the Mind*. London: Thames and Hudson.

Molloy, Maureen. 1990. "Considered Affinity: Kinship, Marriage and Social Class in New France." *Social Science History* 14 (1): 2–26.

Molnar, Stephen. 2006. *Human Variation: Races, Types, and Ethnic Groups* (6th ed.), Upper Saddle River, NJ: Prentice Hall.

Monaghan, L., L. Hinton, and R. Kephart. 1997. "Can't Teach a Dog to Be a Cat?: A Dialogue on Ebonics." *Anthropology Newsletter* 38 (3): 1, 8, 9.

Monsutti, Alessandro. 2013. "Anthropologizing Afghanistan: Colonial and Postcolonial Encounters." *Annual Review of Anthropology* 42: 269–285.

Montagu, Ashley (Ed.), 1968. *Man and Aggression*. London: Oxford University Press.

———. 1997. *Man's Most Dangerous Myth: The Fallacy of Race* (6th ed.). Walnut Creek, CA: AltaMira Press.

Moore, Andrew M. T., Gordon C. Hillman, Anthony J. Legge. 2000. *Village on the Euphrates: From Foraging to Farming at Abu Hureyra*. Oxford: Oxford University Press.

Moran, Emilio F. 2007. *Human Adaptability: An Introduction to Ecological Anthropology* (3rd ed.). Boulder: Westview Press.

———. 2000. *Human Adaptability: An Introduction to Ecological Anthropology* (2nd ed.). Boulder: Westview Press.

Morgan, Lewis Henry. [1877] 1964. *Ancient Society*. Cambridge, MA: Harvard University Press.

Moro, Andrea. 2008. *The Boundaries of Babel: The Brain and the Enigma of Impossible Languages*. Current Studies in Linguistics. Cambridge: MIT Press.

Morris, Ian. 2010. *Why the West Rules – For Now: The Patterns of History, and What They Reveal about the Future*. New York: Farrar, Straus, and Giroux.

———. 2013. *The Measure of Civilization: How Social Development Decides the Fate of Nations*. Princeton: Princeton University Press.

Morrison, K. D. 2006. "Historicizing Foraging in South Asia: Power, History, and Ecology of Holocene Hunting and Gathering." In Miriam Stark (Ed.), *Archaeology of Asia*, pp. 279–302. Malden, MA.: Blackwell.

Morton, D. Holmes, Caroline S. Morton, Kevin A. Strauss, Donna L. Robinson, Erik G. Puffenberger, Christine Hendrickson, Richard I. Kelley. 2003. "Pediatric Medicine and the Genetic Disorders of the Amish and Mennonite People of Pennsylvania". *American Journal of Medical Genetics* 121C (1): 5 (June).

Morwood, M. J., T. Sutikna, Jatmiko, and E. W. Saptomo. 2009. "Homo Floreisensis: A Cladistic Analysis." *Journal of Human Evolution* 57 (5): 623–639.

Moseley, Michael E., and James B. Richardson. 1992. "Doomed by Natural Disaster." *Archaeology* 45 (6): 44–45.

Mosher, Steven W. 1983. *The Broken Earth: The Rural Chinese*. Glencoe, IL: Free Press.

Motulsky, Arno. 1971. "Metabolic Polymorphisms and the Role of Infectious Diseases in Human Evolution." In Laura Newell Morris, (Ed.), *Human Populations, Genetic Variation, and Evolution*. San Francisco: Chandler.

Mountain, Joanna L. 1998. "Molecular Evolution and Modern Human Origins." *Evolutionary Anthropology* 7 (1): 21–38.

Moyá-Solá, S., M. Köhler, D. M. Alba, I. Casanovas-Vilar, and J. Galindo. 2004. "*Pierolapithecus catalaunicus*: A New Middle Miocene Great Ape from Spain." *Science*, 306 (5700): 1339–1344.

Muhly, James D. 2003. "Metalworking/Mining in the Levant." In Suzanne Richard (Ed.), *Near Eastern Archaeology*, pp. 174–183. Eisenbrauns: Winona Lake, IN.

Mukerjee, Madhusree. 1999. "Out of Africa, into Asia." *Scientific American* 280 (1): 24.

Mukhopadhyay, Carol C., Rosemary Henze, and Yolanda T. Moses. 2014. *How Real Is Race: A Sourcebook on Race, Culture, and Biology*. Lanham and Boulder: AltaMira Press.

Muller, Richard. 2002. *Measurement of the Lunar Impact Record for the Past 3.5 Billion Years, and Implications for the Nemesis Theory*. Geological Society of America Special Paper 356, pp. 659–665.

Mumford, Lewis. 1961. *The City in History: Its Origins, Its Transformations, and Its Prospects*. New York: Harcourt, Brace & World.

Munro, Natalie D. 2009. Epipaleolithic Subsistence Intensification in the Southern Levant: The Faunal Evidence. In M. J. Richards and J. J. Hublin (Eds.),*The Evolution of Hominid Diets: Integrating Approaches to the Study of Paleolithic Subsistence*, pp. 141–155. New York: Springer Verlag,

Munson, Henry. 2008. "'Fundamentalisms' Compared." *Religion Compass* 2 10 (1111/): 1–18.

Munson, P. J. 1981. "A Late Holocene (c. 4500–2300 BP) Climate Chronology for the Southwestern Sahara." *Palaeoecology of Africa* 13: 53–60.

Murdock, George. 1945. "The Common Denominator of Cultures." In Ralph Linton (Ed.), *The Science of Man in the World Crisis*, pp. 123–142. New York: Columbia University Press.

———. 1949. *Social Structure*. New York: Macmillan.

———. 1959. *Africa: Its Peoples and Their Culture History*. New York: McGraw Hill.

———. 1967. "Ethnographic Atlas: A Summary." *Ethnology* 6: 109–236.

———. 1968. "The Current Status of the World's Hunting and Gathering Peoples." In Richard Lee and Irven DeVore (Eds.), *Man the Hunter*, pp. 13–20. Chicago: Aldine.

———. 1981a. *Atlas of World Cultures*. Pittsburgh: University of Pittsburgh Press.

———. 1981b. *Ethnographic Atlas*. Pittsburgh: University of Pittsburgh Press.

Murphy, Michael Dean. 2008. "Roman Catholicism" In Raymond Scupin (Ed.), *Religion and Culture: An Anthropological Focus*. (2nd ed.)., pp. 370–401. Upper Saddle River, NJ: Pearson Prentice Hall .

Murphy, Robert. F., and Lawrence Kasdan. 1959. "The Structure of Parallel Cousin Marriage." *American Anthropologist* 61: 17–29.

Murray, R. D., and Smith, E. O. 1983. "The Role of Dominance and Intrafamilial Bonding in the Avoidance of Close Inbreeding." *Journal of Human Evolution* 12: 481–486.

Murtagh, Ben de. 2013. *Genders and Sexualities in Indonesian Cinema: Constructing Gay, Lesbi and Waria Identities on Screen*. London: Routledge.

Myers, David G. 2002. *Intuition: Its Powers and Perils*. New Haven: Yale University Press.

———. 2011. *Psychology* (10th ed.). New York: Worth Publishers.

———. 2012. *Exploring Psychology* (9th ed.). New York: Worth Publishers.

Nakoinz, Oliver. 2010. "Concepts of Central Place Research in Archaeology." In *Landscapes and Human Development: the Contribution European Archaeology*. Bonn: Kiel Graduate School, pp. 251–264.

Nanda, Serena. 1990. *Neither Man nor Woman: The Hijras of India*. Belmont, CA: Wadsworth.

———. 2000. *Gender Diversity: Crosscultural Variations*. Prospect Heights, IL: Waveland Press.

Naranjo, Tessie. 1995. "Thoughts on Two Worldviews." *Federal Archaeology*. Offprint Series, Fall/Winter: 8.

Nash, June. 1997. "The Fiesta of the Word: The Zapatista Uprising and Radical Democracy in Mexico." *American Anthropologist* 99 (2): 261–274.

Nash, Manning. 1989. *The Cauldron of Ethnicity in the Modern World*. Chicago: University of Chicago Press.

National Opinion Research Center. 2001. *General Social Surveys. 1972–2000: Cumulative Codebook.* Chicago: University of Chicago.

———. 2012. **Tom Smith.** "Beliefs About God Across Time and Country." Chicago: University of Chicago Press.

Neale, Walter. 1976. *Monies in Societies.* San Francisco: Chandler.

Needham, Rodney. 1967. "Percussion and Transition." *Man* 2: 606–614.

Nettle, Daniel. 2009. "Beyond Nature Versus Culture: Cultural Variation as an Evolved Characteristic." *Journal of the Royal Anthropological Institute* N.S. 15: 223–240.

Newman, R. W., and E. H. Munro. 1955. "The Relation of Climate and Body Size in U.S. Males." *American Journal of Physical Anthropology* 13: 1–17.

Nisbett, Richard. 2009. *Intelligence and How to Get It: Why Schools and Culture Count.* New York: W.W. Norton & Co.

Nguyen, Vinh-Kim, and Karine Peschard. 2003. "Anthropology, Inequality, and Disease: A Review." *Annual Review of Anthropology* 32: 447–474.

Noel Hume, Ivor. 1983. *Historical Archaeology: A Comprehensive Guide.* New York: Knopf.

Noonan, James P., Graham Coop, Sridhar Kdaravalli, Doug Smith, Johannes Krause, Joe Alessi, Feng Chen, Darren Platt, Svante Pääbo, Jonathan K. Pritchard, and Edward M. Rubin. 2006. "Sequencing and Analysis of Neanderthal Genomic DNA." *Science* 314 (5802): 1113–1118.

Norget, Kristin. 1996. "Beauty and the Feast: Aesthetics and the Performance of Meaning in the Day of the Dead, Oaxaca, Mexico." *Journal of Latin American Lore* 19: 53–64.

———. 2006. *Days of Death, Days of Life: Ritual in the Popular Culture of Oaxaca.* New York: Columbia University Press.

Norton, Heather L., Rick A. Kittles, Esteban Parra, Paul McKiegue, Xianyun Mao, Keith Cheng, Victor A. Canfield, Daniel G. Bradley, Briand Mccoy, and Mark D. Shriver. 2007. "Genetic Evidence for the Convergent Evolution of Light Skin in Europeans and East Asians." *Molecular Biology and Evolution* 24(3): 710–722.

Obeyeskere, Gananath. 1992. *Apotheosis of Captain Cook: European Mythmaking in the Pacific.* Princeton, NJ: Princeton University Press.

Officer, C. B. 1990. "Extinctions, Iridium, and Shocked Minerals Associated with the Cretaceous/Tertiary Transition." *Journal of Geological Education* 38: 402–425.

Ohnuki-Tierney, Emiko. 1998. "A Conceptual Model for the Historical Relationship Between the Self and the Internal and External Others: The Agrarian Japanese, the Ainu, and the Special Status People." In Dru Gladney (Ed)., *Making Majorities: Constituting the Nation in Japan, Korea, China, Malaysia, Fiji, Turkey, and the United States.* Stanford: Stanford University Press.

———. 2006. "McDonald's in Japan: Changing Manners and Etiquette." In James L. Watson (Ed.), *Golden Arches East: McDonald's in East Asia* (2nd ed.). Stanford: Stanford University Press.

Okigbo, Bede N. 1988. "Food: Finding Solutions to the Crisis." *Africa Report*, September-October.

Oliver, Douglas. 1955. *A Solomon Island Society: Kinship and Leadership among the Siuai of Bougainville.* Cambridge, MA: Harvard University Press.

———. 1974. *Ancient Tahitian Society*, 3 vols. Honolulu: University of Hawaii Press.

Olmos, M. F. 1997. *Sacred Possessions: Vodou, Santeria, Obeah, and the Caribbean.* New Brunswick, NJ: Rutgers University Press.

Olsen, Dale. 2004. *The Chrysanthemum and the Song: Music, Memory and Identity in the South American Japanese Diaspora.* Gainesville: University of Florida Press.

O'Meara, Tim J. 1990. *Samoan Planters: Tradition and Economic Development in Polynesia.* New York: Holt, Rinehart and Winston.

Omohundro, John. 1998. *Careers in Anthropology.* Mountain View, CA: Mayfield.

Ong, Aihwa. 2006. *Neoliberalism as Exception: Mutations in Citizenship and Sovereignty.* Durham, NC: Duke University Press.

Orlando L., Ludovic Orlando, Pierre Darlu, Michel Toussaint, Dominique Bonjean, Marcel Otte, and Catherine Hänni. 2006. "Revisiting Neandertal Diversity with a 100,000 Year Old mtDNA Sequence." *Current Biology* 16: 400–402.

Orser, Charles E. 2004. *Historical Archaeology.* Upper Saddle River, NJ: Pearson Education.

Ortner, Sherry. 1974. "Is Female to Male as Nature Is to Culture?" In Michelle Zimbalist Rosaldo and Louise Lamphere (Eds)., *Woman, Culture, and Society*, pp. 67–87. Stanford, CA: Stanford University Press.

———. 1996. *Making Gender: The Politics and Erotics of Culture.* Boston: Beacon Press.

———. 2001. *Life and Death on Mt. Everest: Sherpas and Himalayan Mountaineering.* Princeton: Princeton University Press.

Oswalt, Wendell H. 1972. *Other Peoples, Other Customs: World Ethnography and Its History.* New York: Holt, Rinehart & Winston.

———. 1976. *An Anthropological Analysis of Food-Getting Technology.* New York: John Wiley.

———. 1999. *Eskimos and Explorers* (2nd ed.). Lincoln: University of Nebraska Press.

Otterbein, Keith. 1970. *The Evolution of War.* New Haven, CT: HRAF Press.

———. 1974. "The Anthropology of War." In John Honigmann (Ed.), *Handbook of Social and Cultural Anthropology.* pp. 923–958. Chicago: Rand McNally.

———. 1994. *Feuding and Warfare: Selected Works of Keith F. Otterbein.* Langhorne, PA: Gordon and Breach.

———. 1999. "Historical Essay: A History of the Research on Warfare in Anthropology." *American Anthropologist* 101 (4): 794–805.

———. 2000. "The Doves Have Been Heard From, Where Are the Hawks?" *American Anthropologist* 102 (4): 841–844.

Paigen, B., L. R. Goldman, J. H. Magnant, J. H. Highland, and A. T. Steegman. 1987. "Growth and Children Living Near the Hazardous Waste Site, Love Canal." *Human Biology* 59: 489–508.

Palakornkul, Angkab. 1972. *A Sociolinguistic Study of Pronominial Strategy in Spoken Bangkok Thai.* Doctoral Dissertation, University of Texas, Austin.

Paley, W. 1828. *Natural Theology* (2nd ed.). Oxford: J. Vincent.

Palmore, Erdman Ballagh. 1975. *The Honorable Elders: A Cross-Cultural Analysis of Aging in Japan.* Durham, NC: Duke University Press.

Parker Pearson, M. 2012. *Stonehenge: Exploring the Greatest Stone Age Mystery.* New York: Simon and Schuster.

Parkins, David. 2007. "The Accidental in Religious Instruction: Ideas and Convictions." In Berliner, David, and

Ramon Sarró (Eds.), *Learning Religion. Anthropological Approaches.* pp. 49–64. New York: Berghahn Books.

Parkinson, William, A., and Michael L. Galaty. 2007. "Secondary States in Perspective: An Integrated Approach to State Formation in Prehistoric Aegean." *American Anthropologist* 109 (1): 113–129.

Parpola, Asko. 1994. *Deciphering the Indus Script.* New York: Cambridge University Press.

Parra, Esteban J. 2007. "Human Pigmentation Variation: Evolution, Genetic Basis, and Implications for Public Health." *Yearbook of Physical Anthropology* 50: 85–105.

Parrinder, Geoffrey. 1983. *World Religions: From Ancient History to the Present.* New York: Hamlyn Publishing Group.

Parry, Jonathan. 1980. "Ghosts, Greed and Sin: The Occupational Identity of the Benares Funeral Priests." *Man* 21: 453–473.

Passingham, R. E. 1982. *The Human Primate.* San Francisco: W. H. Freeman.

Pasternak, Burton. 1976. *Introduction to Kinship and Social Organization.* Englewood Cliffs, NJ: Prentice Hall.

Patterson, Francine, and Donald Cohn. 1978. "Conversations with a Gorilla." *National Geographic* 154: 454–462.

Patterson, Francine, and Eugene Linden. 1981. *The Education of Koko.* New York: Holt, Rinehart and Winston.

Patterson, Mary. 2000. "Sorcery and Witchcraft." In Raymond Scupin (Ed.), *Religion and Culture: An Anthropological Focus.* Upper Saddle River, NJ: Prentice Hall.

Pauketat, Timothy R. 2007. *Chiefdoms and Other Archaeological Delusions.* Walnut Creek: AltaMira Press.

Pauketat, Timothy, Lucretia S. Kelly, Gayle J. Fritz, Neal H. Lopinot, Scott Elias, and Eve Hargrave. 2002. "The Residues of Feasting and Public Ritual at Cahokia." *American Antiquity* 67(2): 257–279

Paul, Robert A. 1989. "Psychoanalytic Anthropology." *Annual Review of Anthropology* 18: 177–202.

———. 1996. *Moses and Civilization: The Meaning Behind Freud's Myth.* New Haven: Yale University Press.

Peacock, James. 1986. *The Anthropological Lens: Harsh Light, Soft Focus.* Cambridge: Cambridge University Press.

Pearsall, D. M. 1992. "The Origins of Plant Cultivation in South America." In C. Wesley Cowan and Patty Jo Watson, (Eds.), *The Origins of Agriculture: An International Perspective,* pp. 173–205. Washington, DC: Smithsonian Institution Press.

Pennisi, Elizabeth. 2002. "A Shaggy Dog History." *Science* 298 (5598): 1540–1542.

———.2013 "More Genomes from Denisova Cave Show Mixing of Early Human Groups", *Science* 340: 799.

Pennock, Robert T. 2003. "Creationism and Intelligent Design." *Annual Review of Genomics and Human Genetics* 4: 143–163.

Petto, Andrew J., and Laurie R. Godfrey (Eds.), 2007. *Scientists Confront Intelligent Design and Creationism.* New York: W.W. Norton & Company.

Pfeiffer, John. 1985. *The Emergence of Man* (4th ed.). New York: Harper & Row.

Phillipson, David W. 1993. *African Archaeology.* New York: Cambridge University Press.

Photos, E. 1989. "The Question of Meteoritic versus Smelted Nickel-Rich Iron: Archaeological Evidence and Experimental Results." *World Archaeology* 20 (3): 403–421.

Pickering, Travis Rayne and Manuel Domínguez-Rodrigo. 2010. "Chimpanzee Referents and the Emergence of Human Hunting." *Open Anthropology Journal* 3, 107–113.

Pickett, J. M. 1999. *Acoustics of Speech Communication: The Fundamentals, Speech Perception Theory, and Technology.* Boston: Allyn & Bacon.

Pickford, Martin, Brigette Senut, Dominique Gommercy, and Jacque Treil. 2002. "Bipedalism in *Orrorin tugenensis* Revealed by Its Femora." *Compes Rendu de l'Académie des Science des Paris: Palevol* 1: 1–13.

Piddocke, Stuart. 1965. "The Potlatch System of the Southern Kwakiutl: A New Perspective." *Southwestern Journal of Anthropology* 21: 244–264.

Pierpont, Claudia Roth. 2004. "The Measure of America: How a Rebel Anthropologist Waged a War on Racism." *The New Yorker,* March 8: 48–63.

Pieterse, Jan Nederveen. 2002. *Globalization and Culture: Global Melange.* Lanham, MD: Rowman and Littlefield.

Pike, Douglas. 1990. "Change and Continuity in Vietnam." *Current History* 89 (545): 117–134.

Pikirayi, Innocent. 2001. *The Zimbabwe Culture: Origins and Decline of Southern Zambezian States.* Walnut Creek, CA: AltaMira Press.

Pilbeam, David. 1972. *The Ascent of Man.* New York: Macmillan.

Pinker, Steven. 1994. *The Language Instinct: How the Mind Creates Language.* New York: HarperCollins.

Pitts, Michael. 2001. *Hengeworld.* London: Arrow Books.

Plastino, W., L. Kaihola, P. Bartolomei, and F. Bella, 2001. "Cosmic Background Reduction in the Radiocarbon Measurement by Scintillation Spectrometry at the Underground Laboratory Of Gran Sasso." *Radiocarbon* 43 (2A): 157–161.

Pollard, Mark, Catherine Batt, Ben Stern, Suzanne M. M. Young. 2007. *Analytical Chemistry in Archaeology.* New York: Cambridge University Press.

Polyani, Karl. 1944. *The Great Transformation.* New York: Rinehart.

Pope, Geoffrey. 1989. "Bamboo and Human Evolution." *Natural History* 10: 49–56.

Popline: World Population News Service. 1993. "1993 State of World Population Edition," Vol. 15, July–August.

Population Reference Bureau. 1986. *Population Data Sheet.* Washington, DC: Population Reference Bureau.

———. 1991. *World Population Data Sheet.* Washington, DC: Population Reference Bureau.

Posnansky, Merrick. 1984. "Early Agricultural Societies in Ghana." In J. Clark and Steven A. Brandt (Eds.), *From Hunter to Farmer,* pp. 147–151. Berkeley: University of California Press.

Pospisil, Leonard. 1963. *The Kapauku Papuans of West New Guinea.* New York: Holt, Rinehart and Winston.

———. 1967. "The Attributes of Law." In Paul Bohannon (Ed.)., *Law and Warfare: Studies in the Anthropology of Conflict.* pp. 25–42. Garden City, NY: Natural History Press.

Potter, David, and Paul Knepper. 1998. "Comparing Official Definitions of Race in Japan and the United States." In Joan Ferrante and Prince Brown, Jr.,(Eds.), *The Social Construction of Race and Ethnicity in the United States.* pp. 139–156. New York: Longman Press.

Potts, Richard. 1988. *Early Hominid Activities at Olduvai.* New York: Aldine de Gruyter.

———. 1991. "Why the Oldowan? Plio-Pleistocene Toolmaking and the Transport of Resources." *Journal of Anthropological Research* 47: 153–176.

———. 1993. "Archaeological Interpretations of Early Hominid Behavior and Ecology." In D. Tab Rasmussen (Ed.), *The*

Origins and Evolution of Humans and Humanness, pp. 49–74. Boston: Jones and Barlett.

Potts, Richard, and Pat Shipman. 1981. "Cutmarks Made by Stone Tools from Olduvai Gorge, Tanzania." *Nature* 291: 577–580.

Powdermaker, Hortense. 1966. *Stranger and Friend: The Way of an Anthropologist*. New York: W. W. Norton.

Poznik, G. David, Brenna M. Henn, Muh-Ching Yee, Elzbieta Sliwerska, Ghia M. Euskirchen, Alice A. Lin, Michael Snyder, Lluis Quintana-Murci, Jeffrey M. Kidd, Peter A. Underhill, Carlos D. Bustamante. 2013. "Sequencing Y Chromosomes Resolves Discrepancy in Time to Common Ancestor of Males Versus Females." *Science* 341(6145): 562–565.

Prag, John, and Richard Neave. 1997. *Making Faces*. College Station: Texas A&M University Press.

Prendergast M. E., Yuan J., and Bar-Yosef O. 2009. "Resource Intensification in the Late Upper Paleolithic: A View from Southern China." *Journal of Archaeological Science* 36(4):1027–1037.

Price, David, H. 2011. *Weaponizing Anthropology: Social Service of the Militarized State*. **Oakland, CA: AK Press.**

Price, Douglas T., and James A. Brown. 1985. *Prehistoric Hunter-Gatherers: The Emergence of Cultural Complexity*. New York: Academic Press.

Prieto, N. I. 1997. *Beautiful Flowers of the Maquiladora: Life Histories of Women Workers in Tijuana*. Austin: University of Texas Press.

Pringle, Heather. 2006. *Master Plan: Himmler's Scholars and the Holocaust* (Paperback edition). *New York:* HarperCollins.

Prothero, Donald R. 1989. *Interpreting the Stratigraphic Record*. New York: W. H. Freeman.

Pusey, Anne. 2004. "Inbreeding Avoidance in Primates." In Arthur Wolf and William Durham (Eds)., *Inbreeding, Incest, and the Incest Taboo*. Stanford: Stanford University Press.

Quale, Robin G. 1988. *A History of Marriage Systems*. New York: Greenwood Press.

Quigley, Declan. 1999. *The Interpretation of Caste*. Oxford: Oxford University Press.

Quinn, Naomi, and Dorothy Holland. 1987. "Culture and Cognition." In D. Holland and N. Quinn, (Eds)., *Cultural Models in Language and Thought*. Cambridge: Cambridge University Press.

Quintyn, C. 2009 "The Naming of New Species in Hominin Evolution: A Radical Proposal—A Temporary Cessation in Assigning New Names." *HOMO: Journal of Comparative Human Biology* 60: 307–341.

Radcliffe-Brown, A. R. [1922] 1964. *The Andaman Islanders*. New York: Free Press.

Radinsky, Leonard. 1967. "The Oldest Primate Endocast." *American Journal of Physical Anthropology* 27: 358–388.

Raheja, Gloria. 1988. *The Poison in the Gift: Ritual, Prestation, and the Dominant Caste in a North Indian Village*. Chicago: University of Chicago Press.

Ramsey, Jeffress F. 2010. *Global Studies: Africa* (13th ed.). Guilford: Dushkin Publishing Group.

Rappaport, Roy. 1979. *Ecology, Meaning, and Religion*. Richmond, VA: North Atlantic Books.

———. 1984. *Pigs for the Ancestors: Ritual in the Ecology of a New Guinea People*. New Haven, CT: Yale University Press.

Rasmussen, Tab D., and Elwyn L. Simons. 1988. "New Species of *Oligopithecus savagei*, Early Oligocene Primate from the Fayum, Egypt." *Folia Primatology* 51: 182–208.

Rathbun, T. A., and J. E. Buikstra. 1984. *Human Identification: Case Studies in Forensic Anthropology*. Springfield, IL: Charles C Thomas.

Rathje, William. 1971. "The Origin and Development of Lowland Classic Maya Civilization." *American Antiquity* 36: 275–285.

———. 1984. "The Garbage Decade." *American Behavioral Scientist* 28 (1): 9–29.

———. 1992 *Rubbish!: The Archaeology of Garbage*, New York: HarperCollins.

Rathje, William L., and Cheryl K. Ritenbaugh. 1984. "Household Refuse Analysis: Theory, Method, and Applications in Social Science." *American Behavioral Scientist* 28 (1): 5–153.

Raup, D. M., and J. J. Sepkoski, Jr. 1984. "Periodicity of Extinctions in the Geologic Past." *Proceedings of the National Academy of Science* 81 (3): 801–805.

Raup, David M. 1999. *The Nemesis Affair: A Story of the Death of the Dinosaurs and the Ways of Science*. New York: W. W. Norton.

Raven, Peter H., Linda R. Berg, and George B. Johnson. 1993. *Environment*. Fort Worth, TX: Saunders College Publishing.

Rayner, Steve. 1989. "Fiddling While the Globe Warms." *Anthropology Today* 5 (6): 1–2.

Redfield, Robert. 1930. *Tepotzlan: A Mexican Village: A Study of Folk Life*. Chicago: University of Chicago Press.

Re Cruz, Alicia. 2003." Milpa as an Ideological Weapon: Tourism and Maya Migration to Cancún." In *Ethnohistory* 50(3): 489–502.

Redfield, Robert. 1930. *Tepotzlan: A Mexican Village: A Study of Folk Life*. Chicago: University of Chicago Press.

Redfield, Robert, and Alfonso Villa Rojas. 1934. *Chan Kom, A Maya Village*. Washington, DC: Carnegie Institute.

Reddy, Gayatri. 2005. *With Respect to Sex: Negotiating Hijra Identity in South India*. Chicago: University of Chicago Press.

Reich, Robert B. 2003. "High-Tech Jobs Are Going Abroad! But 'That's Okay.'" *Washington Post*, Outlook, 11 March.

Reichs, Kathleen J. 1998. *Forensic Osteology: Advances in the Identification of Human Remains* (2nd ed.). Springfield, IL: Charles C. Thomas.

Relethford, John H. 2003. *Reflections of Our Past*. Boulder: Westview Press.

———.2013. *The Human Species: An Introduction to Biological Anthropology* (9th ed). Boston: McGraw-Hill.

Rendell, L., R. Boyd, D. Cownden, M. Enquist, K. Eriksson, M. W. Feldman, L. Fogarty, S. Ghirlanda, T. Lillicrap, and K. N. Laland. 2010. "Why Copy Others? Insights from the Social Learning Tournament." *Science* 9:328 (5975): 208–213.

Renfrew, Colin. 1989. *Archaeology and Language: The Puzzle of Indo-European Origins*. Cambridge: Cambridge University Press.

Renfrew, Colin, J. Dixon, and J. Cann. 1966. "Obsidian and Early Cultural Contact in the Near East." *Proceedings of the Prehistoric Society* 2: 30–72.

Renfrew, Colin, and K. L. Cooke. 1979. *Transformations: Mathematical Approaches to Culture Change*. New York: Academic Press.

Renfrew, Colin and Paul Bahn. 2012. Archaeology *Theories, Methods and Practice*, 6th Edition London : Thames & Hudson

Rennie, John. 2002. "Answers to Creationist Nonsense." *Scientific American*, July, pp. 78–85.

Repcheck, Jack. 2003. *The Man Who Found Time: James Hutton and the Discovery of the Earth's Antiquity*. New York: Perseus Books.

Reyna, Stephen. 2012. "NeoBoasianism, a Form of Critical Structural Realism: It's Better Than the Alternative." *Anthropological Theory* 12 (1): 73–99.

Rice, Prudence M. 1987. *Pottery Analysis: A Sourcebook.* Chicago: University of Chicago Press.

Richard, Alison F. 1985. *Primates in Nature.* New York: W. H. Freeman.

Richerson, Peter J., and Robert Boyd. 2005. *Not By Genes Alone: How Culture Transformed Human Evolution.* Chicago: University of Chicago Press.

———. 2008. "The Evolution of Free-Enterprise Values." In Zak, P. (Ed.), *Moral Markets.* P. 107. .Princeton: Princeton University Press.

Richmond, D. G., D. R. Begu, and D. S. Strait. 2001. "Origin of Human Bipedalism." *Yearbook of Physical Anthropology* 44 (S33): 70–105.

Rickford, John R. 1997. "Suite for Ebony and Phonics." *Discovery* 18 (2): 82–87.

Ridley, Matt. 1996. *The Origins of Virtue: Human Instincts and the Evolution of Cooperation.* New York: Viking Press.

———. 2010. *The Rational Optimist: How Prosperity Evolves.* New York: Harper Collins.

Riesenfeld, Alphonse. 1973. "The Effect of Extreme Temperatures and Starvation on the Body Proportions of the Rat." *American Journal of Physical Anthropology* 39: 427–459.

Rightmire, G. P. 1981. "Patterns in the Evolution of *Homo erectus.*" *Paleobiology* 7: 241–246.

———.1993. *The Evolution of Homo Erectus: Comparative Anatomical Studies of an Extinct Human Species.* New York: Cambridge University Press.

———. 1997. "Human Evolution in the Middle Pleistocene: The Role of *Homo heidelbergensis.*" *Evolutionary Anthropology* 6: 218–227.

Rindos, David. 1984. *The Origins of Agriculture: An Evolutionary Perspective.* New York: Academic Press.

Riner, Reed. 1981. "The Supranational Network of Boards of Directors." *Current Anthropology* 22 (2): 167–172.

Ritzer, George. 2010. *The McDonaldization of Society* (6th ed.). Thousand Oaks: Pine Forge Press.

Rivers, W. H. O. [1906] 1967. *Todas.* London: Macmillan.

Robarchek, C. A., and C. J. Robarchek. 1998. *Waorani: The Contexts of Violence and War.* Fort Worth, TX: Harcourt Brace.

Robbins, Richard H. 2013. *Global Problems and the Culture of Capitalism* (6th ed.). Upper Saddle River, NJ: Pearson.

Roberson, Debi. 2010. "Color in Mind, Culture, and Language." In Schaller, Mark, Ara Norenzayan, Steven J. Heine, Toshio Yamagishi, and Tatsuya Kameda (Eds.) *Evolution, Culture, and the Human Mind.* New York: Psychology Press.

Roberson, Debi, Ian Davies, and Jules Davidoff. 2000. "Colour Categories Are Not Universal: Replications and New Evidence from Stone Age Culture." *Journal of Experimental Psychology* 129 (3): 369–398.

Roberson, Debi, J. Davidoff, and Shapiro, I. 2002. "Squaring the Circle: the Cultural Relativity of Good Shape." *Journal of Culture and Cognition* 2: 29–52.

Roberts, John M. 1967. "Oaths, Autonomic Ordeals, and Power." In Clellan S. Ford (Ed.), *Cross-Cultural Approaches: Readings in Comparative Research.* New Haven, CT: HRAF Press.

Robertson, Claire C. 1984. "Women in the Urban Economy." In Margaret Jean Hay and Sharon Stichter (Eds)., *African Women South of the Sahara.* London: Longman.

Robertson, Ian. 1990. *Sociology* (4th ed.). New York: Worth Publishers.

Rodning, Christopher. 2009. "Place, Landscape, and Environment: Anthropological Archaeology in 2009." *American Anthropologist* 112 (2): 180–190.

Rohde, R. A., and Muller, R. A. 2005. "Cycles in Fossil Diversity." *Nature* 434 (7030): 209–210.

Romanucci-Ross, Lola. 1973. *Conflict, Violence and Morality in a Mexican Village.* Palo Alto, CA: National Press Books.

Romer, John. 2007. *The Great Pyramid: Ancient Egypt Revisited.* Cambridge University Press, Cambridge.

Romero, Simon. 2008. "Rain Forest Tribe's Charge of Neglect is Shrouded by Religion and Politics." *New York Times,* October 7, 2008, P.A6.

Roscoe, Paul B. 1993. "The Brokers of the Lord: The Ministrations of a Christian Faith in the Sepik Basin of Papua New Guinea." In V. Lockwood, T. Harding, and B. Wallace (Eds.), *Contemporary Pacific Societies: Studies in Development and Change.* pp. 289–301. Upper Saddle River, NJ: Prentice Hall.

———. 1994. "Amity and Aggression: A Symbolic Theory of Incest." *Man* 28: 1–28.

———. 2013. "War, Collective Action, and the 'Evolution' of Human Polities" In David M. Carbello (Ed.), *Cooperation & Collective Action: Archaeological Perspectives.* Boulder: University Press of Colorado.

———. 2014. "A Changing Climate for Anthropological and Archaeological Research? Improving the Climate Change Models." *American Anthropologist* 116 (3): 535–548.

Roscoe, Will. 1994. "How to Become a Berdache: Towards a Unified Analysis of Gender Diversity." In Herdt, G. (Ed.), *Third Sex, Third Gender: Beyond Sexual Dimorphism in Culture and History,* pp. 329–372. New York: Zone.

Roseberry, William. 1982. "Balinese Cockfights and the Seduction of Anthropology." *Social Research* 49: 1013–1038.

Rosenberg, Michael. 1990. "The Mother of Invention: Evolutionary Theory, Territoriality, and the Origins of Agriculture." *American Anthropologist* 92 (2): 399–415.

Rosman, Abraham, and Paula G. Rubel. 1986. *Feasting with Mine Enemy: Rank and Exchange among Northwest Coast Societies.* Prospect Heights, IL: Waveland Press.

Ross, Norbert. 2004. *Culture and Cognition: Implications for Theory and Method.* Thousand Oaks, CA: Sage.

Rossano, Matt, J. 2010. "Making Friends, Making Tools, and Making Symbols." *Current Anthropology* 51 (Supplement 1): S89–S98.

Rossides, Daniel W. 1990a. *Comparative Societies: Social Types and Their Interrelations.* Upper Saddle River, NJ: Prentice Hall.

———. 1990b. *Social Stratification: The American Class System in Comparative Perspective.* Upper Saddle River, NJ: Prentice Hall.

Rostow, Walter W. 1978. *The World Economy: History and Prospect.* Austin: University of Texas Press.

Rothenberg, Jerome. 1985. *Technicians of the Sacred: A Range of Poetries from Africa, Asia, Europe, and Oceania.* Berkeley: University of California Press.

Rousseau, Jean Jacques. [1762] 1973. *The Social Contract.* London: Dent.

Roux, Valentine and Pierre de Miroschedji. 2009. "Revisiting the History of the Potter's Wheel in the Southern Levant." *Levant* 41(2): 155–173.

Rowley-Conwy, Peter. 1993. "Was There a Neanderthal Religion?" In G. Burenhult, (Ed.)., *The First Humans: Human Origins and History to 10,000 BC,* p. 70. New York: HarperCollins.

Royal, Charmaine D. M., and Georgia M. Dunston. 2004. "Changing the Paradigm from 'Race' to Human Genome Variation." *Nature Genetics* 36 (11): S5–S7.

Rozin, Paul. 2010. "Towards a Cultural/Evolutionary Psychology." In Schaller, Mark, Ara Norenzayan, Steven J. Heine, Toshio Yamagishi, and Tatsuya Kameda (Eds.), *Evolution, Culture, and the Human Mind.* New York: Psychology Press.

Rubenstein, Robert A., Kerry Fisher, and Clementine Fujimoro (Eds),. 2012. *Practicing Military Anthropology: Beyond Expectations and Traditional Boundaries.* Sterling, VA: Kumarian Press.

Rudwick, Martin J. S. 1997. *Georges Cuvier, Fossil Bones, and Geological Catastrophes: New Translations and Interpretations of the Primary Texts.* Chicago: University of Chicago Press.

Rumbaugh, D. M. 1977. *Language Learning by a Chimpanzee: The Lana Project.* New York: Academic Press.

Rusell, D. E. H. 1986. *The Secret Trauma: Incest in the Lives of Girls and Women.* New York: Basic Books.

Rushton, J. P. 2000. *Race, Evolution, and Behavior: A Life History Perspective* (3rd ed.). Port Huron, MI: Charles Darwin Research Institute Press.

Sabloff, Jeremy, and C. C. Lamberg-Karlovsky (Eds.), 1975. *Ancient Civilization and Trade.* Albuquerque: University of New Mexico Press.

Sackett, James R. 1982. "Approaches to Style in Lithic Archaeology." *Journal of Anthropological Archaeology* 1: 59–112.

Safa, Helen I. 1974. *The Urban Poor of Puerto Rico: A Study in Development and Inequality.* New York: Holt, Rinehart & Winston.

Sahlins, Marshall. 1958. *Social Stratification in Polynesia.* Monograph of the American Ethnological Society. Seattle: University of Washington Press.

———. 1965. "On the Sociology of Primitive Exchange." In M. Banton, (Ed.), *The Relevance of Models for Social Anthropology,* pp. 139–227. London: Tavistock.

———. 1968b. *Tribesmen.* Englewood Cliffs, NJ: Prentice Hall.

———. 1972. *Stone Age Economics.* Chicago: Aldine.

———. 1985. *Islands of History.* Chicago: University of Chicago Press.

———. 1995. *How "Natives" Think, About Captain Cook, For Example.* Chicago: University of Chicago Press.

Saler, Benson. 1993. *Conceptualizing Religion: Immanent Anthropologists, Transcendent Natives, and Unbound Categories.* Leiden: E. J. Brill.

Salisbury, R. F. 1962. *From Stone to Steel: Economic Consequences of a Technological Change in New Guinea.* Cambridge: Cambridge University Press.

Salmon, Merrilee H. 1997. "Ethical Considerations in Anthropology and Archaeology, or Relativism and Justice for All." *Journal of Anthropological Research* 53: 47–63.

Salzman, Philip. 1989. "The Lone Stranger and the Solitary Quest." *Anthropology Newsletter* 30 (5): 16, 44.

———. 2000. "Hierarchical Image and Reality: The Construction of a Tribal Chiefship." *Comparative Study of Society and History* 42 (1): 49–66.

———. 2004. *Pastoralists: Equality, Hierarchy, and the State.* Boulder: Westview Press.

Sanday, Peggy Reeves. 2002. *Women at the Center: Life in a Modern Matriarchy.* Ithaca: Cornell University Press.

Sanders, W. T., G. Mastache, and R. Cobean (Eds.), 2003. *Urbanization in Mesoamerica,* Vol. 1. State College: Pennsylvania State University; Mexico City: Instituto Nacional de Antropologia e Historia.

Sanderson, Stephen. 1999. *Social Transformations: A General Theory of Historical Development.* Lanham, MD: Rowman and Littlefield.

Sapolsky, Robert. 2006. "Social Culture among Nonhuman Primates" *Current Anthropology* 47 (4): 641–656.

Sardesai, D. R. 1989. *Southeast Asia: Past and Present.* Boulder, CO: Westview Press.

Sarich, V. M., and A. C. Wilson. 1967. "Rates of Albumen Evolution in Primates." *Proceedings of the National Academy of Sciences* 58: 142–148.

Sauer, Carl O. 1952. *Agricultural Origins and Dispersals.* New York: American Geographical Society.

Sauer, Norman J., William A. Lovis, Mark E. Blumer, and Jennifer Fillion. 2003. "The Contributions of Archaeology and Physical Anthropology to the John McRae Case." In Dawnie Wolfe Steadman, (Ed.), *Hard Evidence: Case Studies in Forensic Anthropology,* pp. 117–126. Upper Saddle River, NJ: Prentice Hall.

Savage-Rumbaugh, Sue E. 1986. *Ape Language from Conditioned Response to Symbol.* New York: Columbia University Press.

Sayers, Ken and C. Owen Lovejoy. 2008. "The Chimpanzee Has No Clothes: A Critical Examination of *Pan troglodytes* in Models of Human Evolution." *Current Anthropology* 39(1): 87–114.

Scarr, S., and R. A. Weinberg. 1978. "Attitudes, Interests, and IQ." *Human Nature* 1 (4): 29–36.

Schafft, Gretchen. 1999. "Professional Denial." *Anthropology Newsletter* 40 (1): 56–57.

Schaller, George. 1976. *The Mountain Gorilla—Ecology and Behavior.* Chicago: University of Chicago Press.

Schell, Lawrence M., and Melinda Denham. 2003. "Environmental Pollution in Urban Environments and Human Biology." *Annual Review of Anthropology* 32: 111–134.

Schepartz, L. A. 1993. "Language and Modern Human Origins." *Yearbook of Physical Anthropology* 36: 1–126.

Schick, K. D., and N. Toth. 1993. *Making Silent Stones Speak: Human Evolution and the Dawn of Technology.* New York: Simon and Schuster.

Schick, Kathy D. 1986. *Stone Age Sites in the Making: Experiments in the Formation and Transformation of Archaeological Occurrences.* Oxford: BAR International Series, 319.

Schieffelin, Bambi B. 1990. *The Give and Take of Everyday Life: Language Socialization of Kaluli Children.* New York: Cambridge University Press.

Schieffelin, Bambi, and Elinor Ochs (Eds.), 1987. *Language Socialization Across Cultures.* Studies in the Social and Cultural Foundations of Languages, No 3. Cambridge: Cambridge University Press.

Schiffer, Michael B. 1987. *Formation Processes of the Archaeological Record.* Albuquerque: University of New Mexico Press.

Schildkrout, Enid, and Adrienne L. Kaeppler. 2004. "From Tattoo to Piercing: Body Art as Visual Language." In Ruth Osterweiss Selig, Marilyn R. London, and P. Ann Kaupp, (Eds.),, *Anthropology Explored: Revised and Expanded: The Best of Smithsonian Anthronotes.* pp. 101–103. Washington, DC: Smithsonian Books.

Schlegel, Alice, and Rohn Eloul. 1988. "Marriage Transactions: Labor, Property, and Status." *American Anthropologist* 90 (2): 291–309.

Schmidt, Peter R., Matthew C. Curtis, and Zelalem Teka (Eds.),. 2008. *The Archaeology of Ancient Eritrea.* Trenton: The Red Sea Press.

Schmidt, Peter R., and McIntosh, Roderick J. (Eds.), 1996. *Plundering Africa's Past*. Bloomington: Indiana University Press.

Schneider, David. 1953. "A Note on Bridewealth and the Stability of Marriage." *Man* 53: 55–57.

Schneider, Nancy. 2013. "Hacking the World: An Anthropologist in the Midst of a Geek Insurgency." *Chronicle of Higher Education* April 1, 2013.

Schusky, Ernest L. 1990. *Culture and Agriculture*. New York: Bergin and Garvey.

Schwartz, Richard, and James C. Miller. 1975. "Legal Evolution and Societal Complexity." In Ronald L. Akers and James C. Miller, (Eds.), *Law and Control in Society*. pp. 52–62. Englewood Cliffs, NJ: Prentice Hall.

Scott, Eugenie C. 2004. *Evolution vs. Creationism: An Introduction*. Westport, CT: Greenwood Press.

Scott, James. 1976. *The Moral Economy of the Peasant: Rebellion and Subsistence in Southeast Asia*. New Haven: Yale University Press.

Scudder, Thayer, and Elizabeth Colson. 1979. "Long-Term Research in Gwembe Valley, Zambia." In G. Foster, (Ed.), *Long-Term Field Research in Social Anthropology*. pp. 227–254. New York: Academic Press.

Scupin, Raymond. 1988. "Language, Hierarchy and Hegemony: Thai Muslim Discourse Strategies." *Language Sciences* 10 (2): 331–351.

———. 2003c. "The Anthropology of Islam as Applied Anthropology." *Reviews in Anthropology* 32: 141–158.

———, (Ed.), 2006. *Peoples and Cultures of Asia*. Upper Saddle River, NJ: Prentice Hall.

———. 2006a. "Mainland Southeast Asia." In Raymond Scupin (Ed.) *Peoples and Cultures of Asia*. pp. 335–378. Upper Saddle River, NJ: Prentice Hall.

———, (Ed.), 2008a. *Religion and Culture: An Anthropological Focus* (2nd ed). Upper Saddle River, NJ: Prentice Hall.

———. 2008b. "Islam." In Raymond Scupin (Ed.) *Religion and Culture: An Anthropological Focus* (2nd ed.). pp. 430–454. Upper Saddle River, NJ: Pearson Prentice Hall.

———, (Ed.), 2012a. *Race and Ethnicity: The United States and the World* (2nd ed.). Upper Saddle River, NJ: Prentice Hall.

———, 2012b. "Ethnicity." In Raymond Scupin (Ed.) *Race and Ethnicity: The United States and the World* (2nd ed.). pp. 58–78. Upper Saddle River, NJ: Pearson Prentice Hall.

———. 2012c. "U.S. Ethnic Relations: Anglos and the White Ethnics." In Raymond Scupin (Ed.) *Race and Ethnicity: The United States and the World* (2nd ed.). pp. 129–151. Upper Saddle River, NJ: Pearson Prentice Hall.

———, 2012d. "Asia" In Raymond Scupin (Ed.) *Race and Ethnicity: The United States and the World*.,(2nd ed.). pp. 363–384. Upper Saddle River, NJ: Pearson Prentice Hall.

Sear, Rebecca and David Coall. 2011. "How Much Does Family Matter: Cooperative Breeding and the Demographic Transition." *Population and Development Review* 37 (Supplement): 81–112.

Sebeok, Thomas A., and Jean Umiker-Sebeok (Eds.), 1980. *Speaking of Apes: A Critical Anthology of Two-Way Communication with Man*. New York: Plenum Press.

Sedley, D. N. 2007. *Creationism and Its Critics in Antiquity*. Berkeley: University of California Press.

Semaw, S., M. J. Rogers, J. Quade, P. R, Renne, R. F. Butler, M. Domínguez-Rodrigo, D. Stout, W. S. Hart, T. Pickering, et al. 2003. "2.6-Million-Year-Old Stone Tools and Associated Bones from OGS-6 and OGS-7, Gona, Afar, Ethiopia." *Journal of Human Evolution* 45 (2): 169–177.

Senghas, Kita S., and A. Ozyurek. 2004. "Children Creating Core Properties of Language: Evidence from an Emerging Sign Language in Nicaragua." *Science* 305 (5691): 1779–1795.

Senut, B., M. Pickford, D. Gommery, P. Mein, K. Cheboi, and Y. Coppens. 2001. "Premier Hominidé du Miocène (Formation de Lukeino, Kenya)." *Comptes Rendus de l' Académie des Sciences, Série IIa* 332: 137–144.

Serageldin, Ismail, and June Taboroff, eds. 1994. "Culture and Development in Africa," *Environmentally Sustainable Development Proceedings Series* No. 1. Washington, DC: International Bank for Reconstruction and Development.

Serrat, M. A., King D., Lovejoy C.O. 2008. "Temperature Regulates Limb Length in Homeotherms by Directly Modulating Cartilage Growth." *Proceedings of the National Academy of Sciences of the United States of America* 105 (49): 19348–19353.

Service, Elman. 1960. "The Law of Evolutionary Potential." In Marshall D. Sahlins and Elman R. Service, (Eds.), *Evolution and Culture*, pp. 93–122. Ann Arbor: University of Michigan Press.

———. [1962] 1971. *Primitive Social Organization: An Evolutionary Perspective*. New York: Random House.

———. 1975. *Origins of the State and Civilization: The Process of Cultural Evolution*. New York: W. W. Norton.

———. 1978a. "Classical and Modern Theories of the Origin of Government." In Ronald Cohen and E. R. Service, (Eds)., *Origins of the State: The Anthropology of Political Evolution*. Philadelphia: Institute for Study of Human Issues.

———. 1978b. *Profiles in Ethnology*. New York: Harper & Row.

———. 1979. *The Hunters* (2nd ed). Englewood Cliffs, NJ: Prentice Hall.

Shahrani, M. Nazif. 1981. "Growing in Respect: Aging among the Kirghiz of Afghanistan." In P. Amoss and S. Harrell, (Eds)., *Other Ways of Growing Old: Anthropologist Perspectives*. Stanford, CA: Stanford University Press.

Shahrani, M. Nazif, and Robert Canfield (Eds.), 1984. *Revolutions and Rebellions in Afghanistan: Anthropological Perspectives*. Berkeley: University of California Press.

Shankman, Paul. 1975. "A Forestry Scheme in Samoa." *Natural History* 84 (8): 60–69.

———. 1978. "Notes on a Corporate 'Potlatch': The Lumber Industry in Samoa." In A. Idris-Soven, E. Idris-Soven, and M. K. Vaugh (Eds), *The World as a Company Town: Multinational Corporations and Social Change*. The Hague: Mouton World Anthropology Series.

———. 1990. Personal Correspondence.

———. 1998. "Margaret Mead, Derek Freeman, and the Issue of Evolution." *Skeptical Inquirer* 22 (6): 35–39.

———. 2000. "Development, Sustainability, and the Deforestation of Samoa." *Pacific Studies* 22 (3/4): 167–188.

———. 2001. "Requiem for a Controversy: Whatever Happened to Margaret Mead?" *Skeptic* 9: 48–53.

———. 2009a. "The Trashing of Margaret Mead: How Derek Freeman Fooled Us All with an Alleged Hoax." *Skeptic* 15 (3): 2–5.

———. 2009b. *The Trashing of Margaret Mead: Anatomy of an Anthropological Controversy*. Madison: University of Wisconsin Press.

———. 2013. "The Fateful 'Hoaxing' of Margaret Mead: A Cautionary Tale." *Current Anthropology* 54 (1): 51–70.

Shanks, Niall. 2004. *God, the Devil, and Darwin: A Critique of Intelligent Design Theory*. New York: Oxford University Press.

Shanks, Niall, and Karl Joplin. 1999. "Redundant Complexity: A Critical Analysis of Intelligent Design in Biochemistry." *Philosophy of Science* 66: 268–282.

Shannon, Thomas Richard. 1988. *An Introduction to the World-System Perspective*. Boulder, CO: Westview Press.

Sharer, Robert J., and Loa P. Traxler. 2006. *The Ancient Maya*. Stanford, CA: Stanford University Press

Shaw, Thurstan. 1986. "Whose Heritage?" *Museum* 149: 46–48.

Shea, B. T., and A. M. Gomez. 1988. "Tooth Scaling and Evolutionary Dwarfism: An Investigation of Allometry in Human Pygmies." *American Journal of Physical Anthropology* 77: 117–132.

Shenk, Mary, K., Monique Borgerhoff Mulder, Jan Veises, Gregory Clark, William Irons, Donna Leonetti, Bobbi S. Low, Samuel Bowles, Tom Hertz, Adrian Bell, and Patrizio Piraino. 2010. "Intergenerational Wealth Transmission among Agriculturalists: Foundations of Agrarian Inequality." *Current Anthropology* 51 (1): 65–83.

Shennan, Stephen. 2008. "Evolution in Archaeology." *Annual Review of Anthropology* 37(1): 75–91.

Shepher, Joseph. 1983. *Incest: A Biosocial View*. New York: Academic Press.

Shi, Lihong. 2013. "Raising One Successful Child: Parental Aspirations and Investments in Rural Northeast China." (Paper read at AAA meetings, November, 2013).

Shimizu, Akitoshi. 1987. "*Ie* and *Dozuku*: Family and Descent in Japan." *Current Anthropology* 2 8(4): S85–S90.

Shipman, Pat. 1984. "Scavenger Hunt." *Natural History* 4 (84): 20–27.

———. 1986a. "Baffling Limb on the Family Tree." *Discover* 7 (9): 86–93.

———. 1986b. "Scavenging or Hunting in Early Hominids: Theoretical Frameworks and Tests." *American Anthropologist* 88: 27–43.

———. 1994. *The Evolution of Racism*. New York: Simon and Schuster.

Shirk, Martha, and O'Dell Mitchell, Jr. 1989. "One Company Evolving in Two Lands." *St. Louis Post-Dispatch*, June 25.

Shostak, Marjorie. 1981. *Nisa: The Life and Words of a !Kung Woman*. New York: Vintage Books, Random House.

Shweder, Richard. 1991. *Thinking Through Cultures: Expeditions in Cultural Psychology*. Cambridge, MA: Harvard University Press.

———. 2003. *Why Do Men Barbeque?: Recipes for Cultural Psychology*. Cambridge, MA: Harvard University Press.

———. 2013. "The Goose and the Gander: the Genital Wars." *Global Discourse: An Interdisciplinary Journal of Current Affairs and Applied Contemporary Thought* 3 (2): 348–366.

Sidky, H. 2004. *Perspectives on Culture: A Critical Introduction to Theory in Cultural Anthropology*. Upper Saddle River, NJ: Prentice Hall.

Sidky, H., and Deborah Akers. 2006. "Afghanistan." In Raymond Scupin, (Ed.), *Peoples and Cultures of Asia*. pp. 14–92. Upper Saddle River, NJ: Prentice Hall.

Sillitoe, Paul. 2001. "Pig Men and Women, Big Men and Women: Gender and Production in the New Guinea Highlands." *Ethnology* 40 (3): 171–193.

Silverman, Philip, and Robert J. Maxwell. 1983. "The Role and Treatment of the Elderly in 95 Societies." In Jay Sokolovsky (Ed.), *Growing Old in Different Cultures*, pp. 43–55. Belmont, CA: Wadsworth.

Simmons, Leo. 1945. *The Role of the Aged in Primitive Society*. London: Oxford University Press.

Simon, Julian L. 1981. *The Ultimate Resource*. Princeton, NJ: Princeton University Press.

Simons, Elwyn L. 1972. *Primate Evolution: An Introduction to Man's Place in Nature*. New York: Macmillan.

———. 1984. "Ancestor: Dawn Ape of the Fayum." *Natural History* 93(5): 18–20.

———. 1989a. "Description of Two Genera and Species of Late Eocene *Anthropoidea* from Egypt." *Proceedings of the National Academy of Science* 86: 9956–9960.

———. 1989b. "Human Origins." *Science* 245: 1343–1350.

———. 1990. "Discovery of the Oldest Known Anthropoidean Skull from the Paleogene of Egypt." *Science* 247: 1567–1569.

Simons, Elwyn L., and D. Rasmussen. 1990. "Vertebrate Paleontology of the Fayum: History of Research, Faunal Review, and Future Prospects." In R. Said (Ed.), *The Geology of Egypt*, pp. 627–638. Rotterdam: Balkema Press.

Simpson, J. A., and E. S. C. Wiener. 1989. "Ethnic." *Oxford English Dictionary* (2nd ed.), Vol. 5. Oxford: Clarendon Press.

Singer, R., and J. Wymer. 1982. *The Middle Stone Age at Klasies River Mouth in South Africa*. Chicago: Chicago University Press.

Singleton, Theresa A. 1999. "I, Too, Am America." *Archaeological Studies in African American Life*. Charlottesville: University of Virginia Press.

Skidmore, Thomas E., and Peter H. Smith. 2005. *Modern Latin America* (6th ed). New York: Oxford University Press.

Slagter, Robert, and Harold R. Kerbo. 2000. *Modern Thailand*. Boston: McGraw-Hill.

Small, Meredith. 1993. *Female Choices: Sexual Behavior of Female Primates*. Ithaca, NY: Cornell University Press.

———. 1995. *What's Love Got to Do with It? The Evolution of Human Mating*. New York: Anchor Books.

———. 1998. *Our Babies: Ourselves*. New York: Anchor Books.

———. 2001. *Kids: How Biology and Culture Shape the Way We Raise Our Children*. New York: Doubleday.

Smart, Alan, and Josephine Smart. 2003. "Urbanization and the Global Perspective." *Annual Reviews of Anthropology* 32 (1): 263–285.

Smith, Adam. [1776] 1937. *An Inquiry into the Nature and Causes of the Wealth of Nations*. New York: The Modern Library.

Smith, Andrew B. 1984. "Origins of the Neolithic in the Sahara." In Desmond J. Clark and Steven A. Brandt, (Eds.), *From Hunter to Farmer*, pp. 84–92. Berkeley: University of California Press.

———. 2005. *African Herders: Emergence of Pastoral Traditions*. Walnut Creek, CA: AltaMira Press.

Smith, Anthony. 1986. *The Ethnic Origins of Nations*. Oxford: Blackwell.

Smith, Bruce D. 1989. "Origins of Agriculture in Eastern North America." *Science* 246: 1566–1571.

———. 1995. *The Emergence of Agriculture*. New York: Scientific American Library.

Smith, Craig B. 2004. *How the Great Pyramid Was Built*. Washington, DC: Smithsonian Books.

Smith, Eric Alden. 2013. "Agency and Adaptation: New Directions in Evolutionary Anthropology." *Annual Review of Anthropology* 42: 103–120.

Smith, Eric Alden, Kim Hill, Frank W. Marlowe, David Nolin, Polly Weisner, Michael Gurven, Samuel Bowles, Monique Borgerhoff Mulder, Tom Hertz, and Adrian Bell. 2010a. "Wealth Transmission and Inequality among Hunter-Gatherers." *Current Anthropology* 51 (1): 19–34.

Smith, Eric Alden, Monique Borgerhoff Mulder, Samuel Bowles, Michael Gurven, Tom Hertz, and Mary K. Shenk. 2010b. "Production Systems, Inheritance, and Inequality in Premodern Societies: Conclusions." *Current Anthropology* 51 (1): 85–94.

Smith, F. H. 1984. "Fossil Hominids from the Upper Pleistocene of Central Europe and the Origin of Modern Europeans." In F. H. Smith and F. Spencer (Eds.), *The Origins of Modern Humans: A World Survey of Fossil Evidence*, pp. 137–210. New York: Alan R. Liss.

Smith, Huston. *The Religions of Man*. New York: Harper & Row.

Smith, M. G. 1965. "The Hausa of Northern Nigeria." In James L. Gibbs, Jr., (Ed.), *Peoples of Africa*. pp. 121–155. New York: Holt, Rinehart & Winston.

Smith, Margo L. 1986. "Culture in International Business: Selecting Employees for Expatriate Assignments." In Hendrick Serrie, (Ed.), *Anthropology and International Business*. Williamsburg, VA: William and Mary University.

Smith, Michael, E. 2004. "The Archaeology of Ancient State Economies." *Annual Review of Anthropology* 33: 73–102.

Smith, Neil. 1999. *Chomsky: Ideas and Ideals*. Cambridge: Cambridge University Press.

Smith, Stuart T. 1990. "Administration at the Egyptian Middle Kingdom Frontier: Sealings from Uronarti and Askut." *Aegaeum* 5: 197–219.

Smith-Ivan, Edda. 1988. "Introduction." In Edda Smith-Ivan, Nidhi Tandon, and Jane Connors, (Eds.), *Women in Sub-Saharan Africa*, Report No. 7. London: Minority Rights Group.

Smuts, Barbara. 1995. "Apes of Wrath." *Discover* 16 (8): 35–37.

Snow, C. C., and M. J. Bihurriet. 1992. "An Epidemiology of Homicide: Ning'n Nombre Burials in the Province of Buenos Aires from 1970 to 1984." In T. B. Jabine and R. P. Claude, (Eds.), *Human Rights and Statistics: Getting the Record Straight*, pp. 328–363 Philadelphia: University of Pennsylvania Press.

Snow, C. C., E. Stover, and K. Hannibal. 1989. "Scientists as Detectives Investigating Human Rights." *Technology Review* 92:2.

Soares P, Ermini L, Thomson N., *et al.* 2009. "Correcting for Purifying Selection: An Improved Human Mitochondrial Molecular Clock." *American Journal of Human Genetics* 84 (6): 740–759.

Soficaru, A., Doboş, A. and Trinkaus, E. 2006. "Early Modern Humans from the Peştera Muierii, Baia de Fier, Romania." *Proceedings of the National Academy of Sciences of the United States* 103 (46): 17196–17201.

Solecki, Ralph S. 1971. *Shanidar: The First Flower People*. New York: Knopf.

Solheim, William. 1972. "An Earlier Agricultural Revolution." *Scientific American* 226 (4): 34–41.

Sorensen, Clark. 2006. "Korea (North and South)" In Raymond Scupin (Ed.), *Peoples and Cultures of Asia*. pp. 279–331. Upper Saddle River, NJ: Prentice Hall Press.

Southall, Aidan. 1956. *Alur Society: A Study in Processes and Types of Domination*. Cambridge: Heffer.

South Asia Online Briefing Program. 2000. June/August. Accessed at http://www.thp.org/sac/unit4/cycle.htm.

Sowell, Thomas. 1994. *Race and Culture*. New York: Basic Books.

———. 1995. "Ethnicity and IQ." In Steven Fraser, (Ed.), *The Bell Curve Wars: Race, Intelligence and the Future of America*. New York: Basic Books.

Spencer, Charle, S. and Elsa M. Redmond. 2004. "Primary State Formation in Mesoamerica." *Annual Review of Anthropology* 33: 173–199.

Sperber, Dan. 1996. *Explaining Culture: A Naturalistic Approach*. Oxford: Blackwell Publishers.

Sperber, Dan, and Deirdre Wilson. 1996. *Relevance: Communication and Cognition*. Hoboken, NJ: Wiley-Blackwell.

Sperber, Dan, and Lawrence Hirschfeld. 1999. "Culture, Cognition, and Evolution." In Robert Wilson & Frank Keil (Eds.) *MIT Encyclopedia of the Cognitive Sciences* (Cambridge, Mass. MIT Press, 1999), pp. cxi–cxxxii.

Spiro, Melford. 1952. "Ghosts, Ifaluk, and Teleological Functionalism." *American Anthropologist* 54: 497–503.

———. 1971. *Buddhism and Society: A Great Tradition and Its Burmese Vicissitudes*. Berkeley: University of California Press.

———. 1982. *Oedipus in the Trobriands*. Chicago: University of Chicago Press.

———. 1993. "Is the Western Conception of the Self "Peculiar" Within the Context of World Cultures." *Ethos* 21 (2): 107–153.

Sponsel, Leslie. 1996. "Human Rights and Advocacy Anthropology." In Melvin. Ember and David. Levinson, (Eds.), *Encyclopedia of Cultural Anthropology*, Vol. 2. pp. 602–607. New York: Henry Holt and Company.

———. 1998. "Yanomami: An Arena of Conflict and Aggression in the Amazon." *Aggressive Behavior* 24: 97–122.

———. 2012. *Spiritual Ecology: A Quiet Revolution*. New York: Praeger.

Srinivas, Tulasi. 2002. "A Tryst with Destiny: The Indian Case of Cultural Globalization." In Peter Berger and Samuel Huntington (Eds.), *Many Globalizations: Cultural Diversity in the Contemporary World*. pp. 89–116. Oxford: Oxford University Press.

Stack, Carol B. 1975. *All Our Kin: Strategies for Survival in a Black Community*. New York: Harper & Row.

Stanford, Craig B. 2012. "Chimpanzees and the Behavior of *Ardipithecus ramidus*" *Annual Review of Anthropology*, Vol. 41: 139–149.

Stanish, Charles. 2001. "The Origins of States in South America." *Annual Review of Anthropology* 30: 41–64.

Stanner, W. E. H. 1979. "The Dreaming." In W. A. Lessa and E. Z. Vogt (Eds.), *Reader in Comparative Religion* (4th ed.), pp. 513–523. New York: Harper & Row.

Starkweather, Katherine and Raymond Hames. 2012. "A Survey of Non-Classical Polyandry." *Human Nature* 23 (2): 149–172.

Starrett, Gregory. 1998. *Putting Islam to Work: Education, Politics, and Religious Transformation in Egypt*. Berkeley: University of California Press.

Starrett, Gregory. 2004. "Culture Never Dies: Anthropology at Abu Ghraib." *Anthropology News*, September: 10–11.

Stavenhagen, Rodolfo. 1975. *Social Classes in Agrarian Societies*. Garden City, NY: Anchor Press.

Stavrianos, L. S. 1995. *A Global History: From Prehistory to the Present* (6th ed.). Upper Saddle River, NJ: Prentice Hall.

Steadman, Dawnie W. 2009 *Hard Evidence: Case Studies in Forensic Anthropology*. New York: Pearson.

Steinmetz, Paul. 1980. *Pipe, Bible and Peyote among the Oglala Lakota*. Stockholm: Almquist and Wiksell International.

Steudel, K. L. 1994. "Locomotor Energetics and Hominid Evolution." *Evolutionary Anthropology* 3: 40–48.

Steven, Rob. 1983. *Classes in Contemporary Japan*. Cambridge: Cambridge University Press.

Steward, Julian H. 1955. *Theory of Culture Change: The Methodology of Multilinear Evolution.* Urbana: University of Illinois Press.

Stewart, Kathleen, and Susan Harding. 1999. "Bad Endings: American Apocalypsis." *Annual Review of Anthropology* 28: 285–310.

Stewart, T. D (Ed.), 1970. *Personal Identification in Mass Disasters.* Washington, DC: Smithsonian Institution Press.

Stiebing, William H., Jr. 1984. *Ancient Astronauts: Cosmic Allusions and Popular Theories About Man's Past.* Buffalo, NY: Prometheus Books.

———. 1994. *Uncovering the Past: A History of Archaeology.* New York: Oxford University Press.

Stock, Jill Kamil. 1993. *Aswan and Abu Simbel: History and Guide.* Cairo: American University in Cairo Press. pp. 141–142.

Stone, Glen. 2002. "Both Sides Now: Fallacies in the Genetic-Modification Wars, Implications for Developing Countries, and Anthropological Perspectives."*Current Anthropology* 43 (4): 611–630.

———. 2005. "A Science of the Gray: Malthus, Marx, and the Ethics of Studying Crop Biotechnology." In L. Meskell and P. Pels, (Eds.), *Embedding Ethics: Shifting Boundaries of the Anthropological Profession*, pp. 197–217. Oxford: Berg.

———. 2010. "The Anthropology of Genetically Modified Crops." *Annual Review of Anthropology* 39: 381–400.

Stone, Linda. 2000. *Kinship and Gender: An Introduction.* Boulder: Westview Press.

———,(Ed.). 2001. *New Directions in Anthropological Kinship.* Lanham, MD: Rowman and Littlefield.

———. 2005. *Kinship and Gender: An Introduction* (3rd ed.). Boulder: Westview Press.

———. 2010. *Kinship and Gender: An Introduction* (4th ed.). Boulder, CO: Westview Press.

Stone, Livia. 2013. "Citizenship, *Compañerismo,* and the New Transnational Anarchism: A Perspective from Mexico." (Paper Read at AAA meetings, Chicago, November 2013).

Stoneking, M., K. Bhatia, and A. C. Wilson. 1987. "Rate of Sequence Divergence Estimated from Restricted Maps of Mitochondrial DNAs from Papua, New Guinea." *Cold Spring Harbor Symposia on Quantitative Biology* 51: 433–439.

Stover, E. 1981. "Scientists Aid Search for Argentina's 'Desaparacidos.'" *Science* 211 (4486): 6.

———. 1992. "Unquiet Graves: The Search for the Disappeared in Iraqi Kurdistan." A report published by Middle East Watch and Physicians for Human Rights.

Strada, Michael J. 2003. *Through the Global Lens: An Introduction to the Social Sciences* (2nd ed.). Upper Saddle River, NJ: Prentice Hall.

Strasser, Elizabeth, and Marian Dagosto (Eds.), 1988. *The Primate Postcranial Skeleton: Studies in Adaptation and Evolution.* New York: Academic Press.

Strathern, Marilyn. 1984. "Subject or Object? Women and the Circulation of Valuables in Highland New Guinea." In Renée Hirschon (Eds.), *Women and Property, Women as Property.* New York: St. Martins.

———. 1988. *The Gender of the Gift: Problems with Women and Problems with Society in Melanesia.* Berkeley: University of California Press.

Strauss, Claudia. 1992. "Models and Motives." In R. D' Andrade and C. Strauss, (Eds.), *Human Motives and Cultural Models.* pp. 1–20. Cambridge: Cambridge University Press.

Strier, Karen B. 2003. *Primate Behavioral Ecology* (2nd ed.). New York: Allyn and Bacon.

Stringer, C. B. 1985. "Middle Pleistocene Hominid Variability and the Origin of Late Pleistocene Humans." In E. Delson, (Ed.), *Ancestors: The Hard Evidence,* pp. 289–295. New York: Alan R. Liss.

———. 2001. "Modern Human Origins—Distinguishing the Models." *African Archaeological Review* 18(2): 67–75.

Stringer, C. B., and P. Andrews. 1988. "Genetic and Fossil Evidence for the Origin of Modern Humans." *Science* 239: 1263–1268.

———. 2005. *The Complete World of Human Evolution.* New York: Thames and Hudson Inc.

Struever, Stuart (Ed.), 1970. *Prehistoric Agriculture.* Garden City, NY: Natural History Press.

Strug, David L. 1986. "The Foreign Politics of Cocaine: Comments on a Plan to Eradicate the Coca Leaf in Peru." In Deborah Pacini and Christine Franquemont (Eds.), *Coca and Cocaine: Effects on People and Policy in Latin America,* Cultural Survival Report 23. Cambridge, MA: Cultural Survival, Inc.; Latin American Studies Program, Cornell University.

Stull, Donald D., and Michael J. Broadway. 2004. *Slaughterhouse Blues: The Meat and Poultry Industry in North America.* Belmont, CA: Wadsworth/Thompson.

Stutley, Margaret. 2003. *Shamanism: An Introduction.* London: Routledge.

Sudarkasa, Niara. 1989. "African and Afro-American Family Structure." In Johnetta Cole, (Ed.), *Anthropology for the Nineties: Introductory Readings,* pp. 132–160. New York: Free Press.

Sullivan, Lynne P., and Christopher P. Rodning. 2001. "Gender, Tradition, and the Negotiation of Power Relationships in Southern Appalachian Chiefdoms." In Timothy Pauketat (Ed.), *The Archaeology of Traditions: Agency and History before and after Columbus.,* pp. 107–120. Gainesville: University Press of Florida.

Survival International. 2010. "News: Outrage as Botswana Bushmen Denied Access to Water." http://www.survivalinternational.org/news/6257. July 21, 2010.

Sussman R. L. 1994. Fossil Evidence for Early Hominid Tool Use. *Science* 265: 1570–1573.

Sussman, Robert W. 1991. "Primate Origins and the Evolution of the Angiosperms." *American Journal of Primatology* 23 (4): 209–223.

Sutton, Mark Q. 2011. *An Introduction to Native North America* (4th ed.). Boston: Pearson Education/Allyn & Bacon.

Swadesh, Morris. 1964. "Linguistics as an Instrument of Prehistory." In Dell H. Hymes, (Ed.), *Language and Society.* pp. 100–107. New York: Harper & Row.

Sweet, Louise. 1965. "Camel Raiding of North Arabian Bedouin: A Mechanism of Ecological Adaptation." *American Anthropologist* 67: 1132–1150.

Swindler, Daris R. 2002. *Primate Dentition: An Introduction to the Teeth of Non-human Primates.* New York: Cambridge University Press.

Swisher, C. C., G. H. Curtis, T. Jacob, A. G. Getty, and A. Suprijo Widiasmoro. 1994. "Age of the Earliest Known Hominids in Java, Indonesia." *Science* 263: 1118–1121.

Symons, Donald. 1979. *The Evolution of Human Sexuality.* Oxford, England: Oxford University Press.

Szabo, G. 1967. "The Regional Anatomy of the Human Integument with Special Reference to the Distribution of Hair Follicles, Sweat Glands and Melanocytes." *Philosophical Transactions of the Royal Society of London* 252B: 447–485.

Tainter, Joseph A. 1990. *The Collapse of Complex Societies.* Cambridge: Cambridge University Press.

———. 2006. "Archaeology of Overshoot and Collapse" *Annual Review of Anthropology* 35: 59–74.

Takaki, Ronald. 1990a. *Iron Cage: Race and Culture in 19th Century America.* New York: Oxford University Press.

———. 1990b. *Strangers from a Different Shore: A History of Asian Americans.* New York: Penguin.

Takashi, Imomata. 2006. "Plazas, Performers, and Spectators: Political Theaters of the Classic Maya." *Current Anthropology* 47 (5): 805–842.

Talmon, Yonina. 1964. "Mate Selection in Collective Settlements." *American Sociological Review* 29: 491–508.

Tambiah, Stanley J. 1976. *World Conqueror and World Renouncer: A Study of Buddhism and Polity in Thailand against a Historical Background.* Cambridge: Cambridge University Press.

———. 1989. "Bridewealth and Dowry Revisited: The Position of Women in Sub-Saharan Africa and North India." *Current Anthropology* 30 (4): 413–435.

———. 1991. *Sri Lanka: Ethnic Fratricide and the Dismantling of Democracy.* Chicago: University of Chicago Press.

———. 1996. *Leveling Crowds: Ethnonationalist Conflicts and Collective Violence in South Asia.* Berkeley: University of California Press.

Tandon, Nidhi. 1988. "Women in Rural Areas." In Edda Smith-Ivan, Nidhi Tandon, and Jane Connors (Eds.)., *Women in Sub-Saharan Africa*, Report No. 77, p. 9. London: Minority Rights Group

Tanner, Nancy M. 1981. *On Becoming Human.* London: Cambridge University Press.

———. 1987. "Gathering by Females: The Chimpanzee Model Revisited and the Gathering Hypothesis." In Warren G. Kinsey (Ed.).,*The Evolution of Human Behavior*, pp. 3–27. Albany: State University of New York Press.

Tappan, Martha. 2001. Deconstructing the Serengeti. In C. Stanford and H. T. Brunn (Eds.), *Meat Eating and Human Evolution.* Oxford: Oxford University Press.

Tapper, Richard, and Nancy Tapper. 1992, 1993. "Marriage, Honor, and Responsibility: Islamic and Local Models in the Mediterranean and Middle East." *Cambridge Anthropology* 16 (2): 3–21.

Tarling, D. H. 1985. *Continental Drift and Biological Evolution.* Burlington, NC: Carolina Biological Supply Co.

Tattersall, Ian. 1986. "Species Recognition in Human Paleontology." *Journal of Human Evolution* 15: 165–175.

———. 1998. *Becoming Human.* New York: Harcourt Brace and Company.

Tax, Sol. 1953. *Penny Capitalism: A Guatemalan Indian Economy.* Smithsonian Institution, Institute of Social Anthropology, Publication No. 16. Washington, DC: U.S. Government Printing Office.

Taylor, R. E. 1995. "Radiocarbon Dating: The Continuing Revolution." *Evolutionary Anthropology* 4 (5): 169–181.

Taylor R. E and J. Southon, 2007. "Use of Natural Diamonds to Monitor 14C AMS Instrument Backgrounds." *Nuclear Instruments and Methods in Physics Research B* 259:282–328.

Telles, Edward Eric. 2004. *Race in Another America: The Significance of Skin Color in Brazil.* Princeton, NJ: Princeton University Press.

Templeton, Alan R. 1993. "The 'Eve' Hypothesis: A Genetic Critique and Reanalysis." *American Anthropologist* 95 (1): 51–72.

———. 1998. "Human Races: A Genetic and Evolutionary Perspective." *American Anthropologist* 100 (3): 632–650.

———. 2002. "Out of Africa Again and Again." *Nature* 416: 45–51.

Terrace, Herbert S. 1986. *Nim: A Chimpanzee Who Learned Sign Language.* New York: Columbia University Press.

Testart, Alain. 1988. "Some Major Problems in the Social Anthropology of Hunter-Gatherers," Roy Willis (Trans.),. *Current Anthropology* 29 (1): 1–31.

Thieme, H. 1997. "Lower Paleolithic Hunting Spars from Germany." *Nature* 385: 807–8 10.

Thomas, David Hurst. 1999. *Exploring Ancient Native America: An Archaeological Guide.* New York: Routledge.

Thomas, Elizabeth, Marshall. 1958. *The Harmless People.* New York: Random House.

Thomas, J. 1999. *Understanding the Neolithic.* London: Routledge.

Thomas, Jolyon Baraka. 2014. "The Concept of Religion in Modern Japan: Imposition, Invention, or Innovation?" *Religious Studies in Japan* 2:3–21.

Thomason, Sarah G., and Terrence Kaufman. 1988. *Language Contact, Creolization, and Genetic Linguistics.* Berkeley: University of California Press.

Thomson, David S. 2003. "The Sapir–Whorf Hypothesis: Worlds Shaped by Words." In James Spradley and David McCurdy (Eds.), *Conformity and Conflict: Readings in Cultural Anthropology.* Boston: Allyn & Bacon.

Thorne, A., and M. H. Wolpoff. 1992. "The Multiregional Evolution of Humans." *Scientific American* 266: 76–83.

Thorpe, I. J. N. 2003. "Anthropology, Archaeology, and the Origin of Warfare." *World Archaeology*, 35 (1): 145–165.

Throckmorton, Peter. 1962. "Oldest Known Shipwreck Yields Bronze Age Cargo." *National Geographic* 121 (5): 697–711.

Tiano, S. 1994. *Patriarchy on the Line: Labor, Gender, and Ideology in the Mexican Maquila Industry.* Philadelphia: Temple University Press.

Tibi, Bassam. 1990. *Islam and the Cultural Accommodation of Social Change.* Clare Kojzl (Trans.). Boulder, CO: Westview Press.

Tierney, Patrick. 2000. *Darkness in El Dorado: How Scientists and Journalists Devastated the Amazon.* New York: W. W. Norton.

Time Almanac. 2000. Boston: Information Please.

Titma, Mikk, and Nancy Brandon Tuma. 2001. *Modern Russia.* Boston: McGraw-Hill.

Tite, M. S. 1972. *Methods of Physical Examination in Archaeology.* London: Seminar Press.

Tobias, P. V. 1998. "Evidence for the Early Beginnings of Spoken Language." *Cambridge Archaeological Journal* 1: 72–78.

Tomasello, Michael., and J. Call. 1997. *Primate Cognition.* New York: Oxford University Press.

Tomasello, Michael., M. Carpenter, J. Call, T. Behne, and H. Moll. 2005. "Understanding and Sharing Intentions: The Origins of Cultural Cognition." *Behavioral and Brain Sciences* 28: 675–691.

Toth, Nicholas, and Kathy Schick (Eds.), 2004. *The Oldowan: Case Studies into the Earliest Stone Age.* Bloomington, IN: Stone Age Institute Press.

———. 2009. "The Oldowan: The Tool Making of Early Hominins and Chimpanzees Compared." *Annual Review of Anthropology* 38: 289–305.

Toth, Nicholas, Kathy Schick, and Sileshi Semaw. 2004. "A Comparative Study of the Stone Tool-Making Abilities of *Pan*, *Australopithecus*, and *Homo sapiens*." In Nicholas Toth and Kathy Schick (Eds.), *The Oldowan: Case Studies into the Earliest Stone Age.* Bloomington, IN: Stone Age Institute Press.

Trigger, Bruce. 1993. *Early Civilizations: Ancient Egypt in Context.* Cairo: American University in Cairo Press.

————.2006. **A History of Archaeological Thought** (*2nd ed.*). **Cambridge: Cambridge University Press.**

Trinkaus, Erik. 2006. Modern Human versus Neandertal Evolutionary Distinctiveness. *Current Anthropology* 47(4): 597–620.

Trinkaus, Erik and Shipman, Pat. 1993. *The Neandertals: Changing the Image of Mankind.* New York: Alfred A. Knopf Pub.

————. 1994. *The Neandertals.* New York: Random House.

Tripcevich, Nicholas and Steven A. Wernke. 2010. "On-Site Recording of Excavation Data Using Mobile GIS." *Journal of Field Archaeology* 35(4): 380–397.

Trouillot, Michel-Rolph. 2002. "Adieu, Culture: A New Duty Arises." In Richard Fox and Barbara J. King (Eds.), *Anthropology beyond Culture,*. pp. 37–60. Oxford, England: Berg.

Tshombe, Richard Key. 2001. "The Case of the Okapi Faunal Reserve in the Northeastern Democratic Republic of Congo." *People and Natural Resources: Changes in Times of Crisis.* Okapi Faunal Reserve Zoning Program. (http://www.cerc.Columbia.edu/elf/ ELF2001CS/TshombeCS).

Tung, T. A. 2007. "Trauma and Violence in the Wari Empire of the Peruvian Andes: Warfare, Raids, and Ritual Fights." *American Journal of Physical Anthropology* 133: 941–956.

Turnbull, Colin. 1963. *The Forest People: A Study of the Pygmies of the Congo.* New York: Simon & Schuster.

————. 1983. *The Mbuti Pygmies: Change and Adaptation.* New York: Holt, Rinehart & Winston.

Turner, Jonathan, and Alexandra Maryanski. 2005. *Incest: Origins of the Taboo.* Boulder, CO: Paradigm Publishers.

Turner, Victor. 1957. *Schism and Continuity in an African Society: A Study of Ndembu Village Life.* Manchester: Manchester University Press.

————. 1967. *The Forest of Symbols: Aspects of Ndembu Ritual.* Ithaca, NY: Cornell University Press.

————. 1969. *The Ritual Process: Structure and Anti-Structure.* Ithaca, NY: Cornell University Press.

————. 1974. *Dramas, Fields, and Metaphors: Symbolic Action in Human Society.* Ithaca, NY: Cornell University Press.

Turton, Andrew. 1980. "Thai Institutions of Slavery." In James L. Watson, (Ed.)., *Asian and African Systems of Slavery,* pp. 251–292. Berkeley: University of California Press.

Tweddell, Colin E., and Linda Amy Kimball. 1985. *Introduction to the Peoples and Cultures of Asia.* Englewood Cliffs, NJ: Prentice Hall.

Tyler, Stephen A. 1986. *India: An Anthropological Perspective.* Prospect Heights, IL: Waveland Press.

Tylor, Edward B. 1871. *Primitive Culture.* London: J. Murray.

————. 1889. "On a Method of Investigating the Development of Institutions, Applied to Laws of Marriage and Descent." *Journal of the Royal Anthropological Institute* 18: 245–272.

Ubelaker, Douglas H. 1988. "North American Indian Population Size, A.D. 1500 to 1985." *American Journal of Physical Anthropology* 77: 289–294.

Uchendu, Victor C. 1965. *The Igbo of Southeast Nigeria.* New York: Holt, Rinehart & Winston.

Ucko, Peter J., and G. W. Dimbleby. 1969. *The Domestication and Exploitation of Plants and Animals.* Chicago: Aldine.

UN News Center. 2010. "Number of Refugees Returning Home Drops to Lowest in 20 Years." http://www.un.org/apps/news/story.asp?NewsID=35026.

Urciuoli Bonnie. 1996. *Exposing Prejudice: Puerto Rican Experiences of Language, Race, and Class.* Boulder: Westview Press.

————. 2003. "Boundaries, Language, and the Self: Issues faced by Puerto Ricans and other Latina/o College Students." *The Journal of Latin American Anthropology* 8 (2): 152–173.

————. 2008. "Skills and Selves in the New Workplace." *American Ethnologist* 35 (2): 211–229.

U.S. Census Bureau. 2000. *Statistical Abstracts of the United States.* U.S. Census Bureau. 2006. *Statistical Abstracts of the United States.*

————. 2006. *Statistical Abstract of the United States: 2006.* Washington, DC: U.S. Government Printing Office.

————. 2008. *Facts For Features.* CB09-FF.01 (December 2, 2008). Washington, DC: U.S. Census Bureau News, U.S. Department of Commerce.

————. 2010. *Statistical Abstract of the United States. 2010.* Washington, DC: U.S. Government Printing Office.

U.S. Committee on Global Change. 1988. *Toward an Understanding of Global Change.* Washington, DC: National Academy Press.

Vaccaro, Ismael. 2010. "Theorizing Impending Peripheries: Postindustrial Landscapes at the Edge of Hypermodernity's Collapse."*Journal of International and Global Studies* 1 (2): 22–44.

Vago, Steven. 1995. *Law and Society* (2nd ed.). Upper Saddle River, NJ: Prentice Hall.

Valeri, Valerio. 1985. *Kingship and Sacrifice: Ritual and Society in Ancient Hawaii,* Paula Wissing (Trans.). Chicago: University of Chicago Press.

van den Berghe, Pierre. 1979. *Human Family Systems: An Evolutionary View.* New York: Elsevier Science Publishing Co.

————. 1980. "Incest and Exogamy: A Sociobiological Reconsideration." *Ethology and Sociobiology* 1: 151–162.

————. 1981. *The Ethnic Phenomenon.* New York: Elsevier Science Publishing Co.

van den Berghe, Pierre, and David Barash. 1977. "Inclusive Fitness Theory and the Human Family." *American Anthropologist* 79: 809–823.

Van Der Veen, Marijke. 2010. "Agricultural Innovation: Invention and Adoption or Change and Adaptation?" *World Archaeology* 42 (1): 1–12.

Van Esterik, Penny (Ed.), 1996. *Women of Southeast Asia.* DeKalb: Northern Illinois University.

Van Gennep, Arnold. 1960. *The Rites of Passage.* Chicago: University of Chicago Press.

Van Schaik, C. P., M. Ancrenaz, G. Borgen, B. Galdikas, C.D. Knott, I. Singleton, A. Suzuki, S. S. Utami, M. Merrill, M. et al. 2003. "Orangutan Cultures and the Evolution of Material Culture." *Science* 299 (5603): 102–105.

Van Willigen, John, and V. C. Channa. 1991. "Law, Custom, and Crimes against Women: The Problem of Dowry Death in India." *Human Organization* 50 (4): 369–377.

Vayda, Andrew P. 1961. "Expansion and Warfare among Swidden Agriculturalists." *American Anthropologist* 63: 346–358.

————, **(Ed.)** 1969. *Environment and Cultural Behavior.* Garden City, NY: Natural History Press.

Vekua, Abesalom, David Lordkipanidze, G. Philip Rightmire, Jordi Agusti, Reid Ferring, Givi Maisuradze, Alexander Mouskhelishvili, et al. 2002. "A New Skull of Early *Homo* from Dmanisi, Georgia." *Science* 297: 85–89.

Verdery, Katherine. 1996. *What Was Socialism, and What Comes Next?* Princeton: Princeton University Press.

Vianna, N. J., and A. K. Polan. 1984. "Incidence of Low Birth Weight among Love Canal Residents." *Science* 226: 1217–1219.

Villa, Paola. 1983. *Terra Amata and the Middle Pleistocene Archaeological Record of Southern France.* Berkeley: University of California Press.

Vincent, Joan. 2002. *The Anthropology of Politics: A Reader in Ethnography, Theory, and Critique*. Blackwell Anthologies in Social and Cultural Anthropology: Oxford: Blackwell Publishers.

von Daniken, Erich. 1970. *Chariots of the Gods*. New York: Bantam.

Von Frisch, Karl. 1967. *The Dance Language and Orientation of Bees*, trans. L. E. Chadwick. Cambridge, MA: Harvard University Press.

von Holdt, Bridgett M., John P. Pollinger, Kirk E. Lohmueller, Eunjung Han, Heidi G. Parker, Pascale Quignon, Jeremiah D. Degenhardt, et al. 2010. "Genome-wide SNP and Haplotype Analyses Reveal a Rich History Underlying Dog Domestication."*Nature* 464, 898–902.

von Humboldt, W. [1836] 1972. *Linguistic Variability and Intellectual Development*, C. G. Buck and F. Raven, (Trans.). Philadelphia: University of Pennsylvania Press.

Vygotsky, L. S. 1986. *Thought and Language*, A. Kozulin (Trans.). Cambridge, MA: MIT Press.

Wafer, Jim. 1991. *The Taste of Blood: Spirit Possession in Brazilian Candomble*. Contemporary Ethnography Series. Philadelphia: University of Pennsylvania Press.

Wagner, Donald B. 1993. *Iron and Steel in Ancient China*. Leiden: Brill.

Walker, A. C., and M. Pickford. 1983. "New Post-Cranial Fossils of *Proconsul africanus* and *Proconsul nyanzae*." In R. L. Ciochon and R. Corruccini (Eds.), *New Interpretations of Ape and Human Ancestry*, pp. 325–352. New York: Plenum Press.

Walker, A. R., E. Leakey, J. M. Harris, and F. H. Brown. 1986. "2.5 MYR *Australopithecus boisei* from West of Lake Turkana, Kenya." *Nature* 322: 517–522.

Walker, Anthony. 1986. *The Toda of South India: A New Look*. Delhi: Hindustan Publishing Company.

Wallace, Anthony K. C. 1972. "Mental Illness, Biology, and Culture." In Francis Hsu (Ed.), *Psychological Anthropology*. Cambridge, MA: Schenkman.

Walker, P. L. 2001. "A Bioarchaeological Perspective on the History of Violence." *Annual Review of Anthropology* 30: 573–596.

Wallerstein, Immanuel. 1974. *The Modern World-System: Capitalist Agriculture and the Origins of the European World-Economy in the Sixteenth Century*. New York: Academic Press.

———. 1979. *The Capitalist World-Economy*. New York: Cambridge University Press.

———. 1980. *The Modern World-System: II. Mercantilism and the Consolidation of the European World-Economy, 1600–1750*. New York: Academic Press.

———. 1986. *Africa and the Modern World*. Trenton, NJ: Africa World Press.

Wang, Cheng gang. 1999. "China's Environment in the Balance." In Susan Ogden, (Ed.), *China* (9th ed). Guilford, CT: McGraw-Hill/Dushkin.

Wang, W-M, J. L. Ding, J. W. Shu, and W. Chen. 2010. Exploration of Early Rice Farming in China. *Quaternary International* 227(1): 22–28.

Ward, Martha. 2003. *World Full of Women* (3rd ed.). Boston: Allyn and Bacon.

Warner, W. 2000. "Flexible Production, Households, and Fieldwork: Multisited Zapotec Weavers in the Era of Late Capitalism." *Ethnology* 39 (2): 133–149.

Warshaw, Steven. 1988. *Southeast Asia Emerges*. Berkeley, CA: Diablo Press.

———. 1989. *India Emerges*. Berkeley, CA: Diablo Press.

Washburn, Sherwood. 1960. "Tools and Human Evolution." *Scientific American* 203 (3): 67–75.

Watson, James L. 1980. "Slavery as an Institution, Open and Closed Systems." In James L. Watson (Ed., *Asian and African Systems of Slavery*. pp. 1–15. Berkeley: University of California Press.

Watson, Patty Jo. 1984. *Archaeological Explanation: The Scientific Method in Archaeology*. New York: Columbia University Press.

Watson, Patty Jo, Steven A. LeBlanc, and Charles L. Redman. 1971. *Explanation in Archaeology: An Explicitly Scientific Approach*. New York: Columbia University Press.

Watters, Ethan. 2010. *Crazy Like Us: the Globalization of the American Psyche*. New York: The Free Press.

Waugespack, Nicole M. 2005. "The Organization of Male and Female Labor in Foraging Societies: Implications for Early Paleoindian Archaeology." *American Anthropologist* 107 (4): 666–676.

Wax, Dustin. 2008. *Anthropology at the Dawn of the Cold War*. London: Pluto.

Wax, Murray. 2003. "Wartime Dilemmas of an Ethical Anthropology." *Anthropology Today* 19 (3): 24–25.

Wax, Rosalie. 1971. *Doing Fieldwork: Warnings and Advice*. Chicago: University of Chicago Press.

Weatherford, Jack. 1988. *Indian Givers: How the Indians of the Americas Transformed the World*. New York: Crown.

Weiner, Annette B. 1976. *Women of Value, Men of Renown*. Austin: University of Texas Press.

———. 1987. *The Trobrianders of Papua New Guinea*. New York: Holt, Rinehart & Winston.

Weiner, J. 1994. *The Beak of the Finch*. New York: Knopf.

Weiner, J. S. 1955. *The Piltdown Forgery*. London: Oxford University Press.

Weiner, Steve, Qinqi Xu, Paul Goldberg, Jinyi Liu, and Ofer Bar-Yosef. "Evidence for the Use of Fire at Zhoukoudian, China." *Science* **10 July** 1998: Vol. 281. no. 5374, pp. 251–253.

Weisgrau, Maxine. 2008. "Vedic and Hindu Traditions." In Raymond Scupin, (Ed.), *Religion and Culture: An Anthropological Focus* (2nd ed.). pp. 249–272. Upper Saddle River, NJ: Pearson, Prentice Hall.

Weiss, Anita M. 2006. "Pakistan." In Raymond Scupin, (Ed.), *Peoples and Cultures of Asia*. pp. 143–181. Upper Saddle River, NJ: Pearson, Prentice Hall.

Weissner, Polly. 2002. "Hunting, Healing, and Hxaro Exchange: A Long-Term Perspective on !Kung (Ju/'hoansi) Large-Game Hunting." *Evolution and Human Behavior* 23: 407–436.

Weitz, Eric D. 2003. *A Century of Genocide: Utopias of Race and Nation*. Princeton, NJ: Princeton University Press.

Welcher, Laura. 2009. "Human Language as a Secret Weapon." *Rosetta Project* http://rosettaproject.org/blog/02009/nov/25/human-language-secret-weapon/.

Wells, Spencer. 2010. *Pandora's Seed: The Unforeseen Cost of Civilization*. New York: Random House.

Wendorf, Fred, and Romuald Schild. 1981. "The Earliest Food Producers." *Archaeology* 34 (5): 30–36.

———. 1984. "The Emergence of Food Production in the Egyptian Sahara." In Desmond J. Clark and Steven A. Brandt (Eds.). *From Hunter to Farmer*, pp. 93–101. Berkeley: University of California Press.

West, Fred. 1975. *The Way of Language: An Introduction*. New York: Harcourt Brace Jovanovich.

Wheeler, P. E. 1991. "The Thermoregulatory Advantage of Hominid Bipedalism in Open Equatorial Environments: The Contribution of Increased Convective Heat Loss and Cutaneous Evaluative Cooling." *Journal of Human Evolution* 21: 117–136.

———. 1992. "The Influence of the Loss of Functional Body Hair on the Water Budgets of Early Hominids." *Journal of Human Evolution* 23, 379–388.

———. 1994. "The Thermoregulatory Advantages of Heat Storage and Shade-Seeking Behavior to Hominids Foraging in Equatorial Savannah Environments." *Journal of Human Evolution* 26, 339–350.

White, Douglas. 1988. "Rethinking Polygyny: Co-Wives, Codes, and Cultural Systems." *Current Anthropology* 29 (4): 529–553.

White, John Peter. 1993. "The Settlement of Ancient Australia." In G. Burenhult, (Ed.), *The First Humans: Human Origins and History to 10,000 BC*, pp. 147–70. New York: HarperCollins.

White, John Peter, and James F. O'Connell. 1982. *A Prehistory of Australia, New Guinea and Sahul*. New York: Academic Press.

White, Leslie. [1949] 1971. "The Symbol: The Origin and Basis of Human Behavior." In Leslie White, (Ed.)., *The Science of Culture: A Study of Man and Civilization*. pp. 22–39. New York: Farrar, Straus & Giroux.

———. 1959. *The Evolution of Culture*. New York: McGraw-Hill.

White, Randall. 1982. "Rethinking the Middle/ Upper Paleolithic Transition." *Current Anthropology* 23: 169–192.

White, Tim D. 1995. "Early Hominids—Diversity or Distortion?" *Science* 299: 1994–1997.

White, Tim D., B. Asfaw, D. DeGusta, H. Gilbert, G. D. Richards, G. Suwa, and F. C. Howell. 2003. "Pleistocene Homo sapiens from Middle Awash, Ethiopia." *Nature* 423: 742–747.

White, Tim D., B. Asfaw, Y. Beyene, Y. Haile-Selassie, C. O. Lovejoy, G. Suwa, G. WoldeGabriel. 2009. "*Ardipithecus ramidus and the Paleobiology of Early Hominids*". *Science* 326 (5949): 75–86.

White, Tim D., B. Asfaw, D. DeGusta, H. Gilbert, G. D. Richards, G. F. C. Howell. 2003. "Pleistocene *Homo sapiens* from Middle Awash, Ethiopia." *Nature* 423 (6491): 742–747,

Whitehouse, Harvey. 2004. *Modes of Religiosity: A Cognitive Theory of Religious Transmission*. Walnut Creek, CA: AltaMira Press.

Whitehouse, Harvey and Luther H. Martin. 2004. *Theorizing Religions Past: Archaeology, History, and Cognition*. Walnut Creek, CA: AltaMira Press.

Whitley, David S., and Ronald I. Dorn. 1993. "New Perspectives on the Clovis vs. Pre-Clovis Controversy." *American Antiquity* 58 (4): 626–647.

Whorf, Benjamin. 1956. *Language, Thought, and Reality: The Selected Writings of Benjamin Lee Whorf*. Cambridge, MA: MIT Press.

Wikan, Unni. 1991. *Behind the Veil in Arabia: Women in Oman*. Chicago: University of Chicago Press.

Wilk, Richard R. 1995. "Consumer Goods as Dialogue about Development: Colonial Time and Television Time in Belize." In J. Friedman (Ed.), *Consumption and Identity*, pp. 97–118. Chur, Switzerland: Harwood Academic.

———. 1996. *Economies and Cultures: Foundations of Economic Anthropology*. Boulder, CO: Westview Press.

Wilkinson, Caroline D. 2004 *Forensic Facial Reconstruction*. New York : Cambridge University Press.

Williams, Holly Ann. 1990. "Families in Refugee Camps." *Human Organization* 49 (2): 100–109.

Williams, Robin M., Jr. 1970. *American Society: A Sociological Interpretation* (3rd ed.). New York: Knopf.

Williams, Stephen. 1991. *Fantastic Archaeology: The Wild Side of North American Prehistory*. Philadelphia: University of Pennsylvania Press.

Williams-Blangero, S., and J. Blangero. 1992. "Quantitative Genetic Analysis of Skin Reflectance: A Multivariate Approach." *Human Biology* 64: 35–49.

Wilson, A. C., and R. L. Cann. 1992. "The Recent African Genesis of Humans." *Scientific American* 266 (4): 68–73.

Wilson, B., C. Grigson, and S. Payne (Eds.), 1982. *Aging and Sexing Animal Bones from Archaeological Sites*. Oxford: British Archaeological Reports, International Series 109.

Wilson, Caroline. 2010 "Eating, Eating is Always There; Food Consumerism and Cardiovascular Disease: Some Evidence from Kerala, South India." *Anthropology and Medicine* 17 (3): 261–275.

Wilson, E. O. (Ed.), 1988. *Biodiversity*. Washington, DC: Smithsonian Institution, National Academy of Sciences.

——— **(Ed.),** 1989. *Biodiversity*. Washington, DC: National Academy Press.

———. 1992. *The Diversity of Life*. Cambridge, MA: Harvard University Press.

Wilson, E. O., and Laura Simonds Southworth. 1996. *In Search of Nature*. New York: Island Press.

Wilson, Michael L., Marc D. Hauser, and Richard Wrangham. 2001. "Does Participation in Intergroup Conflict Depend on Numerical Assessment, Range Location, or Rank for Wild Chimpanzees?" *Animal Behavior* 61: 1203–1216.

Wilson, Michael L., and Richard Wrangham. 2003. "Intergroup Relations in Chimpanzees." *Annual Review of Anthropology* 32: 363–92.

Wilson, Monica. 1951. *Good Company: A Study of Nyakyusa Age-Villages*. Boston: Beacon Press.

Wilson, William Julius. 1980. *The Declining Significance of Race: Blacks and Changing American Institutions* (2nd ed.). Chicago: University of Chicago Press.

———. 1997. *When Work Disappears: The World of the New Urban Poor*. New York: Knopf.

Winchester, Simon. 2002. *The Map That Changed the World: William Smith and the Birth of Modern Geology*. New York: HarperCollins.

Winzeler, Robert L. 1996. "Sexual Status in Southeast Asia: Comparative Perspectives on Women, Agriculture and Political Organization." In Penny Van Esterik, (Ed.)., *Women of Southeast Asia*. Occasional Paper No. 17. DeKalb: Northern Illinois University, Center for Southeast Asian Studies.

Wittfogel, Karl W. 1957. *Oriental Despotism: A Comparative Study of Total Power*. New Haven, CT: Yale University Press.

Wolf, Arthur. 1970. "Childhood Association and Sexual Attraction: A Further Test of the Westermarck Hypothesis." *American Anthropologist* 72: 503–515.

———. 2004. "Introduction." In Arthur Wolf and William Durham (Eds.), *Inbreeding, Incest, and the Incest Taboo*. Stanford: Stanford University Press.

Wolf, Arthur, and William Durham. 2004. *Inbreeding, Incest, and the Incest Taboo*. Stanford: Stanford University Press.

Wolf, E. R., and S. Mintz. 1950. "An Analysis of Ritual Coparenthood (*Compadrazgo*)." *Southwestern Journal of Anthropology* 6. Reprinted in Jack A. Potter, May Diaz, and George Foster (Eds.), 1967. *Peasant Society: A Reader*, pp. 174–199. Boston: Little, Brown.

Wolf, Eric R. 1955a. "Closed Corporate Communities in Mesoamerica and Java." *Southwestern Journal of Anthropology* 13 (1): 1–18.

———. 1955b. "Types of Latin American Peasantry: A Preliminary Discussion." *American Anthropologist* 57 (3): 452–471.

———. 1958. "The Virgin of Guadalupe: A Mexican National Symbol." *Journal of American Folklore* 71: 34–39.

———. 1959. *Sons of the Shaking Earth.* Chicago: University of Chicago Press.

———. 1964. *Anthropology.* Englewood Cliffs, NJ: Prentice Hall.

———. 1966. *Peasants.* Englewood Cliffs, NJ: Prentice Hall.

———. 1969. *Peasant Wars of the Twentieth Century.* New York: Harper & Row.

———. [1982] 1997. *Europe and the People Without History.* Berkeley: University of California Press.

———. 1987. "Cycles of Violence: The Anthropology of War and Peace." In Kenneth Moor, (Ed.), *Waymarks: The Notre Dame Inaugural Lectures in Anthropology*, pp. 127–151. Notre Dame, IN: University of Notre Dame Press.

———. 1999. *Envisioning Power: Ideologies of Domination and Crisis.* Berkeley: University of California Press.

Wolf, Eric. R., and Sidney Mintz. 1950. "An Analysis of Ritual Coparenthood (*Compadrazgo*)." *Southwestern Journal of Anthropology* 6. Reprinted in Jack A. Potter, May Diaz, and George Foster (Eds.), 1967. *Peasant Society: A Reader*, 174–199. Boston: Little Brown.

Wolfe, Alvin. 1977. "The Supranational Organization of Production: An Evolutionary Perspective." *Current Anthropology* 18: 615–635.

———. 1986. "The Multinational Corporation as a Form of Sociocultural Integration Above the Level of the State." In Hendrick Serrie, (Ed.), *Anthropology and International Business*, Publication No. 28. Williamsburg, VA: Studies in Third World Societies.

——— 2006. "Supranational Networks: States and Firms." *Peace and Conflict Studies* 13 (1): 68–80.

Wolpoff, Milford H. 1980. *Paleoanthropology.* New York: Knopf.

———. 1983. "*Ramapithecus* and Human Origins: An Anthropologist's Perspective of Changing Interpretations." In R. L. Ciochon and R. Corruccini (Eds.), *New Interpretations of Ape and Human Ancestry*, pp. 651–676. New York: Plenum Press.

Wolpoff, Milford., and Rachel Caspari. 1997. *Race and Human Evolution.* Boulder, CO: Westview Press,.

———. 2002. *Race and Human Evolution: A Fatal Attraction.* New York: Simon and Schuster.

Wolpoff, Milford H., John Hawks, B. Senut ,M. Pickford, and J. Ahern. 2006. "An Ape or *the* Ape: Is the Toumaï Cranium TM 266 a Hominid?" *PaleoAnthropology*, 2006: 36–50.

Wong, Kate. 2003. "An Ancestor to Call Our Own." *Scientific American*, January: 56–65.

Wood, B. A. 2002. "Palaeoanthropology: Hominid revelations from Chad." *Nature* 418, 133–135.

Woodburn, James. 1982. "Egalitarian Societies." *Man* 17: 431–451.

Workman, P. L., B. S. Blumberg, and A. J. Cooper. 1963. "Selection, Gene Migration and Polymorphic Stability in a U.S. White and Negro Population." *American Journal of Human Genetics* 15: 71–84.

World Book Online Infofinder. 2014. "Mexico City." Chicago: World Book.

World Economic Forum. 2014. *Global Risks 2014 report.* Davos, Switzerland.

World Factbook. 2012. Washington, DC: CIA. https://www.cia.gov/cia/publications/ factbook/index.html

Worsley, Peter. 1957. *The Trumpet Shall Sound.* New York: Schocken.

———. 1984. *The Three Worlds: Culture and World Development.* Chicago: University of Chicago Press.

Wrangham, R. W. 1987. "The Significance of African Apes for Reconstructing Human Social Evolution." In W. G. Kinsey (Ed.), *The Evolution of Human Behavior: Primate Models*, pp. 51–71. Albany, NY: State University of Albany Press.

Wright, Henry T. 1977. "Recent Researches of the Origin of the State." *Annual Review of Anthropology* 6: 355–370.

Wright, Henry T., and G. Johnson. 1975. "Population, Exchange, and Early State Formation in Southwestern Iran." *American Anthropologist* 77: 267–289.

Wright, Rita P. 2010. *The Ancient Indus: Urbanism, Economy, and Society.* New York: Cambridge University Press.

Wright, Robert. 2000. *Non-Zero: The Logic of Human Destiny.* New York: Pantheon Books.

Wu, R., and S. Lin. 1983. Peking Man. *Scientific American* 248: 78–86.

Wynn, T. 1995. "Handaxe enigmas." *World Archaeology* 27: 10–24.

———. 1998. "Did *Homo erectus* speak?" *Cambridge Archaeological Journal* 1: 78–81.

Xu Z., L. Jing, D. Yu, and X. Xu. 2000. "Air Pollution and Daily Mortality in Shenyang, China." *Architecture and Environmental Health* 55: 115–120.

Yan, Yunxiang. 2006. "McDonalds in Beijing: The Localization of Americana." In James L. Watson (Ed.), *Golden Arches East: McDonald's in East Asia* (2nd ed.). pp. 39–76. Stanford: Stanford University Press.

Yang, Z. 2002. "Likelihood and Bayes estimation of ancestral population sizes in hominoids using data from multiple loci."*Genetics* 162: 1811–1823.

Yangisako, Sylvia J., and Jane F. Collier. 1990. "The Mode of Reproduction in Anthropology." In Deborah Rhode (Ed.), *Theoretical Perspectives on Sexual Difference.* pp. 131–144. New Haven, CT: Yale University Press.

Yellen, J. E., A. S. Brooks, E. Cornelissen, M. J. Mehlman, and K. Stewart. 1995. "A Middle Stone Age Worked Bone Industry from Katanda, Upper Semliki Valley, Zaire." *Science* 268: 553–556.

Yellen, John. 1985. "Bushmen." *Science* 85: 40–48.

Yelvington, Kevin. 2001. "The Anthropology of Afro-Latin America: Diasporic Dimensions." *Annual Review of Anthropology* 30: 227–260.

Yengoyan, Aram A. 1986. "Theory in Anthropology: On the Demise of the Concept of Culture." *Comparative Studies in Society and History* 28 (2): 357–374.

Yoffee, Norman. 1979. "The Decline and Rise of Mesopotamian Civilization." *American Antiquity.* 44: 5–35.

Yokoyama Y, C. Falguères, F. Sémah, F Jacob, and R. Grün. 2008."Gamma-ray Spectrometric Dating of Late Homo erectus Skulls from Ngandong and Sambungmacan, Central Java, Indonesia." *Journal of Human Evolution* **55(2):** 274–277.

Young, Christian C., and Mark A. Largent. 2007. *Evolution and Creationism: A Documentary and Reference Guide*. Westport: Greenwood Press.

Yorburg, Betty. 2002. *Family Realities: A Global View*. Upper Saddle River, NJ: Prentice Hall.

Yoshino, Kosaku. 1997. *Japan's Minorities: The Illusion of Homogeneity*. London: Routledge.

———. 1998. "The Discourse on Blood and Racial Identity in Contemporary Japan." In Dru Gladney (Ed.). *Making Majorities: Constituting the Nation in Japan, Korea, China, Malaysia, Fiji, Turkey, and the United States*. pp. 13–30. Stanford: Stanford University Press.

Zeder, Melinda A. 1997. *The American Archaeologist: A Profile*. Walnut Creek, CA: AltaMira Press.

———. 2011. Pathways to Animal Domestication. In A. Damania and P. Gepts (Eds.),*Harlan II: Biodiversity in Agriculture: Domestication, Evolution, & Sustainability*. University of California: Davis.

———. 2012. The Broad Spectrum Revolution at 40: Resource Diversity, Intensification, and an Alternative to Optimal Foraging Explanations. *Journal of Anthropological Archaeology* 31(3): 241–264.

Zhu, Zhiqun. 2009. *Understanding East Asia's Economic Miracles*. Key Issues in Asian Studies. Ann Arbor: Association for Asian Studies, Inc.

Credits

Chapter 1 Page 1: Dr. Raymond B. Hames; 2: dtopal/Shutterstock.com; 4: John Hawkes; 5: Education Images/Universal Images Group Limited/Alamy; 6: Christopher DeCorse; 7: Kelley Hays-Gilpin at the Museum of Northern Arizona front entrance, Photo by Michele Mountain, © 2006 Museum of Northern Arizona; 8: Courtesy of Christina Dames; 8: Nancy L. Ford Photography; 10: Courtesy of Scott Atran; 11: Courtesy of A.H. Peter Castro; 16: Christopher DeCorse

Chapter 2 Page 19: Christopher Ricciardi; 21: Christopher R. DeCorse; 26: Merrick Posnansky; 27: Institute of Nautical Archaeology; 28: Press Association/AP Images; 29: AP Photo/Jae C. Hong; 29: Reuters/Corbis; 30: Courtesy of Matthew Johnson; 31: NASA; 32: Courtesy of Laurence Kruckman; 32: Courtesy of Laurence Kruckman; 33: Courtesy of Douglas V. Armstrong, Syracuse University; 34: J.D. Dallet/AGE Fotostock; 34: Courtesy of Marek E. Jasinski, Institute of Historical Studies, Archaeology Programme Norwegian University of Science and Technology; 39: Christopher R. DeCorse; 39: Denny Ellis/Alamy; 39: Pics/Fotolia

Chapter 3 Page 42: Bob Ainsworth/Getty Images; 44: Erich Lessing/Art Resource, NY; 47: bpk, Berlin/ Art Resource, NY ; 47: akg-images/Newscom; 48: Hulton Archive/Getty Images; 48: Courtesy of Rodney Livingston; 48: Christopher R. DeCorse; 48: sbarabu/Shutterstock.; 49: AKG/Science Source; 57: U.S. Department of Agriculture

Chapter 4 Page 67: Mejn/Fotolia; 73: santiago silver/Fotolia; 76: holbox/Shutterstock; 77: GeroF/Fotolia; 78: Christopher R. DeCorse; 82: Tom McHugh/Photo Researchers Inc.; 82: Parnumas Na Phatthalung/Shutterstock; 83: Sjaak van den Nieuwendijk/Steve Bloom Images; 84: Christopher R. DeCorse; 85: Liam White/Alamy

Chapter 5 Page 90: John Reader/Science Source; 90: Courtesy of the American Museum of Natural History; 97: Christopher R. DeCorse; 97: Christopher R. DeCorse; 98: John Reader/Science Source; 99: Christophe Boisvieux/Eureka/Corbis; 99: Pearson Education/PH College; 100: Christopher R. DeCorse; 102: Christopher R. DeCorse; 103: Christopher R. DeCorse; 104: Christopher R. DeCorse; 108: Christopher R. DeCorse; 114: Christopher R. DeCorse; 115: Christopher R. DeCorse

Chapter 6 Page 120: Jupiterimages/Stockbyte/Getty Images; 126: John Moss/Science Source; 126: Cindy Hopkins/Alamy; 128: Jackie Lewin, Royal Free Hospital/Science Source; 130: John Warburton-Lee/Getty Images; 130: H. Mark Weidman Photography/Alamy; 132: George Holton/Science Source; 133: Peter Menzel/Science Source; 137: National Archives and Records Administration

Chapter 7 Page 143: Robert Harding Picture Library Ltd/Alamy; 145: Bruce Coleman/Photoshot; 154: Pamela Willoughby; 154: Pamela Willoughby; 155: Album/sfgp/Newscom; 158: Arjun Clarry; 160: Clement Philippe/Arterra Picture Library/Alamy; 161: Pascal Goetgheluck/Science Source; 164: Christopher DeCorse; 165: Kenneth Garrett/National Geographic Creative; 165: Tom McHugh/Photo Researchers Inc.; 166: Amy Nichole Harris/Fotolia

Chapter 8 Page 170: Â© Matthew Jacques/Shutterstock.com; 172: Adam Woolfitt/Encyclopedia/Corbis; 174: The Trustees of the British Museum/Art Resource, NY; 175: Brian M. Fagan; 177: James King-Holmes/Science Source; 178: Courtesy of the Everson Museum; 184: www.BibleLandPictures.com/Alamy; 185: Christopher DeCorse; 191: Robert S. Peabody Museum of Archaeology, Phillips Academy, Andover, Massachusetts. All Rights Reserved; 192: Caitlin Mirra/Shutterstock

Chapter 9 Page 198: David Whitley; 202: Georg Gerster/Science Source; 203: Courtesy of the Everson Museum of Art, Syracuse, New York; 204: Courtesy of the Corning Museum of Glass; 204: Courtesy of the Corning Museum of Glass; 204: Courtesy of the Corning Museum of Glass; 205: Courtesy of the Corning Museum of Glass; 209: Kazuyoshi Nomachi/Pacific Press/Photo Researchers Inc.; 214: Courtesy of Special Collections Research Center, Syracuse University Libraries; 217: Peter Horree/Alamy; 218: Christopher R. DeCorse; 219: Christopher R. DeCorse; 220: Courtesy of the Library of Congress; 221: Sacsahuman Incan Fortress (photo), ./Cuzco, Peru/Photo Â© Boltin Picture Library/Bridgeman Images

Chapter 10 Page 226: Jon Bower Thailand/Alamy; 228: Courtesy: CSU Archives/Everett Collection/Alamy; 228: Tom McHugh/Science Source; 229: Lawrence Migdale/Science Source; 231: Beren Patterson/Alamy; 234: Ali Mubarak/Grapheast/Alamy; 236: Connie Bransilver/Science source; 237: Loretta Wardrip; 239: Pictorial Press Ltd/Alamy; 240: Donald E. Brown

Chapter 11 Page 243: Design Pics/Newscom; 246: William Perry/123RF; 248: Vassar College Art Gallery/Library; 249: Courtesy of Library of Congress; 252: Creativa/Fotolia; 254: Sarit Uzieli/ASAP/Science Source; 255: Raymond Scupin; 259: Chlaus Lotscher/PhotoLibrary/Getty Images

Chapter 12 Page 269: Michael DeFreitas Middle East/ Alamy; 271: Susan Kuklin/Science Source; 272: Kay & Karl Ammann/BRUCE COLEMAN INC./Alamy; 278: Good-luz/Shutterstock; 279: Anette Selmer-Andresen/Alamy; 280: Angela Hampton Picture Library/Alamy; 281: Ed Kashi/ Encyclopedia/Corbis; 283 Edward S. Curtis/Cor-bis; 289: Pawel Bienkowski/Alamy; 289: Robin Laurance/ Alamy; 290: Hoang Van Danh/Bettmann/Corbis; 290: JackF/Fotolia; 290: Platslee/Shutterstock; 290: Rob/Fotolia

Chapter 13 Page 293: Morandi Bruno/Hemis.fr/ Alamy; 294: Library of Congress Prints and Photographs Division[LC-USZC4-8725]; 296: Time & Life Pictures/Getty Images; 297: North Wind Picture Archives/Alamy; 297: Ian Stewart/Shutterstock; 299: SPL/Science Source; 300: Mary Evans Picture Library/Alamy; 305: Stefan Ember/123RF

Chapter 14 Page 311: Karl Johaentges/Alamy; 313: Hay-tham Pictures/Alamy; 319: Pegaz/Alamy; 323: joyfull/ Shutterstock

Chapter 15 Page 326: Ton Koene/ Horizons WWP/ Alamy; 332: Martin Harvey/Photolibrary/Getty Images; 333: Ton Koene/Horizons WWP/Alamy; 336: Arco Im-ages GmbH/Alamy; 337: Historical/Corbis; 344: Vasina Nazarenko/Fotolia

Chapter 16 Page 347: Blickwinkel/Alamy; 352: Nigel Pavitt/John Warburton-Lee Photography/Alamy; 359: Winter & Pond/Museum of History and Industry/Corbis; 360: Chistopher DeCorse; 364: Gabriella Coleman; 365: Bryan Smith/ZUMA Press, Inc./Alamy; 367: Bettmann/ Corbis

Chapter 17 Page 371: Christopher Arnesen/The Image Bank/Getty Images; 379: Anthony Bannister/Gallo Images/Corbis; 391: J. Tim O'Meara; 394: Y. Layma/ Explorer/Science Source; 395: Mrakor/Fotolia; 395: sydeen/ Shutterstock; 403: nyul/Fotolia; 406: david mbiyu/Alamy

Chapter 18 Page 411: irishphoto.com/Alamy; 417: George Holton/Science Source; 421: duncan1890/Getty Images; 427: German Day in Nuremberg, 1923; the SA is lined up, from 'Germany Awakened' (colour litho), German School, (20th century)/Private Collection/The Stapleton Collec-tion/Bridgeman Images; 429: Photo12 Collection /Alamy

Chapter 19 Page 432: Design Pics/Getty Images; 435: Andres Rodriguez/Fotolia; 440: blickwinkel/Alamy; 441: Nancy L. Bridges; 442: Universal Images Group/ DeAgostini/Alamy; 444: Nancy L. Bridges; 446: Cahokia Mounds State Historical Site, painting by William R. Iseminger; 454: Christopher DeCorse; 456: Peter Horree/ Alamy; 457: Martin Thompson/Lebrecht Music and Arts Photo Library/Alamy

Chapter 20 Page 461: Jamil Bittar/Reuters/Landov; 462: dpa/Alamy; 463: HotNYCNews/Alamy; 464: Fredrik Renander/Alamy; 465: Akg-images/Newscom; 471: Courtesy of Sydel Silverman Wolf; 475: Nick Greaves/ Alamy; 481: Library of Congress Prints and Photographs Division[Trager and Kuhn/LC-USZ62-116812]; 484: AP Photo/Ronen Zilberman; 486: Doug Steley C/Alamy; 486: Dailin/Shutterstock

Chapter 21 Page 490: Andrew Woodley/Alamy; 496: Tom Salyer/Alamy; 497: Charles O. Cecil/Alamy; 498: Christoph Henning/Das Fotoarchiv/Black Star/Alamy; 500: Gallo Images/Foto24/Alamy; 502: AP Images; 507: frans lemmens/Alamy; 508: Marmaduke St. John/Alamy; 509: Alamer/Iconotec/Alamy; 514: Charles Harker/ Shutterstock

Chapter 22 Page 518: Paul Cowan/Shutterstock; 524: David Longstreath/AP Images; 526: Dinodia Photos/ Alamy; 527: World History Archive/Alamy; 527: akg-images/Newscom; 528: YASSER AL-ZAYYAT/Getty Images; 529: R.T. Nowitz/Photo Researchers Inc.; 532: gezzeg/Shutterstock; 538: Yu Zhang/Shutterstock; 538: Courtesy of Susan Brownell; 543: Stringer/Afghanistan/ Reuters/Corbis; 544: Courtesy of Akbar Ahmed

Chapter 23 Page 547: Rawpixel/Shutterstock; 548: Jay Premack/ZUMA Press/Newscom; 553: guatebrian/Alamy; 558: Kristy-Anne Glubish/Design Pics/Getty Images; 561: Monkey Business Images/Shutterstock; 562: Monkey Business Images/Shutterstock; 564: Blend Images/123RF; 564: ZouZou/Shutterstock

Chapter 24 Page 569: Kristin Smith/Shutterstock; 572: Gavin Hellier/Robert Harding World Imagery/Alamy; 584: jeremy sutton-hibbert/Alamy; 587: Oleksiy Maksy-menko Photography/Alamy

Chapter 25 Page 593: Hamilton Wright/Photo Research-ers Inc.; 596: Courtesy of Gene O'Donnell, FBI; 596: Cour-tesy of Federal Bureau of Investigation; 596: Federal Bureau of Investigation; 596: Federal Bureau of Investigation; 597: Jacinski; 597: AP Images/Victor Ruiz C; 600: xixinxing/ Fotolia; 603: CASBS Archives; 605: Courtesy of teh General Services Administration; 605: Courtesy of the General Services Administration; 605: Rick Shupper /Ambient Images Inc./Alamy; 608: Christopher R. DeCorse; 610: The Trustees of The British Museum/Art Resource, NY; 614: John L. McCreery; 615: Design Pics/Alberto Arzoz/Alberto Arzoz/Newscom; 616: Library of Congress ; 619: Adam Kazmierski/Getty Images; 620: Napoleon Chagnon

Index